Paul's Letter to the Romans

Paul's Letter to the Romans

A COMMENTARY

Arland J. Hultgren

WILLIAM B. EERDMANS PUBLISHING COMPANY

GRAND RAPIDS, MICHIGAN / CAMBRIDGE, U.K.

Published 2011 by
Wm. B. Eerdmans Publishing Co.
2140 Oak Industrial Drive N.E., Grand Rapids, Michigan 49505 /
P.O. Box 163, Cambridge CB3 9PU U.K.

Printed in the United States of America

17 16 15 14 13 12 11   7 6 5 4 3 2 1

Library of Congress Cataloging-in-Publication Data

Hultgren, Arland J.
Paul's letter to the Romans: a commentary / Arland J. Hultgren.
p.   cm.
ISBN 978-0-8028-2609-1 (cloth: alk. paper)
1. Bible. N.T. Romans — Commentaries. I. Title.

BS2665.53.H85   2011
227'.107 — dc22

2010052131

www.eerdmans.com

Contents

Preface

Paul's Letter to the Romans is inspiring, challenging, and often puzzling. The primary purpose of a commentary on Romans should therefore be to walk with the reader through the letter, illumining the text with helpful comment, giving detailed attention to major puzzles where necessary, and — hopefully — not diminishing those features of the biblical book that are inspiring and challenging.

Few books of the Bible have received more comment and scholarly analysis than Romans. That makes the research and writing of a commentary on it a daunting task, requiring the author to search through previous work to the extent possible and helpful. Inevitably the research will be selective.

While working on the present volume, I had to make some major decisions. The first had to do with the amount of detail that I should give to various sections and specific verses within the letter. What may have seemed obvious to me will inevitably receive lighter treatment than those portions that are more difficult to figure out. But I had to make judgment calls, and what may seem obvious to me may not be as clear to the reader. Another major decision I had to make had to do with balance. How is one to balance descriptive work, analytical work, documentation, summation, and theological engagement? In the present commentary I have attempted to involve all of those concerns and more. To be sure, that is true of other commentaries as well. But more than is typical of some, this commentary gives sustained attention to the theological claims of the letter. That is justified by the sheer fact that Romans is one of the most important theological documents ever written.

There are many commentaries and studies of Romans, each of which has it own approach. Many interpreters hold that in this letter Paul takes on live issues within the house churches in Rome, seeking to create a more peaceful situation there by his intervention as an apostle. Moreover, a number of them regard

Romans as Paul's final theological statement, even a retrospective summary of his earlier work.

My approach in this commentary is different. It takes seriously those passages written by Paul at the beginning and end of the letter in which he speaks of mutual edification upon his planned arrival in Rome and makes an appeal for his readers' support for a mission to Spain. By means of the letter Paul prepares for his arrival by setting forth the basics of his message, telling his readers what he expects that they would want to hear from him. He had been involved in controversies prior to his planned trip to Rome, and he was known to have strong views on various topics. The Christian believers in Rome could certainly have had serious concerns about what Paul might say and do within their own community. By means of this letter Paul is able to take up and discuss sensitive issues that were common within early Christianity, and in which he has been involved. Moreover, rather than being Paul's final statement of his theology, the letter projects a theological vision for his future work as he arrives in Rome, seeks support from his readers, and goes on from there to Spain. It is more forward looking than retrospective.

I owe special thanks to many persons who contributed to the production of this work. Having taught Romans many times over in a theological seminary, I have gained immeasurable stimulation through classroom interaction with students and in conversations and symposia with colleagues over the years. In addition, the Board of Directors of Luther Seminary granted a year-long sabbatical for research and writing early on in the process. As usual, but not to be taken for granted, the fine staff of the library of Luther Seminary was helpful in acquiring research materials beyond the holdings of the library.

ARLAND J. HULTGREN
Asher O. and Carrie Nasby
Professor of New Testament
Luther Seminary

General Abbreviations

Ancient Sources

Old Testament Pseudepigrapha

Apoc. Abr.	*Apocalypse of Abraham*
Apoc. Bar.	*Apocalyse of Baruch*
Apoc. Mos.	*Apocalypse of Moses*
Jos. Asen.	*Joseph and Aseneth*
Jub.	*Jubilees*
Let. Arist.	*Letter of Aristeas*
Odes Sol.	*Odes of Solomon*
Pss. Sol.	*Psalms of Solomon*
Sib. Or.	*Sibylline Oracles*
T. Abr.	*Testament of Abraham*
T. Ash.	*Testament of Asher*
T. Benj.	*Testament of Benjamin*
T. Dan	*Testament of Dan*
T. Gad	*Testament of Gad*
T. Iss.	*Testament of Issachar*
T. Jud.	*Testament of Judah*
T. Levi	*Testament of Levi*
T. Moses	*Testament of Moses*
T. Naph.	*Testament of Naphtali*
T. Reuben	*Testament of Reuben*
T. Zeb.	*Testament of Zebulun*

Philo

Abr.	*De Abrahamo*
Aet.	*De Aeternitate Mundi*

Cher.	*De Cherubim*
Conf.	*De Confusione Linguarum*
Cont.	*De Vita Contemplativa*
Decal.	*De Decalogo*
Deus	*Quod Deus Sit Immutabilis*
Ebr.	*De Ebrietate*
Flacc.	*In Flaccum*
Fug.	*De Fuga et Inventione*
Gig.	*De Gigantibus*
Her.	*Quis Rerum Divinarum Heres Sit*
Jos.	*De Josepho*
Leg. All.	*Legum Allegoriae*
Legat.	*Legatio ad Gaium*
Migr.	*De Migratione Abrahami*
Mos.	*De Vita Mosis*
Mut.	*De Mutatione Nominum*
Op.	*De Opificio Mundi*
Post.	*De Posteritate Caini*
Praem.	*De Praemiis et Poenis*
Sacr.	*De Sacrificiis Abelis et Caini*
Somn.	*De Somniis*
Spec. Leg.	*De Specialibus Legibus*
Virt.	*De Virtutibus*

Josephus

Ag. Ap.	*Against Apion*
Ant.	*Jewish Antiquities*
J. W.	*The Jewish War*

Dead Sea Scrolls

1QH	*Thanksgiving Hymns*
1QM	*War Scroll*
1QpHab	*Pesher Habakkuk*
1QS	*Rule of the Community*
4Q504	*Words of the Luminaries*
CD	*Damascus Document*

Rabbinic Works

Abod. Zar.	*Abodah Zarah*
Aboth R. Nat.	*Aboth de Rabbi Nathan*
b.	*Babylonian Talmud*
B. Bat.	*Baba Batra*

Ber.	*Berakhot*
B. Mes.	*Baba Mesia*
Eduy.	*Eduyyoth*
Gen. Rab.	*Genesis Rabbah*
Git.	*Gittim*
m.	*The Mishnah*
Ned.	*Nedarim*
Nid.	*Niddah*
Pes.	*Pesahim*
Qidd.	*Qiddušin*
Sanh.	*Sanhedrin*
Shab.	*Shabbat*
Taan.	*Taanit*
t.	*Tosefta*
y.	*Palestinian Talmud*

Early Christian Literature

Barn.	*Epistle of Barnabas*
Ignatius, *Eph.*	*Epistle to the Ephesians*
Ignatius, *Magn.*	*Epistle to the Magnesians*
Ignatius, *Phld.*	*Epistle to the Philadelphians*
Ignatius, *Pol.*	*Epistle to Polycarp*
Ignatius, *Rom.*	*Epistle to the Romans*
Ignatius, *Smyrn.*	*Epistle to the Smyrnaeans*
Ignatius, *Trall.*	*Epistle to the Trallians*

Other Ancient Literature

Aelius Lampridius, *Elag.*	Aelius Lampridius, *Elagabalus*
Appian, *Bell. civ.*	Appian, *Bella civilia (Civil Wars)*
Aristotle, *Eth. eud.*	*Eudaemonian Ethics*
Aristotle, *Eth. nic.*	*Nichomachean Ethics*
Aristotle, *Rhet.*	*Rhetoric*
Athenaeus, *Deipn.*	Athenaeus, *Deipnosophistae*
Cassius Dio, *Rom. Hist.*	Cassius Dio, *Roman History*
Cicero, *Dom.*	Cicero, *De domo sua*
Dionysius of Halicarnassus, *Ant. rom.*	Dionysius of Halicarnasus, *Roman Antiquities*
Epictetus, *Dis.*	Epictetus, *Discourses*
Firmicus Maturnus, *Math.*	Firmicus Maturnus, *Mathesis*
Heraclitus, *All.*	Heraclitus, *Allegories (Questiones Homericae)*
Herodotus, *Hist.*	Herodotus, *History*
Homer, *Od.*	Homer, *Odyssey*

Juvenal, *Sat.*	Juvenal, *Satires*
Longus, *Daphn.*	Longus, *Daphnis and Chloe*
Lucian, *Dial. meretr.*	Lucian, *Dialogues of the Courtesans*
Lucian, *Dial. mort.*	*Dialogi mortuorum (Dialogues of the Dead)*
Lucian, *Merc. cond.*	*De mercede conductis (Salaried Posts in a Great House)*
Lucian, *Ver. hist.*	*Vera historia (A True Story)*
Musonius Rufus, *Frag.*	Musonius Rufus, *Fragments*
Orosius, *Hist.*	Orosius, *Historiae adversus paganos*
Pindar, *Pyth.*	Pindar, *Pythian Odes*
Plato, *Apol.*	*Apology*
Plato, *Leg.*	*Laws*
Plato, *Phaedr.*	*Phaedrus*
Plato, *Resp.*	*Republic*
Plato, *Symp.*	*Symposium*
Plato, *Tim.*	*Timaeus*
Plutarch, *Adv.*	*Advice about Keeping Well*
Plutarch, *Mor.*	*Moralia*
Plutarch, *Rom.*	*Romulus*
Ps.-Aristotle, *Cosm.*	Pseudo-Aristotle, *On the Cosmos*
Ps.-Lucian, *Forms*	Pseudo-Lucian, *Forms of Love*
Strabo, *Geogr.*	Strabo, *Geography*
Strato of Sardis, *Mus.*	Strato of Sardis, *Musa puerilis*
Tacitus, *Ann.*	Tacitus, *Annals*
Thucydides, *Hist.*	Thucydides, *History*
Xenophon, *Mem.*	Xenophon, *Memorabilia*

Journals, Reference Works, and Serials

AASF	Annales Academicae scientiarum fennicae
AB	Anchor Bible
AbCJD	Abhandlungen zum christlich-judischen Dialog
ABD	*The Anchor Bible Dictionary,* ed. David N. Freedman, 6 vols., ABRL (New York: Doubleday, 1992)
ABRL	Anchor Bible Reference Library
ACCS.NT	Ancient Christian Commentary on Scripture: New Testament
ACNT	Augsburg Commentary on the New Testament
AGAJU	Arbeiten zur Geschichte des antiken Judentums und des Urchristentums
AGSJU	Arbeiten zur Geschichte des späteren Judentums und des Urchristentums
AJT	*American Journal of Theology*
AKG	Arbeiten zur Kirchengeschichte
AnBib	Analecta biblica

ANRW	*Aufstieg und Niedergang der römischen Welt,* ed. Wolfgang Haase and Hildegard Temporini (Berlin: Walter de Gruyter, 1895–)
ANTC	Abingdon New Testament Commentaries
ArB	The Aramaic Bible
ASE	*Annali de storia dell'esegesi*
ASeign	*Assemblées du seigneur*
ASNU	Acta seminarii neotestamentici upsaliensis
ASTI	*Annual of the Swedish Theological Institute*
ASV	American Standard Version
AT	Arbeiten zur Theologie
ATANT	Abhandlungen zur Theologie des Alten und Neuen Testaments
ATRSup	Anglican Theological Review Supplements
AusBR	*Australian Biblical Review*
AusS	Ausgewählte Schriften
AUSS	*Andrews University Seminary Studies*
AUUSDCU	Acta Universitatis Upsaliensis, Studia Doctrinae Christianae Upsaliensia
AYB	Anchor Yale Bible
AzTh	Arbeiten zur Theologie
BA	*Biblical Archaeologist*
BabT	*The Babylonian Talmud,* ed. Isidore Epstein, 34 vols. (London: Soncino Press, 1935-48)
BBR	*Bulletin of Biblical Research*
BBET	Beiträge zur biblischen Exegese und Theologie
BCBC	Believers Church Bible Commentary
BDAG	Walter Bauer, *A Greek-English Lexicon of the New Testament and Other Early Christian Literature,* 3d ed., rev. and ed. Frederick W. Danker; previously with W. F. Arndt and F. W. Gingrich (Chicago: University of Chicago Press, 2000)
BDF	Friedrich Blass, Albert Debrunner, and Robert W. Funk, *A Greek Grammar of the New Testament and Other Early Christian Literature* (Chicago: University of Chicago Press, 1961)
BECNT	Baker Exegetical Commentary on the New Testament
BETL	Bibliotheca ephemeridum theologicarum lovaniensium
BEvT	Beiträge zur evangelischen Theologie
BFCT	Beiträge zur Förderung christlicher Theologie
BHT	Beiträge zur historischen Theologie
Bib	*Biblica*
BibInt	*Biblical Interpretation*
BibIntS	Biblical Interpretation Series
BibLeb	*Bibel und Leben*
BiblSac	*Bibliotheca sacra*
BibS	*Biblical Studies*
BibSem	Biblical Seminary

BibSF	Biblische Studien (Freiburg)
BibSym	Biblica et symbiotica
BiO	Bibliotheque oecumenique
BiTod	*The Bible Today*
BIS	Biblical Interpretation Series
BJRL	*Bulletin of the John Rylands Library*
BJS	Brown Judaic Studies
BLT	*Brethren Life and Thought*
BN	*Biblische Notizen*
BNTC	Black's New Testament Commentaries
BR	*Biblical Research*
BSt	Biblische Studien
BT	*The Bible Translator*
BTB	*Biblical Theology Bulletin*
BTH	Bibliothèque de théologie historique
BThSt	Biblisch-Theologische Studien
BTN	Bibliotheca Theologica Norvegica
BWANT	Beiträge zur Wissenschaft vom Alten und Neuen Testament
BZ	*Biblische Zeitschrift*
BZNW	Beihefte zur Zeitschrift für die neutestamentliche Wissenschaft
CBC	Cambridge Bible Commentary
CBET	Contributions to Biblical Exegesis and Theology
CBQ	*Catholic Biblical Quarterly*
CBQMS	Catholic Biblical Quarterly Monograph Series
CCT	Chalice Commentaries for Today
CH	Calwer Hefte
CIG	*Corpus inscriptionum graecarum,* ed. August Boeckh et al., 5 vols. (Berlin: Officina Academica, 1828-77).
CII	*Corpus inscriptionum iudaicarum,* ed. Jean-Baptiste Frey, 2 vols. (Vatican City: Institute of Christian Archaeology, 1936-52).
CJ	*Classical Journal*
CJA	Christianity and Judaism in Antiquity
CJT	*Canadian Journal of Theology*
ConBNT	Coniectanea biblica, New Testament
ConBOT	Coniectanea biblica, Old Testament
ConNT	Coniectanea neotestamentica
Colloq	*Colloquium*
ConJ	*Concordia Journal*
CRBR	*Critical Review of Books in Religion*
CRINT	Compendia rerum iudaicarum ad novum testamentum
CSCT	Columbia Studies in the Classical Tradition
CSEL	Corpus scriptorum ecclesiasticorum latinorum
CTJ	*Calvin Theological Journal*
CTM	*Concordia Theological Monthly*

CTQ	*Concordia Theological Quarterly*
CUANTS	Catholic University of America New Testament Studies
CurrBS	*Currents in Research: Biblical Studies*
CurTM	*Currents in Theology and Mission*
CV	*Communio viatorum*
DRev	*Downside Review*
DTT	*Dansk teologisk tidsskrift*
EBib	Études bibliques
ECDSS	Eerdmans Commentary on the Dead Sea Scrolls
ECLS	Early Christian Literature Series
EdF	Erträge der Forschung
EDNT	*Exegetical Dictionary of the New Testament,* ed. Horst Balz and Gerhard Schneider, 3 vols. (Grand Rapids: Wm. B. Eerdmans, 1990-93)
EGLMBSP	*Eastern Great Lakes and Midwest Biblical Societies Proceedings*
ÉgThéol	*Église et théologie*
EHS.T	Europäische Hochschulschriften Theologie
EJT	*European Journal of Theology*
EKKNT	Evangelisch-katholischer Kommentar zum Neuen Testament
EncJud	*Encyclopedia Judaica,* 2d ed., ed. Fred Skolnik, 22 vols. (Detroit: Thomson Gale, 2007).
EncRel	*Encyclopedia of Religion,* 2d ed., ed. Lindsay Jones, 15 vols. (Farmington Hills: Thomson Gale, 2005).
EpComm	Epworth Commentaries
EPRO	Etudes préliminaires aux religions orientales dans l'empire romain
ESEC	Emory Studies in Early Christianity
ESTNT	Exegetische Studien zur Theologie des Neuen Testaments
ESV	English Standard Version
ETL	*Ephemerides theologicae lovanienses*
ETR	Études théologiques et religieuses
ETS	Erfurter theologische Studien
EvQ	*Evangelical Quarterly*
EvT	*Evangelische Theologie*
ExAud	*Ex auditu*
ExpTim	*Expository Times*
FB	Forschung zur Bibel
FBBS	Facet Books, Biblical Series
FC	Fathers of the Church
FCNTECW	Feminist Companion to the New Testament and Early Christian Writings
FGS	Forum German Series
FilNeot	*Filologia neotestamentaria*
FM	*Faith and Mission*
FRLANT	Forschungen zur Religion und Literatur des Alten und Neuen Testaments

FV	*Foi et vie*
FzAT	Forschungen zum Alten Testament
GCT	Gender, Culture, Theory
GNS	Good News Studies
GP	Gospel Perspectives
GTA	Göttinger theologische Arbeiten
HBT	*Horizons in Biblical Theology*
HDB	*Harvard Divinity Bulletin*
HDR	Harvard Dissertations in Religion
HeyJ	*Heythrop Journal*
HNT	Handbuch zum Neuen Testament
HNTC	Harper's New Testament Commentary
HO	Handbuch der Orientalistik
HT	Helps for Translators
HTKNT	Herders theologischer Kommentar zum Neuen Testament
HTR	*Harvard Theological Review*
HTS	Harvard Theological Studies
HTS	*Hervormde teologiese studies*
HUTh	Hermeneutische Untersuchungen zur Theologie
IBC	Interpretation: A Biblical Commentary for Preachers and Teachers
IBS	*Irish Biblical Studies*
ICC	International Critical Commentary
IDB	*The Interpreter's Dictionary of the Bible,* ed. George A. Buttrick, 4 vols. (Nashville: Abingdon Press, 1962)
IDBSup	*The Interpreter's Dictionary of the Bible: Supplementary Volume,* ed. Keith Crim (Nashville: Abingdon Press, 1976)
IJST	*International Journal of Systematic Theology*
IKZ	*Internationale kirchliche Zeitschrift*
Int	*Interpretation*
ISBE	*International Standard Bible Encyclopedia,* ed. Geoffrey W. Bromiley, 4 vols. (Grand Rapids: Wm. B. Eerdmans, 1979-88).
ITQ	*Irish Theological Quarterly*
IVPNTCS	InterVarsity Press New Testament Commentary Series
JAAR	*Journal of the American Academy of Religion*
JAC	*Jahrbuch für Antike und Christentum*
JB	Jerusalem Bible
JBL	*Journal of Biblical Literature*
JBT	Jahrbuch für biblische Theologie
JCE	*Journal of Christian Ethics*
JETS	*Journal of the Evangelical Theological Society*
JNES	*Journal of Near Eastern Studies*
JR	*Journal of Religion*
JRS	*Journal of Roman Studies*
JSJ	*Journal for the Study of Judaism*

JSJSup	Supplements to the Journal for the Study of Judaism
JSNT	*Journal for the Study of the New Testament*
JSNTSup	Journal for the Study of the New Testament — Supplement Series
JSPSup	Journal for the Study of the Pseudepigrapha — Supplement Series
JSS	*Journal of Semitic Studies*
JST	*Journal for the Study of Judaism*
JTS	*Journal of Theological Studies*
JTSA	*Journal of Theology for Southern Africa*
Jud	*Judaica*
KBANT	Kommentare und Beiträge zum Alten und Neuen Testament
KD	*Kerygma und Dogma*
KEK	Kritische-evangelischer Kommentar über das Neue Testament
KGMG	Kirchengeschichte als Missionsgeschichte
KJV	King James Version
KNT	Kommentar zum Neuen Testament
KuD	*Kerygma und Dogma*
LBS	Linguistic Biblical Studies
LCL	Loeb Classical Library
LD	Lectio divina
LEC	Library of Early Christianity
LN	Johannes Louw and Eugene A. Nida, *Greek-English Lexicon of the New Testament Based on Semantic Domains,* 2d ed. (New York: United Bible Societies, 1989)
LNTS	Library of New Testament Studies
LPS	Library of Pauline Studies
LS	*Louvain Studies*
LSJ	Henry G. Liddell and Robert Scott, *A Greek-English Lexicon,* rev. Henry S. Jones (Oxford: Clarendon Press, 1968)
LSTS	Library of Second Temple Studies
LTJ	*Lutheran Theological Journal*
LTPM	Louvain Theological and Pastoral Monographs
LTQ	*Lexington Theological Quarterly*
LUÅ	*Lunds universitets årsskrift*
LuthW	*Luther's Works,* ed. Jaroslav Pelikan, Helmut T. Lehmann, et al., 55 vols. (St. Louis: Concordia Publishing House; Philadelphia: Muhlenberg Press, 1955-76)
LV	*Lumen vitae*
LW	*Lutheran World*
LXX	The Septuagint
LZ	*Lebendiges Zeugnis*
m.	*The Mishnah*
MBPS	Mellen Biblical Press Series
MdB	Le monde de la Bible
MeyerK	Meyer Kommentar

MM	James H. Moulton and George Milligan, *The Vocabulary of the Greek Testament* (Grand Rapids: Wm. B. Eerdmans, 1930; reprinted, Peabody: Hendrickson Publishers, 1997)
MNTS	McMaster New Testament Studies
MT	Masoretic Text
MTZ	*Münchener theologische Zeitschrift*
NAB	New American Bible
NASV	New American Standard Version
NCB	New Century Bible
NCBC	New Century Bible Commentary
NCCS	New Covenant Commentary Series
NEB	New English Bible
NEchtB	Neue Echter Bibel
Neot	*Neotestamentica*
NESTTR	*Near Eastern School of Theology Theological Review*
NET	New English Translation (NET Bible)
NIB	*The New Interpreter's Bible,* ed. Leander E. Keck, 12 vols. (Nashville: Abingdon Press, 1994-2004)
NIBCNT	New International Biblical Commentary, New Testament
NICNT	New International Commentary on the New Testament
NIDB	*The New Interpreter's Dictionary of the Bible,* ed. Katharine Doob Sakenfeld, 5 vols. (Nashville: Abingdon Press, 2006–).
NIGTC	New International Greek Testament Commentary
NIV	New International Version
NJB	New Jerusalem Bible
NKJV	New King James Version
NKZ	*Neue kirchliche Zeitschrift*
NorTT	*Norsk teologisk tidsskrift*
NovT	*Novum Testamentum*
NovTSup	Novum Testamentum Supplements
NPAJ	New Perspectives on Ancient Judaism
NPNF	*A Select Library of the Nicene and Post-Nicene Fathers,* ed. Philip Schaff, 14 vols. (New York: Christian Literature Company, 1888-90)
NRSV	New Revised Standard Version
NRT	*Nouvelle revue théologique*
NStB	Neukirchener Studienbücher
NSBT	New Studies in Biblical Theology
NT	New Testament
NTAbh	Neutestamentliche Abhandlungen
NTApoc	*New Testament Apocrypha,* ed. Wilhelm Schneemelcher, 2d ed., 2 vols. (Louisville: Westminster John Knox, 1991)
NTD	Das Neues Testament Deutsch
NTG	New Testament Guides
NTL	New Testament Library

NTM	New Testament Message
NTMs	New Testament Monographs
NTOA	Novum Testamentum et orbis antiquus
NTR	*New Theology Review*
NTRG	New Testament Reading Guide
NTS	*New Testament Studies*
NTSR	New Testament for Spiritual Reading
NTT	*Norsk teologisk tidsskrift*
NTTS	New Testament Tools and Studies
OCD	*Oxford Classical Dictionary,* ed. Simon Hornblower and Anthony Spawforth, rev. 3d ed. (New York: Oxford University Press, 2003)
OEANE	*Oxford Encyclopedia of Archaeology in the Near East,* ed. Eric M. Meyers, 5 vols. (New York: Oxford University Press, 1997)
OED	*The Oxford English Dictionary,* 2d ed., ed. J. A. Simpson and E. S. C. Weiner, 20 vols. (Oxford: Clarendon Press, 1989)
OT	Old Testament
OTL	Old Testament Library
OTP	*The Old Testament Pseudepigrapha,* ed. James H. Charlesworth, 2 vols. (Garden City: Doubleday and Company, 1983-85)
PAST	Pauline Studies
PBM	Paternoster Biblical Monographs
PCC	Paul in Critical Contexts
PEccl	*Pro Ecclesia*
PG	*Patrologia graeca,* ed. Jacques-Paul Migne, 161 vols. (Turnhout, Belg.: Brepols [and other imprints], 1857-66)
PGL	*A Patristic Greek Lexicon,* ed. G. W. H. Lampe (Oxford: Clarendon Press, 1961)
PIBA	*Proceedings of the Irish Biblical Association*
PL	*Patrologia latina,* ed. Jacques-Paul Migne, 217 vols. (Turnhout, Belg.: Brepols [and other imprints], 1844-55)
PMS	Patristic Monograph Series
PNTC	Pillar New Testament Commentary
ProtoBib	*Protokolle zur Bibel*
PRS	*Perspectives in Religious Studies*
PS	Patristic Studies
PSB	*Princeton Seminary Bulletin*
PSBSup	Princeton Seminary Bulletin Supplement Series
PTMS	Pittsburgh Theological Monograph Series
PVTG	Pseudepigrapha veteris Testamenti Graece
QD	Quaestiones disputatae
QR	*Quarterly Review*
RB	*Revue biblique*
REB	Revised English Bible
RefRev	*Reformed Review*

ResQ	*Restoration Quarterly*
RevExp	*Review and Expositor*
RevQ	*Revue de Qumran*
RGG⁴	*Religion in Geschichte und Gegenwart,* 4th ed., ed. Hans D. Betz (Tübingen: J. C. B. Mohr [Paul Siebeck], 1998–)
RHCS	Romans through History and Culture Series
RHPR	*Revue d'histoire et de philosophie religieuses*
RivB	*Rivista biblica*
RL	*Religion in Life*
RNT	Regensburger Neues Testament
RRef	*Revue réformée*
RRBS	Recent Research in Biblical Studies
RSPT	*Revue des sciences philosophiques et théologique*
RSV	Revised Standard Version
RTR	*Reformed Theological Review*
RVV	Religionsgeschichtliche Versuche und Vorarbeiten
SAIS	Studies in the Aramaic Interpretation of Scripture
SANT	Studien zum Alten und Neuen Testament
SB	Sources bibliques
SBEC	Studies in the Bible and Early Christianity
SBLAB	Society of Biblical Literature Academia Biblica
SBLDS	Society of Biblical Literature Dissertation Series
SBLRBS	Society of Biblical Literature Resources for Biblical Study
SBLSBS	Society of Biblical Literature Sources for Biblical Study
SBLSCS	Society of Biblical Literature Sources for Septuagint and Cognate Studies
SBLSP	Society of Biblical Literature Seminar Papers
SBLSS	Society of Biblical Literature Semeia Series
SBLSymS	Society of Biblical Literature Symposium Series
SBL.TT	Society of Biblical Literature Texts and Translations
SBS	Stuttgarter Bibelstudien
SBT	Studies in Biblical Theology
SC	Sources chrétiennes
SCJ	*Stone-Campbell Journal*
SD	Studies and Documents
SE	*Studia Evangelica*
SEÅ	*Svensk exegetisk årsbok*
SESJ	Suomen eksegeettisen seuran julkaisuja
SF	Studia fribirgensia
SFSHJ	South Florida Studies in the History of Judaism
SHBC	Smyth and Helwys Bible Commentary
SHLL	Societatis humaniorum litterarum Lundensis
SIGU	Studien zur interkulturellen Geschichte des Urchristentums
SJLA	Studies in Judaism in Late Antiquity

SJT	*Scottish Journal of Theology*
SJTOP	Scottish Journal of Theology Occasional Papers
SKHVL	Skrifter utgivna av Kungliga Humanistika vetenskapssamfundet Lund
SKKNT	Stuttgarter kleiner Kommentar, Neues Testament
SM	*Studia missionalia*
SNT	Studien zum Neuen Testament
SNTSMS	Society for New Testament Studies Monograph Series
SNTW	Studies of the New Testament and Its World
SNTU	Studien zum Neuen Testament und seiner Umwelt
SPB	Studia Post-Biblica
SPS	Sacra Pagina Series
SR	*Studies in Religion/Sciences religieuses*
SSEJC	*Studies in Early Judaism and Christianity*
SSRH	Sociological Studies in Roman History
SST	Studies in Sacred Theology
ST	*Studia theologica*
STDJ	Studies on the Texts of the Desert of Judah
Str-B	Hermann L. Strack and Paul Billerbeck, *Kommentar zum Neuen Testament aus Talmud und Midrasch,* 6 vols. (Munich: C. H. Beck'sche, 1922-61)
StudBL	Studies in Biblical Literature
StudBT	*Studia biblica et theologica*
StudNeot	Studia neotestamentica
SuppJSJ	Supplements to the Journal for the Study of Judaism
SVTQ	*St. Vladimir's Theological Quarterly*
TBei	*Theologische Beiträge*
TBü	Theologische Bücherei
TBC	Torch Bible Commentaries
TBN	Themes in Biblical Narrative
TBT	*The Bible Today*
TD	*Theology Digest*
TDNT	*Theological Dictionary of the New Testament,* ed. Gerhard Kittel and Gerhard Friedrich, 10 vols. (Grand Rapids: Wm. B. Eerdmans, 1964-76)
TDOT	*Theological Dictionary of the Old Testament,* ed. G. Johannes Botterweck, Helmer Ringgren, et al., 15 vols. (Grand Rapids: Wm. B. Eerdmans, 1974-2006)
TEH	Theologische Existenz Heute
TEV	Today's English Version
TGl	*Theologie und Glaube*
Theol	*Theology*
THNT	Theologischer Handkommentar zum Neuen Testament
ThR	*Theologische Rundschau*
ThStud	Theologische Studien

ThViat	*Theologia viatorum*
TJ	*Trinity Journal*
TJT	*Toronto Journal of Theology*
TK	*Texte und Kontexte*
TLG	*Thesaurus linguae graecae*
TLOT	*Theological Lexicon of the Old Testament*, ed. Ernst Jenni and Claus Westermann, 3 vols. (Peabody: Hendrickson Publishers, 1997)
TLZ	*Theologische Literaturzeitung*
TNTC	Tyndale New Testament Commentary
TPINTC	Trinity Press International New Testament Commentaries
TQ	*Theologische Quartalschrift*
TR	Theology and Religion
TRE	*Theologische Realenzyklopädie*, ed. Gerhard Krause et al. (New York: Walter de Gruyter, 1977–)
TS	*Texts and Studies*
TS	*Theological Studies*
TSK	*Theologische Studien und Kritiken*
TSR	*Trinity Seminary Review*
TST	Toronto Studies in Theology
TTK	*Tidsskrift for Teologi og Kirke*
TTZ	*Trierer theologische Zeitschrift*
TU	Texte und Untersuchungen
TUGAL	Texte und Untersuchungen zur Geschichte der altchristlichen Literatur
TW	Theologische Wissenschaft
TynB	*Tyndale Bulleltin*
TZ	*Theologische Zeitschrift*
UNT	Untersuchungen zum Neuen Testament
VC	*Vigiliae christianae*
VD	*Verbum domini*
VTSup	Vetus Testamentum Supplements
WBC	Word Biblical Commentary
WTJ	*Westminster Theological Journal*
WD	*Wort und Dienst*
WMANT	Wissenschaftliche Monographien zum Alten und Neuen Testament
WUNT	Wissenschaftliche Untersuchungen zum Neuen Testament
WW	*Word and World*
WWSup	Word and World Supplement Series
ZAW	*Zeitschrift für die alttestamentliche Wissenschaft*
ZEE	*Zeitschrift für evangelische Ethik*
ZNT	*Zeitschrift für Neues Testament*
ZNW	*Zeitschrift für die neutestamentliche Wissenschaft*
ZST	*Zeitschrift für systematische Theologie*
ZTK	*Zeitschrift für Theologie und Kirche*
ZWT	*Zeitschrift für wissenschaftliche Theologie*

Abbreviations for Frequently Cited Commentaries and Studies

P. Achtemeier, *Romans*   Paul J. Achtemeier, *Romans,* IBC (Atlanta: John Knox Press, 1985)

C. K. Barrett, *Romans*   C. K. Barrett, *The Epistle to the Romans,* 2d ed., BNTC (Peabody: Hendrickson Publishers, 1991)

K. Barth, *Romans*   Karl Barth, *The Epistle to the Romans* (London: Oxford University Press, 1968)

E. Best, *Romans*   Ernest Best, *The Letter of Paul to the Romans,* CBC (Cambridge: Cambridge University Press, 1967)

M. Black, *Romans*   Matthew Black, *Romans,* 2d ed., NCBC (Grand Rapids: Wm. B. Eerdmans, 1989)

R. Brown, *Introduction*   Raymond E. Brown, *An Introduction to the New Testament,* ABRL (New York: Doubleday, 1997)

F. F. Bruce, *Romans*   F. F. Bruce, *The Epistle of Paul to the Romans,* TNTC 6 (London: Tyndale Press, 1963)

E. Brunner, *Romans*   Emil Brunner, *The Letter to the Romans: A Commentary* (Philadelphia: Westminster Press, 1959)

B. Byrne, *Romans*   Brendan Byrne, *Romans,* SPS 6 (Collegeville: Liturgical Press, 1996)

J. Cobb and D. Lull, *Romans*   John B. Cobb Jr. and David Lull, *Romans,* CCT (St. Louis: Chalice Press, 2005)

C. Cranfield, *Romans*   C. E. B. Cranfield, *A Critical and Exegetical Commentary on the Epistle to the Romans,* ICC, 2 vols. (Edinburgh: T&T Clark, 1979)

C. H. Dodd, *Romans*   C. H. Dodd, *The Epistle to the Romans* (New York: Long & Smith, 1932)

J. Dunn, *Romans*   James D. G. Dunn, *Romans,* WBC 38, 2 vols. (Dallas: Word Books, 1988)

P. Esler, *Romans*   Philip F. Esler, *Conflict and Identity in Romans: The Social Setting of Paul's Letter* (Minneapolis: Fortress Press, 2003)

J. Fitzmyer, *Romans*	Joseph A. Fitzmyer, *Romans,* AB 33 (New York: Doubleday, 1993)
K. Haacker, *Römer*	Klaus Haacker, *Der Brief des Paulus an die Römer,* THNT 6 (Leipzig: Evangelische Verlagsanstalt, 1999)
R. Harrisville, *Romans*	Roy A. Harrisville, *Romans,* ACNT (Minneapolis: Augsburg Publishing House, 1980)
J. Heil, *Romans*	John P. Heil, *Paul's Letter to the Romans: A Reader-Response Commentary* (New York: Paulist Press, 1987)
L. Johnson, *Romans*	Luke Timothy Johnson, *Reading Romans: A Literary and Theological Commentary* (New York: Crossroad, 1997)
E. Käsemann, *Romans*	Ernst Käsemann, *Commentary on Romans* (Grand Rapids: Wm. B. Eerdmans, 1980)
C. Keener, *Romans*	Craig S. Keener, *Romans,* NCCS 6 (Eugene: Cascade Books, 2009)
J. Knox, *IB (Romans)*	John Knox, *Romans,* in *The Interpreter's Bible,* ed. George Buttrick, 12 vols. (Nashville: Abingdon Press, 1955), 9:355-668.
W. Kümmel, *Introduction*	Werner G. Kümmel, *Introduction to the New Testament* rev. ed. (Nashville: Abingdon Press, 1975)
O. Kuss, *Römer*	Otto Kuss, *Der Römerbrief,* 2d ed., RNT 6, 3 vols. (Regensburg: F. Pustet, 1963)
M.-J. Lagrange, *Romains*	Marie-Joseph Lagrange, *Saint Paul: Épître aux Romains,* 4th ed., ÉBib (Paris: J. Gabalda, 1931; reprinted 1950)
S. Légasse, *Romains*	Simon Légasse, *L'épître de Paul aux Romains,* LD 10 (Paris: Cerf, 2002)
E. Lohse, *Römer*	Eduard Lohse, *Der Brief an die Römer,* KEK 4 (Göttingen: Vandenhoeck & Ruprecht, 2003)
M. Luther, *Romans*	Martin Luther, *Lectures on Romans,* in *Luther's Works,* ed. Jaroslav Pelikan et al., 55 vols. (St. Louis: Concordia Publishing House; Philadelphia: Fortress Press, 1955-76), 25:1-560.
F. Matera, *Romans*	Frank J. Matera, *Romans,* Paideia Commentaries on the New Testament (Grand Rapids: Baker Academic, 2010)
B. Metzger, *TCGNT*	Bruce M. Metzger, *A Textual Commentary on the Greek New Testament,* 2d ed. (Stuttgart: Deutsche Bibelgesellschaft, 1994)
O. Michel, *Römer*	Otto Michel, *Der Brief an die Römer,* 11th ed., KEK 4 (Göttingen: Vandenhoeck & Ruprecht, 1957)
D. Moo, *Romans*	Douglas J. Moo, *The Epistle to the Romans,* NICNT (Grand Rapids: Wm. B. Eerdmans, 1996)
L. Morris, *Romans*	Leon Morris, *The Epistle to the Romans,* PNTC (Grand Rapids: Wm. B. Eerdmans, 1988)
J. Murray, *Romans*	John Murray, *The Epistle to the Romans,* 2 vols. (Grand Rapids: Wm. B. Eerdmans, 1959)

A. Nygren, *Romans*	Anders Nygren, *A Commentary on Romans* (Philadelphia: Muhlenberg Press, 1949)
J. O'Neill, *Romans*	John C. O'Neill, *Paul's Letter to the Romans* (Harmondsworth: Penguin, 1975)
G. Osborne, *Romans*	Grant R. Osborne, *Romans,* IVPNTCS (Downers Grove: InterVarsity Press, 2004)
W. Sanday and A. Headlam, *Romans*	William Sanday and Arthur C. Headlam, *A Critical and Exegetical Commentary on the Epistle to the Romans,* 5th ed., ICC (Edinburgh: T&T Clark, 1902)
A. Schlatter, *Romans*	Adolf Schlatter, *Romans: The Righteousness of God* (Peabody: Hendrickson Publishers, 1995)
H. Schlier, *Römer*	Heinrich Schlier, *Der Römerbrief: Kommentar,* HTKNT 6 (Freiburg im Breisgau: Herder, 1977)
W. Schmithals, *Römer*	Walter Schmithals, *Der Römerbrief: Ein Kommentar* (Gütersloh: Gütersloher Verlagshaus Gerd Mohn, 1988)
T. Schreiner, *Romans*	Thomas R. Schreiner, *Romans* (Grand Rapids: Baker Book House, 1998)
P. Stuhlmacher, *Romans*	Peter Stuhlmacher, *Paul's Letter to the Romans: A Commentary* (Louisville: Westminster/John Knox, 1994)
C. Talbert, *Romans*	Charles H. Talbert, *Romans,* SHBC (Macon: Smyth & Helwys Publishing, 2002)
M. Theobald, *Römerbrief*	Theobald, Michael. *Römerbrief.* SKKNT 6, 2 vols. (Stuttgart: Verlag Katholisches Bibelwerk, 1992-93)
J. Toews, *Romans*	John E. Toews, *Romans,* BCBC (Scottdale: Herald Press, 2004)
U. Wilckens, *Römer*	Ulrich Wilckens, *Der Brief an die Römer,* EKK 6, 3 vols. (Neukirchen-Vluyn: Neukirchener Verlag, 1978-82)
B. Witherington, *Romans*	Ben Witherington III, *Paul's Letter to the Romans: A Socio-Rhetorical Commentary* (Grand Rapids: Wm. B. Eerdmans, 2003)
N. T. Wright, *NIB (Romans)*	N. Thomas Wright, *Romans,* in *The New Interpreter's Bible,* ed. Leander E. Keck, 12 vols. (Nashville: Abingdon Press, 1994-2004), 10:395-770.
D. Zeller, *Römer*	Dieter Zeller, *Der Brief an die Römer übersetz und erklärt,* RNT (Regensburg: Friedrich Pustet, 1985)
J. Ziesler, *Romans*	John A. Ziesler, *Paul's Letter to the Romans,* TPINTC (Philadelphia: Trinity Press International, 1989)

Introduction

The Letter to the Romans is the longest of the letters attributed to Paul the apostle, and it stands — probably for that very reason — first in the usual sequence of his letters in the NT.[1] In fact, it is the longest of all the letters in the NT and also stands first among them.

Romans is also the most well known and most widely investigated of Paul's letters by those who seek to know his gospel and theology. Furthermore, within the history of the church, no other book in the NT (with the possible exception of any of the four gospels) has exceeded Romans for its theological claims and impact. The constructive theological work and reforming activities of major figures in church history — such as Augustine, Martin Luther, John Wesley, and Karl Barth — cannot be explained except that those persons were ignited and affected deeply by the study of Paul's Letter to the Romans.[2]

Introductory questions concerning Romans that need to be addressed have to do with the time, place, and purpose of the letter, but the question of authorship need not be, except in reference to certain portions of the letter. That is taken up below (section 3, "Romans 16 in Light of Textual Criticism"). Other than that, one can say that if there ever was an apostle Paul, and if he wrote anything that has remained for subsequent generations, he wrote Romans. Paul's authorship of the letter has never been seriously disputed. It remains as one of

---

1. On the ordering of the letters of Paul and others in the New Testament, cf. H. Gamble, "The Canon of the New Testament," 201-43, and the various works cited there.

2. The history of interpretation is covered in part in essays in the book edited by J. Greenman and T. Larsen, *Reading Romans through the Centuries: From the Early Church to Karl Barth*. Various facets in the history of interpretation are discussed in M. Reasoner, *Romans in Full Circle*. Cf. also R. Jewett, "Major Impulses in the Theological Interpretation of Romans since Barth," 1-31, and the long list of commentaries provided by J. Fitzmyer, *Romans*, 173-214.

the seven "undisputed" letters of Paul along with 1 and 2 Corinthians, Galatians, Philippians, 1 Thessalonians, and Philemon.[3]

1. Time and Place of Composition

It is widely accepted that the letter falls late in Paul's career. It reflects a mature Paul. As various interpreters have pointed out, topics taken up in Romans appear in his other letters, but here they are less polemic in tone and consist of more seasoned reflections.[4]

Most information concerning the time and place of composition comes from 15:14-33. At 15:19 Paul says that he has preached the gospel from Jerusalem to Illyricum. The latter area lies west of Macedonia, encompassing much of modern Albania. By saying that he has done missionary work between these two points, Paul implies that he has worked within Asia Minor, Greece, and Macedonia. He says that there is no more room for him to continue working in the East (15:23). Moreover, he indicates that he wishes now to travel to Rome and on to Spain (15:24, 28). But first he must go to Jerusalem with a collection from the churches of Macedonia (Philippi and Thessalonica) and Achaia (Corinth), which he had intended to obtain (Gal 2:10) and has now concluded (15:25-26).

The information in Romans can be supplemented from other sources. According to Acts 20:3, Paul resided for three months in Greece prior to his going to Jerusalem. The location within Greece was probably Corinth, since he had written in 1 Corinthians that he would receive a collection from the community there upon his arrival and would then go on to Jerusalem (1 Cor 16:1-4). From what Paul says in Romans, the contribution from Corinth has already been acquired, and he is ready to go to Jerusalem (15:25-26). Corinth emerges, then, as a quite likely place for Paul to have written Romans. That is confirmed by Paul's references to two other persons at the time of writing Romans. The first is a man named Gaius who sends greetings to Rome. Paul says that this man is "host (ξένος) to me and to the whole church" (16:23). Since Gaius sends greetings by way of the letter, he is clearly Paul's host at the time that Paul writes

---

3. Concerning the distinction between "undisputed" and "disputed" letters of Paul, scholarly opinions differ. Nevertheless, there has been a growing consensus in modern scholarship to include the seven letters mentioned as "undisputed." The question whether any of the "disputed" letters were written by Paul in whole or in part continues. For discussion, see W. Kümmel, *Introduction,* 250-387; R. Brown, *Introduction,* 585-680; or C. Roetzel, *The Letters of Paul,* 133-60.

4. G. Bornkamm, *Paul,* 93-94, lists seven topics and themes in Romans that appear in other undisputed letters of Paul; he lists 16 in his essay, "The Letter to the Romans," 23-24. J. Fitzmyer, *Romans,* 71-73, lists 64 phrases and themes that appear in other letters of Paul. References to previous positions that Paul had taken and are referred to in various letters of Paul, prior to and including Romans, have been gathered by J. Plevnik, "Pauline Presuppositions," 51-53.

the Letter to the Romans. The Gaius mentioned is most likely the person by that name whom Paul had baptized in Corinth (1 Cor 1:14).[5] He was then still living in Corinth when Paul wrote the letter.

The other person of note to mention is Phoebe (Rom 16:1-2). She is called a deacon (διάκονος) of the church at Cenchreae, the port of Corinth, and benefactor (προστάτις) of Paul and other Christians. Paul asks the Roman Christians to receive her and to help her in whatever she needs. It is highly likely that she is the bearer of the letter.[6] That would also mean that she was entrusted by Paul to comment on anything in the letter that could not be understood, making her the first exegete of the Letter to the Romans. Moreover, she would be able to supplement the letter on behalf of Paul whenever the need arose, filling in any gaps, telling the members of the Roman house churches of Paul's views and plans in more detail. Since Cenchreae was the port of ancient Corinth, that points again to Corinth or its environs as the place of composition of the letter.

There is widespread agreement that Paul wrote the letter somewhere between A.D. 55 and 58 from Corinth.[7] That fits well with data in the NT and beyond, including references to Prisca (called Priscilla in Acts) and Aquila, Jewish Christians, to whom Paul sends greeting in his letter to Rome (16:3). The emperor Claudius had expelled Jews (both Christian Jews and Jews who did not convert) from Rome, as mentioned in both Acts (18:2-3) and the writings of Suetonius.[8] That event would have happened in A.D. 49.[9] According to Suetonius, the expulsion was due to disturbances (*tumultuantes*) among Jews concerning "Chrestus." The event most likely refers to a highly contentious dis-

5. He could also be the Gaius of Derbe mentioned by Luke (Acts 20:6).

6. Illustrations from the Oxyrhynchus Papyri demonstrate that in antiquity letter carriers were routinely expected to provide additional information and explanations of the letters that they carried. Cf. P. Head, "Named Letter-Carriers among the Oxyrhynchus Papyri," 279-99.

7. Cf. W. Kümmel, *Introduction*, 311 (Corinth, "spring of 55 or 56"); E. Käsemann, *Romans*, 14 (Corinth, but no date given); C. Cranfield, *Romans*, 12-16 (Corinth, 55-56 or 56-57); E. Best, *Romans*, 8 (Corinth, 55-59); R. Harrisville, *Romans*, 15 (Corinth, 58); J. Dunn, *Romans*, xliii-xliv (Corinth, "late 55/early 56 or late 56/early 57"); J. Fitzmyer, *Romans*, 85-88 (Corinth, mid to late 50s); D. Zeller, *Römer*, 12-15 (Corinth, 55-57); A. Wedderburn, *The Reasons for Romans*, 63 (Corinth, 57 or 58); J. Ziesler, *Romans*, 18-19 (Corinth, mid to late 50s); B. Byrne, *Romans*, 8-9 (Corinth, 54-59, early 58 "most likely"); E. Lohse, *Römer*, 42 (Corinth, 56); G. Theissen, *Introduction*, 56 (Corinth, "55/56"); U. Schnelle, *Apostle Paul*, 305; R. Jewett, *Romans*, 18 (Corinth, "winter of 56-57 C.E. or the early spring of 57"); F. Matera, *Romans*, 5 (Corinth, late winter/early spring of 56).

8. Suetonius, *Claudius* 25.15: "Iudaeos impulsore Chresto assidue tumultuantes Roma expulit."

9. The source concerning this claim is a statement of the fifth-century historian Orosius, *Hist.* 7.6.15-16, where he comments on the account of Suetonius and places the expulsion in the ninth year of the reign of Claudius, which would have run from January 25 of the year 49 through January 24 of the year 50.

pute, causing civil disruptions, between Jews who had become Christians and Jews who had not, a controversy concerning whether Jesus was the Christ.[10] It would have been after that event that Paul met Prisca and Aquila in Corinth. They were Jewish Christians from Italy (Acts 18:2), Luke says. And it would have been during that time that Paul could have learned considerable details about the situation of the Christians in Rome.

In addition to referring to Paul's being in Rome at the same time as Prisca and Aquila, Luke writes that Paul was present in Corinth when Gallio was proconsul of Achaia (Acts 18:12). Gallio's term of office is known to have been from the spring of A.D. 51 to the spring of 52.[11] Moreover, Luke indicates that Paul was there for eighteen months (18:11). Those eighteen months could have begun as early as the autumn of 49 and ended as early as the spring of 51, or they could have begun as late as the spring of 52 and extended to the fall of 53 — or anywhere in between. Following upon that time, Paul's travels took him to Ephesus, Syria, Jerusalem, and Antioch (Acts 18:18-22). Then he traveled through Asia Minor (18:23) and settled in Ephesus for two to three years (19:10; 20:31). Finally, he entered into Macedonia and went on to Greece (20:1-2), where he stayed for three months (20:3), presumably in Corinth, the most certain location for the writing of his Letter to the Romans. Allowing for several months of travel and visitations prior to his stay in Ephesus, the time of his residing there could have been anywhere from A.D. 52 to 56, and his arrival in Corinth shortly after his departure from Ephesus.

One more historical matter adds to what can be known concerning the date of writing the letter. After the death of Claudius in 54, Jews and Jewish Christians began to return to Rome.[12] Among them were Prisca and Aquila, the first on the list of the persons to whom Paul sends greetings (16:3), and who are already heading a house church when Paul greets them (Rom 16:3-5). This would place the earliest date for writing the letter at some time after the return of Jews and Jewish Christians to Rome. On the other hand, the latest date of writing the letter would be just prior to Paul's final trip from Corinth to Jerusalem with the collection. The time of writing could have been any time between A.D. 55 and 58.

---

10. A thorough exegesis of the text of Suetonius is provided by P. Lampe, *From Paul to Valentinus*, 11-16, and a detailed discussion is carried on by J. Barclay, *Jews in the Mediterranean Diaspora*, 303-6. A brief survey of interpretations of the text of Suetonius has been made by L. Rutgers, "Roman Policy toward the Jews," 105-6. Perhaps the most forceful rejection of the usual interpretation is that of D. Slingerland, "Chrestus: Christus?" 133-43, who has proposed that Chrestus was the name of the instigator of the expulsion. A response to his proposal has been made by D. Noy, *Foreigners at Rome*, 42-43.

11. For information and discussion, cf. Klaus Haacker, "Gallio," *ABD* 2:901-3.

12. H. Lichtenberger, "Jews and Christians in Rome in the Time of Nero," 2168.

2. Character and Purpose of the Letter

In recent years there have been various proposals concerning the kind of letter Romans appears to be within the general sphere of ancient epistolography. Interpreters have suggested various models to help understand it. Robert Jewett has called it an "ambassadorial letter" in which Paul expresses a missionary diplomacy to enlist the Roman Christians in his mission to Spain.[13] M. Luther Stirewalt has called it a "letter essay,"[14] while Joseph Fitzmyer has suggested that it is an "essay letter."[15] But one wonders how fruitful the suggestions are among the multitude of possible epistolary types of the ancient world.[16] According to Pseudo-Demetrius, whose work comes anywhere from the second century B.C. to the third century A.D., no fewer than 21 types of letters were common in antiquity, and according to Pseudo-Libanius, whose work comes from the fourth to sixth centuries A.D., 41 types could be found.[17] Perhaps it is sufficient to follow Gerd Theissen, who has called Romans "a treatise in the form of a letter."[18] It has epistolary features, especially at the beginning and the end, but much of it is a discourse on matters of faith.

Other interpreters have opted to speak of Romans in light of ancient rhetorical models, saying that Romans is an epideictic (or demonstrative) letter, in which an orator or author celebrates values held in common between the addressee and himself.[19] Nevertheless, the letter does not necessarily fit into any model precisely.[20] Furthermore, as one observer has remarked, it is "not what conforms to the rules, but what seems at variance with them" that "often proves

---

13. R. Jewett, "Romans as an Ambassadorial Letter," 5-20; idem, "Following the Argument of Romans," 266; idem, *Romans*, 42-46. In the latter Jewett speaks of a fusion of the ambassadorial letter with other subtypes, such as a paraenetic letter and a philosophical diatribe.

14. M. L. Stirewalt, *Paul the Letter Writer*, 107-12. On the form, see his essay, "The Form and Function of the Greek Letter-Essay," 147-71.

15. J. Fitzmyer, *Romans*, 69-71.

16. The study of ancient epistolary types can be illustrative, but one must also recognize the limitations that the types represent for comparative work in the study of letters in early Christianity; so S. Stowers, *Letter Writing in Greco-Roman Antiquity*, 56.

17. For texts, cf. Pseudo-Demetrius, "Epistolary Types," and Pseudo-Libanius, "Epistolary Styles," in A. Malherbe, *Ancient Epistolary Theorists*, 30-31 and 66-67, respectively.

18. G. Theissen, *Introduction*, 81, 87. Similarly, L. Keck, *Romans*, 23, has called it "a discourse within a letter."

19. W. Wuellner, "Paul's Rhetoric of Argumentation," 134-35, 139; B. Byrne, *Romans*, 16-18; L. Keck, *Romans*, 22.

20. In terms of the other options among ancient rhetorical models (judicial and deliberative), as set out by ancient rhetorical theorists, the epideictic is probably the closest to describe Romans. Types of rhetoric and references to ancient theorists are surveyed by D. Aune, *The New Testament in Its Literary Environment*, 198-99.

most instructive for the interpretation."[21] Paul uses a large number of rhetorical and other literary conventions (such as diatribe, paraenesis, creedal formulas, and epistolary *topoi* [commonplaces]) to persuade and otherwise communicate with his readers, and these should be noticed as the letter is read.

Why Paul's Letter to the Romans should ever have come into being — and what it was for — has been a puzzle for interpreters for a long time. In his *Loci communes* of 1521 Philip Melanchthon called it a *doctrinae Christianae compendium* ("compendium of Christian doctrine").[22] That view is no longer generally held, but what to replace it with is debated. There have been monographs on the question of Paul's purpose in writing the letter,[23] and every major commentary takes up the question. In order to discern Paul's purpose in writing the letter, it is important to attend to some of the basic data within the letter and then to consider Paul's situation and that of his readers.

2.1. Basic Data in the Letter

Chapters 1 and 15 contain some clear notations about Paul's purpose in writing to the Christians at Rome. Paul tells his readers that he intends to come to their city and then go on from there to Spain (15:24, 28). In fact, he says that he has been planning to do so for many years (15:23; cf. 1:10, 15). At the time of writing, he expresses the hope that he will be received by the Roman Christians (15:29), anticipates the enjoyment of their company for a while (15:24, 32; cf. 1:12), and hopes that they will speed him on from there as he goes to Spain (15:24). From these basic data, it is clear that the most explicit purpose of the letter was to inform the Roman community of Paul's plan to arrive in Rome eventually and to go on from there to Spain.

When Paul writes that he hopes to be "sent on" (προπεμφθῆναι) to Spain by the Christians in Rome (15:24), it can mean only one thing. He is hoping to obtain financial support from them, since the word translated "to send on" (προπέμπω) means "to assist someone in making a journey, send on one's way with food, money, by arranging for companions, means of travel, etc." (cf. 1 Cor 16:6, 11; 2 Cor 1:16; Titus 3:13; 3 John 6).[24]

---

21. C. Classen, *Rhetorical Criticism of the New Testament*, 27.

22. Philip Melanchthon, *Loci communes 1521*, in *Melanchthons Werke*, ed. Hans Engelland, 7 vols. (Gütersloh: C. Bertelsmann Verlag, 1951-75), 2.7.25; English ed., *The Loci Communes of Philipp Melanchthon*, trans. Charles L. Hill (Boston: Meador Publishing Company, 1944), 69.

23. These include A. Wedderburn, *The Reasons for Romans*; L. Jervis, *The Purpose of Romans*; L-k. Lo, *Paul's Purpose in Writing Romans*; and J. Miller, *The Obedience of Faith*. Many of the essays in *The Romans Debate*, ed. K. Donfried, take up the question of purpose as well.

24. BDAG 873 (προπέμπω).

2.2. Paul's Situation

In addition to saying that he is going to Jerusalem with the collection raised in his churches in Macedonia and Greece (15:25-26), Paul asks for the prayers of the Roman Christians that his travels in Judea will be safe and that the church at Jerusalem will accept the gift he brings (15:30-31). It is important for him that the collection be received as a sign of unity between the Jerusalem church and his Gentile congregations.[25] He speaks explicitly of his collection as a sign of "fellowship" (κοινωνία) on two occasions (2 Cor 8:4; 9:13).

2.3. The Christian Community in Rome

The community of Christians was located within a large international population at Rome. Estimates of the total population in Rome during the first century run from 440,000 to 1,000,000.[26] The Jewish population within the city was anywhere from 20,000 to 50,000.[27] There is evidence from inscriptions that at least five synagogues existed in Rome at the beginning of the first century A.D.[28] (and there could certainly have been more[29]), plus additional places for prayer,[30] and as many as thirteen or fourteen synagogues from the second or third centuries.[31] Moreover, it appears that there were close connections between the Jews of Rome and those of Jerusalem and Palestine, since many of the Roman Jews were descendants of immigrants and captives brought there in the first century B.C.[32]

The origins of the Christian community are obscure. Paul himself never

---

25. Cf. D. Georgi, *Remembering the Poor*, 33-42; G. Bornkamm, *Paul*, 41; B. Holmberg, *Paul and Power*, 35-43; K. Nickle, *The Collection*, 111-29; J. Munck, *Paul and the Salvation of Mankind*, 287-97; and U. Wilckens, *Römer*, 3:124-25.

26. D. Noy, *Foreigners at Rome*, 15-16. The population was 1,000,000 by the end of the reign of Caesar Augustus (A.D. 14), according to C. Wells, *The Roman Empire*, 88.

27. The figure of 40,000 to 50,000 is proposed by H. Leon, *The Jews of Rome*, 15, and J. Jeffers, "Jewish and Christian Families in First-Century Rome," 129. R. Brändle and E. Stegemann, "The Formation of the First 'Christian Congregations' in Rome," 120, set the figure at 20,000. On issues concerning the question of organization, cf. S. Appelbaum, "The Organization of the Jewish Communities of the Diaspora," 492-502.

28. P. Richardson, "Augustan-Era Synagogues in Rome," 19-29.

29. Anywhere from 11 to 15 may have existed in the first century A.D., according to H. Leon, *The Jews of Ancient Rome*, 135-66.

30. Philo, *Legat.* 23.155–57, refers to various προσευχαί (places of prayer) existing in Rome.

31. P. Lampe, *From Paul to Valentinus*, 431-32, concludes that there were 14 as a maximum; there is inscriptional evidence for 13, according to P. Richardson, "Augustan-Era Synagogues in Rome," 19-29.

32. M. Stern, "The Jewish Diaspora," 1:160-70; D. Noy, *Foreigners at Rome*, 256-57.

speaks of the entire community of Roman Christians as a church, although he does mention a church (ἐκκλησία) that meets in the home of Prisca and Aquila (16:5). The apostle simply calls his readers "God's beloved in Rome" and "saints" (1:7). In this regard it is better to think in terms of a number of cells or house churches within the city. Estimates of how many house churches existed have ranged anywhere from three to eight.[33]

Paul had never been in Rome previously. Yet, if we consider Romans 16:1-23 integral to the letter sent to Rome, which seems to be gaining more support than it had in the mid to last part of the twentieth century,[34] it indicates that Paul knew a fairly large number of persons within the Roman Christian community. He sends greetings to 26 persons (19 men and 7 women) whom he names, as he does to two additional women known to him but whom he does not name, the mother of Rufus and the sister of Nereus (16:13, 15). The result is that he actually greets 28 persons known to him (19 men and 9 women). The first persons whom he names are Prisca and Aquila, who had been expelled from Rome during the time of Claudius, and whom Paul knew from contacts with them in Corinth (Acts 18:1-2) and Ephesus (1 Cor 16:19; Acts 18:26). They would have been prime sources of information for Paul concerning the community in Rome when he was with them at Corinth and Ephesus, and now they would be prime sources of information at Rome about Paul. Paul also greets another Jewish Christian couple, Andronicus and Junia (16:7), who were considered prominent within the circle of the apostles.[35] Paul indicates that they had become Christians even prior to his own becoming such, which would put their becoming Christians in the early 30s. Paul says too that they had been prisoners along with him at some point. We are left in the dark as to whether they were a part of the early Christian community in Rome,[36] were expelled, and have now returned, or whether they had migrated there later. Since they had been imprisoned with Paul, they must have been associated with him in an unspecified place to the east, and since Paul says that they were prominent within the circle of the apostles, that too points to their origins in the East, most likely in Jerusalem. It is therefore unlikely that they

---

33. E. Judge, *Social Pattern of the Christian Groups in the First Century*, 36; and Abraham J. Malherbe, *Social Aspects of Early Christianity*, 70, 100, identify three. P. Lampe, *From Paul to Valentinus*, 359, and L. White, "House Churches," 119, conclude that there would have been seven or eight, respectively, at the time of writing Romans.

34. For discussion, see section 3, "Romans 16 in Light of Textual and Historical Criticism."

35. For an exhaustive study of the evidence in favor of Junia as an apostle, and for both her and Andronicus as "within" the apostolic circle, cf. L. Belleville, "Ἰουνιαν . . . ἐπίσημοι ἐν τοῖς ἀποστόλοις," 231-49.

36. F. Watson, "The Two Roman Congregations," 210, suggests that Andronicus and Junia were founders of the church at Rome.

had ever been a source of information for Paul concerning Rome. But they would have been a source of information for the community at Rome about Paul.

The Christian community would have had its beginnings prior to the expulsion of Jews and Jewish Christians in A.D. 49. Since the community was large enough to be involved in a disturbance at that time, we can conclude that it must have originated quite a few years earlier. In addition, when Paul wrote his letter in the mid-50s, he says that he had been wishing to come to Rome "for many years" (ἀπὸ πολλῶν ἐτῶν, 15:23; cf. 1:13), and that the faith of the Romans was known throughout the world (1:8). In light of these phenomena, it is commonly suggested that the community had its beginnings in the early 40s,[37] but even that is not necessarily the earliest possible date. According to Luke, there were "visitors from Rome, both Jews and proselytes" at Pentecost (Acts 2:10), from which one might conclude that the Christian message came to Rome early on. He calls the Roman visitors in Jerusalem ἐπιδημοῦντες (RSV, NIV, NRSV: "visitors"), a Greek participle that normally refers to persons in transit, either coming or going,[38] not permanent residents or persons stationed abroad. Whatever we are to make of that reference in Acts, it is apparent that when Luke wrote his account late in the first century, he thought that the earliest Christian community at Rome could be traced back to a founding by converts (formerly Jews and proselytes), and that they had a connection with Jerusalem. Luke's understanding can be taken seriously to the extent that the beginnings of the Christian community at Rome can most likely be attributed to converts who had migrated from the East.[39]

The community of Christians at Rome seems to have been of mixed Jewish and Gentile composition by the time Paul wrote his letter. Although some interpreters of Romans have claimed that the Christian community there was entirely Gentile or that, regardless of its actual composition, the letter was written to an implied audience of Gentile Christians alone,[40] those views are difficult to sustain in light of much within the letter. Insofar as the letter provides clues to the Roman community of believers being addressed,[41] that community must have repre-

---

37. R. Brown and J. Meier, *Antioch and Rome*, 102-3; R. Brown, *Introduction*, 562; P. Lampe, "Paths of Early Christian Mission in Rome," 143, 148.

38. BDAG 370 (ἐπιδημέω).

39. E. Judge and G. Thomas, "The Origin of the Church at Rome," 81-94.

40. N. Elliott, *The Rhetoric of Romans*, 56-59, 66-67, 271-75; S. Stowers, *A Rereading of Romans*, 21-33; M. Nanos, *The Mystery of Romans*, 78-84; P. Achtemeier, "Unsearchable Judgments and Inscrutable Ways," 3-21; A. Das, *Solving the Romans Debate*, 6, 53-114, 264.

41. Using a rhetorical approach, A. Guerra, *Romans and the Apologetic Tradition*, 171, *et passim*, concludes that those being addressed include Jewish Christians. That the community was made up of at least a minority of Jewish Christians, and that they are addressed in the letter,

sented a more conservative ethos and theological position than what one finds in congregations founded by Paul himself. Its oldest nucleus would have consisted of Hellenistic Jewish Christians who had been shaped largely by the Jerusalem community, who held the latter in high regard, and who, to some degree at least, continued contacts with the church in Jerusalem.[42] At a later stage its leaders, including Prisca and Aquila, were banished by Claudius.[43] When Paul writes to the community there, he addresses at least five Christians who are of Hellenistic Jewish heritage (Prisca, Aquila, Andronicus, Junia, and Herodion[44]), and within the letter Paul takes up issues that both bind and divide Christians and Jews. Christianity at Rome at the time of Paul's writing still preserved its Jewish roots, since Jewish symbols and traditions need no explanation (such as the word ἱλαστήριον, "mercy seat" [3:25] and frequent references to Abraham [4:1-3, 9, 12-13, 16; 9:7; 11:1] and Moses [5:17; 9:15; 10:5, 19]). The Aramaic address to God as "Abba" is familiar (8:15), and the Scriptures of Israel can be referred to as authoritative. Quotations from Scripture and allusions to them can be made as though they are familiar to the readers (of the 89 quotations from the OT in all of Paul's letters, 51 [or 57%] are in Romans,[45] and allusions are countless). That Christianity at Rome tended to preserve Jewish features can be documented beyond Romans itself and in its aftermath. The Letter to the Hebrews is commonly thought to have been sent to the Christian community of Rome,[46] and 1 Peter may have been composed there.[47] The letter known as *1 Clement* was written from Rome near the end of the first century.[48] All of these demonstrate a high degree of interest and loyalty to Jewish tradition.[49] When Ignatius of Antioch addresses the community at Rome, he speaks of it as "united in flesh and spirit in every one of [God's] command-

is widely held. Among others, cf. R. Brown, *Introduction,* 562-63; P. Lampe, *From Paul to Valentinus,* 69-79; W. Lane, "Social Perspectives on Roman Christianity," 202-14; R. Jewett, *Romans,* 70-72; and C. Keener, *Romans,* 11-13.

42. Cf. R. Brown and J. Meier, *Antioch and Rome,* 110-14; J. Fitzmyer, *Romans,* 33-34.

43. One should also entertain the possibility that a few Jewish Christians at Rome were from what appears to have been an Aramaic-speaking synagogue, the "Synagogue of the Hebrews" (συναγωγὴ τῶν ἑβραίων, CIG 4:9909; CII 1:291, 317, 510, 535).

44. The woman named Mary (Rom 16:6) may or may not have been of Jewish heritage. Since the name is found in pagan inscriptions at Rome, she may have been of Gentile origin. See the commentary on 16:6.

45. D.-A. Koch, *Die Schrift als Zeuge des Evangeliums,* 21-24.

46. R. Brown and J. Meier, *Antioch and Rome,* 142-49; W. Lane, *Hebrews,* lviii-lx; C. Koester, *Hebrews,* 49-50.

47. In the sentence "your sister church in Babylon . . . sends you greetings" (1 Pet 5:13), "Babylon" is code language for Rome, and a date between 70 and 100 is probable. Cf. E. Best, *1 Peter,* 32-36, 64-65; P. Achtemeier, *1 Peter,* 43-64; and J. Elliott, *1 Peter,* 131-38.

48. The letter is usually considered to have been composed ca. A.D. 96 in Rome. For discussion, cf. Laurence L. Welborn, "Clement, First Epistle of," *ABD* 1:1055-60.

49. W. Lane, "Social Perspectives on Roman Christianity," 196-244.

ments."[50] In the fourth century Ambrosiaster reported that those Jews in Rome who had come to believe in Christ passed on to those who became Christians subsequently the tradition of keeping the law, and the latter "received the faith . . . although in a Jewish manner."[51]

By the time Paul wrote his Letter to the Romans two major shifts had taken place. The first was the expulsion of Jewish Christians from the city, leaving the Gentiles to become the major component of the Christian community there. But what can one conclude from that theologically? The remaining Gentiles could already have become accustomed to observing many Jewish Christian traditions. The second was the return of Jewish Christians a half-dozen years later. But what can one conclude from that theologically? Some of them, such as Prisca and Aquila, had come to know the apostle Paul while they were away, and Andronicus and Junia had known him even earlier. Then too Epaenetus, a convert of Paul and probably a Gentile (16:5), had arrived in Rome as well. Paul and his gospel were therefore known and represented in Rome to some extent. In any case, when Paul wrote his letter, the majority of Christians in Rome were Gentiles.[52] Of the twenty-six persons to whom he sends greetings by name in chapter 16, only four can be identified as Jewish Christians for certain (Aquila, Andronicus, Junia, and Herodion), although two more (Prisca and Mary) might be (see the exegesis of Rom 16:3-16). In addition to that, much of the letter appears to be addressed primarily to persons of Gentile background (1:5-6, 13-15; 11:13, 17-24, 28, 30-31; 15:7-9, 15-16, 18). But even those of the Jewish minority were obviously sympathetic to Paul too. With variety comes a degree of tension, but not necessarily division.

2.4. Some Proposals concerning the Purpose of Romans

In light of the situation of the Christian community at Rome, various scholars have made proposals concerning the purpose of Romans. During the last half

---

50. Ignatius, *Romans* (Preface).

51. Ambrosiaster, Preface, *Commentary on Romans* (PL 17:46): "ritu licet Judaico."

52. An analysis by use of several approaches to the question of "Jewish and Gentile Christians" is provided by P. Lampe, *From Paul to Valentinus*, 69-79; idem, "The Romans Christians of Romans 16," 224-25. For an earlier analysis, cf. S. Johnson, "Jews and Christians in Rome," 51-58. E. P. Sanders, *Paul, the Law, and the Jewish People*, 183, writes that "scholars universally and doubtless correctly conclude that Rome was a mixed church" (of Jewish and Gentile Christians). According to S. Stowers, *A Rereading of Romans*, 29-33, Paul's audience was exclusively Gentile. He grants that Prisca, Aquila, and at least three others mentioned in chapter 16 were Jewish, but he does not consider them among the "encoded readers." But surely Jewish Christians would have been included among those addressed (explicitly, e.g., at 2:17-29) as members of a community of Jewish and Gentile Christians. A thorough response is given by R. Hays, "'The Gospel Is the Power of God for Salvation to Gentiles Only'?" 27-44.

of the twentieth century proposals concerning the purpose of Romans tended to fall into two major types.[53] The first was that Romans should be understood *a priori* like all the other letters of Paul, and that is that in all of them Paul addresses specific issues and concerns of his readers. They are instances of apostolic intervention. By analogy, Romans must have been directed to a concrete, historical, and troublesome situation at Rome (with reference particularly to the matter of civil obedience in 13:1-7 and "the weak and the strong" in 14:1–15:13), and that situation called forth much of the contents of the letter as a response. Here once can cite the proposals of Paul Minear, J. Christiaan Beker, Wolfgang Wiefel, Karl Donfried, Robert Jewett, William S. Campbell, William Lane, Anthony J. Guerra, Mark D. Nanos, Lung-kwong Lo, Mark Seifrid, Peter Stuhlmacher, Raymond Brown, Leander Keck, Francis Watson, N. T. Wright, Craig Keener, and others.[54] Jewett, for example, has suggested that Paul seeks to unify the competing house churches in Rome so that they will be willing to cooperate in a mission to Spain.[55] According to him, "the Gentile and Jewish Christians continued to shame each other," and the house and tenement churches needed to "overcome their conflicts and accept one another as honorable servants of the same master (14:4)" in order to "participate in a credible manner in the mission to extend the gospel to the end of the known world."[56]

The other leading type of proposal has been that Romans is unlike the other letters of Paul; it was situational but not in the usual sense. Specifically, it had to do more with Paul's situation and plans than it did with troubleshooting in Rome. In the words of Günther Bornkamm, "we should have reservations about looking to the Roman church as the reason for the exceptional content in the letter to the Romans."[57] Here one can cite the proposals of C. H. Dodd,

53. This is based on the typology proposed by K. Donfried, "False Presuppositions," 102; cf. also his "Introduction 1991: The Romans Debate since 1977," in *Romans Debate*, xlix. A modification of this approach and a survey are provided by L. Jervis, *The Purpose of Romans*, 14-28.

54. P. Minear, *The Obedience of Faith*, 8-17; J. Beker, *Paul the Apostle*, 59-93; idem, "The Faithfulness of God," 327-29; W. Wiefel, "The Jewish Community in Ancient Rome and the Origins of Roman Christianity," 96; K. Donfried, "False Presuppositions," 102-25; R. Jewett, "Following the Argument of Romans," *Romans Debate*, 265; W. Campbell, "Romans III as a Key," 260-62; W. Lane, "Social Perspectives on Roman Christianity," 198-202; A. Guerra, *Romans and the Apologetic Tradition*, 22-42; M. Nanos, *The Mystery of Romans*, 75-84; L-k. Lo, *Paul's Purpose in Writing Romans* (especially p. 247): Paul wrote to solve problems between the Jewish and Gentile Christians in Rome before arriving there; M. Seifrid, *Justification by Faith*, 207; P. Stuhlmacher, "The Purpose of Romans," 231-42; idem, *Romans*, 3-10; R. Brown, *Introduction*, 559-64; L. Keck, *Romans*, 30-32; F. Watson, *Paul, Judaism, and the Gentiles*, 163-91; N. T. Wright, *NIB (Romans)*, 406 (there was an "uneasy coexistence" among Jewish and Gentile Christians); C. Keener, *Romans*, 15-16, 160.

55. R. Jewett, "Following the Argument of Romans," 266; idem, *Romans*, 88-91.

56. R. Jewett, *Romans*, 88.

57. G. Bornkamm, "The Letter to the Romans as Paul's Last Will and Testament," 20.

Bornkamm, John Drane, C. E. B. Cranfield, Robert Karris, Anders Nygren, Werner Kümmel, Helmut Koester, Jacob Jervell, L. Ann Jervis, and Christopher Bryan.[58] Probably the best known of the proposals of this kind is that of Bornkamm, who proposed that Paul wrote Romans as his "Last Will and Testament." According to that view, Paul expected conflicts in Jerusalem, so he might not get to Rome and Spain. He gathered up themes from earlier letters (and preaching) and presented a summary.[59] Earlier he had dealt with things in polemical situations. Here he is more calm. The letter "elevates his theology above the moment of definite situations and conflicts into the sphere of the eternally and universally valid."[60] Somewhat similarly, and for comparable reasons, Eduard Lohse speaks of Romans as "a summary of the gospel."[61] Another proposal along these lines (i.e., in which Paul takes up his own immediate concerns) is that of Jacob Jervell, who has contended that Romans is actually Paul's "letter to Jerusalem." Here Paul sets forth what he will say when he gets to Jerusalem.[62]

In actual practice the typology of either a Roman-specific situational letter or a non-Roman specific situational letter has become strained to the breaking point. Hardly anyone speaks of one purpose of Romans any more.[63] Generally interpreters have tended to speak of more than one purpose, and they often combine elements of both approaches. In their commentaries on Romans, for example, Joseph Fitzmyer and John Ziesler suggest that Paul wrote Romans to introduce himself to the Roman Christians, to seek their support for his mission to Spain, and to solicit their prayers for his trip to Jerusalem, but also to deal with some concrete problems.[64] And A. J. M. Wedderburn suggests a cluster of purposes, such as preparing the way for his visit to Rome, affirming his apostolic responsibility for the church there, and taking up live issues between Judaizers and law-free Christians.[65]

---

58. C. H. Dodd, *Romans*, xxiv-xxv; G. Bornkamm, "The Letter to the Romans as Paul's Last Will and Testament," 27-28; J. Drane, "Why Did Paul Write Romans?" 223-24; C. Cranfield, *Romans*, 814-23; R. Karris, "The Occasion of Romans," 125-27; A. Nygren, *Romans*, 5-9; W. Kümmel, *Introduction*, 311-14; H. Koester, *Introduction*, 2:142; Jacob Jervell, "The Letter to Jerusalem," 53-64; L. Jervis, *The Purpose of Romans*, 163-64; C. Bryan, *Preface to Romans*, 20 (cf. p. 32).

59. Cf. n. 4 above.

60. G. Bornkamm, "The Letter to the Romans as Paul's Last Will and Testament," 28; cf. idem, *Paul*, 96. The view of Bornkamm is endorsed by W. Kümmel, *Introduction*, 312-14; and G. Theissen, *Introduction*, 87-88.

61. E. Lohse, *Römer*, 46 ("einer Summe des Evangeliums"), with illustrations of themes and concerns from previous letters on pp. 46-48.

62. Jacob Jervell, "The Letter to Jerusalem," 60.

63. K. Donfried, "Introduction 1991," *The Romans Debate*, lxx, acknowledges this.

64. J. Fitzmyer, *Romans*, 79; J. Ziesler, *Romans*, 3-16.

65. A. J. M. Wedderburn, *The Reasons for Romans*, 96-98, 102, 142. Cf. also U. Schnelle, *Apostle Paul*, 308-9, who lists five reasons for the letter.

2.5. *The Purpose Reconsidered*

One of the questions to be considered in determining the purpose of writing Romans is why the letter is so long. If Paul wrote simply to announce his hoped-for arrival in Rome and his intent to go from there to Spain, he needed only a fraction of the space he took in writing this letter. If he sought to settle problems in Rome, one can explain chapters 13–15 and more, but why did he produce all that is in chapters 1 through 8? If he sought to raise his teaching to the level of "the eternally valid and universal" as in a "last will and testament" of his theology, why did he involve himself in the particulars of chapters 12 though 15? Furthermore, if the letter was actually Paul's last will and testament, why would he send it to Rome — a place to which he had never gone and where he had not founded a church?

The letter itself is evidence that Paul had to set forth basic theological convictions to a community of diverse house churches in Rome, a place he had never been. A few individuals there knew who he was and what he preached, but others did not. Moreover, as he himself wrote, there had been rumors about his preaching and its implications (Rom 3:8; 6:1). Some had false impressions of him, and those had to be addressed.

There must have been several purposes in writing Romans. But was there an overriding one, *without which the writing and sending of the letter cannot be explained?* Is there a purpose that makes all the other identifiable purposes secondary and yet necessary in light of the primary one? Why would Paul enlist Phoebe to make the arduous and no doubt dangerous journey from Corinth to Rome with such a letter? Why did he have to send her, a trusted coworker, to interpret and expand upon the letter? Why was it so urgent to write this letter?

One can begin with the explicit data in the letter. Accordingly, Paul wrote Romans to announce his coming, his plans to go on to Spain, his hope for their support, and his appeal for their prayers as he was about to set out for Jerusalem.

But more can be said. While writing the letter, Paul anticipated problems in Jerusalem concerning his Gentile mission. James the Lord's brother was still the leading figure there (Gal 2:1-12). Moreover, Paul had rather recently written his Letter to the Galatians, in which he had spoken harshly against certain persons (conventionally called "Judaizers") who carried on a mission among Gentiles, and those persons seem to have emanated from, or at least had strong associations with, the church in Jerusalem.[66] That letter, if known in Jerusalem, could only have served to drive the wedge between Paul and the Jerusalem community of believers even wider.

---

66. W. Kümmel, *Introduction*, 300-301; R. Brown, *Introduction*, 469; J. L. Martyn, *Galatians*, 18.

In light of all this, the primary purpose for the writing of Romans, without which it cannot be explained at all, is that Paul wrote the letter to prepare the groundwork at Rome for his mission to Spain in case a crisis should happen in Jerusalem. If the Jerusalem church rejected him and his collection, branding him as a false apostle, repudiating his theology, and essentially declaring that his Gentile converts could not be considered part of the people of God in the fullest sense, that would have repercussions among the more conservative members of the Christian community in Rome and make his hope for support of his mission to Spain difficult, if not impossible. The fact that he asked for intercessory prayers for himself as he set out for Jerusalem, asking the Christians at Rome to pray that his ministry might be acceptable to the leaders of the church in Jerusalem, shows how anxious he was (15:31).[67] From this a number of interpreters suggest that Paul sought to enlist the support of the church at Rome to aid his case in Jerusalem.[68] But actually the direction of Paul's gaze should be reversed; his gaze was toward Rome, not Jerusalem. It is not likely that the opinion of the Christians at Rome would have much influence in Jerusalem, and any organized expression of such support would take a lot of time to reach Jerusalem. But a rejection of Paul's ministry in Jerusalem would have been catastrophic for Paul in Rome, and his mission to Spain would become impossible.

Therefore, it can be said that Paul wrote Romans not only to inform the Roman Christians of his plans but also to set forth a theological statement. He wanted the support of the Christians in Rome as allies in his mission to Spain. He made a first installment of his theological views so that, in case of a crisis in Jerusalem, he would not have to defend himself when he arrived in Rome, for his message would have been shown to be in keeping with common Christian tradition shared by both him and the Roman Christians (what Paul calls "each others' faith, both yours and mine," Rom 1:12; and "the teaching" that they had been taught, 16:17). In Romans, therefore, Paul set forth a summary of major themes of his teaching. One must entertain the possibility that even those pas-

67. Acts confirms that Paul's anxieties were well founded, but it gives an interpretation of its own. In a gathering before James and the elders there, Luke says, Paul was spoken to bluntly with the words: "You see, brother, how many thousands of believers there are among the Jews, and they are all zealous for the law. They have been told about you that you teach all the Jews living among the Gentiles to forsake Moses, and you tell them not to circumcise their children or observe the customs" (Acts 21:20-21). The problem with Paul in the eyes of the Jerusalem apostles, according to Luke, was that in his law-free mission to Gentiles, he went to excess, and Jews converting to Christianity were adopting Gentile ways. Luke's version of what was thought of Paul in Jerusalem might be correct, but it does not seem to be what Paul anticipated.

68. E. Käsemann, *Romans,* 405; C. Cranfield, *Romans,* 823; A. Wedderburn, *The Reasons for Romans,* 139, 141-42; K. Yinger, *Paul, Judaism and Judgment according to Deeds,* 144.

sages that appear to be troubleshooting have to do as much with Paul, or even more so, as they do about live, immediate issues at Rome. The most explicit passages are those that speak of the future of Israel (9:1–11:36), civil obedience (13:1-7), and the weak and the strong (14:1–15:13). These have to be taken into account in any discussion of the purpose of the letter, including the discussion here.

The first two can be taken together. There had been civil disturbance in Rome earlier, leading to the expulsion of the Jewish population (or at least much of it), and that had to do with controversy concerning Christ, leading to offense against the larger non-Christian Jewish population. The question could be raised in Rome: Could it be the case that when Paul arrives, he will enter synagogues and proclaim the gospel of the Christ, as he had done before (cf. Acts 9:20; 13:5, 14; 14:1; 17:1-2, 10, 17; 18:4, 19; 19:8), and so the controversy will be played out all over again? Moreover, during the years of Nero's reign (the time that this letter was written) there were growing complaints within the general population about the tax system in place.[69] Either of these could become a basis for a civil disturbance once more. Paul responds that every person should be subject to the powers that be (13:1-7) and that God has not rejected his people, a people that will be saved purely by God's grace beyond history (Romans 9–11).

The third issue that appears to entail troubleshooting at length is the section on the "weak and the strong" (Rom 14:1–15:13), the identity of which is widely disputed among interpreters.[70] In any case, Christians at Rome, probably without exception, would have known that Paul was a zealous proclaimer of a radical version of the gospel, in which the observance or nonobservance of days and foods should count for nothing (1 Cor 8:8; 10:25; Gal 4:10). For Paul, such matters are adiaphora, and one is free in regard to them. On the other hand, when Paul had taken up the matter of food offered to idols at Corinth (1 Cor 8:1-13; 10:23-30), he concluded that one should not cause offense by eating such foods (1 Cor 10:28). In light of that position, filtered through various channels, some at Rome could reasonably think of Paul as a legalist. Either position — freedom or an alleged legalism — could be used in a campaign against Paul, either by opponents of the apostle or by persons who simply do not understand him. So what will happen when Paul arrives at Rome and is in the midst of persons who are not of one mind on this issue and perhaps others?

What the Christians at Rome would be thinking on all this is actually beside the point. What is important is that Paul himself obviously sensed a need to address the matter of foods and days. Although he writes a rather lengthy

---

69. Tacitus, *Ann.* 13.50-51; Suetonius, *Nero* 10.1.

70. A survey is provided in section "8. The Weak and the Strong." Cf. also M. Reasoner, *The Strong and the Weak,* 1-23.

paraenetic section (14:1–15:13), there is actually nothing in it that signifies active apostolic intervention in a troubled situation. There are only three places where Paul uses the second person imperative in this section, and those are at 14:1 ("Welcome those who are weak in faith, but not for the purpose of quarreling over opinions"), 14:13b ("Resolve never to put a stumbling block or hindrance in the way of another"), and finally at 15:7 ("Welcome one another, therefore, just as Christ has welcomed you, for the glory of God"). These are rather general admonitions, by which Paul gives assurances to the Roman Christians. The same is true of the use of the plural hortatory subjunctive in this section on two occasions, namely, at 14:13a ("Let us therefore no longer pass judgment on one another") and at 14:19 ("Let us then pursue what makes for peace and for mutual upbuilding").[71] More on all this and related issues is discussed in "8. The Weak and the Strong."

In these sections of Romans Paul seems to be saying precisely what he thinks the Roman Christians would have no quarrel with — things that they would even want to hear from him. It is not necessary to conclude that whenever a writer expresses a point of view in hortatory language, the aim is to combat an opponent or an opposing viewpoint. As in modern times, so in antiquity, the aim of the one speaking or writing in hortatory language is often to gain rapport and support, couched in diplomatic expressions,[72] and often having as its aim the confirming of mutually held values.[73] Going beyond the undisputed letters of Paul, for example, one need only point to a passage like Ephesians 5:15-21. There the author calls upon his readers not to be foolish, not to get drunk with wine, and to sing psalms and spiritual songs. One need not conclude that the writer of the letter considers the readers to be foolish, prone to drunkenness, or persons who do not sing psalms and spiritual songs. On the contrary, the writer is more likely giving encouragement to his readers and reinforcing the values common among them and shared with himself. One of the most concentrated hortatory sections within Romans itself is 12:9-21, where Paul, in nearly staccato manner, calls for genuine love, patience in suffering, blessing

---

71. Other imperatives are in second person singular (14:15b, 20, 22), or third person singular (14:3 [twice], 5, 16; 15:2).

72. C. Bjerkelund, *Parakalô*, 109-11, 188.

73. L. Perdue, "The Social Character of Paraenesis," 23; S. Stowers, *Letter Writing in Greco-Roman Writing*, 92: "advice and exhortation to continue in a certain way of life"; Benjamin Fiore, "Parenesis and Protreptic," *ABD* 5:164: "what Paul writes is not new but is a reminder of what his correspondents already know, so that they might continue along their chosen path"; T. Tobin, *Paul's Rhetoric in Its Contexts*, 77: "[Paul] needed to persuade [his readers] that his gospel was indeed based on convictions they held in common." Cf. also the statement concerning paraclesis by Johannes Thomas, "παρακαλέω," *EDNT* 3:25: it "(almost) always assumes a believing or assenting response," and C. Bjerkelund, *Parakalô*, 173, 188.

persecutors, associating with the lowly, refraining from revenge, living at peace with one another, and much more. That does not imply that Paul is seeking to correct conditions at Rome that are the opposite of these; on the contrary, one can assume that the community at Rome and communities elsewhere share these values along with him.

There are additional matters that need to be brought into the discussion of the letter's purpose, including one passage where Paul appears to denounce possible opponents. At 16:17-20 Paul appeals to the Roman Christians to avoid those who cause dissensions and offenses. But there are no particular charges against such persons beyond that. Nothing is said about the theological position or teachings of those persons. No apostolic intervention concerning anything specific appears to be needed.[74] The section appears to be rather general exhortation (see the exegesis of that passage).

Apart from those sections already reviewed, it is noteworthy that, when Paul speaks directly to his readers in second person plural elsewhere in the letter, the tone is very positive (1:8, 12; 6:17; 15:14, 30, 32), particularly in the following passages:

> 1:8, "I thank my God through Jesus Christ for all of you, because your faith is proclaimed throughout the world."
>
> 1:11-12, "For I am longing to see you so that I may share with you some spiritual gift to strengthen you — or rather so that we may be mutually encouraged by each other's faith, both yours and mine."
>
> 6:17, "But thanks be to God that you, having once been slaves of sin, have become obedient from the heart to the standard of teaching to which you were entrusted."
>
> 15:14, "I myself feel confident about you, my brothers and sisters, that you yourselves are full of goodness, filled with all knowledge, and able to instruct one another."

Chapter 16, with all its greetings, can be explained within this discussion of purpose as well. Paul sends greetings to everyone he knows in order to have them, or at least some of them, vouch for him and his anticipated presence within the larger community there. If they need not or cannot vouch for him, they would at least be pleased, even flattered, to have been mentioned by the apostle, who thereby makes a strategic move. Moreover, Paul can count on Phoebe to explain any remaining issues.

Any discussion of the purpose of Romans has to account for all that is

---

74. This point is also made in the rhetorical study of Romans by M. Debanné, *Enthymemes in the Letters of Paul*, 169-70.

present in chapters 1 through 8. Why all of this? It is necessary for Paul to present his gospel with clarity in a community of Christians assembling in house churches who have mixed feelings and thoughts concerning Paul, his apostleship, and his message. Each of the topics taken up serves to demonstrate Paul's thinking about the faith and life of Christians. Paul does not take up matters that have specifically corporate or institutional aspects, such as the Lord's Supper, conduct at worship, or benevolence, as he does in his other letters. Instead he focuses on more comprehensive topics, such as the wrath and righteousness of God, the work of God in Christ, and the new life that arises from being incorporated into Christ. It is remarkable that at the very opening of the letter Paul seeks rapport with his readers by repeating back to them a Christological formula that had apparently originated in the Roman community (see the exegesis of 1:3-4).

Finally, the proposal described here fits well with another important item in Paul's letter. He assures his readers that when he arrives in Rome, he will not establish another congregation (or house church) that could be called (although the terms are anachronistic) "Pauline" and "apostolic," and that could rival those communities already in existence in Rome.[75] To paraphrase what he says in 15:20, he does not plant churches where they exist already. That is an important assurance on Paul's part as the Romans Christians anticipate his arrival.

Although one would not speak of Romans today as a "compendium of Christian doctrine," as Melanchthon did, it can nevertheless be considered a summation and projection of Paul's primary theological convictions delivered to a community that knew him only in part but whose support he so ardently sought for his mission to Spain. And if it is a summation and projection of Paul's primary convictions, made as he looks to a hoped-for, future mission to Spain and perhaps beyond, Romans should not be regarded simply as Paul's "last will and testament," as though it summed up for all time everything that he could possibly say. On the contrary, when Paul wrote the letter, he anticipated an entirely new era of missionary work in distant Spain. There he would meet

---

75. That Paul seeks to create a Pauline congregation on the basis of his gospel is contended by A. Reichert, *Der Römerbrief als Gratwanderung*, 96-97, but that viewpoint is not supported by the evidence. Equally unpersuasive are four other views: G. Klein, "Paul's Purpose in Writing the Epistle to the Romans," 29-43: for Paul, the church at Rome lacked an "apostolic" foundation, which Paul intended to rectify; J. Suh, *The Gospel of Paul*, 115: it would be possible for Paul to consider the community at Rome a "church" only when it accepts his gospel; B. Byrne, *Romans*, 19: Paul sought to bring "the basically Gentile Roman community into the sphere of his own responsibility" so that it "will be in the same relationship to himself as the communities he has personally founded"; and F. Watson, "The Two Roman Congregations," 207: Paul wrote "with the aim of converting Jewish Christians to his point of view so as to create a single 'Pauline' congregation in Rome."

new circumstances for further theological work. While he had set out his primary theological convictions in Romans, he did not thereby close down the possibility of ever new theological work in new situations.

Romans remains unique among the letters of Paul. The others that he wrote to churches he had founded are necessarily more occasional and retrospective. Romans is occasional too, as all letters are, but it sets forth Paul's primary theological convictions and is future-oriented in a way that the others are not, calling for the proclamation of the gospel among the Gentiles and for a fresh start in Christian-Jewish relationships. In this letter, too, Paul aims to be ecumenical insofar as he seeks a hearing among Christian communities that he had not founded. But the special character of the letter is its powerful claims concerning God's grace in Christ for the world and God's call to those who live in Christ to be a people obedient to his will in the world.

3. Romans 16 in Light of Textual and Historical Criticism

The last chapter of Romans has been the subject of extensive research and debate. That is so on two fronts. First, there has been the question whether the chapter as a whole concluded Paul's Letter to the Romans. That question is complicated by the fact that no fewer than 15 different endings of Romans exist in the ancient textual witnesses.[76] Second, there are text-critical questions within the chapter. We shall begin with the latter.

3.1. Integrity within the Chapter

Three issues have been at the forefront regarding material *within* chapter 16. These are as follows:

1. Is Romans 16:24 is to be included or omitted? Some Greek texts, including the Majority Text, have a benediction at this point: ἡ χάρις τοῦ κυρίου ἡμῶν Ἰησοῦ Χριστοῦ μετὰ πάντων ὑμῶν. ἀμήν ("The grace of our Lord Jesus Christ be with you all. Amen"). Consequently the verse appears in some English versions that rely heavily on the Majority Text (KJV, NKJ, and ASV).

The material does not, however, appear at this place in earlier, superior texts (𝔓[61], ℵ, A, B, C, and others), and should be omitted.[77] It is not included in

---

76. The evidence is provided in a list by K. Aland, "Der Schluss," 286-90.

77. Cf. B. Metzger, *TCGNT* 476; K. Aland and B. Aland, *The Text of the New Testament,* 296, 310; H.-J. Klauck, *Ancient Letters,* 461-62. H. Gamble, *Textual History,* 129-32, maintains that 16:24 should be included. For a response, cf. L. Hurtado, "The Doxology at the End of Romans," 194-99.

the text of the Nestle-Aland Greek NT (27th ed.) and in modern English versions (such as ESV, RSV, NAB, NIV, and NRSV).

2. The authenticity of Romans 16:25-27, as printed in modern English versions (e.g., RSV, NIV, and NRSV), has been questioned. It has been said that it poses the most difficult of textual problems for the NT text critic.[78] The unit is printed in brackets within the Nestle-Aland Greek text (27th ed.), indicating that its authenticity is doubtful. The material consists of a doxology, and it appears in most known manuscripts, but at different places. Six different textual conditions exist. The doxology appears: (1) after 14:23 and followed by 15:1–16:24 (Majority Text); (2) after both 14:23 and 16:23 (so twice); (3) after 16:24 (but 15:1–16:23 is lacking); (4) after 15:33 and followed by 16:1-23 ($\mathfrak{P}^{46}$); (5) after 16:23; or (6) not at all.

Of these, reading 1 (after 16:23 alone) has the best attestation ($\mathfrak{P}^{61}$, ℵ, B, C, and other witnesses).[79] The inclusion of the doxology at this point is a concession to the weight of the textual tradition. But there is a strong and broad consensus among interpreters that the doxology — in its present form — is deutero-Pauline.[80] One team of major text critics has written forthrightly that "not only 16:24 . . . but also 16:25-27 . . . are not a part of the letter in its original form."[81] The passage consists of one long sentence of 53 words in Greek (as printed in the Nestle-Aland text) — which is highly uncharacteristic of Paul's writing habits — and its vocabulary and phraseology are not typical of Paul. To be sure, it must be admitted that the letter would end in an odd manner if 16:23 were the end of it. But proposed solutions to the apparent problem are unsatisfactory. It might be argued, for example, that a shorter doxology existed from the beginning, but it was replaced with this long and flowing, highly liturgical doxology early in the career of the letter. But even though doxologies do in fact appear within Pauline letters (e.g., at Rom 11:36; Gal 1:5; Phil 4:20), they never appear at the very end of an undisputed Pauline letter; what appears instead is a benediction.[82] See the commentary for details regarding the

---

78. K. Aland, "Der Schluss," 284.

79. B. Metzger, *TCGNT*, 471, 476-77.

80. Among others who contend this, cf. J. K. Elliott, "The Language and Style of the Concluding Doxology to the Epistle to the Romans," 124-30; R. Collins, "The Case of a Wandering Doxology: Rom 16,25-27," 293-303; H.-J. Klauck, *Ancient Letters*, 462; and others cited in the commentary on 16:25-27. That it is genuinely Pauline is maintained by W. Sanday and A. Headlam, *Romans*, lxxxv-xcviii, 433, and others cited in the commentary on 16:25-27. That its authenticity is still an open question is held by L. Hurtado, "The Doxology at the End of Romans," 185-99; J. Weima, *Neglected Endings*, 141-44, 218-19, includes it within his study of the ending of Romans, but recognizes that there are problems with claims for its authenticity.

81. K. Aland and B. Aland, *The Text of the New Testament*, 310.

82. W. Walker, *Interpolations*, 194-95. For benedictions, cf. 1 Cor 16:23; 2 Cor 13:14; Gal 6:18; Phil 4:23; 1 Thess 5:28; Phlm 25.

expressions and phrases that do not otherwise appear in the undisputed letters of Paul.

3. In addition to questions of authenticity raised concerning Romans 16:24 and 16:25-27, there have been some concerning Romans 16:17-20.[83] But the reasons for questioning in this case are fewer. For one thing, 16:17-20 is firmly attested in the textual tradition of the letter. The basis for claiming that 16:17-20 cannot be a part of an original letter to Rome rests primarily on the observation that it would have been strange for Paul to admonish his readers in Rome — a community he is trying to win for support of himself, and a community which he praises elsewhere in his letter for its faith and life (Rom 1:8; 15:14) — about false teachers. But that is not sufficient for most interpreters to consider the unit to be an interpolation.

3.2. The Chapter as a Whole

One of the most fascinating questions about the text of Romans is whether the last chapter (meaning 16:1-23) belonged to the earliest form of the letter, the one that Paul sent to the Christians at Rome.

Although not the first to raise the issue, T. W. Manson put forth the theory in an essay published first in 1948 that chapter 16 was not originally a part of the letter that Paul sent to Rome.[84] His thesis was that Paul's Letter to the Romans existed in two forms: (1) the original actually sent to Rome (1:1–15:33); and (2) an expanded form (1:1–16:27) that Paul sent to the church at Ephesus. The grounds for this view were partly text-critical — claiming on the basis of the various endings of Romans that no fewer than three forms of the letter existed in antiquity (the two already mentioned, plus that of Marcion, 1:1–14:23) — but also that chapter 16 contains (1) a large number of greetings for a church Paul had never visited; (2) names of persons associated with Ephesus; and (3) the exhortations of 16:17-20, which seem odd when addressed to a church Paul had not visited, but natural for a church in which he had worked several

---

83. J. Knox, *IB (Romans)*, 9:664; W. Schmithals, "The False Teachers of Romans 16:17-20," 219-38; J. O'Neill, *Romans*, 252, 248; W.-H. Ollrog, "Die Abfassungsverhältnisse von Röm 16," 232-34; B. Byrne, *Romans*, 446-47, 455-56; L. Keck, *Romans*, 27-28, 377-78; R. Jewett, "Ecumenical Theology for the Sake of Mission," 90, 105-8; idem, *Romans*, 986-98. For a rejoinder to Jewett, cf. J. Sampley, "Romans in a Different Light," 127-28. That the passage is not an interpolation, cf. U. Wilckens, *Römer*, 3:140; J. Dunn, *Romans*, 901-2; H. Gamble, *Textual History*, 52-53, 94; J. Fitzmyer, *Romans*, 745; E. Lohse, *Römer*, 411-12.

84. T. W. Manson, "St. Paul's Letter to the Romans — and Others," 3-15. Manson mentions a predecessor, David Schulz, who questioned whether Rom 16 is integral to the letter as early as 1829.

years.[85] Manson's arguments are impressive, and a number of scholars have adopted his viewpoint (or at least have agreed with him that the chapter is not integral to the letter).[86]

The arguments, however, are not conclusive. While there are named persons who are associated with Ephesus (Epaenetus is called the "first convert of Asia" at Rom 16:5; on Prisca and Aquila at Ephesus, cf. 1 Cor 16:19; Acts 18:18-19), there is no good reason why Prisca and Aquila could not have returned to Rome — from which they had come when Paul first met them in Corinth — after the death of Claudius, accompanied by Epaenetus. Moreover, persons are greeted who appear to have been longtime residents of Rome, particularly Aristobulus, Narcissus, and Rufus (see the exegesis regarding them at 16:10-11, 13). Finally, if the inclusion of chapter 16 is a problem for a letter to Rome, it is even more difficult to imagine that Paul would end a letter without any greetings at all to the Roman Christians. After all, if at all possible, he needs to acquire support and recommendations from persons who know him prior to his arrival at a place he has never been. Recent major commentaries and other works have tended to be of one mind, and that is that Romans 16 was part of the letter from the beginning, and that Romans 1–16 (minus the interpolations discussed above) was sent to Rome.[87] That is the viewpoint presupposed in the current work.

4. Outline of the Letter to the Romans

Romans can be outlined in various ways. Once the epistolary opening and closing have been identified (1:1-17 and 16:1-27), there are three major parts to the let-

---

85. T. W. Manson, "St. Paul's Letter to the Romans — and Others," 12-13.

86. These include such persons as E. J. Goodspeed, "Phoebe's Letter," 55-57; A. McNeile, *An Introduction to the Study of the New Testament*, 154-58; H. Koester, *Introduction to the New Testament*, 2:138-39; G. Bornkamm, *Paul*, 79-80, 247; C. Roetzel, *The Letters of Paul*, 103; R. Fuller, *Introduction to the New Testament*, 51-54; W. Marxsen, *Introduction to the New Testament*, 107-8 (contending that Rom 16 is a fragment of a letter to Ephesus); N. Petersen, "On the Ending(s) to Paul's Letter to Rome," 337-47; G. Theissen, *Introduction*, 82; and B. Malina and J. Pilch, *Social-Science Commentary on the Letters of Paul*, 291-92. N. Perrin, *The New Testament*, 114, held to the theory, but in the 2d ed. of the same book (1982), he and his coauthor Dennis C. Duling allow that it might well be a part of Romans (pp. 187, 197). That Rom 16 was actually a separate, independent letter has been proposed by J. McDonald, "Was Romans xvi a Separate Letter?" 369-72.

87. Among many others, these include K. Donfried, "A Short Note," 44-52; W. Kümmel, *Introduction*, 314-20; B. Kaye, "'To the Romans and Others' Revisited," 37-77; C. Cranfield, *Romans*, 8-11; J. Dunn, *Romans*, 884-85; U. Wilckens, *Römer*, 1:24-27; J. Fitzmyer, *Romans*, 50; P. Stuhlmacher, *Romans*, 244-46; B. Byrne, *Romans*, 29; H. Gamble, *Textual History*, 56-95; W.-H. Ollrog, "Die Abfassungsverhältnisse von Röm 16," 244; A. Wedderburn, *The Reasons for Romans*, 13-18; J. Fitzmyer, *Romans*, 59-64; D. Moo, *Romans*, 7-8; P. Lampe, *From Paul to Valentinus*, 153-64; J. Weima, *Neglected Endings*, 215-17; R. Brown, *Introduction*, 575-76; G. Osborne, *Romans*, 22-23.

ter.[88] The first part (1:18–8:39) consists primarily of proclamation and paraenesis. Paul sets forth his proclamation of the wrath of God, the righteousness of God, and his explication of the Christian life. The second part (9:1–11:36) consists of a lengthy discussion of the place of unbelieving Israel in the purposes of God. Paul takes up the question whether the Jewish people have been rejected by God because of their unbelief in the gospel of Christ. The third part (12:1–15:33) consists of various exhortations concerning life within the Christian community and within the Roman Empire and discloses Paul's missionary work and intentions as these relate to the Roman community of believers. The detailed outline that follows presupposes this more general outline, but as a topical outline it gives subject heads as aids for a closer reading of the text and comment on it.

1. **Opening, 1:1-17**
   1.1. Salutation, 1:1-7
   1.2. Thanksgiving, 1:8-15
   1.3. *Propositio:* Overture to the Letter, 1:16-17
2. **The Revelation of the Wrath of God, 1:18–3:20**
   2.1. Wrath against the Gentile World, 1:18-32
   2.2. God's Impartial Judgment, 2:1-16
   2.3. Boasting in the Law Is Excluded, 2:17-29
   2.4. Advantages without Privileges, 3:1-8
   2.5. The Universal Judgment of God, 3:9-20
3. **The Revelation of the Righteousness of God, 3:21–4:25**
   3.1. The Revelation of the Saving Righteousness of God in Christ, 3:21-26
   3.2. The Universality of Justification by Grace Alone, 3:27-31
   3.3. Abraham as Illustration and Forebear of Justification by Faith, 4:1-25
4. **The New Life in Christ, 5:1–8:39**
   4.1. Peace with God through Justification, 5:1-11
   4.2. Adam and Christ, 5:12-21
   4.3. Free and Alive in Christ: The Struggle against Sin, 6:1-11
   4.4. Free to Serve God as Slaves of Righteousness, 6:12-23
   4.5. The Law and Christ, 7:1-6
   4.6. The Law and Sin, 7:7-13
   4.7. The Law and the Flesh, 7:14-25

88. Within their more formal analyses of the letter, various interpreters propose the following parts: *Prescript,* 1:1-7; *Exordium,* 1:8-17; *Argumentatio,* 1:18–11:36; *Exhortatio,* 12:1–15:13; and *Postscript,* 15:14–16:23. Cf. D. Zeller, *Römer,* 8-9; D. Aune, *The New Testament in Its Literary Environment,* 210; H. Hübner, "Die Rhetorik und die Theologie," 169; D. Dormeyer, "The Hellenistic Letter-Formula," 83-84.

5. Paul's Theology in Romans: An Orientation

Although one can speak of a theology of Paul, at least in the sense that there is a coherence to the theological convictions set forth in his letters as a whole, each letter was written for a particular readership and has its own theological characteristics. In the case of Romans, Paul writes to a community of believers that he had not founded, and he writes without having to exercise apostolic intervention. He writes to introduce himself or represent himself and his gospel anew for the sake of his anticipated arrival in Rome and his subsequent journey to Spain. His letter is to a large degree an elaboration of the gospel he proclaims.

Throughout history there has been a tendency to read Romans from an anthropocentric and individualistic viewpoint. That is to say, the letter has been read from the perspective of the human predicament, particularly the predicament of the individual, and how that is resolved through faith in Christ. That approach to Romans is conditioned largely by the common view that Paul's primary concern is how persons can "get in" and "stay in" the people of God, or to be assured of the favor of God, and thus become those who are (or are being) saved. The matter has been expressed with precision by E. P. Sanders:

> Much of what Paul wrote falls within a framework which I call "getting in and staying in." The framework, besides those two topics, includes what happens to those who do not "get in" and what happens to those who get in but who do not behave in the way which Paul considers appropriate to life in the Spirit.[89]

But a fresh assessment of Romans on its own terms does not lead to that way of thinking. The question for Paul in Romans is not how the individual person "gets in and stays in" the company of those who are saved. The question that preoccupies Paul is not primarily anthropocentric, although anthropocentrism does surface frequently. The primary question in Romans is theocentric: How can God reclaim the creation? In terms of humanity alone, two major questions come to the surface. How can God include Gentiles? Paul declares that God justifies the ungodly, which includes the Gentiles who believe in Christ. So God has resolved the problem of the Gentiles; he can get them in. But if justification is by faith in Christ, how can God save the people of Israel, his chosen? Is there a way that they can stay in? Paul resolves that by declaring that the commitments God has made to Israel remain.

Paul's theological horizons and assertions in this letter are dynamic and dialectical. He speaks of the wrath of God upon all humanity (1:18–3:20) and how all of humanity is subject to God's judgment either on the basis of their own behavior or Adam's disobedience, in which all are implicated (2:6, 16; 5:18-19; 11:32; 14:10). On the other hand, he speaks audaciously of God as the one who justifies the ungodly (4:5), and he declares that ultimately God's

---

89. E. P. Sanders, *Paul, the Law, and the Jewish People,* 6; for similar expressions, cf. his *Paul and Palestinian Judaism,* 544.

mercy is upon all, a declaration to which he appends a poetic — but, on that account, no less theological — outburst of praise of God's grace and mercy (11:30-36). What Adam has brought upon humankind has been countered by God's act in Christ for the justification of all (5:12-21). And while the creation as a whole has been subjected by God to futility and is bound to decay (8:20-21), it will be set at liberty and enjoy the freedom of the glory of the children of God (8:21).

Specific theological concerns within the larger theocentric framework are taken up during the discussion of the letter and in appendices that follow. The theological convictions expressed in the letter frequently provoke reactions in the mind of the interpreter, and one soon comes to realize that Paul did not deal with all the questions that an interpreter — any interpreter — might bring to the text. His theology is visionary and suggestive as much as it is clear and conclusive. The implication of that is that any interpretation of the letter is tentative and conditioned by the time and place of the interpreter. That should call for humility on the part of the interpreter, but it should not lead to despair. This letter, one of the most important theological documents ever written, will always invite attention and the best efforts of the interpreter.

BIBLIOGRAPHY

Achtemeier, Paul J. *1 Peter: A Commentary on First Peter.* Hermeneia. Minneapolis: Fortress Press, 1996.

———. "Unsearchable Judgments and Inscrutable Ways: Reflections on the Discussion of Romans." In *Pauline Theology 4: Looking Back, Pressing On,* 3-21. Ed. E. Elizabeth Johnson and David M. Hay. SBLSS 4. Atlanta: Scholars Press, 1997.

Aland, Kurt. "Der Schluss und die ursprüngliche Gestalt des Römerbriefes." In his *Neutestamentliche Entwürfe,* 284-301. TBü 63. Munich: Chr. Kaiser Verlag, 1979.

Aland, Kurt, and Barbara Aland. *The Text of the New Nestament: An Introduction to the Critical Editions and to the Theory and Practice of Modern Texual Criticism.* Rev. ed. Grand Rapids: Wm. B. Eerdmans, 1989.

Alexander, Philip S. "Epistolary Literature." In *Jewish Writings of the Second Temple Period,* 579-96. Ed. Michael E. Stone. Philadelphia: Fortress Press, 1984.

Appelbaum, Shimon. "The Organization of the Jewish Communities of the Diaspora." In *The Jewish People in the First Century: Historical Geography, Political History, Social, Cultural and Religious Life and Institutions,* 1:464-503. Ed. Shemuel Safrai and Menachem Stern. CRINT 1. 2 vols. Philadelphia: Fortress Press, 1974-76.

Aune, David E. *The New Testament in Its Literary Environment.* LEC 8. Philadelphia: Westminster Press, 1987.

Bacon, Benjamin W. "The Doxology at the End of Romans." *JBL* 18 (1899): 167-76.

Barclay, John M. G. *Jews in the Mediterranean Diaspora from Alexander to Trajan (323 BCE–117 CE).* Edinburgh: T&T Clark, 1996.

Beker, J. Christiaan. *Paul the Apostle: The Triumph of God in Life and Thought*. Philadelphia: Fortress Press, 1980.

Belleville, Linda. "Ἰουνιαν . . . ἐπίσημοι ἐν τοῖς ἀποστόλοις: A Re-examination of Romans 16.7 in Light of Primary Source Materials." *NTS* 51 (2005): 231-49.

Best, Ernest. *1 Peter*. NCBC. Grand Rapids: Wm. B. Eerdmans, 1982.

Birdsall, J. Neville. "The Recent History of the New Testament Textual Criticism (from Westcott and Hort, 1881, to Present)." *ANRW* II.26.1 (1992): 99-197.

Bjerkelund, Carl J. *Parakalô: Form, Funktion und Sinn der parakalô-Sätze in den paulinischen Briefen*. BTN 1. Oslo: Universitetsforlaget, 1967.

Bornkamm, Günther. "The Letter to the Romans as Paul's Last Will and Testament." In *The Romans Debate*, 16-28. 2d ed. Ed. Karl P. Donfried. Peabody: Hendrickson Publishers, 1991.

———. *Paul*. New York: Harper & Row, 1971; reprinted, Minneapolis: Fortress, 1995.

Brändle, Rudolf, and Ekkehard W. Stegemann. "The Formation of the First 'Christian Congregations' in Rome in the Context of the Jewish Congregations." In *Judaism and Christianity in First-Century Rome*, 117-27. Ed. Karl P. Donfried and Peter Richardson. Grand Rapids: Wm. B. Eerdmans, 1998.

Brown, Raymond E., and John P. Meier. *Antioch and Rome: New Testament Cradles of Catholic Christianity*. New York: Paulist Press, 1983.

Bruce, F. F. "The Romans Debate — Continued." In *The Romans Debate*, 175-94. 2d ed. Ed. Karl P. Donfried. Peabody: Hendrickson Publishers, 1991.

Bryan, Christopher. *Preface to Romans: Notes on the Epistle in Its Literary and Cultural Setting*. New York: Oxford University Press, 2000.

Campbell, William S. "Martin Luther and Paul's Epistle to the Romans." In *The Bible as Book: The Reformation*, 103-14. Ed. Orlaith O'Sullivan. New Castle: Oak Knoll Press, 2000.

———. "Romans III as a Key to the Structure and Thought of the Letter." In *The Romans Debate*, 251-64. 2d ed. Ed. Karl P. Donfried. Peabody: Hendrickson Publishers, 1991.

Campbell, William S., Peter S. Hawkins, and Brenda Deen Schildgen, eds. *Medieval Readings of Romans*. RHCS 6. New York: T&T Clark, 2007.

Cappelletti, Silvia. *The Jewish Community of Rome: From the Second Century B.C. to the Third Century C.E.* JSJSup 113. Leiden: E. J. Brill, 2006.

Classen, Carl J. *Rhetorical Criticism of the New Testament*. WUNT 128. Tübingen: J. C. B. Mohr (Paul Siebeck), 2000.

Collins, Raymond F. "The Case of a Wandering Doxology: Rom 16,25-27." In *New Testament Textual Criticism and Exegesis: Festschrift J. Delobel*, 293-303. Ed. Adelbert Denaux. BETL 161. Leuven: Peeters, 2002.

Crafton, Jeffrey A. "Paul's Rhetorical Vision and the Purpose of Romans: Toward a New Understanding." *NovT* 32 (1990): 317-39.

Das, A. Andrew. *Solving the Romans Debate*. Minneapolis: Fortress Press, 2007.

Debanné, Mark J. *Enthymemes in the Letters of Paul*. LNTS 303. New York: T&T Clark, 2006.

Donfried, Karl P. "A Short Note on Romans 16." In *The Romans Debate*, 44-52. 2d ed. Ed. Karl P. Donfried. Peabody: Hendrickson Publishers, 1991.

————. "False Presuppositions in the Study of Romans." In *The Romans Debate*, 102-23. 2d ed. Ed. Karl P. Donfried. Peabody: Hendrickson Publishers, 1991.

————, ed. *The Romans Debate*. Rev. ed. Peabody: Hendrickson Publishers, 1991.

————. "A Short Note on Romans 16." *JBL* 89 (1970): 441-49; reprinted in *The Romans Debate*, 44-52. Ed. Karl P. Donfried. Rev. ed. Peabody: Hendrickson Publishers, 1991.

Donfried, Karl P., and Peter Richardson, eds. *Judaism and Christianity in First-Century Rome*. Grand Rapids: Wm. B. Eerdmans, 1998.

Dormeyer, Detlev. "The Hellenistic Letter-Formula and the Pauline Letter-Scheme." In *The Pauline Canon*, 59-93. Ed. Stanley E. Porter. PAST 1. Boston: E. J. Brill, 2004.

Doty, William G. "The Classification of Epistolary Literature." *CBQ* 31 (1960): 183-99.

————. *Letters in Primitive Christianity*. Philadelphia: Fortress Press, 1973.

Drane, John W. "Why Did Paul Write Romans?" In *Pauline Studies: Essays Presented to F. F. Bruce on His 70th Birthday*, 208-27. Ed. Donald A. Hagner and Murray J. Harris. Grand Rapids: Wm. B. Eerdmans, 1980.

Elliott, James K. "The Language and Style of the Concluding Doxology to the Epistle to the Romans." *ZNW* 72 (1981): 124-30.

Elliott, John H. A. *1 Peter*. AB 37B. New York: Doubleday, 2000.

Elliott, Neil. *The Rhetoric of Romans: Argumentative Constraint and Strategy and Paul's Dialogue with Judaism*. JSNTSup 45. Sheffield: JSOT Press, 1990; reprinted, Minneapolis: Fortress Press, 2006.

Exler, Francis X. J. *The Form of the Ancient Greek Letter: A Study in Greek Epistolography*. Washington, D.C.: Catholic University of America, 1923.

Fuller, Reginald H. *Introduction to the New Testament*. London: Gerald Duckworth, 1966.

Gaca, Kathy L., and Laurence L. Welborn, eds. *Early Patristic Readings of Romans*. RHCS. Edinburgh: T&T Clark, 2005.

Gamble, Harry Y. "The Canon of the New Testament." In *The New Testament and Its Modern Interpreters*, 201-43. Ed. Eldon J. Epp and George W. MacRae. Philadelphia: Fortress Press, 1989.

————. *The Textual History of the Letter to the Romans: A Study in Textual and Literary Criticism*. SD 42. Grand Rapids: Wm. B. Eerdmans, 1977.

Georgi, Dieter. *Remembering the Poor: The History of Paul's Collection for Jerusalem*. Nashville: Abingdon, 1992.

Goodspeed, Edgar J. "Phoebe's Letter of Introduction." *HTR* 44 (1951): 55-57.

Greenman, Jeffrey P., and Timothy Larsen. *Reading Romans through the Centuries: From the Early Church to Karl Barth*. Grand Rapids: Brazos Press, 2005.

Guerra, Anthony J. *Romans and the Apologetic Tradition: The Purpose, Genre and Audience of Paul's Letter*. New York: Cambridge University Press, 1995.

Hays, Richard B. "'The Gospel Is the Power of God for Salvation to Gentiles Only'? A Critique of Stanley Stowers' *A Rereading of Romans*." *CRBR* 9 (1996): 27-44.

Head, Peter M. "Named Letter-Carriers among the Oxyrhynchus Papyri." *JSNT* 31 (2009): 279-99.

Holmberg, Bengt. *Paul and Power: The Structure of Authority in the Primitive Church as Reflected in the Pauline Epistles*. ConBNT 11. Lund: C. W. K. Gleerup, 1978.

Hübner, Hans. "Die Rhetorik und die Theologie: Der Römerbrief und die rhetorische

Kompetenz des Paulus." In *Die Macht des Wortes: Aspekte gegenwärtiger Rhetorik-forschung,* 165-79. Ed. Carl J. Classen and H. J. Müllenbrock. Ars Rhetorika 4. Marburg: Koch, 1992.

Hurtado, Larry W. "The Doxology at the End of Romans." In *New Testament Textual Criticism: Its Significance for Exegesis: Essays in Honour of Bruce M. Metzger,* 185-99. Ed. Eldon J. Epp and Gordon D. Fee. New York: Oxford University Press, 1981.

Jeffers, James S. "Jewish and Christian Families in First-Century Rome." In *Judaism and Christianity in First-Century Rome,* 128-50. Ed. Karl P. Donfried and Peter Richardson. Grand Rapids: Wm. B. Eerdmans, 1998.

Jervell, Jacob. "The Letter to Jerusalem." In *The Romans Debate,* 53-64. 2d ed. Ed. Karl P. Donfried. Peabody: Hendrickson Publishers, 1991.

Jervis, L. Ann. *The Purpose of Romans: A Comparative Letter Structure Investigation.* JSNTSup 55. Sheffield: Sheffield Academic Press, 1991.

Jewett, Robert. "Ecumenical Theology for the Sake of Mission: Romans 1:1-17 + 15:14–16:24." In *Pauline Theology,* vol. 3: *Romans,* 89-108. Ed. David M. Hay and E. Elizabeth Johnson. Minneapolis: Fortress Press, 1995.

———. "Following the Argument of Romans." In *The Romans Debate,* 265-77. 2d ed. Ed. Karl P. Donfried. Peabody: Hendrickson Publishers, 1991.

———. "Major Impulses in the Theological Interpretation of Romans since Barth." *Int* 34 (1980): 1-31.

———. "Romans as an Ambassadorial Letter." *Int* 36 (1982): 5-20.

Johnson, Sherman E. "Jews and Christians in Rome." *LTQ* 17 (1982): 51-58.

Judge, Edwin A. *The First Christians in the Roman World.* Ed. James R. Harrison. WUNT 229. Tübingen: J. C. B. Mohr (Siebeck), 2008.

———. "Judaism and the Rise of Christianity: A Roman Perspective." *TynB* 45 (1994): 355-68.

———. *Social Distinctiveness of the Christians in the First Century.* Ed. David M. Scholer. Peabody: Hendrickson Publishers, 2007.

———. *Social Pattern of the Christian Groups in the First Century.* London: Tyndale Press, 1960.

Judge, Edwin A., and G. S. R. Thomas. "The Origin of the Church at Rome: A New Solution." *RefRev* 25 (1966): 81-94.

Kamlah, Erhard. "Traditionsgeschichtliche Untersuchungen zur Schlussdoxologie des Römerbriefes." Unpublished doctoral diss., University of Tübingen, 1955.

Karris, Robert J. "The Occasion of Romans: A Response to Prof. Donfried." In *The Romans Debate,* 125-27. 2d ed. Ed. Karl P. Donfried. Peabody: Hendrickson Publishers, 1991.

———. "Romans 14:1–15:13 and the Occasion of Romans." In *The Romans Debate,* 65-84. 2d ed. Ed. Karl P. Donfried. Peabody: Hendrickson Publishers, 1991.

Kiefer, René. "The Interpretation of the Letter to the Romans in Melanchthon's *Loci Communes* from 1521." In *Paul and His Theology,* 381-92. Ed. Stanley E. Porter. PAST 3. Boston: E. J. Brill, 2006.

Kaye, Bruce N. "'To the Romans and Others' Revisited." *NovT* 18 (1976): 37-77.

Klauck, Hans-Josef. *Ancient Letters and the New Testament: A Guide to Context and Exegesis.* Waco: Baylor University Press, 2006.

Knox, John. "A Note on the Text of Romans." *NTS* 2 (1955-56): 191-93.

Koch, Dietrich-Alex. *Die Schrift als Zeuge des Evangeliums: Untersuchungen zur Verwendung und zum Verständnis der Schrift bei Paulus.* BHT 69. Tübingen: J. C. B. Mohr (Paul Siebeck), 1986.

Koester, Craig. *Hebrews.* AB 36. New York: Doubleday, 2001.

Koester, Helmut. *Introduction to the New Testament.* 2 vols. Philadelphia: Fortress Press, 1982.

Lampe, Peter. *From Paul to Valentinus: Christians at Rome in the First Two Centuries.* Minneapolis: Fortress Press, 2003.

———. "Paths of Early Christian Mission in Rome: Judeo-Christians in the Households of Pagan Masters." In *Celebrating Romans: Template for Pauline Theology: Essays in Honor of Robert Jewett,* 143-48. Ed. Sheila E. McGinn. Grand Rapids: Wm. B. Eerdmans, 2005.

———. "The Roman Christians of Romans 16." In *The Romans Debate,* 216-30. 2d ed. Ed. Karl P. Donfried. Peabody: Hendrickson Publishers, 1991.

———. "Zur Textgeschichte des Römerbriefes." *NovT* 27 (1985): 273-77.

Lane, William L. *Hebrews.* WBC 47. 2 vols. Dallas: Word Books, 1991.

———. "Social Perspectives on Roman Christianity during the Formative Years from Nero to Nerva: Romans, Hebrews, *1 Clement.*" In *Judaism and Christianity in First-Century Rome,* 196-244. Ed. Karl P. Donfried and Peter Richardson. Grand Rapids: Wm. B. Eerdmans, 1998.

Leon, Harry J. *The Jews of Ancient Rome.* Philadelphia: Jewish Publication Society of America, 1960; reprinted, Peabody: Hendrickson Publishers, 1995.

Lichtenberger, Hermann. "Jews and Christians in Rome in the Time of Nero: Josephus and Paul in Rome." *ANRW* II.26.3 (1996): 2142-76.

Lo, Lung-kwong. *Paul's Purpose in Writing Romans: The Upbuilding of a Jewish and Gentile Christian Community in Rome.* Jian Dao Dissertation Series 6; Bible and Literature 4. Hong Kong: Alliance Bible Seminary, 1998.

McDonald, James I. H. "Was Romans xvi a Separate Letter?" *NTS* 16 (1969/70): 369-72.

Malherbe, Abraham J. *Ancient Epistolary Theorists.* SBLSBS 19. Atlanta: Scholars Press, 1988.

———. *Social Aspects of Early Christianity.* 2d ed. Philadelphia: Fortress Press, 1983.

Malina, Bruce J., and John J. Pilch. *Social-Science Commentary on the Letters of Paul.* Minneapolis: Fortress Press, 2006.

Manson, T. W. "St. Paul's Letter to the Romans — and Others," *BJRL* 31 (1948): 224-40; reprinted in *Romans Debate,* 3-15. 2d ed. Ed. Karl P. Donfried. Peabody: Hendrickson Publishers, 1991. References are to the latter publication.

Marcus, Joel. "The Circumcision and Uncircumcision in Rome." *NTS* 35 (1989): 67-81.

Marshall, I. Howard. "Romans 16:25-27 — An Apt Conclusion." In *Romans and the People of God: Essays in Honor of Gordon D. Fee on the Occasion of His 65th Birthday,* 170-84. Ed. Sven K. Soderlund and N. T. Wright. Grand Rapids: Wm. B. Eerdmans, 1999.

Martyn, J. Louis. *Galatians.* AB 33A. New York: Doubleday, 1997.

Marxsen, Willi. *Introduction to the New Testament.* Philadelphia: Fortress Press, 1968.

McNeile, A. H. *An Introduction to the Study of the New Testament.* Rev. C. S. C. Williams. New York: Oxford University Press, 1953.

Miller, James C. *The Obedience of Faith, the Eschatological People of God, and the Purpose of Romans.* SBLDS 177. Atlanta: Society of Biblical Literature, 2000.

Minear, Paul S. *The Obedience of Faith: The Purpose of Paul in the Epistle to the Romans.* SBT 2/19. Naperville: Alec R. Allenson, 1971.

Munck, Johannes. *Paul and the Salvation of Mankind.* Atlanta: John Knox Press, 1959.

Nanos, Mark D. "The Jewish Context of the Gentile Audience Addressed in Paul's Letter to the Romans." *CBQ* 61 (1999): 283-304.

————. *The Mystery of Romans: The Jewish Context of Paul's Letter.* Minneapolis: Fortress Press, 1996.

Nickle, Keith F. *The Collection: A Study in Paul's Strategy.* SBT 48. London: SCM Press, 1966.

Noy, David. *Foreigners at Rome: Citizens and Strangers.* London: Gerald Duckworth & Company, 2000.

Ollrog, Wolf-Henning. "Die Abfassungsverhältnisse von Röm 16." In *Kirche: Festschrift für Günther Bornkamm zum 75. Geburtstag,* 221-44. Ed. Dieter Lührmann and Georg Strecker. Tübingen: J. C. B. Mohr (Paul Siebeck), 1980.

Perdue, Leo G. "The Social Character of Paraenesis and Paraenetic Literature." In *Paraenesis: Act and Form,* 5-39. Semeia 50. Atlanta: Scholars Press, 1990.

Perrin, Norman. *The New Testament: An Introduction.* New York: Harcourt Brace Jovanovich, 1974.

Perrin, Norman, and Dennis C. Duling. *The New Testament: An Introduction.* 2d ed. New York: Harcourt Brace Jovanovich, 1982.

Petersen, Norman R. "On the Ending(s) to Paul's Letter to Rome." In *The Future of Early Christianity: Essays in Honor of Helmut Koester,* 337-47. Ed. Birger A. Pearson. Minneapolis: Fortress Press, 1991.

Plevnik, Joseph. "Pauline Presuppositions." In *The Thessalonian Corespondence,* 50-61. Ed. Raymond F. Collins. BETL 87. Leuven: Leuven University Press, 1990.

Porter, Stanley E. "Did Paul Have Opponents in Rome and What Were They Opposing?" In *Paul and His Opponents,* 149-68. Ed. Stanley E. Porter. PAST 2. Leiden: E. J. Brill, 2005.

Reasoner, Mark. *Romans in Full Circle: A History of Interpretation.* Louisville: Westminster John Knox, 2005.

————. *The Strong and the Weak: Romans 14.1–15.13 in Context.* SNTSMS 103. Cambridge: Cambridge University Press, 1999.

Reichert, Angelika. *Der Römerbrief als Gratwanderung: Eine Untersuchung zur Abfassungsproblematik.* FRLANT 194. Göttingen: Vandenhoeck & Ruprecht, 2001.

Richardson, Peter. "Augustan-Era Synagogues in Rome." In *Judaism and Christianity in First-Century Rome,* 17-29. Ed. Karl P. Donfried and Peter Richardson. Grand Rapids: Wm. B. Eerdmans, 1998.

Roetzel, Calvin J. *The Letters of Paul,* 5th ed. Louisville: Westminster John Knox Press, 2009.

Rutgers, Leonard V. *The Jews in Late Ancient Rome: Evidence of Cultural Interaction in the Roman Diaspora*. Leiden: Boston: E. J. Brill, 1995.

———. "Roman Policy toward the Jews: Expulsions from the City of Rome during the First Century C.E." In *Judaism and Christianity in First-Century Rome*, 93-116. Ed. Karl P. Donfried and Peter Richardson. Grand Rapids: Wm. B. Eerdmans, 1998.

Sampley, J. Paul. "Romans in a Different Light: A Response to Robert Jewett." In *Pauline Theology*, vol. 3, *Romans*, 109-29. Ed. David M. Hay and E. Elizabeth Johnson. Minneapolis: Fortress Press, 1995.

Sanders, E. P. *Paul and Palestinian Judaism: A Comparison of Patterns of Religion*. Philadelphia: Fortress Press, 1977.

———. *Paul, the Law, and the Jewish People*. Philadelphia: Fortress Press, 1983.

Schmithals, Walter. "Römer 16." In his *Der Römerbrief als historisches Problem*, 125-51. Gütersloh: Gerd Mohn, 1975.

Schnelle, Udo. *Apostle Paul: His Life and Theology*. Grand Rapids: Baker Academic, 2003.

Seifrid, Mark A. *Justification by Faith: The Origin and Development of a Central Pauline Theme*. NovTSup 68. Leiden: E. J. Brill, 1992.

Slingerland, Dixon. "Chrestus: Christus?" In *The Literature of Early Rabbinic Judaism: Issues in Talmudic Redaction and Interpretation*, 133-44. Ed. Alan J. Avery-Peck. NPAJ 4. Lanham: University Press of America, 1989.

———. *Claudian Policymaking and the Early Imperial Repression of Judaism at Rome*. SFSHJ 160. Atlanta: Scholars Press, 1997.

———. "Suetonius, *Claudius* 25.4 and the Account of Cassius Dio." *JQR* 79 (1989): 305-22.

Smiga, George. "Romans 12:1-2 and 15:30-32 and the Occasion of the Letter to the Romans." *CBQ* 53 (1991): 257-73.

Stern, Menachem. "The Jewish Diaspora." In *The Jewish People in the First Century: Historical Geography, Political History, Social, Cultural and Religious Life and Institutions*, 1:17-83. Ed. Shemuel Safrai and Menachem Stern. CRINT. 2 vols. Assen: Van Gorcum, 1974-76.

Stirewalt, M. Luther, Jr. "The Form and Structure of the Greek Letter-Essay." In *The Romans Debate*, 147-71. 2d ed. Ed. Karl P. Donfried. Peabody: Hendrickson Publishers, 1991.

———. *Paul, the Letter Writer*. Grand Rapids: Wm. B. Eerdmans, 2003.

Stowers, Stanley K. *Letter Writing in Greco-Roman Antiquity*. LEC 5. Philadelphia: Westminster Press, 1986.

———. *A Rereading of Romans: Justice, Jews, and Gentiles*. New Haven: Yale University Press, 1994.

Stuhlmacher, Peter. "The Purpose of Romans." In *The Romans Debate*, 231-42. 2d ed. Ed. Karl P. Donfried. Peabody: Hendrickson Publishers, 1991.

Suh, Joong Suk. *The Gospel of Paul*. StudBL 56. New York: Peter Lang, 2003.

Theissen, Gerd. *Fortress Introduction to the New Testament*. Minneapolis: Fortress Press, 2003.

Tobin, Thomas H. *Paul's Rhetoric in Its Contexts: The Argument of Romans*. Peabody: Hendrickson Publishers, 2004.

Theobald, Michael. "Warum schrieb Paulus den Römerbrief?" In his *Studien zum Römerbrief*, 2-14. WUNT 136. Tübingen: J. C. B. Mohr (Paul Siebeck), 2001.

Vorster, Johannes N. "The Context of the Letter to the Romans: A Critique on the Present State of Research." *Neot* 28 (1994): 127-45.

Walker, William O., Jr. *Interpolations in the Pauline Letters*. JSNTSup 213. Sheffield: Sheffield Academic Press, 2001.

———. "Interpolations in the Pauline Letters." In *The Pauline Canon*, 189-235. Ed. Stanley E. Porter. PAST 1. Boston: E. J. Brill, 2004.

Watson, Francis. *Paul, Judaism and the Gentiles: Beyond the New Perspective*. Rev. ed. Grand Rapids: Wm. B. Eerdmans, 2007.

———. "The Two Roman Congregations: Romans 14:1–15:13." In *The Romans Debate*, 203-15. 2d ed. Ed. Karl P. Donfried. Peabody: Hendrickson Publishers, 1991.

Wedderburn, A. J. M. "Purpose and Occasion of Romans Again." In *The Romans Debate*, 195-202. 2d ed. Ed. Karl P. Donfried. Peabody: Hendrickson Publishers, 1991.

———. *The Reasons for Romans*. Studies of the New Testament and Its World. Edinburgh: T&T Clark, 1988.

Weima, Jeffrey A. D. *Neglected Endings: The Significance of the Pauline Letter Closings*. JSNTSup 101. Sheffield: JSOT Press, 1994.

Wells, Colin. *The Roman Empire*, 2d ed. Cambridge: Harvard University Press, 1992.

White, John L. *The Form and Function of the Body of the Greek Letter: A Study of the Letter-Body in the Non-literary Papyri and in Paul the Apostle*. SBLDS 2. Missoula: Scholars Press, 1972.

———. "New Testament Epistolary Literature in the Framework of Ancient Epistolography." *ANRW* II.25.2 (1984): 1730-56.

———. "Saint Paul and the Apostolic Letter Tradition." *CBQ* 45 (1983): 433-44.

White, L. Michael. "House Churches," *OEANE* 3:118-21.

Wiefel, Wolfgang. "The Jewish Community in Ancient Rome and the Origins of Roman Christianity." In *The Romans Debate*, 85-101. 2d ed. Ed. Karl P. Donfried. Peabody: Hendrickson Publishers, 1991.

Williams, Margaret. "Being a Jew in Rome: Sabbath Fasting as an Expression of Romano-Jewish Identity." In *Negotiating Diaspora: Jewish Strategies in the Roman Empire*, 8-18. Ed. John M. G. Barclay. New York: T&T Clark, 2004.

———. "The Shaping of the Identity of the Jewish Community in Rome in Antiquity." In *Christians as a Religious Minority in a Multicultural City: Modes of Interaction and Identity Formation in Early Imperial Rome*, 33-46. Ed. Jürgen Zangenberg and Michael Labahn. JSNTSup 243. London: T&T Clark, 2004.

Wuellner, Wilhelm. "Paul's Rhetoric of Argumentation in Romans: An Alternative to the Donfried-Karris Debate over Romans." In *The Romans Debate*, 128-46. 2d ed. Ed. Karl P. Donfried. Peabody: Hendrickson Publishers, 1991.

Yinger, Kent L. *Paul, Judaism and Judgment according to Deeds*. SNTSMS 105. Cambridge: Cambridge University Press, 1999.

Young, Frances M. "Romans 16: A Suggestion." *ET* 47 (1935-36): 44.

CHAPTER 1

Opening, 1:1-17

Most letters, ancient and modern, begin with some preliminary remarks prior to getting on with the matters that are of utmost concern for the author in writing. It comes as no surprise, therefore, that in this longest and most theological of Paul's writings, written to a community he has neither founded nor visited previously, the apostle would employ some rather conventional forms in order to introduce himself, speak about his intended relationship with his addressees, and give some kind of introduction, however brief, of his essential message. The opening section of his letter to Rome accomplishes those three purposes, and it can be divided into three parts corresponding to them. They also correspond in part with ancient conventions in letter writing. Each of the three parts is discussed in more detail subsequently, but in bare outline they can be described as follows.

1. The letter begins with an address and greeting (1:1-7), which is called more formally the prescript (Latin *praescriptio*). Its purpose is to identify the writer (named in the *superscriptio*), name the addressee (identified in the *adscriptio*), and convey a greeting (the *salutatio*).[1]

2. The prescript is followed by a thanksgiving section (1:8-15), in which Paul gives thanks for the faith of those being addressed and sketches out briefly his plans concerning them and himself. Typically, an ancient letter contains a prayer petition or a wish for health at this place,[2] but thanksgiving sections do exist in some ancient letters outside the NT.[3] The thanksgiving corresponds

---

1. These compare with the "standard letter components" of ancient letters; cf. H.-J. Klauck, *Ancient Letters and the New Testament*, 17-18.

2. These are amply illustrated by F. Exler, *The Form of the Ancient Greek Letter*, 101-12.

3. These are discussed and illustrated by P. Schubert, *The Form and Function of the Pauline Thanksgivings*, 158-79.

largely to the *exordium* used at the outset of orations to secure the goodwill of those who are assembled.[4]

3. The third segment of the opening is the *propositio* (1:16-17), in which Paul sets forth a focused statement concerning what is to come later in the letter.[5]

Although it is to be expected that exegetical and theological work will always focus on the body of the letter (1:18–15:13), the opening is compact with words and phrases whose meanings are important for the remainder of the letter, such as "gospel," "Son of God," "grace," "faith," "salvation," and "righteousness of God." Moreover, those words and phrases are essential for comprehending the message and theology of the apostle Paul. A comprehensive theology of Paul cannot be derived from Romans alone, but any description of his theology will be largely dependent upon that letter and upon the use and development of words and phrases employed already in the first seventeen verses.

BIBLIOGRAPHY

Aune, David E. "Letters." In *The Westminster Dictionary of New Testament and Early Christian Literature and Rhetoric.* Louisville: Westminster John Knox, 2003.

Doty, William G. *Letters in Primitive Christianity.* Philadelphia: Fortress Press, 1973.

Exler, Francis X. J. *The Form of the Ancient Greek Letter of the Epistolary Papyri (3rd c. B.C.–3rd c. A.D.).* Chicago: Ares Publishers, 1976.

Klauck, Hans-Josef. *Ancient Letters and the New Testament: A Guide to Context and Exegesis.* Waco: Baylor University Press, 2006.

Lausberg, Heinrich. *Handbook of Literary Rhetoric: A Foundation for Literary Study.* Boston: E. J. Brill, 1998.

Legrand, Lucien. "Rm 1.11-15 (17): *Proemium* ou *Propositio?*" NTS 49 (2003): 566-72.

O'Brien, Peter T. *Introductory Thanksgivings in the Letters of Paul.* NovTSup 49. Leiden: E. J. Brill, 1977.

Schubert, Paul. *The Form and Function of the Pauline Thanksgivings.* BZNW 20. Berlin: Alfred Töpelmann, 1939.

Stowers, Stanley K. *Letter Writing in Greco-Roman Antiquity.* LEC 5. Philadelphia: Westminster Press, 1986.

1.1. Salutation, 1:1-7

1Paul, a servant of Jesus Christ, called to be an apostle, set apart for the gospel of God, 2which he promised beforehand through his prophets in the holy scrip-

---

4. H. Lausberg, *Handbook of Literary Rhetoric,* 121-36.

5. H.-J. Klauck, *Ancient Letters and the New Testament,* 303; P. O'Brien, *Introductory Thanksgivings in the Letters of Paul,* 198, 202. L. Legrand, "Rm 1.11-15 (17)," 566-72, considers 1:8-15 to be the *propositio.*

tures ₃concerning his Son, who was descended from David according to the flesh ₄but designated Son of God in power according to the Spirit of holiness by resurrection from the dead, Jesus Christ our Lord, ₅through whom we have received grace and apostleship to bring about the obedience of faith among all the nations for the sake of his name, ₆among whom you also are called to belong to Jesus Christ; ₇to all God's beloved in Rome, who are called to be saints: Grace to you and peace from God our Father and the Lord Jesus Christ.

Notes on the Text and Translation

1:1 On the preference for the term "slave" over "servant," see the discussion in the Detailed Comment.

The word order "Christ Jesus" (NEB, NIV, NASV, ESV, and NET; and Χριστοῦ Ἰησοῦ in the 27th ed. of the Nestle-Aland Greek text) is to be preferred over "Jesus Christ" (KJV, RSV, and NRSV). Although the textual evidence is almost equally divided, that is the word order in similar passages by which Paul introduces himself at the outset of letters (1 Cor 1:1; 2 Cor 1:1; Phil 1:1; Phlm 1).[6] In terms of frequency, Paul uses the two word orders almost equally.[7] Theologically the word order is of no significance; the expressions are used interchangeably by Paul.[8]

1:7 Some important witnesses (including G and Origen) lack the words ἐν Ῥώμῃ ("in Rome"). The reason may be accidental, or the omission may have been deliberate to give the letter a general, not local, significance.[9]

General Comment

In these seven verses, comprising one long sentence, Paul identifies himself, greets his readers, and begins immediately to proclaim the gospel, summarizing with an economy of words the story of God's redemptive work culminating in the death and resurrection of Jesus Christ. Writing to believers in Rome, a city he had not yet visited, he alludes already to his anticipated visit among them. His wording is formal, but it is also diplomatic and warmhearted — diplomatic in that he makes use of language familiar to the community and the common Christian tradition (such as references to the "holy scriptures," the

---

6. The opening lines of Gal 1:1 and 1 Thess are constructed more elaborately and do not provide true parallels. The reading of 1 Cor 1:1 also has the variant, but with less support.

7. Basing statistics on the Nestle-Aland Greek text (27th ed.), Paul uses "Jesus Christ" 57 times, and "Christ Jesus" 49 times.

8. N. Dahl, "The Messiahship of Jesus in Paul," 38.

9. Cf. B. Metzger, *TCGNT* 446.

promises of God, the lineage of Jesus from David, and Jesus' resurrection from the dead), and warmhearted in that he extends a blessing ("grace and peace") and calls his readers "God's beloved."

The letter opens with a greeting modeled largely on the form typical of Greco-Roman letters of antiquity from the third century B.C. to the third century A.D. That form consisted of the name of the author, then the addressee, followed by a verb of greeting (so, A to B, χαίρειν, "greetings").[10] But Paul's greeting differs from the typical one in two ways: (1) instead of using the verb of greeting (χαίρειν), he uses the noun for "grace" (χάρις); and (2) he adds the commonly used Jewish (and Jewish Christian) greeting (שָׁלוֹם, "shalom" [šālôm] in Hebrew) and the Greek word for "peace" (εἰρήνη). It is possible that Paul was the first to compose such a greeting.[11] The common greeting, "peace," appears by itself in the sources (e.g., Judg 6:23; 19:20; Dan 10:19; Tob 12:17; Luke 24:36; John 20:19), but not in combination with "grace" in the LXX or NT.[12] It is, however, combined with the verb "to be merciful" (ἐλεέω) in the Benediction of Aaron (Num 25-26). The formal parts of the greeting consist, then, of "Paul . . . to God's beloved in Rome, who are called to be saints: Grace to you and peace from God our Father and the Lord Jesus Christ."

Insofar as Paul has a greeting at all, and at this place, he is dependent upon the typical Hellenistic letter form. It is too facile to say, however, that Paul has simply substituted the one expression for the traditional one. He writes as an apostle and mediates revelation from the risen Christ and God the Father, just as he can on occasion reveal a divine "mystery" (11:25; 1 Cor 15:51).[13] As in the case of the Beatitudes (Matt 5:1-11), in which Jesus declares eschatological blessings proleptically upon those named, so here the apostle, exercising authority, declares the eschatological gifts of grace and peace from God to his readers; it is a performative utterance.

Modern English versions present 1:1-7 as one long sentence. The verses do

---

10. The form is discussed in the work of W. Doty, *Letters in Primitive Christianity*, 29-31. It is illustrated from a papyrus text (BGU 27) in *Hellenistic Commentary to the New Testament*, ed. M. Boring et al., 335.

11. Cf. BDAG 288 (εἰρήνη, 2, a): "A new and characteristic development is the combination of the Greek epistolary greeting χαίρειν with a Hebrew expression in the Pauline and post-Pauline letters χάρις καὶ εἰρήνη."

12. E. Käsemann, *Romans*, 16, cites 2 *Apoc. Bar.* 78.2 as a precedent in Jewish tradition. But (1) that document is regarded as being written in the early part of the second century A.D. (cf. A. F. J. Klijn, "2 Baruch," *OTP* 1:615-17); and (2) the expression is not the same; the Greek version reads: "mercy and peace (ἔλεος καὶ εἰρήνη) be with you," according to Pierre Bogaert, *Apocalypse de Baruch*, 2 vols., SC 144-45 (Paris: Éditions du Cerf, 1969), 2:142. Cf. "grace, mercy, and peace" in 1 Tim 1:2, 2 Tim 1:2, and 2 John 3.

13. F. Schnider and W. Stenger, *Studien*, 25-26, who cite the work of K. Berger, "Apostelbrief und apostolische Rede," 193-96.

not comprise a complete sentence, however, since there is no verb. Moreover, what begins at 1:1 can formally end at 1:7a, since the greeting in 1:7b begins with "grace and peace" in the nominative. Nevertheless, the greeting relates to what precedes rather than what follows (the Thanksgiving section, 1:8-15), and thereby concludes 1:1-7 as a unit.[14] The greeting is spoken on behalf of God to the readers of the letter.

Detailed Comment

1:1 Paul calls himself a "servant of Christ Jesus" (δοῦλος Χριστοῦ Ἰησοῦ). The term δοῦλος has usually been translated as "servant" in English versions (as in KJV, RSV, NEB, JB, TEV, NAB, NIV, and NRSV). An alternative, "slave," is sometimes suggested (as in footnotes to RSV and NRSV). The latter is preferred by various commentators and in more recent literature.[15]

What would the phrase have meant to Paul and his readers at Rome? Interpreters disagree. Common to several is the view that when Paul uses the term δοῦλος as a self-designation here (cf. Phil 1:1; Gal 1:10), he is drawing imagery from his social world, in which a high number of persons (estimated to be as many as 20 percent or more)[16] were in fact slaves, subject to legal ownership by their masters. But from this point onward, interpreters have come to differing conclusions: (1) In using the phrase Paul designates himself as completely bound to Christ in an analogous manner, and "slave" is a title of humiliation.[17] (2) The metaphor would serve as a title of leadership. Although slavery was an abhorrent institution in antiquity, it actually was an avenue for some slaves to gain upward mobility, obtain managerial roles, and reflect the status of their masters.[18] By use of the phrase, then, Paul exercises his authoritative leadership; he is the "slave of Christ."[19] (3) The phrase is a technical one, by which

---

14. J. Louw, *Semantics of New Testament Greek*, 141-42.

15. J. Knox, *IB (Romans)*, 9:379-80; C. Cranfield, *Romans*, 48-51; C. K. Barrett, *Romans*, 17; J. Dunn, *Romans*, 7-8; N. T. Wright, *NIB (Romans)*, 10:415; BDAG 259-60; Alfons Weiser, "δουλεύω," *EDNT* 1:352; D. Martin, *Slavery as Salvation*, 51-52, 59; I. Combes, *Metaphor of Slavery*, 77-94; S. Scott Bartchy, "Slavery," *ABD* 6:72; J. Byron, *Slavery Metaphors in Early Judaism and Pauline Christianity*, 231-33.

16. W. G. Rollins, "Slavery in the NT," *IDBSup* 830. The estimates for Rome range from 20 to 40 percent, according to P. Lampe, "The Roman Christians of Romans 16," 228.

17. J. Knox, *IB (Romans)*, 9:380; K. Bradley, *Slavery and Society at Rome*, 152; I. A. H. Combes, *Metaphor of Slavery*, 77-94 (esp. 83, 89, 92); R. Jewett, *Romans*, 100.

18. Dale B. Martin, *Slavery as Salvation*, 1-49. But cf. P. Garnsey, *Ideas of Slavery*, 186: "Slavery for most slaves was . . . anything but an avenue of upward mobility"; and the critique of Martin's position by K. Bradley, *Slavery and Society at Rome*, 152.

19. D. Martin, *Slavery as Salvation*, 51-52.

Paul identified himself with certain members of the *familia Caesaris* (the imperial household in Rome) who were slaves and members of the Roman church. By using a creative rhetorical tactic, Paul makes a connection between his ministry as a slave of Christ and the lives of imperial slaves, thereby having an entrée into the congregation.[20]

The imagery of slavery in the world of Paul and his readers, however, is not the only possible basis for the term. Its background could be the familiar use of the term in Hellenistic Judaism for the people of God. From this point on, two other possibilities emerge: (4) The people of Israel are designated as "servants" or "slaves" (δοῦλοι) of God in the Old Testament and other Jewish writings (LXX Deut 32:36; Josh 14:7; Isa 48:20; 2 Macc 7:33; 8:29);[21] they are a people who "serve" (δουλεύειν) God in their worship and in their corporate lives of covenant fidelity in the world (Judg 2:7; 1 Sam 7:4; 12:20; Pss 2:11; 100:2; 102:22 [LXX 99:2; 101:22]).[22] Paul therefore picks up a venerable term from Hellenistic Judaism, identifying himself with the people of Israel,[23] but with a twist; he is a servant of Israel's Messiah. (5) The term is used in the OT especially in reference to major figures, such as Abraham (Ps 105:42 [LXX 104:42]), Moses (Ps 105:26 [LXX 104:26]; 2 Kgs 18:12), Joshua (Josh 24:29 [LXX 24:30]; Judg 2:8), David (2 Sam 7:5; Ps 78:70 [LXX 77:70]), and the prophets (Jer 25:4; Amos 3:7; Zech 1:6). Since that is so, Paul links himself with other major figures in the history of Israel, using an honorific title (designating an office, parallel to "apostle") that sets him apart from other Christians.[24]

In considering the possibilities, two other considerations are needed: (1) Paul does not restrict the term "servant" to himself. He uses the term δοῦλος for other believers (1 Cor 7:22; Phil 1:1), and he speaks of them as persons who

---

20. Cf. M. Brown, "Paul's Use of Δοῦλος Χριστοῦ Ἰησοῦ in Romans 1:1," 723-37. Brown's view is dependent upon his prior claim that Philippians was written at Rome and that "those of the imperial household" (Phil 4:22) "formed part of the Roman congregation" (p. 725). The provenance of that letter is disputed, however. It is frequently thought to have been written in Ephesus. Cf. R. Brown, *Introduction*, 494-96.

21. For extrabiblical texts that speak of the Jewish people as servants (δοῦλοι) of God, cf. Philo, *Mut.* 5.46; *Her.* 2.7; Josephus, *Ant.* 11.90.

22. Extrabiblical texts with the verb include Josephus, *Ant.* 7.367; 8.257; Philo, *Cher.* 31.107; *Somn.* 2.100.

23. C. K. Barrett, *Romans*, 18; C. Cranfield, *Romans*, 50; E. Käsemann, *Romans*, 5; L. Morris, *Romans*, 37; J. Dunn, *Romans*, 7.

24. Karl H. Rengstorf, "δοῦλος," *TDNT* 2:276-77; A. Weiser, "δουλεύω," *EDNT* 1:352; J. Fitzmyer, *Romans*, 228-29; P. Stuhlmacher, *Romans*, 19; S. Bartchy, "Slavery," 6:72; P. Garnsey, *Ideas of Slavery*, 184; R. Horsley, "Paul and Slavery," 169; C. Keener, *Romans*, 19. Cf. Philip Melanchthon, *Commentary on Romans* (St. Louis: Concordia Publishing House, 1992), 60: "Paul here is not speaking of private servitude, but of his office. He calls himself a servant, that is, a minister performing an office pertaining to the kingdom of Christ."

"serve" (δουλεύειν) Christ (Rom 12:11; 14:18; 16:18), God (1 Thess 1:9), or the Lord (Rom 12:11). In calling himself a "servant" of Christ," therefore, Paul identifies himself at the outset of his letter as a fellow servant with all other Christians, including those at Rome. (2) Paul is not the only NT writer to use the imagery. The terms δοῦλος ("servant") and συνδοῦλος ("fellow servant") of Christ are used widely by other writers in the NT for Christian believers (Eph 6:6; Col 1:7; 4:7, 12; Jas 1:1; 2 Pet 1:1; Jude 1; Rev 1:1; 6:11; 19:10; 22:9).[25] Writing to a church he has never visited and certainly did not establish, Paul seeks to establish a commonality with his readers immediately. He does that in lines to follow later on (1:8-15), but he anticipates that by using the phrase "servant of Jesus Christ" in reference to himself. With these considerations in mind, it can be concluded that the term recalls the ancient term of Israelite identity, but with a Christianized nuance. The "servant of Christ" is a member of the people of God, particularly a servant of Israel's Messiah.

It is after this use of the metaphor has been established that one can return to the social world of the apostle Paul. According to Philo, most of the Jewish inhabitants of Rome during the reign of Augustus (29 B.C.–A.D. 14) had been brought there as slaves and were subsequently freed by manumission.[26] Moreover, out of the 26 persons named in Romans 16 to whom Paul sends greetings, as many as two-thirds are likely either to have been slaves themselves or to have been freed from slavery.[27] Consequently, when Paul wrote his letter to Rome, the Christian community of that city would have had in its membership both slaves and persons who had formerly been slaves, both Jewish and Gentile. With such an intimate connection with slavery, and having been known as δοῦλοι in common life, such persons could consider themselves (and others within their own Christian circles) "servants" or "slaves of Christ," thereby indicating their ultimate loyalty. Using that self-designation, Paul would be establishing rapport with his readers by using a phrase known to them. Nevertheless, the fact that Paul uses the term for himself (having never been a servant/slave in the socioeconomic sense) and uses it for believers elsewhere indicates that the term was not derived primarily from the social world, but from the Jewish self-designation of the people of God.

While Paul identifies with his readers at Rome by using the term "servant of Christ Jesus," he distinguishes himself from them, and from Christians in general, by his claim to be "called" (κλητός) as an "apostle" (ἀπόστολος). By designating himself as an apostle, Paul also precludes the possibility of begin-

---

25. Related terms are found as well: slave(s) of God (Acts 16:17; Titus 1:1; 1 Pet 2:16; Rev 7:3; 15:3; 19:5), slave(s) of the Lord (Acts 4:29; 2 Tim 2:24), and slave of the Lamb (Rev 22:3).

26. Philo, *Legat.* 23.155.

27. P. Lampe, "The Roman Christians of Romans 16," 228.

ning this letter in the same manner as he did Philippians: "Paul and Timothy, slaves of Jesus Christ" (Phil 1:1). Even though Timothy is present with Paul at the writing of Romans and sends greetings (Rom 16:21), he was not considered an apostle.

Like the prophets before him, who were called to their prophetic tasks (cf. especially Isa 46:1-6; Jer 1:5), Paul claims to have been called by God to his role as an apostle. That is confirmed not only by the verbal adjective "called" (κλητός), which is equivalent to the divine passive ("called [by God]"), but above all by the language he uses at Galatians 1:15-16 to describe his call more explicitly. It resonates in particular with the language used to speak of the call of Jeremiah. The similarity can be seen by comparing what Paul himself says with the text from Jeremiah in the Septuagint:

Jeremiah 1:5 (LXX):
πρὸ τοῦ με πλάσαι σε ἐν κοιλίᾳ ἐπίσταμαί σε
καὶ πρὸ τοῦ σε ἐξελθεῖν ἐκ μήτρας ἡγίακά σε
προφήτην εἰς ἔθνη τέθεικά σε

Before I formed you in the womb I knew you,
and before you came from your mother I consecrated you;
I appointed you a prophet to the nations.

Galatians 1:15-16:
Ὅτε δὲ εὐδόκησεν [ὁ θεὸς] ὁ ἀφορίσας με ἐκ κοιλίας μητρός μου
καὶ καλέσας διὰ τῆς χάριτος αὐτοῦ ἀποκαλύψαι τὸν υἱὸν αὐτοῦ ἐν ἐμοί,
ἵνα εὐαγγελίζωμαι αὐτὸν ἐν τοῖς ἔθνεσιν. . . .

But when [God], who had set me apart from my mother's womb,
and called me through his grace, was pleased to reveal his son to me,
in order that I might proclaim him among the nations (or Gentiles). . . .

Two items stand out in particular: (1) Paul, as in the text from Jeremiah, speaks of his vocation as having been determined before he was born; and (2) Paul, as in the text from Jeremiah, speaks of that vocation as a divinely given appointment to go to the "nations/Gentiles" as an apostle. What Paul wrote has similarities to the prophetic call of Isaiah 49:1-6 as well, particularly where the latter says that the Lord had called him before he was born in his mother's womb (49:1b, ἐκ κοιλίας μητρός μου ἐκάλεσεν τὸ ὄνομά μου, "He [the Lord] called my name from my mother's womb"). For more on Paul as an apostle to the "nations" or "Gentiles," see the discussion at 15:14-33.

Paul uses the same formulation ("called to be an apostle") at 1 Corinthians 1:1 and, in any case, identifies himself as an apostle at the outset of other letters

(2 Cor 1:1; Gal 1:1). The term "apostle" means "one who is sent" (cf. John 13:16, "the apostle [is not greater than] the one who sent him"). Specifically, at least for Paul, the term "apostle" signifies one who has been sent by the risen Lord, not the earthly Jesus. It cannot therefore be restricted to the Twelve. While Paul grants that the latter were apostles (1 Cor 9:5; Gal 1:17), he speaks of other persons as apostles as well (Rom 16:7; 1 Cor 15:7) who were outside the circle of the Twelve. Clearly the term is a technical one by the time that Paul uses it. Its origins can scarcely be traced but must have been used from the beginning of the Christian movement and mission. The Greek ἀπόστολος appears only once in the LXX (3 Kgdms 14:6; but all of 14:1-20 is missing in some mss, including Vaticanus) as a translation for the Hebrew שָׁלוּחַ, applied to the prophet Ahijah, already having a technical meaning for a messenger from God.[28] By way of contrast, the Greek term appears over 80 times in the NT.

Paul speaks of his call to apostleship more fully in Galatians 1:11-17. There he does not speak of his call to apostleship in a manner that suggests that he went through a "conversion" from Judaism to Christianity. Instead he speaks of himself as one who stands in the long line of succession of those called by the God of Israel — the God of the entire world — for a specific vocation. He, a child of Israel, was called to proclaim the gospel particularly to the Gentiles (Rom 11:13; Gal 1:16; 2:7-9). On his call as apostle to the Gentiles, cf. the comment on 11:13.

Paul speaks of himself as having been "set apart for the gospel of God." The word for "set apart" (ἀφωρισμένος, aorist passive participle of ἀφωρίζω) is used again in Galatians 1:15 (but as an aorist active participle, ἀφορίσας). The divine passive is intended here, for Paul had been "set apart" by God himself for service to the gospel. The echo of Paul's sometimes heated assertions of his apostleship — made over against his opponents in earlier correspondence (2 Cor 11:1-5, 22-29; Gal 1:11-12, 17) — is heard here.

That the "gospel of God" is referred to in the very first sentence of the letter cannot be insignificant. There can be no misunderstanding. Paul's apostleship differs from those forms of apostleship displayed by others who have opposed him. It is an apostleship for the sake of the gospel alone (cf. Gal 1:7-9; 2 Cor 11:5). Moreover, the genitive phrase εὐαγγέλιον θεοῦ ("gospel of God") signifies that God is the originator of the gospel Paul proclaims.[29]

1:2 God, says Paul, "promised the gospel beforehand" (προεπηγγείλατο, first aorist middle of the verb προεπαγγέλλω) "by means of the prophets in the holy scriptures." The "holy scriptures" were frequently designated by Paul's time

---

28. Karl H. Rengstorf, "ἀπόστολος," *TDNT* 1:413-15. In rabbinic Judaism the corresponding term שָׁלִיחַ is used for a commissioned representative (for legal, commercial, or religious matters), but it is not attested prior to the rise of the Christian movement.

29. BDF 90 §163.

as "the law and the prophets" (Prologue to Sirach; Luke 24:44). But the "prophets" in particular conveyed the promises of God. Paul does not cite any particular texts in the prophetic books.[30] For Paul, the Scriptures are the "oracles of God" (Rom 3:2) and the bearers of the promises of God (9:4). The scriptural prophets anticipate and promise a new age, which is a present reality as a result of the resurrection of Jesus from the dead.

1:3-4 The prepositional phrase "concerning his Son" is linked conceptually with the "gospel of God" in 1:1. Paul is thus an apostle of the gospel concerning the Son of God. In 1:3-4 Paul speaks about the identity of the Son. The verses contain two assertions in parallelism:

> He was from the family of David according to the flesh.
> He was designated Son of God in power according to the Spirit of
> holiness from [his] resurrection from the dead.

The two lines are parallel in their structure through their use of participles (τοῦ γενομένου at 1:3 and τοῦ ὁρισθέντος at 1:4) and prepositional phrases (κατὰ σάρκα in 1:3 and κατὰ πνεῦμα ἁγιωσύνης in 1:4). The preposition κατά can be translated as "according to," although alternatives have been suggested.[31] The couplet (beginning with τοῦ γενομένου in 1:3 and ending with νεκρῶν in 1:4) can be considered a pre-Pauline creedal formula, as many interpreters have held.[32] It may well have been known within the Christian communities of Rome, and by reciting it at the very outset of the letter, Paul makes an immediate connection with those to whom he writes.

---

30. It is unlikely that Paul alludes here to specific texts (e.g., Isa 49:1-7), as suggested by J. Dunn, *Romans*, 8.

31. C. F. D. Moule, *An Idiom-Book of New Testament Greek*, 58, suggests for 1:3: "as far as physical descent is concerned"; BDAG 513 (κατά, 6): "with respect to the flesh, physically."

32. J. Weiss, *Earliest Christianity*, 1:118-19; R. Bultmann, *Theology of the New Testament*, 1:49-50; 2:121; C. H. Dodd, *Romans*, 4-5; C. K. Barrett, *Romans*, 20-22; E. Best, *Romans*, 10; J. Knox, *IB (Romans)*, 9:382; V. Neufeld, *The Earliest Christian Confessions*, 51; F. Hahn, *The Titles of Jesus in Christology*, 246; R. Fuller, *The Foundations of New Testament Christology*, 165; H. Conzelmann, *An Outline of the Theology of the New Testament*, 77; C. Burger, *Jesus als Davidssohn*, 27-29; K. Wengst, *Christologische Formeln*, 112-17; W. Kümmel, *The Theology of the New Testament*, 110-11; L. Goppelt, *Theology of the New Testament*, 1:22; O. Michel, *Römer*, 38-39; E. Käsemann, *Romans*, 10-11; D. Zeller, *Römer*, 35-36; M. Hengel, *The Son of God*, 59-60; C. Cranfield, *Romans*, 57; R. Harrisville, *Romans*, 18; J. Fitzmyer, *Romans*, 230; J. Dunn, *Romans*, 5; P. Stuhlmacher, *Romans*, 18; idem, *Biblische Theologie des Neuen Testaments*, 1:186; G. Strecker, *Theology of the New Testament*, 66-69; C. Tuckett, *Christology and the New Testament*, 49-50; C. Talbert, *Romans*, 31-32; L. Keck, *Romans*, 43; and L. Hurtado, *Lord Jesus Christ*, 171. That these verses were composed by Paul from traditional materials is held by V. Poythress, "Is Romans 1:3-4 a *Pauline* Confession after All?" 180-83, and D. Moo, *Romans*, 45-46 (n. 31). J. Scott, *Adoption as Sons of God*, 227-36, concludes that there is no certain basis for the passage to be pre-Pauline.

There are several reasons for concluding that 1:3-4 is a pre-Pauline creedal formula: (1) The term "Spirit of holiness" (πνεῦμα ἁγιωσύνης) is a Semitism[33] that is otherwise not used by Paul or any other NT writer. Paul's terms are "the Holy Spirit,"[34] "the Spirit of God,"[35] "the Spirit of Christ,"[36] "the Spirit of his [= God's] Son,"[37] or simply (and most commonly) "the Spirit."[38] (2) The work of the Spirit in this passage is not characteristic of Paul's own thinking. Here the Spirit is instrumental in the resurrection of Jesus from the dead,[39] whereas in Paul's thinking it is God (the Father) who raises him from the dead,[40] and the Spirit proceeds from Christ; it does not act upon him.[41] (3) The Spirit/flesh antithesis, as expressed here, is uncharacteristic of Paul. Where an antithesis exists between the Spirit and the flesh in the letters of Paul, it is anthropological (i.e., within the human being), not Christological.[42] (4) The Christological view expressed in the formula is not that of Paul. Paul affirms the preexistence and incarnation of the Son of God, which is presupposed and expressed implicitly already in the first four words of 1:3, composed by Paul (περὶ τοῦ υἱοῦ αὐτοῦ, "concerning his Son"). Paul holds to a three-stage Christology (preexistence, incarnate earthly existence, postresurrection reign). The formula of 1:3-4, however, sets forth a two-stage Christology (earthly existence, postresurrection reign) by which Jesus became Son of God only by his exaltation; the descendant of David was designated Son of God at his resurrection.

The last point is controverted. While interpreters agree that the two

---

33. The same expression (πνεῦμα ἁγιωσύνης) appears in the Greek version of *T. Levi* 18.11. The Hebrew expressions רוּחַ קָדְשְׁךָ and רוּחַ קָדְשׁוֹ appear at Ps 51:13; Isa 63:10-11 (where the LXX [Ps 50:13; Isa 63:10-11] has τὸ πνεῦμα τὸ ἅγιον); the expression in Hebrew appears also at 1QS 4.21; 8.16; 9.3; CD 2.12; 1QH 7.6-7; 9.32.

34. Rom 5:5; 9:1; 14:17; 15:13, 16; 1 Cor 6:19; 12:3; 2 Cor 13:13; 1 Thess 1:5, 6; 4:8.

35. Rom 8:9, 14; 15:19; 1 Cor 2:11, 14; 3:16; 6:11; 7:40; 2 Cor 3:3 ("the Spirit of the living God"); Phil 3:3.

36. Rom 8:9; Phil 1:19 ("the Spirit of Jesus Christ").

37. Gal 4:6.

38. Rom 7:6; 8:4, 5 (twice), 6, 9, 10, 11 (twice), 13, 16, 23, 26 (twice), 27 (twice); 15:30; 1 Cor 2:4, 10 (twice), 12, 13; 12:4, 7, 8 (twice), 9 (twice), 11 (twice), 13; 14:2; 2 Cor 1:22; 3:6, 8, 17 (twice), 18; 5:5; Gal 3:2, 3, 5, 14; 4:29; 5:5, 16, 17 (twice), 18, 22, 25 (twice); 6:1, 8 (twice); Phil 2:1; 1 Thess 5:19.

39. Contra M. Fatehi, *The Spirit's Relation to the Risen Lord in Paul*, 253-54, who interprets the verse to mean that Christ is Lord according to the Spirit *at work among believers* (emphasis mine) after the resurrection.

40. That God raised Jesus from the dead is stated at Rom 4:24; 8:11; 10:9; 1 Cor 6:14; 15:15; 2 Cor 4:14; Gal 1:1; 1 Thess 1:10; that Christ was raised (divine passive) is asserted at Rom 4:25; 6:4, 9; 7:4; 8:34; 1 Cor 15:4, 12, 13, 14, 16, 17, 20; 2 Cor 5:15.

41. E. Käsemann, *Romans*, 11.

42. O. Michel, *Römer*, 39; E. Käsemann, *Romans*, 11; J. Fitzmyer, *Romans*, 230; E. Schweizer, "Röm. 1,3f. und Gegensatz von Fleisch und Geist vor und bei Paulus," 180-81.

verses express a Christology that differentiates between the status of the earthly Jesus and that of the resurrected Jesus, they do not agree on the significance of that differentiation. (1) Some are forthright in saying that the unit expresses a primitive "adoptionism," meaning that in his earthly life Jesus did not have a messianic status but became the Messiah/Son of God at his resurrection, thereby being "adopted" as God's Son.[43] (2) Others do not use the word "adoptionism," but agree that the parallelism asserts that at his resurrection Jesus took on a status and role that he did not have previously.[44] (3) Still others maintain that the passage does not say that the resurrection was the occasion by which Jesus became the Son of God; instead, it was simply the moment at which Jesus (whose preexistence and incarnation are presupposed) began his exalted life.[45]

The three views can be reduced finally to two. The exegetical and theological issue is whether in this couplet the resurrection is said to be the moment of transformation of the earthly Jesus into the exalted Lord (so Jesus was "made" Son of God at Easter), or whether the resurrection was simply the ratification of his sonship and the beginning of his exalted life. In regard to this, the following points can be made: (1) There is an antithesis between the two members of the couplet (an antithetical parallelism),[46] and particularly between the

---

43. J. Weiss, *Earliest Christianity*, 1:118-19; 2:476; R. Bultmann, *Theology*, 1:50; O. Michel, *Römer*, 40; J. Knox, *IB (Romans)*, 9:382; E. Käsemann, *Romans*, 12; F. Hahn, *The Titles of Jesus in Christology*, 248-49; H. Conzelmann, *Outline of New Testament Theology*, 77; L. Goppelt, *Theology of the New Testament*, 2:22; C. Burger, *Jesus als Davidssohn*, 28-29; K. Wengst, *Christologische Formeln*, 115; G. Strecker, *Theology of the New Testament*, 68; R. Jewett, *Romans*, 104. C. K. Barrett, *Romans*, 22, says that the passage has an "adoptionist tinge"; J. Dunn, "Christology (NT)," *ABD* 1:983, notes that the passage has an "adoptionistic" ring.

44. C. H. Dodd, *Romans*, 4-5; E. Best, *Romans*, 11; O. Michel, *Römer*, 38-39; Eduard Schweizer, "πνεῦμα," *TDNT* 6:417; J. Dunn, *Romans*, 14; P. Stuhlmacher, *Romans*, 18; L. Keck, *Romans*, 45; M. de Jonge, *Christology in Context*, 49; C. Tuckett, *Christology and the New Testament*, 50. J. Scott, *Adoption as Sons*, 228, 234, 236, grants that "adoptionistic language" is used, but he says that it refers to Paul's perception ("Paul perceived," p. 243) on the Damascus Road that Jesus was the adopted Son of God in fulfillment of 2 Sam 7:12-14. That view, however, cannot be sustained, for Paul writes concerning something that happened to Jesus, not himself.

45. Origen, *Commentarii in Epistulam ad Romanos*, ed. Theresia Heither, 5 vols. (New York: Herder, 1990-95), 2:194; M. Luther, *Romans*, 147; A. Nygren, *Romans*, 48; L. Goppelt, *Theology of the New Testament*, 2:22-23; C. Cranfield, *Romans*, 58, 62; J. Fitzmyer, *Romans*, 236; idem, "The Christology of the Epistle to the Romans," 85; M. Hengel, *Studies in Early Christology*, 157; M. Fatehi, *The Spirit's Relation to the Risen Lord in Paul*, 248; D. Moo, *Romans*, 48 ("change in status or function").

46. B. Schneider, "Κατὰ Πνεῦμα Ἁγιωσύνης (Romans 1,4)," 361. J. Scott, *Adoption as Sons*, 239, insists that there is a "climactic" parallelism here "that carries forward the sense to its culmination," not an "antithetical" one. But that is to miss the clear force of the antithesis between the two prepositional phrases κατὰ σάρκα and κατὰ πνεῦμα.

46

two sets of prepositional phrases ("according to the flesh"//"according to the Spirit" and "from the family of David"//"from [his] resurrection from the dead"); these antitheses speak in favor of a contrast rather than complementarity. (2) The verb ὁρίζω in 1:4, not otherwise used by Paul, has a rather consistent meaning that should be considered. In classical Greek its basic meaning is to "divide" or "separate from, as a border or boundary,"[47] and in inscriptions and papyri prior to and after Paul's time it has the primary sense of "divide," "separate from," or "set apart."[48] It can thus mean to "separate entities and so establish a boundary."[49] The aorist passive participle τοῦ ὁρισθέντος ("who was designated") is a divine passive, and coupled with the phrase ἐξ ἀναστάσεως νεκρῶν ("from resurrection from the dead"), it signifies that Jesus was "designated" (RSV) Son of God or, indeed, "installed" as Son of God as a result of his resurrection.[50] Some English versions render the verb in question as "to declare" (NIV, NRSV), which leaves options open. Translated that way, the resurrection could be understood either as the moment at which Jesus was "designated" or "appointed" God's Son (for the first time) or in some more explicit way "declared" God's Son (which he had always been) as he entered into his postresurrection reign. The rigor of the verb, however, speaks in favor of "designated," "installed," or "appointed."

Whether one insists upon the term "adoptionism" or not is not a major issue. Adoptionism, as it is known in the history of doctrine (also known as dynamic monarchianism), was articulated in the second- and third-century teachings of Theodotus of Byzantium (ca. A.D. 190) and Paul of Samosata (ca. A.D. 260-70), whose teachings were condemned at the Council of Antioch (A.D. 268). The reason that the term "adoptionism" might be considered inappropriate here is that it is anachronistic. The adoptionists consciously opposed a three-stage Christology, whereas presumably neither Paul nor the composer(s) of the pre-Pauline formula of Romans 1:3-4 would have done so.[51] Nevertheless, with that caution in mind, and as a convenient shorthand, it can be helpful to speak of a "primitive adoptionism" here that is expressed elsewhere in the NT as well — whether the moment of "adoption" is the exaltation (or resurrection) of Jesus (Acts 2:36; 3:13; 5:30; 10:39-42; 13:33) or his baptism (Mark 1:9-11). Christology has a history not only after the NT all the way to the Council of Chalcedon (A.D. 451), when the two-nature Christology was formulated, but also prior

47. LSJ 1250.
48. MM 457.
49. BDAG 723.
50. Gerhard Schneider, "ὁρίζω," *EDNT* 2:532: "Since the point in time from which the sonship dates is given, here ὁρίζω must mean install." Cf. F. Hahn, *Titles of Jesus*, 250; K. Wengst, *Christologische Formeln*, 114-15.
51. J. Dunn, *Romans*, 14; P. Stuhlmacher, *Biblische Theologie*, 1:188.

to the NT and within it. The adoptionism spoken of in regard to these passages must be considered more functional than ontological. Whereas the great Christological debates to come were about the nature of Christ, here the focus is temporal and related to the earthly ministry and the postresurrection reign in sequence.

Interpreters have differed on the question whether the verses contain the pre-Pauline formula intact — or whether Paul added words or phrases. Some have suggested that Paul added the prepositional phrase κατὰ σάρκα ("according to the flesh"), which is used frequently (but not exclusively) by Paul among NT writers,[52] and κατὰ πνεῦμα ἁγιωσύνης ("according to the Spirit of holiness").[53] But the wording of the latter phrase, so uncharacteristic of Paul, speaks against his having composed that and, in turn, its antecedent antithetical phrase in 1:3. Some have suggested that Paul has inserted the phrase ἐν δυνάμει ("in power") in 1:4.[54] A decision on this is more difficult. There seem to be no compelling reasons for holding that it is a Pauline insertion.[55] In any case, interpreters have asserted that the phrase cannot be considered adverbial, modifying "designated," but attaches rather to "Son of God."[56] That is probable, for the exaltation is not simply a sign of the power of God, but rather an act of investiture of the Son with power.[57] Accordingly, the clause then speaks of the Son's investiture with power from the time of "resurrection from the dead."[58] Moreover, the preposition ἐν ("in") can be considered to have the sense of "with," as often in the NT (particularly in Semitisms where ἐν is colored by the double meaning of בְּ as both "in" and "with"), including the letters of Paul.[59]

52. Besides here, it is used at Rom 4:1; 8:12; 9:3, 5; 1 Cor 1:26; 10:18; 2 Cor 1:17; 5:16; 10:2, 3; 11:18; Gal 4:23, 29. It is also found, however, in the deutero-Pauline letters (Eph 6:5; Col 3:22) and at John 8:15.

53. Both are pre-Pauline additions according to R. Bultmann, *Theology of the New Testament*, 1:49; G. Strecker, *Theology of the New Testament*, 67; K. Wengst, *Christologische Formeln*, 113-14; E. Schweizer, "Röm. 1,3f. und Gegensatz von Fleisch und Geist vor und bei Paulus," 180-89; and R. Fuller, *The Foundations of New Testament Christology*, 165.

54. R. Fuller, *The Foundations of New Testament Christology*, 165; K. Wengst, *Christologische Formeln*, 113-14.

55. Cf. remarks by F. Hahn, *The Titles of Jesus*, 247.

56. O. Michel, *Römer*, 39-40; C. Cranfield, *Romans*, 62; J. Dunn, *Romans*, 14; J. Fitzmyer, *Romans*, 235; M. Fatehi, *The Spirit's Relation to the Risen Lord in Paul*, 247. In BDAG 330 (ἐν, 11), however, the phrase is considered adverbial, equivalent to "powerfully" with references also to Mark 9:1; Col 1:29; 2 Thess 1:11.

57. Cf. O. Michel, *Römer*, 40.

58. The prepositional phrase ἐξ ἀναστάσεως probably has a temporal meaning (so "from the time of [his] resurrection"), as held by F. Hahn, *The Titles of Jesus*, 250; C. Cranfield, *Romans*, 62; J. Fitzmyer, *Romans*, 236; J. Scott, *Adoption as Sons*, 242 (n. 80); G. Schneider, "ὁρίζω," *EDNT* 2:532.

59. Cf. BDAG 328 (ἐν, 5); BDF 117-18 (§219).

The usage speaks in favor of the inclusion of the phrase within the pre-Pauline formula, although not decisively. The only clear additions that Paul made to the formula are the introductory words of 1:3 ("concerning his Son") and the closing words of 1:4 ("Jesus Christ our Lord").

Descent from David designates a royal lineage and dignity elsewhere in the NT,[60] as well as in pre-Christian Jewish literature,[61] but here and at 2 Timothy 2:8 it signifies Jesus' earthly existence and lowliness.[62]

Although Christ's own resurrection is meant in 1:4, the term "his" does not appear in that verse for good reason. For Paul, and presumably for his readers, the resurrection of Jesus and the general resurrection of the dead cannot be separated. The "resurrection of the dead" was inaugurated at the moment of Christ's own resurrection, the "first fruits"; the remainder of the resurrection of the dead is yet to come (cf. 1 Cor 15:20-28). The significance of this is that the resurrection of Jesus from the dead was not just a turning point for him, a passing from death to life, but for humanity as a whole.[63] What God has in store for humanity has taken place proleptically in the resurrection of Jesus; the resurrection of the dead and the era of the Messiah have burst forth.

How Paul would have become acquainted with the Christological formula of 1:3-4 and why he used it in his letter to Rome are matters of interest and speculation. It is commonly thought to have had its origins in a Hellenistic Jewish Christian community.[64] It is possible that the formula was familiar at Rome itself and was made known to Paul from his acquaintances there (e.g., Prisca and Aquila).[65] If so, when Paul makes use of it at the very outset of the letter, he is not only establishing rapport with his readers, to be sure, but is also signaling that his own understanding of the gospel can accommodate its use. The formula presupposes a primitive, functional Christology that might well have been in keeping with the faith of the more conservative Jewish community at Rome.[66] Paul is then already participating in the mutual encouragement of faith that he goes on to speak of (1:12).

The formula expresses the fact that the promises of 2 Samuel 7:8-17 (and

---

60. Mark 10:47-48//Matt 20:30-31//Luke 18:38-39; Matt 1:1; 9:27; 21:9; 2 Tim 2:8.

61. *Pss. Sol.* 17.21.

62. F. Hahn, *The Titles of Jesus*, 248.

63. Cf. Augustine, *Unfinished Commentary on the Epistle to the Romans* 5.11; A. Nygren, *Romans*, 48-51.

64. C. Burger, *Jesus als Davidssohn*, 27-30, 41; K. Wengst, *Christologische Formeln*, 116.

65. C. H. Dodd, *Romans*, 5; C. K. Barrett, *Romans*, 20; R. Bultmann, *Theology of the New Testament*, 1:49; E. Best, *Romans*, 10; C. Cranfield, *Romans*, 57; C. Burger, *Jesus als Davidssohn*, 30, 41; C. Tuckett, *Christology and the New Testament*, 50.

66. On the conservative character of the Roman church, cf. R. Brown and J. Meier, *Antioch and Rome*, 87-210; J. Ropes, "The Epistle to the Romans and Jewish Christianity," 353-65.

its parallel in 1 Chr 17:7-15) concerning the house of David have been fulfilled in the resurrection of Jesus from the dead and his consequent enthronement as Son of God. In that passage the prophet Nathan is instructed to declare to David that the Lord will raise up his offspring or "seed," σπέρμα (7:12), and establish his kingdom, and the promise is given: "I will be a father to him, and he shall be a son (υἱός) to me" (7:14). These promises (Rom 1:2) are now declared to have been fulfilled through Jesus' coming into the world and his resurrection (Rom 1:3-4). The passage in 2 Samuel 7 is decisive for the contents of Romans 1:3-4. Except for its parallel in 1 Chronicles 17, which is dependent on it, it is the only known source that combines in one place the terms "seed" (σπέρμα) and "son" (υἱός) in reference to the Messiah and the concept of the Messiah as Son of David.[67] Further, the divine promise to raise (ἀναστήσω) the "offspring" of David (2 Sam 7:12//1 Chr 17:11) can be taken to refer to the resurrection of Jesus, which has now taken place.

1:5-6 On Paul's claim to apostleship, see the comment on 1:1. That Paul would also claim to have received "grace" (along with "apostleship") for his mission to the nations sounds at once unusual, since the word "grace" so customarily denotes divine favor in the letters of Paul, not an enabling power. But in fact Paul speaks elsewhere of having received grace as authorization, power, and capacity to carry out his apostolic mission (cf. Rom 12:3; 15:15; 1 Cor 3:10; 15:10).[68] His apostolic mission is to bring about the "obedience of faith" (ὑπακοὴν πίστεως) "among all the nations for his name's sake."

The phrase "obedience of faith," which appears again in the Pauline corpus only at 16:26 (deutero-Pauline; see comment there), is not likely to mean "obedience to the faith" (KJV, i.e., the Christian message), but signifies instead "faith that consists of obedience" (NIV: "the obedience that comes from faith"). The Greek term πίστεως ("of faith") is a genitive of apposition. Paul's mission is thus to bring people to faith in Christ and its attendant obedience to him.[69]

Paul conducts his mission ἐν πᾶσιν τοῖς ἔθνεσιν. This prepositional phrase is translated as "among all the *nations*" in the RSV and ESV ("among all nations" in KJV and "in all nations" in NEB), but as "among all the *Gentiles*" in the NIV, NRSV, and NET. The former is to be preferred. If Paul had been *an* or

---

67. The term "son of David" is applied to the Messiah in *Pss. Sol.* 17.21.

68. BDAG 1080 (χάρις, 4); J. Nolland, "Grace as Power," 26-31. The relationship between grace and charisma in Paul is discussed by H. von Lips, "Der Apostolat des Paulus," 305-34.

69. On this there is virtual consensus among major interpreters; cf. A. Schlatter, *Romans*, 11; C. K. Barrett, *Romans*, 22; C. Cranfield, *Romans*, 66; J. Dunn, *Romans*, 17; J. Fitzmyer, *Romans*, 237; D. Moo, *Romans*, 51-53. Cf. also J. Knox, *IB (Romans)*, 9:380: "the obedience [to Christ] which comes from faith"; R. Jewett, *Romans*, 110: "obedience produced by the gospel"; D. Garlington, *Faith, Obedience, and Perseverance*, 30: "the obedience which consists in faith, and the obedience which is the product of faith."

even *the* "apostle to the Gentiles," he would not have had to travel outside of Palestine and Syria. His mission was to all the "nations" known to him. The time of the Messiah has arrived, and it is time for the nations of the world to turn from idolatry to the worship of the God of Israel, indeed the God of the whole world; and that turning and worship can occur for the (Gentile) "nations" of the world without circumcision and Torah observance. It is only when Paul is understood to be an apostle to the "nations" that one can make sense of his far-flung travels in Syria, Asia Minor, Greece, Macedonia, and now to the lands of the West. At this place (1:5) he indicates that he works for the sake of Jesus' name "among all the nations" known to him.[70]

Paul goes on to address his readers with the words: "among whom [referring back to the nations (ἔθνεσιν)] you also are called to belong to Jesus Christ" (1:6). It is at Rome that "all the nations" are represented, and "among whom" the house churches of that city are located.[71] The Christians at Rome, though living "among" the nations, are persons who have been "called" (the verbal adjective κλητός is used again, as in 1:1; cf. 8:28) from the nations, i.e., they have been called by God in the era of the Messiah to belong to Christ. Just as Israel of old had been a people whom God called (Isa 41:8-9; 42:6; 48:12),[72] and could not have been God's people otherwise, so now those who belong to Christ are a people called into being (Rom 8:28; 1 Cor 1:1-2, 24; Jude 1; Rev 17:14). That also means that they are numbered among those characterized by faith and obedience, even though they have not come to that through Paul's own mission. It would not be fitting for Paul to be referring to the Christians at Rome here as "Gentiles," for the church at Rome did not consist only of Gentiles; it had a (presumably minority) Jewish membership as well (cf. 4:1, 12; 7:1; 16:3-4, 7).[73]

1:7 The addressees in Rome are God's "beloved" and "called [to be]

---

70. This and related matters are discussed further in A. Hultgren, "The Scriptural Foundations for Paul's Mission to the Gentiles," 21-44, and in the exegetical commentary on Rom 15:14-21.

71. Cf. A. Schlatter, *Romans,* 11; O. Michel, *Römer,* 42; and J. Scott, *Paul and the Nations,* 122, who favors "nations" on the basis of Rom 1:13-15.

72. Cf. also 4Q509 97-98.6-8: "You have chosen a people in the period of your favour, because you remembered your covenant. You established them . . . to make them holy among all the nations. And you have renewed your covenant with them. . . ." Quoted from *The Dead Sea Scrolls: Study Edition,* ed. Florentino García Martínez and Eibert J. C. Tigchelaar, 2 vols. (Grand Rapids: Wm. B. Eerdmans, 1997-98), 2:1027.

73. On the mixed (Jewish-Gentile) character of the church(es) of Rome, cf. C. Cranfield, *Romans,* 1:16-21; J. Fitzmyer, *Romans,* 76-80; R. Brown, *Introduction,* 559-64; and Peter Lampe, "The Roman Christians of Romans 16," 224-25. The translation of ἔθνεσιν in 1:5 as "nations" is supported by A. Schlatter, *Romans,* 11; O. Michel, *Römer,* 42; and K. Haacker, *Römer,* 20, 28. Others contend that it should be translated "Gentiles": E. Käsemann, *Romans,* 15; C. K. Barrett, *Romans,* 23; C. Cranfield, *Romans,* 67; J. Dunn, *Romans,* 18; J. Fitzmyer, *Romans,* 238.

saints." The term ἀγαπητοῖς θεοῦ ("God's beloved") appears only here in Paul's letters for a Christian community. The only other time he speaks of a community that is "beloved" by God, he refers to Israel (Rom 11:28). At other times the "beloved" are persons "beloved" by Paul, referring either to a community (Rom 12:19; 1 Cor 4:14; 10:14; 15:58; 2 Cor 7:1; 12:19; Phil 2:12; 4:1) or to individuals (Rom 16:5-12; 1 Cor 4:17; Phlm 1, 16). Those addressed have been summoned by God to be "saints" (cf. 1 Cor 1:2, 24), i.e., persons who — by virtue of belonging to Christ — are set apart, sanctified, from the common lot of humanity. Augustine put it so succinctly: "One should not think that 'called to be saints' indicates that they were called because they were holy. Rather, they were made holy because they were called."[74]

The concept of being a people called and holy is traditional in Israel's heritage (Lev 19:2; Deut 7:6; 14:2, 21; Isa 48:12; 62:12), but here the people called are both Jewish and Gentile, for the gospel is for both, and the community of believers embraces both.[75]

BIBLIOGRAPHY

Agnew, Francis H. "On the Origin of the Term *Apostolos*." *CBQ* 38 (1976): 49-53.

———. "The Origin of the NT Apostle-Concept: A Review of Research." *JBL* 105 (1986): 75-96.

Allen, Leslie C. "The Old Testament Background of (προ)ὁρίζειν in the New Testament." *NTS* 17 (1970-71): 104-8.

Barnett, Paul W. "Romans and the Origins of Paul's Christology." In *History and Exegesis: New Testament Essays in Honor of Dr. E. Earle Ellis,* 90-103. Ed. S. Aaron Son. Edinburgh: T&T Clark, 2006.

Barrett, C. K. "Shaliach and Apostle." In *Donum Gentilicium: New Testament Studies in Honour of David Daube,* 88-102. Ed. Ernst Bammel et al. Oxford: Clarendon Press, 1978.

Bartsch, Hans-Werner. "Zur vorpaulinischen Bekenntnisformel im Eingang des Römerbriefs." *TZ* 23 (1967): 329-39.

Beasley-Murray, Paul. "Romans 1:3f.: An Early Confession of Faith in the Lordship of Jesus." *TynB* 31 (1980): 147-54.

Berger, Klaus. "Apostelbrief und apostolische Rede: Zum Formular frühchristlicher Briefe." *ZNW* 63 (1974): 190-231.

Boismard, Marie-Émile. "Constitué fils de Dieu (Rom. 1:4)." *RB* 60 (1953): 5-17.

---

74. Augustine, *Unfinished Commentary on the Epistle to the Romans* 7.7; quoted from *Augustine on Romans: Propositions from the Epistle to the Romans; Unfinished Commentary on the Epistle to the Romans,* ed. Paula Fredriksen Landes, SBL.TT 23 (Chico: Scholars Press, 1982), 61-63.

75. A. Schlatter, *Romans,* 11.

Bolt, Peter, and Mark Thompson, eds. *The Gospel to the Nations: Perspectives on Paul's Mission: In Honour of Peter T. O'Brien.* Downers Grove: InterVarsity Press, 2000.

Boring, M. Eugene, Klaus Berger, and Carsten Colpe, eds. *Hellenistic Commentary to the New Testament.* Nashville: Abingdon Press, 1995.

Bradley, Keith R. *Slaves and Masters in the Roman Empire: A Study in Social Control.* New York: Oxford University Press, 1987.

—————. *Slavery and Society at Rome.* Cambridge: Cambridge University Press, 1994.

Brandt, Wilhelm. *Dienst und Dienen im Neuen Testament,* N.T.F. 2/5. Gütersloh: C. Bertelsmann, 1931.

Brown, Michael J. "Paul's Use of Δοῦλος Χριστοῦ Ἰησοῦ in Romans 1:1." *JBL* 120 (2001): 723-37.

Brown, Raymond E., and John P. Meier, *Antioch and Rome: New Testament Cradles of Catholic Christianity.* New York: Paulist Press, 1983.

Buckland, W. W. *The Roman Law of Slavery: The Condition of the Slave in Private Law from Augustus to Justinian.* Cambridge: Cambridge University Press, 1908; reprinted, New York: AMS Press, 1969.

Bultmann, Rudolf. *Theology of the New Testament.* 2 vols. New York: Charles Scribner's Sons, 1951-55.

Burger, Christoph. *Jesus als Davidssohn: Eine traditionsgeschichtliche Untersuchung.* FRLANT 98. Göttingen: Vandenhoeck & Ruprecht, 1970.

Byron, John. *Recent Research on Paul and Slavery.* RRBS 3. Sheffield: Sheffield Phoenix Press, 2008.

—————. *Slavery Metaphors in Early Judaism and Pauline Christianity: A Traditio-Historical and Exegetical Examination.* WUNT 2/162. Tübingen: J. C. B. Mohr (Paul Siebeck), 2003.

Byrskog, Samuel. "Epistolography, Rhetoric and Letter Prescript: Romans 1.1-7 as a Test Case." *JSNT* 65 (1997): 27-46.

Campbell, William S. "'All God's Beloved in Rome!' Jewish Roots and Christian Identity." In *Celebrating Romans: Template for Pauline Theology: Essays in Honor of Robert Jewett,* 67-82. Ed. Sheila E. McGinn. Grand Rapids: Wm. B. Eerdmans, 2005.

Combes, I. A. H. *The Metaphor of Slavery in the Writings of the Early Church: From the New Testament to the Beginning of the Fifth Century.* JSNTSup 156. Sheffield: Sheffield Academic Press, 1998.

Conzelmann, Hans. *An Outline of the Theology of the New Testament.* New York: Harper & Row, 1969.

Dahl, Nils. "The Messiahship of Jesus in Paul." In his *The Crucified Messiah and Other Essays,* 37-47. Minneapolis: Augsburg Publishing House, 1975.

Davies, Glenn N. *Faith and Obedience in Romans: A Study in Romans 1-4.* JSNTSup 39. Sheffield: Sheffield Academic Press, 1990.

Dickson, John P. "Gospel as News: εὐαγγελ- from Aristophanes to the Apostle Paul." *NTS* 51 (2005): 212-30.

Doty, William G. *Letters in Primitive Christianity.* Philadelphia: Fortress Press, 1973.

Du Toit, Andreas B. "'God's Beloved in Rome' (Rm 1:7): The Genesis and Socio-Economic

Situation of the First Generation Christian Community in Rome." *Neot* 32 (1998): 367-88.

Dunn, James D. G. "Jesus — Flesh and Spirit: An Exposition of Romans 1:3-4." *JTS* 24 (1973): 40-68.

Ehrensperger, Kathy. *Paul and the Dynamics of Power: Communication and Interaction in the Early Christ-Movement.* LNTS 325. London: T&T Clark, 2007.

Fatehi, Mehrdad. *The Spirit's Relation to the Risen Lord in Paul: An Examination of Its Christological Implications.* WUNT 2/128. Tübingen: J. C. B. Mohr (Paul Siebeck), 2000.

Fee, Gordon D. *God's Empowering Presence: The Holy Spirit in the Letters of Paul.* Peabody: Hendrickson Publishers, 1994.

———. *Pauline Christology: An Exegetical-Theological Study.* Peabody: Hendrickson Publishers, 2007.

Fitzmyer, Joseph A. "The Christology of the Epistle to the Romans." In *The Future of Christology: Essays in Honor of Leander E. Keck,* 81-90. Ed. Abraham J. Malherbe and Wayne A. Meeks. Minneapolis: Fortress Press, 1993.

Fuller, Reginald H. *The Foundations of New Testament Christology.* New York: Charles Scribner's Sons, 1965.

Funk, Robert W. "The Apostolic *Parousia:* Form and Significance." In *Christian History and Interpretation: Studies Presented to John Knox,* 249-86. Ed. William R. Farmer et al. Cambridge: Cambridge University Press, 1967.

Garlington, Don B. *Faith, Obedience, and Perseverance: Aspects of Paul's Letter to the Romans.* WUNT 79. Tübingen: J. C. B. Mohr (Paul Siebeck), 1994.

———. *'The Obedience of Faith' — A Pauline Phrase in Historical Context.* WUNT 2/38. Tübingen: J. C. B. Mohr (Paul Siebeck), 1991.

Garnsey, Peter. *Ideas of Slavery from Aristotle to Augustine.* Cambridge: Cambridge University Press, 1996.

Gathercole, Simon J. *Where Is Boasting? Early Jewish Soteriology and Paul's Response in Romans 1–5.* Grand Rapids: Wm. B. Eerdmans, 2002.

Glancy, Jennifer A. *Slavery in Early Christianity.* Minneapolis: Fortress Press, 2006.

Goppelt, Leonhard. *Theology of the New Testament.* 2 vols. Grand Rapids: Wm. B. Eerdmans, 1981-82.

Gordon, Mary L. "The Nationality of Slaves under the Early Roman Empire." *JRS* 14 (1924): 93-111.

Greenlee, J. Harold. "Some 'Called' People: Romans 1:1, 6-7." *Notes on Translation* 11/3 (1997): 49-51.

Haacker, Klaus. "Exegetische Probleme des Römerbriefs." *NovT* 20/1 (1978): 1-21.

Hahn, Ferdinand. *The Titles of Jesus in Christology: Their History in Early Christianity.* Cleveland: World Publishing Company, 1969.

Harrill, J. Albert. *Slaves in the New Testament: Literary, Social, and Moral Dimensions.* Minneapolis: Fortress Press, 2006.

Harrison, James R. *Paul's Language of Grace in Its Graeco-Roman Context.* WUNT 2/172. Tübingen: J. C. B. Mohr (Paul Siebeck), 2003.

Hengel, Martin. "Präexistenz bei Paulus." In *Jesus Christus als die Mitte der Schrift: Studien zur Hermeneutik des Evangeliums*, 479-518. Ed. Christof Landmesser et al. BZNW 86. New York: Walter de Gruyter, 1997.

————. *The Son of God: The Origin of Christology and the History of Jewish-Hellenistic Religion*. Philadelphia: Fortress Press, 1976.

————. *Studies in Early Christology*. Edinburgh: T&T Clark, 1995.

Herron, Robert W., Jr. "The Origins of the New Testament Apostolate." *WTJ* 45 (1983): 101-31.

Hester, James D. "The Rhetoric of *Persona* in Romans: Re-reading Romans 1:1-12." In *Celebrating Romans: Template for Pauline Theology: Essays in Honor of Robert Jewett*, 83-105. Ed. Sheila E. McGinn. Grand Rapids: Wm. B. Eerdmans, 2005.

Holtz, Traugott. "Zum Selbstverständnis des Apostels Paulus." *TLZ* 91 (1966): 322-30.

Hooke, S. H. "The Translation of Romans i.4." *NTS* 9 (1962-63): 370-71.

Hooker, Morna D. "A Partner in the Gospel: Paul's Understanding of His Ministry." In *Theology and Ethics in Paul and His Interpreters: Essays in Honor of Victor Paul Furnish*, 83-100. Ed. Eugene H. Lovering Jr. and Jerry L. Sumney. Nashville: Abingdon Press, 1996.

Hopkins, Keith. *Conquerors and Slaves*. SSRH 1. Cambridge: Cambridge University Press, 1978.

Horsley, Richard A. "Paul and Slavery: A Critical Alternative to Recent Readings." In *Slavery in Text and Interpretation*, 153-200. Ed. Allen D. Callahan et al. *Semeia* 83/84. Atlanta: Society of Biblical Literature, 1998.

————. "The Slave Systems of Classical Antiquity and Their Reluctant Recognition by Modern Scholars." In *Slavery in Text and Interpretation*, 18-66. Ed. Allen D. Callahan, Richard A. Horsley, and Abraham Smith. *Semeia* 83/84. Atlanta: Society of Biblical Literature, 1998.

Hultgren, Arland J. "The Scriptural Foundations for Paul's Mission to the Gentiles." In *Paul and His Theology*, 21-44. Ed. Stanley E. Porter. PAST 3. Boston: E. J. Brill, 2006.

Hurtado, Larry W. "Jesus' Divine Sonship in Paul's Epistle to the Romans." In *Romans and the People of God: Essays in Honor of Gordon D. Fee on the Occasion of His 65th Birthday*, 217-33. Ed. Sven K. Soderlund and N. T. Wright. Grand Rapids: Wm. B. Eerdmans, 1999.

————. *Lord Jesus Christ: Devotion to Jesus in Earliest Christianity*. Grand Rapids: Wm. B. Eerdmans, 2003.

Jewett, Robert. "Ecumenical Theology for the Sake of Mission: Romans 1:1-17+15:14–16:24." In *Pauline Theology*, vol. 3, *Romans*, 89-108. Ed. David M. Hay and E. Elizabeth Johnson. Minneapolis: Fortress Press, 1995.

————. "The Redaction and Use of an Early Christian Confession in Romans 1:3-4." In *The Living Text: Essays in Honor of Ernest W. Saunders*, 99-122. Ed. Dennis E. Groh and Robert Jewett. Lanham: University Press of America, 1985.

Jonge, Marinus de. *Christology in Context: The Earliest Christian Response to Jesus*. Philadelphia: Westminster Press, 1988.

Kümmel, Werner G. *The Theology of the New Testament: According to Its Main Witnesses: Jesus — Paul — John*. Nashville: Abingdon Press, 1973.

Lampe, Peter. "The Roman Christians of Romans 16." In *The Romans Debate,* 216-30. Rev. ed. Ed. Karl P. Donfried. Peabody: Hendrickson Publishers, 1991.

Légasse, Simon. "Fils de David et Fils de Dieu: Note sur Romains 1,3-4." *NRT* 122 (2000): 564-72.

Levison, John R. *The Spirit in First-Century Judaism.* AGAJU 29. New York: E. J. Brill, 1997.

Lieu, Judith M. "'Grace to You and Peace': The Apostolic Greeting." *BJRL* 86 (1985): 161-78.

Linnemann, Eta. "Tradition und Interpretation in Rom. 1,3f." *EvT* 31 (1971): 264-75.

Lips, Hermann von. "Der Apostolat des Paulus — ein Charisma? Semantische Aspekte zu charis-charisma und anderen Wortpaaren im Sprachgebrauch des Paulus." *Bib* 66 (1985): 305-34.

Longenecker, Bruce W. *Eschatology and the Covenant: A Comparison of 4 Ezra and Romans I–II.* JSNTSup 57. Sheffield: Academic Press, 1991.

Lohse, Eduard. "Εὐαγγέλιον Θεοῦ: Paul's Interpretation of the Gospel in His Epistle to the Romans." *Bib* 76 (1995): 127-40.

—————. "Das Präskript des Römerbriefes als theologisches Programm." In *Paulus, Apostel Jesu Christi: Festschrift für Günter Klein zum 70. Geburtstag,* 65-78. Ed. Michael Trowitzsch. Tübingen: J. C. B. Mohr (Paul Siebeck), 1998.

Louw, Johannes P. *Semantics of New Testament Greek.* SBLSS. Philadelphia: Fortress Press, 1982.

Lyall, Francis. *Slaves, Citizens, Sons: Legal Metaphors in the Epistles.* Grand Rapids: Zondervan Publishing House, 1984.

MacMullen, Ramsay. *Roman Social Relations 50 B.C. to A.D. 284.* New Haven: Yale University Press, 1974.

Martin, Dale B. *Slavery as Salvation: The Metaphor of Slavery in Pauline Christianity.* New Haven: Yale University Press, 1990.

Miller, James C. *The Obedience of Faith, The Eschatological People of God, and the Purpose of Romans.* SBLDS 177. Atlanta: Scholars Press, 2000.

Minear, Paul S. *The Obedience of Faith: The Purposes of Paul in the Epistle to the Romans.* SBT 2/19. London: SCM, 1971.

Moule, C. F. D. *An Idiom-Book of New Testament Greek.* 2d ed. Cambridge: Cambridge University Press, 1960.

Mullins, Terence Y. "Greeting as a New Testament Form." *JBL* 87 (1968): 418-26.

Munck, Johannes. "La vocation de l'Apôtre Paul." *ST* 1 (1947): 131-45.

Neufeld, Vernon. *The Earliest Christian Confessions.* NTTS 5. Grand Rapids: Wm. B. Eerdmans, 1963.

Nickelsburg, George W. E. "An ἘΚΤΡΩΜΑ, though Appointed from the Womb: Paul's Apostolic Self-Description in 1 Corinthians 15 and Galatians 1." *Christians among Jews and Gentiles: Essays in Honor of Krister Stendahl on His Sixty-fifth Birthday,* 198-205. Ed. George W. E. Nickelsburg and George W. MacRae. Philadelphia: Fortress Press, 1986.

Nolland, John. "Grace as Power." *NovT* 28 (1986): 26-31.

Olsson, Birger. "Rom 1:3f enligt Paulus." *SEÅ* 37-38 (1972-73): 255-73.

Osiek, Carolyn. "Slavery in the Second Testament World." *BTB* 22 (1992): 174-79.

Pesch, Rudolf. "Das Evangelium Gottes über seinen Sohn: Zur Auslegung der Tradition in

Röm 1,1-4." In *Christus bezeugen: Festschrift für Wolfgang Trilling zum 65. Geburtstag,* 208-17. Ed. Karl Kertelge et al. ETS 59. Leipzig: St. Benno, 1989.

Polaski, Sandra Hack. *Paul and the Discourse of Power.* BibSem 62. London: T&T Clark, 1999.

Poythress, Vern S. "Is Romans 1.3-4 a *Pauline* Confession after All?" *ExpTim* 87 (1976): 180-83.

Rollins, Wayne. "Greco-Roman Slave Terminology and Pauline Metaphors for Salvation." In *Society of Biblical Literature 1987 Seminar Papers,* 100-110. Ed. Kent H. Richards. SBLSP 26. Atlanta: Scholars Press, 1987.

Ropes, James H. "The Epistle to the Romans and Jewish Christianity." In *Studies in Early Christianity,* 353-65. Ed. Shirley J. Case. New York: Century, 1928.

Russell, Kenneth C. "Slavery as Reality and Metaphor in the Pauline Letters." Ph.D. diss., Pontifical Biblical University, Rome, 1968.

Sandnes, Karl Olav. *Paul — One of the Prophets?* WUNT 2/43. Tübingen: J. C. B. Mohr (Paul Siebeck), 1991.

Sass, Gerhard. "Zur Bedeutung von δοῦλος bei Paulus." *ZNW* 40 (1941): 24-32.

Satake, Akira. "Apostolat und Gnade bei Paulus." *NTS* 15 (1968-69): 96-107.

Schlier, Henrich. "Eine christologische Credo-Formel der römischen Gemeinde. Zu Röm. 1,3f." In *Neues Testament und Geschichte: Historisches Geschehen und Deutung im Neuen Testament. Oscar Cullmann zum 70. Geburtstag,* 207-18. Ed. Heinrich Baltensweiler and Bo Reicke. Tübingen: J. C. B. Mohr (Paul Siebeck), 1972.

Schmithals, Walter. *The Office of Apostle in the Early Church.* Nashville: Abingdon, 1969.

Schneider, Bernardin. "Κατὰ Πνεῦμα Ἁγιωσύνης (Romans 1,4)." *Bib* 48 (1967): 359-87.

Schnider, Franz, and Werner Stenger. *Studien zum Neutestamentlichen Briefformular.* NTTS 11. New York: E. J. Brill, 1987.

Schütz, John H. *Paul and the Anatomy of Apostolic Authority.* SNTSMS 26. Cambridge: Cambridge University Press, 1975.

Schweizer, Eduard. "Röm. 1,3f, und Gegensatz von Fleisch und Geist vor und bei Paulus," *EvT* 15 (1955): 563-71; reprinted in his *Neotestamentica: Deutsche und englische Aufsätze,* 180-89. Zurich: Zwingli Verlag, 1963. Page references are to the latter.

Scott, James M. *Adoption as Sons of God: An Exegetical Investigation into the Background of ΥΙΟΘΕΣΙΑ in the Pauline Corpus.* WUNT 2/48. Tübingen: J. C. B. Mohr (Paul Siebeck), 1992.

―――. *Paul and the Nations: The Old Testament and Jewish Background of Paul's Mission to the Nations with Special Reference to the Destination of Galatians.* WUNT 84. J. C. B. Mohr (Paul Siebeck), 1995.

Spallek, Andrew J. "The Origin and Meaning of *Euangelion* in the Pauline Corpus." *CTQ* 57 (1993): 177-90.

Strecker, Georg. *Theology of the New Testament.* Louisville: Westminster John Knox Press, 2000.

Stuhlmacher, Peter. *Biblische Theologie des Neuen Testaments.* 2 vols. Göttingen: Vandenhoeck & Ruprecht, 1992-99.

―――. "Theologische Probleme des Römerbriefpräskripts." *EvT* 29 (1967): 374-89.

Thébert, Yvon. "The Slave." In *The Romans,* 138-74. Ed. Andrea Giardina. Chicago: University of Chicago Press, 1993.

Theobald, Michael. "'Dem Juden zuerst und auch dem Heiden'. Die paulinische Auslegung der Glaubensformel Röm 1,3f." In his *Studien zum Römerbrief,* 102-18. WUNT 136. Tübingen: J. C. B. Mohr (Paul Siebeck), 2001.

————. "'Sohn Gottes' als christologische Grundmetapher bei Paulus." *TQ* 174 (1994): 185-207.

Tuckett, Christopher M. *Christology and the New Testament: Jesus and His Earliest Followers.* Westminster John Knox Press, 2001.

Watson, Alan. *Roman Slave Law.* Baltimore: Johns Hopkins University Press, 1987.

Wegenast, Klaus. "Römer 1,3f." In his *Das Verständnis der Tradition bei Paulus und in den Deuteropaulinen,* 70-76. Neukirchen-Vluyn: Neukirchener Verlag, 1962.

Weiss, Johannes. *Earliest Christianity: A History of the Period A.D. 30-150.* 2 vols. New York: Harper & Row, 1937.

Wengst, Klaus. *Christologische Formeln und Lieder des Urchristentums.* SNT 7. Gütersloh: Gütersloher Verlagshaus Gerd Mohn, 1972.

White, John L. "New Testament Epistolary Literature in the Framework of Ancient Epistolography." *ANRW* II.25.2 (1984): 1730-56.

Whitsett, Christopher G. "Son of God, Seed of David: Paul's Messianic Exegesis in Romans [1]:3-4." *JBL* 119 (2000): 661-81.

Wiedemann, Thomas. *Greek and Roman Slavery.* Baltimore: Johns Hopkins University Press, 1981.

Wright, Benjamin G., III. "'*Ebed/Doulos*: Terms and Social Status in the Meeting of Hebrew Biblical and Hellenistic Roman Culture." In *Slavery in Text and Interpretation,* 83-111. Ed. Allen D. Callahan et al. *Semeia* 83/84. Atlanta: Society of Biblical Literature, 1998.

1.2. Thanksgiving, 1:8-15

8*To begin with, I give thanks to my God through Jesus Christ for all of you, for your faith is well attested throughout the world.* 9*For God, whom I serve with my spirit in the gospel of his Son, is my witness, that I mention you* 10*always in my prayers without ceasing, asking whether somehow I might now at last make my way by the will of God to come to you.* 11*For I desire to see you, in order that I may impart to you some spiritual gift in order for you to be strengthened,* 12*that is, that I may receive encouragement together with you through our mutual faith, both yours and mine.* 13*But I do not want you to be uninformed, brothers and sisters, for I have desired frequently to come to you (and I have been hindered up to now), in order that I might reap some fruit among you also, as even among the other Gentiles.* 14*I am under obligation to both Greeks and barbarians, wise and simple;* 15*thus my eagerness to proclaim the gospel also to you who are in Rome.*

Notes on the Text and Translation

1:7, 15 Majuscule G (ninth century) lacks "in Rome" in both of these verses. The phrase may have been dropped to enable the letter more readily to be a general letter to all Christian communities.

1:8 The phrase "to begin with" is a rendition of the adverb πρῶτον, usually rendered simply as "first" (KJV, RSV, NIV, NRSV), which is in keeping with its frequent semantic usage (cf. Rom 1:16; 2:9-10; 1 Cor 15:46, etc.). But in this case there are no succeeding points. The term can have the meaning "to begin with," "above all," or "first of all" (cf. Rom 3:8; 1 Cor 11:18) to mark a transition to what follows.[76]

1:9 The word ὡς can be rendered as "how" (as in the ASV and NIV), but "that" is to be preferred (as in KJV, RSV, and NRSV).[77]

1:13 The term ἀδελφοί has been translated as "brethren" (KJV, ASV, RSV) or "brothers" (NIV) in older English versions, but as "brothers and sisters" in the NRSV. Since the meaning of the word in context is gender inclusive, and since there are other biblical and extrabiblical texts that are unambiguously gender inclusive,[78] that is preferable here and elsewhere in Romans.

The clause "and have been hindered up to now" can be regarded as parenthetical. Consequently, the ἵνα-clause goes with προεθέμην.[79]

1:14 The substantive ἀνόητος is translated as "foolish" in several major English versions (ASV, RSV, NIV, NRSV; KJV has "unwise"). But "foolish" can be represented by other words known to Paul, namely, ἄφρων (1 Cor 15:36; 2 Cor 11:16, 19; 12:6, 11) and μωρός (1 Cor 4:10; cf. the related word μωρία ["foolishness"] at 1 Cor 1:18, 21, 23, etc.). The contrast in this verse appears to be not so much between the wise and those who do foolish things, but between those who are wise (persons of high culture) and those who are uneducated, persons who are "simple and uneducated, whose power of thought is undeveloped."[80] The NEB has "simple," which has also been adopted here. The term can have a negative connotation (cf. Gal 3:1, 3; Titus 2:3), but not in this instance.

It has been suggested that "both Greeks and barbarians, wise and simple" should be understood as standing in apposition to "the rest of the Gentiles," and that "I am under obligation" should begin a new clause with "to proclaim the

---

76. BDF 232 (§447, 4).

77. BDAG 1105 (ὡς, 5): "that" after verbs of knowing and saying.

78. Illustrations from nonbiblical Greek, as well as in the NT, are provided in BDAG 18 (ἀδελφός).

79. Cf. BDF 242-43 (§465, 1).

80. Johannes Behm, "ἀνόητος," *TDNT* 1:962.

gospel."[81] One of the consequences of that is an extreme piling up of conjunctions: "also (καί) among you, as even (καί) among the other Gentiles, both (postpositive τε) Greeks and (καί) barbarians, both (τε) wise and (καί) simple." The reading is much smoother when there is a period after "Gentiles," as in the Nestle-Aland text (27th ed.). In addition, support of the alternative requires that the phrase τὸ κατ' ἐμὲ πρόθυμον in 1:15 be treated adverbially (e.g., "as far as I am concerned").[82] But as indicated in the next notation, the phrase can serve as the subject of the sentence, introduced by "thus."

1:15 The preposition κατά with accusative can express a possessive or subjective genitive in Hellenistic Greek. So τὸ κατὰ ἐμὲ πρόθυμον = ἡ ἐμὴ προθυμία (τὸ πρόθυμον = ἡ προθυμία), "my eagerness."[83]

General Comment

At this point, following the opening, the typical Greco-Roman letter contains a prayer petition or a wish for the health of its addressee(s).[84] But Paul substitutes a thanksgiving for such a convention. The thanksgiving section provides an opportunity for Paul to gain rapport with his readers, giving thanks for their faith and witness, and to anticipate, however elliptically, what is to come later in the letter.[85] Such a section appears in five of the undisputed letters of Paul; the exceptions are 2 Corinthians, which contains a blessing of God (1:3-7) and his Letter to the Galatians,[86] in which an irate Paul simply launches into the body of his letter after its opening, unable to give thanks for the behavior of his recipients.[87]

The thanksgiving clearly begins at 1:8, but where does it end? According to some interpreters, the thanksgiving consists of a rather brief section of the letter, such as 1:8-9[88] or 1:8-12.[89] According to others, it consists of 1:8-17.[90] What

---

81. R. Thorsteinsson, "Paul's Missionary Duty," 531-47, who cites the earlier essay of H. Parkin, "Romans i.13-15," 95. Cf. also B. Gaventa, "'To Preach the Gospel,'" 183-85.

82. As suggested by C. F. D. Moule, *An Idiom-Book of New Testament Greek*, 58.

83. BDF 120 (§224, 1).

84. For illustrations, cf. F. Exler, *The Form of the Ancient Greek Letter*, 101-12.

85. Major works on thanksgiving sections in Paul are by P. Schubert, *The Form and Function of the Pauline Thanksgivings*, and P. O'Brien, *Introductory Thanksgivings in the Letters of Paul*.

86. The thanksgiving sections are at 1 Cor 1:4-9; Phil 1:3-11; 1 Thess 1:2-10; and Phlm 4-7.

87. J. L. Martyn, *Galatians*, 106-7.

88. J. Fitzmyer, *Romans*, 98, 242-43.

89. Terence Y. Mullins, "Disclosure," 49, and J. White, "Introductory Formulae in the Body of the Pauline Letter," 97; idem, *The Form and Function of the Body of the Greek Letter*, 76, 84; R. Jewett, *Romans*, 117.

90. P. Schubert, *The Form and Function of the Pauline Thanksgivings*, 31-33; P. O'Brien,

is clear is that the body of the letter does not commence until 1:18. The most debatable question concerning the extent of the thanksgiving section is whether the two verses of 1:16-17, which set forth the theme of the letter, belong to it or whether they should be considered a separate unit. One can argue either way. It has been maintained that 1:16 continues what is said prior to it (based on vocabulary, thought, and the conjunction γάρ ["for"]); therefore the two verses belong to the thanksgiving.[91] On the other hand, there is a shift at 1:16 from Paul's attention to his readers to a programmatic statement concerning the gospel that he preaches. Though the two verses do not begin the body proper, and therefore can be considered a part of the thanksgiving, they serve as a thematic "bridge passage" into the body of the letter.[92] Because of their singular significance, introducing or at least including key concepts in Paul's letter and theology (such as "gospel," "salvation," "the righteousness of God," "faith," and Paul's use of the OT), they merit being treated as a unit by themselves.

In this particular thanksgiving Paul gives thanks for the faith of the believers in Rome, saying that it is exemplary and well known. But he also uses the opportunity to announce that he is planning to travel there for the sake of mutual sharing of faith, which will include the proclamation of the gospel. He gives no hint here about his intentions to go on from Rome to Spain. That is not revealed until 15:24. One gets the initial impression that he is planning to arrive in Rome before many more weeks have passed. The community at Rome would have no idea of his plans beyond his visit to them. Will he reside there permanently, or will he return to the eastern Mediterranean where he has founded churches (e.g., at Corinth, Ephesus, Philippi, Thessalonica, and Galatia), resided, and has friends? If Phoebe was the bearer of the letter, which seems likely (cf. the exegesis of 16:1-2), she would be able to provide information about Paul's intentions even prior to their reading of the letter. In any case, the community would become familiar with Paul's plans as it neared the end of the letter.

All that aside, the Roman believers in Christ are praised by Paul for their faith, which is not based on his prior proclamation. He is willing to accommodate himself to their distinct expressions of faith, and he is eager to share his own with them. He expects that the result will be mutual edification and encouragement.

Introductory Thanksgivings, 200-202. Commentaries that include 1:16-17 in the thanksgiving (or, using different language, within the same larger unit) include those of E. Käsemann, *Romans*, 21; C. Cranfield, *Romans*, 27, 87; U. Wilckens, *Römer*, 1:76-77; J. Dunn, *Romans*, 37; P. Stuhlmacher, *Romans*, 17; B. Byrne, *Romans*, 27, 48; E. Lohse, *Römer*, 70-78. Cf. also W. Doty, *Letters in Primitive Christianity*, 43, and C. Roetzel, *The Letters of Paul*, 66.

91. P. Schubert, *The Form and Function of the Pauline Thanksgivings*, 32.

92. C. K. Barrett, *Romans*, 27; P. O'Brien, *Introductory Thanksgivings*, 202, 261. D. Starnitzke, *Die Struktur paulinischen Denkens im Römerbrief*, 21, considers 1:16-17 an introduction to the body of the letter; cf. also L. Keck, *Romans*, 50.

Detailed Comment

1:8 After the relatively long opening (1:1-7), the term πρῶτον ("to begin with")
marks a transition into the thanksgiving, catching the attention of those who
hear the letter being read to them. It strikes the ear, signifying that what is to
come is highly important. Paul is writing to a community that he has not
founded. To give thanks for their faith, as a phenomenon widely known in the
Roman world, is to testify (and at the same time concede) that not all communities of faith need to resemble those that he has founded. There is nothing
lacking at Rome, for the people there are filled with goodness and knowledge
and are able to instruct one another (15:14).

The thanksgiving in this letter differs in content — and has to differ —
from those written by Paul to churches that he has founded. Paul must solicit
trust and goodwill from his readers at the outset. And so he speaks not only of
the sturdiness of their faith (1:12) but also of their reputation "throughout the
world" and his desire to be their guest (1:10, 13).

To give thanks to God "through Jesus Christ" (cf. 7:25 for the same expression) appears to be a liturgical expression already in existence.[93] In any
case, the formulation affirms that Jesus Christ is the mediator who carries the
thanksgivings of believers in Christ to the Father.[94] Although on occasion Paul,
like other NT writers, addresses prayers to the risen Christ, it is more characteristic of him to address prayer to God.[95] But to pray "through" or "in the name of
Christ" is a way of affirming that one may enter the presence of God with confidence. "God in Christ has reconciled us; therefore it is through Christ that we
draw near."[96] Paul's thanksgiving for "all of you" indicates that, even if he is
aware of possible tensions among the Christians at Rome, he hereby affirms
forthrightly that he has all of them in mind as persons for whom he is grateful.
They are persons of faith and witness.

The degree to which the faith of the Roman Christians could be "well attested throughout the world" can hardly be measured. As in similar phrases
elsewhere (Rom 16:19; 2 Cor 2:14; 1 Thess 1:8), there may be hyperbole here,[97]
but not entirely. What is certain is that the Christian faith had existed in Rome
for some time prior to Paul's writing his letter. Beyond that, the faith of the
Romans was known in such places such as Corinth and Ephesus where Roman
Christians had been exiled (Acts 18:2; 1 Cor 16:19), and it would have been

---

93. C. F. D. Moule, *Worship in the New Testament*, 71-73.
94. J. Jungmann, *The Place of Christ in Liturgical Prayer*, 133-40.
95. L. Hurtado, *At the Origins of Christian Worship*, 74-76.
96. C. F. D. Moule, *Worship in the New Testament*, 71.
97. C. Cranfield, *Romans*, 75 (n. 2); J. Fitzmyer, *Romans*, 244; B. Witherington, *Romans*,
42.

known in Palestine, particularly in Jerusalem, because of the linkages between the two communities, both commercial and cultural. How well Roman Christianity was known elsewhere is more conjectural. Christian communities existed already in Antioch of Syria, Asia Minor, and perhaps in Alexandria by the time of Paul's letter, and contacts between Christians in Rome and in these other places by the time of the writing of Romans cannot be ruled out.

1:9 To speak of God as one's witness is equivalent to taking an oath. It has an OT background prior to Paul (Gen 31:44; Wis 1:6), and he uses it elsewhere as well (Phil 1:8; 1 Thess 2:5; cf. 2 Cor 1:23).

The verb λατρεύω ("to worship" or "to serve") appears three times (Rom 1:9, 25; Phil 3:3) and its noun cognate λατρεία twice (Rom 9:4; 12:1) in the letters of Paul. Both are linked to God as the object of worship, except for one case (Rom 1:25) where the reference is to idolatry. Paul's worship (or service) to God is "with [his] spirit in the gospel of his Son." The phrase "with my spirit" refers to the human spirit, as elsewhere in the letters of Paul (e.g., Rom 8:16; 1 Cor 2:11; 5:4; 7:34; 14:14, etc.), not the Holy Spirit. One worships God by means of the human spirit, the "spiritual" aspect of human existence.[98] The cultic and pneumatic terminology being used is taken out of the confines of worship itself to speak of Paul's life and being in the world. His way of serving/worshiping God is to proclaim the gospel concerning God's Son.[99]

Paul steps on dangerous ground when he claims God as a witness concerning his prayers. How long and how often has Paul actually prayed for what he claims? Actually the claim that Paul makes is in present tense; his prayers are intense in the present. It is not necessarily the case that he has been praying for a long time. Nevertheless, the statement must be taken as a diplomatic one, in which Paul's expression is more earnest than it is descriptive.

1:10 The verse contains a "petitionary prayer report," including a summary of the petitionary prayer of Paul. It differs from others in thanksgivings, however, in that the request articulated does not concern the addressees, but Paul himself (that he might get to Rome).[100] The impression he conveys is that he has been wanting to travel to Rome for some time. The phraseology used is reticent and filled with qualifications ("whether somehow I might now at last"[101] and "by the will of God"). On the face of it, Paul speaks as though he can only surmise that his prayers might be answered. But he has been able to say, in

---

98. Eduard Schweizer, "πνεῦμα," *TDNT* 6:434-36.

99. The genitive is an objective genitive. It is not the message from Jesus, but the message about him. This is agreed upon by interpreters generally. Cf. BDAG 403 (εὐαγγέλιον, 1, b, β, ℵ); U. Wilckens, *Römer*, 1:78; J. Fitzmyer, *Romans*, 245; J. Dunn, *Romans*, 29; P. O'Brien, *Introductory Thanksgivings*, 213.

100. P. O'Brien, *Introductory Thanksgivings*, 197.

101. BDAG 434 (ἤδη, 2): "whether now at last I may perhaps succeed in coming."

any case, what his wish is, and that is to travel to Rome and, by implication — since he can arrive there only if God wills it — be received there. The content of the prayer and the anticipated journey are thus blended.

1:11-12 Paul uses the language of longing (ἐπιποθέω), which he uses elsewhere to express the desire — either his or someone else's — to see other persons known intimately (2 Cor 9:14; Phil 1:8; 2:26; 1 Thess 3:6). The longing to see the persons at Rome is followed by a purpose clause: "that I may impart to you some spiritual gift in order for you to be strengthened." The kind of "spiritual gift" that Paul would impart is left indefinite. Interpreters have sought to fill in the blank, suggesting that the spiritual gift would be any or all of the gifts described in 1 Corinthians 12 to 14 (prophecy, tongues, interpretation, knowledge, faith, etc.),[102] the charismatic effects that come from his proclamation of the gospel,[103] or even the presence of Paul himself as a benefit.[104] It is probably best to leave the possibilities open, as the Romans themselves would have had to do. In any case, it is clear from the context that Paul will proclaim the gospel at Rome (1:15), and his proclamation will be a means by which members of the community will be strengthened. Paul uses a passive form of the verb (στηριχθῆναι, "to be strengthened"), indicating that it is not he who will do the strengthening, but God (so a divine passive here).

1:12 The RSV and NRSV translations ("that we may be mutually encouraged by each other's faith, both yours and mine") does not capture the full effect of the clause. A more literal reading is: "that I may receive encouragement together with you through our mutual faith, both yours and mine." To be sure, there is a mutuality in either case, but the latter translation allows for Paul to be a recipient of the faith of the Romans more than does the RSV/NRSV translation. Paul signals that he will be a beneficiary of the faith of believers at Rome; they are not the only ones who will have something to gain.

1:13 The opening phrase, "I do not want you to be uninformed," appears elsewhere in the letters of Paul (1 Cor 10:1; 12:1; 1 Thess 4:13) to indicate the importance of what is to be said. In this case it will be about the obstacles that have stood in the way of his coming to Rome previously.

Paul addresses his readers as ἀδελφοί ("brothers and sisters"). The term is used in its various forms (singular, plural, masculine, or feminine) 113 times in the undisputed letters of Paul for Christian believers,[105] and can be considered

---

102. W. Sanday and A. Headlam, *Romans*, 21.

103. E. Käsemann, *Romans*, 19; U. Wilckens, *Römer*, 1:79 (n. 82).

104. C. Cranfield, *Romans*, 79.

105. The word count does not include references to the (natural) brothers of Jesus (1 Cor 9:5; Gal 1:10), a relative (Rom 16:15), or Israel (Rom 9:3). The figure differs slightly from that (112) of David G. Horrell, "From ἀδελφοί to οἶκος θεοῦ," 299, 311. Our figures are 19 in Rom, 40 in 1 Cor, 12 in 2 Cor, 10 in Gal, 9 in Phil, 18 in 1 Thess, and 5 in Phlm.

Paul's favorite way of referring to those to whom he writes.[106] The use of the terminology can be found in the OT and other literature of Jewish origin, in traditions of Jesus concerning his hearers or disciples (Matt 28:10; Mark 3:34-35; John 20:17), and in literary sources of Gentile origin in the ancient world.[107] It is the language of primary groups, and the use of the term conveys a sense of affection, mutual responsibility, and solidarity.[108] It also implies an ethic of relativization and reciprocity. The natural ties of family are relativized so that the spiritual brotherhood/sisterhood is stronger than relationships between spouses, parent and child, and siblings; and there is reciprocity in the sense of mutual aid and support, based on the principle that the need of the other person today could be one's own tomorrow ("was heute dir mangelt, kann morgen mir mangeln"[109]). Typically Paul uses the terminology to challenge his readers to give to their fellow Christians a degree of consideration, respect, and care that is lacking, but which should be evident because they are "brothers and sisters" in Christ.[110]

In this particular instance, however, the term functions in a way that it does not in the other letters of Paul. Since Paul had not founded the Roman church, his relationship with its members was more tenuous, even ambiguous.[111] He needs to establish a relationship that has not existed heretofore. He uses fictive siblingship, then, to call that relationship into being. Since they are mutually persons of faith, he stresses the unity that they already have in Christ, which should lead those at Rome to give him a hearing.

Paul says that he has been "hindered" from coming to Rome. The verb is in the passive voice, which is likely to mean the divine passive, since it is only by "the will of God" that he can come to Rome (1:10). At 15:22-23 he repeats the matter of being hindered, adding that he had been planning to come to Rome for years. In addition, he adds there the "outward" reason for his being hindered: he has been heavily engaged in his work in the eastern sphere of the Mediterranean world (15:19-23).

The verse includes a purpose clause telling the reason for Paul's coming to Rome: "in order that I might reap some fruit among you also, as even among the other Gentiles." Although the suggestion has been made that the "fruit"

---

106. Robert Banks, *Paul's Idea of Community*, 50-51.

107. For the wide range of usage in various literary sources, cf. Hans F. von Soden, "ἀδελφός," *TDNT* 1:44-46.

108. D. Horrell, "From ἀδελφοί to οἶκος θεοῦ," 299. On the basis of a study of papyri and literary sources, A. Clarke, "Equality or Mutuality?" 151-64, contends that the term signifies mutuality, not equality.

109. M. Weber, "Zwischenbetrachtung," 1:543.

110. D. Horrell, "From ἀδελφοί to οἶκος θεοῦ," 300, 309.

111. R. Aasgaard, *"My Beloved Brothers and Sisters,"* 271.

sought by Paul is a contribution to the collection for Jerusalem,[112] it is more likely that it refers metaphorically to results of his anticipated proclamation.[113]

1:14 Paul claims to be "under obligation" (RSV and NAB) or to be "a debtor" (KJV, ASV, and NRSV) to Greeks, barbarians, the wise, and the simple. Being indebted or obligated to these is due to his being an apostle commissioned to reach the Gentiles (Rom 1:5-6; 11:13). It is as though he "owes" them something, and that is the gospel. Although his primary indebtedness is to God for God's saving work through Christ, Paul is "under obligation" to proclaim the gospel to the Gentiles, to whom God had sent him.[114] The term "Greeks" does not specify a particular ethnic group, but to Greek-speaking persons. Moreover, the term can be a substitute for "Gentiles," such as at other places where "Greeks" are contrasted with "Jews" (Rom 1:16; 2:9-10; 3:9; 10:12; 1 Cor 1:22, 24; 10:32; 12:13). "Barbarians" are non-Greek-speaking persons. The Greek term for "barbarian" (βάρβαρος) is onomatopoetic in origin, presumably imitating the sounds that a non-Greek uttered in speech, according to Greeks themselves.[115] What is of note here is that Paul does not speak of Greeks (or Gentiles) and Jews, as he normally does, but rather of "Greeks and barbarians," a phrase that typically signifies all people in Hellenistic speech.[116] For Paul, however, the terms in combination would refer not to all people, but to Gentiles in general; he does not include Jews in this instance. His inclusion of "barbarians" means that he envisions the evangelization of persons of linguistic groups other than Greek, many of which would have resided in Rome itself (including Latin-speaking persons, although it is unlikely that any Romans would consider themselves to be barbarians![117]). Paul has already evangelized persons of foreign speech (Acts 14:8-18), and he envisions further work in the West as he moves on to Spain (Rom 15:24, 28). The following combination of "wise" and "simple" is not necessarily synthetic parallelism to the first set. It is a sweeping combination concerning the Gentiles. It includes both those of high culture and those who are uneducated. By naming all four groups of people, Paul includes virtually every imaginable Gentile person.

1:15 Paul plans to proclaim the gospel in Rome. He has already indicated that he wants to "reap some fruit" there (1:13). Two problems arise, however, as soon as one compares these statements with what Paul writes at 15:20-23. First,

---

112. M. Kruger, "TINA KARPON," 167-73.

113. That is clearly the case in the deutero-Pauline use at Col 1:6.

114. Cf. P. Minear, "The Mission (Romans)," 240.

115. Cf. Hans Windisch, "βάρβαρος," *TDNT* 1:546: The term has Sanskrit origins, replicating stammering.

116. Cf. BDF 137 §262 (2) and references in Joseph H. Thayer, *A Greek-English Lexicon of the New Testament* (New York: American Book Company, 1889), 95.

117. Cf. BDAG 166 (βάρβαρος, 2, b) for references.

in 15:20-23 he says that he aspires (φιλοτιμέομαι) to evangelize *not* where Christ has been named, and *not* to build on another's foundation. But in fact Christ has been named at Rome, and the foundations of that church reach back many years. The impression given in 15:24 is that he will simply enjoy the company of the Roman Christians as he passes through on his way to Spain.

The tension between 1:13-15 and 15:20-24 can, however, be resolved. The latter must be taken as Paul's working principle. His intent is not to start a new congregation (house church) in Rome, nor will he transform the church there into a "Pauline" church.[118] There is no hint that he considers the church in Rome as in need of transformation.[119] He and the Roman Christians will mutually enrich each other, and he will not take up residence there for any length of time; he comes as a visitor — and as an apostle, to be sure — not a future resident and founder of a congregation. He will proclaim the gospel, yes, but as an ally of the church and its leaders, not their competitor. Although some interpreters seek to go further by saying that in this verse Paul speaks of a previous plan that had been hindered, and not what he means to do at the time he wrote Romans,[120] that does not seem necessary. Moreover, the problem of Paul's proclaiming where the gospel has already been preached is then simply moved back to an earlier point in time.

The second problem that a comparison yields is that Paul does not mention his plan to go on to Spain in 1:8-15, as he does in 15:24, 28. In fact, one could say that he springs it on his readers as a surprise in 15:24. On the other hand, to bring up the matter at the outset might have seemed impolite and repellent to the readers. The travel plans of Paul are rather detailed at this point in his career (he is on his way to Jerusalem, which needs explanation, will then head for Rome, and then go on to Spain). It seems fitting that, with even rudimentary planning of the composition of this letter, all those details should be postponed until the closing portion.

---

118. Contra A. Reichert, *Der Römerbrief als Gratwanderung,* 96-97, who claims that Paul sought to create a Pauline congregation on the basis of his gospel.

119. Contra G. Klein, "Paul's Purpose in Writing the Epistle to the Romans," 39, who says that Paul considers "an apostolic effort in Rome because he does not regard the local Christian community there as having an apostolic foundation." Other proposals demonstrate a wide divergence on the matter, e.g., those by F. Watson, "The Two Roman Congregations," 212-14, that Gentile Christianity at Rome was of Pauline origin (consequently, Paul did not have to build on another's foundation at Rome, since the Gentile Christians there were "converts and fellow workers of Paul") and B. Gaventa, "'To Preach the Gospel,'" 188, that in his letter Paul is "enlarging, extending their understanding of the gospel," for "they have not heard the gospel preached in its cosmic apocalyptic fullness" (p. 179).

120. P. Stuhlmacher, "The Purpose of Romans," 236-37; idem, *Romans,* 26; B. Byrne, *Romans,* 50-51; J. Dickson, "Gospel as News," 224-28.

BIBLIOGRAPHY

Aasgaard, Reider. *My Beloved Brothers and Sisters: Christian Siblingship in the Apostle Paul.* JSNTSup 265. Edinburgh: T&T Clark, 2003.

Baird, William. "Romans 1:8-17." *Int* 33 (1979): 398-403.

Banks, Robert. *Paul's Idea of Community: The Early House Churches in Their Cultural Setting.* Rev. ed. Peabody: Hendrickson Publishers, 1994.

Bartsch, Hans Werner. "Concept of Faith in Paul's Letter to the Romans." *BR* 13 (1968): 41-53.

Baumert, Norbert. "Charisma und Amt bei Paulus." In *L'Apôtre Paul: Personnalité, style et conception du ministère,* 203-228. Ed. Albert Vanhoye. Louvain: Peeters, 1986.

Campbell, William S. "Determining the Gospel through Rhetorical Analysis in Paul's Letter to the Roman Christians." In *Gospel in Paul: Studies on Corinthians, Galatians and Romans for Richard N. Longenecker,* 315-36. Ed. L. Ann Jervis and Peter Richardson. JSNTSup 108. Sheffield: Sheffield Academic Press, 1994.

————. *Paul's Gospel in an Intercultural Context: Jew and Gentile in the Letter to the Romans.* SIGU 69. New York: Peter Lang, 1991.

Clarke, Andrew D. "Equality or Mutuality? Paul's Use of 'Brother' Language." In *The New Testament in Its First-Century Setting: Essays in Context and Background in Honour of B. W. Winter on His 65th Birthday,* 151-64. Ed. P. J. Williams et al. Grand Rapids: Wm. B. Eerdmans, 2004.

Corsani, Bruno. "ΕΚ ΠΙΣΤΕΩΣ in the Letters of Paul." In *The New Testament Age: Essays in Honor of Bo Reicke,* 1:87-93. Ed. William C. Weinrich. 2 vols. Macon: Mercer University Press, 1984.

Dickson, John P. "Gospel as News: εὐαγγελ- from Aristophanes to the Apostle Paul." *NTS* 51 (2005): 212-30.

————. *Mission-Commitment in Ancient Judaism and in the Pauline Communities.* WUNT 2/159. Tübingen: J. C. B. Mohr (Paul Siebeck), 2003.

Doty, William G. *Letters in Primitive Christianity.* Philadelphia: Fortress Press, 1973.

Eichholz, Georg. "Der ökumenische und missionarische Horizont der Kirche: Eine exegetische Studie zu Röm. 1,8-15." *EvT* 21 (1961): 15-27.

Exler, Francis X. J. *The Form of the Ancient Greek Letter of the Epistolary Papyri (3rd c. B.C.– 3rd c. A.D.).* Chicago: Ares Publishers, 1976.

Funk, Robert W. "The Apostolic Parousia: Form and Significance." In *Christian History and Interpretation: Studies Presented to John Knox,* 249-68. Ed. William R. Farmer et al. Cambridge: Cambridge University Press, 1967.

Gaventa, Beverly Roberts. "'To Preach the Gospel': Romans 1,15 and the Purposes of Romans." In *The Letter to the Romans,* 179-95. Ed. Udo Schnelle. BETL 226. Walpole: Peeters, 2009.

Harland, Philip A. "Familial Dimensions of Group Identity: 'Brothers' (Ἀδελφοί) in Associations of the Greek East." *JBL* 124 (2005): 491-513.

Horrell, David G. "From ἀδελφοί to οἶκος θεοῦ: Social Transformation in Pauline Christianity." *JBL* 120 (2001): 293-311.

Hurtado, Larry W. *At the Origins of Christian Worship: The Context and Character of Earliest Christian Devotion.* Grand Rapids: Wm. B. Eerdmans, 1999.

Jungmann, Joseph A. *The Place of Christ in Liturgical Prayer.* Collegeville: Liturgical Press, 1989.

Kilgallen, John J. "Reflections on Charisma(ta) in the New Testament." *SM* 41 (1992): 289-323.

Klein, Günter. "Paul's Purpose in Writing the Epistle to the Romans." In *The Romans Debate,* 29-43. Rev. ed. Ed. Karl P. Donfried. Peabody: Hendrickson Publishers, 1991.

Kraftchick, Steve. "Paul's Use of Creation Themes: A Test of Romans 1–8." *ExAud* 3 (1987): 72-87.

Kruger, M. A. "*TINA KARPON,* 'Some Fruit' in Romans 1:13." *WTJ* 49 (1987): 167-73.

Lyonnet, Stanislas. "Deum cui servio in spiritu meo (Rom 1,9)." *VD* 41 (1963): 52-59.

————. "De justitia Dei in epistola ad Romanos 1,17 et 3,21-22." *VD* 25 (1947): 23-34.

Marquardt, Friedrich-Wilhelm. *Die Juden im Römerbrief.* ThStud 107. Zurich: Theologischer Verlag, 1971.

Martyn, J. Louis. *Galatians.* AB 33A. New York: Doubleday, 1997.

McKnight, Scot. *A Light among the Gentiles: Jewish Missionary Activity in the Second Temple Period.* Minneapolis: Fortress Press, 1991.

Minear, Paul S. "The Mission (Romans)." In his *The Bible and the Historian: Breaking the Silence about God in Biblical Studies,* 239-45. Nashville: Abingdon Press, 2002.

Moule, C. F. D. *An Idiom-Book of New Testament Greek.* 2d ed. Cambridge: Cambridge University Press, 1960.

————. *Worship in the New Testament.* Ecumenical Studies in Worship 9. Richmond: John Knox Press, 1961.

Mullins, Terence Y. "Disclosure: A Literary Form in the New Testament." *NovT* 7 (1964-65): 44-50.

O'Brien, Peter T. *Introductory Thanksgivings in the Letters of Paul.* NovTSup 49. Leiden: E. J. Brill, 1977.

Ochsenmeier, Erwin. "Romans 1,11-12: A Clue to the Purpose of Romans?" *ETL* 83 (2007): 395-406.

————. "Thanksgiving and the Gospel in Paul." *NTS* 21 (1974-75): 144-55.

Parkin, Harry. "Romans i.13-15." *ExpTim* 79 (1967-68): 95.

Reichert, Angelika. *Der Römerbrief als Gratwanderung: Eine Untersuchung zur Abfassungsproblematik.* FRLANT 194. Göttingen: Vandenhoeck & Ruprecht, 2001.

Reid, Marty L. "A Consideration of the Function of Romans 1:8-15 in Light of Greco-Roman Rhetoric." *JETS* 38 (1995): 181-91.

Roetzel, Calvin J. *The Letters of Paul.* 5th ed. Louisville: Westminster John Knox Press, 2009.

Sanders, Jack T. "The Transition from Opening Epistolary Thanksgiving to Body in the Letters of the Pauline Corpus." *JBL* 81 (1962): 348-62.

Schubert, Paul. *The Form and Function of the Pauline Thanksgivings.* BZNW 20. Berlin: Alfred Töpelmann, 1939.

Starnitzke, Dierk. "'Griechen und Barbaren . . . bin ich verpflicht' (Röm 1,14). Die Selbstdefinition der Gesellschaft und die Individualität und Universalität der paulinischen Botschaft." *WD* 24 (1997): 187-207.

————. *Die Struktur paulinischen Denkens im Römerbrief: Eine linguistische-logische Untersuchung.* BWANT 8/3. Stuttgart: W. Kohlhammer, 2004.

Stuhlmacher, Peter. "The Purpose of Romans." In *The Romans Debate,* 231-42. Rev. ed. Ed. Karl P. Donfried. Peabody: Hendrickson Publishers, 1991.

Thorsteinsson, Runar M. "Paul's Missionary Duty towards Gentiles in Rome: A Note on the Punctuation and Syntax of Rom 1.13-15." *NTS* 48 (2002): 531-47.

Watson, Francis. "The Two Roman Congregations: Romans 14:1–15:13." In *The Romans Debate,* 203-15. Rev. ed. Ed. Karl P. Donfried. Peabody: Hendrickson Publishers, 1991.

Weber, Max. "Zwischenbetrachtung: Theorie der Stufen und Richtungen religiöser Weltablehnung." In his *Gesammelte Aufsätze zur Religionssoziologie,* 1:536-73. 3 vols. Tübingen: J. C. B. Mohr (Paul Siebeck), 1920.

Weima, Jeffrey A. D. "Preaching the Gospel in Rome: A Study of the Epistolary Framework of Romans." In *Gospel in Paul: Studies on Corinthians, Galatians and Romans for Richard N. Longenecker,* 337-66. Ed. L. Ann Jervis and Peter Richardson. Sheffield: Sheffield Academic Press, 1994.

White, John L. "Introductory Formulae in the Body of the Pauline Letter." *JBL* 90 (1971): 91-97.

————. *The Form and Function of the Body of the Greek Letter: A Study of the Letter-Body in the Nonliterary Papyri and in Paul the Apostle.* 2d ed. SBLDS 2. Missoula: Scholars Press, 1972.

Wiles, Gordon P. *Paul's Intercessory Prayers: The Significance of the Intercessory Prayer Passages in the Letters of St. Paul.* SNTSMS 24. Cambridge: Cambridge University Press, 1974.

1.3. *Propositio:* Overture to the Letter, 1:16-17

16For I am not ashamed of the gospel, for it is God's power for salvation to everyone who believes, Jew first and also Greek. 17For God's righteousness is revealed in it from faith to faith, as it has been written, "The one who is righteous by faith will live."

Notes on the Text and Translation

1:16 Some Greek witnesses (D [corrector], Ψ, and the Majority Text) include τοῦ Χριστοῦ after τὸ εὐαγγέλιον, resulting in the reading "the gospel of Christ," which is followed in the KJV but not by other major versions. The textual evidence ($\mathfrak{P}^{26}$, ℵ, B, and others), however, is strongly against the additional words.

On the translation of Ἰουδαῖος as "Jew" here and subsequently (2:9-10, 17, 28-29; 3:1; 10:12) rather than as "Judean," as proposed by some interpreters,[121] see the note regarding 2:17.

121. BDAG 478-79 (Ἰουδαῖος, 2, a); P. Esler, *Romans,* 62-74.

1:17 The expression "from faith to faith" is a literal translation of the Greek phrase (ἐκ πίστεως εἰς πίστιν). Alternatives in English versions include "by faith from first to last" (NIV) and "through faith for faith" (RSV and NRSV). See the Exegetical Commentary for the reasoning behind the translation proposed here.

The quotation from Habakkuk in this verse is translated as "The righteous will live by faith" in the NIV and as "The one who is righteous will live by faith" in the NRSV. The Greek is ambiguous. For justification of the translation used here, see the exegesis of 1:17.

General Comment

The two verses make up a "bridge passage," expressing the theme of the letter,[122] the gospel of the righteousness of God in Christ. They function as an overture does in some works of classical music. In formal rhetorical analysis, the passage has been called the *propositio,* which summarizes in thesis form the central thought of what is to follow.[123] Formally the verses are part of the thanksgiving section of the letter, but they can be regarded as a separate paragraph, as they usually are in modern English versions.

After giving thanks for the faith of the believers in Rome and referring to the gospel three times already in the space of fifteen verses (1:3, 9, 15), Paul declares that he is not ashamed of it. He does not explain why he might have reason to be ashamed, but he knows very well that some persons find the gospel to be abhorrent, since it is about a crucified "savior" who was rejected by the highest authorities in Roman Palestine. He goes on to explore essential dimensions of the word "gospel," claiming it to be a "power of salvation" and the means by which God's saving righteousness is revealed in the world, dominated by the city and empire of Rome.

Detailed Comment

1:16 Paul declares that he is not "ashamed of the gospel." The term for being ashamed (ἐπαισχύνομαι) appears in both the LXX (Ps 118:6 [MT 119:6]; Job 34:19; Isa 1:29) and the NT (Mark 8:38//Luke 9:26; Rom 6:21; 2 Tim 1:8, 12, 16; Heb 2:11; 11:16). In the NT it takes on the function of confessional language,[124]

---

122. P. O'Brien, *Introductory Thanksgivings,* 198, 202.
123. H.-J. Klauck, *Ancient Letters and the New Testament,* 219, 303.
124. Axel Horstmann, "αἰσχύνομαι," *EDNT* 1:42.

rooted in a wide confessional stream related to the preaching of Jesus.[125] To be ashamed is to deny or renounce, as in being ashamed of Christ (Mark 8:38// Luke 9:26; 2 Tim 1:8). In saying that he is not ashamed of the gospel, Paul is saying that he is a robust confessor of it. It is not likely that he is making a statement over against the Christians in Rome. On the contrary, he continues what he has said in 1:15 — that he is eager to proclaim the gospel at Rome. Proclaiming the gospel is his passion, and it is something of which he is not ashamed. Though the gospel is foolishness to many (1 Cor 1:18-25), for Paul it is the power of God unto salvation.

The gospel is "God's power for salvation to everyone who believes." For Paul, the word "gospel" (εὐαγγέλιον) does not refer to a narrative of the life, teachings, death, and resurrection of Jesus, but essentially to good news that is delivered in proclamation. It is a message of dynamic "power" (δύναμις), a "powerful message," and so a "performative utterance" that accomplishes something. Preaching is an event in which good news is not just conveyed; it also sets free. The hearer becomes a new creation (2 Cor 5:17).

The term εὐαγγέλιον is pre-Pauline, for the apostle nowhere explains its meaning in his letters, and he assumes that even his Roman readers know the term. Moreover, early pre-Pauline usage of the term accounts for its having different nuances among different NT writers.[126] The background of the term has been explored in the LXX, the writings of subsequent Hellenistic Jewish writers, the proclamation of Jesus, and nonbiblical Greek sources. A background in the emperor cult, in which the "good tidings" of the dawn of a new era are proclaimed with the accession of an emperor to the throne, is likely.[127] It has been suggested that that is the primary basis for the term,[128] and that, indeed, "The NT use of εὐαγγέλιον does not derive from the LXX."[129] But that view is misleading. Strictly speaking, the term εὐαγγέλιον does not show up in the LXX. But the plural form εὐαγγέλια appears once (2 Sam 4:10). And although it is usually rendered there as "reward for good news" (ASV, RSV, NIV, and NRSV), there is no reason why it cannot be translated as "good news."[130] Furthermore, the feminine form ἡ εὐαγγέλια is used on several occasions to

---

125. C. K. Barrett, "I Am Not Ashamed of the Gospel," 116-43.

126. Cf. the surveys of Gerhard Friedrich, "εὐαγγέλιον," TDNT 2:727-35, and Georg Strecker, "εὐαγγέλιον," EDNT 2:70-74.

127. For references, cf. G. Friedrich, "εὐαγγέλιον," TDNT 2:724-25.

128. G. Friedrich, "εὐαγγέλιον," TDNT 2:724, and G. Strecker, "εὐαγγέλιον," EDNT 2:71. On the other hand, P. Stuhlmacher, Romans, 25, says that the usage in the imperial cult had "no influence" on the NT meaning.

129. G. Friedrich, "εὐαγγέλιον," TDNT 2:725.

130. In context, David is making a sarcastic remark. He says that he gave "good news" (death) to a messenger who claimed to bring good news about the death of Saul.

signify "good news" (2 Sam 18:20, 22, 25, 27; 2 Kgs 7:9). More to the point, the verbal form εὐαγγελίζομαι ("to proclaim good news") is used nearly two dozen times in the LXX.[131] The term is used to proclaim the good news of victory in a more general sense (1 Sam 31:9), but particularly the good news of God's victory for his people, signifying that they are safe and secure, and that a new era has now begun (2 Sam 18:19, 31; Pss 39:10; 67:12; 95:2 [MT 40:9; 68:11; 96:2]; Isa 40:9; 52:7; 61:1; Nah 2:1 [MT 1:15]). Among these is the eloquent declaration "How beautiful upon the mountains are the feet of the messenger who announces peace, who brings good news, who announces salvation, who says to Zion, 'Your God reigns!'" (Isa 52:7), a passage known well to Paul and quoted by him (Rom 10:15). This will mean that for Paul the gospel is the good news of salvation. It is the good news that in the Christ event God has defeated the powers of the old age (sin and death) that have kept humanity in bondage. The new era has come. Those who hear and receive the gospel are free and safe. The gospel is not then simply information, even though it does have a content (cf. 1 Cor 15:1-8), but it is first of all news that sets people free. As a performative utterance, it declares to people that the bondage to sin and death, under which they have been living, is gone. To hear and accept that news is life-giving. The gospel is therefore "God's power for salvation to everyone who believes."

As with the word "gospel," so with the word "salvation" (σωτηρία), Paul does not give a definition. Surprisingly, he does not speak of salvation explicitly as being saved from sin, death, and the power of the devil or — in the positive sense — as being saved for life in heaven after death. The primary way that he uses the language of salvation is to signify being saved from the wrath of God on the day of final judgment (Rom 5:9; 1 Thess 1:10; 5:9; cf. 2 Cor 5:10).[132] It is on that basis that he can speak of salvation derivatively as the antithesis of "perishing" that leads to death (1 Cor 1:18; 2 Cor 2:15) and as deliverance from bondage to "the present evil age" (Gal 1:4). Furthermore, by implication, salvation will still be from sin and death, since these are what hold persons in bondage (Rom 3:9; 5:12, 17, 21; 6:6, 9-14; 8:38). In regard to the positive meaning of salvation, it indicates that one is a child of God, adopted, and redeemed (Rom 8:23-24), reconciled to God (Rom 5:10-11), living in the new age (Rom 5:17), and being conformed to the image of God's Son (Phil 3:20-21; Rom 8:29).

---

131. 1 Sam 31:9; 2 Sam 1:20; 4:10; 18:19, 20 (twice), 26, 31; 1 Kgs 1:42; 1 Chr 10:9; Pss 39:10; 67:12; 95:2; Joel 3:5; Nah 2:1; Isa 40:9 (twice) 52:7 (twice); 60:6; 61:1; Jer 20:15. Cf. also *Pss. Sol.* 11.1.

132. At Rom 5:9 the Greek text speaks only of being saved "from the wrath" (as in the KJV and NAB), not "from the wrath of God." But the context clearly means divine wrath (as at 1 Thess 1:10; 5:9). Therefore various modern English versions (ASV, RSV, NIV, NRSV, ESV, and NET) have "God's wrath" or "the wrath of God."

Paul can speak of salvation as both future (Rom 5:9-10; 10:9; 13:11; 1 Cor 5:5; 1 Thess 5:9) and present (Rom 1:16; 1 Cor 1:18; 2 Cor 2:15; 6:2). Once he speaks of it as past (using an aorist passive verb, ἐσώθημεν), referring to the work of God in Christ on the cross, which remains the believer's hope (Rom 8:24). Taking the passages (with their various tenses) together, the stress is primarily on the future, but the assurance of future salvation fills the present with new significance. Believers receive the future gift now — at least in part — a down payment, so to speak.

The phrase "Jew first and also Greek" is puzzling. Paul uses the same expression in the letter twice more (2:9-10), and there — as well as here — the combination of "Jew" and "Greek" means essentially all people. But the word "first" (πρῶτον) must be considered. While it may well have a temporal meaning — i.e., that the gospel had its hearing and effects among Jews "first" and then among Gentiles — that is not likely the whole of the matter. There must be a theological matter at stake. The phrase as a whole signifies that, for Paul, the Jews have had precedence among those to whom the gospel has been preached, and that is for the sake of the continuity of salvation history. It is to them that the gospel was "promised beforehand through [God's] prophets in the holy scriptures" (Rom 1:2). Now that the promise has been fulfilled, they are the ones to whom the gospel should be proclaimed first. Therefore Paul can speak of a priority (in principle, not just in the passing of time) of proclamation to the Jews.[133]

But there is a double edge to the expression. On the one hand, Paul reminds his Gentile readers at Rome that the gospel is for the Jews "first" as recipients of the promises of God; the gospel is not simply for Gentiles. On the other hand, by saying "also Greek," he is saying that the gospel is God's power for salvation for all people. Priority, not privilege, is the operative way of thinking. As apostle to the Gentiles (Rom 11:13), Paul can never relinquish his insistence that the gospel is for them; but at the same time he can never abandon the thought of continuity within the history of salvation.

The words "Jew first and also Greek" stand in apposition to "everyone who believes." Here it is important to notice that Paul's declaration concerning the gospel as the "power for salvation" to every believer is an indicative, descriptive statement. Paul does not say here that faith is a precondition for salvation in the sense that one must first be disposed to believe in the gospel in order to be saved.[134] The emphasis in the verse is on the gospel itself as a *power* that

---

133. In various ways this viewpoint is found in the works of C. K. Barrett, *Romans,* 29; E. Käsemann, *Romans,* 23; C. Cranfield, *Romans,* 91; J. Fitzmyer, *Romans,* 257; and P. Stuhlmacher, *Romans,* 28; D. Moo, *Romans,* 68-69.

134. For a fine survey of interpreters who speak of faith as a "precondition" for salvation in Paul and a critique of them, cf. A. Nygren, *Romans,* 67-72.

brings salvation to those who accept it. It is the power that makes salvation possible for those who believe.[135] For "faith comes from what is heard, and what is heard comes through the word of Christ" (Rom 10:17), the gospel concerning the crucified and risen Christ. Consequently, faith itself is evidence that the gospel has exercised its power. The gospel is the power that brings life, and wherever one hears it and accepts it, salvation is present. The gospel is the good news that God has reconciled the world to himself through the death and resurrection of Christ (2 Cor 5:19). The only problem remaining in the divine-human relationship is for humanity to hear that good news and accept it. The gospel is a message of reconciliation, and the herald of the gospel calls upon hearers to accept it and therefore be reconciled to God (2 Cor 5:20). God has declared amnesty toward the world; what remains is for the people of the world to declare amnesty toward God in return. The response of faith in the good news completes the reconciliation offered already from the divine side. The gospel is thus a power for salvation insofar as it declares the amnesty of God, thereby enabling everyone to let down their defenses against God, unseat any other god in their lives, and let God be their one and only God.

1:17 The gospel can be called the "power for salvation" because "the righteousness of God" is revealed in it. To reveal (ἀποκαλύπτω) is to "disclose, bring to light, make fully known."[136] And so the good news (the εὐαγγέλιον) concerning what God has done in Christ discloses "the righteousness of God." Right away, then, the latter phrase must be taken as one that relates directly to salvation. The idea that God's "righteousness" at this place is an expression of God's wrath or justice would be misleading. The Vulgate's translation of the phrase as "*iustitia Dei*" can be taken to mean "the justice of God," and that is how Martin Luther understood the phrase initially prior to his breakthrough. He thought that it meant that "God is righteous and punishes the unrighteous sinner."[137] But Luther came to understand it as a phrase that speaks of the righteousness by which God justifies, i.e., a gift of righteousness from God to one who has faith in the gospel.[138]

The Pauline phrase concerning "the righteousness of God" has been debated in recent decades, and it is discussed more fully than here in an appendix ("The 'Righteousness of God' in Paul"). Essentially, however, the righteousness of God signifies God's saving work, setting right the relationship between humanity and himself. The Greek word δικαιοσύνη is used frequently in the LXX

---

135. P. Gräbe, *The Power of God in Paul's Letters*, 177. Cf. A. Nygren, *Romans*, 71: "It is not man's faith that gives the gospel its power; quite the contrary, it is the power of the gospel that makes it possible for one to believe."

136. BDAG 112 (ἀποκαλύπτω).

137. Martin Luther, "Preface to Latin Writings," in *LuthW*, 34:336.

138. Martin Luther, "Preface to Latin Writings," in *LuthW*, 34:337.

to translate the Hebrew words for "righteousness" (צֶדֶק and צְדָקָה), meaning not simply an attribute of God, but God's saving activity. God shows God's righteousness by delivering his people from their enemies (Pss 31:1 [LXX 31:2]; 70:15 [LXX 71:15]; 98:2 [LXX 97:2]; 143:11; Isa 41:10; 45:8; 46:12-13; 51:5; 59:17). Furthermore, the passage contains terms found in Psalm 98:2 (LXX 97:2), such as the verb "reveal" and the noun "righteousness," and in that place the term "righteousness" is in synonymous parallelism with "salvation."

The expression "from faith to faith" has been interpreted in several ways, being rendered as (among other things): (1) from less faith to more (as faith matures);[139] (2) "faith from beginning to end," virtually equivalent to "*sola fide* (by faith alone)";[140] (3) "from [God's] faithfulness to [a person's] faith";[141] (4) a movement from Judaism to Christianity, "from the faith of the Old Testament believer to the faith of the New Testament believer";[142] and (5) "from the faith of the Jews first, and now growing also among the Gentiles" ("Jews" being Christian Jews).[143] There are only a few parallel constructions in the OT and in the writings of Paul that can be brought into the discussion. Psalm 84:7 has the expression "from strength to strength" (LXX 83:8, ἐκ δυνάμεως εἰς δύναμιν), and Jeremiah has "from evil to evil" (LXX 9:3, ἐκ κακῶν εἰς κακά). Paul himself uses the "from . . . to" idiom twice in one passage. At 2 Corinthians 2:16 he writes concerning: "a fragrance from death to death" (ὀσμὴ ἐκ θανάτου εἰς θάνατον) and of "a fragrance from life to life" (ὀσμὴ ἐκ ζωῆς εἰς ζωήν). Elsewhere he speaks of being transformed "from glory unto glory" (ἀπὸ δόξης εἰς δόξαν, 2 Cor 3:18). These passages speak of growth or progression, and that is often the case in extrabiblical sources as well.[144]

In seeking the meaning of the phrase here, it would seem that interpretations 3 through 5 can be excluded, for it is difficult to imagine (without further

---

139. J. Calvin, *Romans*, 65; W. Sanday and A. Headlam, *Romans*, 28.

140. BDAG 819 (πίστις, 2, d, α); C. H. Dodd, *Romans*, 13-14; A. Nygren, *Romans*, 78 ("something like *sola fide*"); C. K. Barrett, *Romans*, 31; J. Knox, *IB (Romans)*, 9:394; E. Käsemann, *Romans*, 31; C. Cranfield, *Romans*, 100; J. Fitzmyer, *Romans*, 263; B. Byrne, *Romans*, 60; E. Lohse, *Römer*, 78 (emphasizing "*sola fide*").

141. K. Barth, *Romans*, 41; B. Corsani, "ΕΚ ΠΙΣΤΕΩΣ," 92-93; J. Dunn, *Romans*, 44, 48 (who cites still others); C. Talbert, *Romans*, 41; G. Davies, *Faith and Obedience in Romans*, 43, 112. L. Keck, *Romans*, 53-54, interprets ἐκ πίστεως Christologically, so that it speaks of the faithfulness of Christ.

142. C. Quarles, "From Faith to Faith," 19.

143. J. Taylor, "From Faith to Faith," 348. Cf. U. Wilckens, *Römer*, 1:88; R. Jewett, *Romans*, 144, for whom the two phrases are used in a more general sense to speak of the universal outreach or expansion of the gospel.

144. C. Quarles, "From Faith to Faith," 13, summarizing from a search in *TLG*: the expression can express "range, duration, repetition, source and destination, previous state and new state, or progression."

clues) that Paul has two different subjects of faith in mind when using the expression (such as [1] God and the believer; [2] Judaism and Christianity; [3] the Jewish Christian and the Gentile Christian). Moreover, the following portion of the verse — the quotation from Habakkuk 2:4 — has to be taken into consideration, in which ἐκ πίστεως is present once again, and there the phrase refers to the faith of a believer.[145] Although this is not decisive, one should expect that the two uses of ἐκ πίστεως are identical or at least similar. But that the expression designates a maturing of faith or that it is for emphasis only (interpretations 1 and 2 above) seems insufficient. In context, a far richer explanation is called for. That is that, for Paul, the righteousness of God is revealed in the gospel, perceived by faith (ἐκ πίστεως), and directed to faith (εἰς πίστιν) which receives it. When the righteousness of God is exercised, perceived, and received by faith, God's saving work is done. Eschatological salvation is proleptically realized in the life of the believer. That will mean that the verse speaks of a progression, to be sure, but it is the progression of the righteousness of God to accomplish what God seeks to do, not the progression of faith in the individual believer or in the spread of faith in the world.

Paul's quotation from Habakkuk 2:4 in 1:17b poses problems on three fronts. These include: (1) textual alterations by Paul from the LXX (already different from MT); (2) translation; and (3) OT meaning and NT application.[146]

1. Textual alterations: The Greek text of Romans 1:17b reads: ὁ δὲ δίκαιος ἐκ πίστεως ζήσεται. Paul writes virtually the same (with one less word, δέ) at Galatians 3:11: ὁ δίκαιος ἐκ πίστεως ζήσεται. In neither case does Paul quote the LXX exactly,[147] which reads: ὁ δὲ δίκαιος ἐκ πίστεώς μου ζήσεται. ("But the righteous [person] shall live by my [= God's] faithfulness" or "But the righteous [person] shall live by faith in me [= God]").[148] The LXX differs from the MT,

---

145. Contra those who maintain that it refers to the faith or faithfulness of Christ: L. Johnson, "Romans 3:21-26," 90; R. Hays, *The Faith of Jesus Christ*, 132-41, 279-81, *et passim*; I. Wallis, *The Faith of Jesus Christ in Early Christian Traditions*, 111; D. Campbell, "Romans 1:17," 280-85; and D. Heliso, *Pistis and the Righteous One*, 146-54, 254, *et passim*. The Greek phrase ἐκ πίστεως is used frequently by Paul; leaving aside the contested passages in the "*Pistis Christou* Debate" (Rom 1:17; 3:26; 4:16; Gal 2:16; 3:11, 22), it is most often used in passages concerning justification; and in those it refers consistently to the faith of the believer (Rom 3:30; 5:1; 9:30, 32; 10:6; Gal 3:8, 24) — which is also true of other passages where justification is not being discussed (Rom 14:23; Gal 3:12; 5:5). In addition, as J. Taylor, "From Faith to Faith," 339-41, points out, Hab 2:4 is interpreted as the faith of the believer in Jewish texts (Qumran pesher and the targum); it does not have a messianic meaning.

146. For discussion of these and other issues, cf. S. Hultgren, *Habakkuk 2:4 in Early Judaism, in Hebrews, and in Paul* (forthcoming).

147. Nor does the author of Hebrews quote the LXX exactly: ὁ δὲ δίκαιός μου ἐκ πίστεως ζήσεται (10:38).

148. This is based on the early major majuscles, including A, B, W, Q, and S. There is a vari-

which reads: וְצַדִּיק בֶּאֱמוּנָתוֹ יִחְיֶה ("But the righteous [person] shall live by his faith" or "his faithfulness"), which corresponds to the consonantal text at Qumran.[149] The difference may be due not to an interpretive alteration by the LXX translator but to reading the final ו (*waw*) of בֶּאֱמוּנָתוֹ in the Hebrew text ("his faith") as a י (*yod*), resulting in "my faithfulness" or "faith in me."[150] By way of summary, the LXX differs from the MT (and Qumran text) by reading "my faithfulness" (or "faith in me") over against "his faithfulness" (or "his faith"), and Paul's version does not have the possessive pronoun μου ("my") of the LXX.

2. Translation: Both the Hebrew and LXX versions of the OT have an adverbial use of the prepositional phrase, "by faith." That is, it modifies the Hebrew or Greek verb represented by the English expression "shall live."

English versions of Romans 1:17b, however, differ. Some have an adverbial rendering of the phrase; others have an adjectival one, as follows (differences illustrated here by the / marker):

Adverbial sense: ὁ δὲ δίκαιος/ἐκ πίστεως ζήσεται.

KJV (1611): "The just shall live by faith."
ASV (1901): "But the righteous shall live by faith."
JB (1966): "The upright man finds life through faith."
NAB (1970): "The just man shall live by faith."
NASV (1971): "But the righteous man shall live by faith."
NIV (1973): "The righteous will live by faith."
NRSV (1989): "The one who is righteous will live by faith."

Adjectival sense: ὁ δὲ δίκαιος ἐκ πίστεως/ζήσεται.

RSV (1946): "He who through faith is righteous shall live."
NEB (1961): "He shall gain life who is justified by faith."
TEV (1966): "He who is put right with God through faith shall live."
NET (2005): "The righteous by faith will live."
Note in NRSV (alternative reading): "The one who is righteous through
    faith will live."

---

ant, ὁ δὲ δίκαιος ἐκ πίστεως ζήσεται. This reading is attested by a corrector of W and by minuscles 763 (eleventh century), 130 (twelfth-thirteenth century), and 106 (fourteenth century). The variant could be attributed to scribal aligning of Habakkuk with the writings of Paul (primarily Rom 1:17 and secondarily Gal 3:11). Cf. *Septuaginta: Duodecim prophetae*, ed. J. Ziegler, 264.

149. 1QpHab 7.17 (וצדיק באמונתו יחיה). The Hebrew text is presented and translated into English in *The Dead Sea Scrolls Study Edition*, ed. Florentino García Martínez and Eibert J. C. Tigchelaar, 2 vols. (Grand Rapids: Wm. B. Eerdmans, 1997-98), 1:16-17.

150. F. Andersen, *Habakkuk*, 211.

Interpreters also favor one or the other position. There are advocates for the adverbial reading,[151] and advocates for the adjectival one.[152]

A decision on which reading should be chosen cannot be made on the basis of grammar and syntax, but only by paying attention to context and considering various exegetical possibilities. The adjectival sense is to be preferred for a number of reasons: (1) the immediate context is righteousness/salvation by faith; (2) the larger context (3:21–4:25) is righteousness by faith (to which 1:17 is an overture); (3) Galatians 3:11 employs Habakkuk 2:4 to affirm righteousness by faith (over against righteousness by works of the law); and (4) Paul speaks of righteousness by faith in other passages in Romans (4:11, 13; 5:1; 9:30; 10:6). To be sure, a person doesn't "get" righteousness by faith, but by faith in the gospel (rather than faith in one's works), one is rightwised and (consequently) lives. The adverbial sense can be ruled out, for Paul is not talking about a way of life (i.e., that a righteous person lives by his or her faith in God or by faith in the gospel) at this point in his letter.

3. OT Meaning and NT Application: According to the Hebrew text, the prophet Habakkuk contrasts the righteous one, who shall live by fidelity to the Lord (an adverbial usage!), to the proud (the Chaldean oppressors). By a strange twist (perhaps due to an error in reading the Hebrew text), the LXX translator has "helped" the reader to know that it is not simply his fidelity (πίστις) in the abstract, but his fidelity to the Lord that is the means of having life. Paul (quoting from memory, citing a text no longer available, or making an alteration to the Greek text as we know it via the LXX) "reads" Scripture in light of the gospel. Habakkuk 2:4 confirms that by faith in the righteousness (saving activity) of God, announced in the gospel, one shall live (have eschatological salvation).

This is an interesting case study for the relationship between the testaments. In both texts the accent is on faith as fidelity and/or trust in God (Habakkuk) or the righteousness of God (Paul) as a means to life in its fullest sense. Paul takes Habakkuk 2:4 (future tense verb) as being fulfilled in his time. The OT text is surpassed but not distorted.

---

151. Included here are W. Sanday and A. Headlam, *Romans,* 28; O. Michel, *Romans,* 44, 55; J. Murray, *Romans,* 1:32-33; D. Smith, "Ὁ ΔΕ ΔΙΚΑΙΟΣ ΕΚ ΠΙΣΤΕΩΣ ΖΗΣΕΤΑΙ," 13-25; H. Cavallin, "The Righteous Shall Live by Faith," 33-43; J. Fitzmyer, *Romans,* 265; C. Talbert, *Romans,* 42; E. Lohse, *Römer,* 82; R. Jewett, *Romans,* 146; M. Seifrid, "Paul's Use of Habakkuk 2:4," 135.

152. A. Nygren, *Romans,* 84-92; C. K. Barrett, *Romans,* 27; J. Knox, *IB (Romans),* 9:395; E. Käsemann, *Romans,* 32; C. E. B. Cranfield, *Romans,* 102; U. Wilckens, *Römer,* 1:89-90; P. Stuhlmacher, *Romans,* 29; B. Byrne, *Romans,* 60-61; D.-A. Koch, *Die Schrift als Zeuge des Evangeliums,* 290-91.

BIBLIOGRAPHY

Andersen, Francis I. *Habakkuk.* AB 25. New York: Doubleday, 2001.

Barrett, C. K. "I Am Not Ashamed of the Gospel." In *Foi et salut selon S. Paul (Épître aux Romains 1,16)*, 19-50. Ed. Marcus Barth et al. AnBib 42. Rome: Pontifical Biblical Institute, 1970; reprinted in his *New Testament Essays*, 116-43. London: SPCK, 1972. References are to the latter version.

Barth, Markus, et al., eds. *Foi et salut selon S. Paul (Épître aux Romains 1,16)*. AnBib 42. Rome: Pontifical Biblical Institute Press, 1970.

Bartsch, Hans-Werner. "Concept of Faith in Paul's Letter to the Romans." *BR* 13 (1968): 41-53.

Berger, Klaus. "Neues Material zur 'Gerechtigkeit Gottes.'" *ZNW* 68 (1977): 266-75.

Bonneau, Norman. "Stages of Salvation History in Romans 1:16–3:26." *ÉgThéol* 23 (1992): 177-94.

Brauch, Manfred T. "Perspectives on 'God's Righteousness' in Recent German Discussion." In E. P. Sanders, *Paul and Palestinian Judaism: A Comparison of Patterns of Religion*, 523-42. Philadelphia: Fortress Press, 1977.

Brindle, Wayne A. "'To the Jew First': Rhetoric, Strategy, History, or Theology?" *BiblSac* 159 (2002): 221-33.

Broz, Ludek. "The Faith of Ours Which Is Not Ours." *CV* 28 (1985): 33-46.

Campbell, Douglas A. "False Presuppositions in the ΠΙΣΤΙΣ ΧΡΙΣΤΟΥ Debate: A Response to Brian Dodd." *JBL* 116 (1997): 713-19.

———. "The Meaning of Πίστις and Νόμος in Paul: A Linguistic and Structural Perspective." *JBL* 111 (1992): 91-103.

———. "Romans 1:17 — A *Crux Interpretum* for the Πίστις Χριστοῦ Debate." *JBL* 113 (1994): 265-85.

Campbell, William S. *Paul's Gospel in an Intercultural Context: Jew and Gentile in the Letter to the Romans.* SIGU 69. New York: Peter Lang, 1991.

Cambier, Jules. "Justice de Dieu, salut de tous les hommes et foi." *RB* 71 (1964): 537-83.

———. "L'évangile, révélation de la justice de Dieu." In *L'Évangile de Dieu selon l'épître aux Romains*, 11-59. Tome I: L'évangile dela justice et de la grâce. Bruges: Desclée de Brouwer, 1967.

Cavallin, H. C. C. "'The Righteous Shall Live by Faith': A Decisive Argument for the Traditional Interpretation." *ST* 32 (1978): 33-43.

Conzelmann, Hans. "Die Rechtfertigungslehre des Paulus: Theologie oder Anthropologie?" *EvT* 28 (1968): 389-404.

Corrigan, Gregory M. "Paul's Shame for the Gospel." *BTB* 16 (1986): 23-27.

Corsani, Bruno. "ΕΚ ΠΙΣΤΕΩΣ in the Letters of Paul." In *The New Testament Age: Essays in Honor of Bo Reicke*, 1:87-93. Ed. William C. Weinrich. 2 vols. Macon: Mercer University Press, 1984.

Davies, Glenn N. *Faith and Obedience in Romans: A Study of Romans 1–4.* JSNTSup 39. Sheffield: Sheffield Academic Press, 1990.

Dockery, David S. "Romans 1:16-17." *RevExp* 86 (1989): 87-91.

Dodd, Brian. "Romans 1:17 — A *Crux Interpretum* for the Πίστις Χριστοῦ Debate?" *JBL* 114 (1995): 470-73.

Donge, Gloria van. "In What Way Is Paul's Gospel *(Euangelion)* of Freedom Theology of the Cross *(Theologia Crucis)*?" *Coll* 21 (1988): 19-33.

Du Toit, Andreas B. "Forensic Metaphors in Romans and Their Soteriological Significance." In *Salvation in the New Testament: Perspectives on Soteriology*, 213-46. Ed. Jan G. van der Watt. NovTSup 121. Boston: E. J. Brill, 2005.

Feuillet, Andreas. "La citation d'Habacuc 2:4 et les huit premiers chapteres de l'Epître aux Romains." *NTS* 6 (1959-60): 52-80.

Fitzmyer, Joseph A. "Habakkuk 2:3-4 and the New Testament." In his *To Advance the Gospel: New Testament Studies*, 236-46. New York: Crossroad, 1981.

———. "Paul and the Dead Sea Scrolls." In *The Dead Sea Scrolls after Fifty Years: A Comprehensive Assessment*, 2:599-621. Ed. Peter W. Flint and James C. Vanderkam. 2 vols. Boston: E. J. Brill, 1998-99.

Fridrichsen, Anton. "Aus Glauben zum Glauben, Röm. 1,17." In *Walter Bauer Gottingensi viro de Novi Testamenti philologia optime merito sacrum*, 54. ConBNT 12. Lund: C. W. K. Gleerup, 1948.

Globitza, Otto. "Von der Scham des Gläubigen: Erwägungen zu Röm. 1 14-17." *NovT* 4 (1960-61): 74-80.

Gräbe, Petrus. *The Power of God in Paul's Letters*. WUNT 2/123. Tübingen: J. C. B. Mohr (Paul Siebeck), 2000.

Grayston, Kenneth. "'Not Ashamed of the Gospel'. Romans I,16a, and the Structure of the Epistle." *SE* 2 (1964): 569-73.

Haacker, Klaus. "Evangelium ohne Scham." *TBei* 30 (1999): 23-31.

Hays, Richard B. *The Faith of Jesus Christ: The Narrative Substructure of Galatians 3:1–4:11*. 2d ed. Grand Rapids: Wm. B. Eerdmans, 2002.

———. "ΠΙΣΤΙΣ and Pauline Theology: What Is at Stake?" In *Society of Biblical Literature 1991 Seminar Papers*, 714-29. Ed. Eugene H. Lovering. SBLSP 30. Atlanta: Scholars Press, 1991; reprinted in his *The Faith of Jesus Christ: The Narrative Substructure of Galatians 3:1–4:11*, 272-97. 2d ed. Grand Rapids: Wm. B. Eerdmans, 2002.

———. "'The Righteous One' as Eschatological Deliverer: A Case Study in Paul's Apocalyptic Hermeneutics." In *Apocalyptic and the New Testament: Essays in Honor of J. Louis Martyn*, 191-215. Ed. Joel Marcus and Marion L. Soards. JSNTSup 24. Sheffield, JSOT Press, 1989; reprinted as "Apocalyptic Hermeneutics: Habakkuk Proclaims 'The Righteous One.'" In his *The Conversion of the Imagination: Paul as an Interpreter of Israel's Scripture*, 119-42. Grand Rapids: Wm. B. Eerdmans, 2005.

Heliso, Desta. *Pistis and the Righteous One: A Study of Romans 1:17 against the Background of Scripture and Second Temple Jewish Literature*. WUNT 2/235. Tübingen: Mohr Siebeck, 2007.

Herold, Gerhart. *Zorn und Gerechtigkeit Gottes bei Paulus: Eine Untersuchung zu Röm. 1,16-18*. Europäische Hochschulschriften 23.14. Bern: Herbert Lang, 1973.

Hultgren, Stephen J. *Habakkuk 2:4 in Early Judaism, in Hebrews, and in Paul*. Cahiers de la Revue Biblique. Paris: J. Gabalda, forthcoming.

Hvalvik, Reidar. "'For jøde først og så for greker': Til betydningen av Rom 1,16b." *TTK* 60 (1989): 189-96.

Janzen, J. Gerald. "Habakkuk 2:2-4 in the Light of Recent Philological Advances." *HTR* 73 (1980): 53-78.

Johnson, Luke Timothy. "Romans 3:21-26 and the Faith of Jesus." *CBQ* 44 (1982): 77-90.

Klaiber, Walter. "Rechtfertigung. II. Neues Testament." *RGG* 7:98-103.

Klauck, Hans-Josef Klauck. *Ancient Letters and the New Testament: A Guide to Context and Exegesis.* Waco: Baylor University Press, 2006.

Klein, Günter. "Gottes Gerechtigkeit als Thema der neuesten Paulus-Forschung." In his *Rekonstruktion und Interpretation: Gesammelte Aufsätze zum Neuen Testament,* 225-36. Munich: Kaiser Verlag, 1969.

Koch, Dietrich-Alex. *Die Schrift als Zeuge des Evangeliums: Untersuchungen zur Verwendung und zum Verständnis der Schrift bei Paulus.* BHT 96. Tübingen: J. C. B. Mohr (Paul Siebeck), 1986.

————. "Der Text von Hab 2:4b in der Septuagint und im Neuen Testament." *ZNW* 76 (1985): 68-85.

Kuhn, Heinz-Wolfgang. "The Impact of the Qumran Scrolls on the Understanding of Paul." In *The Dead Sea Scrolls: Forty Years of Research,* 327-39. Ed. Devorah Dimant and Uriel Rappaport. STDJ 10. New York: E. J. Brill, 1992.

Lee, Jae Hyun. *Paul's Gospel in Romans: A Discourse Analysis of Rom 1:16–8:39.* LBS 3. Boston: E. J. Brill, 2010.

Leonard, Bill J. "A Place to Believe: Romans 1:16-18." *RevExp* 86 (1989): 93-98.

Lohse, Eduard. "Das Evangelium für Juden und Griechen: Erwägungen zur Theologie des Römerbriefes." *ZNW* 92/3-4 (2001): 168-84.

Manson, T. W. "The Argument from Prophecy." *JTS* 46 (1945): 129-36.

Mason, Steve. "'For I Am Not Ashamed of the Gospel' (Rom. 1.16): The Gospel and the First Readers of Romans." In *Gospel in Paul: Studies on Corinthians, Galatians and Romans for Richard N. Longenecker,* 254-87. Ed. L. Ann Jervis and Peter Richardson. JSNTSup 108. Sheffield: Sheffield Academic Press, 1994.

Michel, Otto. "Zum Sprachgebrauch von ἐπαισχύνομαι in Röm 1:16." In *Glaube und Ethos: Festschrift für Professor d. dr. Georg Wehrung zum 60. Geburtstag am 6. Oktober 1940,* 36-53. Ed. Rudolf Paulus. Stuttgart: W. Kohlhammer Verlag, 1940.

Moody, R. M. "The Habakkuk Quotation in Romans 1:17." *ExpTim* 92 (1981): 205-8.

O'Brien, Peter T. *Introductory Thanksgivings in the Letters of Paul.* NovTSup 49. Leiden: E. J. Brill, 1977.

Olson, Stanley N. "Epistolary Uses of Expressions of Self-Confidence." *JBL* 103 (1984): 585-97.

Plutta-Messerschmidt, Elke. *Gerechtigkeit Gottes bei Paulus.* HUTh 14. Tübingen: J. C. B. Mohr (Paul Siebeck), 1973.

Prete, Benedetto. "La formula *dunamis Theou* in Rom. 1.16 e sue motivationi." *RivB* 23 (1975): 299-328.

Quarles, Charles. "From Faith to Faith: A Fresh Examination of the Prepositional Series in Romans 1:17." *NovT* 45 (2003): 1-21.

Rad, Gerhard von. "Faith Reckoned as Righteousness." In *The Problem of the Hexateuch and Other Essays,* 125-30. New York: McGraw-Hill, 1966.

Reumann, John, *"Righteousness" in the New Testament: "Justification" in the United States Lutheran-Roman Catholic Dialogue*. Philadelphia: Fortress Press, 1982.

Ropes, James Hardy. "Righteousness in the Old Testament and in St. Paul." *JBL* 22 (1903): 211-27.

Sanders, James A. "Habakkuk in Qumran, Paul, and the Old Testament." In *Paul and the Scriptures of Israel*, 98-117. Ed. Craig A. Evans and James A. Sanders. JSNTSup 83/ SSEJC 1. Sheffield: Sheffield Academic Press, 1993.

Schulz, Siegfried, "Zur Rechtfertigung aus Gnaden in Qumran und bei Paulus," *ZTK* 56 (1959): 155-85.

Seifrid, Mark. "Paul's Use of Habakkuk 2:4 in Romans 1:17: Reflections on Israel's Exile in Romans." In *History and Exegesis: New Testament Essays in Honor of Dr. E. Earle Ellis for His 80th Birthday*, 133-49. Ed. Sang-Won (Aaron) Son. Edinburgh: T&T Clark, 2006.

Septuaginta: Duodecim prophetae. Ed. Joseph Ziegler. 2d ed. Göttingen: Vandenhoeck & Ruprecht, 1967.

Smith, D. Moody. "Ο ΔΕ ΔΙΚΑΙΟΣ ΕΚ ΠΙΣΤΕΩΣ ΖΗΣΕΤΑΙ." In *Studies in the History and Text of the New Testament in Honor of Kenneth Willis Clark*, 13-25. Ed. B. L. Daniels and M. J. Suggs. SD 29. Salt Lake City: University of Utah Press, 1967.

Soards, Marion L. "The Righteousness of God in the Writings of the Apostle Paul." *BTB* 15 (1985): 104-9.

Stockmeier, Peter. "Christlicher Glaube und antike Religiosität." *ANRW* II.23.2 (1980): 871-909.

Strobel, August. *Untersuchungen zum eschatologischen Verzögerungsproblem: Auf Grund der spätjüdisch-urchristlichen Geschichte von Habakuk 2,2ff.* NovTSup 2. Leiden: E. J. Brill, 1961.

Stubblefield, Jon. "What Is the Gospel?" In *Proceedings of the Conference on Biblical Interpretation, 1988*, 183-89. Ed. Richard Jackson et al. Nashville: Broadman, 1988.

Taylor, John W. "From Faith to Faith: Romans 1:17 in the Light of Greek Idiom." *NTS* 50 (2004): 337-48.

Trudinger, Peter. "Two Ambiguities in Habakkuk's 'Unambiguous' Oracle." *DRev* 113 (1995): 282-83.

Van Daalen, David H. "The Revelation of God's Righteousness in Romans 1:17." In *Studia Biblica 1978: Sixth International Congress on Biblical Studies, Oxford, 3-7 April 1978*, 3:383-89. Ed. Elizabeth A. Livingstone. 3 vols. Sheffield: JSOT Press, 1979-80.

Vorster, Johannes N. "Strategies of Persuasion in Romans." In *Rhetoric and the New Testament*, 152-70. Ed. Stanley E. Porter et al. Sheffield: JSOT Press, 1993.

Wallis, Ian G. *The Faith of Jesus Christ in Early Christian Traditions*. SNTSMS 84. Cambridge: Cambridge University Press, 1995.

Wallis, W. B. "The Translation of Romans 1:17 — A Basic Motif in Paulinism." *JETS* 16 (1973): 17-23.

Watts, Rikki E. "'For I Am Not Ashamed of the Gospel': Romans 1:16-17 and Habakkuk 2:4." In *Romans and the People of God: Essays in Honor of Gordon D. Fee on the Occasion of His 65th Birthday*, 3-25. Ed. Sven K. Soderlund and N. T. Wright. Grand Rapids: Wm. B. Eerdmans, 1999.

Waetjen, Herman C. "The Trust of Abraham and the Trust of Jesus Christ: Romans 1:17."
     CurrTM 30 (2003): 446-54.
Westerholm, Stephen. "The Righteousness of the Law and the Righteousness of Faith in
     Romans." *Int* 58 (2004): 253-64.
Zorn, Walter D. "The Messianic Use of Habakkuk 2:4a in Romans." *SCJ* 1 (1998): 213-30.

CHAPTER 2

The Revelation of the Wrath of God, 1:18–3:20

The body of the letter begins formally at this point and proceeds from here through 15:33.[1] It begins with an indictment of Paul against the entire world (1:18–3:20). He establishes that all persons, Jew and Gentile alike, are under the power of sin (3:9). Paul is not taking up live issues at Rome but is doing a theological analysis of the human situation before God apart from the grace of God revealed in Christ. He mentions Christ only once in this long section (2:16).

Much of the section is cast in the form of a "diatribe" (from the Greek word διατριβή). When it is used in oratory, the speaker confronts and debates an imaginary opponent, typically using second person singular, in order to persuade those who are assembled. The speaker raises hypothetical questions and responds to them or states false conclusions and goes on to refute them.[2] The form is also used in literary works, including Greco-Roman sources prior to and contemporary with Paul,[3] and its features appear vividly as Paul:

1. Cf. P. Schubert, *The Form and Function of the Pauline Thanksgivings*, 31-32; P. O'Brien, *Introductory Thanksgivings*, 200-202; and C. Roetzel, *The Letters of Paul*, 66, for whom the thanksgiving gives way to the body at 1:18. Cf. also, among commentators, C. Cranfield, *Romans*, 27, 103; U. Wilckens, *Römer*, 1:93; P. Stuhlmacher, *Romans*, 14, 33; B. Byrne, *Romans*, 27; D. Moo, *Romans*, 33; E. Lohse, *Römer*, 8; R. Jewett, *Romans*, vii, 148. According to J. White, *The Form and Function of the Body of the Greek Letter*, 76, 84, the body opening starts at 1:13 with the phrase "I want you to know. . . ." But that formulation appears elsewhere well along (beyond body openings) in Paul's letters (Rom 11:25; 1 Cor 10:1; 12:1; 2 Cor 1:8; 1 Thess 4:13) to stress the importance of what is being said. That is illustrated and discussed further by J. Sanders, "The Transition from Opening Epistolary Thanksgiving to Body," 349-52. J. Dunn, *Romans*, lix, says that the "main body" consists of 1:16–15:13, but later speaks of the "treatise" as beginning at 1:18 (p. 50). For L. Keck, *Romans*, 23, the "discourse part" of the letter begins at 1:16.

2. J. Bailey and L. Vander Broek, "Diatribe," 38-39; D. Aune, "The Greco-Roman Diatribe," 200.

3. Illustrated and discussed by R. Bultmann, *Der Stil der paulinischen Predigt und die*

Addresses an imaginary opponent (2:1, 17)
Uses second person singular (2:1, 4, 17)
Demonstrates the ignorance of the opponent (2:4)
Refutes false conclusions (3:1-2, 3-4, 9)

Somewhat in the fashion of Amos before him, who declares God's judgment first upon the nations surrounding Israel (1:3–2:5), and then against Israel itself (2:6-16), Paul begins his indictment against the Gentiles (1:18-32) before he takes up the case of the Jewish people (2:17–3:20). What distinguishes him from Amos is that he composes a section on God's impartial judgment in between (2:1-16).

BIBLIOGRAPHY

Aune, David E. "The Greco-Roman Diatribe." In his *The New Testament in Its Literary Environment*, 200-202. Louisville: Westminster/John Knox, 1987.

Bailey, James L., and Lyle D. Vander Broek. "Diatribe." In their *Literary Forms in the New Testament: A Handbook*, 38-42. Louisville: Westminster/John Knox, 1992.

Bultmann, Rudolf. *Der Stil der paulinischen Predigt und die kynisch-stoische Diatribe*. FRLANT 13. Göttingen: Vandenhoeck & Ruprecht, 1910.

O'Brien, Peter T. *Introductory Thanksgivings in the Letters of Paul*. NovTSup 49. Leiden: E. J. Brill, 1977.

Sanders, Jack T. "The Transition from Opening Epistolary Thanksgiving to Body in the Letters of the Pauline Corpus." *JBL* 81 (1962): 348-62.

Schubert, Paul. *The Form and Function of the Pauline Thanksgivings*. BZNW 20. Berlin: Alfred Töpelmann, 1939.

Stowers, Stanley K. *The Diatribe and Paul's Letter to the Romans*. SBLDS 57. Chico: Scholars Press, 1981.

White, John L. *The Form and Function of the Body of the Greek Letter: A Study of the Letter-Body in the Non-literary Papyri and in Paul the Apostle*. SBLDS 2. Missoula: Scholars Press, 1972.

2.1. Wrath against the Gentile World, 1:18-32

18*For the wrath of God is being revealed from heaven against all human ungodliness and wickedness of those who suppress the truth by their unrighteousness, because what can be known about God is plain to them.* 19*For God has made it evident to them.* 20*For since the creation of the world his invisible attributes — his*

---

kynisch-stoische Diatribe, 10-64, and S. Stowers, *The Diatribe and Paul's Letter to the Romans*, 48-78.

eternal power and divinity — have been perceived, because they are understood in the things that have been made, so that they are without excuse. 21For although they knew God, they did not honor God or give thanks to him, but they became foolish in their thoughts, and their senseless hearts were darkened. 22Although they claimed to be wise, they became fools, 23and exchanged the glory of the immortal God for an image resembling mortal human beings, birds, four-footed animals, or reptiles.

24Therefore God gave them over in the lusts of their hearts to impurity, that their bodies might be degraded among themselves. 25They exchanged the truth about God for a lie and worshiped and served the creature rather than the Creator, who is blessed forever! Amen.

26Therefore God gave them over unto degrading passions, for their females exchanged natural intercourse for unnatural; 27likewise also the males, abandoning natural intercourse with the female, became inflamed in their inordinate passion for one another, males carrying on disgraceful conduct among males and receiving among themselves the penalty, which it was necessary [for them to receive] from their error.

28And since they did not see fit to acknowledge God, God gave them over to a depraved mind, to do what should not be done. 29They were filled with every kind of wickedness, maliciousness, greed, and malice; full of envy, murder, strife, deceit, and craftiness, they are gossips, 30slanderers, haters of God, insolent, arrogant, braggarts, contrivers of all kinds of evil, disobedient to parents, 31senseless, untrustworthy, hardhearted, and merciless. 32Although they know God's decree that those who do such things are worthy of death, they not only do them but approve those who practice them.

Notes on the Text and Translation

1:18 The term ἀποκαλύπτεται, a present passive, is typically rendered "is revealed" (KJV, RSV, NRSV), but it is translated here as "is being revealed" (as in the NIV). Either is correct, but the latter carries a more active nuance in the present.

1:23 The verb ἀλλάσσω (and compounds, "to exchange") is conventionally followed by the direct object (in this case, "the glory of God") and the preposition ἐν, meaning "to exchange something for."[4]

1:25 The prepositional phrase (παρά and an accusative) can be equivalent to "instead of."[5]

---

4. BDF 97 (§179, 2).
5. BDF 124 (§236, 2).

1:28 Here the conjunction καθώς ("as," "just as," "because," or "since") has the sense of "since."[6]

1:29 There are four textual variants for this verse: (1) κακία πονηρία πλεονεξία (a different word order: "malice, maliciousness, greed"), (2) πονηρία κακία πλεονεξία (another case of a different word order: "maliciousness, malice, greed"), (3) πορνεία πονηρία πλεονεξία κακία (an additional word: "impurity, maliciousness, greed, malice"); and (4) πλεονεξία κακία (one less word, resulting in: "greed, malice"). Of these, the second (attested by a) and third (attested by Ψ and the Majority Text) have the greatest support as possible alternative readings. But the textual reading has the support of B and other witnesses. The addition might be due to the conflation of earlier witnesses, of which some contained the usual πονηρία and others by mistake contained the nearly identical word πορνεία.[7]

General Comment

In the initial portion of this long indictment Paul declares that the wrath of God is being exercised against the Gentiles (1:18-32).[8] The Gentiles spoken of are pagans, not Christians, for they are described as idolaters (1:23, 25). At 2:17–3:8 Paul turns to the standing of the Jewish people before God.

The revelation of divine wrath (ἀποκαλύπτεται . . . ὀργὴ θεοῦ, 1:18) stands in parallel to the revelation of God's righteousness (δικαιοσύνη . . . θεοῦ . . . ἀποκαλύπτεται, 1:17). The fact that the revelation of God's wrath is being revealed "from heaven" does not mean that such revelation is but another aspect of proclamation.[9] The phrase "from heaven" stands, rather, in contrast to "in the gospel,"[10] and it is but a circumlocution for "from God." The "righteousness of God" and the "wrath of God" are related to one another, but they are antithetical. While the former is being revealed in the proclamation of the gospel, the latter is being revealed in divine actions being played out in the world against those who disdain God and his will. That does not mean that every per-

---

6. BDF 236 (§453, 2).

7. For additional discussion, cf. B. Metzger, *TCGNT* 447.

8. For references to other interpreters who claim that 1:18-32 is directed against Gentiles, see the appendix, "Romans 1:26-27 and Homosexuality" (n. 1).

9. Contra K. Barth, *A Shorter Commentary on Romans*, 24-25; A. Schlatter, *Romans*, 29-30; C. Cranfield, *Romans*, 110; U. Wilckens, *Römer*, 1:101-2; K. Haacker, *Römer*, 47; E. Lohse, *Römer*, 86; R. Jewett, *Romans*, 151.

10. G. Bornkamm, "The Revelation of God's Wrath," 47-49, 63-64; E. Käsemann, *Romans*, 35; J. Fitzmyer, *Romans*, 277; P. Stuhlmacher, *Romans*, 35-36; D. Moo, *Romans*, 101-2; C. Talbert, *Romans*, 58-59.

son can perceive it in nature and in the course of history, for the revelation is
known only because of the prophetic and apocalyptic message from God's apostolic witness.

For moderns, the concept of the revelation of the final judgment in the
present may seem to be extremely foreign. But it has been revived from time to
time after the NT. It was revived, for example, in the Reformation era on several
fronts, and it is expressed in a hymn of the American Civil War era composed
by Julia Ward Howe: "He [= God] is trampling out the vintage where the grapes
of wrath are stored; He has loosed the fateful lightning of his terrible swift
sword." It is as though the wrath of God is being revealed in the present as never
before — and as never again.

For Paul, the wrath of God is being revealed in the present,[11] and that is
exhibited — for those who have eyes to see — in God's giving over (παραδίδωμι) the Gentiles to their own ways of sinful behavior in consequence of
their idolatry (1:24, 26, 28). It is exercised, too, in God's judgment upon the Jewish people, charging that all are under the power of sin (3:9), which is documented no less in the Scriptures of Israel (3:10-18). The result is that the entire
world is accountable to God (3:19).

Detailed Comment

1:18 The opening verse of the section sets the tone and theme for what is to follow from here to 3:20, a discourse on the wrath of God. "The wrath of God" or
simply "the wrath," meaning divine wrath, is an expression used 12 times in
Romans (1:18; 2:5 [twice], 8; 3:5; 4:15; 5:9; 9:22 [twice]; 12:19; 13:4, 5) and three times
elsewhere by Paul's letters (1 Thess 1:10; 2:16; 5:9). The term "wrath (ὀργή)," referring to a divine disposition, appears frequently in the OT (e.g., Exod 4:14; 15:7;
32:10; Pss 2:12; 6:1 [LXX 6:2]; 78:31 [LXX 77:31]; Isa 9:19; Mic 7:9; Hab 3:2). It appears particularly where disloyalty to God and the worship of other gods is taking
(or has taken) place (e.g., Deut 6:15; 7:4; 13:18; Josh 7:1; 22:18; Isa 57:6; Mic 5:15
[LXX 5:14]). Sometimes the exercise of the wrath of God is a future expectation
(e.g., Ps 110:5 [LXX 109:5]; Isa 13:9, 13; 26:21; Mic 5:15 [LXX 5:14]; Zeph 1:15, 18; Sir
5:7), and at other times it is being exercised in the present (Pss 90:7 [LXX 89:7];
79:6 [78:6]; Sir 5:6; Isa 9:19 [LXX 9:18]; 10:6; 34:2; 60:10; 63:6). This double perspective is found also in the letters of Paul. Usually when Paul speaks of it, he declares that the wrath of God will be revealed at the last day as punitive judgment
(Rom 2:5, 8; 3:5; 5:9; 9:22; 1 Thess 1:10; 5:9), but he says that the wrath of God can

---

11. Contra H.-J. Eckstein, "'Denn Gottes Zorn wird vom Himmel her offenbar warden,'"
83-86, for whom the reference is future (at the parousia).

be seen already in the effects of the law (i.e., divine judgment, Rom 4:15) and in the punishment of wrongdoers by temporal rulers (Rom 13:4-5).

The declaration of the revelation of the wrath of God at 1:18 is expressed in the language of apocalyptic.[12] The expectation in the OT that God will exercise his wrath is now taking place. The OT expectation typically meant judgment within history, as in the case of Isaiah: "Behold, the day of the LORD comes, cruel, with fury and wrath (θυμὸς καὶ ὀργή), to make the earth a desolation and to destroy its sinners from it" (13:9). For Paul, that time is now at hand. For him, nothing less than the revelation of the wrath of God is taking place in the present. It consists in God's not stopping or rescuing people in their wrongdoing. Its consequences will be described in the verses that follow. Because of their idolatry, God has "given up" (1:24, 26, 28) the Gentiles to a life devoid of the divine presence and filled with wickedness of all kinds.

Present judgment by God upon the earth is expressed outside Paul's own writings most eloquently in *1 Enoch* 91:7, a document from anywhere between the second century B.C. to the first A.D.:

> When sin, oppression, blasphemy, and injustice increase, crime, iniquity, and uncleanliness shall be committed and increase (likewise). Then a great plague shall take place from heaven upon all these; the holy Lord shall emerge with wrath and plague in order that he may execute judgment upon the earth.[13]

In a similar manner Paul declares that the wrath of God is directed against a collective consisting of "all human ungodliness and wickedness of those who suppress the truth by their unrighteousness." The word for "ungodliness" (ἀσέβεια) means essentially to lack reverence for God, and the word for "wickedness" (ἀδικία) can also mean "unrighteousness."[14] The suppression of truth by the wicked is to make hidden that which has been revealed.

The Pauline view of wrath as directed toward wickedness stands in continuity with the OT, in which wrath is not a divine attribute but is always provoked,[15] and that makes it very different from divine love. The same is true in the NT: "Wrath is not a permanent attribute of God. For whereas love and holiness are part of his essential nature, wrath is contingent upon human sin: if there were no sin, there would be no wrath."[16]

---

12. Cf. D. Lührmann, *Offenbarungsverständnis bei Paulus,* 145-48.

13. Quoted from the translation by E. Isaac in *OTP* 1:72.

14. BDAG 141 (ἀσέβεια) and 20 (ἀδικία), respectively.

15. A. Heschel, *The Prophets,* 279-306; T. Fretheim, "Theological Reflections on the Wrath of God," 17.

16. Stephen H. Travis, "Wrath of God (NT)," *ABD* 6:997.

1:19-21 Paul goes on to account more fully for the reason that the wrath of God is being revealed. The reason is that, among the Gentiles, all have turned aside and refuse to worship God. The results of that are devastating, for the loss of the worship of God means a loss of self to self-centeredness, illusions, and disorientation.

Beginning with 1:19b, and running all the way through 1:27, the indicative verbs are in the aorist (simple past) tense in Greek. The effect is that Paul carries on his discourse as though he is talking about something that happened at some point in the past (*in illo tempore*, "in that time" of mythical origins) that explains the present (so an etiological myth); the "primal sin of rebellion against the Creator . . . finds repeated and universal expression."[17] In effect, Paul says that the way to account for Gentile misbehavior in the present is that "since the creation of the world" (1:20) the Gentiles have had the opportunity to worship God, but instead they have been idolatrous; and their misbehavior flows from that.

When Paul says that "what can be known about God" is plain to all, he does not go so far as to affirm that a person can know God through the observation of nature and/or unaided reason alone, a view that in fact existed in both Jewish and non-Jewish traditions in his day (but see below),[18] so much so that Philo, for example, could say that a person could (mentally) ascend, contemplate, and form a conception of God through reason.[19] Paul does not think in that way, but affirms a general revelation (rather than a natural theology).[20] For him, that which can be known about God has been made known by God himself (1:19), not simply by human observation or reason.[21] Consequently it is all the more true that the Gentiles are "without excuse" (1:20).[22] For Paul, as for

---

17. E. Käsemann, *Romans*, 47.

18. Plato, *Tim.* 27c-30c; Epictetus, *Dis.* 1.6.19; 1.9.4-6; 1.14.1-17; 1.15-21; Pseudo-Aristotle, *Cosm.* 399b; Josephus, *Ant.* 1.155-56; *Ep. Arist.* 132; Philo, *Migr.* 35.192-95; *Decal.* 12.58; 14.69; *Praem.* 7.43; Wis 13: 5. For several references to Stoic literature, cf. S. Schulz, "Die Anklage," 162-63, and D. Lührmann, *Offenbarungsverständnis bei Paulus*, 21-26; for citation and discussion of texts in both Jewish and Greco-Roman sources, cf. C. Talbert, *Romans*, 59-62, 72-73. For a discussion of how Paul subverts natural theology, cf. D. Campbell, "Natural Theology in Paul?" 231-52; cf. also R. Bell, *No One Seeks for God*, 90-102.

19. Philo, *Praem.* 7.43.

20. C. Talbert, *Romans*, 62.

21. This view is also found in Philo, *Abr.* 17.80; *Sib. Or.* 3.13-19; 1QH 2.16-19. G. Bornkamm, "Faith and Reason in Paul," 33: the knowledge of God "is grounded very simply and definitely in the sovereign decision of God" (1:19); cf. also M. Bockmuehl, *Jewish Law in Gentile Churches*, 130.

22. Cf. Wis 13:8-9. R. Young, "The Knowledge of God," 695-707, suggests that here Paul means a rather vague awareness of God (not full knowledge), sufficient to lead one to obtain knowledge; so the Gentiles are without excuse.

others before and after him, a wondrous awe of the creation — known through what came later to be called "general revelation" — should lead to the worship of the Creator, a view that is expressed already in the NT (Acts 17:27-28) and in subsequent Christian theology. But Paul goes a step further. For him that means that there is no excuse for idolatry.[23] As he goes on to say concerning the Gentiles, "they knew God" (1:21), and therefore had no excuse for their idolatry and consequent behavior. Whatever they knew about God is grounds for an indictment.[24]

Paul's sweeping, general statement that God has revealed to the Gentiles "what can be known about God" himself is astonishing. Surely he cannot mean that God has revealed *everything* that can be known. There is more to be revealed through God's sending of his Son. Presumably Paul would have shared the traditional Jewish view that God, even though he reveals himself, is elusive and unknowable in himself.[25] But he would also have shared the traditional view that God can be known in part through general revelation,[26] and that is all that he needs to affirm at this place in his letter. He limits his claim of knowledge by all to the majesty and power of God, which should elicit right worship by all. God's "eternal power and divinity (δύναμις καὶ θειότης)" have been "perceived" and "understood" in those things that God has made. The term for God's "divinity" (θειότης) appears only here in the NT, and, coupled with "power," it signifies God's majestic rule in nature and history. Although they remain "invisible" in the traditional sense — for God cannot be seen directly — they have been "clearly perceived, being understood in the things that have been made." The use of both καθορᾶται ("perceived") and νοούμενα ("being understood") makes the point emphatic; the Gentiles are without excuse. Although having knowledge of God, they did not honor or give thanks to God, which are basic to right worship. On the contrary, "they became foolish in their thoughts, and their senseless hearts ["minds" in the RSV, NRSV, and NAB; "hearts" is retained in the KJV, NIV, and NET] were darkened." When they turned away from the worship of God, their thinking — now directed to false gods — was foolish or futile. Although for moderns the "mind" is the seat of thinking, for Paul and other NT writers the "heart" is often considered the "seat of physical, spiritual and mental life"; as such it is the "center and source of the whole inner life," including "its thinking, feeling, and volition."[27]

1:22-25 The claim to be "wise" (σοφός, 1:22) is a symptom of the arro-

---

23. On the contrast between the theology of Paul and that of Acts 17, cf. P. Vielhauer, "On the 'Paulinism' of Acts," 33-50.

24. Similarly, Wis 13:8-9; 2 *Apoc. Bar.* 54.17-19; *Sib. Or.* 3.8-45.

25. Exod 33:20; Sir 43:31; *Sib. Or.* 3.13-19; Philo, *Somn.* 1.66; *Post.* 16.

26. Job 36:22-25; Ps 19:1-6; *Sib. Or.* 3.15-16.

27. BDAG 508 (καρδία, 1, b).

gance that is characteristic of those who seek to know God through human wisdom (1 Cor 1:20-25) but miss the mark because they do not perceive what has been revealed.

Beginning with 1:23 and extending through 1:28 there is a structural pattern built around two key terms: ἤλλαξαν (or μετήλλαξαν, "exchanged") in 1:23, 25, and 26 and παρέδωκεν ("gave over") in 1:24, 26, and 28. The structure can be seen in the following outline:

> The Gentiles *exchanged* (ἤλλαξαν) the glory of God for images (1:23). Therefore God *gave* them *over* (παρέδωκεν) to impurity, to degrading their bodies (1:24).
>
> The Gentiles *exchanged* (μετήλλαξαν) the worship of God for idolatry (1:25). Therefore God *gave* them *over* (παρέδωκεν) to degrading passions (1:26a).
>
> The Gentiles *exchanged* (μετήλλαξαν) natural relations for unnatural (1:26b-27). Since they did not acknowledge God, God *gave* them *over* (παρέδωκεν) to a base mind and improper conduct (1:28).

The idolatry of the Gentile world has provoked the divine wrath, which expresses itself in God's abandoning that world to its own destructive behavior. The threefold pairing of the verbs "exchanged" and "gave [them] over" in 1:23-24, 1:25-26a, and 1:26b-28 should be taken as one dynamic, expressed in three different ways, rather than as a sequence of three occasions.[28]

Instead of worshiping "the immortal God," the Gentiles have turned to idolatry. Paul picks up the language of a psalm to describe what they have done: "They exchanged their glory for the image of an ox that eats grass" (Ps 106:20; καὶ ἠλλάξαντο τὴν δόξαν αὐτῶν ἐν ὁμοιώματι μόσχου ἔσθοντος χόρτον [LXX 105:20]).[29] The similarity is so great that Paul even uses the expression ἐν ὁμοιώματι that is in the psalm. His use of the term ὁμοίωμα here can have the meaning of "likeness" or "copy,"[30] and it is followed by the noun εἰκών ("icon," "image") in genitive form. A literal translation would be "in the likeness of an image."

Paul uses sweeping terms to characterize, and even perhaps ridicule, the idols that they have constructed. Drawing perhaps from observation, but certainly from OT texts, Paul says that their idols have been made to resemble the likenesses of human beings (Deut 4:16), birds (Deut 4:17), animals (Deut 4:17;

---

28. So already, Origen, *Commentary on Romans* on 1:26; text in Origen, *Commentarii in Epistulam ad Romanos*, ed. Theresia Heither, 6 vols. (New York: Herder, 1990-99), 1:156, 158.

29. Cf. also the use of the phrase ἠλλάξατο τὴν δόξαν in Jer 2:11.

30. BDAG 707 (ὁμοίωμα); Traugott Holtz, "ὁμοίωμα," *EDNT* 2:513.

Ps 106:20; Wis 11:15; 12:24), and reptiles (Deut 4:17; Wis 11:15).[31] Speaking in traditional, Jewish terms, Paul says that "the glory of God" has been replaced by idols. The expression "the glory of God" is reverential. Paul could simply say that "God" has been replaced, but "the glory of God" emphasizes God's majesty. God's "glory" is God's presence (e.g., in theophanies, Exod 24:15-18), but to speak of his "glory" also emphasizes his transcendence (cf. Ezek 1:28). Contrary to worshiping the eternal God, to be held in reverence, the Gentiles have chosen to worship humanly made idols.

The first of the three instances of the divine "giving up" appears in 1:24. Is this to be understood primarily as simple resignation by God (with no retribution intended) or primarily as divine punishment? The first has been suggested,[32] but it is hardly adequate, for the verse is introduced with the conjunction διό ("therefore"), indicating the effect from some prior cause. Clearly the note of judgment is sounded in this verse. The result is that God has delivered the idolatrous Gentiles to their own ways. The act echoes lines from the Psalms: "He gave them (παρέδωκεν αὐτούς) into the hand of the nations, so that those who hated them ruled over them" (Ps 106:41; LXX 105:41) and "So I gave them over (ἐξαπέστειλα αὐτούς) to their stubborn hearts, to follow their own counsels" (Ps 81:12).[33] In the contexts of both passages God's judgment against the people of Israel is due to their turning away from him to worship foreign gods. Paul echoes those words while speaking of God's making a charge against the Gentiles for their idolatry. Although it cannot be said that God abandoned the Gentiles forever (Paul's gospel makes that clear), the fact of his giving them over entails a form of punishment.[34] Since they wish to serve idols, they are free to do so and to pursue the ways of life that follow. As a

31. Less convincing is the claim that Paul alludes here to Gen 1:20-27, as suggested by N. Hyldahl, "A Reminiscence," 285-88, and M. Hooker, "Adam in Romans 1," 76-77, and "A Further Note on Romans 1," 85. J. Fitzmyer, *Romans*, 274, expresses doubt that there are "echoes of the Adam stories in Genesis" here. The suggestion of J. Levison, "Adam and Eve," 519-34, that Paul used some form ("presumably written but possibly oral," p. 523) of the narrative in the *Life of Adam and Eve* in the composition of Romans at this point, based on some linguistic similarities, seems plausible but can hardly be demonstrated. The earliest manuscript of the *Life* is from the ninth century A.D. Although the time of composition is unclear, "toward the end of the first Christian century" is probable, according to Marshall D. Johnson, "Life of Adam and Eve," *OTP* 2:252.

32. Wiard Popkes, "παραδίδωμι," *EDNT* 3:20.

33. God's "giving over" a people as punishment is also expressed in the Qumran scrolls at 1QH 2.16-19.

34. So most interpreters (though variously expressed), including M. Luther, *Romans*, 11-12; C. K. Barrett, *Romans*, 38; E. Käsemann, *Romans*, 47; C. Cranfield, *Romans*, 121; J. Fitzmyer, *Romans*, 284; J. G. D. Dunn, *Romans*, 62-63, 73; P. Stuhlmacher, *Romans*, 36-37; K. Haacker, *Römer*, 51-52; N. T. Wright, *NIB (Romans)*, 10:433; E. Lohse, *Römer*, 89; and S. Gathercole, "Sin in God's Economy," 162.

consequence of God's giving over the Gentiles to their own ways, abusive and evil behaviors follow.

The verb translated "to give over" (παραδίδωμι) has a wide range of meanings. Often, in regard to persons, it has the meaning of turning someone over to another. That can be for protection, betrayal, or custody.[35] In the present instance Paul says that, in keeping with the "desires of their hearts," God gave the Gentiles over to ἀκαθαρσία ("impurity"), a term that frequently refers to sexual immorality.[36]

The remainder of 1:24 consists of an articular infinitive in passive voice (τοῦ ἀτιμάζεσθαι). Typically it is translated as active within a purpose clause (so "to the degrading of their bodies among themselves," NRSV), but the passive voice (and sense) can be retained, and the clause can be rendered: God gave them over to impurity, "that their bodies might be degraded among themselves."[37] The implication is that the act of giving them over does not include divine degradation, for that is carried on by the Gentiles themselves among themselves.

The exchange of truth for falsehood was accompanied by worshiping and serving "the creature rather than the Creator" (1:25). It is conventional Jewish teaching that a turn to idolatry leads consequently to all manner of wickedness, especially sexual immorality, as expressed in the Wisdom of Solomon — "the worship of idols . . . is the beginning, cause, and end of every evil" and "For the idea of making idols was the beginning of fornication, and the invention of them was the corruption of life" (14:27, 12) — and elsewhere.[38] Over against the idolatry of the Gentiles, the Creator is the "Blessed One," as expressed in the form of a benediction (for others by Paul, cf. Rom 9:5; 2 Cor 11:31). Paul praises the One against whom the Gentiles have rebelled.

1:26-27 The "degrading passions" (πάθη ἀτιμίας) — passions that disgrace a person[39] — follow God's giving the Gentiles over to their own ways, beginning with their idolatry and leading to all manner of foolish thinking, destructive behaviors, and abuse. Over against the usual way of thinking, for Paul, "moral perversion is the result of God's wrath, not the reason for it."[40] At the top of Paul's list are these two verses concerning sexual misconduct. That Paul

---

35. BDAG 761-63 (παραδίδωμι).

36. BDAG 34 (ἀκαθαρσία, 2).

37. BDAG 148-49 (ἀτιμάζω). C. K. Barrett, *Romans*, 38, suggests that the clause is epexegetic, but the verb in the first clause is active, the second is passive, and the subject of each differs.

38. Philo, *Abr.* 26.135; *Spec. Leg.* 1.4.21–5.31; 2.14.50; 2 *Enoch* 10.4; *T. Levi* 17.11; *T. Naph.* 3.3-7; Josephus, *Ant.* 10.50; *Ag. Ap.* 2.132-38; Wis 14:22-27; *Sib. Or.* 3.8-45; cf. Eph 5:5; Col 3:5.

39. BDAG 149 (ἀτιμία), 748 (πάθος). Cf. C. Cranfield, *Romans*, 125: "passions which bring dishonour."

40. E. Käsemann, *Romans*, 47.

should take up sexual misconduct at the outset is not surprising, since it was a commonplace in Jewish tradition that the idolatry of the Gentiles has led them to sexual perversions of all kinds.[41] The verses are located within the section 1:22-31 in which Paul speaks of the mythological past of the Gentiles, using aorist (past tense) indicative verbs all the way through.[42] He is not therefore addressing specific conduct at Rome or anywhere else, although the conduct of which he speaks was clearly known by Paul to exist, and he passes a negative judgment against it.

Concerning the conduct of women, Paul says only that they "exchanged natural intercourse for unnatural (μετήλλαξαν τὴν φυσικὴν χρῆσιν εἰς τὴν παρὰ φύσιν)." The terms translated here as "natural intercourse" (τὴν φυσικὴν χρῆσιν) can have various meanings. The simplest meaning of the word χρῆσις is "use" or "usage," but it had taken on the meaning of sexual relations prior to the rise of Christianity.[43] More controversial is the meaning of φυσική ("natural") and the accompanying phrase παρὰ φύσιν (translated here as "unnatural," as in RSV, NIV, NRSV, but "against nature" in KJV). Clearly the term φύσις would not refer here simply to the physical universe in general — although it could refer to the ordering of such — since it has to do with conduct. The usual opposite of παρὰ φύσιν in Hellenistic traditions is κατὰ φύσιν ("according to nature," especially common in Stoic literature),[44] a phrase known to Paul (Rom 11:21, 24). In fact, Paul himself sets the two phrases in opposition to one another later on in the letter (11:24), although not in a moral context.

Romans 1:26 suggests a range of possibilities for the term φύσις:[45] (1) at a minimum it refers to something that is customary (as in 1 Cor 11:14), familiar, usual, and accepted;[46] (2) more than that, it refers to the natural order of

---

41. Wis 14:22-27; Philo, *Abr.* 26.133-35; *Sib. Or.* 3.43-45; 3.586-600; *T. Levi* 17.11; *2 Enoch* 10.4.

42. According to P. Esler, "The Sodom Tradition in Romans 1:18-32," 4-16, Paul draws upon collective memories of the "Sodom tradition" from various ancient texts that reflect an oral culture. But the proposal is not convincing, since specific elements of the Sodom story in Genesis are not made explicit in these verses. Instead Paul portrays a mythical past concerning the Gentiles that does not have, nor need to have, an OT or legendary base in Jewish traditions.

43. The word is used for sexual relations by Plato, *Leg.* 841a, Plutarch, *Mor.* 905a, and Philo, *Mut.* 19.111-12. Additional references are provided in BDAG 1089 (χρῆσις).

44. For references to uses of the phrase, cf. Helmut Koester, "φύσις," *TDNT* 9:262-65. The phrase appears only once in the LXX (4 Macc 5:25); Josephus, *Ag. Ap.* 2.199, uses the phrase to speak of the relationship of husband and wife.

45. Regarding Paul's own use of the term (seven times): it can refer to one's origins ("we who are Jews by nature," Gal 2:15); deny legitimacy to something ("beings that by nature are not gods," Gal 4:8); mean little more than a custom (1 Cor 11:14); be done "instinctively" (Rom 2:14, NRSV); and be consistent with the order of things (Rom 2:27; 11:21, 24).

46. M. Nissinen, *Homoeroticism*, 105. According to O. Wischmeyer, "ΦΥΣΙΣ und ΚΤΙΣΙΣ

things;[47] or (3) even more, it refers to the divinely created order, echoing the creation story of Genesis 1.[48] Of these, the first possibility seems too weak at this point, following upon the moral tone of "degrading passions" in the previous clause. The third is unlikely, for there is no clear reference to the creation story here, which is surprising if such is intended.[49] Instead, the language used is in keeping with the familiar tradition in both Jewish and non-Jewish Hellenism, as well as Paul himself (Rom 2:27; 11:21, 24), concerning what is "natural." Such traditions affirm that there is a natural order, and that that order can be discerned by observation and reason. The result is that, for Paul, the kind of sexual relations to which he is referring do not conform to what is "natural."

Before proceeding further, it is important for interpreting these verses to notice the tone of the language and specific words being used in them. One phrase has been noted already, namely, "degrading passions." But there are other terms as well. Paul writes that the men became "inflamed (ἐξεκαύθησαν)," a term used only here in the NT. The verb means to be consumed by fire. That is how it is used dozens of times in OT and Hellenistic Jewish texts.[50] It is often used metaphorically to express wrath and rage.[51] In regard to sexual matters, it is used at Sirach 23:16 (LXX 23:17) in the saying: "A fornicator will not cease until fire consumes him." The verb is unusually harsh; elsewhere when Paul refers to sexual passion, he uses another, more familiar term in Hellenistic usage (πυρόω, "to be aflame," 1 Cor 7:9).[52] Moreover, the term translated as "inordinate passion" (ὄρεξις, 1:27), found only here in the NT, has a pejorative, negative connotation.[53]

Returning to the language concerning φύσις, the meaning of παρὰ φύσιν in general and in this particular context is contested. The prepositional phrase employing παρά followed by an accusative noun (φύσις in this case) can — on

---

bei Paulus," 371, whatever is in accord with nature is true to its type, customary, or according to the rules; according to R. Jewett, *Romans,* 177, "nature" is "culturally subjective," reflecting cultural norms.

47. H. Koester, "φύσις," 9:273; BDAG 1070 (φύσις); J. Dunn, *Romans,* 1:64; J. Fitzmyer, *Romans,* 286; B. Byrne, *Romans,* 69; E. Lohse, *Römer,* 88.

48. O. Michel, *Römer,* 68; C. Cranfield, *Romans,* 126; R. Gagnon, *The Bible and Homosexual Practice,* 290; D. Moo, *Romans,* 115; T. Schreiner, *Romans,* 94-97; K. Holter, "A Note on the Old Testament Background of Rom 1,23-27," 21-23; J. Nolland, "Romans 1:26-27," 49, 51-52; U. Mauser, "Creation and Human Sexuality," 11-13.

49. Cf. a similar judgment by R. Scroggs, *The New Testament and Homosexuality,* 114-15; V. Furnish, "The Bible and Homosexuality," 30; M. Nissinen, *Homoeroticism,* 107.

50. Josephus, *J.W.* 3.201; *Ant.* 7.169; in the LXX, e.g., at Exod 21:6; Num 11:1; Judg 15:5; 2 Sam 22:9, 13; Pss 105:18 (MT 106:18); 117:12 (MT 118:12); Jer 51:6; Dan 3:27.

51. Examples in the LXX include Deut 29:20; 32:22; 2 Sam 22:9, 13; 2 Chr 34:21, 25.

52. For its familiar use in Hellenistic texts, cf. LSJ 1558.

53. Josephus, *Ant.* 7.169; 4 Macc 1:33, 35; Sir 18:3 23:6; Wis 14:2; 16:2.

the basis of syntax alone — have the meaning of "against nature" (so the KJV), since παρά followed by an accusative noun can have the meaning of "against" or "contrary to," such as "against the teaching" (παρὰ τὴν διδαχήν, Rom 16:17). On the other hand, the same preposition plus an accusative noun can mean "more than" and "beyond," as in "beyond [their] means" (παρὰ δύναμιν, 2 Cor 8:3).[54] In either case, the statement that women exchanged natural intercourse for that which is παρὰ φύσιν would mean that the latter is "unnatural" or "deviating from nature."[55] But there is a meaningful difference. In the first instance the exchange would be "against nature" in the sense that only intercourse between males and females is in keeping with nature.[56] In the second instance the exchange would be "beyond nature" in the sense that the women exceeded the bounds of what is natural or normal.[57] Coupled with the terminology in 1:27 highlighted above, it is most likely that in these verses Paul is speaking not so much about same-gender sexual relationships per se (although he surely is referring to them) as he is about the behavior flowing from the "degrading passions" that, in turn, have come into being due to idolatry, which is the cause of disorientation. The "degrading passions" exceed what is natural, overreaching the bounds of normalcy; they are indeed παρὰ φύσιν, leading to inordinate, lustful behaviors that virtually destroy the self (being consumed with passion) and abuse others. Pelagius put it with an economy of expression: "Lust, once unbridled, knows no limit."[58]

The term παρὰ φύσιν appears in several contexts. Sometimes it appears without reference to sexual matters and simply means "unnatural" (or deviating from what is natural),[59] such as uncharacteristic behavior, the ownership of slaves, irregularities in nature, and passions leading to wars and covetousness.[60]

---

54. BDAG 757-58 (παρά, C, 3).

55. This is the translation of παρὰ φύσιν suggested by T. Hubbard, *Homosexuality in Greece and Rome,* 245 (n. 134).

56. That only sexual intercourse between a male and female is in accord with nature (κατὰ φύσιν) is asserted by Plato, *Leg.* 636c, and Josephus, *Ag. Ap.* 2.199. According to Josephus, sexual activity is only for the purpose of procreation. The same is attested in the works of Plato, *Leg.* 838e; such intercourse is κατὰ φύσιν. For this viewpoint in Plato and its terminological consequences for what is natural and unnatural in later traditions in Hellenism and Paul, cf. R. Ward, "Why Unnatural?" 263-84.

57. D. Martin, "Heterosexism and the Interpretation of Romans 1:18-22," 342; D. Fredrickson, "Natural and Unnatural Use in Romans 1:24-27," 205-6.

58. Pelagius, *Commentary on Romans* on 1:27. Quoted from *Pelagius' Commentary on St. Paul's Epistle to the Romans,* trans. Theodore S. de Bruyn (Oxford: Oxford University Press, 1993), 67.

59. Some examples include Philo, *Abr.* 5.27; *Decal.* 28.142; *Spec. Leg.* 4.14.79; *Cont.* 9.70; *Aet.* 7.32, 24; Plutarch, *Mor.* 125c; 134b; 731c; 993d-e; 995d; 996b.

60. Respectively, in Thucydides, *Hist.* 6.17.1; Philo, *Cont.* 9.70; *Aet.* 7.32, 34; *Abr.* 5.27; *Decal.* 28.142.

In cases where sexual matters are involved, the phrase can refer to rape,[61] same-gender sexual intercourse,[62] and pederasty.[63] In the present case it most likely refers to female same-gender sexual activities. That is not said explicitly in 1:26, but the fact that the next verse begins with "and likewise" (ὁμοίως τε καί) and speaks of same-gender sexual relationships between men gives specificity to 1:26.[64] But the question remains whether that which is considered "unnatural" is same-gender activity in itself, or whether it refers to a woman's abandoning her traditional gender role (passivity) and adopting an active sexual role within a sexual encounter with another person, male or female, which tradition had reserved for men.[65] Perhaps it is best to combine the two; that is, the reference is to same-gender activity, in which women take on an active sexual role. Here, as in 1:27, Paul uses a broad brush to portray Gentile behavior as idolatrous and abusive, a theme that runs through 1:18-32.

In 1:27 the "exchange" of males consists of "abandoning natural intercourse with the female" and "carrying on disgraceful conduct among males" due to their "inordinate passion for one another." Typically the term for "disgraceful conduct" (ἀσχημοσύνη) has a public nuance to it, indicating that the conduct spoken of is not simply private, but a cause for public concern,[66] and that is fitting in the present context. The conduct referred to cannot be pederasty alone,[67] but since that was the most public, visible, and controversial form of same-gender sexual activity among males,[68] it would certainly be included in the scope of what Paul refers to here, and would in fact be primary. In addition, the "disgraceful conduct" existing "among males" could refer to a sexual encounter in which one of them takes on the role of a female. In that case Paul could have thought much like his contemporary Philo, for whom it was an

61. Appian, *Bell. civ.* 1.109; Dionysius of Halicarnassus, *Ant. rom.* 16:4.3 (attempted rape of a boy).

62. Plato, *Leg.* 636c; *Resp.* 466d; Josephus, *Ag. Ap.* 2.273-75; Plutarch, *Mor.* 751d-e; Musonius Rufus, *Frag.* 12.

63. Philo, *Spec. Leg.* 3.7.37-39; *Cont.* 7.59-61; Athenaeus, *Deipn.* 13.605d.

64. Cf. B. Brooten, *Love between Women*, 249. J. Banister, "Ὁμοίως and the Use of Parallelism in Romans 1:26-27," 569-90, discusses other possibilities but stops short of certainty on any.

65. M. Nissinen, *Homoeroticism*, 107-8. J. Miller, "The Practices of Romans 1:26," 1-11, contends that the reference is to unnatural heterosexual practices. L. White, "Does the Bible Speak about Gays or Same-Sex Orientation?" 23, concludes that "*their* women" shame their husbands by means of same-gender sexual activity.

66. Cf. BDAG 147 (ἀσχημοσύνη).

67. Contra R. Scroggs, *The New Testament and Homosexuality*, 116; J. Miller, "Pederasty and Romans 1:27," 861-66. For critique, cf. M. Smith, "Ancient Bisexuality," 225-28, 43-44, and R. Jewett, "The Social Context," 235.

68. R. Scroggs, *The New Testament and Homosexuality*, 126 (*et passim*); M. Nissinen, *Homoeroticism*, 96-97; R. Gagnon, *The Bible and Homosexual Practice*, 162.

"emasculation of their bodies" (τὰ σώματα μαλακότητι) for a male "to play the part of a woman" in such an encounter, for that is to act "without respect for the sexual nature (φύσις) which the active partner shares with the passive."[69] In short, gender roles are distorted, and effeminization of the passive partner takes place.[70] For Paul, as with Philo, any form of effeminization was considered to be "against nature" to one degree or another. And so Paul asks elsewhere: "Does not nature itself (αὐτὴ ἡ φύσις) teach you that if a man wears long hair, it is degrading to him (ἀτιμία αὐτῷ)?" (1 Cor 11:14). Effeminacy might also be an issue for Paul when he includes among those who will not enter the kingdom of God those whom he calls the μαλακοί (1 Cor 6:9; KJV: "effeminate"; Luther: "Weichlinge," meaning "effeminate" or "sissies"; but NRSV: "male prostitutes").

The degree to which 1 Corinthians 6:9-11 should be included within a discussion of Romans 1:26-27 is unclear. The meaning of two words there (μαλακοί and ἀρσενοκοῖται) are themselves contested in terms of their respective meanings. The first of them means, literally, "soft," a term that since Aristotle at least could refer also to persons who lack moral self-control.[71] The second, which has not been documented in Greek literature prior to Paul, might have been coined by the apostle himself from ἄρσην and κοίτη, terms that appear in LXX Leviticus 18:22 and 20:13, and meaning "male" and "bed," but the latter being a euphemism for sexual relations.[72] The combination of the two terms could indicate a sexual relationship between two males in general, the former the passive partner, and the latter the active one.[73] But it need not. No actual relationship may be implied between the persons called μαλακοί and ἀρσενοκοῖται, as illustrated in a major lexicon in which it is said that the "formal equivalents" for the two words are, respectively, "effeminate" and "pederasts."[74] Paul uses two terms that, more likely, refer to two different groups of persons. If he was referring to men who engage in same-sex activity in general, and if he had the Leviticus passages in mind, it would be more natural for him to use the term ἀρσενοκοῖται ("male bedders") alone to refer to both of them.

69. Philo, *Abr.* 26.135-36; text and translation from F. H. Colson, *Philo*, LCL, 10 vols. (Cambridge: Harvard University Press, 1929-62), 6:70-71.

70. J. Elliott, "No Kingdom of God for Softies?" 28: the expression "'exchanging natural relations for unnatural' meant males behaving as females and females behaving as males."

71. Aristotle, *Eth. nic.* 7.7.1-4.

72. BDAG 554 (κοίτη).

73. C. K. Barrett, *A Commentary on the First Epistle to the Corinthians*, 140; H. Conzelmann, *1 Corinthians*, 106; J. Fitzmyer, *First Corinthians*, 250 ("homosexual acts of males"), 255-58.

74. BDAG 613 (μαλακός, 2); 135 (ἀρσενοκοίτης). That italicized words are considered "formal equivalents" in this lexicon, cf. the "Foreword," viii.

The fact that he also uses μαλακοί ("soft ones") in his vice list suggests some differentiation between two kinds of persons. Consequently, interpreters have argued that he is referring in this particular passage either to pederasts and their boy partners[75] or to men who have sexual relationships with male prostitutes and the prostitutes themselves.[76] Perhaps the wisest course is to conclude that the precise meaning of the terms is inconclusive, but that from the context it is clear that they are examples of persons who exploit others.[77] While this passage in 1 Corinthians needs attention in the interpretation of Romans 1:26-27, the latter is more general, and the fact that it includes female same-gender sexual activity breaks down any direct parallel between the two passages. Nevertheless, the passage in 1 Corinthians highlights the point that when Paul speaks of same-gender sexual activity, he is speaking of prominent, common, and visible behaviors in the Greco-Roman world that were practiced by Gentiles of pagan background (cf. 6:11, "and this is what some of you used to be"), and that were exploitive.

Exegesis of 1:26-27 requires attention to language and concepts both in antiquity and in modern times. That 1:26-27 is about "homosexuality" or "homosexual behavior" per se is excluded,[78] since the concepts of "heterosexuality," "homosexuality," and "sexual orientation" were unknown in Paul's day. To be sure, there were those in the Greco-Roman world who were aware that some people were attracted to persons of their own gender.[79] But that having been said, there is no evidence in his letters that Paul himself had such an awareness. In light of the modern awareness of sexual orientation, four things should be added here. First, it has to be said that Paul does not speak here about persons

75. W. Schrage, *Der erste Brief an die Korinther,* 1:431-32; G. Fee, *The First Epistle to the Corinthians,* 243-44; J. Sampley, *The First Letter to the Corinthians,* 10:858-59; C. Wolff, *Der erste Brief des Paulus an die Korinther,* 118; M. Theobald, "Röm. 1:26f.," 512.

76. R. Scroggs, *The New Testament and Homosexuality,* 106-9; G. Snyder, *First Corinthians,* 72-73; V. Furnish, *The Moral Teaching of Paul,* 80-83 (other possibilities: "the 'receptive' and 'aggressive' males in any homoerotic encounter," or "effeminate males" and "males who have sex with males"; in any case, behavior associated with Gentile idolaters).

77. Nissinen, *Homoeroticism in the Biblical World,* 113-18.

78. That the passage is about "homosexuality" is routinely stated in various commentaries, e.g., E. Käsemann, *Romans,* 48; J. Ziesler, *Romans,* 78; P. Stuhlmacher, *Romans,* 37; that it concerns "homosexual conduct" (or activity or practice) is stated in others, e.g., C. K. Barrett, *Romans,* 39; J. Dunn, *Romans,* 64-65; J. Fitzmyer, *Romans,* 275-76, 285-88.

79. Cf. Pindar, *Pyth.* 10.59-61; Aristotle, *Eth. nic.* 7.5.3-5; Pseudo-Lucian, *Forms* 9; Firmicus Maturnus, *Math.* 3.6.4-6; and the statement of Longus, *Daphn.* 4.11, concerning a person whom he calls "a pederast by nature (φύσει παιδεραστὴς ὤν)." For texts, cf. T. Hubbard, *Homosexuality in Greece and Rome,* 49, 259-60, 509, 531, and 487, respectively. Hubbard indicates that the term "homosexuality" in the title of his book is "problematic" but has been adopted "as a convenient shorthand linking together a range of different phenomena involving same-gender love and/or sexual activity" (p. 1).

who are homosexual (a small percentage of the population with an abiding orientation), but makes a broadside indictment of the Gentiles as a whole in a world where heterosexual persons (in modern understanding) knowingly and voluntarily exchanged their normal sexual roles for same-gender activities.[80] Moreover, the context and wording indicate that Paul refers to excessive, public same-gender sexual activity. Second, as indicated earlier, the passage falls within a section (1:18-32) about abusive behaviors of all kinds, and that should inform one's reflections on these verses. In light of that, one must ask whether they speak unilaterally of all types of same-gender sexual relationships. That they speak of *all* nonabusive ones between persons of homosexual orientation (in modern understanding) can be legitimately challenged. Third, as soon as one brings the concepts of what is "natural" and "unnatural" into the discussion, it has to be granted that such concepts change over time. In Paul's day the concept would presumably have to do primarily with anatomical differences,[81] and one could appeal to the animal world (as Plato does) to speak of same-gender sexual relationships as deviations from nature on the (mistaken) assumption that such does not occur among animals.[82] In the modern era, however, other factors (physiological, genetic, psychological, sociological, and more) will be included in seeking to understand human nature. Whatever is made of the meaning of "nature" or "natural" in Paul's writings, must that meaning be considered normative in theology and ethical discourse for all time? And finally, any discussion of homosexuality in the church or wider culture must, if it is to be faithful to this text, pay attention to the particular behaviors that Paul refers to and ask whether and where behaviors in the contemporary world correspond to them. At that point Paul's concern and judgment can be legitimately shared.

In the final portion of 1:27 the "penalty" (ἀντιμισθία) does not refer to sexually transmitted diseases (even if they were known in Paul's day as possible consequences of sexual activity), but to the life of folly and abuse — sexual perversion in particular — due to the error (πλάνη) of idolatry by the Gentiles.[83] The translation of πλάνη as "perversion" in the NIV (so "the due penalty [ἀντιμισθία] for their perversion [πλάνη]") misses the point, since it is the per-

<hr />

80. The term "same-gender" is more fitting than "homosexual," since the latter term presupposes an orientation that may or may not exist in "same-gender" activities.

81. R. Gagnon, *The Bible and Homosexual Practice*, 254, uses the phrase: "the material shape of the created order."

82. Plato, *Leg.* 836c.

83. C. Cranfield, *Romans*, 126-27; J. Dunn, *Romans*, 65; K. Haacker, *Römer*, 54; contra B. Brooten, *Love between Women*, 258, who interprets the term to mean venereal disease, and N. T. Wright, *NIB (Romans)*, 10:434, who speaks here of "physical ailments" resulting from "homosexual practice."

version itself that is due to the πλάνη ("error") of idolatry. There is a similar sentiment, using similar language, in the Wisdom of Solomon, where it is said of the Egyptians that "they went far astray on the paths of error (τῶν πλάνης ὁδῶν μακρότερον ἐπλανήθησαν), accepting as gods those animals that even their enemies despised; they were deceived like foolish infants" (Wis 12:24).

For additional comment on these verses and hermeneutical considerations, see the appendix, "Romans 1:26-27 and Homosexuality."

1:28-31 Once more the divine "giving up" of the Gentiles as a consequence of their idolatry is reiterated. They have exchanged the glory of God for idols (1:23); they have exchanged the truth about God for a lie (1:25); and they have not seen fit to acknowledge God as God (1:28). They have been bound over, then, by God to having depraved minds, doing all manner of things that should not be done. Paul continues with his indictment of the depravity of the Gentiles, becoming specific concerning additional abusive, destructive, and selfish behaviors.

The next three verses (1:29-31) contain a "vice list." Such lists are found elsewhere in the NT as well (Rom 13:13; 1 Cor 5:10-11; 6:9-10; 2 Cor 6:14; Gal 5:19-21; Eph 4:31-32; 5:3-4; 1 Col 3:5-8; Tim 1:9-10; 6:4; 2 Tim 3:2-4; 1 Pet 4:3). The lists tend to be stereotypical, and, as with the lists of virtues, "in every case the virtues or vices listed are not characteristics of the particular community addressed."[84] Paul is not therefore speaking of particular problems of behavior at Rome. Instead he picks up and uses a standard form of speech in his day. It is not likely that Paul quoted from a pre-formed "vice list" at hand, since the difficult syntax suggests that he composed the list from words that came to mind. Those words, however, are typical of what existed in vice lists, and to that extent Paul was dependent upon lists familiar to him.

The vice list has four different syntactical constructions, indicating that Paul must have composed it orally, while dictating his letter to Tertius (16:22), rather than in writing. The first part (1:29a) is governed by a passive participle (πεπληρωμένους, "filled") that is followed by a series of four abstract nouns in the dative case ("with every kind of wickedness, maliciousness, greed, and malice").

The second part (1:29b) is governed by an adjective (μεστούς, "full") that is followed by five other nouns in the genitive case ("of envy, murder, strife, deceit, and craftiness").

The third part (1:29b-30) marks a syntactical shift. It consists of a list of nouns and adjectives as substantives — both nouns and adjectives in the accusative case, in agreement with their antecedent αὐτούς ("them") in 1:28 — that

---

84. W. Doty, *Letters in Primitive Christianity*, 57; cf. B. Easton, "New Testament Ethical Lists," 1-12; O. J. F. Seitz, "Lists, Ethical," *IDB* 3:137-39.

designate persons as malicious ("gossips, slanderers, haters of God, insolent, arrogant, braggarts, contrivers of all sorts of evil, disobedient to parents").

The fourth part (1:31) consists of a string of adjectives in the accusative case — and all of them alpha-privative in Greek, corresponding to the English prefix "un-," or "non-," or the suffix "less" — that, presumably, describe the entire lot ("senseless, untrustworthy, hardhearted, and merciless").

There are some slight observable differences among the vices found within these different syntactical expressions. The first two portions tend to refer to attitudinal matters or a mind-set; the Gentiles are "filled with" or "full of" these evil inclinations. The third lists persons who behave in certain ways. The fourth tends to be descriptive of the character of the Gentiles. The whole list, however, has to be taken as a unit. Only as the whole list of things is read intact can the impact be heard.

The wording of the vice list contains some clever wordplays in Greek (not visible in English), such as the use of assonance in 1:29 (φθόνου φόνου, "envy, murder") and in 1:31 (ἀσυνέτους ἀσυνθέτους, "senseless, untrustworthy"). Such wordplays are typical of the diatribe.

The words in the list can be found in Hellenistic vice lists, both Jewish and non-Jewish. There is nothing about them that is particularly "biblical" (i.e., derived from the OT). They belong to the common lot of the vices of humanity. Although some of the terms listed recall commandments in the Decalogue (Exod 20:3-17; Deut 5:7-21) in their content (e.g., the commandments to serve and, by implication, to love God; to honor parents; and to refrain from murder, slander, and coveting), they do not correspond in actual wording to the specific commandments. Most of the 21 terms are found in both the LXX and NT. But there are exceptions. Three terms appear in the LXX but only here in the NT: κακοήθεια, ἀσυνθέτους, and ἀνελεήμονας ("craftiness," "untrustworthy," and "merciless," respectively). Four other terms appear in neither the LXX nor the NT: ψιθυριστάς, καταλάλους, θεοστυγεῖς, and ἐφευρετὰς κακῶν ("gossips," "slanderers," "haters of God," and "contrivers of all sorts of evil"). Although the two words in the expression γονεῦσιν ἀπειθεῖς ("disobedient to parents") appear independently elsewhere in the LXX and NT, the combination of them does not.

1:32 Paul closes the section with a rhetorical flourish. In saying that those who offend by means of their vices are "worthy of death," Paul is hardly saying, literally, that they should face the death penalty. Instead, he says that, before God, and because of their misbehavior, the Gentiles stand condemned. God's "decree (δικαίωμα)" is taken very broadly here. The word cannot be equivalent to a specific commandment in the OT, for the Gentiles would not "know" such a decree. More generally, it has to mean that the Gentiles, being "without excuse" (1:20), know God's will sufficiently, and that the vices and abuses spoken of are against his will. Subsequently Paul will go on to affirm that Gentiles are capable of knowing what God requires of them (2:14-15).

In the final part of the verse Paul says that the same persons (he does not actually refer here to others outside that group)[85] not only practice the behaviors listed in the previous verses, but applaud one another for doing so. Not only actions, but thoughts and attitudes are involved. The lives of the Gentiles are in bondage to the powers of evil, leading to abusive behaviors that get approval.

BIBLIOGRAPHY

Adams, Edward. "Abraham's Faith and Gentile Disobedience: Textual Links between Romans 1 and 4." *JSNT* 65 (1997): 47-66.

Aune, David E. *The New Testament in Its Literary Environment.* LEC. Philadelphia: Westminster Press, 1987.

Balch, David L. "Romans 1:24-27, Science, and Homosexuality." *CurrTM* 25 (1998): 433-40.

Banister, Jamie A. "Ὁμοίως and the Use of Parallelism in Romans 1:26-27." *JBL* 128 (2009): 569-90.

Barrett, C. K. *A Commentary on the First Epistle to the Corinthians.* 2d ed. BNTC. London: A. & C. Black, 1971.

Barth, Karl. *A Shorter Commentary on Romans.* Richmond: John Knox Press, 1959.

Bell, Richard H. *No One Seeks for God: An Exegetical and Theological Study of Romans 1:18–3:20.* WUNT 106. Tübingen: J. C. B. Mohr (Paul Siebeck), 1999.

Bietenhard, Hans. "Natürliche Gotteserkenntnis der Heiden? Eine Erwägung zu Röm 1." *TZ* 12 (1956): 275-88.

Bockmuehl, Marcus. *Jewish Law in Gentile Churches: Halakhah and the Beginning of Christian Public Ethics.* Edinburgh: T&T Clark, 2000; reprinted, Grand Rapids: Baker Book House, 2003.

Bornkamm, Günther. "Faith and Reason in Paul." In his *Early Christian Experience,* 29-46. New York: Harper & Row, 1969.

———. "The Revelation of God's Wrath: Romans 1–3." In his *Early Christian Experience,* 47-70.

Boswell, John. *Christianity, Social Tolerance, and Homosexuality: Gay People in Western Europe from the Beginning of the Christian Era to the Fourteenth Century.* Chicago: University of Chicago Press, 1980.

Brooten, Bernadette J. "Liebe zwischen Frauen im frühen Christentum." *ZNW* 2 (1999): 31-39.

———. *Love between Women: Early Christian Responses to Female Homoeroticism.* Chicago: University of Chicago Press, 1996.

———. "Patristic Interpretations of Romans 1.26." In *Studia Biblica XVIII,* 287-91. Ed. Elizabeth A. Livingston. Kalamazoo: Cistercian Publications, 1985.

85. Contra C. K. Barrett, *Romans,* 40.

————. "Paul's Views on the Nature of Women and Female Homoeroticism." In *Homosexuality and Religion and Philosophy*, 61-87. Ed Wayne R. Dynes and Stephen Donaldson. New York: Garland, 1992.

Bultmann, Rudolf. *Der Stil der paulinischen Predigt und die kynisch-stoische Diatribe*. FRLANT 13. Göttingen: Vandenhoeck & Ruprecht, 1910.

Campbell, Douglas A. "Natural Theology in Paul? Reading Romans 1:19-20." *IJST* 3 (1999): 231-52.

Campbell, J. Y. "Great Texts Reconsidered: Romans 1,18." *ExpTim* 50 (1938-39): 229-33.

Coffey, David M. "Natural Knowledge of God: Reflections on Romans 1:18-32." *TS* 31 (1970): 674-91.

Conzelmann, Hans. *1 Corinthians*. Hermeneia. Philadelphia: Fortress Press, 1975.

Cranfield, C. E. B. "Romans 1.18." *SJT* 21 (1968): 330-35.

Dabourne, Wendy. *Purpose and Cause in Pauline Exegesis: Romans 1.16–4.25 and a New Approach to the Letters*. SNTSMS 104. Cambridge: Cambridge University Press, 1999.

Davies, Margaret. "New Testament Ethics and Ours: Homosexuality and Sexuality in Romans 1:26-27." *BibInt* 3 (1995): 315-31.

Debel, Hans. "'Unnatural Intercourse' in Rom 1,26-27: Homosexual or Heterosexual?" In *The Letter to the Romans*, 631-40. Ed. Udo Schnelle. BETL 226. Walpole: Peeters, 2009.

DeYoung, James B. "The Meaning of 'Nature' in Romans 1 and Its Implications for Biblical Proscriptions of Homosexual Behaviour." *JETS* 31 (1988): 429-41.

Doty, William G. *Letters in Primitive Christianity*. Philadelphia: Fortress Press, 1973.

Dover, Kenneth J. *Greek Homosexuality*. Cambridge: Harvard University Press, 1978.

Duby, Georges, and Michelle Perrot, eds. *A History of Women in the West*. 5 vols. Cambridge: Belknap Press, 1992-94.

Du Toit, Andreas B. "Forensic Metaphors in Romans and Their Soteriological Significance." In *Salvation in the New Testament: Perspectives on Soteriology*, 213-46. Ed. Jan G. van der Watt. NovTSup 121. Boston: E. J. Brill, 2005.

Easton, Burton S. "New Testament Ethical Lists." *JBL* 51 (1932): 1-12.

Eckstein, Hans-Joachim. "'Denn Gottes Zorn wird vom Himmel her offenbar werden': Exegetische Erwägungen zu Röm 1,18." *ZNW* 78 (1987): 74-89.

Ellens, J. Harold. *Sex in the Bible: A New Consideration: Psychology, Religion, and Spirituality*. Westport: Praeger, 2006.

Elliott, John H. "No Kingdom of God for Softies?" *BTB* 34 (2004): 17-40.

Esler, Philip F. "The Sodom Tradition in Romans 1:18-32." *BTB* 34 (2004): 4-16.

Fee, Gordon. *The First Epistle to the Corinthians*. NICNT. Grand Rapids: Wm. B. Eerdmans, 1987.

Feuillet, André. "La connaissance naturalle de Dieu par les hommes, d'aprés Romains 1,18-23." *LV* 14 (1954): 63-80.

Finamore, Steve. "The Gospel and the Wrath of God in Romans 1." In *Understanding, Studying, and Reading: New Testament Essays in Honour of John Ashton*, 140-45. Ed. Christopher Rowland and Crispin H. T. Fletcher-Lewis. JSNTSup 153. Sheffield: Sheffield Academic Press, 1998.

Fitzgerald, John T. "Virtue/Vice Lists." *ABD* 6:857-69.

Fitzmyer, Joseph A. *First Corinthians.* AYB. New Haven: Yale University Press, 2008.

Flückiger, Felix. "Zur Unterscheidung von Heiden und Juden in Röm. 1,18–2,3." *TZ* 10 (1954): 154-58.

Fredrickson, David E. "Natural and Unnatural Use in Romans 1:24-27: Paul and the Philosophic Critique of Eros." In *Homosexuality, Science, and the "Plain Sense" of Scripture,* 197-222. Ed. David L. Balch. Grand Rapids: Wm. B. Eerdmans, 2000.

Fretheim, Terence E. "Theological Reflections on the Wrath of God in the Old Testament." *HBT* 24 (2002): 1-26.

Furnish, Victor P. "The Bible and Homosexuality: Reading the Texts in Context." In *Homosexuality in the Church: Both Sides of the Debate,* 18-35. Ed. Jeffrey S. Siker. Louisville: Westminster John Knox Press, 1994.

———. *The Moral Teaching of Paul: Selected Issues.* 3d ed. Nashville: Abingdon Press, 2009.

Gagnon, Robert A. J. *The Bible and Homosexual Practice: Texts and Hermeneutics.* Nashville: Abingdon Press, 2001.

Gathercole, Simon J. "Sin in God's Economy: Agencies in Romans 1 and 7." In *Divine and Human Agency in Paul and His Cultural Environment,* 158-72. Ed. John M. G. Barclay and Simon J. Gathercole. LNTS 335. New York: T&T Clark, 2008.

Gaventa, Beverly R. "God Handed Them Over: Reading Romans 1:18-32 Apocalyptically." *AusBR* 53 (2005): 42-53.

Hays, Richard B. "Awaiting the Redemption of Our Bodies: Drawing on Scripture and Tradition in the Church Debate on Homosexuality." *Sojourners* 20 (1991): 17-21.

———. *The Moral Vision of the New Testament: Community, Cross, New Creation: A Contemporary Introduction to New Testament Ethics.* San Francisco: HarperSanFrancisco, 1996.

———. "Relations Natural and Unnatural: A Response to John Boswell's Exegesis of Romans 1." *JCE* 14 (1986): 184-215.

Helminiak, Daniel A. "Ethics, Biblical and Denominational: A Response to Mark Smith." *JAAR* 65 (1997): 855-59.

Heschel, Abraham J. *The Prophets.* New York: Harper & Row, 1962.

Holter, Knut. "A Note on the Old Testament Background of Rom 1,23-27," *BN* 69 (1993): 21-23.

Hooker, Morna D. "Adam in Romans 1." *NTS* 6 (1959-60): 297-306; reprinted in her *From Adam to Christ: Essays on Paul,* 73-84. Cambridge: Cambridge University Press, 1990. References are to the latter publication.

———. "A Further Note on Romans 1." *NTS* 13 (1966-67): 181-83; reprinted in her *From Adam to Christ: Essays on Paul,* 85-87. Cambridge: Cambridge University Press, 1990. References are to the latter publication.

Hubbard, Thomas K., ed. *Homosexuality in Greece and Rome: A Sourcebook of Basic Documents.* Berkeley: University of California Press, 2003.

Hultgren, Arland J. "Being Faithful to the Scriptures: Romans 1:26-27 as a Case in Point." *WW* 14 (1994): 315-25.

Hyldahl, Niels. "A Reminiscence of the Old Testament at Romans i.23." *NTS* 2 (1955-56): 285-88.

Jewett, Robert. "The Social Context and Implications of Homoerotic References in Romans 1:24-27." In *Homosexuality, Science, and the "Plain Sense" of Scripture,* 223-41. Ed. David L. Balch. Grand Rapids: Wm. B. Eerdmans, 2000.

Keck, Leander E. "Romans 1:18-23." *Int* 40 (1986): 402-6.

Levison, John R. "Adam and Eve in Romans 1.18-25 and the Greek *Life of Adam and Eve.*" *NTS* 50 (2004): 519-34.

Lincoln, Andrew T. "From Wrath to Justification: Tradition, Gospel, and Audience in the Theology of Romans 1:18–4:25." In *Pauline Theology,* vol. 3, *Romans,* 130-59. Ed. David M. Hay and E. Elizabeth Johnson. Minneapolis: Fortress Press, 1995.

Lührmann, Dieter. *Das Offenbarungsverständnis bei Paulus und in paulinischen Gemeinden.* WMANT 16. Neukirchen-Vluyn: Neukirchener Verlag, 1965.

Macgregor, G. H. C. "The Concept of the Wrath of God in the New Testament." *NTS* 7 (1960-61): 101-9.

Martin, Dale B. "*Arsenokoitēs* and *Malakos:* Meanings and Consequences." In *Biblical Ethics and Homosexuality: Listening to Scripture,* 117-36. Ed. Robert L. Brawley. Louisville: Westminster John Knox, 1996.

———. "Heterosexism and the Interpretation of Romans 1:18-32." *BibInt* 3 (1995): 332-55.

Mauser, Ulrich W. "Creation and Human Sexuality in the New Testament." In *Biblical Ethics and Homosexuality: Listening to Scripture,* 3-16. Ed. Robert L. Brawley. Louisville: Westminster John Knox, 1996.

McKenzie, John L. "Natural Law in the New Testament." *BR* 9 (1964): 3-13.

Miller, James E. "Pederasty and Romans 1:27: A Response to Mark Smith." *JAAR* 65 (1997): 861-66.

———. "The Practices of Romans 1:26: Homosexual or Heterosexual?" *NovT* 37 (1995): 1-11.

Nissinen, Martti. *Homoeroticism in the Biblical World: A Historical Perspective.* Minneapolis: Fortress Press, 1998.

Nolland, John. "Romans 1:26-27 and the Homosexuality Debate." *HBT* 22 (2000): 32-57.

O'Rourke, John J. "Romans 1,20 and Natural Revelation." *CBQ* 23 (1961): 301-6.

Phipps, William E. "Paul on 'Unnatural' Sex." *CurTM* 29 (2002): 128-31.

Popkes, Wiard. "Zum Aufbau und Charakter von Römer 1.18-32." *NTS* 28 (1982): 490-501.

Porter, Calvin L. "Romans 1:18-32: The Role in the Developing Argument." *NTS* 40 (1994): 210-28.

Sampley, J. Paul. *The First Letter to the Corinthians.* In *The New Interpreter's Bible,* 10:771-1003. Ed. Leander E. Keck. 12 vols. Nashville: Abingdon Press, 1994-2002.

Schaller, Berndt. "Zum Textcharakter der Hiobzitate im paulinischen Schrifttum." *ZNW* 71 (1980): 21-26.

Schlier, Heinrich. "Über die Erkenntnis Gottes bei den Heiden (nach dem Neuen Testament)." *EvT* 2 (1935): 9-26.

———. "Von den Heiden: Römer 1,18-22." *EvT* 5 (1938): 113-24.

Schmeller, Thomas. *Paulus und die 'Diatribe': Eine vergleichende Stilinterpretation.* NTAbh 19. Munster: Aschendorff, 1987.

Schrage, Wolfgang. *Der erste Brief an die Korinther.* EKKNT 7. 4 vols. Neukirchen-Vluyn: Neukirchener Verlag, 1991-2001.

Schulz, Siegfried. "Die Anklage in Röm. 1,18-32." *TZ* 14 (1958): 161-73.

Scroggs, Robin. *The New Testament and Homosexuality: Contextual Background for Contemporary Debate.* Philadelphia: Fortress Press, 1983.

Seifrid, Mark A. "Unrighteous by Faith: Apostolic Proclamation in Romans 1:18–3:20." In *Justification and Variegated Nomism,* 2:105-45. Ed. D. A. Carson, Peter T. O'Brien, and Mark Seifrid. 2 vols. Grand Rapids: Baker Academic, 2001-4.

Sissa, Giulia. *Sex and Sensuality in the Ancient World.* New Haven: Yale University Press, 2008.

Smith, Abraham. "The New Testament and Homosexuality." *QR* 11 (1991): 18-32.

Smith, Mark D. "Ancient Bisexuality and the Interpretation of Romans 1:26-27." *JAAR* 64 (1996): 223-56.

Snyder, Graydon F. *First Corinthians: A Faith Community Commentary.* Macon: Mercer University Press, 1992.

Stegemann, Wolfgang. "Homosexualität — Ein moderne Konzept." *ZNT* 2 (1988): 61-68.

Stowasser, Martin. "Homosexualität und die Bibel. Exegetische und hermeneutische Überlegungen zu einem schwierigen Thema." *NTS* 43 (1997): 503-26.

Swart, Gerhard. "Why without Excuse? An Inquiry into the Syntactic and Semantic Relations of Romans 1:18-21." *Neot* 39 (2005): 389-407.

Theobald, Michael. "Röm 1,26f.: Eine paulinische Weisung zur Homosexualität? Plädoyer für einen vernüftigen Umgang mit der Schrift." In his *Studien zum Römerbrief,* 511-18. WUNT 136. Tübingen: J. C. B. Mohr (Paul Siebeck), 2001.

Thielman, Frank. "Law and Liberty in the Ethics of Paul." *Ex Auditu* 11 (1995): 63-75.

Thomas, Yan. "The Division of the Sexes in Roman Law." In Georges Duby and Michelle Perrot, gen. eds., *A History of Women in the West,* vol. 1, *From Ancient Goddesses to Christian Saints,* 83-137. Ed. Pauline Schmitt Pantel. Cambridge: Belknap-Harvard University Press, 1992.

Tobin, Thomas H. "Controversy and Continuity in Romans 1:18–3:20." *CBQ* 55 (1993): 298-318.

Vielhauer, Philipp. "On the 'Paulinism' of Acts." In *Studies in Luke-Acts,* 33-50. Ed. Leander E. Keck and J. Louis Martyn. Nashville: Abingdon Press, 1966.

Walker, William O. "Romans 1.18–2.29: A Non-Pauline Interpolation?" *NTS* 45 (1999): 533-52.

Ward, Roy B. "Why Unnatural? The Tradition behind Romans 1:26-27." *HTR* 90 (1997): 263-84.

Wengst, Klaus. "Paulus und die Homosexualität: Überlegungen zu Röm 1,26f." *ZEE* 31 (1987): 72-81.

White, John L. *The Form and Function of the Body of the Greek Letter: A Study of the Letter-Body in the Nonliterary Papyri and in Paul the Apostle.* SBLDS 2. Missoula: Scholars Press, 1972.

White, Leland J. "Does the Bible Speak about Gays or Same-Sex Orientation? A Test Case in Biblical Ethics." *BTB* 25 (1995): 14-23.

Wischmeyer, Oda. "ΦΥΣΙΣ und ΚΤΙΣΙΣ bei Paulus: Die paulinische Rede von Schöpfung und Natur." *ZTK* 93 (1996): 352-75.

Wolff, Christian. *Der erste Brief des Paulus an die Korinther.* THNT 7. Leipzig: Evangelische Verlagsanstalt, 1996.

Young, Richard A. "The Knowledge of God in Romans 1:18-23: Exegetical and Theological Reflections." *JETS* 43 (2000): 695-707.

2.2. God's Impartial Judgment, 2:1-16

1*Therefore you are without excuse, whoever you are, when you judge someone else. For on the basis by which you judge another person, you condemn yourself, for you who judge are doing the same things.* 2*And we know that God's judgment is in accord with truth against those who do such things.* 3*But do you realize — you who judge those who do such things and do them — that you shall not escape God's judgment?* 4*Or do you despise the riches of his kindness, forbearance, and patience, not knowing that God's kindness leads you to repentance?* 5*But because of your stubbornness and unrepentant heart, you are storing up for yourself wrath on the day of wrath and the revelation of the righteous judgment of God,* 6*who "will render to each according to his deeds":* 7*eternal life to those who, by perseverance in good works, seek glory, honor, and immortality,* 8*but wrath and fury to those who from selfish ambition disobey the truth but obey wickedness.* 9*There will be affliction and distress for every person who does evil, for the Jew first and also the Greek;* 10*but glory, honor, and peace for everyone who does good, for the Jew first and also the Greek;* 11*for there is no partiality with God.*

12*For as many as have sinned apart from the law will perish apart from the law, and as many as have sinned under the law will be judged by the law.* 13*For it is not the hearers of the law that are righteous before God, but it is those who are doers of the law that will be justified.* 14*For when Gentiles, who do not have the law, do by nature what the law requires, they are a law unto themselves, even though they do not possess the law.* 15*They show that the works of the law are written on their hearts, while their conscience bears witness and their conflicting thoughts condemn or even defend them* 16*on the day when, according to my gospel, God judges human secrets through Christ Jesus.*

Notes on the Text and Translation

2:1 The expression "whoever you are" (NRSV and NET) is used here as a rendering of the Greek expression ὦ ἄνθρωπε, which has often been translated as "O man" (KJV, ASV, RSV, ESV). To render the term as "O person" to be inclusive is unsatisfactory. The NRSV is more satisfactory, even though it may lack the directness of the Greek. The NIV is inclusive by means of reordering the sentence: "You, therefore, have no excuse, you who pass judgment. . . ."
     2:12 The clause καὶ ὅσοι ἐν νόμῳ ἥμαρτον is translated here to read "and

as many as have sinned under the law." The words ἐν νόμῳ can be rendered "in the law" or, as a Semitism, "by the law," which must be its meaning here. Modern English versions (RSV, NIV, NRSV, ESV, and NET) often translate the phrase as "under the law." Although that is appropriate, it should not be assumed that it represents the phrase ὑπὸ νόμον ("under the law") that Paul uses elsewhere (Rom 6:14-15; 1 Cor 9:20; Gal 3:23; 4:4-5, 21; 5:18).[86]

2:15 The Greek clause καὶ μεταξὺ ἀλλήλων τῶν λογισμῶν κατηγορούντων ἢ καὶ ἀπολογουμένων is difficult to translate. The entire clause involves a genitive absolute construction. The main problem is how to render μεταξὺ ἀλλήλων τῶν λογισμῶν. The preposition μεταξύ followed by a noun in the genitive case typically means "between" or "among." The phrase μεταξὺ ἀλλήλων could therefore mean "among one another" or "among themselves."[87] There are two translation possibilities. One is that the "thoughts" are among the Gentiles, i.e., the thoughts of some condemn, while the thoughts of others defend, so "while among them [their] thoughts accuse or even defend [them]." The other is that the thoughts are the inward thoughts within the Gentiles as a whole, so "while [their] thoughts among themselves condemn or even defend [them]." Within the context here, stressing the inward life (such as "conscience"), it is best to follow the latter way of thinking. There is merit in rendering the Greek phrase as "their conflicting thoughts," as in the RSV, NAB, and NRSV.

General Comment

Modern versions of the Bible begin a new paragraph at 2:1 and a new chapter as well. It is agreed that there is a rhetorical shift at 2:1, in which Paul turns from a vice list to a diatribe. The question debated is the identity of the interlocutor at 2:1 and following. Some, probably most, interpreters see the opponent as an imaginary Jewish hearer. According to this viewpoint, the discussion concerning the Gentiles and their sinful behavior was rounded off with a flourish at 1:32, and 2:1-16 marks a transition in which the impartiality of God is discussed.[88] Others contend that the use of the conjunction διό ("therefore" or "wherefore") at the outset of 2:1 indicates that a continuity is intended between what has gone before in 1:18-

---

86. J. Marcus, "'Under the Law,'" 72-83, suggests that the prominence of the phrase in Gal indicates that it originated with Paul's opponents in Galatia.

87. BDAG 641 (μεταξύ, 2).

88. C. H. Dodd, *Romans*, 30; A. Nygren, *Romans*, 113; J. Murray, *Romans*, 1:54-56; E. Käsemann, *Romans*, 52; C. Cranfield, *Romans*, 136, 138-39; J. O'Neill, *Romans*, 46-479; E. Best, *Romans*, 24; U. Wilckens, *Römer*, 1:121; H. Räisänen, *Paul and the Law*, 97-98; J. Dunn, *Romans*, 78-82; P. Stuhlmacher, *Romans*, 38; C. Talbert, *Romans*, 79; E. Lohse, *Römer*, 97; S. Gathercole, *Where Is Boasting?* 197-200; L. Keck, *Romans*, 74.

32 and what follows; the word draws a conclusion from what was said in 1:18-32. Furthermore, it is not until 2:17 that Paul's indictment of the Jewish people begins explicitly. Therefore, according to this point of view, one should understand the imaginary hearer to be a Gentile.[89] Finally, there are those who maintain that Paul addresses humanity in general at this point.[90]

While it is true that the identity of the imaginary opponent becomes explicit at 2:17, it is equally the case that the diatribe moves along from the beginning (2:1) on the basis of Jewish presuppositions,[91] replete with traditional Jewish terms and allusions to the OT and other Jewish texts (see comments below). The imaginary interlocutor can hear and appreciate what is being said only if that person is either Jewish or else is a Gentile who is willing to debate on Jewish terms. To that extent, the diatribe envisions an opponent with a Jewish point of view.

What is important to underscore, however, is that Paul is addressing Christians in Rome, using diatribe to explicate what he wants to convey to them. His indictment in 1:18–3:20 has to do with the entire world, made up of Jews and Gentiles. He seeks to show that there is no hope of salvation for anyone apart from the redemptive work of God in Christ. What he is driving at is said explicitly in 2:11: "God shows no partiality." Such a statement undercuts any presumed Jewish privilege based on election or confidence in one's ability to observe the law. It would also undercut any presumed moral superiority among Gentiles, although that does not seem to be an issue anywhere in 2:1-16. God's judgment, Paul says, is fundamentally according to works. On *that* basis alone, some are found righteous, others guilty — in principle, if not in fact. This entire diatribe concerns judgment apart from Christ, whom Paul mentions only once, and that is at the end of the section (2:16).

Judgment according to works stands in tension with justification by faith. They are alike in one respect, and that is that in both cases God shows no distinction between Jews and Gentiles.[92] Paul's purpose in this section is not, however, to endorse righteousness according to works as the basis for salvation, but to make a rhetorical case for what is to follow, and that is that if the criterion for the final judgment will be righteousness according to good works, all people

89. S. Stowers, *A Rereading of Romans*, 11-15, 37, 101, 103, 128; B. Witherington, *Romans*, 73-77; R. Thorsteinsson, *Paul's Interlocutor in Romans 2*, 188-94.

90. C. K. Barrett, *Romans*, 42; R. Harrisville, *Romans*, 41; J. Bassler, *Divine Impartiality*, 122, 136; M. Winninge, *Sinners and the Righteous*, 283; T. Engberg-Pedersen, *Paul and the Stoics*, 201-2; O. Wischmeyer, "Römer 2.1-24," 356-76. According to N. Elliott, *The Rhetoric of Romans*, 191, the specific identity of the accused cannot be determined.

91. Cf. E. P. Sanders, *Paul, the Law, and the Jewish People*, 129; H. Räisänen, *Paul and the Law*, 98; G. Carras, "Romans 2:1-29," 183-207; K. Yinger, *Paul, Judaism, and Judgment according to Deeds*, 149.

92. J. Bassler, *Divine Impartiality*, 166-70, 186-88.

will certainly fail the test. The only hope for anyone is the grace of God extended in the redemptive death of Christ. God is impartial, and that is fundamental to understanding both his judgment and his grace.

Detailed Comment

2:1 The conjunction διό ("therefore") draws an inference from what has gone before.[93] Since God's wrath has been poured out in judgment on the world, each person stands under his judgment. The switch to the singular "you," common in diatribe, is particularly effective rhetorically. That and the phrase "whoever you are" (representing ὦ ἄνθρωπε, literally, "O man," but see the Note above on this verse for the translation here) are often used in diatribe.[94] Paul's use of these expressions (διό and ὦ ἄνθρωπε) initiate the diatribe that follows. At the outset Paul declares that anyone who passes judgment on another person receives the same judgment, since the one judging does the same as the one being judged. That is a rather strange charge if it is to be taken literally. It is possible for a person to pass judgment on another who is, for example, "disobedient to parents" (1:30) without being such oneself. But when the vice list is taken as a unity, declaring a broad range of offensive attitudes and behaviors, the charge makes sense. Everyone can find something of the self within the vice list at one place or another. Those who judge others seek to excuse themselves, but they are no better than the others. There is a resonance here with what is said in the Sermon on the Mount: "Do not judge, so that you may not be judged. For with the judgment you make you will be judged" (Matt 7:1-2).

2:2-3 The NRSV (but not other modern versions) makes an interpretive move at 2:2 by inserting the words "You say." The effect is that Paul then introduces a statement by the imaginary opponent into the discussion: "You say, 'We know that God's judgment on those who do such things is in accordance with truth.'" The Greek text (followed by other modern versions) lacks a basis for the additional words, and can be rendered simply as: "And we know that God's judgment is in accord with truth against those who do such things." Limiting the statement to the opponent (as in the NRSV) is overreaching what the Greek text has. According to what is actually written, the imaginary opponent is included, but is not alone, among those who think in a certain way about God's judgment. The statement itself would be axiomatic: God's judgment is true

93. BDAG 250 (διό). Cf. D. Starnitzke, *Die Struktur paulinischen Denkens im Römerbrief,* 86.

94. Stanley K. Stowers, "Diatribe," *ABD* 2:193; idem, *Diatribe and Romans,* 78-118; for many illustrations in texts from Epictetus, cf. R. Thorsteinsson, *Paul's Interlocutor in Romans 2,* 188-89 (including footnotes).

(Tob 3:2; Pr Azar 1:8; 2 Esdr 7:104). In 2:3, however, Paul addresses the opponent again and, once more, uses the style of the diatribe within a question — second person singular in Greek, plus the words ὦ ἄνθρωπε ("O man," as in KJV, ASV, RSV; "whoever you are" in NRSV). The question is direct, expecting a negative answer. Surely no one can escape divine judgment who judges others but does the same thing as the one who is judged. In fact the offense can be considered worse, since it is accompanied by hypocrisy.

2:4-5 One cannot take the goodness of God for granted, a goodness that is spelled out and emphasized by the use of three terms in succession ("kindness, forbearance, and patience"). The divine goodness is a check upon the divine wrath. Those who judge and do the very things they condemn others for are worthy of God's condemning wrath. But God holds it in check in order to provide time for repentance, a point made elsewhere by Paul (Rom 9:22) and by other writers (Wis 11:23; 2 Pet 3:9, 15; 2 *Apoc. Bar.* 21.20).

But having made that point, Paul insists that the withholding of God's wrath cannot be taken for granted either. Indeed, a "day of wrath" is coming, and then the "righteous judgment of God" will be revealed to all the world. The image of the "day of wrath," when God's anger and righteous judgment will be revealed, is a familiar one in the OT (Job 20:28; 21:30; Ps 110:5; Prov 11:4; Isa 13:9 Ezek 7:19; Zeph 1:15, 18; 2:2, 3; Sir 18:24). For Paul, that day is near, since the events of the last day are present, and the wrath of God is being revealed (Rom 1:18). Speaking to the imaginary opponent, Paul declares that that person is storing up God's wrath for the day of wrath by refusing to repent. The imagery of "storing up" implies that the person is accumulating a list of charges against himself or herself that will be revealed on the day of judgment (cf. 2:16). It can also be used elsewhere to refer to an accumulation of righteous deeds (Matt 6:20; *Pss. Sol.* 9.5).

2:6-11 These verses speak of judgment according to the deeds of each. As various interpreters have contended,[95] the presentation can be set out chiastically:

> A: 2:6, divine judgment is according to deeds
> > B: 2:7, doing good/seeking glory leads to eternal life
> > > C: 2:8, obeying wickedness leads to wrath and fury
> > > C': 2:9, doing evil leads to affliction and distress
> > B': 2:10, doing good leads to glory, honor, and peace
> A': 2:11, there is no partiality with God

---

95. K. Grobel, "A Chiastic Retribution-Formula," 255-61; J. Fitzmyer, *Romans*, 302-3; K. Yinger, *Paul, Judaism, and Judgment according to Deeds*, 153. Some interpreters include only 2:7-10 in the chiastic structure, including J. Jeremias, "Chiasmus in den Paulusbriefen," 282; C. Cranfield, *Romans*, 149; and J. Dunn, *Romans*, 78.

2:6 Paul declares flat out that God "will render to each according to his deeds." That is to assert the truth. How else can God make judgments except on the basis of one's deeds in this world? Yet interpreters have had difficulty with the verse in light of Paul's doctrine of justification by faith (not works). Three examples can be cited: (1) justification "belongs properly to the beginning, not to the end of the Christian's career,"[96] so that (apparently) unless there is a transformation, justification by faith counts for nothing, and judgment will depend on works; (2) Paul is speaking here of judgment in Jewish understanding for the Jewish people (as though the section has to do with an indictment of Jews only);[97] and (3) "Here 'by works alone' in fact coincides with 'by faith alone.'"[98]

Attempts of this kind to harmonize the verse with other elements of Paul's theology are misleading. In this particular instance the statement must be taken as a universal principle concerning God's righteous judgment.[99] It is only later in the letter that Paul will speak of the justifying work of God in Christ (3:21-26). Here Paul continues to engage in diatribe, exposing everyone to the judgment of God. All ideas of privilege are ruled out, whether they be election (in the case of Israel), presumed intellectual and moral superiority (in the case of Hellenism), or standing before others as their judge.[100] The verse is virtually (but not exactly) a quotation from Psalm 62:13 (LXX 61:13): "For you [= God] will render to each according to his deeds" (ὅτι σὺ ἀποδώσεις ἑκάστῳ κατὰ τὰ ἔργα αὐτοῦ). A similar statement appears at Proverbs 24:12. Paul does not use any introductory formula to indicate that he is quoting from the Scriptures, and the saying could easily have become common enough by Paul's day to have become a popular maxim. Nevertheless, Paul may well have been aware that he was quoting Scripture, and he could have assumed that others would recognize it as such. Parallels appear elsewhere in the OT (Job 34:11; Ezek 33:20; Hos 12:2; Sir 16:12; cf. Eccl 12:14; Jer 17:10), in non-canonical Jewish sources,[101] and in other NT contexts (Matt 16:27; 1 Pet 1:17), including elsewhere in the letters of Paul (Rom 14:10-12; 2 Cor 5:10).

2:7-10 The implications of judgment according to one's works are spelled out. Paul follows traditional teaching concerning divine judgment. There are two ways of living, and two consequences from those ways. The traditional

96. W. Sanday and A. Headlam, *Romans*, 57.

97. U. Wilckens, *Römer*, 1:126.

98. E. Käsemann, *Romans*, 58. Cf. L. Mattern, *Das Verständnis des Gerichtes bei Paulus*, 136-38, 151.

99. K. Donfried, "Justification and Last Judgment in Paul," 140-52; P. Stuhlmacher, *Romans*, 41; A. Lincoln, "From Wrath to Justification," 141; E. Lohse, *Römer*, 100.

100. Cf. A. Lincoln, "From Wrath to Justification," 141-44; B. Byrne, *Romans*, 82-83; K. Yinger, *Paul, Judaism, and Judgment according to Deeds*, 181.

101. *1 Enoch* 100.7; *Jos. Asen.* 28.3.

teaching is colored by Jewish terminology. Paul uses language concerning the judgment of the living God, known from the OT, who extends his blessing upon those who do good (2:7, 10), but who is also capable of visiting his "wrath and fury" upon the disobedient (2:8-9). The combination of the two words "wrath and fury" (ὀργὴ καὶ θυμός) is rather traditional, for it appears in the OT (Deut 29:28; Ps 2:5; Jer 21:5; cf. Sir 48:10), as does "affliction and distress" (θλῖψις καὶ στενοχωρία) to a lesser extent (Deut 28:53, 55, 57; Isa 8:22; Add Esth 11:8). The blessing and concept of "eternal life" (ζωὴν αἰώνιον) is spoken of only once in the OT (Dan 12:2), once more in the apocryphal/deuterocanonical books (4 Macc 15:3), and then in other Jewish sources.[102] It appears elsewhere in the NT many times to represent the final and finest blessing that God can give (e.g., Matt 19:16, 29; Luke 10:25; John 3:15; Acts 13:46; 1 Tim 1:16; 1 John 1:2, etc.). No matter how much humanity can achieve or enjoy in this life, particularly in relationship to God, there is always a residue of what cannot be known, experienced, or accomplished. But eternal life is not simply one more human ambition, and it is certainly not an achievement. It is the gift of God given for the sake of God's own love for humanity. God is not willing to cease a relationship with his own.

Twice in these verses (2:2-10) Paul uses the phrase "the Jew first and also the Greek," which he has used previously (1:16). The phrase means all people ("Greek" meaning Gentile), but when "first" is inserted, the phrase carries with it the idea that God's righteous judgment will begin with the Jewish people, who are heirs to the promises, and then it will be exercised on the Gentiles.

2:11 The assertion that there is no partiality with God restates as briefly as possible what has been said in the previous verses, and it corresponds particularly to what was said in 2:6. God's judgment — whether resulting in "eternal life" or in "wrath and fury" — is fair, and no one has any privileges. Even though Israel is God's elect, the judgment of God is even-handed, based on the principle put forth in 2:6. Paul also speaks of divine impartiality at Galatians 2:6, albeit in different language. The theme appears, too, in Acts (10:34) and in 1 Peter (1:17), using different terminology. It is also found in two deutero-Pauline letters (Eph 6:9; Col 3:25) that use the word προσωπολημψία, as Paul does in the passage under discussion here (Rom 2:11).

2:12 In 2:12-16 Paul elaborates on what he has already said. He brings the law into the discussion at the very outset in 2:12. Among the various meanings of ὁ νόμος ("the law") in Paul, here it has the meaning of the Torah, both written and oral.[103] In Jewish understanding, the Torah is to be kept, and in so do-

---

102. *Pss. Sol.* 3.12; *Jos. Asen.* 8.11; *Sib. Or.* 2.336; *Odes Sol.* 11.16; Philo, *Fug.* 78; Josephus, *J.W.* 1.650.

103. This is the view also of H. Räisänen, *Paul and the Law*, 25-26.

ing there is fullness of life and righteousness (Lev 18:5). Anticipating the final judgment, Paul divides the human race into two parts. There are those who will have "sinned apart from the law" (Gentiles), and there are those who will have "sinned under the law" (Jews). And, he says, both will be judged on the basis of whether they are "apart from" or "under" the law. That Jews will be judged "under" the law (the Torah) is clear implicitly from their own tradition, and sometimes it is made explicit.[104] That Gentiles will be judged "apart" from the law seems only fair, since they do not have the Torah as a standard by which to be judged. Yet for Paul to make such a statement without qualification is rather astounding. Generally the Jewish view was that Gentiles will be judged on a portion of the law that concerns them, i.e., the Noachic laws.[105]

As with parables, so also with diatribe, not everything said, or put forcefully, should be raised to the level of doctrine. Paul does not put forth his views concerning the Gentiles in the final judgment here. He is making a point of another kind, and that is to make clear — and elaborate on — his statement that there is no partiality with God.

2:13-14 In these verses Paul speaks of Gentiles as capable of doing what is right in the eyes of God every bit as much as Jews. What he is doing rhetorically is to create a level playing field among Jews and Gentiles. Gentiles do not have the Torah as a guide for their lives, but at least theoretically it is possible for them to "do by nature what the law requires (φύσει τὰ τοῦ νόμου ποιῶσιν; literally, "do by nature the things of the law")." Paul would not mean here all the laws of the Mosaic tradition. That would be impossible, since many of the laws (particularly the ceremonial laws) would not be known to the Gentiles.[106] And by saying that "they are a law unto themselves," Paul is not speaking of them as "lawless," as the phrase has come to mean in later history. That they are a law unto themselves can only mean that they are self-regulated in ways that are moral. So they do "by nature" (KJV, ASV, RSV, and NIV; "instinctively," NRSV) what the law requires. There is then an overlap between what God has given through the law (the Torah) and the moral consciousness of the Gentiles. The degree to which Paul, by using "by nature" (φύσει), maintains a theology of natural law at this point is debatable. Within the context of diatribe it is not necessary for him to reflect on the

104. Ps 119:80; *Jub.* 5.13; *2 Apoc. Bar.* 48.47; 1QpHab 5.5.

105. These laws are articulated in *Jub.* 7.20 (2d century B.C.) and then in later works, such as *t. Abod. Zar.* 8.4; *b. Sanh.* 56a; and *Gen. Rab.* 34.8. Cf. also Acts 15:20; 21:35. For discussion, cf. Steven S. Schwarzschild, "Noachide Laws," *EncJud* 12:1189-90, who sums up the seven laws: prohibitions against idolatry, blasphemy, bloodshed, sexual sins, theft, eating a living animal; and instituting a legal system.

106. This has been recognized early on in the history of interpretation; for example, cf. Origen, *Commentarii in Epistulam ad Romanos* 2:14. Among modern authors, cf. H. Räisänen, *Paul and the Law*, 26.

issue whether there can be natural knowledge of the will of God by unaided human reason (cf. the exegesis of 1:19-23). But Paul takes for granted that even though Gentiles do not know the actual commandments, they are capable of a high moral standard that coincides with the teachings set forth by the moral commandments.[107] That is sufficient for the rhetorical point being made. Paul undercuts any notions of Jewish moral superiority. On this point, one may contrast what Paul says with what the author of 2 Esdras declares (3:34-36):

> Now therefore weigh in a balance our iniquities and those of the inhabitants of the world; and it will be found which way the turn of the scale will incline. When have the inhabitants of the earth not sinned in your sight? Or what nation has kept your commandments so well? You may indeed find individuals who have kept your commandments, but nations you will not find.

Anticipating what will be declared in 3:9 (that all, both Jews and Gentiles, are under the power of sin) and in 3:19 (that the whole world is accountable before God), Paul says, in effect, that no one has a privileged position before God in terms of moral standing. The expression "doers of the law" (2:13) occurs also in the Dead Sea Scrolls.[108] Elsewhere in his letters Paul speaks of doing "the works of the law" (Rom 3:28; Gal 2:16; 3:2, 5, 12).

2:15 The concept of the law being written on human hearts has an OT background (Isa 51:7; Jer 31:33).[109] At Jeremiah 31:33 it is spoken of as a future expectation (νόμους μου . . . ἐπὶ καρδίας αὐτῶν γράψω, "I will write my laws upon their hearts"), and therefore it has been suggested that here Paul has Christian Gentiles, not pagans, in mind when he refers to Gentiles.[110] But that need not follow.[111] It is certainly possible for Paul — in a diatribe where he seeks to create a level playing field between Jews and Gentiles in the eyes of God — to pick up the language and imagery of the OT and have it refer to Gentiles in general.

The term "conscience" (συνείδησις), rare in the LXX (Eccl 10:20; Wis 17:10), appears 14 times (of the 30 NT occurrences) in the letters of Paul.[112]

---

107. Cf. T. Donaldson, *Paul and the Gentiles*, 146-47; M. Bockmuehl, *Jewish Law in Gentile Churches*, 131. N. T. Wright, "The Law in Romans 2," 146, contends that the Gentiles spoken of are Christian Gentiles, but that does not seem to be warranted, since Paul says that what the law requires is innate.

108. 1QpHab 8.1 (עושי התורה, "observing the law"); text in *The Dead Sea Scrolls: Study Edition*, trans. Florentino García Martínez and Eibert J. C. Tigchelaar, 2 vols. (Grand Rapids: Wm. B. Eerdmans, 1997-98), 1:16-17.

109. It appears also in Qumran literature, as at 4Q504 1-2.2.13.

110. C. Cranfield, *Romans*, 158-59; N. T. Wright, "The Law in Romans 2," 146; R. Bergmeier, "Gesetzeserfüllung ohne Gesetz und Beschneidung," 26-40.

111. Cf. E. P. Sanders, *Paul, the Law, and the Jewish People*, 126; L. Keck, *Romans*, 80.

112. Rom 2:15; 9:1; 13:5; 1 Cor 8:7, 10, 12; 10:26, 27, 28, 29 (2x); 2 Cor 1:12; 4:2; 5:11.

Here, as at 2 Corinthians 1:12, the term signifies that moral awareness, common to many, that can testify for or against a person.[113] It "bears witness" within and to the self concerning one's conduct. On the difficult phrase "and their conflicting thoughts condemn or even defend them," see the Notes on the Translation above. With reference to both the witnessing conscience of Gentiles and their conflicting thoughts, Paul affirms that Gentiles are capable, in principle, of doing the will of God, in spite of their not having the Torah, just as the Jews are.

2:16 But all will be disclosed only at the final judgment. The "day" will come when God will judge all the secrets of humanity (τὰ κρυπτὰ τῶν ἀνθρώπων), as indicated also in an apocalyptic saying of Jesus (Mark 4:22// Matt 10:26//Luke 8:17). Nothing can be hidden before God: "For God will bring every deed into judgment, including every secret thing, whether good or evil" (Eccl 12:14). In the *Psalms of Solomon,* from the first century B.C. and possibly of Pharisaic origin, it is said that the Messiah will "condemn sinners by the thoughts of their hearts" (17.25, ἐν λόγῳ καρδίας αὐτῶν).[114] Christ, says Paul, brings all things to light. For more on the day of judgment, cf. the exegesis of 2:5, in which it is said that people are "storing up" charges that will be revealed on the day of judgment. The use of the phrase "according to my gospel" within the context of a statement about divine judgment can seem out of place. Yet divine judgment is good news in that it means an end to injustice in the world. Furthermore, the judgment of God will be exercised by Jesus Christ, as stated elsewhere by Paul (1 Cor 4:5; 2 Cor 5:10; cf. 1 Cor 15:24-28) and by other NT writers (Acts 10:42; 2 Thess 2:8). This is the only time Christ is mentioned in 1:18–3:20, and it offers a moment of relief from the diatribe and its indictments that Paul has been pouring forth. More than that, it makes a claim concerning the whole world. God alone can judge the world, but that judgment will be exercised by Christ on the last day. Implicit in the claim is that judgment will not in the end concern conduct alone, but will also include matters of the heart, conscience, and thoughts about the right and wrong that one has done.

BIBLIOGRAPHY

Abegg, Martin G., Jr. "Paul and James on the Law in Light of the Dead Sea Scrolls." In *Christian Beginnings and the Dead Sea Scrolls,* 63–74. Acadia Studies in Bible and Theology. Grand Rapids: Baker Book House, 2006.

113. Cf. Gerd Lüdemann, "συνείδησις," *EDNT* 3:302.
114. Quoted from the translation of R. B. Wright, *OTP* 2:667. Wright places the *Pss. Sol.* in the first century B.C. (pp. 640-41). That these psalms are of Pharisaic origin is affirmed by L. Rost, *Jewish Literature outside the Hebrew Canon,* 119, and G. Nickelsburg, *Jewish Literature between the Bible and the Mishnah,* 203-4. Wright is less certain.

————. "Paul, 'Works of the Law' and MMT." *BAR* 20 (1994): 52-55, 82.

Aletti, Jean-Noël. *Israël et la loi dans la lettre aux Romains*. LD 173. Paris: Cerf, 1998.

————. "Rm. 1,18–3,20: Incohérence ou cohérence de l'argumentation paulinienne?" *Bib* 69 (1988): 47-62.

————. "Romains 2: Sa cohérence et sa fonction." *Bib* 77 (1996): 153-77.

Barclay, John M. G. "Paul and the Law: Observations on Some Recent Debates." *Themelios* 12 (1986-87): 5-15.

Barton, Stephen C. "'All Things to All People': Paul and the Law in the Light of I Corinthians 9.19-23." In *Paul and the Mosaic Law*, 271-85. Ed. James D. G. Dunn. WUNT 89. Tübingen: J. C. B. Mohr (Paul Siebeck), 1996.

Bassler, Jouette M. *Divine Impartiality: Paul and a Theological Axiom*. SBLDS 59. Chico: Scholars Press, 1982.

————. "Divine Impartiality in Paul's Letter to the Romans." *NovT* 26/1 (1984): 43-58.

Bergmeier, Roland. *Das Gesetz im Römerbrief und andere Studien zum Neuen Testament*. WUNT 121. Tübingen: J. C. B. Mohr (Paul Siebeck), 2000.

————. "Gesetzeserfüllung ohne Gesetz und Beschneidung." In *Das Gesetz im frühen Judentum und im Neuen Testament: Festschrift für Christoph Burchard zum 75. Geburtstag*, 26-40. Ed. Dieter Sänger and Matthias Konradt. NTOA 57. Göttingen: Vandenhoeck & Ruprecht, 2006.

Bockmuehl, Markus. *Jewish Law in Gentile Churches: Halakhah and the Beginning of Christian Public Ethics*. Edinburgh: T&T Clark, 2000.

Boers, Hendrikus. "We Who Are by Inheritance Jews: Not from the Gentiles, Sinners." *JBL* 111/1 (1992): 273-81.

Bornkamm, Günther. "Gesetz und Natur, Röm 2,14-16." In his *Studien zu antike und Urchristentum: Gesammelte Aufsätze II*, 93-118. BEvT 28. Munich: Kaiser Verlag, 1959.

Bosman, Philip. *Conscience in Philo and Paul: A Conceptual History of the* Synoida *Word Group*. WUNT 2/166. Tübingen: Mohr Siebeck, 2003.

Bultmann, Rudolf. "Glossen im Römerbrief." *TZ* 72 (1947): 197-202.

Byrne, Brendan. "The Problem of Νόμος and the Relationship with Judaism in Romans." *CBQ* 62 (2000): 294-309.

Cambier, Jules-M. "Le jugement des tous les hommes par Dieu seul, selon la vérité dans Rom 2:1–3:20." *ZNW* 67 (1976): 187-213.

Carras, George P. "Romans 2,1-29: A Dialogue on Jewish Ideals." *Bib* 73 (1992): 183-207.

Cosgrove, Charles H. "Justification in Paul: A Linguistic and Theological Reflection." *JBL* 106 (1987): 653-70.

Cranfield, C. E. B. "Has the Old Testament Law a Place in the Christian Life? A Response to Professor Westerholm." *IBS* 15 (1993): 50-64; reprinted in his *On Romans and Other New Testament Essays*, 109-24. Edinburgh: T&T Clark, 1998.

————. "St. Paul and the Law." *SJT* 17 (1964): 43-68; reprinted in *New Testament Issues*, 148-72. Ed. Richard A. Batey. New York: Harper & Row, 1970.

————. "The Works of the Law in the Epistle to the Romans." *JSNT* 43 (1991): 89-101; reprinted in his *On Romans and Other New Testament Essays*, 1-14. Edinburgh: T&T Clark, 1998.

Dewey, Arthur J. *Spirit and Letter in Paul*. SBEC 33. Lewiston: Edwin Mellen Press, 1996.

Dodd, C. H. "Natural Law in the New Testament." In his *New Testament Studies*, 129-42. Manchester: Manchester University Press, 1953.

Donaldson, Terence L. *Paul and the Gentiles: Remapping the Apostle's Convictional World*. Minneapolis: Fortress Press, 1997.

Dunn, James D. G. "Was Paul against the Law? The Law in Galatians and Romans: A Test-Case of Text in Context." In *Texts and Contexts: Biblical Texts in Their Textual and Situational Contexts: Essays in Honor of Lars Hartman*, 455-75. Ed. Tord Fornberg and David Hellholm. Oslo: Scandinavian University Press, 1995.

—————. "What Was the Issue between Paul and 'Those of the Circumcision'?" In *Paulus und das antike Judentum*, 295-317. Ed. Martin Hengel and Ulrich Heckel. Tübingen: J. C. B. Mohr (Paul Siebeck), 1991.

—————. "Yet Once More — 'Works of the Law': A Response." *JSNT* 46 (1992): 99-117.

—————. "4QMMT and Galatians." *NTS* 43 (1997): 147-53.

Du Toit, Andreas B. "Forensic Metaphors in Romans and Their Soteriological Significance." In *Salvation in the New Testament: Perspectives on Soteriology*, 213-46. Ed. Jan G. van der Watt. NovTSup 121. Boston: E. J. Brill, 2005.

Eckstein, Hans-Joachim. *Der Begriff* Syneidesis *bei Paulus*. WUNT 2/10. Tübingen: J. C. B. Mohr (Paul Siebeck), 1983.

—————. *Verheissung und Gesetz*. WUNT 86. Tübingen: J. C. B. Mohr (Paul Siebeck), 1996.

Elliott, Neil. *The Rhetoric of Romans: Argumentative Constraint and Strategy and Paul's Dialogue with Judaism*. JSNTSup 45. Sheffield: JSOT Press, 1990; reprinted, Minneapolis: Fortress Press, 2006.

Engberg-Pedersen, Troels. *Paul and the Stoics*. Louisville: Westminster John Knox Press, 2000.

Frid, Bo. "How Does Romans 2.1 Connect to 1.18-32?" *SEÅ* 71 (2006): 109-30.

Gaston, Lloyd. "Works of Law as a Subjective Genitive." *SR* 13 (1984): 39-46.

Gathercole, Simon J. "A Law unto Themselves: The Gentiles in Romans 2.14-15 Revisited." *JSNT* 85 (2002): 27-49.

—————. *Where Is Boasting? Early Jewish Soteriology and Paul's Response in Romans 1-5*. Grand Rapids: Wm. B. Eerdmans, 2002.

Grelot, Pierre. "Les oeuvres de la Loi (A propos de 4Q394-398)." *RevQ* 16 (1994): 441-48.

Grobel, Kendrick. "A Chiastic Retribution-Formula in Romans 2." In *Zeit und Geschichte: Dankesgabe an Rudolf Bultmann zum 80. Geburtstag*, 255-61. Ed. Erich Dinkler. Tübingen: J. C. B. Mohr (Paul Siebeck), 1964.

Haacker, Klaus. "Der 'Antinomianism' des Paulus im Kontext antiker Gesetzestheorie." In *Geschichte — Tradition — Reflexion: Martin Hengel zum 70. Geburtstag*, 3:387-404. Ed. Hubert Cancil, Hermann Lichtenberger, and Peter Schäfer. 3 vols. Tübingen: J. C. B. Mohr (Paul Siebeck), 1996.

—————. "Exegetische Probleme des Römerbriefs." *NovT* 20 (1978):1-21.

Hübner, Hans. *Law in Paul's Thought*. Edinburgh: T&T Clark, 1984.

Ito, Akio. "Romans 2: A Deuteronomistic Reading." *JSNT* 59 (1995): 21-37.

Jackson, Bernard S. "The Concept of Religious Law in Judaism." *ANRW* II.19.1 (1979): 33-52.

Jeremias, Joachim. "Chiasmus in den Paulusbriefen." In his *Abba: Studien zur neutestamentlichen Theologie und Zeitgeschichte*, 276-90. Göttingen: Vandenhoeck & Ruprecht, 1966.

Jewett, Robert, "Conscience." *IDBSup* 173-74.

Jolivet, Ira J., Jr. "An Argument from the Letter and Intent of the Law as the Primary Argumentative Strategy in Romans." In *The Rhetorical Analysis of Scripture: Essays from the 1995 London Conference*, 309-34. Ed. Stanley E. Porter and Thomas H. Olbricht. JSNTSup 146. Sheffield: Sheffield Academic Press, 1997.

Kuhr, Friedrich. "Römer 2.14f. und die Verheissung bei Jeremia 31.31ff." *ZNW* 55 (1964): 243-61.

Lamp, Jeffrey S. "Paul, the Law, Jews, and Gentiles: A Contextual and Exegetical Reading of Romans 2:12-16." *JETS* 42 (1999): 37-51.

Lincoln, Andrew T. "From Wrath to Justification: Tradition, Gospel, and Audience in the Theology of Romans 1:18–4:25." In *Pauline Theology*, vol. 3, *Romans*, 130-59. Ed. David M. Hay and E. Elizabeth Johnson. Minneapolis: Fortress Press, 1995.

Longenecker, Bruce W. "Lifelines: Perspectives on Paul and the Law." *Anvil* 16 (1999): 125-30.

Maertens, Philip. "Une étude de Rm 2.12-16." *NTS* 46 (2000): 504-19.

Malherbe, Abraham. "Hellenistic Moralists and the New Testament." *ANRW* II.26.1 (1992): 267-333.

Marcus, Joel. "'Under the Law': The Background of a Pauline Expression." *CBQ* 63 (2001): 72-83.

Marmorstein, Arthur. *The Doctrine of Merits in the Old Rabbinical Literature*. New York: Ktav Publishing Company, 1968.

Martens, John W. "Romans 2:14-16: A Stoic Reading." *NTS* 40 (1994): 55-67.

Mattern, Lieselotte. *Das Verständnis des Gerichtes bei Paulus*. ATANT 47. Zürich: Zwingli Verlag, 1966.

McKenzie, John L. "Natural Law in the New Testament." *BR* 9 (1964): 1-13.

Moo, Douglas J. "Paul and the Law in the Last Ten Years." *SJT* 49 (1987): 287-307.

———. "Romans 2: Saved apart from the Gospel?" In *Through No Fault of Their Own? The Fate of Those Who Never Heard*, 137-45. Ed. William V. Crockett and James G. Sigountos. Grand Rapids: Baker Book House, 1991.

Müller, Karlheinz. "Gibt es ein Judentum hinter den Juden? Ein Nachtrag zu Ed Parish Sanders' Theorie vom 'Covenantal Nomism.'" In *Das Urchristentum in seiner literarischen Geschichte: Festschrift für Jürgen Becker zum 65. Geburtstag*, 473-86. Ed. Ulrich Mell and Ulrich B. Müller. BZNW 100. Berlin: Walter de Gruyter, 1999.

Nickelsburg, George W. E. *Jewish Literature between the Bible and the Mishnah*. Philadelphia: Fortress Press, 1981.

Ortlund, Dane. "Justified by Faith, Judged according to Works: Another Look at a Pauline Paradox." *JETS* 52 (2009): 323-39.

Pierce, Claude A. *Conscience in the New Testament: A Study of* Syneidesis *in the New Testament*. SBT 15. London: SCM Press, 1955.

Porter, Calvin L. "God's Justice and the Culture of the Law: Conflicting Traditions in Paul's Letter to the Romans." *Encounter* 59 (1998): 135-55.

Rad, Gerhard von. "The Origin of the Concept of the Day of Yahweh." *JSS* 4 (1959): 97-108.

Räisänen, Heikki. *Jesus, Paul, and Torah: Collected Essays.* JSNTSup 43. Sheffield: JSOT Press, 1992.

————. *Paul and the Law.* Philadelphia: Fortress Press, 1983.

Reicke, Bo. "Natürliche Theologie bei Paulus." *SEÅ* 22-23 (1957-58): 154-67.

————. "*Syneidēsis* in Röm. 2,15." *TZ* 12 (1956): 157-61.

Rhyne, C. Thomas. *Faith Establishes the Law.* SBLDS 55. Chico: Scholars Press, 1981.

Rost, Leonhard. *Jewish Literature outside the Hebrew Canon: An Introduction to the Documents.* Nashville: Abingdon Press, 1976.

Sandberg, Ruth N. *Development and Continuity in Jewish Law.* Lanham: University Press of America, 2002.

Sanders, E. P. *Paul, the Law, and the Jewish People.* Philadelphia: Fortress Press, 1983.

Schnabel, Eckhard J. *Law in Wisdom from Ben Sira to Paul.* WUNT 2/16. Tübingen: J. C. B. Mohr (Paul Siebeck), 1985.

Schreiner, Thomas R. "Did Paul Believe in Justification by Works? Another Look at Romans 2." *BBR* 3 (1993): 131-55.

————. *The Law and Its Fulfillment: A Pauline Theology of Law.* Grand Rapids: Baker Book House, 1993.

Seifrid, Mark A. "Natural Revelation and the Purpose of the Law in Romans." *TynB* 49 (1998): 115-29.

Snodgrass, Klyne R. "Justification by Grace — to the Doers: An Analysis of the Place of Romans 2 in the Theology of Paul." *NTS* 32 (1986): 72-93.

Starnitzke, Dierk. *Die Struktur paulinischen Denkens im Römerbrief: Eine linguistische-logische Untersuchung.* BWANT 8/3. Stuttgart: W. Kohlhammer, 2004.

Stendahl, Krister. "Justification and the Last Judgment." *LW* 8 (1961): 1-7.

Stowers, Stanley K. *The Diatribe and Paul's Letter to the Romans.* SBLDS 57. Chico: Scholars Press, 1981.

————. *A Rereading of Romans: Justice, Jews, and Gentiles.* New Haven: Yale University Press, 1994.

Stuhlmacher, Peter. "The Law as a Topic in Biblical Theology." In his *Reconciliation, Law, and Righteousness: Essays in Biblical Theology,* 110-33. Philadelphia: Fortress Press, 1986.

————. "Paul's Understanding of the Law in the Letter to the Romans." *SEÅ* 50 (1985): 87-104.

Thorsteinsson, Runar M. *Paul's Interlocutor in Romans 2: Function and Identity in the Context of Ancient Epistolography.* ConBNT 40. Stockholm: Almqvist & Wiksell, 2003.

Thrall, Margaret. "The Pauline Use of *Syneidēsis.*" *NTS* 14 (1967-68): 118-25.

Tomson, Peter J. *Paul and the Jewish Law: Halakha in the Letters of the Apostle to the Gentiles.* CRINT 3:1. Minneapolis: Fortress Press, 1990.

Walker, Rolf. "Die Heiden und das Gericht: Zur Auslegung von Röm 2:12-16." *EvT* 29 (1960): 302-14.

Watson, Nigel M. "Justified by Faith; Judged by Works — An Antinomy?" *NTS* 29 (1983): 209-21.

Westerholm, Stephen. *Perspectives Old and New on Paul: The "Lutheran" Paul and His Critics.* Grand Rapids: Wm. B. Eerdmans, 2004.

———. "Torah, *Nomos,* and Law." In *Law in Religious Communities in the Roman Period: The Debate over Torah and Nomos in Postbiblical Judaism and Early Christianity,* 45-56. Ed. Peter Richardson, Stephen Westerholm, et al. Waterloo: Wilfrid Laurier University Press, 1991.

Winger, Michael. "Meaning and Law." *JBL* 117 (1998): 105-10.

Winninge, Mikael. *Sinners and the Righteous: A Comparative Study of the Psalms of Solomon and Paul's Letters.* ConBNT 26. Stockholm: Almqvist & Wiksell, 1995.

Winter, Michael. "The Law of Christ." *NTS* 46 (2000): 537-46.

Wischmeyer, Oda. "Römer 2.1-24 als Teil der Gerichtsrede des Paulus gegen die Menschheit." *NTS* 52 (2006): 356-76.

Wright, N. T. "4QMMT and Paul: Justification, 'Works,' and Eschatology." In *History and Exegesis: New Testament Essays in Honor of Dr. E. Earle Ellis,* 104-32. Ed. Sang-Won (Aaron) Son. Edinburgh: T&T Clark, 2006.

———. "The Law in Romans 2." In *Paul and the Mosaic Law,* 131-50. Ed. James D. G. Dunn. Grand Rapids: Wm. B. Eerdmans, 2001.

Yinger, Kent L. *Paul, Judaism and Judgment according to Deeds.* SNTSMS 105. Cambridge: Cambridge University Press, 1999.

Zeller, Dieter. "Der Zusammenhang von Gesetz und Sünde im Römerbrief: Kritischer Nachvollzug der Auslegung von Ulrich Wilckens." *TZ* 38 (1982): 193-212.

2.3. Boasting in the Law Is Excluded, 2:17-29

17*But if you call yourself a Jew and rely upon the law and boast of your relationship to God* 18*and know his will and discern what is of importance, because you are instructed from the law,* 19*and if you are convinced that you are a guide to the blind, a light to those in darkness,* 20*an instructor of those lacking knowledge, a teacher of children, having in the law the correct formulation of knowledge and truth,* 21*you then who teach others, do you not teach yourself? You who preach against stealing, do you steal?* 22*You who say that one must not commit adultery, do you commit adultery? You who despise idols, do you rob temples?* 23*You who boast in the law dishonor God by transgressing the law!* 24*"For the name of God is blasphemed among the nations because of you," just as it is written.*

25*Circumcision indeed is of value if you observe the law; but if you are a transgressor of the law, your circumcision has become uncircumcision.* 26*So, if a man who is uncircumcised keeps the requirements of the law, will not his uncircumcision be regarded as circumcision?* 27*And the uncircumcised man who keeps the law will condemn you who has the written code and circumcision as a transgressor of the law.* 28*For a person is not a Jew who is one outwardly, nor is circumcision something external in the flesh.* 29*But one is a Jew who is one inwardly,* *and circumcision is a matter of the heart, spiritual not literal, whose praise is not from people but from God.*

Notes on the Text and Translation

2:17 The term Ἰουδαῖος is translated here as "Jew," although some interpreters suggest that it be translated as "Judean."[115] But the term does not refer simply to a resident or former resident of Judea, as is evident in the present passage (as well as in many others). Nor is it pejorative (as contemporary examples of self-identification attest). It is a term, for Paul, that refers to persons who claim beliefs and ways of life that stem from Israel's Mosaic and prophetic tradition. Cf. especially Romans 3:1; 10:12; and Galatians 2:14.

2:20 The Greek word ἄφρων is usually translated "foolish" (KJV, ASV, RSV, NIV, and NRSV). But here, as in 1:14, that can be misleading. Foolish persons lack sound judgment. But in context here, the term refers to persons who lack knowledge and have to be taught.[116] The term is translated then as "those lacking knowledge."

2:23 The verse is sometimes written out as a question (as in KJV, ASV, RSV, NIV, and NRSV), but it should be written as an indicative statement (as in NEB, ESV, and NJB),[117] making a charge, which the scriptural quotation following in 2:24 proves.

General Comment

At 2:17 Paul makes a rhetorical turn. He now indicts the Jewish person who knows the law, claiming thereby to know the will of God, and who ostensibly has all that is needed to teach others about it.[118] That person has "in the law the

---

115. BDAG 478-79 (Ἰουδαῖος); P. Esler, *Romans*, 62-74.

116. LN 1:387 offer this as a possibility but actually prefer "foolish."

117. The view that it is an indicative statement is expressed also by various interpreters, including W. Sanday and A. Headlam, *Romans*, 66; C. K. Barrett, *Romans*, 54; H. Schlier, *Römer*, 86; C. Cranfield, *Romans*, 170; J. Dunn, *Romans*, 113; J. Fitzmyer, *Romans*, 318; D. Moo, *Romans*, 165. The interrogative form is favored by R. Jewett, *Romans*, 229.

118. Contra R. Thorsteinsson, *Paul's Interlocutor in Romans 2*, 163, 196-211, who claims that Paul continues his indictment of Gentiles throughout Rom 2, speaking of persons of Gentile origin who want to call themselves Jews. Thorsteinsson's insistence that all of Romans was directed to Gentile readers only, even if correct, would not preclude a rhetorical indictment of stock Jewish caricatures to make his point that, in the eyes of God, all stand on an equal footing; and ultimately all fail to do the will of God. That Paul's imaginary opponent is the Jewish teacher of the law is the dominant view among interpreters, e.g., J. Fitzmyer, *Romans*, 315; B. Byrne, *Romans*, 96; T. Berkley, *From a Broken Covenant to Circumcision of the Heart*, 116.

correct formulation of knowledge and truth," a claim that Paul does not deny. But he goes on to ask in a series of questions whether such a person actually observes the law of Moses himself, implying that he does not truly keep it (cf. 2:3). Even Scripture (Isa 52:5) shows that to be true. Consequently such a person can hardly claim superiority to Gentiles.

Paul also raises the issue whether those who are ritually circumcised but do not obey the law remain in a special, favored relationship with God. He charges that their circumcision is, in effect, void, thereby questioning the favored status of the Jew and even the security of belonging to the covenant between God and Israel (to which he will return in chapters 9–11). He goes even further by saying that those persons who are not circumcised, but who keep the essential requirements of the law, can be regarded just as favorably by God as those who are circumcised. In a manner that is absolutely breathtaking, Paul says that such persons actually represent the spirit of the Jewish tradition and the spiritual significance of circumcision: "For a person is not a Jew who is one outwardly, nor is circumcision something external in the flesh. But one is a Jew who is one inwardly, and circumcision is a matter of the heart, spiritual not literal" (2:28-29).

Detailed Comment

2:17 The features of the diatribe appear again, and the imaginary opponent is now the Jewish person ('Ιουδαῖος) explicitly. Two features of the diatribe in particular stand out: (1) the imaginary opponent is addressed, and (2) the second person singular is used.[119] Paul goes on to speak of relying on the law and (literally) boasting in God (or in one's relationship to God); later, at 2:23, he speaks of boasting in the law. The verb "to rely on" (ἐπαναπαύομαι) can have the sense of finding rest, comfort, or support,[120] and to find such in the law of Moses would be normal for Jewish piety. According to tradition, the law is a delight, and in it one finds strength (Deut 4:5-8; Pss 1:2-3; 119:97, 165; Sir 2:16; 33:3).[121] Here, however, Paul is setting up a rhetorical trap,[122] portraying a person who can be toppled in the final judgment. He strengthens that point by adding the verb "to boast" (καυχάομαι) in regard to one's relationship to God.

---

119. J. Bailey and L. Vander Broek, "Diatribe," 38-39; D. Aune, "The Greco-Roman Diatribe" and "Romans," 200, 219.

120. BDAG 358 (ἐπαναπαύομαι).

121. On the extolling of the law in other Jewish texts, see 4 Macc 5:14-38; Philo, *Legat.* 1.210; 2 *Apoc. Bar.* 48.22-24.

122. W. Loader, "Paul and Judaism," 11-20: Paul paints a caricature of a Jew in this section of Romans.

For Paul, boasting can have a positive connotation when it is truly boasting in God or God's work (Rom 15:17; cf. Pss 44:8; 106:47 [LXX 43:9; 105:46]; Jer 9:23-24), and even in the present context it appears to have that connotation, since Paul writes, literally, about boasting "in God" (καυχᾶσαι ἐν θεῷ). The turn of phrase is undoubtedly intended. For the present moment the statement is complimentary, and it is only as the sentences go on that the reader catches on to realize that Paul is building a case, an indictment. Then it becomes clear that the boasting spoken of is a boasting of one's relationship to God, which is actually a boasting about the self. And in that case, as elsewhere in Paul's letters, whenever boasting refers to self-confidence in one's standing before God on the basis of a presumed righteousness under the law, it has a negative meaning (Rom 3:27; 4:2; 1 Cor 1:29; 4:7).[123] The verse begins a long conditional sentence which extends from 2:17 through 2:21a.

2:18-20 Continuing the paradosis of his interrogative sentence, Paul sets forth a series of phrases having to do precisely with those matters in which a Jew with knowledge of, and devotion to, the law can be expected to excel. Such a person should be able to know God's will, since it is revealed in the Torah (Pss 19:7; 119:1; Jer 5:5; Sir 17:11; 45:5; cf. Hos 4:6), and be able to discern "what is of importance," i.e., "the things that really matter."[124] Being a "guide to the blind" (the opposite of being a "blind guide," as at Matt 15:14; 23:16, 24; cf. Luke 6:39) is an attribute of God himself (Isa 42:16), and it is a role to be played by the nation as a whole (Isa 42:6-7).[125] Likewise, the vocation of being a light to the nations belongs peculiarly to Israel (Isa 42:6, 16; 49:6; 51:4; Wis 18:4), and to no other nation on the earth. Here that vocation is accredited to the individual who is schooled in the Torah. The phrase "instructor of those lacking knowledge" contributes to a crescendo of flattery concerning the person confident of a proper and righteous standing before God on the basis of the law. And being "a teacher of children" implies that such a person enjoys tremendous trust from others, but it also implies carrying out a duty as a faithful Israelite (Deut 4:10; 11:19; Ps 78:5 [LXX 77:5]). All these attributes are possible because of one's confidence that one has in the Torah the "correct formulation of knowledge and truth." The correct formulation is presumably at hand for the person who is devoted to the Torah, and to possess that formulation is all-sufficient as a guide for a life that is fulfilling and honorable. The Greek word μόρφωσις ("correct formulation") is often translated as "embodiment" (RSV, NIV, and NRSV), implying that the Torah is a de-

---

123. An extensive discussion is provided by S. Gathercole, *Where Is Boasting?* 197-215.

124. BDAG 239 (διαφέρω, 4, citing Rom 2:18). The translation "determine what is best" (NRSV) can be misleading, for the person described would not be able to "determine" in the sense of deciding and declaring, but would only claim to know what is right, as revealed in the Torah.

125. For other ancient texts expressing this view, see *Sib. Or.* 3.195; *1 Enoch* 105.1.

posit of knowledge and truth. As much as that might be so, nevertheless the Greek term has to do as much with form as it does with sheer corporality.[126] Therefore "correct formulation" is more accurate. The Torah has knowledge and truth in codified form, and to study it in all its intricacies is the way of knowing both divine and human matters (4 Macc 1:17; cf. Sir 39:1; Ps 119; Bar 4:1-4).

2:21-23 Now comes the apodosis of the interrogative sentence, which is made up of a series of questions, beginning with a general one: "Do you not teach yourself?" With the question comes an implied judgment. Surely, if a person knows the will of God by means of the law and, moreover, can boast of having a special relationship with God, such a person can be expected to live a life that is above reproach and free of transgressions in every way. But the questions that follow can be compared to a searchlight that reveals things hidden in the darkness of night. Paul recalls three commandments in the Decalogue, i.e., the commandments against stealing (Exod 20:15), adultery (20:14), and making graven images (20:4). In the latter case, the issue is not actually the making of idols, but taking ready-made idols from pagan worship sites and possessing them, as though they have some religious value,[127] which is also prohibited in the Torah (Deut 7:25). Even though the law of God is clear, Paul implies that those who rely upon it for righteousness, and who accuse others of sinful behavior in light of the law, are themselves guilty of transgressing it, and he sums up his case by his declaration in 2:23: "You who boast in the law dishonor God by transgressing the law!"[128] The implication is that righteousness by observing the law is impossible. The corollary is that boasting in the law as a way of life is futile, for the law is transgressed continually even by those persons who boast in it as their own faithful and right guide for living.

2:24 Implicitly Paul insists that what he says is not a matter of personal opinion. He cites Isaiah 52:5 to show that the Scriptures themselves testify against Israel. His wording is slightly different from the LXX reading, as shown here:

---

126. Cf. BDAG 660 (μόρφωσις): "the state of being formally structured, embodiment, formulation, form."

127. The verb ἱεροσυλέω can have the more general sense "to commit sacrilege," but in this passage Paul seems to be referring more specifically to matters related to Jewish law, "to rob temples." The same trio of offenses (stealing, committing adultery, and robbing temples) is spoken of by Philo, *Conf.* 163. Josephus, *Ant.* 4.207, includes an admonition against robbing foreign temples (συλᾶν ἱερὰ ξενικά). D. Garlington, "ʹΙΕΡΟΣΥΛΕΙΝ and the Idolatry of Israel (Romans 2:22)," 148, maintains that Paul refers here to "Israel's idolatrous attachment to the law" and that the Torah is "the new idol." But that is not persuasive within this context of Romans, listing public offenses.

128. Some modern versions (RSV, NIV, and NRSV) render 2:23 as a question, but it is better to let it stand as a statement (as in NET and ESV); cf. W. Sanday and A. Headlam, *Romans*, 66; C. Cranfield, *Romans*, 170; J. Dunn, *Romans*, 108, 115; J. Fitzmyer, *Romans*, 318; B. Byrne, *Romans*, 95. R. Jewett, *Romans*, 229, considers it a question.

LXX Isa 52:5: δι᾽ ὑμᾶς διὰ παντὸς τὸ ὄνομά μου βλασφημεῖται ἐν τοῖς ἔθνεσιν. ("Because of you my name is continually blasphemed among the nations.")

Rom 2:24: τὸ γὰρ ὄνομα τοῦ θεοῦ δι᾽ ὑμᾶς βλασφημεῖται ἐν τοῖς ἔθνεσιν, καθὼς γέγραπται. ("For the name of God is blasphemed among the nations because of you.")

Paul's wording differs from the LXX in four ways: (1) the addition of the conjunction γάρ ("for"); (2) the necessary substitution of τοῦ θεοῦ ("of God") for μου ("my"); (3) the moving of the phrase δι᾽ ὑμᾶς ("because of you") so that it comes after τοῦ θεοῦ ("of God"); and (4) the lack of διὰ παντός ("continually"). The effect is to make a statement that is even more emphatic than what the LXX has in two major ways: (1) the conjunction γάρ ("for") functions to introduce a conclusion, based on scriptural proof;[129] and (2) the clause "because of you" is placed between "the name of God" and "is blasphemed," a construction that can be expressed well in Greek but cannot translate well into English.

The passage in Isaiah spoke originally to the blaspheming of the name of God by the oppressors of the Israelites, and the phrase δι᾽ ὑμᾶς ("because of you" in our translation) could have been understood in the sense of "because of your misfortune." But Paul uses the verse to witness to God's case against Israel. This is a case where there is a "stunning misreading of the text" of Isaiah,[130] or else it is a case where Paul quotes a text from memory, unaware of its context at the moment, and adapting it for his purpose at this point in his letter. Paul uses the OT passage to prove his point that those who "boast in the law" (ἐν νόμῳ καυχᾶσαι) actually dishonor God by breaking the law. In fact, the dishonoring is "among the Gentiles," which is a level of shame that is despicable. How can the Gentiles ever honor God if God's own people do not, and if they even blaspheme God's name?

2:25-29 The rite of circumcision and Torah observance go together as essential to Jewish identity and life. The rite of circumcision is commanded in the Torah (Gen 17:9-14) of every Jewish male, and it has remained as a requirement for those born of Jewish parents and, except in extreme cases,[131] for proselytes

---

129. T. Berkley, *From a Broken Covenant to Circumcision of the Heart*, 137.

130. R. Hays, *Echoes of Scripture in the Letters of Paul*, 45: It is a "stunning misreading" because in Isaiah the passage is part of Yahweh's reassurance of Israel's in exile. Paul transfers it into a word of reproach.

131. There is the famous case of the conversion of Izates, Prince of Adiabene, mentioned by Josephus, *Ant.* 20.17-48. Although he was finally circumcised, his teacher Ananias had told him that he could worship God and observe all the other laws without being circumcised. For a survey of texts that illustrate exceptions for proselytes, cf. N. McEleney, "Conversion, Circumcision and the Law," 319-41; F. Watson, *Paul, Judaism, and the Gentiles*, 74-79. For a response to McEleney, cf. J. Nolland, "Uncircumcised Proselytes?" 1173-94.

entering into the covenant people.[132] The circumcised person takes up the Torah as a way of life that has been described as "covenantal nomism."[133] One is thereby obliged to live a life of Torah observance as a matter of Jewish identity. (For more on the concept of "covenantal nomism" and critique, see the exegesis of 3:28.) To keep "the requirements of the law" (τὰ δικαιώματα τοῦ νόμου) is the ideal of the life of the Jew, and the obligation of the Jew is to keep all of its commands (Lev 18:5; 25:18; Deut 12:1; 30:15-16; Gal 5:3), even though that does not imply perfect fulfillment of it in every respect. The Jew knows that God remains ever faithful and merciful even when a person falls short of fulfilling the law (Pss 25:18; 65:3; 79:9; 130:4; Jer 31:34; Wis 15:1-2). Nevertheless, for Paul, going down that road as a way of life leads to false security. He argues that circumcision is "a matter of the heart," not the flesh, "spiritual and not literal" (Rom 2:29).[134] Indeed, he argues on another occasion (but not here) that believers in the Christian gospel are the true circumcision: "For it is we who are the circumcision, who worship in the Spirit of God and boast in Christ Jesus and have no confidence in the flesh" (Phil 3:3). The statement that Gentiles who keep the law "will condemn" (κρινεῖ) those who possess the "written code" (γράμμα, the Torah, as also at 7:6; 2 Cor 3:6) and practice circumcision is not to be taken as a doctrinal aspect of the final judgment, but as a hyperbolic figure of speech within a diatribe to disclose the folly of confidence in one's status before God on the basis of possessing the Torah and having been circumcised.

Paul is not the first to speak of the circumcision of the heart, for the imagery is rooted in both the law and the prophets (Lev 26:41; Deut 10:16; 30:6; Jer 4:4; 9:26; Ezek 44:7, 9).[135] But there is a difference. The prophets could say that circumcision is a matter of the heart while preaching *within* the Israelite community (the community of the circumcised). They made the point that the true identity of the people of God is moral — *as well as* physical. But Paul maintains that circumcision is a matter of the heart while referring to persons *outside*, as well as within, the Jewish community: "For a person is not a Jew who is one outwardly, nor is circumcision something external in the flesh. But one is a Jew

132. For texts on the importance of circumcision in ancient Judaism, see (in addition to Gen 17:9-14) 1 Macc 2:45-46; *Jub.* 15.25-28; Philo, *Spec. Leg.* 1.1.1–2.11; *Migr.* 89–93. On its importance in subsequent history, including references to Jewish literature, see Cecil Roth, "Circumcision," *EncJud* 5:567-75. The circumcision of proselytes is mentioned in Jdt 14:10; Esth 8:17.

133. E. Sanders, *Paul and Palestinian Judaism*, 75.

134. Although Philo could speak of circumcision in allegorical ways and of its spiritual importance, he does not go as far as Paul toward dispensing with it. On this, cf. J. Barclay, "Paul and Philo on Circumcision," 536-56.

135. The circumcision of the heart is also referred to in Philo, *Spec. Leg.* 1.66.305; *Migr.* 16.92; *Jub.* 1:23; 1QS 5.5; 1QpHab 11.13; 4Q504.4.3.11. Similarly in 1QH 18.20 there is reference to circumcision of the ear, and in 1QS 5.6-7 the circumcision to be performed is of the evil inclination. Biblical passages speak also of uncircumcised lips (Exod 6:12, 30) and ears (Jer 6:10).

who is one inwardly, and circumcision is a matter of the heart, spiritual not literal, whose praise is not from people but from God" (2:28-29; cf. Phil 3:3).[136] The question of who is truly a Jew (among those who claim to be such) can be debated, and has been debated, *within* the Jewish community, just as the question of who is truly a Christian or Muslim can be, has been, and continues to be debated among persons within those communities. But for Paul to assert that Gentiles who are moral ("keep the requirements of the law," 2:26) are, in effect, Jews goes beyond the bounds of what is legally and otherwise permitted within Judaism, for it is to disregard the historic boundary markers existing within Jewish law, tradition, and identity.

The implicit basis for Paul's making such an assertion — and its explicit result — is to create a level playing field for both Jews and Gentiles in the overall redemptive work of God in Christ. Neither Torah observance for the Jew nor claims of moral superiority by the enlightened Hellenized Gentile count before God when justification is being considered. On the one hand, all are sinful; on the other, persons in both categories do good works. But finally, it is God who justifies all on the basis of his redemptive work in Christ for all the world. Wherever the gospel of God's redemptive work in Christ is heard and believed, there is justification, newness of life, and salvation. That is true for both Jew and Gentile. In order for Paul to say that, in the final analysis, in Christ "there is neither Jew nor Greek" (Gal 3:28), he has to argue that, even apart from and prior to Christian faith, there may well be advantages in being Jewish, but there are no privileges.

All of this is disastrous for a theology of election and covenant, in which it is affirmed that God has chosen and made an abiding covenant with a particular people that is permanent until the end of time — and, according to some within the Jewish tradition, even beyond history in the world to come.[137] If God is now incorporating Gentiles along with Jews into the one people of God, and doing so without placing upon them the traditional requirements that were expected of proselytes, God's election and covenant with Israel amount to noth-

---

136. That Paul actually alludes here to the "Christian Gentile . . . rejoicing in the gift of the eschatological Spirit" (J. Dunn, *Romans,* 125), to a circumcision that "springs from the Spirit of Christ" (J. Fitzmyer, *Romans,* 323), or "to Christians" (D. Moo, *Romans,* 175) is doubtful. The diatribe is against the self-confidence of those who are physically circumcised but do not practice its implications. Paul is not making a case in this place for a "spiritual circumcision" per se that can be identified with Christian faith, as he implies in Phil 3:3. The writer of *Odes Sol.* 11.2 writes of God as having circumcised him by the Holy Spirit.

137. This would be implied in the case of those teachers and sages who contended that the Torah would abide in the "age to come," which was not the teaching of others, who held that the Torah is for the present age only. On this, cf. W. D. Davies, *Torah in the Messianic Age and/or the Age to Come,* 50-83.

ing. That is not the end of the discussion of election and covenant, however, for Paul returns to it in 9:1–11:36 and rescues the concepts of election and covenant on the basis of God's grace. But for the time being, in this portion of the letter, the point has been made that Gentiles are equally capable of having a positive standing before God. Such a person is worthy of praise (ἔπαινος) or approval from God. That is a backhand way of saying, consequently, that boasting in the law and circumcision, as though they are inherently and sufficiently grounds for salvation by themselves, are excluded.

BIBLIOGRAPHY

Aune, David E. "The Greco-Roman Diatribe" and "Romans." In his *The New Testament in Its Literary Environment,* 200-202, 219-21. Louisville: Westminster/John Knox Press, 1987.

Bailey, James L., and Lyle D. Vander Broek. "Diatribe." In their *Literary Forms in the New Testament: A Handbook,* 38-42. Louisville: Westminster/John Knox Press, 1992.

Barclay, John M. G. "Paul and Philo on Circumcision: Romans 2:25-29 in Social and Cultural Context." *NTS* 44 (1998): 536-56.

Berkley, Timothy W. *From a Broken Covenant to Circumcision of the Heart: Pauline Intertextual Exegesis in Romans 2:17-29.* SBLDS 175. Atlanta: Society of Biblical Literature, 2000.

Borgen, Peder. "Debates on Circumcision in Philo and Paul." In his *Paul Preaches Circumcision and Pleases Men,* 15-32. Trondheim: Tapir, 1983.

Davies, W. D. *Torah in the Messianic Age and/or the Age to Come.* SBLMS 7. Philadelphia: Society of Biblical Literature, 1952.

Derrett, J. Duncan M. "'You Abominate False Gods; but Do You Rob Shrines?' Rom 2.22b." *NTS* 40 (1994): 558-71.

Elliott, Neil. "'Blasphemed among the Nations': Pursuing an Anti-Imperial 'Intertextuality' in Romans." In *As It Is Written: Studying Paul's Use of Scripture,* 213-33. Ed. Stanley E. Porter and Christopher D. Stanley. SBLSymS 50. Atlanta: Society of Biblical Literature, 2008.

Fraikin, Dan. "The Rhetorical Function of the Jews in Romans." In *Anti-Judaism in Early Christianity,* 1:91-105. Ed. Peter Richardson and David Granskou. 2 vols. Waterloo: Wilfrid Laurier University Press, 1986.

Garlington, Don B. "ΊΕΡΟΣΥΛΕΙΝ and the Idolatry of Israel (Romans 2:22)." *NTS* 36 (1990): 142-51.

Gathercole, Simon J. *Where Is Boasting? Early Jewish Soteriology and Paul's Response in Romans 1–5.* Grand Rapids: Wm. B. Eerdmans, 2002.

Hagner, Donald A. "Paul and Judaism: The Jewish Matrix of Early Christianity: Issues in the Current Debate." *BBR* 3 (1993): 111-30.

Hays, Richard B. *Echoes of Scripture in the Letters of Paul.* New Haven: Yale University Press, 1989.

Krentz, Edgar. "The Name of God in Dispute: Romans 2:17-29." *CurTM* 17 (1990): 429-39.

Loader, William R. G. "Paul and Judaism: Is He Fighting Strawmen?" *Colloquium* 16 (1984): 11-20.

Lyonnet, Stanislas. "La circoncision du couer' celle qui relève de l'Esprit et non de la lettre." In *L'Évangile hier et aujourd'hui: Melanges offerts au professeur Franz-J. Leenhardt*, 87-97. Geneve: Éditions Labor et Fides, 1968.

McEleney, Neil J. "Conversion, Circumcision and the Law." *NTS* 20 (1973-74): 319-41.

Nolland, John. "Uncircumcised Proselytes?" *JSJ* 12 (1981): 173-94.

Sanders, E. P. *Paul and Palestinian Judaism: A Comparison of Patterns of Religion.* Philadelphia: Fortress Press, 1977.

Thorsteinsson, Runar M. *Paul's Interlocutor in Romans 2: Function and Identity in the Context of Ancient Epistolography.* ConBNT 40. Stockholm: Almqvist & Wiksell, 2003.

Watson, Francis. *Paul, Judaism, and the Gentiles: Beyond the New Perspective.* Rev. ed. Grand Rapids: Wm. B. Eerdmans, 2007.

2.4. Advantages without Privileges, 3:1-8

1*Then what advantage has the Jew? Or what is the value of circumcision?* 2*Much in every way. To begin with, they have been entrusted with the oracles of God.* 3*What then? If some were unfaithful, does their unfaithfulness nullify God's faithfulness?* 4*By no means! Let God be true — and every person a liar, as it is written: "That you may be justified in your words and prevail when you judge."* 5*But if our unrighteousness demonstrates the righteousness of God, what shall we say? That God is unjust for inflicting wrath? (I speak in human terms.)* 6*By no means! If so, how could God judge the world?* 7*But if, in spite of my falsehood, the truth of God abounds unto his glory, why am I still being condemned as a sinner?* 8*And why not say, as we are being slandered, and as some claim that we say, "Let us do evil in order that good may come"? Their condemnation is just!*

Notes on the Text and Translation

3:2 The phrase "to begin with" is a translation of πρῶτον μέν, which could be translated as "first." But as at 1:8 (and 1 Cor 11:18), there are no succeeding points (second, third, etc.). The term can have the meaning "to begin with," "above all," or "first of all" to mark a transition to what follows.[138]

3:4 Some ancient witnesses (including B) have the verb νικήσῃς ("[that] you may prevail"; second person, singular, aorist, subjunctive) instead of νικήσεις (which can also be rendered as "[that] you may prevail";[139] second

---

138. BDF 232 (§447, 4).
139. A future tense verb in the indicative can follow a subjunctive followed by καί in the

person, singular, future, indicative) in this verse. The former is the easier read-ing for two reasons: (1) it is grammatically correct in a purpose clause, and (2) it conforms to the reading of the LXX at Psalm 50:6, which is being quoted. The other reading, however, is attested in equally important ancient witnesses (in-cluding ℵ and A), is the more difficult reading, and is to be preferred.

At the end of the verse, the verb in the phrase ἐν τῷ κρίνεσθαί σε (an ar-ticular infinitive) should be understood as middle in voice and, consequently, rendered as "when you judge" (as in the NIV; similarly, the NRSV has "in your judging"). Furthermore, that is also the meaning of the OT phrase being quoted (Ps 51:4; LXX 50:6). The verb is understood (erroneously) to be passive by the translators of the KJV, ASV, and RSV ("and prevail when thou art judged").

General Comment

At the close of the previous chapter, Paul has placed Jew and Gentile on a level playing field. True circumcision, he says, is a spiritual, not simply a physical, matter. That means that the Gentile who keeps the precepts of the law is every bit as acceptable to God as the Jew who does the same. But as soon as Paul makes that point, he must surely realize that he has caused a problem for him-self that an imaginary opponent could seize upon. He continues the diatribe with an imaginary Jewish opponent,[140] taking up the obvious question that must be faced: What advantage is there then in being Jewish?

Paul could never doubt, even as an apostle of Christ, but that there are ad-vantages for the Jewish people in being heirs to the heritage of Israel, which he will enumerate in more detail at 9:4-5. God had elected the people of Israel, which is an advantage in itself. But what Paul lifts up for emphasis is that God gave to Israel the Torah, a special revelation that speaks of that election, the promises, and God's will for life in the world. Moreover, even on those occa-sions when Israel failed to be faithful to God, God has always been faithful to Israel.

That claim, however, can lead to another misunderstanding that Paul ad-dresses immediately in this section. Having emphasized the faithfulness of God to Israel, in spite of Israel's lapses into infidelity, the imaginary opponent could now accuse Paul of being a purveyor of antinomianism. It is clear from 3:8 (and perhaps 6:1, indirectly) that Paul was accused of teaching antinomianism — or at least that his gospel leads to it. Whether such persons existed in Rome is not

---

same sentence (as in this case, δικαιωθῇς . . . καὶ νικήσεις) to express purpose. Cf. BDF 186 (§369, 3).

140. S. Stowers, "Paul's Dialogue with a Fellow Jew in Romans 3:1-9," 707-22.

clear, although that claim has been made.[141] But the declaration at the end of 3:8 ("Their condemnation is just!") speaks against any group within the community itself, for that would undercut any attempts that Paul would be making in the letter either to promote goodwill within a mixed (Jewish/Gentile) community or to promote it between himself and the community there. It is more likely that the charge against Paul was from some other arena (such as from his opponents in Galatia, Corinth, and elsewhere), and that it was sufficiently well known even in Rome.[142] Although not endorsing the charge itself, persons who had been with Paul previously (such as Prisca, Aquila, Epaenetus, and others mentioned in 16:3-16) must have been aware of it, and others in Rome might have heard of it in some way. In any case, it was to Paul's advantage to take up the charge at some point, and this place in the letter provided an excellent opportunity.

Detailed Comment

3:1-2 Questions of advantage and value arise in the diatribe. What advantage is there in being Jewish (= being among the elect) if circumcision is a spiritual matter only, and if by implication "true" circumcision can therefore be attributed to any Gentile who keeps the moral teachings of the law? Why should anyone undergo circumcision at all? Moreover, if the Jew has no advantage, and if circumcision apparently counts for nothing, was God's election of Israel for no purpose after all?

There is no way that Paul could negate the value of election and circumcision. But by implication, even if not explicitly, Paul focuses on the meaning of the term περισσόν ("advantage"). On the one hand, an advantage can be understood as a privilege that one has by virtue of a status given; but on the other hand, it can be understood simply as a benefit or gain for which one should be grateful. It is in the latter sense that Paul answers the question. The Jew has some advantages, even if no privileges.

If there is an advantage, what is it? Above all, the Jews have been entrusted with "the oracles of God" (τὰ λόγια τοῦ θεοῦ), an expression that appears only a few times in the LXX (Ps 107:11, LXX 106:11; Num 24:4, 16, the latter without the article τά) and elsewhere in the NT (Heb 5:12; 1 Pet 4:11). For Paul, the oracles would be those divine utterances expressed in the law and the

---

141. W. Campbell, "Romans III as a Key to the Structure and Thought of the Letter," 36, suggests that they were Gentile Christians at Rome who attributed their own antinomianism to Paul's gospel of grace; I. Canales, "Paul's Accusers in Romans 3:8 and 6:1," 244, maintains that they were "Judaizers" in Rome.

142. Cf. J. Dunn, *Romans*, 137; B. Byrne, *Romans*, 110; D. Moo, *Romans*, 195; and P. Stuhlmacher, *Romans*, 51.

prophets.[143] To possess the oracles is a tremendous advantage, for they provide clarity concerning the will of God.

3:3-4 Without warning, Paul seems to switch to another topic, the unfaithfulness of the Jewish people and the faithfulness of God. But he has not actually jumped to another topic after all. He is continuing his diatribe, saying that human folly and transgression have existed and continue to exist, and that would seem to be sufficient cause for God to relinquish his special relationship with the Jewish people. But no, that is impossible. In spite of human infidelity, the fidelity of God abides.

Paul asks rhetorically, "If some" — meaning some of the people of Israel — "were unfaithful, does their unfaithfulness nullify God's faithfulness?" And then he responds with his famous μὴ γένοιτο, translated as "By no means!" (RSV and NRSV), "Not at all!" (NIV), or even as in the less literal "God forbid!" (KJV). The expression is found 13 times in the letters of Paul in this way,[144] i.e., as a strong negation after a rhetorical question (Rom 3:4, 6, 31; 6:2, 15; 7:7, 13; 9:14; 11:1, 11; 1 Cor 6:15; Gal 2:17; 3:21), and only once by another NT writer (Luke 20:16). The expression appears fairly frequently, however, in other ancient works.[145] Paul uses the expression regularly to object to a possible false conclusion and then follows up with a reason for rejecting the false conclusion.[146]

The expression "the faithfulness of God" (ἡ πίστις τοῦ θεοῦ) is not used elsewhere in the writings of Paul, nor does it appear again in the Greek Bible. Nevertheless, the claim that God is faithful is firmly established in the OT (Deut 7:9; 32:4; Ps 33:4 [LXX 32:4]; Isa 49:7; Hos 2:20) and in Jewish literature generally,[147] and it is affirmed elsewhere by the use of other expressions in the writings of Paul (1 Cor 1:9; 10:13; 1 Thess 5:24). God's saving purpose for humanity continues in spite of Israel's unfaithfulness. Human infidelity cannot nullify God's faithfulness.

As a parallel to the unfaithfulness of the Jewish people and faithfulness of God, Paul now speaks more generally, switching the sequence of terms. He contrasts God and "every person" (πᾶς ἄνθρωπος). God is "true" (ἀληθής), even though every person is "false" (RSV) or, more literally, "a liar" (ψεύστης), as in

---

143. According to U. Wilckens, *Römer,* 1:163-64; J. Dunn, *Romans,* 130-31; J. Fitzmyer, *Romans,* 326; D. Moo, *Romans,* 182; and J. Doeve, "Some Notes with Reference to ΤΑ ΛΟΓΙΑ ΤΟΥ ΘΕΟΥ in Romans iii, 2," 111-23, the expression refers to the OT as a whole. C. Cranfield, *Romans,* 179, concludes that the term must be taken "in the widest sense," including the OT and possibly more; similarly, D. Hall, "Romans 3:1-8 Reconsidered," 185.

144. The only other use of the expression at Gal 6:14 differs: ἐμοὶ δὲ μὴ γένοιτο καυχᾶσθαι εἰ μὴ ἐν τῷ σταυρῷ τοῦ κυρίου ἡμῶν Ἰησοῦ Χριστοῦ ("may I never boast of anything except the cross of our Lord Jesus Christ").

145. Several references are provided in BDAG 197 (γίνομαι, 4, a).

146. A. Malherbe, "ΜΗ ΓΕΝΟΙΤΟ in the Diatribe and Paul," 231-40.

147. *Pss. Sol.* 14:1; 17:10; Philo, *Her.* 18.93; *Leg. All.* 3.204; *Sacr.* 28.93.

NIV and NRSV. Once again the apostle picks up a familiar theme in both the OT and the NT, in which God is spoken of as true (ἀληθής or ἀληθινός: Exod 34:6; Isa 65:16; 3 Macc 6:18; Wis 15:1; John 3:33; 1 Thess 1:9; 1 John 5:20; Rev 15:3).

Furthermore, Paul says, God has every right to judge and express wrath against the world. He quotes a portion of Psalm 51:4 (LXX 50:6) to make a point, quoting the words of David to God. Omitting the main clause of the Davidic saying, Paul achieves all that he wants to by quoting only the purpose clause that follows the main clause: "That you may be justified in your words and prevail when you judge." The quotation shows that, according to the Scriptures, God's pronouncements are righteous and his judgments are on the mark. The quotation corresponds to the LXX reading, except that Paul uses a different tense and mood of the Greek verb translated above (and in RSV, NIV, and NRSV) as "prevail." While the LXX has an aorist subjunctive (νικήσῃς), which one ordinarily expects in a purpose clause, Paul has a future indicative (νικήσεις). For more on this, see the text-critical note above.

3:5-6 Paul sets up a contrast in 3:5 between humanity and God, but key terms referring to each are translated and interpreted in different ways. The two terms are ἀδικία (within ἡ ἀδικία ἡμῶν) and δικαιοσύνη (within θεοῦ δικαιοσύνην), respectively, and have been translated as follows in major English versions:

> KJV: But if *our unrighteousness* commend the *righteousness of God,* what shall we say?
>
> ASV: But if *our unrighteousness* commendeth the *righteousness of God,* what shall we say?
>
> RSV: But if *our wickedness* serves to show the *justice of God,* what shall we say?
>
> NEB: If *our injustice* serves to bring out *God's justice,* what are we to say?
>
> NIV: But if *our unrighteousness* brings out *God's righteousness* more clearly, what shall we say?
>
> NRSV: But if *our injustice* serves to confirm the *justice of God,* what should we say?
>
> ESV: But if *our unrighteousness* serves to show the *righteousness of God,* what shall we say?
>
> NET: But if *our unrighteousness* demonstrates the *righteousness of God,* what shall we say?

The term in reference to God is familiar from prior use in the letter (1:17) and elsewhere (3:21, 22; 10:3 [twice]; 2 Cor 5:21; Phil 3:9).[148] In the present in-

---

148. For further discussion, see the appendix, "The Righteousness of God in Paul."

stance, it could be interpreted to mean the "justice of God," as in RSV, NIV, and among some interpreters,[149] since Paul goes on to argue that God is not "unjust" to inflict wrath and will judge the world. Yet the familiar translation of "righteousness of God" is preferable, for the phrase is expressed within the context of statements concerning the faithfulness and truthfulness of God (3:3-4).[150] As Paul contrasts human unfaithfulness (ἀπιστία) and the faithfulness of God (ἡ πίστις τοῦ θεοῦ) in 3:3, so he contrasts human unrighteousness (ἀδικία) and God's righteousness (θεοῦ δικαιοσύνη) in 3:5.

It is precisely because of Paul's claim that God is faithful, true, and righteous — in contrast to human unrighteousness — that one might go on to maintain (falsely) that God cannot therefore exercise judgment and expend wrath against the world (3:5a). Indeed, to follow this line of reasoning, it could be concluded (falsely) that God would be unjust to inflict wrath on humanity. For if God is a redeeming God, he should not be a God of wrath and judgment. One cannot have it both ways; either God is a God of grace and compassion, rescuing the lost, or God is a God of judgment and wrath, casting transgressors away. But such thinking, Paul insists, is entirely wrong. He affirms that God, though righteous, can still inflict wrath. God remains and can be judge of all (3:6), a common theme within Jewish and Christian teachings known at Rome and elsewhere (Pss 9:8; 96:10, 13; 98:9; Isa 34:5; Wis 12:12-13; Tob 3:2; Heb 10:30; 1 Pet 1:17). But that does not diminish the righteousness of God, understood as the saving power of God, God's setting relationships right between humans and himself. On the expression "By no means!" see the comments on 3:4.

3:7 At this point in his diatribe Paul draws back from what is general to something more specific, making a rhetorical shift, speaking of himself personally as a particular case, but still representing humanity in general. It is not likely that Paul is being autobiographical only, making no reference to and inclusion of others along with himself. As in Romans 7:7-25, so also here, Paul is able to generalize concerning the human condition in light of the gospel by use of the first person singular. The "truth of God" (ἡ ἀλήθεια τοῦ θεοῦ) — a phrase that Paul also uses at Rom 15:8 (and in a different sense at 1:25) — exists even when "I" am false, failing to be the person I should be. The term translated

---

149. Among those who interpret the phrase in this sense are C. H. Dodd, *Romans*, 45; L. Morris, *Romans*, 157-59 (God's righteousness means "God's justice"); T. Schreiner, *Romans*, 156 ("God's judging righteousness"). According to J. Piper, "The Righteousness of God in Romans 3:8, 15," the term includes God's "punitive judgment on sin."

150. Included here are M. Luther, *Romans*, 27, 200-201; W. Sanday and A. Headlam, *Romans*, 72; C. K. Barrett, *Romans*, 61; C. Cranfield, *Romans*, 184; E. Käsemann, *Romans*, 79; U. Wilckens, *Römer*, 1:165-66; J. Dunn, *Romans*, 129, 134; B. Byrne, *Romans*, 113; J. Ziesler, *Romans*, 97-98; D. Moo, *Romans*, 189-91; P. Stuhlmacher, *Romans*, 51-52; E. Lohse, *Römer*, 118; L. Keck, *Romans*, 91; R. Jewett, *Romans*, 247-48.

here as "truth" (in reference to God) has the connotation of integrity and dependability,[151] and it echoes what Paul has said about God already at 3:4. God remains true to God's own self and character as the creating and redeeming God, even though human beings are not capable of remaining true to themselves. The truth of God enhances his glory (ἡ δόξα αὐτοῦ), that is, his renown as a being of truth and fidelity. But I, Paul says, am condemned as I stand alone in the presence of God. In spite of God's righteousness — his saving activity by which he justifies sinners — that does not make one less a sinner on one's own before the glorious and righteous God and in light of one's actual life in the world.

3:8 But if all that is true, and it is, a new problem lurks and needs to be addressed. If God is true and faithful, and if the love and mercy of God overcome human unrighteousness, which for Paul is beyond question, one could conclude: "the greater the evil of humanity, the greater the grace of God." So the question follows: "Why not say, 'Let us do evil in order that good may come'"? The charge of antinomianism is inescapable.

The question expressed by Paul at this point in his letter was not simply theoretical. It was clearly a live issue, as indicated here when Paul says that some persons have slandered him, and apparently continue to do so, charging that he teaches what he actually abhors. The issue is brought up again at 6:1 where Paul asks whether believers in Christ should "continue in sin that grace may abound." In both instances Paul responds with a strong negative reply. At 3:8 he declares that those who slander him are worthy of condemnation. There can hardly be a harsher reply than that.

BIBLIOGRAPHY

Achtemeier, Paul J. "Romans 3:1-8: Structure and Argument." In *Christ and His Communities: Essays in Honor of Reginald H. Fuller,* 77-87. Ed. Arland J. Hultgren and Barbara Hall. ATRSup 11. Cincinnati: Forward Movement Publications, 1990.

Barton, John. *Oracles of God.* London: Darton, Longman and Todd, 1986.

Boers, Hendrikus. "The Problem of Jews and Gentiles in the Macro-Structure of Romans." *Neot* 15 (1981): 1-11.

Bornkamm, Günther. "Theologie als Teufelskunst: Römer 3,1-9." In his *Geschichte und Glaube,* 140-48. BEvT 53. Munich: Kaiser Verlag, 1971.

Campbell, William S. "Romans III as a Key to the Structure and Thought of the Letter." *NovT* 23 (1981): 21-40.

Canales, Isaac J. "Paul's Accusers in Romans 3:8 and 6:1." *EvQ* 57 (1985): 237-45.

Cerfaux, Lucien. "Le privilège d'Israël sel. s. Paul." *ETL* 17 (1950): 5-26.

---

151. BDAG 42 (ἀλήθεια).

Cosgrove, Charles H. "What If Some Have Not Believed? The Occasion and Thrust of Romans 3:1-8." *ZNW* 78 (1987): 90-105.

Doeve, Jan W. "Some Notes with Reference to ΤΑ ΛΟΓΙΑ ΤΟΥ ΘΕΟΥ in Romans iii, 2." In *Studia paulina in honorem Johannis de Zwaan septuagenarii,* 111-23. Ed. Jan N. Sevenster and W. C. van Unnik. Haarlem: Bohn, 1953.

Dunn, James D. G. "The Justice of God: A Renewed Perspective on Justification by Faith." *JTS* 43 (1992): 1-22.

Fridrichsen, Anton. "Nochmals Römer 3,7-8." *ZNW* 34 (1935): 306-8.

Giesen, Heinz. "Gottes Treu angessichts menschlicher Untreu (Röm 3,1-9): Zugleich ein Beitrag zum Röm 1,17." *SNTU* 31 (2006): 61-88.

Hall, David R. "Romans 3.1-8 Reconsidered." *NTS* 29 (1983): 188-97.

Hays, Richard B. "Psalm 143 and the Logic of Romans 3." *JBL* 99 (1980): 107-15; reprinted as "Psalm 143 as Testimony to the Righteousness of God," in his *The Conversion of the Imagination: Paul as an Interpreter of Israel's Scripture,* 50-60. Grand Rapids: Wm. B. Eerdmans, 2005.

———. "Three Dramatic Roles: The Law in Romans 3–4." In *Paul and the Mosaic Law,* 151-64. Ed. James D. G. Dunn. WUNT 89. Tübingen: J. C. B. Mohr (Paul Siebeck), 1996; reprinted in his *The Conversion of the Imagination: Paul as an Interpreter of Israel's Scripture,* 85-100. Grand Rapids: Wm. B. Eerdmans, 2005.

Ljungvik, Herman. "Zum Römerbrief 3,7-8." *ZNW* 32 (1933): 207-10.

Malherbe, Abraham J. "ΜΗ ΓΕΝΟΙΤΟ in the Diatribe and Paul." *HTR* 73 (1980): 231-40.

Myers, Charles D. "Chiastic Inversion in the Argument of Romans 3–8." *NovT* 35 (1993): 30-47.

Piper, John. "The Righteousness of God in Romans 3:1-8." *TZ* 36 (1980): 3-16.

Räisänen, Heikki. "Zum Verständnis von Röm 3:1-8." *SNTU* 10 (1985): 93-108.

Stowers, Stanley K. "Paul's Dialogue with a Fellow Jew in Romans 3:1-9." *CBQ* 46 (1984): 707-22.

Wright, N. T. "New Exodus, New Inheritance: The Narrative Structure of Romans 3–8." In *Romans and the People of God: Essays in Honor of Gordon D. Fee on the Occasion of His 65th Birthday,* 26-35. Ed. Sven K. Soderlund and N. T. Wright. Grand Rapids: Wm. B. Eerdmans, 1999.

2.5. The Universal Judgment of God, 3:9-20

9*What then? Are we better off? No, not at all; for we have already charged that all, both Jews and Greeks, are under sin,* 10*as it is written:*

"No one is righteous, not even one; 11*no one understands;*
     no one seeks God.
12*All have turned aside, together they have become depraved;*
     no one shows kindness, not even one."
13*"Their throats are opened graves; they deceive with their tongues";*

"the poison of asps is under their lips."
14*"Their mouths are full of cursing and bitterness."*
15*"Their feet are swift to shed blood;* 16*ruin and misery are in their paths,*
    17*and the way of peace they have not known."*
18*"There is no fear of God before their eyes."*

19*We know that whatever the law says, it speaks to those under the law, in order that every mouth may be silenced, and the entire world may be held accountable to God.* 20*For no human being will be justified before him by works prescribed by the law, for through the law comes knowledge of sin.*

Notes on the Text and Translation

3:9 The wording προεχόμεθα; οὐ πάντως ("Are we better off? No, not at all") reflects some text-critical and translation choices. The Greek wording here is the best attested,[152] although there are several variants, and it is the wording printed in the Greek NT editions of Westcott-Hort and Nestle-Aland (27th ed.). Questions arise concerning the translation of the verb προεχόμεθα. In form it could be a middle or a passive. If it is a middle, the usual meaning would be, "Are we protecting ourselves?" If it is a passive, it would mean, "Are we excelled?" or (cf. NRSV marginal note), "Are we at any disadvantage?"[153] Normally one would expect that, in order to express "Are we better off?," the apostle would have used the active form of the verb (writing προέχομεν).[154] Nevertheless, the strong assertion of the rest of the verse that Jew and Gentile are on the same level before God and the string of scriptural quotations that follow indicate that Paul seeks to undermine any thoughts of advantages that persons of Jewish heritage might harbor. The expression "Are we better off" is fitting in context (cf. RSV, NIV, NRSV, and NET).[155]

The RSV begins with the question: "Are we Jews any better off?" Actually the word "Jews" does not appear in that sentence. But it is found in the next.

3:12 Both the NIV and the NRSV render the verb ἠχρεώθησαν as "become worthless." That seems like an unfortunate translation, for one can hardly

---

152. This is contested by N. Dahl, "Romans 3:19," 184-204, and J. Dunn, *Romans*, 144-47. But in order to support their viewpoint, the textual evidence of ℵ, B, and other early versions has to be set aside in favor of a single ninth-century majuscule (P).

153. Favored by W. Sanday and A. Headlam, *Romans*, 76; J. Fitzmyer, *Romans*, 330; L. Keck, *Romans*, 94; R. Jewett, *Romans*, 253, 257.

154. See discussion in BDAG 869 (προέχω).

155. The rendering favored here is supported by C. E. B. Cranfield, *Romans*, 189; E. Käsemann, *Romans*, 85-86; U. Wilckens, *Römer*, 1:172; J. Ziesler, *Romans*, 101-2; E. Lohse, *Römer*, 120-21.

say that, according to the scriptural tradition as a whole, anyone becomes worthless in the eyes of God. The verb is the aorist passive of ἀχρειόω, which can mean "become depraved." The verb appears only here in the NT. It appears within the LXX passages being conflated here (Pss 13:3; 52:4; cf. also Jer 11:16; Dan 6:12).

General Comment

Paul has established in the previous section that there are indeed advantages to being Jewish, since it is to the Jews that the Scriptures have been given, but there are no privileges. He maintains that God is true and faithful, and that his saving righteousness remains constant in spite of human disobedience. In this section Paul expands upon the theme of disobedience, forming a catena (or chain) of scriptural passages to make his point. The catena demonstrates that Paul's portrayal of the human condition is not simply a matter of Paul's own opinion; it is rooted and revealed in the Scriptures. He establishes "beyond all possible doubt the affirmation that God is just in his judgment of the world."[156]

Paul also establishes that both "Jews and Greeks" are under the power of sin. Beginning the section with a quotation from the OT that says that "no one" is righteous, and following that with other quotations that, in Paul's use, are not specifically about Jews or Gentiles, he universalizes. He is no longer indicting the person of Jewish heritage, as in 2:17–3:8, but humanity as a whole. He concludes his diatribe at 3:20 with the apodictic statement that no one will be justified in God's sight "by works prescribed by the law." That is followed by an explanation, beginning with the conjunction γάρ ("for"). From what has gone before, one might expect him to say: "for all fail to live up to the prescriptions." But what he says is far more serious. He turns from the human subject to say something about the dark side of the law itself: "for through the law comes knowledge of sin." With all its prescriptions the law is not only impossible to observe; it also exposes and brings to light "sin" (singular) as an operative power in the life of every person.

Detailed Comment

3:9 Persons of Jewish heritage, Paul insists, are no better off than any other, for all people, both Jews and Greeks (= Gentiles), are "under sin" (ὑφ' ἁμαρτίαν), that is, under its domination. For Paul there are two possibilities for anyone, being under sin (Rom 3:9; 7:14) or under grace (Rom 6:14-15). Variations on the

---

156. R. Hays, *Echoes of Scripture in the Letters of Paul*, 50.

two ways exist, such as being under the law (Rom 2:12; 3:19; 6:14-15; 7:6; Gal 3:23; 4:5, 21; 5:18), which guides the life of the Jewish person but is a form of bondage for Gentiles leading to condemnation and death, or else one is under the lordship of Christ (Rom 6:11; 8:10; 1 Cor 9:21; 2 Cor 13:5; cf. Gal 2:4), sharing his destiny and becoming conformed to him by growth in grace.

For Paul to claim that all people are under the power of sin (i.e., that sin itself is a power) is to assert something that is not familiar in Jewish tradition. According to the most familiar core of Jewish tradition, God's demands in the Torah are not unreasonable, not obscure, and not too difficult to obey. These assertions are plain from Deuteronomy 30:11-14 and Leviticus 18:5, leading to the view that a person can therefore become confident of being righteous under the law. Even Paul had once entertained such confidence about himself (Phil 3:6). On the other hand, there is a well-established tradition within Judaism that all people are sinful without exception.[157] And for Paul that can be established not simply by deference to that tradition, but to passages from the Scriptures, including such major books as the Psalms and Isaiah.

3:10-18 The OT passages cited appear to be of mixed origin. Some correspond to the wording in the LXX. In other cases Paul seems to have used versions of the OT not available to us, or he quoted from memory and not exactly from known versions. To complicate matters further, for the most part Paul offers only fragments, using lines or wordings sufficient to make his case, thereby showing that the Scriptures themselves bear witness against Israel. The data are as follows, comparing the Pauline quotations with the LXX (and in the case of the Psalms using the LXX numbering system):

> 3:10 Perhaps quoted from Ecclesiastes 7:20, but not exactly. Paul has: "No one is righteous, not even one" (οὐκ ἔστιν δίκαιος οὐδὲ εἷς). The OT text reads: "no one on earth is righteous" (οὐκ ἔστιν δίκαιος ἐν τῇ γῇ). A similar charge appears in Psalm 13:1 and 52:1: "there is no one who does good" (οὐκ ἔστιν ποιῶν ἀγαθόν). Similar claims are made in other Jewish literature.[158]
>
> 3:11: Quoted from identical portions of Psalms 13:2 and 52:2, but not exactly. Paul has: "no one understands; no one seeks God" (οὐκ ἔστιν ὁ συνίων, οὐκ ἔστιν ὁ ἐκζητῶν τὸν θεόν). The OT text reads: "The Lord [Ps 13:2, but "God" in 52:2] looks down from heaven on humankind to see if there are any who are wise, who seek after God" (. . . εἰ ἔστιν συνίων ἢ ἐκζητῶν τὸν θεόν).

157. Eccl 7:21; Sir 25:24; Wis 2:24; 2 Esdr 3:21-22, 26; 2 Apoc. Bar. 54.15; 23.4.

158. 2 Esdr 7:68; 8:35; 1QH 9.14-15. On the sinfulness of every person in the Qumran texts, cf. H.-W. Kuhn, "The Impact of the Dead Sea Scrolls on the Understanding of Paul," 333.

3:12: Quoted from Psalm 13:3, almost exactly, which reads: "All have turned aside, together they have become depraved; no one shows kindness, not even one" (πάντες ἐξέκλιναν ἅμα ἠχρεώθησαν· οὐκ ἔστιν ποιῶν χρηστότητα οὐκ ἔστιν ἕως ἑνός). Paul adds the relative pronoun ὁ ("who"), which is omitted in some ancient witnesses to make the correspondence exact. Nearly the same wording appears at Psalm 52:4, but in that verse the Psalmist had the word "good" (ἀγαθόν) rather than "kindness" (χρηστότητα).

3:13a-b: Quoted exactly from Psalm 5:10: "Their throats are opened graves; they deceive with their tongues" (τάφος ἀνεῳγμένος ὁ λάρυγξ αὐτῶν, ταῖς γλώσσαις αὐτῶν ἐδολιοῦσαν).

13c: Quoted exactly from Psalm 139:4: "the poison of asps is under their lips" (ἰὸς ἀσπίδων ὑπὸ τὰ χείλη αὐτῶν).

3:14-18: Quoted exactly from Psalm 13:1-3 (the sentences are not contained in the Hebrew text of Ps 14:1-7): "Their mouths are full of cursing and bitterness. Their feet are swift to shed blood; ruin and misery are in their paths, and the way of peace they have not known. There is no fear of God before their eyes" (ὧν τὸ στόμα ἀρᾶς καὶ πικρίας γέμει, ὀξεῖς οἱ πόδες αὐτῶν ἐκχέαι αἷμα, σύντριμμα καὶ ταλαιπωρία ἐν ταῖς ὁδοῖς αὐτῶν, καὶ ὁδὸν εἰρήνης οὐκ ἔγνωσαν. οὐκ ἔστιν φόβος θεοῦ ἀπέναντι τῶν ὀφθαλμῶν αὐτῶν). There are other OT texts that have sentences or phrases similar to those in 3:14-18,[159] probably due to intra-OT quotations, but what Paul has written corresponds to the continuous text of LXX Psalm 13:1-3, and the latter alone can be considered the basis for his own composition.

Whether there is any particular scheme underlying the verses quoted that determines their sequence is difficult to determine. Perhaps the only obvious cases are those in 3:10-12. The very first, in which Paul declares that no one is righteous, follows the indictment that he has made since 1:18, declaring that no one in all the world is righteous. The quotation in 3:11 (Ps 13:2 and 52:2) follows naturally after that in 3:10 (Ps 13:1 and 52:1), since it follows the sequence of the psalm verses. Notable, too, is that each of the verses in 3:10-12 contains the words οὐκ ἔστιν ("there is no one," five times over). The other passages quoted could be in random order, but all serve together to present God's indictment against the world within the larger sustained theological exposition of 1:18–3:20.[160] Interpreters have suggested that Paul may have used here a collection or

159. Rom 3:15 has similarities with Prov 1:16; Rom 3:17 with Isa 59:7; and Rom 3:18 with LXX Ps 35:2.

160. L. Keck, "The Function of Romans 3.10-18," 152.

"catena" (chain) of OT passages created previously by himself or someone else.[161] It is possible that Paul made use here of a catena of passages used previously in missionary proclamation within synagogues (Acts 13:13-52; 14:1-5; 17:1-5, 10-14, 17; 18:4-8, 18-21, 26; 19:8-9). The passages quoted expose the sinful condition of those who hear the case being made from Scripture, make clear the need for their repentance, and anticipate the ensuing atonement, which has actually been made in the death of Christ upon the cross (3:25).[162]

3:19-20 Although Paul speaks now of "whatever the law says," none of the passages just quoted are actually from the "law" (νόμος), the Torah. All are from that portion of Scripture known as the "writings" (with possible allusions to the "prophets"). Nevertheless, Paul can use the term "law" in a general sense to refer to the Scriptures of Israel (cf. 1 Cor 14:21), and that is the case here. The message of the Scriptures applies, he says, to "those under the law," i.e., the Jewish people.[163] That means that no one is excused from judgment; no one is exempt. Every mouth is thereby stopped; there can be no boasting (2:17, 23). The entire world is "accountable" (ὑπόδικος, a term used only here in the NT and LXX) to God.

Paul concludes his long diatribe (1:18–3:20) with the sweeping statement: "For no human being will be justified before [God] by works prescribed by the law, for through the law comes knowledge of sin" (3:20). The first clause recalls a line from Psalm 143:2 (LXX 142:2): ὅτι οὐ δικαιωθήσεται ἐνώπιόν σου πᾶς ζῶν ("for no living person will be justified before you [= God]"), which Paul has modified slightly, changing πᾶς ζῶν ("every living person") to πᾶσα σάρξ ("every human being"). Moreover, he adds the words ἐξ ἔργων νόμου ("by works prescribed by the law"), words that do not appear in the verse from the Psalms.

By this apodictic statement Paul declares that justification — being put right in relationship to God — is impossible for anyone by means of Torah observance. It is impossible because it has been established firmly from Scripture itself that no person is righteous, not even those who are "under the law" and seek righteousness by its guidance. The phrase "works prescribed by the law" is a rendering of ἐξ ἔργων νόμου (more literally, "from works of the law"). The entire phrase ἐξ ἔργων νόμου appears six other times in the letters of Paul (Gal 2:16 [three times]; 3:2, 5, 10); a similar expression, χωρὶς ἔργων νόμου ("apart from works prescribed by the law"), appears once as well (Rom 3:28). The phrases refer to a way of life in which righteousness is sought through the ob-

---

161. L. Keck, "The Function of Romans 3.10-18," 141-57; idem, *Romans*, 95-96; J. Fitzmyer, *Romans*, 334; R. Jewett, *Romans*, 254.

162. For further discussion, cf. A. Hultgren, *Paul's Gospel and Mission*, 47-81 (esp. 62-65).

163. Contra H. Bowsher, "To Whom Does the Law Speak?" 295-303, who maintains that Gentiles are included.

servance of the commandments presented in the law (the Torah).[164] For a discussion of this important phrase in detail, see the exegesis at 3:28.

Paul concludes with the statement that "through the law comes knowledge of sin." The phrase "through the law" (διὰ νόμου) most likely refers to one's encounter with the law as a body of instruction, including its commandments. The person who gives attention to the law in all its details finds more there than one can adopt and apply to life as a way of achieving righteousness.[165] The result is the "knowledge of sin" in one's own life. The same point is made at 7:7 and obliquely at 5:20. At 5:13 Paul provides the obverse: "sin is not counted when the law is not present."

BIBLIOGRAPHY

Bowsher, Herbert. "To Whom Does the Law Speak? Romans 3:19 and the Works of the Law Debate." *WTJ* 68 (2006): 295-303.

Carter, Timothy L. *Paul and the Power of Sin: Redefining "Beyond the Pale."* SNTSMS 115. Cambridge: Cambridge University Press, 2002.

Cosgrove, Charles H. "Justification in Paul: A Linguistic and Theological Reflection." *JBL* 106 (1987): 653-70.

Cranfield, C. E. B. "'The Works of the Law' in the Epistle to the Romans." *JSNT* 43 (1991): 89-101; reprinted in his *On Romans and Other New Testament Essays*, 1-14. Edinburgh: T&T Clark, 1998.

Dahl, Nils A. "Romans 3:9: Text and Meaning." In *Paul and Paulinism: Essays in Honour of C. K. Barrett,* 184-206. Ed. Morna D. Hooker and S. G. Wilson. London: SPCK, 1982.

Davies, W. D. "Paul and the Law: Reflections on Pitfalls in Interpretation." In *Paul and Paulinism: Essays in Honour of C. K. Barrett,* 4-16. Ed. Morna D. Hooker and S. G. Wilson. London: SPCK, 1982.

De Roo, Jacqueline C. R. *"Works of the Law" at Qumran and in Paul.* NTMs 13. Sheffield: Sheffield Phoenix Press, 2007.

Dunn, James D. G. "Works of the Law and the Curse of the Law (Galatians 3:10-14)." *NTS* 31 (1985): 523-42.

———. "Yet Once More — 'The Works of the Law': A Response." *JSNT* 46 (1991): 99-117.

164. According to P. Owen, "The 'Works of the Law,'" 553-77, when Paul uses the phrase "works of the law," he employs a subjective genitive construction. The expression denotes "the effects of the Law's activity" (p. 554), and Paul considers "the Law as an agent on which the Jews rely for their righteousness before God" (p. 570). Consequently, he translates Rom 3:20 as: "no one will be justified . . . by what is produced by the Law" (p. 556). But clearly it is the one striving ("no one" in this case), not the law itself, that seeks to do "the works" and is the agent that seeks righteousness. Cf. the diatribe at Rom 2:13: "It is those who are doers of the law (οἱ ποιηταὶ νόμου) that will be justified."

165. To that extent the claim of the Apology of the Augsburg Confession 4.128 that *lex semper accusat* ("the law always accuses") those who seek righteousness under the law has a basis in Paul's theology.

Feuillet, André. "La situation privilégiée des Juifs d'après Rom. 3:9: Comparison avec Rom. 1:16 et 3:1-2." *NRT* 105 (1983): 33-46.

Fitzmyer, Joseph A. "Paul and the Dead Sea Scrolls." In *The Dead Sea Scrolls after Fifty Years: A Comprehensive Assessment*, 2:599-621. Ed. Peter W. Flint and James C. VanderKam. 2 vols. Boston: E. J. Brill, 1998-99.

———. "Paul's Jewish Background and the Deeds of the Law." In his *According to Paul: Studies in the Theology of the Apostle*, 18-35. New York: Paulist Press, 1993.

Gaston, Lloyd. *Paul and the Torah*. Vancouver: University of British Columbia Press, 1987.

Gaventa, Beverly R. "The Cosmic Power of Sin in Paul's Letter to the Romans." *Int* 58 (2004): 229-40.

Hays, Richard B. *Echoes of Scripture in the Letters of Paul*. New Haven: Yale University Press, 1989.

———. "Psalm 143 and the Logic of Romans 3." *JBL* 99 (1980): 107-15.

Hübner, Hans. "Was heist bei Paulus 'Werke des Gesetzes'?" In *Glaube und Eschatologie: Festschrift für Werner Georg Kümmel zum 80. Geburtstag*, 123-33. Ed. Erich Grässer and Otto Merk. Tübingen: J. C. B. Mohr (Paul Siebeck), 1985.

Hultgren, Arland J. *Paul's Gospel and Mission: The Outlook from His Letter to the Romans*. Philadelphia: Fortress Press, 1985.

Kampen, John. "4QMMT and New Testament Studies." In *Reading 4QMMT: New Perspectives on Qumran Law and History*, 129-44. Ed. John Kampen and Moshe J. Bernstein. SBLSymS 2. Atlanta: Scholars Press, 1996.

Keck, Leander E. "The Function of Romans 3.10-18: Observations and Suggestions." In *God's Christ and His People: Studies in Honour of Nils Alstrup Dahl*, 141-57. Ed. Jacob Jervell and Wayne A. Meeks. Oslo: Universitetsforlaget, 1977.

Kuhn, Heinz-Wolfgang. "Qumran und Paulus: Unter traditionsgeschichtlichem Aspekt ausgewählte Parallelen." In *Das Urchristentum in seiner literarischen Geschichte: Festschrift für Jürgen Becker zum 65. Geburtstag*, 227-46. Ed Ulrich Mell and Ulrich B. Müller. BZNW 100. Berlin: Walter de Gruyter, 1999.

———. "The Impact of the Qumran Scrolls on the Understanding of Paul." In *The Dead Sea Scrolls: Forty Years of Research*, 327-39. Ed. Devorah Dimant and Uriel Rappaport. STDJ 10. New York: E. J. Brill, 1992.

Moyise, Steve. "The Catena of Romans 3:10-18." *ExpTim* 106 (1995): 367-70.

Owen, Paul L. "The 'Works of the Law' in Romans and Galatians: A New Defense of the Subjective Genitive." *JBL* 129 (2007): 553-77.

Schreiner, Thomas R. "'Works of Law' in Paul." *NovT* 33 (1991): 217-44.

Synge, Francis C. "The Meaning of προσεχόμεθα in Romans 3:9." *ExpTim* 81 (1969-70): 351.

Tyson, Joseph B. "'Works of Law' in Galatians." *JBL* 92 (1973): 423-31.

Walter, Nikolaus. "Gottes Erbarmen mit 'Allem Fleisch' (Röm 3,20/Gal 2,16) — Ein 'femininer' Zug im paulinischen Gottesbild?" *BZ* 35 (1991): 99-102.

Wilckens, Ulrich. "Was heisst bei Paulus: 'Aus Werken des Gesetzes wird kein Mensch gerecht.'" In his *Rechtfertigung als Freiheit: Paulusstudien*, 77-109. Neukirchen-Vluyn: Neukirchener Verlag, 1974.

CHAPTER 3

The Revelation of the Righteousness of God,
3:21–4:25

In 1:18–3:20, Paul indicts the whole world, employing all manner of rhetorical skills, theological reasoning, and the use of Scripture. On the one hand, he declares that the wrath of God is being poured out upon the Gentiles for their idolatry, which leads to extremes of abusive behavior. On the other hand, he assails those of Jewish heritage who claim to know the will of God through the law but do not keep it. He establishes that all persons, Jew and Gentile alike, are under the power of sin (3:9). As one schooled in the Jewish tradition, he backs up his indictment of all humanity by using scriptural passages.

At 3:21, however, Paul makes an abrupt and extraordinary turn. The theme of the "wrath of God" (ὀργὴ θεοῦ) is suspended and overcome by his taking up again the theme, first mentioned in the overture at 1:17, of the "righteousness of God" (δικαιοσύνη θεοῦ). The "righteousness of God" has been revealed dramatically and decisively in God's redemptive work in Christ (3:21), crucified and raised from the dead. In this portion of the letter Paul discloses what, for him, is crucial in understanding the righteousness of God. It is God's activity by which he justifies, or sets relationships right, between humanity and himself. As a consequence, humanity has been set free from the power of sin (3:9), a freedom that is received proleptically by faith (3:25). (See the appendix, "The 'Righteousness of God' in Paul.")

Paul insists that God's redemptive work in Christ has occurred as sheer gift. Therefore no boasting is possible (3:27-31). One cannot be justified on the basis of doing works of the law. Justification comes about as one accepts by faith the good news of what God has done in Christ. Justification is by faith. This is demonstrated in the OT in the case of Abraham, who was considered righteous (or justified) because he believed in the promises of God, anticipating the justification of all those who believe in the God who raised Jesus from the dead (4:1-25).

149

BIBLIOGRAPHY

Gaston, Lloyd. "Abraham and the Righteousness of God." *HBT* 2 (1980): 39-68.

Gathercole, Simon J. "Justified by Faith, Justified by His Blood: The Evidence of Romans 3:21–4:25." In *Justification and Variegated Nomism*, 2:147-84. Ed. D. A. Carson, Peter T. O'Brien, and Mark Seifrid. 2 vols. Grand Rapids: Baker Academic, 2001-4.

Hays, Richard B. "Three Dramatic Roles: The Law in Romans 3–4." In *Paul and the Mosaic Law*, 151-64. Ed. J. D. G. Dunn. WUNT 89. Tübingen: J. C. B. Mohr (Paul Siebeck), 1996; reprinted in his *The Conversion of the Imagination: Paul as an Interpreter of Israel's Scripture*, 85-100. Grand Rapids: Wm. B. Eerdmans, 2005.

Klein, Günter. "Exegetische Probleme in Römer 3,21–4,25." *EvT* 24 (1964): 676-83.

Meecham, Henry G. "Romans iii.25f., iv.25 — the Meaning of διά c. acc." *ExpTim* 50 (1938-39): 564.

Wilckens, Ulrich. "Zu Römer 3,21–4,25: Antwort an G. Klein." *EvT* 11 (1964): 586-610.

3.1. The Revelation of the Saving Righteousness of God in Christ, 3:21-26

21*But now, apart from the law, the righteousness of God has been manifested, although borne witness to by the law and the prophets,* 22*the righteousness of God through faith in Jesus Christ for all who believe. For there is no distinction.* 23*Since all have sinned and fall short of the glory of God,* 24*they are justified freely by his grace through the redemption that is in Christ Jesus,* 25*whom God put forth as a mercy seat by his blood, to be received by faith. He did this to demonstrate his righteousness for the sake of the remission of the sins committed previously* 26(*during the time of his divine forbearance); it was to show his righteousness at the present time, that he himself is righteous, and that he justifies the one who has faith in Jesus.*

Notes on the Text and Translation

3:22 The phrase διὰ πίστεως Ἰησοῦ Χριστοῦ has been translated "through faith in Jesus Christ." A footnote to the NRSV text sets forth an alternative translation, "through the faith of Jesus Christ." For a discussion of the issues involved and a defense of "through faith in Jesus Christ," see the appendix, "*Pistis Christou*: Faith in or of Christ?"

3:25 The term ἱλαστήριον, translated here as "mercy seat," has been translated and interpreted in various ways (for some examples, cf. KJV: "a propitiation"; RSV: "an expiation"; NIV and NRSV: "a sacrifice of atonement"). For a discussion of the terms proposed and used, and justification for "mercy seat," see the appendix, "The Imagery of Romans 3:25."

The ancient witnesses differ in regard to the prepositional phrase (as printed in the Nestle-Aland 27th edition) διὰ [τῆς] πίστεως. The article τῆς ("the") is present in some witnesses (apparently in 𝔓⁴⁰, B, and others, including the Majority Text) but is lacking in others (including ℵ, C, D, and others). As the brackets indicate, it is doubtful whether it should appear in the text.

3:26 The phrase δικαιοῦντα τὸν ἐκ πίστεως Ἰησοῦ is translated here as "he justifies the one who has faith in Jesus." The NRSV footnote reads as an alternative: "he justifies the one who has the faith of Jesus." For a discussion of the issues here, see the appendix, *"Pistis Christou: Faith in or of Christ?"*

General Comment

Having established that all of humanity is under the power of sin, that no one can be justified by performing deeds of the law, and therefore that all stand under divine judgment, Paul now makes an abrupt and extraordinary shift. He composes a powerfully strident and highly significant section of his letter in which he celebrates the "righteousness of God" and its effects for humanity. In this brief portion of the letter, Paul presents his understanding of the meaning of the death of Christ for human redemption. It is the most provocative statement in the entire letter — indeed in all of Paul's letters — concerning the redemptive work of God in Christ. Moreover, every atonement theory in the history of theology has had to come to terms with what Paul says in these verses.

The section is tightly packed with words that are highly charged theologically, and the syntax is more complicated than usual in Paul's writings. Because of that and other factors, some interpreters have suggested that it contains a pre-Pauline confessional formula, to which Paul has added words and phrases. According to the most widely accepted theory, the pre-Pauline formula consisted of 3:24-26a, as printed in the Nestle-Aland Greek text (27th ed.), but which is actually 3:24-25 in widely used English versions (RSV, NIV, and NRSV). The Pauline insertions, according to most proponents of this view, include the phrases δωρεὰν τῇ αὐτοῦ χάριτι ("by his grace as a gift") and διὰ [τῆς] πίστεως ("effective through faith"). Quoting from the NRSV, but placing ellipses in place of the suggested interpolations, the proposed pre-Pauline formula reads as follows:[1]

---

1. R. Bultmann, *Theology of the New Testament,* 1:46; E. Käsemann, "Zum Verständnis von Römer 3,24-26," 150-54; idem, *Romans,* 96-99; O. Michel, *Römer,* 89; A. Hunter, *Paul and His Predecessors,* 120-22; P. Stuhlmacher, *Gerechtigkeit Gottes bei Paulus,* 86-91; idem, "Recent Exegesis of Romans 3:24-26," 94; H. Conzelmann, *An Outline of the Theology of the New Testament,* 166; K. Kertelge, *"Rechtfertigung" bei Paulus,* 48-62; W. Kümmel, *The Theology of the New Testament,* 198; and J. Fitzmyer, *Romans,* 342-43. A survey of the German discussion is provided

24. . . . they are now justified . . . through the redemption that is in Christ Jesus, 25whom God put forward as a sacrifice of atonement by his blood. . . . He did this to show his righteousness, because in his divine forbearance he had passed over the sins previously committed.

In terms of the Greek text, the pre-Pauline formula would begin with the participle δικαιούμενοι ("being justified") and end with the phrase ἐν τῇ ἀνοχῇ τοῦ θεοῦ ("in the forbearance of God").

A major reason for proposing that this was a pre-Pauline tradition incorporated by Paul into his letter is that it contains a densely packed concentration of terms that — when limiting one's search to the undisputed letters of Paul — are found only here, such as ἱλαστήριον ("mercy seat"), πάρεσις ("remission"), and προγίνομαι ("previously happened"), or at least seldom, such as προτίθημι ("set forth," only here and at 1:13), ἔνδειξις ("display," only here and at 2 Cor 8:24; Phil 1:28), ἁμάρτημα ("sin," only here and at 1 Cor 6:18), and ἀνοχή ("forbearance," only here and at Rom 2:4).

All of these terms, however, appear in 3:25-26a, and none in 3:24. In fact, 3:24 contains typical Pauline terminology and phrases. For that reason, some interpreters have maintained that the interpolation consists of 3:25-26a only.[2] In that case, the formula would have begun with the relative pronoun ὅν ("whom") at the beginning of 3:25. To strengthen this case, it can be added that NT creedal formulations often begin with a relative pronoun,[3] referring to Christ as antecedent in a previous phrase which has been replaced by the NT author with his own introduction. As one might expect, other interpreters conclude that even less of the material in 3:24-26 is pre-Pauline.[4] Another proposal is that there is no pre-Pauline tradition here at all, but that 3:25-26 is in fact an interpolation placed into the text late in the first century.[5] The proposal has not, however, been accepted very much by others.[6]

by J. Reumann, "The Gospel of the Righteousness of God," 432-52; cf. also idem, *"Righteousness" in the New Testament,* 36-38.

2. U. Wilckens, *Römer,* 1:183; E. Lohse, *Märtyrer und Gottesknecht,* 149-50; idem, *Römer,* 129; B. Meyer, "Pre-Pauline Formula in Rom. 3.25-26a," 198-208; J. Dunn, *Romans,* 163-64; W. Kraus, *Der Tod Jesu als Heiligtumsweihe,* 10-20.

3. Cf. Rom 4:25; Phil 2:6; 1 Tim 3:16; 1 Pet 2:22, 23, 24.

4. That only 3:25 is pre-Pauline is maintained by K. Wengst, *Christologische Formeln und Lieder des Urchristentums,* 87-91, and not all of that by G. Strecker, "Befreiung und Rechtfertigung," 501-2.

5. C. Talbert, "A Non-Pauline Fragment," 287-96; and G. Fitzer, "Der Ort der Versöhnung nach Paulus," 161-83.

6. A major critique has been provided by S. Williams, "The Meaning of Jesus' Death," 6-11. The proposal is not even mentioned by C. Talbert in his subsequent commentary, *Romans,* 105-28, while discussing 3:21–4:25.

As intriguing as the theory is that Paul inserted a pre-formed, pre-Pauline tradition at 3:24-26a, it cannot be maintained for certain, and arguments can be made against it. For one thing, there are only three words within these verses (all in 3:25) that are not used elsewhere by Paul (ἱλαστήριον, πάρεσις, and προγίνομαι), but they could certainly have been within his linguistic range. For that reason, various interpreters have concluded that no pre-Pauline formula has been inserted here at all.[7]

It must be granted that many words and phrases were stock-in-trade for early Christians, not all of them are used by NT writers, and that Paul would have picked them up and used them when and where necessary, both orally and in writing. Therefore another approach can be taken. That is that all of Rom 3:21-26 was composed by Paul at the time of the writing of his letter to Rome, but he employed words and phrases that he himself had used previously in missionary proclamation within synagogues,[8] and that some of them are embedded particularly in 3:24-26. In his preaching it would have been necessary on various occasions to show how the promises of the OT had been fulfilled in Jesus as the Messiah who had been crucified, and he would have had to show then how the death of the crucified Messiah had an atoning effect. Drawing upon the imagery in lessons related to the Day of Atonement — since they are the most specific and familiar concerning atonement — Paul could declare that redemption and forgiveness of sins have now been secured through God's offering of his Son as the "mercy seat" (כַּפֹּרֶת, kappōreth; ἱλαστήριον, hilastērion in Greek). In the crucified Christ the ἱλαστήριον has been set forth to manifest the presence of God among his people. Atonement has been made at the "place of atonement," and that "place of atonement" is the crucified, blood-spattered Messiah Jesus. On the imagery used here concerning the ἱλαστήριον at Romans 3:25, see the appendix, "The Imagery of Romans 3:25."

Detailed Comment

3:21 Paul begins with the emphatic νυνὶ δέ ("but now!"). The expression appears elsewhere in Paul's writings a dozen times.[9] In some cases it marks a

---

7. O. Kuss, *Römer,* 1:160-61; S. Lyonnet, "Notes sur l'exegèsè de l'Épître aux Romains," 59; H. Schlier, *Römer,* 107 (n. 8); C. Cranfield, *Romans,* 200 (n. 1); D. Campbell, *The Rhetoric of Righteousness,* 57; D. Moo, *Romans,* 220. J. Ziesler, *The Meaning of Righteousness,* 192-94, 209-10, works on the assumption that the passage is Pauline, but grants that "something like Käsemann's view is not implausible" (p. 210).

8. On Paul's missionary proclamation in synagogues, cf. Acts 13:13-52; 14:1-5; 17:1-5, 10-14, 17; 18:4-8, 18-21, 26; 19:8-9. Although Paul does not speak explicitly of such activities, they explain why he received the floggings five times over that he mentions (2 Cor 11:24).

9. Rom 6:22; 7:6, 17; 15:23, 25; 1 Cor 12:18; 13:13; 15:20; 2 Cor 8:11, 22; Phlm 9, 11.

sharp contrast (e.g., 1 Cor 12:18; NRSV: "but as it is"), and in other places it has a purely temporal meaning (e.g., Rom 15:23, 25). At 3:21 the expression most certainly signifies both.[10] In terms of expressing a contrast, νυνὶ δέ marks a total reversal between what is to follow and what has preceded in 1:18–3:20. At 1:18 Paul declared that *the wrath of God* (ὀργὴ θεοῦ) is being revealed from heaven, doing its work of judgment, but now he declares that *the righteousness of God* (δικαιοσύνη θεοῦ) has been made manifest in the crucifixion and resurrection of Christ. In terms of time, the expression "but now" marks the arrival of the "eschatological now" or the "already" of the revelation of God's righteousness in Christ. The promise of the prophets that God's righteousness would be revealed with the coming of the Messiah (or the messianic age) has *now* been fulfilled.

The "righteousness of God" (δικαιοσύνη θεοῦ), now revealed, is not "God's justice" (a possible translation of the Greek words when context is disregarded),[11] nor is it a divine standard that must be met by all people at the final judgment, for God's righteousness is revealed *in the gospel* (1:17). The righteousness of God is God's saving activity, setting the relationship right between humanity and himself. For more on the concept, see the exegesis of 1:17 and the appendix, "The 'Righteousness of God' in Paul."

The righteousness of God has been revealed, Paul declares, "apart from the law" (χωρὶς νόμου). Paul is rooted in Jewish tradition, and for that tradition the prime medium of divine revelation is the Torah (Rom 3:19). But now, says Paul, revelation has come by means of something else, and that is God's sending his Son into the world, whose life, death, and resurrection was a manifestation of God's saving work. Backing up, as if to catch himself from being misunderstood after saying that all this is "apart from the law," Paul goes on to assert that the righteousness of God, to be sure, has been "borne witness to by the law and the prophets." In other words, this is not something that would surprise Moses and the prophets, as though the Christian movement had its origins in Gentile paganism. In fact, the law and the prophets (the scriptural tradition of Israel)[12] anticipated the coming of the Messiah (or messianic age) and the advent of righteousness attending him. The law and the prophets bore witness to the advent of the righteousness of God. The promises they gave have now been fulfilled.

3:22-23 God's righteousness, now revealed in Christ, is apprehended and

---

10. Gustav Stählin, "νῦν," *TDNT* 4:1117 (n. 70); C. Cranfield, *Romans*, 201; J. Dunn, *Romans*, 164; K. Haacker, *Römer*, 86; E. Lohse, *Römer*, 129-30. Contra J. Woyke, "'Einst' und 'Jetzt,'" 185-206, for whom the expression at Rom 3:21 has a rhetorical function only.

11. The Vulgate has *iustitia Dei*, and "justice of God" is the translation in the Douay-Rheims version (1899), the JB (1966), the NJB (1985), and the NAB of 1970 (the NAB of 1986 has "righteousness of God").

12. The expression "the law and the prophets" is found, e.g., in 2 Macc 15:9; 4 Macc 18:10; Sir Prologue 1:1; Matt 7:12; 11:13; 22:40; Luke 16:16; John 1:45, and elsewhere.

made effective proleptically "through faith in Jesus Christ for all who believe." It has been proposed that the phrase διὰ πίστεως Ἰησοῦ Χριστοῦ should be translated "through the faith (or faithfulness) of Jesus Christ" (a subjective genitive reading) and that to leave it as "through faith in Jesus Christ" makes the rest of the sentence ("for all who believe") redundant.[13] But the case for a subjective genitive reading here has not been convincing to many,[14] as shown in the appendix, "*Pistis Christou:* Faith in or of Christ?" And rather than seeing a redundancy here, it is more fitting to interpret what Paul has written as an emphasis on the universality of redemption, which he does by means of the phrase "for all who believe." The "all" is emphasized by the following phrase, "for there is no distinction." Paul has affirmed earlier that God shows no partiality (2:11).

The "all" is picked up again in 3:23. All have sinned, and all fall short of the glory of God. The verb for "sinned" (ἥμαρτον) is in the aorist tense, but need not be translated as simple past ("all sinned"). As in other places, the perfect tense "have sinned" is required in English translation (Job 7:20; Ps 51:4 [LXX 50:6]; Sir 27:1; Matt 27:4; Luke 15:18, 21; Acts 25:8; Rom 2:12). To fall short of the glory of God, a puzzling phrase, is to fail to share that perfect communion with God for which humanity was created. According to Jewish sources roughly contemporary with Paul, that communion with God existed prior to the fall, but was lost when Adam and Eve transgressed the command of God not to eat from the forbidden tree.[15] According to Paul, it will be restored among the saints in the world to come (Rom 5:2; 8:21; 1 Thess 2:12; cf. Heb 2:10),[16] but for now it is elusive and reached by no one. At 5:2 Paul will declare that, being justified by faith, believers have the hope of sharing the glory of God once again.

---

13. See the footnote in the NRSV and the studies of various proponents, including S. Williams, "The 'Righteousness of God' in Romans," 274; idem, "Again *Pistis Christou,* 436 (n. 19); R. Hays, *The Faith of Jesus Christ,* 142, 158; L. Keck, "'Jesus' in Romans," 454-56. Cf. also L. T. Johnson, "Romans 3:21-26," 79, 83; M. Hooker, "Πίστις Χριστοῦ," 166; N. T. Wright, *NIB (Romans),* 10:470.

14. Among others, these include A. Hultgren, "The *Pistis Christou* Formulation in Paul," 248-63; C. Cranfield, "On the Πίστις Χριστοῦ Question," 81-97; J. Dunn, "Once More, ΠΙΣΤΙΣ ΧΡΙΣΤΟΥ," 249-71; J. Fitzmyer, *Romans,* 345-46; B. Byrne, *Romans,* 124, 130; K. Haacker, *Römer,* 87; D. Moo, *Romans,* 224-26; E. Lohse, *Römer,* 131; R. Jewett, *Romans,* 277-78.

15. In *Apoc. Mos.* 21.6 Adam says to Eve: "O evil woman! Why have you wrought destruction among us? You have estranged me from the glory of God." Cf. *3 Apoc. Bar.* 4.16: "Adam through this tree was condemned and was stripped of the glory of God" (translations by M. D. Johnson, *OTP* 2:281, and H. E. Gaylord, *OTP* 1:669, respectively). These works are commonly considered to be from the first century A.D. and first to third centuries A.D., respectively. That Adam was fashioned in the image of God's glory is asserted in 4Q504.8.1.4.

16. For a similar view in Jewish sources, cf. *1 Enoch* 50.1; *2 Apoc. Bar.* 51.3; 1QS 4.23; 1QH 17.15; CD 3.20.

3:24 The verse begins with a passive participle (δικαιούμενοι, "being justified"), the antecedent of which is πάντες ("all") in the previous verse. That being the case, Paul is saying that all are justified freely by God's grace. Justification cannot be considered an achievement that is won, for it is God's action by which humanity is set in right relationship with God once again, and so it is totally a matter of grace (χάρις), meaning undeserved favor.[17] The statement is modified by the adverb δωρεάν ("freely" or "as a gift")[18] to emphasize the point. The justifying work of God takes place by means of the "redemption" (ἀπολύτρωσις) that God has accomplished in Christ. The term ἀπολύτρωσις appears two more times in the writings of Paul (Rom 8:23; 1 Cor 1:30) and then in other NT passages (Luke 21:28; Eph 1:7, 14; 4:30; Col 1:14; Heb 9:15; 11:35). It carries a range of meanings ("redemption," "acquittal," "release," and "deliverance").[19] In this particular case it signifies being set free from the power of sin as the dominating condition of humanity (Rom 3:9) and, as a consequence, being set free from the divine wrath at the final judgment (Rom 5:9). Although some interpreters take the phrase "in Christ Jesus" (ἐν Χριστῷ Ἰησοῦ) to refer to those for whom redemption is accomplished (i.e, for those "in Christ," meaning Christians),[20] the clause does not actually say that much but speaks instead of the "redemption that is in Christ Jesus" (which the relative pronoun τῆς ["that" or "which"] makes clear, referring to ἀπολύτρωσις as its antecedent). The phrase in question speaks of the way that God has accomplished redemption, i.e., through the crucified and risen Christ.[21] The "in Christ" formulation is used by Paul dozens of times in his letters, and frequently in reference to persons who are in union with Christ through faith (i.e., persons who are Christians, Rom 8:1; 16:7, 9; 1 Cor 15:8; 2 Cor 5:17). But it can have the instrumental use as well, particularly in contexts where Paul is speaking of the redemptive work of God by means of Christ (Rom 6:23; 1 Cor 1:4; 15:22; 2 Cor 5:19; Gal 3:14), and that is the case here.

3:25 As printed in the Nestle-Aland Greek NT (27th edition), the material in 3:25-26 continues a lengthy, 74-word sentence that began at 3:22b (οὐ γάρ ἐστιν διαστολή, "for there is no distinction") and ends at the close of 3:26 (πίστεως Ἰησοῦ, "faith in Jesus"). English versions break the sentence up into shorter units in attempts to make it more comprehensible.

Verse 3:25 begins with the relative pronoun ὅν ("whom"), referring back to "Christ Jesus" at the close of 3:24, and what follows is a clause that — once again — speaks of divine action. God is the subject, Christ the object, and the

---

17. BDAG 1079 (χάρις, 2, a).
18. BDAG 268 (δωρεάν, 1).
19. BDAG 117 (ἀπολύτρωσις).
20. J. Dunn, *Romans*, 170; J. Fitzmyer, *Romans*, 348.
21. U. Wilckens, *Römer*, 1:190; E. Käsemann, *Romans*, 96; C. Cranfield, *Romans*, 208.

rest of the clause speaks of the redemptive work of God that was accomplished by means of the crucified Christ.

There is a second object in the clause as well, which has been translated here as "mercy seat." It comes from the Greek term ἱλαστήριον. Although the term has been translated "mercy seat" in at least one modern version (NET), it is usually translated with other terms, such as "propitiation" (KJV and ASV), "expiation" (RSV), and "sacrifice of atonement" (NIV and NRSV). Of these possibilities, "mercy seat" is the most fitting, as at Hebrews 9:5, which is the only other place in the NT where the word appears. The Greek term is extremely rare. It appears 28 times in the LXX, of which 21 instances refer to the "mercy seat" (כַּפֹּרֶת, kappōreth) of the OT (Exod 25:17-22; Lev 16:11-17), the lid (or cover) over the ark of the covenant, which was sprinkled with blood for the sin offering by the high priest within the Holy of Holies on the Day of Atonement. Here Paul makes a connection between the "mercy seat" of the OT as a "type" and the crucified Christ as the "antitype."[22] The crucified Christ is the ἱλαστήριον, the "mercy seat," that God has put forth publicly for an atoning purpose. The crucified Christ is the place at which atonement is made for all of humanity. Furthermore, since God has promised to be present at the mercy seat (Exod 25:22; Lev 16:2; Num 7:89), God has now fulfilled the promise of his presence in effecting atonement. Whoever would look for the presence of God need look no further than to the crucified Christ. Paul says, in effect, that the crucified Christ is the one whom God has put forth to show his righteousness once and for all, and whose death was prefigured in the OT ritual at the mercy seat on the Day of Atonement. By this means God has shown forth his righteousness "at the present time" (ἐν τῷ νῦν καιρῷ, Rom 3:26). In the atoning death of Jesus the OT promise has been fulfilled: "For on this day atonement shall be made for you, to cleanse you; from all your sins you shall be clean before the LORD" (Lev 16:30).

Although it must be granted that an interpretation of this verse as a case in which Paul makes a typological connection to the OT may seem obscure to the modern reader, it must also be granted that the typological interpretation is the "classical" one, for it is found in the writings of various ancient interpreters whose language was Greek. Moreover, since the Christians at Rome were composed partly of persons of Jewish heritage, the typological correlation would have been the most obvious within that community. Nevertheless, there are many issues to explore in regard to the term in its context. For further discussion, see the appendix, "The Imagery of Romans 3:25."

The verb προέθετο ("put forth," aorist indicative of προτίθημι) appears in

---

22. The typological interpretation appears frequently in early Christian writings, as illustrated in the appendix, "The Imagery of Romans 3:25."

the LXX in places where it refers to cultic actions, in which a presentation is made before God and/or the people (Exod 29:23; 40:23; Lev 24:8; 1 Chr 29:6, 9, 17; 2 Macc 1:8). Here then it refers to God's putting forth his Son for a redemptive purpose in his death. The phrase "by his blood" (ἐν τῷ αὐτοῦ αἵματι) need not mean any more than "by his death."[23] The word ἐν (usually meaning "in") is instrumental at this place, corresponding to Hebrew constructions with בְּ (b^e),[24] and therefore is best translated as "by." The phrase διὰ [τῆς] πίστεως is translated here as "to be received by faith" (as in RSV; NRSV has "effective through faith").

The KJV and NIV follow the word order of the Greek text, rendering the two prepositional phrases διὰ πίστεως ("through faith") and ἐν τῷ αὐτοῦ αἵματι ("in his blood") as "through faith in his blood." Although that is understandable when following the word order, the prepositional phrase "through faith" should not be connected to "in his blood" as though the latter is the object of faith; it should be connected rather to the earlier part of the clause, which speaks of the divine action. The divine action of putting forth Christ as the mercy seat is apprehended by faith, and effective for faith. One gets the impression that Paul's diction at this point is both halting and staccato, as though a phrase comes to mind that he wants included while composing the main thrust of what he wants to say.

This act of God in the death of Christ, says Paul, was "to demonstrate [God's] righteousness for the sake of the remission of the sins committed previously" (3:25b). The terminology of this half-verse is loaded with theological terms, some of which are familiar, but others not at all, in Paul's letters. The wording for "to demonstrate" is a prepositional phrase in Greek that, literally, means "unto a demonstration"; the noun "demonstration" (ἔνδειξις) appears again already at Romans 3:26, then at 2 Corinthians 8:24, and also at Philippians 1:28. The term translated "remission" (πάρεσις) is used only here in the NT (and is not used in the LXX). It can have the meaning of "passing over" or "overlooking" sins in the past,[25] but it more likely has the meaning here for "remission" or "forgiveness" of sins.[26] It is therefore a synonym of the more famil-

---

23. The term προέθετο ("put forth") would not then include the resurrection of Christ within the divine action as well, as suggested by D. Brandos, *Paul on the Cross*, 131.

24. BDF 118 (§219, 2).

25. BDAG 776 (πάρεσις). That meaning is preferred by W. Sanday and A. Headlam, *Romans*, 90; C. Cranfield, *Romans*, 211; Cyril Blackman, "Romans 3:26a," 203-4; J. Dunn, *Romans*, 173; S. Gathercole, "Justified by Faith," 180.

26. W. Kümmel, "Πάρεσις and ἔνδειξις," 3-4. Cf. also Rudolf Bultmann, "ἀφίημι," *TDNT* 1:511-12; E. Käsemann, *Romans*, 98; U. Wilckens, *Römer*, 1:196; N. Dahl, "Promise and Fulfillment," 129; J. Ziesler, *Romans*, 115-16; B. Meyer, "The Pre-Pauline Formula in Rom. 3.25-26a," 204; S. Travis, "Christ as Bearer of Divine Judgment," 339-40; and J. Fitzmyer, *Romans*, 351.

iar word ἄφεσις ("forgiveness"), which Paul himself never uses.[27] The word for "sins" (ἁμαρτήματα) appears again — in singular, not plural, form — only at 1 Corinthians 6:18; the usual term, used over 50 times by Paul, is ἁμαρτία (e.g., at Rom 3:9, 20; 5:12, 13; or its plural, 1 Cor 15:3, etc.). The word προγίνομαι (προγεγονότων in the text, a perfect participle, translated here as "committed previously") appears nowhere else in the NT, but it appears three times in the LXX (Wis 19:13; 2 Macc 14:3; 15:8). In the present instance Paul would be referring to sins committed prior to the sending of Christ,[28] that is, sins committed during the time of God's patience — prior to the expression of God's wrath (Rom 1:18–3:20) and prior to the expression of God's righteousness in Christ (3:21-26).

In this half-verse, then, Paul declares that *now*,[29] since God has put forth his Son, the day of salvation has arrived. Through his presentation of Christ crucified, God has made atonement "to demonstrate his righteousness for the sake of the remission of the sins committed previously" since the world began, which includes not only the sins of those who have died long ago but also those in the present. By saying this, Paul declares that the eschatological forgiveness of sins — the forgiveness to be exercised heretofore in the final judgment by the God who is righteous — has been revealed and exercised in the present. In the days prior to God's sending forth his Son, the Day of Atonement could provide only provisional atonement, leaving the full "remission of the sins committed formerly" by anyone (between the annual day and that person's death) to the final judgment.[30] (A similar treatment of the Day of Atonement as provisional, always needing repetition, is found in Heb 9:25-28.) But *now,* says Paul, God has remitted the sins committed prior to the final judgment in the display of his righteousness through the death of Christ.

The force of the preposition διά followed by an accusative noun (διὰ τὴν πάρεσιν) is disputed. Some see it as having the meaning of "through" (so "through the remission of the sins committed previously").[31] But an analogy where Paul uses διά plus accusative, and is speaking of the saving work of God in Christ, is Romans 4:25a. There Paul writes that Christ "was put to death *for* [διά plus accusative] our trespasses." So God demonstrates his righteousness (or saving activity) "for the sake of the remission of the sins committed previ-

27. The term appears, however, in the deutero-Paulines (Eph 1:7; Col 1:14).

28. Such is the view also of D. Stanley, "The Atonement," 170.

29. Both the νυνί ("now!") of Rom 3:21 and the νῦν ("now") of 3:26 speak of a shift to the eschatological age. Cf. Gustav Stählin, "νῦν," *TDNT* 4:1117; E. Käsemann, *Romans,* 92; O. Michel, *Römer,* 89; C. Cranfield, *Romans,* 201; and U. Wilckens, *Römer,* 1:184.

30. On the provisional character of the Day of Atonement, see T. Gaster, *Festivals of the Jewish Year,* 145-46.

31. W. Kümmel, "Πάρεσις and ἔνδειξις," 10-11; U. Wilckens, *Römer,* 1:196.

ously" (cf. LXX Isa 53:5).[32] The display has one intended purpose and effect: the forgiveness of sins.

Although there are no verbal links to show dependence, Paul speaks here of the activity of God in a way that is reminiscent of Micah 7:18-20. The author of that book asks rhetorically of God: "Who is a God like you, pardoning iniquity and passing over the ungodly deeds (LXX: ὑπερβαίνων ἀσεβείας) of the remnant of your possession?" He then goes on to say about God: "He does not retain his anger forever, because he delights in showing mercy. He will again have compassion upon us; he will tread our iniquities under foot." Then the prophet addresses God again: "You will cast all our sins into the depths of the sea. You will show faithfulness to Jacob and unswerving loyalty to Abraham, as you have sworn to our ancestors from the days of old." The character of God envisioned by Micah has been confirmed in the death and resurrection of Christ, and the anticipated activity of God to pass over sins has been fulfilled.

The phrase "during the time of his divine forbearance" (ἐν τῇ ἀνοχῇ τοῦ θεοῦ) is usually contained within 3:25 in English versions of the NT (e.g., KJV, ASV, RSV, NIV, and NRSV), but it is actually the opening portion of 3:26 in the Westcott-Hort and Nestle-Aland editions of the Greek NT. The phrase modifies the words immediately before it, i.e., "the sins committed previously." The effect is to say that in the sending of his Son for redemption, God has forgiven those sins committed during the time of his "forbearance," "patience," or "restraint." It is a parenthetical phrase to clarify what sins Paul has in mind. They are those sins committed ever since creation and prior to the exercise of God's wrath against the world at the close of the present age (Rom 1:18–3:20) and the present manifestation of his righteousness in sending his Son to redeem (3:21-26).

3:26 This saving activity of God in Christ, Paul says, demonstrates God's righteousness in the present moment (ἐν τῷ νῦν καιρῷ) as well. The expression "the present time" (ὁ νῦν καιρός) is used elsewhere by Paul as well, and in each case it signifies the present era in which he and all of humanity reside, prior to the parousia (Rom 8:18; 11:5; 2 Cor 8:14). God is righteous (δίκαιος) and justifies (δικαιοῦντα, a present active participle from δικαιόω, "to justify" or "to set right") the person who has faith in Jesus, crucified and risen. The νῦν ("now") of 3:26 recalls and echoes the νυνί ("now!") of 3:21. God's righteousness (i.e., God's saving activity) has been revealed in the Christ event, and it is effective in the present for all believers, those who trust in all that God has done in Christ, the manifestation of God's righteousness. On rendering the closing line as

---

32. On the meaning of "for the sake of" in the use of διά plus accusative, cf. BDAG 225 (διά, B, 2, a); similarly, J. Fitzmyer, *Romans*, 351, and W. Kraus, *Der Tod Jesu als Heiligtumsweihe*, 149.

"[God] justifies the one who has faith in Jesus" (rather than "[God] justifies the one who has the faith of Jesus") see the appendix, "*Pistis Christou*: Faith in or of Christ?"

BIBLIOGRAPHY

Bailey, Daniel P. "Jesus as the Mercy Seat: The Semantics and Theology of Paul's Use of *Hilastērion* in Romans 3:25." Ph.D. diss., University of Cambridge, 1999.

———. "Jesus as the Mercy Seat: The Semantics and Theology of Paul's Use of *Hilastērion* in Romans 3:25." *TynBul* 51 (2000): 155-58.

Bird, Michael F. *The Saving Righteousness of God: Studies on Paul, Justification and the New Perspective.* Colorado Springs: Paternoster, 2007.

Blackman, Cyril. "Romans 3:26b: A Question of Translation." *JBL* 87 (1968): 203-4.

Brondos, David A. *Paul on the Cross: Reconstructing the Apostle's Story of Redemption.* Minneapolis: Fortress Press, 2006.

Buchanan, George W. "The Day of Atonement and Paul's Doctrine of Redemption." *NovT* 32 (1990): 236-49.

Bultmann, Rudolf. *Theology of the New Testament.* 2 vols. New York: Charles Scribner's Sons, 1951-55.

Byrne, Brendan. "Universal Need of Salvation and Universal Salvation by Faith in the Letter to the Romans." *Pacifica* 8 (1995): 123-39.

Cadman, W. H. "Δικαιοσύνη in Romans 3,21-26." *SE* 2 (= TU 87, 1964): 532-34.

Campbell, Douglas A. "False Presuppositions in the ΠΙΣΤΙΣ ΧΡΙΣΤΟΥ Debate: A Response to Brian Dodd." *JBL* 116 (1997): 713-19.

———. *The Rhetoric of Righteousness in Romans 3.21-26.* JSNTSup 65. Sheffield: Sheffield Academic Press, 1992.

———. "Romans 1:17 — A *Crux Interpretum* for the Πίστις Χριστοῦ Debate." *JBL* 113 (1994): 265-85.

Campbell, William S. "Romans III as a Key to the Structure and Thought of the Letter." *NovT* 23 (1981): 21-40; reprinted in *The Romans Debate,* 251-64. Rev. ed. Ed. Karl P. Donfried. Peabody: Hendrickson Publishers, 1991.

Carroll, John T., and Joel Green. *The Death of Jesus in Early Christianity.* Peabody: Hendrickson Publishers. 1995.

Carter, Warren C. "Rome (and Jerusalem): The Contingency of Romans 3:21-26." *IBS* 11 (1989): 54-68.

Choi, Richard R. "The Problem of Translating ἐν τῷ αὐτοῦ αἵματι in Romans 3:25a." *AUSS* 38 (2000): 199-201.

Conzelmann, Hans. *An Outline of the Theology of the New Testament.* New York: Harper & Row, 1969.

Cosgrove, Charles H. "Justification in Paul: A Linguistic and Theological Reflection." *JBL* 106 (1987): 653-70.

Cousar, Charles B. *A Theology of the Cross: The Death of Jesus in the Pauline Letters.* Minneapolis: Fortress Press, 1990.

Cranfield, C. E. B. "On the Πίστις Χριστοῦ Question." In his *On Romans and Other New Testament Essays,* 81-97. Edinburgh: T&T Clark, 1998.

Creed, J. M. "ΠΑΡΕΣΙΣ in Dionysius of Halicarnassus and in St. Paul." *JTS* 41 (1940): 28-30.

Dahl, Nils A., "Promise and Fulfillment." In his *Studies in Paul,* 121-36. Minneapolis: Augsburg Publishing House, 1977.

Dodd, Brian. "Romans 1:17 — A *Crux Interpretum* for the Πίστις Χριστοῦ Debate?" *JBL* 114 (1995): 470-73.

Dodd, C. H. "Atonement." In his *The Bible and the Greeks,* 82-95. London: Hodder & Stoughton, 1935; reprinted (and renamed) from his essay "ΙΛΑΣΚΕΣΘΑΙ, Its Cognates, Derivatives and Synonyms in the Septuagint." *JTS* 32 (1931): 352-60.

Donfried, Karl P. "Justification and Last Judgment in Paul." *Int* 30 (1976): 140-52.

———. "Justification and Last Judgment in Paul — Twenty-Five Years Later." In his *Paul, Thessalonica and Early Christianity,* 279-92. Grand Rapids: Wm. B. Eerdmans, 2002.

———. "Romans 3:21-28." *Int* 34 (1980): 59-64.

Dugandzic, Ivan. "Das Zeugnis von 'Gesetz und Propheten' für die sich in Christus offenbarende Gerechtigkeit Gottes: Rom 3,21-4,22: Die Erklärung von 3,21-31." In his *Das 'Ja' Gottes in Christus: Eine Studie zur Bedeutung des Alten Testaments für das Christusverständnis des Paulus,* 158-77. FB 26. Würzburg: Echter Verlag, 1977.

Dunn, James D. G. "Once More, ΠΙΣΤΙΣ ΧΡΙΣΤΟΥ." In *Society of Biblical Literature 1991 Seminar Papers,* 730-44. Ed. Eugene H. Lovering. SBLSP 30. Atlanta: Scholars Press, 1991; reprinted in Richard B. Hays, *The Faith of Jesus Christ: The Narrative Substructure of Galatians 3:1–4:11,* 249-71. 2d ed. Grand Rapids: Wm. B. Eerdmans, 2002. References are to page numbers there.

Dupont, Jacques. "The Conversion of Paul and Its Influence on His Understanding of Salvation by Faith." In *Apostolic History and the Gospel: Biblical and Historical Essays Presented to F. F. Bruce on His 60th Birthday,* 176-94. Ed. W. Ward Gasque and Ralph P. Martin. Exeter: Paternoster Press, 1970.

Du Toit, Andreas B. "Forensic Metaphors in Romans and Their Soteriological Significance." In *Salvation in the New Testament: Perspectives on Soteriology,* 213-46. Ed. Jan G. van der Watt. NovTSup 121. Boston: E. J. Brill, 2005.

Ekem, John D. K. "A Dialogical Exegesis of Romans 3.25a." *JSNT* 30 (2007): 75-93.

Fahy, Thomas. "Exegesis of Romans 3:25f." *ITQ* 23 (1956): 69-73.

Finlan, Stephen. *The Background and Content of Paul's Cultic Atonement Metaphors.* SBLAB 19. Atlanta: Society of Biblical Literature, 2004.

Fitzer, Gottfried. "Der Ort der Versöhnung nach Paulus: Zu der Frage des 'Suhnopfers Jesu.'" *TZ* 22 (1966): 161-83.

Fitzmyer, Joseph A. "Paul and the Dead Sea Scrolls." In *The Dead Sea Scrolls after Fifty Years: A Comprehensive Assessment,* 2:599-621. Ed. Peter W. Flint and James C. VanderKam. 2 vols. Boston: E. J. Brill, 1998-99.

Frey, Jörg, and Jens Schrötter, eds. *Deutungen des Todes Jesu im Neuen Testament.* WUNT 181. Tübingen: J. C. B. Mohr (Paul Siebeck), 2005.

Fryer, Nico S. L. "The Meaning and Translation of *Hilastērion* in Romans 3:25." *EvQ* 59 (1987): 99-116.

Garlington, Don. "Paul's 'Partisan ἐκ' and the Question of Justification in Galatians." *JBL* 127 (2008): 567-89.

Gaster, Theodor H. *Festivals of the Jewish Year.* New York: William Sloane, 1952.

Gathercole, Simon J. "The Doctrine of Justification in Paul and Beyond: Some Proposals." In *Justification in Perspective: Historical Developments and Contemporary Challenges,* 219-41. Ed. Bruce L. McCormack. Grand Rapids: Baker Academic, 2006.

———. "Justified by Faith, Justified by His Blood: The Evidence of Romans 3:21–4:25." In *Justification and Variegated Nomism,* 2:147-84. Ed. D. A. Carson, Peter T. O'Brien, and Mark Seifrid. 2 vols. Grand Rapids: Baker Academic, 2001-4.

Genest, Olivette. *Le discourse du Nouveau Testament sur la mort de Jésus: Épîtres et Apocalypse.* Sainte-Foy, Québec: Presses de l'Université Laval, 1995.

Greenwood, David. "Jesus as *Hilastērion* in Romans 3:25." *BTB* 3 (1973): 316-22.

Hays, Richard B. *The Faith of Jesus Christ: The Narrative Substructure of Galatians 3:1–4:11,* 272-97. 2d ed. Grand Rapids: Wm. B. Eerdmans, 2002.

———. "PISTIS and Pauline Theology." In E. H. Lovering, ed., *Society of Biblical Literature 1991 Seminar Papers,* 714-29. Atlanta: Scholars Press, 1991; reprinted in his *The Faith of Jesus Christ: The Narrative Substructure of Galatians 3:1–4:11,* 272-97. 2d ed. Grand Rapids: Wm. B. Eerdmans, 2002. References to this essay are to page numbers in the latter volume.

———. "Psalm 143 and the Logic of Romans 3." *JBL* 99 (1980): 107-15.

Henten, Jan Willem van. *The Maccabean Martyrs as Saviours of the Jewish People: A Study of 2 and 4 Maccabees.* JSJSup 57. Leiden: E. J. Brill, 1997.

———. "The Tradition-Historical Background of Rom. 3.25: A Search for Pagan and Jewish Parallels." In *From Jesus to John: Essays on Jesus and New Testament Christology in Honour of Marinus de Jonge,* 101-28. Ed. Martinus C. de Boer. JSNTSup 84. Sheffield: JSOT Press, 1993.

———, and Friedrich Avemarie. *Martyrdom and Noble Death: Selected Texts from Graeco-Roman, Jewish and Christian Antiquity.* London: Routledge, 2002.

Hooker, Morna D. "Πίστις Χριστοῦ." *NTS* 35 (1989): 321-42; reprinted in her *From Adam to Christ: Essays on Paul,* 165-86. Cambridge: Cambridge University Press, 1990. Page references are to the latter.

Howard, George. "Romans 3:21-31 and the Inclusion of the Gentiles." *HTR* 63 (1970): 223-33.

Hübner, Hans. "Rechtfertigung und Sühne bei Paulus: Eine hermeneutische und theologische Besinnung." *NTS* 39 (1993): 80-93.

———. "Sühne und Versöhnung: Anmerkungen zu einem umstritten Kapital biblischer Theologie." *KD* 29 (1983): 284-305.

Hultgren, Arland J. "The *Pistis Christou* Formulation in Paul." *NovT* 22 (1980): 248-63.

Hunter, Archibald M. *Paul and His Predecessors.* Rev. ed. Philadelphia: Westminster Press, 1961.

Johnson, Luke Timothy. "Romans 3:21-6 and the Faith of Jesus." *CBQ* 44 (1982): 77-90.

Käsemann, Ernst. "Justification and Salvation History in the Epistle to the Romans." In his *Perspectives on Paul,* 60-78. Philadelphia: Fortress Press, 1971.

————. "'The Righteousness of God' in Paul." In his *New Testament Questions of Today,* 168-82. London: SCM Press, 1969.

————. "The Saving Significance of the Death of Jesus in Paul." In his *Perspectives on Paul,* 32-59. Philadelphia: Fortress Press, 1971.

————. "Zum Verständnis von Römer 3,24-26." *ZNW* 43 (1950-51): 150-54.

Keck, Leander E. "'Jesus' in Romans." *JBL* 108 (1989): 443-60.

Kertelge, Karl. *"Rechtfertigung" bei Paulus. Studien zur Struktur and zum Bedeutungsgehalt des paulinischen Rechtfertigungsbegriffs.* NTAbh 3. Münster: Aschendorff, 1966.

Klumbies, Paul-Gerhard. "Der Eine Gott des Paulus. Röm 3,21-31 als Brennpunkt paulinischer Theologie." *ZNW* 85 (1994): 192-206.

Kraus, Wolfgang. *Der Tod Jesu als Heiligtumsweihe: Eine Untersuchung zum Umfeld der Sühnevorstellung in Römer 3:25-26a.* WMANT 66. Neukirchen: Neukirchener Verlag, 1991.

Kümmel, Werner G. "Πάρεσις and ἔνδειξις: A Contribution to the Understanding of the Pauline Doctrine of Justification." In *Distinctive Protestant and Catholic Themes Reconsidered,* 1-13. Ed. Robert W. Funk. New York: Harper & Row, 1967.

————. *The Theology of the New Testament.* Nashville: Abingdon Press, 1973.

Kuhn, Heinz-Wolfgang. "The Impact of the Qumran Scrolls on the Understanding of Paul." In *The Dead Sea Scrolls: Forty Years of Research,* 327-39. Ed. Devorah Dimant and Uriel Rappaport. STDJ 10. New York: E. J. Brill, 1992.

Lohse, Eduard. "Die Gerechtigkeit Gottes in der paulinischen Theologie." In *Battesimo e giustizia in Rom 6 e 8, 7-26.* Ed. Lorenzo de Lorenzi. Rome: Abbazia S. Paolo, 1974.

Longenecker, Bruce W. "Πίστις in Romans 3.25: Neglected Evidence for the 'Faithfulness of Christ'?" *NTS* 39 (1993): 478-80.

Lyonnet, Stanislas. "Notes sur l'exégése de l'épître aux Romans." *Bib* 38 (1957): 35-61.

Manson, T. W. "ἱλαστήριον." *JTS* 46 (1945): 1-10.

Meyer, Ben F. "The Pre-Pauline Formula in Rom. 3.25-26a." *NTS* 29 (1983): 198-208.

Morris, Leon. "The Meaning of ΙΛΑΣΤΗΡΙΟΝ in Romans III. 25." *NTS* 2 (1955-56): 33-43.

Mussner, Franz. "Die Offenbarung der Gerechtigkeit Gottes." In his *Tod und Auferstehung: Fastenpredigten über Römerbrieftext,* 9-20. Regensburg: Pustet, 1967.

Nygren, Anders. "Christus, der Gnadenstuhl." In *In Memoriam Ernst Lohmeyer,* 89-93. Ed. Werner Schmauch. Stuttgart: Evangelisches Verlag, 1951.

Piper, John. "The Demonstration of the Righteousness of God in Romans 3:25, 26." *JSNT* 7 (1980): 2-32; reprinted in *The Pauline Writings,* 175-202. Ed. Stanley E. Porter and Craig A. Evans. BibSem 34. Sheffield: Sheffield Academic Press, 1995.

Pollard, Paul. "The 'Faith of Christ' in Current Discussion." *ConJ* 23 (1997): 213-28.

Price, James L. "God's Righteousness Shall Prevail." *Int* 28 (1974): 259-80.

Pryor, John W. "Paul's Use of Ἰησοῦς: A Clue for the Translation of Romans 3:26?" *Coll* 16 (1983): 31-45.

Reumann, John H. P. "The 'Gospel of the Righteousness of God': Pauline Reinterpretation in Romans 3:21-31." *Int* 20 (1966): 433-52.

————. *"Righteousness" in the New Testament: "Justification" in the United States Lutheran–Roman Catholic Dialogue.* Philadelphia: Fortress Press, 1982.

Robeck, Cecil M., Jr. "What Is the Meaning of HILASTĒRION in Romans 3:25?" StudBT 4 (1974): 21-36.

Schnackenburg, Rudolf. "Notre justification par la foi en Jesus Christ sans les oeuvres de la loi (Rm 3)." ASeign 40 (1973): 10-15.

Schrage, Wolfgang. "Römer 3:21-26 und die Bedeutung des Todes Jesu Christi bei Paulus." In Das Kreuz Jesu: Theologische Überlegungen, 65-88. Ed. Paul Rieger. FGS 12. Göttingen: Vandenhoeck & Ruprecht, 1969.

Schreiber, Stefan. "Das Weihegeschenk Gottes: Eine Deutung des Todes des Jesu in Röm 3,25." ZNW 97 (2006): 88-110.

Schroeder, Christoph. "'Standing in the Breach': Turning Away the Wrath of God." Int 52 (1998): 16-23.

Searle, David. "The Righteousness of God, Romans 3:21-22." EJT 8 (1999): 13-22.

Seeley, David. "The Rhetoric of Righteousness in Romans 3:21-26." CBQ 55 (1993): 572-73.

Stanley, David M. "The Atonement as a Manifestation of God's Justice." In his Christ's Resurrection in Pauline Soteriology, 166-71. AnBib 13. Rome: Pontifical Biblical Institute, 1961.

Stökl, Daniel Ben Ezra. The Impact of Yom Kippur on Early Christianity: The Day of Atonement from Second Temple Judaism to the Fifth Century. WUNT 163. Tübingen: J. C. B. Mohr (Paul Siebeck), 2003.

Strecker, Georg. "Befreiung und Rechtfertigung: Zur Stellung der Rechtfertigungslehre in der Theologie des Paulus." In Rechtfertigung: Festschrift für Ernst Käsemann zum 70. Geburtstag, 479-508. Ed. Johannes Friedrich et al. Tübingen: J. C. B. Mohr (Paul Siebeck), 1976.

Stuhlmacher, Peter. Gerechtigkeit Gottes bei Paulus, FRLANT 87. Göttingen: Vandenhoeck & Ruprecht, 1965.

————. "Recent Exegesis of Romans 3:24-26." In his Reconciliation, Law, and Righteousness: Essays in Biblical Theology, 94-109. Philadelphia: Fortress Press, 1986.

Talbert, Charles H. "A Non-Pauline Fragment at Romans 3:24-26?" JBL 85 (1966): 287-96.

Theobald, Michael. "Das Gottesbild des Paulus nach Röm 3,21-31." In his Studien zum Römerbrief, 30-67. WUNT 136. Tübingen: J. C. B. Mohr (Paul Siebeck), 2001.

Thornton, T. C. G. "Propitiation or Expiation? Ἱλαστήριον and Ἱλασμός in Romans and 1 John." ExpTim 80 (1968-69): 53-55.

Travis, Stephen H. "Christ as Bearer of Divine Judgment in Paul's Thought about the Atonement." In Jesus of Nazareth, Lord and Christ: Essays on the Historical Jesus and New Testament Christology, 332-45. Ed. Joel B. Green and Max Turner. Grand Rapids: Wm. B. Eerdmans, 1994.

Ulrichs, Karl F. Christusglaube: Studien zum Syntagma πίστις Χριστοῦ und zum paulinischen Verständnis von Glaube und Rechtfertigung. WUNT 2/227. Tübingen: Verlag Mohr Siebeck, 2007.

VanLandingham, Chris. Judgment and Justification in Early Judaism and the Apostle Paul. Peabody: Hendrickson Publishers, 2006.

Wengst, Klaus. Christologische Formeln und Lieder des Urchristentums. SNT 7. Gütersloh: Gütersloher Verlagshaus Gerd Mohn, 1972.

Williams, Sam K. "Again Pistis Christou." CBQ 49 (1987): 431-47.

———. "The Meaning of Jesus' Death in Romans 3:24-26." In his *Jesus' Death as Saving Event: The Background and Origin of a Concept*, 5-58. HDR 2. Missoula: Scholars Press, 1975.

———. "The 'Righteousness of God' in Romans." *JBL* 99 (1980): 241-90.

Wonneberger, Reinhard. *Syntax und Exegese: Eine generative Theorie der griechischen Syntax und ihr Beitrag zur Auslegung des Neuen Testaments, dargestellt an 2. Korinther 5,2f und Römer 3,21-26.* BBET 13. Frankfurt: Peter Lang, 1979.

Woyke, Johannes. "'Einst' und 'Jetzt' in Röm 1-3? Zur Bedeutung von νυνὶ δέ in Röm 3:21." *ZNW* 92 (2001): 185-206.

Young, Norman H. "Did St. Paul Compose Romans iii,24f?" *AusBR* 22 (1974): 23-32.

———. "The Impact of the Jewish Day of Atonement upon the New Testament." Ph.D. diss., University of Manchester, 1973.

Ziesler, John A. *The Meaning of Righteousness in Paul: A Linguistic and Theological Inquiry.* SNTSMS 20. Cambridge: Cambridge University Press, 1972.

———. "Salvation Proclaimed: IX. Romans 3.21-26." *ExpTim* 93 (1982): 356-59.

3.2. The Universality of Justification by Grace Alone, 3:27-31

27*Where then are the grounds for boasting? They are excluded! By what principle? Of works? No, but on the principle of faith.* 28*For we hold that a person is justified by faith apart from works of the law.* 29*Or is God the God of Jews only? Is he not God of Gentiles too? Yes, also of the Gentiles,* 30*since God is one, who justifies the circumcision by faith and the uncircumcision through faith.* 31*Do we therefore abolish the law through faith? By no means! Instead, we uphold the law.*

Notes on the Text and Translation

3:27 The term νόμος can be translated either as "law" (as in the KJV, ASV, and NRSV) or as "principle" (as in the RSV and NIV). Although there is some advantage in using "law," for it allows a play on words, the connotation here is clearly that of a "principle" at stake. The word "principle" comes across in this context more strongly than does "law." For more, see the commentary below.

3:28 According to the Luther Bible (*Lutherbibel*, 1984), a person is justified apart from works of the law, by faith *alone* ("ohne des Gesetzes Werke, allein durch den Glauben"). When Martin Luther translated the NT into German (1522), he inserted the word *"allein"* (alone). The word has no textual basis in the Greek NT, but exists as an emphasis, and is found in no other modern version.[33] It is ironic that "by faith alone" *(sola fide)* is used in a negative sense

---

33. Although Luther introduced the term "alone" into the actual text of a version of the

in a NT book that Luther considered "an epistle of straw," James 2:24: "You see that a person is justified by works and not by faith alone" (οὐκ ἐκ πίστεως μόνον).[34] It is also significant for ecumenical concerns to see that some Roman Catholic interpreters have commended Luther's understanding of the text (as provided by his insertion) or at least concluded that it poses no difficulty for theology.[35]

General Comment

Having established that God has manifested his saving righteousness in the atoning death of his Son, Paul goes on to say that any boasting of one's own observance of the law is totally impossible. Gentile believers in God's saving righteousness in Christ, who do not possess the law in the first place, are also included among those who are justified. Paul affirms a gospel that is fit for both Jews and Gentiles. Immediately that means that he runs up against the problem of the status of the law. If Gentiles are justified "through faith," does that mean that the law is abolished "through faith"? Paul cannot for a moment allow such a thought to be entertained seriously. He seems to brush the thought aside at this point, but he takes up the question in the following chapter.

A primary exegetical question is whether the term "faith" (πίστις) in this section, as in the preceding one, is the faith of the believer or that of Christ (meaning either his "faith" or his "faithfulness"). In seeking a solution to the question, it is important to see that the section is a bridge passage between the previous paragraph (3:21-26) and the following chapter (4:1-25). It reflects back on the former and anticipates the latter. Seen in that larger context, the term in question refers clearly to the faith of the believer. Just as Abraham is the model of one who is justified by believing God, the one who believes now in the God who raised the crucified Jesus from the dead is the one who is justified (4:24). For more on the question of the believer's faith in this passage, see the appendix, "*Pistis Christou:* Faith in or of Christ?"

Bible, he was not the first to consider the adverb appropriate. J. Fitzmyer, *Romans*, 360-61, lists several Latin writers (providing the texts) prior to Luther who used *sola* (alone) in their commentaries or comments on the text.

34. For Luther's remark on James, cf. Martin Luther, "Prefaces to the New Testament," *LuthW* 35:362 (written in 1522).

35. D. Zeller, *Römer*, 93 (the word is appropriate as a supplement); J. Fitzmyer, *Romans*, 362 ("no difficulty"); B. Byrne, *Romans*, 137, says that the insertion provides a correct understanding of the phrase, but he considers the entire verse as "an aside," summing up what has gone before in 3:21-26 as a basis for the exclusion of boasting in 3:27.

Detailed Comment

3:27 The Greek reads in clipped fashion: "Where then is the boasting?" Boasting (καύχησις) is possible only where a person can claim some accomplishment, advantage, or privilege. The term need not always have a negative connotation, for it can sometimes mean pride in a modest or at least realistic self-assessment within Paul's letters (Rom 15:17; 1 Cor 15:31; 2 Cor 7:4, 14; 8:24; 11:10; 1 Thess 2:19). But here, as at 2 Corinthians 11:17, the term has a decidedly negative connotation. It refers to the pride that can arise in one's possessing the Torah, relying upon it as a means of a favored relationship with God, and thus boasting of that special relationship, which is not available to Gentiles (2:17, 2).[36] This anticipates the play on words to follow, making use of the word νόμος ("law" or "principle") and the question that Paul poses two verses later: "Or is God the God of Jews only?" (3:29).

Boasting is excluded. Since justification is God's doing, not one's own, no one has reason to boast. Paul asks διὰ ποίου νόμου; τῶν ἔργων; ("By what principle? Of works?"). Implicit in the way Paul puts the two questions (using the word νόμος in particular) is that he is alluding to the law of Moses, the Torah, as the "law of works."[37] Nevertheless, Paul continues with the words οὐχί, ἀλλὰ διὰ νόμου πίστεως ("No, but on the principle of faith"), a clause in which the word νόμος cannot be translated as "law." To be sure, some interpreters translate it as "law" and mean by that the law of Moses as seen by the eyes of faith.[38] But to translate the word as "law" leads to confusion, and to understand it to signify the law of Moses compounds the difficulties. Paul makes use of a clever play on words, using a noun that has a broad range of meanings (including "law," "principle," "rule," "norm," "ordinance," "habitual practice," "custom," "usage," and more[39]), as also three times over in a single verse elsewhere in this letter where the term is usually (and best) translated "law" but signifies

---

36. Interpreters are divided on whether Paul is speaking of the boasting that is possible universally in anyone's relationship to God or specifically of that which is possible within the Jewish tradition. The former is held by E. Käsemann, *Romans,* 102; R. Jewett, *Romans,* 296; the latter by C. K. Barrett, *Romans,* 78; J. Dunn, *Romans,* 185; P. Stuhlmacher, *Romans,* 65-66; D. Moo, *Romans,* 246; and Josef Zmijewski, "καυχάομαι," *EDNT* 2:278.

37. O. Michel, *Römer,* 155; J. Dunn, *Romans,* 186; H. Hübner, *Law in Paul's Thought,* 138; H. Räisänen, *Paul and the Law,* 171; E. P. Sanders, *Paul, the Law, and the Jewish People,* 32-33; J. Fitzmyer, *Romans,* 363; D. Moo, *Romans,* 249; E. Lohse, *Römer,* 137.

38. G. Friedrich, "Das Gesetz des Glaubens Röm. 3.27," 401-17; C. Cranfield, *Romans,* 220; U. Wilckens, *Römer,* 1:245; H. Hübner, *Law in Paul's Thought,* 138; J. Dunn, *Romans,* 186-87; R. Hays, "Three Dramatic Roles," 153-54; R. Jewett, *Romans,* 297. A. Ito, "ΝΟΜΟΣ (ΤΩΝ) ΕΡΓΩΝ and ΝΟΜΟΣ ΠΙΣΤΕΩΣ," 257, suggests a different, idiosyncratic view: "the law of faith described in that part of the Torah concerning Abraham's faith."

39. BDAG 677-78 (νόμος); LSJ 1180 (νόμος).

what is typical (constant, regular) concerning the self, the mind, and sin: "I see in my members another law (νόμος) that wages war with the law (νόμος) of my mind and makes me captive to the law (νόμος) of sin that dwells in my members" (Rom 7:23). It is clear that, in the present instance, Paul makes a contrast between two ways of thinking: the way of works and the way of faith. What he declares is that the way of apprehending God's righteousness and of accepting one's own justification is, in principle,[40] by faith, not by observance of the law. Paul uses the term "in the broader sense of the divine ordinance"[41] by which it is faith in the righteousness of God, not works of the law, that justifies (3:26, 28).

3:28 The phrase translated here as "for we hold" (λογιζόμεθα γάρ), consisting of the verb λογιζόμεθα ("we hold") and the conjunction γάρ ("for"), expresses a particularly solemn pronouncement (cf. 8:18; 2 Cor 11:5), a "judgment of faith" that the gospel entails,[42] and to which all believers (so the plural "we") can be expected to give assent. That is that one is justified "by faith" (πίστει, a dative of means) "apart from works of the law" (χωρὶς ἔργων νόμου). The expression "by faith" cannot mean "by faith as a virtue" or "by faith as a power from within." On the contrary, it can mean for Paul only a trust that looks away from the self, turning to God alone as the one who sets the relationship right by means of the atoning work he has done in the crucified Christ. On the place of justification in Paul's theology, see the discussion within the exegesis of 5:1-11.

The expression χωρὶς ἔργων νόμου ("apart from works of the law"; cf. χωρὶς νόμου ["apart from the law"] at 3:21; 7:8-9) means setting aside observance of the law (the Torah), given to the people of Israel, as a means of justification.[43] If justification is by means of "works of the law," the corollary is that only the people of Israel could qualify for justification and ultimate salvation. The verse is strikingly similar in thought to that at Galatians 2:16: "we know that a person is justified not by the works of the law (ἐξ ἔργων νόμου) but through faith in Jesus Christ (διὰ πίστεως Ἰησοῦ Χριστοῦ)." The phrase "works of the law" appears eight times in the letters of Paul (χωρὶς ἔργων νόμου ["apart from works of the law"] here; ἐξ ἔργων νόμου ["by works of the law"] at Rom 3:20; Gal 2:16 [three times]; 3:2, 5, 10).

The meaning of "works of the law" is disputed. Proponents of the "new

40. Walter Gutbrod, "νόμος," *TDNT* 4:1071; R. Bultmann, *Theology of the New Testament*, 1:259; E. Käsemann, *Romans*, 102-3; H. Schlier, *Römer*, 116; H. Räisänen, "Das 'Gesetz des Glaubens' (Rom. 3.27) und das 'Gesetz des Geistes' (Rom. 8.2)," 101-17; idem, *Paul and the Law*, 51-52; E. P. Sanders, *Paul, the Law, and the Jewish People*, 32-33; M. Winger, *By What Law?* 85; E. Lohse, *Römer*, 137.

41. W. Gutbrod, "νόμος," 1071.

42. Hans W. Heidland, "λογίζομαι," *TDNT* 4:288.

43. Cf. R. Rapa, *The Meaning of "Works of the Law,"* 244-50.

perspective" on Paul, which had its origins in the 1970s,[44] have presented a challenge to the commonly held view that Judaism in Paul's day was a religion of "works righteousness" by which one would gain favor with God, and that Paul opposed that way of thinking. According to James D. G. Dunn, for example, doing "works of the law" does not mean keeping the (Mosaic) law to win or preserve divine favor (or "merits"), but designates rather one's living in obedience to a pattern of life, including circumcision, Sabbath, and food laws, that provides social boundaries between Jews and Gentiles.[45] The reason that Paul was opposed to doing "works of the law" was that, for him, the Jewish people had taken over this pattern of life "too completely," leading to "a misplaced emphasis on boundary-marking ritual."[46] That could not be continued within the Christian community, increasingly made up of Gentiles.

One can grant that there have been descriptions of ancient Judaism that have portrayed it as extremely legalistic and to have been a religion in which good works are necessary for salvation. In one of his descriptions of ancient Judaism, for example, Rudolf Bultmann speaks of it as having "regulations" that "went into detail to the point of absurdity"; "to take them seriously meant making life an intolerable burden"; and then the "consequence of the legalistic conception of obedience was that the prospect of salvation became highly uncertain"; and so "in the end the whole range of man's relation with God came to be thought of in terms of merit, including faith itself."[47] Such a description is surely a one-sided caricature of ancient Judaism. Altogether missing are those accents within the sources themselves on the "delight" one has in the Torah (Ps 1:2) and how it makes the heart rejoice (Ps 19:8). It is to the credit of the "new perspective" movement that it has modified and corrected the picture of ancient Judaism. The work of E. P. Sanders has been important in this regard, in which he speaks of the "all-pervasive view" of ancient Judaism as being summarized in the term "covenantal nomism," which he explains in this way: "Briefly put, covenantal nomism is the view that one's place in God's plan is established on the basis of the covenant and that the covenant requires as the proper response of man his obedience to its commandments, while providing means of atonement for transgression."[48] And

---

44. The beginning date is often traced to the publication of E. P. Sanders, *Paul and Palestinian Judaism*, in 1977. But the term "new perspective" is typically attributed (at least for its popularity) to J. Dunn, "The New Perspective on Paul," 95-122, published in 1983. It should be noted, however, that the term was used 20 years earlier (1963) within a presentation by K. Stendahl on "The Apostle Paul and the Introspective Conscience of the West," reprinted in his *Paul among Jews and Gentiles,* where the term appears on p. 95.

45. J. Dunn, *Romans,* lxxii; cf. 186. Cf. also M. Abegg, "Paul and James on the Law," 63-74.

46. J. Dunn, *Romans,* lxxii.

47. R. Bultmann, *Primitive Christianity in Its Contemporary Setting,* 65-66, 70-71.

48. E. P. Sanders, *Paul and Palestinian Judaism,* 75; cf. also pp. 236 and 544.

Dunn has added: "Judaism's whole religious self-understanding was based on the premise of grace — that God had freely chosen Israel and made his covenant with Israel, to be their God and they his people. This covenant relationship was regulated by the law, not as a way of entering the covenant, or of gaining merit, but as the way of living *within* the covenant."[49]

The revised portrayal of ancient Judaism has been extremely important for understanding Judaism itself, but also for interpreting Paul. Having said that, however, it has to be said, too, that ancient Judaism had many strands of tradition, and one can rightly speak of it as variegated and diverse, particularly in the Second Temple era.[50] Some ancient Jewish sources do in fact speak of doing good works for justification or salvation, representing certain strands of Jewish tradition. These sources appear in ancient Jewish sources both prior to and after Paul.[51] Indeed, the expression "works of the law" appears in the Dead Sea Scrolls.[52] Although it must be granted (and even insisted) that the following passage in 2 Esdras 8:33 was most likely composed after the destruction of Jerusalem and its Temple in A.D. 70 — and therefore was post-Pauline in origin — it reflects a viewpoint that its author and his community would have considered traditional for themselves.

> For the righteous, who have many works laid up *(operae multae repositae)* with [God], shall receive their reward in consequence of their own deeds *(ex propriis operibus).*[53]

It should be noted that Paul speaks not only of "works of the law" but of doing "the whole law" (ὁ πᾶς νόμος, Gal 5:14), and in that instance he is speaking not simply of boundary markers but of the love commandment as fulfilling

---

49. J. Dunn, *Romans*, lxv.

50. J. Neusner, *Judaism in the Beginning of Christianity*, 25-30. Some speak of "Judaisms" (plural) as characteristic of the first century, e.g., S. Cohen, "The Modern Study of Ancient Judaism," 55-73; R. Deines, "The Pharisees between 'Judaisms' and 'Common Judaism,'" 443-504; and H. Lichtenberger, "The Understanding of the Torah in the Judaism of Paul's Day," 7-23.

51. Relevant texts usually thought to have been composed prior to Paul include *Pss. Sol.* 9.4-5; 14.1-5; 15.1-13. Texts usually thought to have been composed contemporary with, or later than, Paul include 2 Esdr 7:24, 35; 8:33-36; 9:7-13; *2 Bar.* 14.12-13; 51.1-6; 57.2; *T. Abr.* A.12.12–14.8; B.9.8; *T. Abr.* B.9.8–10.16.

52. 4Q398 (4QMMT); 4QHalakhic Letter 14-17.ii.2-3 (מעשי התורה, "works of the Torah") and 1QS *(Rule of the Community)* 5.21 (מעשין בתורה, "deeds in law"); cf. also 1QpHab 8.1 (עושי התורה, "observing the law"). For texts, cf. *The Dead Sea Scrolls: Study Edition*, trans. Florentino García Martínez and Eibert J. C. Tigchelaar, 2 vols. (Grand Rapids: Wm. B. Eerdmans, 1997-98), 2:802-3; 1:80-81; 1:16-17, respectively. For discussion, cf. J. Fitzmyer, "Paul and the Dead Sea Scrolls," 2:614; H.-W. Kuhn, "Qumran und Paulus," 232; J. de Roo, *Works of the Law at Qumran and in Paul*, 4-25; N. T. Wright, "4QMMT and Paul," 104-32.

53. Quoted from *OTP* 1:543 (NRSV is identical) with Latin inserted from the Vulgate.

the law of Moses. While a theoretical distinction can be made between moral, dietary, and ritual commandments, the Jew is to observe all of them in a comprehensive manner; in fact, the person who lives according to the law is obliged to keep all the commandments (Lev 26:14-15; Num 15:40; Deut 8:1-20; 30:8; 2 Chr 33:8). One must take Paul as an important witness to first-century views concerning the law, and there one finds evidence that, for this former Pharisee, Torah observance had been the way of righteousness in the community he knew (Rom 9:31; 10:5; Phil 3:9). Moreover, those practices were not simply "boundary markers" of Jewish identity — which they were — but, at least for some, a basis for justification and final salvation as well.[54]

In speaking of the "works of the law" at this place, the term "law" (νόμος) refers to the Mosaic Torah, i.e., the compendium of commandments to be observed both as a mark of Jewish identity and as a pattern of the life of the Jew who seeks to be obedient to the will of God. The entire discussion of the righteousness of God — ever since 3:21 — has been carried on by Paul to demonstrate that Jew and Gentile stand at the same place before God. Observing the Torah, while it may indeed be a sign of one's identity among the elect, and while it is expected of such a person, is finally not the basis for a right relationship with God. The apostle has declared already that the entire world is fallen and subject to divine wrath (3:9), and even those who possess the Torah do not in fact observe it, even as the law and the prophets attest (3:10-20). The only way that the relationship can be restored is by means of God's own activity, and that is through the redemption accomplished in the death and resurrection of God's own Son.

3:29-30 That God is one (meaning that there is but one God, the God of the patriarchs and of the entire world) is common to Jewish and Christian theology, as expressed in the Shema of Israel's faith (Deut 6:4; cf. Isa 54:5; Zech 14:9), and echoed in the NT several times over (Mark 12:29; 1 Cor 8:4, 6; Gal 3:20; Eph 4:6; 1 Tim 2:5; Jas 2:19). And since that is the case, God is God of Jews and Gentiles alike.

On that basis, Paul asserts that God justifies the Jewish believer ("the circumcision") "by faith" (ἐκ πίστεως) and the Gentile ("the uncircumcision") "through faith" (διὰ τῆς πίστεως). Is there a distinction between the two prepo-

---

54. Cf. J. Fitzmyer, "Paul's Jewish Background and the Deeds of the Law," 18-35; idem, "Paul and the Dead Sea Scrolls," 2:614; S. Gathercole, "Justified by Faith," 2:154. There are many critiques of the "new perspective." A major work is that of S. Westerholm, *Perspectives Old and New on Paul*, 183-93 *et passim*; excellent, brief discussions are those of D. Hagner, "Paul and Judaism," 75-105, and K. Haacker, "Merits and Limits of the 'New Perspective on the Apostle Paul,'" 275-89. On the other hand, J. Dunn has written an extensive essay that responds to his critics (including extensive bibliography), "The New Perspective on Paul: Whence, What, and Whither?" in his *The New Perspective on Paul*, 1-97.

sitional phrases? The difference between them is no doubt purely rhetorical or stylistic.[55] Up to this point Paul has been consistent in his emphasis that there is no distinction between Jew and Gentile in regard to justification, so it is unlikely that he would make any distinction at this point.

3:31 But now Paul has found himself to be in a tight spot. He indulges in a bit of wordplay to set up a question. He has just said that Gentiles are justified "through faith" (διὰ τῆς πίστεως). He repeats the prepositional phrase, asking whether one can now abolish the law "through faith" (διὰ τῆς πίστεως). The question is inevitable. For if the distinction between Jewish and Gentile believers has been abolished, and if justification is by grace apart from works of the law, one could easily draw the conclusion that the law is no longer valid. Has it therefore been abolished? Paul will not allow any such conclusion. He uses his sharp reply, "By no means!" (μὴ γένοιτο); on this expression, see the exegesis of 3:4. He says that he and others of like mind "uphold" the law. The verb used here (ἱστάνω) means to confirm or validate something, particularly in regard to traditions.[56] Paul does not explain here how the law can still be considered upheld through what he has said. Instead he turns at 4:1 to illustrate and to establish justification by faith apart from the law through the story of Abraham. Although he refers to the law in the next three chapters (4:13-16; 5:13, 20; 6:14-15), it is not until 7:1 that Paul returns to the significance of the law and can go on to claim that it is holy, spiritual, and good (7:12, 14, 16).

This verse has been particularly vexing to interpreters.[57] Unless Paul is simply inconsistent,[58] any interpretation has to fulfill the following criteria in the present context of the letter: (1) the law referred to has to be the Mosaic law (the Pentateuch);[59] (2) that law is valid, expressing the will of God; and (3) it has

55. So Augustine, *De spiritu et littera* 29.50; C. K. Barrett, *Romans*, 80; E. Käsemann, *Romans*, 104; C. Cranfield, *Romans*, 222; J. Dunn, *Romans*, 189; J. Fitzmyer, *Romans*, 365; B. Byrne, *Romans*, 140; D. Moo, *Romans*, 252; E. Lohse, *Römer*, 139. A distinction is made by S. Stowers, "ΕΚ ΠΙΣΤΕΩΣ and ΔΙΑ ΤΗΣ ΠΙΣΤΕΩΣ in Romans 3:30," 665-74: the phrase διὰ τῆς πίστεως applies to Gentiles, while ἐκ πίστεως applies to Jews and Gentiles. But the first of these is used in passages that speak of redemption of both Jews and Gentiles as well (Rom 3:22, 25).

56. BDAG 482 (ἵστημι/ἱστάνω, A, 4).

57. Surveys of proposals are provided by H. Hübner, *Law in Paul's Thought*, 141-42; C. Rhyne, *Faith Establishes the Law*, 26-30, 71-74; D. Moo, *Romans*, 252-55.

58. H. Räisänen, *Paul and the Law*, 72, claims such.

59. So most interpreters, e.g., W. Sanday and A. Headlam, *Romans*, 96; C. Cranfield, *Romans*, 223 (n. 4; the Pentateuch or OT); E. Käsemann, *Romans*, 105; E. P. Sanders, *Paul, the Law, and the Jewish People*, 102-3; J. Fitzmyer, *Romans*, 367; C. Rhyne, *Faith Establishes the Law*, 71; D. Moo, *Romans*, 254; E. Lohse, *Romans*, 139. Contra R. Jewett, *Romans*, 302-3, for whom the term "law" here can mean Jewish or Roman law. According to B. Byrne, *Romans*, 140, the term signifies the Scriptures; for H. Hübner, *The Law in Paul's Thought*, 142, the will of God in the OT; for R. Hays, "Three Dramatic Roles," 155, "Scripture taken as a *narrative* whole," and so "the gospel is the narrative completion" of the law (= Scripture).

to accommodate the theme of the righteousness of God, received by faith. The verse can then be considered a bridge passage between what has gone before and what is to follow. In both instances Paul makes assertions about the law: (1) no one can be justified before God by deeds prescribed by the law, as the law itself teaches (3:20); and (2) one is justified by faith, as the story of Abraham within the Torah illustrates (4:3, quoting Gen 15:6); he had no reason to boast on the basis of works (4:2). By those claims, Paul confirms that the heritage, the law of Moses, stands and is valid. That point has to be made not only because of Paul's emphasis on justification by faith, but also over against any possible claims that he is an antinomian (3:8; 6:1-2).

BIBLIOGRAPHY

Abegg, Martin G., Jr. "Paul and James on the Law in Light of the Dead Sea Scrolls." In *Christian Beginnings and the Dead Sea Scrolls,* 63-74. Ed. John J. Collins and Craig A. Evans. Acadia Studies in Bible and Theology. Grand Rapids: Baker Book House, 2006.

Aune, David E., ed. *Rereading Paul Together: Protestant and Catholic Perspectives on Justification.* Grand Rapids: Baker Academic, 2006.

Barrett, C. K. "Boasting (καυχάομαι, κτλ.) in the Pauline Epistles." In *L'Apôtre Paul: Personnalité, style et conception du ministère,* 363-68. Ed. Albert Vanhoye. BETL 73. Leuven: Leuven University Press, 1986.

Bultmann, Rudolf. *Primitive Christianity in Its Contemporary Setting.* Cleveland: World Publishing Company, 1956.

————. *Theology of the New Testament.* 2 vols. New York: Charles Scribner's Sons, 1951-55.

Cohen, Shaye J. D. "The Modern Study of Ancient Judaism." In *The State of Jewish Studies,* 55-73. Ed. S. Cohen and Edward L. Greenstein. Detroit: Wayne State University Press, 1990.

Cosgrove, Charles H. "Justification in Paul: A Linguistic and Theological Reflection." *JBL* 106 (1987): 653-70.

Cranfield, C. E. B. "The Works of the Law in the Epistle to the Romans." *JSNT* 43 (1991): 89-101; reprinted in his *On Romans and Other New Testament Essays,* 1-14. Edinburgh: T&T Clark, 1998.

Dahl, Nils A. "The One God of Jews and Gentiles." In his *Studies in Paul: Theology for the Early Christian Mission,* 178-91. Minneapolis: Augsburg Publishing House, 1977.

Deines, Roland. "The Pharisees between 'Judaisms' and 'Common Judaism.'" In *Justification and Variegated Nomism,* 1:443-504. Ed. D. A. Carson et al. 2 vols. Grand Rapids: Baker Academic, 2001-4.

De Roo, Jacqueline C. R. *"Works of the Law" at Qumran and in Paul.* Sheffield: Sheffield Phoenix Press, 2007.

Donfried, Karl P. "Justification and Last Judgment in Paul." *Int* 30 (1976): 140-52.

Dunn, James D. G. "The New Perspective on Paul." *BJRL* 65 (1983): 95-122; reprinted in *The*

Romans Debate, 299-308. Ed. Karl P. Donfried. Rev. ed. Peabody: Hendrickson Publishers, 1991, and in *The New Perspective on Paul* (next entry), 99-120.

―――. *The New Perspective on Paul*. Rev. ed. Grand Rapids: Wm. B. Eerdmans, 2008.

―――. "Works of the Law and the Curse of the Law (Galatians 3:10-14)." *NTS* 31 (1985); 523-42.

―――. "Yet Once More — 'The Works of the Law': A Response." *JSNT* 46 (1992): 99-117.

Fitzmyer, Joseph A. "Paul and the Dead Sea Scrolls." In *The Dead Sea Scrolls after Fifty Years: A Comprehensive Assessment*, 2:599-621. Ed. Peter W. Flint and James C. VanderKam. 2 vols. Boston: E. J. Brill, 1998-99.

―――. "Paul's Jewish Background and the Deeds of the Law." In his *According to Paul: Studies in the Theology of the Apostle*, 18-35. New York: Paulist Press, 1993.

Friedrich, Gerhard. "Das Gesetz des Glaubens Röm. 3.27." *TZ* 10 (1954): 401-17.

Garlington, Don. *Studies in the New Perspective on Paul: Essays and Reviews*. Eugene: Wipf & Stock, 2008.

Gathercole, Simon. "Justified by Faith, Justified by His Blood: The Evidence of Romans 3:21–4:25." In *Justification and Variegated Nomism*, 2:147-84. Ed. D. A. Carson et al. 2 vols. Grand Rapids: Baker Academic, 2001-4.

―――. *Where Is Boasting? Early Jewish Soteriology and Paul's Response in Romans 1–5.* Grand Rapids: Wm. B. Eerdmans, 2002.

Grässer, Erich. "'Ein einziger ist Gott' (Röm 3,30). Zum christologischen Gottesverständnis bei Paulus." In *"Ich will euer Gott werden": Beispiele biblischen Redens von Gott*, 177-205. Ed. Norbert Lohfink. SBS 100. Stuttgart: Katholisches Bibelwerk, 1981.

Grelot, Pierre. "Les oeuvres de la Loi (A propos de 4Q394-398)." *RevQ* 16 (1994): 441-48.

Gundry, Robert H. "Grace, Works, and Staying Saved in Paul." *Bib* 66 (1985): 1-38.

Haacker, Klaus. "Merits and Limits of the 'New Perspective on the Apostle Paul.'" In *History and Exegesis: New Testament Essays in Honor of Dr. E. Earle Ellis for His 80th Birthday*, 275-89. Ed. Sang-Won (Aaron) Son. Edinburgh: T&T Clark, 2006.

Hagner, Donald A. "Paul and Judaism: Testing the New Perspective." In Peter Stuhlmacher, *Revisiting Paul's Doctrine of Justification: A Challenge to the New Perspective*, 75-105. Downers Grove: InterVarsity Press, 2001.

Hays, Richard B. "Three Dramatic Roles: The Law in Romans 3–4." In *Paul and the Mosaic Law*, 151-64. Ed. James D. G. Dunn. Grand Rapids: Wm. B. Eerdmans, 2001.

Hübner, Hans. *Law in Paul's Thought*. Edinburgh: T&T Clark, 1984.

Ito, Akio. "ΝΟΜΟΣ (ΤΩΝ) ᾿ΕΡΓΩΝ and ΝΟΜΟΣ ΠΙΣΤΕΩΣ: The Pauline Rhetoric and Theology of ΝΟΜΟΣ." *NovT* 45 (2003): 237-59.

Kuhn, Heinz-Wolfgang. "The Impact of the Qumran Scrolls on the Understanding of Paul." In *The Dead Sea Scrolls: Forty Years of Research*, 327-39. Ed. Devorah Dimant and Uriel Rappaport. STDJ 10. New York: E. J. Brill, 1992.

―――. "Qumran und Paulus: Unter traditionsgeschichtlichem Aspekt ausgewählte Parallelen." In *Das Urchristentum in seiner literarischen Geschichte: Festschrift für Jürgen Becker zum 65. Geburtstag*, 227-46. Ed Ulrich Mell and Ulrich B. Müller. BZNW 100. Berlin: Walter de Gruyter, 1999.

Lambrecht, Jan. "Paul's Logic in Romans 3:29-30." *JBL* 119 (2000): 526-28.

―――. "Why Is Boasting Excluded? A Note on Rom 3:27 and 4:2." *ETL* 61 (1985): 365-69.

————, and Richard W. Thompson, *Justification by Faith: The Implications of Romans 3:27-31*. Wilmington: Michael Glazier, 1989.

Lichtenberger, Hermann. "The Understanding of the Torah in the Judaism of Paul's Day: A Sketch." In *Paul and the Mosaic Law*, 7-23. Ed. James D. G. Dunn. WUNT 89. Tübingen: J. C. B. Mohr (Paul Siebeck), 1996.

Neusner, Jacob. *Judaism in the Beginning of Christianity*. Philadelphia: Fortress Press, 1984.

Räisänen, Heikki. "Das 'Gesetz des Glaubens' (Rom. 3.27) und das 'Gesetz des Geistes' (Rom. 8.2)." *NTS* 26 (1979): 101-17.

————. *Paul and the Law*. Philadelphia: Fortress Press, 1986.

Rapa, Robert K. *The Meaning of "Works of the Law" in Galatians and Romans*. StudBL 31. New York: Peter Lang, 2001.

Rhyne, C. Thomas. *Faith Establishes the Law*. SBLDS 55. Chico: Scholars, 1981.

Sanders, E. P. *Paul and Palestinian Judaism: A Comparison of Patterns of Religion*. Philadelphia: Fortress Press, 1977.

Scott, James M. "'For as Many as Are of Works of the Law Are under a Curse' (Galatians 3.10)." In *Paul and the Scriptures of Israel*, 187-221. Ed. Craig A. Evans and James A. Sanders. JSNTSup 83/SSEJC 1. Sheffield: Sheffield Academic Press, 1993.

Seifrid, Mark A. *Justification by Faith: The Origin and Development of a Central Pauline Theme*. NovTSup 68. Leiden: E. J. Brill, 1992.

Stendahl, Krister. "The Apostle Paul and the Introspective Conscience of the West." *HTR* 56 (1963): 199-215; reprinted in his *Paul among Jews and Gentiles and Other Essays*, 78-96. Philadelphia: Fortress Press, 1976.

Stowers, Stanley K. "ΕΚ ΠΙΣΤΕΩΣ and ΔΙΑ ΤΗΣ ΠΙΣΤΕΩΣ in Romans 3:30." *JBL* 108 (1989): 665-74.

Stuhlmacher, Peter. *Revisiting Paul's Doctrine of Justification: A Challenge to the New Perspective*. Downers Grove: InterVarsity Press, 2001.

Tamez, Elsa. "Justification as Good News for Women: A Re-reading of Romans 1–8." In *Celebrating Romans: Template for Pauline Theology: Essays in Honor of Robert Jewett*, 177-89. Ed. Sheila E. McGinn. Grand Rapids: Wm. B. Eerdmans, 2005.

Thompson, Richard W. "The Alleged Rabbinic Background of Rom 3:31." *ETL* 63 (1987): 136-48.

————. "The Inclusion of the Gentiles in Rom 3,27-30." *Bib* 69 (1988): 543-46.

————. "Paul's Double Critique of Jewish Boasting: A Study of Rom 3:27 in Its Context." *Bib* 67 (1986): 520-31.

Westerholm, Stephen. "The New Perspective at Twenty-Five." In *Justification and Variegated Nomism*, 2:1-38. Ed. D. A. Carson, Peter T. O'Brien, and Mark A. Seifrid. 2 vols. Grand Rapids: Baker Academic, 2001-4.

————. *Perspectives Old and New on Paul: The "Lutheran" Paul and His Critics*. Grand Rapids: Wm. B. Eerdmans, 2004.

————. "The Righteousness of the Law and the Righteousness of Faith in Romans." *Int* 58 (2004): 253-64.

Winger, Michael. *By What Law? The Meaning of Νόμος in the Letters of Paul*. SBLDS 128. Atlanta: Scholars Press, 1992.

————. "Meaning and Law." *JBL* 117 (1998): 105-10.

Wright, N. T. "4QMMT and Paul: Justification, 'Works,' and Eschatology." In *History and Exegesis: New Testament Essays in Honor of Dr. E. Earle Ellis for His 80th Birthday*, 104-32. Ed. Sang-Won (Aaron) Son. Edinburgh: T&T Clark, 2006.

3.3. Abraham as Illustration and Forebear of Justification by Faith, 4:1-25

1*What then shall we say that Abraham, our forefather according to the flesh, discovered?* 2*For if Abraham was justified by works, he has something to boast about, but not before God.* 3*For what do the Scriptures say? "And Abraham believed God, and it was accredited to him as righteousness."* 4*Wages are not paid to the person who works on the basis of grace, but according to what is owed.* 5*And to the person who does not work but trusts in the one who justifies the ungodly, his faith is accredited to him as righteousness.* 6*Just so, David also pronounces a blessing upon the person to whom God accredits righteousness apart from works:*

7*Blessed are those whose iniquities are forgiven,*
and whose sins are covered;
8*Blessed is the one to whom the Lord will not reckon his sin.*

9*Is this blessing for the circumcised or also for the uncircumcised? For we say, "Faith was accredited to Abraham as righteousness."* 10*How then is it accredited? Was it while he was circumcised or uncircumcised? It was not while he was circumcised, but while he was uncircumcised.* 11*And he received the sign of circumcision as a seal of the righteousness of faith that he had while uncircumcised, in order that he might be the father of all who believe without being circumcised, that righteousness might be accredited to them,* 12*and the father of the circumcised who are not only circumcised but also follow the example of the faith of our father Abraham while he was uncircumcised.*

13*For the promise to Abraham and his descendants that they would inherit the world did not come through the law but through the righteousness of faith.* 14*For if the adherents of the law are heirs, faith is empty and the promise is nullified.* 15*For the law brings wrath, but where there is no law, neither is there transgression.*

16*For this reason it is by faith, in order that it may be by grace that the promise may be certain to every descendant — not only to the adherent of the law, but also to the adherent of the faith of Abraham, who is the father of us all,* 17*as it is written, "I have made you the father of many nations" — in the presence of the God in whom he believed, who gives life to the dead and calls into being those things that are not.*

18*Against hope he believed with hope in order that he would become the fa-*

ther of many nations in accord with what had been said: "So shall your descendants be," and 19without becoming weak in faith, he considered his own body as dead — since he was about one hundred years old — and the death of Sarah's womb. 20He did not waver in unbelief concerning the promise of God, but became stronger in faith, giving glory to God, 21having become fully convinced also that [God] was also able to do what had been promised. 22So indeed it was accredited to him as righteousness. 23But "It was accredited to him" was written not only for his sake, 24but for our sake also, to whom it will be accredited, who believe in the one who raised from the dead Jesus our Lord, 25who was given over for our trespasses and was raised for our justification.

Notes on the Text and Translation

4:1 There are several variants to the text as printed in the Nestle-Aland 27th edition, εὑρηκέναι Ἀβραὰμ τὸν προπάτορα ἡμῶν ("Abraham our forefather discovered"). The most important of them are the omission of the verb εὑρηκέναι (perfect, active infinitive of the verb "to discover") in B and the use of πατέρα ("father") instead of προπάτορα ("forefather," "ancestor") in some major "corrected" texts (ℵ¹ and C³), D, other majuscules, and in the Majority Text, which is reflected in the KJV. The reading provided, however, has strong support in the original readings of ℵ, C, as well as in A and minuscules.

4:19 The Western Text, as provided in D and in Old Latin witnesses, and the Majority Text read οὐ κατενόησεν ("he did not consider"), which is reflected in the KJV: "he [Abraham] considered not his own body now dead." But the word οὐ ("not") is lacking in major Alexandrian majuscules (including ℵ, A, and B), Syriac, and Coptic witnesses, resulting in "he considered his own body as dead." The word was probably added to avoid portraying Abraham as somehow lacking in faith.

General Comment

Although chapter 4 can be broken down into smaller units, it is read best as one continuous section of the letter concerning justification by faith in light of the story of Abraham. Paul continues the thought of 3:27-31, namely, that any boasting in one's ability to keep the law as a means of justification is excluded, and he offers the story of Abraham as a proof. Abraham, he declares, was justified by God while he was still a Gentile (i.e., prior to his being circumcised). The basis for that was simply that Abraham believed God, and God declared him justified, righteous, in a right relationship. For Paul, this shows that God deals with the *whole* world on an equal basis as far as justification is concerned. Against all human expectations, God justifies the ungodly, the nonpious, those who have nothing to claim before God. Those who believe his promise are the ones who are the children of Abraham, and upon whom God's promise of righteousness rests.

By the time the chapter ends, Paul has maintained that the "faith of Abraham" not only (1) anticipates Christian faith but (2) is shown to have been identical to it. All this serves to show that the exclusive claim of Judaism to God's promises cannot stand. There is a continuity between Abraham and the Christian.

Detailed Comment

4:1-8 Paul begins with that familiar rhetorical question — familiar in Romans, but appearing nowhere else in his letters — that he uses six other times in diatribe within Romans (cf. 3:5; 6:1; 7:7; 8:31; 9:14, 30): "What then shall we say?" (τί οὖν ἐροῦμεν;), although here he does not leave the question by itself, followed by another question, which is his usual pattern. Here he continues with a clause concerning Abraham, thereby asking a question concerning Abraham, "our forefather according to the flesh." What did Abraham himself discover?[60] Here the phrase "according to the flesh" (κατὰ σάρκα), as in some other places (Rom 1:3; 9:3, 5; 1 Cor 10:18), simply means biological descent.[61] The answer to the question is spelled out in the following verses. He was not justified "by works" (ἐξ ἔργων), which is shorthand for the entire expression used previously (3:20),

---

60. It has been proposed that the question of 4:1 be translated as "What then shall we say? Have we found Abraham to be our forefather according to the flesh?" with an implied negative answer; so R. Hays, "Abraham as Father of Jews and Gentiles," 61-84; idem, *Echoes of Scripture in the Letters of Paul*, 54; similarly, M. Palmer, "τί οὖν; The Inferential Question," 211. But the verses following have to do precisely with what Abraham (not "we") discovered, i.e., that there is no basis for boasting, and that his faith in the promises of God was accredited to him as righteousness. For other critical responses, cf. J. Dunn, *Romans*, 199; R. Harrisville, *The Figure of Abraham in the Epistles of St. Paul*, 22; D. Moo, *Romans*, 259 (n. 13); T. Tobin, *Paul's Rhetoric in Its Contexts*, 146 (n. 52); G. Visscher, *Romans 4 and the New Perspective on Paul*, 135-40. It has also been asserted by F. J. A. Hort, *Prolegomena to St. Paul's Epistles to the Romans and the Ephesians*, 23-24, that κατὰ σάρκα belongs to τί οὖν ἐροῦμεν, thrown to the end for emphasis, but that is unconvincing. A survey of various proposals is provided by B. Schliesser, *Abraham's Faith in Romans 4*, 321-27.

61. In other places the phrase can have a negative meaning, referring to a life contrary to that which would be Spirit led (Rom 8:4-5) or, in general, a life lived or a judgment made without reference to the life in Christ and its ways of understanding (Rom 8:12-13; 1 Cor 1:26; 2 Cor 5:16; 10:2).

"by works prescribed by the law" (ἐξ ἔργων νόμου). If he had been justified by works, Paul says, he would have something to boast about, ἀλλ᾽ οὐ πρὸς θεόν. The latter is typically rendered as "but not before God" (KJV, RSV, NIV, NRSV, and NET), as here. The prepositional phrase πρὸς θεόν has the connotation of "toward God" (as in the ASV) or (in the πρός of reference construction) "in reference to God" or "in relationship to God." The sense of the verse is that, if Abraham had been justified by works of the law, he would have something to boast about indeed among his companions *(coram hominibus)*, but he would have no reason to boast in the presence of God *(coram deo)*.[62] His boasting would be self-congratulation. On distinctions between two kinds of boasting in Paul's letters, see the exegesis of 2:17.

Paul asserts that Abraham was justified by believing the promises of God (cf. also Gal 3:6). He argues his point on the basis of Scripture, quoting Genesis 15:6. The quotation corresponds to the text of the LXX with two slight differences: (1) while the LXX has καὶ ἐπίστευσεν ("and [he] believed"), Paul has ἐπίστευσεν δέ (a variation of the same, "and [he] believed"), and (2) while the LXX has Αβραμ (the earlier name of the patriarch, "Abram," transliterated from the name אַבְרָם at this place in Genesis), Paul has Ἀβραάμ ("Abraham," the name given to the patriarch later at Gen 17:5, אַבְרָהָם). The latter is the version of the name that appears consistently in the NT (73 times, 19 of which are in the undisputed letters of Paul).

In 4:4-5 Paul makes a distinction between "the person who works" (ὁ ἐργαζόμενος) and "the person who does not work" (ὁ μὴ ἐργαζόμενος). The first is an allusion to the person who seeks justification on the basis of observing the law, doing "the works prescribed by the law." The second alludes to the person who does not do that but is open to receive justification by grace. The difference is spelled out by an analogy to the payment of wages. Wages are paid to "the person who works," and they are paid "according to what is owed" (κατὰ ὀφείλημα). They are not paid "on the basis of grace" (κατὰ χάριν).

The difference between the two phrases regarding payment is absolute; they are totally antithetical. Paul's composition at this point is somewhat elliptical. One would expect him to compose in 4:5 a statement parallel to that in 4:4, completing the thought he is expressing, so that 4:5 would read: "So also gifts are not given freely to the person who works according to what is owed, but on the basis of grace." And then he would go on to say that, just so, God justifies on the basis of grace, not on the basis of what is owed. Paul implies that in what he says, but he rushes on to say that it is the person who trusts in God, "who justifies the ungodly" — and does so apart from doing works prescribed by the law — whose faith is "accredited to him as righteousness."

---

62. E. Grässer, "Der ruhmlose Abraham (Röm 4.2)," 16-17.

Here, by implication, Paul begins to take what pertained specifically to Abraham in the biblical text and to apply it to other persons. Earlier in the letter he maintained that persons are justified by God's grace as a gift through the redemptive work of God in Christ for all (3:24), received by faith. In order to give biblical warrant to that claim, he invokes the story of Abraham, showing that if such was the case there, so it is the case everywhere. Furthermore, lest it be argued that Abraham was a special case, since he was surely not only the patriarch but the epitome of righteousness — a person who in legends was observant of the law even prior to the giving of the law through Moses (Sir 44:20: "He kept the law of the Most High")[63] — Paul implicitly includes him among the "ungodly" at this point. He is able to do that since Abraham was declared justified at Genesis 15:6, prior to his being circumcised, which does not occur until two chapters later in Genesis (17:24). And as it was with Abraham, so it is with others; whoever trusts God, who justifies the ungodly, is justified freely apart from doing the works prescribed by the law.

The claim that God justifies the "ungodly" (4:5) is radical, indeed extreme, even when it is measured within its biblical context. The term translated "ungodly" is ἀσεβής,[64] and it is used consistently in the Bible (apart from Paul's own use) in a very negative sense. In the OT (taking canonical and deuterocanonical texts together) the "ungodly" are generally regarded as wicked (Gen 18:23, 25; Ps 1:6; Prov 3:33; 11:23; Jer 25:31), are hated by God (Wis 14:9), and will surely perish in the judgment (Pss 1:4-6; 31:17 [LXX 30:18]; Isa 11:4; 13:11; Wis 3:10; 14:9; Sir 7:17; 12:6). Never, with the possible exception of Psalm 51:13 (LXX 50:15),[65] is any hope expressed for them. The same is true in other ancient Jewish sources,[66] and it is true without fail in the writings of other NT authors as well, for when they refer to persons with the term ἀσεβής, they do so with the view that such persons stand condemned (1 Tim 1:9; 1 Pet 4:18; 2 Pet 2:5-6; 3:7; Jude 4, 15). Surely Paul must have been aware of the highly negative connotation of the word in both Jewish and early Christian usage, but here he speaks of God as justifying the "ungodly," and at Romans 5:6 he declares that Christ died for the "ungodly."

What can Paul possibly mean by the term ἀσεβής? To translate it as "ungodly," as often in English versions (KJV, ASV, RSV, and NRSV) without further

---

63. For other references to Abraham as an observer of the law, cf. 2 Apoc. Bar. 57.1-2; Jub. 11.14–23.7; Philo, Abr. 276; m. Qidd. 4.14; b. Yoma 28b; b. Ned. 32a. Although these texts were written after Paul's day, the legends may well be from earlier times, as Sir 44:20 confirms.

64. BDAG 141 (ἀσεβής): "violating norms for a proper relation to deity, irreverent, impious, ungodly."

65. LXX Ps 50:15 reads: "I will teach transgressors your ways, and sinners (ἀσεβεῖς) will return to you."

66. Philo, Her. 18.90; Leg. All. 3.9; Conf. 117, 152; T. Zeb. 10.3. Werner Foerster, "ἀσεβής," TDNT 7:188: In the LXX ἀσέβεια "expresses complete contempt for God and His will."

ado, begs questions.[67] Does Paul mean (1) persons who have a general lack of respect for God (irreverent, impious persons), (2) more specifically, persons who do not rely upon observing the law for justification, or (3) persons who are actually "wicked" (NIV), as in many other passages (OT, NT, and other ancient writings)? The answer can be found in what was said earlier within the same verse. The antithesis of "the one who trusts in the one who justifies the ungodly" is "the person who works" (the ἐργαζόμενος), meaning the one who seeks to gain righteousness by observing the law. The person referred to as the "ungodly" is therefore one who does not seek to gain God's favor by performing "works prescribed by the law." Such a person stands ready to be declared righteous by God, and thereby to be in a right relationship with God, purely on the basis of God's justifying work in Christ.

Paul draws upon another biblical text (Ps 32:1-2) to strengthen his case even more. In this case the text does not contain the language of justification (forms of the verb δικαιόω) as in Romans 4:2 and 4:5, or of righteousness (δικαιοσύνη) as in 4:3 and 4:6, but it contains terms that are closely related. The choice of the text is most likely due to Paul's employment of the so-called *gezera shawa* principle, which became codified in later rabbinic rules for biblical interpretation.[68] According to that principle, two texts using the same word can be brought together, and what is taught in the one can be applied to the other as well. In this particular instance Paul has made a word association between a form of the verb λογίζεσθαι ("to accredit" or "to reckon") in Genesis 15:6 (ἐλογίσθη), which he has quoted at 4:3, with another form of that verb in Psalm 32:1-2 (LXX 31:2: λογίσηται), which he quotes in 4:7-8. Paul's quotation of the psalm corresponds exactly in wording with the LXX version, except that he omits 31:2b, οὐδὲ ἔστιν ἐν τῷ στόματι αὐτοῦ δόλος ("nor is there deceit in his mouth").

On the face of it, the psalm does not seem to help Paul's case that righteousness is accredited to a person "apart from works" (χωρὶς ἔργων), which is the phrase that Paul uses in the verse leading into his quotation of the psalm (4:6), and which the quotation is meant to prove. But for Paul the status of being "blessed" (4:7-8) and that of being justified are identical, which becomes particularly clear at 4:9. The term for "blessed" is μακάριος, which appears also in the Beatitudes of the Sermon on the Mount (Matt 5:1-12) and the Sermon on the Plain (Luke 6:20-23). As in the Beatitudes, so here in a letter of Paul, the beatitudes are "anticipated eschatological verdicts."[69] Those who are called the "blessed ones" are declared to be the righteous ones whom God favors. For Paul

---

67. The NEB has "the guilty," which is equally ambiguous.

68. On this and other rules, cf. Louis Jacobs, "Hermeneutics," *EncJud* 8:366-72; on Paul's use, cf. C. Plag, "Paulus und die *Gezera schawa*," 135-40.

69. The term is used by H. Betz, *The Sermon on the Mount,* 94.

the "blessed ones" are those whose sins have been forgiven by God. Moreover, although there is no obvious connection between the passage in Genesis and the psalm, aside from the use of forms of the verb λογίζεσθαι, in both cases there is no mention of works as a means of a right relationship with God. In the first case it is said that Abraham was justified by faith. In the second it is said that a person is blessed by God's forgiveness, God's covering up of sin, and by God's not counting a person's sin. In both cases divine grace is operative.

4:9-12 Paul raises a question, asking whether the "blessing" (μακαρισμός, equivalent to being declared righteous) of which David speaks in the psalm applies only to persons who have been ritually circumcised, or whether it could apply to the uncircumcised as well. In order to answer the question, Paul refers to texts in Genesis once more. He points out that Abraham was declared righteous *before* he had been circumcised. That means, in effect, that Abraham was circumcised while he was still a Gentile. The implication to be drawn is that even the uncircumcised can be justified as they accept the promises of God, the gospel.

Paul uses a fascinating argument. The passage where Abraham is declared righteous is at Genesis 15:6. That passage precedes the commandment concerning circumcision (Gen 17:10-14) and the actual circumcision of Abraham (17:24). There is no indication in Genesis concerning the age of Abraham at the event of 15:6, when he was declared righteous, but there is a notice concerning his age at the time of his circumcision, and that is that he was 99 (17:24). Between these two events there is one indicator of age, and that is that at the time Ishmael was born, Abraham was 86 (16:16). According to rabbinic tradition,[70] Abraham was 70 years old at the time that the promise of 15:6 was given, which was also the time that he was declared to be justified. That means that Abraham was a justified-by-faith Gentile for twenty-nine years prior to his circumcision. Whether that tradition existed at the time of Paul, and whether he was aware of it or not, cannot be known. What is certain is that Paul was aware of the general time-frame, and he made a point of it, namely, that the promise to Abraham, and the declaration of his righteousness by faith in the divine promise, was prior to his circumcision. Therefore circumcision was not a precondition for righteousness. In an interesting wording of the matter at 4:11, Paul speaks not of circumcision itself, but of the "sign of circumcision" (σημεῖον περιτομῆς) that Abraham received as "a seal of the righteousness of faith (σφραγῖδα τῆς δικαιοσύνης τῆς πίστεως) that he had while uncircumcised." Circumcision is thereby spoken of as a ritual subsequent to Abraham's being declared righteous. And that has important consequences. Abraham is to be regarded, then, as "the father of all who believe without being circumcised." In other words, according to the scriptural account concerning parents and children, Gentile believers are

---

70. *Olam Rabbah* 1; quoted in Str-B 3:203.

children of Abraham. They have become his children for a purpose, and that is that they, too, might be justified by faith.

Paul cannot of course for a moment assert that while Gentiles who believe the promises of God have become children of Abraham, Jews are such no longer (a concern that arises again in 11:17-24). To do so would be to dismiss the promise of Genesis 15:5 and its interpretation through the ages. To avoid any misunderstanding, Paul declares at 4:12 that Abraham is (or remains) father of the circumcised "who follow the example of the faith of our father Abraham while he was uncircumcised." To be sure, the qualification does limit the scope of those whom Paul counts as descendants of Abraham. They consist of those who follow the example of the faith of Abraham prior to his circumcision. Just who those persons are is not spelled out in detail. One can only surmise that Paul has Christian Jews in mind, for he will go on to argue later that they, like Paul himself, are the true descendants of Abraham, the remnant chosen by grace (11:1-7). In both instances — both here and in chapter 11 — Paul is able to maintain that the promises of God continue and cannot be broken.

Nevertheless, what Paul has written here concerning Gentiles goes against Jewish tradition. For Judaism, Abraham was the father of all Jews and proselytes. But for Paul, the justifying work of God in Christ opens the way for believing Gentiles to become children of Abraham. That means that in Christ God has dealt with the whole world in a new way. No longer is Israel alone a witness to the world, but Israel itself is enlarged potentially to contain the whole world.

4:13-15 The promise to Abraham is now said by Paul to consist of inheriting the world on the part of Abraham and his descendants. The clause "that they would inherit the world" does not appear in the stories concerning Abraham in Genesis. What does appear is that the promise (actually the "promises," plural) consists of land (12:7; 13:14-15; 17:8), posterity (12:2; 13:16; 15:5; 18:18; 22:16-18), and having a great name (12:2). But in later Jewish writings the promise given to Abraham was apparently considered to be a world-encompassing one. So in Sirach 44:21 the Lord tells Abraham that he will bestow upon Abraham's descendants "an inheritance from sea to sea and from the Euphrates to the ends of the earth." And in *Jubilees* it is said that the descendants of Jacob will fill the earth (19.21).

The main point that Paul makes, however, is not about the extent of the inheritance promised to Abraham and his descendants, but how the promise came to him and his descendants in the first place. It came to him, says Paul, through the righteousness of faith, not through the law. Here Paul introduces a stark antithesis between νόμος ("law") and πίστις ("faith"), "an antithesis which was unheard-of in Jewish theology."[71] The promise could not have come

---

71. H. Moxnes, *Theology in Conflict*, 255.

through the law (διὰ νόμου), since the law had not yet been given. Normally the provisions for inheritances — ancient or modern — are stated in the law. The specific promises of what is to be inherited and by whom are typically written and are protected by law. But, Paul says, at the time of Abraham no such matters of law existed. The promise was given directly by God to Abraham, who received it by faith. Having accepted the promise, Abraham had trusted God and was therefore rightly related to God, and he was declared justified (rightwised). In short, "the righteousness of faith" was operative. There was no doing of the works prescribed by the (subsequent) law of Moses that qualified Abraham and his descendants to receive the promise of God.

At 4:14 Paul says, in so many words, that the story of Abraham would have to be declared totally untrue if the inheritance promised to him depended upon the prior existence of the law and Abraham's having to do something to fulfill it. If "adherents of the law" are heirs of the promises — i.e., the circumcised who observe the law — then the promise of God to (the uncircumcised) Abraham prior to the law's very existence would have been an empty one, and Abraham's response by faith would have amounted to nothing.

The statement of 14:15 concerning the law ("For the law brings wrath, but where there is no law, neither is there transgression") seems out of place, as though it is an apodictic saying out of the blue concerning the law. But the connection to what has been said previously becomes clear if it is related to what Paul wrote two verses previously (14:13, "For the promise to Abraham and his descendants that they would inherit the world did not come through the law but through the righteousness of faith"). The law, in other words, was not a conduit for the promises from God to Abraham and his descendants, but it is an instrument for disclosing God's wrath. The term "wrath" (ὀργή), which stands alone in the text (rather than the full phrase "the wrath of God"), most certainly is shorthand for the "wrath of God" (ὀργὴ θεοῦ, 1:18), as it is elsewhere (Rom 5:9; 12:19; 13:5; 1 Thess 2:16). Since the law conveys God's wrath, not God's promises, it is totally impossible that the promise to Abraham and his descendants depended on the law in any sense. On the other hand, Paul says, "where there is no law, neither is there transgression." There was no way for Abraham to make claims upon God by obeying the law, which would have been a form of transgression.

4:16-22 The antithesis of obtaining the promise of God through the law is to receive it "by faith" (ἐκ πίστεως), which allows it to be "by grace" (κατὰ χάριν) and, furthermore, be assured to every descendant of Abraham, both "the adherent of the law" (τῷ ἐκ τοῦ νόμου) and "the adherent of the faith of Abraham" (τῷ ἐκ πίστεως Ἀβραάμ).

The two expressions in 4:16b, τῷ ἐκ τοῦ νόμου and τῷ ἐκ πίστεως Ἀβραάμ, designate two groups of persons. Each begins with a definite article (τῷ), which is followed by the preposition ἐκ and a noun (or a series of two nouns) in the genitive (either τοῦ νόμου or πίστεως Ἀβραάμ) to speak of a person's identity (a sect or a persuasion).[72] Instances of similar syntactical usage appear at Romans 4:14 (οἱ ἐκ νόμου, "those of the law" or "the adherents of the law"); 4:16 (τῷ ἐκ τοῦ νόμου, "the adherent of the law"); 1 Corinthians 15:23 (οἱ τοῦ Χριστοῦ, "those of Christ" or "those who belong to Christ"); Galatians 2:12 (τοὺς ἐκ περιτομῆς, "those of the circumcision"); 3:7 and 3:9 (οἱ ἐκ πίστεως, "the people of faith," "those who believe," i.e., believers in Christ). Accordingly, Paul speaks here of two groups: those who adhere to the law, and those who adhere to the faith of Abraham (the "Abrahamic faith," which can now include Gentile believers). The latter are those who believe the promises of God that were given to Abraham and (through him) to his descendants. That faith was expressed by Abraham even before he was circumcised (4:10-12). In light of his syntactical usage elsewhere (and illustrated here), the proper way for Paul to refer to a true (spiritual) descendant of Abraham is to speak of that person as ὁ ἐκ πίστεως Ἀβραάμ, and that is precisely what he does in this verse.

Paul concedes that "the adherent of the law" is to be counted among the descendants of Abraham. The question that arises is whether by that term he means Jews as Jews or Jews who are Christians. Interpreters vary in their conclusions. Some conclude that when Paul speaks of "the adherent of the law" he means the Jewish Christian, and when he speaks of "the adherent of the faith of Abraham," he means a Gentile who is a Christian.[73] That view can be defended on the grounds that Paul has been arguing throughout the chapter that the true descendants of Abraham are persons who believe in the promises of God. But it has to be conceded that there is a sharp antithesis in the verse. Paul says "not only to the adherent of the law but also to the adherent of the faith of Abraham" (οὐ τῷ ἐκ τοῦ νόμου μόνον ἀλλὰ καὶ τῷ ἐκ πίστεως Ἀβραάμ). He seeks to stress that the latter is "also" (καί) an heir of the promise. That the latter would be an heir of the promises goes without saying on the basis of what has been said already, and by the same discussion that category would include both Jews and Gentiles who believe. It is therefore more likely that Paul has a separate category in mind when he speaks of "the adherent of the law" and concedes here, as he finally must, that the Jewish people retain their right to be called descendants of Abraham and heirs with him of the promises given to Abraham their father.[74] The matter is taken up again in chapter 11, where Paul says that the promises to the patriarchs remain valid (11:28). He can conclude, then, that

---

72. Cf. N. Turner, *Grammar*, 3.15, 260.

73. Included here are C. Cranfield, *Romans*, 242; L. Morris, *Romans*, 207; E. Käsemann, *Romans*, 121; U. Wilckens, *Römer*, 1:271-72; D. Moo, *Romans*, 278-79; B. Schliesser, *Abraham's Faith in Romans 4*, 373-75.

74. Included here are J. G. D. Dunn, *Romans*, 216; H. Schlier, *Römer*, 131; J. Fitzmyer, *Romans*, 385; T. Tobin, *Paul's Rhetoric in Its Contexts*, 150-51; R. Jewett, *Romans*, 331.

Abraham is "the father of us all," not only the father of those who adhere to the law, *but also* to all who are now, by faith, admitted into the inheritance.

At 4:17, to establish what he has just said, Paul quotes Genesis 17:5, containing God's word to Abraham: "I have made you the father of many nations" (πατέρα πολλῶν ἐθνῶν τέθεικά σε). Paul's wording corresponds exactly to that of the LXX. The wording opens up for Paul an important insight into the purposes of God. The Greek word translated "nations" (ἔθνη, *ethnē*) can also be translated "Gentiles," and the same is true with the Hebrew term in Genesis (גוֹיִם, *gôyim*), for it, too, can be translated as either "nations" or "Gentiles." The distinction is not as great in Greek as it is in English. In any case, Paul understands the term as referring to Gentiles at this place, and specifically to Gentiles who become believers in Christ. Therefore, he concludes, the promise to Abraham bursts asunder the circle of God's people.

Following the quotation from Genesis 17:5 a statement is juxtaposed concerning the manner in which Abraham received the promise from God. He received the promise with an assured awareness of the presence of God ("in the presence of the God in whom he believed," 4:17b). Then a confessional formula follows that is appropriate for Abraham, as illustrated in the story concerning him and Sarah, but also a basis for what is to follow concerning Christian faith. The God in whom Abraham placed his trust is the God "who gives life to the dead and calls into being those things that are not."

This is the first time in the letter that Paul has referred to God as giving life to the dead (or raising the dead), except for the Christological formula of 1:3-4 where he refers to the resurrection of Jesus. The claim that God brings forth life out of death will appear again in the letter (5:21; 6:4; 7:6; 8:11), just as it has in other letters (1 Cor 15:22, 42-58; 2 Cor 1:9). The expectation of the resurrection of the dead developed late in the history of Israel's religious life. Limiting a survey to the Hebrew books of the OT alone, there are only two passages that can be said to affirm resurrection of the dead unambiguously (Isa 26:19; Dan 12:1-3).[75] In addition, the expectation is affirmed in some apocryphal/deuterocanonical and pseudepigraphal texts.[76] The expectation was that God will raise the dead at the last day, followed by the final judgment.[77] But for Paul, as for other early Christians, there was an awareness already that the resurrection of the dead had commenced with the resurrection of Jesus from the dead. Typically the language of Paul concerning resurrection is that God raises the dead (Rom 4:24; 8:11; 10:9;

75. G. von Rad, *Old Testament Theology,* 1:407; 2:350. He declares that the prediction that God will raise the dead is found "only peripherally" in the OT (2:350).

76. 2 Macc 7:9, 14, 23, 29; *1 Enoch* 104:2-6; *T. Jud.* 25:1; *T. Benj.* 10:6-9; *Pss. Sol.* 3.11-16.

77. On resurrection in Jewish theology, see George W. E. Nickelsburg, "Resurrection: Early Judaism and Christianity," *ABD* 5:684-91; idem, *Resurrection, Immortality, and Eternal Life in Intertestamental Judaism.*

1 Cor 6:14; 15:15; 2 Cor 1:9; 4:14; Gal 1:1; 1 Thess 1:10), or that the dead are raised (Rom 4:25; 6:4, 9; 7:4; 8:34; 1 Cor 15:4, 12-14, 16-17, 20, 43-44, 52; 2 Cor 5:15), using the divine passive, meaning that they are raised by God.[78]

Paul makes a close link and correspondence between the faith of Abraham and the faith of believers in Christ. Although he and Sarah were old and beyond child-bearing age, Abraham accepted the promise of God, "who gives life to the dead" (4:17b), believing firmly that he would have an heir. Likewise, Christian faith is faith in "the one who raised from the dead Jesus our Lord" (4:24). The connection is typological:

OT Type	*Antitype*
Abraham believed	Christians believe
in God who	in God who
gives life to the dead.	raised Jesus from the dead.

This demonstrates that the faith of Abraham not only anticipates the faith of Christians but is identical to it. Or, turning the connection around, believers in Christ, Jewish and Gentile alike, share in the faith of Abraham (4:12, 16). As he was justified by faith, so are all those who believe in the God who gives life to the dead. For, Paul says, all this "was written not only for [Abraham's] sake, but for our sake also, to whom it will be accredited, who believe in the one who raised from the dead Jesus our Lord" (4:23-24).

Along with resurrection language, Paul employs creation language,[79] declaring that God "calls into being those things that are not" (καλοῦντος τὰ μὴ ὄντα ὡς ὄντα).[80] The concept of calling into being those things that are not is rooted already in the Scriptures of Israel (Gen 1:1–2:3, creation by God's word; Isa 48:12-13, divine summons to the heavens and the earth), and it is affirmed widely in apocryphal/deuterocanonical and pseudepigraphal sources.[81] Within the Hebrew OT itself, including the passages just cited, it is unlikely that a concept of *creatio ex nihilo* ("creation out of nothing") can actually be found.[82] But

78. An exception to these expressions is at 1 Thess 4:14, where Paul says that Jesus rose from the dead.

79. Resurrection and creation are linked together also in 2 Macc 7:28-29; cf. O. Hofius, "Eine altjüdische Parallele zu Röm. iv.17b," 93-94.

80. The specific language referring to "things that are not" (τὰ μὴ ὄντα) is used by Paul once more in his letters (1 Cor 1:28) but nowhere else in the Bible.

81. Sir 16:26–17:8; 42:15–43:33; Bar 3:32-37; 2 Esdr 6:38-54; 2 Macc 7:28; 2 *Apoc. Bar.* 21:4; 48:8; *1 Enoch* 69:16-24; *Jub.* 2:1-33; *Sib. Or.* 1.8-37.

82. Bernhard W. Anderson, "Creation," *IDB* 1:728. On the other hand, "the idea of *creatio ex nihilo* is connected with [the wording of Gen 1:1]," according to G. von Rad, *Old Testament Theology*, 1:142.

the concept appears at 2 Maccabees 7:28, where the mother of the seven martyrs declares to her youngest son prior to his death that God did not make heaven, earth, and all that is in them, "out of things that existed" (ὅτι οὐκ ἐξ ὄντων ἐποίησεν αὐτὰ ὁ θεός). Similarly, Philo says: "for [God] calls things that do not exist into being" (τὰ γὰρ μὴ ὄντα ἐκάλεσσεν εἰς τὸ εἶναι).[83] And the author of Hebrews declared: "By faith we understand that the worlds were prepared by the word of God, so that what is seen was made from things that are not visible" (τὸ μὴ ἐκ φαινομένων τὸ βλεπόμενον γεγονέναι, 11:3).

Paul shares this Hellenistic Jewish view of creation out of nothing. Yet it needs to be underscored that Paul does not enter here into the question of cosmological origins for its own sake. His twin emphases on resurrection from the dead and creation out of nothing serve to highlight the character of Abraham's faith, i.e., a faith that believes that God is capable of fulfilling his promises, whether that be making Abraham the father of many nations or justifying him and all his descendants through faith in the promises of God. Elsewhere Paul declares: "God chose what is low and despised in the world, things that are not (τὰ μὴ ὄντα), to reduce to nothing things that are, so that no one might boast in the presence of God" (1 Cor 1:28-29). It is precisely those who are open to God's grace that are the chosen ones. "This puts an end to every . . . possibility of human self-glorification."[84]

Abraham, Paul says, not only believed the promise of God, but he hoped confidently and patiently that the promise would be fulfilled (4:18). The expression παρ᾽ ἐλπίδα ἐπ᾽ ἐλπίδι consists of two prepositional phrases, and if the last of the two (ἐπ᾽ ἐλπίδι) is taken to modify the verb (ἐπίστευσεν), as it should, the phrase can be translated: "against hope he believed with hope." The stress is upon Abraham's faith. He continued against all odds, against what could reasonably be believed, believing with hope that the promise would be fulfilled. The meaning of hope is important here. In common speech "hope" can mean wish, desire, or wishful thinking, but in the NT the word for "hope" (ἐλπίς) has the meaning of expectation, trust, confidence, and patient waiting.[85] Such was the confidence of Abraham, which was lived out in his patient waiting. He awaited the fulfillment of the promise, which he had believed, as stated in Genesis 15:5: "So shall your descendants be" (οὕτως ἔσται τὸ σπέρμα σου, quoted exactly as in the LXX). The NRSV wording ("So numerous shall your descendants be") catches the sense of the OT text, but it is paraphrastic.

In 4:19-20 Paul describes the physical condition of Abraham and his wife Sarah. In the first case, says Paul, Abraham was "about one hundred years old."

83. Philo, *Spec. Leg.* 4.187.
84. H. Conzelmann, *1 Corinthians*, 51.
85. Rudolf Bultmann, "ἐλπίς," *TDNT* 2:531.

The statement cannot refer to the time that the promise was first given and the promise just quoted in 4:18b ("So shall your descendants be," Gen 15:5-6), for at that point in the narrative Abraham was surely not a hundred years old. He would have had to be eighty-six or less at that point (cf. Gen 16:16). For details, see the comments above on 4:10-11. But Paul picks up the narrative at Genesis 17:17, where Abraham asks God, after being told that he will have a son with Sarah, "Can a child be born to a man who is a hundred years old? Can Sarah, who is ninety years old, bear a child?" At this point Abraham has not yet been circumcised; that occurs later, and then he is said to be ninety-nine (17:24). The birth of Isaac their son, followed by the notation of his circumcision on the eighth day, is recorded later (21:1-4). Then follows the report: "Abraham was a hundred years old when his son Isaac was born to him" (21:5).

Abraham is frequently the exemplar of faith in the Bible.[86] That is attested and illustrated by Paul when he says that the patriarch did not weaken in faith, even though "he considered his own body as dead" (νενεκρωμένον, literally, "to have been put to death"), i.e., incapable of life itself, but then also incapable of generating it. The "death" (νέκρωσις) of Sarah's womb would have taken place many years previously, since she was a ninety-year-old woman when the promise of having a son was made.

In 4:20-22 Paul extends his discussion of the faith of Abraham. What he presents is a brief midrash, by which Paul "fills in" between the lines of the narrative in Genesis.[87] Not only did Abraham not waver in unbelief; he became even stronger in faith. He knew that God would deliver on the promise made. The midrash is hagiographic, in which the subject — Abraham in this case — never doubts, grows ever stronger in faith, and gives glory to God. Following that, Paul brings the discussion of Abraham to a close, summarizing once again what he has been saying, and recalling the line from Genesis that has been cited before. Abraham's faith "was accredited to him as righteousness" (cf. 4:3, 9-10).

4:23-25 Using typology, Paul asserts that Abraham is the type, and the believer in the God who raised Jesus from the dead is the antitype.[88] The words of justification ("It [= righteousness] was accredited to him") apply to the latter as well as to the former. The cases of Abraham and that of the believer are tightly drawn by Paul. Abraham had believed in God, "who gives life to the

---

86. Cf. surveys and discussion by T. Fretheim, *Abraham*, 144-79. Although not so frequent in the OT, the theme of Abraham's faith or faithfulness is emphasized in intertestamental literature and the NT. Among texts cited (some allude to Abraham's faith only implicitly) are Gen 26:3-5, 24; Neh 9:8; Ps 105:43; Isa 41:8; 1 Macc 2:51-52; 2 Macc 1:2; 4 Macc 16:20-22; Jdt 5:6-10; Heb 11:8, 11; Jas 2:23.

87. On this and other functions of midrash, cf. Gary G. Porton, "Midrash," *ABD* 4:818-22.

88. On typology in the NT, see John E. Alsup, "Typology," *ABD* 6:682-85, and studies cited there.

dead and calls into being those things that are not" (4:17), and that took on concreteness in the case of his faith in God to do what God claimed possible in spite of his own body and that of Sarah's, both of which were "dead" in terms of reproductive power. Likewise, the person of Christian faith believes in the God who brings life out of death. There is a likeness, then, between Abraham and his children. Abraham believed in God, who gives life (the birth of Isaac); the children of Abraham are like their father, since they believe in God, who gives life (the resurrection of Christ). The expression "to believe in the one who raised from the dead Jesus our Lord" is confessional language,[89] and it represents the essential confession of Christian faith (Acts 3:15; 4:10; Rom 8:11; 1 Cor 15:15; 2 Cor 4:14; Gal 1:1; Eph 1:20; 1 Thess 1:10; 1 Pet 1:21).

The section ends at 4:25 with what is generally regarded as a creedal formula concerning Christ: he "was given over for our trespasses and was raised for our justification" (4:25).[90] The common features of a confessional formula (as generally understood) are present, including the use of the relative pronoun "who" (ὅς) at the outset, referring to Christ in the previous verse (cf. Phil 2:6; Col 1:15, 18; 1 Tim 3:16; Titus 2:14; 1 Pet 2:24); the antithethical parallelism between being handed over to death and being raised from death (cf. Acts 2:36; 3:15; 4:10; Rom 14:9; 1 Cor 15:3-4; 1 Thess 4:14); and the use of the verb παρεδόθη itself, which is used in confessional formulas (Rom 8:32; cf. Mark 9:31; 10:33, par.).[91] The confessional formula appears to have been formulated with reference to Isaiah 52:13–53:12 (the Fourth Servant Song).[92] There the Lord's Servant is portrayed as one who suffers for the sins of others, as in 53:12: "he was given over for their sins" (διὰ τὰς ἁμαρτίας αὐτῶν παρεδόθη) and in related passages that express the same theme, e.g., 53:5, "he was wounded for our iniquities" (ἐτραυματίσθη διὰ τὰς ἀνομίας ἡμῶν), and 53:6, "the Lord gave him up for our sins" (κύριος παρέδωκεν αὐτὸν ταῖς ἁμαρτίαις ἡμῶν). In any case, the confessional formula used by Paul speaks of the death of Christ as atoning ("for our trespasses") and his resurrection as the means of justification ("for our justification").[93] Both are expressed in Greek by prepositional phrases beginning with the preposition διά ("for") followed by nouns in the accusative case. There is a difference in meaning, however. In the first case the phrase means "on account

89. O. Michel, *Römer*, 112; V. Neufeld, *The Earliest Christian Confessions*, 46-48.

90. O. Michel, *Römer*, 112; V. Neufeld, *Earliest Christian Confessions*, 46-49; K. Wengst, "Römer 4,25," 80-82; F. Hahn, *The Titles of Jesus in Christology*, 59-61; C. Cranfield, *Romans*, 251; Wiard Popkes, "παραδίδωμι," *EDNT* 3:20; R. Jewett, *Romans*, 342.

91. N. Perrin, "The Use of *(Para)didonai* in Connection with the Passion of Jesus in the New Testament," 94-103; C. Cranfield, *Romans*, 251.

92. The other Servant Songs are at Isa 42:1-4; 49:1-6; and 50:4-11.

93. This means that the resurrection also, and not only the cross, is the basis for justification, as maintained by M. Bird, "'Raised for Our Justification,'" 31-46.

of our trespasses" (a phrase expressing cause), and in the second it means "in order that we might be justified" (a phrase expressing purpose).[94]

The formula is generally regarded as pre-Pauline. But that is not certain. The first clause appears to express the common language concerning the death of Christ and could therefore be pre-Pauline. The second clause, however, uses the language of justification (δικαίωσις), which appears only in Paul's writings in the entire NT (Rom 4:25; 5:18). Since that word is a rather distinctive Pauline one, it is possible that Paul composed the formula, taking a traditional line first and then amplifying it with the second. The alternative is that Paul was not the first to speak of justification as a consequence of the death and resurrection of Jesus, and what follows from that is that Paul was not an innovator at this point, nor was he idiosyncratic.

BIBLIOGRAPHY

Adams, Edward. "Abraham's Faith and Gentile Disobedience: Textual Links between Romans 1 and 4." *JSNT* 19 (1997): 47-66.
Bailey, Kenneth E. "St. Paul's Understanding of the Territorial Promise of God to Abraham: Romans 4:13 in Its Historical and Theological Context." *NESTTR* 15 (1994): 59-69.
Baird, William. "Abraham in the New Testament: Tradition and the New Identity." *Int* 42 (1988): 367-79.
Behrens, Achim. "Gen 15,6 und das Vorverständnis des Paulus." *ZAW* 109 (1997): 327-41.
Berger, Klaus. "Abraham in den paulinischen Hauptbriefen." *MTZ* 17 (1966): 47-89.
Betz, Hans D. *The Sermon on the Mount.* Hermeneia. Minneapolis: Fortress Press, 1995.
Bird, Michael F. "'Raised for Our Justification': A Fresh Look at Romans 4:25." *Coll* 35 (2003): 31-46.
Brawley, Robert L. "Multivocality in Romans 4." In *Society of Biblical Literature 1997 Seminar Papers,* 284-305. Atlanta: Scholars Press, 1997; reprinted in *Reading Israel in Romans: Legitimacy and Plausibility of Divergent Interpretations,* 74-95. Ed. Cristina Grenholm and Daniel Patte. RHCS 1. Harrisburg: Trinity Press International, 2000.
Bruce, F. F. "Abraham Our Father (Romans 4)." In his *The Time is Fulfilled: Five Aspects of the Fulfillment of the Old Testament in the New,* 57-74. Exeter: Paternoster Press, 1978.
Calvert-Koyzis, Nancy. *Paul, Monotheism and the People of God: The Significance of Abraham Traditions for Early Judaism and Christianity.* JSNTSup 273. London: T&T Clark, 2005.
Conzelmann, Hans. *1 Corinthians.* Hermeneia. Philadelphia: Fortress Press, 1975.
Cranford, Michael. "Abraham in Romans 4: The Father of All Who Believe." *NTS* 41 (1995): 71-88.

94. For the distinction, cf. BDAG 225 (διά, B, 2, a).

Das, A. Andrew. "Paul and Works of Obedience in Second Temple Judaism: Romans 4:4-5 as a 'New Perspective' Case Study." *CBQ* 71 (2009): 795-812.

Dietzfelbinger, Christian. *Paulus und das Alte Testament: Die Hermeneutik des Paulus, untersucht an seiner Deutung der Gestalt Abrahams.* TEH 95. Munich: C. Kaiser Verlag, 1961.

Du Toit, Andreas B. "Gesetzesgerechtigkeit und Glaubensgerechtigkeit in Röm 4:13-25: In Gesprach mit E. P. Sanders." *HTS* 44/1 (1988): 71-80.

Ehrhardt, Arnold. "Creatio ex nihilo." In his *The Framework of the New Testament Stories,* 200-223. Cambridge: Harvard University Press, 1964.

Fahy, Thomas. "Faith and the Law: Epistle to the Romans Ch. 4." *ITQ* 28 (1961): 207-14.

Forman, Mark. "The Politics of Promise: Echoes of Isaiah 54 in Romans 4.19-21." *JSNT* 31 (2009): 301-24.

Fretheim, Terence E. *Abraham: Trials of Family and Faith.* Columbia: University of South Carolina Press, 2007.

Furnish, Victor P. "'He Gave Himself [Was Given] Up . . .': Paul's Use of a Christological Assertion." In *The Future of Christology: Essays in Honor of Leander E. Keck,* 109-21. Ed. Abraham J. Malherbe and Wayne A. Meeks. Minneapolis: Fortress Press, 1993.

Gaston, Lloyd. "Abraham and the Righteousness of God." *HBT* 2 (1980): 39-68.

Goppelt, Leonhard. "Paulus und die Heilsgeschichte: Schlussfolgerungen aus Röm. iv und I Kor. x.1-13." *NTS* 13 (1966-67): 31-42.

Guerra, Anthony J. "Romans 4 as Apologetic Theology." *HTR* 81 (1988): 251-70.

Grässer, Erich. "Der ruhmlose Abraham (Röm 4,2): Nachdenkliches zu Gesetz und Sünde bei Paulus." In *Paulus, Apostel Jesu Christi: Festschrift für Günter Klein zum 70. Geburtstag,* 3-22. Ed. Michael Trowitzsch. Tübingen: J. C. B. Mohr (Paul Siebeck), 1998.

Hahn, Ferdinand. "Genesis 15:6 im Neuen Testament." In *Probleme biblischer Theologie: Gerhard von Rad zum 70. Geburtstag,* 90-107. Ed. Hans W. Wolff. Munich: C. Kaiser Verlag, 1971.

———. *The Titles of Jesus in Christology: Their History in Early Christianity.* Cleveland: World Publishing Company, 1969.

Hanson, Anthony T. "Abraham the Justified Sinner." In his *Studies in Paul's Technique and Theology,* 52-66. London: SPCK, 1974.

Harrisville, Roy A., III. *The Figure of Abraham in the Epistles of St. Paul: In the Footsteps of Abraham.* Lewiston: Mellen Research University Press, 1992.

Hays, Richard B. *Echoes of Scripture in the Letters of Paul.* New Haven: Yale University Press, 1989.

———. "'Have We Found Abraham to Be Our Forefather according to the Flesh?' A Reconsideration of Rom 4:1." *NovT* 27 (1985): 76-98; reprinted as "Abraham as Father of Jews and Gentiles." In his *The Conversion of the Imagination: Paul as an Interpreter of Israel's Scripture,* 61-84. Grand Rapids: Wm. B. Eerdmans, 2005.

———. "Three Dramatic Roles: The Law in Romans 3-4." In *Paul and the Mosaic Law,* 151-64. Ed. J. D. G. Dunn. WUNT 89. Tübingen: J. C. B. Mohr (Paul Siebeck), 1996; reprinted in his *The Conversion of the Imagination: Paul as an Interpreter of Israel's Scripture,* 85-100. Grand Rapids: Wm. B. Eerdmans, 2005.

Hester, James D. *Paul's Concept of Inheritance.* SJTOP 14. Edinburgh: Oliver and Boyd, 1968.

Hofius, Otfried. "Eine altjüdische Parallele zu Röm. iv.17b." *NTS* 18 (1972-73): 93-94.

Holst, Richard. "The Meaning of 'Abraham Believed in God' in Romans 4:3." *WTJ* 59 (1997): 319-26.

Hooker, Morna D. "Raised for Our Acquittal (Rom 4,25)." In *Resurrection in the New Testament: Festschrift J. Lambrecht,* 323-41. Ed. Reimund Bieringer et al. BETL 165. Leuven: Leuven University Press, 2002.

————. "'Who died for our sins, and was raised for our acquittal': Paul's Understanding of the Death of Christ." *SEÅ* 68 (2003): 59-71.

Hort, F. J. A. *Prolegomena to St. Paul's Epistles to the Romans and the Ephesians.* New York: Macmillan, 1895.

Hübner, Hans. "Abraham und die Beschneidung in Röm 4." In his *Das Gesetz bei Paulus: Ein Beitrag zum Werden der paulinischen Theologie,* 44-50. Göttingen: Vandenhoeck & Ruprecht, 1978.

Johnson, Bo. "Who Reckoned Righteousness to Whom?" *SEÅ* 51-52 (1986-87): 108-15.

Käsemann, Ernst. "The Faith of Abraham in Romans 4." In his *Perspectives on Paul,* 79-101. Philadelphia: Fortress Press, 1971.

Klein, Günter. "Heil und Geschitchte nach Römer iv." *NTS* 13 (1966-67): 43-47.

————. "Römer 4 und die Idee der Heilsgeschichte." *EvT* 23 (1963): 424-47.

Kolenkow, Anitra. "The Ascription of Romans 4:5." *HTR* 60 (1967): 228-30.

Lincoln, Andrew. "Abraham Goes to Rome: Paul's Treatment of Abraham in Romans 4." In *Worship, Theology, and Ministry in the Early Church: Essays in Honor of Ralph P. Martin,* 163-79. Ed. Michael J. Wilkins and Terence Paige. Sheffield: JSOT Press, 1992.

Longenecker, Richard N. "The 'Faith of Abraham' Theme in Paul, James and Hebrews: A Study in the Circumstantial Nature of New Testament Teaching." *JETS* 20 (1977): 203-12.

Lowe, Bruce A. "Oh διά! How Is Romans 4:25 to Be Understood?" *JTS* 57 (2006): 149-57.

McNeil, Brian. "Raised for Our Justification." *ITQ* 42 (1975): 97-105.

Meecham, Henry G. "Romans iii.25f., iv.25 — The Meaning of διά c. acc." *ExpTim* 50 (1938-39): 564.

Moore, Richard K. "Romans 4:5 in TEV: A Plea for Consistency." *BT* 39 (1988): 126-29.

Moxnes, Halvor. *Theology in Conflict: Studies in Paul's Understanding of God in Romans.* NovTSup 53. Leiden: E. J. Brill, 1980.

Neufeld, Vernon. *The Earliest Christian Confessions.* NTTS 5. Grand Rapids: Wm. B. Eerdmans, 1963.

Nickelsburg, George W. E. *Resurrection, Immortality, and Eternal Life in Intertestamental Judaism.* HTS 26. Cambridge: Harvard University Press, 1972.

Noort, Edward, and Eibert J. C. Tigchelaar, eds. *The Sacrifice of Isaac: The Aqedah (Genesis 22) and Its Interpretation.* TBN 4. Boston: E. J. Brill, 2002.

O'Rourke, John J. "*Pistis* in Romans." *CBQ* 35 (1973): 188-94.

Palmer, Michael W. "τί οὖν; The Inferential Question in Paul's Letter to the Romans with a Proposed Reading of Romans 4.1." In *Discourse Analysis and Other Topics in Biblical*

Greek, 200-218. Ed. Stanley E. Porter and D. A. Carson. JSNTSup 113. Sheffield: Sheffield Academic Press, 1995.

Parker, Thomas D. "Abraham, Father of Us All, in Barth's Epistle to the Romans." In *Reading Israel in Romans: Legitimacy and Plausibility of Divergent Interpretations*, 57-73. Ed. Cristina Grenholm and Daniel Patte. RHCS 1. Harrisburg: Trinity Press International, 2000.

Patsch, Hermann. "Zum alttestamentlichen Hintergrund von Römer 4,25 und I Petrus 2,24." *ZNW* 60 (1969): 273-79.

Perrin, Norman. "The Use of *(Para)didonai* in Connection with the Passion of Jesus in the New Testament." In his *A Modern Pilgrimage in New Testament Christology*, 94-103. Philadelphia: Fortress Press, 1974.

Plag, Christoph. "Paulus und die *Gezera schawa*: Zur Übernahme rabbinischer Auslegungskunst." *Judaica* 50 (1994): 135-40.

Rad, Gerhard von. *Old Testament Theology*. 2 vols. New York: Harper & Row, 1962-65.

Sandmel, Samuel. *Philo's Place in Judaism: A Study of Conceptions of Abraham in Jewish Literature*. Cincinnati: Hebrew Union College Press, 1956.

Sasson, Jack M. "Circumcision in the Ancient Near East." *JBL* 85 (1966): 473-76.

Schliesser, Benjamin. *Abraham's Faith in Romans 4: Paul's Concept of Faith in Light of the History of Reception of Genesis 15:6*. WUNT 2/224. Tübingen: Verlag Mohr Siebeck, 2007.

Swetnam, James. "The Curious Crux at Romans 4,12." *Bib* 61 (1980): 110-15.

Tobin, Thomas H. *Paul's Rhetoric in Its Contexts: The Argument of Romans*. Peabody: Hendrickson Publishers, 2004.

————. "What Shall We Say That Abraham Found? The Controversy behind Romans 4." *HTR* 88 (1995): 437-52.

Turner, Nigel. *Syntax*. Vol. 3 of *A Grammar of New Testament Greek* by James H. Moulton. 3 vols. Edinburgh: T&T Clark, 1908-63.

Visscher, Gerhard H. *Romans 4 and the New Perspective on Paul: Faith Embraces the Promise*. StudBL 122. New York: Lang, 2009.

Wengst, Klaus. *Christologische Formeln und Lieder des Urchristentums*. SNT 7. Gütersloh: Gütersloher Verlagshaus Gerd Mohn, 1972.

————. "Römer 4,25." In his *Das Verständnis der Tradition bei Paulus und in den Deuteropaulinien*, 80-82. WMANT 8. Neukirchen-Vluyn: Neukirchener Verlag, 1962.

White, John L. *The Apostle of God: Paul and the Promise of Abraham*. Peabody: Hendrickson Publishers, 1999.

Wilckens, Ulrich. "Die Rechtfertigung Abrahams nach Römer 4." In *Studien zur Theologie der alttestamentlichen Überlieferungen: Gerhard von Rad zum 60. Geburtstag*, 111-27. Ed. Rolf Rendtorff and Klaus Koch. Neukirchen: Neukirchener Verlag, 1961.

Wyschograd, Michael. *Abraham's Promise: Judaism and Jewish-Christian Relations*. Ed. R. Kendall Soulen. Grand Rapids: Wm. B. Eerdmans, 2004.

CHAPTER 4

The New Life in Christ, 5:1–8:39

Romans 5:1–8:39 can be considered a major block of material in the letter. Alternative views have been proposed,[1] but there are good reasons for considering chapters 5 through 8 as a major section of the letter.[2] Having completed the section on Abraham as an example of one justified by faith, Paul makes a transition at 5:1 that sums up the significance of 3:21–4:25: "Therefore, since we have been justified by faith, we have [or "let us have"; see the the appendix, "The Text of Romans 5:1"] peace with God." And he goes on in that chapter and in those following to explicate the meaning of justification by means of a theological and ethical treatment of the new life in Christ. Although there is no discrete treatment of a series of topics in these chapters as self-contained units — for themes overlap among them — in each of the four chapters Paul affirms the freedom of the believer at some point: freedom from the wrath of God in chapter 5 (5:9-11); freedom from the power of sin in chapter 6 (6:14); freedom from the law in chapter 7 (7:4-6); and freedom from death in chapter 8 (8:9-11, 37-39).[3]

1. J. Dunn, *Romans*, 242-44, U. Wilckens, *Römer*, 1:181, and P. Stuhlmacher, *Romans*, 14, 57 maintain that 3:21–5:21 should be taken as a unit; C. Talbert, *Romans*, 129, 144, considers 1:18–5:11 and 5:12–8:39 to be major units; P. Achtemeier, *Romans*, 25, 87, regards 4:23–8:39 as a unit; L. Keck, *Romans*, 102, divides the letter into 3:21–5:11 and 5:12–8:39; T. Pulcini, "In Right Relationship with God," 63, connects 5:1-11 with what goes before in chapter 4, considering 5:12 through chapter 8 a separate section. Other proposals are reviewed by J. Fitzmyer, *Romans*, 96-97.

2. This is the view of, among others, H. Schlier, *Römer*, 13-15, 137-38; A. Nygren, *Romans*, 188; O. Michel, *Römer*, 129; C. H. Dodd, *Romans*, 71; N. Dahl, "A Synopsis of Romans 5:1-11 and 8:1-39," 88-90; C. Cranfield, *Romans*, 252-54; E. Käsemann, *Romans*, 131; J. White, *Form and Function of the Body of the Greek Letter*, 95; J. Ziesler, *Romans*, 135; R. Harrisville, *Romans*, 75; J. Fitzmyer, *Romans*, 97, 393; B. Byrne, *Romans*, 162-64; J. C. Beker, *Paul the Apostle*, 78-86; D. Moo, *Romans*, 32, 290-95; T. Schreiner, *Romans*, 245-49; R. Longenecker, "The Focus of Romans," 64-65; E. Lohse, *Römer*, 163-65; R. Jewett, *Romans*, 346.

3. This is a modification of the pattern set forth by A. Nygren, *Romans*, 188. The need for its modification is spelled out forcefully by J. Beker, *Paul the Apostle*, 66.

Since there are thematic connections between this section (5:1–8:39) and what has been written prior to it, one should not set it off from what has gone before by being bound by the restraints of a neatly ordered outline. The opening portion of this section (5:1-11) has been called a "rhetorical bridge" and a "hinge" between the previous chapters and what is developed subsequently.[4] There are at least three major connections to justify such claims. (1) The opening statement concerning justification by faith (5:1) depends on what has been said since 3:21; (2) Paul's declaration that, due to justification, believers will be saved from the wrath of God (5:9) responds to what was said earlier about the wrath of God against the world apart from God's gracious act in Christ (1:18); and (3) the phrase "justified by his blood" (5:9) recalls the previously used language of justification and atonement "by his blood" (3:24-25).

Yet chapters 5 through 8 make up a unified section. Many of the terms and concepts that Paul uses in 5:1-11 appear again in 8:12-39, so that the latter provides an *inclusio*.[5] These include:

Terms	5:1-11	8:12-39
Justified/justify	5:1, 9	8:30, 33
"In hope"	5:2	8:20, 24
Glory/glorify	5:2	8:17
Suffering/suffer	5:3	8:17, 35-36
Endurance	5:3	8:25
Hope	5:4	8:24-25
God's/Christ's love	5:5	8:35, 39
Holy Spirit	5:5	8:14-16
Christ died	5:6, 8, 10	8:34
Christ was raised	5:10	8:34
Saved from God's wrath	5:9	8:31-34
Through/in Christ	5:11	8:39

In addition to these verbal and conceptual connections between the beginning of chapter 5 and the end of chapter 8, there are other items to notice that bind these chapters together. First, and most obvious, each of the chapters closes with the refrain that binds them together: "through [or "in"] Jesus Christ our Lord" (5:21; 6:23; 7:25; 8:39).[6] Second, there is a shift from Paul's

---

4. P. McDonald, "Romans 5:1-11 as a Rhetorical Bridge," 81-82; L. Keck, *Romans*, 133, calls it a "hinge."

5. For other demonstrations of connections, cf. N. Dahl, "A Synopsis of Romans 5:1-11 and 8:1-39," 88-89; D. Moo, *Romans*, 292-95; and R. Longenecker, "The Focus of Romans," 65.

6. The phrase appears also at 5:11 in reference to the reconciling work of God. Paul is obliged by his theology to declare that that is so through the death and resurrection of Christ (5:10).

making a case in 3:21–4:25 for justification by faith to confessional and hortatory matters that belong to the life of faith; in this regard there is a striking increase in the use of first person plural verbs and pronouns.[7] And, finally, it is in these chapters that Paul carries on a sustained theological analysis of the life of faith around key terms, such as sin, death, the law, the Spirit, and life. He deals with the relationship between sin, the law, the inability to do the will of God in one's life, and death, on the one hand. On the other, he speaks eloquently of justification, grace, the Spirit, and life. As one illustration of this, while the noun "life" appears only twice in Romans 1–4, it appears 16 times in chapters 5 through 8.

BIBLIOGRAPHY

Beker, J. Christiaan, *Paul the Apostle: The Triumph of God in Thought and Life*. Philadelphia: Fortress Press, 1980.

Cousar, Charles B. "Continuity and Discontinuity: Reflections on Romans 5–8." In *Pauline Theology*, vol. 3, *Romans*, 196-210. Ed. David M. Hay and E. Elizabeth Johnson. Minneapolis: Fortress Press, 1995.

Dahl, Nils A. "A Synopsis of Romans 5:1-11 and 8:1-39" and "The Argument in Romans 5:12-21." In his *Studies in Paul: Theology for the Christian Mission*, 88-91. Minneapolis: Augsburg Publishing House, 1977.

Jipp, Joshua W. "Rereading the Story of Abraham, Isaac, and 'Us' in Romans 4." *JSNT* 32 (2009): 217-42.

Knox, John. *Life in Christ Jesus: Reflections on Romans 5–8*. Greenwich: Seabury Press, 1961.

Longenecker, Richard N. "The Focus of Romans: The Central Role of 5:1–8:39 in the Argument of the Letter." In *Romans and the People of God: Essays in Honor of Gordon D. Fee on the Occasion of His 65th Birthday*, 49-69. Ed. Sven K. Soderlund and N. T. Wright. Grand Rapids: Wm. B. Eerdmans, 1999.

Minear, Paul S. "'Life for All Men': The Dialectic of 5.1–8.39." In his *The Obedience of Faith: The Purpose of Paul in the Epistle to the Romans*, 57-71. SBT 19. Naperville: Alec R. Allenson, 1971.

Olson, Stanley N. "Romans 5–8 as Pastoral Theology." *WW* 6 (1986): 390-97.

Osten-Sacken, Peter von der. "Die Bedeutung von Röm 5–7 für die Interpretation von Röm 8." In his *Römer 8 als Beispiel paulinischer Soteriologie*, 160-225. FRLANT 112. Göttingen: Vandenhoeck & Ruprecht, 1975.

Pulcini, Theodore. "In Right Relationship with God: Present Experience and Future Fulfillment: An Exegesis of Romans 5:1-11." *SVTQ* 36 (1992): 61-85.

Thielman, Frank, "The Story of Israel and the Theology of Romans 5–8." In *Pauline Theol-*

---

7. D. Moo, *Romans*, 292 (n. 9): "Paul uses first person plural verbs 13 times in Rom. 1–4, mainly editorially or as a stylistic device; in Rom. 5–8, however, there are 48 first person plural verbs."

ogy, vol. 3, *Romans,* 169-95. Ed. David M. Hay and E. Elizabeth Johnson. Minneapolis: Fortress Press, 1995.

White, John L. *The Form and Function of the Body of the Greek Letter: A Study of the Letter-Body in the Nonliterary Papyri and in Paul the Apostle.* SBLDS 2. Missoula: Scholars Press, 1972.

4.1. Peace with God through Justification, 5:1-11

₁*Therefore, since we have been justified by faith, let us be at peace with God through our Lord Jesus Christ, ₂through whom we have indeed obtained access to this grace in which we stand, and let us rejoice on the basis of our hope of sharing the glory of God. ₃And not only that, but let us rejoice in our sufferings, knowing that suffering produces endurance, ₄and endurance produces character, and character produces hope, ₅and hope does not disappoint us, because God's love has been poured into our hearts through the Holy Spirit, which has been given to us.*

₆*For while we were still helpless, at the right time Christ died for the ungodly. ₇For ordinarily one will not die for a righteous person; indeed, one hardly dares to die even for a good person. ₈But God demonstrates his love for us in that while we were still sinners, Christ died for us. ₉Therefore much more surely, since we have now been justified by his blood, shall we be saved through him from the wrath. ₁₀For if while we were enemies we were reconciled to God through the death of his Son, how much more, since we have been reconciled, will we be saved by his life. ₁₁And not only that, but let us also rejoice in God through our Lord Jesus Christ, through whom we have now received reconciliation.*

Notes on the Text and Translation

5:1 The translation is based on a text-critical choice for the word ἔχωμεν ("let us have," the hortatory subjunctive) rather than ἔχομεν ("we have," the indicative). For discussion, see the appendix, "The Text of Romans 5:1."

The expression "be at peace" is used to render the verb ἔχω with the preposition πρός, which could be translated "to have" and "in reference to" an object. But the verb ἔχω can signify "to be" in certain circumstances, including those where πρός follows.[8]

5:2 Some major texts (including ℵ, C, Ψ, and others) and the Majority Text include the phrase τῇ πίστει ("by faith"), which is reflected in various English versions, as in the NIV: "through whom we have gained access by faith."

---

8. BDAG 522 (ἔχω, 10, b).

Other versions having "by faith" include the KJV, ASV, NASV, and NET; the NAB has it in parenthesis. Other major texts (including B, D, F, G, and others) lack the phrase. Although the evidence is almost evenly balanced, and the phrase could either have been added (for emphasis) or dropped (because it was considered redundant in light of 5:1), the shorter reading may be the better choice. In any case, the meaning is not changed either way. Versions that omit the phrase include the RSV and NRSV.

5:2, 3, 11 How the Greek term καυχώμεθα in 5:2, 3 and its participial form καυχώμενοι in 5:11 are to be translated depends on what lexical meaning is given to the verb καυχάομαι and how one is to understand the mood of the verb in 5:2, 3. The verb can be translated "to rejoice" or "to boast."[9] The latter is the rendering in the NRSV,[10] but "to rejoice" is favored in the ASV, RSV, NIV, ESV, and NET.[11] The KJV has "rejoice," "glory," and "to joy" in the three verses, respectively. Furthermore, the verb form καυχώμεθα can be either an indicative (so either "we rejoice" or "we boast") or subjunctive (so either "let us rejoice" or "let us boast"). Here it is understood to be a hortatory subjunctive (as in the case of ἔχωμεν in 5:1).[12] The result is that the verb is translated in the three verses here as "let us rejoice," for it has a doxological meaning in its contexts.[13]

5:6 The word ἀσθενής is frequently translated as "weak" (ASV, RSV, NRSV), but it can also have the meaning of "helpless" in moral contexts,[14] as here.

5:7b The conjunction γάρ, usually translated as "for" (as in 5:7a), is translated here as "but," which makes good sense contextually as in other instances.[15]

5:9 Although various English versions read "the wrath of God" (ASV, RSV, NIV, NRSV) instead simply of "the wrath," the latter is the actual reading of the Greek text. Undoubtedly, however, the "wrath of God" is meant. The NEB has "final retribution."

9. BDAG 536 (καυχάομαι) does not list "to rejoice," but does include "to glory" along with "to boast" and related words. The sense of "to boast" is appropriate at Rom 2:17, 23.

10. This is also the sense favored by various interpreters, e.g., E. Käsemann, *Romans*, 133; J. Dunn, *Romans*, 249, 261; J. Fitzmyer, *Romans*, 396-97, 401; J. Ziesler, *Romans*, 137-38; B. Byrne, *Romans*, 164-65; and R. Jewett, *Romans*, 344; cf. E. Lohse, *Römer*, 165-67: "wir rühmen uns."

11. Cf. C. Cranfield, *Romans*, 256: "to exult"; it "denotes exultant rejoicing, jubilation" (p. 259).

12. The hortatory subjunctive is favored by the NEB ("let us exult") and by O. Kuss, *Römer*, 1:200, 203; T. Pulcini, "In Right Relationship with God," 68-69; and R. Jewett, *Romans*, 344, 351. Most interpreters, however, prefer the indicative.

13. Even if the verb is translated to signify boasting, it would mean theocentric boasting, a confessional use of the term, expressing trust that God will fulfill promises. Cf. D. Watson, "Paul and Boasting," 95-96.

14. BDAG 142-43 (ἀσθενής, 2, c).

15. BDAG 189 (γάρ, 2).

General Comment

Having established that justification is by faith (3:21–4:25), and that therefore Gentiles have a place in God's saving purposes — apart from their observing the law — Paul turns to a theological treatment of the new life in Christ, which extends from 5:1 through 8:39 (see 4, "The New Life in Christ, Romans 5:1–8:39"). The opening verses of 5:1-11 produce a "rhetorical bridge" from what has been said previously to what he will be saying in this and the three chapters to follow.[16] Paul makes a dramatic change in the subject of his sentences. No longer is it third person. Now it is first person plural throughout 5:1-11. At 5:12 he goes back to third person as he writes concerning sin and grace, Adam and Christ, and condemnation and justification.

Within these verses Paul, on the basis of justification, calls upon his readers to claim and enjoy the peace that is theirs with God. By reconciling those in Christ, and indeed even the world, unto himself (Rom 5:10; 2 Cor 5:19), God has declared amnesty and therefore peace to the world. The problem remaining is that humanity is not at peace with God. Moreover, Paul calls upon his readers to rejoice in their sufferings. Although they are justified, that does not mean that they are exempt from suffering. Moreover, even suffering leads ultimately to hope, grounded in God's love. Christ has died "for the ungodly" (ὑπὲρ ἀσεβῶν, 5:6; cf. 4:5). Believers are "justified by his blood," for sin has been condemned at the cross (Rom 8:3). They are "reconciled" (Rom 5:10a) and therefore shall be saved at the final judgment (5:10b). Paul does not claim that salvation and the new age have already come *en toto*. There is still suffering now, and there is a final judgment to come. In spite of the "already" of justification, the "not yet" of salvation remains a future expectation in the present.

Detailed Comment

5:1 Justification by faith has been the theme since 3:21, and it is developed further in 5:1-21. The actual phrase "justification by faith" never appears in Paul's letters. What does appear is the verbal expression "justified by faith." That appears in this verse (δικαιωθέντες ἐκ πίστεως, "since we have been justified by faith") and three more times in Paul's letters (Rom 3:28; Gal 2:16; 3:24), but not always in the same form of expression. When Paul speaks of justification, the following forms of expression are used:

---

16. P. McDonald, "Romans 5:1-11 as a Rhetorical Bridge," 81-82. Cf. L. Keck, *Romans,* 133, who calls 5:1-11 a "hinge" between preceding and subsequent discourse; similarly, K. Sandnes, "Abraham, the Friend of God," 124-28.

1. He uses a passive form of the verb δικαιόω ("to justify") followed by the prepositional phrase ἐκ πίστεως ("by faith," Rom 5:1; Gal 2:16; 3:24).

2. He uses a passive form of the verb δικαιόω ("to justify") followed by the dative form of the word for "faith," used in an instrumental sense, πίστει ("by faith," Rom 3:28).

3. He uses the verb in the active voice, followed by the prepositional phrase ἐκ πίστεως ("by faith," Rom 3:30; Gal 3:8).

4. He uses the verb in the active voice, followed by the prepositional phrase διὰ τῆς πίστεως ("through faith," Rom 3:30).

Interpreters of Paul's letters are not of one mind concerning the importance of justification by faith in Paul's theology. Some continue to maintain its centrality,[17] but others place it further on the periphery, considering it a side and subsidiary teaching in comparison to something else,[18] a polemical doctrine,[19] or a doctrine with the limited purpose of admitting Gentiles into the people of God.[20] Methodologically, it is important to make a distinction: what is central to Romans, and what might preoccupy him there, might not be central to Paul's theology *en toto*.

Surely the center of Paul's consciousness would not have been a doctrine but a person — Christ, crucified and resurrected, who had appeared to him and transformed his life (1 Cor 9:1; 15:8; Gal 1:16). But from that point as a beginning, there have been a number of suggestions concerning a possible "center" to his thinking. As one interpreter has written, "These include God, Christ or Christology, justification by faith, salvation history, reconciliation, apocalyptic, (mystical) participation in Christ, the cross, anthropology and salvation, resurrection and/or exaltation, ethics, and gospel, among others."[21] Moreover, Paul held an array of convictions from his Jewish heritage and the common Christian tradition available to him, such as the exaltation of Jesus as the Christ, his present reign, and the expectation of his coming again in glory.[22] Yet insofar as

17. G. Bornkamm, *Paul*, 116; E. Käsemann, "Justification and Salvation History in the Epistle to the Romans," 74; idem, "Some Thoughts on the Theme 'The Doctrine of Reconciliation in the New Testament,'" 63; M. Seifrid, *Justification by Faith*, 270 *et passim*; H. Hübner, "Pauli Theologiae Proprium," 445-73; idem, *Law in Paul's Thought*, 7; J. Reumann, '*Righteousness' in the New Testament*, 105-20; E. Lohse, "Christus, das Gesetzes Ende," 18-32.

18. A. Schweitzer, *The Mysticism of Paul the Apostle*, 22: "The doctrine of righteousness by faith is therefore a subsidiary crater, which has formed within the rim of the main crater — the mystical doctrine of redemption through the being-in-Christ."

19. W. Wrede, *Paul*, 123-24, 127.

20. K. Stendahl, *Paul among Jews and Gentiles*, 2.

21. S. Porter, "Is There a Center to Paul's Theology?" 9-11. Porter provides extensive documentation, which has been omitted here.

22. J. Plevnik, "The Center of Pauline Theology," 461-78.

Paul was a theologian, reflecting on the significance of the Christ who had appeared to him, he could not think otherwise than to place the appearance of Christ into the larger framework of Jewish understandings about God. In his theology as discourse concerning what God has done in Christ, Paul makes use of a wide array of terms and images, such as: "justification, salvation, reconciliation, expiation, redemption, freedom, sanctification, transformation, new creation, and glorification."[23] In spite of the different imageries that these terms convey, however, there is a commonality among them as well.[24] At the center of Paul's theological reflection — aside from the experiential aspects of his faith — was the conviction that God has set humanity free from sin and death through his redemptive work in Christ's death and resurrection, and that persons are restored to a right relationship with God through faith in that which God has done in Christ. Although the specific language of justification by faith is not used in each of Paul's letters, one cannot determine its importance by counting the frequency of words or phrases. It is accompanied by similar expressions that imply the same. It is present implicitly wherever Paul makes a contrast between justification by works prescribed by the law or by grace (Rom 3:24; cf. Gal 5:4), speaks of justification as a gift from faith in Christ (Rom 3:26; 10:10; Gal 2:16; 3:11), or declares that persons are "justified in the name of the Lord Jesus Christ and in the Spirit of our God" (1 Cor 6:11). The concept of justification thus permeates much of Paul's theology, and one cannot imagine a theology of Paul without it. Perhaps the term "center" is a problem for some interpreters. If we mean by the word "center" that which dominates Paul's *letters* as a centerpiece to all of them, it is not appropriate to speak of justification as the center. On the other hand, its place in his *theology* is another matter. The justification of the ungodly is the theological expression of both the memory and the indelible image of Christ's appearing to Paul, a persecutor of the church who considered himself "the least of the apostles" (1 Cor 15:8-9) and for whom all attempts to gain righteousness had become loss and rubbish because of the surpassing value of knowing Christ as Lord (Phil. 3:8). It must be conceded that Paul's theology, as expressed in his writings, would be diffuse without justification providing a "centering" to it.

Paul issues a summons to his readers in 5:1: Since they have been justified by faith, they are called upon to join him in being at peace with God. God has reconciled the world unto himself (to be mentioned at 5:11). There is no longer any reason to fear the wrath of God; it is time to put down one's fears, defenses,

---

23. J. Fitzmyer, "Justification by Faith in Pauline Thought," 82.

24. J. Fitzmyer, "Justification by Faith in Pauline Thought," 82. J. Fitzmyer says that the ten terms are but different ways of conceiving "the basic mystery of Christ and his role." He suggests conceiving of the Christ-event as "a decahedron, a ten-sided solid figure. . . . Each of the ten panels expresses one aspect of the whole."

and even hostility against God (to be mentioned in 5:10) in order to be truly at peace with God. All is well on the divine side's disposition toward humanity; what remains is for humanity to accept the good news, trust God for his grace extended to all in Christ's redemptive death, and to rejoice in the communion that God offers. For additional comment on 5:1, see the appendix, "The Text of Romans 5:1."

5:2 It is "through" (διά) Christ that believers have obtained access into the grace in which they stand. The term translated here as "access" (προσ-αγωγή) has been understood as having its background either in the royal court or in cultic language of the OT. If the former is the background, the term has to do with a person's "introduction to the presence-chamber of a monarch."[25] If the latter, the term would refer to "unhindered access to the sanctuary as the place of God's presence."[26] But since the term (or its verbal form, προσάγω, "to bring forward") appears in both contexts in Greco-Roman literature,[27] one need not make an exclusive choice between the two.[28] The point is that it is through the crucified and risen Christ that "access" has been provided for believers to the grace in which they stand (cf. similar concepts in Heb 10:19-20; 1 Pet 3:18). "Grace" in its most basic sense means divine favor.[29] To stand within grace is a striking metaphor, conjuring up the picture of one standing in a room or a garden, and signifying that one is surrounded by grace on all sides.

On the form and meaning of the term καυχώμεθα, rendered here as "let us rejoice," see the Notes on the Text and Translation above. Paul calls upon his readers to rejoice with him on the basis of the hope that they have.[30] The word is doxological, and it expresses "a triumphant, rejoicing confidence" in God.[31] The "hope" spoken of is not that of wishful or wistful thinking but of assurance and expectation.[32] And that is the hope of sharing the glory of God.

The expression "sharing the glory of God" is singular in the NT and begs for an explanation. By itself, the phrase "glory of God" (ἡ δόξα τοῦ θεοῦ), as used here, is rooted in the OT. Within the LXX the phrase is used to translate the expression כְּבֹד אֵל, כְּבֹד אֱלֹהִים ("glory of God," Ps 19:1 [LXX 18:1]; Prov 25:2; Ezek 9:3; 10:19; 11:22), or כְּבוֹד יְהוָה ("glory of the LORD," Exod 24:16-17; Isa

---

25. W. Sanday and A. Headlam, *Romans*, 121; cf. B. Byrne, *Romans*, 170.

26. E. Käsemann, *Romans*, 133; U. Wilckens, *Römer*, 1:289.

27. BDAG 875-76 (προσάγω, προσαγωγή); Karl L. Schmidt, "προσαγωγή," *TDNT* 1:131-34; Udo Borse, "προσαγωγή," *EDNT* 3:161.

28. Cf. J. Dunn, *Romans*, 247-48; J. Fitzmyer, *Romans*, 396; R. Jewett, *Romans*, 349-50.

29. BDAG 1080 (χάρις, 3, b).

30. Josef Zmijewski, "καυχάομαι," *EDNT* 2:276: at Rom 5:2 ἐπ' plus the dative should be rendered to express the cause, so ἐπ' ἐλπίδι should be translated "because of our hope."

31. C. K. Barrett, *Romans*, 96.

32. BDAG 320 (ἐλπίς, 1, b, β).

58:8). The "glory of God" shines forth in theophanies, such as at Mount Sinai (Exod 24:15-18). Ezekiel emphasizes the brightness of the glory of God (Ezek 1:28; 43:2). The phrase comes to signify the presence of God in splendor.[33] This is shown to be the case in the Isaiah Targum. At Isaiah 6:1 the MT text can be rendered: "I saw the LORD sitting on a throne, high and lofty." But the Targum has, "I saw the glory of the LORD resting upon a throne." Then again at 6:5, instead of the MT reading, "my eyes have seen the King, the LORD of hosts," the Targum has, "my eyes have seen the glory of the Shekinah of the eternal king, the LORD of hosts."[34] The phrase "glory of God" is also an expression for the divine presence in the Dead Sea Scrolls.[35]

The experience of being in the presence of the glory of God becomes a future hope in portions of the OT (Ps 102:15-16; Isa 24:23 [within the postexilic Isaiah Apocalypse, 24–27]) and postbiblical Judaism.[36] For Paul it is an eschatological "hope" (ἐλπίς), an assured expectation based on having been justified. Believers are thus summoned by Paul to rejoice in the hope of sharing the divine presence (cf. also Titus 2:13; Rev 21:23).

5:3-4 Nevertheless, while rejoicing in that assured expectation, believers are "between the times." The present is a time of suffering, which leads to endurance, character, and hope. There is an ascending order of conditions in these two verses: from physical and mental suffering, to endurance in that suffering, on to the even more admirable quality of character, and finally to eschatological hope.

The message that believers are not exempt from suffering is in keeping with the history of the people of God. The term translated here as "suffering" (θλῖψις) can also be translated as "tribulation." Within the LXX the term is used to translate various Hebrew nouns, and it signifies the sufferings or tribulations that both the people as a whole and righteous individuals experience.[37] In the case of the people as a whole, it is used to describe the oppression of Israel in Egypt (Exod 4:31; Judg 6:9; cf. Acts 7:10-11 in the NT, reflecting back), the experience of the exile (Deut 4:29; 28:53; Isa 63:9), the suffering of the Maccabean era (1 Macc 9:27), and much more concerning the suffering of Israel in general (Judg 10:14; 1 Kgdms 10:19; 4 Kgdms 19:3). It is particularly the righteous of Israel who experience suffering for their fidelity to God (LXX Pss 33:19; 36:39; 49:15; 76:2; 137:7; 4 Macc 18:15). In the NT the term is used in the gospels to speak of end-time sufferings which are most certain to come (Mark 13:19, 24)

---

33. G. von Rad, *Old Testament Theology,* 1:239-41.

34. Quoted from Bruce D. Chilton, *The Isaiah Targum: Introduction, Translation, Apparatus and Notes,* The Aramaic Bible 11 (Wilmington: Michael Glazier, 1987), 14.

35. 1QpHab 10.14; 1QM 4.6, 8; 1Q19.13.1; 4Q377.2.9; 11Q5.18.3.

36. 2 Esdr 7:42, 91; *Pss. Sol.* 17.34-35; CD 20.26.

37. Heinrich Schlier, "θλῖψις," *TDNT* 3:140-43.

and which are, in fact, necessary in the present age (John 16:33). Paul assumes that suffering will be the normal lot of the believer (Rom 8:35; 12:12; 2 Cor 4:17), and in that he is joined by other NT writers as well (Col 1:24; Heb 10:33; 1 Pet 5:9-10; Rev 2:10; 7:14).

Rejoicing in suffering is possible because of the end in view, the hope that does not disappoint. Along the way, in light of the "hope" (ἐλπίς) or assured expectation in store, the believer's struggle results in ὑπομονή, typically translated as "endurance," an ability to bear up in the face of difficulty.[38] Moreover, "endurance" or "steadfastness" is a characteristic of Christian hope (1 Thess 1:3, ἡ ὑπομονὴ τῆς ἐλπίδος, "the steadfastness of hope"). That kind of endurance results, in turn, in δοκιμή, which is often translated as "character" (ASV, RSV, NIV, NRSV, NET, and ESV), but in this instance seems to denote the evidence of being able to stand firm in testing (cf. NASV: "proven character");[39] the word signifies the result of having shown one's trustworthiness.[40] Paul writes with a bold imagination, supported by his own experience of suffering (2 Cor 1:7-8; 6:4; 11:23-27; Phil 3:8-10; 1 Thess 2:2), to declare that believers can rejoice in their sufferings because they result in characteristics that outwardly mark the life of discipleship and lead a person to place all trust and hope in God. Since suffering is capable of misinterpretation, the believer's existence that is bound up with faith in God can be one of hope.[41]

5:5 And "hope does not disappoint us," Paul declares, referring directly to that hope in God, who is a "God of hope" (ὁ θεὸς τῆς ἐλπίδος, Rom 15:13). Although the phrase οὐ καταισχύνει has been rendered "not to put [us] to shame" (as in KJV, ASV, and ESV),[42] it is more commonly rendered "does not disappoint [us]" (RSV, NIV, NAB, NET, NASV, and NRSV).[43] The verb can certainly mean "to shame" in some contexts (as at Rom 9:33; 10:11; cf. ἐπαισχύνομαι, "to be ashamed," at 1:16), but in the present instance it is more appropriately translated "to disappoint."[44] (To be sure, one would be ashamed if one's hopes failed, but it is not the hope itself that would cause shame.) The phrase recalls lines from the LXX in which hope, placed in God, cannot be disappointed (Pss 21:6; 30:2; 24:29; 70:1; 118:31; Jer 31:13). The hope that one has is not illusory, since "God's love has been poured into our hearts through the Holy Spirit, which has

38. BDAG 1039 (ὑπομονή, 1)

39. BDAG 256 (δοκιμή, 2).

40. Gerd Schunack, "δοκιμή," *EDNT* 1:342.

41. R. Harrisville, *Romans*, 78.

42. Cf. also E. Käsemann, *Romans*, 135; C. Cranfield, *Romans*, 261-62; D. Moo, *Romans*, 304; R. Jewett, *Romans*, 344.

43. Cf. also W. Sanday and A. Headlam, *Romans*, 125; J. Fitzmyer, *Romans*, 393, 397-98; J. Ziesler, *Romans*, 139.

44. BDAG 517 (καταισχύνω, 3, a).

been given to us." The "heart" is the faculty of understanding, knowing, and will.[45] It knows God's love in a personal, intimate way due to the Holy Spirit's work within. To know God's love (mentioned here for the first time in the letter) is to know God's reality, faithfulness, and presence.[46] Since nothing can separate the believer from God's love in Christ (Rom 8:39), nothing can separate one from God and his faithfulness. Hope will not and cannot be disappointed, nor can anything prevent one from sharing in the glorious presence of God despite the sufferings of the present and to come.

5:6 Within 5:6-11 Paul describes the human condition with four terms. The first two are adjectives: "helpless" (ἀσθενής, 5:6) and "ungodly" (ἀσεβής, 5:6); the last two are nouns, portraying humanity as consisting of "sinners" (ἁμαρτωλοί, 5:8), and "enemies" (ἐχθροί, 5:10) of God. They are arranged in descending order of gravity concerning the human situation before God. Being helpless is rather benign compared to the other three conditions. Being enemies toward God is the most severe.

Each of the terms is used by Paul elsewhere in his writings. They express the powerlessness, the unworthiness, and the actual offensiveness of each human being toward God. On the other hand, since they speak within their contexts of the need which the redemptive work of God in Christ has met, the terms reveal the abundance of God's grace and love for humanity. The four words constitute a backdrop of dark colors on which the glorious gospel of God's redemptive work in Christ stands out in brilliant contrast.

The adjective rendered here as "helpless" (ἀσθενής) appears 13 times in the letters of Paul.[47] Sometimes the word is better translated "weak," as in bodily weakness (1 Cor 11:30; 2 Cor 10:10) or in references to those who are weak in faith or whose consciences are weak (1 Cor 8:7, 9, 10; 9:22; 1 Thess 5:14).[48] In the present context, however, it designates the helplessness of humanity as a whole in its relationship to God. Paul has already asserted, and shown from Scripture, that humanity is under the power of sin (Rom 3:9) and by implication cannot free it-

---

45. Alexander Sand, "καρδία," *EDNT* 2:250.

46. According to Augustine, *De spiritu et littera* 32.56, and *De peccatorum meritis et remissione* 2.17.27, "the love of God" is an objective genitive; love originates in God and is transmitted by the Holy Spirit, and only then can one love God and others. For a discussion and reference to additional texts, cf. M. Reid, *Augustinian and Pauline Rhetoric in Romans Five*, 51-59. M. Luther, *Romans*, 293-96, follows Augustine. Modern interpreters have usually taken it to be a subjective genitive (God's love for us). Cf. W. Sanday and A. Headlam, *Romans*, 125; A. Nygren, *Romans*, 196-99; C. Cranfield, *Romans*, 262; U. Wilckens, *Römer*, 1:293; J. Dunn, *Romans*, 252; J. Fitzmyer, *Romans*, 398; and many others.

47. Rom 5:6; 1 Cor 1:25, 27; 4:10; 8:7, 9, 10; 9:22; 11:30; 2 Cor 10:10; 12:22; Gal 4:9; 1 Thess 5:14. On the various uses of the term, cf. BDAG 142-43 (ἀσθενής).

48. At Rom 14:1-2 a participial form of ἀσθενέω is used to speak of those who are weak in faith.

self from sin's dominion. Nevertheless, Paul declares, even while humanity was in that condition, "at the right time" (κατὰ καιρόν) Christ died "for the ungodly" (ὑπὲρ ἀσεβῶν) and for a redemptive purpose.

The two prepositional phrases used in the verse carry theological concepts forged out of Paul's understanding of Scripture and the redemptive act of God in Christ. The first of them (κατὰ καιρόν) is found only here in the NT, but six times in the LXX (Num 9:7; 23:23; Job 5:26; 39:18; Isa 60:22; Jer 5:24). It speaks of the "right time" in the sense of God's appointed time. It does not refer to a time determined by human history, whether that be its apparent progress or decline; nor does it take into account the spiritual and cultural readiness — or lack thereof — of humanity.[49]

The other prepositional phrase in 5:6 is "for the ungodly" (ὑπὲρ ἀσεβῶν). Paul makes use of a number of kerygmatic formulas that use a subject ("God" or "Christ"), an aorist verb ("sent," "died," or "was put to death"), a prepositional phrase ("for," "on behalf of"), and an object (someone or something). The basic formula that has Christ as the subject, who died on behalf of others, is found with slight variations in Paul's letters (Rom 5:6, 8; 14:15; 1 Cor 8:11; 2 Cor 5:15; 1 Thess 5:10) and can be regarded as pre-Pauline in its origins.[50] In addition to Χριστὸς . . . ὑπὲρ ἀσεβῶν ἀπέθανεν ("Christ died for the ungodly," used here), the formulations include:

> Christ died "for us" (ὑπὲρ ἡμῶν, Rom 5:8; 1 Thess 5:10)
> God made Christ to be sin "for us" (ὑπὲρ ἡμῶν, 2 Cor 5:21)
> Christ became a curse "for us" (ὑπὲρ ἡμῶν, Gal 3:13)
> Christ died "for all" (ὑπὲρ πάντων, 2 Cor 5:14-15)
> Christ died "for our sins" (ὑπὲρ τῶν ἁμαρτιῶν ἡμῶν, 1 Cor 15:3)
> Christ gave himself "for our sins" (ὑπὲρ τῶν ἁμαρτιῶν ἡμῶν, Gal 1:4)
> God sent his son "for sin" (περὶ ἁμαρτίας, Rom 8:3)
> God gave Christ up "for us all" (ὑπὲρ ἡμῶν πάντων, Rom 8:32)

In these formulas the preposition ὑπέρ means "on behalf of" or "for the sake of" persons or sins.[51] The ὑπέρ-formula (in the sense of a person dying for another or for others) has a long and widespread usage in both Jewish and pagan

---

49. BDAG 497 (καιρός, 1, b): concerning this verse, κατὰ καιρόν "is more naturally construed with ἀπέθανεν than with ἀσεβῶν." That is how it is construed in the KJV, ASV, RSV, and NRSV ("at the right time Christ died for the ungodly"). The NEB has the phrase modify the previous clause ("for at the very time when we were still powerless"). The NIV maintains an ambiguity ("at just the right time, when we were still powerless, Christ died for the ungodly").

50. Cf. the discussion in V. Neufeld, *The Earliest Christian Confessions*, 48; K. Wengst, *Christologische Formeln und Lieder des Urchristentums*, 78-90.

51. BDAG 1030 (ὑπέρ, A, 1, a, ε); Harald Riesenfeld, "ὑπέρ," *TDNT* 8:508-9.

Hellenistic sources.[52] In each case within the NT the death of Christ is referred to as an event in past history that is complete and sufficient as the redemptive work of God. As indicated, the formula is sometimes for the sake of people (as in Rom 5:6, 8), but in other cases it is for the sake of sin or sins (Rom 8:3; 1 Cor 15:3; Gal 1:4). It has been suggested that the phrase "for us" is earlier and that "for our sins" is a more developed interpretation.[53] But that is not likely. The kerygmatic formula that Paul claims to have received must be considered among the earliest, and according to that, "Christ died for our sins" (1 Cor 15:3). Moreover, within the OT the language of atonement is parallel to that found in the letters of Paul. Atonement can be made for sins (Exod 32:30; Num 29:11) or for people (Lev 4:20; 16:30; 23:28). In the letters of Paul the death of Christ can be a means of doing away with sin and its power (Rom 5:20-21; 6:18; 2 Cor 5:19), and therefore it is also the means by which the weak and ungodly are rescued (Rom 5:6, 8).

The term "ungodly" (ἀσεβής) in our verse (5:6) always has a negative connotation in the Bible, except twice in Romans (4:5 and here), and surely Paul must have been aware of that. It normally refers to the wicked, who will not stand in the judgment. See further the comments on 4:5; there the term refers to the person who does not seek to gain God's favor by performing "works prescribed by the law." Here at 5:6, however, by his use of the first person plural ("we" in English) — and as the generalizing context shows — Paul applies the term to all humans everywhere. Before God, all humans are actually without sufficient righteousness to stand in a right relationship with God. Nevertheless, in spite of that, Christ died for all — "ungodly" though they be — for an atoning purpose.

5:7 The verse is parenthetical in function. Christ has died for those who are "helpless" and "ungodly." To do so is beyond normal expectations. A person will "not ordinarily" (μόλις) die for a righteous person; in fact, a person "hardly" (τάχα) dares to die even for a good person. There is no need to attempt to discern a difference between a "righteous person" and a "good person" in this verse.[54] The clauses are composed in parallel fashion, which is rhetorically effective, and more visible in Greek than in English:

---

52. J. Gibson, "Paul's 'Dying Formula,'" 22: "I found that equivalents to Paul's 'dying formula' occur well over one hundred times in Greco-Roman literature." It is also found in Hellenistic Jewish texts, e.g., 2 Macc 7:9; 8:21; 4 Macc 1:8; Sir 29:15; Josephus, *Ant.* 13.1.1 §§5-6; cf. idem, *J.W.* 2.201.

53. W. Kramer, *Christ, Lord, Son of God*, 26.

54. F. Wisse, "The Righteous Man and the Good Man in Romans v.7," 91-93. According to A. Clarke, "The Good and the Just in Romans 5:7," 128-42, the designation "good" could signify a benefactor, for whom one might be willing to die. But that would undercut the argument somewhat. Paul says, in effect, that a person can hardly be expected to die even for a good person. More to the point, C. Black, "Pauline Perspectives on Death in Romans 5–8," 420, contends that Paul makes use of the classical Greek motif of the heroic death.

μόλις γὰρ ὑπὲρ δικαίου τις ἀποθανεῖται·
ὑπὲρ γὰρ τοῦ ἀγαθοῦ τάχα τις καὶ τολμᾷ ἀποθανεῖν·

For ordinarily one will not die for a righteous person;
Indeed, one hardly dares to die even for a good person.

The second line essentially repeats the thought of the first, but it also advances the thought a step further by its use of the modifiers "hardly," "even," and "dare." The result is to draw back even further from any thought that a person would find it easy to die for another person whose life is worth preserving. Such a self-sacrificing act is rare and cannot be expected. And since that is the case, how much more should one not expect Christ to die for the "weak" and "ungodly." Within this parenthetical phrase, Paul is making an implicit use of the *qal wa-ḥomer* ("from minor to major") form of argument, which was commonly used in rabbinic literature.[55] If one would not normally die for the worthy person, how much more would one not die for the unworthy one. And yet that is what has happened. Christ's dying for the weak and ungodly demonstrates a love that surpasses normal human experience. God's love in Christ is not based on the worthiness of the object loved, but on the character of the one who loves. It is God's nature so to love.

5:8 That love for humanity has been demonstrated in a radical way.[56] Christ's death occurred when "we" — meaning all persons — were "still" (ἔτι) "sinners" (ἁμαρτωλοί). He did not die for persons who had reformed, but for persons who were "still sinners." The term "sinners," like the term "ungodly," is used throughout the Bible as a term of reproach for persons who have rebelled against God (Isa 1:28; Tob 13:8) and God's commandments (Ps 50:16-17 [LXX 49:16-17]; Rom 5:19) or, more generally, for persons who are considered wicked (Pss 11:2; 37:14; 68:2 [LXX 10:2; 36:14; 67:3]). Within the NT the term ἁμαρτωλοί is applied also, according to Pharisaic standards, to persons who cannot or will not keep the commands of the Torah according to the Pharisaic interpretation of them (Matt 9:10; Mark 2:15; Luke 15:1).[57] Yet, Paul declares, it is precisely for the "sinners" of the world, meaning humanity as a whole, that Christ died.

Paul uses the "for us" (ὑπὲρ ἡμῶν) formula in this verse to speak of the death of Jesus as atoning (cf. 2 Cor 5:21; Gal 3:13; 1 Thess 5:10). Commentary on this and other formulas has been made at 5:6. The "us" of which Paul speaks has been identified by now in the passage as the "helpless," the "ungodly," and "sinners." Paul will add too that Christ died when we were "enemies" of God, mean-

---

55. On the *qal waḥomer* form of argumentation, see Louis Jacobs, "Hermeneutics," *EncJud* 8:367; H. Strack and G. Stemberger, *Introduction to the Talmud and Midrash*, 21, 27.
56. L. Keck, *Romans*, 139: *"This is Paul's Christology in a nutshell"* (italics his).
57. Cf. Karl H. Rengstorf, "ἁμαρτωλός," *TDNT* 1:328.

ing hostile toward God (5:10). For such persons there can ordinarily be no hope. But Christ has died for such persons nevertheless. No greater love can be displayed than that.

5:9 Now Paul makes explicit use of the *qal waḥomer* ("from minor to major") form of argumentation (cf. also 5:10, 15, 17), employing the introductory words "much more" (πολλῷ μᾶλλον). Since justification has come about through the death of Christ (ἐν τῷ αἵματι αὐτοῦ, an instrumental use of ἐν, so "by his blood"), which was beyond what anyone could expect in the first place, one can most certainly expect salvation "through him" (δι' αὐτοῦ) from the (final) wrath (of God). If this much (justification) has happened already, what follows (salvation) will most surely occur. Here salvation is from wrath (literally, "from the wrath" [ἀπὸ τῆς ὀργῆς]), meaning the divine wrath at the final judgment, for the verb is future (σωθησόμεθα, "we shall be saved").[58] Concerning the tenses of salvation (past, present, and future), see the discussion in the commentary on 1:16. Salvation is primarily in the future, and it means deliverance from the divine wrath at the final judgment (as here). In an extended sense, salvation can also be deliverance from bondage to sin (Rom 6:18-22; 8:2) and from perishing (1 Cor 1:18; 2 Cor 2:15), which leads to death.

5:10-11 When Paul speaks of "enemies" (ἐχθροί) here, he means by implication "enemies of God." That, in turn, means persons who are hostile to God, not persons to whom God is hostile.[59] As things stand, "the mind that is set on the flesh is hostile to God" (Rom 8:7). But in spite of such hostility, God has reconciled the world to himself (cf. 2 Cor 5:19). God's enemies "were changed into his reconciled friends."[60] God is well disposed to humanity. One problem remains, and that is for human beings to lay aside their hostility and to be at peace with God.

Once again Paul makes use of the *qal waḥomer* form of argumentation, using the "much more" (πολλῷ μᾶλλον) formulation. If it is possible for reconciliation to have happened (κατηλλάγημεν, past tense [aorist passive indicative], "we were reconciled") even when humanity was hostile to God, now that reconciliation has taken place (καταλλαγέντες, past tense [aorist passive participle], "having been reconciled"), it is self-evident that salvation will follow (fu-

---

58. Contra R. Jewett, *Romans,* 367, who claims that Paul speaks of salvation from current tribulations.

59. The wording and context make this clear. It is puzzling that some interpreters claim that Paul speaks here of a mutual hostility between God and humanity, e.g., C. Cranfield, *Romans,* 267; J. Dunn, *Romans,* 258; J. Fitzmyer, *Romans,* 401; D. Moo, *Romans,* 312. Against such, cf. U. Wilckens, *Römer,* 1:298; R. Jewett, *Romans,* 364 ("the theme of God's hatred is alien to this passage, which has repeatedly stressed divine grace, love, sacrifice, and salvation from wrath").

60. C. Breytenbach, "The 'For Us' Phrases in Pauline Soteriology," 183.

ture tense, σωθησόμεθα, "we shall be saved"). The language of reconciliation is not frequent in Paul, and no other NT writer uses it in reference to the divine-human relationship. But it does exist at crucial points in Paul's letters. He uses both the verb καταλλάσσω ("to reconcile," Rom 5:10; 2 Cor 5:18-20) and the noun καταλλαγή ("reconciliation," Rom 5:11; 11:15; 2 Cor 5:18-19) to express the reestablishment of a broken relationship between God and humanity. Never does he say that God must be reconciled to humanity (contra some later theological traditions), for it is humanity that is estranged from God — not the other way around — and in need of reconciliation. That has been accomplished in the redemptive work of God in the crucified Christ. It is on the basis of God's redemptive work in Christ that there is rejoicing (5:11). That rejoicing is in God who has acted through his Son, by whom reconciliation has now been accomplished and secured.

What Paul has written in verses 9 and 10 can be reduced to two affirmations, which are parallel in structure:

> Since we have been justified by his blood, we shall be saved through him from the wrath.
> Since we have been reconciled to God through the death of his Son, we will be saved by his life.

The symmetry between the two verses can be seen more clearly when portions are presented side by side in Greek. In each case the emphasis is on the saving work of God in the death and resurrection of Christ:

5:9	*5:10*
πολλῷ μᾶλλον	πολλῷ μᾶλλον
δικαιωθέντες	καταλλαγέντες
ἐν τῷ αἵματι αὐτοῦ,	διὰ τοῦ θανάτου τοῦ υἱοῦ αὐτοῦ,
σωθησόμεθα.	σωθησόμεθα.
Much more	Much more
having been justified	having been reconciled
by his blood,	through the death of his Son,
we shall be saved.	we shall be saved.

On the basis of the parallelism, one might conclude that, for Paul, justification and reconciliation are "equivalents of one another."[61] But reconciliation

---

61. J. Dunn, *Romans*, 259. Cf. also C. K. Barrett, *Romans*, 100; E. P. Sanders, *Paul and Palestinian Judaism*, 469-71.

is more fitting within the present context, and that demonstrates how the two terms differ. Justification applies to being set within a right relationship in spite of sin. Reconciliation applies to the restoring of a relationship where enmity has existed. Furthermore, reconciliation involves a risk that is not obvious in the case of justification. It requires that one of the parties, usually the one who has caused offense, take the initiative to restore the relationship, and the initiative can be rejected by the other party. But Paul declares here that the offended party, God, is the one who has taken the initiative; humanity is the offending party ("enemies of God").[62]

In this entire section (5:6-11) Paul stresses divine initiative and activity in the death of Christ. He uses forms of the verb ἀποθνῄσκω ("to die") four times (5:6, 7 [twice], 8). He comes close to a theory of the atonement.[63] Christ, he says, "died for the ungodly" (ὑπὲρ ἀσεβῶν ἀπέθανεν, 5:6) and "died for us" (ὑπὲρ ἡμῶν ἀπέθανεν, 5:8). These passages fit within a constellation of passages in Paul's letters concerning the death of Christ and its benefits for humanity:

> Galatians 3:13: "Christ redeemed us from the curse of the law by becoming a curse for us — for it is written, 'Cursed is everyone who hangs on a tree'" (quoting Deut 21:23).
>
> 2 Corinthians 5:14: "because we are convinced that one has died for all; therefore all have died."
>
> 2 Corinthians 5:21: "[God] made him to be sin who knew no sin, so that in him we might become the righteousness of God."
>
> Romans 8:3: "By sending his own Son in the likeness of sinful flesh, and to deal with sin, [God] condemned sin in the flesh."
>
> Romans 8:32: "He who did not withhold his own Son, but gave him up for all of us. . . ."

Although it can be methodologically misguided to blend passages together in the letters of Paul in order to distill from them a theological concept, there is sufficient consistency in the passages cited, together with what he says in 5:6-11, to assert that, for Paul, God has focused his wrath against humanity upon Jesus. The punishment has been exercised at the cross, carried out once and for all. Humanity is thus relieved of the wrath and punishment due at the final judgment. Amnesty has been declared; liberty has come. In Christ's atoning death God has reconciled the world unto God's own self (2 Cor 5:19). The basis for reconciliation from the divine side has been accomplished. What re-

---

62. J. Fitzgerald, "Paul and Paradigm Shifts," 254; R. Jewett, *Romans*, 366.

63. A more complete discussion of Paul's redemptive Christology is presented in A. Hultgren, *Christ and His Benefits*, 47-57.

mains is for people to hear the good news of that event, to accept it, and put away any enduring hostility toward God. The apostolic mission consists in announcing the good news to the world and calling upon the world to believe. "So," Paul writes, "we are ambassadors for Christ, since God is making his appeal through us; we entreat you on behalf of Christ, be reconciled to God" (2 Cor 5:20). That imperative ("be reconciled") follows the indicative ("in Christ God was reconciling the world to himself, not counting their trespasses against them, and entrusting the message of reconciliation to us," 5:19).

Bibliography

Alkier, Stefan, Hans-Joachim Eckstein, and Hendrikus Boers, "Die Stellung der Rechtfertigungslehre in der paulinischen Theologie." *ZNW* 7 (2004): 40-54.

Bammel, C. P. "Patristic Exegesis of Romans 5:7." *JTS* 47 (1996): 532-42.

Barrett, C. K. "Boasting (καυχᾶσθαι, κτλ.) in the Pauline Epistles." In *L'Apôtre Paul: Personnalité, style et conception du ministère*, 363-68. Ed. Albert Vanhoye. BETL 73. Leuven: Leuven University Press, 1986.

Bieringer, Reimund. "Aktive Hoffnung im Leiden: Gegenstand, Grund und Praxis der Hoffnung nach Röm 5,1-5." *TZ* 51 (1995): 305-25.

Black, C. Clifton, II. "Pauline Perspectives on Death in Romans 5–8." *JBL* 103 (1984): 413-33.

Blank, Josef. "Röm 5,10." In his *Paulus und Jesus: Eine theologische Grundlegung*, 280-87. Munich: Kösel Verlag, 1968.

Bornkamm, Günther. *Paul.* Minneapolis: Fortress Press, 1994.

Brandos, David. *Paul on the Cross: Reconstructing the Apostle's Story of Redemption.* Minneapolis: Fortress Press, 2006.

Breytenbach, Cilliers. "'Christus starb für uns': Zur Tradition und paulinischen Rezeption der sogenannten 'Sterbeformeln.'" *NTS* 49 (2003): 447-75.

———. "The 'For Us' Phrases in Pauline Soteriology: Considering Their Background and Use." In *Salvation in the New Testament: Perspectives on Soteriology*, 163-85. Ed. Jan G. van der Watt. NovTSup 121. Boston: E. J. Brill, 2005.

Clarke, Andrew D. "The Good and the Just in Romans 5:7." *TynBul* 41 (1990): 128-42.

Crabtree, A. R. "Translation of Romans 5:1 in the Revised Standard Version of the New Testament." *RevExp* 43 (1946): 436-39.

Dahl, Nils A. "A Synopsis of Romans 5:1-11 and 8:1-39." In his *Studies in Paul: Theology for the Christian Mission*, 88-90. Minneapolis: Augsburg Publishing House, 1977.

Fitzgerald, John T. "Paul and Paradigm Shifts: Reconciliation and Its Linkage Group." In his *Cracks in an Earthen Vessel: An Examination of the Catalogues of Hardships in the Corinthian Correspondence.* SBLDS 99. Atlanta: Scholars Press, 1988.

Fitzmyer, Joseph A. "Justification by Faith in Pauline Thought: A Catholic View." In *Rereading Paul Together: Protestant and Catholic Perspectives on Justification*, 77-94. Ed. David E. Aune. Grand Rapids: Baker Academic, 2006.

———. "Reconciliation in Pauline Theology." In his *To Advance the Gospel: New Testament Studies*, 162-85. Rev. ed. Grand Rapids: Wm. B. Eerdmans, 1998.

Fryer, Nico S. L., "Reconciliation in Paul's Epistle to the Romans." *Neot* 15 (1981): 34-68.

Gibson, Jeffrey B. "Paul's 'Dying Formula': Prolegomena to an Understanding of Its Import and Significance." In *Celebrating Romans: Template for Pauline Theology: Essays in Honor of Robert Jewett,* 20-41. Ed. Sheila E. McGinn. Grand Rapids: Wm. B. Eerdmans, 2004.

Harrisville, Roy A., III. "Romans 5:1-15." *Int* 45 (1991): 181-85.

Hays, Richard B. "Christ Died for the Ungodly: Narrative Soteriology in Paul?" *HBT* 26 (2004): 48-68.

Hübner, Hans. *Law in Paul's Thought.* Edinburgh: T&T Clark, 1984.

———. "Pauli Theologiae Proprium." *NTS* 26 (1990): 445-73.

Hultgren, Arland. *Christ and His Benefits: Christology and Redemption in the New Testament.* Philadelphia: Fortress Press, 1987.

Jervis, L. Ann. *At the Heart of the Gospel: Suffering in the Earliest Christian Message.* Grand Rapids: Wm. B. Eerdmans, 2007.

Käsemann, Ernst. "Justification and Salvation History in the Epistle to the Romans." In his *Perspectives on Paul,* 60-78. Philadelphia: Fortress Press, 1971.

———. "Some Thoughts on the Theme 'The Doctrine of Reconciliation in the New Testament.'" In *The Future of Our Religious Past: Essays in Honour of Rudolf Bultmann,* 49-64. Ed. James M. Robinson. New York: Harper & Row, 1971.

Keck, Leander E. "The Post-Pauline Interpretation of Jesus' Death in Rom. 5:6-7." In *Theologia Crucis — Signum Crucis: Festschrift für Erich Dinkler,* 237-48. Ed. Carl Andresen and Günter Klein. Tübingen: J. C. B. Mohr (Paul Siebeck), 1979.

Klein, Günter. "Der Friede Gottes und der Friede der Welt: Eine exegetische Vergewisserung am Neuen Testament." *ZTK* 83 (1986): 325-55.

Kümmel, Werner G. "Interpretation of Romans 5:1-11." In *Exegetical Method: A Student's Handbook,* 49-58. Ed. Otto Kaiser and Werner G. Kümmel. New York: Seabury Press, 1963.

Leivestad, Ragnar. "Rom. 5,7." *NorTT* 57 (1956): 245-48.

Levison, John R. *The Spirit in First-Century Judaism.* AGAJU 29. New York: E. J. Brill, 1997.

Lohse, Eduard. "Christus, das Gesetzes Ende? Die Theologie des Apostels Paulus in kritischer Perspektive." *ZNW* 99 (2008): 18-32.

Maartens, Pieter J. "The Relevance of 'Context' and 'Interpretation' to the Semiotic Relations of Romans 5:1-11." *Neot* 29 (1995) 75-108.

Martin, Ralph P. *Reconciliation: A Study of Paul's Theology.* Atlanta: John Knox Press, 1981.

———. "Reconciliation: Romans 5:1-11." In *Romans and the People of God: Essays in Honor of Gordon D. Fee on the Occasion of His 65th Birthday,* 36-48. Ed. Sven K. Soderlund and N. T. Wright. Grand Rapids: Wm. B. Eerdmans, 1999.

Martin, Troy W. "*The Good* as God (Romans 5:7)." *JSNT* 25 (2002): 55-70.

McDonald, Patricia M. "Romans 5:1-11 as a Rhetorical Bridge." *JSNT* 40 (1990): 81-96.

Moo, Douglas J. "Israel and the Law in Romans 5–11: Interaction with the New Perspective." In *Justification and Variegated Nomism,* 2:185-216. Ed. D. A. Carson, Peter T. O'Brien, and Mark Seifrid. 2 vols. Grand Rapids: Baker Academic, 2001-4.

Myers, Charles D. "The Place of Romans 5:1-11 within the Argument of the Epistle." Ph.D. diss., Princeton Theological Seminary, 1985.

Neufeld, Vernon. *The Earliest Christian Confessions.* NTTS 5. Grand Rapids: Wm. B. Eerdmans, 1963.

Plevnik, Joseph. "The Center of Pauline Theology," *CBQ* 51 (1989): 461-78.

Porter, Stanley E. "The Argument of Romans 5: Can a Rhetorical Question Make a Difference?" *JBL* 110 (1991): 655-77.

———. "Is There a Center to Paul's Theology? An Introduction to the Study of Paul and His Theology." In *Paul and His Theology*, 1-19. Ed. Stanley E. Porter. Boston: E. J. Brill, 2006.

———. "Paul's Concept of Reconciliation, Twice More." In *Paul and His Theology*, 131-52. Ed. Stanley E. Porter. Boston: E. J. Brill, 2006.

Pulcini, Theodore. "In Right Relationship with God: Present Experience and Future Fulfillment: An Exegesis of Romans 5:1-11." *SVTQ* 36 (1993): 61-85.

Rad, Gerhard von. *Old Testament Theology.* 2 vols. New York: Harper & Row, 1962-65.

Reid, Marty L. *Augustinian and Pauline Rhetoric in Romans Five: A Study in Early Christian Rhetoric.* MBPS 30. Lewiston: Mellen Biblical Press, 1996.

———. "A Rhetorical Analysis of Romans 1:1–5:21 with Attention to the Rhetorical Function of 5:1-21." *PRS* 19 (1992): 255-72.

Reumann, John. *'Righteousness' in the New Testament: Justification in the United States Lutheran-Roman Catholic Dialogue.* Philadelphia: Fortress Press, 1982.

Sanders, E. P. *Paul and Palestinian Judaism: A Comparison of Patterns of Religion.* Philadelphia: Fortress Press, 1977.

Sandnes, Karl O. "Abraham, the Friend of God, in Rom 5: A Short Notice." *ZNW* 99 (2008): 124-28.

Schweitzer, Albert. *The Mysticism of Paul the Apostle.* New York: Seabury Press, 1931.

Seifrid, Mark A. *Justification by Faith: The Origin and Development of a Central Pauline Theme.* NovTSup 68. Leiden: E. J. Brill, 1992.

Seitz, Erich. "Korrigiert sich Paulus? Zu Röm 5,6-8." *ZNW* 91 (2000): 279-87.

Stendahl, Krister. *Paul among Jews and Gentiles and Other Essays.* Philadelphia: Fortress Press, 1976.

Strack, Herman, and Günter Stemberger. *Introduction to the Talmud and Midrash.* Minneapolis: Fortress Press, 1992.

Wanamaker, Charles A. "Christ as Divine Agent in Paul." *SJT* 39 (1986): 517-28.

Watson, Duane F. "Paul and Boasting." In *Paul in the Greco-Roman World: A Handbook*, 77-100. Ed. J. Paul Sampley. Harrisburg: Trinity Press International, 2003.

Wengst, Klaus. *Christologische Formeln und Lieder des Urchristentums.* SNT 7. Gütersloh: Gütersloher Verlagshaus Gerd Mohn, 1972.

Wisse, Fredrik. "The Righteous Man and the Good Man in Romans v.7." *NTS* 19 (1972-73): 91-93.

Wolter, Michael. *Rechtfertigung und zukünftiges Heil: Untersuchungen zu Röm 5,1-11.* BZNW 43. New York: Walter de Gruyter, 1978.

Wrede, William. *Paul.* Boston: American Unitarian Association, 1908.

4.2. Adam and Christ, 5:12-21

12*Therefore, just as sin entered the world through one man, and death through sin, so also death came to all people, because all have sinned.* 13*For prior to the law, sin was in the world, but sin is not counted when the law is not present,* 14*but death reigned from Adam to Moses, even over those who did not sin in the manner of Adam's transgression, who is a type of the one who was to come.*

15*But the free gift is not like the trespass. For if by the trespass of one man many died, how much more surely have the grace of God and the free gift in the grace of that one man, Jesus Christ, abounded for many.* 16*And the free gift is not like the consequence of that one man's sin. For judgment, resulting from one trans-gression, led to condemnation, but the free gift from many transgressions leads to justification.* 17*For if, by the transgression of the one man, death reigned through the one, how much more surely will those who receive the abundance of grace and the free gift of righteousness reign in life through the one, Jesus Christ!*

18*Therefore just as the trespass of one person led to condemnation for all, so the act of righteousness of one person leads to justification resulting in life for all.* 19*For as the many were made sinners through the disobedience of one man, so also the many will be made righteous through the obedience of one man.*

20*The law came in, in order that the trespass might increase; but where sin increased, grace was present in greater abundance,* 21*in order that, as sin reigned in death, so also grace might reign through righteousness unto eternal life through Jesus Christ our Lord.*

Notes on the Text and Translation

5:15-16 It has been suggested that 5:15a and 5:16a can be rendered as rhetorical questions (cf. the use of οὐχ at the outset of each, which is then understood to be interrogative): "But does not the free gift operate just like the trespass did?" (5:15a); "And is not the free gift transmitted in the same way as sin was transmit-ted by the one who sinned?" (5:16a). Consequently, Paul then speaks of a com-parison (not a contrast) between Adam and Christ.[64] But in both 5:17 and 5:18-19 sharp contrasts are made between Adam and Christ. Both 5:15a and 5:16a should be seen in light of that. See further discussion below.

---

64. C. Caragounis, "Romans 5.15-16 in the Context of 5.12-21," 142-48 (quotations from p. 145). O. Hofius, "The Adam–Christ Antithesis and the Law," 165-205, emphasizes the contrast.

General Comment

Up to this point, Paul has established a number of points. He has declared that all humanity stands under the wrath of God, under the power of sin, and is unable to be justified through works of the law (1:18–3:20). But God has manifested his righteousness in Christ in order to justify both Jew and Gentile on a foundation other than the law, and that is his own righteousness, which is received by faith alone as God's justifying power (3:21-31). This claim has a scriptural basis to it in the story of Abraham, who was reckoned as righteous by God when he believed the promises of God, even before he was circumcised (i.e., while he was technically a Gentile); so it is clear that those who believe the promises of God are, like Abraham, the justified ones (4:1-25). Believers know that they are justified, reconciled, and saved from the wrath of God for the world to come (5:1-11), even though that does not preclude suffering in the present.

The following section (5:12-21) opens with διὰ τοῦτο ("therefore"),[65] which has no clear antecedent. Presumably Paul thinks that what he goes on to say has a relationship to what has been said in 5:1-11. And, to be sure, there is a linkage in his use of justification language in the two sections (cf. 5:1, 9 and 5:16, 18). Moreover, in each section Paul makes use of the *qal waḥomer* ("how much more") form of argumentation, drawing theological corollaries of eschatological significance from the death of Christ (5:9, 10) or of the reversal of the death-dealing effects of Adam's trespass (5:15, 17). In any case, throughout 5:1-11 Paul had used the first person plural, but now he switches to third person and continues that mode through 5:12-21. He does not merely continue the previous discussion, but uses the "therefore" (5:12) to mark a transition, drawing consequences from what has been said but moving on to another topic.[66] The transition is strengthened by the immediate onset of the ὥσπερ ("just as") plus οὕτως ("so") construction. The only other occurrences of this formal construction (ὡς/ὥσπερ plus οὕτως) are found at Romans 6:4, 19 and 11:30-31.[67] Paul allows himself to recast his thinking and presentation in light of what has gone before in a new way, and that turns out to be a discussion of the effects of Adam and Christ upon humanity.

Paul has established that through God's act of righteousness in Christ

---

65. The phrase is used also at Rom 1:26; 4:16; 13:6; 15:9; 1 Cor 4:17; 11:10, 30; 2 Cor 4:1; 7:13; 13:10; 1 Thess 2:13; 3:5, 7; and Phlm 15.

66. The question of the relationship of Rom 5:12-21 to 5:1-11 is treated in detail particularly by R. Bultmann, "Adam and Christ according to Romans 5," 153; C. K. Barrett, *Romans*, 102; R. Scroggs, *The Last Adam*, 77; N. Dahl, "The Argument in Romans 5:12-21," 90-91; O. Hofius, "The Adam–Christ Antithesis and the Law," 176-79; and S. Porter, "The Argument of Romans 5," 670-71. See also the discussion in "4. The New Life in Christ, Romans 5:1–8:39."

67. R. Erickson, "The Damned and the Justified in Romans 5.12-21," 287.

there is justification, reconciliation, and final salvation (life) for all who believe. But now he takes a different approach to the matter of "justification" and "life." Without denying or amending what has already been said, he goes on to treat justification and life under the broader horizons of their theocentric origins. There is a change of focus. While the earlier discussion was based on the situation of humankind before God, and taking issue with the claims of those who would argue for justification before God through works of the law, now his discussion is based on the apocalyptic view of the ages and what God has done in the crucified and risen Christ. The situation of humanity under the wrath of God has been altered in the new aeon, which has dawned upon the world through the advent of the "one who was to come" (5:14), and who brings justification and life for humanity.

The universality of sin, says Paul, has been countered by the universality of grace. The correlation between Adam (by whom sin entered the world) and Christ (by whom grace has come) has received considerable attention. Some interpreters have suggested that here (as well as at 1 Cor 15:22, 45-59) Paul is dependent on — and was reacting to — either the writings of Philo or Gnostic traditions concerning a "first" and "second" Adam, the one heavenly and the other earthly.[68] Other interpreters, however, have found these proposals insufficient.[69] A more plausible background is a traditional Palestinian Jewish interpretation of Adam (as expressed in later rabbinic literature) to which Paul resorted following upon his experience of the risen Christ.[70] In any case, it is likely that the concept of Christ as a "last Adam" (1 Cor 15:45) or "second man" who is "from heaven" (15:47) was introduced to the church by Paul himself.[71] Paul makes a creative interpretive move in light of his understanding of the redemptive work of God in Christ. Christ is not simply an idealized man (an ideal Adam), the model of what God has created humanity to be.[72] The correspondence between Adam and Christ is not anthropological, having to do with the nature of humanity. In fact, the attention given to Adam is not related to the

---

68. Interpreters favoring a Philonic background include W. Schrage, *Der erste Brief an die Korinther*, 303; A. Thiselton, *The First Epistle to the Corinthians*, 1284; those favoring a Gnostic background include E. Käsemann, *Leib und Leib Christi*, 163; E. Brandenburger, *Adam und Christus*, 70-71; W. Schmithals, *Gnosticism in Corinth*, 169-70.

69. Cf. S. Hultgren, "The Origins of Paul's Doctrine of the Two Adams," 343-70. He includes references to the work of additional interpreters who analyze the proposals and find them unsatisfactory.

70. S. Hultgren, "The Origins of Paul's Doctrine of the Two Adams," 359-70. Rabbinic sources are discussed on pp. 359-66.

71. W. D. Davies, *Paul and Rabbinic Judaism*, 44. U. Wilckens, *Römer*, 1:314, speaks of the entire unit (Rom 5:12-21) as original work by Paul.

72. On Adam as the ideal man, cf. Philo, *Op.* 46.134, and rabbinic works cited in Str-B 4:940-41, 947, 1126.

creation accounts in Genesis 1 and 2 at all, as in the usual Adam speculations, but to Genesis 3 (the fall),[73] which had universal consequences under the old aeon. Likewise, the attention given to Christ is not about his becoming what Adam failed to be, but upon his redemptive work, which has universal consequences as well, the beginning of a new era of life. Each of these two persons is head of a humanity, either that of the old aeon (leading to sin and death) or of the new (leading to righteousness and life). Adam and Christ appear therefore not simply as comparable or complementary figures, but in contrast to one another,[74] and "the world is changed by both."[75]

Detailed Comment

5:12-14 Paul speaks in these verses concerning sin, death, the law, and accountability. Sin came into the world through Adam, he says, and on that point Paul recalls what had existed in Jewish thought prior to his own time.[76] But sin's advent into the world was not the end of the matter, for "death" arrived "through sin" (5:12). Sin entered when Adam disobeyed the commandment of God (Gen 2:16-17; 3:3) and thereby sought to be "as God" (Gen 3:5). The sentence of death followed (Gen 3:19), and "death came to all people, because all have sinned." The view that sin leads to death is pre-Pauline, appearing in Jewish sources prior to and contemporary with Paul.[77]

The clause translated as "because all have sinned" in 5:12 is a rendering of an expression that has preoccupied interpreters intensely over the centuries.[78] That expression is ἐφ' ᾧ πάντες ἥμαρτον. It was translated in the Old Latin and Vulgate versions as *in quo omnes peccaverunt* ("in whom all sinned"), in which *in quo* ("in whom" or "in which") represents the prepositional phrase ἐφ' ᾧ, and

---

73. D. Stanley, "Paul's Interest in the Early Chapters of Genesis," 1:248. Cf. also U. Wilckens, *Römer,* 1:310-11, and J. Muddiman, "Adam," 101-10.

74. Cf. the discussion by R. Erickson, "The Damned and the Justified in Romans 5.12-21," 292-94, who contends that there is a contrast (not simply a comparison) between Christ and Adam. He writes: "the construction εἰ + πολλῷ μᾶλλον most naturally implies a contrast, an intent to indicate a difference" (p. 293). Cf. also K. Barth, *Romans,* 166; A. Nygren, *Romans,* 208; E. Käsemann, *Romans,* 151; B. Byrne, *Romans,* 180.

75. E. Käsemann, *Romans,* 144.

76. The concept is found in Jewish literature prior to Paul, e.g., in Wis 2:24; Sir 25:24. It is also found in other sources that are later, e.g., in 2 Esdr 3:21-26; 4:30; 7:48, 118; 8:35; 2 *Apoc. Bar.* 23:4; 54:15.

77. Cf. Wis 2:24; 1 *Enoch* 5.9; 4 *Ezra* 7.62-131; Philo, *Mos.* 2.147. For additional references, cf. C. Black, "Pauline Perspectives on Death in Romans 5–8," 414-16.

78. C. Cranfield, *Romans,* 274-75, lists six possible meanings; J. Fitzmyer, *Romans,* 413-16, lists eleven possibilities.

the antecedent of "whom" is usually taken to be Adam. From that rendering, Augustine of Hippo (A.D. 354-430) interpreted the verse to mean that all of humanity sinned in Adam. They sinned not as individuals but as participants in human nature existing at that time in Adam.[79] The verse was foundational for the development of the doctrine of original sin.

The clause has been translated in modern English versions as "because all have sinned," "because all sinned," or the like (KJV, ASV, RSV, NIV, NRSV, NET). The issue at hand — from all points of view in interpretation — is what to make of the prepositional phrase ἐφ' ᾧ. The phrase consists of the contraction (and the use of the letter φ in place of π prior to the following vowel) of the Greek preposition ἐπί ("upon"), followed by the relative pronoun ᾧ (dative case, "whom" or "which"). The phrase appears within biblical Greek 15 times, and in many cases it means simply "upon whom" or "on which."[80] Within the letters of Paul it appears on three other occasions (2 Cor 5:4; Phil 3:12; 4:10), and in those instances — as well as in some other Greek sources — it is a contraction for ἐπὶ τούτῳ ὅτι, meaning "for the reason that" (comparable to the English expression "in that") or simply "because."[81] Since that is how Paul uses the term elsewhere, it is most likely his meaning here, as various interpreters contend.[82]

But to render the passage as "because all have sinned" may seem at first glance to mean that, according to Paul, there is no causal or organic connection

---

79. Augustine, *City of God* 13.14; 16.27. Cf. also these works of Augustine: *On the Merits and Forgiveness of Sins and Infant Baptism* 1.10; *Against Julian* 7.24; 20.63; and *Tractates on the Gospel of John* 49.12.23. For a discussion of Augustine's exegesis of Rom 5:12, cf. M. Reid, *Augustinian and Pauline Rhetoric in Romans Five*, 69-76. Augustine's construal of the verse continues to appear in one form or another in modern works, e.g., A. Nygren, *Romans*, 214-15 ("If we are to keep the translation 'because all men have sinned,' we shall have to understand it as Augustine did, 'all men have sinned in Adam'"); and W. Manson, "Notes on the Argument of Romans (Chapters 1–8)," 159.

80. Examples include Gen 38:30; Isa 25:9; 37:10; 62:8; Jer 7:14; Acts 7:33.

81. BDAG 365 (ἐπί, 6, c). Cf. BDF 123 (#235). At least one passage in the LXX has this meaning (Josh 5:15).

82. R. Bultmann, "Adam and Christ according to Romans 5," 153; O. Michel, *Römer*, 122; E. Käsemann, *Romans*, 147-48; U. Wilckens, *Römer*, 1:316; C. Cranfield, *Romans*, 279; J. Dunn, *Romans*, 273; D. Moo, *Romans*, 321-22. B. Byrne, *Romans*, 173, 177, 183, renders the expression "on this basis, namely, that," which is much the same as "because"; similarly, C. Talbert, *Romans*, 148, who renders it as "from which it follows that." J. Fitzmyer, *Romans*, 405, 416, renders the phrase as "with the result that" (equivalent to ὥστε, "so that"), and he cites some evidence for that usage in Hellenistic texts. He is followed by T. Schreiner, *Romans*, 273-77. But that rendering implies that death preceded sin, instead of the reverse (which Schreiner is aware of and explains well for that point of view). But the usage of Paul elsewhere in his own letters should carry more weight. R. Jewett, *Romans*, 369, 376, suggests: "on which [world] all sinned," which requires that the pronoun ᾧ refer back to τὸν κόσμον. While grammatically possible, it is better to take the phrase ἐφ' ᾧ as a familiar expression for "because."

between the sin of Adam and that of "all" other people. In other words, it might be argued that, since no causal relationship is stated, each person commits sin on his or her own; no one is affected by the sin of Adam. Any concept of "original sin" (however that is transmitted)[83] is then out of the question. Moreover, even if the specific doctrine of "original sin" is set aside, any concept of the universal sinfulness of humanity due to the fall of Adam is irrelevant. Each person is punished by the sentence of death because of his or her own sin. The view of Pelagius (ca. A.D. 354-418) would then seem to be true to Paul: it is theoretically possible for anyone not to sin.[84] So when Paul claims that "all have sinned," he means only that they have sinned by their own volition and, at best, by imitation of Adam,[85] and not by any inherent and irrepressible inclination to do so.

That need not, however, be the consequence of the translation. Paul simply states that death has spread to all of humanity, "because all have sinned." Since all have sinned, that does not preclude the idea that people are sinful to begin with. There are at least five reasons for that view. (1) The "all" of the verse implies that all are incapable of not sinning, as in the view of Augustine and the classical Christian tradition of the West,[86] even if not always of the East.[87] (2) The οὕτως ("so") in 5:12b corresponds to the word ὥσπερ ("just as") in 5:12a, so that the

83. E. Brunner, *Romans*, 44: "Paul is not concerned with giving an instructive presentation of original sin in the sense of the later teaching of the Church. The physical moment of hereditary transmission is just not stressed by Paul — that element which since Augustine has penetrated into the teaching of the Church from ways of thought alien to the Bible and governed it." For an example of the latter, cf. Philip Melanchthon, *Commentary on Romans*, trans. Fred Kramer (St. Louis: Concordia Publishing House, 1992), 132-33.

84. Pelagius, *Commentary on Romans* at 3:18; 6:7; 8:3. For texts, see *Pelagius' Commentary on St. Paul's Epistle to the Romans*, trans. Theodore S. de Bruyn (Oxford: Oxford University Press, 1993), 80, 97, 107. Cf. also the remarks on Pelagius by Augustine, *On Nature and Grace* 8; idem, *On the Grace of Christ* 1.4.

85. According to Pelagius, commenting on Rom 5:12, when Paul claims that "all have sinned," he means that they have sinned "by example or by pattern" (imitation) of Adam. For text, cf. *Pelagius' Commentary on St. Paul's Epistle to the Romans*, ed. T. de Bruyn, 92. According to de Bruyn, "The idea that sin is passed on from Adam 'by example or by pattern', emphasized by Pelagius in reaction to traducianist interpretations of the fall, came to be regarded as a trademark of his thought" (p. 92, n. 19).

86. Augustine, *Against Julian* 20.63; *City of God* 16.27. Prior to Augustine, Irenaeus, *Against Heresies* 5.3.1; 5.16.3; 5.17.3, and Cyprian, *Epistles* 64.5, affirmed the universality of sin due to the fall.

87. According to D. Weaver, "The Exegesis of Romans 5:12 among the Greek Fathers," 133-59, 231-57, the prevailing view among the Greek fathers was that sins are freely committed personal acts, and that humanity's inheritance from Adam was limited to mortality and corruption. Cf. John Chrysostom, *Homilies on Romans* 10.1. Nevertheless, that all humanity is sinful due to Adam's rebellion is affirmed in one way or another by Melito of Sardis, *On Pascha* 54-55; Origen, *Commentary on Romans* 5.9; Athanasius, *Orations against the Arians* 1.51; and Theodoret of Cyrrhus, *Interpretation of the Letter to the Romans* 5.12.

sense of the verse is: ". . . just as sin entered the world through one man [i.e., Adam], and death through sin, *so too* death came to all people [through one man, Adam]."[88] What is true of the latter (death) is therefore true of the former (sin) as well; the universality of death is parallel to the universality of sin. (3) That sinful behavior is but an imitation of Adam's behavior is ruled out by Paul's statement that the sins of humanity have been committed in spite of their not being like the transgression of Adam (5:14); they have not even been a "copy" or "likeness" (ὁμοίωμα) of Adam's.[89] (4) In 5:17a Paul says that it is actually on account of Adam's rebellion against God that death has exercised its dominion over all of humanity; from the sentence of death for all one can reason that all share in Adamic rebellion. And (5) in 5:18a and 5:19a humanity is said to have been condemned and "made sinners" due to Adam's rebellion. Combining what he says in 5:12b and 5:17a, one can conclude that, for Paul, both Adam and every person ever born are alike in their sinful condition; all rebel against God. Consequently, as in the case of Adam, upon whom the sentence of death was pronounced (Gen 3:19), the sentence of death has been pronounced upon all humanity. The thinking here is that "death comes to man [*sic*] as something for which he was not made, as an offence, cutting short and reducing to meaninglessness all that is highest and distinctive about him, the negation of love and his personal existence and values."[90] Moreover, it can be said:

> The universality of human mortality is Paul's empirical proof of the universality of human sin. It is as useless here to speculate on the biological origins of sin (e.g., in the act of procreation) as it is to speculate on whether apart from sin humans would be immortal. In the present time, to be human for Paul means to be involved in the pain and loss of death, a pain and loss that will be eliminated in the new age (e.g., 8:23; more fully in I Cor 15:51-57). As long as death remains, therefore, sin continues to exercise power in God's creation.[91]

According to what Paul says in 5:12, sin entered the world through Adam, and death was its consequence. Yet, according to modern understanding, death existed long before humans existed, and death is the natural outcome of the life of every biological organism. A helpful approach to the modern question has been expressed this way:

> When we look more closely at what Paul is saying about death, it soon be-

88. J. Kirby, "The Syntax of Romans 5.12," 284.
89. Cf. Traugott Holtz, "ὁμοίωμα," *EDNT* 2:513.
90. J. Robinson, *Wrestling with Romans*, 63.
91. P. Achtemeier, *Romans*, 97.

comes clear that what biologists call death is only loosely related to what Paul calls "death" in Romans. Both death and sin are personified by Paul into spiritual powers, under which humanity is now enthralled. Death is not merely biological in Romans, any more than the life that is given us in Jesus is merely biological. The typological parallel between Adam and Christ makes it clear that mere organic death is not the point. Rather, . . . we should understand death as both spiritual and biological, a powerful force under which humanity is enslaved, body and soul. If we insist on reading Romans 5 in the Augustinian tradition, we will have trouble with Darwin. Yet the gift of Darwin to biblical theology . . . is to get us to pay attention to what the text is saying theologically rather than force it into a literal or "scientific" sense.[92]

The overt act of Adam against God's commandment can be called a "transgression" (παράβασις, Rom 5:14), "trespass" (παράπτωμα, 5:15-18), and "disobedience" (παρακοή, 5:19). But at a deeper level, and at the outset, Paul speaks rather of "sin" (ἁμαρτία, 5:12). This section makes a distinction between "sin" and "transgression."[93] As summarized by C. K. Barrett, "Sin is an inward disposition of rebellion against God arising out of exaltation of the self. . . . Sin is turned into transgression, and becomes visible and assessable, only when a law is given."[94] Thus sin entered the world through Adam's rebellion, and it can be spoken of as "transgression" in consequence of Adam's overstepping of the commandment of God (Rom 5:14).

The era between Adam and Moses is spoken of as a time "before the law was given" (5:13). Therefore it was not a time of "transgression" in the strict sense (except in the case of Adam), "for sin is not counted where there is no law." Nevertheless, says Paul, "sin was in the world" even then. That had to be the case since the sentence of death was carried out against all of humanity. Moreover, unless that were the case, Jesus' redemptive death would be only for those "under the law" rather than for Gentiles as well. Sin was indeed in the world prior to the giving of the law through Moses, and all who lived in that era were sinful. Earlier Paul had declared that all are under the power of sin (3:9), and that would apply to persons of the earlier era as well as the era after the law was given.

One can understand Paul's statement concerning "transgression" prior to the giving of the law in light of the history of law-making in general. An action that is "counted" as illegal in one era might not have been considered illegal in a

---

92. M. Throntveit and A. Padgett, "Reading the Bible after Darwin," 46.

93. Cf. U. Wilckens, *Römer*, 1:317. On the other hand, R. Bultmann, *Theology of the New Testament*, 1:252, finds the distinction unintelligible. Cf. also his essay, "Adam and Christ according to Romans 5," 153-54, and E. P. Sanders, *Paul, the Law, and the Jewish People*, 35-36.

94. C. K. Barrett, *Romans*, 105.

prior one. Nevertheless, the action could have been reprehensible, and the law that was made would have been formulated because of the judgment held against the action in question. So it is with sin. It existed in the world from the beginning. It would not have been "counted" (RSV), "reckoned" (NRSV), or "taken into account" (NIV) prior to the giving of the law in the sense that one could document it according to a code of law, but it was a reality nonetheless.

Paul speaks of Adam as a "type" (τύπος) of the one who was to come (i.e., Christ, 5:14). By means of typology here, Adam is the "type" ("pattern," "model") who foreshadows the "antitype," the second Adam. Due to the "universal havoc" he caused, "Adam is for Paul a τύπος, an advance presentation, through which God intimates the future Adam, namely, Christ in His universal work of salvation."[95] As typical of biblical typology, that which the type anticipates is much greater than itself, for that which is to come is an eschatological event. In its origins the word τύπος designates the raised face of a printing font or a stamp that leaves an impression in printing a text. Paul uses the term in reference to OT persons, events, and institutions that announce the forthcoming, eschatological intervention of God.[96] But what is unusual about the typology in this particular instance is that it is antithetical, and the first member of the antithesis (Adam) is superseded by the second (Christ).[97] The intensification of the antithesis is carried out further in the verses that follow.

5:15-21 A shift occurs at 5:15. While in 5:12-14 the solidarity of all humankind as rebellious like Adam is affirmed, so that "death reigned" (5:14) and exercised its rule over all, in 5:15-21 the "trespass" of Adam becomes itself the factor that leads to the condemnation of all.[98] Here the focus is no longer upon the sinfulness of humanity as such, but upon the effects of Adam's trespass. Now Adam is positioned as the head of humanity. Here Adam becomes much more a symbol, a mythological figure, who symbolizes not only rebellion against God (as one who "sins") but whose "trespass" brought death and condemnation to the whole human race (5:15-16).

The theological shift can be detected, moreover, in the terminology used. In 5:14 Paul had spoken of Adam's "transgression" (παράβασις). But in the following verses he speaks of the "trespass" (παράπτωμα) of Adam (5:15, 17, 18). A distinction can be made. The former term (παράβασις, "transgression") implies transgression of a commandment, and Adam's "transgression" of a commandment is portrayed in Genesis. The word denotes "sin in its relation to law" and

---

95. Leonhard Goppelt, "τύπος," *TDNT* 8:252.

96. Leonhard Goppelt, "τύπος," *TDNT* 8:251-56.

97. Cf. H. Müller, "Der rabbinische Qal-Wachomer-Schluss in paulinischer Typologie," 80-91, who contends that the typology is based on a traditional Adam-Messiah typology, which also appears at 1 Cor 15:45-46.

98. E. Käsemann, *Romans*, 153; U. Wilckens, *Römer*, 1:322-23.

exists only where there is law (4:15).[99] But the latter term (παράπτωμα, "trespass") is a more radical term, an equivalent to "sin" (ἁμαρτία), the disruption of humanity's relationship to God, and it existed prior to the giving of the law.[100] Etymologically the word is related to the verb παραπίπτω ("to fall away" or "to commit apostasy"). That the term is equivalent to sin for Paul can be seen in the parallelism at 5:20 ("the law came in to increase the *trespass* [παράπτωμα]; but where *sin* [ἁμαρτία] increased, grace abounded all the more").

For Paul, then, "sin" entered the world through Adam, the disobedient one, and all persons have "sinned" ever since. That is Paul's teaching in 5:12-14. But there is more. Adam's "trespass" (παράπτωμα) — his fall — has set the whole world into rebellion against God. All of humanity bears the character of Adam as the fallen one. Paul does not think in terms of a biological descent of "original sin" from Adam to successive generations, as in the manner of subsequent theology, but he thinks of Adam as the prototype or head of humanity in its actual character. So he can write that "by one man's trespass, many died" (5:15). The sentence of death upon Adam (Gen 3:19) has been extended to all.

Paul declares, however, that the effects of Christ's obedience are far greater for humankind than the effects of Adam's fall. For the third (5:15) and fourth (5:17) times in this chapter he makes explicit use of the *qal waḥomer* ("from minor to major") form of argument that is commonly used in rabbinic literature,[101] expressed by "much more" (πολλῷ μᾶλλον; cf. earlier use at 5:9, 10). And as in the case of the typology previously used (5:14), here, too, the form of argument is antithetical.[102] The grace of God extended to humanity in the event of Christ's death has abounded "for the many" (5:15b), which corresponds to the "all" of 5:12, 18. The free gift given by God in Christ more than matches the sin of Adam and its effects; it exceeds it.

At the end of 5:16 Paul uses the term δικαίωμα, which normally refers in his writings either to (1) a "regulation, requirement, or commandment" (cf. Rom 1:32; 2:26; 8:4) or (2) a "righteous deed" (Rom 5:18). In the present instance, however, the term can properly be understood to mean "justification," the equivalent of δικαίωσις in 5:18.[103] Although the usage is unusual, it can be

---

99. Johannes Schneider, "παράβασις," *TDNT* 5:739-40.

100. Wilhelm Michaelis, "πίπτω," *TDNT* 6:172.

101. On the *qal waḥomer* form of argumentation, see Louis Jacobs, "Hermeneutics," *EncJud* 8:367; H. Strack and G. Stemberger, *Introduction to the Talmud and Midrash*, 21, 27.

102. Cf. H. Müller, "Der rabbinische Qal-Wachomer-Schluss in paulinischer Typologie," 80-91.

103. BDAG 249-50 (δικαίωμα); Karl Kertelge, "δικαίωμα," *EDNT* 1:335; LSJ 429 (δικαίωμα): "act of justification," referring to Rom 5:16. J. Kirk, "Reconsidering *Dikaiōma* in Romans 5:16," 791, maintains that the term denotes "the reparation demanded by God in the face of transgression," but nowhere else is such a concept found in Paul's letters. The antithetical struc-

explained as a "rhetorical assimilation"[104] to the use of a string of nouns ending with -μα earlier in the sentence (δώρημα, κρίμα, κατάκριμα, and χάρισμα) and in particular as an antithesis to, even opposite of, the word κατάκριμα ("condemnation") in the previous clause. And so Paul writes that "the free gift (τὸ δώρημα) is not like the consequence of that one man's sin."

For judgment (κρίμα) . . . led to condemnation (κατάκριμα),
but the free gift (χάρισμα) . . . leads to justification (δικαίωμα).

Although the contrasts between Adam and Christ are not uniformly developed in exact parallelism throughout 5:12-21,[105] they are spelled out explicitly in parallel in 5:18-19, as can be seen through the use of parallel columns (author's translation):

5:18

ὡς δι᾽ ἑνὸς	οὕτως καὶ δι᾽ ἑνὸς
παραπτώματος	δικαιώματος
εἰς πάντας ἀνθρώπους	εἰς πάντας ἀνθρώπους
εἰς κατάκριμα,	εἰς δικαίωσιν ζωῆς

As through one's [Adam's]	so through one's [Christ's]
trespass	act of righteousness
[there has been]	[there is]
for all persons	for all persons
condemnation,	justification resulting in life.

5:19

ὥσπερ γὰρ διὰ τῆς παρακοῆς	οὕτως καὶ διὰ τῆς ὑπακοῆς
τοῦ ἑνὸς ἀνθρώπου	τοῦ ἑνὸς
ἁμαρτωλοὶ	δίκαιοι
κατεστάθησαν οἱ πολλοί,	κατασταθήσονται οἱ πολλοί.

For as through the disobedience	so also through the obedience
of one man [Adam]	of one [Christ]

---

ture of the verse requires that δικαίωμα signifies the opposite of condemnation and therefore means "acquittal" or "justification." R. Jewett, *Romans*, 382, suggests that the term means "righteous decree" that overcomes the legacy of trespasses. That seems to be the equivalent of forensic justification.

104. E. Käsemann, *Romans*, 154.

105. For example, in 5:12-14 the attention is almost solely on Adam, sin, and death; Christ is alluded to only in 5:14.

the many	the many
were made	will be made
sinners,	righteous.

The contrasts are between Adam's "trespass" (παράπτωμα) or "disobedience" (παρακοή) and Christ's "act of righteousness" (δικαίωμα, or "deed which establishes righteousness")[106] or "obedience" (ὑπακοή). Contrasts are also to be seen in the results of the work of each. Adam's trespass or disobedience has brought condemnation (κατάκριμα, 5:18); through his act many were made sinners (5:19). Christ's "act of righteousness" results in "justification of life" (δικαίωσις ζωῆς) for all (5:18). The term δικαίωσις can be translated as "justification" (NIV, NRSV; but RSV has "acquittal") — the opposite of "condemnation."[107] The word ζωῆς ("of life") is a genitive of result, providing the outcome of justification, so that the phrase may be rendered "justification resulting in life."[108]

The universality of grace in Christ is shown to surpass the universality of sin. Christ's "act of righteousness" is the opposite of Adam's "trespass" and equivalent to Christ's "obedience," which was fulfilled in his being obedient unto death (Phil 2:8). The results of Christ's righteous action and obedience are "justification resulting in life for all persons" (εἰς πάντας ἀνθρώπους, 5:18) and "righteousness" for "many" (5:19). The term "many" in 5:19 is equivalent to "all persons," and that is so for four reasons: (1) the parallel in 5:18 speaks in its favor; (2) even as within 5:19 itself, "many were made sinners" applies to all humankind, so "many will be made righteous" applies to all; (3) the same parallelism appears in 5:15, at which "many" refers to "all"; and (4) the phrase "for many" is a Semitism which means "for all," as in Deutero-Isaiah 52:14; 53:11-12; Mark 6:2; 9:26; 10:45; 14:24; Heb 12:15.[109] The background for Paul's expression is set forth in Deutero-Isaiah, where it is said that "the righteous one" (LXX δίκαιος), the Lord's servant, shall make "many" to be accounted righteous, and he shall bear their sins (LXX τὰς ἁμαρτίας αὐτῶν, Isa 53:11).

It is significant, and even astounding, that justification is said here to be world-embracing. Nothing is said about faith as a prerequisite for justification to be effective, nor about faith's accepting it. To be sure, some interpreters have maintained that faith is assumed to be a condition, usually basing their claim on 5:17, in which Paul says that "those who receive the abundance of grace and the free gift of righteousness" will "reign in life through the one man Jesus

---

106. Karl Kertelge, "δικαίωμα," *EDNT*, 1:335, citing U. Wilckens, *Römer*, 1:326.

107. Gottlob Schrenk, "δικαίωσις," *TDNT* 2:223-24; U. Wilckens, *Römer*, 1:326.

108. BDAG 250 (δικαίωσις): "acquittal that brings life." The construction is variously called a "genitive of apposition," an "epexegetical genitive," or "genitive of purpose." Cf. BDF 92 (§166). The meaning is the same in each case: justification which brings life.

109. Joachim Jeremias, "πολλοί," *TDNT* 6:540-45.

Christ." That, it is said, implies that there is a possibility for justification and life on the basis of Christ's work, but that faith is the condition for receiving such.[110] But does the verse in fact imply restrictions? Other interpreters understand 5:18-19 to envision a universal scope of redemption.[111]

In order to resolve this issue, it is crucial to analyze what Paul says in 5:17. There the apostle writes that the redemptive work of Christ is "much more" in its effects than the "trespass" of Adam. Death, because of Adam's trespass, "reigned through the one" (διὰ τοῦ ἑνός, 5:17a), and its reign was over all. Using the *qal waḥomer* argument, Paul writes "how much more" (πολλῷ μᾶλλον) will the recipients of the "abundance of grace and the free gift of righteousness reign in life through the one (διὰ τοῦ ἑνός), Jesus Christ" (5:17b). The parallel of Adam and Christ is maintained. The parallel of reigning, however, is not. On the one hand, death reigned through Adam; on the other, recipients of grace will reign in life. Death can indeed be said to "reign" over humanity (cf. 5:14), but life cannot be said to "reign," for it is an eschatological gift that is received (passive voice).[112] Paul, therefore, has to replace the expected subject of the clause ("life") with something else, even though that destroys the parallelism. He draws on the traditional language that speaks of the redeemed as reigning in

110. R. Bultmann, "Adam and Christ according to Romans 5," 158; idem, *Theology of the New Testament,* 1:302-3. Cf. also H. Conzelmann, *An Outline of the Theology of the New Testament,* 207-8; J. O'Neill, *Romans,* 97, 106; H. Ridderbos, *Paul,* 340-41; E. Brandenburger, *Adam und Christus,* 230, 242-43; H. Schlier, *Römer,* 174-75; P. Stuhlmacher, *Romans,* 87-88; N. T. Wright, *NIB (Romans),* 10:528-29; D. Moo, *Romans,* 342-44; R. Jewett, *Romans,* 387; R. Erickson, "The Damned and the Justified in Romans 5.12-21," 300-307. J. Dunn, *Romans,* 283-85, tends in this direction, but then (pp. 297-98) opens the possibility of eschatological "universalism" at this point in Paul's letter and in its interpretation. Concerning the parallel at 1 Cor 15:22, and interpreting it as restrictive in meaning, cf. W. Crockett, "The Ultimate Restoration of Mankind," 3:83-87.

111. J. Jeremias, "πολλοί," 6:542: Paul "ascribes the greatest conceivable breadth to οἱ πολλοί; Christ's obedience affects mankind in the same way as does Adam's disobedience." Similarly, cf. A. Schlatter, *Romans,* 129-31; K. Barth, *Christ and Adam,* 70-71, 109-17; O. Michel, *Römer,* 126; C. K. Barrett, *Romans,* 109; W. Michaelis, *Versöhnung des Alles,* 137-39; E. Käsemann, *Romans,* 155-57; U. Wilckens, *Römer,* 1:325-28; O. Hofius, "The Adam–Christ Antithesis and the Law," 188-90; J. Fitzmyer, *Romans,* 421; B. Byrne, *Romans,* 180-82; E. Lohse, *Römer,* 182; H. Müller, "Der rabbinische Qal-Wachomer-Schluss in paulinischer Typologie," 87; M. Boring, "The Language of Universal Salvation in Paul," 283-85; C. Cousar, "Continuity and Discontinuity," 203-4; R. Bell, "Rom 5.18-19 and Universal Salvation," 429; G. Holtz, *Damit Gott ei alles in allem,* 25-35; J. Adam, *Paulus und Versöhnung der Aller,* 332-38. C. Cranfield, *Romans,* writes, on the one hand, that "what God has accomplished in the death of Jesus Christ does not just concern believers but is as universal in its effects as was the sin of Adam" (p. 839), but on the other hand that, while the gift of "justification resulting in life for all" is "offered" to all, "this clause does not foreclose the question whether in the end all will actually come to share it" (p. 290).

112. O. Michel, *Römer,* 125.

life (*Pss. Sol.* 3.8; 1 Cor 6:2; Rev 20:4).[113] The point he makes is that the reign of death is over, since it is superseded by the abundance of grace and the free gift of righteousness streaming forth upon the world by means of God's act "through the one, Jesus Christ." Paul uses the aorist (simple past tense) — "death reigned" (ὁ θάνατος ἐβασίλευσεν) — to speak of an era that is over, just as he does in 5:14 (ἐβασίλευσεν ὁ θάνατος, "death reigned"), 5:15 (οἱ πολλοὶ ἀπέθανον, "many died"), and 5:19 (ἁμαρτωλοὶ κατεστάθησαν οἱ πολλοί, "many were made sinners"). Then he uses the future tense in the main verb of 5:17b — "those who have received . . . shall reign in life" (οἱ . . . λαμβάνοντες ἐν ζωῇ βασιλεύσουσιν) — to speak of a reign that has not yet been realized but remains a future expectation.

But are the recipients of grace, who are to reign, persons standing even outside the circle of believers? Or are believers alone the ones who receive the abundance of grace and the free gift of righteousness? Either way one answers that question, there are difficulties. But there are more exegetical difficulties with an affirmative reply to the latter question (implying a restriction, "believers alone") than the alternative. (1) It overlooks the fact that the past reign of death is over and done with through the reign of grace (5:21) that has come through Christ. (2) It overlooks the nuance of the phrase πολλῷ μᾶλλον in the main clauses of 5:15 and 5:17, which can be translated "how much more surely."[114] That is to say, death has had its reign, but if that is the case — and it is — then how much more surely will reigning take place for the recipients of grace! The contrast is not between the many who have been under the reign of death and the few who will reign in life, but between death's reign — death personified — and the reign of those who are recipients of God's grace. The reign of death is over, and the grace of God has made its grand entry into the world. (3) In 5:15 Paul speaks of God's grace and the free gift of grace in Christ as having abounded "for many" (= for all). That is the obverse of 5:17, so that "those who receive the abundance of grace and the free gift of righteousness" are indeed all persons. As 5:15 speaks of the scope of grace extending to all, so 5:17 speaks of all being under that scope. There is no reason for saying that 5:17 places limitations on the "many" of 5:15 and 19 and upon the "all" of 5:18.[115] Paul's concern is to show that a shift of aeons has taken place. His interest is not primarily anthropological here; it is Christological and eschatological. In the wake of the redemptive work of God in Christ, a division of the ages has taken place: death reigned, but now the righteousness of God has been revealed (3:21)

---

113. A similar switch in subjects is found in 5:15. In the protasis Paul writes, "For if the many died," and in the apodosis, "much more surely have the grace of God and the free gift . . . abounded for the many."

114. BDAG 614 (μᾶλλον, 2, b).

115. O. Hofius, *Paulusstudien*, 2:87-88; G. Holtz, *Damit Gott sei alles in allem*, 32.

in Christ's atoning death and consequent resurrection, and God's act of righteousness leads to justification resulting in life for all persons (5:18). The scope of divine justifying grace extends to all humankind, not simply to believers alone. So Karl Barth has written concerning 5:19: "In the light of this act of obedience there is no man who is not — in Christ. All are renewed and clothed with righteousness, all are become a new subject, and are therefore set at liberty and placed under the affirmation of God."[116]

The extent to which this passage (5:12-21) can be considered the "essence" of Paul's gospel and theology can be debated. Yet it must be pointed out that the theme of God's saving action toward the world in Christ appears in several contexts: (1) in those passages using the ὑπέρ-formula ("for the ungodly," etc.; Rom 5:6, 8; 8:32; 1 Cor 15:3; Gal 1:4; 2:20; 3:13), (2) in the theme of reconciliation (Rom 5:10; 2 Cor 5:19-20), (3) in Paul's gospel of the salvation of Israel (Rom 11:26-31), (4) in his gospel of the mercy of God for all (Rom 11:32), and (5) in his expectation of the redemption of the entire creation (Rom 8:21). Since the death and resurrection of Jesus Christ, a new age has dawned which is world-embracing in its effects. The action of God in Christ toward the world, grounded in God's own love, has canceled the tension between his wrath and his desire to save; there has been a "negation of the negation"[117] through God's self-giving love, by which he has reconciled the world to himself.

The major problem with understanding 5:18-19 as an affirmation of the universal scope of redemption in Christ is that there are passages where Paul speaks of eschatological peril for some persons. Those who reject the gospel are perishing (1 Cor 1:18; 2 Cor 2:15; 4:3-4), dying (2 Cor 2:16), or being destroyed (Phil 1:28; 3:18-19).[118] In light of those passages, there are various possibilities regarding 5:18-19, of which three are the most challenging: (1) By using the term "all," Paul does not mean all people but Jews and Gentiles;[119] (2) by means of "all," he means all those who are "in Christ";[120] and (3) Paul got "carried away by the force of his analogy and argued more than he intended."[121] Yet the term "all" in the verses can hardly be reduced to anything less than referring to all hu-

---

116. K. Barth, *Romans,* 182.

117. U. Wilckens, *Römer,* 1:333.

118. The concepts of hell and eternal torment do not appear in the undisputed letters of Paul.

119. N. T. Wright, "Towards a Biblical View of Universalism," 56; P. Stuhlmacher, *Romans,* 88; I. H. Marshall, "Does the New Testament Teach Universal Salvation?" 317; M. Rapinchuk, "Universal Sin and Salvation in Romans 5:12-21," 428, 433, 440: "all" means persons "without ethnic distinction."

120. J. Murray, *Romans,* 1:202-3; L. Morris, *Romans,* 239; J. Ziesler, *Romans,* 151; D. Moo, *Romans,* 343-44; R. Jewett, *Romans,* 385-87.

121. E. P. Sanders, *Paul and Palestinian Judaism,* 473; somewhat similarly, D. Zeller, *Römer,* 120-21.

manity, for it is used in reference to the effects of Adam as well as to those of Christ. And to suggest that Paul argued more than he intended is not only to speculate on authorial intent but possibly to cut short a full consideration of a theological pattern that exists within a number of texts. Moreover, not to be overlooked is that, on the basis of certain other passages, there is also eschatological peril for believers in Christ in the final judgment, which will be based on their attitudes and conduct (Rom 14:10; 1 Cor 3:16-17; 2 Cor 5:10). One cannot conclude, therefore, that faith in Christ or lack thereof is the major divide between those who are not in peril and those who are.

It is easy for the interpreter to get preoccupied with the question whether or not Paul was a "universalist" and raise questions that moderns ask and with a precision that Paul may not have entertained, such as whether God will save every individual in the end. If so, then where is divine freedom? What is left of human freedom? Where is justice?

What emerges from a study of Paul's letters is that he speaks of both the wrath of God against a sinful humanity (Rom 1:18; 2:5, 8; 1 Thess 1:10) and the redemptive love of God for all (Rom 5:8; 8:32; 2 Cor 5:19; 13:11). But the two are not of equal theological significance.[122] As indicated earlier (see the exegesis of Rom 1:18), the wrath of God is always caused by factors outside of God. If there were no sin, there would be no wrath, judgment, or condemnation. But the love of God is generated from within, a part of God's nature. God loves in spite of human rebellion. While Paul can therefore speak of the wrath and judgment of God against those who oppose him and his will, he can speak of the scope of redemption in sweeping terms, reaching out beyond to the ends of the universe (Rom 8:21) and including humanity as a whole, as he does in 5:18-19 and elsewhere. But that does not mean that there is no distinction between believers and others. What God has in store for the creation (including humanity as a whole) is realized proleptically within the community of believers — those who are justified by faith and are thereby in a right relationship with God. They are participants already in the new creation that has been inaugurated with the resurrection of Jesus from the dead (1 Cor 15:20, 23; 2 Cor 5:17; Gal 6:15). What is theirs already will be given to all at the parousia (Rom 8:18-25; 11:26, 32; 1 Cor 15:24-28). Paul, the opponent of Christ and persecutor of his church, was confronted by the risen Christ, and all defenses gave way (Gal 1:13-17). Likewise, he could envision the parousia of Christ as the moment in which all opposed to him will be transformed and join in universal praise of God (Phil 2:9-11). One

---

122. This contrast between the love of God and the wrath of God seems to work better, since it is rooted in actual Pauline texts, than the contrast made by M. Boring, "The Language of Universal Salvation," 289-92: God as judge (faith in Christ as necessary for salvation) and God as king (royal conquest over sin on behalf of humanity, resulting in universal salvation).

need not, in the end, insist upon a consistent view from Paul on this from all of his letters. Romans 5:12-21, written later in Paul's career, is the most sustained and comprehensive treatment of sin and redemption in his letters, making use of the Adam and Christ contrasting typology, and it could have marked a charismatic breakthrough.

5:20-21 Paul returns now to the matter of the law, which "came in" through Moses. He has already mentioned the law in 5:13, but he mentions it here once more in order that he can make a contrast between sin and grace, which are major themes in the following chapter (6:1-23). In an astonishing statement, Paul says that "the law came in, in order that the trespass (παράπτωμα) might increase" (5:20). Here he is speaking of a purpose of the law, using the standard form of a purpose clause in Greek, including the usual conjunction ἵνα ("in order that"), followed by a subjective verb, πλεονάσῃ ("might increase"). The statement is astonishing, because in common Jewish thought the purpose of the law is to curb trespasses and lead people into the paths of righteousness. One cannot possibly say that the purpose of God in giving the law was to promote trespasses (against the law!) of any kind. Why would God give the law to his people with such a purpose in view?

Paul knows well that the law given to Israel was a good and gracious gift from God (3:2, 31; 7:12; 9:4-5). But he sees the giving of the law in light of a larger panorama and in light of a dialectical dynamic, in which the law operates in two ways. While the law is good and can be a guide, it also exposes sin (3:19). Moreover, it can suggest ways in which a person hostile to God can offend God, which Paul will maintain later in his letter (7:7-11). It is the law's function of exposing sin that Paul has in mind when he writes 5:20 (παράπτωμα ["trespass"] and ἁμαρτία ["sin"] being equivalent). The law makes sin apparent and brings it out into the open. Sins can thus be counted, and their record is one of accumulation. In short, sin increased after the giving of the law.

But, in spite of the increase of sin, Paul says, "grace was present in greater abundance." The verb ὑπερπερισσεύω appears only twice in the NT (here and at 2 Cor 7:4). It designates something increasing to great excess,[123] and so it can be translated as "abounded all the more" (RSV, NRSV) or "increased all the more" (NIV). That happened during the time of God's forbearance (3:25) and up to the time of his redemptive work in Christ.

Paul follows up with a conclusion in 5:21, again using a purpose clause containing both the usual conjunction ἵνα ("in order that") and a subjunctive verb βασιλεύσῃ ("might reign"). By means of the purpose clause he says that grace became greater and greater in order that it might override and overcome sin. Sin leads only to death. But grace leads to eternal life through the saving

---

123. BDAG 1034 (ὑπερπερισσεύω).

work of Christ. The fact that it reigns "through righteousness" means that grace has triumphed over sin. In saying that, however, Paul can hardly mean that grace empowers the believer to be righteous in an empirical sense and thereby qualify for "eternal life," for no one is righteous (3:9-10). Instead, he says, grace reigns by virtue of the "act of righteousness" and "obedience" of Christ (5:18-19). God has done something that the law cannot do in sending his Son for a redemptive purpose (8:3), and the result is the overwhelming reign of grace "through Jesus Christ our Lord."

BIBLIOGRAPHY

Adam, Jens. *Paulus und die Versöhnung Aller: Eine Studie zum paulinischen Heilsuniversalismus*. Neukirchen-Vluyn: Neukirchener Verlag, 2009.

Aletti, Jean-Noël. "Romains 5,12-21: Logique, sens et function." *Bib* 78 (1997): 3-32.

Anderson, Gary A. "Biblical Origins and the Problem of the Fall." *PEccl* 10 (2001): 17-30.

Barclay, William. "Romans v.12-21." *ET* 70 (1959-60): 132-35, 172-75.

Barrett, C. K. "The Significance of the Adam-Christ Typology for the Resurrection of the Dead." In his *Jesus and the Word and Other Essays*, 163-84. PTMS 41. Allison Park: Pickwick Publications, 1995.

Barth, Karl. *Christ and Adam: Man and Humanity in Romans 5*. New York: Collier, 1962.

Bell, Richard H. "Rom 5.18-19 and Universal Salvation." *NTS* 48 (2002): 417-32.

Black, C. Clifton, II. "Pauline Perspectives on Death in Romans 5–8." *JBL* 103 (1984): 413-33.

Black, Matthew. "The Pauline Doctrine of the Second Adam." *SJT* 7 (1954): 170-79.

Blocher, Henri. *Original Sin: Illuminating the Riddle*. Grand Rapids: Wm. B. Eerdmans, 1999.

Boer, Marinus C. de. *The Defeat of Death: Apocalyptic Eschatology in 1 Corinthians 15 and Romans 5*. JSNTSup 22. Sheffield: JSOT Press, 1988.

Boring, M. Eugene. "The Language of Universal Salvation in Paul." *JBL* 105 (1986): 269-92.

Brandenburger, Egon. *Adam und Christus: Exegetisch-religions-geschichtliche Untersuchung zu Röm. 5,12-21 (1. Kor. 15)*. WMANT 7. Neukirchen-Vluyn: Neukirchener Verlag, 1962.

———. "Alter und neuer Mensch, erster und letzer Adam-Anthropos." In *Vom alten zum neuen Adam*, 182-223. Ed. Walter Strolz. Freiburg: Herder, 1986.

Bray, Gerald L. "Adam and Christ (Romans 5:12-21)." *Evangel* 18 (2000): 4-8.

Bultmann, Rudolf. "Adam and Christ according to Romans 5." In *Current Issues in New Testament Interpretation: Essays in Honor of Otto A. Piper*, 143-65. Ed. William Klassen and Graydon F. Snyder. New York: Harper & Brothers, 1962.

———. *Theology of the New Testament*. 2 vols. New York: Charles Scribner's Sons, 1951-55.

Byrne, Brendan. "The Type of the One to Come (Rom 5:14): Fate and Responsibility in Romans 5:12-21." *AusBR* 36 (1988): 19-30.

Cambier, Jules. "Péchés des homes et péché d'Adam en Rom v.12." *NTS* 11 (1964-65): 217-55.

Caragounis, Chrys C. "Romans 5.15-16 in the Context of 5.12-21: Contrast or Comparison?" *NTS* 31 (1985): 142-48.

Condon, Kevin. "The Biblical Doctrine of Original Sin." *ITQ* 34 (1967): 20-36.

Conzelmann, Hans. *An Outline of the Theology of the New Testament.* New York: Harper & Row, 1969.

Cousar, Charles B. "Continuity and Discontinuity: Reflections on Romans 5–8." In *Pauline Theology,* vol. 3, *Romans,* 196-210. Ed. David M. Hay and E. Elizabeth Johnson. Minneapolis: Fortress Press, 1995.

Cranfield, C. E. B. "A Note on Romans 5.20-21." In his *On Romans and Other Essays,* 15-22. Edinburgh: T&T Clark, 1998.

———. "On Some of the Problems in the Interpretation of Romans 5.12." *SJT* 22 (1969): 324-41.

Crockett, William V. "The Ultimate Restoration of Mankind: 1 Corinthians 15:22." In *Studia Biblica 1978: Sixth International Congress on Biblical Studies, Oxford, 3-7 April 1978,* 3:83-87. Ed. Elizabeth A. Livingstone. 3 vols. Sheffield: JSOT Press, 1979-80.

Dahl, Nils A. "The Argument in Romans 5:12-21." In his *Studies in Paul: Theology for the Christian Mission,* 90-91. Minneapolis: Augsburg Publishing House, 1977.

Danker, Frederick W. "Romans v.12: Sin under Law." *NTS* 14 (1967-68): 424-39.

Davidsen, Ole. "Den strukturelle Adam/Kristus-typologi: Om Roberbrevets grundfortaelling." *DTT* 55 (1992): 241-61.

Davies, W. D. *Paul and Rabbinic Judaism.* 4th ed. Philadelphia: Fortress Press, 1980.

De Bruyn, Theodore S. "Pelagius' Interpretation of Rom 5:12-21: Exegesis within the Limits of Polemic." *TJT* 4 (1988): 30-43.

Drummond, Alistair. "Romans 5:12-21." *Int* 57 (2003): 67-69.

Erickson, Richard J. "The Damned and the Justified in Romans 5.12-21: An Analysis of Semantic Structure." In *Discourse Analysis and the New Testament: Approaches and Results,* 282-307. Ed. Stanley E. Porter and Jeffrey T. Reed. JSNTSup 170. Sheffield: Sheffield Academic Press, 1999.

Feuillet, André. "Le nouvel Adam et l'antithèse mort-vie." In his *Le Christ, sagesse de Dieu, d'après les épîtres pauliniennes,* 333-39. Paris: Gabalda, 1966.

———. "Le règne de la mort et le règne de la vie (Rom. v, 12-21)." *RB* 77 (1970): 481-521.

Fitzmyer, Joseph A. "The Consecutive Meaning of ἐφ' ᾧ in Romans 5.12." *NTS* 39 (1993): 321-39.

Friedrich, Gerhard. "Ἁμαρτία οὐκ ἐλλογεῖται: Röm. 5,13." *TLZ* 77 (1952): 523-28.

Giblin, Charles H. "A Qualifying Parenthesis and Its Context." In *To Touch the Text: Biblical and Related Studies in Honor of Joseph A. Fitzmyer, S.J.,* 305-15. Ed. Maurya P. Horgan and Paul J. Kobelski. New York: Crossroad, 1989.

Goppelt, Leonhard. *Typos: The Typological Interpretation of the Old Testament in the New.* Grand Rapids: Wm. B. Eerdmans, 1982.

Grelot, Pierre. *Péché original et rédemption examines à partir de l'épître aux Romains: Essaí théologique.* Paris: Desclée, 1973.

———. "Pour une lecture de Romains 5,12-21." *NRT* 116 (1994): 495-512.

Grundmann, Walter. "Die Übermacht der Gnade: Eine Studie zur Theologie des Paulus." *NovT* 2 (1958): 50-72.

Haag, Herbert. "Röm 5,12-21." In his *Biblische Schöpfungslehre und kirchliche Erbsünden-lehre*, 60-66. Stuttgart: Katholisches Bibelwerk, 1966.

Hamerton-Kelly, Robert. "Sacred Violence and Sinful Desire: Paul's Interpretation of Adam's Sin in the Letter to the Romans." In *The Conversation Continues: Studies in Paul and John: In Honor of J. Louis Martyn*, 35-54. Ed. Robert T. Fortna and Beverly R. Gaventa. Nashville: Abingdon Press, 1990.

Hellholm, David. "Universalität und Partikularität: Die amplifikatorische Struktur von Römer 5,12-21." In *Paulus und Johannes: Exegetische Studien zur paulinischen und johanneischen Theologie und Literatur*, 217-69. Ed. Dieter Sänger, Ulrich Mell, and Jürgen Becker. WUNT 198. Tübingen: Mohr-Siebeck, 2006.

Hillert, Sven. *Limited and Universal Salvation: A Text-Oriented Study of Two Perspectives on Paul*. ConBNT 31. Stockholm: Almqvist & Wiksell, 1999.

Hofius, Otfried. "The Adam–Christ Antithesis and the Law: Reflections on Romans 5:12-21." In *Paul and the Mosaic Law*, 165-205. Ed. James D. G. Dunn. Grand Rapids: Wm. B. Eerdmans, 2001.

————. *Paulusstudien*. 2 vols. WUNT 51, 143. Tübingen: J. C. B. Mohr (Paul Siebeck), 1989, 2002.

Holtz, Gudrun. *Damit Gott seit alles in allem: Studien zum paulinischen und frühjüdischen Universalismus*. BZNW 149. New York: Walter de Gruyter, 2007.

Houlden, Leslie. "Fall and Salvation: A Case of Difficulty." *ExpTim* 109 (1998): 234-37.

Hultgren, Stephen. "The Origin of Paul's Doctrine of the Two Adams in 1 Corinthians 15.45-49." *JSNT* 25 (2003): 343-70.

Johnson, S. Lewis. "Romans 5:12 — An Exercise in Exegesis and Theology." In *New Dimensions in New Testament Study*, 298-316. Ed. Richard N. Longenecker and Merrill C. Tenney. Grand Rapids: Zondervan, 1974.

Jüngel, Eberhard. "Das Gesetz zwischen Adam und Christus: Eine theologische Studie zu Röm 5.12-21." *ZTK* 60 (1963): 43-74; reprinted in his *Unterwegs zur Sache: Theologische Bemerkungen*, 145-72. BEvT 61. Munich: Kaiser Verlag, 1972.

Käsemann, Ernst. *Leib und Leib Christi: Eine Untersuchung zur paulinischen Begrifflichkeit*. BHT 9. Tübingen: J. C. B. Mohr [Paul Siebeck], 1933.

Kertelge, Karl. "The Sin of Adam in the Light of Christ's Redemptive Act according to Romans 5:12-21." *Communio* 18 (1991): 502-13.

Kirby, John T. "The Syntax of Romans 5.12: A Rhetorical Approach." *NTS* 33 (1987): 283-86.

Kirk, J. R. Daniel. "Reconsidering *Dikaiōma* in Romans 5:16." *JBL* 126 (2007): 787-92.

Kister, Menahem. "Romans 5:12-21 against the Background of Torah-Theology and Hebrew Usage." *HTR* 100 (2007): 391-424.

Kline, Meredith G. "Gospel until the Law: Rom 5:13-14 and the Old Covenant." *JETS* 34 (1991): 433-46.

Levison, John R. *Portraits of Adam in Early Judaism: From Sirach to 2 Baruch*. JSPSup 1. Sheffield: JSOT Press, 1988.

Lombard, Herman A. "The Adam-Christ 'Typology' in Romans 5:12-21." *Neot* 15 (1981): 69-100.

Lyonnet, Stanislas. "Le Péché originel et l'exégèse de Rom. 5,12-14." *RSR* 44 (1956): 63-84; translation, abbreviated as "Original Sin and Romans 5:12-14." *TD* 5 (1957): 54-58.

———. "Le Sens de ἐφ' ᾧ en Rom 5,12 et l'exégèse des pères grecs." *Bib* 36 (1955): 436-56; reprinted in his *Études sur l'épître aux Romains*, 185-202. AnBib 120. Rome: Pontifical Biblical Institute Press, 1989.

———. "L'Universalité du péché et son explication par le péché d'Adam: Exégesè des Romains 5, 12-14." In his *Les Étapes du mystère du salut selon l'épître aux Romains*, 55-111. BiO 8. Paris: Éditions du Cerf, 1965.

Malina, Bruce. "Some Observations on the Origin of Sin in Judaism and St. Paul." *CBQ* 31 (1969): 18-34.

Manson, William. "Notes on the Argument of Romans (Chapters 1-8)." In *New Testament Essays: Studies in Memory of T. W. Manson*, 150-64. Ed. A. J. B. Higgins. Manchester: Manchester University Press, 1959.

Marshall, I. Howard. "Does the New Testament Teach Universal Salvation?" In *Christ in Our Place: The Humanity of God in Christ for the Reconciliation of the World: Essays Presented to Professor James Torrance*, 313-28. Ed. Trevor A. Hart and Daniel P. Thimell. Allison Park: Pickwick Publications, 1989.

———. "The New Testament Does *Not* Teach Universal Salvation." In *Universal Salvation: The Current Debate*, 55-76. Ed. Robin A. Parry and Christopher H. Partridge. Grand Rapids: Wm. B. Eerdmans, 2003.

Michaelis, Wilhelm. *Versöhnung des Alles: Die frohe Botschaft von der Gnade Gottes*. Gümlingen (Bern): Verlag Siloah, 1950.

Milne, Douglas J. W. "Genesis 3 in the Letter to the Romans." *RTR* 39 (1980): 10-18.

Muddiman, John. "Adam, the Type of the One to Come." *Theol* 87 (1984): 101-10.

Müller, Heinrich. "Der rabbinische Qal-Wachomer-Schluss in paulinischer Typologie (Zur Adam-Christus Typologie in Rm 5)." *ZNW* 58 (1967): 73-92.

Mussner, Franz. "Adam und Christus." In his *Tod und Auferstehung: Fastenpredigten über Römerbrieftexte*, 34-45. Regensburg: Pustet, 1967.

O'Neill, John C. "Adam, Who Is the Figure of Him That Was to Come: A Reading of Romans 5:12-21." In *Crossing the Boundaries: Essays in Biblical Interpretation in Honour of Michael D. Goulder*, 183-99. Ed. Stanley E. Porter et al. BibIntS 8. Leiden: E. J. Brill, 1994.

Poirier, John C. "Romans 5:13-14 and the Universality of Law." *NovT* 38 (1996): 344-58.

Porter, Stanley E. "The Argument of Romans 5: Can a Rhetorical Question Make a Difference?" *JBL* 110 (1991): 655-77.

———. "The Pauline Concept of Original Sin, in Light of Rabbinic Background." *TynB* 41 (1990): 3-30.

Reid, Marty L. "A Rhetorical Analysis of Romans 1:1–5:21 with Attention to the Rhetorical Function of 5:1-21." *PRS* 19 (1992): 255-72.

———. *Augustinian and Pauline Rhetoric in Romans Five: A Study in Early Christian Rhetoric*. MBPS 30. Lewiston: Mellen Biblical Press, 1996.

Quek, Swee-Hwa. "Adam and Christ according to Paul." In *Pauline Studies: Essays Presented to F. F. Bruce on His 70th Birthday*, 67-79. Ed. Donald A. Hagner and Murray J. Harris. Grand Rapids: Wm. B. Eerdmans, 1980.

Rapinchuk, Mark. "Universal Sin and Salvation in Romans 5:12-21." *JETS* 42 (1999): 427-41.

Ridderbos, Herman. *Paul: An Outline of His Theology.* Grand Rapids: Wm. B. Eerdmans, 1975.

Robinson, John A. T. *Wrestling with Romans.* Philadelphia: Westminster Press, 1979.

Sahlin, Harald. "Adam-Christologie im Neuen Testament." *ST* 41 (1987): 11-32.

Sanders, E. P. *Paul and Palestinian Judaism: A Comparison of Patterns of Religion.* Philadelphia: Fortress Press, 1977.

————. *Paul, the Law, and the Jewish People.* Philadelphia: Fortress Press, 1983.

Schmithals, Walter. *Gnosticism in Corinth: An Investigation of the Letters to the Corinthians.* Nashville: Abingdon Press, 1971.

Schrage, Wolfgang. *Der erste Brief an die Korinther (1 Kor 15,1–16,24).* EKKNT 7.4. Neukirchen: Neukirchener Verlag, 1999.

Scroggs, Robin. *Last Adam: A Study in Pauline Anthropology.* Philadelphia: Fortress Press, 1966.

Stanley, David M. "The Last Adam." *The Way* 6 (1966): 104-12.

————. "Paul's Interest in the Early Chapters of Genesis." In *Studiorum paulinorum congressus internationalis catholicus 1961,* 1:241-52. AnBib 17-18. 2 vols. Rome: Pontifical Biblical Institute Press, 1963.

————. "The Risen Christ as Second Adam: Rom 5,19." In his *Christ's Resurrection in Pauline Soteriology,* 176-80. Rome: Pontifical Biblical Institute Press, 1961.

Strack, Herman, and Günter Stemberger, *Introduction to the Talmud and Midrash.* Minneapolis: Fortress Press, 1992.

Thielman, Frank, "The Story of Israel and the Theology of Romans 5–8." In *Pauline Theology,* vol. 3, *Romans,* 169-95. Ed. David M. Hay and E. Elizabeth Johnson. Minneapolis: Fortress Press, 1995.

Thiselton, Anthony C. *The First Epistle to the Corinthians.* Grand Rapids: Wm. B. Eerdmans, 2000.

Throntveit, Mark A., and Alan G. Padgett. "Reading the Bible after Darwin." *WW* 29 (2009): 39-46.

Tobin, Thomas H. "The Jewish Context of Rom 5:12-14." *Studia Philonica Annual* 13 (2001): 159-75.

Towner, W. Sibley. "Interpretations and Reinterpretations of the Fall." In *Modern Biblical Scholarship: Its Impact on Theology and Proclamation,* 53-85. Ed. F. A. Eigo. Villanova: Villanova University Press, 1984.

Vanhoye, Albert. "Salut universel par le Christ et validité de l'Ancienne Alliance." *NRT* 116 (1994): 815-35.

Vanneste, Alfred. "Le péché originel: Un débat sans issue?" *ETL* 70 (1994): 359-83.

Vanni, Ugo. "L'analisi letteraria del contesto di Rom. v,12-24." *RivB* 11 (1963): 115-44.

Velasco, F. Gómez. "Por un solo hombre: Estudio exegético de Rm 5,12-21." *Mayéutica* 22/1 (1996): 67-128.

Vickers, Brian. "Grammar and Theology in the Interpretation of Rom 5:12." *TJ* 27 (2006): 271-88.

Weaver, David. "The Exegesis of Romans 5:12 among the Greek Fathers and Its Implications for the Doctrine of Original Sin: The 5th-12th Centuries." *SVTQ* 29 (1985): 133-59, 231-57.

Wedderburn, A. J. M. "Adam in Paul's Letter to the Romans." In *Studia Biblica 1978: Sixth International Congress on Biblical Studies, Oxford, 3-7 April 1978*, 3:413-30. Ed. Elizabeth A. Livingstone. 3 vols. Sheffield: JSOT Press, 1979-80.

———. "The Theological Structure of Romans v.12." *NTS* 19 (1972-73): 339-54.

Weder, Hans. "Gesetz und Sünde: Gedanken zu einem qualitativen Sprung im Denken des Paulus." *NTS* 31 (1985): 357-76.

Wright, N. T. "Adam in Pauline Christology." In *Society of Biblical Literature 1983 Seminar Papers*, 359-89. Ed. Kent H. Richards. SBLSP 22. Chico: Scholars Press, 1983.

———. "Towards a Biblical View of Universalism." *Themelios* 4 (1979): 54-58.

4.3. Free and Alive in Christ: The Struggle against Sin, 6:1-11

1*What then shall we say? Are we to remain in sin in order that grace may abound?* 2*By no means! How can we who died to sin go on living in it?* 3*Or do you not know that as many of us as have been baptized into Christ Jesus were baptized into his death?* 4*We have been buried therefore with him through baptism into death, in order that just as Christ was raised from the dead through the glory of the Father, so we too may walk in newness of life.* 5*For if we have become united with the likeness of his death, we shall certainly also be united with the likeness of his resurrection.* 6*We know that our old self was crucified with him, in order that the body of sin might be destroyed, so that we might no longer be enslaved to sin;* 7*for whoever has died is freed from sin.* 8*And if we have died with Christ, we believe that we shall also live with him.* 9*We know that since Christ has been raised from the dead, he will not die again; death no longer has dominion over him.* 10*For the death he died, he died to sin once for all; but the life he lives, he lives to God.* 11*So you also, consider yourselves dead to sin, but alive to God in Christ Jesus.*

Notes on Text and Translation:

6:3 Instead of having the full phrase "[we were] baptized into Christ Jesus" (ἐβαπτίσθημεν εἰς Χριστὸν Ἰησοῦν), Codex Vaticanus and a few other witnesses omit "Jesus." Paul uses a similar expression (omitting "Jesus") at Galatians 3:27. But the quantity and strength of other witnesses to include "Jesus" is overwhelming.

6:5 Major English versions (ASV, RSV, NIV, NRSV, ESV, and NET) insert "with him" into the text, e.g., "For if we have been united *with him* in a death like his" (NRSV). There is no basis for the addition in the Greek text. The phrase has been added to make the verse cohere with what has been said in 6:3a, but if it is left out, it coheres with what has been emphasized in 6:3b.

6:7 The verb in the phrase "is freed from sin" is δεδικαίωται (perfect passive, from δικαιόω, typically used by Paul and others for "to justify"). To render the verb "has been justified from sin" does not work here. The verb can have the meaning of having been released, set free.[124]

6:11 Some important witnesses, including ℵ, C, and the Majority Text, have the additional words τῷ κυρίῳ ἡμῶν ("our Lord") at the end of the sentence. The expression appears in the KJV, but not in other major English versions. The words do not appear in other major witnesses, including 𝔓[46], A, B, and D (nor are they represented in Latin and Syriac versions), which speaks loudly for their omission. The words may be a liturgical expansion that has been modeled after the ending of 6:23.[125]

General Comment

Chapter 6 marks a departure from what has just been said in 5:12-21 in one important respect. The discussion in 5:12-21 had to do with humanity more generally, for Paul spoke there of the effects of Adam on the whole human race and the corresponding redemptive work of God in Christ. But at 6:1 Paul resumes use of the first person plural ("we"), which had been used earlier in the chapter (5:1-11). In doing so, he turns the reader's attention specifically to the Christian community.

But there is also continuity from 5:12-21 into the present chapter. In 5:12-21 Paul asserted that grace triumphs over sin. Therefore a question arises, and Paul takes up the diatribe style to deal with it. The question that one could propose is: Since grace triumphs over sin, which is a good thing, shall we help grace along by continuing in sin? Paul responds by referring to Christian baptism and the consequent new life flowing from it to demonstrate that such a conclusion would be false. Moreover, up to this point Paul has emphasized that the believer in Christ is justified by faith without works of the law (3:21-31; 5:1). He now has to make the case that justification by faith does not lead to moral indifference or depravity.

In constructing his argument on the basis of baptism, Paul sets forth the longest treatment of baptism in the NT (unless one considers all of 1 Peter a

---

124. BDAG 249 (δικαιόω, 3), citing various texts: "to cause someone to be released from personal or institutional claims that are no longer to be considered pertinent or valid, *make free/pure.*"

125. B. Metzger, *TCGNT* 453-54.

baptismal homily). He does not take up baptism as a topic in itself, however. Nor does he necessarily intend to put forth a specifically Pauline doctrine of baptism. He uses the common tradition of baptism, known also at Rome, to illustrate a point, and that has to do with living the new life in Christ, which entails a struggle against sin. It is possible that he does all this to demonstrate to the believers in Rome, lest they have any doubts about him, that he also affirms the common view that there are ethical consequences of baptism.[126]

Detailed Comment

6:1-2 The section opens with a way of questioning that is familiar to diatribal style in Romans (but only there in Paul's letters): τί οὖν ἐροῦμεν ("What then shall we say?"). The question is asked also at 3:5; 7:7; 9:14, 30 (cf. also its use in longer sentences at 4:1; 8:31). From the standpoint of rhetorical criticism, the way of posing the imaginary question is called an "enthymeme," a form of argument in which a false premise or false conclusion is expressed.[127] In the present instance Paul imagines an argument directed against himself in which one would come to a false conclusion. The argument implied by the question would be: If it is the case that "where sin increased, grace was present in greater abundance" (5:20), it follows that we should continue in sinful behavior, increasing sin, in order that grace might abound all the more. What Paul says at 3:8 shows that the charge posed here is not totally imaginary ("And why not say, as we are being slandered, and as some claim that we say, 'Let us do evil in order that good may come'? Their condemnation is just!"). Whether the charge was current in Rome cannot be known on the basis of either 3:8 or 6:1.[128] It is more likely that it has come from elsewhere from persons who accuse him of antinomianism. In both cases, however, Paul expresses (3:8) or alludes to (6:1, 15) the sting that he has experienced from persons who have made the charge against him, whatever the source.

Paul responds to the question with his emphatic "by no means" (μὴ γένοιτο), a strong negation that he often uses after a rhetorical question.[129]

---

126. T. Tobin, *Paul's Rhetoric in Its Contexts*, 198.

127. P. Holloway, "The Enthymeme as an Element of Style in Paul," 337.

128. According to I. Canales, "Paul's Accusers in Romans 3:8 and 6:1," 239, Paul refers to Gentile Christian antinomians at Rome. That he does not refer to any specific persons at Rome, but speaks more generally in diatribe to well-known charges against him, thereby heading off false conclusions, is maintained by various interpreters, e.g., C. Cranfield, *Romans*, 296-97; J. Dunn, *Romans*, 196, 307-8; D. Moo, *Romans*, 356.

129. Besides here, it is used a dozen other times (Rom 3:4, 6, 31; 6:15; 7:7, 13; 9:14; 11:1, 11; 1 Cor 6:15; Gal 2:17; 3:21).

For a discussion of his use of the phrase, see the exegesis of 3:4. Paul then goes on to ask the crucial question, which is the basis for all that follows in this unit: "How can we who died to sin go on living in it?" Those who have died do not live in sin and, consequently, do not behave in sinful ways. And since we have died to sin by our baptism into Christ, he says, it is utterly inconsistent to go on living in sin. It is important to notice that here, as so often elsewhere, Paul speaks of "sin" in the singular and as a power that seeks to control one's life. That use of the term anticipates what is to come later when Paul speaks of being freed from sin (6:7), dead to it (6:11), liberated from it (6:12-14, 18, 22), and becoming slaves of righteousness (6:18) and of God (6:22). For believers to "remain in sin" would mean that they are under its power instead of under the reign of Christ.

6:3-4 The discussion that follows is acutely dependent upon Paul's understanding of the turn of the ages — from old to new — that has come about in the resurrection of Christ from the dead. The passage is saturated with references to events in history, to eschatological events, and to eschatological existence within history. Some of the references are to Christ and his destiny:

> Christ died (aorist), an event in history (6:3, 5, 10).
> Christ was raised from the dead (aorist), an eschatological event that took place within history (6:4, 9).
> Christ has passed into an eternal reign with God and is no longer subject to death, an eschatological event and existence for him (6:4, 9, 10).

Other references are to the baptized person and to that person's destiny with Christ. Baptism is an act in history, but it is also an event that incorporates the believer into Christ, so that the believer belongs to the new age and is no longer subject to the power of the old age:

> Baptism takes place in this world, so one can refer to it and associated metaphors as past historical events (aorist verbs) in the believer's life — baptized (6:3), buried (6:4), united with the likeness of his death (6:5), crucified (6:6), and having died (6:8).
> The baptized person lives in the new age (future verbs or purpose clauses), an eschatological existence, while continuing to live within history: newness of life (6:4), future resurrection (6:5), destruction of the sinful body (6:6), and life with Christ (6:8).

The passage is constructed in such a way that there is an already/not yet dialectic at work:

The "already"	*The "not yet"*
(1) we are enabled to walk in newness of life (6:4)	
	(2) we shall be united with the likeness of his resurrection (6:5)
(3) we are no longer enslaved to sin (6:6)	
	(4) we shall also live with Christ (6:8)

From what Paul says in 6:3a, it can be assumed that baptism "into Christ" is familiar within the Christian community at Rome (as elsewhere; cf. Gal 3:27). What Paul does, however, is take the familiar and explicate what baptism into Christ actually means. The introductory question, "Do you not know?" signals that a particularly solemn teaching is to follow,[130] and that is spelled out in 6:3b: baptism is baptism *into the death of Christ*. Understanding baptism in this way was not necessarily new with Paul and unknown at Rome. On the contrary, he underscored a concept that was probably familiar to his readers,[131] and only if it was familiar or at least acceptable to them would the argument that follows stand. By stressing that baptism is into the death of Christ at the outset of this section, Paul sets up a concept that will become important as the discussion proceeds.

But prior to following that discussion, it is necessary to give attention to some of the terms that Paul uses in 6:3. First, the imagery of baptism into the death of Christ is drastic and is the most radical among the metaphors used in the NT in connection with baptism (such as washing, rebirth, and putting on Christ).[132] The implication is that life in this world with its attendant values and behaviors is now at an end. In the very act of baptism (symbolized by immersion in water) the person being baptized is put to death, but it is not simply the end of personal existence in the world of conventional values and behaviors. By means of the event, the person is joined to Christ.

---

130. For this expression elsewhere, cf. Rom 2:4; 7:1; more commonly Paul asserts that he does not want his readers to be ignorant, as at Rom 1:13; 11:25; 1 Cor 10:1; 12:1; 1 Thess 4:13.

131. That the concept of baptism as "into the death of Christ" was new with Paul is held by U. Wilckens, *Römer*, 2:11. Whether or not that is so, the concept is not found prior to Romans, as stated by H. Betz, "Transferring a Ritual," 109-12. Those who claim that it was traditional include R. Tannehill, *Dying and Rising with Christ*, 22, and D. Hellholm, "Enthymemic Argumentation in Paul," 154-55. Hellholm's summary of arguments is persuasive.

132. Among the various metaphors are the following: washing (Acts 22:16; Eph 5:26; Titus 3:5; Heb 10:22; less explicitly: 1 Cor 6:11; 1 Pet 3:21; John 13:8, 10); rebirth or regeneration (John 3:3, 5; Titus 3:5; 1 Pet 1:3, 23; 1 John 2:29; 3:9; 4:7; 5:1, 18); putting on Christ (Gal 3:27); being enlightened (Heb 6:4; 10:32); being circumcised with a circumcision made without hands (Col 2:11); and being sealed (2 Cor 1:22; Eph 1:13).

A second feature of Paul's language is his use of the preposition εἰς ("into") in connection with baptism. Baptism is "into Christ" (6:3a; Gal 3:27), "into his death" (6:3b), and "into death" (6:4). The use of the preposition in baptismal contexts appears elsewhere in the NT, such as "into the name of the Lord Jesus" (Acts 8:16; 19:5).[133] Paul also uses the preposition when he refers to the people of Israel, saying that "all were baptized into Moses" (πάντες εἰς τὸν Μωϋσῆν ἐβαπτίσθησαν) in connection with the events surrounding the exodus from Egypt (1 Cor 10:2), and he speaks of Christians and himself as "baptized into one body" (εἰς ἓν σῶμα ἐβαπτίσθημεν, 1 Cor 12:13), the church. The preposition is used in these cases to speak of a means by which a shared identity of a people is created, an identity in reference to Moses, Christ, and/or the church. Attempts to find a background for the use of the prepositional phrase in Greco-Roman or Jewish traditions have not been particularly fruitful. The expression has been called "both un-biblical and un-Greek,"[134] meaning that analogous expressions are not found in the Septuagint or in secular Greek. The closest linguistic similarities can be found in the Hebrew expression לְשֵׁם or the Aramaic expression לְשׁוּם. Qumran texts use the expression in the phrase "and unto your name be blessing" (ולשמך הכרכה) and in the entire clause "a city will be built to the name of my Great One" (לשמה די רבי).[135] The latter expression is of particular interest, for it indicates its use in a religious sense, and there it has the basic meaning of designating the one to whom something is dedicated. The expression is used also in rabbinic literature,[136] and there it generally means "in regard to [someone or something]" or "with reference to [someone or something]."[137] It is possible that the phrase was used in proselyte baptism,[138] but it is not clear (1) whether proselyte baptism antedated the rise of Christianity, and (2) even if it did, whether an expression of that type would have been used.[139]

---

133. Cf. also Acts 2:38 and 10:48. In these cases, however, different prepositions (ἐπί and ἐν, respectively) are used.

134. L. Hartman, 'Into the Name of the Lord Jesus,' 39.

135. 1QH 17.20; and 4Q529.9. Texts quoted from The Dead Sea Scrolls: Study Edition, ed. Florentino García Martínez and Eibert J. C. Tigchelaar, 2 vols. (Grand Rapids: Wm. B. Eerdmans, 2000), 1:148-49, 2:1062-63.

136. Texts are quoted in Str-B 1:1055; 4:744. For discussion of the meaning of the phrase in rabbinic literature, cf. J. Jeremias, Infant Baptism, 29 (n. 8); G. Beasley-Murray, Baptism, 90; BDAG 713 (ὄνομα, 1, d, γ, ב).

137. Gustaf Dalman, Aramäisch-Neuhebräisches Wörterbuch zu Targum, Talmud und Midrasch, 2 vols. (Frankfurt: J. Kauffmann, 1901), 1:406.

138. J. Jeremias, Infant Baptism, 29; R. Schnackenburg, Baptism, 20; Hans Bietenhard, "ὄνομα," TDNT 5:275.

139. References to proselyte baptism appear at m. Pes. 8.8; m. Eduy. 5.2; and Sib. Or. 4.165. They may well contain traditions from pre-Christian times. The uncertain date of the origins of proselyte baptism is discussed by G. Moore, Judaism in the First Centuries of the Christian Era,

In some way Christian baptism developed out of the baptismal ministry of John the Baptist (Mark 1:4 and parallels), but just how remains a puzzle, except to say that baptism must have originated among Jewish Christians, some of whom may have been disciples of John.[140] What is more clear is that baptism into the name of Jesus would have differentiated the rite from all other Jewish rites.[141] The formula of being baptized "into Christ" distinguishes the one baptized as belonging exclusively to Christ and sharing his destiny. The saving work of Christ is transferred to the person who is baptized into him or into his death.[142]

The baptized person can be said to be "in Christ" (ἐν Χριστῷ), a term that Paul uses to speak of Christian identity (Rom 8:1; 16:7; 1 Cor 3:1; 2 Cor 5:17; 12:2; Phil 3:8-9). In such passages those things claimed about Christ can be attributed to the Christian as well. For Paul, being "in Christ" is more than a personal identification with him but being joined to him in such a way that what happened to him can be claimed either to have happened to the Christian (e.g., death to sin) or to be promised in the future (e.g., resurrection) in consequence of the existing union.[143] That way of thinking is expressed in particular in a passage that speaks of the "blessed exchange" between Christ and the believer: "For our sake [God] made him to be sin who knew no sin, so that in him we might become the righteousness of God" (2 Cor 5:21).

Although it has been said that Paul speaks of a mystical union with Christ in regard to baptism,[144] that can be misleading, since there are various definitions and understandings of mysticism and mystical union. If one means mysticism in the sense of an absorption into the divine and consequent loss of one's own personal identity or, more broadly, direct knowledge of or communion with the divine,[145] Paul does not fit neatly into the definition of a mystic. Nevertheless, no one definition seems to fit all expressions of mysticism.[146] There are mystical elements in some of the religious experiences that he recounts regarding himself (cf. 2 Cor 12:2-10 in particular), but he does not expect them of

---

1:332-35; and L. Finkelstein, "The Institution of Baptism for Proselytes," 203-11; for more, cf. G. Beasley-Murray, *Baptism*, 23; G. Delling, *Die Taufe im Neuen Testament*, 30-38. According to U. Wilckens, *Römer*, 2:49, proselyte baptism cannot have been the background for Christian baptism.

140. Albrecht Oepke, "βάπτω," *TDNT* 1:539; Otto Böcher, "Johannes der Täufer," *TRE* 17 (1988): 177.

141. L. Hartman, *'Into the Name of the Lord Jesus,'* 44; idem, "Early Baptism," 193.

142. L. Hartman, *'Into the Name of the Lord Jesus,'* 37-50.

143. C. Tuckett, *Christology and the New Testament*, 60-62.

144. A. Deissmann, *Paul*, 147-57; A. Schweitzer, *The Mysticism of Paul the Apostle*, 13-18, 377-79.

145. Peter Moore, "Mysticism," *EncRel* 9:6355.

146. G. Scholem, *Major Trends in Jewish Mysticism*, 6: "There is no mysticism as such, there is only the mysticism of a particular religious system"; cited by U. Luz, "Paul as Mystic," 143.

others. And although he indicates that he has experienced ecstatic speech, he does not commend it to others, and he prefers ordinary speech instead even for himself (1 Cor 14:19). At most one can speak of a distinctive Pauline mysticism that shares some features with other forms but has its own profile.[147]

In regard to the religious backgrounds to Christian baptism in general, assumptions and viewpoints have shifted in modern times. Although it was claimed at one time that Christian baptism as a sacramental act arose out of analogous initiation rites within Hellenistic mystery cults,[148] it can now be said that that view has been put to rest.[149]

Besides being into Christ's death, baptism is a burial with Christ, which anticipates a renewal unto life corresponding with Christ's resurrection (6:4). Paul points back to the resurrection event, affirming that Christ was raised "through the glory of the Father." The prepositional phrase grounds the resurrection of Christ firmly within divine action, a theopractic event (not an act of Christ himself). The term "glory" (δόξα) designates not only the majesty of God, but in certain contexts can refer to the power of God, and that is its meaning here.[150] In fact, Paul speaks elsewhere of the resurrection of Christ in the past and that of believers in the future as a result of God's power (δύναμις) at work (1 Cor 6:14; 2 Cor 13:4). It is characteristic of Paul to assert that God raised Christ from the dead (Rom 4:24; 8:11; 10:9; 1 Cor 6:14; 15:15; 2 Cor 4:14; Gal 1:1; 1 Thess 1:10) or that (using the divine passive) Christ was raised from the dead (Rom 4:25; 6:4, 9; 7:4; 8:34; 1 Cor 15:4, 12-14, 16-17, 20; 2 Cor 5:15).[151]

The actual resurrection of the person baptized into Christ remains future (6:5, 8). But already, since the baptized person has been baptized into Christ's death and shares in its termination of life in accord with sin, a new future has been opened up, and that is to "walk in newness of life" (6:4). Paul's use of the verb περιπατέω ("to walk") is highly significant for his ethics. He uses the word 15 additional times to speak of the way of life expected of the believer.[152] Al-

---

147. U. Luz, "Paul as Mystic," 131-43. Luz discusses six features of what he calls "Pauline mysticism."

148. Cf., e.g., W. Heitmüller, *Taufe und Abendmahl im Urchristentum,* 21-26; W. Bousset, *Kyrios Christos,* 157-58, 193-94.

149. For a survey and conclusions, cf. G. Wagner, *Pauline Baptism and the Pagan Mysteries;* cf. also A. Wedderburn, "Hellenistic Christian Traditions in Romans 6," 337-55; idem, *Baptism and Resurrection,* 396; S. Agersnap, *Baptism and the New Life,* 52-98. According to A. Nock, *Early Gentile Christianity and Its Hellenistic Background,* 60-66, rituals of death and rebirth in Gentile Hellenism can be traced only to the second century A.D.; and for the origins of Christian baptism, "it is . . . not necessary to look outside Judaea" (p. 60).

150. BDAG 257 (δόξα, 1, b), referring also to Philo, *Spec. Leg.* 1.45; Matt. 16:27//Mark 8:38.

151. There is an exception (1 Thess 4:14) where Paul says that Jesus arose.

152. Rom 8:4; 13:13; 14:15; 1 Cor 3:3; 7:17; 2 Cor 4:2; 5:7; 10:3; 12:18; Gal 5:16; Phil 3:17, 18; 1 Thess 2:12; 4:1, 12.

though the term is used (but rarely) among Hellenistic writers generally while discussing conduct, in Paul's case the term's background would have been primarily from within Hellenistic Judaism, for it is there that the verb is used customarily in reference to how one conducts one's life.[153] It is in Jewish tradition in particular that one's manner of life is a "walk," in which one's "steps" are guided by precepts of the Torah (the *halakhot* [הֲלָכוֹת], a term derived from the verb הָלַךְ, "to walk").[154] As Paul the Pharisee would have spoken of "walking" according to the Torah prior to his call, Paul the apostle speaks of "walking" in "newness of life" (Rom 6:4), "by the Spirit" (Rom 8:4; Gal 5:16), and "in love" (Rom 14:15).

6:5-7 Paul speaks next of being united with both the likeness of Christ's death and his resurrection (6:5). Two terms are used here that are crucial. The first is σύμφυτος ("united with") and the other is ὁμοίωμα ("likeness"). The first appears only here in the NT (but in the LXX at 3 Macc 3:22; Amos 9:13; Zech 11:2) and has the basic meaning of "grown together"; in this place it could mean to be "identified with" something.[155] The other term (ὁμοίωμα) appears six times in the NT (Rom 1:23; 5:14; 6:5; 8:3; Phil 2:7; Rev 9:7) and has the meaning "likeness."[156] Paul does not say in this particular verse that the baptized person is "united with Christ" (contra the RSV and NRSV: "united with him in a death like his") but "united with the likeness of his death."[157] The implication is that this clause is parallel to what has been said in 6:3b. Whereas in 6:3a Paul speaks of baptism into Christ, in 6:3b he speaks of the significance of that, and that is being baptized into the death of Christ. The very act of baptism implies an identification with Christ's death. But since Christ's own death can never be repeated, the Christian's baptismal experience can only be one of entering into a "likeness" of the death of Christ, going into the water for a spiritual (and no doubt emotional) drowning.[158] There the old self is put to death, allowing the new to arise.

The second part of the verse (6:5b) is elliptical. If it were stated fully, Paul would say that "we shall also be united with the likeness of his resurrection."[159]

153. Heinrich Seesemann and George Bertram, "πατέω," *TDNT* 5:940-43.

154. The Near Eastern background of the metaphor is explored by J. O. Holloway, ΠΕΡΙΠΑΤΕΩ *as a Thematic Marker for Pauline Ethics* (San Francisco: Mellen University Press, 1992).

155. BDAG 960 (σύμφυτος); for Rom 6:5: "identified with."

156. BDAG 707 (ὁμοίωμα, 1); LSJ 1225 (ὁμοίωμα): "likeness," "resemblance."

157. The syntax of the clause is discussed by H. Betz, "Transferring a Ritual," 114-15.

158. H. Betz, "Transferring a Ritual," 115-16: The ritualized experience of baptism is itself the "likeness" to Christ's death; "The ritual is a ὁμοίωμα." Cf. also Traugott Holtz, "ὁμοίωμα," *EDNT* 2:513.

159. G. Bornkamm, "Baptism and New Life in Paul," 77; J. Dunn, *Romans*, 318; S. Agersnap, *Baptism and the New Life*, 278-80.

That does not mean, however, that the future, actual resurrection of the believer is in question. For to say, "we shall also be united with the resurrection of Christ," is meaningless by itself. One can only be united with something "like" his resurrection (as in NRSV: "a resurrection like his"), something resembling it. As we have been united with the likeness of Christ's death through baptism, being put to death, so we shall be united with the likeness of his resurrection, experiencing a resurrection similar to his. His is a resurrection resulting in lordship. That of believers is a resurrection to eternal communion with him.

Paul moves on in 6:6 with the introductory "we know" (τοῦτο γινώσκοντες), which introduces the meaning and consequences of what has just been said. When the believer has been crucified with Christ, "the body of sin" (τὸ σῶμα τῆς ἁμαρτίας) has been destroyed, and he or she is free from the power of sin. The term "body of sin" is otherwise not used by Paul. The phrase "of sin" is a genitive of quality,[160] modifying "body," but to translate it as "the sinful body" (RSV) can be misleading since it can imply that the human body is itself sinful. In this context and others Paul does not refer specifically to the anatomical body as such. The term refers to the physical-social-spiritual identity of a person. The understanding presupposed is that human life has many aspects (physical, social, spiritual) that cannot be reduced to any one alone. By "the body of sin" in this context Paul refers to the life of the Christian prior to baptism, a life that has now been put to death through baptism into the death of Christ.[161] Crucified, it has been destroyed. Once destroyed, it is no longer enslaved to sin. Sin as a power can enslave the living, as it does, but it cannot enslave that which does not exist. Paul adds, as a recap and explanatory comment in 6:7, that anyone who has died is no longer a slave to sin. The dead cannot be slaves.

6:8-10   In these verses Paul makes a shift. In previous verses he has emphasized the believer's death through baptism, and the verb "to die" and the noun "death" are used five times (verb: 6:2, 7; noun: 6:3, 4, 5); in addition, terms for burial and crucifixion are used (6:4, 6). These terms are used in a highly compressed discussion. Even though that language is continued in 6:8-10, the language of life and resurrection becomes more prominent. The new life of Christ through his resurrection is highlighted (6:9-10), and it is the basis for the new life of the believer with him (6:8). Death's dominion over Christ has been ended. He has been set free for life. The same is possible for the believer in an ethical sense, and already in this world, if that person is joined to Christ through baptismal death and the newness of life that comes from it.

Although there is a shift in emphasis, there are some remarkable like-

---

160. BDF 91-92 (§165).
161. R. Scroggs, "Romans vi.7," 108.

nesses in expression between 6:5-7 and 6:8-10. The first is that in each case Paul begins with conditional sentences (6:5, 8), using εἰ ("if") followed by the indicative verbs γεγόναμεν ("we have become") and ἀπεθάνομεν ("we have died"), and the main clauses ("we shall certainly also be united with the likeness of his resurrection" and "we believe that we shall also live with him"). Although a conditional sentence typically expresses contingency, that is not so in these cases. The conditional sentences actually express certainty, and εἰ could be translated as "since" instead of "if," for what is stated in the initial clause (the protasis) is actually taken to be a certainty (cf. similar usage at Rom 8:31; 15:27).[162]

The second likeness of expression is the way Paul has composed 6:5-7 and 6:8-10 in parallel constructions:[163]

6:5-7	6:8-10
Protasis: 5"For if we have become united with the likeness of his death,"	*Protasis:* 8"And if we have died with Christ,"
Apodosis: "we shall certainly also be united with the likeness of his resurrection."	*Apodosis:* "we believe that we shall also live with him."
Meaning and Consequences: 6"We know that our old self was crucified with him, in order that the body of sin might be destroyed, so that we might no longer be enslaved to sin";	*Meaning and Consequences:* 9"We know that since Christ has been raised from the dead, he will not die again; death has no longer any dominion over him."
Explanation: 7"for whoever has died is freed from sin."	*Explanation:* 10"For the death he died, he died to sin once for all; but the life he lives, he lives to God."

The believer's union with Christ in his death opens up union with him in life. The verb that Paul uses to speak of living with Christ is expressed in the future tense (συζήσομεν, "we shall live"). Paul refers, to be sure, to an eternal existence that will be inaugurated by the resurrection of the dead.[164] But the fact that he does not say "we believe that we shall also be raised with him," which would denote future resurrection from the dead, allows for a double entendre.

---

162. BDAG 278 (εἰ, 3; with additional NT references).

163. Adopted but modified from G. Bornkamm, "Baptism and New Life in Paul," 75.

164. Some interpreters seem to take this to be the only meaning here (rather than life with Christ both prior to and after resurrection), including C. K. Barrett, *Romans,* 118; E. Käsemann, *Romans,* 170; U. Wilckens, *Römer,* 2:18; R. Tannehill, *Dying and Rising with Christ,* 10; J. Dunn, *Romans,* 322, 332; D. Zeller, *Römer,* 126; B. Byrne, *Romans,* 192, 197; P. Stuhlmacher, *Romans,* 92; T. Schreiner, *Romans,* 320; E. Lohse, *Römer,* 192.

To live with Christ can then also mean to live in communion with him already in this life as a consequence of having died in baptism. Paul speaks of the future living with Christ as a matter of faith (πιστεύομεν ὅτι, "we believe that"), using confessional language. That would apply in either case, whether one is referring to life with Christ in one's future pilgrimage on earth or to life with him beyond resurrection. The accent, to be sure, is upon the latter. As an obverse to having died with Christ, any living with him is projected into an eschatological existence beyond actual resurrection. But since the dying that has taken place is in baptism, not in one's physicality, the believer has come up from the water to enter into a new future, living with Christ already in newness of life prior to actual resurrection (cf. 6:4) as well as beyond.[165] That double meaning lays the groundwork for the exhortation that follows in 6:11 concerning life in the world (dead to sin/alive to God).

When Paul speaks of the death of Christ as a death "to sin" (τῇ ἁμαρτίᾳ) in 6:10 — using language virtually identical to that of 6:2, 11 concerning the death of the Christian "to sin" (τῇ ἁμαρτίᾳ) — he does not of course imply that Christ had formerly lived "in sin." Nor does he mean that Christ, sharing the human condition, was subordinate to sin's power.[166] The phrase (using a dative of respect in Greek) must mean that his death was "for sin" or "in respect to sin,"[167] and so the phrase has a soteriological meaning.[168] In other words, Christ has taken to himself the consequences of sin (judgment and the consequent punishment due) on behalf of humanity. (For more on Paul's interpretation of the death of Christ as redemptive, see the exegesis of 5:6-11.) Those who have been baptized have been delivered over to him; they now have the benefits of his redemptive death. This is the presupposition for Paul's treatment of the Christian life. Delivered from the effects of sin, made effective and certified in baptism, Christians can no longer continue to live in sin (6:2), as though nothing has happened. The verse closes with the saying that provides the basis for the ethical exhortation to follow: "but the life he lives, he lives to God." Christ's living "to God" provides the pattern for all who have died with him through baptism and live with him in newness of life.

6:11 The section ends with an exhortation. Christians are to regard

---

165. Cf. M. Luther, *Romans*, 52; J. Murray, *Romans*, 1:223; C. Cranfield, *Romans*, 312-13; G. Bornkamm, "Baptism and New Life in Paul," 78; A. Wedderburn, "Hellenistic Christian Traditions in Romans 6," 339; J. Fitzmyer, *Romans*, 437; J. Ziesler, *Romans*, 161; D. Moo, *Romans*, 377; R. Jewett, *Romans*, 406; S. Agersnap, *Baptism and the New Life*, 328-30.

166. Contra J. Dunn, *Romans*, 323.

167. On this usage, cf. BDF 105-6 (§197); but it is assigned at BDF 101 (§188) to the category of "dative of advantage and disadvantage."

168. S. Agersnap, *Baptism and the New Life*, 345-46; C. Cranfield, *Romans*, 314; U. Wilckens, *Römer*, 2:19.

themselves as dead to sin and alive to God. The imperative "consider your-selves" (λογίζεσθε ἑαυτούς) is not only hortatory. In this context it also reflects the language of faith, not unlike the confessional language at 6:8a ("we believe that"). It is by faith that a believer would reason that he or she is "dead to sin, on the one hand, but alive to God in Christ Jesus on the other" (as one can trans-late the clause with its μὲν . . . δέ construction); being "alive to God *in Christ*" signifies as much. Interestingly, nothing is said here about God's granting power for the new life through the Spirit, although Paul would surely not ex-clude that way of thinking, for he speaks of the Spirit elsewhere as the power that guides the life of the believer (Rom 8:11, 14). But in this particular place the new life is motivated primarily by a new self-understanding.[169] In consequence of one's baptism into the crucified and resurrected Christ, the believer is freed from judgment and the sentence due in consequence of sin.

BIBLIOGRAPHY

Aageson, James W. "'Control' in Pauline Language and Culture: A Study of Rom 6." *NTS* 42 (1996): 75-89.

Agersnap, Søren. *Baptism and the New Life: A Study of Romans 6.1-14.* Aarhus: Aarhus University Press, 1999.

Aland, Kurt. "Die Vorgeschichte der christlichen Taufe." In *Neues Testament und Geschichte: Historische Geschenen und Deutung im Neuen Testament: Oscar Cullmann zum 70. Geburtstag,* 1-14. Ed. Heinrich Baltensweiler and Bo Reicke. Zurich: Theologischer Verlag, 1972.

Arens, Edmund. "Participation and Testimony: The Meaning of Death and Life in Jesus Christ Today." *Concilium* 1 (1997): 112-19.

Barth, Gerhard. *Die Taufe in frühchristlicher Zeit.* BThSt 4. Neukirchen-Vluyn: Neukirchener Verlag, 1981.

Baudry, Gerard-Henry. "Le baptême: Mise au tombeau avec le Christ." *EspVie* 107/6 (1997): 120-27.

Bauer, John A. *A Study of* "Homoioma" *in Romans 6:5.* St. Louis: Concordia Seminary, 1969.

Beasley-Murray, George R. *Baptism in the New Testament.* New York: St. Martin's Press, 1962.

Betz, Hans Dieter. "Transferring a Ritual: Paul's Interpretation of Baptism in Romans 6." In *Paul in His Hellenistic Context,* 84-118. Ed. Troels Engberg-Pedersen. Minneapolis: Fortress Press, 1995.

Bligh, John. "Baptismal Transformation of the Gentile World." *HeyJ* 37 (1996): 371-81.

Boers, Hendrikus. "The Structure and Meaning of Romans 6:1-14." *CBQ* 63 (2001): 664-82.

169. The matter has been stated well by G. Bornkamm, "Baptism and New Life in Paul," 71: "The indicative establishes the imperative, and the imperative follows from the indicative with an absolute unconditional necessity."

Bornkamm, Günther. "Baptism and New Life in Paul." In his *Early Christian Experience,* 71-86. New York: Harper & Row, 1969.

Bousset, Wilhelm. *Kyrios Christos: A History of Belief in Christ from the Beginnings of Christianity to Irenaeus.* Nashville: Abingdon Press, 1970 (German ed., 1913).

Braumann, Georg. *Vorpaulinische christliche Taufverkündigung bei Paulus.* BWANT 5/2. Stuttgart: Kohlhammer Verlag, 1962.

Bultmann, Rudolf. "Glossen im Römerbrief." *TLZ* 72 (1947): 197-202.

Byrne, Brendan. "Living Out the Righteousness of God: The Contribution of Rom 6:1–8:13 to an Understanding of Paul's Ethical Presuppositions." *CBQ* 43 (1981): 557-81.

Canales, Isaac J. "Paul's Accusers in Romans 3:8 and 6:1." *EvQ* 57 (1985): 237-45.

Cranfield, C. E. B. "Romans 6.1-14 Revisited." *ExpTim* 106 (1994-95): 40-43; reprinted in his *On Romans and Other New Testament Essays,* 23-31. Edinburgh: T&T Clark, 1998.

Cullmann, Oscar. *Baptism in the New Testament.* SBT 1. London: SCM, 1950.

Deissmann, Adolf. *Paul: A Study in Social and Religious History.* 2d ed. New York: Harper & Brothers, 1927.

Delling, Gerhard. *Die Taufe im Neuen Testament.* Berlin: Evangelische Verlagsanstalt, 1963.

Dennison, W. "Indicative and Imperative: The Basic Structure of Pauline Ethics." *CTJ* 14 (1979): 55-78.

Dodd, C. H. "Ἔννομος Χριστοῦ." In his *More New Testament Studies,* 134-48. Grand Rapids: Wm. B. Eerdmans, 1968.

Dunn, James D. G. *Baptism in the Holy Spirit: A Re-examination of the New Testament Teaching on the Gift of the Spirit in Relation to Pentecostalism Today.* SBT 2/15. Naperville: Alec R. Allenson, 1970.

———. "Salvation Proclaimed. VI. Romans 6:1-11: Dead and Alive." *ExpTim* 93 (1982): 259-64.

Eckert, Jost. "Indikativ und Imperativ bei Paulus." In *Ethik im Neuen Testament,* 168-89. QD 102. Ed. Karl Kertelge. Freiburg: Herder, 1984.

———. "Die Taufe und das neue Leben: Röm 6,1-11 im Kontext der paulinischen Theologie," *MTZ* 38 (1987): 203-22.

Eckstein, Hans J. "Auferstehung und gegenwärtiges Leben nach Röm 6,1-11." *TBei* 28 (1997): 8-23.

Fape, M. Olusina. *Paul's Understanding of Baptism and Its Present Implications for Believers: Walking in the Newness of Life.* TST 78. Lewiston: Edwin Mellen Press, 1999.

Finkelstein, Louis. "The Institution of Baptism for Proselytes." *JBL* 52 (1933): 203-11.

Fogelman, William J. "Romans 6:3-14." *Int* 47 (1993): 294-98.

Frankemölle, Hubert. *Das Taufverständnis des Paulus: Taufe, Tod und Auferstehung nach Röm 6.* SBS 47. Stuttgart: Katholisches Bibelwerk, 1970.

Frid, Bo. "Römer 6.4-5." *BZ* 30 (1986): 188-203.

Fridrichsen, Anton. "Zu Röm. 6,7." In *Gunnaro Rudberg, septuagenario amicitiae munusculum,* 6-8. ConNT 7. Uppsala: Seminarium neotestamenticum upsaliense, 1942.

Gäumann, Niklaus. *Taufe und Ethik. Studien zu Römer 6.* BevT 47. Munich: Kaiser Verlag, 1967.

Gillman, Florence M. *A Study of Romans 6:5a: United to a Death like Christ's.* Lewiston: Edwin Mellen Press, 1993.

Güttgemanns, Erhardt. "Der Tod-Jesu als Heilsereignis in Röm. 6." In his *Der leidende Apostel und sein Herr: Studien zur paulinischen Christologie*, 210-25. FRLANT 90. Göttingen: Vandenhoeck & Ruprecht, 1966.

Hagen, Wayne H. "Two Deutero-Pauline Glosses in Romans 6." *ExpTim* 92 (1980-81): 364-67.

Hartman, Lars. "Baptism." *ABD* 1:583-94.

———. "Early Baptism — Early Christology." In *The Future of Christology: Essays in Honor of Leander E. Keck*, 191-201. Ed. Abraham J. Malherbe and Wayne A. Meeks. Minneapolis: Fortress Press, 1993.

———. "'Into the Name of Jesus': A Suggestion concerning the Earliest Meaning of the Phrase." *NTS* 20 (1974/75): 432-40.

———. *'Into the Name of the Lord Jesus': Baptism in the Early Church*. SNTW. Edinburgh: T&T Clark, 1997.

Haufe, Günter. "Das Geistmotiv in der paulinischen Ethik." *ZNW* 85 (1994): 183-91.

Heitmüller, Wilhelm. *Taufe und Abendmahl im Urchristentum*. Tübingen: J. C. B. Mohr (Paul Siebeck), 1911.

Hellholm, David. "Enthymemic Argumentation in Paul: The Case of Romans 6." In *Paul in His Hellenistic Context*, 119-79. Ed. Troels Engberg-Pedersen. Minneapolis: Fortress Press, 1995.

Holloway, Paul A. "The Enthymeme as an Element of Style in Paul." *JBL* 120 (2001): 329-39.

Holloway, Joseph O. *ΠΕΡΙΠΑΤΕΩ as a Thematic Marker for Pauline Ethics*. San Francisco: Mellen University Press, 1992.

Howard, James Keir. "'. . . into Christ': A Study of the Pauline Concept of Baptismal Union." *ExpTim* 79 (1967-68): 147-51.

———. *New Testament Baptism*. London: Pickering & Inglis, 1970.

Hultgren, Arland J. "Baptism in the New Testament: Origins, Formulas, and Metaphors." *WW* 14 (Winter 1994): 6-11.

Jackson, Ryan. *New Creation in Paul's Letters: A Study of the Historical and Social Setting of a Pauline Concept*. WUNT 2/272. Tübingen: Mohr Siebeck, 2010.

Jeremias, Joachim. *Infant Baptism in the First Three Centuries*. Philadelphia: Westminster Press, 1960.

Kaye, Bruce N. "βαπτίζειν εἰς with Special Reference to Romans 6." In *SE* 6 (1973): 281-86.

———. *The Thought Structure of Romans with Special Reference to Chapter 6*. Austin: Schola Press, 1979.

Kearns, Conleth. "The Interpretation of Romans 6:7." In *Studiorum paulinorum congressus internationalis catholicus 1961*, 301-7. AnBib 17-18. 2 vols. Rome: Pontifical Biblical Institute Press, 1963.

Kertelge, Karl. "Der neue Lebenswandel nach Rö 6." In his *"Rechtfertigung" bei Paulus: Studien zur Struktur und zum Bedeutunggsgehalt des paulinischen Rechtfertigungsbegriffs*, 263-75. Münster: Aschendorff, 1966.

Klaar, Erich. "Röm 6,7: ὁ γὰρ ἀποθανὼν δεδικαίωται ἀπὸ τῆς ἁμαρτίας." *ZNW* 59 (1968): 131-34.

Klostergaard, Anders. "Shedding New Light on Paul's Understanding of Baptism: A Ritual-Theoretical Approach to Romans 6." *ST* 52 (1998): 3-28.

Koperski, Veronica. "Resurrection Terminology in Paul." In *Resurrection in the New Testament: Festschrift J. Lambrecht,* 265-81. Ed. Reimund Bieringer et al. BETL 165. Leuven: Leuven University Press, 2002.

Kuhn, Karl G. "Rm 6,7: ὁ γὰρ ἀποθανὼν δεδικαίωται ἀπὸ τῆς ἁμαρτίας." *ZNW* 30 (1931): 305-10.

Kuss, Otto. "Zu Röm 6,5a." *TGl* (1951): 430-37.

——. "Zur paulinischen und nachpaulinischen Tauflehre." *TGl* 42 (1932): 401-25.

Langevin, Paul-Émile. "Le Baptême dans la mort-résurrection: Exégèse de Rm 6,1-5." *ScEc* 17 (1965): 29-65.

Lawrence, Jonathan D. *Washing in Water: Trajectories of Ritual Bathing in the Hebrew Bible and Second Temple Literature.* SBLAB 23. Atlanta: Society of Biblical Literature, 2006.

Légasse, Simon. "Être baptisé dans la mort du Christ: Étude de Romains 6:1-14." *RB* 98 (1991): 544-59.

Lohse, Eduard. "Taufe und Rechtfertigung bei Paulus." In his *Die Einheit des Neues Testaments,* 228-44. ESTNT 1. Göttingen: Vandenhoeck & Ruprecht, 1973.

——. "Der Wandel der Christen im Zeichen der Auferstehung: Zur Begründung der Ethik im Römerbrief." In *Resurrection in the New Testament: Festschrift J. Lambrecht,* 315-22. Ed. Reimund Bieringer et al. BETL 165. Leuven: Leuven University Press, 2002.

Marcus, Joel. "Let God Arise and End the Reign of Sin: A Contribution to the Study of Pauline Parenesis." *Bib* 69 (1988): 386-95.

Marshall, I. Howard. "The Meaning of the Verb 'Baptize.'" In *Dimensions of Baptism: Biblical and Theological Studies,* 8-24. Ed. Stanley E. Porter and Anthony R. Cross. JSNTSup 234. Sheffield: Sheffield Academic Press, 2002.

Moo, Douglas J. "Exegetical Notes: Romans 6:1-14." *TJ* 3 (1982): 215-20.

Moore, George F. *Judaism in the First Centuries of the Christian Era.* 3 vols. Cambridge: Harvard University Press, 1927-30.

Morgan, Florence A. "Romans 6,5a: United to a Death like Christ's." *ETL* 59 (1983): 267-302.

Moule, C. F. D. "Death 'to Sin,' 'to Law,' and 'to the World': A Note on Certain Datives." In *Mélanges bibliques en homage au R. P. Béda Rigaux,* 367-75. Ed. Albert-Louis Descamps and R. P. Andre de Halleux. Gembloux: Duculot, 1970.

Mussner, Franz. "Taufe auf Christus." In his *Tod und Auferstehung: Fastenpredigten über Römerbrieftexte,* 46-57. Regensburg: Pustet, 1967.

——. "Zur paulinischen Tauflehre in Röm 6:1-6." In his *Praesentia Salutis: Gesammelte Studien zu Fragen und Themen des Neuen Testaments,* 189-96. Düsseldorf: Patmos, 1967.

Neugebauer, Fritz. *In Christus, EN ΧΡΙΣΤΩΙ: Eine Untersuchung zum paulinischen Glaubensverständnis.* Göttingen: Vandenhoeck & Ruprecht, 1961.

Nock, Arthur D. *Early Gentile Christianity and Its Hellenistic Background.* New York: Harper & Row, 1964.

Ostmeyer, Karl-Heinrich. *Taufe und Typos.* WUNT 2/118. Tübingen: J. C. B. Mohr (Paul Siebeck), 2000.

Pelser, G. M. M. "The Objective Reality of the Renewal of Life in Romans 6:-11." *Neot* 15 (1981): 101-17.

Perkins, Pheme. "Paul and Ethics." *Int* 38 (1984): 268-80.

Petersen, Norman R. "Pauline Baptism and 'Secondary Burial.'" *HTR* 79 (1986): 217-26.

Porter, Stanley E., Michael A. Hayes, and David Tombs, eds. *Resurrection*. Sheffield: Sheffield Academic Press, 1999.

Price, James L. "Romans 6:1-14." *Int* 4 (1980): 65-69.

Przybylski, Benno. "The Spirit: Paul's Journey to Jesus and Beyond." In *From Jesus to Paul: Studies in Honour of Francis Wright Beare*, 157-67. Ed. Peter Richardson and John C. Hurd. Waterloo: Wilfrid Laurier Press, 1984.

Purvis, Sally. "Following Paul: Some Notes on Ethics Then and Now." *WW* 16 (1996): 413-19.

Reese, James M. "The Thought Structure of Romans with Special Reference to Chapter 6." *CBQ* 55 (1982): 512-13.

Quanbeck, Warren A. "Justification and Baptism in the New Testament." *LW* 8 (1961): 8-15.

Sabou, Sorin. *Between Horror and Hope: Paul's Metaphorical Language of 'Death' in Romans 6:1-11*. PBM. Waynesboro: Paternoster Press, 2005.

Schelkle, Karl-Hermann. "Taufe und Tod: Zur Auslegung von Römer 6,1-11." In *Vom christlichen Mysterium: Gesammelte Arbeiten zum Gedächtnis von Odo Casel O.S.B.*, 9-21. Ed. Anton Mayer et al. Düsseldorf: Patmos, 1951.

Schlier, Heinrich. "Die Taufe nach dem 6. Kapitel des Römerbriefes." In his *Die Zeit der Kirche: Exegetische Aufsätze und Vorträge*, 47-56. 5th ed. Freiburg im Breisgau: Herder, 1972.

Schnackenburg, Rudolf. *Baptism in the Thought of St. Paul*. Oxford: Basil Blackwell, 1964.

———. "Der locus classicus Röm 6,1-11." In his *Das Heilsgeschehen bei der Taufe nach dem Apostel Paulus: Eine Studie zur paulinischen Theologie*, 26-56. München: Zink, 1950.

———. "Die umstrittene Wendung βαπτίζειν εἰς Χριστόν." In his *Das Heilsgeschehen bei der Taufe nach dem Apostel Paulus: Eine Studie zur paulinischen Theologie*, 18-23. München: Zink, 1950.

Scholem, Gershom. *Major Trends in Jewish Mysticism*. New York: Schocken Books, 1954.

Schrage, Wolfgang. "Ist die Kirche das 'Abbild seines Todes'? Zu Röm 6,5." In *Kirche: Festschrift für Günther Bornkamm zum 75. Geburtstag*, 205-19. Ed. Dieter Lührmann and Georg Strecker. Tübingen: J. C. B. Mohr (Paul Siebeck), 1980.

Scroggs, Robin. "Romans vi.7: Ο ΓΑΡ ΑΠΟΘΑΝΩΝ ΔΕΔΙΚΑΙΩΤΑΙ ΑΠΟ ΤΗΣ ΑΜΑΡΤΙΑΣ." *NTS* 10 (1963): 104-8.

Schweitzer, Albert. *The Mysticism of Paul the Apostle*. London: A. & C. Black, 1931; reprinted, Baltimore: Johns Hopkins University Press, 1998.

Schweizer, Eduard. "Dying and Rising with Christ." *NTS* 14 (1967-68): 1-14.

Steward, Roy A. "Engrafting: A Study in New Testament Symbolism and Baptismal Application." *EvQ* 50 (1978): 8-22.

Strecker, Georg. "Indicative and Imperative according to Paul." *BR* 35 (1987): 60-72.

Styler, G. M. "The Basis of Obligation in Paul's Christology and Ethics." In *Christ and Spirit in the New Testament: In Honour of Charles Francis Digby Moule*, 175-87. Ed.

Barnabas Lindars and Stephen S. Smalley. Cambridge: Cambridge University Press, 1973.

Talbert, Charles H. "Tracing Paul's Train of Thought in Romans 6–8." *RevExp* 100 (2003): 53-63.

Tanghe, Vincent. "Die Vorlage in Römer 6." *ETL* 73 (1997): 411-14.

Tannehill, Robert C. *Dying and Rising with Christ: A Study in Pauline Theology.* BZNW 32. Berlin: Alfred Töpelmann, 1967.

Thiering, Barbara E. "Qumran Initiation and New Testament Baptism." *NTS* 27 (1980-81): 615-31.

Thrall, Margaret E. "Paul's Understanding of Continuity between the Present Life and the Life of the Resurrection." In *Resurrection in the New Testament: Festschrift J. Lambrecht,* 283-300. Ed. Reimund Bieringer et al. BETL 165. Leuven: Leuven University Press, 2002.

Tobin, Thomas H. *Paul's Rhetoric in Its Contexts: The Argument of Romans.* Peabody: Hendrickson Publishers, 2004.

Tuckett, Christopher M. *Christology and the New Testament: Jesus and His Earliest Followers.* Louisville: Westminster John Knox Press, 2001.

Villiers, Jan de. "Adolf Deissmann: A Reappraisal of His Work, Especially His Views on the Mysticism of Paul." In *Paul and His Theology,* 393-422. PAST 3. Ed. Stanley E. Porter. Boston: E. J. Brill, 2006.

Wagner, Günter. *Pauline Baptism and the Pagan Mysteries: The Problem of the Pauline Doctrine of Baptism in Romans VI.1-11, in the Light of Its Religio-Historical "Parallels."* London: Oliver & Boyd, 1967.

Wedderburn, Alexander J. M. *Baptism and Resurrection: Studies in Pauline Theology against Its Graeco-Roman Background.* WUNT 44. Tübingen: J. C. B. Mohr (Paul Siebeck), 1987.

———. "Hellenistic Christian Traditions in Romans 6?" *NTS* 29 (1983): 337-55.

———. "Some Observations on Paul's Use of the Phrases 'in Christ' and 'with Christ.'" *JSNT* 25 (1985): 83-97.

———. "The Soteriology of the Mysteries and Pauline Baptismal Theology." *NovT* 29 (1987): 53-72.

Winandy, Jacques. "La mort de Jésus: Une morte au péché?" *ETL* 76 (2000): 433-34.

4.4. Free to Serve God as Slaves of Righteousness, 6:12-23

12*Therefore do not let sin reign in your mortal bodies to obey their passions.* 13*Do not present your members as instruments of unrighteousness to sin, but present yourselves to God as having come to life from the dead and your members as instruments of righteousness to God.* 14*For sin will have no dominion over you, because you are not under law but under grace.*

15*What then? Should we sin because we are not under law but under grace? By no means!* 16*Do you not know that, if you present yourselves to anyone as obe-*

dient slaves, you are slaves of the one you obey, either of sin resulting in death or of obedience resulting in righteousness? 17But thanks be to God that, although you were slaves of sin, you have become obedient from the heart to the standard of teaching to which you were entrusted, 18and having been set free from sin, you have become slaves of righteousness. 19(I am speaking in human terms because of the weakness of your flesh.) For just as you once presented your members as slaves to impurity and increasing lawlessness, so now present your members as slaves to righteousness leading to sanctification.

20For when you were slaves of sin, you were free in regard to righteousness. 21So what benefit did you gain, then, from the things of which you are now ashamed? For the end of those things is death. 22But now, since you have been freed from sin and have become enslaved to God, the benefit you gain is sanctification, and the end is eternal life. 23For the wages of sin is death, but the gift of God is eternal life in Christ Jesus our Lord.

Notes on the Text and Translation

6:12 Paul begins with a strange mixture of singular and plural terms: ὑμῶν ("your," plural), σῶμα ("body," singular), αὐτοῦ ("its," singular), and ἐπιθυμίαι ("passions," plural). Since he is clearly speaking to the community as a whole, as the subsequent plurals show, it is appropriate to transform the singulars into plurals ("your bodies . . . their passions"), as in some major versions (RSV, NRSV, and ESV). Others (NIV and NET) let the singular "body" and "its" stand ("your body . . . its desires").

Some major witnesses (including 𝔓⁴⁶ and D) have αὐτῇ ("it," referring to ἁμαρτία, "sin"), but ἐπιθυμίαις αὐτοῦ ("its desires") is attested more strongly by others (including ℵ, A, B, and C). The Textus Receptus conflates the two (along with the insertion of ἐν, "in") to read αὐτῇ ἐν ταῖς ἐπιθυμίαις αὐτοῦ, which is reflected in the KJV reading: "it in the lusts thereof." The reading ἐπιθυμίαις αὐτοῦ ("its desires") is to be preferred.[170]

6:17 The expression τύπον διδαχῆς is translated in various ways: "form of doctrine" (KJV), "standard of teaching" (RSV and ESV), "form of teaching" (ASV, NIV, and NRS), and "pattern of teaching" (NET). The term τύπος can be translated by a wide range of words: "type," "pattern," "form," "mark," "image," "content," "model," "character," and more.[171] In the present context the term has to do with content, not simply the "type" of teaching, for it has to do with some-

---

170. B. Metzger, *TCGNT* 454.
171. LSJ 1835 (τύπος); BDAG 1019-20 (τύπος). For Rom 6:17, BDAG suggests "pattern of teaching."

thing with which the readers are acquainted and to which they have given their assent. While there are other possibilities, "standard of teaching" may offer the best rendering of the phrase.

General Comment

The section is dominated by exhortation, and second person address ("you" and "your," plural) is both explicit and plentiful. That does not mean that Paul is carrying on an argument with the Christian community at Rome, or even with some actual opponent there. In fact, he declares at 6:17 that his readers are "obedient from the heart to the standard of teaching" to which they had been entrusted, the common tradition of belief and behavior of the Christian faith. Making use of hortatory language, he makes the case for his understanding of the life of faith, thinking that there will be agreement with him in Rome.

Detailed Comment

6:12-14 Although those who have been baptized into Christ, and consequently into his death, have been set free from the power of sin (6:7) and are enabled "to walk in newness of life" (6:4), it is still possible for sin to "reign" in their lives, if it is allowed to do so. The lives of believers are therefore always perilous. Although they belong to Christ and have been transferred from being under the powers of the present age to being under Christ's lordship (Gal 1:4), that does not mean that they are free from the spiritual limitations that exist or from bodily desires that are common to all people. Paul says, therefore, that one must resist the power of sin. He does not speak of "sins" (plural), but "sin" as a power that can "reign" in anyone's life, unless there is some means of resistance. The "body" of which Paul speaks includes the physical aspect of a person, but it cannot be reduced to that. It is the "self" within the complex of human relationships of earthly existence.[172] As such, the body is "mortal," and that means that it is subject to all the conditions of mortality. That includes death (cf. 8:11) but also all those human weaknesses that make a person prone to selfish desires and behaviors.[173] Therefore, if "sin" is able to reign within anyone, it will lead that person to obey, or become subject to, those passions that are common to all, but which are controlled by some, not by others. In light of what is said here,

---

172. Cf. Eduard Schweizer, "σῶμα," *EDNT* 3:323.

173. R. Bultmann, *Theology of the New Testament*, 1:197; R. Gundry, *Sōma in Biblical Theology*, 29-31.

if sin reigns, no one can control his or her passions; on the contrary, the various passions will have the upper hand and be in control.

Paul goes on to elaborate. He makes a contrast. Speaking directly to his readers, he says in effect: "You have a choice. You can either present your members to sin, or you can present yourselves and your members to God." In speaking that way, Paul does not set up an exact parallel. The implication is that one cannot present one's "members" to God without first presenting oneself to God. In a strict sense, the word for "members" (τὰ μέλη) refers to parts of the human body, including feet, hands, eyes, and ears (cf. 1 Cor 12:14-24), but it need not be limited to them in this particular case.[174] It can refer to the whole range of human capacities,[175] for in this context the members and the self are intimately interrelated. There are two possibilities for the use of those capacities. One can give them over to "sin" (as a power) to serve as "instruments of unrighteousness" (ὅπλα ἀδικίας). But that is not the way of the life in Christ. The other way is for the readers of the letter to present themselves "as having come to life from the dead" and their members to God to serve as "instruments of righteousness" (ὅπλα δικαιοσύνης). The expression "as having come to life from the dead" is rather singular for Paul; he does not use anything quite like it elsewhere. But it conveys the viewpoint that has been finding its expression earlier in this chapter, i.e., that the believer who has come out of the water of baptism has been incorporated into the crucified and risen Christ, is capable of walking in newness of life (6:4), and is "dead to sin, but alive to God in Christ Jesus" (6:11).

The expression "no longer" at 6:13 in the NRSV ("No longer present your members . . .") has no basis in the Greek text. It implies a contrast, making Paul say that right up into the present time the Roman Christians have in fact been offering their members to sin. The probable basis for the translation is Paul's discussion in 6:17-23 of slavery to sin in the past. But the NRSV misses a nuance. Paul exhorts his readers afresh at 6:13, making no judgment about their present condition in regard to this whole matter. In fact, he goes on to say at 6:17 that his readers are obedient from the heart to the Christian gospel and way of life.

Paul concludes this little section with the astonishing claim that sin (as a power) will have no dominion over his readers since they are under grace, not law. What is said in the latter clause makes the former possible. Being baptized into Christ, believers are "under grace," for they are Christ's own. That is clear enough. But to be "not under law" is a radical departure for anyone who has been raised in the Jewish tradition. For Paul, however, all is a matter of either/

---

174. The NIV makes such a limitation by its unfortunate rendering: "the parts of your body."

175. Cf. C. Cranfield, *Romans,* 317-18.

or. One is either under the Torah, which Paul considers a way of life that cannot bring certainty of salvation but instead brings accusation of sin (7:7-11; 1 Cor 15:56), or in Christ, a way of life that relies upon the grace of God alone.

But how can the new situation of being in Christ make it possible for sin not to have dominion? The response is that Christ has dominion over one's life. Moreover, through baptism the Christian belongs to Christ and to his destiny. Although there may in fact be instances of sin making inroads into the life of the believer, ultimately that person shares in the destiny of the resurrected Lord. That is something on which one can rely. Paul uses the language of promise, saying that sin will not be lord; the law will not be one's overlord either. The one who is in Christ is "under grace," free from the reign of the law in one's life that leads to a foreboding sense of ultimate condemnation in God's judgment, and free from the power of sin.

While it is true that, for Paul, there is a paradox to Christian life in that the believer is set free from the power of sin but is never considered by him to be without sin, it is possible that if he had thought of it, he might have maintained the Reformation doctrine of *simul iustus et pecccator,* i.e., that the Christian is "at the same time justified and a sinner."[176] What is more certain, however, is that Paul thinks in terms of another *simul,* and that has to do with the two ages. The person who is in Christ has been transferred from the old era of sin and death into the new era of righteousness and life; at the same time, the power of the old age still assails that person. It may be accurate to say, then, that the one who is in Christ is *simul novus et vetus* ("at the same time new and old"); i.e., one actually belongs to Christ and his destiny, but also lives in the old world of sin and death, which are still present, are effective in thwarting the life of righteousness, and must be overcome.

6:15-19 Paul resumes with a question prompted by what has just been concluded in 6:14. The question is not unlike the one in 6:1 and, like it, is posed in the style of diatribe, rejecting an incorrect conclusion. If we are under grace, should we sin? The response is predictable in light of what has gone before: "By no means!" (μὴ γένοιτο). On this expression, see the exegesis of 3:4. But Paul does not leave the matter there. He makes an argument to back it up. The argu-

---

176. As maintained by C. K. Barrett, *Romans,* 120, and J. Ziesler, *Romans,* 192. The expression itself was used by Martin Luther in his lectures on Galatians in 1535; for text, cf. *LuthW* 26:232; cf. also *LuthW* 27:231, where he uses a similar phrase as early as 1519 in reference to Job in the OT. Cf. the excursus, "Simul justus et peccator," in E. Lohse, *Römer,* 225-27, maintaining that it appears within the structure of Paul's theology, and N. Dahl, "In What Sense Is the Baptized Person 'simul justus et peccator' according to the New Testament?" 231: "According to Paul the baptized person is at one and the same time righteous and a sinner, because his righteousness is and remains the 'alien' righteousness of faith. . . . The baptized person remains carnal; he is exposed to temptation and sin; and indeed he does this all too often."

ment is about the consequences of being enslaved either to "sin" or to "obedience," which implies obedience to God (although it is not said explicitly). The former results in death, and the other in righteousness.

Paul implies in 6:17 that members of the Christian community at Rome had at one time been "slaves of sin." In saying that, he must refer primarily (but not only) to the majority of Christians there who came out of Gentile backgrounds. Nevertheless, he says that they have become obedient to the "standard of teaching" (τύπον διδαχῆς) to which they had been entrusted. Interestingly, Paul does not say that that "standard of teaching" had been entrusted to them, as though they are custodians of it, but that they had been entrusted to it, resulting in their having become committed to it. The way Paul expresses the matter, there is a "standard of teaching" that is common to all believers, and to which they give assent.[177] Persons are delivered over to it, rather than the other way around, which takes place in catechesis. Moreover, Paul declares that his readers have "become obedient from the heart" to this standard. They have therefore given their wholehearted assent to it. They have done so freely, turning from their former slavery to sin to the freedom of obedient assent.

Once more (6:18) Paul speaks of the community of believers as "set free from sin," an assertion that he has made before (6:7, 14) and will make again (6:22; 8:2). Those who have died through baptism are no longer under the power of sin, for they are under grace and share the destiny of the risen Christ. Moreover, since they have been transferred by faith and baptism from slavery under sin to live under the lordship of Christ, they have become slaves of righteousness. No longer slaves of sin but slaves of righteousness, they seek to please God.

What Paul says at the outset of 6:19 appears to be a parenthetical explanation. The expression ἀνθρώπινον λέγω can be translated literally as "I speak humanly" or, more fitting in English, "I speak in human terms," i.e., "as people do in daily life."[178] In saying that, Paul must be referring to his use of slavery as a metaphor, even though he recognizes that it may be inadequate.[179] He provides his readers with a reason for his use of metaphorical language: "because of

177. U. Wilckens, *Römer*, 2:35-36; J. Fitzmyer, *Romans*, 449-50; B. Byrne, *Romans*, 206; R. Jewett, *Romans*, 418-19; E. Lohse, *Römer*, 200-201; contra J. Dunn, *Romans*, 343-44, for whom the "pattern of teaching" is Christ. According to Leonhard Goppelt, "τύπος," *TDNT* 8:250, the expression means teaching as a mold or norm that shapes a person. Somewhat similarly, R. Gagnon, "Heart of Wax and a Teaching That Stamps," 687, suggests: "the imprint stamped by teaching, to which (imprint) you were handed over."

178. BDAG 80 (ἀνθρώπινος, a).

179. U. Wilckens, *Römer*, 2:37-38; J. Dunn, *Romans*, 345; B. Byrne, *Romans*, 206; according to C. Cranfield, 325, J. Fitzmyer, *Romans*, 450, and R. Jewett, *Romans*, 419-20, Paul makes an apology here for using the metaphor, but why then does Paul go on so boldly to speak of his reason for doing so (the weakness of his readers' flesh), since that would only compound the alleged offense?

the weakness of your flesh (σάρξ)." The term σάρξ ("flesh"), so important for Paul's understanding of human existence (a term used 72 times in his letters, 26 times in Romans alone), is used here for the first time in this letter. When used in a theological sense by Paul, the term refers to that realm of human existence that is hospitable to sin, the world, and any other forces opposed to God.[180] It seems strange, then, for Paul to say that he uses metaphorical language because of the weakness of the flesh of his readers. One should not be surprised, therefore, that modern versions of the NT tone the expression down somewhat by using other phrases, such as "because of your natural limitations" (RSV, NRSV, and ESV) or "because you are weak in your natural selves" (NIV). Yet it is plausible that, for Paul, one's understanding of the matters discussed in this section of the letter can be misunderstood apart from his making sharp contrasts — either persons are slaves of sin or they are slaves of righteousness. The "flesh" is always ready to make concessions and compromises.[181] But that cannot be done. And so Paul follows up with an exhortation, extending the use of the metaphor of slavery. The past is over; the present is a new day: "For just as you once presented your members as slaves to impurity and increasing lawlessness, so now present your members as slaves to righteousness leading to sanctification." Moreover, Paul uses an additional metaphor — one that he has used also at 6:13 — i.e., the term μέλη ("members"). Ordinarily the term refers to members or limbs of the human body. But in the present instance, as at 6:13, it is used to refer to the whole range of human capacities. The use of all of one's capacities in slavery to righteousness leads εἰς ἁγιασμόν ("to sanctification"). The term ἁγιασμός can have a variety of meanings, such as "holiness," "consecration," or "sanctification." Moreover, it can refer either to the process of becoming holy or to the state of being holy, i.e., the end result.[182] In the present instance the term is used in contrast to ἀκαθαρσίᾳ καὶ τῇ ἀνομίᾳ εἰς τὴν ἀνομίαν (literally, "to impurity and to lawlessness unto lawlessness" or "to impurity and increasing lawlessness"), a process of going from one stage to another that is worse. Paul must intend, therefore, to have sanctification as a process in mind,[183] and the term for "sanctification" must have a moral sense to it in this case. The same kind of contrast is made at 1 Thessalonians 4:7: "For God did not call us to impurity but in holiness (ἐπὶ ἀκαθαρσίᾳ ἀλλ' ἐν ἁγιασμῷ)." In another place in Paul's writings sanctification (or being sanctified) is a state of being for those who are baptized into Christ, and it is coterminous with justification: "But you were

180. Alexander Sand, "σάρξ," *EDNT* 3:231.
181. It is not sufficient, then, to say that by means of the phrase Paul refers "primarily to intellectual difficulty," as maintained by B. Byrne, *Romans*, 206.
182. BDAG 10 (ἁγιασμός).
183. C. Cranfield, *Romans*, 327; D. Moo, *Romans*, 405; contra J. Murray, *Romans*, 1:234 (n. 21).

washed, you were sanctified (ἡγιάσθητε), you were justified (ἐδικαιώθητε) in the name of the Lord Jesus Christ and in the Spirit of our God" (1 Cor 6:11). In the present instance (Rom 6:19) the term for "sanctification" carries with it the sense of living out one's baptismal identity in a struggle against immoral behavior, "the daily task of the living out of justification."[184]

6:20-23 Going back to the imagery of slavery to sin (6:6, 12, 16-17), Paul reminds his readers that when they were in such a condition, they were free in one sense. They were "free in regard to righteousness (δικαιοσύνη)"; i.e., they did not give righteousness any serious attention. It had no claim upon them; it was not something for which to strive, not like the striving that a slave does for a master. But freedom from righteousness was actually an illusory freedom, not freedom at all, for it all leads to death, not to an abundant life.

By way of contrast, at 6:22 Paul opens the final verses of this section with the adversative νυνὶ δέ ("but now"), as at 3:21. Those who are "in Christ" have been "freed from sin and have become enslaved to God." That is true freedom, for the result of the new enslavement to God is "sanctification" (ἁγιασμός), "and the end is eternal life (τὸ δὲ τέλος ζωὴν αἰώνιον)." In this context "sanctification" is conceived of as a state of being holy, not as a process (contra what it was at 6:19). It is the proleptic eschatological holiness that is bestowed upon those who are enslaved to God. And the "end" of all that — the word τέλος meaning "end," not "goal," in this place[185] — is eternal life. The brief sentence stands in contrast to what was said in 6:21: τὸ γὰρ τέλος ἐκείνων θάνατος ("for the end of those things is death"). The final verse (6:23) recapitulates what has been said. A contrast is made between what sin and God, respectively, can confer. The one is death; the other is eternal life for those who are in Christ.

The question needs to be asked whether Paul expected ethical perfection from the one who had been baptized and incorporated into the community of faith in Christ. It has been said that for Paul, since Christians have been liberated from the bondage to sin, "henceforth they were to remain pure and blameless while awaiting the Lord's coming."[186] But what can such a statement mean? Did Paul actually expect his readers to be pure and blameless? There are instances where he uses that terminology. He informs the Philippians that he

---

184. E. Käsemann, *Romans*, 183. The ethical implications are also stressed by R. Bultmann, "The Problem of Ethics in Paul," 213 (the justified person "is therefore also subject to the moral imperative"); J. Dunn, *Romans*, 347; J. Fitzmyer, *Romans*, 451; B. Byrne, *Romans*, 206.

185. Hans Hübner, "τέλος," *EDNT* 3:348 (regarding Rom 6:21-22, "the result emerging necessarily from a certain manner of existence"); C. Cranfield, *Romans*, 328; J. Fitzmyer, *Romans*, 452; J. Dunn, *Romans*, 349 ("the end result"); D. Moo, *Romans*, 407; E. Lohse, *Römer*, 203. BDAG 999 (τέλος, 3) suggests on Rom 6:21-22: "the final *goal* toward which persons and things are striving, or the *outcome* or *destiny* which awaits them in accordance with their nature."

186. E. P. Sanders, *Paul, the Law, and the Jewish People*, 106.

prays for them, hoping that their love may overflow with knowledge and insight "to help [them] determine what is best, so that in the day of Christ [they] may be pure and blameless (εἰλικρινεῖς καὶ ἀπρόσκοποι)" (1:10). Elsewhere he speaks of the strength that Christ supplies, so that the Corinthians may be blameless (ἀνεγκλήτους) at the coming of the Lord (1 Cor 1:8). And at still other places he exhorts his readers to be blameless (ἄμεμπτοι) until the Lord's coming (Phil 2:15; 1 Thess 3:15; 5:23). Nevertheless, it is not certain that Paul expected believers to be actually "pure and blameless" in an empirical sense within this world and in the presence of God. The point of being set free from sin is that a person is no longer under its power. Then, out from under its power, one can fight against it. The struggle against it must go on. It is precisely because sinful behavior continues that Paul admonishes his readers to persevere in faith and obedience. He calls upon them to examine themselves (1 Cor 11:28; 2 Cor 13:5), which implies that imperfections and transgressions occur in the life of the believer. He also says that they should not be overconfident in their own strength or wisdom (1 Cor 10:12; cf. Rom 12:3, 16; Gal 5:26); not be judgmental or denigrating of others (Rom 14:10); not be envious of one another (Gal 5:26); and not repay evil for evil (Rom 12:17; 1 Thess 5:15). He calls upon the Corinthians to cease being factious (1 Cor 11:17-19). And he encourages instead the practice of goodness (Rom 12:9, 17; 1 Thess 5:15, 21), mutual upbuilding (Rom 14:19; 1 Cor 14:12), generosity (Rom 12:13), and exhibiting the fruits of the Spirit (Gal 5:22-26). It is likely, too, that when Paul speaks of the tortured ego and its inability to do what is right (Rom 7:18-19), he is speaking of the life of the believer. (See the exegesis of that passage.) All of these references to human behavior are what one can expect while life goes on in the world as anyone knows it, including Paul, who seems to have some misgivings even about his own righteousness (1 Cor 4:3-5; Phil 3:12-16).[187] The apostle works in a dialectical manner:

> You are free from the power of sin (6:14, 22).
> In fact, you have become slaves of righteousness (6:18-19).
> But sinful behavior is still a possibility (6:15).
> Therefore withstand the power of sin (6:12-13).

The struggle continues as long as life is lived within the confines of this world and within the limits of human capability, albeit aided by the Spirit. Being freed from the power of sin, however, the believer baptized into Christ is ultimately secure and can expect final salvation due to the grace of God.[188]

---

187. M. Winninge, *Sinners and the Righteous*, 333-34.
188. Cf. J. Gundry Volf, *Paul and Perseverance*, 283-87.

BIBLIOGRAPHY

Agersnap, Søren. "Rom 6,12 og det paulinske imperative." *DTT* 43 (1980): 36-47.

Beare, Francis W. "On the Interpretation of Romans vi.17." *NTS* 5 (1958-59): 206-10.

Bjerkelund, Carl J. "'Nach menschlicher Weise rede ich': Funktion und Sinn des paulinischen Ausdrucks." *ST* 26 (1972): 63-100.

Bultmann, Rudolf. "The Problem of Ethics in Paul." In *Understanding Paul's Ethics: Twentieth-Century Approaches*, 195-216. Ed. Brian S. Rosner. Grand Rapids: Wm. B. Eerdmans, 1995.

———. *Theology of the New Testament.* 2 vols. New York: Charles Scribner's Sons, 1951-55.

Dahl, Nils A. "In What Sense Is the Baptized Person 'simul justus et peccator' according to the New Testament?" *LW* 9 (1962): 219-31.

Gagnon, Robert A. J. "Heart of Wax and a Teaching That Stamps: ΤΥΠΟΣ ΔΙΔΑΧΗΣ (Rom 6:17b) Once More." *JBL* 112 (1993): 667-87.

Gundry, Robert H. Sōma *in Biblical Theology: With Emphasis on Pauline Anthropology.* SNTSMS 29. New York: Cambridge University Press, 1976.

Gundry Volf, Judith M. *Paul and Perseverance: Staying In and Falling Away.* WUNT 2/37. Tübingen: J. C. B. Mohr (Paul Siebeck), 1990; reprinted, Louisville: Westminster John Knox Press, 1991.

Hagen, Wayne H. "Two Deutero-Pauline Glosses in Romans 6." *ExpTim* 92 (1980-81): 364-67.

Käsemann, Ernst. "Römer 6,19-23." In his *Exegetische Versuche und Besinnungen*, 1:263-66. 2d ed. 2 vols. Göttingen: Vandenhoeck & Ruprecht, 1960.

Kürzinger, Josef. "Τύπος διδαχῆς und der Sinn von Röm 6,17f." *Bib* 39 (1958): 156-76.

Marcus, Joel. "'Under the Law': The Background of a Pauline Expression." *CBQ* 63 (2001): 72-83.

Michael, J. Hugh. "The Text of Romans 6:13 in the Chester Beatty Papyrus." *ExpTim* 49 (1937-38): 235.

Moffatt, James. "The Interpretation of Romans 6:17-18." *JBL* 48 (1929): 233-38.

Sanders, E. P. *Paul, the Law, and the Jewish People.* Philadelphia: Fortress Press, 1983.

Schweizer, Eduard. "Die Sünde in den Gliedern." In *Abraham unser Vater: Juden und Christen im Gespräch über die Bibel: Festschrift für Otto Michel zum 60. Geburtstag*, 437-39. Ed. Otto Betz et al. AGAJU 5. Leiden: E. J. Brill, 1963.

Trimaille, Michel. "Encore le 'typos didachès' de Romains 6,17." In *La Vie de la parole: De l'Ancien au Nouveau Testament: Études d'exégèse et d'herméneutique bibliques offertes à Pierre Grelot*, 269-80. Paris: Desclée, 1987.

Winninge, Mikael. *Sinners and the Righteous: A Comparative Study of the Psalms of Solomon and Paul's Letters.* ConBNT 26. Stockholm: Almqvist & Wiksell, 1995.

4.5. The Law and Christ, 7:1-6

1*Or do you not know, brothers and sisters — for I am speaking to those who know the law — that the law has authority over a person as long as that person* lives? 2For a married woman is bound by law to her husband while he is living, but if her husband dies, she is released from the law concerning her husband. 3Consequently, if she is joined to another man while her husband is alive, she will be called an adulteress; but if her husband dies, she is free from that law, and if she is joined to another man, she is not an adulteress.

4In the same way, my brothers and sisters, you also were put to death to the law through the body of Christ, in order that you might belong to another, to him who has been raised from the dead, in order that we may bear fruit for God. 5For when we were in the flesh, our sinful passions, aroused by the law, were at work in our members in order to bear fruit for death. 6But now, since we have died to that by which we were bound, we have been released from the law, so that we may serve in the newness of the Spirit and not in the obsolescence of the letter.

Notes on the Text and Translation

7:2 The expression ὕπανδρος γυνή can be translated as "a married woman." The adjective ὕπανδρος means, literally, being "under the power of or subject to a man," and so "married."[189] It appears only here in the NT, but it appears four times in the LXX (Prov 6:24, 29; Sir 9:9; 41:23) where, combined with various forms of γυνή, it means a "married" woman.[190]

7:4 The translation "you were put to death" is based on Paul's use of the aorist passive verb (ἐθανατώθητε). Major English versions have "you died" (RSV, NIV, NRSV); an exception is the NAB. The aorist passive highlights the death inflicted upon the believer through incorporation into the body of Christ.

The Greek clause εἰς τὸ γενέσθαι ὑμᾶς ἑτέρῳ is translated here as "*in order that* you may belong to another," expressing purpose, although modern versions (RSV, NRSV, ESV, and NET) typically translate the clause as "*so that* you may belong to another" or the like, expressing result. Although the use of εἰς τό and the infinitive can express either purpose or result,[191] the fact that the clause preceding speaks of being put to death speaks in favor of purpose.

7:6 The first two clauses have been transposed for ease of following the thoughts expressed.

189. BDAG 1029 (ὕπανδρος).

190. P. Spitaler, "Analogical Reasoning in Romans 7:2-4," 721-22, seeks to broaden the adjective to encompass legal and hierarchical possibilities beyond "married." For more on this, see the exegesis.

191. BDF 207 (§402, 2).

General Comment

It is not immediately obvious why Paul now (in chapter 7 as a whole) turns to the topic of the law. But in fact it is incumbent upon him to do so. In chapter 6 he had gone to great lengths to maintain that the one who is baptized into Christ has been set free from the bondage to sin. In addition, he maintained that the freedom gained does not free a person from moral obligations. The person who has been baptized and has become a member of the body of Christ must oppose the power of sin and its consequent behaviors as long as he or she resides in the present age. It is expected that such a person will be devoted to a life of righteousness (6:18-19) and a common and recognizable standard of teaching that has been received (6:17).

But all of that begs a question. How does a believer in Christ live in righteousness and in opposition to sin? What guidance can be found? What is the standard? The quickest and simplest response would be that the standard to follow is the law of Moses. If one is a Jewish Christian, one should continue observing the ancestral law. If one is a Gentile Christian, one should adopt the law (at least its moral teachings) as the basis for a life of righteousness.

The quick and easy answer, however, is not Paul's. He has already said concerning the Christians at Rome: "you are not under law but under grace" (6:14). That claim complicates matters tremendously. Since he is a son of the people of Israel, it is impossible for Paul to claim here or anywhere else that the law of Moses was given for no purpose at all or that it fails to teach righteousness. What he has to do, then, is to maintain that the law has had an important function in the history of salvation and that "the law is holy, and the commandment [concerning covetousness] is holy, just, and good" (7:12). He begins his discussion to show that the law of Moses has no abiding authority in the life of the Christian, and he does so by using an analogy.

Detailed Comment

7:1 Here and elsewhere (already at 7:4 again) Paul addresses his readers as "brothers and sisters." For comment on the term, see the exegesis at 1:13.

The question "Do you not know?" is familiar from 6:3, where Paul takes up the basis for what follows in 6:3-25: "Do you not know that as many of us as have been baptized into Christ Jesus were baptized into his death?" The question introduces a solemn pronouncement both there and here.[192] When he goes

---

192. Cf. also Rom 2:4; more commonly Paul asserts that he does not want his readers to be ignorant, as at Rom 1:13; 11:25; 1 Cor 10:1; 12:1; 1 Thess 4:13.

on to speak of "those who know the law," that does not mean that he is addressing only Jewish Christians in what follows. Paul can assume that his readers, whether of Jewish or Gentile background, would have enough knowledge of the law of Moses to follow what he goes on to say.[193] He then gets to his point: "the law has authority over a person as long as that person lives." That is a truism no matter what system of law one is talking about. But here "the law" (ὁ νόμος) has the specific meaning of the law of Moses.[194] Although the issue was debated (at least within rabbinic Judaism) as to whether the law has an abiding significance in the world to come,[195] the meaning is clear here. Once a person has died in this age, he or she is not subject to the law.

7:2-4 Paul makes use of an analogy from laws concerning marriage. The analogy does not actually work if one is looking for strict parallels between the two parts,[196] but one can discern from it what Paul tries to argue. The point is that, just as a widowed woman is no longer bound by the law of Moses concerning her husband, but is free to marry again, the Christian is not bound by the law of Moses to keep its precepts but is free to belong to Christ. Paul does not refer to any explicit precept in the law of Moses concerning marriage. But according to the law of Moses, while a husband can divorce his wife (Deut 24:1-4), nowhere is there a provision for a wife to divorce her husband, so by implication she is bound to her husband as long as he lives (unless he divorces her). If he is still alive and she lives with another man (ἐὰν γένηται ἀνδρὶ ἑτέρῳ), she will be considered an adulteress (7:3), Paul says, echoing in part language from the law being cited (καὶ ἀπελθοῦσα γένηται ἀνδρὶ ἑτέρῳ, "and if she goes and becomes another man's wife," Deut 24:2). It is quite possible, however, that Paul refers here to "an apostolic marriage law,"[197] according to which a woman cannot divorce her husband (1 Cor 7:10: "To the married I give this command — not I but the Lord — that the wife should not separate from her husband").

193. R. Brändle and E. Stegemann, "The Formation of the First 'Christian Congregations' in Rome," 124.

194. On this there is agreement by a wide range of interpreters, e.g., C. Cranfield, *Romans*, 333; U. Wilckens, *Römer*, 2:64; J. Fitzmyer, *Romans*, 456; J. Dunn, *Romans*, 359; B. Byrne, *Romans*, 213; D. Moo, *Romans*, 412; T. Schreiner, *Romans*, 358; E. Lohse, *Römer*, 206; R. Jewett, *Romans*, 430; W. Diezinger, "Unter Toten Freigeworden," 268-98; contra E. Käsemann, *Romans*, 187 ("the legal order" prevailing at Rome).

195. W. D. Davies, *Torah in the Messianic Age and/or the Age to Come.*

196. As discussed by H. Räisänen, *Paul and the Law*, 61-62; and in detail by J. A. Little, "Paul's Use of Analogy," 82-90.

197. P. Tomson, "What Did Paul Mean by 'Those Who Know the Law'? (Rom 7.1)," 580. Tomson maintains that the "apostolic marriage law" would have "had its origins in the teachings of Jesus." The basis for that could be Mark 10:12, which assumes that a woman can divorce her husband. But that verse may be an accommodation to Roman law rather than a saying of Jesus. Cf. A. Hultgren, *Jesus and His Adversaries*, 119-23.

Necessarily, in his use of the analogy, Paul's argument is limited to the experience of the Jewish person who becomes a Christian through baptism:

> Marital history of a woman according to law:
>> A woman is bound to her husband until *his* death;
>>> then she is free to be bound to another.

> History of the Christian formerly under the law:
>> You were bound to the law until your incorporation into Christ,
>>> *your* death;
>> now you are free to be bound to Christ.

There have been attempts to correct the problem of an otherwise unsuccessful analogy. One way is to raise the question regarding the translation and consequent interpretation of the first clause of 7:2a (ἡ γὰρ ὕπανδρος γυνὴ τῷ ζῶντι ἀνδρὶ δέδεται νόμῳ). The question is: To whom or to what is the married woman bound? Is it to her husband (τῷ ζῶντι ἀνδρὶ δέδεται, "bound to the husband while he is living")? Or is it to the law (νόμῳ, "bound to the law" regarding her husband)? The former is stated or implied in major versions of the NT (ASV, NAB, NET, RSV, NIV, NRSV), but the latter has been proposed, resulting in this translation about the woman: she is "bound to the law by way of the man who is alive."[198] The advantage of such a translation is that, according to it, the woman is "bound to the law" (not the husband), and it would make an analogy between the outcome of a change in circumstances in each case. The married woman is bound to the law until her husband dies, and the Christian who has been under the law has been bound to the law until baptism. In this way, being "bound to the law" is parallel in the two cases, even if the changes of circumstances are not, except for the "until" ("until her husband dies"//"until baptism").

Nevertheless, the simplest and most likely reading is that the first dative (τῷ ζῶντι ἀνδρί, "to the husband while he is living") is the direct object of the verb δέδεται (literally, "has been bound"),[199] and that the second dative (νόμῳ, "by law") is instrumental,[200] resulting in the translation: "for a married woman is bound by law to her husband while he is living." Moreover, what follows in 7:2b ("but if her husband dies, she is released from the law concerning her hus-

---

198. P. Spitaler, "Analogical Reasoning in Romans 7:2-4," 717, 734 (with discussion of the syntax on pp. 726-34).

199. On the use of the dative for a direct object, cf. A. T. Robinson, *A Grammar of the Greek New Testament in the Light of Historical Research*, 5th ed. (New York: Harper & Brothers, 1931), 539-41.

200. On the instrumental dative, cf. BDF 104 (§195, 2).

band")[201] confirms that translation; she is free from her obligation to her husband and can marry again. Finally, the idea that a woman is bound to her husband throughout his lifetime is said forthrightly (and in similar language) by Paul at 1 Corinthians 7:39: γυνὴ δέδεται ἐφ’ ὅσον χρόνον ζῇ ὁ ἀνὴρ αὐτῆς ("a woman is bound to her husband as long as he lives"). In both of these verses (Rom 7:2; 1 Cor 7:39) Paul states what would have been familiar in Jewish tradition, as codified later in the Mishnah: "[The married woman] acquires her freedom by a bill of divorce or by the death of her husband."[202]

It is self-evident that a person who has died is free from observing the law.[203] Paul says that the death of the believer is through the body of Christ (διὰ τοῦ σώματος τοῦ Χριστοῦ). This is the first time that he uses the term "body of Christ" in this letter, but not the last (cf. 12:5), and he has used it previously in his letters as a primary image for the church.[204] The term has received an enormous amount of scholarly attention and will be treated more fully in the exegesis of 12:5 and in an appendix ("The Church as the Body of Christ in the Letters of Paul"). At this point, however, when Paul speaks of the death of a believer "through the body of Christ," he does not use the expression in an ecclesial sense.[205] It has an instrumental function. In baptism the believer is joined to the body of the crucified Christ and, being incorporated into him, the believer has died to the law, free to belong to Christ and his destiny.

Paul switches from second person plural "you" to first person plural "we" as he concludes the sentence, apparently because he, too, belongs to the body of Christ. In any case, all this, he says, has a purpose in the larger scheme of things. That is that "we" may bear fruit for God. The expression concerning fruit-bearing is familiar in both the OT and elsewhere in the NT.[206] It signifies doing good. But the basis for doing good is not a matter of keeping the law. Doing good in analogy to fruit-bearing is a matter of expressing outwardly what is within: a good tree bears good fruit (cf. the Q saying, Matt 7:18//Luke 6:43).

7:5-6 Who is the "we" of these two verses? It appears that Paul simply

---

201. In the phrase ἀπὸ τοῦ νόμου τοῦ ἀνδρός Paul uses the objective genitive: "from the law about the husband"; cf. James H. Moulton, Wilbert F. Howard, and Nigel Turner, *A Grammar of New Testament Greek,* 4 vols. (Edinburgh: T&T Clark, 1949-63), 3:212.

202. *M. Qidd.* 1.1; quoted from *The Mishnah,* ed. Herbert Danby (Oxford: Oxford University Press, 1933), 321.

203. The obvious is stated in *b. Shab.* 30a: "Once a man dies, he becomes free of the Torah and good deeds"; quoted from *BabT* (tractate *Shab.,* 2 vols.), 1:132.

204. 1 Cor 10:16; 12:12-13, 23, 27.

205. Contra C. H. Dodd, *Romans,* 101-2; A. Nygren, *Romans,* 274; J. Robinson, *The Body,* 47. That the expression is not ecclesial is maintained by, among others, C. Cranfield, *Romans,* 336; E. Käsemann, *Romans,* 189; J. Fitzmyer, *Romans,* 458; R. Harrisville, *Romans,* 101; R. Jewett, *Romans,* 434.

206. E.g., 2 Kgs 19:30; Ps. 1:3; Isa 37:31; Jer 17:8; Matt 3:8, 10; Mark 4:20; John 15:2; Col 1:10.

continues the "we" expressed at the end of the previous verse. He is being instructive, using what might be called a "pedagogical we" to speak as if he is an insider along with his readers. He goes on to make a contrast. But to get at what he says, it helps to dismantle his syntax. He says, in effect, that life under the law of Moses is life "in the flesh." The latter phrase is pejorative here, equivalent to life "according to the flesh" (κατὰ σάρκα) in other passages (Rom 8:4-5, 12-13; 2 Cor 1:17; 10:2-3; 11:18). Consequently, Paul does not refer here simply to physical life in the world, but life which is oriented toward the self and its desires; it is the opposite of a life that is oriented according to the Spirit.[207] Paul says that life under the law is equivalent to life according to the flesh, because the law arouses sinful passions. It gives sin (as power) the opportunity to rebel, which Paul will explain at 7:8-11. In short, the law helps sin fulfill its mission. That whole way of living leads to death.

But now, Paul asserts, we are not under the law. The reason for saying that is that "we have died to that by which we were bound," i.e., the law of Moses. The clause picks up what was said earlier: those who have "died to the law" belong to Christ and his body (7:4), not the law. Those who belong to Christ and his body serve "in the newness of the Spirit." They do not serve "in the obsolescence of the letter" of the law. That contrast between the letter (γράμμα) and the Spirit (πνεῦμα) is made by Paul elsewhere (Rom 2:29; 2 Cor 3:6). In the present instance "the letter" refers to the written law of Moses in its entirety, not simply to a strict literalism. That becomes clear with its antithesis, living "in the newness of the Spirit," i.e., the Holy Spirit, which has not been mentioned since 5:5. The emphasis on "newness" (καινότης) had also been made at 6:4, where Paul speaks of believers as those "who walk in newness of life." At 8:4 he will speak of them as those who "walk not according to the flesh but according to the Spirit." The Christian is thus one who has "died to the law" by baptism into Christ and been made alive again by the Holy Spirit. The law of Moses no longer has a ruling function in the life of the believer, and it lacks power to lead one to righteousness before God. The life of the believer has been renewed, and it is directed by the Holy Spirit.

BIBLIOGRAPHY

Bornkamm, Günther. "Sin, Law and Death (Romans 7)." In his *Early Christian Experience*, 87-104. New York: Harper & Row, 1969.

Brändle, Rudolf, and Ekkehard W. Stegemann. "The Formation of the First 'Christian Congregations' in Rome in the Context of the Jewish Congregations." In *Judaism and Christianity in First-Century Rome*, 117-27. Ed. Karl P. Donfried and Peter Richardson. Grand Rapids: Wm. B. Eerdmans, 1998.

207. Alexander Sand, "σαρξ," *EDNT* 3:231.

Bultmann, Rudolf. "Romans 7 and the Anthropology of Paul." In his *Existence and Faith: Shorter Writings of Rudolf Bultmann*, 147-57. New York: Meridian Books, 1960.

Burton, Keith A. "The Argumentative Coherence of Romans 7:1-6." In *Society of Biblical Literature 2000 Seminar Papers*, 452-64. SBLSPS 38. Atlanta: Society of Biblical Literature, 2000.

———. *Rhetoric, Law, and the Mystery of Salvation in Romans 7:1-6*. Lewiston: Edwin Mellen, 2001.

Davies, Donald M. "Free from the Law: An Exposition of the Seventh Chapter of Romans." *Int* 7 (1953): 156-62.

Davies, W. D. *Torah in the Messianic Age and/or the Age to Come*. SBLMS 7. Philadelphia: Society of Biblical Literature, 1952.

Deming, Will. *Paul on Marriage and Celibacy: The Hellenistic Background of I Corinthians 7*. Cambridge: Cambridge University Press, 1995.

Derrett, J. Duncan M. "Romans vii.1-4: The Relationship with the Resurrected Christ." In his *Law in the New Testament*, 461-71. London: Darton, Longman & Todd, 1970.

Diezinger, Walter. "Unter Toten Freigeworden: Eine Untersuchung zu Röm. iii-viii." *NovT* 5 (1962): 268-98.

Earnshaw, John D. "Reconsidering Paul's Marriage Analogy in Romans 7:1-4." *NTS* 40 (1994): 68-88.

Gale, Herbert M. *The Use of Analogy in the Letters of Paul*. Philadelphia: Westminster Press, 1964.

Hellholm, David. "Die argumentative Funktion von Römer 7.1-6." *NTS* 43 (1997): 385-411.

Hultgren, Arland J. *Jesus and His Adversaries: The Form and Function of the Conflict Stories in the Synoptic Tradition*. Minneapolis: Augsburg Publishing House, 1979.

Jewett, Robert. "Spirit," *IDBSup*, 839-41.

Kruijf, Th. C. de. "The Perspective of Romans vii." In *Miscellanea Neotestamentica*, 1:127-41. Ed. Titze Baarda et al. 2 vols. NovTSup 47-48. Leiden: E. J. Brill, 1978.

Little, Joyce A. "Paul's Use of Analogy: A Structural Analysis of Romans 7:1-6." *CBQ* 46 (1984): 82-90.

Lyonnet, Stanislas. "L'Histoire du salut selon le chapitre VII de L'Épître aux Romains." *Bib* 43 (1962): 117-51; reprinted in his *Études sur l'épître aux Romains*, 203-30. AnBib 120. Rome: Pontifical Biblical Institute Press, 1989.

Räisänen, Heikki. *Paul and the Law*. Philadelphia: Fortress Press, 1986.

———. "Paul's Theological Difficulties with the Law." In *Studia Biblica 1978: Sixth International Congress on Biblical Studies, Oxford, 3-7 April 1978*, 3:301-20. Ed. Elizabeth A. Livingstone. 3 vols. Sheffield: JSOT Press, 1979-80.

Rehmann, Luzia Sutter, and Brian McNeil. "The Doorway into Freedom: The Case of the 'Suspected Wife' in Romans 7.1-6." *JSNT* 79 (2000): 91-94.

Robinson, John A. T. *The Body: A Study in Pauline Theology*. SBT 5. Chicago: H. Regnery Company, 1952.

Roetzel, Calvin J. "Paul and the Law: Whence and Whither?" *CurrBS* 3 (1995): 249-75.

Sand, Alexander. *Der Begriff "Fleisch" in den paulinischen Hauptbriefen*. Regensburg: Pustet, 1967.

Spitaler, Peter. "Analogical Reasoning in Romans 7:2-4: A Woman and the Believers in Rome." *JBL* 125 (2006): 715-47.

Stanley, David M. "The Christian's Liberation from the Law. Rom 7,4-6." In his *Christ's Resurrection in Pauline Soteriology*, 186-88. Rome: Pontifical Biblical Institute Press, 1961.

Thimmes, Pamela. "'She Will Be Called an Adulteress . . .': Marriage and Adultery Analogies in Romans 7:1-4." In *Celebrating Romans: Template for Pauline Theology: Essays in Honor of Robert Jewett*, 190-203. Ed. Sheila E. McGinn. Grand Rapids: Wm. B. Eerdmans, 2005.

Tomson, Peter J. "What Did Paul Mean by 'Those Who Know the Law'? (Rom 7.1)." *NTS* 49 (2003): 573-81.

Turner, Nigel. *Syntax*. Vol. 3 of *A Grammar of New Testament Greek* by James H. Moulton. 3 vols. Edinburgh: T. & T. Clark, 1908-63.

Westerholm, Stephen. "Letter and Spirit: The Foundation of Pauline Ethics." *NTS* 30 (1984): 229-48.

4.6. The Law and Sin, 7:7-13

7 *What, then, shall we say? Is the law sin? By no means! But I would not have known sin except through the law. I would not have known what it is to covet except that the law said, "You shall not covet."* 8 *But sin, seizing an opportunity through the commandment, produced in me all kinds of covetousness. For apart from the law, sin is dead.* 9 *At one time I was alive apart from the law, but when the commandment came, sin became alive,* 10 *and I died, and the commandment that was intended for life proved to be a cause for death to me.* 11 *For sin, seizing an opportunity through the commandment, deceived me and through it killed me.* 12 *So then, the law is holy, and the commandment is holy, just, and good.* 13 *Did that which is good, then, become death to me? By no means! But sin, in order that it would be shown to be sin, produced death in me through what is good, in order that, through the commandment, sin might truly become sinful.*

Notes on the Text and Translation

7:10 The verb in the clause εὑρέθη μοι ἡ ἐντολὴ εἰς θάνατον is an aorist passive ("[it] was found"); it is followed by a dative for an indirect object (μοι, "to me"); and a form of the verb "to be" is required in translation. A translation more literal than that of the RSV, NIV, and NRSV is provided in BDAG: "the commandment proved to be a cause for death to me."[208]

---

208. BDAG 412 (εὑρίσκω, 2).

7:13 The translation of the purpose clause ἵνα γένηται καθ' ὑπερβολὴν ἁμαρτωλὸς ἡ ἁμαρτία διὰ τῆς ἐντολῆς is notoriously difficult. In the NRSV it is rendered "in order that sin might be shown to be sin, and through the commandment might become sinful beyond measure." That seems to imply a two-step process. The NET rendering is better and concise: "that through the commandment sin would become utterly sinful." A major problem is how to translate the preposition καθ' ὑπερβολὴν (typically, "to an extraordinary degree, beyond measure, utterly")[209] in the present context and come out with a clause that reads well in modern English. The translation adopted above is an attempt to do that.

General Comment

Beginning with 7:7 the question inevitably rises concerning the identity of the "I" (ἐγώ) being discussed from 7:7 through 7:25. On the surface it appears that Paul is speaking of himself and his experience under the law, past and present: in the past within 7:7-13 and in the present within 7:14-25. But the meaning (or meanings) of Paul's use of the pronoun "I" in this section of Romans is one of the most contested issues in the interpretation of the letter. It is difficult to do justice to all the positions and nuances that have been offered. The issues are discussed in an appendix ("The Identity of the 'I' in Romans 7"). That discussion need not be repeated here. Its results are assumed, and that is that in 7:7-25 Paul speaks of what it means to live under the law in order to be righteous, taking insights from his own life experience in the past under the law as paradigmatic, and seeing all from the perspective of one who is now "in Christ."

The issue was not taken up in Romans 7:7-25 arbitrarily. Paul had said in 7:4-6 that believers have been freed from bondage to life under the law, for they belong to Christ, and they now serve God in the newness of the Spirit. But that assertion could be misunderstood. As Paul himself indicates at 3:8; 6:1, 15, there were people who thought of him as an antinomian, and since he mentions those charges, they must have been known at Rome. Furthermore, to make matters more complicated, and even worse for himself, at 7:5 Paul had said that "our sinful passions" were "aroused by the law." From that, one could conclude that, according to Paul, the law is the source of sin; it arouses "our sinful passions." What follows in 7:7-25 can be understood as Paul's drawing back to make a clear and forthright defense of the law. From his own Jewish background, and considering the Jewish Christian background of the community at Rome, their legacy, and their continuing presence — for whom the law was considered a

---

209. BDAG 1032 (ὑπερβολή), rendering Rom 7:13 as "sinful in the extreme."

good gift from God — it is not surprising that Paul would feel compelled to do as he did. He had to correct any false impressions that readers might acquire from what he had said in 7:5.

It is not self-evident where the unit beginning at 7:7 ends. If we follow the division of paragraphs in modern versions, it ends either at 7:12 (RSV and NRSV) or at 7:13 (NIV). The latter corresponds to the paragraph ending in the Nestle-Aland Greek NT (27th ed.). One can consider 7:13 as a bridge between what comes prior to it (7:7-12) and what follows (7:14-25), for it concludes the discussion about the question whether the law brings sin and death, but to some degree it also anticipates the discussion about sin at work over against the law. Since the former is more obvious, however, it is wise to consider 7:13 the conclusion to 7:7-13 as a unit.

Detailed Comment

7:7-8a Paul begins with the rhetorical question that has become familiar by now in the letter (cf. 3:5; 4:1; 6:1; for later uses, cf. 8:31; 9:14, 30): τί οὖν ἐροῦμεν; ("What, then, shall we say?"). That is followed by an additional question: ὁ νόμος ἁμαρτία; ("Is the law sin?"). The latter is asked in order to provide Paul the opportunity to head off a false inference. The question can legitimately be raised in light of the connection he has made in 7:5 between "our sinful passions" and "the law." Since the law has aroused sinful passions, does it mean that the law itself could be called sin, or at least be a source of it? Paul responds to his own question with his familiar: μὴ γένοιτο ("By no means!"), a strong negation that he uses after rhetorical questions. On this expression, see the exegesis of 3:4.

Having said that, Paul maintains that, nevertheless, it is through the law of Moses that a person gains knowledge of sin. This is not the first time he has made that point. He made the same point at 3:20: "for through the law comes knowledge of sin" (cf. also 5:20). Sin is present in a person's life at all times, but when a person is confronted by the law, and hears what it says, he or she becomes aware of sin in its particulars. By way of illustration, Paul says that all one has to do is think for a moment about the commandment against covetousness (Exod 20:17; Deut 5:21) and how it exposes one's sinfulness. He does not provide all the details of the commandment that are listed in the OT texts (which prohibit coveting the neighbor's wife, house, servants, etc.), but simply quotes the words οὐκ ἐπιθυμήσεις ("You shall not covet"), which he does also at 13:9 when he summarizes the Decalogue. Philo of Alexandria, when speaking of the commandment concisely, does the same.[210] In referring to that com-

---

210. Philo, *Spec. Leg.* 4.78. Cf. also 4 Macc 2:6. In both Hebrew and Greek texts and tradi-

mandment, Paul refers to the commandment that in some Jewish traditions was considered "the essence and origin of all sin,"[211] indeed, "the sin from which all others flow."[212] That is because, while the other commandments have to do with outward actions, the commandment against covetousness speaks of an inner disposition, "desire" (ἐπιθυμία). The term ἐπιθυμία can signify a longing for that which is good (Phil 1:23; 1 Thess 2:17), but more often for Paul it means a craving for that which is forbidden, evil, or undesirable (Rom 6:12; 13:14; Gal 5:24; 1 Thess 4:5),[213] and so ἐπιθυμία as "covetousness" (in this instance) is the basis for sinful actions.

Although the law is not sin, there is a connection between the two. Due to sin as a power, the human being is by nature rebellious against God. And the way to act out rebellion against God is to disobey the commandments. If the commandments demand or prohibit a certain course of action, the reaction of a rebellious and sinful self is to defy what is expected. And so, Paul says, since the commandment prohibits covetousness, sin finds "opportunity" (ἀφορμή) in it to produce covetousness of every kind within a person. The commandment against covetousness provides sin with a base of operations.[214]

7:8b-11 "Apart from the law, sin is dead." The expression "apart from the law" (χωρὶς νόμου) appears only in the letters of Paul within the NT. Moreover, it does not appear in the LXX or in any of the works of Hellenistic Jewish writers of antiquity.[215] Paul himself uses the expression only three times (3:21; 7:8, 9).[216] In the present instance Paul means that, if the law is unknown or disregarded, sin is "dead." It is unknown, or, as Augustine wrote, it is "hidden,"[217] for it is only through the law that sin is known at all (3:20; 7:7). And if it is not

---

tions, the Ten Commandments are referred to as the "ten words." Cf. Raymond F. Collins, "Ten Commandments," *ABD* 6:383.

211. J. Ziesler, *Romans*, 185.

212. J. Ziesler, "The Role of the Tenth Commandment in Romans 7," 44. As references, he lists Philo, *Spec. Leg.* 4.84-94; *Decal.* 28.142, 150-53; 33.173; *Apoc. Mos.* 19.3; *Apoc. Abr.* 24.10.

213. BDAG 372 ἐπιθυμία).

214. BDAG 158 (ἀφορμή). Cf. S. Romanello, "Rom 7,7-25 and the Impotence of the Law," 517; P. von Gemünden, "Der Affekt der ἐπιθυμία und der νόμος," 69-71.

215. There are 116 instances of the use of the phrase indicated by an electronic search, using the *TLG*. All are in the works of Christian theologians who cite Paul or at least echo his words. The same is true if one adds the article (χωρὶς τοῦ νόμου); there are nine instances within early Christian literature.

216. In addition, Paul uses the phrase "apart from works of the law" (χωρὶς ἔργων νόμου) at Rom 3:28.

217. Augustine, *Propositions from the Epistle to the Romans* 37.4: "When Paul says, 'Without the Law sin lies dead,' he did not mean that sin does not exist, but that it lies hidden." Quoted from *Augustine on Romans: Propositions from the Epistle to the Romans; Unfinished Commentary on the Epistle to the Romans,* ed. Paula Fredriksen Landes, SBL.TT 23 (Chico: Scholars Press, 1982), 15.

known, it cannot be recognized in anyone or counted against a person in any particular case (cf. 5:13). Sin has no opportunity to produce a transgression against the law if the law does not exist. But when the law is present, sin seizes the opportunity to defy God's express will. There is material here for the psychologist and the theologian alike. Origen (ca. A.D. 185-254) put the matter precisely: "I do not know why it is, but things which are forbidden are desired all the more."[218]

At 7:9 Paul begins to use the first person singular pronoun (ἐγώ) for emphasis (the first of eight times in 7:7-25). He speaks of himself as having lived once "apart from the law" (χωρὶς νόμου). It is difficult not to think that Paul is drawing here upon his own experience in part. But his overall purpose is not to disclose an era of his younger years with accuracy for its own sake, but to construct an argument. He portrays himself as having an idyllic childhood,[219] when he had not yet taken on the obligation of the law in its entirety and in a formal way.[220] Paul reflects Jewish tradition here, as expressed explicitly in later Mishnaic and Talmudic texts. Although there is actually no time in the life of a Jewish male when he is not under obligation to observe the law, it is at the age of 13 years and a day that he assumes religious and legal obligations in a prescribed and publicly recognized way.[221] According to the saying attributed to Judah ben Tema (late second century):[222] "At five years old [one is fit] for the Scripture, at ten years for the Mishnah, at thirteen for [the fulfilling of] the commandments."[223] The tradition is echoed in a rather oblique way within the rabbinic work known as *Aboth de Rabbi Nathan,* where it is said: "The impulse to do evil is thirteen years older than the impulse to do good. From the mother's womb it

---

218. Origen, *Commentarii in Epistulam ad Romanos* 7.8; quoted from *Ancient Christian Commentary on Scripture,* vol. 6, *Romans,* ed. Gerald Bray (Downers Grove: InterVarsity Press, 1998), 183.

219. Cf. C. H. Dodd, *Romans,* 110: Paul "is describing a happy childhood — happier and freer in retrospect, no doubt, than it ever really was."

220. Other interpreters reject the possibility that Paul is speaking in any way here about himself. According to them, he is speaking of humanity more generally. Cf. C. Cranfield, *Romans,* 351: "man's situation before the giving of the law"; J. Dunn, *Romans,* 382: "the childhood of man"; N. T. Wright, *NIB (Romans),* 10:563: "Israel in the pre-Mosaic state, corresponding to Adam in the garden." For the view taken here, see the appendix, "The Identity of the 'I' in Romans 7."

221. Zvi Kaplan, "Bar Mitzvah, Bat Mitzvah," *EncJud* 4:243-44, citing *m. Nid.* 5.6; *b. B. Mes.* 96a. Cf. also Str.-B 3:237, citing *Aboth R. Nat.* 16. Kaplan adds that, prior to the thirteenth year, a father was responsible for the deeds of his son.

222. There is uncertainty whether the saying was original to the text of *m. Abot.* Some authorities maintain that it is a later addition, e.g., R. Herford, *Pirke Aboth,* 143-44.

223. *M. Aboth* 5.21; quoted from *The Mishnah,* ed. Herbert Danby (Oxford: Oxford University Press, 1933), 458.

grows and develops with a person. . . . After thirteen years the impulse to do good is born."[224]

But then, says Paul, after living "apart from the law" in those younger days, "the commandment came" and "sin became alive." He does not say which "commandment" he has in mind, or how it came, but within the context of this section it has to be the commandment against covetousness (7:7),[225] and in regard to its coming, it comes to everyone who hears the Torah. The use of the phrase ἐλθούσης δὲ τῆς ἐντολῆς ("but when the commandment came")[226] need not refer to a particular moment in the history of Israel (e.g., the giving of the law on Sinai),[227] but can have a more specific meaning here, i.e., "when the commandment came *to me*."[228] It was only when that particular commandment declared that covetousness is sinful that sin itself, previously "dead" (7:8), came to life.

The result is death. At 7:10 Paul declares that the promise had been given in the Torah that by keeping the commandments one shall live (Lev 18:5: "You shall keep my statutes and my ordinances; by doing so one shall live"), a promise that Paul knows well, since he cites it twice more in his letters (Rom 10:5; Gal 3:12).[229] Keeping the commandment against coveting, as well as keeping all the rest of them, should bring life. But the opposite is the case. It brings death, because no one can observe it. To be sure, none of the commandments was intended to bring death. But the commandments offer opportunities for sin to fulfill its mission of defying God. Persons become implicated with sin (as a power) and sin's aim to be disobedient. Therefore, they are under the sentence of death, since sin results in death (Rom 5:12, 21; 6:16, 23; 7:13; 1 Cor 15:56).

7:12 While the law does provide opportunities for sin to have its way,

---

224. *Aboth R. Nat.* 16.3.1. Quoted from *The Fathers according to Rabbi Nathan,* trans. Jacob Neusner, BJS 114 (Atlanta: Scholars Press, 1986), 116. J. Neusner adds the comment: "the impulse to do evil is more deeply seated than the impulse to do good."

225. J. Fitzmyer, *Romans,* 467; R. Jewett, *Romans,* 451. Some interpreters maintain that the commandment in question is the command given to Adam not to eat from the forbidden tree (Gen 2:16-17). These include E. Käsemann, *Romans,* 196; U. Wilckens, *Römer,* 2:80; J. Dunn, *Romans,* 383; G. Theissen, *Psychological Aspects of Pauline Theology,* 207; P. Stuhlmacher, *Romans,* 106-8. C. Cranfield, *Romans,* 352; J. Ziesler, *Romans,* 187; and L. Keck, *Romans,* 183, include both that and the commandment against covetousness.

226. Cf. BDAG 394 (ἔρχομαι, 3): "to change place or position, with implication of being brought, be brought" (with Rom 7:9 as an example).

227. Contra B. Byrne, *Romans,* 223; D. Moo, *Romans,* 430. For a critical response, cf. T. Schreiner, *Romans,* 362-63,

228. Similarly, T. Schreiner, *Romans,* 364; somewhat similarly, R. Jewett, *Romans,* 451: when the commandment became an obligation for Paul.

229. According to P. Sprinkle, *Law and Life,* 186 (n. 82), Rom 7:10 does not satisfy his "criteria for detecting an allusion to Lev 18:5." But the criteria (pp. 14-20) may be too restrictive. An allusion is affirmed by others, e.g., J. Fitzmyer, *Romans,* 468; J. Dunn, *Romans,* 384, 402; R. Jewett, *Romans,* 452.

there is no way possible to say that "the law is sin" (7:7). Paul cannot, even for a moment, contemplate such a thought. He makes it clear that the law (νόμος) is "holy," meaning in this case the entire law of Moses, and the "commandment" (ἐντολή, specifically the commandment against covetousness) is "holy, just, and good." Here Paul stands within the mainstream of Jewish tradition, joining the voices of others who speak of the law in glowing terms, praising it for its perfection and goodness (Deut 4:8; Wis 18:9; 2 Macc 6:23; 2 Esdr 9:30-37).[230]

7:13 In order to head off another possible false conclusion, Paul asks another rhetorical question: "Did that which is good, then, become death to me?" He answers with his familiar and emphatic: μὴ γένοιτο ("By no means!"). It is a fair question. Paul has already made it clear that although the law can arouse sinful passions (7:5), the law itself is not sin, i.e., not a power or agent that draws one into sinful behavior (7:7). The law does, however, provide an opportunity for sin to carry out its mission, leading to death (7:8, 11). Can one say, then, that, in spite of the fact that it is good, the law turns out to be deadly? That would seem to be a possible conclusion. Even though the law promises life to those who keep it, its commandments bring death, since in fact no one can keep them (7:10; cf. 3:20).

Even though one might take such a viewpoint, it is impossible for Paul to let such a false conclusion stand. The problem, once more, is sin. As said before, sin works through the law, "through what is good," to produce death in a person. What the law does is to make clear that sin is a recognizable reality, for sin can be documented by means of the commandments of the law. Here Paul reiterates a view that he has made explicit before: "Sin is not counted when the law is not present" (5:13); and "where there is no law, neither is there transgression" (4:15). But when the law is present, sin becomes obvious. Sin, says Paul, has produced death through what is good, i.e., through the law, "in order that, through the commandment, sin might truly become sinful."

The way the argument is presented is convoluted. By way of summary, Paul has asked the rhetorical question whether the law brings death. To paraphrase him, the answer is no, the law was intended for life, but sin works through the (good) law for my death. By means of the law, sin is exposed for what it is, lest it be trivialized or ignored. It is truly sinful and therefore produces death in me.

BIBLIOGRAPHY

Aletti, Jean-Noël. "Rm 7.7-25 encore une fois: Enjeux et propositions." *NTS* 48 (2002): 358-76.

---

230. Similar expressions appear in Philo, *Mos.* 2.3.14, and *3 Enoch* 11; cf. 4Q400.1.i.15: "holy precepts."

————. "Romans 7,7-25: Rhetorical Criticism and Its Usefulness." *SEÅ* 61 (1996): 77-95.

Anz, Wilhelm. "Zur Exegese von Römer 7 bei Bultmann, Luther, Augustine." In *Theologia Crucis, Signum Crucis: Festschrift für Erich Dinkler zum 70. Geburtstag*, 1-15. Ed. Carl Andresen and Günter Klein. Tübingen: J. C. B. Mohr (Paul Siebeck), 1979.

Benoit, Pierre. "The Law and the Cross according to St Paul, Romans 7:7–8:4." In his *Jesus and the Gospel*, 2:11-39. 2 vols. New York: Herder & Herder, 1973.

Betz, Hans D. "The Concept of the 'Inner Human Being' (ὁ ἔσω ἄνθρωπος) in the Anthropology of Paul." *NTS* 46 (2000): 315-41.

————. "The Human Being in the Antagonisms of Life according to the Apostle Paul." *JR* 80 (2000): 557-75.

Borgen Peder. "The Contrite Wrongdoer — Condemned or Set Free by the Spirit? Romans 7:7–8:4." In *The Holy Spirit and Christian Origins: Essays in Honor of James D. G. Dunn*, 181-92. Ed. Graham N. Stanton et al. Grand Rapids: Wm. B. Eerdmans, 2004.

Bornkamm, Günther. "Sin, Law and Death (Romans 7)." In his *Early Christian Experience*, 87-104. New York: Harper & Row, 1969.

Braun, Herbert. "Römer 7,7-25 und das Selbstverständnis des Qumran-Frommen." *ZTK* 56 (1959): 1-18; reprinted in his *Gesammelte Studien zum Neuen Testament und seiner Umwelt*, 100-119. Tübingen: J. C. B. Mohr (Paul Siebeck), 1962.

Busch, Austin. "The Figure of Eve in Romans 7:5-25." *BibInt* 12 (2004): 1-36.

Campbell, William S. "The Identity of ἐγώ in Romans 7:7-25." In *Studia Biblica 1978: Sixth International Congress on Biblical Studies, Oxford, 3-7 April 1978*, 3:57-64. Ed. Elizabeth A. Livingstone. 3 vols. Sheffield: JSOT Press, 1979-80.

Cranfield, C. E. B. "Romans 7 Reconsidered." *ExpTim* 65 (1953-54): 221.

Doutre, Jean. "Le 'moi' dominé par la péché et le 'nous' libéré dans le Christ: Deux paradigms simultanés pour penser le sujet en Rm 7,7–8,30." In *"Christ est mort pour nous": Études sémiotiques en l'honneur d'Olivette Genest*, 157-77. Ed. Alain Gignac and Anne Fortin. Montreal: Médiaspaul, 2005.

Fuchs, Ernst. "Existentiale Interpretation von Röm 7,7-12 und 21-23." *ZTK* 59 (1962): 285-314; reprinted in his *Glaube und Erfahrung: Zum christologischen Problem im Neuen Testament*, 364-401. Tübingen: J. C. B. Mohr (Paul Siebeck), 1965.

Fung, Ronald Y. K. "The Impotence of the Law: Towards a Fresh Understanding of Romans 7:14-25." In *Scripture, Tradition and Interpretation: Essays Presented to Everett F. Harrison*, 34-48. Ed. W. Ward Gasque and William S. LaSor. Grand Rapids: Wm. B. Eerdmans, 1978.

Gathercole, Simon J. "Sin in God's Economy: Agencies in Romans 1 and 7." In *Divine and Human Agency in Paul and His Cultural Environment*, 158-72. Ed. John M. G. Barclay and Simon J. Gathercole. LNTS 335. New York: T&T Clark, 2008.

Gemünden, Petra von. "Der Affekt der ἐπιθυμία und der νόμος: Affektkontrolle und soziale Identifitätsbildung im 4. Makkabäerbuch mit einem Ausblick auf den Römerbrief." In *Das Gesetz im frühen Judentum und im Neuen Testament: Festschrift für Christoph Burchard zum 75. Geburtstag*, 55-74. Ed. Dieter Sänger and Matthias Konradt. NTOA 57. Göttingen: Vandenhoeck & Ruprecht, 2006.

Gundry, Robert H. "The Moral Frustration of Paul before His Conversion: Sexual Lust in Romans 7:7-25." In *Pauline Studies: Essays Presented to Professor F. F. Bruce on His*

70th Birthday, 228-45. Ed. Donald A. Hagner and Murray J. Harris. Grand Rapids: Wm. B. Eerdmans, 1980.

Heckel, Theo K. *Der innere Mensch: Die paulinische Verarbeitung eines platonischen Motives.* Tübingen: J. C. B. Mohr (Paul Siebeck), 1993.

Herford, R. Travers. *Pirke Aboth: The Ethics of the Talmud: Sayings of the Fathers.* New York: Schocken Books, 1962.

Jervis, L. Ann. "'The Commandment Which Is for Life' (Romans 7.10): Sin's Use of the Obedience of Faith." *JSNT* 27 (2004): 193-216.

Jewett, Robert. "The Basic Human Dilemma: Weakness or Zealous Violence (Romans 7:7-25 and 10:1-18)." *Ex Auditu* 13 (1997): 96-109.

Joest, Wilfried. "Paulus und das lutherische simul Iustus et Peccator." *KuD* 1 (1955): 269-320.

Jolivet, Ira J., Jr. "An Argument from the Letter and Intent of the Law as the Primary Argumentative Strategy in Romans." In *The Rhetorical Analysis of Scripture: Essays from the 1995 London Conference,* 309-34. Ed. Stanley E. Porter and Thomas H. Olbricht. JSNTSup 146. Sheffield: Sheffield Academic Press, 1997.

Karlberg, Mark W. "Israel's History Personified: Romans 7:7-13 in Relation to Paul's Teaching on the 'Old Man.'" *TJ* 7 (1986): 65-74.

Kertelge, Karl. "Exegetische Überlegungen zum Verständnis der paulinischen Anthropologie nach Römer 7." *ZNW* 62 (1971): 105-14.

Krarup, Katrine. "Det apologetiske sigte i Paulus' apologi for loven." *DTT* 57 (1994): 199-216.

Kümmel, Werner G. *Römer 7 und die Bekehrung des Paulus.* UNT 17. Leipzig: J. C. Hinrichs'sche Buchhandlung, 1929.

———. *Römer 7 und das Bild des Menschen im Neuen Testament: Zwei Studien.* TBü 53. Munich: C. Kaiser Verlag, 1974.

Lambrecht, Jan. "Man before and without Christ: Rom 7 and Pauline Anthropology." *LS* 5 (1974-75): 18-33.

———. *The Wretched 'I' and Its Liberation: Paul in Romans 7 and 8.* Grand Rapids: Wm. B. Eerdmans, 1993.

Lichtenberger, Hermann. *Das Ich Adams und das Ich der Menschheit: Studien zum Menschenbild in Römer 7.* WUNT 164. Tübingen: J. C. B. Mohr (Paul Siebeck), 2004.

Luck, Ulrich. "Das Gute und das Böse in Römer 7." In *Neues Testament und Ethik: Für Rudolf Schnackenburg,* 220-37. Ed. Helmut Merklein. Freiburg im Breisgau: Herder, 1989.

Lyonnet, Stanislas. "Tu ne convoiteras pas (Rom. 7:7)." In *Neotestamentica et Patristica: Eine Freundesgabe, Herrn Professor Dr. Oscar Cullmann zu seinem 60. Geburtstag überreicht,* 157-66. Ed. Willem C. van Unnik. NovTSup 6. Leiden: E. J. Brill, 1962.

Martin, Brice L. "Some Reflections on the Identity of the ἐγώ in Rom 7:14-25." *SJT* 34 (1981): 39-47.

Meyer, Paul W. "The Worm at the Core of the Apple: Exegetical Reflections on Romans 7." In *The Conversation Continues: Studies in Paul and John: In Honor of J. Louis Martyn,* 62-84. Ed. Robert Fortna and Beverly R. Gaventa. Nashville: Abingdon Press, 1990; reprinted in *The Word in This World: Essays in New Testament Exegesis and Theology,* 78-94. Ed. John T. Carroll. NTL. Louisville: Westminster John Knox Press, 2004. Page references are to the latter.

Middendorf, Michael P. *The "I" in the Storm: A Study of Romans 7.* St. Louis: Concordia Academic Press, 1997.

Milne, Douglas J. W. "Romans 7:7-12: Paul's Pre-conversion Experience." *RTR* 43 (1984): 9-17.

Mitton, Charles L. "Romans 7 Reconsidered." *ExpTim* 65 (1953-54): 78-81, 99-103, 132-35.

Moo, Douglas J. "Israel and Paul in Romans 7:7-12." *NTS* 32 (1986): 122-35.

Napier, Daniel. "Paul's Analysis of Sin and Torah in Romans 7:7-25." *ResQ* 44 (2002): 15-32.

Nickle, Keith F. "Romans 7:7-25." *Int* 33 (1979): 181-87.

Osten-Sacken, Peter von der. *Die Heiligkeit der Tora: Studien zum Gesetz bei Paulus.* Munich: Kaiser Verlag, 1989.

Romanello, Stefano. "Rom 7,7-25 and the Impotence of the Law: A Fresh Look at a Much-Debated Topic Using Literary-Rhetorical Analysis." *Bib* 84 (2003): 510-30.

Russell, Walt. "Insights from Postmodernism's Emphasis on Interpretive Communities in the Interpretation of Romans 7." *JETS* 37 (1994): 511-27.

Sanders, E. P. "Romans 7 and the Purpose of the Law." *PIBA* 7 (1983): 44-59.

Schnackenburg, Rudolf. "Römer 7 im Zusammenhang des Römerbriefes." In *Jesus und Paulus: Festschrift für Georg Kümmel,* 283-300. Ed. E. Earle Ellis and Erich Grässer. Göttingen: Vandenhoeck & Ruprecht, 1975.

Sprinkle, Preston M. *Law and Life: The Interpretation of Leviticus 18:5 in Early Judaism and in Paul.* WUNT 2/241. Tübingen: Mohr Siebeck, 2008.

Stowers, Stanley K. "Romans 7.2-25 as a Speech-in-Character (προσωποποιία)." In *Paul in His Hellenistic Context,* 180-202. Ed. Troels Engberg-Pedersen. Edinburgh: T&T Clark, 1994.

Strelan, John G. "A Note on the Old Testament Background of Romans 7:7." *LTJ* 15 (1981): 23-25.

Theissen, Gerd. "Gesetz und Ich: Beobachtungen zur persönlichen Dimension des Römerbriefs." In *Das Gesetz im frühen Judentum und im Neuen Testament: Festschrift für Christoph Burchard zum 75. Geburtstag,* 261-85. Ed. Dieter Sänger and Matthias Konradt. NTOA 57. Göttingen: Vandenhoeck & Ruprecht, 2006.

————. *Psychological Aspects of Pauline Theology.* Edinburgh: T&T Clark, 1987.

Trudinger, Peter. "An Autobiographical Digression? A Note on Romans 7:7-25." *ExpTim* 107 (1996): 173-74.

Ziesler, John A. "The Role of the Tenth Commandment in Romans 7." *JSNT* 33 (1988): 41-56; reprinted in *The Pauline Writings,* 137-52. Ed. Stanley E. Porter and Craig A. Evans. BibSem 34. Sheffield: Sheffield Academic Press, 1995.

4.7. The Law and the Flesh, 7:14-25

14*For we know that the law is spiritual, but I am of the flesh, sold under sin.*
15 *For I do not understand what I am doing. In fact, that which I do not will to do*

is what I do, but that which I hate is what I do. 16And if I do that which I do not will, I agree in regard to the law, that it is good. 17Consequently, it is no longer I that do it, but sin that dwells within me. 18For I know that nothing good dwells within me, that is, in my flesh. For willing what is good is close at hand, but not the doing of it. 19For I do not do the good that I will, but the evil I do not will is what I do. 20And if I do that which I do not will, it is no longer I that do it, but sin that dwells within me.

21So I discover the principle that when I will to do good, evil is close at hand. 22For I delight in the law of God in my inner being, 23but I see in my members another law that wages war with the law of my mind and makes me captive to the law of sin that dwells in my members.

24Wretched man that I am! Who will rescue me from this body of death? 25But thanks be to God through Jesus Christ our Lord! So then, with my mind I serve the law of God, but with my flesh I serve the law of sin.

Notes on the Text and Translation

7:17 The Greek νυνὶ δέ is rendered here as "consequently" (cf. "so then" in RSV; "but in fact" in NRSV). The frequent temporal meaning of νυνί is not being employed here.[231] The context implies the making of a logical conclusion.

7:20 The pronoun ἐγώ ("I") appears twice within this verse in some versions (including ℵ, A, and the Majority Text), but the first occurrence does not appear in others (including B). The evidence is quite evenly divided. The Nestle-Aland text (27th ed.) has the pronoun in brackets, indicating that the word is of doubtful authenticity. Its presence or absence makes no difference in meaning or in English translation.

7:22 According to Vaticanus (B), and contrary to all other Greek witnesses, Paul says, "I delight in the law of [my] mind" (τῷ νόμῳ τοῦ νοός), instead of, "I delight in the law of God" (τῷ νόμῳ τοῦ θεοῦ). That may have been due to an eye skip to 7:23, which has the alternative.

7:25 The reading adopted in the Nestle-Aland text (27th ed.) is χάρις δὲ τῷ θεῷ, and that is the basis for "Thanks be to God" in major English versions (RSV, NIV, and NRSV). The major alternative is εὐχαριστῶ τῷ θεῷ, which is the basis for "I thank God" in the KJV. The textual basis for either is about even, but slightly more weight can be given to the former.[232]

---

231. BDAG 682 (νυνί, 2): "the idea of time weakened or entirely absent, *now, as it is.*"
232. Cf. B. Metzger, *TCGNT* 455.

General Comment

Paul continues his discussion concerning the self, the law, and sin. But there are three differences in regard to language and issues between 7:14-25 and the previous discussion of 7:7-13. First, in 7:7-13 all the verbs related to the "I" are in past tense, whereas in 7:14-25 they are all in the present tense (with the exception of the future in 7:24). Second, the issues that Paul takes up are related, but they are not quite the same. In 7:7-13 the question dealt with is that posed at 7:7, "Is the law sin?" The answer is no. Sinful passions are indeed aroused by the law, but that is because sin finds opportunities in the law to disobey God. The discussion in 7:14-25 does not continue that line of thinking, but turns to the problem of human weakness in the presence of the power of sin that dwells within the self. In going in that direction, Paul probes more deeply into the human condition. Finally, in 7:7-13 Paul speaks of the law as an instrument used by sin as a power, but in 7:14-25 he does not. The law is held up by Paul as worthy of one's respect, a goal to strive for, and something that is spiritual and good (7:14, 16), even a delight (7:22), but it sets forth an impossible ideal, which one cannot finally attain.

The issues surrounding the identity of the first person singular ἐγώ ("I") used in this passage (7:14, 17, 20, 24, 25) are discussed in an appendix ("The Identity of the 'I' in Romans 7"). Although several proposals have been made, the viewpoint taken here is that in 7:7-25 as a whole, in spite of the differences cited between 7:7-13 and 7:14-25, Paul speaks of what it means to live under the law in order to be righteous, taking insights from his own life experience in the past under the law as paradigmatic, and seeing all from the perspective of one who is now "in Christ."

Romans 7:14-25 is a classic text of Scripture, making a profound analysis of the self. Within it Paul describes the great struggle that goes on within himself and, by implication, others who have heard the gospel of Christ and live in him. There is a theoretical desire (will) to serve God (7:15, 18, 19, 20, 21, 22, 25). But one cannot do it (7:18). In fact, such a person is very much aware that he or she does what is contrary to the will of God (7:15, 19, 23).

The discussion should not, however, be considered primarily an analysis of the self. Paul's main argument here concerns the law of God. Known to some as an antinomian (3:8; 6:1, 15), and having said that one's "sinful passions" can be aroused by the law, so as to have specific ways to act out one's rebellion against God, Paul argues that the law itself is not defective. On the contrary, the law given by God is holy (7:12), good (7:13, 16), spiritual (7:14), and a delight (7:22). The problem of doing that which is not willed and not doing what is willed is due to human weakness. Sin as a power moves in, takes up residence, and leads the self away from doing the will of God.

Detailed Comment

7:14 Continuing his praise of the law (called "holy" in 7:12), Paul now speaks of the law of Moses as "spiritual" (πνευματικός), a term that can designate something of heavenly origin (as at 1 Cor 10:3-4).[233] The law is of divine origin and belongs to the realm of the Spirit.[234] Paul was hardly the first to make a connection between the law and the Spirit. Philo speaks of Moses as being filled with the Holy Spirit as he delivered the law to Israel,[235] and in 2 Esdras the prophet Ezra calls upon God to send to him the Holy Spirit in order that he might write the words of the law (14:22). To be sure, Paul has made a contrast earlier in this letter between the law and the Spirit, setting in opposition the serving of God "in the newness of the Spirit" over against serving "in the obsolescence of the letter" (7:6). That contrast echoes what Paul has also made elsewhere between "the Spirit" that gives life and "the letter" of the old covenant that kills (2 Cor 3:6). Nevertheless, there is no contradiction between those assertions and the assertion here that the Torah has been given by God, and that it can be considered a "spiritual" reality as such. If observance of the law cannot be attained, and the result is death, that does not diminish the holiness of the law, nor does it lessen its "spiritual" origins and character. Paul begins here to set up what is to follow, an analysis of the human situation, in which there is a struggle between the will to serve God and the inability to do it.

In contrast to the "spiritual" character of the law, Paul knows himself as "of the flesh" (σαρκικός, RSV: "carnal"; NIV and NET: "unspiritual"), a term signifying weakness. The term used is related to the word σάρξ ("flesh"), that aspect of human nature that connotes weakness within the Bible (Ps 56:4; Rom 8:3) and Jewish traditions,[236] and is associated "with passions and desires" (σὺν τοῖς παθήμασιν καὶ ταῖς ἐπιθυμίαις) by Paul (Gal 5:24) and other ancient writers, both Jewish and Gentile.[237] By speaking of himself as "of the flesh," the apostle is saying that he is unable to attain the expectations that are set forth for him in the law of Moses.

Since Paul writes in this same verse that he is "sold under sin," interpreters have often concluded that he could not be speaking about himself here and,

233. Cf. also Philo, *Abr.* 22.113.

234. Cf. Eduard Schweizer, "πνεῦμα," *TDNT* 6:437: "When the νόμος is called πνευματικός in R. 7:14, it is characterized thereby as the νόμος θεοῦ (v. 22, 25) which comes from the world of God and not from that of man."

235. Philo, *Decal.* 23.175; cf. *Mos.* 2.51.291.

236. 4 Macc 7:18; *T. Jud.* 19.1-4; *T. Zeb.* 9.7; 1QS 11.9-10; 1QH^a 4.29-30; 12.29-31.

237. For the association with passions, cf. 4 Macc 7:18; with desires, cf. Plutarch, *Mor.* 1096c; Diogenes Laertius, *Lives* 10.145. Cf. also the association with pleasures in Plutarch, *Mor.* 101b; Philo, *Deus* 30.143; *Gig.* 7.29-30.

in fact, is not being autobiographical in Romans 7:7-25 in any sense, for Paul has declared unequivocally that those "in Christ" have "died to sin" (Rom 6:2) and have been freed from it (6:7, 18, 22); sin no longer has dominion (6:14).[238] In light of those declarations, it is impossible for him, then, to say that he is "sold under sin." But that concern for consistency should not preclude the actual introspective analysis that Paul has set forth here, for it is an analysis that applies not only to himself but to all who have experienced the presence of God as the Holy One.[239] It is only by faith, not inner experience, that one knows the self to be delivered from the power of sin. And it is by that same faith that one has the freedom and the ability to speak of the self as known to one's own mind and heart. It is precisely when one has the certainty of divine pardon that one can confess one's own sinfulness (Ps 51:3). Moreover, in spite of the declaration of freedom from sin for those who are in Christ, Paul nevertheless still finds it necessary to exhort his readers to consider themselves dead to sin (6:11) and to work at "actualizing this condition" (6:12-13).[240] The history of Christian experience illustrates that those who know themselves to be justified and at peace with God continue to consider themselves in ordinary, empirical life as being in bondage to sin and in need of forgiveness and freedom.

7:15-16 Here Paul outlines the struggle that takes place within his own life and that of others who are "in Christ." On the one hand, one might very well have a theoretical desire (will) to serve God (7:15, 18, 19, 20, 21, 22, 25). But the fact remains that one cannot do it (7:18); instead, one ends up doing what is contrary to the will of God (7:15, 19, 23). Paul says, in effect, that his understanding of himself has failed (7:15), and he says more explicitly that, above all, his will fails him constantly (7:15, 18, 19, 20). Although he does not use the noun "will" (θέλημα) or the full phrase "the will of God" (τὸ θέλημα τοῦ θεοῦ) in this section (a phrase that appears at Rom 12:2; Gal 1:4; 1 Thess 4:3; 5:18), he uses the active verb "to will" (θέλω), which is translated in modern versions (including the RSV, NIV, and NRSV) as "to want." The verb "to want," however, misses the intensity of the verb "to will" something in the moral sphere. To want is to long for or to desire something, a matter of the heart as well as the mind, and often more so. But to will within the moral sphere is to have a mental resolve to do something, as expressed at 7:23 (referring to the "mind" in its capacity to delight in God's law), or to refrain from something, in a conscious way.[241] It re-

---

238. E. Käsemann, *Romans,* 200; P. Stuhlmacher, *Romans,* 115; B. Byrne, *Romans,* 231. According to others, such as B. Byrne, *Romans,* 231, and L. Keck, *Romans,* 187, Paul cannot be speaking here of Christian experience.

239. Cf. C. Cranfield, *Romans,* 356; J. Ziesler, *Romans,* 195-96.

240. Cf. J. Espy, "Paul's 'Robust Conscience' Re-examined," 173; C. Cranfield, *Romans,* 346-47; J. Dunn, *Romans,* 389.

241. BDAG 448 (θέλω, 2).

quires effort. Paul wills to do what is "good" (ἀγαθόν), but he is incapable of doing it.

What Paul says here is similar to what was spoken by others, such as the pagan authors Ovid (43 B.C.–A.D. 17) and Epictetus (A.D. 55–135). The former (writing in Latin) declared: "I see the better and approve it, but I follow the worse."[242] The language of Epictetus is very similar to that of Paul. According to him, a person who is strong in argument and effective in persuasion should be able to show another person "how he is not doing what he wishes, and is doing what he does not wish" (πῶς ὃ θέλει οὐ ποιεῖ καὶ ὃ μὴ θέλει ποιεῖ).[243]

Similar anxieties are spoken in Jewish traditions. Typically those texts speak of an evil impulse that can or should be held in check,[244] which is somewhat different and more optimistic than what Paul has written. But there are postbiblical texts that illustrate the kind of struggle that Paul speaks about. A particularly striking passage is that spoken by Rabbi Tanhum bar Scholasticus (fourth century A.D.) in a prayer. Within that prayer he speaks of humanity as created to do God's will, and indeed being willing to do it, but the "evil inclination" prevents people from doing it:

> And may it be thy will, Lord my God, God of my fathers, that you break the yoke of the evil inclination and vanquish it from our hearts. For you created us to do your will. And we are obliged to do your will. You desire [that we do your will]. And we desire [to do your will]. And what prevents us? That bacteria [the evil inclination]. . . . It is obvious to you that we do not have the strength to resist it. So let it be thy will, Lord my God, and God of my fathers, and you vanquish it from before us, and subdue it, so that we may do thy will as our own will, with a whole heart.[245]

Another rabbinic passage speaks of the nation Israel as unable to do God's will because of some difficulty. Rabbi Alexandri (third century A.D.) says to God in a prayer that it is "perfectly obvious to you that our will is to do your will," and goes on to ask, "What prevents it?" He does not find the fault within the nation itself, however, but blames Israel's inability on its subjugation by the pagan kingdoms. He then concludes: "May it be pleasing before you, O Lord our God,

---

242. Ovid, *Metamorphoses* 7.19-20; quoted from *Ovid: Metamorphoses,* trans. Frank J. Miller, LCL, 2 vols. (Cambridge: Harvard University Press, 1916), 1:343.

243. Epictetus, *Dis.* 2.26.4; quoted from *Epictetus,* trans. W. A. Oldfather, LCL, 2 vols. (New York: G. P. Putnam's Sons, 1926-28), 1:432-33.

244. Among Qumran texts, cf. 1QH^a 19.19-22; among rabbinic texts, *y. Taan.* 66c; *b. Qidd.* 30b.

245. *Y. Ber.* 4.2; quoted from *The Talmud of the Land of Israel: Berakhot,* trans. Tzvee Zahavy (Chicago: University of Chicago Press, 1989), 169-70. The ellipses indicate texual uncertainties.

to save us from their power so that we may return to carry out the rules that please you with a whole heart."[246]

In Paul's own case, the will to do good is frustrated by sin as a power that dwells within the self ("in my flesh," 7:18), so that he is incapable of doing the very thing that he wills. In this respect, Paul can say that "the law is good," i.e., it teaches the will of God (cf. 2:18). Even though sin finds opportunity in the law to oppose God's will (7:8), the law itself is not sinful. On the contrary, it is from the law — which is holy, spiritual, and a delight (7:12, 14, 22) — that one is guided into knowing the perfect will of God.

7:17 Here Paul looks at the conflict from a different perspective. Although he admits to doing that which he does not will, he says that that "doing" is not actually his own. It is "sin dwelling within me" (ἡ οἰκοῦσα ἐν ἐμοὶ ἁμαρτία) that is at fault; the Greek clause appears twice in exactly the same form (7:17, 20). The assertion does not mean that Paul thereby excuses himself from doing that which is contrary to what he wills. Two things are being said here in light of the entire paragraph. First, Paul makes a distinction between his own enlightened will, which seeks the good (7:15, 19), and the power of sin within the self that continues to oppose that will. And, second, the self (the "I," ἐγώ) is inhabited by sin as a power in the present era. The ἐγώ is not itself an instrument of sin, but sin as a power occupies the self and dominates one's life so that one fails to do the good and does what one does not will to do. In the case of those who are "in Christ," the self is liberated from that power in principle and is destined to share all that faith in Christ entails, but while living in the present era the power of sin is still real, and it makes itself known in one's inability to do what God wills and even what the enlightened self wills in harmony with the will of God. Sin is not simply an external power that leads a person into disobedience to the conscience; it is a power that dwells within a person, cohabiting with the will and opposing the will, thereby causing one to fail to do the good that the will seeks to do.

7:18-20 Continuing the metaphor of indwelling, Paul says flatly that "nothing good dwells within me, that is, in my flesh." The latter phrase ("that is, in my flesh") appears to be an afterthought as though Paul realized that, of course, the will to do the good does reside in himself. The point to be made is that it does not reside in that aspect of human nature that is weak and transitory, "the flesh" (ἡ σάρξ). The best evidence for that is that, in spite of the fact that willing to do the good "is close at hand," Paul says that the ability to do it is not. The term for being close at hand (παράκειμαι) is rare, used only here and at 7:21 in the NT. Paul repeats what he has said before in 7:16-17. If a portion of the latter is left out, the language in the two verses is identical:

---

246. Ber. 17a; quoted from *The Talmud of Babylonia: An American Translation,* vol. 1, *Tractate Berakhot,* trans. Jacob Neusner (Chico: Scholars Press, 1984), 130.

7:16-17: εἰ δὲ ὃ οὐ θέλω τοῦτο ποιῶ, . . . οὐκέτι ἐγὼ κατεργάζομαι αὐτὸ
ἀλλὰ ἡ οἰκοῦσα ἐν ἐμοὶ ἁμαρτία.

7:20: εἰ δὲ ὃ οὐ θέλω [ἐγὼ] τοῦτο ποιῶ, οὐκέτι ἐγὼ κατεργάζομαι αὐτὸ
ἀλλὰ ἡ οἰκοῦσα ἐν ἐμοὶ ἁμαρτία.

And if I do that which I do not will, it is no longer I that do it, but sin that
dwells within me.

7:21-23 What follows from that is the declaration by Paul: "So I discover the
principle (νόμος) that when I will to do good, evil is close at hand." Here Paul
uses the term νόμος, usually translated "law," to mean a "principle" (as in the
NASV, but "law" in RSV, NIV, and NRSV).[247] The term has that meaning also at
3:27. That is to say, Paul has discovered a certain and regular pattern in his life
(and that of others): in spite of the effort to do good, evil is close at hand. The
contrast could hardly be made more precisely.

There is a dichotomy between the "delight in the law of God," located
within Paul's "inner being" (ἔσω ἄνθρωπος), and some "other law" (ἕτερος
νόμος) that conducts warfare against "the law" of his "mind" (νοῦς). The anthropological aspects appear rather imprecise. What becomes clearest of all is
that the "other law" of which Paul speaks is sin ("the law of sin"), which dwells
in the "members" (μέλη) of the body (7:23).

Interpretation is helped along, however, when one realizes that there is a
wordplay in 7:22-23 with the fourfold use of the word "law": the law of God (ὁ
νόμος τοῦ θεοῦ), another law (ἕτερος νόμος), the law of my mind (ὁ νόμος τοῦ
νοός μου), and the law of sin (ὁ νόμος τῆς ἁμαρτίας). In order to keep the
wordplay intact, English versions customarily and rightly translate the term
νόμος as "law." But except for the first of these ("the law of God"), the term νόμος
could be translated in such a way as to emulate what law does in life. When law is
at work, it imposes an ordering and regularity upon those who are subject to it.
Or, alternatively, one can say that the law gives expression to the same, as in "the
laws of nature" or "economic laws," all of which are metaphorical uses of the
word "law." Paul's usage in 7:23 is metaphorical as well. The phrases "the law of
my mind" and "the law of sin" can be regarded as figures of speech that reflect
what is typical (constant, regular) of "the mind" and "sin." Paul is not speaking of
a code or a particular legal prescription by use of the term.

The "inner being" that delights in the law cannot be located with precision,
but obviously the term refers to a consciousness that is capable of knowing and is
aware of the emotions. There is an ongoing struggle between that "inner being"

---

247. BDAG 677 (νόμος, 1). The translation of N. T. Wright, *NIB (Romans)*, 10:570, "this is
what I find about the law," referring to the Torah, does not work syntactically.

and "my members." The former accommodates the "mind," which affirms the goodness of the law,[248] while the latter is the locus of "sin." The term "members" (plural) refers to the body as the sum of its parts,[249] and in this instance the "members" of the body are associated with "the flesh" (σάρξ), as made evident in the explicit statement at 7:25b ("with my flesh I serve the law of sin"), that aspect of human nature that connotes weakness (cf. 7:14). Sin resides within the "members" of the body and takes a person captive to its own rule ("the law of sin").

7:24-25a Paul concludes with his famous cry of wretchedness, using a term (ταλαίπωρος, "wretched," "miserable") that is the antonym of "blessedness" (μακάριος, "blessed").[250] Since sin is such a power, and because it prevents one from being able to do that which one really wills to do — to do the good (7:19) — rescue is needed. The phrase "body of death" is stark, for it acknowledges that one is finite, bound toward death. There are no resources from within by which one can prevent the inexorable march toward death. But for Paul the term has an existential meaning as well. Death symbolizes an estrangement from all that one is created to be. To speak of the self as the resident of the "body of death" means that one's entire existence, physical and spiritual, is doomed to pass away into oblivion. Rescue is the only way out.

Having asked the question, Paul provides the self-evident answer immediately. As a child of Jewish heritage, he gives thanks to God, but as one who is "in Christ" the thanks to God is "through (the mediation of) Jesus Christ our Lord." The thanksgiving is thoroughly Pauline in vocabulary and expression; Paul uses the same or similar thanksgivings (all beginning with χάρις τῷ θεῷ, "thanks be to God") on five other occasions (Rom 6:17; 1 Cor 15:57; 2 Cor 2:14; 8:16; 9:15).

7:25b Paul sums up what has gone before. He repeats terms and concepts, affirming that in terms of his mind, he is devoted to the law of God, but that he is actually a slave of sin.

It has been maintained by some that 7:25b is a post-Pauline gloss added to the text of Romans.[251] The grounds for that claim is that Paul can hardly call himself "a slave to the law of sin," for that contradicts what has been written in 6:6 (". . . no longer . . . enslaved to sin"). Others have suggested that 7:25b would

248. H. Betz, "The Concept of the 'Inner Human Being' (ἔσω ἄνθρωπος) in the Anthropology of Paul," 338: "The νοῦς is the element of the ἔσω ἄνθρωπος that sees and is able to understand the human predicament." It has "the capacity of 'seeing (βλέπειν) another law,' antagonistic to God's law, at work in the bodily members" (p. 337).

249. BDAG 628 (μέλος, 1).

250. BDAG 988 (ταλαίπωρος).

251. R. Bultmann, "Glossen in Römerbrief," 198-99; G. Bornkamm, "Sin," 99; E. Käsemann, *Romans*, 211-12; J. O'Neill, *Romans*, 131-32, 268, 273; U. Wilckens, *Römer*, 2:97. According to R. Jewett, *Romans*, 473, Paul added 7:25b-c as a gloss himself.

originally have been located prior to 7:24, but was moved to the present place by scribes.[252] But there is no textual basis for the latter. Concerning the former, it is totally conceivable that Paul would draw the discussion to a close with a sweeping *inclusio* that recapitulates what has gone before.

BIBLIOGRAPHY

Althaus, Paul. "Zur Auslegung von Röm. 7,14ff.: Antwort an Anders Nygren." *TLZ* 77 (1952): 475-80.

Banks, Robert. "Romans 7:25a: An Eschatological Thanksgiving." *AusBR* 26 (1978): 34-42.

Beasley-Murray, George R. "Flesh and Spirit." *BI* 3/1 (1976): 38.

Betz, Hans D. "The Concept of the 'Inner Human Being' (ὁ ἔσω ἄνθρωπος) in the Anthropology of Paul." *NTS* 46 (2000): 315-41.

———. "The Human Being in the Antagonisms of Life according to the Apostle Paul." *JR* 80 (2000): 557-75.

Borgen, Peder. "The Contrite Wrongdoer — Condemned or Set Free by the Spirit? Romans 7:7–8:4." In *The Holy Spirit and Christian Origins: Essays in Honor of James D. G. Dunn*, 181-92. Ed. Graham N. Stanton et al. Grand Rapids: Wm. B. Eerdmans, 2004.

Bultmann, Rudolf. "Glossen im Römerbrief." *TLZ* 72 (1947): 197-202; reprinted in his *Exegetica: Aufsätze zur Erforschung des Neuen Testaments*, 278-84. Ed. Erich Dinkler. Tübingen: J. C. B. Mohr (Paul Siebeck), 1967.

Burgland, Lane A. "Eschatological Tension and Existential *Angst*: 'Now' and 'Not Yet' in Romans 7:14-25 and 1QS 11 (Community Rule, Manual of Discipline)." *CTQ* 61 (1997): 163-76.

Byskov, Martha. "Simul Iustus et Peccator: A Note on Romans vii.25b." *ST* 30 (1976): 75-87.

Catchpole, David. "Who and Where Is the 'Wretched Man' of Romans 7, and Why Is 'She' Wretched?" In *The Holy Spirit and Christian Origins: Essays in Honor of James D. G. Dunn*, 168-80. Ed. Graham N. Stanton et al. Grand Rapids: Wm. B. Eerdmans, 2004.

Dahl, Nils A. "Confession and Comments in Rom. 7:14-25." In his *Studies in Paul: Theology for the Christian Mission*, 92-94. Minneapolis: Augsburg Publishing House, 1977.

Dunn, James D. G. "Rom. 7,14-25 in the Theology of Paul." *TZ* 31 (1975): 257-73; reprinted in *Essays on Apostolic Themes: Studies in Honor of Howard M. Ervin*, 49-70. Ed. Paul Elbert. Peabody: Hendrickson Publishers, 1985.

Espy, John M. "Paul's 'Robust Conscience' Re-examined." *NTS* 31 (1985): 161-88.

Fung, Ronald Y. K. "The Impotence of the Law: Towards a Fresh Understanding of Romans 7:14-25." In *Scripture, Tradition and Interpretation: Essays Presented to Everett F. Harrison*, 34-48. Ed. W. Ward Gasque and William S. LaSor. Grand Rapids: Wm. B. Eerdmans, 1978.

Garlington, Don B. "Romans 7:14-25 and the Creation Theology of Paul." *TJ* 11 (1990): 197-235.

---

252. C. H. Dodd, *Romans*, 114-15; F. Müller, "Zwei Marginalien," 249-54.

Hofius, Otfried. *Paulusstudien.* 2d ed. 2 vols. WUNT 51, 143. Tübingen: J. C. B. Mohr (Paul Siebeck), 1989-94.

Hommel, Hildebrecht. "Das 7. Kapital des Römerbrief im Licht antiker Überlieferung." In his *Sebasmata: Studien zur antiken Religionsgeschichte und zum frühen Christentum,* 141-73. 2 vols. Tübingen: J. C. B. Mohr (Paul Siebeck), 1983-84.

Huggins, Ronald V. "Alleged Classical Parallels to Paul's 'What I Want to Do I Do Not Do, But What I Hate, I Do.'" *WTJ* 54 (1992): 153-61.

Jewett, Robert. "Flesh in the New Testament." *IDBSup,* 339-40.

Jonas, Hans. "Philosophical Meditation on the Seventh Chapter of Paul's Epistle to the Romans." In *The Future of Our Religious Past: Essays in Honour of Rudolf Bultmann,* 333-50. Ed. James M. Robinson. New York: Harper & Row, 1971.

Kümmel, Werner G. *Römer 7 und das Bild des Menschen im Neuen Testament: Zwei Studien.* TBü 53. Munich: Christian Kaiser Verlag, 1974.

Kürzinger, Josef. "Der Schlussel zum Verständnis von Röm 7." *BZ* 7 (1963): 270-74.

Laato, Timo. *Paulus und das Judentum: Anthropologische Erwägungen.* Åbo: Åbo Academy Press, 1991.

Lambrecht, Jan. "The Line of Thought in Romans 7,15-20." *Bib* 85 (2004): 393-98.

———. *The Wretched 'I' and Its Liberation: Paul in Romans 7 and 8.* Grand Rapids: Wm. B. Eerdmans, 1993.

Lichtenberger, Hermann. "Der Beginn der Auslegungsgeschichte von Römer 7: Röm 7,25b." *ZNW* 88 (1997): 284-95.

Martin, Brice L. "Some Reflections on the Identity of the ἐγώ in Rom. 7:14-25." *SJT* 34 (1981): 39-47.

Müller, Friedrich. "Zwei Marginalien im Brief des Paulus an die Römer." *ZNW* 40 (1941): 249-54.

Packer, James I. "The 'Wretched Man' in Romans 7." *SE* 2 (1964): 621-27.

———. "The 'Wretched Man' Revisited: Another Look at Romans 7:14-25." In *Romans and the People of God: Essays in Honor of Gordon D. Fee on the Occasion of His 65th Birthday,* 70-81. Ed. Sven K. Soderlund and N. T. Wright. Grand Rapids: Wm. B. Eerdmans, 1999.

Porter, Stanley E. "The Pauline Concept of Original Sin, in Light of Rabbinic Background." *TynB* 41 (1990): 3-30.

Roetzel, Calvin J. "Paul and the Law: Whence and Whither?" *CurrBS* 3 (1995): 249-75.

Schrage, Wolfgang. "Israel nach dem Fleisch." In *'Wenn nicht jetzt': Aufsätze für Hans-Joachim Kraus zum 65. Geburtstag,* 143-51. Ed. Hans-Georg Geyer et al. Neukirchen-Vluyn: Neukirchener Verlag, 1983.

Schmithals, Walter. *Die theologische Anthropologie des Paulus: Auslegung von Röm 7,17–8,39.* Stuttgart: W. Kohlhammer, 1980.

Schweizer, Eduard. "Die Sünde in den Gliedern." In *Abraham unser Vater: Juden und Christen im Gespräch über die Bibel: Festschrift für Otto Michel zum 60. Geburtstag,* 437-39. Ed. Otto Betz et al. AGAJU 5. Leiden: E. J. Brill, 1963.

Seifrid, Mark A. "The Subject of Rom 7:14-25." *NovT* 34 (1992): 313-33.

Shogren, Gary S. "The 'Wretched Man' of Romans 7:14-25 as Reductio ad absurdum." *EvQ* 72 (2000): 119-34.

Smith, Edgar W. "The Form and Religious Background of Romans VII 24-25a." *NovT* 13 (1971): 127-35.

Stiegman, Emero. "Rabbinic Anthropology." *ANRW* II.19.2 (1979): 487-579.

Theissen, Gerd. *Psychological Aspects of Pauline Theology.* Edinburgh: T&T Clark, 1987.

Ziesler, John A. "The Role of the Tenth Commandment in Romans 7." *JSNT* 33 (1988): 41-56.

4.8. Liberation from Sin and Life in the Spirit, 8:1-11

1*Therefore, there is now no condemnation for those who are in Christ Jesus.* 2*For the law of the Spirit of life in Christ Jesus has set you free from the law of sin and death.*

3*For that which was impossible for the law to do, because it was weakened through the flesh, God has done. By sending his own Son in the likeness of sinful flesh, and for sin, he condemned sin in the flesh,* 4*in order that the just requirement of the law might be fulfilled in us who walk not according to the flesh but according to the Spirit.* 5*For those who are of the flesh think the thoughts of the flesh, but those who are of the Spirit think the thoughts of the Spirit.* 6*To set the mind on the flesh is death, but to set the mind on the Spirit is life and peace.* 7*For the mind that is set on the flesh is hostile to God; it does not obey the law of God, nor can it.* 8*Indeed, those who are in the flesh are not able to please God.*

9*But you are not in the flesh but in the Spirit, since the Spirit of God dwells in you. But if anyone does not have the Spirit of Christ, that person does not belong to him.* 10*But if Christ is in you, the body is dead on account of sin, but the Spirit is life on account of righteousness.* 11*And if the Spirit of him who raised Jesus from the dead dwells in you, he who raised Christ from the dead will also give life to your mortal bodies through his Spirit that dwells in you.*

Notes on the Text and Translation

8:1 Some ancient witnesses include the words μὴ κατὰ σάρκα περιπατοῦσιν, and still others continue with the clause ἀλλὰ κατὰ πνεῦμα. The Majority Text includes both, and the inclusion of both is reflected in the KJV ("who walk not after the flesh, but after the Spirit"). The clauses appear to have been taken from 8:4b, thereby providing a moral qualification to the otherwise sweeping statement of Paul. The clauses do not appear in the earliest witnesses, including ℵ, B, and D, and should not be included.

8:2 The word for "you" in this verse is the singular σέ in Greek. That is the reading of some of the earliest witnesses, including ℵ and B, supported by some Old Latin witnesses (a and b) as well, and that is represented in some widely used English versions (e.g., NSRV, NASV, ESV, and NET). But other important ancient witnesses have μέ ("me"). These include A and D, having support from other Old Latin texts. That reading is represented in other widely used English versions (e.g., KJV, RSV, and NIV). The decision is a difficult one, but the reading "you" has slightly more support among the ancient witnesses.[253] There is another variant, ἡμᾶς ("us"), but support for that is weak.

8:6-7 Three times over in these verses Paul uses the noun φρόνημα, which can be translated as "way of thinking" or "mind-set."[254] The term conveys the sense of the outcome of a thinking process (φρόνησις). The NET renders it as "outlook." It seems to imply in context a mentality or fixation that has resulted from contemplation. That seems to apply well to the dynamics regarding the flesh, but to speak of the "mentality" or "fixation" of the Spirit would not be appropriate. How to achieve parallelism is a challenge. It seems that one can do no better than the RSV and NRSV in using the circumlocution "to set the mind on."

8:11 Some texts read Χριστὸν Ἰησοῦν ("Christ Jesus") in 8:11b — with various word orders among them — instead of the word Χριστόν alone. Important witnesses support both. The inclusion of Ἰησοῦν could be due to its presence in a very similar phrase in 8:11a. The shorter reading is, therefore, preferable. The inclusion of both words is represented in the RSV, NASV, and ESV. The KJV, NIV, NET, and NRSV have simply the word "Christ."

In the same verse important ancient witnesses are divided between διὰ τοῦ ἐνοικοῦντος αὐτοῦ πνεύματος ἐν ὑμῖν (ℵ, A, and C, "through his Spirit that dwells in you") and διὰ τὸ ἐνοικοῦν αὐτοῦ πνεῦμα ἐν ὑμῖν (B, D, F, and the Majority Text, "on account of his Spirit that dwells in you"). Although the evidence is quite evenly balanced, the former is the more probable in context (cf. the repeated emphases in 8:8-11 on how the indwelling Spirit gives life).[255] The latter reading is reflected in the KJV, but the former is represented in other major English versions (ASV, RSV, NIV, NET, and NRSV) and is to be preferred.

General Comment

It is not immediately obvious how chapter 8 follows from what has gone before it in the previous chapter. Yet a link does exist. Within chapter 7 Paul main-

---

253. For additional discussion and evaluation of the variants, cf. B. Metzger, *TCGNT* 456.

254. BDAG 1066 (φρόνημα). "Mind-set" is favored by B. Byrne, *Romans*, 244, and J. Dunn, *Romans*, 426 (or "way of thinking"). J. Fitzmyer, *Romans*, opts for "concern." R. Jewett, *Romans*, 474, 487, simply uses "mind," but that seems too static.

255. B. Metzger, *TCGNT* 456; C. Cranfield, *Romans*, 391; U. Wilckens, *Römer*, 2:134 (n. 551); J. Dunn, *Romans*, 414; contra R. Jewett, *Romans*, 475.

tained that the law, though a good gift from God, cannot be kept by anyone because of the weakness of the "flesh." Moreover, although the law itself promised life to all who would observe its commandments (Lev 18:5), sin finds opportunity in those commandments to act contrary to the will of God. The result is the wretchedness of which Paul speaks in 7:24.

But that is not the end of the matter. For Paul has maintained earlier that, in spite of human weakness and the power of sin, the power of sin has been overcome. Those who are "in Christ" have been set free from its power and share in the destiny of the risen Lord (6:6-7, 14, 18, 22). Therefore, Paul can bring an end to his discussion of the conspiracy between sin and the flesh to lead a person toward death — and do so with a joyful outburst. It is God who delivers human beings from the body of death through Jesus as Christ and Lord (7:25).

The previous discussion of the law and the weakness of the flesh is not totally over at the end of chapter 7. At 8:3 Paul resumes what he has said before concerning human weakness, saying that living in accord with the law is impossible; at 8:4 he mentions its precepts ("just requirements"); and at 8:7-8 he speaks of the failure of those who are "in the flesh" to please God, since they will not submit to "the law of God."

Detailed Comment

8:1-2 Those who are "in Christ" are no longer under condemnation. The "now" (νῦν) is the eschatological "now" of the new age that has arrived with the resurrection of Jesus from the dead (as also at 3:21, 26; 5:9, 11; 6:19). The judgment against sin has been exercised at the cross (Rom 5:6, 8, 15; 6:10; 8:3; 1 Cor 15:3; 2 Cor 5:14), and for those who are "in Christ" the eschatological verdict has been passed proleptically. There is no condemnation (κατάκριμα) for them. The term κατάκριμα carries with it not only the sense of a judicial pronouncement of guilt, but also the punitive sentence that goes with it.[256] In this case the sentence would have been death, for that is the most suitable punishment for sin (5:12, 17; 6:16, 23; 1 Cor 15:56).

Paul uses here his familiar designation for Christians, i.e., those who are "in Christ" (ἐν Χριστῷ), a term that Paul uses to speak of Christian identity (Rom 16:7; 1 Cor 3:1; 2 Cor 5:17; 12:2; Phil 3:8-9). The phrase is more than a means of identification, a boundary marker in society, even though it most certainly is that. It carries with it the connotation of a personal union with Christ. The person "in Christ" shares in the destiny of the crucified and risen Lord Jesus. What has happened to him (death to sin and resurrection from the dead)

---

256. BDAG 518 (κατάκριμα).

becomes one's own; it is known as one's own in faith, despite all conditions and indications to the contrary. For more on the "in Christ" formula, see the exegesis of 6:3.

The basis for there being no condemnation is set out in 8:2. Paul uses a lengthy figure of speech ("the law of the Spirit of life in Christ Jesus") as the subject of the sentence and an almost equally lengthy phrase at the end ("the law of sin and death"). The phrases continue the play on words begun in 7:21-25 ("the law of my mind" and "the law of sin"), in which the term "law" (νόμος) is used metaphorically to speak of an ordered and regular behavior of its subject (the "mind" and "sin"). The phrases used here then speak of the patterns of how the Spirit, sin, and death operate.[257] Once the circumlocutions are trimmed away, Paul is saying that the Spirit sets one free from sin and death.

Seen in this way, it is probable that Paul had the end of his sentence in view well before he uttered it. He had just spoken of "the law of sin" (7:23), and now expands it to "the law of sin and death." In speaking, then, of the Spirit as the intended subject of the sentence, he creates the circumlocution that we have. Furthermore, by speaking of "the law" as the actual subject of the sentence, Paul is able to express an irony. The intent of the law was indeed to bring life (Lev 18:5), but that does not happen. It is the Spirit that brings life (Rom 8:10-11; 2 Cor 3:6). In fact, when Paul speaks of the law and the Spirit, he can set them in contrast (Rom 7:6; Gal 5:18). In the present instance Paul is able to bring the terms together, and the result is not only playful but effective. He has already said that the law is spiritual (7:14), and that is so because it came from heaven. But now, with the coming of the age of Christ and the Spirit, the Spirit has broken in to provide the life that the law could not give.

The "Spirit of life" is a Semitism for "the life-giving Spirit" (as the NET renders it), referring to the Holy Spirit as the one who gives life (2 Cor 3:6; cf. Job 33:4; John 6:63).

Since the Spirit has given life to the believer, the latter has been set free from sin and death. It is rather odd that the "you" spoken of is in the singular (σέ). Yet this is not the only place in Romans where one might expect the plural (cf. 2:4, 27; 11:18, 22).

---

257. This means that the term νόμος does not mean the Torah in this context. But interpreters are divided on the issue. Those who maintain that it does include U. Wilckens, *Römer*, 2:122; J. Dunn, *Romans*, 416-17; E. Lohse, *Römer*, 229; and R. Jewett, *Romans*, 480-81. Those who reject that view and understand the term as a figure of speech include C. Cranfield, *Romans*, 375-76; J. Fitzmyer, *Romans*, 482-83; D. Moo, *Romans*, 473-77; H. Räisänen, *Paul and the Law*, 52; L. Keck, "The Law and 'the Law of Sin and Death' (Rom 8:1-4), 41-57; and M. Winger, *By What Law?* 195. That Paul uses wordplay here is affirmed by E. P. Sanders, *Paul, the Law, and the Jewish People*, 26, 98. It is interpreted as "principle" or "rule" by J. Bertone, "*The Law of the Spirit*," 178-79.

8:3-4 The syntax of 8:3-4 is complex, consisting of 46 words within one long sentence in the Greek text. The sentence begins with the phrase τὸ γὰρ ἀδύνατον τοῦ νόμου, which can be translated, "For that which was impossible for the law."[258] The adjective ἀδύνατον ("impossible") with the article (τό) becomes the subject of the clause. Yet the clause is elliptical and can only be rescued by supplying an additional verb ("to do").[259] The main clause is yet to come, beginning with ὁ θεός ("God") as the subject, followed by an aorist participle (πέμψας, "having sent") and a main verb late in the sentence (κατέκρινεν, "he condemned"). But the sentence remains extremely difficult to follow. The best way to relieve the difficulty is to supply once again a form of the verb "to do" in the main clause (cf. "God has done" in the RSV and NRSV, "God did" in NIV) and divide the long sentence into two, as follows: "For that which was impossible for the law to do, because it was weakened through the flesh, God has done. By sending his own Son in the likeness of sinful flesh, and for sin, he condemned sin in the flesh." That relieves the difficulty to the end of the main clause in 8:3, even though that is still not the end of the matter, for a purpose clause follows in the Greek text that fills out an entire additional verse (8:4). But what is said in 8:3 calls for more immediate attention.

Paul has made positive comments about the law, such as how it is holy (7:12), good (7:13), and spiritual (7:14). It therefore strikes the ear as strange to hear him say that the law "was weakened through the flesh."[260] How could the law itself be "weakened" when in fact it is human weakness that fails to do what the law commands? There are two possibilities. One possibility is that, according to Paul, the law itself was weakened, or became ineffective, in the face of human resistance. It could no longer have power over humanity, much less over the power of sin, and was therefore weakened;[261] it fell from its former authoritative place and was truly diminished. The other, more likely possibility is that, although the law itself remains holy, good, and spiritual, humanity (due to the power of sin) is incapable of observing it, so the law is frustrated, made ineffective, and thus weakened as a force in human life.[262]

Because of the weakness due to the flesh (human weakness), God has entered into the human sphere for a saving purpose. Paul says that God sent his

258. The translation is adapted from BDAG 22 (ἀδύνατος, 2, b): "what was impossible for the law (God has done)."

259. Cf. NIV: "For what the law was powerless to do."

260. The expression ἐν ᾧ ἠσθένει in 8:3 can be rendered "because it was weakened." The phrase ἐν ᾧ regularly has the meaning "because" in the letters of Paul. For discussion, see exegesis of 5:12. Cf. also BDAG 365 (ἐπί, 6, c); BDF 123 (§235).

261. J. Fitzmyer, *Romans*, 484; somewhat similarly, B. Byrne, *Romans*, 236.

262. Cf. C. Cranfield, *Romans*, 397; J. Ziesler, *Romans*, 203; L. Keck, *Romans*, 197-98; R. Jewett, *Romans*, 483.

Son "for sin" (περὶ ἁμαρτίας), an expression used only here in the letters of Paul, but commonly employed by other writers (Heb 10:6, 8; 1 Pet 3:18; 1 John 2:2; 4:10). Elsewhere Paul uses a different prepositional phrase in Greek, also meaning "for sin" (ὑπὲρ τῶν ἁμαρτιῶν ἡμῶν, 1 Cor 15:3; Gal 1:4, literally, "for our sins"). Noticeable, too, are the different subjects of the sentences in the various formulas.[263] At times Paul makes Christ the subject: Christ died "for us" (Rom 5:8; Gal 3:13; 1 Thess 5:10), "for all" (2 Cor 5:14-15), "for the ungodly" (Rom 5:6), and "for our sins" (1 Cor 15:3; Gal 1:4). On the other hand, Paul uses "God" as the subject of the sentence in "sending" formulas, as in the present passage (Rom 8:3: "God, . . . sending his own Son") and later in the chapter (Rom 8:32: "God . . . gave him up for us all"). God is also the subject of a sentence where he makes Christ sin "for us" (2 Cor 5:21). These formulas are in agreement with Paul's declaration also that "in Christ God was reconciling the world to himself" (2 Cor 5:19). Paul's theology of redemption is primarily theopractic, and it could be no other for this son of Israel and its scriptural heritage. That is to say, while Christ is the means by which redemption is carried out, the God of Israel — and of the whole world — is the primary actor in the drama. One cannot derive from Paul any theory of the atonement that implies that the Son has to appease the wrath of God (the Father). The work of redemption is the work of God in Christ.

God sent his Son, says Paul, "in the likeness of sinful flesh" (ἐν ὁμοιώματι σαρκὸς ἁμαρτίας). The word "likeness" (ὁμοίωμα, used by Paul also at Rom 1:23; 5:14; 6:5; and Phil 2:7) is used to speak of the similarity of Jesus with sinful humanity. The words following ("of sinful flesh") do not imply that he was himself sinful. Paul simply means that "Jesus in his earthly career was similar to sinful humans and yet not totally like them";[264] God sent his Son to the very place in which sin had set up its power: "in the worldly-physical sphere to which all human beings belong without exception."[265] There he experienced the effects of sin; he suffered death, the result of sin.[266] By the sending of his Son and the consequent crucifixion of the Son, God "condemned sin in the flesh." As Paul puts it elsewhere, God made Christ to be sin "for us" (ὑπὲρ ἡμῶν, 2 Cor 5:21), and he gave him up "for us all" (ὑπὲρ ἡμῶν πάντων, Rom 8:32). In short, the wrath of God has been expended in the death of Jesus upon the cross, an event that is complete and sufficient as the redemptive work of God for the world.

263. These distinctions have been highlighted by W. Kramer, *Christ, Lord, Son of God*, 127.

264. BDAG 707 (ὁμοίωμα, 3); cf. Traugott Holtz, "ὁμοίωμα," *EDNT* 2:513; F. Gillman, "Another Look at Romans 8:3," 604, responding to V. Branick, "The Sinful Flesh of the Son of God (Rom. 8:3)," 246-62, for whom there is, according to Paul, no distinction between Christ and sinful flesh.

265. Alexander Sand, "σάρξ," *EDNT* 3:231.

266. J. Fitzmyer, *Romans*, 485.

The purpose clause in 8:4 is dependent on what has gone previously. By dealing with sin, abolishing its effects, Jesus has fulfilled "the just requirement" (δικαίωμα) of the law for those who are beneficiaries of his atoning death. The logic flows along these lines: (1) the law requires righteousness; (2) humanity falls short of it because of its weakness; (3) the consequence of falling short is condemnation; (4) but God has exercised his judgment and wrath at the cross. There is therefore no further need for those "who walk . . . according to the Spirit" to seek to fulfill "the just requirement." It is fulfilled "in us" (ἐν ἡμῖν), Paul says, people of the new age, the era of the Spirit, who are bound to Christ and his destiny and who walk by the Spirit. The Spirit is "a shared experience which forms their common bond."[267] If the requirement has been fulfilled in the crucified Christ, it has been fulfilled in his people as well. For more on the atoning work of God in Christ, see the exegesis of 5:6-11.

Those who are in Christ walk "according to the Spirit" rather than "according to the flesh." Paul uses the verb περιπατέω ("to walk") 15 additional times to speak of the way of life expected of the believer.[268] Here, as in other instances where the verb is used, the conduct of one's life is portrayed as a "walk." The walk is not, however, in accord with precepts within the Torah (the halakhot [הֲלָכוֹת], derived from the verb "to walk" [הָלַךְ]). Paul preserves the verb from Hellenistic Jewish tradition,[269] but for him the "walk" is in "newness of life" (Rom 6:4), "by the Spirit" (Rom 8:4; Gal 5:16), and "in love" (Rom 14:15). Paul cannot therefore be charged with libertinism (contra the charge echoed in 3:8; cf. 6:1, 15).[270] The believer's life is not guided by the Torah, to be sure, but it is led by the Spirit (Rom 8:14; Gal 5:18). For further discussion of the verb "to walk," see the exegesis of 6:4.

8:5-8 In these verses Paul describes the antitheses between two courses of life; there is no third. The first way is a life "according to the flesh"; the other is life "according to the Spirit." The first is characterized by having one's thoughts set on things of the flesh, bringing death, hostility toward God, and an inability to please God. The second is characterized by having one's thoughts set on things of the Spirit, bringing life and peace. Similar antitheses between the flesh and the Spirit appear elsewhere in Paul's letters (Gal 3:3; 5:16-26; 6:8; Phil 3:3).

For Paul the term "flesh" has a wide range of meanings. The concept of

---

267. J. Dunn, *Romans*, 424.

268. Rom 6:4; 13:13; 14:15; 1 Cor 3:3; 7:17; 2 Cor 4:2; 5:7; 10:3; 12:18; Gal 5:16; Phil 3:17, 18; 1 Thess 2:12; 4:1, 12.

269. Cf. 2 Kgs 20:3; Prov 8:20; Eccl 11:9. Often other verbs are used for "walking" in the way of the Lord, righteousness, or the law; cf. Exod 16:4; Lev 18:4; Deut 13:4 Prov 28:6; LXX Ps 77:10; Philo, *Gig.* 1.13 (§58); *Migr.* 1.26 (§143, 146); *Spec. Leg.* 2.28 (§160).

270. A. Wedderburn, "Pauline Pneumatology and Pauline Theology," 154.

life in the flesh can express the normal manner of earthly existence (Gal 2:20; 2 Cor 10:3; Phil 1:22, 24; Phlm 16); typical human standards of thought and action (1 Cor 1:26; 2 Cor 1:17; 5:16; Gal 3:3); or the arena in which sinful inclinations reside. It is not, like both the Spirit and sin, a power per se, but if "the flesh" becomes the norm by which a person directs one's life, it becomes a power that shapes that life.[271] A person is enticed to put trust in the flesh, and the result is that it takes on "the character of a power which is opposed to the working of the Spirit."[272] Living "according to the flesh" (8:5) includes "the pursuit of the merely human, the earthly-transitory,"[273] but it ends up being more than that, for it is finally "hostile to God" (8:7). It goes without saying, then, that such a person does not obey the law of God (which Paul regards as holy, 7:12), nor can that person please God.

Living according to the Spirit, however, is totally different. Paul operates here under the assumption that all believers are recipients of the Spirit and its various gifts (1 Cor 12:1-13; Gal 3:3; 5:25). Liberated from the life according to the flesh, leading toward death, the believer is open to the power of God and is, in fact, empowered by the Spirit to live in the newness of life available through faith in Christ (Rom 6:4).

8:9-11 In these verses the apostle speaks of believers as both dwelling within the Spirit and as being possessed by it as a power that lives within them. The two expressions appear in close proximity at 8:9 and 8:11:

8:9a: "You [plural: ὑμεῖς] are in the Spirit."
8:9b: "The Spirit of God dwells in you [plural: ἐν ὑμῖν]."
8:11: "The Spirit is in you [plural: ἐν ὑμῖν]."

This is parallel to Christ-language. Paul can speak of persons "in Christ," and he can speak of Christ in various persons:

Persons are in Christ:	*Christ is in persons:*
Rom 8:1 (τοῖς ἐν Χριστῷ Ἰησοῦ).	Rom 8:10 (Χριστὸς ἐν ὑμῖν)
2 Cor 5:17 (τις ἐν Χριστῷ)	2 Cor 13:5 (Χριστὸς ἐν ὑμῖν)
2 Cor 12:2 (ἄνθρωπον ἐν Χριστῷ)	Gal 2:20 (ἐν ἐμοὶ Χριστός)

The question can be raised as to whether there is a distinction between the two forms of expression, whether that be the Christological ("in Christ" or "Christ in" a person) or the pneumatological expressions ("in the Spirit," "Spirit in" a

---

271. Eduard Schweizer, "σάρξ," *TDNT* 7:132.
272. Eduard Schweizer, "σάρξ," *TDNT* 7:133.
273. R. Bultmann, *Theology of the New Testament*, 1:238.

person). Although they are not identical, they are closely related. A dynamic identity of Christ and the Spirit is made by Paul in his declaration that "the Lord is the Spirit" (2 Cor 3:17; cf. 1 Cor 15:45). Finally, one can say that, for Paul, "Christ and Spirit are perceived in experience as one."[274]

That Paul uses plural forms for "you" in 8:9-11 begs the question whether he speaks of the Spirit and the individual or, by contrast, only of the Spirit and the church corporately. If the latter is meant alone, the first expression (8:9a) could remain as it is, but the latter two (8:9b, 11) could be translated as "The Spirit of God dwells among you" and "The Spirit is among you" or "in your midst."[275] Paul can be understood as speaking to his readers corporately about a reality that is both corporate and individual. This becomes clear from the statement in 8:9c, in which individualizing takes place within the paragraph: "But if anyone [Greek: singular τις] does not have the Spirit of Christ, that person [singular οὗτος, literally, "this one"] does not belong to him."

In 8:9 Paul uses two expressions concerning the Spirit: "the Spirit of God" and "the Spirit of Christ." Of these, he uses the former eight times in his undisputed letters (Rom 8:9, 14; 15:19; 1 Cor 2:11; 6:11; 7:40; 12:3; Phil 3:3), plus two other equivalent phrases (Rom 8:11: "the Spirit of him who raised Jesus from the dead"; and 2 Cor 3:3: "the Spirit of the living God"). The "Spirit of Christ" or its equivalent is used less frequently. Paul employs the phrase "the Spirit of Jesus Christ" (Phil 1:19), "the Spirit of his Son" (Gal 4:6), and more oblique expressions, such as "the Spirit of the Lord" (2 Cor 3:17) and "a life-giving Spirit" (referring to Christ, 1 Cor 15:45). Often Paul uses simply the term "the Spirit" (Rom 8:27; 15:30; 1 Cor 2:10; Gal 3:5) or "the Holy Spirit" (Rom 14:17; 15:13, 16; 1 Cor 6:19; 2 Cor 13:14; cf. Rom 1:4). For him, the Spirit is associated with both God and Christ. God is the giver or sender of the Spirit (Rom 5:5; 2 Cor 1:22; 5:5; Gal 3:5; 4:6; 1 Thess 4:8), and so the Spirit can rightfully be called "the Spirit of God." In this understanding Paul's view of the Spirit is rooted directly in the OT, where God fills a person with the Spirit (Exod 31:3) or pours it out (Joel 2:28); it comes upon persons to carry out various activities (Num 24:2; Judg 3:10).[276] In the present context the Spirit is the power of God that animates the life of the Christian in the earthly struggle (8:11, 13b).

The expression "the Spirit of Christ" is used by only one other NT writer (1 Pet 1:11).[277] It does not signify any other power than the Holy Spirit itself. It is another designation of the one Spirit, which can be known more fully from its

274. J. Dunn, *Romans*, 430.

275. Cf. R. Jewett, *Romans*, 474, 489, 492 (opposing the "individualistic construal," p. 489, n. 160).

276. Cf. G. Fee, "Christology and Pneumatology," 317.

277. The "Spirit of Christ" passages in Paul's letters are discussed in detail by A. Gabriel, "Pauline Pneumatology," 355-60.

association with Christ and the redemption that God has accomplished through him. "Paul sees Christ as having conveyed the life and activity of God, so that now the Spirit is defined by Christ."[278] It is only by the work of the Spirit that anyone can make the confession that Jesus is Lord (1 Cor 12:3); believers are baptized by the one Spirit into Christ (1 Cor 12:13); and it is by the work of the Spirit that believers know themselves to be children of God and joint heirs with Christ (Rom 8:15-17). The works and enlightenment of the Spirit do not operate apart from Christ, who is Lord of the Spirit (2 Cor 3:18),[279] distributing the Spirit and the Spirit's gifts as he wills. Not to have the Spirit of Christ, Paul says, is not to belong to him. On the question whether being "in Christ" or being possessed by the Spirit implies that Paul was a mystic (which it does not), see the exegesis of Romans 6:3-4.

Having declared that his readers are "in the Spirit" (8:9a), Paul goes on to affirm that the Spirit is the "Spirit of God." The word εἴπερ (8:9b, "since" in the NRSV) can have the meaning "if indeed," introducing a conditional clause, as in some modern versions (KJV, RSV, NIV, and NET), and favored by some interpreters.[280] But it can also mean "since,"[281] as in the NRSV. The latter fits the context better at this place, for it need not make the main clause conditional.[282] Paul has just declared that his readers are "not in the flesh" but "in the Spirit." It is unlikely that he would go on to qualify that declaration with a condition that expresses a degree of doubt.

Both 8:10 and 8:11 begin with conditional sentences ("if Christ is in you" and "if the Spirit . . . dwells in you"), but they do not thereby imply doubt. They are instances where the conjunction εἰ ("if") has the nuance of "since" (as at Rom 6:8; 15:27).[283]

The first of these verses (8:10) poses a major problem. Does the term τὸ πνεῦμα mean "the Spirit" (the Holy Spirit) — as in the KJV, NRSV, ESV, and NET — which is favored by some interpreters,[284] or does it mean "the spirit"

---

278. J. Ziesler, *Romans*, 210.

279. Although the risen Christ is Lord of the Spirit, it is the Spirit of God who raised Jesus from the dead (8:11). Cf. A. Wedderburn, "Pauline Pneumatology and Pauline Theology," 153.

280. J. Dunn, *Romans*, 428; J. Fitzmyer, *Romans*, 490.

281. BDAG 279 (εἰ, 6, 1). Paul uses the term at 3:30, where it clearly means "since," but also uses it at 8:17, where it appears to have the meaning of "if indeed."

282. Cf. C. Cranfield, *Romans*, 388; R. Harrisville, *Romans*, 125. Cf. R. Jewett, "The Question of the 'Apportioned Spirit' in Paul's Letters," 195-96 (translating the term as "so indeed"); idem, *Romans*, 489 ("since indeed").

283. BDF 189 (§372.1); 237 (§454.2); cf. BDAG 278 (εἰ, 3), although Rom 8:10-11 is not cited.

284. U. Wilckens, *Römer*, 2:132; C. Cranfield, *Romans*, 390; E. Käsemann, *Romans*, 224; J. Murray, *Romans*, 1:289; J. Dunn, *Romans*, 431; B. Byrne, *Romans*, 245; D. Moo, *Romans*, 492; R. Jewett, *Romans*, 491; E. Lohse, *Römer*, 235-36.

(the human spirit) — as in the ASV, RSV, and NIV — which is favored by others?[285] Initially one might seek to resolve the issue by noticing that the clauses within the verse are set in an almost perfectly styled parallelism:

τὸ μὲν σῶμα νεκρὸν διὰ ἁμαρτίαν
τὸ δὲ πνεῦμα ζωὴ διὰ δικαιοσύνην.

On the one hand, the body is dead on account of sin,
But on the other hand, the spirit [or Spirit] is life on account of
    righteousness.

The parallel between the word σῶμα ("body") and its counterpart, πνεῦμα ("spirit"), would seem to indicate that the latter refers to the human spirit. But the parallelism is not quite perfect. If a true parallelism were intended, the second line should not have the noun ζωή ("life") but an adjective or adjectival participle, such as ζῶν ("living," a term which Paul uses elsewhere, Rom 6:11; 7:3, 9; 1 Thess 4:15, 17). Literally, what Paul says is that "the spirit (or Spirit) is life," and such a statement makes sense only if Paul is speaking here of the Holy Spirit. By implication the clause means that the presence of the Spirit results in life for believers. Where the Spirit is, there is life. This coheres with what Paul has declared earlier in the chapter. At 8:2 he speaks of the Spirit as "the Spirit of life," and at 8:6 he says that setting the mind on the Spirit is "life and peace." Furthermore, the Spirit brings newness of life to believers (7:6), and Paul will go on to say to his readers: "if by the Spirit you put to death the deeds of the body, you will live" (8:13).

The twin, parallel phrases "on account of sin" and "on account of righteousness" in this verse pose difficulties for interpretation as well. The first is used in connection with the "body" which is now "dead," and that is because of sin. The body must have in this context its most elementary meaning — the physical, corporal aspect of the self.[286] Because of sin, and without the redemption brought by God's act in Christ, the self is bound to die (cf. Rom 5:12-21; 7:24). But, Paul declares, Christ dwells within believers, and the Spirit brings life "on account of righteousness," referring to the righteousness of God that attends the coming of Christ into the world for redemption, and is bestowed upon believers, "the righteousness from God based on faith" (Phil 3:9).[287] Christ, the Spirit, and the righteousness of God are all means of conferring life:

---

285. W. Sanday and A. Headlam, *Romans*, 198; J. Fitzmyer, *Romans*, 491.

286. R. Bultmann, *Theology of the New Testament*, 1:192-95.

287. Cf. C. Cranfield, *Romans*, 390; J. Ziesler, *Romans*, 212; U. Wilckens, *Römer*, 2:133; J. Dunn, *Romans*, 432, 444; J. Fitzmyer, *Romans*, 491; D. Moo, *Romans*, 492; R. Jewett, *Romans*, 492; E. Lohse, *Römer*, 236. According to B. Byrne, *Romans*, 245, however, it is "the ethical righteousness created in believers through the operation of the Spirit."

Christ is the one through whom life is given (Rom 5:17, 21); the Spirit is the source of new life (Rom 7:6; 8-2; 2 Cor 3:6); and the justifying, rightwising action of God in the redemptive death of Christ is the means by which salvation is secured (Rom 1:17; 3:21), leading to life (5:17-18).

The final verse in this section (8:11) is compact with theological, Christological, pneumatological, and soteriological terms: "And if the Spirit of him who raised Jesus from the dead dwells in you, he who raised Christ from the dead will also give life to your mortal bodies through his Spirit that dwells in you" (8:11). One can hardly avoid noticing that, even prior to later formulations in which God is understood as triune, there are assertions here concerning the unity of God, Christ, and the Spirit. They are not coequal in majesty, however, since God (the Father) is the middle term of their interrelationships. The Holy Spirit is the Spirit of God, and God is the one who raised Jesus from the dead.

Paul's interest here is not to define these relationships; he seems to be drawing phrases from traditional formulations already known to him and perhaps to his readers. His interest is to speak of the saving work of God in Christ. The Spirit dwells in believers, and by that Spirit God will continue to animate their lives in the earthly struggle. The term "mortal bodies" refers once again to the physical, corporate aspect of people's lives, which is subject to death. But, says Paul, God will give life to those in whom the Spirit dwells, both in the earthly struggle and through resurrection. The former can be implied by what has been said previously in the chapter concerning life in the present, particularly the walking by the Spirit that comes to those whose minds are set upon the Spirit (8:4-6; cf. 8:13). The latter — an assertion concerning resurrection — can be implied by the double reference in the verse to God's raising Jesus from the dead and by his use of the future tense verb ζῳοποιήσει ("[God] will give life"). Paul uses a form of the same verb elsewhere to speak of God's raising the dead: "For as in Adam all die, so also in Christ shall all be made alive (ζῳοποιηθήσονται)" (1 Cor 15:22; cf. Rom 4:17; 1 Cor 15:35-36).

It would seem that the final prepositional phrase διὰ τοῦ ἐνοικοῦντος αὐτοῦ πνεύματος ἐν ὑμῖν ("through his Spirit that dwells in you") is superfluous. It would be sufficient to say that "he [= God] who raised Christ from the dead will also give life to your mortal bodies." Why does he seem to have a need to add the phrase? Moreover, the phrase appears to be redundant. Paul has referred to the indwelling of the Spirit among believers already at the beginning of the verse ("if the Spirit of him who raised Jesus from the dead dwells in you"). One solution is that it is simply a "cumbersome repetition."[288] But if one removes the introductory clause, what remains has the appearance of a creedal formula in two respects: (1) the familiar use of ὁ followed by a participle at the beginning ("he

288. J. Dunn, *Romans*, 433.

who" or the like), which is used in creedal formulas elsewhere;[289] and (2) the parallelism of verbs (ἐγείρας//ζωοποιήσει; "who raised"//"will give life"):

> ὁ ἐγείρας Χριστὸν ἐκ νεκρῶν
> ζωοποιήσει καὶ τὰ θνητὰ σώματα ὑμῶν
>   διὰ τοῦ ἐνοικοῦντος αὐτοῦ πνεύματος ἐν ὑμῖν.

> He who raised Christ from the dead
> will also give life to your mortal bodies
>   through his Spirit that dwells in you.

The formula speaks of the instrumentality of the Spirit in the resurrection of the dead, as though God's Spirit, dwelling within those who belong to Christ, revivifies them in the resurrection. This is somewhat comparable in conceptuality to the vision in Ezekiel 37:1-14, in which the Spirit (or breath) of the Lord breathes life into the dry bones, bringing them to life. In any case, what Paul writes shares the viewpoint of the early creedal formula of Romans 1:3 concerning the resurrection of Jesus, in which the Spirit is instrumental in the resurrection of Jesus from the dead (see the exegesis there for discussion). This formula is not, then, likely to have originated with Paul. It can be considered a pre-Pauline kerygmatic formula that Paul has incorporated into his letter. But for him the formula is no longer solely one that speaks of resurrection. As indicated already, for Paul the formula is also used for the life of service in the world. The Spirit dwells within the community of believers, and through the Spirit God empowers its members to "walk not according to the flesh but according to the Spirit" (8:4).

BIBLIOGRAPHY

Bayes, J. F. "The Translation of Romans 8:3." *ExpTim* 111 (1999): 14-16.

Bertone, John A. *"The Law of the Spirit": Experience of the Spirit and Displacement of the Law in Romans 8:1-16.* StudBL 86. New York: Peter Lang, 2005.

Branick, Vincent P. "The Sinful Flesh of the Son of God (Rom. 8:3): A Key Image of Pauline Theology." *CBQ* 47 (1985) 246-62.

Breytenbach, Cilliers. "The 'For Us' Phrases in Pauline Soteriology: Considering Their Background and Use." In *Salvation in the New Testament: Perspectives on Soteriology,* 163-85. Ed. Jan G. van der Watt. NovTSup 121. Boston: E. J. Brill, 2005.

Bultmann, Rudolf. *Theology of the New Testament.* 2 vols. New York: Charles Scribner's Sons, 1951-55.

Christoph, Monika. *Pneuma und das neue Sein der Glaubenden: Studien zur Semantik und Pragmatik der Rede von Pneuma in Röm 8.* EHS.T 23/813. Frankfurt am Main: Peter Lang, 2005.

289. Rom 1:3; 4:25; Phil 2:6; 1 Tim 2:6; 3:16; 2 Tim 1:9.

Coetzer, W. C. "The Holy Spirit and the Eschatological View in Romans 8." *Neot* 15 (1981): 180-98.

Cranfield, C. E. B. "The Freedom of the Christian according to Romans 8.2." In *New Testament Christianity for Africa and the World: Essays in Honour of Harry Sawyer*, 91-98. Ed. M. E. Glasswell and E. W. Fasholé-Luke. London: SPCK, 1974.

———. "Paul's Teaching on Sanctification, with Special Reference to the Epistle to the Romans." *RefRev* 48 (1994-95): 217-29; reprinted in his *On Romans and Other New Testament Essays*, 33-49. Edinburgh: T&T Clark, 1998.

———. "St. Paul and the Law." *SJT* 17 (1964): 43-68.

Dahl, Nils A. "A Synopsis of Romans 5:1-11 and 8:1-39." In his *Studies in Paul: Theology for the Christian Mission*, 88-90. Minneapolis: Augsburg Publishing House, 1977.

Dillon, Richard J. "The Spirit as Taskmaster and Troublemaker in Romans 8." *CBQ* 60 (1998): 687-702.

Engberg-Pedersen, Troels. "The Material Spirit: Cosmology and Ethics in Paul." *NTS* 55 (2009): 179-97.

Fee, Gordon D. "Christology and Pneumatology in Romans 8:9-11 — and Elsewhere: Some Reflections on Paul as a Trinitarian." In *Jesus of Nazareth: Lord and Christ: Essays on the Historical Jesus and New Testament Christology*, 312-31. Ed. Joel B. Green and Max Turner. Grand Rapids: Wm. B. Eerdmans, 1994.

———. *God's Empowering Presence: The Holy Spirit in the Letters of Paul*. Peabody: Hendrickson Publishers, 1994.

———. "Translational Tendenz: English Versions and Πνεῦμα in Paul." In *The Holy Spirit and Christian Origins: Essays in Honor of James D. G. Dunn*, 349-59. Ed. Graham N. Stanton et al. Grand Rapids: Wm. B. Eerdmans, 2004.

Finlan, Stephen. *The Background and Content of Paul's Cultic Atonement Metaphors.* SBLAB 19. Atlanta: Society of Biblical Literature, 2004.

Fitzmyer, Joseph A. "Paul and the Dead Sea Scrolls." In *The Dead Sea Scrolls after Fifty Years: A Comprehensive Assessment*, 2:599-621. Ed. Peter W. Flint and James C. VanderKam. 2 vols. Boston: E. J. Brill, 1998-99.

Fortna, Robert T. "Romans 8:10 and Paul's Doctrine of the Spirit." *ATR* 41 (1959): 77-84.

Fuchs, Ernst. "Der Anteil des Geistes am Glauben des Paulus: Ein Beitrag zum Verständnis von Römer 8." *ZTK* 72 (1975): 293-302.

Gabriel, Andrew K. "Pauline Pneumatology and the Question of Trinitarian Presuppositions." In *Paul and His Theology*, 347-62. Ed. Stanley E. Porter. PAST 3. Boston: E. J. Brill, 2006.

Gillman, Florence Morgan. "Another Look at Romans 8:3: 'In the Likeness of Sinful Flesh.'" *CBQ* 49 (1987): 597-604.

Greene, M. Dwaine. "A Note on Romans 8:3." *BZ* 35 (1991): 103-6.

Hamilton, Neill Q. *The Holy Spirit and Eschatology in Paul*. SJTOP 6. Edinburgh: Oliver and Boyd, 1957.

Hendricks, William L. "Paul's Use of 'Flesh.'" *BI* 92 (1983): 50-52.

Hermann, Ingo. *Kyrios und Pneuma: Studien zur Christologie der paulinischen Hauptbriefe.* Munich: Kösel Verlag, 1961.

Horn, Friedrich W. *Das Angeld des Geistes: Studien zur paulinischen Pneumatologie.* FRLANT 154. Göttingen: Vandenhoeck & Ruprecht, 1992.

Jewett, Robert. "The Question of the 'Apportioned Spirit' in Paul's Letters: Romans as a Case Study." In *The Holy Spirit and Christian Origins: Essays in Honor of James D. G. Dunn,* 193-206. Ed. Graham N. Stanton et al. Grand Rapids: Wm. B. Eerdmans, 2004.

Käsemann, Ernst. "The Cry for Liberty in the Worship of the Church." In his *Perspectives on Paul,* 122-37. Philadelphia: Fortress Press, 1971.

Keck, Leander E. "The Law and 'the Law of Sin and Death' (Rom 8:1-4): Reflections on the Spirit and Ethics in Paul." In *The Divine Helmsman: Studies on God's Control of Human Events, Presented to Lou H. Silberman,* 41-57. Ed. James L. Crenshaw and Samuel Sandmel. New York: KTAV Publishing House, 1980.

Keesmaat, Sylvia C. "Exodus and the Intertextual Transformation of Tradition in Romans 8:14-30." *JSNT* 54 (1994): 29-56.

Kramer, Werner R. *Christ, Lord, Son of God.* SBT 50. London: SCM Press, 1966.

Kuhn, Karl G. "New Light on Temptation, Sin, and Flesh in the New Testament." In *The Scrolls and the New Testament,* 94-113. Ed. Krister Stendahl. New York: Harper & Brothers, 1957.

Lambrecht, Jan. "The Implied Exhortation in Romans 8,5-8." *Greg* 81 (2000): 441-51.

Levison, John R. *Filled with the Spirit.* Grand Rapids: Wm. B. Eerdmans, 2009.

———. *The Spirit in First-Century Judaism.* AGAJU 29. New York: E. J. Brill, 1997.

Loane, Marcus L. *The Hope of Glory: An Exposition of the Eighth Chapter in the Epistle to the Romans.* London: Hodder and Stoughton, 1968.

Lohse, Eduard. "Ὁ νόμος τοῦ πνεύματος τῆς ζωῆς. Exegetische Anmerkungen zu Röm 8,2." In *Neues Testament und christliche Existenz: Festschrift für Herbert Braun,* 287-97. Ed. Hans D. Betz and Luise Schottroff, 279-87. Tübingen: J. C. B. Mohr (Paul Siebeck), 1973.

———. "Zur Analyse und Interpretation von Röm. 8,1-17." In *The Law of the Spirit in Romans 7 and 8,* 129-66. Ed. Lorenzo de Lorenzi. Rome: St. Paul's Abbey, 1976.

Lowe, Chuck. "There Is No Condemnation (Romans 1:8): But Why Not?" *JETS* 42 (1999): 231-50.

Luz, Ulrich. "Paul as Mystic." In *The Holy Spirit and Christian Origins: Essays in Honor of James D. G. Dunn,* 131-43. Ed. Graham N. Stanton et al. Grand Rapids: Wm. B. Eerdmans, 2004.

Lyonnet, Stanislas. "Christian Freedom and the Law of the Spirit according to Paul." In *The Christian Lives by the Spirit,* 145-74. Ed. Ignace de la Potterie and Stanislas Lynonnet. Staten Island: Alba House, 1971.

———. "Le Nouveau Testament à la lumière de l'Ancien, à propos de Rom 8,2-4." *NRT* 87 (1965): 561-87.

McLean, Bradley H. *The Cursed Christ: Mediterranean Expulsion Rituals and Pauline Soteriology.* JSNTSup 126. Sheffield: Sheffield Academic Press, 1996.

Menzies, Robert. *The Development of Early Christian Pneumatology.* JSNTSup 54. Sheffield: Sheffield Academic Press, 1991.

Meyer, Paul W. "The Holy Spirit in the Pauline Letters: A Contextual Exploration." *Int* 33 (1979): 3-18.

Moule, C. F. D. "'Justification' in Its Relation to the Condition κατὰ πνεῦμα (Rom 8:1-11)." In *Battesimo e giustizia in Rom 6 e 8*, 177-87. Ed. Lorenzo de Lorenzi. Rome: St. Paul's Abbey, 1974.

Osten-Sacken, Peter von der. *Römer 8 als Beispiel paulinischer Soteriologie*. FRLANT 112. Göttingen: Vandenhoeck & Ruprecht, 1975.

Paulsen, Henning. *Überlieferung und Auslegung in Römer 8*. WMANT 43. Neukirchen-Vluyn: Neukirchener Verlag, 1974.

Philip, Finny. *The Origins of Pauline Pneumatology: The Eschatological Bestowal of the Spirit upon Gentiles in Judaism and in the Early Development of Paul's Theology*. WUNT 2/194. Tübingen: J. C. B. Mohr (Paul Siebeck), 2005.

Räisänen, Heikki. "Das 'Gesetz des Glaubens' (Röm. 3.27) und das 'Gesetz des Geistes' (Röm. 8.2)." *NTS* 26 (1979): 101-17; reprinted in his *Torah and Christ: Essays in German and English on the Problem of the Law in Early Christianity*, 95-118. SESJ 45. Helsinki: Finnish Exegetical Society, 1986.

———. *Paul and the Law*. Philadelphia: Fortress Press, 1983

Sanders, E. P. *Paul, the Law, and the Jewish People*. Philadelphia: Fortress Press, 1983

Schweizer, Eduard. "Was meinen wir eigentlich wenn wir sagen, 'Gott sandte seinen Sohn . . .'? *NTS* 37 (1991): 204-24.

———. "Zum religionsgeschichtlichen Hintergrund der 'Sendungformel' Gal 4,4f. Rm 8,3f. Joh 3,16f. 1 Joh 4,9." *ZNW* 57 (1966): 199-210; reprinted in his *Beiträge zur Theologie des Neuen Testaments: Neutestamentliche Aufsätze (1955-1970)*, 83-95. Zurich: Zwingli Verlag, 1970.

Stanley, David M. "The Atonement as a Work Proper to God as Father, to Christ as Son: Rom 8:3-4." In his *Christ's Resurrection in Pauline Soteriology*, 189-92. Rome: Pontifical Biblical Institute Press, 1961.

Theobald, Michael. "'Sohn Gottes' als christologische Grundmetapher bei Paulus." *TQ* 174 (1994) 185-207.

Thompson, Richard W. "How Is the Law Fulfilled in Us? An Interpretation of Rom 8:4." *LS* 11 (1986): 31-40.

Thornton, T. C. G. "The Meaning of καὶ περὶ ἁμαρτίας in Romans viii. 3." *JTS* 22 (1971): 515-17.

Wedderburn. Alexander J. M. "Pauline Pneumatology and Pauline Theology." In *The Holy Spirit and Christian Origins: Essays in Honor of James D. G. Dunn*, 144-56. Ed. Graham N. Stanton et al. Grand Rapids: Wm. B. Eerdmans, 2004.

Wilder, William N. *Freed from the Law to Be Led by the Spirit*. StudBL 23. New York: Peter Lang, 2001.

Winger, Michael. *By What Law? The Meaning of Νόμος in the Letters of Paul*. SBLDS 128. Atlanta: Scholars Press, 1992.

Wright, N. T. "The Meaning of περὶ ἁμαρτίας in Romans 8:3." In *Studia Biblica 1978: Sixth International Congress on Biblical Studies, Oxford, 3-7 April 1978*, 3:453-59. Ed. Elizabeth A. Livingstone. 3 vols. Sheffield: JSOT Press, 1979-80; reprinted in his *The Climax of the Covenant: Christ and the Law in Pauline Theology*, 220-25. Minneapolis: Fortress Press, 1992.

Yates, John W. *The Spirit and Creation in Paul.* WUNT 2/251. Tübingen: Mohr Siebeck, 2008.

Ziesler, John A. "The Just Requirement of the Law (Romans 8:4)." *AusBR* 35 (1987): 77-82.

4.9. Adoption as Children of God, 8:12-17

12*So then, brothers and sisters, we are not debtors to the flesh in order to live according to the flesh — * 13*for if you live according to the flesh, you are destined to die; but if by the Spirit you put to death the deeds of the body, you will live.* 14*For as many as are led by the Spirit of God are children of God.* 15*For you did not receive a Spirit of slavery leading again to fear, but you received a Spirit of adoption, by whom we cry, "Abba! Father!"* 16*The Spirit itself bears witness with our spirit that we are children of God.* 17*And if we are children, we are also heirs — heirs of God and fellow heirs with Christ — if, in fact, we suffer with him in order that we may also be glorified with him.*

Notes on the Text and Translation

8:12 On Paul's use of "brothers and sisters," see the comment on 1:13. The Greek word ἀδελφοί is translated here as inclusive of siblings, as in the NRSV and NET.

8:13 Some ancient witnesses (D, F, and others) have πράξεις τῆς σάρκος ("deeds of the flesh") instead of πράξεις τοῦ σώματος ("deeds of the body"). That is understandable, for in light of the use of σάρξ ("flesh") in the first part of the verse, it is usually "the flesh" that is antithetical to the Spirit. But the reading of the text is far better attested. See also the exegesis below.

8:14 The sequence of the Greek words in the 26th and 27th editions of the Nestle-Aland text (υἱοὶ θεοῦ εἰσιν) differs from that of the 25th (υἱοί εἰσιν θεοῦ) and the Majority Text (εἰσιν υἱοὶ θεοῦ). The evidence for each of the first two is strong. But the translation would be the same in any of the three cases.

8:15 Some English versions (RSV and NRSV) begin a new sentence toward the end of this verse, understanding the Greek words ἐν ᾧ κράζομεν as a subordinate clause (translated as "when we cry") that introduces what follows in the remainder of 8:15 and all of 8:16. That requires a period after πνεῦμα υἱοθεσίας ("spirit of adoption"). This is also favored by some interpreters.[290] The alternative, favored by the punctuation in the 27th edition of the Nestle-Aland Greek text and other major English versions (KJV, ASV, NIV, NAB, ESV,

---

290. C. H. Dodd, *Romans,* 128; C. K. Barrett, *Romans,* 153-54.

and NET), is to keep the clause with the preceding words and to render it "by whom we cry" (ESV and NET), "through which we cry" (NAB), "whereby we cry" (KJV and ASV). NIV begins a new sentence but renders the words as "by him we cry." The rendering "by whom we cry" (or similarly) is sound, for it is likely that the phrase ἐν ᾧ refers back to the word πνεῦμα, a view favored by various interpreters.[291]

8:17b This half-verse consists of two clauses — a simple conditional clause (εἴπερ συμπάσχομεν ["if, in fact, we suffer with him"]) and a purpose clause (ἵνα καὶ συνδοξασθῶμεν ["in order that we may also be glorified with him"]). The second (the purpose clause) is dependent upon the first (the conditional clause); the first can stand without the second, but the second cannot exist without the first. In both clauses the prepositional phrase "with him" is implied but not actually represented in the Greek text.

General Comment

According to some interpreters, 8:12-13 should be understood as linked thematically to 8:1-11;[292] according to others, it rightfully begins a new section.[293] While Paul does continue here his discussion of the Spirit and the flesh, he turns it more directly to ethics. There are echoes here of what he said in 6:12-14 concerning the use of the body, resisting the passions, and using one's members as "instruments of righteousness." That ethical concern is resumed in the present passage. Paul insists that those who are "in Christ" and are "led by the Spirit" can and should put to death "the deeds of the body" and live as children of God, persons of God's household, who are in communion with God through the Spirit, doing the bidding of God.

The communal cry, "Abba Father!" (8:15), echoing the prayer language of Jesus (see below), is evidence that believers are united with him and led by the Spirit. It testifies, too, that they are indeed children of God, heirs of his promises. Whatever Christ has received, it is shared with believers, for they are "fellow heirs" with him.

There is another echo to what Paul himself has said previously. In 8:17 he speaks of suffering together with Christ. In 5:1-11 Paul wrote that believers, though justified and anticipating their sharing in the glory of God, are not ex-

---

291. E. Käsemann, *Romans*, 225; U. Wilckens, *Römer*, 2:118; C. Cranfield, *Romans*, 398; J. Dunn, *Romans*, 452; J. Fitzmyer, *Romans*, 501; P. Stuhlmacher, *Romans*, 128; E. Lohse, *Römer*, 237; R. Jewett, *Romans*, 474.

292. J. Fitzmyer, *Romans*, 492; B. Byrne, *Romans*, 235; D. Moo, *Romans*, 493.

293. W. Sanday and A. Headlam, *Romans*, 202; E. Käsemann, *Romans*, 225; C. Cranfield, *Romans*, 394; J. Dunn, *Romans*, 447; E. Lohse, *Römer*, 237.

empt from suffering in the present era (5:3). In this passage he speaks forthrightly to the suffering that comes from one's incorporation into Christ through baptism and the consequences of it as one lives in union with Christ.

Detailed Comment

8:12-13 Once again Paul addresses his readers as "brothers and sisters," an address that appears some 119 times in the undisputed letters, to express a spiritual kinship that is stronger than that of natural relationships. See the commentary at 1:13 for details. He goes on to speak of two possible ways of life that lead to two contrasting outcomes. To live according to the flesh ends in death (cf. similarly his discussion at 8:4-9), while putting to death the deeds of the body by the power of the Spirit results in life. The contrast is clear. What Paul says here resonates with his exhortation at Galatians 5:16-17: "Live by the Spirit, I say, and do not gratify the desires of the flesh. For what the flesh desires is opposed to the Spirit, and what the Spirit desires is opposed to the flesh; for these are opposed to each other, to prevent you from doing what you want." Living according to the flesh is to live for that which is transient, "a life of self-reliant pursuit of one's own ends,"[294] being bound to the power of sin, hostile to God, and therefore heading toward judgment and death.[295]

The alternative is to put to death "the deeds of the body." Here, as previously, Paul associates the body (σῶμα) with human weakness; it is mortal, and although it is not sinful itself, it is the place where sin seeks to have dominion (6:12; 8:10; cf. 7:24).[296] Paul is confident that the believer can put the deeds of the body to death "by the Spirit" (πνεύματι, instrumental dative). Although he uses a conditional sentence, there can be no doubt that the believer in Christ will be capable of engaging in the struggle against sinful deeds. The conditional sentence actually implies life in the Spirit as a present reality (see the exegesis of 8:11), and as such is the basis for the implied imperative of the verse, i.e., that one is to put to death the deeds of the body by means of the Spirit. And so Paul can say: "If we live by the Spirit, let us also be guided by the Spirit" (Gal 5:25).

8:14 The verse opens with the Greek relative pronoun ὅσοι ("as many as," but often translated "all who," as in RSV, NRSV, and NET), which implies an inclusive summary statement.[297] All who are led by the Spirit are by definition in

---

294. R. Bultmann, *Theology of the New Testament,* 1:241.
295. Alexander Sand, "σάρξ," *EDNT* 3:231.
296. Eduard Schweizer, "σῶμα," *EDNT* 3:323.
297. BDAG 729 (ὅσος, 2).

Christ and reconciled to God. Therefore, they can be counted as "children of God" (υἱοὶ θεοῦ). Several widely used English versions (e.g., KJV, RSV, NIV, ESV, and NET) render the phrase as "sons of God." But the context calls for the inclusive "children of God" (as in NRSV), men and women alike. If they are "led by the Spirit of God," they are reconciled to God and have an intimacy comparable to that of a parent and child. This is amplified in the next verse, in which Paul reminds his readers that the language of the believer's worship of God includes the language that a child uses while addressing a parent.

8:15-16 The connective word γάρ ("for") in 8:15 indicates in this instance the reason for what has just been said.[298] In order to verify that those in Christ are children of God, Paul makes a contrast and then his main point. In regard to the contrast, he says, those in Christ did not receive "a Spirit of slavery" (πνεῦμα δουλείας) but "a Spirit of adoption" (πνεῦμα υἱοθεσίας). In each case the prepositional phrases ("of slavery" and "of adoption") define the spirit/Spirit to which Paul refers, and the first is essentially a "rhetorical foil" for the second.[299] By speaking of reception of the Spirit in the aorist (ἐλάβετε), Paul must be referring to the Holy Spirit, which believers have received in baptism.[300] As such, the Spirit is not a Spirit of slavery that leads to fear; for the Spirit brings freedom ("where the Spirit of the Lord is, there is freedom," 2 Cor 3:17).

The Spirit is the Spirit of adoption. Through their baptism into Christ, believers have received the Spirit ("all were made to drink one Spirit," 1 Cor 12:13; cf. 2 Cor 1:22) and are adopted as children of God (cf. 8:23; Gal 4:5). Although the word υἱοθεσία ("adoption") does not appear in the LXX,[301] Paul does not hesitate to use it at 9:4 to speak of Israel's election, and similar terms are used in Hellenistic Judaism.[302] Moreover, the concept is implicit in the OT wherever the people of Israel are spoken of as children whom God has taken as his own (e.g., Exod 4:22; Deut 4:34; 2 Sam 7:14; Isa 1:2; Jer 31:9; Hos 11:1). The term is used here by Paul to speak of the new relationship that believers have with God through faith and baptism.[303] The analogy Paul uses probably comes primarily from Greco-Roman culture, in which the term is used in a legal sense,[304] but theologi-

298. BDAG 189 (γάρ, 1, e); B. Byrne, *Sons of God*, 98.

299. B. Byrne, *Sons of God*, 99 (n. 75).

300. Cf. E. Käsemann, *Romans*, 227; C. Cranfield, *Romans*, 396; B. Byrne, *Sons of God*, 99; J. Scott, *Adoption as Sons of God*, 262-63.

301. Although adoption was practiced in ancient Israel, instances of it are few in the OT. For a survey, cf. Frederick W. Knobloch, "Adoption," *ABD* 1:76-79.

302. For example, Philo refers to the adoption of Moses by Pharaoh's daughter, using the expression υἱὸν ποιεῖται (*Mos.* 1.19); for this and other instances, cf. J. Scott, *Adoption as Sons of God*, 75-79.

303. R. Aasgaard, "Paul as a Child," 132-33, contends that the relationship is of such intensity that to speak of it as metaphorical alone is not sufficient.

304. For texts, cf. J. Scott, *Adoption as Sons of God*, 3-57.

cally it is related to Israel's becoming God's son, or the people of Israel's becoming God's children, through election.[305] The concept is used, then, in a typological sense. As God elected Israel as a people of his own, so now those who are in Christ have been adopted as children of God through the power of the Spirit.

The evidence of the adoption as children is plain. It is children in particular who make use of the term "abba" to address their earthly fathers. The Greek word αββα (unaccented in the 26th and 27th editions of the Nestle-Aland Greek text, but accented as ἀββά in the 25th edition and in the Westcott-Hort Greek New Testament) is transliterated here by Paul from Aramaic (אַבָּא). It is less formal than the word for "father" (אָב), for it was used as a colloquialism in the home, and could also be used in reference to older or other distinguished men in the community.[306] The term was used in the prayers of Jesus (as attested at Mark 14:36), invoking God as "abba" and thereby indicating an intimate relationship with God. Although it has been claimed that the use of the term as an address to God was an innovation with Jesus,[307] that is not certain. Calling upon God as "Father" exists in Jewish sources before and after the time of Jesus,[308] and that usage could have encouraged the use of "abba" as well. What is more certain is that Jesus adopted the Father imagery for God, existing already among a broad range of names for God in the OT and Jewish tradition, even though not often,[309] and he placed it into the center of his proclamation and prayers.

Since the word "abba" has come into the Greek NT in both the gospel tradition and in the letters of Paul (Mark 14:36; Rom 8:16; Gal 4:6), it can be concluded that Aramaic-speaking Christians in Palestine and elsewhere continued its use in prayer, and then it was adopted as a traditional term for calling upon God even among Greek-speaking Christians. Paul himself may have introduced it into the churches of Galatia, for he uses it as a familiar term in his letter to them (Gal 4:6), but it must have been used already at Rome, as this passage suggests, and would probably have been introduced there by early Christians arriving from Palestine.

305. Those who are adopted have no choice in the matter; they are chosen by the one who adopts them and makes them heirs.

306. BDAG 1 (ἀββά). Cf. *m. Ned.* 11.4; *Git.* 7.6; *B. Bat.* 9.3; *b. Taan.* 23b.

307. J. Jeremias, *The Central Message of the New Testament,* 20; idem, *New Testament Theology,* 66. For critique, cf. J. Grieg, "Abba and Amen," 5-7.

308. Isa 63:16; Jer 3:19; Sir 23:1-4; 51:10; Wis 14:3; 3 Macc 6:3; 1QH[a] 17.35; Targum on Ps 89:27; text in *The Targum of Psalms,* trans. David M. Stec (Collegeville: Liturgical Press, 2004), 169. Cf. Ps 89:26 (MT 89:27): David shall say, "You are my Father (אָבִי), my God, and the Rock of my salvation!"

309. Helmer Ringgren, "אָב," *TDOT* 1:17: "Yahweh is called father very rarely in the OT." Examples include Deut 32:6; Pss 89:26; 103:13; Isa 63:11; Jer 3:19; 31:9; Mal 2:10; 3 Macc 2:21; 5:6; 7:6; Tob 13:4; 2 Esdr 1:29. A survey of "Israelite and Jewish" usage of "Father" (including rabbinic works) is provided by G. Dalman, *The Words of Jesus,* 184-89.

In Galatians Paul declares that the Spirit cries "Abba! Father!" but in Romans he says that it is believers themselves who cry "Abba! Father!" Even in the latter case, however, it is "the Spirit itself" that "bears witness with our spirit that we are children of God." Consequently, some interpreters have concluded that the address to God as "abba" originated in ecstatic speech.[310] Others, however, have claimed that it would have been used regularly in liturgical formulas.[311] The first of these claims has some basis in the passage from Galatians ("God has sent the Spirit of his Son into our hearts, crying, 'Abba! Father!'" 4:6). Moreover, the verb that Paul uses to describe the utterance (κράζω, "cry," "cry out") can have the meaning of shrieking.[312] But it can also have the sense of fervency in prayer.[313] The use of the term "Father" within invocations for God in both the OT (אָב) and Hellenistic Judaism (πατήρ) provided a precedent for the liturgical use of "father" terminology in the prayers of early Christianity. Moreover, since "abba" would have been a term that would have to be taught to new believers and was apparently used widely, it must have had a regular place in corporate worship. Although one can expect that "abba" would have been used in ecstatic speech, that does not mean that it originated there. The term must have been used more generally by Christians due to its previous, originating use by Jesus in place of more formal terms. By using it, Jewish Christians would have distinguished themselves from non-Christian Jews, among whom the term does not seem to have been used regularly or often, and they would have differentiated themselves from Gentiles, for whom Zeus could be called πατήρ,[314] but not "abba." The addition of ὁ πατήρ ("Father") immediately after "abba" (also in Mark 14:36 and Gal 4:6) does not necessarily signify the need for translation at Rome (or Galatia), for it could have been appended for emphasis.[315] Use of the two terms together is particularly effective rhetorically.

The fact that believers in Christ call upon God with the language of a child, and are prompted by the Spirit to do so, testifies that they are children of God. The Spirit bears witness with the human spirit that it is so. At the close of this verse Paul uses the expression τέκνα θεοῦ for "children of God," which he does one other time in his letters (Phil 2:15). There is a slight difference in meaning between that and υἱοὶ θεοῦ, which was used above in 8:14 (cf. also Gal 3:26). The latter can be used for mature adults (cf. 9:26, quoting Hos 2:23), while

---

310. E. Käsemann, *Romans*, 227-28; U. Wilckens, *Römer*, 2:137; J. Dunn, *Romans*, 453; D. Moo, *Romans*, 502 (n. 34); R. Jewett, *Romans*, 499; W. Meeks, *The First Urban Christians*, 88.

311. Gerhard Kittel, "ἀββά," *TDNT* 1:6; J. O'Neill, *Romans*, 140; J. Fitzmyer, *Romans*, 501; B. Byrne, *Romans*, 250; E. Lohse, *Römer*, 241.

312. BDAG 563 (κράζω, 1).

313. BDAG 564 (κράζω, 2, b, α); Herbert Fendrich, "κράζω," *EDNT* 2:313-14.

314. For references to Greek texts, cf. BDAG 787 (πατήρ, 6, c).

315. Cf. C. Cranfield, *Romans*, 400.

the former is limited to actual children. The expression is fitting, then, in connection with the use of "abba," traditionally associated with the call of children upon their earthly fathers.

8:17 Paul takes an additional step concerning the relationship of believers to God. They are not only children of God but "heirs of God." Paul had made that step previously in his letter to the Galatians. There he wrote that those who are in Christ are "Abraham's offspring, heirs according to promise" (3:29), and he asserted that any child is also an heir (4:7). All who accept the promises of God by faith are heirs of divine blessings. Here in Romans Paul declares that believers are heirs of God's blessings and calls them "joint heirs with Christ." He takes for granted that Christ is an "heir of God,"[316] which would have its basis in various OT texts concerning God's declaring the king (messiah) to be his son (2 Sam 7:14; Pss 2:7; 89:27 [LXX 88:28]). And if Christ is an heir of God, all who are "in Christ" share in his sonship.[317] This will be emphasized later in the letter where Paul speaks of Christ as the "firstborn among his brothers and sisters" (8:29).

The structure of this verse is complex. It consists of a sentence that contains two conditions and a purpose clause: "And if (εἰ) we are children, we are also heirs — heirs of God and fellow heirs with Christ — if, in fact (εἴπερ), we suffer with him in order that (ἵνα) we may also be glorified with him." The first of the conditions is simple enough; children are heirs of their parents. It is the second condition that prompts questions. Is it the case that believers are children and heirs of God only if they suffer with Christ? Is an *imitatio Christi* way of life necessary in order for the believer to appropriate his benefits? Is not the redemptive work of God in the crucified and risen Christ sufficient? Surely Paul would not deny the sufficiency of Christ's suffering, death, and resurrection.

In spite of his use of the conditional and purpose clauses,[318] Paul does not say here that the suffering of believers is meritorious. It does not add anything to the redemptive work accomplished in Christ. Instead the suffering with Christ of which Paul speaks is the suffering of a disciple that arises out of faith in him, loyalty to him, in all circumstances.[319] It is comparable to what Paul

---

316. In Hebrews Christ is "heir of all things" (1:2). The term "joint heir" (κληρονόμος) appears also at Eph 3:6 and 1 Pet 3:7, but not in the Pauline sense. In those places joint heirs are, respectively, Gentiles and Jews and husbands and wives.

317. J. Scott, *Adoption as Sons of God*, 254-55.

318. The fact that Paul uses a purpose clause speaks in favor of the translation of εἴπερ as "if, in fact," which sets up a condition, rather than as "since," stating a fact, as in the NRSV and maintained by R. Jewett, *Romans*, 592, and L. Jervis, *At the Heart of the Gospel*, 104. The range of meanings for the word in BDAG 279 (εἴπερ, under εἰ, 6, 1) are: "if indeed," "if after all," "since," and "provided that."

319. Cf. P. Stuhlmacher, *Romans*, 130-31. J. Fitzmyer, *Romans*, 502, says that "Paul does not

speaks of elsewhere when he says that by means of baptism believers have been joined to Christ in the likeness of his death (Rom 6:5), and it reflects the tradition that the disciple bears the cross of Jesus (Mark 8:34).[320] Paul himself can say forthrightly that in his apostolic ministry he carries the death of Jesus in his body and is being given up to death for Jesus' sake (2 Cor 4:10-12). The term εἴπερ ("if, in fact" or "if indeed"), which introduces a second condition,[321] is translated in the RSV as "provided that," giving the condition a hortatory sense, which is favored also by various interpreters,[322] and appropriately so, for Paul speaks here of the believer's looking toward the future, anticipating the path of discipleship.

Although the Greek text does not refer specifically to suffering with Christ, virtually every major English version has "with him" (KJV, RSV, NEB, ESV, NET, and NRSV; NIV: "share in his sufferings") after the verb for suffering with another (συμπάσχω). Paul uses the verb only one other time, and there it means to suffer with other persons (1 Cor 12:26). But here it most certainly refers to suffering with Christ. The verb appears in a series of compound words with the prefix συν/συμ/συγ ("with"), all referring to Christ because of the first of them, which is explicitly related to Christ.[323] They have a rhetorical effect in Greek that is missed in English translation: we are "fellow heirs with Christ" (συγκληρονόμοι . . . Χριστοῦ), provided that "we suffer with" (συμπάσχομεν) [him], that "we might be glorified with" (συνδοξασθῶμεν) [him].

Suffering is still to be expected in the present age. Earlier Paul had written that believers rejoice on the basis of their hope of sharing the glory of God (Rom 5:2), the divine presence. But that does not mean that they will be exempt from suffering. On the contrary, still living in the old age of sin and death, they will experience suffering, which leads to endurance, character, and even greater hope (5:3-5). To be "glorified with Christ" (συνδοξασθῶμεν, used only here in the NT) means to share in his glory in the presence of God, made possible by resurrection. Through his own resurrection, Jesus has been glorified, and believers bound to him will share his destiny. But all that is still future. "Christians are heirs, not possessors, as their present suffering demonstrates."[324]

---

play down the cooperation of Christians with Christ," and that "because of it, they are guaranteed a share . . . in his glory." This seems to express later formulations, going beyond what Paul actually says. For further discussion, cf. A. Hultgren, "Suffering Together with Christ," 120-26.

320. J.-M. Cambier, "La liberté du Spirituel dans Romains 8.12-17," 217, speaks of communion in the passion of Christ through faith.

321. BDF 237 (§454.2) provides additional examples; all appear only in the Pauline corpus of the NT (Rom 3:30; 8:9, 17; 1 Cor 8:5; 15:15; 2 Thess 1:6).

322. E. Käsemann, Romans, 229; J. Dunn, Romans, 456; B. Byrne, Romans, 253-54.

323. Wilhelm Michaelis, "συμπάσχω," TDNT 5:925.

324. J. Ziesler, Romans, 216.

BIBLIOGRAPHY

Aasgaard, Reidar. "Paul as a Child: Children and Childhood in the Letters of the Apostle." *JBL* 126 (2007): 129-59.

Barr, James. "'Abba, Father' and the Familiarity of Jesus' Speech." *Theology* 91 (1981): 173-79.

———. "'Abbā Isn't 'Daddy.'" *JTS* 39 (1988): 28-47.

Baulès, Robert. "Fils et héritiers de Dieu dans l'Esprit: Rm 8,14-17." *ASeign* 31 (1973): 22-27.

Bultmann, Rudolf. *Theology of the New Testament.* 2 vols. New York: Charles Scribner's Sons, 1951-55.

Burke, Trevor J. *Adopted into God's Family: Exploring a Pauline Metaphor.* NSBT 22. Downers Grove: InterVarsity Press, 2006.

———. "Adoption and the Spirit in Romans 8." *EvQ* 70 (1998): 311-24.

———. "The Characteristics of Paul's Adoptive-Sonship *(Huiothesia)* Motif." *IBS* 17 (1995): 62-74.

———. "Pauline Adoption: A Sociological Approach." *EvQ* 73 (2001): 119-34.

Byrne, Brendan. *"Sons of God" — "Seed of Abraham": A Study of the Idea of the Sonship of God of All Christians in Paul against the Jewish Background.* AnBib 83. Rome: Pontifical Biblical Institute Press, 1979.

Cambier, Jules-M. "La liberté du Spirituel dans Romains 8.12-17." In *Paul and Paulinism: Essays in Honour of C. K. Barrett,* 205-20. Ed. Morna D. Hooker and S. G. Wilson. London: SPCK, 1982.

Dalman, Gustaf. *The Words of Jesus.* Edinburgh: T&T Clark, 1902.

Dunn, James D. G. "Spirit Speech: Reflections on Romans 8:12-27." In *Romans and the People of God: Essays in Honor of Gordon D. Fee on the Occasion of His 65th Birthday,* 82-91. Ed. Sven K. Soderlund and N. T. Wright. Grand Rapids: Wm. B. Eerdmans, 1999.

Fahy, Thomas. "St. Paul: Romans 8:16-25." *ITQ* 23 (1956): 178-81.

Fitzmyer, Joseph A. "*Abba* and Jesus' Relation to God." In *À cause de L'Évangile: Études sur les Synoptiques et les Actes offertes au P. Jacques Dupont, O.S.B. à l'occasion de son 70ᵉ anniversaire,* 15-38. Ed. Robert Gantoy. LD 123. Paris: Cerf, 1985.

Grassi, Joseph A. "Abba, Father." *TBT* 21 (1983): 320-24.

Grieg, J. C. G. "Abba and Amen: Their Relevance to Christology." *SE* 5 (1968): 3-13.

Hester, James D. *Paul's Concept of Inheritance: A Contribution to the Understanding of Heilsgeschichte.* SJTOP 14. Edinburgh: Oliver and Boyd, 1968.

Hodge, Caroline Johnson. *If Sons, Then Heirs: A Study of Kinship and Ethnicity in the Letters of Paul.* New York: Oxford University Press, 2007.

Hultgren, Arland J. "Suffering Together with Christ: A Study of Romans 8:17." In *God, Evil, and Suffering: Essays in Honor of Paul R. Sponheim,* 120-26. Ed. Terence E. Fretheim et al. WWSup 4. St. Paul: Luther Seminary, 2000.

Jeremias, Joachim. *The Central Message of the New Testament.* New York: Charles Scribner's Sons, 1965; reprinted, Philadelphia: Fortress Press, 1965; reprinted as an essay in his *Jesus and the Message of the New Testament,* 62-110. Ed. K. C. Hanson. Minneapolis: Fortress Press, 2002.

———. *New Testament Theology: The Proclamation of Jesus.* New York: Charles Scribner's Sons, 1971.

Jervis, L. Ann. *At the Heart of the Gospel: Suffering in the Earliest Christian Message*. Grand Rapids: Wm. B. Eerdmans, 2007.

Keesmaat, Sylvia C. "Exodus and the Intertextual Transformation of Tradition in Romans 8:14-30." *JSNT* 54 (1994): 29-56.

————. *Paul and His Story: (Re)Interpreting the Exodus Tradition*. JSNTSup 181. Sheffield: JSOT Press, 1999.

Lyall, Francis. "Roman Law in the Writings of Paul — Adoption." *JBL* 88 (1969): 458-66.

McCasland, S. Vernon. "'Abba, Father." *JBL* 72 (1953): 79-91.

Meeks, Wayne A. *The First Urban Christians: The Social World of the Apostle Paul*. 2d ed. New Haven: Yale University Press, 2003.

Obeng, Emmanuel A. "Abba, Father: The Prayer of the Sons of God." *ExpTim* 99 (1987-88): 363-66.

Rensburg, J. J. Janse van. "The Children of God in Romans 8." *Neot* 15 (1981): 139-79.

Rossel, William H. "New Testament Adoption — Graeco-Roman or Semitic?" *JBL* 71 (1952): 233-34.

Scott, James M. *Adoption as Sons of God: An Exegetical Investigation into the Background of ΥΙΟΘΕΣΙΑ in the Pauline Corpus*. WUNT 2/48. Tübingen: J. C. B. Mohr (Paul Siebeck), 1992.

Taylor, Theophilis M. "Abba, Father and Baptism." *SJT* 11 (1958): 62-71.

Tonstad, Sigve. "The Revolutionary Potential of 'Abba, Father' in the Letters of Paul." *AUSS* 45 (2007): 5-18.

Vos, Johan S. *Traditionsgeschichtliche Untersuchungen zur paulinischen Pneumatologie*. Assen: van Gorcum, 1973.

Watson, Nigel M. "'And if children, then heirs' (Rom 8:17): — Why Not Sons?" *AusBR* 49 (2001): 53-56.

Wolter, Michael. "Der Apostel und seine Gemeinden als Teilhaber am Leidengeschick Jesu Christi: Beobachtungen zur paulinischen Leidenstheologie." *NTS* 36 (1990): 535-57.

4.10. Cosmic Redemption, 8:18-30

18*For I consider that the sufferings of the present time are not to be compared with the glory about to be revealed to us.* 19*For the eager expectation of the creation awaits the revealing of the children of God.* 20*For the creation was subjected to futility, not of its own will but by the will of the one who subjected it in hope,* 21*because the creation itself will be set free from its bondage to decay and will obtain the glorious freedom of the children of God.* 22*For we know that the entire creation has been groaning and suffering in agony until now;* 23*and not only that, but we ourselves, who have the first fruits of the Spirit, groan inwardly as we wait for adoption, the redemption of our bodies.* 24*For in hope we have been saved. But hope that is seen is not hope. For who hopes for that which he sees?* 25*But if we hope for that which we do not see, we wait for it with patience.*

26*Likewise the Spirit helps us in our weakness; for we do not know how to*

pray as we ought, but the Spirit itself intercedes with inexpressible groanings.
27And he who searches hearts knows what is the mind of the Spirit, because the
Spirit intercedes for the saints according to the will of God.

28And we know that to those who love God, who are called according to his
purpose, he works for good in respect to everything. 29For those whom he foreknew
he also predestined to be conformed to the image of his Son, in order that he might
be the firstborn among many brothers and sisters. 30And those whom he predestined he also called; and those whom he called he also justified; and those whom
he justified he also glorified.

Notes on the Text and Translation

8:21 Unlike the ASV, NIV, NRSV, NET, and ESV, but like the KJV and RSV, I
have translated the word ὅτι here as "because" (not "that"), which is also favored by various interpreters; see the comment below. Some ancient witnesses
(including ℵ and D) have διότι ("because") in place of ὅτι, clearly favoring "because" rather than "that." The 25th edition of the Nestle-Aland Greek text has
διότι, but the preferred reading is ὅτι,[325] as in the 27th edition of the Nestle-
Aland Greek text.

8:28 The verse poses both text-critical and translation problems. Major
witnesses support two different readings. The longer of the two readings (τοῖς
ἀγαπῶσιν τὸν θεὸν πάντα συνεργεῖ ὁ θεὸς εἰς ἀγαθόν) is supported by 𝔓46, A,
B, 81, Sahidic texts, and Origen. The shorter (τοῖς ἀγαπῶσιν τὸν θεὸν πάντα
συνεργεῖ εἰς ἀγαθόν) is supported by ℵ, C, D, the Majority Text, Latin witnesses,
Syriac and Bohairic texts, and Clement of Alexandria. This is the reading of the
27th edition of the Nestle-Aland Greek New Testament. The latter has the support of both Alexandrian and Western readings. It is also the shorter reading. It
is more likely that ὁ θεός ("God") is a scribal addition. The shorter reading is to
be preferred.[326] For translation possibilities, see the discussion below.

General Comment

The reference to suffering in 8:17 seems to have triggered in Paul a need to explore its significance more. Believers continue to live in the old age (ὁ νῦν
καιρός, "the present time") where suffering exists. The opposite is the glory that
is to be revealed by God, which means eternal fellowship with God face-to-face

---

325. Cf. B. Metzger, *TCGNT* 456; contra R. Jewett, *Romans*, 504, who favors διότι.
326. Cf. B. Metzger, *TCGNT* 458.

(5:2). But that time is not yet. Paul places the suffering of believers within the larger context of the suffering of the creation as a whole, concluding that hope for redemption is certain (8:19-25). Recognizing, however, that believers remain spiritually weak, he goes on to speak of the sustaining power of the Spirit (8:26-27) and the purposes of God that are being worked out for believers (8:28-30).

On the basis of the saving work of God in Christ, which has been made known to those "who have the first fruits of the Spirit" (8:23), believers are summoned to a larger vision. The entire creation, of which they are a part, will share in the redemption which they know already. To be sure, the creation shares in the fallen state of humanity in the present era, but it has not been cast off by God, for God has subjected it to its present state only for this era. Using anthropomorphic imagery, Paul portrays the creation as anticipating its own liberation. The creation looks forward to redemption, which will take place subsequent to the revealing of the children of God. When they are seen as children of God, redeemed, then the renewal of creation will take place too.

Detailed Comment

8:18-19 Living still in "the present time" (ὁ νῦν καιρός, the era that is passing away), Paul knows well that suffering not only exists but will continue to do so; it is a given. It is to be expected in particular for those who witness to Christ in the world (2 Cor 4:10-12). Nevertheless, believers live in expectation of the glory that is to be revealed by God, which means eternal fellowship with God face-to-face (see the exegesis of 5:2). But they are not there yet. They live within the "creation" (κτίσις), and the creation itself lives in eager expectation of redemption. Here and in 8:20 the word "creation" signifies the created world as a whole, not just those who believe in the gospel. That becomes clear at 8:23, where the "creation" and "we" (believers) are distinguished. Some interpreters conclude that the "creation" signifies only that which is usually called "subhuman" or "nonhuman,"[327] but there is no reason to limit the term in that way. It can refer to all of creation, both human and subhuman.[328]

Using anthropomorphic imagery, Paul speaks of the creation as looking forward in longing for "the revealing of the children of God" when its suffering will be resolved. The Greek wording, translated literally, reads: "the eager ex-

---

327. C. Cranfield, *Romans,* 412; U. Wilckens, *Römer,* 2:153; J. Dunn, *Romans,* 469 ("focused primarily on nonhuman creation"); J. Fitzmyer, *Romans,* 506; P. Stuhlmacher, *Romans,* 134; C. Talbert, *Romans,* 214; R. Jewett, *Romans,* 511 ("primarily," as in Dunn). Least of all does it mean "the new creation," i.e., believers.

328. E. Käsemann, *Romans,* 233; B. Gaventa, *Our Mother Saint Paul,* 53-55 (with extensive discussion).

pectation of the creation (ἡ γὰρ ἀποκαραδοκία τῆς κτίσεως) awaits the revealing of the children of God." Various English versions (e.g., RSV, NIV, NRSV, and NET) make "the creation" the subject of the sentence, as in the NRSV: "For the creation waits with eager longing for the revealing of the children of God." The change allows for an easier reading, comparable to "the creation's eager expectation awaits," which would be more cumbersome. Paul attributes the expectation of the redemption or renewal of creation to creation itself (using anthropomorphism). Elsewhere, however, it is an expectation that humans have concerning it, based on the promises of God.[329]

Awaiting "the revealing of the children of God" presupposes that the children of God (believers) are not yet to be seen; that appearance is yet to come. That would be at the parousia of Christ (1 Thess 3:13). In the present era (the "not yet" of Christian existence) they are subject to the same suffering as the rest of the creation; there is nothing about them, from the point of view of the creation, that would mark them off as different from the rest of humanity or, in regard to suffering, the rest of the created order. Suffering is all around, and it affects all in one way or another and at some time or other. But at his parousia Christ will appear in glory, and those who belong to him (his fellow heirs, 8:17) will accompany him. They will be revealed for what they are, and thereby be vindicated, shown to the whole world to be the children of God.[330] And it is then that the creation's longing for redemption will be at an end, for the creation itself will be set free from its bondage to decay (8:21).

8:20-21 During the present age, and ever since its beginning, the creation has been subjected (by God, using the divine passive) to futility (8:20, alluding to Gen 3:17-19, the curse upon the ground).[331] The fall of Adam affected the entire creation. As Paul has stated previously, "sin entered the world through one man, and death through sin" (5:12).[332] The term for "futility" (ματαιότης) refers at least to the transitory nature of the creation, but undoubtedly also its seeming lack of purpose,[333] reflecting the language and thought of

---

329. Isa 65:17; 2 Esdr 7:75; 13:26; *1 Enoch* 45.4-5; 72.1; 1QS 4.25; 1QH 11.13-14.

330. A similar expectation is projected by the author of 1 John: "Beloved, we are God's children now; what we will be has not yet been revealed. What we do know is this: when he is revealed, we will be like him, for we will see him as he is" (3:2).

331. This is almost universally the view of major interpreters, e.g., C. Cranfield, *Romans*, 413; J. Knox, *IB (Romans)*, 9:518-19; E. Käsemann, *Romans*, 233; U. Wilckens, *Römer*, 2:154; J. Dunn, *Romans*, 470; D. Moo, *Romans*, 515; J. Ziesler, *Romans*, 220; B. Byrne, *Romans*, 260; idem, "Creation Groaning," 195-99; N. T. Wright, *NIB (Romans)*, 10:596; L. Keck, *Romans*, 210-11; R. Jewett, *Romans*, 513; E. Lohse, *Römer*, 247. Contra C. Southgate, *The Groaning of Creation*, 96, who calls for a "fall-free reading" of the text. D. Tsumura, "An OT Background to Rom 8.22," 620-21, suggests that the background is Gen 3:16a. But the "curse" there is upon the woman, not the ground.

332. Cf. L. Keck, *Romans*, 211.

333. BDAG 621 (ματαιότης).

Ecclesiastes. Moreover, Paul echoes the view already present in Jewish tradition that Adam's transgression brought condemnation and harmful consequences for the creation as a whole.[334]

There is a translation problem in these verses. In 8:20 Paul writes that "the creation was subjected to futility . . . by the will of the one who subjected it," meaning God. But from there it is possible to translate the end of 8:20 and the beginning of 8:21 in either of two ways, as illustrated by the RSV and NRSV renderings:

> RSV: [God subjected the creation] "in hope; *because* (ὅτι) the creation itself will be set free. . . ."
> NRSV: [God subjected the creation] "in hope *that* (ὅτι) the creation itself will be set free. . . ."

As indicated above ("Notes on the Text and Translation"), the reading "because" (as in the KJV and RSV) has been chosen here. It makes more sense, for it explains why the creation was subjected by God "in hope." In was subjected by God in hope precisely *because* it will be set free by God's own redemptive work.[335] The alternative (as in the NRSV, but also in the NIV) leaves the matter less certain, for the hope expressed in that rendering can signify little more than a wish (a "hope that . . ."). The reading chosen here expresses an expectation that is certain. That would seem to be the only mode of hope that is fitting for God.

8:22-23 By means of the expression "for we know that . . ." (οἴδαμεν γὰρ ὅτι; cf. similarly at 2:2; 3:19; 7:14; 2 Cor 5:1), Paul does not claim a knowing that is based on observation or reason. Typically the phrase is used to express what is commonly accepted.[336] But what he goes on to say is known only to believers; it is known from faith in God's power to bring to a conclusion what has been inaugurated by Christ's resurrection.

Paul uses a metaphor. Presently, he says, the whole creation is groaning and suffering in agony. The verbs (συστενάζω ["to groan together"] and συνωδίνω ["to suffer in agony together"]), both rare in Greek literature and used only here in the NT, are in the present tense, but the addition ἄχρι τοῦ νῦν ("until now") requires that they be translated as perfects.[337] The prefix συ/συν

---

334. Wis 2:23-24; 2 Esdr 3:7, 21; 7:11-14; *Gen. Rab.* 12.6.

335. The conjunction ὅτι is interpreted as "because" (not "that") also by C. Cranfield, *Romans*, 415; J. Dunn, *Romans*, 471; J. Fitzmyer, *Romans*, 509; J. Ziesler, *Romans*, 217; P. Stuhlmacher, *Romans*, 134; R. Jewett, *Romans*, 504; C. Osburn, "The Interpretation of Romans 8:23," 99-109; and as "denn" (= "for," "because") by U. Wilckens, *Römer*, 2:155, and E. Lohse, *Römer*, 247; but "that" is favored by B. Byrne, *Romans*, 261.

336. BDAG 693 (οἶδα, 1, e).

337. As in the RSV, NIV, NRSV, and ESV; contra KJV, ASV, and NET.

("together") signifies the various parts of the creation; all of its components suffer together. The imagery suggested, particularly from the verb συνωδίνω, is that of a woman giving birth.[338] This imagery is already familiar in Jewish tradition for distress among the people (Isa 13:8; 21:3; 26:17-18; Jer 4:31; 6:24; 22:23; Hos 13:13; Mic 4:9-10) or among some at the final judgment.[339] In other NT and rabbinic texts, and possibly a Qumran text,[340] the imagery is used to signify the suffering that precedes the coming of a redemptive or messianic era.[341] In the present instance, however, it is not the nation of Israel or humanity alone that suffers in agony. It is the creation in its entirety that suffers. The present is a time for waiting, for something is about to happen. Finally, the entire creation will share what believers in Christ themselves shall have in its fullness — adoption as children of God, redemption. The "redemption of our bodies" signifies the renewal of believers in their totality, including bodily existence. The expectation of a new era to come, in which creation is renewed, is expressed already in the OT (Isa 65:17 in particular), other Jewish sources (2 Esdr 7:75; 13:26), and elsewhere in the NT (Rev 21:1).

In 8:23 Paul says that those in Christ have the "first fruits of the Spirit." The Greek word translated "first fruits" is ἀπαρχή, a term used in both pagan Hellenism and in the LXX for the "firstlings" of an offering. The word is related to the verb ἀπάρχομαι, meaning "to make a beginning" in sacrifice. It was used to designate first fruits of any kind (produce or animals) that were presented to a god, or to the God of Israel, prior to the use of the rest (Exod 23:19; 25:2, 3; Lev 22:12; Num 18:12; Deut 12:6).[342] In the present context it would therefore designate the first installment of what is to come. Being enlivened by the Spirit and baptized into Christ, believers experience the Spirit as it directs their steps (Rom 8:4) and as it prompts them to call upon God as "Abba! Father!" and to know that they are his children (8:14-16). As such, having been endowed with the eschatological gift of the Spirit already, believers experience proleptically (as "first fruits of the Spirit") that which the creation as a whole does not yet know. But the "already" and the "not yet" cannot simply be assigned to believers and the rest of the creation, respectively. They characterize the life of the believer as well and en toto. The "already" of the believer's joy in the Spirit is tem-

---

338. The verb is used in that sense in Heraclitus, *All.* 39. It can also mean to feel the pain of another, as in Euripides, *Helen* 727; Aristotle, *Eth. eud.* 7.6 §1240a.

339. *1 Enoch* 62.4. Links between Rom 8:19-22 and Isa 24-27 are explored in detail by J. Moo, "Romans 8.19-22 and Isaiah's Cosmic Covenant," 83-88.

340. 1QH 3.7-10. Does this refer to "the birth-pangs of the Messiah or the messianic people," as suggested by M. Black, *Romans*, 116-17? It is not clear.

341. Mark 13:8; John 16:21-22; for rabbinic texts, cf. Georg Bertram, "ὠδίν," *TDNT* 9:671-72.

342. BDAG 98 (ἀπαρχή).

pered by the "not yet" of life in the world. It is the lot of believers to share in the experience of the creation. So, says Paul, "we ourselves, who have the first fruits of the Spirit, groan inwardly as we wait for adoption, the redemption of our bodies." The groaning inwardly is antiphonal to the groaning of creation.

8:24-25 Paul's declaration at the outset of 8:24, τῇ γὰρ ἐλπίδι ἐσώθημεν ("for in hope we have been saved"), is the only instance where he speaks of being saved as a past event. The tenses elsewhere are consistently either present or future.[343] (For details, see the exegesis of 1:16.) By using the past tense (an aorist passive) in this particular place, accompanied by the phrase "in hope,"[344] Paul says that God's saving action in Christ has taken place already, but it is not yet fully realized; its full effects remain a future hope, something not yet seen. In fact, if it were seen (or experienced in any way) it would not be an object of hope but a tangible reality. Believers, having been saved, live "in hope," and they must wait patiently.

8:26-27 Paul's brief comments here about the Spirit can be accounted for by what he has said about the already/not yet antithesis in 8:23.[345] The opening word ὡσαύτως ("likewise") links the "groanings" of 8:26 with those of 8:22-23. Believers possess the gift of the Spirit, but they also experience an inward groaning as they await final redemption. Living in the weakness of earthly existence and sharing in the groaning of creation, they are spiritually impoverished and unable to pray in a proper way. But, Paul says, the Spirit "intercedes with inexpressible groanings." The groanings of believers are overridden by the intercessions of the Spirit. Although it has been claimed that Paul refers here to glossolalia,[346] that is not the only possibility, and it can be rejected.[347] The words στεναγμοῖς ἀλαλήτοις ("with inexpressible groanings") are not what one would expect for glossolalia and can mean "inexpressible" or even "unspoken groanings." Moreover, that the Spirit "intercedes" is singularly important. Paul does not say that the Spirit prompts prayer or empowers it from within the believer. However much the Spirit is "in" believers (cf. Rom 8:9b, 11; 1 Cor 3:16), in this instance Paul envisions the Spirit as external, praying on their behalf. None of this activity of the Spirit need be heard, for it takes place within the larger life of God. God, "who searches hearts," answers the prayer of the Spirit. The entire

---

343. Paul speaks of salvation as present at Rom 1:16; 1 Cor 1:18; 2 Cor 2:15; 6:2 and as future at Rom 5:9-10; 10:9; 13:11; 1 Cor 5:5; 1 Thess 5:9.

344. The expression τῇ ἐλπίδι is a dative of manner; hence, "in hope" or "by hope." Cf. BDF 106 (198.4).

345. It is inappropriate, then, to call these verses an "alien body," as E. Käsemann, *Romans*, 239, does.

346. E. Käsemann, *Romans*, 239-41; he lists various other interpreters.

347. C. Cranfield, *Romans*, 422; U. Wilckens, *Römer*, 2:161; J. Dunn, *Romans*, 479; J. Ziesler, *Romans*, 223; P. Stuhlmacher, *Romans*, 133; E. Lohse, *Römer*, 250.

emphasis is on God, the life of God, from start to finish. God the Spirit helps those in Christ in their earthly suffering and consequent groaning, and God the Father responds. That the Spirit intercedes for the saints is affirmed only here by Paul. Later on he says that Christ also intercedes for them (8:34).

8:28 The clause reading τοῖς ἀγαπῶσιν τὸν θεὸν πάντα συνεργεῖ εἰς ἀγαθόν can be translated in two major ways (see the "Notes on the Text and Translation" concerning the presence or absence of ὁ θεός ["God"]), depending on how one construes the syntax and makes a choice concerning the subject. Grammatically it is possible that the subject is πάντα ("all things"), taking it to be the neuter nominative plural of πάν. That is possible, because a neuter nominative plural noun takes a third person singular verb (which συνεργεῖ ["works together"] is).[348] On the other hand, it is possible that πάντα is a neuter accusative plural. In that case, it could be an accusative of respect,[349] and the subject of the clause would then be "he" (meaning "God").[350] Modern translations go in both directions. Those in the former group include:

> KJV: "And we know that all things work together for good to them that love God."
>
> ASV: "And we know that to them that love God all things work together for good."
>
> NAB: "We know that all things work for good for those who love God."
>
> NRSV: "We know that all things work together for good for those who love God."
>
> NET: "And we know that all things work together for good for those who love God."
>
> ESV: "And we know that for those who love God all things work together for good."

Those in the latter group (some of which insert "God" for clarification) include:

> RSV: "We know that in everything God works for good with those who love him."
>
> NEB: "And in everything, as we know, he cooperates for good with those who love God."

---

348. This construal is favored by C. K. Barrett, *Romans*, 158; E. Käsemann, *Romans*, 220; U. Wilckens, *Römer*, 2:162-63; C. Cranfield, *Romans*, 425-27; J. Fitzmyer, *Romans*, 521, 523-24; J. Dunn, *Romans*, 481; B. Byrne, *Romans*, 271-72; D. Moo, *Romans*, 527-28; P. Stuhlmacher, *Romans*, 136; and E. Lohse, *Römer*, 252.

349. On the accusative of respect, cf. BDF 87-88 (§160).

350. This construal is favored by C. H. Dodd, *Romans*, 137-38; J. O'Neill, *Romans*, 142; J. Ziesler, *Romans*, 225; L. Keck, *Romans*, 216; J. Ross, "*Panta synergei*," 82-85.

NIV: "And we know that in all things God works for the good of those who love him."

NASV: "And we know that God causes all things to work together for good to those who love God."

The latter course is to be preferred. The primary reason for that is that "he" (= "God") is the subject of verses both prior to and after this one (8:27; 8:29-30). One can expect that "he" would be the subject of this clause as well.[351] Those ancient scribes who added ὁ θεός ("God") as the subject must have sought to clarify the sentence, which the translators of the RSV and NIV did as well, making similar judgments. And even though it has been said that the difference in meaning is not great, since either reading expresses confidence in the sovereignty of God,[352] there is actually a profound difference. In the first instance, Paul is saying that everything works out well for those who love God.[353] This has the ring of the optimism of modern times, although it need not, for it could mean that all that one endures (even suffering) works together for a good outcome, which could include final salvation. Still, in the final analysis, the "all" then appears to transpire for good with or without God's involvement. In the second instance, however, Paul is saying that God works for the good of all who love him in every conceivable situation. Whatever one faces (including suffering), God is present and active to work for a good outcome, which may well be realized only eschatologically in final salvation, but ultimately the promise is sure.[354] That perspective coheres theologically with the rest of this section (8:18-30), which sees suffering — both on the part of humans and of the rest of creation — in light of eschatological hope.[355]

8:29-30 In these verses Paul uses a series of six verbs ("foreknew," "predestined," "conformed," "called," "justified," and "glorified") and vivid imagery in quick succession to speak of the solidarity between the "fellow heirs with

351. This is also the major reason why one should not adopt the view that Paul intended τὸ πνεῦμα ("the Spirit") to be supplied as the subject by the reader, which has been proposed by J. Wilson, "Romans viii.28," 110-11, and endorsed by M. Black, *Romans*, 118; E. Best, *Romans*, 100; and R. Jewett, "The Question of the 'Apportioned Spirit' in Paul's Letters," 204; idem, *Romans*, 527.

352. Cf. the comment of C. Cranfield, *Romans*, 427, against C. H. Dodd.

353. This rendering is favored by C. K. Barrett, *Romans*, 158; C. Cranfield, *Romans*, 425-28; E. Käsemann, *Romans*, 230, 243; J. Dunn, *Romans*, 466, 480-81; U. Wilckens, *Römer*, 2:147, 162-63; J. Fitzmyer, *Romans*, 522-24; B. Byrne, *Romans*, 271-72; D. Moo, *Romans*, 527-28; E. Lohse, *Römer*, 251-52.

354. This rendering is favored by C. H. Dodd, *Romans*, 137-38; J. Knox, *IB (Romans)*, 9:524-25; J. Ziesler, *Romans*, 225; L. Keck, *Romans*, 216.

355. Cf. also the subsequent saying attributed to R. Akiba, *b. Ber.* 60b: "Whatever the All-Merciful does is for good"; quoted from *BabT (Berakoth)*, 380.

Christ" (8:17) and Christ himself. The subject and main verb of 8:29 are "he [= God] predestined," and those whom he predestined are those whom "he foreknew." There can hardly be much difference between the verbs in the two clauses. Paul speaks here of those who have been "called," "justified," and "glorified" (cf. 8:30), meaning believers in Christ, but he moves back beyond the stage of human history, indeed prior to all human knowing and observing, to the eternal purposes of God. Paul stands within those traditions of the OT and Judaism that affirm that God is an electing God, whose purposes surpass human understanding.[356] Above all, in regard to the coming to faith in the heart and mind of believers — from the point of view of the believers themselves — it must be so. Coming to faith is so astonishing and unexpected, so seemingly serendipitous, that it can be accounted for only in a supernatural way. That had been Paul's own experience (Gal 1:15). God chose those whom he willed to become believers and thus "to be conformed to the image of his Son."

Although Paul affirms that believers are those whom God "foreknew," what he says in 8:29 is about more than election as commonly taught in later theology.[357] He uses two verbs in the sentence, and attention should be fastened primarily on the verb in the main clause, and that is προώρισεν (aorist of the verb προορίζω, "to predestine" or "to decide beforehand, to predetermine").[358] That verb has both a direct object ("those whom he foreknew") and a purpose. God determined a purpose for those persons, i.e., that they be conformed to the image of his Son. In all this, Paul speaks of believers in a comprehensive, corporate manner. The passage has less to do with the predestination of individuals to salvation (or condemnation).[359]

The other verb is located within the clause concerning those whom God predestined for their glorification. That is the verb προέγνω (aorist of the verb προγινώσκω, "to foreknow," to "choose beforehand"[360]). By using this word Paul signifies that, prior to their coming to faith, and purely by grace, God knew those whom he would predestine; he elected them. Election, then, is for

---

356. Gen 18:17-19; Exod 19:4-6; Deut 7:6; Isa 44:21; Amos 3:2; *T. Moses* 1.14; *Jub.* 1.17; 1QS 4.22-23; 11.7-8; 1QM 3.2.5-6.

357. Cf. Augustine, *Propositions from the Epistle to the Romans* 55.4-5: "For not all who are called are called according to the purpose, for that purpose pertains to the foreknowledge and predestination of God. Nor did God predestine anyone except him whom he knew would believe and would follow the call. Paul designates such persons 'the elect.' For many do not come, though they have been called; but no one comes who has not been called"; quoted from *Augustine on Romans: Propositions from the Epistle to the Romans; Unfinished Commentary on the Epistle to the Romans*, ed. Paula Fredriksen Landes (SBL.TT 23; Chico: Scholars Press, 1982), 27-29.

358. BDAG 873 (προορίζω).

359. Cf. J. Fitzmyer, *Romans*, 522.

360. BDAG 866 (προγινώσκω, 2).

something greater than the personal privilege of the elect. It is in large part for the creation of a people of witness.[361] The elect were predestined for a purpose, and that was to be "conformed to the image of his Son." Through their being conformed to the image of Christ, they have been forged into a company that surrounds the Son, sharing in his likeness, being joint heirs with him (8:17), and among them he is preeminent. He is the πρωτότοκος (the "firstborn") "among many brothers and sisters," the new humanity, and that company of brothers and sisters, fellow heirs, is devoted to him as its Lord. In common speech the term πρωτότοκος refers to birth order, but since status, privileges, and rights of inheritance accrue to the "firstborn," the term can also refer metaphorically to the special status of Jesus as God's Son (cf. Heb 1:6),[362] the background of which is in Psalm 89:27-28 (LXX 88:28-29), where the Lord speaks concerning David as king: "And I will make him the firstborn (κἀγὼ πρωτότοκον θήσομαι αὐτόν), the highest of the kings of the earth. Forever I will keep my steadfast love for him, and my covenant with him will stand firm."[363]

But the Christological claim does not stand alone, for there is also an ecclesial one. Jesus is first among the many who make up the company around him who share in the inheritance and in his destiny. Without a company of believers to worship Jesus as the Son, he would be known in the world only as an itinerant sage who was the victim of crucifixion. But with the company to worship him as the Son, Jesus is made known to the world as the risen Lord. There can be no Christ in any meaningful way in the world unless there is a community that worships Jesus as the Christ, Lord, and Son of God.

Bibliography

Aasgaard, Reidar. 'My Beloved Brothers and Sisters!': Christian Siblingship in Paul. JSNTSup 265. New York: T&T Clark, 2004.

Allen, Leslie C. "The Old Testament Background of (προ)ὁρίζειν in the New Testament." NTS 17 (1970-71): 104-8.

Balz, Horst R. Heilsvertrauen und Welterfahrung: Strukturen der paulinischen Eschatologie nach Römer 8,18-39. BEvT 59. Munich: Kaiser Verlag, 1971.

Bauer, Johannes B. "Τοῖς ἀγαπῶσιν τὸν θεὸν, Rm 8,28 (1 Cor 2,9; 1 Cor 8,3)." ZNW 50 (1959): 106-12.

361. Gary S. Shogren, "Election: New Testament," ABD 2:441. P. Hanson, The People Called, 539, speaks of election in the OT as "based on a call to a self-transcending task and dedicated solely to God's purpose and God's glory." Cf. G. Wright, God Who Acts, 50-51.

362. BDAG 894 (πρωτότοκος, 1, 2). Various Hellenistic Jewish texts that exhibit the metaphorical sense are reviewed by R. Aasgaard, 'My Beloved Brothers and Sisters,' 142.

363. J. Scott, Adoption as Sons of God, 252; R. Aasgaard, 'My Beloved Brothers and Sisters,' 142-43.

Beasley-Murray, George R. "Intercession." *BI* 3/1 (1976): 43.

Beker, J. Christiaan. "Suffering and Triumph in Paul's Letter to the Romans." *HBT* 7 (1985): 105-19.

—————. "Vision of Hope for a Suffering World: Romans 8:17-30." *PSB* 3 (1994): 26-32.

Benoit, Pierre. "'We Too Groan Inwardly as We Wait for Our Bodies to Be Set Free,' Romans 8:23." In his *Jesus and the Gospel*, 2:40-50. 2 vols. New York: Seabury Press, 1974.

Bindermann, Walther. *Die Hoffnung der Schöpfung: Römer 8,18-27 und die Frage einer Theologie der Befreiung von Mensch und Natur*. NStB 14. Neukirchen-Vluyn: Neukirchener Verlag, 1983.

Black, Matthew. "The Interpretation of Romans viii 28." In *Neotestamentica et patristica: Eine Freundesgabe, Herrn Professor Dr. Oscar Cullmann zu seinem 60. Geburtstag überreicht*, 166-72. NovTSup 6. Leiden: E. J. Brill, 1962.

Bolt, John. "The Relation between Creation and Redemption in Romans 8:18-27." *CTJ* 30 (1995): 34-51.

Boyd, Robert F. "The Work of the Holy Spirit in Prayer: An Exposition of Romans 8:26, 27." *Int* 8 (1954): 35-42.

Braaten, Laurie J. "All Creation Groans: Romans 8:22 in Light of the Biblical Sources." *HBT* 28 (2006): 131-59.

Bultmann, Rudolf. "Römer 8,18-27." In his *Marburger Predigten*, 60-70. Tübingen: J. C. B. Mohr (Paul Siebeck), 1956.

Byrne, Brendan. "Creation Groaning: An Earth Bible Reading of Romans 8:19-21." In *Readings from the Perspective of Earth*, 193-203. Ed. Norman Habel. Cleveland: Pilgrim Press, 2000.

—————. "Universal Need of Salvation and Universal Salvation by Faith in the Letter to the Romans." *Pacifica* 8 (1995): 123-39.

Cambier, Jules. "La Prière de l'Esprit, foundement de l'espérance: Rm 8,26-27." *ASeign* 47 (1970): 11-17.

Christoffersson, Olle. *The Earnest Expectation of the Creature: The Flood-Tradition as Matrix of Romans 8,18-17*. ConBNT 23. Stockholm: Almqvist & Wiksell, 1990.

Cipriani, Settimio. "ΚΤΙΣΙΣ: Creazione o genere umano?" *RB* 44 (1996): 337-40.

Cranfield, C. E. B. "Romans 8.28." *SJT* 19 (1966): 204-15.

—————. "The Creation's Promised Liberation: Some Observations on Romans 8.19-21." In *Reconciliation and Hope: New Testament Essays on Atonement and Eschatology Presented to L. L. Morris on His 60th Birthday*, 224-30. Ed. Robert J. Banks. Exeter: Paternoster Press, 1974; reprinted in his *The Bible and Christian Life: A Collection of Essays*, 94-104. Edinburgh: T&T Clark, 1985.

Denton, D. R. "ἀποκαραδοκία." *ZNW* 73 (1982): 138-40.

Dietzel, Armin. "Beten im Geist: Eine religionsgeschichtliche Parallele aus den Hodajot zum paulinischen Gebet im Geist." *TZ* 13 (1957): 12-32.

Dinkler, Erich. "Prädestination bei Paulus: Exegetische Bemerkungen zum Römerbrief." In *Festschrift Günther Dehn zum 75. Geburtstag am 18. April 1957*, 81-102. Ed. Wilhelm Schneemelcher. Neukirchen-Vluyn: Erziehungsverein, 1957; reprinted in his *Signum crucis*, 249-61. Tübingen: J. C. B. Mohr (Paul Siebeck), 1967.

Eastman, Susan. "Whose Apocalypse? The Identity of the Sons of God in Romans 8:19." *JBL* 121 (2002): 263-77.

Fahy, Thomas. "Romans 8:29." *ITQ* 23 (1956): 410-12.

Forde, Gerhard O. "Romans 8:18-27." *Int* 38 (1984): 281-85.

Gaventa, Beverly Roberts. *Our Mother Saint Paul.* Louisville: Westminster John Knox, 2007.

Gibbs, John G. *Creation and Redemption: A Study in Pauline Theology.* NovTSup 26. Leiden: E. J. Brill, 1971.

Gignilliat, Mark S. "Working Together with Whom? Text-Critical Contextual, and Theological Analysis of συνεργεῖ in Romans 8:28." *Bib* 87 (2006): 511-15.

Goedt, Michel de. "The Intercession of the Spirit in Christian Prayer (Rom. 8.26-27)." *Concilium* 79 (1972): 26-38.

Grässer, Erich. "Das Seufzen der Kreatur (Röm 8,19-22): Auf der Suche nach einer 'biblischen Tierschutzethik.'" In *Schöpfung und Neuschöpfung,* 93-117. Ed. Ingo Baldermann et al. JBT 5. Neukirchen-Vluyn: Neukirchener Verlag, 1990.

Grayston, Kenneth. "The Doctrine of Election in Romans 8,28-30." *SE* 2 (1964): 574-83.

Gundry Volf, Judith M. *Paul and Perserverance.* Louisville: Westminster/John Knox Press, 1990.

Hahne, Harry A. *The Corruption and Redemption of Creation: Nature in Romans 8:19-22 and Jewish Apocalyptic Literature.* LNTS 336. New York: T&T Clark, 2006.

Hanson, Paul D. *The People Called: The Growth of Community in the Bible.* 2d ed. Louisville: Westminster John Knox Press, 2001.

Hommel, Hildebrecht. "Denen, die Gott Lieben: Erwägungen zu Römer 8:28." *ZNW* 80 (1989): 126-29.

Jervell, Jacob. "Zu Röm 8,29f." In his *Imago Dei: Gen 1,26f im Spätjudentum in der Gnosis und in den paulinischen Briefen,* 271-84. FRLANT 76. Göttingen: Vandenhoeck & Ruprecht, 1960.

Jewett, Robert. "The Question of the 'Apportioned Spirit' in Paul's Letters: Romans as a Case Study." In *The Holy Spirit and Christian Origins: Essays in Honor of James D. G. Dunn,* 193-206. Ed. Graham N. Stanton et al. Grand Rapids: Wm. B. Eerdmans, 2004.

Jocz, Jakob. *A Theology of Election.* London: SPCK, 1958.

Johnson, Elisabeth A. "Waiting for Adoption: Reflections on Romans 8:12-25." *WW* 22 (2002): 308-12.

Jüngel, Eberhard. "Predigt über Rom 8,18ff." In *In Verantwortung für den Glauben: Beiträge zur Fundamentaltheologie und Ökumenik: Für Heinrich Fries,* 391-98. Ed. Peter Neuner and Harald Wagner. Freiburg: Herder, 1992.

Käsemann, Ernst. "The Cry for Liberty in the Worship of the Church." In his *Perspectives on Paul,* 122-37. Philadelphia: Fortress Press, 1971.

Kehnscherper, Günther. "Romans 8:19 — On Pauline Belief and Creation." In *Studia Biblica 1978: Sixth International Congress on Biblical Studies, Oxford, 3-7 April 1978,* 3:233-43. Ed. Elizabeth A. Livingstone. 3 vols. Sheffield: JSOT Press, 1979-80.

Kürzinger, Josef. "Σύμμορφους τῆς εἰκόνος τοῦ υἱοῦ αὐτοῦ (Röm 8,29)." *BZ* 2 (1958): 294-99.

Kuhn, Heinz-Wolfgang. "Qumran und Paulus: Unter traditionsgeschichtlichem Aspekt ausgewählte Parallelen." In *Das Urchristentum in seiner literarischen Geschichte: Festschrift für Jürgen Becker zum 65. Geburtstag*, 227-46. Ed. Ulrich Mell and Ulrich B. Müller. BZNW 100. Berlin: Walter de Gruyter, 1999.

Lambrecht, Jan. "The Groaning Creation: A Study of Rom 8:18-30." *LS* 15 (1990): 3-18.

———. "Paul and Suffering." In *God and Human Suffering*, 47-67. Ed. J. Lambrecht et al. LTPM 3. Leuven: Peeters, 1989.

Lampe, G. W. H. "The New Testament Doctrine of *Ktisis*." *SJT* 17 (1964): 449-62.

Larsson, Edvin. *Christus als Vorbild: Eine Untersuchung zu den paulinischen Tauf- und Eikontexten*. ASNU 23. Uppsala: Almqvist & Wiksell, 1962.

Leaney, A. R. C. "'Conformed to the Image of His Son' (Rom. V.iii.29)." *NTS* 10 (1964-65): 470-79.

Lewis, Edwin. "A Christian Theodicy: An Exposition of Romans 8:18-39." *Int* 11 (1957): 405-20.

MacRae, George W. "A Note on Romans 8:26-27." *HTR* 73 (1980): 227-30.

———. "Romans 8:26-27." *Int* 34 (1980): 288-92.

Mayer, Bernhard. *Unter Gottes Heilsratschluss: Prädestinationsaussagen bei Paulus*. FB 15. Würzburg: Echter Verlag, 1974.

McCasland, S. Vernon. "'The Image of God' according to Paul." *JBL* 69 (1950): 85-100.

Michaelis, Willhelm. "Die biblische Vorstellung von Christus als dem Erstgeborenen." *ZST* 23 (1954): 137-57.

Michaels, J. Ramsey. "The Redemption of Our Body: The Riddle of Romans 8:12-22." In *Romans and the People of God: Essays in Honor of Gordon D. Fee on the Occasion of His 65th Birthday*, 92-114. Ed. Sven K. Soderlund and N. T. Wright. Grand Rapids: Wm. B. Eerdmans, 1999.

Moo, Jonathan. "Romans 8.19-22 and Isaiah's Cosmic Covenant." *NTS* 54 (2008): 74-89.

Moore, Brian. "Suffering: A Study on Romans 8:19-30." In *Pulpit and People: Essays in Honour of William Still on His 75th Birthday*, 141-48. Ed. Nigel M. de S. Cameron and Sinclair E. Ferguson. Edinburgh: Rutherford House, 1986.

Niederwinner, Kurt. "Das Gebet des Geistes, Röm. 8,26f." *TZ* 20 (1964): 252-65.

Obeng, Emmanual A. "The Origins of the Spirit Intercession Motif in Romans 8.26." *NTS* 32 (1986): 621-32.

———. "The Spirit Intercession Motif in Paul." *ExpTim* 95 (1983-84): 360-64.

O'Brien, Peter T. "Romans 8:26, 27: A Revolutionary Approach to Prayer?" *RTR* 46 (1987): 65-73.

Oke, C. Clare. "A Suggestion with Regard to Romans 8:23." *Int* 11 (1957): 455-60.

Osburn, Carroll D. "The Interpretation of Romans 8:28." *WTJ* 44 (1982): 99-109.

Paulsen, Henning. *Überlieferung und Auslegung in Römer 8*. WMANT 43. Neukirchen: Neukirchener Verlag, 1974.

Poellot, Luther. "The Doctrine of Predestination in Rom. 8:26-39." *CTM* 23 (1952): 342-53.

Rickards, Raymond. R. "The Translation of *tē astheneia hēmōn* ('in our weakness') in Romans 8:26." *BT* 28 (1977): 247-48.

Rodgers, Peter R. "The Text of Romans 8:28." *JTS* 46 (1995): 547-50.

Ross, John M. "*Pánta synergeî*, Rom. VIII.28." *TZ* 34 (1978): 82-85.

Schlier, Heinrich. "Das worauf alles wartet: Eine Auslegung von Römer 8,18-30." In *Inter-*

pretation der Welt: Festschrift Romano Guardini zum achtizigsten Geburtstag, 599-616. Ed. Helmut Kuhn. Würzburg: Echter Verlag, 1965; reprinted in his *Das Ende der Zeit: Exegetische Aufsätze und Vorträge,* 250-70. Freiburg: Herder, 1971.

Schrage, Wolfgang. "Bibelarbeit über Röm 8,18-23." In *Versöhnung mit der Natur,* 150-66. Ed. Jürgen Moltmann. Munich: C. Kaiser Verlag, 1986.

Scott, James M. *Adoption as Sons of God: An Exegetical Investigation into the Background of* ΥΙΟΘΕΣΙΑ *in the Pauline Corpus.* WUNT 2/48. Tübingen: J. C. B. Mohr (Paul Siebeck), 1992.

Sloan, Robert. "'To predestine' (Προορίζω): The Use of a Pauline Term in Extrabiblical Tradition." In *Good News in History: Essays in Honor of Bo Reicke,* 127-35. Ed. Ed L. Miller. Atlanta: Scholars Press, 1993.

Smith, Geoffrey. "The Function of 'Likewise' (ὡσαύτως) in Romans 8:26." *TynB* 49 (1998): 29-38.

Southgate, Christopher. *The Groaning of Creation: God, Evolution, and the Problem of Evil.* Louisville: Westminster John Knox, 2008.

Stacy, W. David. "God's Purpose in Creation — Romans viii.22-23." *ExpTim* 69 (1957-58): 178-81.

Stanley, David M. "The Cosmic Effects of the Christian's Adoptive Sonship: Rom 8:9-23." In his *Christ's Resurrection in Pauline Soteriology,* 192-95. Rome: Pontifical Biblical Institute Press, 1961.

Stendahl, Krister. "Paul at Prayer." *Int* 34 (1980): 240-49; reprinted in his *Meanings: The Bible as Document and as Guide,* 151-61. Philadelphia: Fortress Press, 1984.

Swetnam, James. "On Romans 8,23 and the 'Expectation of Sonship.'" *Bib* 48 (1967): 102-8.

Tabor, James D. "Firstborn of Many Brothers: A Pauline Notion of Apotheosis." In *Society of Biblical Literature 1984 Seminar Papers,* 295-303. Ed. Kent H. Richards. SBLSP 23. Atlanta: Scholars Press, 1984.

Tostengard, Sheldon. "Light in August: Romans 8:18-39." *WW* 7 (1987): 316-22.

Tsumura, David-Toshio. "An OT Background to Rom 8.22." *NTS* 40 (1994): 620-21.

Vögtle, Anton. *Das Neue Testament und die Zukunft des Kosmos.* Düsseldorf: Patmos Verlag, 1970.

Vollenweider, Samuel. "Der Geist Gottes als Selbst der Glaubenden: Überlegungen zu einem ontologischen Problem in der paulinischen Anthropologie." *ZTK* 93 (1996): 163-92.

Wedderburn, A. J. M. "Romans 8:26 — Towards a Theology of Glossolalia?" *SJT* 28 (1975): 369-77.

Wilson, James P. "Romans viii.28: Text and Interpretation." *ExpTim* 60 (1948-49): 110-11.

Wischmeyer, Oda. "ΦΥΣΙΣ und ΚΤΙΣΙΣ bei Paulus: Die paulinische Rede von Schöpfung und Natur." *ZTK* 93 (1996): 352-75.

———. "ΘΕΟΝ ΑΓΑΠΑΝ bei Paulus: Eine traditionsgeschichtliche Miszelle." *ZNW* 78 (1987): 141-44.

Wood, Herbert G. "God's Providential Care and Continual Help — Rom. V.iii. 28." *ExpTim* 69 (1957-58): 292-95.

Wright, G. Ernest. *God Who Acts: Biblical Theology as Recital.* SBT 8. London: SCM Press, 1952.

Wu, Julie L. "The Spirit's Intercession in Romans 8:26-27: An Exegetical Note." *ExpTim* 105 (1993): 13.

4.11. Confidence in God's Love in Christ, 8:31-39

31*What, then, shall we say about these things? If God is for us, who is against us?* 32*He who did not withhold his own Son, but gave him up for us all, will he not also give us all things with him?* 33*Who will bring charges against God's elect? It is God who justifies.* 34*Who is it that will condemn? Christ Jesus is the one who died, yes, rather was raised, who is also at the right hand of God, who indeed intercedes for us.* 35*Who shall separate us from the love of Christ? Shall tribulation, or distress, or persecution, or famine, or nakedness, or peril, or sword?* 36*As it is written,*

> *"For your sake we are being killed all day long; we are regarded as sheep to be slaughtered."*

37*But in all these things we are more than conquerors through him who loved us.* 38*For I am convinced that neither death, nor life, nor angels, nor rulers, nor things that are present, nor things to come, nor powers,* 39*nor height, nor depth, nor any other creature, shall be able to separate us from the love of God which is in Christ Jesus our Lord.*

Notes on the Text and Translation

8:34 The RSV has the second sentence as a question ("Is it Christ Jesus, who died, yes, who was raised from the dead, who is at the right hand of God, who indeed intercedes for us?"), which is noted in the NRSV as a possible alternative.[364] But other major English versions (KJV, ASV, NIV, NAB, NET, NRSV, ESV) have a declarative sentence ("It is Christ . . ."), as do the standard Greek NT texts (Westcott-Hort, Nestle-Aland [27th ed.]).[365] To make the sentence into a question destroys the parallelism (see below).

8:35 There are two major textual variants for this verse. Instead of Χριστοῦ, codex ℵ reads θεοῦ, resulting in "the love of God," and codex B has θεοῦ τῆς ἐν Χριστῷ Ἰησοῦ, resulting in "the love of God which is in Christ Jesus," as in 8:39. But in spite of the importance of these witnesses, Χριστοῦ has

364. Some interpreters favor this as well, e.g., C. K. Barrett, *Romans*, 162; P. Achtemeier, *Romans*, 149; J. Fitzmyer, *Romans*, 530; and R. Jewett, *Romans*, 531, 541.

365. Interpreters who favor this include E. Käsemann, *Romans*, 245; U. Wilckens, *Römer*, 2:170; C. Cranfield, *Romans*, 437-38; J. Dunn, *Romans*, 496; and D. Moo, *Romans*, 537.

the support of other major Greek texts (A, C, D, and the Majority Text) and other ancient versions (including Old Latin). The variants are probably due to scribal harmonization with 8:39.[366]

General Comment

Paul now concludes his discussion of the dynamic and saving work of God in Christ and through the Spirit. He has declared that God has predestined, called, justified, and glorified a people, the community of believers. He turns now to speak concerning the future of believers before and with God, confident in the love of God shown forth in Christ.

After the introductory question in 8:31a, the passage can be divided into three main parts. The first (8:31b-34) concerns God's being "for us." The second (8:35-37) begins with the question: "Who shall separate us from the love of Christ?" The answer to that question is that no human forces can prevail. The third part (8:38-39) insists that not even any cosmic force can "separate us from the love of God which is in Christ Jesus our Lord." The inability of any forces to "separate" (χωρίζειν, 8:35, 39) believers from God's love binds the second and third sections together.[367]

The passage builds up to a crescendo on the love of God in Christ. It is not surprising that some interpreters have suggested that the passage can be considered a hymn or a catechetical composition.[368] Attempts to demonstrate that, however, have not been satisfactory. It is better to say that the passage contains liturgical, hymnic, and confessional elements which have been brought together by the apostle to exult in the love of God expressed in Christ and to form a fitting conclusion to the chapters that have gone before.[369] The section consists of a series of rhetorical questions employed "to express vivid emotion" and "joyous elation."[370]

366. B. Metzger, *TCGNT* 458.

367. There are other ways, too numerous to mention, in which interpreters have divided the section. Examples can be found in critical commentaries, e.g., C. Cranfield, *Romans,* 434; E. Käsemann, *Romans,* 246; U. Wilckens, *Römer,* 2:170-71; J. Fitzmyer, *Romans,* 529; B. Byrne, *Romans,* 275; and R. Jewett, *Romans,* 532-43. What is provided here does not correspond to any of those listed.

368. J. Weiss, "Beiträge zur paulinischen Rhetorik," 195-96 (a hymn of four stanzas); H. Paulsen, *Überlieferung und Auslegung in Römer 8,* 133-77 (a pre-Pauline hymn); P. von der Osten-Sacken, *Römer 8,* 45-52 (a catechetical formulary with questions and answers reworked by Paul; see p. 47); J. Fitzmyer, *Romans,* 529 ("a jubilant hymn of praise").

369. So E. Käsemann, *Romans,* 246; J. Dunn, *Romans,* 497-98; E. Lohse, *Römer,* 254; R. Jewett, *Romans,* 532-33.

370. BDF 262 (§496).

Detailed Comment

8:31a Paul's initial question ("What, then, shall we say about these things?") begs a question. What does he mean by "these things" (ταῦτα)? It is possible that he is referring back simply to the previous verse, in which he sums up what has gone before in that chapter (8:30). More likely, however, Paul puts forth the question to introduce a dramatic conclusion to the whole discussion that has gone on since 5:1[371] or, indeed, of the entire body of the letter (beginning at 1:16) to this point.[372] It is not likely that Paul sought here to be as precise as one might demand in doing an outline of the letter on a page. As indicated earlier, however, there is language in this section that forms an *inclusio* to that which appears in 5:1-11. See the discussion in "4. The New Life in Christ, Romans 5:1–8:39."

8:31b-34 These verses consist of questions and responses. Three questions are raised concerning the human condition in the presence of God, and each receives a response indicating that God and his Christ are favorably disposed and have acted, or continue to act, redemptively. The questions and responses (including an interrogative reply in 8:32, which implies a positive response) can be presented in parallel statements as follows:

> 31bIf God is for us, who is against us?
>> 32He who did not withhold his own Son, but gave him up for us all, will he not also give us all things with him?
> 33Who will bring charges against God's elect?
>> It is God who justifies.
> 34Who is it that will condemn?
>> Christ Jesus is the one who died, yes, rather was raised, who is also at the right hand of God, who indeed intercedes for us.

The message of Paul in this entire section is that God is "for us." The "for us" (ὑπὲρ ἡμῶν) phrase appears no fewer than three times (8:31, 32, 34). The first time it is within the protasis ("If God is for us") of a present conditional sentence (εἰ + present indicative). Most often a conditional sentence expresses contingency, but in this case it is used to express certainty. It is one of those instances where one might use "since" instead of "if," for the matter at hand is taken as a supposition (cf. Rom 6:8; 15:27).[373] The clause ("If God is for us"), consisting of only five words in both Greek and English, is a massive summary of what has been said in the previous chapters. God is for us, Paul can say, be-

---

371. Cf. E. Käsemann, *Romans*, 246; U. Wilckens, *Römer*, 2:172; B. Byrne, *Romans*, 279; E. Lohse, *Römer*, 254; R. Jewett, *Romans*, 535.

372. Cf. C. Cranfield, *Romans*, 434; J. Dunn, *Romans*, 499; J. Fitzmyer, *Romans*, 529.

373. BDAG 278 (εἰ, 3; with additional NT references).

cause we are justified, reconciled, saved from the wrath of God, and freed from the power of sin, the law, and death itself (5:1–8:30). Since that is the case, what more could one possibly expect? There is nothing that could possibly call God's love into question, a fact that will be resoundingly affirmed in 8:39.

At 8:32 Paul writes that God "did not withhold his own Son" (ἰδίου υἱοῦ οὐκ ἐφείσατο). There may be an allusion here to Genesis 22:16, which follows the story of the near sacrifice of Isaac by Abraham. At that place in Genesis the Lord speaks to Abraham through an angel and says that, because he "did not withhold his beloved son" (ἐφείσω τοῦ υἱοῦ σου τοῦ ἀγαπητοῦ), he would bless him and make his descendants great and a blessing to the nations (Gen 22:16-18). In both cases, forms of the same Greek verb (φείδομαι, "to withhold," "to spare") are used. The allusion is possible, if not certain. If there is an actual allusion here, the implication is that, although Abraham did not have to go through with the sacrifice of his son, God has indeed done so in the sacrifice of his own Son.[374] Furthermore, since God "gave him up for us all," the blessing is now extended directly to the nations of the world through Christ as they come to believe. In any case, whether the allusion is firm or not, the point Paul makes is that, if God has gone so far as not to spare his own Son for our sake, most certainly he will "give us all things with him."

The saying that God "gave him up for us all" contains two expressions derived from pre-Pauline creedal traditions. The first of these (ὑπὲρ ἡμῶν πάντων, "for us all") can be considered one of several kerygmatic formulas that

---

374. It has been suggested that Paul was aware of the "Akedah" (or "Aqedat Yishaq," "Binding of Isaac") tradition in ancient Judaism. According to that tradition, Abraham's willingness to offer his son Isaac had an atoning significance, and consequently the event was recalled in prayers asking that God might remember it to the benefit of Israel. If Paul recalls the Akedah tradition here, he extends it by saying that God has now completed the sacrifice for the benefit of all humankind, not simply Israel. The sources for the Akedah tradition, however, do not antedate the apostle Paul. The tradition appears explicitly in Tannaitic sources and only later in Christian sources (Tertullian, *Adversus Marcionem* 3.18; Clement of Alexandria, *Paedagogus* 1.5). On this, cf. Louis Jacobs and Avi Sagi, "Akedah," *EncJud* 1:555-58. Those who see an allusion include N. Dahl, "The Atonement," 151-53, and R. Daly, "The Soteriological Significance of the Sacrifice of Isaac," 45-75. Those who conclude that no such allusion can be found here include P. Davies and B. Chilton, "The Aqedah," 514-46, who consider the Akedah to be a second-century-A.D. creation; E. Meile, "Isaaks Opferung," 111-28; D. Schwartz, "Two Pauline Allusions," 259-68; and E. Kessler, *Bound by the Bible*, 121-23. G. Vermes, "New Light on the Sacrifice of Isaac," 140-46, contends that elements of the Akedah can be traced to the first century. Although that may be, the concept of a meritorious sacrifice does not appear to be pre-Christian, according to A. Segal, "He Who Did Not Spare His Own Son," 171-72, 179; and J. Fitzmyer, "The Sacrifice of Isaac in Qumran Literature," 220-27. For a survey, cf. R. Hayward, "The Present State of Research," 127-50. On the "Binding of Isaac" in the OT, cf. T. Fretheim, *Abraham,* 118-37; in other texts, E. Noort and E. Tigchelaar, *The Sacrifice of Isaac* (essays primarily on postbiblical sources).

Paul uses.[375] For discussion, see the exegesis at 5:6. The second (παρέδωκεν αὐτόν, "he gave him up") appears in the passion narratives of the gospels on several occasions: the betrayal of Jesus by Judas (Mark 14:10), the delivery of Jesus by the Sanhedrin to Pilate (Mark 15:1), the turning of Jesus over to the will of the people (Luke 23:25), and giving him over to death by Pilate (Matt 27:26// Mark 15:15; John 19:16).[376] The fact that the phrase appears in various traditions — not only in the letters of Paul, the Synoptic Gospels, and the Fourth Gospel, but also in specific passion predictions (Mark 9:31; 10:33; Luke 9:44) and within the Pauline eucharistic tradition as well (1 Cor 11:23) — confirms that it arose early as a kerygmatic expression concerning the death of Jesus.[377] But what is striking about Paul's expressions here is that the handing over to death was by God. The same may be expressed at Romans 4:25. In that verse, since God is the implied subject of 4:25b (the divine passive in the clause "[he] was raised for our justification"), the same may be implied in 4:25a ("[he] was given over [παρεδόθη] for our trespasses"). God, who sent his Son "in the likeness of sinful flesh, and for sin, condemned sin in the flesh" (Rom 8:3). God is the one, then, who delivered him up to death on behalf of humanity.

The questions asked in 8:33 and 8:34 speak, as in a court of law, of charges and condemnation that could be brought forth at the final judgment. The word translated "to bring charges" (ἐγκαλέω) is a legal term for making accusations and carrying on a prosecution in a court.[378] Paul asks who it could possibly be that would bring charges against "the elect." The term "elect" (ἐκλεκτός) appears in the OT to refer to the people of Israel (1 Chr 16:13; LXX Pss 88:4; 104:6, 43; Isa 65:9, 15, 23),[379] and it refers specifically to the Qumran community in the Dead Sea Scrolls.[380] Paul is not likely the first to have used it as a designation for Christians, since it is used by other NT writers as well (Matt 24:22; Mark 13:27; 2 Tim 2:10; 1 Pet 1:1).

---

375. Paul uses ὑπὲρ ἡμῶν ("for us") at Rom 5:8; 2 Cor 5:21; Gal 3:13; 1 Thess 5:10; he uses ὑπὲρ πάντων ("for all") at 2 Cor 5:14-15. For similar expressions, see the discussion at 5:6. On the pre-Pauline nature of these expressions, cf. V. Neufeld, *The Earliest Christian Confessions,* 48; and K. Wengst, *Christologische Formeln und Lieder des Urchristentums,* 78-90.

376. The expression also appears at Mark 3:19 concerning the betrayal of Jesus by Judas.

377. F. Hahn, *The Titles of Jesus in Christology,* 59-61; N. Perrin, "The Use of *(Para)didonai* in Connection with the Passion of Jesus in the New Testament," 94-103; C. Cranfield, *Romans,* 251; Wiard Popkes, "παραδίδωμι," *EDNT* 3:20. B. Gaventa, "Interpreting the Death of Jesus Apocalyptically," 127, has proposed that, for Paul, "God handed [Jesus] over to *anti-god powers*" (italics hers). But the expression is a widespread, pre-Pauline, kerygmatic one, and therefore it is not likely to imply all that is proposed.

378. BDAG 273 (ἐγκαλέω); various references are provided.

379. For additional references, including intertestamental and other Jewish texts, cf. Gottlob Schrenk, "ἐκλεκτός," *TDNT* 4:182-84.

380. CD 4.3-4; 1QS 8.6; 1QH 2.13.

The only party that would have the legal competence to bring charges against the elect would be God.[381] But, Paul declares, God is the one who justifies. If God is for us in the act of justification, it is impossible to think ultimately of God as a prosecutor at the final judgment. It is possible that Paul alludes here to the words of Isaiah 50:8 (LXX): "He who vindicates me is near. Who will judge me?" (ἐγγίζει ὁ δικαιώσας με τίς ὁ κρινόμενός μοι). Similarly, one cannot expect condemnation from Christ, since he has died, been raised, and intercedes "for us." In this verse (8:34) it is likely that Paul is using pre-Pauline liturgical or creedal language.[382] If so, it is remarkable, for it goes beyond what is usually stated (that Christ died and was raised) to include intercession "for us" by him in heaven. Earlier Paul had said that the Spirit intercedes "for the saints" (Rom 8:26-27), but this is the only place where he says that the risen and exalted Christ intercedes for believers. The claim is not limited to Paul, however, since the exalted Christ is intercessor also in Hebrews 7:25 and 1 John 2:1.

One cannot attribute to Paul later understandings of God, as expressed in the ecumenical creeds. But to the degree that there is communion between the Father, Son, and Spirit in his thinking here, it is not limited to an inner life of God that is remote from God's relationship to the world. The Son and the Spirit intercede "for us" or "for the saints," Paul says, as though there is a fellowship among Father, Son, and Spirit with redemption in view, regardless of any other life or communion that there may be among them.

That Christ is at the right hand of God (δεξιᾷ τοῦ θεοῦ) recalls the opening line of Psalm 110, at which the Lord addresses the king: "Sit at my right hand (κάθου ἐκ δεξιῶν μου) until I make your enemies your footstool." That line from the psalm is applied to the risen and exalted Christ within many parts of the NT, representing more breadth across NT authorship than any other (Matt 22:44; Acts 2:34-35; 1 Cor 15:25; Eph 1:20; Col 3:1; Heb 1:3, 13). By using the phrase Paul attributes to the risen Christ a status not only of honor but also of authority.

8:35-37 Finally the question waiting to be answered is raised, "Who shall separate us from the love of Christ?" The question gets a resounding response in all that follows: "No one!" The nouns are run together and have a powerful rhetorical effect. No human forces can separate believers from Christ's love for them. The seven forces mentioned are particularly related to the experience of Christians in persecution: tribulation, distress, persecution, famine, nakedness, peril, and sword. Paul himself had experienced all of them except the sword, al-

---

381. Paul does not seem to consider the possibility of Satan as accuser (cf. that role for Satan in Job 1:6–2:8; Zech 3:1-2).

382. P. von der Osten-Sacken, *Römer 8*, 20-43; H. Paulsen, *Überlieferung und Auslegung in Römer 8*, 141-47, 172.

though that would finally be his fate under Nero. By the time he wrote Romans he had experienced the other things listed. He uses each of the terms in prior letters when speaking about his own suffering as an apostle: θλῖψις ("tribulation," 2 Cor 1:4, 8), στενοχωρία ("distress," 2 Cor 6:4; 12:10), διωγμός ("persecution," 2 Cor 12:10), λιμός ("famine" or "hunger," 2 Cor 11:27), γυμνότης ("nakedness," 1 Cor 4:11; 2 Cor 11:27), and κίνδυνος ("peril," 1 Cor 15:30; 2 Cor 11:26). And there was even more. He had written to the Corinthians previously, saying (1 Cor 4:11-12):

> To the present hour we are hungry and thirsty, we are poorly clothed and beaten and homeless, and we grow weary from the work of our own hands. When reviled, we bless; when persecuted, we endure.

Moreover, he had written to them about his perils (2 Cor 11:25-26):

> Three times I was beaten with rods. Once I received a stoning. Three times I was shipwrecked; for a night and a day I was adrift at sea; on frequent journeys, in danger from rivers, danger from bandits, danger from my own people, danger from Gentiles, danger in the city, danger in the wilderness, danger at sea, danger from false brothers and sisters.

Romans 8:36 makes the allusion to suffering under persecution even more clear.[383] Paul quotes Psalm 44:22 (LXX 43:23), and the wording in Romans is exactly like that of the LXX:

> For your sake we are being killed all day long;
> we are regarded as sheep to be slaughtered.

Nevertheless, in spite of such horrible treatment, nothing that persecutors or oppressors ever do can overcome those who are in Christ's loving embrace (8:37). In all these things, Paul says (translating literally), "we hyper conquer" (ὑπερνικῶμεν); we are more than victors (NET: "we have complete victory"); or "we are winning a most glorious victory."[384] Ultimately, all such social-political realities, which are powers of the old age, are doomed to pass away (1 Cor 2:6).

8:38-39 But it is not only hostile powers on earth that assail and seek to overcome those in Christ. Spiritual and cosmic powers are at work too, seeking to destroy them and to sever them from the love of God in Christ. What Paul goes on to speak of here has a background in both Jewish thought and in

---

383. Passages in Str-B 3:259-60 indicate that this psalm was used in rabbinic literature in reference to the persecution of Jewish martyrs in Maccabean and Hadrianic times; cited by C. Cranfield, *Romans*, 440; J. Dunn, *Romans*, 505.

384. BDAG 1034 (ὑπερνικάω).

Greco-Roman traditional beliefs.[385] In Jewish thought God created the world and gave ruling power to the sun and the moon (Gen 1:14-19); they "rule" day and night. Moreover, cosmic powers (angels, principalities, and powers) rule over humanity for good or ill.[386] In pagan Hellenism the stars and planets are divinities (gods) that rule over the universe (as in astrology). Although both Judaism and Christianity deny that the stars and planets are gods,[387] they can grant that there are cosmic powers.

Paul lists ten potential threats that cannot separate believers from God's love in Christ. Eight of them are paired as opposites; the exceptions are "powers" (δυνάμεις) and "any other creature" (τις κτίσις ἐτέρα):

death (θάνατος)	life (ζωή)
angels (ἄγγελοι)	rulers (ἀρχαί)
things present (ἐνεστῶτα)	things to come (μέλλοντα)
powers (δυνάμεις)	
height (ὕψωμα)	depth (βάθος)
any other creature (τις κτίσις ἐτέρα)	

In his list of potential threats Paul includes three that are presumably supernatural and hostile beings (or at least beings that impede a relationship with God), the "angels (ἄγγελοι)," "rulers (ἀρχαί)," and "powers (δυνάμεις)."[388] A similar list is provided — again designating supernatural powers — at 1 Corinthians 15:24: "every ruler (ἀρχή) and every authority (ἐξουσία) and power (δύναμις)." But the other seven listed cannot be called supernatural beings. "Death" and "life" are more appropriately considered existential and spiritual realities. Death is a threat, the "last enemy" (1 Cor 15:26). It is less evident to say that life is a threat to one's existence. It is quite possible that Paul includes the term in order to create the antithetical schema and, at the same time, to speak of the whole of existence (cf. 1 Cor 3:22 for a similar usage). In any case, life can be perilous as one contemplates the future. "Things present," "things to come" (the

385. For a general discussion, cf. T. Hegedus, *Early Christianity and Ancient Astrology*, 223-26.

386. Cf. Philo, *Gig.* 16; *Somn.* 1.190; Josephus, *J.W.* 5.388; *T. Levi* 19.3; *1 Enoch* 6.1–11.2; 69.2-25; *2 Apoc. Bar.* 56.11-15; *Jub.* 5.6-11; Matt 25:41; Rev 12:9. For discussion of OT and later Jewish texts, cf. Carol A. Newsom, "Angels: Old Testament," *ABD* 1:248-53, and Clinton E. Arnold, "Principalities and Powers," *ABD* 5:467.

387. Philo, *Migr.* 32.181; 1 Cor 8:5-6; Gal 4:8-11.

388. Cf. C. Cranfield, *Romans*, 442; U. Wilckens, *Römer*, 2:177; B. Byrne, *Romans*, 280-81; W. Wink, *Naming the Powers*, 49; but J. Fitzmyer, *Romans*, 535, allows that they could be good or bad. Similarly, W. Carr, *Angels and Principalities*, 112-14, claims that there are no references to hostile forces in this passage. Yet if they are forces that seek to separate persons from God's love, they are hostile.

two are together also at 1 Cor 3:22), "height," and "depth" cover the entire time-space continuum in which every person is enclosed in this life; the terms "height" and "depth" are derived from ancient astronomy and signify the extremities of the created comos.[389] The final line concerning "any other creature" serves to close the list, lest anything else be left out.

Some interpreters have sought to locate the origins of Paul's list of hostile forces in astrological traditions of the ancient Near East or Hellenism[390] or within Gnosticism.[391] But the list is probably Pauline and eclectic, in which Paul makes reference not only to supernatural powers but even more to existential realities of human life. These point to the transitory nature of human existence (death and life) and its limitations (temporal and spatial). The focus of interest is primarily anthropological, not astrological. And the anthropological is located within the sphere of the theocentric: the love of God in Christ, which will have its way, preserving God's beloved in an eternal fellowship.

Paul declares that no forces, human or cosmic, can separate believers in Christ from the love of God that has been shown forth in Christ. The declaration is a certain and personal comfort to anyone who is "in Christ." The bond between God and believers is so great that it can never be broken. But what, then, can one say about persons who are not "in Christ"? Paul takes up that issue in the next three chapters.

BIBLIOGRAPHY

Argyle, A. W. "Romans 8,32." *JTS* 4 (1953): 214-15.

Balz, Horst R. *Heilsvertrauen und Welterfahrung: Strukturen der paulinischen Eschatologie nach Römer 8,18-39.* BEvT 59. Munich: Kaiser Verlag, 1971.

Beker, J. Christiaan. "Romans 9–11 in the Context of the Early Church." In *The Church and Israel: Romans 9–11: The 1989 Frederick Neumann Symposium on the Theological Interpretation of Scripture,* 40-55. Ed. Daniel Migliore. PSBSup 1. Princeton: Princeton Theological Seminary, 1990.

Blank, Josef. "Röm 8,32." In his *Paulus und Jesus: Eine theologische Grundlegung,* 294-98. SANT 18. Munich: Kösel Verlag, 1968.

Bultmann, Rudolf, *Primitive Christianity in Its Contemporary Setting.* Cleveland: World Publishing Company, 1956.

Caird, George B. *Principalities and Powers: A Study in Pauline Theology.* Oxford: Clarendon Press, 1956.

---

389. August Strobel, "βάθος," *EDNT* 1:190; Georg Bertram, "ὕψωμα," *TDNT* 8:614.

390. W. L. Knox, *St. Paul and the Church of the Gentiles,* 106-7; G. Caird, *Principalities and Powers,* 74; Konrad Weiss, "ἀρχή," *EDNT* 1:162. According to R. Reitzenstein, *Poimandres,* 80, Paul himself groaned under the influence of a fatalistic religion in writing Rom 8:38-39.

391. R. Bultmann, *Primitive Christianity,* 190.

Carr, Wesley. *Angels and Principalities: The Background, Meaning and Development of the Pauline Phrase* hai archai kai exousiai. SNTSMS 42. Cambridge: Cambridge University Press, 1981.

Charlesworth, James H. "Jewish Interest in Astrology during the Hellenistic and Roman Period." *ANRW* II.20.2 (1987): 926-50.

Dahl, Nils A. "The Atonement: An Adequate Reward for the Akedah? (Rom 8:32)." In his *The Crucified Messiah and Other Essays*, 146-60. Minneapolis: Augsburg Publishing House, 1974; reprinted from *Neotestamentica et Semitica: Studies in Honour of Matthew Black*, 15-29. Ed. E. Earle Ellis and Max Wilcox. Edinburgh: T&T Clark, 1969

Daly, Robert J. "The Soteriological Significance of the Sacrifice of Isaac." *CBQ* 39 (1977): 45-75.

Davies, Philip R., and Bruce D. Chilton. "The Aqedah: A Revised Tradition History." *CBQ* 40 (1978): 514-46.

Delling, Gerhard. "Die Entfaltung des 'Deus pro nobis' in Röm 8,31-39." *SNTU* 4 (1979): 76-96.

Dibelius, Martin. *Die Geisterwelt im Glauben des Paulus*. Göttingen: Vandenhoeck & Ruprecht, 1909.

Du Toit, Andreas B. "Forensic Metaphors in Romans and Their Soteriological Significance." In *Salvation in the New Testament: Perspectives on Soteriology*, 213-46. Ed. Jan G. van der Watt. NovTSup 121. Boston: E. J. Brill, 2005.

Fahy, T. "Romans 8:34." *ITQ* 25 (1958): 387.

Fiedler, Peter. "Röm 8,31-39 als Brennpunkt paulinischer Frohbotschaft." *ZNW* 68 (1977): 23-34.

Fitzmyer, Joseph A. "The Sacrifice of Isaac in Qumran Literature." *Bib* 83 (2002): 211-29.

Fredrickson, David. "Paul: Hardship and Suffering." In *Paul in the Greco-Roman World*, 172-98. Ed. J. Paul Sampley. Harrisburg: Trinity Press International, 1989.

Fretheim, Terence E. *Abraham: Trials of Family and Faith*. Columbia: University of South Carolina Press, 2007.

Furnish, Victor P. "'He Gave Himself [Was Given] Up . . .': Paul's Use of a Christological Assertion." In *The Future of Christology: Essays in Honor of Leander E. Keck*, 109-21. Ed. Abraham J. Malherbe and Wayne A. Meeks. Minneapolis: Fortress Press, 1993.

Gaventa, Beverly Roberts. "Interpreting the Death of Jesus Apocalyptically: Reconsidering Romans 8:32." In *Jesus and Paul Reconnected: Fresh Pathways into an Old Debate*, 125-45. Ed. Todd D. Still. Grand Rapids: Wm. B. Eerdmans, 2007.

Hahn, Ferdinand. *The Titles of Jesus in Christology: Their History in Early Christianity*. Cleveland: World Publishing Company, 1969.

Hayward, Robert. "The Present State of Research into the Targumic Account of the Sacrifice of Isaac." *JSS* 32 (1981): 127-50.

Hegedus, Tim. *Early Christianity and Ancient Astrology*. PS 6. New York: Peter Lang, 2007.

Hengel, Martin. "Psalm 110 und die Erhöhung des Auferstandenen zur Rechten Gottes." In *Anfänge der Christologie: Festschrift für Ferdinand Hahn zum 65. Geburtstag*, 43-73. Ed. Cilliers Breytenbach and Henning Paulsen. Göttingen: Vandenhoeck & Ruprecht, 1991.

Hodgson, R. "Paul the Apostle and First-Century Tribulation Lists." *ZNW* 74 (1983): 59-80.

Jaquette, James L. "Life and Death, Adiaphora, and Paul's Rhetorical Strategies." *NovT* 28 (1996): 330-54.

Jeffrey, G. J. "Paul's Certainties: The Love of God in Christ — Romans viii. 38, 39." *ExpTim* 69 (1957-58): 359-61.

Jewett, Robert. "Impeaching God's Elect: Romans 8:33-36 in Its Rhetorical Situation." In *Paul, Luke and the Graeco-Roman World: Essays in Honour of Alexander J. M. Wedderburn*, 37-58. Ed. Alf Christophersen et al. JSNTSup 217. Sheffield: Sheffield Academic Press, 2002.

Kessler, Edward. *Bound by the Bible: Jews, Christians and the Sacrifice of Isaac.* Cambridge: Cambridge University Press, 2004.

Knox, Wilfred L. *St. Paul and the Church of the Gentiles.* Cambridge: Cambridge University Press, 1961.

Kooten, George H. van. *Cosmic Christology in Paul and the Pauline School: Colossians and Ephesians in the Context of Graeco-Roman Cosmology, with a New Synopsis of the Greek Texts.* WUNT 2/171. Tübingen: J. C. B. Mohr (Paul Siebeck), 2003.

Kugler, Robert A., and James C. VanderKam. "A Note on 4Q225 (4Qpseudo-Jubilees)." *RevQ* 20 (2001): 109-16.

Laarman, Edward, "Power, Might." *ISBE*, 3:926-29.

Levi, Israel. "Le sacrifice d'Isaac et la mort de Jesus." *REJ* 64 (1912): 161-84.

Loader, W. R. G. "Christ at the Right Hand — Ps xc 1 in the New Testament." *NTS* 24 (1978): 199-217.

Loane, Marcus L. *The Hope of Glory: An Exposition of the Eighth Chapter of the Epistle to the Romans.* London: Hodder & Stoughton, 1968.

Lyonnet, Stanislas. "L'Amour efficace du Christ: Rm 8,35.37-39." *ASeign* 49 (1971): 12-16; reprinted in his *Études sur l'épître aux Romains*, 260-63. AnBib 120. Rome: Pontifical Biblical Institute Press, 1989.

Maartens, Pieter J. "The Vindication of the Righteous in Romans 8:31-39: Inference and Relevance." *HerTS* 51 (1995): 1046-87.

McCasland, S. V., "Power." *IDB* 3:854-55.

Meile, Eva. "Isaaks Opferung: Eine Note an Nils Alstrup Dahl." *Studia Theologica* 34 (1980): 111-28.

Münderlein, G. "Interpretation einer Tradition: Bemerkungen zu Röm. 8,35f." *KuD* 11 (1965): 136-42.

Neufeld, Vernon. *The Earliest Christian Confessions.* NTTS 5. Grand Rapids: Wm. B. Eerdmans, 1963.

Noort, Edward, and Eibert J. C. Tigchelaar, eds. *The Sacrifice of Isaac: The Aqedah (Genesis 22) and Its Interpretation.* TBN 4. Boston: E. J. Brill, 2002.

Osten-Sacken, Peter von der. *Römer 8 als Beispiel paulinischer Soteriologie.* FRLANT 112. Göttingen: Vandenhoeck & Ruprecht, 1975.

Parlier, Isabelle. "La folle justice de dieu (Romains 8,31-39)." *FV* 68 (1992): 103-10.

Paulsen, Henning. *Überlieferung und Auslegung in Römer 8.* WMANT 43. Neukirchen-Vluyn: Neukirchener Verlag, 1974.

Perrin, Norman. "The Use of *(Para)didonai* in Connection with the Passion of Jesus in the

New Testament." In his *A Modern Pilgrimage in New Testament Christology*. Philadelphia: Fortress Press, 1974.

Reitzenstein, Richard. *Poimandres: Studien zur griechisch-ägyptischen und frühchristlichen Literatur*. Leipzig: Teubner, 1904.

Romaniuk, Kazimierz. "L'Origine des formulas pauliniennes 'Le Christ s'est livré pour nous,' 'Le Christ nous a aimés et s'est livré pour nous.'" *NovT* 5 (1962): 55-76.

Rossow, Francis C. "The Hound of Heaven, A Twitch upon the Thread, and Romans 8:31-39." *ConJ* 23 (1997): 91-98.

Schaller, Berndt. "Zum Textcharakter der Hiobzitate im paulinischen Schrifttum." *ZNW* 71 (1980): 21-26.

Schille, Gottfried. "Die Liebe Gottes in Christus: Beobachtungen zu Rm 8,31-39." *ZNW* 59 (1968): 230-44.

Schlier, Heinrich. *Principalities and Powers in the New Testament*. Freiburg: Herder, 1961.

Schoeps, Hans-Joachim. "The Sacrifice of Isaac in Paul's Theology." *JBL* 65 (1946): 385-92.

Schwartz, Daniel R. "Two Pauline Allusions to the Redemptive Mechanism of the Crucifixion." *JBL* 102 (1983): 259-68.

Segal, Alan F. "'He Who Did Not Spare His Own Son . . .': Jesus, Paul and the Akedah." In *From Jesus to Paul: Studies in Honour of Francis Wright Beare*, 169-84. Ed. Peter Richardson and J. C. Hurd. Waterloo: Wilfrid Laurier University Press, 1984.

Smith, Jonathan Z. "Towards Interpreting Demonic Powers in Hellenistic and Roman Antiquity." *ANRW* II.16.1 (1978): 425-39.

Snyman, Andreas H. "Style and Meaning in Romans 8:31-39." *Neot* 18 (1984): 94-103.

———. "Style and the Rhetorical Situation of Romans 8.31-39." *NTS* 34 (1988): 2218-31.

Spiegel, Shalom. *The Last Trial*. New York: Schocken Books, 1969.

Swetnam, James. *Jesus and Isaac*. AnBib 94. Rome: Pontifical Biblical Institute Press, 1981.

Tisdale, Leonora Tubbs. "Romans 8:31-39." *Int* 42 (1988): 68-72.

Vermes, Geza. "New Light on the Sacrifice of Isaac from 4Q225." *JJS* 47 (1996): 140-46.

———. "Redemption and Genesis xxii — The Binding of Isaac and the Sacrifice of Jesus." In his *Scripture and Tradition in Judaism*, 193-227. 2d ed. SPB 4. Leiden: E. J. Brill, 1973.

Weiss, Johannes. "Beiträge zur paulinischen Rhetorik." In *Theologische Studien: Herrn Professor D. Bernhard Weiss zu seinem 70. Geburtstage dargebracht*, 165-247. Ed. Caspar R. Gregory et al. Göttingen: Vandenhoeck & Ruprecht, 1897.

Wengst, Klaus. *Christologische Formeln und Lieder des Urchristentums*. SNT 7. Gütersloh: Gütersloher Verlagshaus Gerd Mohn, 1972.

Wink, Walter, *Naming the Powers: The Language of Power in the New Testament*. Philadelphia: Fortress Press, 1984.

Wood, J. E. "Isaac Typology in the New Testament." *NTS* 14 (1967-68): 583-89.

CHAPTER 5

Israel in God's Plan, 9:1–11:36

Romans 9–11 makes up a section that can hardly be treated as a series of units lifted out of their contexts. It reads as one large unit, and it must be read in its entirety. Too often in the history of interpretation it has been the practice of interpreters to stop along the way between the beginning and the end and then draw out a theological position attributable to Paul on a particular topic (e.g., predestination, election, or the rise of faith from hearing) or to describe his views on some matter (such as an alleged spiritual obduracy of the Jewish people). But to isolate smaller units as providing Paul's last word on any matter is to do violence to the argument being made in the section as a whole.

There are at least three features of this portion of Romans that demand attention at the outset. The first is that the section follows immediately after the crescendo of 8:31-39, which concludes with the words: "For I am convinced that neither death, nor life, nor angels, nor rulers, nor things present, nor things to come, nor powers, nor height, nor depth, nor anything else in all creation, will be able to separate us from the love of God which is in Christ Jesus our Lord" (8:38-39). Such a strong affirmation of the love of God in Christ could have prompted the question in Paul's mind about the fate of those who do not have faith in Christ, particularly the Jewish people. The fact that such a prompting occurred is confirmed by what Paul says at the outset of the section, in which he expresses great sorrow for the Jewish people (9:2-3) for not accepting the gospel.

A second feature is the sheer length of Romans 9–11. The section consists of 90 verses, unrivaled by its length in all of the rest of Paul's undisputed letters.[1] It covers about 20 percent of the 432 verses of the Nestle-Aland Greek text

---

1. Even if 1 Cor 12:1–14:40 is considered a treatment of a single theme, it is not as long (84 verses).

(27th ed.) and the NRSV (both of which lack 16:24). One is thereby struck by the importance that its discussion must have had for Paul.

A third major feature of the section is that it contains an unusually large number of quotations from the OT. Within its 90 verses are 35 direct quotations from the OT (39% of the verses) plus many more allusions and summaries of OT material.[2] The percentage of quotations is much higher than what appears in the rest of the letter and in the writings of Paul generally. There are a total of 51 OT quotations in Romans itself and 89 in all of Paul's undisputed letters.[3] That means that about 69 percent of the OT quotations within Romans are in chapters 9 through 11 and, indeed, about 39 percent of all the quotations in Paul's letters. A couple of implications can be drawn from that phenomenon. First, Paul works very hard here. To weave so many biblical texts into an argument as technical and detailed as the one in this section requires extraordinary mental effort. Second, it is obvious that Paul seeks to base his discussion concerning the Jewish people upon a ground that is common between them and himself. He cannot make assertions out of the air, but must tie his discussion to the actual texts of the Scriptures.

The question has often been raised whether Romans 9–11 is truly integral to the entire letter. C. H. Dodd, for example, maintained that the section consists of an earlier sermon which Paul inserted into the letter, having no organic connection with the rest of the letter, since "the epistle could be read without any sense of a gap if these chapters were omitted."[4] But that view is generally, and rightly, regarded as extreme. The integrity of the section is affirmed by a wide spectrum of interpreters, even if for differing reasons.[5] It would seem that the reason stated above — the question of the future and fate of the Jewish people in light of Christ — would be sufficient. But, in addition, as Paul seeks to gain support for his mission beyond Rome to Spain, he conveys to his readers at Rome that, although he is an ardent exponent of the gospel of Christ, he is also committed to the coexistence of those Jews who have accepted the gospel and those who have remained opposed to it. Only a few years earlier (in A.D. 49) the

---

2. The figure of 35 quotations is based on a count of verses identified as OT quotations in the 27th edition of the Nestle-Aland Greek NT. A complete list is printed in A. Maillot, "Essai sur les citations vétérotestamentaires," 57-58. Maillot lists four additional verses (9:21, 22; 11:1, 33) that have not been considered in the count here, which would bring the number to 39, but not all can be considered actual quotations. Quotations can be seen at 9:7, 9, 12, 13, 15, 17, 20, 25, 26, 27, 28, 29, 33; 10:5, 6, 7, 8, 11, 13, 15, 16, 18, 19, 20, 21; 11:2, 3, 4, 8, 9, 10, 26, 27, 34, 35.

3. The statistics are those of D. A. Koch, *Die Schrift als Zeuge des Evangeliums*, 21-24.

4. C. H. Dodd, *Romans*, 149.

5. Johannes Munck, *Christ and Israel*, 27; A. Nygren, *Romans*, 353-60; E. Käsemann, *Romans*, 257; K. Stendahl, *Paul among Jews and Gentiles*, 4; N. Dahl, "The Future of Israel," 137-58; J. Fitzmyer, *Romans*, 540-41; J. Ziesler, *Romans*, 37-39; J. Beker, "The Faithfulness of God," 328-29; P. Stuhlmacher, *Romans*, 144.

tumult in Rome over "Chrestus" (= Christ) between the two groups had led to their expulsion by Claudius (see Introduction, pp. 3-4). Paul would have been known among the Christians at Rome as one who could debate fellow Jews concerning the significance of Christ. But, Paul is saying in so many words, there is no cause for his readers in Rome to worry that the events of 49 will be repeated with his coming among them. Although he would prefer that those Jews who hear the gospel would come to trust in Christ (Rom 11:14; 1 Cor 9:20), Paul is willing in this section of Romans to leave them in the hands of a merciful God who will remain faithful to his promises to Israel. The subject is an intricate one, requiring lengthy discussion, skill in argumentation, and proficiency in the use of Scripture.

The section 9:1–11:36 has been outlined in various ways. It is commonly divided into four major sections (with subunits) consisting of 9:1-5 (Paul's Sorrow over Israel); 9:6-29 (God's Free Election by Grace); 9:30–10:21 (Israel's Disobedience); and 11:1-36 (God's Faithfulness to Israel).[6] Others have divided the section into five parts: 9:1-5; 9:6-29; 9:30–10:21; 11:1-32; and 11:33-36.[7] The latter is an improvement, since it takes seriously the shift to a doxology in 11:33-36. Still others have proposed a division of the letter into smaller, additional units.[8] In the discussion that follows the material is divided into seven sections, of which some deal with implicit questions, as follows:

Paul's Sorrow (9:1-5)
What Shall We Say about God? (9:6-29)
What Shall We Say about Israel? (9:30–10:21)
Has God Rejected Israel? (11:1-12)
How Should Gentile Christians Think in the Present Situation? (11:13-24)
Consider a Mystery (11:25-32)
God Is Vindicated (11:33-36)

If one wants to press the point, there may be a chiastic structure here. For example, the first and last sections conclude with an "Amen" (9:5; 11:36), both have to do with Paul's sorrow (present and removed), and the fourth section is central: God has not rejected Israel. Yet chiastic structures are often more in the eye of the beholder than in the text.

6. W. Sanday and A. Headlam, *Romans*, 226; E. Käsemann, *Romans*, 257; U. Wilckens, *Römer*, 2:vii; J. Fitzmyer, *Romans*, x-xi; E. Lohse, *Römer*, 10.

7. C. H. Dodd, *Romans*, x; C. Cranfield, *Romans*, 29; J. Dunn, *Romans*, 2:ix-x; B. Byrne, *Romans*, vii; L. Keck, *Romans*, 9.

8. C. K. Barrett, *Romans*, 164-211, divides the section into ten units; J. Aageson, "Scripture and Structure," 265-89, divides it into eleven.

BIBLIOGRAPHY

Aageson, James W. "Scripture and Structure in the Development of the Argument in Romans 9–11." *CBQ* 48 (1986): 265-89.

———. "Typology, Correspondence, and the Application of Scripture in Romans 9–11." *JSNT* 31 (1987): 51-72; reprinted in *The Pauline Writings*, 76-97. Ed. Stanley E. Porter and Craig A. Evans. BibSem 34. Sheffield: Sheffield Academic Press, 1995.

Abasciano, Brian J. *Paul's Use of the Old Testament in Romans 9.1-9: An Intertextual and Theological Exegesis.* LNTS 301. New York: T&T Clark, 2005.

Barth, Marcus. *Israel and the Church.* Richmond: John Knox Press, 1969.

———. *The People of God.* JSNTSup 5. Sheffield: JSOT Press, 1983.

———. "Die Stellung des Paulus zu Gesetz und Ordnung." In *Die Israelfrage nach Röm 9–11*, 245-87. Ed. Lorenzo de Lorenzi. Rome: Abtei von St. Paul, 1977.

Baum, Gregory. *The Jews and the Gospel: A Reexamination of the New Testament.* Westminster: Newman Press, 1961.

Beck, Norman A. *Mature Christianity in the 21st Century: The Recognition and Repudiation of the Anti-Jewish Polemic of the New Testament.* New York: Crossroad, 1994.

Beker, J. Christiaan. "The Faithfulness of God and the Priority of Israel in Paul's Letter to the Romans." In *The Romans Debate*, 327-32. Ed. Karl P. Donfried. Rev. ed. Peabody: Hendrickson Publishers, 1991.

Blackman, Edwin C. "Divine Sovereignty and Missionary Strategy in Romans 9–11." *CJT* 11 (1965): 124-25.

Bovon, Francois. "Israel in the Theology of the Apostle Paul." In his *Studies in Early Christianity*, 178-91. Grand Rapids: Baker Academic, 2003.

Caird, George B. "Expository Problems: Predestination — Romans ix.–xi." *ExpTim* 68 (1956-57): 324-27.

Campbell, William S. "The Place of Romans ix–xi within the Structure and Thought of the Letter." *SE* 7/TU 126 (1982): 211-31.

Chilton, Bruce. "Romans 9–11 as Scriptural Interpretation and Dialogue with Judaism." *ExAud* 4 (1988): 27-37.

Cosgrove, Charles H. *Elusive Israel: The Puzzle of Election in Romans.* Louisville: Westminster John Knox, 1997.

———. "Rhetorical Suspense in Romans 9–11: A Study in Polyvalence and Hermeneutical Election." *JBL* 115 (1996): 271-87.

Cranford, Michael. "Election and Ethnicity: Paul's View of Israel in Romans 9.1-13." *JSNT* 50 (1993): 27-41.

Dahl, Nils A. "The Future of Israel." In his *Studies in Paul: Theology for the Early Christian Mission*, 137-58. Minneapolis: Augsburg Publishing House, 1977.

Davies, W. D. "Paul and the People of Israel." *NTS* 24 (1977-78): 4-39; reprinted in his *Jewish and Pauline Studies*, 123-52. Philadelphia: Fortress Press, 1984.

Donaldson, Terence L. "Jewish Christianity, Israel's Stumbling and the *Sonderweg* Reading of Paul." *JSNT* 29 (2006): 27-54.

Evans, Craig A. "Paul and the Hermeneutics of 'True Prophecy': A Study of Romans 9–11." *Bib* 65 (1984): 560-70.

Gadenz, Pablo T. *Called from the Jews and from the Gentiles: Pauline Ecclesiology in Romans 9-11.* WUNT 2/267. Tübingen: Mohr Siebeck, 2009.

Getty, Mary Ann. "Paul and the Salvation of Israel: A Perspective on Romans 9-11." *CBQ* 50 (1988): 456-69.

Giblin, Charles H. "General Survey of the Argument in Romans 9-11." In his *In Hope of God's Glory: Pauline Theological Perspectives,* 264-310. New York: Herder and Herder, 1970.

Hofius, Otfried. "Das Evangelium und Israel: Erwägungen zu Römer 9-11." *ZTK* 83 (1986): 297-324; reprinted in his *Paulusstudien,* 1:175-202. 2 vols. WUNT 51, 143. Tübingen: J. C. B. Mohr (Paul Siebeck), 1994-2002.

Hübner, Hans. *Gottes Ich und Israel: Zum Schriftgebrauch des Paulus in Römer 9-11.* FRLANT 136. Göttingen: Vandenhoeck & Ruprecht, 1984.

Johnson, E. Elizabeth. *The Function of Apocalyptic and Wisdom Traditions in Romans 9-11.* SBLDS 109. Atlanta: Scholars Press, 1989.

―――. "Romans 9-11: The Faithfulness and Impartiality of God." In *Pauline Theology,* vol. 3, *Romans,* 211-39. Ed. David M. Hay and E. Elizabeth Johnson. Minneapolis: Fortress Press, 1995.

Kim, Johann D. *God, Israel, and the Gentiles: Rhetoric and Situation in Romans 9-11.* SBLDS 176. Atlanta: Society of Biblical Literature, 2000.

Koch, Dietrich-Alex. *Die Schrift als Zeuge des Evangeliums: Untersuchungen zur Verwendung und zum Verständnis der Schrift bei Paulus.* BHT 69. Tübingen: J. C. B. Mohr (Paul Siebeck), 1986.

Lloyd-Jones, D. M. *Romans: An Exposition of Chapter 9: God's Sovereign Purpose.* Grand Rapids: Zondervan, 1992.

Lodge, John G. *Romans 9-11: A Reader-Response Analysis.* University of South Florida International Studies in Formative Christianity and Judaism 6. Atlanta: Scholars Press, 1996.

Longenecker, Bruce W. "On Israel's God and God's Israel: Assessing Supersessionism in Paul." *JTS* 58 (2007): 26-44.

Lorenzi, Lorenzo de, ed. *Die Israelfrage nach Röm. 9-11.* Rome: St. Paul's Abbey, 1977.

Lübking, Hans-Martin. *Paulus und Israel im Römerbrief: Eine Untersuchung zu Römer 9-11.* EHS.T 23.260. Frankfurt am Main: Peter Lang, 1986.

Maillot, Alphonse. "Essai sur les citations vétérotestamentaires contenues dans Romains 9 à 11: Ou comment se server de la Torah pour montrer que le 'Christ est la fin de la Torah.'" *ETR* 57 (1982): 55-73.

Meeks, Wayne A. "On Trusting an Unpredictable God: A Hermeneutical Meditation on Romans 9-11." In *Faith and History: Essays in Honor of Paul W. Meyer,* 15-24. Ed. John T. Carroll et al. Atlanta: Scholars Press, 1990.

Minear, Paul Sevier "The Eternal Triangle: Rebuttal in 9-11." *The Obedience of Faith: The Purpose of Paul in the Epistle to the Romans,* 72-81. SBT 19. Naperville: Alec R. Allenson, 1971.

Munck, Johannes. *Christ and Israel: An Interpretation of Romans 9-11.* Philadelphia: Fortress Press, 1967.

Mussner, Franz. "Die 'Verstockung' Israels nach Röm 9-11." *TTZ* 109 (2000): 191-98.

————. "Die Psalmen im Gedankengang des Paulus in Röm 9–11." In *Freude an der Weisung des Herrn: Beiträge zur Theologie der Psalmen: Festgabe zum 70. Geburtstag von Heinrich Gross*, 243-63. Ed. Ernst Haag and Frank-Lothar Hossfeld. Stuttgart: Katholisches Bibelwerk, 1986.

Oropeza, B. J. "Paul and Theodicy: Intertextual Thoughts on God's Justice and Faithfulness to Israel in Romans 9–11." *NTS* 53 (2007): 57-80.

Plag, Christoph. *Israels Weg zum Heil: Eine Untersuchung zu Römer 9 bis 11*. AT 40. Stuttgart: Calwer Verlag, 1969.

Quesnel, Michel. "La figure de Moïse en Romains 9–11." *NTS* 45 (2003): 321-35.

Räisänen, Heikki. "Paul, God, and Israel: Romans 9–11 in Recent Research." In *The Social World of Formative Christianity and Judaism: Essays in Tribute to Howard Clark Kee*, 178-206. Ed. Jacob Neusner et al. Philadelphia: Fortress Press, 1988.

————. "Römer 9–11: Analyse eines geistigen Ringens." *ANRW* II.25.4 (1987): 2891-2939.

————. "Romans 9–11 and the 'History of Early Christian Religion.'" In *Texts and Contexts: Biblical Texts in Their Textual and Situational Contexts: Essays in Honor of Lars Hartman*, 743-65. Ed. Tord Fornberg and David Hellholm. Oslo: Scandinavian University Press, 1995.

Refoulé, François. "Cohérence ou Incohérence de Paul in Romains 9–11." *RB* 36 (1991): 51-79

Rese, Martin. "Israel und Kirche in Römer 9." *NTS* 34 (1988): 208-17.

Romerowski, Sylvain. "Israël dans le plan de Dieu." *RRef* 51/206 (2000): 51-68.

Ruether, Rosemary Radford. *Faith and Fratricide: The Theological Roots of Anti-Semitism*. New York: Seabury Press, 1974.

Siegert, Folker. *Argumentation bei Paulus: Gezeigt an Röm 9–11*. WUNT 34. Tübingen: J. C. B. Mohr (Paul Siebeck), 1985.

Sigel, Phillip. "Aspects of Dual Covenant Theology: Salvation." *HBT* 5/2 (1983): 1-48.

Skoven, Anne Vig. "Romerbrevet kap. 9–11 som eksegetisk spejl og gåde." *DTT* 65 (2002): 15-39.

Sneen, Donald. "The Root, the Remnant, and the Branches." *WW* 6/4 (1986): 398-409.

Stendahl, Krister. "Missiological Reflections of a Former Zealot: Romans 9–11." In his *Final Account: Paul's Letter to the Romans*, 33-44. Minneapolis: Fortress Press, 1995.

————. *Paul among Jews and Gentiles and Other Essays*. Philadelphia: Fortress Press, 1976.

Theobald, Michael. "Kirche und Israel nach Röm 9–11." In his *Studien zum Römerbrief*, 324-49. WUNT 136. Tübingen: J. C. B. Mohr (Paul Siebeck), 2001.

Thielman, Frank. "Unexpected Mercy: Echoes of a Biblical Motif in Romans 9–11." *SJT* 47 (1994): 169-81.

Wagner, Günter. "The Future of Israel: Reflections on Romans 9–11." In *Eschatology and the New Testament: Essays in Honor of George Raymond Beasley-Murray*, 77-112. Ed. W. Hulitt Gloer. Peabody: Hendrickson Publishers, 1988.

Walter, Nikolaus. "Zur Interpretation von Römer 9–11." *ZTK* 81 (1984): 172-95.

Westerholm, Stephen. "Paul and the Law in Romans 9–11." In *Paul and the Mosaic Law*, 215-37. Ed. James D. G. Dunn. Grand Rapids: Wm. B. Eerdmans, 2001.

Wilk, Florian, and J. Ross Wagner, eds. *Between Gospel and Election: Explorations in the Interpretation of Romans 9–11*. WUNT 257. Tübingen: Mohr Siebeck, 2010.

Zeller, Dieter. *Juden und Heiden in der Mission des Paulus: Studien zum Römerbrief.* FB 1. Stuttgart: Verlag Katholisches Bibelwerk, 1973.

5.1. Paul's Sorrow, 9:1-5

1*I am speaking the truth in Christ; I am not lying. My conscience bears witness to me in the Holy Spirit,* 2*that I have great sorrow and unceasing anguish in my heart.* 3*For I could wish that I myself were accursed, cut off from Christ, for the sake of my brothers and sisters, my kindred according to the flesh,* 4*who are Israelites, and to them belong the adoption, the glory, the covenants, the giving of the law, the worship, and the promises;* 5*to them belong the fathers, and from them, according to the flesh, is the Christ. May he who is God over all be blessed for ever. Amen.*

Notes on the Text and Translation

9:4 The textual evidence is almost equally divided between the plural αἱ διαθῆκαι ("the covenants") and the singular ἡ διαθήκη ("the covenant"). The former is supported by ℵ, C, ψ, and others (including Old Latin texts having the plural), while the latter has the support of such important witnesses as 𝔓⁴⁶, B, and D. The plural is probably to be preferred. It is more likely that the noun was altered to the singular to conform with other nouns in the verse than that it would have been changed from singular to plural.[9]

9:5 The punctuation within this verse is a matter of debate.[10] The earliest Greek NT manuscripts lack punctuation, leaving it to the modern editor of the Greek text and with the translator. The issue in this particular instance is how ὁ ὢν ἐπὶ πάντων θεὸς εὐλογητὸς εἰς τοὺς αἰῶνας should be considered in relationship to the rest of the verse and, consequently, how it should be translated. There are three major ways to render it:[11]

1. The clause can be considered independent of what goes before it, resulting in a doxology: "and from them, according to the flesh, is the Christ. May he who is God over all be blessed forever" (cf. the RSV: "and of their race, according to the flesh, is the Christ. God who is over all be blessed forever"). In

---

9. B. Metzger, *TCGNT* 459.

10. For the punctuation adopted in the 27th edition of the Nestle-Aland text, see B. Metzger, *TCGNT* 459-62.

11. There are actually more possibilities. C. Cranfield, *Romans,* 465, provides six different possibilities. B. Metzger, "The Punctuation of Rom. 9:5," 95-96, reviews eight.

this case there is a distinction between Christ and God. This way of rendering the clause is favored by a good many interpreters.[12]

2. It is possible to consider the Greek expression ὁ ὤν as "who is," referring back to Christ and making a bold Christological affirmation: "and from them, according to the flesh, is the Christ, who is God over all, blessed for ever" (cf. the NIV: "from them is traced the human ancestry of Christ, who is God over all, forever praised"). In this instance Paul speaks of Christ as God. This way of rendering is favored by a large number of interpreters also.[13]

3. It is possible to translate the clause in such a way as to allow for either interpretation. That is to consider the Greek expression ὁ ὤν as "who is," referring back to Christ, but to rearrange the phrases within the clause to make a Christological affirmation, followed by a doxology that could refer to Christ as God, but not necessarily so, depending on where one places a period or semicolon, as in the two following translations. (1) The doxology does not imply that Christ is God in the following: "and from them, according to the flesh, is the Christ, who is over all; God be blessed for ever." (2) But it could imply that Christ is called "God" if the verse is rendered this way: "and from them, according to the flesh, is the Christ, who is over all, God be blessed for ever" (cf. the NRSV: "and from them, according to the flesh, comes the Messiah, who is over all, God blessed forever"). Although this rendering is represented in the NRSV and is reflected in an alternative reading in the NEB, it has not actually received support in recent scholarly literature.[14]

The fact that Christ is never spoken of as "God" elsewhere in the undisputed letters of Paul speaks against any translation that would do so here, particularly in a portion of Romans where the apostle uses theological expressions

12. Among others, the following support this rendering: C. H. Dodd, *Romans,* 152; J. Knox, *IB (Romans),* 9:540; E. Käsemann, *Romans,* 259-60; O. Kuss, "Zu Römer 9,5," 291-303; U. Wilckens, *Römer,* 2:189; J. Dunn, *Romans,* 528-29; R. Harrisville, *Romans,* 143-44; M. de Jonge, *Christology in Context,* 122-23; C. Tuckett, *Christology and the New Testament,* 64-65; K.-J. Kuschel, *Born before All Time?* 301-3; H. Betz, "Geschichte und Selbstopfer," 83; P. Stuhlmacher, *Romans,* 145; B. Byrne, *Romans,* 288; E. Lohse, *Römer,* 269-70; G. Fee, *Pauline Christology,* 272-77.

13. Among others, the following support this rendering: W. Sanday and A. Headlam, *Romans,* 233-38; O. Cullmann, *The Christology of the New Testament,* 312-13; A. Nygren, *Romans,* 358-59; A. Schlatter, *Romans,* 202-3; J. Murray, *Romans,* 216, 245-48; O. Michel, *Römer,* 228-29; B. Metzger, "The Punctuation of Rom. 9:5," 95-112; Raymond E. Brown, *Jesus, God and Man: Modern Biblical Reflections* (New York: Macmillan, 1967), 20-22; C. Cranfield, *Romans,* 464-70; J. Fitzmyer, *Romans,* 548-49; M. Harris, *Jesus as God,* 143-72; D. Moo, *Romans,* 565-68; T. Schreiner, *Romans,* 486-89; N. T. Wright, *NIB (Romans),* 10:629-31; C. Talbert, *Romans,* 248-49; B. Abasciano, *Paul's Use of the Old Testament in Romans 9.1-9,* 138-42; H.-C. Kammler, "Die Prädikation Jesu Christi als 'Gott,'" 164-80; R. Jewett, *Romans,* 555, 566-68.

14. An exception is C. K. Barrett, *Romans,* 167-68, who concludes that the question of whether the clause refers to God the Father or Christ should be left open.

that characterize and celebrate the Jewish heritage. Although Paul can speak of Christ as not regarding "equality with God as something to be exploited" (Phil 2:6), and emptied himself to take the form of a slave, the saying implies a distinction (i.e., Christ did not seize the equality). Likewise, although Paul could speak of Jesus as "Lord," a distinction is made between Jesus as Lord, on the one hand, and the God of Israel, on the other, in the following saying: "if you confess with your lips that Jesus is Lord and believe in your heart that God raised him from the dead, you will be saved" (Rom 10:9). Finally, the wordings of doxologies concerning God the Father used elsewhere by Paul are virtually the same as here: ὁ θεὸς . . . ὁ ὢν εὐλογητὸς εἰς τοὺς αἰῶνας ("God . . . who is blessed for ever," 2 Cor 11:31) and ὁ κτίζων, ὅς ἐστιν εὐλογητὸς εἰς τοὺς αἰῶνας ("the Creator, who is blessed forever," Rom 1:25). The reading adopted (as in the RSV and among many interpreters) presents the fewest problems, syntactically, contextually, and theologically. See additional comments below.

General Comment

This little section reveals the inner, personal feelings of Paul more than any other in his Letter to the Romans. It exudes with ethnic and religious pride that he has for his Jewish heritage. He recounts all that that heritage has to offer and has bequeathed to the Jewish people down to his own time. As a Pharisee and as one who had exceeded so many of his era in knowledge and zeal for his ancestral tradition (Gal 1:14; 2 Cor 11:21-22; Phil 3:4-6), he was also more aware than most of his contemporaries of everything that the tradition had to offer. To the degree that this passage displays his feelings, few of his time could have known and loved the Jewish tradition more than he.

At the same time, the most obvious and unmistakable feature of this passage is that it displays Paul's extreme sorrow concerning the Jewish people. For him, the most upsetting fact and conundrum in his life had been that, in spite of their rich heritage, the overwhelming majority of people of his generation — his "own people," as he calls them (9:3) — had not accepted the gospel of Jesus as the Messiah. His hopes for their acceptance of the gospel had been dashed from the beginning of his apostolic call and commission. Although he was commissioned to be an apostle to the Gentiles (Rom 11:13), he had always hoped for the salvation of the Jewish people through their acceptance of the gospel (1 Cor 9:20-21; Rom 11:11-16). As indicated through the discussion that follows in chapters 9 through 11, however, by the time he wrote 9:1-5 he had concluded that his hopes would most likely not be realized in the foreseeable future. And so he expresses his great sorrow.

Detailed Comment

9:1 Paul begins with a solemn declaration concerning truthful speech, followed by two parenthetical comments, saying that he is not lying, and that his conscience bears witness to him in the Holy Spirit. As elsewhere in his writings (2 Cor 1:12), the term "conscience" (συνείδησις) signifies a moral awareness, common to all humankind, that can testify for or against a person in his or her thoughts (cf. Rom 2:15). It bears witness concerning Paul's conduct, and in the present case bears witness to the truthfulness of what he is about to say. But there is an added emphasis. Paul speaks of his conscience as bearing witness "in the Holy Spirit." Guided by the Spirit, his conscience cannot go wrong. The phrase "in the Holy Spirit" is attached by Paul to his activities in other places as well (Rom 14:17; 2 Cor 6:6; 1 Thess 1:5). His being the beneficiary of God the Father as bearing witness to his testimony is declared in 2 Corinthians 11:31.

9:2-3 Paul declares his great sorrow and anguish for his "kindred according to the flesh" (τῶν συγγενῶν μου κατὰ σάρκα), the Jewish people in general. By calling them his "brothers and sisters" (otherwise only in reference to other Christians, no fewer than 113 times; see comment on 1:13) and by speaking of them as his "kindred," Paul indicates that he has not abandoned his Jewish identity; still, the phrase "according to the flesh" expresses an implied spiritual distancing of himself from them. Although Paul does not say why he has feelings of sorrow and anguish, the reason is obvious. They have not accepted the gospel. For "the sake of" (ὑπέρ followed by a genitive) such persons, says Paul, he would virtually lose all the benefits he has derived for being a person in Christ. The extent to which he is willing to go includes being (literally) "accursed from Christ" (ἀνάθεμα . . . ἀπὸ τοῦ Χριστοῦ), i.e., separated from Christ and all that he has to offer. The term ἀνάθεμα, related to the verb form (ἀνατίθημι, "to set up"), has a primary meaning in Hellenistic Judaism for a votive offering to a divinity (2 Macc 2:13; Philo, *Mos.* 1.253), but then in reference to a thing accursed (Num 21:3; Deut 7:26; Josh 6:17; 7:12; Judg 1:17; Zech 14:11).[15] It is only in the latter sense that Paul uses the term (1 Cor 12:3; 16:22; Gal 1:8-9). The expression αὐτὸς ἐγώ ("I myself") is intensive and is seldom used by Paul except in most solemn pronouncements (Rom 7:12; 15:14; 2 Cor 10:1; 12:13). That Paul is willing to become separated from Christ and thus subject to divine judgment against him shows how intense his feelings were concerning the eventual salvation of the Jewish people.

9:4-5a The attributes and possessions of the Jewish people are listed. But before listing them, Paul speaks of the Jewish people as "Israelites." The term is an honorary one here, just as it is at 11:1 (cf. 2 Cor 3:7), signifying that the Jewish

---

15. BDAG 63 (ἀνάθεμα); Johannes Behm, "ἀνατίθημι," *TDNT* 1:353-56.

people are the descendants of and current members of the venerated people of OT tradition. The term Ἰουδαῖοι ("Jews") was commonly used in the first century as an appropriate ethnic and religious term for adherents to the Mosaic and prophetic tradition, but the term Ἰσραηλῖται ("Israelites") had been in use since after the exile as a self-designation, expressing the claim of continuing the heritage of the elect since Abraham.[16] The designation is used precisely in that way in 4 Maccabees: "O Israelite children, offspring of the seed of Abraham" (18:11). In the Acts of the Apostles it is a term of respect in addresses to Jewish audiences (2:22; 3:12; 5:35; 13:16; 21:28).

The list of attributes and possessions in 9:4-5 provides a catalogue of advantages that the Jewish people have had, which should have prepared them for receiving the gospel. There are eight items in the list:

(1) They have "the adoption" (ἡ υἱοθεσία; RSV: "sonship") as those whom God has claimed as his children by election (Deut 14:1; Hos 11:1).

(2) Theirs is "the glory" (ἡ δόξα), the presence of the God whose "glory" appeared at Sinai and in the wilderness (Exod 16:10; 24:15-18). This God abides with them even now (on "glory," see comment on 5:2).

(3) They possess "the covenants" (αἱ διαθῆκαι), by which God has bound himself to Israel, and Israel is bound to God (Gen 17:10; Jer 31:32; 1 Macc 2:20; Heb 8:9). Paul speaks of "covenants" in the plural (αἱ διαθῆκαι), as does the writer of Sirach (44:12, 18). Which covenants he means is not said. Within his own writings he refers to the covenants of God with Abraham (Rom 4:17; Gal 3:17) and with Israel at Mount Sinai (2 Cor 3:14), and both of these are no doubt included in the plural term. Whether other covenants are meant to be included is less clear.[17] But of the two mentioned, the covenant with Abraham is treated by Paul as particularly important soteriologically. At the end of his long discourse on the salvation of Israel in Romans 9 through 11, Paul concludes that "all Israel will be saved" (11:26). That salvation will not come about by Israel's righteousness under the law of Moses (i.e., keeping the Mosaic covenant) but purely by the grace of God, whose covenantal act will "banish ungodliness from Jacob" (= Israel) and "take away their sins" (11:26-27, perhaps recalling Jer 31:34). All this will be due to God's remaining faithful to his covenant with the patriarchs (11:28), particularly the covenant with Abraham.

(4) To them is "the giving of the law" (ἡ νομοθεσία), which is a divine gift mediated by Moses to Israel (2 Macc 6:23: "the holy God-given law"; 4 Macc 17:16: "the divine legislation"). It was given on Mount Sinai (Exod 20:1-17; Deut

---

16. Karl G. Kuhn, "Ἰσραήλ," *TDNT* 3:359-69.

17. The range of possibilities is treated by C. Cranfield, *Romans*, 462; J. Dunn, *Romans*, 527; and J. Fitzmyer, *Romans*, 546. C. Roetzel, "Διαθῆκαι in Romans 9,4," 390, suggests even other possibilities beyond formal covenants, such as ordinances, commandments, and oaths.

5:1-21) for instruction leading to life (Deut 5:24; Lev 18:5). Whether the emphasis here is on the act of giving the law or on the law as that which was given is not said, but in context (a series of gifts received by Israel) it seems that the law as gift is more important than the act of giving it per se.[18]

(5) They have "the worship" (ἡ λατρεία), the worship of the God of Israel. The term appears in the LXX for ritual acts of worship in general (Josh 22:27; 1 Chr 28:13) and for the Yahwistic religious system in its entirety (cf. 1 Macc 1:43; 2:19, 22, where the NRSV translates the term as "religion"). When Paul wrote to the Romans, the Jerusalem Temple was still standing. The cultus of the Temple in all its grandeur is no doubt in the mind of both the writer and the recipients as the word is uttered or heard. Paul speaks of it as a good gift to Israel. He uses cultic imagery, which has been fulfilled in the death of Christ (Rom 3:25; 1 Cor 5:7).

(6) They are those to whom "the promises" (αἱ ἐπαγγελίαι) were given. Those include the promises to Abraham and his descendants of land (Gen 12:7; 13:14-15; 17:8), posterity (12:2; 13:16; 15:5; 18:18; 22:16-18), and having a great name (12:2). Additional promises were given to Isaac and his descendants (Gen 26:1-5) and to Jacob and his descendants (Gen 28:13-15). Moreover, God promised to raise up a prophet like Moses for his people (Deut 18:15-18), and he promised through David that he would raise up a kingdom from one of his descendants to rule over an everlasting kingdom (2 Sam 2:4-17).

(7) Theirs are "the fathers" (οἱ πατέρες), which would include the patriarchs Abraham, Isaac, and Jacob, the ancestors of the Israelites to whom the promises were given, and who are exemplars of faith and fidelity to God. But the term need not be limited to them; cf. 4 Macc 13:17, where a distinction is made between them and "the fathers" in a more general sense. The word for "patriarch" (πατριάρχης) existed in the world of Paul and could have been used if that was what he intended (4 Macc 7:19; Acts 2:29; 7:8-9; Heb 7:4). While various English versions use the term "patriarchs" at this place (RSV, NIV, NRSV), "fathers" is more suitable (as in KJV and ASV) and can include more than the patriarchs alone (1 Kgs 8:58; Jer 11:10; 27:7; 31:32; Acts 3:13; 1 Cor 10:1; Heb 1:1).[19]

(8) From them is "the Christ according to the flesh" (ὁ Χριστὸς τὸ κατὰ σάρκα). The descent of the Christ from among the people of Israel is not only the traditional expectation, but it has now been fulfilled in Jesus, a descendant of the Israelite nation.

9:5b The doxology is fitting at this place. Interpreters who posit a Christological statement here (instead of a doxology; see "Notes on the Text

---

18. C. Cranfield, *Romans,* 462-63. E. Epp, "Jewish-Gentile Continuity in Paul," 89, opts for the other view.

19. Cf. also *Pss. Sol.* 9.10; Josephus, *Ant.* 13.297.

and Translation") have claimed that a doxology would be out of place at the end of a paragraph expressing sorrow and anguish.[20] But that is to miss the sense of what has gone immediately before. Paul has listed no fewer than eight attributes and possessions of the Jewish people. Great are the gifts that God has bestowed! Paul never ceases to take pride in being an heir to the Jewish tradition (2 Cor 11:22). It is fitting that at this point he would bless God for all the gifts bestowed upon the Jewish people: "May he who is God over all be blessed forever" (cf. 2 Cor 11:31 for a similar doxology).

BIBLIOGRAPHY

Abasciano, Brian J. *Paul's Use of the Old Testament in Romans 9:1-9: An Intertextual and Theological Exegesis.* LNTS 301. New York: T&T Clark, 2005.

Bartsch, Hans Werner. "Röm 9:5 und 1 Clem 32:4: Eine notwendige Kojektur im Römerbrief." *TZ* 21 (1965): 401-9.

Betz, Hans D. "Geschichte und Selbstopfer: Zur Interpretation von Römer 9,1-5." In Ἐπιτομὴ τῆς οἰκουμένης: *Studien zur römischen Religion in Antike und Neuzeit: Für Hubert Cancik und Hildegard Cancik-Lindemaier,* 75-87. Ed. Hubert Cancik et al. Potsdamer altertumswissenschaftliche Beiträge 6. Stuttgart: Franz Steiner Verlag, 2002.

Brown, Raymond E. *Jesus God and Man: Modern Biblical Reflections.* New York: Macmillan, 1967.

Christiansen, Ellen Juhl. *The Covenant in Judaism and Paul: A Study of Ritual Boundaries as Identity Markers.* AGAJU 27. New York: E. J. Brill, 1995.

Cullmann, Oscar. *The Christology of the New Testament.* Rev. ed. Philadelphia: Westminster Press, 1963.

Dunn, James D. G. "Did Paul Have a Covenant Theology? Reflections on Romans 9:4 and 11:27." In *Celebrating Romans: Template for Pauline Theology: Essays in Honor of Robert Jewett,* 3-19. Ed. Sheila E. McGinn. Grand Rapids: Wm. B. Eerdmans, 2005.

Eckstein, Hans-Joachim. *Der Begriff* Syneidēsis *bei Paulus.* WUNT 2/10. Tübingen: J. C. B. Mohr (Paul Siebeck), 1983.

Epp, Eldon Jay. "Jewish-Gentile Continuity in Paul: Torah and/or Faith (Romans 9:1-5)." *HTR* 79 (1986): 80-90.

Fahy, Thomas. "A Note on Romans 9:1-18." *ITQ* 32 (1965): 261-62.

Fee, Gordon D. *Pauline Christology: An Exegetical-Theological Study.* Peabody: Hendrickson Publishers, 2007.

Harris, Murray J. *Jesus as God: The New Testament Use of of* Theos *in Reference to Jesus.* Grand Rapids: Baker Book House, 1992.

Jonge, Marinus de. *Christology in Context: The Earliest Christian Response to Jesus.* Philadelphia: Westminster Press, 1988.

---

20. J. Fitzmyer, *Romans,* 549; T. Schreiner, *Romans,* 488; B. Abasciano, *Paul's Use of the Old Testament in Romans 9.1-9,* 140-41; R. Jewett, *Romans,* 568.

Kammler, Hans-Christian. "Die Prädikation Jesu Christi als 'Gott' und die paulinische Christologie: Erwägungen zur Exegese von Röm 9,5b." *ZNW* 94 (2003): 164-80.

Kuschel, Karl-Josef. *Born before All Time? The Dispute over Christ's Origins.* New York: Crossroad, 1992.

Kuss, Otto. "Zu Römer 9,5." *Rechtfertigung: Festschrift für Ernst Käsemann zum 70. Geburtstag,* 291-303. Ed. Johannes Friedrich et al. Tübingen: J. C. B. Mohr (Paul Siebeck), 1976.

Lorimer, W. L. "Romans ix.3-5." *NTS* 13 (1966-67): 385-86.

Metzger, Bruce M. "The Punctuation of Rom. 9:5." In *Christ and Spirit in the New Testament: In Honour of Charles Francis Digby Moule,* 95-112. Ed. Barnabas Lindars and S. S. Smalley. Cambridge: Cambridge University Press, 1973.

Piper, John. *The Justification of God: An Exegetical and Theological Study of Romans 9:1-23.* 2d ed. Grand Rapids: Baker Book House, 1993.

Roetzel, Calvin. "Διαθῆκαι in Romans 9,4." *Bib* 51 (1970): 377-90.

Thrall, Margaret. "The Pauline Use of ΣΥΝΕΙΔΗΣΙΣ." *NTS* 14 (1967-68): 118-25.

Tuckett, Christopher M. *Christology and the New Testament: Jesus and His Earliest Followers.* Louisville: Westminster John Knox, 2001.

5.2. What Shall We Say about God? 9:6-29

6*It is not as though the word of God has failed. For not all who are descended from Israel truly belong to Israel,* 7*and not all of Abraham's descendants are his children; but "It is through Isaac that descendants shall be named for you."* 8*That is, it is not the children of the flesh that are the children of God, but the children of the promise are considered descendants.* 9*For the word of the promise is this: "At the appointed time I shall return, and Sarah will have a son."*

10*And not only that, but also Rebecca conceived by one man, our ancestor Isaac.* 11*And yet, before they were born or had done anything good or bad — in order that the purpose of God that operates by selection might continue,* 12*not by works but by the one who calls — she was told, "The elder shall serve the younger."* 13*As it is written, "Jacob I loved, but Esau I hated."*

14*What, then, shall we say? Is there injustice on God's part? By no means!* 15*For he says to Moses, "I will have mercy on whom I have mercy, and I will have compassion on whom I have compassion."* 16*Consequently it is not a matter of one's will or exertion, but of God who shows mercy.* 17*For the scripture says to Pharaoh, "I have raised you up for this very purpose, that my power may be shown in you, and that my name may be proclaimed in all the earth."* 18*So then he has mercy on whomever he wills, and he hardens the heart of whomever he wills.* 19*You will say to me then, "Why, then, does he still find fault? For who has resisted his will?"* 20*But who indeed are you, a human being, who answers back to God? Shall what is molded say to the molder, "Why have you made me like this?"* 21*Or* *has the potter no right over the clay, to make out of the same lump one vessel for special use and another for ordinary use?* 22*And what if God, wanting to show his wrath and to make known his power, has endured with patience vessels of wrath prepared for destruction,* 23*and what if he has done so in order to make known the riches of his glory upon vessels of mercy, which he has prepared beforehand for glory,* 24*even us whom he has called — not from Jews only, but also from Gentiles?* 25*So he even says to Hosea:*

> *"Those who were 'not my people' I shall call 'my people,'*
>   *and the one who was not beloved I shall call 'beloved.'"*
> 26*"And in the place where it was said to them, 'You are not my*
>   *people,'*
>   *there they shall be called 'children of the living God.'"*

27*And Isaiah cries out on behalf of Israel,*

> *"Even if the number of the children of Israel be as the sand of the*
>   *sea,*
>   *a remnant will be saved.*
> 28*For by acting decisively and quickly,*
>   *the Lord will carry out his sentence on the earth."*

29*And as Isaiah predicted:*

> *"If the Lord of hosts had not left survivors for us,*
>   *we would have become like Sodom and would have resembled*
>   *Gomorrah."*

Notes on the Text and Translation

9:9 The phrase κατὰ τὸν καιρὸν τοῦτον is variously translated as "about this time" (RSV and NRSV) or as "at the appointed time" (NIV). A more literal rendering would be, "at this appointed time." The citation (not an exact quotation) is from Genesis 18:10, where a promise is made to Abraham. The Lord promises to return to him at "this appointed time" in the future, about a year away, when Sarah would have a son. The time reference is difficult to catch apart from the narrative in Genesis. Therefore "at the appointed time" serves sufficiently.[21]

9:11 The phrase ἡ κατ᾽ ἐκλογὴν πρόθεσις τοῦ θεοῦ is rendered in modern versions as "God's purpose of election" (RSV, NRSV, and ESV) or as "God's purpose in election" (NIV). But the word "election" has a meaning in the his-

---

21. Cf. BDAG 498 (καιρός, 3, a), which has "at this time" for Rom 9:9.

tory of theology that may or may not be intended here. The Greek can be translated simply as "selection," and the phrase can thereby be rendered as "the purpose of God which operates by selection."[22]

9:19 The RSV and NRSV have the wording, "For who can resist his will?" Actually the verb "can" is not in the text, and its presence may raise theological issues that are not at stake. The main verb is ἀνθέστηκεν (perfect of ἀνθίστημι, meaning "to resist"). A more literal translation is provided here.

9:27 Although modern versions (RSV, NIV, NRSV, NET, ESV, but not the KJV and ASV) often contain the word "only" (so "only a remnant"), that is an insertion, not representing the wording in the Greek text.

9:28 Some Greek manuscripts, including the Textus Receptus, have additional wording in this verse: ἐν δικαιοσύνῃ ὅτι λόγον συντετμημένον (in context, "in righteousness, because [his] decree being completed"). For alternative translations, see the KJV and the footnote in the NRSV. By the inclusion of the additional words, Paul's text is conformed more closely to the LXX reading of Isaiah 10:22-23. The additional wording is not present in the earliest, major manuscripts (including 𝔓⁴⁶, ℵ [original hand], and B). The shorter reading is to be preferred because of the external evidence and because conforming the text to the LXX is more likely than the reverse.[23]

General Comment

Although it has been suggested that 9:6-29 is a midrash,[24] it is better to say that it has midrashic features. To be sure, the meaning of the term "midrash" is not settled, but generally it refers to a type of literature that has its starting point in a fixed canonical text.[25] In the case of 9:6-29, however, the biblical text is not actually the starting point, but the reference point within a larger discussion. It is Paul's discussion, having features of the diatribe, that prompts him to make use of a series of biblical texts.

The message of this portion of Romans can be summed up as follows. The fact that the Jewish people have not — overwhelmingly not, in fact — accepted the gospel prompts the question of God's competence. So, Paul asks in effect, "What shall we say about God?" It is not, he insists, that God's word (of promise) has failed. It might appear that way. For if God's saving promises have been confirmed in Jesus, but the Jewish people reject their fulfillment in him,

22. That is the rendering of the phrase in BDAG 306 (ἐκλογή, 1).

23. For these and other reasons, cf. B. Metzger, *TCGNT* 462.

24. W. Stegner, "Romans 9:6-29 — A Midrash," 37-52; B. Abasciano, *Paul's Use of the Old Testament in Romans 9.1-9*, 213.

25. G. Porton, "Midrash," 4:819; idem, "Defining Midrash," 1:62.

and it is primarily Gentiles who have responded to the gospel, it appears that God's word has missed the mark.

But for Paul that cannot be. According to him, one can look at the story of Israel itself. God has always elected whomever he wishes for a response. That is so through Isaac and Jacob, and it is so today when God calls us "not from Jews only but also from Gentiles" (9:24). Paul cites Hosea 2:23; 1:10 to show that it had been prophesied long ago that Gentiles would become God's people, and he cites Isaiah 10:22 to show that out of Israel only a remnant would be saved. So God has not failed, nor have his promises failed. If many Gentiles accept the gospel, and only a few Jews do, that is no surprise.

Detailed Comment

9:6-7a It would be impossible for Paul to think for a moment that the word of God has somehow failed, which would mean that God himself has failed. The meaning of the expression "the word of God" (ὁ λόγος τοῦ θεοῦ), so familiar in Christian tradition as a reference to both Scripture and proclamation, is contested in this verse. Several proposals have been made. According to one point of view, "the word of God" refers to Christian proclamation, which is a familiar use of the expression elsewhere in Paul's letters (1 Cor 14:36; Phil 1:14; 1 Thess 2:13).[26] So it is important for Paul that the gospel has indeed been proclaimed among the Jewish people (10:18) with some positive results. Although it has been rejected by the great majority (10:19-21), it has been believed by some, a remnant, of whom he is a member (11:1, 6). The point is, Paul says, that not all the people of Abrahamic descent are Israelites in the truest sense. According to another point of view, "the word of God" means the declared purpose of God in electing Israel.[27] According to still other interpreters, the phrase means the promises of God proclaimed to Israel and fulfilled in Christ;[28] or, as a slight variant, the promises as proclaimed and recorded in the Scriptures.[29]

Another possibility is favored here. Two observations help to substantiate it. First, Paul makes use of the perfect tense of the verb (ἐκπέπτωκεν, "has

---

26. E. Güttgemanns, "Heilsgeschichte bei Paulus oder Dynamik des Evangeliums," 40-42; H. Schlier, *Römer*, 290; R. Kotansky, "A Note on Romans 9:6," 27; A. Reichert, *Der Römerbrief als Gratwanderung*, 189-90; R. Jewett, *Romans*, 574.

27. W. Sanday and A. Headlam, *Romans*, 240; O. Michel, *Römer*, 231; C. Cranfield, *Romans*, 472-73; N. T. Wright, *NIB (Romans)*, 10:635; L. Keck, *Romans*, 230.

28. A. Nygren, *Romans*, 361; J. Munck, *Christ and Israel*, 34; J. Knox, *IB (Romans)*, 9:541; E. Käsemann, *Romans*, 262; U. Wilckens, *Römer*, 2:191-92; J. Dunn, *Romans*, 539; J. Fitzmyer, *Romans*, 559; C. Talbert, *Romans*, 249; E. Lohse, *Römer*, 272.

29. H. Schlier, *Römer*, 290; B. Byrne, *Romans*, 293; D. Moo, *Romans*, 573; B. Abasciano, *Paul's Use of the Old Testament in Romans 9.1-9*, 178-79.

failed"), indicating the continuing effect of a completed action,[30] or in this case an ongoing condition: "It is not as though the word of God has failed."[31] Second, throughout these chapters the passages from Scripture are often in first person speech where God addresses his people (9:9, 13-14, 17, 25, 33; 10:19-20; 11:4, 27) in the manner of divine oracles (cf. 3:2, τὰ λόγια τοῦ θεοῦ) and twice in second person address (9:7, 26) to the same effect.[32] All of these statements, Paul implies, have come true. In constructing a careful and credible argument, Paul reviews the record of what God has said. All this serves to show that God's word has not failed. On the contrary, God's word has been vindicated.

Paul has indicated already in 9:4-5 that the people of Israel have been beneficiaries of the promises and gifts of God, including their adoption, glory, covenants, the law, worship, the patriarchs, and the Messiah. All of these are due to "the word of God," but that word has not failed. It can be shown not to have failed. And so the expression "the word of God" includes not only all the promises of the past, now written in Scripture, but also the words of rebuke, which are also written in Scripture and are called forth in Romans 9–11. The statement of Paul about the word of God as not having failed (9:6a) is therefore thematic throughout chapters 9 through 11.

Paul goes on in 9:6b-7a to make a point that he will substantiate in the verses to follow. He asserts that physical descent from Abraham has never been the sole basis for belonging to the people of Israel, i.e., Israel in any true sense.

9:7b-9 In order to show that the word of God has not failed, the first proof to be made is that God's word has in fact had a positive hearing among some of the historic, faithful people of Israel. Paul's use of the negative ("not all" in 9:7a) should not overshadow what he says in a positive way. He emphasizes that God is an electing God. Even before the beginning of the corporate life of the people Israel, God had made a decision. It would not be the children of Abraham and Hagar (Ishmael and his descendants), but those descended from Abraham and Sarah (Isaac and his descendants) that would be the people to whom the promises to Abraham would be fulfilled. At 9:7b Paul quotes Genesis 21:12, and his wording is exactly like that of the LXX.

Only the descendants of Isaac can rightly be called "the children of the promise." Not all the "children of the flesh" — i.e., not all who are descended from Abraham — can be considered "children of God" by virtue of biological descent. The "children of God" or the "children of the promise" are a smaller,

---

30. BDF 175-76 (§§340, 342).

31. Paul does not make use of the aorist tense of the verb (ἐξέπεσεν, "failed"), indicating past action that is complete, so as to say: "It is not as though the word of God failed" (or even more emphatic, as in the RSV and NRSV: "It is not as though the word of God had failed").

32. To be sure, there are exceptions to first and second person speech (9:27, 29; 10:21; 11:8-10, 26, 34-35), but these do not diminish the importance of those cited.

restricted circle within the larger one. Paul uses the expression "children of God" elsewhere in an even more restrictive sense, referring to Christians (Rom 8:16-17, 21; Phil 2:15), but in the present case he applies it to those persons, descended from Isaac, who comprise the faithful community of Israel. Paul uses the term "children of promise" (ἐπαγγελίας τέκνα) on one other occasion only in his writings, again referring to Christians explicitly, who are, like Isaac, the heirs of the promise of God given to Abraham (Gal 4:28).

The promise spoken of is the promise of God to Abraham in Genesis 18:10 and repeated in 18:14. The Hebrew readings (as rendered in the NRSV) are: "I will surely return to you in due season, and your wife Sarah shall have a son" and "At the set time I will return to you, in due season, and Sarah shall have a son." The LXX version of each of these differs slightly from both the Hebrew and from Paul's quotation. The LXX texts are provided here, and elements from each that appear in Paul's text are italicized:

Genesis 18:10 (LXX):

ἥξω πρὸς σὲ *κατὰ τὸν καιρὸν τοῦτον εἰς ὥρας*
καὶ ἔξει υἱὸν Σαρρα ἡ γυνή σου.

I shall come to you at this appointed time,
and Sarah your wife will have a son.

Genesis 18:14 (LXX):

εἰς *τὸν καιρὸν τοῦτον* ἀναστρέψω πρὸς σὲ εἰς ὥρας
καὶ ἔσται τῇ Σαρρα υἱός.

I shall return to you at this appointed time,
and Sarah shall have a son.

Perhaps Paul quoted from memory, conflating phrases from both texts, or from a Greek version otherwise not known, since his wording is neither a translation from the Hebrew text nor a quotation from the LXX. His rendering (9:9) is as follows:

κατὰ τὸν καιρὸν τοῦτον ἐλεύσομαι
καὶ ἔσται τῇ Σαρρᾳ υἱός.

At this appointed time I shall return,
and Sarah will have a son.

Accordingly, Paul continues to build his case. Isaac was a child of promise; Ishmael was not. So it follows that right from the beginning of Israel's life a decision and a promise had been made. One can therefore expect that the entire history of Israel will consist of God's electing some, perhaps even a minority, from the larger body of descendants of Abraham to be those who are true heirs to the promise.

9:10-13 Continuing his discussion concerning the way of God, Paul moves on to the next generation of the patriarchs. He uses the story of Isaac, Rebecca, and their children, Jacob and Esau (Gen 25:19–27:40). Even the trickery of Jacob over his brother was by divine design. Prior to the birth of her twins, Rebecca had been told by the Lord that "the elder shall serve the younger" (Rom 9:12), as said at Genesis 25:23. The wording of the Greek in Romans is exactly like that in the LXX (καὶ ὁ μείζων δουλεύσει τῷ ἐλάσσονι, "and the elder shall serve the younger"). God's choice of Jacob over Esau, says Paul, had nothing to do with rewards or punishment for good or bad behavior. The twins had not yet been born when God's word to Rebecca was given. All that happened was according to God's own decision. In this case the revelation from God was given to the mother of the children to be born. The annunciation by an angel of the Lord to Mary can be regarded as another rare instance of the same (Luke 1:26-38).

The OT quotation in 9:13 concerning the love of God for Jacob over Esau corresponds to the reading in the LXX version of Malachi 1:2-3, except for the word order. The text in Malachi reads as: ἠγάπησα τὸν Ιακωβ, τὸν δὲ Ησαυ ἐμίσησα ("I loved Jacob, but Esau I hated"), which follows the word order of the Hebrew text,[33] whereas Paul's version has the direct object ("Jacob") at the outset of the first clause: τὸν Ἰακὼβ ἠγάπησα, τὸν δὲ Ἡσαῦ ἐμίσησα ("Jacob I loved, but Esau I hated"). An interesting feature of Paul's version is that it is more typically "Semitic" in style than the OT versions are. His version has true parallelism in the ordering of the words, while the Hebrew and LXX versions do not.

9:14-18 The question concerning the justice of God in 9:14 is entirely appropriate in the diatribe. Paul begins with the question used by him in diatribal style seven times within Romans: "What then shall we say?" (τί οὖν ἐροῦμεν; cf. 3:5; 4:1; 6:1; 7:7; 8:31; 9:30). This is followed by the question specific to his diatribe at this place, as Paul seeks to prevent a misunderstanding: "Is there injustice (ἀδικία) on God's part?" Paul replies with his famous and emphatic μὴ γένοιτο, "By no means!" (as in the RSV and NRSV). As elsewhere, so here, Paul uses the expression to object to a possible false conclusion and then follows up with a reason for rejecting the false conclusion. For further discussion of the expression, see the exegesis at 3:4.

One should not for a moment conclude that God is unjust. God had said to Moses back at Exodus 33:19: "I will have mercy on whom I have mercy, and I will

---

33. The word order in the Hebrew text is: וָאֹהַב אֶת־יַעֲקֹב וְאֶת־עֵשָׂו שָׂנֵאתִי.

have compassion on whom I have compassion." The Greek text corresponds to that of the LXX. The saying from the Lord to Moses was spoken in the wilderness at the tent of meeting, where Moses sought to have God display his glory. The response was that no one shall be able to see God, but that God will have mercy on whomever he wishes. The context there has no obvious bearing on the present one, but there is a theological connection. God's elusive presence and activity are ongoing from the days of Moses to the present. There is a consistency in God's ways with humanity. Above all, God reserves to himself the freedom of election, and election is a result of divine love, not divine injustice.

A specific illustration of God's acting with mercy on whomever he wills follows in 9:17, where Paul draws upon Exodus 9:16 to make his point. The passage in Exodus relates a scene where God speaks to Moses between the plague of boils and the plague of hail (the sixth and seventh plagues). God orders Moses to address Pharaoh on his behalf, saying, "This is why I have let you live: to show you my power, and to make my name resound through all the earth" (NRSV). Paul's citation of the verse differs slightly from the wording of both the Hebrew and the LXX, making the purpose of God more clear and emphatic. Whereas the LXX has the Lord commanding Moses to say to Pharaoh on God's behalf: "on account of this you have been preserved" (ἕνεκεν τούτου διετηρήθης), Paul has him say to Pharaoh: "I have raised you up for this very purpose" (εἰς αὐτὸ τοῦτο ἐξήγειρά σε). That purpose, says Paul, was to display God's "power" (δύναμις; the LXX has ἰσχύς, "strength") and to make known God's name everywhere. God made use of Pharaoh — otherwise an opponent of his will and purpose — as an instrument of his purpose. And in order to do so, he had mercy on Pharaoh ("he has mercy on whomever he wills," 9:18).

But there are also instances where God "hardens the heart of whomever he wills" (9:18b). The matter of "hardening" will be taken up again at 11:7 in reference to the unbelief of the vast majority of the people of Israel, although at that place the verb used to express "to harden" (πωρόω) is different from the one being used here (σκληρύνω). What is used here coincides with the verb used in the LXX wherever there are accounts of God's hardening the heart of Pharaoh. There can be little doubt but that those stories have come to Paul's mind at this point since he has just referred to Pharaoh — and that in a positive way. But there is the other side to the stories of Pharaoh. Over and again in Exodus it is said that God hardened the heart of Pharaoh (4:21; 7:3, 22; 8:19; 9:12, 35; 10:1, 20, 27; 11:10; 14:4, 8) or the Egyptians (14:13) to impede the freeing of the people of Israel from their bondage. Paul is saying, then, that God can have mercy on whomever he wills (as in the case of Pharaoh) but can also harden such a person's heart to oppose the will and work of God (also as in the case of Pharaoh).[34]

34. Andreas K. Schuele, "Harden the Heart," NIDB 2:735-36.

The thinking behind the comment of John Calvin concerning 9:14 has had far-reaching effects in the history of Christian thought: "Before men are born their lot is assigned to each of them by the secret will of God."[35] Whatever other factors might be involved in the making of such a statement, it can hardly be considered Paul's point at this place. Paul is speaking here of dynamics within history by which God seeks to achieve his purposes. He is not speaking of some eternal, "secret will" that determines the destiny of each individual that is born.

9:19 What Paul has sketched out to this point seems to portray a God who controls all things. And if that is so, there is no room for human responsibility. If God directs all things in such an exacting way, the reader may rightfully ask, "Why, then, does he still find fault? For who has resisted his will?" Paul thus begins in diatribe style, having an imaginary opponent raise a critical question.

9:20-21 Paul responds, addressing his imaginary opponent (ὦ ἄνθρωπε, literally, "O man") and then using the Greek particle μενοῦνγε, which can be translated roughly as "indeed." The particle appears twice more in the letters of Paul (Rom 10:18; Phil 3:8), but nowhere else in the NT or in the LXX. Paul uses it for emphasis (Phil 3:8) or to correct an incorrect point of view (Rom 10:18).[36] No person should talk back to God in such a manner as that.

The imagery of the potter and his clay in 9:20b-21 recalls the message of Jeremiah 18:2-11 (the potter and the clay) and lines from Isaiah 29:16; 45:9; and 64:8. Paul quotes the former verse from Isaiah exactly as in the LXX: μὴ ἐρεῖ τὸ πλάσμα τῷ πλάσαντι ("Shall what is molded say to the molder?") expecting a negative answer by the use of the introductory μή. Then he continues with "Why have you made me like this?" which recalls Isaiah 45:9 but differs from the LXX (and does not actually represent the Hebrew MT). Implying a negative answer already, Paul goes on to assert that the potter has a right to design things out of the clay as that person wishes. The potter can create vessels that are special (or honorable) and others that are rather ordinary. This leads to a theological inquiry.

9:22-24 A hypothetical question is posed, beginning with "what if . . . ?" in 9:22 that is repeated in 9:23, increasing the hypothetical nature of the inquiry. The implication that one could draw from the imagery of the potter making ordinary vessels (that can easily be destroyed) and special ones (that should be preserved) is that God is responsible for the existence of some people (as collec-

---

35. Quoted from John Calvin, *The Epistles of Paul the Apostle to the Romans and to the Thessalonians,* trans. Ross MacKenzie, Calvin's Commentaries 8 (Grand Rapids: Wm. B. Eerdmans, 1995), 203. Cf. also on Rom 9:20: "[God] assigns whatever fate He pleases to His creatures by His own right" (p. 209).

36. BDF 234 (§450, 4).

tives, such as nations) that he intends to destroy and of some that he will save. In the case of the former, he has endured them with patience; in the case of the latter, he has prepared them for glory. And who are the latter? Here Paul turns from hypothetical discussion to actuality, referring to what has happened in history (employing the aorist verb, ἐκάλεσεν, "he called").[37] He responds that the latter are "even us whom he has called — not from Jews only, but also from Gentiles," those who have been called by God to hear and believe the gospel. For Paul the basis for belief in the gospel is divine call (Rom 8:28, 30; 1 Cor 1:9, 24; 1 Thess 2:12). And those called consist of both Jews (of which Paul is himself an example) and Gentiles.

9:25-26 The OT quotations that follow are from Hosea 2:23 (2:25 in the LXX) and 1:10 (2:1 in the LXX), but the first of them is by no means exact. Paul uses the two passages in his own distinctive way to further his argument. Within their own contexts the OT passages refer to apostate Israel, having repented and then been brought back into God's favor; God claims the repentant as "my people." But Paul applies the passages more generally and in a new context. Now they refer both to those Jews who, though initially resisting the gospel, have subsequently heard it and believed it, and also to those Gentiles who have been incorporated into the people of God. So Paul writes: "Those who were 'not my people' I shall call 'my people.'" (The Hebrew and LXX read: "And I shall say to 'Not my people' you are 'My people.'") The following part of what appears to be a quotation ("and the one who was not beloved I shall call 'beloved'") does not appear in the OT. The quotation in 9:26 corresponds exactly to Hosea 2:1 (1:10 in Hebrew and English versions) in the LXX: καὶ ἔσται ἐν τῷ τόπῳ οὗ ἐρρέθη αὐτοῖς· οὐ λαός μου ὑμεῖς, ἐκεῖ κληθήσονται υἱοὶ θεοῦ ζῶντος ("And in the place where it was said to them, 'You are not my people,' there they shall be called 'children of the living God'").

In each of the three verses of 9:24-26 variations of the verb "to call" (καλέω) appear. The term can mean simply to name someone or something (as in Matt 1:21; Luke 1:59; 10:39; John 1:42), but the verb also has the sense of God's creativity (as in Rom 4:17; 8:30). When Paul writes here about God's calling, he speaks of God's creative actions in fashioning or refashioning a people. Paul indicates that God is creatively bringing about a new humanity in Christ by calling people through the gospel.

9:27-28 Paul calls upon Isaiah as a witness concerning the people of Israel. Various modern translations render the opening phrase ὑπὲρ τοῦ Ἰσραήλ as "concerning Israel" (KJV, RSV, NIV, and NRSV), but it can also be translated as "on behalf of Israel." That is better, for here Paul is saying that, in spite of disobedience, a portion of Israel will be saved, the remnant (meaning Jews like

---

37. Cf. C. Cosgrove, *Elusive Israel*, 35.

himself who confess Jesus as the Christ). Just as the previous quotations show that God calls Gentiles, so this one shows that he also calls Jews.[38]

Although Paul asserts at 9:27 that he is quoting from Isaiah, the first line of the verse is not actually from Isaiah but from Hosea 1:10 (LXX, 2:1), which reads: ὁ ἀριθμὸς τῶν υἱῶν Ισραηλ ὡς ἡ ἄμμος τῆς θαλάσσης ("The number of the people of Israel [shall be] as the sand of the sea"). Then he quotes the remainder of Isaiah 10:22-23, but not exactly as in the LXX. The two verses in Isaiah read as follows:

καὶ ἐὰν γένηται ὁ λαὸς Ισραηλ ὡς ἡ ἄμμος τῆς θαλάσσης,
τὸ κατάλειμμα αὐτῶν σωθήσεται.
λόγον γὰρ συντελῶν καὶ συντέμνων ἐν δικαιοσύνῃ
ὅτι λόγον συντετμημένον ποιήσει ὁ θεὸς ἐν τῇ οἰκουμένῃ ὅλῃ.

And even if the people of Israel become as the sand of the sea,
a remnant of them shall be saved.
For [God will] carry out his sentence decisively in righteousness
since God will accomplish his decree with dispatch in the entire world.

Paul's text consists of a blending of the passages in Hosea and (parts of) Isaiah:

ἐὰν ᾖ ὁ ἀριθμὸς τῶν υἱῶν Ἰσραὴλ ὡς ἡ ἄμμος τῆς θαλάσσης,
τὸ ὑπόλειμμα σωθήσεται·
λόγον γὰρ συντελῶν καὶ συντέμνων
ποιήσει κύριος ἐπὶ τῆς γῆς.

Even if the number of the children of Israel be as the sand of the sea,
a remnant will be saved.
For by acting decisively and quickly,
the Lord will carry out his sentence on the earth.

At this place Paul introduces the "remnant" concept from the OT explicitly for the first time. For the term "remnant" he uses ὑπόλειμμα, which is a synonym of κατάλειμμα in the LXX text of Isaiah. Paul is the only NT writer to use the former term, and at this place only, but it appears eight times in the LXX. The latter term appears 19 times in the LXX, but not in the NT at all.[39] At 11:5 Paul will reintroduce the "remnant" concept and use the briefer form λεῖμμα, found only there in the NT and not in the LXX at all.

The "remnant" concept appears in the OT at places where Israel as an en-

---

38. R. Hays, *Echoes of Scripture in the Letters of Paul*, 68.

39. The textual variant κατάλειμμα for 9:27 is not taken into consideration here. See "Notes on the Text and Translation" above.

tire nation is under threat, and it is probably in such historical circumstances that the concept originated.[40] It can have a negative connotation, as when the nation suffers a catastrophe so great due to divine punishment that only a "remnant" of it survives (2 Kgs 21:13-15; Jer 8:3; Ezek 15:1-8; Amos 3:12; 5:3). Or it can have a positive connotation, as when God holds out the promise (usually through a prophet) that a "remnant" will survive for the sake of God's purposes in the future (Gen 45:7; 1 Kgs 19:18; Isa 28:5-6; Jer 23:3-4; Amos 5:15; Joel 2:32; Mic 2:12; Zeph 3:13).[41] It is applied to those who remain faithful to God in spite of oppression from foreign powers and the temptation to follow other gods (Isa 11:16; 37:4, 31-32; Zeph 3:12-13; Sir 44:17). At Qumran it becomes a term for the community's understanding of itself.[42]

Paul understands the prophets as speaking not only in the past but also to present circumstances. The prophet declares that (only) "a remnant will be saved." Therefore, one cannot expect that the people of Israel as a whole in the present era will turn and accept the gospel. After all, Paul has said, "not all descended from Israel truly belong to Israel" (9:6), and "it is not the children of the flesh that are the children of God, but the children of the promise [who are] considered descendants" (9:8). The remnant are precisely the children of promise, for God has promised their salvation. That remnant consists of those who have accepted the gospel, a theme that Paul takes up again in 11:5.

As indicated above (see "Notes on the Text and Translation"), there are text-critical problems with 9:28. In addition to those problems, the verse is notoriously difficult to translate and interpret. It consists of a conflation of quotations from Isaiah. Paul writes:

λόγον γὰρ συντελῶν καὶ συντέμνων ποιήσει κύριος ἐπὶ τῆς γῆς.

"For by acting decisively and quickly, the Lord will carry out his sentence on the earth."

The first five words in Greek are identical to wording in Isaiah 10:22 (LXX: λόγον γὰρ συντελῶν καὶ συντέμνων), but the last five have resemblances (not similarities) to wording in both Isaiah 10:23 (ποιήσει ὁ θεὸς ἐν τῇ οἰκουμένῃ ὅλῃ) and 28:22 (ποιήσει ἐπὶ πᾶσαν τὴν γῆν). It is unlikely that Paul quotes from an existing Greek text. It is more likely that the conflating and altering of the texts was his own,[43] perhaps quoting from memory.

---

40. G. Hasel, *The Remnant*, 402. According to R. Clements, "'A Remnant Chosen by Grace,'" 111, the beginning of the concept can be traced at least as far back as the eighth-century Syro-Ephraimite war, as articulated at Isa 10:20-23.

41. Lester V. Meyer, "Remnant," *ABD* 5:670.

42. 1QpHab 10.13; 1QH 6.8; 1QM 13.8; CD 1.4-5; 1QS 8.6.

43. J. Wagner, *Heralds of the Good News*, 97; that the possibility of the variation is due to

The main clause of 9:28 is λόγον ποιήσει κύριος, which can be translated "the Lord will enact (or carry out) his sentence." The two participles (συντελῶν καὶ συντέμνων) clearly modify "the Lord" but have an adverbial function, modifying the action of the Lord. The verbs συντελέω and συντέμνω can be translated as "to fulfill" or "to accomplish" in the first case and "to cut short" or "to shorten" in the second.[44] They modify the main clause so that the Lord's carrying out his sentence "on the earth" is done decisively and, presumably, within a limited time[45] (RSV: "with rigor and dispatch"; NIV: "with speed and finality"; NRSV: "quickly and decisively"; NET: "completely and quickly"). Paul renders the wording in such a way that, whatever its original meaning in Isaiah, he declares that (1) God's decisive judgment to save only the "remnant" (referred to in the previous verse) is witnessed to in the Scriptures of Israel, and that (2) the division within Israel taking place in the present is therefore to be expected. That is his interest within the context of this portion of Romans.[46] It will not be his last word; that remains to be said at 11:25-36.

9:29 Paul quotes from Isaiah again — specifically, Isaiah 1:9 — and exactly as in the LXX, except that the LXX has the initial word καί ("and"). In the present context Paul employs the quotation to further the point that the very existence of a remnant is due to the purposes of God in history. Without that, the remnant would not exist. To become like Sodom and to resemble Gomorrah would be to perish entirely, leaving no remnant at all, for the two cities were totally annihilated (Gen 19:24-25). The existence of the remnant is God's own doing and a sign of his perpetual favor.

BIBLIOGRAPHY

Abasciano, Brian J. *Paul's Use of the Old Testament in Romans 9.1-9: An Intertextual and Theological Exegesis*. LNTS 301. New York: T&T Clark, 2005.

Brandenburger, Egon. "Paulinische Schriftauslegung in der Kontroverse um das Verheissungswort Gottes (Röm 9)." *ZNW* 82 (1985): 1-47.

Burchard, Christoph. "Römer 9:25 ἐν τῷ Ὡσηέ." *ZNW* 76 (1985): 131.

Campbell, J. C. "God's People and the Remnant." *SJT* 3 (1950): 78-85.

Clements, Ronald. E. "'A Remnant Chosen by Grace' (Romans 11:5): The Old Testament Background and Origin of the Remnant Concept." In *Pauline Studies: Essays Pre-*

Paul, a Greek text, or both is held by S.-L. Shum, *Paul's Use of Isaiah in Romans*, 207. E. Käsemann, *Romans*, 275, suggests that a mistake may have occurred in copying.

44. BDAG 975 (συντελέω, 2, and συντέμνω).

45. Gerhard Delling, "συντελέω," *TDNT* 8:64: the verb connotes the swiftness of God's act.

46. Various interpretations are listed by C. Cranfield, *Romans*, 502; J. Fitzmyer, *Romans*, 574.

sented to Professor F. F. Bruce on His 70th Birthday, 106-21. Ed. Donald A. Hagner and Murray J. Harris. Grand Rapids: Wm. B. Eerdmans, 1980.

Cosgrove, Charles H. *Elusive Israel: The Puzzle of Election in Romans.* Louisville: Westminster John Knox Press, 1997.

Ellingworth, Paul. "Translation and Exegesis: A Case Study (Rom 9,22ff.)." *Bib* 59 (1978): 396-402.

Grindheim, Sigurd. *The Crux of Election: Paul's Critique of the Jewish Confidence in the Election of Israel.* WUNT 2/202. Tübingen: J. C. B. Mohr (Paul Siebeck), 2005.

Güttgemanns, Erhardt. "Heilsgeschichte bei Paulus oder Dynamik des Evangeliums: Zur strukturellen Relevanz von Röm 9–11 für die Theologie des Römerbriefes." In his *Studia linguistica neotestamentica: Gesammelte Aufsätze zur linguistischen Grundlage einer Neutestamentlichen Theologie.* BEvT 60. Munich: C. Kaiser, 1971.

Hanson, Anthony T. "Vessels of Wrath or Instruments of Wrath? Romans IX.22-23." *JTS* 32 (1981): 433-43.

Hasel, Gerhard F. *The Remnant: The History and Theology of the Remnant Idea from Genesis to Isaiah.* AUSS 5. 2d ed. Berrien Springs: Andrews University Press, 1974.

Hays, Richard B. *Echoes of Scripture in the Letters of Paul.* New Haven: Yale University Press, 1989.

Heil, John P. "From Remnant to Seed of Hope for Israel: Romans 9:27-29." *CBQ* 64 (2002): 703-20.

Huebsch, Robert W. "The Understanding and Significance of the 'Remnant' Motif in Qumran Literature: Including a Discussion of the Use of This Concept in the Hebrew Bible, the Apocrypha and the Pseudepigrapha." Ph.D. diss., McMaster University, 1981.

Klein, William W. "Paul's Use of *Kalein:* A Proposal." *JETS* 27 (1984): 53-64.

Kotansky, Roy D. "A Note on Romans 9:6: *HO LOGOS TOU THEOU* as the Proclamation of the Gospel." *StudBT* 7 (1977): 24-30.

Munck, Johannes. *Christ and Israel: An Interpretation of Romans 9–11.* Philadelphia: Fortress Press, 1967.

Neusner, Jacob. *What Is Midrash?* Philadelphia: Fortress Press, 1987.

Porton, Gary C. "Defining Midrash." In *The Study of Ancient Judaism,* 1:55-92. Ed. Jacob Neusner. 2 vols. New York: KTAV Publishing House, 1981.

———. "Midrash." *ABD* 4:818-22.

Reichert, Angelika. *Der Römerbrief als Gratwanderung: Eine Untersuchung zur Abfassungsproblematik.* FRLANT 194. Göttingen: Vandenhoeck & Ruprecht, 2001.

Schaller, Berndt. "Zum Textcharakter der Hiobzitate im paulinischen Schrifttum." *ZNW* 71 (1980): 21-26.

Seitz, Erich. "λόγον συντέμνων — Eine Gerichtsankündigung? (Zu Römer 9,27/28)." *BN* 109 (2001): 56-82.

Shum, Shiu-Lun. *Paul's Use of Isaiah in Romans: A Comparative Study of Paul's Letter to the Romans and the Sibylline and Qumran Sectarian Texts.* WUNT 2/156. Tübingen: J. C. B. Mohr (Paul Siebeck), 2002.

Stegemann, Ekkehard W. "Alle von Israel, Israel und der Rest: Paradoxie als argumentative-rhetorische Strategie in Römer 9,6." *TZ* 62 (2006): 125-57.

Stegner, William R. "Romans 9:6-29 — A Midrash." *JSNT* 22 (1984): 37-52.

Wagner, J. Ross. *Heralds of the Good News: Isaiah and Paul in Concert in the Letter to the Romans.* NovTSup 101. Boston: E. J. Brill, 2002.

Watts, James W. "The Remnant Theme: A Survey of New Testament Research, 1921-1987." *PRS* 15 (1988): 109-29.

5.3. What Shall We Say about Israel? 9:30–10:21

30*What, then, shall we say? Shall we say that the Gentiles, who did not pursue righteousness, received it, that is, righteousness by faith;* 31*but Israel, although pursuing the law of righteousness, did not attain it?* 32*For what reason? Because pursuing it not by faith, but as if it were possible on the basis of works, they rejected the stone of stumbling,* 33*as it is written,*

> *"Behold, I am laying a stone of stumbling in Zion, even a rock of offense,*
> *and whoever believes in him will not be put to shame."*

1*Brothers and sisters, my heart's desire and prayer to God for them is for their salvation.* 2*For I bear witness to them that they have a zeal for God, but it is not in accord with knowledge.* 3*For, being ignorant of the righteousness that comes from God, and seeking to establish their own, they have not become subject to the righteousness of God.* 4*For Christ is the end of the law unto righteousness for everyone who believes.*

5*For Moses writes concerning the righteousness that is from the law: "The person who does these things shall live by them."* 6*But the righteousness that is from faith says this: "Do not say in your heart, 'Who will ascend into heaven?'"* *(that is, to bring Christ down)* 7*"or 'Who will descend into the abyss?'" (that is, to bring Christ up from the dead).* 8*But what does it say? "The word is near you, in your mouth and in your heart" (that is, the word of faith that we proclaim);* 9*because if you confess with your mouth that Jesus is Lord and believe in your heart that God raised him from the dead, you will be saved.* 10*For one believes with the heart and so is justified, and one confesses with the mouth and so is saved.* 11*The scripture says, "Everyone who believes in him will not be put to shame."* 12*For there is no distinction between Jew and Greek; for the same Lord is Lord of all, and he is generous toward all who call on him.* 13*For "everyone who calls on the name of the Lord shall be saved."*

14*But how are they to call upon one in whom they have not believed? And how will they believe in one of whom they have not heard? And how will they hear without someone to proclaim him?* 15*And how will they proclaim him unless they are sent? As it is written, "How timely is the arrival of those who proclaim good* news." 16But not all have obeyed the gospel. For Isaiah says, "Lord, who has believed our message?" 17Consequently, faith comes from what is heard, and what is heard comes through the word of Christ.

18But, I ask, have they not heard? Indeed they have:

> "Their voice has gone out to all the earth,
>   and their words to the ends of the world."

19But, I ask, did Israel not understand? First, Moses says,

> "I will make you jealous of a people not a nation;
>   with a senseless nation I will make you angry."

20Then Isaiah is bold to say,

> "I have been found by those who have not sought me;
>   I have become known to those who did not ask for me."

21But of Israel he says,

> "All day long I have held out my hands
>   to a disobedient and obstinate people."

Notes on the Text and Translation

9:32 The translation of the phrase ὡς ἐξ ἔργων into "as if it were possible on the basis of works" is comparable to the NRSV ("as if it were based on works"), but takes more fully into account the use of ὡς in this instance as a marker to "focus on what is objectively false or erroneous."[47]

Some important texts, including the Majority Text (reflected in the KJV), read ἔργων νόμου ("works of the law"), but the superior texts (including 𝔓46, ℵ, and B) lack νόμου ("of the law"). The longer reading is probably due to conforming it to readings elsewhere in the letters of Paul (Rom 3:28; Gal 2:16; 3:2, 5, 10). The shorter reading is to be preferred.[48]

10:9, 10 Some versions speak of confessing with the "lips" in either both verses (RSV) or at least in 10:9 (NRSV). But Paul actually writes of confessing with one's στόμα ("mouth," KJV, NIV, and NET) in both verses.

10:12 The use of the verb πλουτέω ("to be rich"), followed by the preposition εἰς, can mean "rich (and generous) toward" an object, in this case "all" (πάντας).[49]

---

47. BDAG 1105 (ὡς, 3, β, c).
48. B. Metzger, *TCGNT* 462-63.
49. BDAG 831 (πλουτέω, 2).

10:15 The word ὡραῖος is usually translated "beautiful" (KJV, RSV, NIV, and NRSV, so "how beautiful the feet . . ."). But the word more properly means (as its root suggests) "coming at the right time/timely," and so it is suggested that the quotation from Isaiah 52:7 be rendered as: "How timely is the arrival of those who proclaim good news!"[50] To be sure, the timeliness of a herald with good news for an oppressed people evokes the sense of welcome or beauty.

  Some texts (including a scribal revision of ℵ and the Majority Text) have the additional words τῶν εὐαγγελιζομένων εἰρήνην ("of those who proclaim peace") after πόδες ("feet"), which is reflected in the KJV, but the phrase is not in the superior texts (𝔓⁴⁶, ℵ [original hand], and B), and its existence is probably due to conforming it more fully to the LXX.[51]

  10:17 Instead of διὰ ῥήματος Χριστοῦ ("through the word of Christ"), some texts have διὰ ῥήματος θεοῦ ("through the word of God"). This rendering is witnessed in the Majority Text, which is reflected in the KJV. But major witnesses (including 𝔓⁴⁶, ℵ, and B) have the former reading, which is preferable and therefore followed by more recent English versions (such as the RSV, NIV, NRSV, and NET).

  10:21 The phrase πρὸς δὲ τὸν Ἰσραὴλ λέγει could be translated: "but to Israel he says" (cf. KJV). But it is more likely that πρός followed by an accusative is a "πρός of reference" construction at this place.[52] And so God is not speaking directly to Israel, but "about Israel" ("concerning Israel" or "of Israel," as in RSV, NIV, NRSV, ESV, and NET).

General Comment

In the previous section (9:6-29) Paul established that, in spite of Israel's rejection of the gospel, one cannot conclude that God has somehow failed. God has promised to preserve a remnant within Israel, and that remnant exists in the present, consisting of Jews like Paul himself who are believers, and believing Gentiles who have been added to them (9:24).

  But how does one account for the continuing unbelief of the majority of Israel? In other words, what shall we say about Israel? The people of Israel are the recipients of adoption by God, the law of Moses, right worship, and the promises to the patriarchs (9:4-5). Since all of those have been given, how is it possible for the people of Israel to reject the gospel?

---

50. BDAG 1103 (ὡραῖος, 1). Cf. NET; J. Dunn, *Romans*, 621-22; J. Fitzmyer, *Romans*, 597.
51. B. Metzger, *TCGNT* 463.
52. BDAG 874-75 (πρός, 3, d, β, a) with references not only to this passage but also to Mark 12:12; Luke 20:19, and others.

Paul's immediate response in 9:30–10:4 is that Israel has not pursued the righteousness that comes from God through faith, which is revealed in the gospel (3:22), but has sought to establish righteousness through the law, even though that avenue was one of failure (9:31). God's free offer of righteousness is made effective through faith in the gospel concerning Christ. But unfortunately Christ is a "stone of stumbling," which Isaiah foresaw (9:32-33, citing Isa 28:16). Paul goes on to claim that "Christ is the end of the law unto righteousness for everyone who believes" (10:4).

This discussion is followed in 10:5-13 by a brief one on "the righteousness that is from faith." Paul maintains that righteousness by faith is available to all, Jew and Gentile alike (10:12). It is effective on the basis of faith in Christ, crucified and resurrected. He quotes two passages from the OT (Isa 28:16; Joel 2:32) that verify that believers — and for Paul those are believers in the gospel of Christ — will be saved.

Paul does not leave the matter at that, i.e., the contrast between righteousness by the law, which leads to failure, and righteousness by faith in the gospel, which brings justification and life. He puts a charitable construction upon Israel's not having accepted the gospel. In 10:14-21 he entertains the possibility that, while Israel has pursued righteousness in a way that will not work, it could well be that the alternative way of righteousness through faith has not been made known to its people. In short, it is certainly possible that there is a very good reason for the unbelief of the Jewish people; simply put, the people of Israel have not heard the gospel. But no, Paul says, the gospel has gone out to the whole world. The problem of unbelief is that the Jewish people have not heeded the gospel (10:16). They have heard "the word of Christ" (10:18-19), but they have been disobedient and contrary (10:21), while Gentiles have accepted it (10:19-20).

Detailed Comment

9:30-33 The question "What, then, shall we say?" (τί οὖν ἐροῦμεν) sets up the critical issue that follows from the case made in 9:6-29.[53] Paul has argued that the word of God — and therefore God — has not failed in calling the people of Israel to faith in Israel's Messiah, thus saving them. God has been at work mightily in the history of the Israelite people, working out the divine purpose. So now, in the face of the continuing rejection of the gospel by the Jewish people, a new question has to be raised. Could it be that it is not God who has

---

53. The diatribal question ("What, then, shall we say?") appears also at Rom 3:5; 4:1; 6:1; 7:7; 8:31; 9:14. For discussion of its function, see the exegesis of 6:1.

failed, but that the recipients of God's word have not, for whatever reason, been able to hear it?

Paul turns immediately to the matter of "righteousness" (δικαιοσύνη).[54] In doing so, he refers to righteousness in the theological sense, i.e., the right relationship between persons and God. The key verb in 9:30-31, used twice, is διώκω (NIV and RSV: "pursue"; NRSV: "strive for"). A dichotomy is set up, which would normally seem preposterous: Gentiles, not pursuing righteousness, have attained it; but Israel, pursuing righteousness by the only way made known to its people (conforming life to Torah), has failed. In the latter case Paul uses an unusual expression, one that he does not use elsewhere (νόμος δικαιοσύνης, "law of righteousness"). If Paul intends to speak of righteousness by observing the law (of Moses), one could expect a more expansive phrase. But what he writes can be taken in that very sense, for pursuing the "law of righteousness" would imply a way of life in which a person seeks to conform all of life to the law, a law that demands righteousness and, by observing it, is the means to achieve it. In that way of thinking (in principle, if not in reality), righteousness comes from law (the observing of it), so it can be called a "law of righteousness."[55]

Paul makes contrasts: Gentiles (meaning Gentile Christians), not pursuing righteousness, have received it; Jews, pursuing righteousness, have not received it. How can this be? Paul asserts that Gentile Christians have received a particular kind of righteousness, the "righteousness of faith" (cf. similar expressions at Rom 4:11, 13; 10:6), i.e., by way of faith in the gospel. The people of Israel, on the other hand, have pursued righteousness by observing the law, but that has not been effective, for Israel could "not attain the law" (εἰς νόμον οὐκ ἔφθασεν; NRSV: "Israel . . . did not succeed in fulfilling that law").[56]

It was assumed in 9:31 that to "attain the law" (i.e., to observe it in its details) would result in righteousness. The way of Torah, in Paul's understanding of Judaism, is not, then, simply a matter of religious and ethnic identity,[57] but a way of life that should lead to righteousness before God, at least theoretically. Whatever various strands of Judaism taught in his day, Paul's own view of Jewish life was that the Torah presents a standard that is to be met for righteousness, but in fact no one can meet its demands.

---

54. According to O. Michel, *Römer,* 249, and J. Lambrecht, "The Caesura," 141-47, 9:30-33 belong to the previous section, and 10:1 begins a new one. But striving for "righteousness" (9:30) and pursuing it (10:3) are a thematic link.

55. C. Rhyne, "Nomos Dikaiosynēs," 489.

56. For another instance of the use of εἰς after the verb φθάνω, cf. Phil 3:16.

57. Contra the "New Perspective" in Pauline studies. For an example of the latter, cf. J. Dunn, *Romans,* lxiii-lxxii, in which the law is considered to have functioned as an "identity marker" and "boundary" for the Jewish people (see especially p. lxix).

Why the failure? In 9:32 there is a switch of objects. Now the attention is specifically on "righteousness" (instead of "law"), even though the term is not in the sentence. The people of Israel have failed to achieve righteousness because they pursued it "as if it were possible on the basis of works," not on the basis of "faith." Pursuing righteousness on the basis of "works" is to presume that one can fulfill all the commandments set forth in the Torah, which is impossible (3:20, 23). On the phrase "works of the law," see the exegesis of Romans 3:28.

Interpreters are not agreed on the meaning of the "stone of stumbling" and "rock of offense" that Paul mentions in 9:33. A few consider it to be the law,[58] but the vast majority affirm that it is Christ.[59] The issue will be taken up below, but first it is necessary to examine the texts.

Paul's quotation at 9:33 is composite and unlike the wording of any known versions of the OT. The first portion (9:33a) is based on Isaiah 28:16, but it differs in several respects from the LXX (as well as from the MT and Qumran versions):[60]

LXX version:
ἰδοὺ ἐγὼ ἐμβαλῶ εἰς τὰ θεμέλια Σιων λίθον πολυτελῆ ἐκλεκτὸν ἀκρογωνιαῖον ἔντιμον εἰς τὰ θεμέλια αὐτῆς.

Behold, I am laying for the foundations of Zion a costly stone, an elect, precious cornerstone for its foundations.

Romans 9:33a:
ἰδοὺ τίθημι ἐν Σιὼν λίθον προσκόμματος καὶ πέτραν σκανδάλου.

Behold, I am laying a stone of stumbling in Zion, even a rock of offense.

Paul's expressions λίθον προσκόμματος ("stone of stumbling") and πέτραν σκανδάλου ("rock of offense") appear to have been drawn from Isaiah 8:14 (the LXX containing the former explicitly and a slight variation of the latter).

The second portion of the quotation (9:33b) is almost identical to the text

58. C. K. Barrett, "Romans 9:30–10:21," 144-45; P. Meyer, "Romans 10:4 and the End of the Law," 84-85; L. Keck, *Romans*, 245. Cf. also the note in the *The New Oxford Annotated Bible*, ed. Michael D. Coogan, 3d ed. (New York: Oxford University Press, 2001), 257 (NT section); and *The Harper Collins Study Bible*, ed. Wayne A. Meeks (New York: Harper Collins, 1993), 2129.

59. W. Sanday and A. Headlam, *Romans*, 280; C. H. Dodd, *Romans*, 164; J. Munck, *Christ and Israel*, 80; O. Michel, *Römer*, 251; U. Wilckens, *Römer*, 2:213-14; E. Käsemann, *Romans*, 278-79; C. Cranfield, *Romans*, 512; P. Stuhlmacher, *Romans*, 151-53; D. Moo, *Romans*, 628-30; B. Byrne, *Romans*, 310; N. T. Wright, *NIB (Romans)*, 10:650; C. Talbert, *Romans*, 254. According to J. Fitzmyer, *Romans*, 579; K. Haacker, *Römer*, 200; and R. Jewett, *Romans*, 613, the reference is to the gospel (concerning Christ).

60. Cf. T. Lim, *Holy Scripture in the Qumran Commentaries and Pauline Letters*, 148-49.

of the LXX (Isa 28:16b). The LXX has the more emphatic negation, using οὐ μή followed by an aorist subjunctive (in this case passive),[61] whereas Paul uses the simple οὐ followed by an indicative future passive:

LXX version:
καὶ ὁ πιστεύων ἐπ' αὐτῷ οὐ μὴ καταισχυνθῇ.

And whoever believes on it [or "in him"] will not be put to shame.

Romans 9:33b:
καὶ ὁ πιστεύων ἐπ' αὐτῷ οὐ καταισχυνθήσεται.

And whoever believes on it [or "in him"] will not be put to shame.

The combination of the two passages from Isaiah appears also at 1 Peter 2:6-8, at which the Christological reference is clear.[62] Some interpreters have concluded that, since the same two verses from Isaiah have been combined in these two places in the NT, there must have been a precanonical collection of *testimonia* (OT texts that are understood to witness to Christ), from which Paul and the author of 1 Peter have drawn.[63] But the differences between the two citations are sufficient to call into question that they are drawn from a common source.[64] It is more likely that Paul combined the passages himself, and that his doing so had a lasting effect on the church at Rome where 1 Peter was composed at a later time, even though the latter did not quote explicitly from Romans.[65]

The question remains whether the quotation from the OT is used in a Christological sense by Paul in Romans. Some interpreters have sought support for such by claiming that there was a basis for it in a messianic interpretation of Isaiah 28:16 in Jewish tradition prior to Paul.[66] The arguments rest on two basic points. The first is that the LXX, in two of its major textual witnesses (ℵ and A), differs from the MT by adding ἐπ' αὐτῷ ("on it" or "in him") in the last line. The MT has simply "the one who trusts" without the prepositional phrase, which is lacking in the other major textual witness of the LXX as well (B). It has been

---

61. On the construction, familiar in both classical and NT Greek, cf. BDF 184 (§365).

62. Isa 28:16a is also quoted in a Christological context at *Barn.* 6.2-3, corresponding more closely to the LXX than in Paul's case. The rest of the verse (Isa 28:16b) reads differently: "Whoever hopes upon him shall live forever." Isa 8:14 is not combined with 28:16 in this passage.

63. C. H. Dodd, *According to the Scriptures,* 41-43; B. Lindars, *New Testament Apologetic,* 177-79; E. E. Ellis, *Paul's Use of the Old Testament,* 89; J. Dunn, *Romans,* 584.

64. P. Achtemeier, *1 Peter,* 151.

65. R. Brown and J. Meier, *Antioch and Rome,* 136; J. Elliott, *1 Peter,* 38; S.-L. Shum, *Paul's Use of Isaiah in Romans,* 214-15.

66. E. Käsemann, *Romans,* 278; C. Cranfield, *Romans,* 511; J. Dunn, *Romans,* 584; P. Stuhlmacher, *Romans,* 152; E. Lohse, *Römer,* 288.

conjectured that this addition to the LXX reflects "the oldest example of Messi-anic interpretation of an OT stone statement."[67] But whether one can be so certain of that conclusion on such slim evidence is debatable. One must also consider that the addition of the phrase is due to Christian interpolation into the LXX (i.e., into א and A, but not B) in light of Paul's rendering of it.

The other argument is that Isaiah 28:16 is interpreted messianically in the Isaiah Targum. There the word "king" replaces "stone," and the passage is most likely messianic:

> Thus says the LORD God, "Behold I am appointing in Zion a king, a strong, mighty and terrible king. I will strengthen him and harden him," says the prophet, "and the righteous who believe in these things will not be shaken when distress comes."[68]

The dating of the traditions in the *Targum of Isaiah*, however, is notoriously difficult. While the Targum possibly reflects an interpretive tradition that precedes the advent of the Christian movement, it appears that it is the product of generations of interpreters who flourished after the rise of Christianity.[69] The fact that at Qumran the Isaiah passage was interpreted as referring to the "council of the community" (1QS 8.7-8) speaks against the view that there was an established tradition of interpreting it messianically.

In light of the uncertainties about a pre-Christian messianic interpretation, and even if such did exist, the question of Paul's use of the Isaiah texts is best resolved within the context of Romans itself. Since there is no clear reference to Christ in the context, none since 9:5, that gives credence to the view that Paul is referring to the misuse of the law for gaining righteousness as the stone of stumbling.[70] Nevertheless, the references to righteousness received by faith (9:30, 32) presuppose a particular kind of faith, and that is faith in Christ. It is not unusual for the phrase "in Christ" to be lacking in the lines cited, since Paul often speaks of the believer's being justified by faith without the phrase "in Christ" following the noun πίστις ("faith"; e.g., Rom 3:28, 30; 5:1; Gal 3:8, 24; Phil 3:9b) and even on a couple of occasions without "Christ" following the verb πιστεύω ("believe in," Rom 10:4, 10). Yet in each of these cases the faith or believing spoken about is in Christ. Moreover, at 10:11 the apostle quotes Isaiah 28:16b again, and at that place there is no ambiguity; the phrase ἐπ' αὐτῷ within the clause πᾶς ὁ πιστεύων ἐπ' αὐτῷ ("everyone who believes in him") means "in Christ."

67. Joachim Jeremias, "λίθος," *TDNT* 4:272.

68. Quoted from Bruce D. Chilton, *The Isaiah Targum: Introduction, Translation, Apparatus and Notes*, ArB 11 (Wilmington: Michael Glazier, 1987), 56.

69. Bruce D. Chilton, *The Isaiah Targum*, xx-xxv.

70. L. Keck, *Romans*, 245.

Paul sets up a contrast. Those who seek righteousness by means of the law fail to see righteousness (= a right relationship between a person and God) as a gift, which has now been given freely to all in Christ, and appropriated proleptically by faith in him. God has sent forth his Son, whom Paul calls elsewhere a "stumbling block" (σκάνδαλον) to Jews and "foolishness" (μωρία) to Gentiles (1 Cor 1:23). But "whoever believes in him [Christ]," trusting in the gospel of God's reconciling work in Christ, "will not be put to shame."

10:1-4 Paul returns to what is on his heart (as at 9:2). His desire and prayer to God is that the Jewish people might be saved. In spite of their rejection of "the stone of stumbling," Paul continues in hope that they will be set once more in a right relationship with God. He acknowledges their "zeal" (ζῆλος) for God, a disposition that is admirable in the OT (Num 25:11; 2 Kgs 10:16; Ezra 7:23; Ps 69:9; Jdt 9:14; Bar 4:28; 1 Macc 2:24, 26, 50, 58; 4 Macc 18:12) and in Jewish traditions,[71] signifying one's dedication to God (or, in some cases, to the Torah). But what Paul gives with one hand, he takes back with the other. He says that the zeal of the Jewish people is "not in accordance with (real) knowledge" (οὐ κατ᾽ ἐπίγνωσιν).[72] The reason for that is that they do not know the righteousness that comes freely from God, God's own saving activity expressed above all in the sending forth of his Son, a righteousness that becomes one's own through accepting it. On "The 'Righteousness of God' in Paul," see the appendix with that title. Instead, the Jewish people have sought to establish their own righteousness by the only way they actually know, and that is by observance of the law. And while there is actual righteousness in observing the law — that cannot be disputed — nevertheless, that is a way that leads to the exclusion of most of humanity from a living relationship with God. By sending his Son, God has demonstrated his righteousness, his saving activity, which embraces all of humanity. But by refusing to accept the gospel concerning God's Son, the Jewish people have not "become subject to the righteousness of God." They have not adopted the way that God has provided for all, a trusting relationship with God through hearing and believing the good news of God's reconciling work in Christ.

The next verse (10:4) flows directly out of what has gone before and should therefore not be separated from it. Debates over the meaning of the Greek word τέλος ("end") have so preoccupied interpreters that it is often taken out of context. Does the term mean "end" in the sense of "termination," "cessation," or "abolition"?[73] Or does it mean "end" in the sense of "goal," "culmina-

---

71. Josephus, *Ant.* 13.244; *J.W.* 2.230; *Ag. Ap.* 2.271; *T. Ash.* 4.5

72. As translated in BDAG 369 (ἐπίγνωσις). Cf. K. Sullivan, "ΕΠΙΓΝΩΣΙΣ," 405-16.

73. This view is favored, among others, by C. H. Dodd, *Romans,* 176; R. Bultmann, "Christ the End of the Law," 36-37; C. K. Barrett, *Romans,* 184; idem, "Romans 9:30–10:21," 147;

tion," or "fulfillment"?[74] Could it mean both? It is possible, as various interpreters have maintained, to hold that even if the term means "termination," that does not exclude the meaning of "goal."[75] The question remains, then, whether "termination" can be excluded. As a lexical item without any particular context, the term τέλος can be defined in the sense of either "termination" or "goal,"[76] and interpreters have differed on its meaning for centuries, often dividing on theological and confessional grounds.[77]

It is important not to divide the sentence in such a way that the phrase "Christ is the end of the law" is taken as a theological topic by Paul in its own right, for that necessitates a broad-ranging discussion of the general topic of "Paul and the law." The phrase has a limited function in the present context, and that is that Christ is the end of the law "unto righteousness for everyone who believes." In other words, observing the law (meaning the Torah) is no longer the means by which one who knows and believes the gospel can obtain righteousness. Paul is speaking explicitly here of believers in Christ. For them, Christ has replaced the Torah, and righteousness is therefore not a matter of Torah observance but of receiving the righteousness that God extends to all, and which is received proleptically in the present by faith. The believer lives "in

---

J. Munck, *Christ and Israel,* 83; O. Michel, *Römer,* 362; H. Schlier, *Römer,* 311; E. Käsemann, *Romans,* 282-83; H. Räisänen, *Paul and the Law,* 54; J. Dunn, *Romans,* 589-91; S. Williams, "The Righteousness of God in Romans," 284; F. Refoulé, "Romains x,4: Encore une fois," 321-50; W. Linss, "Exegesis of *telos* in Romans," 5-12; M. Getty, "An Apocalyptic Perspective on Rom 10:4," 100; B. Martin, *Christ and the Law in Paul,* 141; P. Stuhlmacher, *Romans,* 155-56; E. Lohse, *Römer,* 292-93; F. Watson, *Paul and the Hermeneutics of Faith,* 332-33. According to E. P. Sanders, *Paul, the Law, and the Jewish People,* 83, "Paul could think of the law as at an end, at least for Christians"; according to H. Hübner, *Law in Paul's Thought,* 138 (cf. 148-49), "Christ is the end of the misuse of the Law."

74. C. Cranfield, *Romans,* 519; U. Wilckens, *Römer,* 2:223; G. Howard, "Christ the End of the Law," 331-37; R. Badenas, *Christ the End of the Law,* 79-80, 116-18, 155-61; J. Hills, "Christ Was the Goal of the Law," 585-92; P. Meyer, "Romans 10:4," 86; R. Hays, *Echoes of Scripture in the Letters of Paul,* 75-76; N. T. Wright, *Romans (NIB),* 10:655-58; J. Fitzmyer, *Romans,* 582; C. Rhyne, "*Nomos Dikaiosynēs,*" 492; idem, *Faith Establishes the Law,* 103-4; M. Nanos, *The Mystery of Romans,* 22, 316, 364; J. Ziesler, *Romans,* 257-58; B. Byrne, *Romans,* 315; D. Moo, *Romans,* 631; K. Haacker, *Römer,* 206-9; S. Bechtler, "Christ, the Τέλος of the Law," 288-308. L. Keck, *Romans,* 248-50; R. Jewett, *Romans,* 619; I. Gruenwald, "Paul and the Nomos," 412; F. Matera, *Romans,* 245-46.

75. BDAG 998-99 (τέλος, 3); P. Achtemeier, *Romans,* 168; S. Westerholm, "Paul and the Law in Romans 9–11," 233-34; M. Seifrid, *Justification by Faith,* 248; I. Jolivet, "Christ the τέλος in Romans 10:4," 13-30.

76. Both interpretations are presented in BDAG 998-99 (τέλος): "end, termination, cessation" and "end, goal, outcome." For the wide range of meanings of the word, cf. LSJ 1772-74 (τέλος).

77. For a history of interpretation, cf. J. Nestingen, "Christ the End of the Law"; and R. Badenas, *Christ the End of the Law,* 7-37.

Christ," not under the Torah, and the whole of life is guided by the Spirit (Rom 7:6; 8:4, 14; Gal 5:16, 25).

But if Paul refers here specifically to the life of the believer, what significance does the statement in 10:4 have to his overall discussion in this part of the letter about the Jewish people, persons not "in Christ"? Paul has indicated that his desire is the salvation of the Jewish people (10:1), which at this place (even if not at 11:25-32) can be envisioned only on the basis of faith in the crucified and resurrected Jesus. The Jewish people, he says, are zealous for God, but they continue to seek righteousness as though it could be acquired by observing the Torah, and they fail. The result is that they are no better off (in regard to righteousness) than Gentiles (Rom 2:12-16), and that they and everyone else obtain righteousness as a gift from God, received by faith. In regard to obtaining righteousness, therefore, Christ is the end, the termination, of the most obvious and familiar way of achieving it, i.e., observance of the Torah. Paul goes on to say in the verses that follow that Torah observance breaks down in any case. The very next verse (10:5) begins with an explanatory γάρ ("for") that puts forth the standard, and that is that anyone who seeks righteousness by the law must keep the entire Torah.[78] But the implication is that, in the final analysis, no one can keep the Torah, as Paul has stated previously (Rom 3:30; 8:2-3; cf. Gal 2:16; 3:11-13).

Paul does not denigrate the Torah here or anywhere else in his writings. On the contrary, he speaks of the law (the Torah) as "holy" and the specific commandment against covetousness as "holy, just, and good" (Rom 7:12). As a son of Israel, he could not say otherwise. The Torah served well in the past as a guide to life within Israel. It was a "disciplinarian" (NRSV, παιδαγωγός, Gal 3:24-25) until the coming of Christ. But with the coming of Christ a new way of righteousness has been opened up for all humanity. God has demonstrated his righteousness in the sending of his Son, the crucified Messiah, by which he has reconciled the world to himself (2 Cor 5:19). The good news is that this reconciling work has been accomplished. All who hear and accept the good news are not only assured that the news is true, but they have also been grafted thereby into the new humanity coming into being. Through their baptism into Christ they have become new, belonging to the new creation (2 Cor 5:17). The Torah in all its details (moral, dietary, and ceremonial) can no longer be a way of life for all who are in Christ (particularly Gentiles), and therefore it cannot be a means of gaining righteousness. Christ is then the end of the Torah for righteousness.

That said, it does not follow that the Torah is no longer a guide for those who are in Christ. Paul refers to the Decalogue on two occasions, saying that the love commandment fulfills the law (Rom 13:9; Gal 5:14). But he can do so on the prior basis of the believer's life in Christ, and the Decalogue is not the only moral

---

78. Cf. H. Räisänen, *Paul and the Law*, 54.

authority to which he refers. Whatever is in accord with the new life in Christ can be endorsed by Paul as a basis for moral guidance, whether that be sayings of Jesus (1 Cor 7:10; 9:14), the commandments, his own life as a model (1 Cor 4:16; 11:1; Gal 4:12; Phil 4:9), other Christians as models (2 Cor 8:1-6; 9:1-2; 1 Thess 1:7-8; 2:14), or common Hellenistic moral teaching (Phil 4:8; cf. Rom 12:2). But that does not mean that righteousness — in the sense of a right relationship with God, either in the present or in the final judgment — can be based on Torah observance as a way of life and righteousness. Righteousness is a gift from a gracious God, accepted by faith. That was so in the case of Abraham long ago, who believed in the promises of God (4:3, 22), and it is true in the present wherever people believe in the gospel of the crucified and risen Christ as the act by which God has reconciled the world to himself. Just as righteousness in the final judgment is a matter of a trusting relationship with God, based on the redemptive work of God in Christ rather than Torah observance (an impossibility for Gentiles, in spite of its theoretical possibility set forth in diatribe, 2:14), so it is realized proleptically in the present. One is righteous through trusting in the gospel of God's redemptive work through the crucified and resurrected Lord.

10:5-13 In order to authorize his point (that righteousness does not come from Torah observance), Paul refers to the Scriptures of Israel. The connection is underscored by the use of γάρ ("for," indicating a reason) in 10:5: "For Moses writes concerning the righteousness that is from the law." A specific "righteousness" is thus being taken up, i.e., that which is from (observing) the law (the Torah). The quotation attributed to Moses is from Leviticus 18:5. It is a free rendering of the verse, corresponding to neither the MT nor the LXX.

Leviticus 18:5 (MT):

וּשְׁמַרְתֶּם אֶת־חֻקֹּתַי וְאֶת־מִשְׁפָּטַי אֲשֶׁר יַעֲשֶׂה אֹתָם הָאָדָם וָחַי בָּהֶם׃

And you shall keep my statutes and my ordinances; by doing so one shall live by them.

Leviticus 18:5:

καὶ φυλάξεσθε πάντα τὰ προστάγματά μου καὶ πάντα τὰ κρίματά μου καὶ ποιήσετε αὐτά ἃ ποιήσας ἄνθρωπος ζήσεται ἐν αὐτοῖς.

And you shall observe all my commandments and all my judgments, and you shall do them which, if a person does, he shall live by them.

Romans 10:5:

ὁ ποιήσας αὐτὰ ἄνθρωπος ζήσεται ἐν αὐτοῖς.

The person who does these things shall live by them.

385

It is this text that Paul alludes to at 7:10 ("the very commandment that promised life proved to be death to me"), and he quotes it again at Galatians 3:12. Although it promises life, it brings death, for no one can fulfill its demands.

In contrast to this way of righteousness, the way that is based on faith attends to another voice in Scripture. The phrase "the righteousness that is from faith" is personified, having a message of its own, speaking forth from a passage in Deuteronomy 30:11-14. What is missing in Paul's citation of it is any word about its context, although it is precisely that which must have drawn him to it. The passage in Deuteronomy is preceded with promises from God, declaring that if the people of Israel keep his commandments and turn to him with their hearts and souls, he will give them prosperity (30:1-10). Then verses follow in which God says that the commandments are neither too difficult nor too obscure (30:11-14). Just prior to the material quoted by Paul, God says: "This commandment that I am commanding you today is not too hard for you, nor is it too far away" (Deut 30:11). Within the context of the OT, and certainly within the history of Jewish interpretation, this passage can be taken as showing that the commandments given by God are reasonable, not too difficult, and not obscure. Together with Leviticus 18:5, one can conclude that life under Torah can indeed be practiced, for it is not impossible, and it leads to life.

But when Paul cites the passage in Deuteronomy (he alludes to it more than quotes from it), he takes it less as a complement to Leviticus 18:5; he renders it as an alternative.[79] He makes no reference to the commandments as being difficult or far away (and therefore he implies that they are reasonable and at hand), nor does he indicate that the passage, as divine speech, is addressed to Israel. Instead he writes as though the passage in Deuteronomy is the word of God for his own time. In that way he can understand it as having a universalizing significance.[80]

The alternative to "the righteousness that is by the law" is "the righteousness that is from faith" (10:6). According to this kind of righteousness (i.e., this way of relating to God), one need not go "into heaven" or "into the abyss" to acquire God's message to the world. On the contrary, "the word is near" (Deut 30:14; Rom 10:8), the word of God that is being preached.

Within 10:6-9 Paul quotes several portions of Deuteronomy. He quotes a part of Deuteronomy 9:4 when he says, "Do not say in your heart" (Rom 10:6a). He goes on to quote a part of Deuteronomy 30:12, which puts forth the question, "Who will ascend into heaven?" (Rom 10:6b). But when he writes, "Who will descend into the abyss?" (Rom 10:7), he departs from the deuteronomic

---

79. Cf. P. Sprinkle, *Law and Life*, 168-73, who summarizes scholarship and maintains that the passages are "antithetical," not "correlative."

80. Cf. J. Dunn, "'Righteousness from the Law' and 'Righteousness from Faith,'" 223-26.

text (30:13, "Neither is it beyond the sea, that you should say, 'Who will cross to the other side of the sea for us, and get it for us so that we may hear it and observe it?'"). At this place he appears to substitute language from Psalm 107:26 ("they went down to the depths"; LXX 106:26, καταβαίνουσιν ἕως τῶν ἀβύσσων) but also draws upon the wisdom tradition, in which Torah and wisdom have been identified. At Job 28:14 "the deep (ἄβυσσος) says, 'It (σοφία, "wisdom") is not in me,' and the sea says, 'It is not with me.'" It is apparently by means of this way of associating the word of God, the Torah, wisdom, and Christ, as well as associating the abyss and the sea (commonly associated in OT traditions),[81] that Paul makes the connection he does. Finally, at 10:8, after the question ("But what does it say?"), Paul comes back to the text in Deuteronomy; his words correspond to those of Deuteronomy 30:14 LXX almost exactly when he says, "The word is near you, in your mouth and in your heart." The LXX differs only by having an additional word, "very" (σφόδρα), modifying "near."

The imagery of having neither to ascend to heaven nor to descend to the abyss to obtain the Torah (Deut 30:11-14) had already, prior to Paul's day, been transformed and interpreted in the wisdom tradition. There it is said that the divine wisdom cannot be acquired by going into heaven or over the sea (Bar 3:29-30), for God's wisdom has been brought near through the Torah (3:9). Paul makes the association between the divine wisdom and Christ.[82] But he goes a step further. When all is said and done, Paul makes a *tour de force,* taking what applies to the Torah in Deuteronomy 30:11-14 and applying it to the gospel. The divine wisdom — now the word of God, the gospel of Christ — is near at hand, made known in the apostolic preaching.[83]

It appears that, for Paul, the combined imageries and language of Psalm 107:26 and Job 28:14 were more fitting than that of Deuteronomy 30:13. The imagery of descending to the abyss (ἄβυσσος, the underworld realm of the dead) provides the opposite of ascending into heaven. Moreover, the antithesis between heaven above and the abyss below must have been familiar to Paul, since it existed already in Jewish traditions (Ps 107:26; Sir 1:3; 16:18; 24:5; 2 Esdr 4:8; cf. Isa 7:11).

According to Paul, there are two major *a priori* possibilities concerning Christ, who has been crucified. Either he is in the abyss (for those who would

---

81. Job 38:16; 41:31; Pss 33:7; 106:9; 135:6 (LXX 32:7; 105:9; 134:6); Isa 51:10; Sir 24:29; 2 Esdr 4:7; 16:57.

82. M. Suggs, "'The Word Is Near You,'" 304-12; C. Tuckett, *Christology and the New Testament,* 63.

83. That Paul alludes to the proclamation of the gospel, cf. E. Käsemann, *Romans,* 288; U. Wilckens, *Römer,* 2:225-26; C. K. Barrett, *Romans,* 186; C. Cranfield, *Romans,* 526; J. Fitzmyer, *Romans,* 588, 591; P. Stuhlmacher, *Romans,* 154, 156.

deny the resurrection), or he is in heaven (for those who affirm it). But there is a third possibility, and that is that he is present in the apostolic proclamation (10:8b). Paul calls this τὸ ῥῆμα τῆς πίστεως ὃ κηρύσσομεν ("the word of faith that we proclaim"). The Greek wording for "word of faith" is an objective genitive,[84] signifying a message concerning "the faith that we proclaim." Paul will use the term ῥῆμα ("word") again within a clause at 10:17. There he speaks of faith as coming from what is heard, and "what is heard comes by the preaching of Christ" (διὰ ῥήματος Χριστοῦ). There, too, the genitive is objective, so Paul speaks about Christian proclamation concerning Christ (not Jesus' own proclamation).

The word is indeed "near," since it is "in your mouth and in your heart." It is "in your mouth" in a double sense, for it is the word of proclamation (10:8), and it is the word of confession (10:9). It is "in your heart," says Paul, because one believes with the "heart" (10:9, 10). The fact that the word is near intensifies "the paradox of Israel's unbelief. . . . The nearness of the word stands in ironic juxtaposition to Israel's deafness."[85]

The confession "Jesus is Lord" (κύριος Ἰησοῦς, 10:9) is perhaps the earliest of all confessional formulations, having its utterance already among Aramaic-speaking Christians.[86] Paul cites it two other times in his writings (1 Cor 12:3; Phil 2:11) as the essential, basic confession, inspired by the Holy Spirit (1 Cor 12:3). The fact that Paul cites it here indicates that it must have been familiar among believers in Rome. Its origins need not be traced to an opposition to the imperial cult, in which "Caesar is Lord," but to a prior conviction already in Palestinian Christianity that Jesus is the one appointed by God to reign. But the confession could hardly avoid taking on additional significance as a counterconfession to emperor worship. At least that is how it would have been understood in Rome.

But Paul does not seem interested at this point in engaging in polemics against the imperial cult. He is concerned rather about the way of righteousness for all people in the presence of God. The word of Moses that promises life but leads to death (Lev 18:5) is countered by the "word of faith" that is the basis for a

---

84. BDAG 905 (ῥῆμα, 1).
85. R. Hays, *Echoes of Scripture in the Letters of Paul,* 83.
86. J. Fitzmyer, "Paul and the Dead Sea Scrolls," 617 (after showing evidence for the use of the Aramaic term מרא in reference to God at Qumran): "Paul's κύριος . . . simply adopts for the risen Christ a title that Palestinian Jews were already using for Yahweh." Cf. idem, "The Semitic Background of the New Testament Kyrios-Title," 115-42; F. Hahn, *The Titles of Jesus in Christology,* 73-89; R. Fuller, *The Foundations of New Testament Christology,* 156-58; V. Neufeld, *The Earliest Christian Confessions,* 54-56. That its origins cannot be traced to Aramaic-speaking Christianity but only to Gentile Hellenistic worship is claimed by K. Wengst, *Christologische Formeln,* 131-35.

new kind of righteousness, "the righteousness of faith." That word of faith is the gospel proclaimed concerning Jesus, who is Lord, and who has been raised from the dead by God the Father. Believing brings justification (10:10a), and confession brings salvation (10:10b).

At 10:11 Paul quotes again from Isaiah 28:16 (as he did in 9:33b) to confirm his point. The one who believes will not be turned away by God ("will not be put to shame"). The quotation is altered slightly from the Isaiah text (and by what was written in 9:33b) by the insertion of πᾶς ("all" in a collective expression, or "everyone" in an individual one). The sense of "everyone" was present already in the Isaiah text (ὁ πιστεύων, "whoever believes"), but the insertion of πᾶς makes it more emphatic. That, in turn, opens the way for Paul to go on to make the point that "there is no distinction between Jew and Greek," a point that Paul has made before (3:22, 29; cf. Gal 3:28).

Since Paul has spoken the confession "Jesus is Lord" already at 10:9, it is likely that the threefold use of the term κύριος ("Lord") in 10:12b-13 is Christological as well.[87] That Christ is "Lord of all" is affirmed elsewhere (3:29; Phil 2:9-11; 1 Cor 15:25), and that he is generous toward all is affirmed in the proclamation of the gospel concerning the death of Christ as being "for all" (Rom 8:32; 2 Cor 5:14-15). Elsewhere Paul could write: "For you know the generous act (τὴν χάριν) of our Lord Jesus Christ, that though he was rich, yet for your sakes he became poor, so that by his poverty you might become rich" (2 Cor 8:9). He is generous, Paul says, to those who call on (ἐπικαλέω) him. The verb ἐπικαλέω is used in the LXX for calling on God (1 Sam 12:17-18; 2 Sam 22:4, 7; Pss 13:4; 17:3; Isa 55:6; cf. Bar 3:7). Here it is used to call upon Christ as Lord (cf. Acts 2:21; 22:16; 2 Tim 2:22), which leads to salvation. Paul uses the same verb when he addresses the Christians at Corinth as "saints, together with all those who in every place call on (ἐπικαλέω) the name of our Lord Jesus Christ" (1 Cor 1:2). Paul confirms that Christ is gracious to all by quoting from Joel 2:32. His wording corresponds exactly with that of the LXX, except for the addition of γάρ ("for") at the beginning of the sentence (so, πᾶς γὰρ ὅς instead of πᾶς ὅς). Whoever calls upon him in faith will be saved.

10:14-17 Paul raises a series of four questions that flow from the affirmation he has just made. The rhetorical effect of the four is to raise the question whether the Jewish people are in fact to blame for not believing in the gospel. They have not called upon Christ, for that presupposes faith; but they have not believed. Could it be, then, that they have not believed because they have not

---

87. C. Cranfield, *Romans*, 531-32; U. Wilckens, *Römer*, 2:228; D. Capes, *Old Testament Yahweh Texts in Paul's Christology*, 116-23; D. Moo, *Romans*, 600; S.-L. Shum, *Paul's Use of Isaiah in Romans*, 223; C. Rowe, "Romans 10:13," 135-73. For the view that Paul refers to Yahweh, cf. G. Howard, "Tetragram and the New Testament," 63-83.

heard the gospel concerning him? And perhaps they have not heard the gospel because they have not had it proclaimed to them. Moreover, perhaps they have not had the gospel proclaimed to them because God has not commissioned anyone to evangelize them.

Such ways of thinking are quickly excluded by what Paul says from 10:15b to 10:21, which contains various OT passages to prove that the Jewish people are without excuse. He cites Isaiah 52:7, but what he presents is more of a paraphrase than a quotation,[88] and it is closer in wording to the MT than to the LXX: "How timely is the arrival of those who proclaim good news" (Rom 10:16). Moreover, Paul alters the citation in two major ways: (1) he renders the verse in such a way that the proclaimers are now plural (the herald is singular in Isaiah); and (2) he turns what was a salvific word of hope in the text of Isaiah into a word of judgment. God has indeed sent messengers to bring the good news. Therefore, the people of Israel are without excuse. The sending of messengers had been foreseen in the Scriptures, which now speak to the present. The messengers have been proclaiming the gospel right up to the present. The problem is that "not all have obeyed" the gospel. Some have, such as Paul himself, but the overwhelming majority has not. The concept of obeying the gospel, using the verb ὑπακούω ("to obey"), appears one other time in the Pauline corpus, but that is in a letter that is often regarded as deutero-Pauline (2 Thess 1:8).[89] Paul does, however, speak elsewhere of the "obedience of faith" (ὑπακοὴ πίστεως, Rom 1:5).[90] In such cases both the verb and the noun can have the sense of one's becoming subject to the gospel, giving it one's consent, and conforming one's life to it.[91]

Again the point is made that the fault for not hearing, believing, or obeying the gospel is not God's, but Israel's alone. At 10:16 Paul quotes a portion of Isaiah 53:1 (exactly as presented in the LXX), in which the prophet addresses God, complaining that the people of Israel have paid no attention to God's message through the prophet: "Lord, who has believed our message?" The implication is that no one has. So Paul sees the same phenomenon in his own time. The people of Israel do not pay attention to the apostolic message.

The word for "message," that which is heard (ἀκοή), can also mean (the act of) "hearing."[92] There is then a play on the word between 10:16, where it means "message," and 10:17, where it means "hearing." Faith, Paul says, comes from "hearing," but of course that is the hearing of the apostolic "message." That

88. S.-L. Shum, *Paul's Use of Isaiah in Romans,* 223-24.

89. A similar expression, but with a different verb (ἀπειθέω), appears as 1 Pet 4:17.

90. The phrase appears also at Rom 16:26, but that might be a deutero-Pauline passage. See the exegesis of 16:25-27.

91. G. Schneider, "ὑπακούω," *EDNT* 3:394-95.

92. For references and contexts, cf. BDAG 36 (ἀκοή).

is so, says Paul, since the "hearing" takes place "through the word of Christ."
Once again, as at 10:8, the term ῥῆμα ("word") is followed by the genitive — an
objective genitive[93] — signifying the proclamation concerning Christ (not
Christ's own proclamation).

Now, in 10:18-21, a catena of OT passages is constructed in rapid succession to further the argument that the Jewish people are without excuse; there is
no way for anyone to claim that they have not had a chance to hear and believe
the gospel of Christ. The four passages cited are used by Paul as vehicles for a
message about the present. He sees them as speaking directly to his own day
and about the Jewish people of his own generation. The four OT passages
quoted correspond closely to the text of the LXX, but there are differences in
three of the four cases (the very first being the exception).

1. In 10:18 Paul cites Psalm 19:4 (LXX 18:5), corresponding exactly to the
LXX. The expression "their words" (τὰ ῥήματα αὐτῶν) picks up the term ῥῆμα
("word") from 10:17, referring to apostolic preaching. The apostolic proclamation has gone out to the whole world, according to the passage cited. Although
that could not have been considered true in a literal sense, it could be considered valid insofar as the gospel is for both Jew and Gentile.

2. In 10:19 Paul maintains that the people of Israel has understood the
message. The proof of that is that they are jealous of Gentiles who have come to
worship the God of Israel. This is a point that Paul picks up again in 11:11-14, but
for now he cites Deuteronomy 32:21. The quotation differs from the LXX in
making the direct object "you" (plural, ὑμᾶς) rather than "them" (αὐτούς). The
result is that the word proclaimed is direct address to Israel.

3. In 10:20 Paul quotes from Isaiah 65:1 to cite the experience of God, as
spoken by God himself through the prophet, in Isaiah's time and in his own.
That is that God has been found by Gentiles who believe the divine message,
even though the Gentiles have not sought him out. He has indeed become
known (revealed) to people who were not searching for him. That is by divine
grace and unexpected.

Paul's citation of the text differs from the LXX in that the main verbs at
the beginning of the lines are reversed. The Isaiah text reads:

> "I have become known (ἐμφανὴς ἐγενόμην) to those who have not
>   sought me;
>   I have been found (εὑρέθην) by those who have not asked for me."

93. This is confirmed by the use of the word in the next verse (10:18), where it (plural
form) is used for the apostolic preaching. Cf. also W. Sanday and A. Headlam, *Romans,* 298;
J. Fitzmyer, *Romans,* 598; R. Jewett, *Romans,* 642. E. Käsemann, *Romans,* 295: "the word of the
exalted Lord . . . which manifests itself in the apostolic preaching."

Paul's text reads:

"I have been found (εὑρέθην) by those who have not sought me;
    I have become known (ἐμφανὴς ἐγενόμην) to those who did not ask
    for me."

Since neither corresponds to the MT, Paul must have quoted from a Greek version not otherwise known, or else he modified the text at this point himself, which is probably the most likely explanation.[94] Within the context of the book of Isaiah the verse actually applies to the people of Israel being rebellious,[95] but Paul understands it as applying to the Gentiles.

4. In 10:21 Paul quotes the very next verse from Isaiah (Isa 65:2), in which God speaks through the prophet in reference to Israel. As Israel has been stubborn and recalcitrant in the past, so now. The present situation should surprise no one. As it was in the earlier days, so it is now. The quotation corresponds to the LXX for the most part, except that in Paul's version the phrase ὅλην τὴν ἡμέραν ("all day long") has been placed at the beginning of the first line, rather than at the end.

BIBLIOGRAPHY

Achtemeier, Paul. *1 Peter.* Hermeneia. Minneapolis: Fortress Press, 1996.

Badenas, Robert. *Christ the End of the Law: Romans 10:4 in Pauline Perspective.* JSOTSup 10. Sheffield: JSOT Press, 1985.

Barrett, C. K. "Romans 9:30–10:21: Fall and Responsibility of Israel." In his *Essays on Paul,* 132-53. Philadelphia: Westminster Press, 1982.

Bechtler, Steven R. "Christ, the Τέλος of the Law: The Goal of Romans 10:4." *CBQ* 56 (1994): 288-308.

Bekken, Per Jarle. "Paul's Use of Deut 30,12-14 in Jewish Context: Some Observations." In *The New Testament and Hellenistic Judaism,* 183-203. Ed. Peder Borgen and Søren Giversen. Aarhus: Aarhus University Press, 1995.

Bell, Richard H. *Provoked to Jealousy: The Origin and Purpose of the Jealousy Motif in Romans 9–11.* WUNT 2/63. Tübingen: J. C. B. Mohr (Paul Siebeck), 1994.

Bring, Ragnar. "Die Erfüllung des Gesetzes durch Christus: Eine Studie zur Theologie des Apostels Paulus." *KuD* 5 (1959): 1-22.

———. "Die Gerechtigkeit Gottes und das alttestamentliche Gesetz: Eine Untersuchung von Röm. 10,4." In his *Christus und das Gesetz: Die Bedeutung des Gesetzes des Alten Testaments nach Paulus und sein Glauben an Christus,* 35-72. Leiden: E. J. Brill, 1969.

94. Discussion of the various possibilities is carried on by T. Lim, *Holy Scripture in the Qumran Communities and Pauline Letters,* 146-47, and S.-L. Shum, *Paul's Use of Isaiah in the Letter to the Romans,* 226-31.

95. Cf. B. Childs, *Isaiah,* 535.

———. "Das Gesetz und die Gerechtigkeit Gottes: Eine Studie zur Frage nach der Bedeutung des Ausdruckes *telos nomou* in Röm. 10:4." *ST* 20 (1966): 1-36.

———. "Paul and the Old Testament: A Study of the Ideas of Election, Faith and Law in Paul, with Special Reference to Romans 9:30–10:30." *ST* 25 (1971): 21-60.

Brown, Raymond E., and John P. Meier. *Antioch and Rome: New Testament Cradles of Catholic Christianity.* New York: Paulist Press, 1983.

Bultmann, Rudolf. "Christ the End of the Law." In his *Essays Philosophical and Theological,* 36-66. New York: Macmillan, 1955.

Burchard, Christoph. "Christus, 'das Ende des Gesetzes, des Dekalogs und des Liebesgebots?'" *TZ* 63 (2007): 171-74.

Campbell, William S. "Christ the End of the Law: Romans 10:4." In *Studia Biblica 1978: Sixth International Congress on Biblical Studies, Oxford, 3-7 April 1978,* 3:73-81. Ed. Elizabeth A. Livingstone. 3 vols. Sheffield: JSOT Press, 1979-80.

Capes, David B. *Old Testament Yahweh Texts in Paul's Christology.* WUNT 2/47. Tübingen: J. C. B. Mohr (Paul Siebeck), 1992.

———. "YHWH and His Messiah: Pauline Exegesis and the Divine Christ." *HBT* 16 (1994): 121-43.

Childs, Brevard S. *Isaiah.* OTL. Louisville: Westminster John Knox Press, 2001.

Cranfield, C. E. B. "Romans 9.30–10:4." *Int* 34 (1980): 70-74.

———. "Some Notes on Romans 9:30-33." In *Jesus und Paulus: Festschrift für Werner Georg Kümmel zum 70. Geburtstag,* 35-43. Ed. E. Earle Ellis and Erich Grässer. Göttingen: Vandenhoeck & Ruprecht, 1975.

Cullmann, Oscar. *The Earliest Christian Confessions.* London: Lutterworth, 1949.

Delling, Gerhard. "Nahe ist das Wort: Wort–Geist–Glaube bei Paulus." *TLZ* 99 (1974): 402-12.

Dewey, Arthur J. "A Re-Hearing of Romans 10:1-15." In *Orality and Textuality in Early Christian Literature,* 109-27. Ed. Joanna Dewey. SBLSS 65. Atlanta: Scholars Press, 1994.

Dodd, C. H. *According to the Scriptures: The Sub-Structure of New Testament Theology.* New York: Charles Scribner's Sons, 1953.

Dunn, James D. G. "'Righteousness from the Law' and 'Righteousness from Faith': Paul's Interpretation of Scripture in Romans 10:1-10." In *Tradition and Interpretation in the New Testament: Essays in Honor of E. Earle Ellis for His Sixtieth Birthday,* 216-28. Ed. Gerald F. Hawthorne and Otto Betz. Grand Rapids: Wm. B. Eerdmans, 1987.

Eckstein, Hans-Joachim. "'Nahe ist dir das Wort': Exegetische Erwägungen zu Röm 10,8." *ZNW* 79 (1988): 204-20.

Elliott, John H. *1 Peter.* AB 37B. New York: Doubleday, 2000.

Ellis, E. Earle. *Paul's Use of the Old Testament.* Grand Rapids: Wm. B. Eerdmans, 1957; reprinted, Grand Rapids: Baker Book House, 1981.

Fitzmyer, Joseph A. "Paul and the Dead Sea Scrolls." In *The Dead Sea Scrolls after Fifty Years: A Comprehensive Assessment,* 2:599-621. Ed. Peter W. Flint and James C. VanderKam. 2 vols. Boston: E. J. Brill, 1998-99.

———. "The Semitic Background of the New Testament Kyrios-Title." In his *A Wandering Aramean: Collected Aramaic Essays,* 115-42. SBLMS 25. Missoula: Scholars Press, 1971.

Flückiger, Felix. "Christus, der Gesetzes τέλος." *TZ* 11 (1955): 153-57.

Führer, Werner. "'Herr Is Jesus': Die Rezeption der urchristlichen Kyrios-Akklamation durch Paulus Römer 10,9." *KuD* 33 (1987): 137-49.

Fuller, Reginald H. *The Foundations of New Testament Christology.* New York: Charles Scribner's Sons, 1965.

Gaston, Lloyd. *Paul and the Torah.* Vancouver: University of British Columbia Press, 1987.

Getty, Mary Ann. "An Apocalyptic Perspective on Rom 10:4." *HBT* 4 (1983): 79-131.

Gignac, Alain. "Citation de Lévitique 18,5 en Romains 10,5 et Galates 3,12: Deux lectures différentes des rapports Christ-Torah?" *ÉgThéol* 25 (1994): 367-403.

Gordon, T. David. "Why Israel Did Not Obtain Torah-Righteousness: A Translation Note on Rom 9:32." *WTJ* 54 (1992): 163-66.

Gruenwald, Ithamar. "Paul and the *Nomos* in Light of Ritual Theory." *NTS* 54 (2008): 398-416.

Hahn, Ferdinand. *The Titles of Jesus in Christology: Their History in Early Christianity.* New York: World Publishing Company, 1969.

Hanson, Anthony T. "Paul's Interpretation of Scripture." In his *Studies in Paul's Technique and Theology,* 136-68. London: S.P.C.K., 1974.

Hays, Richard B. *Echoes of Scripture in the Letters of Paul.* New Haven: Yale University Press, 1989.

Heil, John P. "Christ, the Termination of the Law (Romans 9:30–10:8)." *CBQ* 63 (2001): 484-98.

Hellbrandt, Hans. "Christus das *Telos* des Gesetzes." *EvT* 3 (1936): 331-46.

Heller, Jan. "Himmel- und Höllenfahrt nach Römer 10,6-7." *EvT* 32 (1972): 478-86.

Hills, Julian V. "Christ Was the Goal of the Law . . ." *JTS* 44 (1993): 585-92.

Howard, George E. "Christ the End of the Law: The Meaning of Romans 10:4ff." *JBL* 88 (1969): 331-37.

———. "The Tetragram and the New Testament." *JBL* 96 (1977): 63-83.

Hübner, Hans. *Law in Paul's Thought.* Edinburgh: T&T Clark, 1984.

———. "τέλος." *EDNT* 3:347-48.

Humphrey, Edith M. "Why Bring the Word Down? The Rhetoric of Demonstration and Disclosure in Romans 9:30–10:21." In *Romans and the People of God: Essays in Honor of Gordon D. Fee on the Occasion of His 65th Birthday,* 129-48. Ed. Sven K. Soderlund and N. T. Wright. Grand Rapids: Wm. B. Eerdmans, 1999.

Ito, Akio. "The Written Torah and the Oral Gospel: Romans 10:5-13 in the Dynamic Tension between Orality and Literacy." *NovT* 48 (2006): 234-60.

Jewett, Robert. "The Law and the Coexistence of Jews and Gentiles in Romans." *Int* 39 (1985): 341-56.

Jolivet, Ira. "Christ the τέλος in Romans 10:4 as Both Fulfillment and Termination of the Law." *ResQ* 51 (2009): 13-30.

Kaiser, Walter C. "Leviticus 18:5 and Paul: Do This and You shall Live (Eternally)." *JETS* 14 (1971): 19-28.

Kundert, Lukas. "Christus als Inkorporation der Tora: τέλος γὰρ νόμου Χριστός: Röm 10,4 vor dem Hintergrund einer erstaunlichen rabbinischen Argumentation." *TZ* 55/1 (1999): 76-89.

Lambrecht, Jan. "The Caesura between Romans 9.30-3 and 10.1-4." *NTS* 45 (1999): 141-47.

Lang, Friedrich. "Erwägungen zu Gesetz und Verheissung in Römer 10,4-13." In *Jesus Christus als die Mitte der Schrift: Studien zur Hermeneutik des Evangeliums*, 579-602. BZNW 86. Ed. Christof Landmesser et al. New York: Walter de Gruyter, 1997.

Langevin, Paul-Émile. "The Christology of Romans 10:3-13." *TD* 28 (1980): 45-48.

Lim, Timothy H. *Holy Scripture in the Qumran Commentaries and Pauline Letters*. Oxford: Clarendon Press, 1997.

Lindars, Barnabas. *New Testament Apologetic: The Doctrinal Significance of the Old Testament Quotations*. Philadelphia: Westminster Press, 1961.

Lindemann, Andreas. "Die Gerechtigkeit aus dem Gesetz: Erwägungen zur Auslegung und zur Textgeschichte von Römer 10,5." *ZNW* 73 (1982): 231-50.

Linss, Wilhelm C. "Exegesis of *telos* in Romans." *BR* 33 (1988): 5-12.

Lohse, Eduard. "Christus, das Gesetzes Ende? Die Theologie des Apostels Paulus in kritischer Perspektive." *ZNW* 99 (2008): 18-32.

Martin, Brice L. *Christ and the Law in Paul*. NovTSup 62. Leiden: E. J. Brill, 1989.

———. "Paul on Christ and the Law." *JETS* 26 (1983): 271-82.

Meyer, Paul W. "Romans 10:4 and the End of the Law." In *The Word in This World: Essays in New Testament Exegesis and Theology*, 78-94. Ed. John T. Carroll. NTL. Louisville: Westminster John Knox, 2004.

Müller, Friedrich. "Zwie Marginalien im Brief des Paulus an die Romer." *ZNW* 40 (1941): 249-54.

Munck, Johannes. *Christ and Israel: An Interpretation of Romans 9–11*. Philadelphia: Fortress Press, 1967.

Nanos, Mark D. *The Mystery of Romans: The Jewish Context of Paul's Letter*. Minneapolis: Fortress Press, 1996.

Nestingen, James A. "Christ the End of the Law: Romans 10:4 as an Historical-Exegetical-Theological Problem." Ph.D. diss., University of Toronto, 1984.

Neufeld, Vernon H. *The Earliest Christian Confessions*. NTTS 5. Grand Rapids: Wm. B. Eerdmans, 1963.

Räisänen, Heikki. *Paul and the Law*. Philadelphia: Fortress Press, 1986.

Refoulé, François. "Note sur Romains ix, 30-33." *RB* 92 (1985): 161-86.

———. "Romains x,4: Encore une fois." *RB* 91 (1984): 321-50.

Reinbold, Wolfgang. "Israel und das Evangelium: Zur Exegese von Römer 10,19-21." *ZNW* 86 (1995): 122-29.

———. "Paulus und das Gesetz: Zur Exegese von Röm 9,30-33." *BZ* 38 (1994): 253-64.

Rhyne, C. Thomas. *Faith Establishes the Law*. SBLDS 55. Chico: Scholars Press, 1981.

———. "*Nomos Dikaiosynēs* and the Meaning of Romans 10:4." *CBQ* 47 (1985): 486-99.

Rickards, Raymond R. "The Translation of *dia rhēmatos Christou* ('through the word of Christ') in Romans 10.17." *BT* 27 (1976): 447-48.

Rowe, C. Kavin. "Romans 10:13: What Is the Name of the Lord?" *HBT* 22 (2000): 135-73.

Sanders, E. P. *Paul, the Law, and the Jewish People*. Philadelphia: Fortress Press, 1983.

Sanders, James A. "Torah and Paul." In *God's Christ and His People: Studies in Honour of Nils Alstrup Dahl*, 132-40. Ed. Jacob Jervell and Wayne A. Meeks. Oslo: Universitetsforlaget, 1977.

Schreiner, Thomas. "Israel's Failure to Attain Righteousness in Romans 9:30–10:3." *TJ* 12 (1991): 209-20.

———. "Paul's View of the Law in Romans 10:4-5." *WTJ* 55 (1993): 113-35.

Seifrid, Mark A. *Justification by Faith: The Origin and Development of a Central Pauline Theme.* NovTSup 68. New York: E. J. Brill, 1992.

Shum, Shiu-Lum. *Paul's Use of Isaiah in Romans: A Comparative Study of Paul's Letter to the Romans and the Sibylline and Qumran Sectarian Texts.* WUNT 2/156. Tübingen: J. C. B. Mohr (Paul Siebeck), 2002.

Sloyan, Gerard S. *Is Christ the End of the Law?* Philadelphia: Westminster Press, 1978.

Sprinkle, Preston M. *Law and Life: The Interpretation of Leviticus 18:5 in Early Judaism and in Paul.* WUNT 2/241. Tübingen: Mohr Siebeck, 2008.

Stuhlmacher, Peter. "'The End of the Law': On the Origin and Beginnings of Pauline Theology." In his *Reconciliation, Law, and Righteousness: Essays in Biblical Theology,* 134-54. Philadelphia: Fortress Press, 1986.

———. "Paul's Understanding of the Law in the Letter to the Romans." *SEÅ* 50 (1985): 87-104.

Suggs, M. Jack. "'The Word Is Near You': Romans 10:6-10 within the Purpose of the Letter." In *Christian History and Interpretation: Studies Presented to John Knox,* 289-312. Ed. Wiliam R. Farmer, C. F. D. Moule, and R. R. Niebuhr. Cambridge: Cambridge University Press, 1967.

Sullivan, Kathryn. "ΕΠΙΓΝΩΣΙΣ in the Epistles of St. Paul." *Studiorum Paulinorum Congressus Internationalis Catholicus, Rome, 1961,* 2:405-16. AnBib 17-18. 2 vols. Rome: Pontifical Biblical Institute Press, 1963.

Tuckett, Christopher M. *Christology and the New Testament: Jesus and His Earliest Followers.* Louisville: Westminster John Knox Press, 2001.

Vos, Johan S. "Die hermeneutische Antinomie bei Paulus (Galater 3.11-12; Römer 10.5-10)." *NTS* 38 (1992): 254-70.

Watson, Francis. *Paul and the Hermeneutics of Faith.* New York: T&T Clark, 2004.

Wengst, Klaus. *Christologische Formeln und Lieder des Urchristentums.* SNT 7. Gütersloh: Gütersloher Verlagshaus Gerd Mohn, 1972.

Westerholm, Stephen. "Paul and the Law in Romans 9–11." In *Paul and the Mosaic Law: The Third Durham-Tübingen Research Symposium on Earliest Christianity and Judaism (Durham, September, 1994),* 215-37. Ed. James D. G. Dunn. Grand Rapids: Wm. B. Eerdmans, 2001.

Williams, Sam K. "The 'Righteousness of God' in Romans." *JBL* 99 (1980): 241-90.

5.4. Has God Rejected Israel? 11:1-12

1*I ask, then, God has not rejected his people, has he? By no means! For I myself am an Israelite, a descendant of Abraham, a member of the tribe of Benjamin. 2God has not rejected his people whom he foreknew. Or do you not know what Scripture says in the case of Elijah, how he pleads with God against Israel?* 3*"Lord,* *they have killed your prophets, they have demolished your altars, and I alone am left, and they are seeking my life." 4But what does the divine reply say to him? "I have kept for myself seven thousand men who have not bowed the knee to Baal." 5So then also at the present time there is a remnant, chosen by grace. 6But if it is by grace, it is no longer from works, since grace would no longer be grace.*

7What then? Israel did not obtain that which it sought, but the elect obtained it. And the rest were hardened, 8as it is written,

> *"God gave them a spirit of stupor,*
> *eyes that do not see and ears that do not hear,*
> *to this very day."*

9And David says,

> *"Let their table become a snare and a trap,*
> *a stumbling block and a retribution for them;*
> *10let their eyes be darkened so that they do not see,*
> *and cause their backs to bend continually."*

11I say, therefore, have they not stumbled in order to fall? By no means. But by their transgression salvation has come to the Gentiles in order to make Israel jealous. 12And if their transgression means riches for the world, and their loss means riches for the Gentiles, how much more will their full inclusion mean?

Notes on the Text and Translation

11:1 The question begins with the word μή ("not"), which implies a negative answer.[96] It is often not translated (RSV, NIV, and NRSV, e.g., do not). The translation here is that of the NET, which employs the negation.

Some witnesses (including 𝔓[46], F, and G) read τὴν κληρονομίαν αὐτοῦ ("his inheritance") instead of the more widely attested τὸν λαόν αὐτοῦ ("his people"). Although that reading has gained some favor,[97] the external support for τὸν λαόν αὐτοῦ is surely stronger; moreover, the variant is likely to be an assimilation to the wording of Psalm 94:13 (LXX 93:14).[98]

11:4 The subject of the sentence in Greek is ὁ χρηματισμός ("the divine statement"),[99] a word used only here in the NT. NRSV and NET have "divine reply" (which is adopted here), while other versions (KJV, RSV, and NIV) simply use "God."

---

96. BDF 220-21 (§427, 2).
97. M. Given, "Restoring the Inheritance in Romans 11:1," 89-96.
98. B. Metzger, *TCGNT* 464.
99. BDAG 1089 (χρηματισμός).

The expression "seven thousand men" is retained in this translation, reflecting the Greek usage of ἄνδρας ("men") at this point (the LXX, similarly, has the genitive form of the same noun, ἀνδρῶν). The Greek word refers to males. The NIV and NRSV read simply "seven thousand" to allow for inclusive understanding, and the NET has "seven thousand people" for the same purpose. But in its OT context it probably does in fact refer to males.

11:6 Some ancient texts have an entire additional sentence (with variations within it) following upon the first. This is reflected in the KJV: "But if it be of works, then is it no more grace: otherwise work is no more work." The late attestation (and variations within it) casts doubt on the originality of any such sentence.[100]

11:12 The word πλήρωμα has been translated here as "full inclusion" (as in the RSV, NRSV, and ESV). It can have the meaning of "full number" or "fulfillment,"[101] and so it has also been translated as "fullness" (NIV) and "full restoration" (NET). It is used in a collective sense here (and in 11:25), so "full number" might be applicable, but a set number is not implied.[102] It stands in contrast to (but not quite as an antithesis of) the "remnant" (λεῖμμα) a few verses earlier (11:5). The rendering of the term as "full inclusion" expresses the contrast well.

General Comment

Romans 11:1-36 consists of a series of units. The three most perceptible are those in the second half of the chapter: (1) 11:17-24, the extended metaphor of the olive tree and its branches; (2) 11:25-32, the disclosure of a mystery concerning the salvation of Israel; and (3) 11:33-36, a doxological conclusion.

Structural analysis of the rest of the chapter (11:1-16) is not so clear. According to one viewpoint, 11:1-16 should be considered a unit concerning the remnant motif.[103] There is, however, a transition and decisive shift at 11:13 ("I am speaking to you Gentiles"). Within 11:1-12 Paul takes up the question whether God has rejected his people due to their disobedience, which is highlighted at the end of chapter 10. The answer to the question is a definite no, for

---

100. B. Metzger, *TCGNT* 464.

101. BDAG 829-30 (πλήρωμα, 3, a; and 4).

102. Differences among interpreters are notable: W. Sanday and A. Headlam, *Romans,* 322: "their full and completed number"; C. K. Barrett, *Romans,* 198: their "full strength"; J. Fitzmyer, *Romans,* 611: "their full number"; R. Jewett, *Romans,* 666: "their full total." Those favoring "their fullness" include C. Cranfield, *Romans,* 553; J. Dunn, *Romans,* 654-55; D. Moo, *Romans,* 689-90; B. Byrne, *Romans,* 345; and L. Keck, *Romans,* 269.

103. D. Johnson, "The Structure and Meaning of Romans 11," 21-103.

the rejection of the gospel is due to Israel's stumbling, but even that serves a divine purpose. Romans 11:1-12 has to do with the people of Israel and their disobedience, and 11:13-36 has to do with the attitude of Gentile Christians and Israel's salvation.

In light of what had just been said in the divine oracles from Isaiah at the close of the previous chapter (10:20-21), one might conclude that, according to Paul, God has rejected the people of Israel. In those texts from Isaiah, God declares that he has been found by those who have not sought him, meaning those Gentiles who have accepted the gospel. On the other hand, God has called the people of Israel disobedient and obstinate. There is good cause, then, to raise the question whether God has rejected Israel.

Paul argues that that is impossible, referring to himself, a child of the Israelite people, as an example of one who is a believer. He resorts to finding a way of speaking of the present situation by referring to the "remnant" concept in the OT.

Within this section Paul puts forth a sequence of salvation history that runs opposite of that which is traditional in Jewish sources. According to tradition, the salvation of Israel is to take place first, followed by that of the Gentiles. For it is through Abraham and his descendants that all the nations will be blessed, learn the ways of the Lord, and thus gain salvation.[104] Moreover, the salvation of Israel as a nation, making possible the salvation of the wider world, depends upon Israel's repentance and returning to the Lord (Isa 30:15; 45:22; Jer 4:14).[105] But here there is a reversal. The usual flow of the history of salvation has been diverted, at least momentarily, for the salvation of the Gentiles. The consequence, intended by God in his wisdom, will be jealousy within Israel, which will prepare her people for hearing the gospel once again. Israel's turning to God is subsequent to and a consequence of the progress of the gospel among the Gentiles.[106]

Detailed Comment

11:1 In answer to his question whether God has rejected his people, Paul replies most emphatically with his customary expression μὴ γένοιτο ("By no means!"). On that expression both here and at 11:11 (as well as at 3:4, 6, 31; 6:2, 15; 7:7, 13), see the exegesis of 3:4. Typically Paul uses the expression to object to a possible

---

104. Cf. Gen 12:3; Pss 22:27; 86:9; Isa 2:2-4; 51:4-5; Zech 8:20-23; Tob 14:6; *Pss. Sol.* 17.30-35; *T. Zeb.* 9.8; *T. Jud.* 24; *T. Benj.* 9.2.

105. *T. Benj.* 10.11; *b. Sanh.* 97b; for discussion, cf. G. Moore, *Judaism in the First Centuries of the Christian Era*, 2:350-62; and D. Allison, "The Background of Romans 11:11-15," 229-32.

106. D. Allison, "Romans 11:11-15," 23-30.

false conclusion. Then he follows up with a reason for rejecting it. That is precisely what he does here.

God has not rejected his people. The fact that Paul has accepted the gospel indicates that God has exercised his saving power among the Jewish people. Paul identifies himself as an "Israelite" ('Ισραηλίτης). While that term can have a special religious meaning in Hellenistic Judaism over against "Jew" ('Ιουδαῖος), thereby referring to the faithful of Israelite heritage,[107] the term here is applied in such a way as to imply no distinction; he uses the honorific term for the Jewish people as a whole. That has to be the case in order for the statement to work rhetorically in this context. Paul is one of those among whom God has been at work. See the commentary at 9:4, where the same term (plural, "Israelites") is applied to the Jewish people as a whole. Paul's claim of his oneness with the Jewish people is made even stronger by his being able to identify his tribal heritage in a specific way; he is of the tribe of Benjamin.

11:2-4 Pointing to himself as an example of divine favor toward the Jewish people, the case has been settled. But his own case is nothing new. Paul goes again to the OT to show a consistency, taking up the case of Elijah in 1 Kings 19:10. Within that context, the prophet Elijah has fled to a cave at Mount Horeb after killing the prophets of Baal at Mount Carmel, and the Lord asks him what he is doing there. The text in the OT continues with Elijah's reply:

> [Elijah] answered, "I have been very zealous for the LORD, the God of hosts; for the Israelites have forsaken your covenant, thrown down your altars, and killed your prophets with the sword. I alone am left, and they are seeking my life, to take it away."

Paul does not quote exactly from either the MT or the LXX. What he writes takes up clauses from Elijah's reply to the Lord in 1 Kings 19:10b, but Paul renders it in his own way: "Lord, they have killed your prophets, they have demolished your altars, and I alone am left, and they are seeking my life" (Rom 11:3).

Three of Paul's clauses correspond exactly to the wording of the LXX: (1) τοὺς προφήτας σου ἀπέκτειναν ("they have killed your prophets"); (2) τὰ θυσιαστήριά σου κατέσκαψαν ("they have demolished your altars"); and (3) καὶ ζητοῦσιν τὴν ψυχήν μου ("and they are seeking my life"). The sequence of clauses differs between the two texts, however. What appears as the second clause here (in Paul) stands first in the sequence of clauses in 1 Kings. The expression "and I alone am left" in the LXX (καὶ ὑπολέλειμμαι ἐγὼ μονώτατος) is expressed differently in Paul's text (κἀγὼ ὑπελείφθην μόνος). The expression "to take it away" at the end of 1 Kings 19:10 does not appear in Paul's text.

---

107. Horst Kuhli, "'Ισραηλίτης," *EDNT* 2:205.

The "divine reply" is based on God's word to Elijah in 1 Kings 19:11. Paul's wording of the divine reply ("I have kept for myself seven thousand men who have not bowed the knee to Baal") is a rather free rendering of the OT passage, corresponding neither to the wording of the LXX nor to that of the MT ("I will leave seven thousand in Israel, all the knees that have not bowed to Baal").

The case of Elijah as a solitary figure of faithfulness in Israel seems extreme, but it is tempered with the divine reply concerning the seven thousand. The latter constitute the "remnant," the faithful of Israel. The term is not used in the OT passage being referred to, but Paul applies it to the seven thousand in 11:5. The divine utterance spoken to Elijah can be taken as both judgment and promise. On the one hand, only seven thousand shall be preserved; the rest, who have been unfaithful, will not. On the other hand, God promises to preserve the remnant. God's purpose in history will continue through those who are faithful and who are preserved.

11:5-6 Drawing from the OT illustration, Paul is able to show that there should be no surprise in the present. There are times when only a "remnant" (λεῖμμα) of the people of Israel is faithful. The present era is one such time, as were the days of Elijah. The term λεῖμμα is found only here in the NT and not at all in the LXX, but compounds exist (κατάλειμμα, ὑπόλειμμα) that have the same sense. These and the remnant concept are discussed in the exegesis of 9:27. The remnant that Paul has in mind are those Jews who have accepted the gospel. They are, he says, "chosen by grace." They have been chosen totally by God's own favor and in accord with God's purposes. Paul would include himself in that group, conscious of his own calling as due to God's grace (Rom 1:5), and he generalizes, applying the concept to others. The claim of being a remnant chosen by grace appears to be a fresh concept with Paul, for among his predecessors there can be no remnant apart from its being established in the law.[108] But for Paul, the very fact that people have come to be believers in the gospel indicates that divine grace has been operative. As God has acted in the history of Israel by grace and mercy (9:6-18), so God acts that way in the present.

11:7 The verse opens with the interrogative, "What then?" One could expect an additional question to follow, but there is a statement instead, consisting of three assertions. Paul declares that "Israel" failed to obtain what it sought; "the elect" obtained it; and "the rest" were hardened. There was a division within "Israel" as a whole between "the elect" and "the rest." The term used for "the elect" (ἡ ἐκλογή) is used elsewhere by Paul to speak of the process or result of election (Rom 9:11; 11:5, 28; 1 Thess 1:4), but here alone it is used for a specific group of persons, a synonym for "the remnant." The term for "the rest" (οἱ λοιποί) in this verse is not otherwise used by Paul. It refers to non-believing Israel, the majority

---

108. R. Clements, "'A Remnant Chosen by Grace,'" 119.

of the Jewish people.[109] Paul has already spoken of the (divine) "hardening" of the rest in 9:18.

11:8-10 In order to amplify the theme of the "hardening" of Israel, Paul goes on to quote from scriptural passages that speak of God's actions leading to Israel's present condition. What is particularly significant about the passages is that they lend themselves to a contemporary application through the use of the phrase "to this very day" and "continually" in two of the OT passages cited.

In 11:8 Paul quotes portions of two OT passages. They include phrases from Deuteronomy 29:3 (ἔδωκεν . . . ὁ θεὸς . . . ὀφθαλμοὺς βλέπειν καὶ ὦτα ἀκούειν, "God has given eyes to see and ears to hear") and Isaiah 29:10 (πνεῦμα κατανύξεως, a "spirit of stupor"), but there are some differences from the LXX.[110] Concerning the former of these portions from the OT, the Pauline version contains some negations (using μή ["not"]) prior to the verbs of seeing and hearing, whereas the OT text has a negation (using οὐκ ["not"]) at the beginning of the sentence (so "the Lord has not given"). The word κατάνυξις ("stupor" or "stupefaction")[111] is found only here in the NT, drawn from the LXX text being quoted (Isa 29:10), and then only one other time in the LXX (Ps 59:5 [MT 60:5; NRSV 60:3]). The quotation from Deuteronomy concludes with the phrase ἕως τῆς ἡμέρας ταύτης ("until this day"); Paul's text reads ἕως τῆς σήμερον ἡμέρας (using σήμερον, "today"; the full phrase can then be translated "until today" or "to this very day").[112]

What Paul says in 11:9-10 includes phrases from Psalm 69:22-23 (LXX 68:23-24). The first of the verses (11:9) differs somewhat from the LXX (Ps 68:23), but the wording of the second (11:10) is identical to it (Ps 68:24). The latter ends with the words: καὶ τὸν νῶτον αὐτῶν διὰ παντὸς σύγκαμψον ("and cause their backs to bend continually"). By including this passage, Paul is able to have the psalm speak to the present (as in "to this very day" in the previous verse), in which the people of Israel are said to be continually bent over. The imagery is puzzling, but could mean, for Paul, that the people of Israel, who are unable to see because of the imposed darkness (11:10a, "let their eyes be darkened so that they do not see"), will continue to grope in the dark.[113]

11:11 In spite of the stumbling of the Jewish people, Paul says, that has not resulted in a permanent condition. Using the familiar image of a person walk-

---

109. The term can also have an opposite meaning, as at Rev 2:24, where it means "the remainder" or "those who are left," equivalent to "the remnant."

110. The theme of having eyes and ears but not perceiving and hearing appears also at Isa 6:9-10; 29:9-10; 42:18-20; 43:8; 44:18; Jer 5:21; Ezek 12:2. On the theme in the letters of Paul specifically, cf. C. Evans, *To See and Not Perceive*, 81-89.

111. So BDAG 523 (κατάνυξις).

112. BDAG 921 (σήμερον).

113. Cf. C. Cranfield, *Romans*, 552; B. Byrne, *Romans*, 336.

ing along who begins to stumble but does not quite fall to the ground, Paul declares that Israel's stumbling (rejecting the gospel) is not the end of the matter. Nor can Gentile Christians thereby think even for a moment that the end of Israel has come.[114] By their stumbling, which is a "transgression" (παράπτωμα) to be sure, salvation comes now to the Gentiles. But that will have an effect on the people of Israel in the long run. It will make them jealous. Jealousy implies envy, and the implication is that the people of Israel will then seek to have that which the Gentiles have received. The expression εἰς τὸ παραζηλῶσαι αὐτούς (εἰς + the articular infinitive) denotes purpose.[115] Since it is God's purpose that is at stake (cf. 10:19), the clause can be rendered: "in order to make Israel jealous." That divine intent can be missed in the more casual rendition of the RSV and NRSV ("so as to make Israel jealous"), since that can be taken to mean a result instead of a purpose.

11:12 The expression "how much more" (πόσῳ μᾶλλον), like its twin expression (πολλῷ μᾶλλον), is used in rabbinic argumentation.[116] It is the *qal waḥomer* ("from minor to major" or vice versa) form of argumentation. For details, see the exegesis of 5:7. It is used effectively in this verse to make a contrast between a worst case and best case scenario. The transgression of Israel brought riches for the world. How much better, then, their "full inclusion"! The verse anticipates what Paul will say in 11:26 about the salvation of all Israel.[117] But from a rhetorical standpoint, Paul is not there yet. What he is saying is that the world (ὁ κόσμος) has benefited greatly from Israel's disobedience, since the gospel has gone out to the Gentiles. How much more, then, would the world benefit if Israel were to become obedient! That means that here "their full inclusion" (τὸ πλήρωμα αὐτῶν) can mean the full participation of the Jewish people in the new humanity as a consequence of hearing the gospel and accepting it.[118] "Paul looks beyond the advantages conferred on the Gentiles by the unbelief of Israel to the far greater eschatological bliss which Israel's return will inaugurate."[119] By the time that Paul arrives at 11:25, however, that is not what he expects to happen. There he speaks of the "hardening"

---

114. J. Munck, *Christ and Israel*, 119.

115. BDF 207 (§402, 2).

116. The former expression is used by Paul also at Rom 11:24 and Phlm 16; the latter at Rom 5:9, 10, 15, 17; 1 Cor 12:22; 2 Cor 3:9, 11; Phil 1:23; 2:12.

117. Similarly (with some variations), C. K. Barrett, *Romans*, 198-99; E. Käsemann, *Romans*, 325; C. Cranfield, *Romans*, 558; J. Dunn, *Romans*, 655; J. Fitzmyer, *Romans*, 611; P. Stuhlmacher, *Romans*, 167. T. Donaldson, "'Riches for the Gentiles' (Rom 11:12)," 93, maintains that the consequences of the "much more" in 11:12 are made explicit in 11:15, the resurrection and parousia.

118. T. Donaldson, "'Riches for the Gentiles' (Rom 11:12)," 94: Paul speaks not of the displacement of Israel, but of opening up some time for its inclusion.

119. C. K. Barrett, *Romans*, 198-99.

of Israel prior to his going on to affirm its salvation, in spite of that hardening, by God's own mercy (11:26-32).

There is an implicit message in what Paul says in 11:11-12, which has been summed up succinctly by Augustine: "the Gentiles ought to take heed all the more lest, when they grow proud, they likewise fall."[120]

BIBLIOGRAPHY

Allison, Dale C., Jr. "The Background of Romans 11:11-15 in Apocalyptic and Rabbinic Literature." *StudBT* 10 (1980): 229-34.

———. "Romans 11:11-15: A Suggestion." *PRS* 12 (1985): 23-30.

Campbell, William S. "Salvation for the Jews and Gentiles: Krister Stendahl and Paul's Letter to the Romans." *StudBT* 3 (1980): 65-72.

Clements, Ronald E. "'A Remnant Chosen by Grace' (Romans 11:5): The Old Testament Background and Origin of the Remnant Concept." In *Pauline Studies: Essays Presented to Professor F. F. Bruce on His 70th Birthday*, 106-21. Ed. Donald A. Hagner and Murray J. Harris. Grand Rapids: Wm. B. Eerdmans, 1980.

Cranfield, C. E. B. "The Significance of διὰ παντός in Romans 11.10." In *Studia Evangelica II*, 546-50. Ed. Frank L. Cross. Berlin: Akademie Verlag, 1964; reprinted in his *The Bible and Christian Life: A Collection of Essays*, 197-202. Edinburgh: T&T Clark, 1985.

Donaldson, Terence L. "'Riches for the Gentiles' (Rom 11:12): Israel's Rejection and Paul's Gentile Mission." *JBL* 112 (1993): 81-98.

Evans, Craig A. *To See and Not Perceive: Isaiah 6.9-10 in Early Jewish and Christian Interpretation*. JSOTSup 64. Sheffield: JSOT Press, 1989.

Given, Mark D. "Restoring the Inheritance in Romans 11:1." *JBL* 118 (1999): 89-96.

Hanson, Anthony T. "Christ and the First Fruits, Christ the Tree." In his *Studies in Paul's Technique and Theology*, 104-25. London: SPCK, 1974.

———. "The Oracle in Romans 11:4." *NTS* 19 (1973): 300-302.

Harding, Mark. "The Salvation of Israel and the Logic of Romans 11:11-36." *AusBR* 46 (1998): 55-69.

Hasel, Gerhard F. *The Remnant: The History and Theology of the Remnant Idea from Genesis to Isaiah*. AUSS 5. 2d ed. Berrien Springs: Andrews University Press, 1974.

———. "Remnant." *IDBSup* 735-36.

Jegher-Bucher, Verena. "Erwählung und Verwerfung im Römerbrief? Eine Untersuchung von Röm 11,11-15." *TZ* 47 (1991): 326-36.

Johnson, Dan G. "The Structure and Meaning of Romans 11." *CBQ* 46 (1984): 91-103.

Merkle, Ben L. "Romans 11 and the Future of Ethnic Israel." *JETS* 43 (2000): 709-21.

Meyer, Lester V. "Remnant." *ABD* 5:669-71.

Moore, George F. *Judaism in the First Centuries of the Christian Era: The Age of the Tannaim*. 3 vols. Cambridge: Harvard University Press, 1927-30.

---

120. Augustine, *Propositions from the Epistle to the Romans* 70.3. Quoted from *Augustine on Romans: Propositions from the Epistle to the Romans; Unfinished Commentary on the Epistle to the Romans*, ed. Paula Fredriksen Landes, SBL.TT 23 (Chico: Scholars Press, 1982), 41.

Munck, Johannes. *Christ and Israel: An Interpretation of Romans 9–11*. Philadelphia: Fortress Press, 1967.

Mussner, Franz. "Fehl- und Falschüberzetungen von Röm 11 in der Einheitsübersetzung." *TQ* 170 (1990): 137-39.

Rese, Martin. "Die Rettung der Juden nach Römer 11." In *L'Apôtre Paul: Personnalité, style et conception du ministère*, 422-30. BETL 73. Ed. Albert Vanhoye. Louvain: Leuven University Press, 1986.

Schuele, Andreas K. "Harden the Heart," *NIDB* 2:735-36.

Stanley, Christopher D. "The Significance of Romans 11:3-4 for the Textual History of the LXX Book of Kingdoms." *JBL* 112 (1993): 43-54.

5.5. How Should Gentiles Think in the Present Situation? 11:13-24

13*I am speaking to you Gentiles. To the extent that I am an apostle to the Gentiles, I glorify my ministry,* 14*if somehow I might make my own people jealous and save some of them.* 15*For if their rejection is reconciliation of the world, what will their acceptance be but life from the dead?* 16*And if the first fruits of dough are holy, so is the whole loaf; and if the root is holy, the branches are too.*

17*But if some of the branches were broken off and you, a wild olive shoot, were grafted in their place and become a participant in the richness of the root of the olive tree,* 18*do not boast over the branches. And if you do boast, consider that you do not support the root, but the root supports you.* 19*Then you will say, "Branches were broken off in order that I might be grafted in."* 20*Well enough. They were broken off on the basis of unbelief, but you stand on the basis of faith. Do not be haughty, but be reverent.* 21*For if God did not spare the natural branches, neither will he spare you.* 22*Notice, then, the kindness and the severity of God: severity toward those who have fallen, but God's kindness toward you, provided you continue in his kindness; otherwise you will be cut off too.* 23*And even the others, if they do not persist in unbelief, will be grafted in, for God is able to graft them in again.* 24*For if you were cut from an olive tree that is wild by nature and grafted, contrary to nature, into a cultivated olive tree, how much more will these natural branches be grafted into their own olive tree.*

Notes on the Text and Translation

11:13 The expression ἐφ' ὅσον is rendered here as "to the extent that,"[121] rather than the more exclusive "inasmuch as" (RSV, NIV, and NRSV). Paul considers

---

121. BDAG 366 (ἐπί, 13): "to the degree that, in so far as."

himself an apostle to the Gentiles, to be sure, but does not exclude some opportunities to evangelize Jews (cf. 1 Cor. 9:20-23).

The Greek phrase (ἐθνῶν ἀπόστολος, Rom 11:13) has been rendered both as "an apostle to the Gentiles" (NRSV and NET) and "the apostle to the Gentiles" (KJV and NIV). The former rendering is to be preferred. The lack of a definite article in Greek is somewhat significant, but the context is also. Paul makes a concession, not a statement concerning his office. He says that, although he is an apostle of the Gentiles, he hopes to make some Jews jealous and thus save them. He has not written Israel off. He hopes for the salvation of some, and his own ministry is evidence that he had sought to win some (1 Cor 9:20).[122] Unfortunately, the NEB has "a missionary to the Gentiles." The term "missionary" hardly does justice to ἀπόστολος.

11:14 Following the NIV and NRSV, "my own people" is used for the sense of Paul's expression, although the Greek text reads μου τὴν σάρκα ("my flesh").

11:16 The words "of dough" have been added to the phrase for the sake of clarity ("the first fruits of dough").[123]

11:21 Some major texts (including 𝔓⁴⁶ and D) read μή πως ("lest somehow" or "perhaps"), which tends to soften the verse to read: "perhaps he will not spare you" (NRSV). The words are missing in other major witnesses (including ℵ, A, and B) and are set in brackets in the Nestle-Aland Greek text (27th edition), indicating that the words are of doubtful authenticity. They are not included in the Westcott-Hort edition and the 25th edition of the Nestle-Aland text. Although a decision is difficult,[124] the words are not translated here. Their presence or absence does not materially affect the meaning of the verse.

11:23 NRSV has "And even those of Israel" at the beginning of the verse. Although that is what is meant, the text reads simply, "and even those" (κἀκεῖνοι δέ).

General Comment

The unit consists of a direct address to the readers of the letter (11:13) followed by hortatory language (11:18, 20-22, 24). At the outset Paul writes concerning

---

122. On the syntax of the verse, cf. BDF 250 (§474, 4). The reading "an apostle" is favored by W. Sanday and A. Headlam, *Romans*, 324; C. K. Barrett, *Romans*, 199; C. Cranfield, *Romans*, 553; B. Byrne, *Romans*, 345; J. Dunn, *Romans*, 655-56; and R. Jewett, *Romans*, 678-79. D. Moo, *Romans*, 691 (n. 40), favors the same but suggests caution, since the term "may be something of a title." C. H. Dodd, *Romans*, 177, J. Munck, *Christ and Israel*, 122, and L. Morris, *Romans*, 409, favor "the apostle." J. Fitzmyer, *Romans*, 612, considers "the apostle of the Gentiles" to be a common epithet concerning Paul.

123. BDAG 98 (ἀπαρχή, 1): "if the first fruits (of dough) are holy, so is the whole lump."

124. B. Metzger, *TCGNT* 464-65.

his ministry and his hopes for Israel (11:13-16). That is followed by his use of an extended metaphor concerning the olive tree and its branches (11:17-24). The two units are related to one another through Paul's use of the metaphor of branches in 11:16 and then again in 11:17.

Paul addresses the Gentile members of the Roman community in particular, although that is not new. He has been doing that all along. Nowhere in these three chapters (9–11) has he addressed Jewish members directly. By mentioning the Gentiles as those whom he is addressing, however, he makes them reflect particularly on what he is about to say about the Jewish people. The people he has in mind are not Jewish Christians but those Jews who have not accepted the gospel.

Paul's most dramatic statement in the entire section is that Gentiles should stand in awe (11:20), for it is precisely Israel's rejection of the gospel that has allowed the salvation of Gentiles. Standing in awe is most appropriate, for one must consider a possible event that would be of massive proportions and consequences. That is that at any time Israel might accept the gospel and be grafted back into the people of God. That would be natural (11:24), as an analogy from horticulture demonstrates. Branches cut from a cultivated olive tree (but not discarded!) can be grafted back into that tree. Likewise, Jews who do not believe now, but who might do so in the future, could be grafted back into the one people of God (11:23). The corollary is that Gentiles, like branches from a wild olive tree, could easily be disposed of. "Notice, then, the kindness and the severity of God: severity toward those who have fallen, but God's kindness toward you, provided you continue in his kindness; otherwise you will be cut off too" (11:22).

Detailed Comment

11:13-14 This is the first and only time that Paul speaks in the letter of himself specifically as "an apostle to the Gentiles." But it is not the only time that he designates himself as such. In his letter to the Galatians, written earlier,[125] he speaks of his commission to proclaim Christ among the Gentiles (1:16) and of his being entrusted with the gospel for them (2:7-9). And in Romans itself Paul speaks of his aim to evangelize Gentiles (1:13; 15:18). Whatever Paul experienced in the Christophany of which he speaks (1 Cor 9:1; 15:8; Gal 1:16), he was convinced that he was commissioned as an apostle to the Gentiles, and that his

---

125. Galatians is generally thought to have been written about A.D. 50 or shortly thereafter. Cf. H. Betz, *Galatians,* 12: "the years between 50 and 55"; J. L. Martyn, *Galatians,* 20 (n. 20): "about A.D. 50."

apostleship among them was to bring about their ingathering into the one new humanity at the dawning of the messianic era, as anticipated in the Scriptures of Israel.[126]

Nevertheless, Paul has continuing sorrow for his own people and their non-acceptance of the gospel. By emphasizing (or glorifying) his own ministry to the Gentiles, and having success in reaching them, he intends to make the Jews jealous. Paul does not explain why they would become jealous. But the sheer fact that they would see that the Gentiles have joy in the fellowship of the gospel would apparently, to Paul, cause it. In any case, Paul thinks that he would be able to "save some" through their acceptance of the gospel.

11:15 The expression "their rejection" (ἡ ἀποβολὴ αὐτῶν) can have either of two meanings: (1) their rejection by God (objective genitive in Greek) or (2) their rejection of the gospel (subjective genitive). The former is favored by most commentators, meaning a temporary rejection until the incoming of the Gentiles has run its course.[127] A minority, however, conclude that a subjective genitive is meant.[128] Likewise, the expression "their acceptance" (ἡ πρόσλημψις, a term used only here in the LXX and NT) can have either of two meanings: (1) their acceptance by God or (2) their acceptance of the gospel.

In working toward a solution, one needs to take three matters into consideration. First, back in 11:1-2 Paul has declared that God has not rejected Israel, so the very idea of God's rejecting Israel in 11:15 does not seem to work. Second, there is a parallel between this verse and what is said in 11:11-12. In those verses Paul declares concerning the Jewish people that "their transgression" and "their loss" (subjective genitives in both cases) have resulted in the extension of the gospel to the Gentiles. Finally, the idea of Israel's rejection of the gospel and possible future acceptance of it coincides well with the rest of what is being said in chapters 9 through 11 (cf. 10:16-21; 11:23). These factors favor understanding the words ἡ ἀποβολὴ αὐτῶν to mean "their rejection" of the gospel.

Israel's rejection of the gospel has made the "reconciliation of the world" possible. That done, Israel's acceptance of the gospel would mean new life, indeed, a transformation from death to life. It is not likely that by the expression

---

126. For a discussion, see A. Hultgren, "The Scriptural Foundations for Paul's Mission to the Gentiles," 21-44.

127. Cf. BDAG 108 (ἀποβολή, 1): "the (temporary) rejection of Israelites by God"; W. Sanday and A. Headlam, *Romans*, 325; J. Munck, *Christ and Israel*, 126; A. Nygren, *Romans*, 397; N. Dahl, "The Future of Israel," 150; U. Wilckens, *Römer*, 2:245; C. Cranfield, *Romans*, 562; J. Dunn, *Romans*, 657; P. Stuhlmacher, *Romans*, 167; B. Byrne, *Romans*, 345; D. Moo, *Romans*, 693.

128. J. Fitzmyer, *Romans*, 612-13; K. Haacker, *Römer*, 227; E. Lohse, *Römer*, 312-13; R. Jewett, *Romans*, 680-81.

"life from the dead" that Paul is referring to the general resurrection,[129] for that seems out of place here. He uses the expression as a metaphor, and as a metaphor in relationship to the Jewish people it must have a more limited meaning. In that context it most likely signifies their salvation. But that in itself, a miraculous event, would be an eschatological event, ushering in the new age of the world's redemption.[130]

11:16 The new life gained through Israel's "yes" to the gospel would have cosmic effects. Drawing upon cultic imagery, Paul speaks of "first fruits" (ἀπαρχή) as holy, referring here to a dough offering (φύραμα) to the Lord (Lev 23:20; Num 15:20-21; Neh 10:39; Ezek 44:30), consisting of dough made into loaves. Specifically, the origin of the imagery can be traced to Numbers 15:20: "From your first batch (ἀπαρχή) of dough (φύραμα) you shall present a loaf as an offering." Metaphorically, the term applies within the OT to Israel, the first fruits of Yahweh's harvest: "Israel was holy (ἅγιος) to the Lord, the first fruits of his harvest" (ἀρχὴ γενημάτων)" (Jer 2:3).[131]

The use of the metaphor presupposes the view in ancient Israel that the holiness of the first fruits assures that the entire loaf is holy.[132] Interpreters differ widely on the meaning of "first fruits," "loaf," "root," and "branches" in this verse. One of the most common interpretations is to take "first fruits" and "loaf" to represent the remnant and unbelieving Israel, respectively; and to take the "root" and the "branches" as the patriarchs and unbelieving Israel.[133] But within this context, where Paul is speaking about the acceptance of the gospel by the Jewish people and the consequent eschatological effects that would entail, those interpretations seem inadequate. A more satisfactory interpretation is that Paul uses the first of the two metaphors here to claim that, just as the holiness of the first fruits of dough assures that the entire loaf is holy, so a believing Israel would sanctify the entire world, including not only themselves but believing Gentiles as well, for Israel's accepting the gospel would bring about the new age and therewith the new humanity. The new humanity of Jews and Gentiles together depends ultimately on the election and faithfulness of the people of Israel. And to

---

129. Contra W. Sanday and A. Headlam, *Romans*, 325-26; C. K. Barrett, *Romans*, 199-200; E. Käsemann, *Romans*, 307; C. Cranfield, *Romans*, 563; J. Dunn, *Romans*, 658; P. Stuhlmacher, *Romans*, 167; B. Byrne, *Romans*, 346; R. Jewett, *Romans*, 681.

130. J. Murray, *Romans*, 2:82-84; J. Fitzmyer, *Romans*, 613; E. Löhse, *Römer*, 313.

131. Richard O. Rigsby, "First Fruits," *ABD* 2:796-97.

132. W. Eichrodt, *Theology of the Old Testament*, 1:152; G. von Rad, *Old Testament Theology*, 1:254.

133. Various interpretations of the metaphors (of which there are several) are surveyed by C. Cranfield, *Romans*, 564, and J. Fitzmyer, *Romans*, 614. According to M. Hartung, "Die kultische bzw. agrartechnisch-biologische Logik," 129-30, the leaven/loaf imagery simply serves as an analogy for the root/branches metaphor: as leaven sanctifies the whole, so the root (Abraham) sanctifies the branches (the Jewish people).

extend the point further, Paul declares that, "if the root is holy, the branches are too." The figure of Israel as a root is familiar from the OT, especially where its writers speak of God's planting Israel as a vine with roots in the land. The psalmist declares: "You cleared the ground for [the vine brought out of Egypt]; it took deep root and filled the land" (Ps 80:9 [LXX 79:10]; cf. Isa 27:6; 2 Kgs 19:30).[134] Israel's acceptance of the gospel (and so becoming holy) would make the entire world of believing Jews and Gentiles holy, extending from the root, Israel itself, into all the branches that make up the world in the new era to come.

11:17-18 That the imagery of the first fruits of the dough and that of the root and its branches have universal effects is developed by the use of another figure of speech, the allegory of the olive tree (11:17-24), which has its basis in the metaphor of the olive tree as a representation of Israel (Jer 11:16-19).[135] Paul speaks here of the grafting of a wild olive shoot (ἀγριέλαιος) into a cultivated olive tree[136] from which the branches have been removed. Although it seems unlikely that a horticulturalist would normally replace natural branches with wild ones, instances exist for the practice in ancient literature as a means to rejuvenate an older tree.[137] It is possible that Paul asserts, then, that the grafting in of the Gentiles can rejuvenate Israel (another expression of the "jealousy" motif).[138] In any case, the allegory serves Paul well in other ways that are more important.

In order for the grafting to take place, Paul says, certain "branches" were broken off, referring to the vast majority of Israel's populace outside of the faithful remnant, i.e., those who have not accepted the gospel. They have been broken off from the tree, and the Gentile believers (the "wild olive shoot") have been grafted in. The contrast between the "cultivated" tree (11:24) and the "wild olive shoot" (11:17, 24) shows that Paul is ever mindful of his Jewish heritage as a matter of ethnic and cultural pride. In any case, the Gentiles have been grafted in and now enjoy the richness of all that comes from the root. The Gentiles have no reason to boast, therefore, for it is the root — the Israelite/Jewish people's spiritual heritage — that provides life to the branches.[139]

---

134. For references to the "planting" of Israel, cf. Ps 92:13; Jer 11:17; *Pss. Sol.* 14.3-4; *1 Enoch* 84.6.

135. Instances of rabbinic use of the metaphor for Israel are cited by A. T. Hanson, *Studies in Paul's Technique and Theology,* 121-24.

136. The term ἀγριέλαιος exists both as an adjective and a noun; see BDF 66 (§120, 3); BDAG 15 (ἀγριέλαιος). Although the KJV renders it as an (entire) "wild olive tree," other versions (RSV, NIV, NRSV, ESV, NET) are probably correct to render it as a "wild olive shoot." A "shoot" in this context would mean, as in the *OED* 15:306 (2.b): a "young branch which shoots out from the main stock of a tree."

137. For references and discussion, cf. J. Munck, *Christ and Israel,* 128-30.

138. A. Baxter and J. Zeisler, "Paul and Arboriculture," 25-32.

139. W. D. Davies, "Paul and the Gentiles," 158-63; C. Johnson Hodge, "Olive Trees and Ethnicities," 85.

It should be emphasized that breaking off the natural branches and replacing them with wild shoots is a fresh metaphor and does not imply the rejection of Israel and replacement by Gentile Christians. A metaphor, and particularly an allegory, is limited in terms of its referentiality. It has been established that God has not rejected Israel (11:1-2), and the language of "rejection" in 11:15 does not undermine that (see the exegesis there). By using the allegory of the olive tree and its branches, Paul does not point to God's rejection of Israel but rather God's acceptance of Gentiles by grace alone in the present era.

11:19-20 Any tendency toward Gentile pride has to be curbed. While it is true that, for the sake of the salvation of the whole world, God has bypassed Israel for the time being so that the gospel can reach the Gentiles, that does not mean total and permanent rejection of Israel. Gentiles must acknowledge that for them all is by grace. There is no basis for being haughty. It is only by Israel's no to the gospel that it has come to the Gentiles. Gentile believers stand within the circle of the new humanity only through faith, not through rights based on natural inheritance.

11:21-22 One should not conclude that God's favor rests now exclusively with the believing Gentiles of the world and that they can take their eternal security for granted. No, Paul asserts, God can lop those off who have been grafted into the tree, and that would be easier than cutting off the natural branches. Gentile believers should recognize that they have received divine favor purely from the "kindness" or "goodness" (χρηστότης) of God extended to them. There are no grounds for pride on their part, nor can any one of them make claims upon God's justice. God has been more than fair.

11:23-24 Paul still holds out hope at this point that the people of Israel will put aside their unbelief and believe the gospel concerning God's redemptive work in Christ. Then they will be counted among the faithful. Though they are like branches that have been cast off temporarily, they can be picked up and grafted back into the tree. Using the argument "from the greater to the lesser" (the familiar rabbinic *qal waḥomer* form of argumentation),[140] Paul establishes that if God has been able to call the Gentiles to faith, grafting them into the tree, he can surely bring the Jewish people to faith, grafting them into their own tree. It can hardly be said that Paul expects the latter to take place within the foreseeable future, but what he says works rhetorically to emphasize that Gentiles have no reason for boasting or assuming that they have any superiority over unbelieving Jews.

---

140. For details, see the exegesis of Rom 5:7. For other instances of the use of the expression by Paul, cf. Rom 5:7, 9, 10, 15, 17; 11:24; 1 Cor 12:22; 2 Cor 3:9, 11; Phil 1:23; 2:12; Phlm 16.

Bibliography

Baker, Murray. "Paul and the Salvation of Israel: Paul's Ministry, the Motif of Jealousy, and Israel's Yes." *CBQ* 67 (2005): 469-84.

Baxter, A. G., and John A. Ziesler. "Paul and Arboriculture: Romans 11:17-24." *JSNT* (1985): 25-32.

Betz, Hans D. *Galatians*. Hermeneia. Philadelphia: Fortress Press, 1979.

Bourke, Myles M. *A Study of the Metaphor of the Olive Tree in Romans XI*. SST 2/3. Washington, D.C.: Catholic University of America, 1947.

Dahl, Nils A. "The Future of Israel." In his *Studies in Paul: Theology for the Early Christian Mission*, 137-58. Minneapolis: Augsburg Publishing House, 1977.

Davies, W. D. "Paul and the Gentiles: A Suggestion concerning Romans 11:13-24." In his *Jewish and Pauline Studies*, 153-63. Philadelphia: Fortress Press, 1984.

Eichrodt, Walther. *Theology of the Old Testament*. 2 vols. Philadelphia: Westminster Press, 1961-67.

Hanson, Anthony T. *Studies in Paul's Technique and Theology*. London: S.P.C.K., 1974.

Hartung, Matthias G. "Die kultische bzw. agrartechnisch-biologische Logik der Gleichnisse von der Teighebe und vom Ölbaum in Röm 11.16-24 und die sich daraus ergebenden theologischen Konsequenzen." *NTS* 45 (1999): 127-40.

Havemann, J. C. T. "Cultivated Olive — Wild Olive: The Olive Tree Metaphor in Romans 11:16-24." *Neot* 31 (1997): 87-106.

Hodge, Caroline Johnson. "Apostle to the Gentiles: Constructions of Paul's Identity." *BibInt* 13 (2005): 270-88.

Hughes, Philip E. "The Olive Tree of Romans XI." *EvQ* 20 (1948): 22-45.

Hultgren, Arland J. "The Scriptural Foundations for Paul's Mission to the Gentiles." In *Paul and His Theology*, 21-44. Ed. Stanley E. Porter. PAST 3. Boston: E. J. Brill, 2006.

Johnson, Dan G. "The Structure and Meaning of Romans 11." *CBQ* 46 (1984): 91-103.

—————. "Olive Trees and Ethnicities: Judeans and Gentiles in Rom. 11.17–24." In *Christians as a Religious Minority in a Multicultural City: Modes of Interaction and Identity Formation in Early Imperial Rome*, 77-89. Ed. Jürgen Zangenberg and Michael Labahn. JSNTSup 243. London: T&T Clark, 2004.

Maartens, Pieter J. "A Criticial Dialogue of Structure and Reader in Romans 11:16-24." *HervTS* 53 (1997): 1030-51.

—————. "Inference and Relevance in Paul's Allegory of the Wild Olive Tree." *HervTS* 53 (1997): 1000-29.

Martyn, J. Louis. *Galatians*. AB 33A. New York: Doubleday, 1997.

Mussner, Franz. "'Wenn sie nicht im Unglauben verharren.' Bemerkungen zu Röm 11,23." *TTZ* 111 (2002): 62-67.

Neubrand, Maria, and Johannes Seidel. "'Eingepfropft in den edlen Ölbaum' (Röm 11,24): Der Ölbaum Ist *nicht* Israel." *BN* 105 (2000): 61-76.

Rad, Gerhard von. *Old Testament Theology*. 2 vols. New York: Harper & Row, 1962-65.

Rengstorf, Karl H. "Das Ölbaum-Gleichnis in Röm 11,16ff: Versuch einer weiterführenden Deutung." In *Donum Gentilicium: New Testament Studies in Honour of David Daube*, 127-64. Ed. Ernst Bammel et al. Oxford: Clarendon Press, 1978.

Riggans, Walter. "Romans 11:17-21." *ExpTim* 98 (1986-87): 205-6.
Shae, Gam S. "Translating 'But Life from the Dead' in Romans 11.15." *BT* 50 (1999): 227-35.
Sneen, Donald. "The Root, the Remnant, and the Branches." *WW* 6 (1986): 398-409.
Spicq, Ceslaus. "ΑΠΑΡΧΗ: Note de lexicographie néo-testamentaire." In *The New Testament Age: Essays in Honor of Bo Reicke*, 2:493-502. Ed. William C. Weinrich. 2 vols. Macon: Mercer University Press, 1984.
Wischmeyer, Oda. "ΦΥΣΙΣ und ΚΤΙΣΙΣ bei Paulus." *ZTK* 93 (1996): 352-75.

5.6. Consider a Mystery, 11:25-32

25For I do not want you to be ignorant, brothers and sisters, concerning this mystery — lest you be wise in your own eyes — that to some extent a hardening has befallen Israel until that time when the fullness of the Gentiles has come in. 26And so all Israel will be saved, as it is written:

"The Deliverer will come out of Zion; he will remove ungodliness from Jacob."
27"And this is my covenant with them, when I take away their sins."

28In regard to the gospel, they are enemies for your sake, but in regard to election, they are beloved for the sake of the patriarchs. 29For the gifts and the call of God are irrevocable. 30For just as you were at one time disobedient to God but have now received mercy because of their disobedience, 31so they have now been disobedient in order that, by the mercy shown to you, they, too, may receive mercy. 32For God has consigned all people to disobedience, in order that he may have mercy upon all.

Notes on the Text and Translation

11:25 The expression "lest you be wise in your own eyes" is admittedly a rather free translation of [παρ'] ἑαυτοῖς φρόνιμοι. The use of the dative after the preposition in this case can signify "in the sight or judgment of someone."[141] Paul borders on sarcasm here, indicating that his readers should not consider themselves wiser than they are. So the NRSV has: "that you may not claim to be wiser than you are," and the NIV has: "that you may not be conceited."

The Greek expression ἀπὸ μέρους has the meaning "in part" or "partially."[142] Here it modifies the process of "hardening" rather than "Israel." See the comments below.

141. BDAG 757 (παρά, B, 2).
142. BDAG 633 (μέρος, 1, c), rendering the phrase "a partial hardening" for this verse.

The translation "until that time when" is based on the Greek expression ἄχρι οὗ, which is used for the longer phrase ἄχρι τοῦ χρόνου οὗ ("until the time of which").[143]

On "brothers and sisters," see the comments on 1:13.

11:26 The expression "and so" (as in KJV, RSV, NIV, NRSV, NET) is an appropriate translation of the Greek expression καὶ οὕτως, referring to what follows (cf. Rom 5:12; 1 Cor 7:17, 36; 11:28; 14:25; 15:4; Gal 6:2; 1 Thess 4:17). It is not simply a temporal expression,[144] which could be expressed better by καὶ τότε ("and then"), an expression that Paul uses elsewhere (1 Cor 4:5; Gal 6:4). There may well be a temporal aspect in this particular context, but it refers more to the manner, not the timing, of Israel's salvation, which is explained in what follows.[145]

11:28 Various texts have "enemies of God" (RSV, NRSV, ESV), but the phrase "of God" is not in the Greek text (so NIV and NET).

The Greek term πατέρας has been translated "fathers" (KJV, ASV), "forefathers" (RSV), and — for the sake of inclusivity — "ancestors" (NRSV). But the term has both a historical and theological specificity in this place, referring to the "patriarchs" (as in NIV).

11:31b Some witnesses (ℵ, B, D, et al.) include νῦν ("now") in the purpose clause of the sentence (thus reading: ἵνα καὶ αὐτοὶ νῦν ἐλεηθῶσιν, "in order that they, too, may now receive mercy"). Others (𝔓46, A, the Majority Text, Old Latin, Vulgate, et al.) do not include the word (and so reading: ἵνα καὶ αὐτοὶ ἐλεηθῶσιν, "in order that they, too, may receive mercy"). In two minuscules (33 and 365) the word ὕστερον ("finally," "later") appears where νῦν appears in ℵ and B. It was probably introduced to replace νῦν, referring to mercy at the last judgment. This reading is not to be regarded as the earliest.

The word νῦν is present in the Westcott-Hort text, but in the 27th edition of the Nestle-Aland text it is placed in brackets (meaning that its authenticity is doubtful).[146] A decision is difficult here, but the word "now" is left out of the translation here for the following reasons. (1) While there are important textual witnesses for both readings (including ℵ and B for its inclusion), the fact that Alexandrian (𝔓46), Western (Old Latin, Vulgate), and Byzantine witnesses

---

143. BDAG 160 (ἄχρι, 1, b, a).

144. Contra O. Michel, *Römer,* 280-81; C. K. Barrett, *Romans,* 206; E. Käsemann, *Romans,* 313; P. van der Horst, "'Only Then Will All Israel Be Saved,'" 521-25; cf. NEB ("when that has happened") and REB ("once that has happened").

145. Cf. W. Sanday and A. Headlam, *Romans,* 335; N. Dahl, "The Future of Israel," 152; H. Hübner, *Gottes Ich und Israel,* 118; U. Wilckens, *Römer,* 2:255; C. Cranfield, *Romans,* 574; J. Dunn, *Romans,* 681; D. Moo, *Romans,* 720; H. Thyen, "Das Mysterium Israel," 310.

146. The word is omitted in *The Greek New Testament,* ed. R. V. G. Tasker (Oxford: Oxford University Press, 1964), 251, the textual basis for the NEB of 1961.

(which normally add rather than omit words) agree in not including νῦν is of major importance on external grounds. (2) The word νῦν could well have been added here to provide a parallel to 11:31a. (3) In a series of clauses speaking of time, and using various adverbial expressions for it (11:25, 30a, 30b, and 31a), it is more likely that an additional temporal adverb was added to this particular clause (filling out a series) than that it was dropped either by "eye-skip" or for a theological purpose (contrast the substitution of the word ὕστερον for νῦν, however). A temporal adverb was not necessary for the clause at the moment of composition. (4) Paul uses an aorist subjunctive with a future meaning in this verse to speak of the mercy that Israel will receive.[147]

The presence or absence of the word does not actually change the meaning. In either case, the Jewish people receive the mercy of God — either now with a view toward the final judgment or simply at the final judgment. The English term "now" appears in some modern versions (ASV, NIV, NRSV, ESV, NET) but not in others (KJV, NEB, NAB, RSV). While a majority of interpreters seem to favor the inclusion of the term,[148] others conclude that a decision is not possible,[149] and still others conclude that the word should be omitted.[150]

11:31b Within the clause ἠπείθησαν τῷ ὑμετέρῳ ἐλέει a dative of purpose is used.[151] It is translated here as "for mercy to be shown to you." It stands prior to the purpose clause (contra the NRSV: "in order that, by the mercy shown to you, they, too, may now receive mercy").

General Comment

It has been suggested that the most dramatic statement within Romans 9–11 — the declaration that "all Israel will be saved" — must have been part of an interpolation (11:25-27).[152] But that view cannot be sustained for several reasons: (1) there is no text-critical basis for making the claim; (2) if these verses are excised from the text, it is hard to explain why Paul would go on to speak of the gifts and call of God through the patriarchs as irrevocable (11:29); there must be

---

147. R. Miller, "The Text of Rom. 11:31," 37-53.

148. W. Sanday and A. Headlam, *Romans,* 338; O. Michel, *Römer,* 284; H. Schlier, *Römer,* 343; E. Best, *Romans,* 133; E. Käsemann, *Romans,* 316; C. Cranfield, *Romans,* 585-86; J. Fitzmyer, *Romans,* 628; B. Byrne, *Romans,* 356; D. Moo, *Romans,* 735; E. Lohse, *Römer,* 323. Cf. also B. Metzger, *TCGNT* 465 (with reservations about its inclusion).

149. J. Dunn, *Romans,* 677. Cf. B. Metzger, *TCGNT* 465.

150. C. Plag, *Israels Weg zum Heil,* 40; U. Wilckens, *Römer,* 2:251, 261-62; J. O'Neill, *Romans,* 189.

151. Cf. BDF 105 (§196): "because God desired to show you mercy."

152. C. Plag, *Israels Weg zum Heil,* 41; J. O'Neill, *Romans,* 177.

some reason why he has to say that (some new element within the discussion, a counterintuitive claim, which 11:26 most surely is); and (3) if these verses are not original to the text, it is virtually impossible to figure out why Paul would become so effusive in his doxology at the end of the section (11:33-36). His praise of God's riches, wisdom, and knowledge needs to be explained, and 11:25-27 provide the grounds for it. Without those verses the basis for Paul's praise would be a rather conventional theological claim, saying that the people of Israel will receive mercy by accepting the gospel. There would be no surprise in that, and Paul's statement that in regard to the gospel the people of Israel are "enemies" undercuts it.

Detailed Comment

11:25a Paul expresses himself here by means of an apocalyptic form of speech, resorting to the language of a "mystery" or "secret" (μυστήριον) of transcendent origin, unknown to the readers of the letter to this point, and now made known for the first time.[153] The term μυστήριον appears in apocalyptic literature to designate the "mystery" (or "mysteries") of God that exists in heaven and will be revealed at the end of time.[154] Such mysteries, however, can be disclosed to prophets and to the wise prior to that time.[155] Here Paul assumes the role of the one to whom a mystery has been given, and he affirms that the time has come to convey it to others. Various suggestions have been made concerning when the mystery had been disclosed to Paul himself,[156] but none can be adopted as certain. He chides his readers somewhat by calling them persons who think of themselves as "wise" (φρόνιμος). The implication is that they do not possess the wisdom that the apostle himself does, for he has a "mystery" to convey to them.

The mystery consists of the entire oracular message of 11:25b-32.[157] It con-

---

153. M. Wolter, "Apokalyptik als Redeform," 183-84.

154. Extensive coverage is provided in R. Brown, *Semitic Background*, 1-30, and Helmut Krämer, "μυστήριον," *EDNT* 2:447. Among texts referred to are *1 Enoch* 38.3; 63.3; 83.7; 103.2-3; 106.9.

155. Dan 2:19; 2:27-29; 2 Esdr 12:36-39; 14:5-6, 45-46; 1QpHab 7.4-5; 1QH 7.27; 11.10; 12.13.

156. Examples include the following. According to S. Kim, "The 'Mystery' of Rome 11.25-6," it would have been from the time of Paul's call as an apostle. According to O. Hofius, "'All Israel Will Be Saved,'" 33-39, it would have originated from scriptural interpretation. C. Cranfield, *Romans*, 574, says that "the contents of this mystery are to be discerned in the OT seen in the light of the gospel events." N. Bockmuehl, *Revelation and Mystery*, 174, speaks of "revelation by exegesis," a "dynamic inter-reaction, [exegetical] tradition, and religious experience."

157. M. Wolter, "Apokalyptik als Redeform," 183-84; D. Aune, *Prophecy in Early Christianity and the Mediterranean World*, 252.

sists of what is stated in the rest of the sentence, namely, the message of a "hardening" of Israel until the full number of Gentiles enters (11:25b), followed by the salvation of all Israel (11:26-32). Since 9:1 Paul's concern has been that Israel might be saved. What he has written to this point would indicate that Israel *as Israel* falls outside the realm of salvation. The only possibility of salvation is a divine act, a miraculous work of God, in spite of Israel's disobedience. And precisely all that is spelled out in 11:26-32, in which Paul discloses a truth beyond human reason and observation.

To begin with, and in diatribe fashion, Paul addresses any possible Gentile mind-set that would gloat over the fact that the gospel has come to and been received by Gentiles, but resisted by the people of Israel in general. Paul seeks to defuse any sense of arrogance by disclosing a mystery on the way that Israel will be saved.

11:25b A "hardening" has befallen Israel "to some extent." Interpreters disagree concerning the expression ἀπὸ μέρους ("in part" or "partially"). Does it refer to the process of "hardening" of which Paul speaks, so "a hardening has occurred in part,"[158] or does it modify "Israel," so "a part of Israel"?[159] Modern English versions differ as well. For example, the NIV and ESV opt for the former in its wording. The NIV has "Israel has experienced a hardening in part," and the ESV has "a partial hardening has come upon Israel." The RSV and NRSV take the expression to modify the noun "Israel"; both versions have "a hardening has come upon part of Israel." But that does not work well, for to speak of a "part of Israel" having been hardened (resistant to the gospel) hardly does justice to the massive portion to which he would be referring. Moreover, Paul uses the expression elsewhere in his letters (Rom 15:15, 24; 2 Cor 1:14; 2:5), and in those cases it never modifies a noun following it but instead functions adverbially. That is most likely the case here as well. Paul declares that a "hardening" has happened "in part," "to some extent," or (less precisely) "by and large" to Israel. It has befallen Israel *as Israel* to some extent, i.e., as Israel carries on its national and religious existence in the world. Paul does not divide Israel into parts here, but speaks of the same Israel he has spoken of in 9:1-5. It has experienced a harden-

---

158. Among others, the following have this understanding: Karl L. and Martin A. Schmidt, "πορόω," *TDNT* 5:1027; W. Sanday and A. Headlam, *Romans*, 334; M. Black, *Romans*, 147; J. Dunn, *Romans*, 679; BDAG 633 (μέρος, 1, c); U. Wilckens, *Römer*, 2:254; J. Fitzmyer, *Romans*, 621; O. Hofius, "'All Israel Will Be Saved,'" 34 (n. 86); P. Stuhlmacher, *Romans*, 172; T. Tobin, *Paul's Rhetoric in Its Contexts*, 371; E. Lohse, *Römer*, 319.

159. Included here are J. Robinson, "ΠΩΡΩΣΙΣ and ΠΗΡΩΣΙΣ," 83; O. Michel, *Römer*, 280; C. K. Barrett, *Romans*, 206; E. Käsemann, *Romans*, 313; B. Byrne, *Romans*, 354; J. Wagner, *Heralds of the Good News*, 278; M. Baker, "Paul and the Salvation of Israel," 481-83; and L. Keck, *Romans*, 279. C. Cranfield, *Romans*, 572, translates the phrase as "part of Israel" but speaks of it on p. 575 as "adverbial," leaving the matter unresolved.

ing of heart to some extent — not enough to be incapable of renewal, but suffi-cient enough to refuse to accept the proclamation of the gospel.

That "hardening" exists for a time, the time allotted "until the fullness (τὸ πλήρωμα) of the Gentiles enters" into the new humanity. The expression τὸ πλήρωμα (also used at 11:12) need not be rendered so precisely as to mean "the full number of the elect,"[160] as though a specific number of individual persons, predetermined by God, must first become Christians before the close of history. On the other hand, the expression "the Gentile world as a whole"[161] is too vague. It is more likely that Paul speaks here in a general way, envisioning the ingather-ing of the nations at the end of the present age (cf. Mark 13:10), in accord with God's purposes. The fullness of the Gentiles can mean, then, the Gentiles with-out restriction, people of all the Gentile "nations" (for the term τὰ ἔθνη means both "Gentiles" and "nations"). Paul does not thereby think that all Gentiles in-dividually throughout the nations will be converted, or a specific number of them, but rather that the "fullness of the nations" will be ushered into the new humanity representatively by those who believe throughout the various nations of the world.[162] The gospel must therefore be preached among them at the dawn of the new age, which has begun with the resurrection of Jesus from the dead. The eschatological expectation of the Scriptures of Israel that in the latter days the nations will come to worship the God of Israel (Isa 2:2-4; 60:3; 66:18; Jer 16:19; Mic 4:1-3; Zech 8:20-23; Pss 2:27; 86:9; Tob 13:11) is thus being realized — with the apostle himself having a pivotal role in the history of salvation.

11:26a Interpreters have disagreed widely concerning the meaning of Paul's statement that "all Israel will be saved."[163] Some have taken "all Israel" to mean a spiritual Israel (Christians, both Jews and Gentiles),[164] and that would mean that Paul is not talking here about the Jewish people as Jews (empirical Is-rael) at all. But that interpretation can be dismissed quickly, for Paul goes on to say that "in regard to the gospel, they [= the people of Israel] are enemies" (11:28). Still other interpreters have claimed that Paul envisions the conversion of the Jewish people through their acceptance of the gospel.[165] That is explicit

160. The phrase is used by both E. Käsemann, *Romans,* 313; and C. Cranfield, *Romans,* 575; somewhat similarly, P. Stuhlmacher, *Romans,* 172 ("the 'full number' of the Gentiles . . . des-tined to salvation"). The view that Paul speaks here of a particular number of individual Gentiles is expressed most explicitly by C. K. Barrett, *Romans,* 206: "the 'number intended by God.'"

161. The phrase is used by W. Sanday and A. Headlam, *Romans,* 335.

162. Cf. J. Munck, *Paul,* 48; idem, *Christ and Israel,* 134-35.

163. Five major ways of interpreting the verse (but differing in detail from what is pro-vided here) are surveyed by C. Zoccali, "'And So All Israel Will Be Saved,'" 289-318.

164. Irenaeus, *Against Heresies* 4.2.7; J. Calvin, *Romans,* 437; H. Ponsot, "Et ainsi tout Is-rael sera sauvé," 406-17.

165. Cyril of Alexandria, *PG* 74:849; Theodoret of Cyrrhus, *PG* 82:180; Augustine, *City of God,* 21.24; M. Luther, *Romans,* 430; C. H. Dodd, *Romans,* 182-83; O. Cullmann, *Christ and*

in the comment by William Sanday and Arthur C. Headlam, who say that Paul "looks forward in prophetic vision to a time when the whole earth, including the kingdoms of the Gentiles . . . and the people of Israel . . . , shall be united in the Church of God."[166] But if the Jewish people will be saved by their acceptance of the gospel within history, there is no "mystery" (or "secret") to speak of at all. Moreover, the "mystery" is not Israel's ultimate salvation but "the way in which Israel will achieve that ultimate salvation."[167] Consequently, still other interpreters conclude that Paul means that the people of Israel will be saved by God's own mercy, expressed after history has ended, without conversion. Then two possibilities open up: the people of Israel will (1) convert at the coming of Christ, confessing him as Lord, thereby being saved by the same confession as Gentile Christians[168] or (2) remain in their refusal to confess Jesus as the Christ but be saved at his parousia purely by the mercy of God.[169] In order to resolve the problem, we need to deal with related issues.[170]

The expression "all Israel" (πᾶς Ἰσραήλ) occurs some 148 times in the OT,[171] in virtually all of its parts, and in Qumran literature.[172] It also appears in other ancient sources that speak of its salvation, such as the *Testament of*

Time, 78 (but see subsequent note 169 concerning Cullmann); D. Zeller, *Juden und Heiden,* 257; R. Hvalvik, "A 'Sonderweg' for Israel," 89, 96; F. Hahn, "Zum Verständnis von Römer 11.26a," 230; C. Stanley, "'The Redeemer Will Come,'" 137-42; N. T. Wright, *NIB (Romans),* 10:689; A. Das, *Paul and the Jews,* 109-13, 115-20, 190; D. Moo, *Romans,* 724-26 ("a large-scale conversion of Jewish people at the end of this age," p. 724); C. Talbert, *Romans,* 264-67.

166. W. Sanday and A. Headlam, *Romans,* 336.

167. N. Dahl, "The Future of Israel," 152; cf. J. C. Beker, *Paul the Apostle,* 334.

168. J. Munck, *Christ and Israel,* 139-41; E. Käsemann, *Romans,* 314-15; H. Hübner, *Gottes Ich und Israel,* 114-17; J. Fitzmyer, *Romans,* 619-20; J. Ziesler, *Romans,* 285-86; P. Stuhlmacher, *Romans,* 172; B. Byrne, *Romans,* 354-55; O. Hofius, "Evangelium und Israel," 1:197; idem, "'All Israel Will Be Saved,'" 36-37; E. Lohse, *Römer,* 320-22; U. Schnelle, *Apostle Paul,* 350-52; R. Jewett, *Romans,* 701-4.

169. C. K. Barrett, *Romans,* 206-10; H. Ridderbos, *Paul,* 358; J. Murray, *Romans,* 2:98-100; U. Wilckens, *Römer,* 2:261, 264-65; O. Cullmann, *Salvation in History,* 162; K. Stendahl, *Paul among Jews and Gentiles,* 4; idem, *Meanings,* 215 (n. 1); N. Dahl, "The Future of Israel," 152-58; P. Achtemeier, *Romans,* 14, 189; F. Mussner, *Tractate,* 34; M. Getty, "Paul and the Salvation of Israel," 464; M. Theobald, *Römerbrief,* 278; B. Oropeza, "Paul and Theodicy," 78; T. Donaldson, "Jewish Christianity, Israel's Stumbling and the *Sonderweg* Reading of Paul," 51-52; J. Flebbe, *Solus Deus,* 401; and S. Eastman, "Israel and the Mercy of God," 384-85.

170. Some interpreters do not fit into the categories outlined here. For F. Refoulé, *"Et ainsi tout Israël sera sauvé,"* 167-77, "all Israel" are the pious remnant within Israel who will eventually come to faith. O. Michel, *Römer,* 281-82, speaks of Israel's salvation with the coming of the Messiah, who will reconcile (unbelieving) Israel to God. L. Keck, *Romans,* 281-82, seems to lean toward divine action, but (as he puts it) not apart from the Christ-event.

171. The figure is taken from J. Fitzmyer, *Romans,* 623.

172. Some examples: Exod 18:25; 40:38; Num 16:34; Deut. 1:1; 5:1; 11:6; 1 Kgs 12:1; Dan 9:11; 1 Macc 2:70; 13:26; 12:52; CD 15.5; 16.1.

Benjamin 10.11 ("All Israel will be gathered to the Lord")[173] and the *Mishnah* tractate *Sanhedrin* 10.1 ("All Israelites have a share in the world to come").[174] In all such instances the expression means the people of Israel as a corporate entity.[175] It need not mean every individual any more than similar expressions of modern times, such as "the whole country is celebrating today." Presumably some individuals would not be included in such an expression (as the exceptions listed in the text from the Mishnah tractate *Sanhedrin* demonstrate).[176] Nevertheless, the expression "all Israel" has to be taken for what it is, and that is that it refers to the people of Israel, the Jewish people, who have not accepted the gospel (again, cf. 11:28).

11:26b-27 Paul offers a proof from Scripture to confirm the point he has made concerning Israel's ultimate salvation. What he presents is a conflation of two texts in Isaiah (59:20-21; 27:9), a conflation probably created by Paul himself,[177] and altered somewhat from the LXX:

ἥξει ἐκ Σιὼν ὁ ῥυόμενος,
    ἀποστρέψει ἀσεβείας ἀπὸ Ἰακώβ.
καὶ αὕτη αὐτοῖς ἡ παρ' ἐμοῦ διαθήκη,
    ὅταν ἀφέλωμαι τὰς ἁμαρτίας αὐτῶν.

The Deliverer will come out of Zion;
    he will remove ungodliness from Jacob.
And this is my covenant with them,
    when I take away their sins.

The texts in the LXX read as follows, and those portions that appear in Paul's text — leaving aside differences among singular and plural nouns and pronouns — are underscored:

---

173. Quoted from the translation by Howard C. Kee in *OTP* 1:828. According to Kee, the *Testaments of the Twelve Patriarchs* (of which this document is one) originated in the second century B.C. (*OTP* 1:777-78).

174. Quoted from *The Mishnah*, ed. Herbert Danby (New York: Oxford University Press, 1933), 397. For the claim that the passage was modeled on Rom 11:26 in polemics over against Jewish Christianity, cf. I. Yuval, "All Israel Have a Portion in the World to Come," 114-38 (esp. pp. 119-20).

175. BDF 143 (§275, 4); cf. BDAG 783 (πᾶς, 4, a).

176. *M. Sanh.* 10.2-6 provides a list of those who do not have a share in the world to come, including those who deny the resurrection, who deny that the Torah is from heaven, and Epicureans. In addition, R. Akiba adds to the list those who read heretical books and utter certain charms, and R. Saul adds those who pronounce the divine name.

177. D.-A. Koch, *Die Schrift als Zeuge des Evangeliums*, 177; J. Wagner, *Heralds of the Good News*, 280.

Isaiah 59:20-21:
καὶ <u>ἥξει</u> ἕνεκεν <u>Σιων</u> ὁ ῥυόμενος,
    καὶ <u>ἀποστρέψει ἀσεβείας ἀπὸ Ιακωβ</u>.
<u>καὶ αὕτη αὐτοῖς ἡ παρ' ἐμοῦ διαθήκη</u>, εἶπεν κύριος.

And <u>the deliverer will come</u> for the sake of <u>Zion</u>
    and <u>remove ungodliness from Jacob</u>.
<u>And this is my covenant with them</u>, says the Lord

Isaiah 27:9:
διὰ τοῦτο ἀφαιρεθήσεται ἡ ἀνομία Ιακωβ,
καὶ τοῦτό ἐστιν ἡ εὐλογία αὐτοῦ,
    <u>ὅταν ἀφέλωμαι αὐτοῦ τὴν ἁμαρτίαν</u>.

Therefore the lawlessness of Jacob will be removed,
and this is his blessing,
    <u>when I take away his sin</u>.

The conflation and consequent modifications of the Isaiah passages in Paul's letter differ in the following respects where material is being quoted: (1) the word καί in Isaiah 59:20 is omitted twice in Paul's text; (2) instead of the phrase ἕνεκεν Σιων ("for Zion's sake"), Paul has ἐκ Σιών ("out of Zion"); and (3) while Isaiah has αὐτοῦ τὴν ἁμαρτίαν ("his sin") in the last line, Paul has τὰς ἁμαρτίας αὐτῶν ("their sins"). Of these differences, the major one is the second (the change of ἕνεκεν Σιων to ἐκ Σιών). Although interpreters have usually attributed the change of wording to Paul[178] or to a predecessor,[179] the fact that such wording exists in some known Greek versions, a Bohairic version, and in quotations by some early Christian writers[180] makes the matter more complicated. On balance, however, since the versions having the alteration are few and late, and the early Christian writers could have been dependent upon Paul, there is no compelling reason to exclude Paul as the one who altered the reading at this point. The alteration can be explained on the basis of different geographical perspectives. While in Isaiah 59:20 the Redeemer is to come to Zion and "for Zion's sake" to save his people, in Paul's view the Redeemer will come from Zion itself. The wording is also suggested by Psalm 14:7 (LXX 13:7): "O that deliverance (σωτήριον) for Israel would come from Zion (ἐκ Σιων)!" The meaning of "Zion" need not be pinned down too precisely, since it simply comes with

178. J. Fitzmyer, *Romans*, 624; J. Dunn, *Romans*, 682; J. Wagner, *Heralds of the Good News*, 284.
179. C. Stanley, "'The Redeemer Will Come,'" 121-26.
180. C. Stanley, "'The Redeemer Will Come,'" 133 (n. 43). Stanley cites certain minuscules "in the LXX tradition" (22c-93, 564, 407, 534); for patristic evidence, Stanley cites Epiphanius, Hilary, and Jerome.

the quotation. Be that as it may, the clause with this noun most likely means that the Redeemer will come from the heavenly realm (as in Gal 4:26; Heb 12:22; Rev 3:12) in an eschatological act of deliverance. To add other meanings to it, such as that the gospel has gone out from Jerusalem, would be to press the imagery too far. The reference is future, not past.

The primary exegetical question concerning the verse is: What is meant by "the deliverer" (ὁ ῥυόμενος)? Does the term refer to God or Christ? Virtually all interpreters consider it to be a reference to Christ at his parousia.[181] Although there is dissent from this view,[182] the fact that Paul uses the same term for Christ at his parousia elsewhere (1 Thess 1:10: Ἰησοῦν τὸν ῥυόμενον ἡμᾶς ἐκ τῆς ὀργῆς τῆς ἐρχομένης ["Jesus, who delivers us from the wrath to come"]) makes it at least possible that he means the same here.

It is important, however, to observe four things prior to making a conclusion. First, Paul can use the term ῥύομαι ("to deliver") in other contexts that have no explicit Christological significance. In those instances where Paul uses the verb, God is the subject, whether explicitly or by implication (Rom 7:24; 15:31; 2 Cor 1:10 [twice]).[183] Second, the entire passage, Romans 9–11, has to do entirely with the work of God in relationship to Israel. Not only has there been no reference to Christ since 9:1-5, but the focus is explicitly theopractic, envisioning divine action, and it is about a God who has not and cannot give up on a living relationship with Israel. Third, the God of Israel is the only one who can "banish ungodliness from Jacob" and who can say, "I [shall] take away their sins," for Israel's salvation is based solely here on its election by God, not on its conversion — either in history or at history's end. Finally, in Paul's own view, all things will be subject to God the Father, including the Son himself, in the last stage of redemptive history when God alone will be all in all (1 Cor 15:24, 28).

In the final analysis, it is difficult to know exactly how precise Paul was —

---

181. E. Käsemann, *Romans,* 314; U. Wilckens, *Römer,* 2:256; O. Hofius, "'All Israel Will Be Saved,'" 36; C. Cranfield, *Romans,* 578; J. Fitzmyer, *Romans,* 624; J. Dunn, *Romans,* 682; E. P. Sanders, *Paul, the Law, and the Jewish People,* 194; F. Mussner, *Tractate,* 31-32; R. Hvalvik, "A 'Sonderweg' for Israel," 92; J. Ziesler, *Romans,* 286; P. Stuhlmacher, *Romans,* 172; B. Byrne, *Romans,* 350; J. Wagner, *Heralds of the Good News,* 297-98; K. Haacker, *Römer,* 242; M. Baker, "Paul and the Salvation of Israel," 482-83; T. Tobin, *Paul's Rhetoric in Its Contexts,* 374; R. Jewett, *Romans,* 703-4; E. Lohse, *Römer,* 321; C. Keener, *Romans,* 137; S. Eastman, "Israel and the Mercy of God," 384; J. Adam, *Paulus und die Versöhnung Aller,* 379-81, 391; F. Matera, *Romans,* 273. The view of C. Stanley, "'The Redeemer Will Come,'" 140-42, that Paul envisions a day in Yahweh's purposes when the Jews will respond to the gospel in history, is less convincing.

182. N. Dahl, "The Future of Israel," 153, has written: "From the quotation in Rom. 11:26-27, one could assume that Christ himself is going to save Israel when he appears at the end of days, but no other passage suggests such a view."

183. Rom 7:24b ("Who will deliver me from this body of death?"), a rhetorical question, is somewhat ambiguous. But the following verse shows Paul's reliance upon God to do that.

and how much precision he intended — in his reference to "the deliverer" when he used these texts from Isaiah. Given the considerations enumerated here, it is possible that he was referring primarily to the God of Israel as Israel's own deliverer. There can be no question about the use of the term in Isaiah 59:20; the deliverer (NRSV: "the Redeemer") is God. But for Paul the act of God's deliverance of Israel may well be through the instrumentality of Christ at his parousia. The fact that Paul speaks of Christ as deliverer at his parousia in one of his earlier letters (1 Thess 1:10) is weighty and finally tilts the scales in favor of concluding that here, too, he makes reference to Christ. In any case, Paul envisions the salvation of Israel purely by the mercy of God at the end of history, even though the confession of Jesus as Lord is not made by its people within history itself. All is by grace alone. Israel's salvation will not be based on Torah observance, nor will it depend on their making the Christian confession, but *sola gratia,* by God's grace.

11:28-29 The people of Israel remain "enemies" in reference to the gospel (i.e., opposed to it; cf. 5:10; 8:7), says Paul,[184] but that is "for your sake," i.e., for the sake of Gentiles who have become Christians. Israel's "no" has provided the opportunity for the gospel to be proclaimed among Gentiles, where it has received a "yes" (cf. 11:11). Yet, God cannot let Israel go. God has bound himself to Israel in covenantal union, based on election (ἐκλογή). Paul has used that term previously in this letter (11:5, 7) in a restrictive way, referring there to those people in Israel, the remnant, who were faithful to God. But here the term applies to the people as a whole.

When Paul writes that the people of Israel "are beloved for the sake of the patriarchs," he does not make up an argument on his own, but picks up a claim within the Scriptures. The author of 2 Kings writes that, when Israel was oppressed by Syria during the days of Jehoahaz (king of Israel, 816-800 B.C.), the Lord "was gracious to [the people of Israel] and had compassion on them; he turned toward them, because of his covenant with Abraham, Isaac, and Jacob" (2 Kgs 13:23). God's covenant with Israel since patriarchal times (Gen 12:1-3, the call of Abraham) meant that God was irrevocably bound to Israel, a theme that reappears in the OT on several occasions. The covenant with Abraham is considered the basis for God's rescue of Israel from Egypt (Exod 2:23-35; 3:15-16) and from exile in Babylonia (Isa 41:8-10). It is the basis for future protection, prosperity, and life on the land (Lev 26:42; Deut 1:8; Judg 2:1; Jer 7:7, 14; 11:5; 30:3 Ezek 36:28; 47:14), and it will not be broken (Judg 2:1; 2 Esdr 3:15; cf. 2 Kgs 13:23). And so Ezra says to God (in an apocryphal text of the first century A.D.) con-

---

184. That it was the Christian Gentiles in Rome who regarded Jews as "enemies of God," and that Paul corrected that view in 11:28b, is maintained by M. Nanos, *The Mystery of Romans,* 101, 114. No, the statement is Paul's own.

cerning Abraham: "You made an everlasting covenant with him, and promised him that you would never forsake his descendants" (2 Esdr 3:15),[185] a theme repeated in other literatures as well.[186] For Paul to say that God's "gifts and call" are "irrevocable" is thus to express what was commonplace in Jewish thought of the era, based on familiar scriptural texts. It is no more emphatic than the declaration of an angel of the Lord to the people of Israel in the days of Joshua: "I brought you up from Egypt, and brought you into the land that I had promised to your ancestors. I said, 'I will never break my covenant with you'" (Judg 2:1).

11:30-31 Paul writes with an intricate parallelism in 11:30-31 that can be mapped out as follows:[187]

ὥσπερ γὰρ ὑμεῖς	ποτε	ἠπειθήσατε	τῷ θεῷ,
	νῦν δὲ	ἠλεήθητε	τῇ τούτων ἀπειθείᾳ,
οὕτως καὶ οὗτοι	νῦν	ἠπείθησαν	τῷ ὑμετέρῳ ἐλέει,
ἵνα καὶ αὐτοὶ	[νῦν]	ἐλεηθῶσιν.	

For just as you	at one time	were disobedient	to God
	but now	have received mercy	by their disobedience,
so also they	now	have been disobedient	for mercy to be
shown to you			
that they also	[now]	may receive mercy.	

The parallelism is intricate, but the logic of the passage is not complicated, consisting of three main assertions: (1) In the past, the Gentiles were disobedient, but now they have received mercy because of Israel's no to the gospel (11:30). (2) Inversely stated, Israel's no to the gospel has meant mercy for the Gentiles, who were formerly disobedient (11:31a). (3) Since Gentile disobedience has led to mercy, the disobedience of Israel can be expected to have the same result. The argument concludes, as if there is a divine plan in all of this, with a purpose clause: "in order that (ἵνα + an aorist subjunctive) they also may receive mercy" (11:31b). The verb is passive, and so the divine passive is meant. In other words, all has taken place in order that God may have mercy on Israel. The point about the Gentiles shows that disobedience does not preclude mercy, and therefore it does not exclude mercy upon Israel in particular. That mercy, whether one includes the "now" of 11:31b or not, has future, eschatological effects according to God's own purpose. From now on the eschatological future that has already begun is open for the inclusion of

185. Concerning scholarship on the composition of 2 Esdras, cf. the introductory essay on it by B. Metzger, *OTP* 1:517-24.

186. Cf. *Jub.* 12.22-24; 15.1-10; 22.1-9; *Pss. Sol.* 9.9-11; *Odes Sol.* 31.13; 4Q225; 4Q503; 4Q504.1-2.9-11; 4Q509; 11QTemple 29.7-8.

187. Slightly altered from the presentation by U. Wilckens, *Römer*, 2:259.

the people of Israel.[188] In light of that, the claims being made in the verses can be diagrammed as follows:

Past	*Present*	*Eschatological Future*
Gentiles were		
disobedient	Gentiles receive *mercy*	
	Israel is *disobedient*	Israel will receive *mercy*

11:32 The conclusion to be drawn is that the charge of "disobedience" applies to both Jews who refuse the gospel in the present and to Gentiles (Paul's primary readership at Rome) who did not honor God in the past (1:20-23). As there are no grounds for boasting by those under the law (2:17-24), so there are no grounds for those who are Gentile Christians either. God has "consigned" (συνέκλεισεν, "enclosed," "confined") all into the category of the disobedient ones. While saying that, Paul is still disclosing the "mystery" (11:25), speaking of God's action, which no one can observe. It has to be revealed, and it is a word of judgment. But Paul, continuing to disclose the mystery as though he knows the mind of God, declares that God will have mercy on all. As he had mercy on the Gentiles, so he will have mercy on the Jewish people beyond history in the new age, when God will redeem the creation.

BIBLIOGRAPHY

Adam, Jens. *Paulus und die Versöhnung Aller: Eine Studie zum paulinischen Heilsuniversalismus.* Neukirchen-Vluyn: Neukirchener Verlag, 2009.

Aune, David E. *Prophecy in Early Christianity and the Mediterranean World.* Grand Rapids: Wm. B. Eerdmans, 1983.

Aus, Roger D. "Paul's Travel Plans to Spain and the 'Full Number of the Gentiles' of Rom. XI 25." *NovT* 21 (1979): 232-62.

Baker, Murray. "Paul and the Salvation of Israel: Paul's Ministry, the Motif of Jealousy, and Israel's Yes." *CBQ* 67 (2005): 469-84.

Batey, Richard. "So All Israel Will Be Saved." *Int* 20 (1966): 218-28.

Beker, J. Christiaan. "The Faithfulness of God and the Priority of Israel in Paul's Letter to the Romans." In *The Romans Debate*, 327-32. Ed. Karl P. Donfried. Rev. ed. Peabody: Hendrickson Publishers, 1991.

———. *Paul the Apostle: The Triumph of God in Life and Thought.* Philadelphia: Fortress Press, 1980.

Bell, Richard H. *The Irrevocable Call of God: An Inquiry into Paul's Theology of Israel.* WUNT 184. Tübingen: J. C. B. Mohr (Paul Siebeck), 2005.

Bloesch, Donald G. "'All Israel Will Be Saved': Supersessionism and the Biblical Witness." *Int* 43 (1989): 130-42.

188. Cf. H. Schlier, *Römer,* 343.

Bockmuehl, Markus N. A. *Revelation and Mystery in Ancient Judaism and Pauline Christianity.* WUNT 2/36. Tübingen: J. C. B. Mohr (Paul Siebeck), 1990.

Brown, Raymond E. *The Semitic Background of the Term "Mystery" in the New Testament.* FBBS 21. Philadelphia: Fortress Press, 1968.

Byrne, Brendan. "Universal Need of Salvation and Universal Salvation by Faith in the Letter to the Romans." *Pacifica* 8 (1995): 123-39.

Campbell, William S. "Salvation for Jews and Gentiles: Krister Stendahl and Paul's Letter to the Romans." In *Studia Biblica 1978: Sixth International Congress on Biblical Studies, Oxford, 3-7 April 1978,* 3:65-72. Ed. Elizabeth A. Livingstone. 3 vols. Sheffield: JSOT Press, 1979-80.

Capes, David B. "YHWH and His Messiah: Pauline Exegesis and the Divine Christ." *HBT* 16 (1994): 121-43.

Cooper, Craig. "Romans 11:25-26." *ResQ* 21 (1978): 84-94.

Coppens, Joseph. "'Mystery' in the Theology of Saint Paul and Its Parallels at Qumran." In *Paul and Qumran,* 132-58. Ed. Jerome Murphy-O'Connor. Chicago: Priory Press, 1968.

Cross, Frank M. "A Christian Understanding of the Election of Israel." *Andover Newton Quarterly* 8 (1968): 237-40.

Cullmann, Oscar. *Christ and Time: The Primitive Christian Conception of Time and History.* Philadelphia: Westminster Press, 1964.

———. *Salvation in History.* New York: Harper & Row, 1967.

Dahl, Nils A. "The Future of Israel." In his *Studies in Paul: Theology for the Early Christian Mission,* 137-58. Minneapolis: Augsburg Publishing House, 1977.

Das, A. Andrew. *Paul and the Jews.* LPS. Peabody: Hendrickson Publishers, 2003.

Davies, W. D. "Paul and the People of Israel." *NTS* 24 (1997-98): 4-39.

Donaldson, Terence L. "Jewish Christianity, Israel's Stumbling and the *Sonderweg* Reading of Paul." *JSNT* 29 (2006): 27-54.

Dunn, James D. G. "Did Paul Have a Covenant Theology? Reflections on Romans 9:4 and 11:27." In *Celebrating Romans: Template for Pauline Theology: Essays in Honor of Robert Jewett,* 3-19. Ed. Sheila E. McGinn. Grand Rapids: Wm. B. Eerdmans, 2005.

Eastman, Susan Grove. "Israel and the Mercy of God: A Re-reading of Galatians 6.16 and Romans 9–11." *NTS* 56 (2010): 367-95.

Evans, Craig A. "The Meaning of *Pleroma* in Nag Hammadi." *Biblica* 65 (1984): 259-65.

Flebbe, Jochen. *Solus Deus: Untersuchungen zur Rede von Gott im Brief des Paulus an die Römer.* BZNW 158. Berlin: de Gruyter, 2008.

Getty, Mary Ann. "Paul and the Salvation of Israel: A Perspective on Romans 9–11." *CBQ* 50 (1998): 456-69.

Glancy, Jennifer A. "Israel vs. Israel in Romans 11:25-32." *USQR* 45 (1991): 191-203.

Glombitza, Otto. "Apostolische Sorge: Welche Sorge Treibt den Apostel Paulus zu den Sätzen Röm. xi 25ff.?" *NovT* 7 (1964-65): 312-18.

Grässer, Erich. *Der alte Bund im Neuen: Exegetische Studien zur Israelfrage im Neuen Testament.* WUNT 35. Tübingen: J. C. B. Mohr (Paul Siebeck), 1985.

———. "Zwei Heilswege: Zum theologischen Verhältnis von Israel und Kirche." In *Kontinuität und Einheit: Für Franz Musser,* 411-29. Ed. Paul-Gerhard Müller und

Werner Stenger. Freiburg im Breisgau: Herder, 1981; reprinted in his *Der Alte Bund im Neuen*, 212-30. WUNT 35. Tübingen: J. C. B. Mohr (Paul Siebeck), 1985.

Guthrie, Shirley C. "Romans 11:25-32." *Int* 38 (1984): 286-91.

Haacker, Klaus. "Das Evangelium Gottes und die Erwählung Israels." *TBei* 13 (1982): 59-72.

Hafemann, Scott. "The Salvation of Israel in Romans 11:25-32: A Response to Krister Stendahl." *Ex Auditu* 4 (1988): 38-58.

Hahn, Ferdinand. "Zum Verständnis von Römer 11:26a: '. . . und so wird ganz Israel gerettet werden.'" In *Paul and Paulinism: Essays in Honour of C. K. Barrett*, 221-36. Ed. Morna D. Hooker and S. G. Wilson. London: SPCK, 1982.

Harding, Mark. "The Salvation of Israel and the Logic of Romans 11:11-36." *AusBR* 46 (1998): 55-69.

Harrington, Daniel J. *Paul on the Mystery of Israel (Rom 11:25-32)*. Collegeville, Minn.: Liturgical Press, 1992.

Hofius, Otfried. "'All Israel Will Be Saved': Divine Salvation and Israel's Deliverance in Romans 9–11." In *The Church and Israel: Romans 9–11: The 1989 Frederick Neumann Symposium on the Theological Interpretation of Scripture*, 19-39. Ed. Daniel Migliore. PSBSup 1. Princeton: Princeton Theological Seminary, 1990.

———. "Das Evangelium und Israel: Erwägungen zu Römer 9–11." In his *Paulusstudien*, 1:175-202. 2 vols. WUNT 51, 143. Tübingen: J. C. B. Mohr (Paul Siebeck), 1994-2002.

Holtz, Traugott. "The Judgment on the Jews and the Salvation of All Israel: 1 Thes 2,15-16 and Rom 11,25-26." In *The Thessalonian Correspondence*, 284-94. Ed. Raymond F. Collins. BETL 87. Leuven: Leuven University Press, 1990.

Horne, Charles M. "The Meaning of the Phrase 'And Thus All Israel Will Be Saved' (Romans 11:26)." *JETS* 21 (1978): 329-34.

Horst, Pieter W. van der. "'Only Then Will All Israel Be Saved': A Short Note on the Meaning of καὶ οὕτως in Romans 11:26." *JBL* 119 (2000): 521-25.

Hübner, Hans. *Gottes Ich und Israel: Zum Schriftgebrauch des Paulus in Römer 9–11*. FRLANT 136. Göttingen: Vandenhoeck & Ruprecht, 1984.

Hvalvik, Reidar. "A 'Sonderweg' for Israel: A Critical Examination of a Current Interpretation of Romans 11:25-27." *JSNT* 38 (1990): 87-107.

Hyldahl, Niels. "Καὶ οὕτως i Rom 11,26." *DTT* 37 (1974): 231-34.

Jeremias, Joachim. "Einige vorwiegend sprachliche Beobachtungen zu Röm 11.25-26." In *Die Israelfrage nach Röm 9–11*, 193-216. Ed. Lorenzo de Lorenzi. Monographische Reihe von "Benedictine" 3. Rome: Abtei von St. Paul von den Mauern, 1977.

Kim, Seyoon. "The 'Mystery' of Rom 11.25-26 Once More." *NTS* 43 (1997): 412-29.

Koch, Dieter-Alex. "Beobachtungen zum christologischen Schriftgebrauch in den vorpaulinischen Gemeinden." *ZNW* 71 (1980): 174-91.

———. *Die Schrift als Zeuge des Evangeliums: Untersuchung zur Verwendung und zum Verständnis der Schrift bei Paulus*. BHT 69. Tübingen: J. C. B. Mohr (Paul Siebeck), 1986.

Lambrecht, Jan. "Grammar and Reasoning in Romans 11,27." *ETL* 79 (2003): 179-83.

Miller, Robert W. "The Text of Rom. 11:31." *FM* 23 (2006): 37-53.

Munck, Johannes. *Christ and Israel: An Interpretation of Romans 9–11*. Philadelphia: Fortress Press, 1967.

————. *Paul and the Salvation of Mankind*. Atlanta: John Knox Press, 1959.

Mussner, Franz. "'Ganz Israel wird gerettet werden' (Röm 11,26): Versuch einer Auslegung." *Kairos* 18 (1976): 241-55.

————. "Heil für alle: Der Grundgedanke des Römerbriefs." *Kairos* 23 (1981): 207-14; reprinted in his *Dieses Geschlecht wird nicht vergehen: Judentum und Kirche*, 29-38.
Freiburg-Basel-Wien: Herder, 1991.

————. *Tractate on the Jews: The Significance of Judaism for Christian Faith*. Philadelphia:
Fortress Press, 1984.

————. "Die 'Verstockung' Israels nach Röm 9–11." *TTZ* 109 (2000): 191-98.

Nanos, Mark. *The Mystery of Romans: The Jewish Context of Paul's Letter*. Minneapolis:
Fortress Press, 1996.

Oropeza, B. J. "Paul and Theodicy: Intertextual Thoughts on God's Justice and Faithfulness to Israel in Romans 9–11." *NTS* 53 (2007): 57-80.

Osborne, William L. "The Old Testament Background of Paul's 'All Israel' in Romans
11:26a." *AJT* 2 (1988): 282-93.

Osten-Sacken, Peter von der. "Heil für die Juden — Auch ohne Christus?" In *Wenn nicht
jetzt, wann dann? Aufsätze für Hans-Joachim Kraus zum 65. Geburtstag*, 169-82. Ed.
Hans-Georg Geyer et al. Neukirchen-Vluyn: Neukirchener Verlag, 1983; reprinted
in his *Evangelium und Tora: Aufsätze zu Paulus*, 256-71. TBü 77. Munich: Kaiser
Verlag, 1987.

Plag, Christoph. *Israels Weg zum Heil: Eine Untersuchung zu Römer 9 bis 11*. AT 40. Stuttgart: Calwer Verlag, 1969.

Ponsot, Hervé. "Et ainsi tout Israël sera sauvé: Rom. XI,26a." *RB* 89 (1982): 406-17.

Räisänen, Heikki. *The Idea of Divine Hardening: A Comparative Study of the Notion of Divine Hardening, Leading Astray and Inciting to Evil in the Bible and the Qur'an*. SESJ
25. Helsinki: Finnish Exegetical Society, 1972.

Refoulé, François. "*. . . Et ainsi tout Israël sera sauvé*": *Romains 11,25-32*. LD 117. Paris: Cerf,
1984.

Reichrath, Hans. "Der Retter wird aus 'Zion kommen.'" *Jud* 49 (1993): 146-55.

Reicke, Bo. "Um der Väter willen, Röm. 11,28." *Judaica* 14 (1958): 106-14.

Rese, Martin. "Die Rettung der Juden nach Römer 11." In *L'Apôtre Paul: Personnalité, style
et conception du ministère*, 422-30. Ed. Albert Vanhoye. BETL 73. Louvain: Leuven
University Press, 1986.

Richardson, Peter. *Israel in the Apostolic Church*. SNTSMS 10. Cambridge: Cambridge University Press, 1969.

Ridderbos, Herman. *Paul: An Outline of His Theology*. Grand Rapids: Wm. B. Eerdmans,
1975.

Robinson, J. Armitage. "ΠΩΡΩΣΙΣ and ΠΗΡΩΣΙΣ." *JTS* 3 (1902): 81-93.

Sanders, E. P. *Paul, the Law, and the Jewish People*. Philadelphia: Fortress Press, 1983.

Sänger, Dieter. "Rettung der Heiden und Erwählung Israels: Einige vorläufige Erwägungen
zu Römer 11,25-27." *KD* 32 (1986): 99-119.

Schaller, Berndt, "ΗΞΕΙ ΕΚ ΣΙΩΝ Ο ΡΥΟΜΕΝΟΣ: Zur Textgestalt von Jes. 59.20-21 in
Röm. 11.26f." In *De Septuaginta: Studies in Honour of John William Wevers on His*

Sixty-Fifth Birthday, 201-6. Ed. Albert Pietersma and Claude Cox. Mississauga, Ont.: Benben Publications, 1984.

Schnelle, Udo. *Apostle Paul: His Life and Theology.* Grand Rapids: Baker Academic, 2003.

Seewann, Maria-Irma. "Semantische Untersuchung zu πώρωσις, veranlasst durch Röm 11,25." *FilNeot* 10 (1997): 139-56.

──────. "'Verstockung', 'Verhärtung' oder 'Nicht-Erkennen'? Überlegungen zu Röm 11,25." *Kirche und Israel* 12 (1997): 161-72.

Sievers, Joseph. "'God's Gifts and Call Are Irrevocable': The Interpretation of Rom 11:29 and Its Uses." In *Society of Biblical Literature 1997 Seminar Papers,* 337-57. SBLSP 36. Atlanta: Scholars Press, 1997; reprinted in *Reading Israel in Romans: Legitimacy and Plausibility of Divergent Interpretations,* 127-73. Ed. Cristina Grenholm and Daniel Patte. Romans through History and Culture Series 1. Harrisburg: Trinity Press International, 2000.

──────. "A History of the Interpretation of Romans 11:29." *ASE* 14/2 (1997): 381-442.

Stanley, Christopher D. "'The Redeemer Will Come ἐκ Σιών': Romans 11.26-27 Revisited." In *Paul and the Scriptures of Israel,* 118-42. Ed. Craig A. Evans and James A. Sanders. JSNTSup 83/SSEJC 1. Sheffield: Sheffield Academic Press, 1993.

Stendahl, Krister. "Judaism and Christianity Then and Now." *HDB* 28 (1963): 1-9.

──────. *Meanings: The Bible as Document and as Guide.* Philadelphia: Fortress Press, 1984.

──────. *Paul among Jews and Gentiles and Other Essays.* Philadelphia: Fortress Press, 1976.

Stuhlmacher, Peter. "Zur Interpretation von Römer 11,25-32." In *Probleme biblischer Theologie: Gerhard von Rad zum 70. Geburtstag,* 555-70. Ed. Hans Walter Wolff. Munich: Kaiser Verlag, 1971.

Thyen, Hartwig. "Das Mysterium Israel (Röm 11,25-32)." In *Das Gesetz im frühen Judentum und im Neuen Testament: Festschrift für Christoph Burchard zum 75. Geburtstag,* 304-18. Ed. Dieter Sänger and Matthias Konradt. NTOA 57. Göttingen: Vandenhoeck & Ruprecht, 2006.

Tobin, Thomas H. *Paul's Rhetoric in Its Contexts: The Argument of Romans.* Peabody: Hendrickson Publishers, 2004.

Uhlig, Torsten. *The Theme of Hardening in the Book of Isaiah: An Analysis of Communicative Action.* FzAT 2/1. Tübingen: Mohr Siebeck, 2009.

Wagner, J. Ross. *Heralds of the Good News: Isaiah and Paul "in Concert" in the Letter to the Romans.* NovTSup 101. Boston: E. J. Brill, 2002.

Walter, Nikolas. "Zur Interpretation von Römer 9–11." *ZTK* 81 (1984): 172-95.

Wolter, Michael. "Apokalyptik als Redeform im Neuen Testament." *NTS* 51 (2005): 171-91.

Yuval, Israel Y. "All Israel Have a Portion in the World to Come." In *Redefining First-Century Jewish and Christian Identities: Essays in Honor of Ed Parish Sanders,* 114-38. Ed. Fabian E. Udoh et al. CJA 16. Notre Dame: University of Notre Dame Press, 2008.

Zeller, Dieter. *Juden und Heiden in der Mission des Paulus: Studien zum Römerbrief.* FB 1. Stuttgart: Verlag Katholisches Bibelwerk, 1973.

Zoccali, Christopher. "'And So All Israel Will Be Saved': Competing Interpretations of Romans 11.26 in Pauline Scholarship." *JSNT* 30 (2008): 289-318.

5.7. God Is Vindicated, 11:33-36

33*O the depth of the riches and wisdom and knowledge of God!*
How unsearchable are his judgments
    and inscrutable his ways!
34*"For who has known the mind of the Lord?*
    Or who has been his counselor?"
35*"Or who has given to him,*
    and it will be paid back to him?"
36*For from him and through him and to him are all things.*
    To him be the glory forever. Amen.

General Comment

God is vindicated! Paul becomes a poet. God has not failed, nor have his promises to the patriarchs failed. God's riches, wisdom, and knowledge are great and beyond comprehending except through special divine revelation. The salvation of Israel will not come about by any means that can be deduced from prior revelation. It will come about another way, disclosed by a mystery that Paul can now celebrate. The doxology shows that Paul's sorrow, of which he spoke in 9:1, has left.

The passage is often referred to as a hymn consisting of nine lines (as presented above).[189] To consider it to have been an actual hymn sung in worship, however, may be going too far. If it is considered a hymn, one is obliged to ask whether it would have been sung in a congregation at worship.[190] Moreover, would it have been sung in a Christian congregation? There is nothing about it that is specifically Christian. Even the word "Lord" (κύριος) in 11:34 refers to the God of Israel, not Christ. If the unit had been a pre-Pauline hymn, it could actually have been used in Jewish worship. It is preferable, then, to speak of the unit as a poetic composition rather than a hymn per se, which concludes with a doxology (11:36). Although it has been suggested that the unit is pre-Pauline,[191] there seem to be no good or necessary reasons for making that claim.[192]

189. The nine-line arrangement of the text presented here follows that of E. Norden, *Agnostos Theos*, 241. That unit is called a hymn by, among others, G. Bornkamm, "The Praise of God," 105; R. Deichgräber, "Römer 11,33-36," 61; C. Cranfield, *Romans*, 589; U. Wilckens, *Römer*, 2:268-69; J. Dunn, *Romans*, 702; P. Stuhlmacher, *Romans*, 174; E. Lohse, *Römer*, 324; R. Jewett, *Romans*, 713.

190. G. Bornkamm, "The Praise of God," 105 ("its original context is that of worship").

191. T. Lim, *Holy Scripture in the Qumran Commentaries and Pauline Letters*, 159.

192. G. Bornkamm, "The Praise of God," 105; C. Cranfield, *Romans*, 589; J. Dunn, *Romans*, 698; J. Fitzmyer, *Romans*, 633; B. Byrne, *Romans*, 358-59; E. Lohse, *Römer*, 325.

The unit is constructed by the piling up of words and phrases in group-ings of three. It begins with three attributes of God ("riches," "wisdom," and "knowledge," 11:33). It continues with three questions (11:34-35). And it con-cludes with an ascription to God with the use of three prepositional phrases ("from him," "through him," and "unto him," 11:36).

Detailed Comment

11:33 Paul bursts out with the introductory exclamatory utterance, "O" (ὦ), which is found particularly in non-Jewish Hellenistic poetic sources, and not elsewhere in the NT in this particular sense.[193] With that exclamation Paul ex-presses strong emotion, going on to speak of the "depth," meaning the inex-haustibility,[194] of the divine attributes. Paul lists three attributes. When he speaks of God's "riches" (πλοῦτος) or "abundance" in his letter previously, he refers to God's kindness, forbearance, and patience (2:4), his generosity to all (10:12), even to the entire world (11:12). And so here he speaks of God's generos-ity once again, triggered by his joy for God's salvation of Israel. "Wisdom" (σοφία) as a divine attribute is familiar in both Jewish and Christian traditions (Job 11:6; 12:13; Dan 2:20; 1 Cor 1:21; 2:7; Eph 3:10; Rev 5:12). Here Paul affirms that God's wisdom is superior to all that humans might possess (cf. 1 Cor 1:21). Although Christ can be spoken of as the wisdom of God (1 Cor 1:24), that is clearly not the meaning here. The depth of the "knowledge of God" (γνῶσις θεοῦ) refers to God's unsurpassing capacity to know all things (a subjective genitive in Greek), not human knowledge of (= about) God (Num 24:16; 1 Sam 2:3; Job 21:22; Ps 94:11; 1 Cor 3:20; cf. 1 John 3:20). And here it indicates that the knowledge of God is indeed greater than what humans could possibly have (cf. Job 21:22), disclosed only as a "mystery" or "secret" to the apostle.

Paul's poetic artistry is displayed further in a play on words that is appar-ent in Greek, but not in English, where he speaks of God's judgments as ἀνεξεραύνητα ("unsearchable") and his ways as ἀνεξιχνίαστοι ("inscrutable"). The words are virtual synonyms in Greek, as are the English renditions used here, an instance of parallelism. The first of the two words is found only here in the NT, and the latter only here and at Ephesians 3:8. That God's "judgments" (κρίματα) are past finding out is not a new assertion by Paul, for that has been said in the OT (Ps 36:6; Wis 17:1; cf. Ps 10:5), but in this case God's judgments are praised for being so unusual and unexpected. That God's ways are inscruta-ble has been declared previously as well (Job 5:9; 9:10), but here they are praised as gracious beyond expectation.

193. R. Deichgräber, "Römer 11,33-36," 62; BDAG 1101 (ὦ, 2, a).
194. BDAG 162 (βάθος, 2).

11:34 The first two questions consist of a quotation from Isaiah 40:13, essentially as it is in the LXX ("Who has known the mind of the Lord, and who has been his counselor who might instruct him?"). Minor differences are Paul's addition of the conjunction γάρ ("for") at the beginning of the first question, the replacement of καί ("and") with ἤ ("or") at the beginning of the second question, and the transposition of the words αὐτοῦ σύμβουλος to the more usual word order σύμβουλος αὐτοῦ ("his counselor"). The major difference is that Paul does not include the last clause of the Isaiah passage of the LXX (ὃς συμβιβᾷ αὐτόν, "who might instruct him"). But the exclusion is understandable, since its inclusion would have interrupted the series of three questions in succession, each beginning with "who?" When he quotes from the same Isaiah text at 1 Corinthians 2:16, he includes that clause but then leaves out the second question ("Or who has been his counselor?"). The two questions of 11:34 are rhetorical, both expecting the same answer: "No one!"

11:35 The third question is based upon (not a quotation from) Job 35:7 ("If you are righteous, what do you give to him; or what does he receive from your hand?").[195] Paul formulates a question, beginning as the others do, asking who it is that would be capable of giving to God in such a way that God is indebted and must give something in return. Again the expected answer is: "No one!" Just as no one can comprehend the mind of God, so no one can surpass the generosity of God.

11:36 Paul rounds off the composition with a thoroughgoing praise of God, a doxology. In speaking of "all things" (τὰ πάντα), he undoubtedly means to include the entire creation (cf. 1 Cor 8:6; 11:12). But at this place, as elsewhere (Rom 8:28; 1 Cor 6:12; 13:7; 15:28; Phil 3:8, 21), the expression need not be limited to that. At this place Paul must include not simply God's creative work, but his saving work as well, exercised above all in the salvation of Israel. In order to give praise to the utmost, Paul uses three prepositional phrases: "from him," "through him," and "unto him." All things come from God. All things have come through God's loving care and grace. And all things belong to God and return to him. Stylistically this threefold use of phrases balances well with the threefold use of terms at the outset of the doxology (riches, wisdom, and knowledge) and the three questions asked in 11:34-35. The doxological praise has parallels in Stoic sources,[196] in which nature and God are one. One of the most striking parallels is a line from the writings of Marcus Aurelius: "All things come from thee, subsist in thee, go back to thee" (ἐκ σοῦ πάντα, ἐν σοὶ πάντα,

---

195. According to B. Schaller, "Zum Textcharacter der Hiobzitate," 21-26, Paul could well be quoting from a Greek version of the text otherwise not known.

196. These are illustrated lavishly by E. Norden, *Agnostos Theos*, 240-50. Norden calls Rom 11:36 "a Stoic doxology in Paul."

εἰς σὲ πάντα).[197] But there are differences. For Paul the "all things" are not only those things that God has created, which can be observed in nature, but also those things that God has done in the history of salvation. Moreover, Stoic pantheism (that all things subsist, or indeed exist, in God, ἐν σοὶ πάντα) is not represented in Paul's doxology. For Paul, all things have come "through him" (δι᾽ αὐτοῦ . . . πάντα) as a God of love and grace.

The doxology makes no mention of Christ, and it is not the only one that does not in the letters of Paul (cf. Phil 4:20: "To our God and Father be glory forever and ever.").[198] The last time Christ was mentioned in chapters 9 through 11 is at 9:1-5. At this place, after working through the problem of the salvation of Israel and gaining an insight that came to him as a divine mystery or secret, Paul ends with the exclamation *Soli Deo gloria* ("Glory to God alone")!

BIBLIOGRAPHY

Barth, Markus. "Theologie — Ein Gebet (Röm 11,33-36)." *TZ* 41 (1985): 330-48.
Bornkamm, Günther. "The Praise of God (Romans 11.33-36)." In his *Early Christian Experience*, 105-11. New York: Harper & Row, 1969.
Deichgräber, Reinhard. "Römer 11,33-36." In his *Gotteshymnus und Christushymnus in der frühen Christenheit*, 61-64. SUNT 5. Göttingen: Vandenhoeck & Ruprecht, 1967.
Lim, Timothy H. *Holy Scripture in the Qumran Commentaries and Pauline Letters*. Oxford: Clarendon Press, 1997.
Norden, Eduard. *Agnostos Theos: Untersuchungen zur Formengeschichte religiöser Rede*. Berlin: Verlag B. G. Teubner, 1913.
Schaller, Berndt. "Zum Textcharakter der Hiobzitate im paulinischen Schrifttum." *ZNW* 71 (1980): 21-26.

197. Marcus Aurelius, *Meditations* 4.23; text and translation from *The Communings with Himself of Marcus Aurelius*, trans. C. R. Haines, LCL (Cambridge: Harvard University Press, 1916), 79-80.
198. Therefore one can hardly say with E. Käsemann, *Romans*, 321, that the passage speaks of "universal redemption . . . with christology at the center."

CHAPTER 6

Serving God and Loving Others, 12:1-21

Romans 12:1 inaugurates a new, major section of the letter that concludes at 15:13. In this section Paul's attention is focused largely on ethical issues, his mission strategy, his plans for travel to Jerusalem, and his hopes for travel to Rome and Spain.

Since the first eleven chapters of the letter are primarily theological, and much of 12:1–15:13 consists of ethical admonitions, it has been maintained that Romans 1 through 11 is the "doctrinal" portion of the letter and chapters 12 through 15 the "ethical" section.[1] There is some basis to that point of view, since the most explicit exhortations in Romans are in chapters 12-15. For example, 31 of 42 imperatives of the letter are in this section, and there are a good number of imperatival infinitives, adjectives, participles, and hortatory subjunctives within it as well.[2]

While the distinction between "doctrinal" and "hortatory" sections is not to be discounted entirely in terms of tendencies, it does not actually hold up in a consistent manner. There are plenty of ethical admonitions in the first eleven chapters (e.g., 2:1; 5:1-5; 6:12-14; 8:12-17), and there are doctrinal affirmations in those that follow (e.g., 12:4-8; 13:9-10; 14:7-9; 15:8-13). Moreover, the admonitions within chapters 12 through 15 presuppose all that has gone before concerning the redemptive work of God in Christ and the new life initiated through baptism into Christ, ending the old life and giving birth to the new; in other words, they indicate what the new life in Christ entails.[3] Therefore, other

---

1. Cf. W. Sanday and A. Headlam, *Romans,* xlvii-l (division between "doctrinal" and "practical and hortatory"); U. Wilckens, *Römer,* 1:15, 21 ("Evangelium" [= "gospel"] in chs. 1–11, while 12–15 is "paränetisch" [= "paraenetic," i.e., hortatory]); J. Fitzmyer, *Romans,* 637 ("doctrinal discussion" in chs. 1–11, followed by "exhortation"); C. Bjerkelund, *Parakalô,* 156 ("theoretisch" [theoretical] part in chs. 1–11, "paränetisch" [paraenetic] part in chs. 12–15).

2. V. Furnish, *Theology and Ethics in Paul,* 99.

3. V. Furnish, *Theology and Ethics in Paul,* 105-6.

interpreters emphasize that, although a shift is made at 12:1, introducing a largely hortatory section (chapters 12 through 15), they do not make such a sharp distinction between that and a discrete doctrinal portion previous to it.[4] The issues that Paul takes up in the closing chapters of the letter point the way for those who are in Christ. The word οὖν ("therefore") in the opening sentence ("I appeal to you, therefore") is a connector to what has gone before.

The entire section of 12:1–15:33 prompts the question of ethical reasoning and discourse in the letters of Paul. What emerges in an analysis of his ethical discourse is that he understands that the Christian lives "in Christ" and not under the law. When Paul thinks of the law, he cannot think otherwise than as a son of the Israelite people. The law is holy, just, and good (Rom 7:12). God would not give to Israel anything less. It consists, however, not only of moral teaching but also of much that is ceremonial and dietary (the dietary being a subset of the ceremonial). One cannot separate these in one's living, even if one can make a distinction for the purposes of discussion. A person is either in or out, observant or nonobservant of the law. The consequence is that the law, so understood, is for those "under the law," the Jewish people, not for humanity as a whole.

Life in Christ is not life under the law. One belongs to Christ and his destiny, free from the law and the power of sin and death. But there are moral obligations, and Paul writes 12:1–15:13 to show that the gospel of grace that he preaches does not exempt anyone from those moral obligations.[5] That charge has been made against him, and it was apparently known in Rome (3:8; 6:1, 15). The one who is in Christ lives under the lordship of Christ and is led by the Spirit. Whatever coheres with that life in Christ can be endorsed and used by Paul within his exhortations. That can include the commandments (13:9), the love commandment above all (Rom 13:8-10; Gal 5:15), the teachings of Jesus (1 Cor 7:10-11; 9:14; 11:23-26), and common Greco-Roman ethical values.

BIBLIOGRAPHY

Bjerkelund, Carl J. *Parakalô: Form, Funktion und Sinn der parakalô-Sätze in den paulinischen Briefen*. BTN 1. Oslo: Universitetsforlaget, 1967.
Bultmann, Rudolf. "The Problem of Ethics in Paul." In *Understanding Paul's Ethics: Twentieth-Century Approaches*, 195-216. Ed. Brian S. Rosner. Grand Rapids: Wm. B. Eerdmans, 1995.
Campbell, William S. "The Rule of Faith in Romans 12:1–15:13: The Obligation of Humble

---

4. Cf. A. Nygren, *Romans*, 411; J. Dunn, *Romans*, lxi-lxiii; R. Harrisville, *Romans*, 189; B. Byrne, *Romans*, 361; P. Stuhlmacher, *Romans*, 185; E. Lohse, *Römer*, 54; R. Jewett, *Romans*, 724-25.

5. C. Roetzel, "Sacrifice in Romans 12–15," 410-19.

Obedience to Christ as the Only Adequate Response to the Mercies of God." In *Pauline Theology*, vol. 3, *Romans*, 259-86. Ed. David M. Hay and Elizabeth Johnson. Minneapolis: Fortress Press, 1995.

Deidun, T. J. *New Covenant Morality in Paul*. Rome: Pontifical Biblical Institute Press, 1981.

Esler, Philip F. "Paul and Stoicism: Romans 12 as a Test Case." *NTS* 50 (2004): 106-24.

————. "Social Identity, the Virtues, and the Good Life: A New Approach to Romans 12:1–15:13." *BTB* 33 (2003): 51-63.

Furnish, Victor Paul. *The Moral Teaching of Paul: Selected Issues*. 3d ed. Nashville: Abingdon Press, 2009.

————. *Theology and Ethics in Paul*. Nashville: Abingdon Press, 1968; new ed. NTL. Louisville: Westminster John Knox, 2009.

Hays, Richard B. *The Moral Vision of the New Testament: A Contemporary Introduction to New Testament Ethics*. San Francisco: HarperSanFrancisco, 1996.

————. "The Role of Scripture in Paul's Ethics." In *Theology and Ethics in Paul and His Interpreters: Essays in Honor of Victor Paul Furnish*, 30-47. Ed. Eugene H. Lovering Jr. and Jerry L. Sumney. Nashville: Abingdon Press, 1996; reprinted in his *The Conversion of the Imagination: Paul as an Interpreter of Israel's Scripture*, 143-62. Grand Rapids: Wm. B. Eerdmans, 2005.

Hooker, Morna D. "Interchange in Christ and Ethics." *JSNT* 25 (1985): 3-17.

Houlden, J. L. *Ethics and the New Testament*. New York: Oxford University Press, 1973.

Jankowski, Gerhard. "Ermutigungen: Paulus an die Römer Kapital 12–15." *TK* 2 (1978): 11-27.

Lee, Michelle V. *Paul, the Stoics, and the Body of Christ*. SNTSMS 137. New York: Cambridge University Press, 2006.

Lohse, Eduard. *Theological Ethics of the New Testament*. Minneapolis: Fortress Press, 1991.

Matera, Frank J. *New Testament Ethics: The Legacies of Jesus and Paul*. Louisville: Westminster John Knox, 1996.

Meeks, Wayne A. *The Moral World of the First Christians*. Philadelphia: Westminster, 1996.

Minear, Paul Sevier. "The Mercies of God: Measuring Faith in 12:1–13:1." In his *The Obedience of Faith: The Purpose of Paul in the Epistle to the Romans*, 82-90. London: SCM, 1971.

Moiser, Jeremy. "Rethinking Romans 12–15." *NTS* 36 (1990): 571-82.

Peng, Kuo-Wei. *Hate the Evil, Hold Fast to the Good: Structuring Romans 12.1–15.13*. LNTS 300. London: T&T Clark, 2006.

Peterson, David. "Worship and Ethics in Romans 12." *TynBul* 44 (1993): 271-88.

Reasoner, Mark. "The Theology of Romans 12:1–15:13." In *Pauline Theology*, vol. 3, *Romans*, 287-99. Ed. David M. Hay and E. Elizabeth Johnson. Minneapolis: Fortress, 1995.

Roetzel, Calvin. "Sacrifice in Romans 12–15." *WW* 6 (1986): 410-19.

Rosner, Brian. "Paul's Ethics." In *The Cambridge Companion to St. Paul*, 212-23. Ed. James D. G. Dunn. Cambridge: Cambridge University Press, 2003.

Samuelson, Peter L. "A New Vision of Rightousness: Paul's Exhortations in Romans 12–15." *WW* 10 (1990): 295-97, 300, 302-3.

Taylor, Walter F. "Obligation: Paul's Foundation for Ethics." *Trinity Seminary Review* 19 (1997): 91-112.

Thompson, Michael B. *Clothed with Christ: The Example and Teaching of Jesus in Romans 12.1–15.13.* JSNTSup 59. Sheffield: JSOT Press, 1991.

Vouga, François. "L'Épître aux Romains comme document ecclésiologique (Rm 12–15)." *ETR* 61 (1986): 485-95.

Walter, Nikolaus. "Christusglaube und heidnische Religiosität in paulinischen Gemeinden." *NTS* 25 (1979): 422-42.

6.1. Worship and the Renewal of the Mind, 12:1-2

1*Brothers and sisters, I appeal to you, therefore, by the mercies of God, to present your bodies as a sacrifice, living, holy, and pleasing to God, which is your spiritual worship. 2And do not be conformed to this age, but be transformed by the renewal of the mind in order that you may discern the will of God, that which is good, pleasing, and perfect.*

Notes on the Text and Translation

12:1 On "brothers and sisters" as a translation of ἀδελφοί, see comment on 1:13.

12:2 Some ancient witnesses (including ℵ) have ὑμῶν ("your") after τοῦ νοός ("of the mind"), which is implied ("your mind"). But it is not present in other important witnesses (including 𝔓⁴⁶ and B). The word most likely was added by scribes to make a parallel to what is said in 12:1.[6] Almost all widely used English versions (KJV, ASV, RSV, ESV, NAB, NET, NIV) read "your mind" at this point, thereby reflecting the longer reading. The NRSV has "your minds" (plural). Although "your mind" appears in many versions, "the mind" is preferred here (see the exegesis).

General Comment

Paul initiates a new, major section of the letter at Romans 12:1 that concludes at 15:13. He addresses his readers as "brothers and sisters" at the outset (12:1), just as he will once again when he begins the next section (15:14). By using this form of address, he expresses affection, mutual responsibility, and solidarity.

The two verses under consideration here form a connection between what has gone before and what is to follow. The second word οὖν ("therefore") of 12:1 acts as a prompter to notice the connection. What follows presupposes all that has been said up to that point. Moreover, it presupposes Paul's thinking concerning the two ages or eras — the old age dominated by sin and death since

6. B. Metzger, *TCGNT* 466.

Adam, and the new age of righteousness and life that has been inaugurated with the resurrection of Christ, and to which all who believe in the gospel share with him. Paul explicitly uses the language of the ages in his appeal not to be "conformed to this age," i.e., the old age of sin and death, but to be "transformed by the renewal of the mind," i.e., gaining a new mind (or way of thinking), transformed by the power of the indwelling Spirit, that is characteristic of those who belong to Christ and his destiny.

On the basis of the identity of those who are in Christ, Paul exhorts them to present their bodies — their very selves — to be living sacrifices to God. The indicative is the basis for the imperative. The remainder of 12:3–15:13 provides a series of applications of bodies and minds leaning into the future of God for life in the world.

Detailed Comment

12:1 The expression "I appeal to you" (παρακαλῶ ὑμᾶς) appears elsewhere in Paul's letters at those places where he is making a particularly important admonition (Rom 15:30; 16:17; 1 Cor 1:10; 4:16; 16:15; 2 Cor 2:8; 10:1). In each case the appeal is a personal petition, but in the present instance Paul appeals "by the mercies of God," thus indicating that he makes his appeal by divine authority.[7] The expression resonates with those in the OT where God is a God of "mercies" (e.g., Exod 34:6; Deut 4:31; 2 Sam 24:14; 1 Chr 21:13; 2 Chr 30:9; LXX Pss 24:6; 85:15), and where the plural of the noun for "mercy" is conventionally used (רַחֲמִים, οἰκτιρμοί, "mercies").[8]

The verse contains cultic terminology, the most obvious of which are the terms παρίστημι ("to present"), which is used in reference to presenting offerings,[9] θυσία ("sacrifice"), and λατρεία ("worship"). Paul calls upon his readers to present their "bodies" to God as living sacrifices. By so doing Paul calls upon them to offer themselves, to be sure, but it is themselves as subjects of the Lord in their earthly existence, not simply in a spiritual sense that loses contact with the world.[10]

Paul writes his appeal while the sacrificial system is still operative in the Jerusalem Temple among Jews, and Gentiles were offering sacrifices at shrines and temples for various deities. But he makes a rather backhanded critique of

---

7. T. Mullins, "Petition as a Literary Form," 53-54. There is a similar expression at 2 Cor 10:1 ("I . . . appeal to you by the meekness and gentleness of Christ").

8. C. Bjerkelund, *Parakalô*, 163-68, cites rabbinic passages as well.

9. Josephus, *J.W.* 2.89; *Ant.* 4.113. For additional references in Hellenistic literature, cf. BDAG 778 (παρίστημι, 1, d).

10. Cf. Eduard Schweizer, "σῶμα," *EDNT* 3:323; E. Käsemann, *Romans*, 327.

any and all sacrifices being made when he says that Christians are to offer themselves as "living sacrifices" in contrast to the offering of animals that have been slain and are no longer living. The living sacrifices are to be "holy," which can have a moral sense but at its base means to be set apart for divine use. And so the living sacrifices will also be "pleasing to God."

The words λογικὴ λατρεία are translated here as "spiritual worship," as in the RSV, NRSV, NAB, and ESV. Other terms are used in other versions, such as "reasonable service" (KJV and NET), "spiritual service" (ASV), and "spiritual act of worship" (NIV). The word λατρεία ("worship," "service") is familiar from the LXX (Exod 12:25-26; 13:5; Josh 22:27), other places in the NT (John 16:2; Rom 9:4; Heb 9:1, 6), and in still other sources, both pagan and Jewish.[11] The word λογικὴ, however, is more difficult to render in connection with "worship." An adjective, its basic meaning in classical Greek is "of or belonging to the reason," "logical,"[12] and the emphasis on discernment in the next sentence (12:2) indicates that the cognitive nuance of the adjective should not be lost. In light of that, one might render the terms as "reasonable service," as has been done. Yet the context (containing various cultic terms) indicates that Paul is speaking here about worship in a metaphorical sense (not simply "service"). It is best, therefore, to keep the language of worship and find an appropriate modifier for it to represent the word λογικὴ. A similar expression, λογικὴ καὶ ἀναίμακτος προσφορά ("a rational [or 'spiritual'] and bloodless offering"), appears in the *Testament of Levi* 3.6, referring to the worship that the angels do. The author of 1 Peter 2:5 exhorts his readers to offer πνευματικὰς θυσίας ("spiritual sacrifices"). Finally, the term λογικὴ θυσία ("a rational [or 'spiritual'] sacrifice") appears in later Gnostic sources.[13] In each case the terms refer to actual acts of worship. Within the context of Romans 12, however, where attention is focused on the life of the believer in the world, the expression λογικὴ λατρεία does not refer to an act of worship but to "daily life determined by faith as the true worship."[14]

Once that point is granted, one searches in vain for a rendering that would be better than "spiritual worship" at this place. As such, it stands over against worship that lacks ethical relationships in the world. Thoughts concerning worship and ethics converge at this point in Romans.[15] In this regard Paul stands within the OT tradition that calls for obedience to God as true worship and sacrifice (Isa 1:10-17; Jer 6:20; 7:21-23; Hos 6:6; Amos 5:20-25; Mal 1:10-14;

---

11. Plato, *Apol.* 23b; *Phaedr.* 244e; Josephus, *J.W.* 2.409; Philo, *Ebr.* 144.

12. LSJ 1056 (λογικός).

13. *Corpus Hermeticum* 1.31; 13.18-19; quoted from *Corpus Hermeticum*, ed. Arthur D. Nock and André Jean Festugière, 2 vols. (Paris: Société d'edition 'Les Belles Lettres,' 1945), 1:19, 208.

14. Hans-Werner Bartsch, "λογικός," *EDNT* 2:355.

15. E. Käsemann, "Worship and Everyday Life," 191.

Sir 34:18-26), an emphasis that is also found in Hellenistic Judaism and at Qumran.[16] But beyond those who went before him, or were his contemporaries at Qumran, Paul would not think of "spiritual worship" apart from obedience to Christ, under whose lordship all belong who have rendered themselves as living sacrifices. Earlier in the letter Paul had recorded that some persons had charged him with antinomianism (3:8; cf. 6:1, 15). But here at the outset of Romans 12:1–15:13, Paul assures his readers that his gospel of grace involves a life given over to God in sacrificial service and obedience.[17] Believers, baptized into Christ, are expected to be "slaves to righteousness" (6:18-19).

12:2 Paul continues his exhortation, calling upon his readers not to be "conformed to this age." Except for the deutero-Pauline author of Ephesians (1:21), Paul is the only other NT writer to use "this age" (ὁ αἰὼν οὗτος and oblique forms) as an expression, which he uses seven times (Rom 12:2; 1 Cor 1:20; 2:6 [twice], 8; 3:18; 2 Cor 4:4); additionally, he uses the expression "the present age" (ὁ αἰὼν ὁ ἐνεστώς) once (Gal 1:4). It presupposes the doctrine of the two aeons derived from Jewish apocalyptic (cf. 2 Esdr 7:113, "But the day of judgment will be the end of this age [*finis temporis huius*] and the beginning of the immortal age to come [*initium futuri inmortalis temporis*], in which corruption has passed away").[18] In Paul's writings "this age" refers to the present world in which people exist, having its own ethos and standards, and which can be characterized as evil (Gal 1:4; cf. 1 Cor 2:6, 8), under the dominion of its own divinity (2 Cor 4:4), and doomed to pass away (1 Cor 2:6). Its passing away allows for the coming of the "new age."[19] Rather than living in conformity to the existing era of sin and death, Paul says, those who are believers in Christ are to be "transformed by the renewal of the mind." The term νοῦς ("mind") is always in the singular in Paul's writings, even when he is speaking to a corporate body, as here (cf. Rom 1:28; 14:35; 1 Cor 1:10). There is no need (contra the NRSV) to make the term plural. Paul speaks to the community, as though it has a shared experience, a shared "mind," a solidarity within a corporate life.[20] The word νοῦς ("mind") has several nuances of meaning in the NT,[21] but here it signifies a mental capacity to discern moral matters, even the will of God.[22]

---

16. Philo, *Spec. Leg.* 1.272; 1.277; 1.290; *Let. Arist.* 234; *T. Levi* 3.5-6; 1QS 9.4-5. For additional references, cf. E. Ferguson, "Spiritual Sacrifice," 1156-62; and J. Baumgarten, "Sacrifice and Worship among the Jewish Sectarians," 141-59.

17. C. Roetzel, "Sacrifice in Romans 12–15," 410-19.

18. The Latin expressions are from the Vulgate.

19. Hermann Sasse, "αἰών," *TDNT* 1:205-6.

20. H. Stoessel, "Notes on Romans 12:1-2," 161-63.

21. BDAG 680 (νοῦς) lists "mind," "intellect," "understanding," "way of thinking," "attitude," "thought," "opinion," and "decree."

22. Alexander Sand, "νοῦς," *EDNT* 2:479.

Paul does not say just how the mind is to be renewed at this place in his letter. The main verb concerning it is μεταμορφοῦσθε ("be transformed"), a passive imperative; it is also plural, indicating once more the corporate scope of the admonition. The fact that Paul speaks of "renewal" (ἀνακαίνωσις) in the same sentence — a word associated with baptism (Titus 3:5) — indicates that, for him, transformation occurs in the life of the baptized through the Spirit, which is given in baptism. It is the indwelling Spirit, bestowed in baptism, that gives life (Rom 8:6, 11), enabling believers to walk in newness of life (Rom 6:4). Paul's imperative is a simple present tense, indicating that the transforming of the mind is to be an ongoing, dynamic process. The imperative is based on the indicative; Paul calls upon his readers to continue to become what they are.

Specifically, those who are in Christ are expected to "discern the will of God," and that is followed by words in apposition: they are to discern "that which is good, pleasing, and perfect." Discerning those things involves observation and reason concerning conflicting and competing values within the old age, this world in which one lives. The verb used for such discerning (δοκιμάζω) has the twin meanings of discovering and approving,[23] and that is where rationality and discretion become necessary. In all of this it is evident that, for Paul, the renewed mind of the believer does not abandon its critical powers but is affected and guided by life under grace and the lordship of Christ.[24] Moreover, it needs to be stressed that, for Paul, rationality, discretion, and other values of the Greco-Roman tradition continue to remain even for those whose minds have been renewed. That is illustrated vividly where Paul, writing to the Philippians, asserts that certain Greco-Roman values known to them are worthy of attention and emulation: "whatever is true, whatever is honorable, whatever is just, whatever is pure, whatever is pleasing, whatever is commendable, if there is any excellence and if there is anything worthy of praise, think about these things" (Phil 4:8).

BIBLIOGRAPHY

Asmussen, Hans. "Das Opfer der Gemeinde." *EvT* 1 (1934-35): 49-55.
Baumgarten, Joseph M. "Sacrifice and Worship among the Jewish Sectarians of the Dead Sea (Qumran) Scrolls." *HTR* 46 (1953): 141-59.
Betz, Hans D. "The Foundation of Christian Ethics according to Romans 12:1-2." In *Witness and Existence: Essays in Honor of Schubert M. Ogden*, 55-72. Ed. Philip E. Devenish and George L. Goodwin. Chicago: University of Chicago Press, 1989.
Bjerkelund, Carl J. *Parakalô: Form, Funktion und Sinn der parakalô-Sätze in den paulinischen Briefen*. BTN 1. Oslo: Universitetsforlaget, 1967.

23. BDAG 255 (δοκιμάζω).
24. Cf. G. Bornkamm, "Faith and Reason in Paul," 41-42.

Blank, Josef. "Zum Begriff des Opfers nach Röm 12,1-2." In *Funktion und Struktur christlicher Gemeinde: Festgabe für Prof. Dr. Heinz Fleckenstein zum 65. Geburtstag,* 35-51. Ed. Heinrich Pompey et al. Würzburg: Echter Verlag, 1971; reprinted in his *Paulus, von Jesus zum Christentum: Aspekte der paulinischen Lehre und Praxis,* 169-91. Munich: Kösel Verlag, 1982.

Bornkamm, Günther. "Faith and Reason in Paul." In his *Early Christian Experience,* 29-46. New York: Harper & Row, 1969.

————. "On the Understanding of Worship." In his *Early Christian Experience,* 161-79. New York: Harper & Row, 1969.

Daly, Robert J. *Christian Sacrifice.* Washington: Catholic University of America Press, 1978.

Esler, Philip F. "Paul and Stoicism: Romans 12 as a Test Case." *NTS* 50 (2004): 106-24.

Evans, Craig F. "Rom 12:1-2: The True Worship." In *Dimensions de la vie chrétienne (Rm 12–13),* 7-33. Ed. Lorenzo de Lorenzi. Rome: St. Paul's Abbey, 1979.

Ferguson, Everett. "Spiritual Sacrifice in Early Christianity and Its Environment." *ANRW* II.23.2 (1980): 1151-89.

Furnish, Victor Paul. *Theology and Ethics in Paul.* Nashville: Abingdon Press, 1968; new ed. NTL. Louisville: Westminster John Knox, 2009.

Giblin, Charles H. "Charismatic Worship in Faith and Love in Paul's Gospel." In his *In Hope of God's Glory,* 224-31. New York: Herder and Herder, 1970.

Gundry, Robert H. *Sōma in Biblical Theology: With Emphasis on Pauline Anthropology,* SNTSMS 29. Cambridge: Cambridge University Press, 1976.

Hubert, Henri, and Marcel Mauss. *Sacrifice: Its Nature and Function.* Chicago: University of Chicago Press, 1964.

Käsemann, Ernst. "Worship and Everyday Life: A Note on Romans 12." In his *New Testament Questions of Today,* 188-95. London: SCM Press, 1969.

Kirchhoff, Renate. "Röm 12,1-2 und der Qualitätsanspruch diakonischen Handelns." In *Das Gesetz im frühen Judentum und im Neuen Testament: Festschrift für Christoph Burchard zum 75. Geburtstag,* 87-98. Ed. Dieter Sänger and Matthias Konradt. NTOA 57. Göttingen: Vandenhoeck & Ruprecht, 2006.

Klauck, Hans-Josef. "Sacrifice and Sacrificial Offerings (NT)." *ABD* 5:886-91.

Koenig, John. "Vision, Self-offering, and Transformation for Ministry (Rom 12:1-8)." In *Sin, Salvation, and the Spirit,* 307-23. Ed. Daniel Durken. Collegeville: Liturgical Press, 1979.

Mullins, Terence Y. "Petition as a Literary Form." *NovT* 5 (1962): 46-54.

Parsons, Michael. "Being Precedes Act: Indicative and Imperative in Paul's Writing." *EvQ* 60 (1900): 99-127; reprinted in *Understanding Paul's Ethics: Twentieth-Century Approaches,* 217-47. Ed. Brian S. Rosner. Grand Rapids: Wm. B. Eerdmans, 1995.

Perdue, Leo G. "The Social Character of Paraenesis and Paraenetic Literature." *Semeia* 59 (1990): 5-39.

Rad, Gerhard von. "The Sacrifices." In his *Old Testament Theology,* 1:250-61. 2 vols. New York: Harper & Row, 1962-65.

Reichert, Angelika. "Gottes universaler Heilswille und der kommunikative Gottesdienst: Exegetische Anmerkungen zu Röm 12,1-2." In *Paulus, Apostel Jesu Christi: Festschrift für Günter Klein zum 70. Geburtstag,* 79-95. Ed. Michael Trowitzsch. Tübingen: J. C. B. Mohr (Paul Siebeck), 1998.

Roetzel, Calvin J. "Sacrifice in Romans 12–15." *WW* 6 (1986): 410-19.

Schweizer, Eduard. "Gottesdienst im Neuen Testament und Kirchenbau heute." In *Beiträge zur Theologie des Neuen Testaments,* 249-61. Zurich: Zwingli Verlag, 1970.

Seidensticker, Philipp. *Lebendiges Opfer (Röm 12,1): Ein Beitrag zur Theologie des Apostels Paulus.* NTAbh 20.1-3. Münster: Aschendorff, 1954.

Stoessel, Horace E. "Notes on Romans 12:1-2: The Renewal of the Mind and Internalizing the Truth." *Int* 17 (1963): 161-75.

Thorsteinsson, Runar M. "Paul and Roman Stoicism: Romans 12 and Contemporary Stoic Ethics." *JSNT* 29 (2006): 139-61.

Young, Frances M. *The Use of Sacrificial Ideas in Greek Christian Writers from the New Testament to John Chrysostom.* PMS 5. Cambridge: Philadelphia Patristic Foundation, 1979.

6.2. Grace and Gifts within the Body of Christ, 12:3-8

3For by virtue of the grace given to me, I say to everyone among you not to think more highly than you ought to think, but to think with sober judgment, according to the measure of faith that God has apportioned to each. 4For as in one body we have many members, but all members do not have the same function, 5so we, who are many, are one body in Christ, and individually we are members of one another, 6but having gifts that differ according to the grace given to us — if prophecy, in agreement with the faith; 7if service, in serving; if one teaches, in teaching; 8if one exhorts, in exhortation; the one who makes contributions, with sincerity; the one who gives aid, with diligence; the one who does acts of mercy, with cheerfulness.

Notes on the Text and Translation

12:3 The preposition διά followed by the genitive can signify instrumentality, and in this case the phrase can be translated as "by virtue of the grace."[25]

12:6 The verse begins with a participle (ἔχοντες, "having") and consists of a subordinate clause that does not end until the close of 12:8. The Nestle-Aland text (27th ed.) has a period after 12:5 and starts a new sentence at 12:6. Modern English versions (KJV, ASV, RSV, NIV, NRSV, ESV, NET) do the same. But that is not necessary and can be misleading, for then one has to supply a main verb (indeed an entire clause) in 12:6, such as "let us use them," and the result is a horta-

25. The translation is suggested in BDAG 225 (διά, 3, e).

tory passage to the end of the paragraph. But syntactically 12:6-8 is one sentence and is descriptive, not prescriptive, of the community of believers.[26]

General Comment

Prior to these verses Paul has called for the transformation of the believer's mind at the beginning of his (mainly) ethical section. That calls for a right judgment concerning one's place within the body of Christ. No one is to be haughty or to fail to recognize the gifts that others have within the body. He goes on to mention the various gifts in 12:6-8.

Paul lists seven gifts of grace. Actually only two gifts are mentioned, strictly speaking (prophecy and service), and they are listed at the beginning. Then Paul enumerates five cases of persons graced by gifts who enact them. Two relate to prophecy, and three to service. Therefore, by using prophecy and service as the primary categories, the seven gifts of grace can be arranged as follows:

> **Gifts expressed through speech:**
> προφητεία ("prophecy"), expressed by
> > ὁ διδάσκων ("the one who teaches")
> > ὁ παρακαλῶν ("the one who exhorts")

> **Gifts expressed through practical service:**
> διακονία ("service"), expressed by
> > ὁ μεταδιδούς ("the one who contributes")
> > ὁ προϊστάμενος ("the one who gives aid")
> > ὁ ἐλεῶν ("the one who does acts of mercy")

Paul does not speak explicitly here of the gifts listed as gifts of the Spirit, but calls them gifts provided by God "according to the grace given to us." In fact, except for "prophecy" in this passage, the gifts listed do not appear in the list of gifts of the Spirit in 1 Corinthians 12:7-11:

> To each is given the manifestation of the Spirit for the common good. To one is given through the Spirit the utterance of wisdom, and to another the utterance of knowledge according to the same Spirit, to another faith by the same Spirit, to another gifts of healing by the one Spirit, to another the

---

26. Cf. B. Byrne, *Romans,* 372; for a survey and analysis, cf. K. Berding, "Romans 12:4-8," 433-39.

working of miracles, to another prophecy, to another the discernment of spirits, to another various kinds of tongues, to another the interpretation of tongues. All these are activated by one and the same Spirit, who allots to each one individually just as the Spirit chooses.

Later in that chapter Paul enumerates divinely given appointments in the church where "prophets" and "teachers" are included (1 Cor 12:28):

And God has appointed in the church first apostles, second prophets, third teachers; then deeds of power, then gifts of healing, forms of assistance, forms of leadership, various kinds of tongues.

There is a noticeable difference between the gifts in Romans 12:6-8 and those in 1 Corinthians 12:7-11, 28. The latter are ecstatic or charismatic in the narrow sense of the term, and they are gifts that manifest themselves in the community at worship, whereas those in Romans are not expressed in moments of ecstasy, and they are exercised within the community of believers for the sake of believers and (at least possibly) non-believers alike. But what is common to both passages on gifts is that, when they are used, they are to be used for the good of all.

Detailed Comment

12:3 Paul claims to have been endowed by a particular "grace" (χάρις) that enables him to speak to the community. In saying that, he recalls what he has said at the beginning of the letter, namely, that he has received "grace and apostleship" from Christ "to bring about the obedience of faith among all the nations for the sake of his name" (1:5). Although the term χάρις usually, or at least typically, has the meaning of divine favor in the letters of Paul,[27] it takes on the meaning of a divine gift (similar to χάρισμα) to empower him and others for the tasks to which they are called (Rom 1:5; 15:15; 1 Cor 3:10; 15:10; Gal 2:9). In fact, Paul declares at 12:6 that the χάρις ("grace") of God manifests itself in various χαρίσματα ("gifts").

As one who has received grace for the task, Paul says that no one should think more highly than one ought to think. Once again, it is not necessary to conclude that Paul addresses a particular problem at Rome. He speaks in the singular ("everyone among you"), as in the form of diatribe. And he does not innovate, for he expresses what belongs to the common Christian tradition,[28]

---

27. Many examples are cited in BDAG 1079 (χάρις, 2, c).
28. Cf. Luke 18:9-14; 1 Cor 4:6; Phil 2:5-8; 1 Pet 5:5-6.

namely, that one ought not to think too highly of oneself (or "be haughty"; the word is ὑπερφρονέω, used only here in the NT), but to think with sober judgment. A more literal translation, which includes all the verbs and the play on words, would be: "not to think more highly (ὑπερφρονεῖν) in comparison to that which it is necessary to think (φρονεῖν), but to think (φρονεῖν) so as to be prudent (σωφρονεῖν)." Moreover, one should think — in this place meaning to consider one's own place and role within the community of faith — "according to the measure of faith (μέτρον πίστεως) that God has apportioned to each." The entire clause is adverbial, spelling out how one ought to think. The expression "measure of faith" in this context does not refer to a quantity of faith (various degrees of faith among individuals), nor is it likely to refer to a "standard of faith," an objective measure against which one would measure one's own faith.[29] Rather the accent is upon God's having "measured out" (ἐμέρισεν, aorist of μερίζω)[30] a "measure of faith" to each individual, and so each has the ability to think with sober judgment.[31] The faith spoken of in the expression is then the faith that each believer possesses, the faith by which one believes (fides qua). But that faith is also a means of Christian discernment. The believer in Christ is endowed with faith sufficient for thinking of the self in a proper way. The admonition is directed against hybris and is repeated in 12:16 ("do not be haughty" and "do not claim to be wiser than you are").[32]

12:4-5 Paul uses the imagery of the church as "the body of Christ" here for the first time in his letter (actually using only the expression "one body" rather than the full phrase, as in 1 Cor 12:27). He had used the expression "the body of Christ" earlier at 7:4, but not in an ecclesial sense (see the exegesis there). He had also used the imagery previously when he wrote to the Corinthians (1 Cor 12:4-31). There he emphasized that, although gifts differ among the members of the community, none is to be despised or considered inferior. The body is to care for all its members.

Here a different accent is made. To be sure, as in his Corinthians correspondence, Paul asserts that the members of the body differ, depending upon the variety of gifts given. But rather than emphasizing the body's caring for its members, here he writes that the members are to employ their gifts for the sake

29. Contra C. Cranfield, "Μέτρον πίστεως in Romans 12:3," 345-51; idem, Romans, 614-15; U. Wilckens, Römer, 3:11; J. Fitzmyer, Romans, 646; P. Stuhlmacher, Romans, 192; and E. Lohse, Römer, 340. R. Jewett, Romans, 736-42, renders the phrase "the measuring rod of faith" and speaks of differentiated "measuring rods" among believers.

30. BDAG 632 (μερίζω, 2, b): "deal out," "assign," "apportion" something to someone.

31. Somewhat similarly, Kurt Deissner, "μέτρον," TDNT 4:634; C. K. Barrett, Romans, 217; J. Dunn, Romans, 721-22; D. Moo, Romans, 761.

32. H. Moxnes, "The Quest for Honor and the Unity of the Community in Romans 12," 222.

of the body.[33] Not all members have the same function, but all are "one body in Christ" and individually "members of one another."

The use of the term "body" (of Christ) as an ecclesiological term in this instance refers not to a congregation (there seems to be no single congregation in Rome at this time) but to the church in its wider sense. Paul can use the term for the local community (cf. 1 Cor 12:27: "you are the body of Christ"), but also in a universal sense (1 Cor 12:13: "we were all baptized into one body"), just as he can use the term "church" in both the local sense (Rom 16:1, 5; 1 Cor 1:2; 1 Thess 1:1) and in the universal sense (1 Cor 10:32; 15:9; Gal 1:13; Phil 3:6). Here at Romans 12:4-5 he speaks of the body in the wider sense, for not all the gifts listed can necessarily be found in any particular congregation (especially an ancient house church), and he includes himself ("we have many members," "we . . . are one body," and "we are members of one another"). For more on the church as the body of Christ, see the appendix, "The Church as the Body of Christ in the Letters of Paul."

12:6   The gifts which God gives differ from one another (cf. 1 Cor 12:11), and all are of value. But it is not surprising that when Paul begins his list of gifts he would start with "prophecy" (προφητεία).[34] In his Corinthian correspondence it is clear that, among the various gifts of the Spirit, prophecy is indispensable (1 Cor 14:1, 5, 39). It is for upbuilding, encouragement, and consolation (14:3-4); it is greater than speaking in tongues (and so is comprehensible, 14:5); it convicts unbelievers (14:24-25); and it includes teaching and encouragement (14:31).

This gift, Paul says, is to be used in a specific way. That is κατὰ τὴν ἀναλογίαν τῆς πίστεως (literally, "according to the analogy of faith"). The meaning of the phrase is disputed. The noun ἀναλογία is used only here in the entire NT. It can mean, and is often translated to mean, "proportion,"[35] so that the phrase κατὰ τὴν ἀναλογίαν has been translated as "according to" or "in proportion to one's faith" (KJV, NIV, NRSV, and NET). In that case, the phrase would refer to the proportion of faith that a person possesses, i.e., the prophet's personal faith (*fides qua creditur,* "the faith by which one believes"). This rendering is favored by several interpreters.[36] On the other hand, it can mean "according to" or "in proportion to [our] faith," meaning the common Christian faith (ASV, RSV, and ESV), some common standard shared within the commu-

---

33. The distinction, however, is not absolute. Paul goes on to emphasize the use of gifts to edify the church at 1 Cor 14:3-5, 12, 26.

34. Contra R. Jewett, *Romans,* 746, who says that "the list as a whole reflects a random sequence."

35. BDAG 67 (ἀναλογία).

36. W. Sanday and A. Headlam, *Romans,* 356-57; J. Dunn, *Romans,* 727-28; R. Jewett, *Romans,* 747; Gerhard Kittel, "ἀναλογία," *TDNT* 1:347-48.

nity of believers (*fides quae creditur,* "the faith that is believed"). This view is shared widely as well.[37]

There are good arguments in each case. In favor of the first of these, Paul is citing gifts that are given individually and that differ, so it could be maintained that Paul describes here "how the act of prophecy comes about — that is, by the prophet speaking forth in proportion to his faith = his dependence on God."[38] But the second viewpoint is to be preferred. The Greek term ἀναλογία has a wide range of meanings within phrases other than "in proportion to," such as "in analogy to," "in relationship to," "in correspondence with," "in agreement with," and the like,[39] and those meanings favor the objective view. Moreover, when Paul speaks of the gifts of grace other than prophecy, he says that they are to be used "with" (Greek: ἐν or ἐν τῇ), but in the case of prophecy he does not say "with faith" (which, on analogy in context, would be ἐν πίστει). Instead, by using the elaborate phrase κατὰ τὴν ἀναλογίαν τῆς πίστεως, he points to something outside the personal faith of the prophet, and that must be the faith shared and passed on in liturgical, catechetical, and baptismal confessions and instructions. The prophetic function is expressed by those who teach and those who exhort within the communities of believers (12:7-8). Their ministries of the word, prophetic though they are, can be expected to be in accord with the faith centered in the crucified and risen Christ. This is not the only time that Paul indicates that those who prophesy have a responsibility to the wider community of believers. To the church at Corinth he declared: "Two or three prophets should speak, and the others should evaluate what is said" (1 Cor 14:29, NET).

12:7 After "prophecy" Paul mentions the gift of διακονία, translated variously as "ministry"/"ministering" (KJV, ASV, NRSV) or "service"/"serving" (RSV, NIV, NET, ESV). Since the term "ministry" has overtones of a form of official ministry that did not yet exist in Paul's day, there seems to be an advantage in rendering the term as "service."[40] This becomes all the more clear with the phrase following (ἐν τῇ διακονίᾳ, "in serving"), apparently referring to charitable service.[41]

Paul switches at 12:7b from the gifts ("prophecy" and "service") given and

---

37. E. Käsemann, *Romans,* 341-42; C. Cranfield, *Romans,* 621; U. Wilckens, *Römer,* 3:14; R. Harrisville, *Romans,* 197; J. Fitzmyer, *Romans,* 647; J. Ziesler, *Romans,* 298-99; P. Stuhlmacher, *Romans,* 193; D. Moo, *Romans,* 765-66; L. Keck, *Romans,* 300; E. Lohse, *Römer,* 342; Rudolf Bultmann, "πίστις," *TDNT* 6:213; D. Aune, *Prophecy,* 204-5, 235.

38. J. Dunn, *Romans,* 728. Cf. BDAG 67 (ἀναλογία): "in proportion to the share of commitment one has."

39. LSJ 111 (ἀναλογία); BDAG 67 (ἀναλογία).

40. Cf. BDAG 230 (διακονία, 5).

41. Alfons Weiser, "διακονέω, διακονία," *EDNT* 1:302-3.

speaks of persons who possess various gifts. He begins with the one who teaches (ὁ διδάσκων). For Paul and others of the first generations of believers, teaching (διδασκαλία), consisting largely of transmitting the tradition of the apostles, was extremely important (Acts 2:42; 1 Cor 11:2, 23-26; 15:3-6; Gal 6:6; 1 Thess 4:1; 2 Thess 2:15; 3:6; Heb 5:12). It would have served as a necessary ingredient and stable (but not static) component of the ministry of the word along with prophecy. The importance of the role of the teacher is emphasized and honored particularly where Paul says that "God has appointed in the church . . . teachers" (1 Cor 12:28). The teacher, Paul says, is to use that gift for teaching — meaning teaching well, whether that be in catechesis or some other function.

12:8 In this verse Paul, using a series of participles, lists four kinds of persons who have gifts to employ in the church. The first is ὁ παρακαλῶν ("the one who exhorts"), who should use the gift ἐν τῇ παρακλήσει, which can mean "in [giving] encouragement" or "in [providing] comfort."[42] The second is ὁ μεταδιδούς ("the one who contributes"), who is to do so ἐν ἁπλότητι, meaning "with sincerity" (NET) or "with sincere concern."[43]

Next Paul lists the person who is ὁ προϊστάμενος. The participle could mean "one who provides leadership" (cf. similar rendering in KJV, ASV, NIV, NRSV, ESV, and NET), but it can also mean "one who gives aid" (cf. RSV).[44] The fact that the term (1) is listed among those functions having to do with service (διακονία) and (2) stands between ὁ μεταδιδούς ("the one who makes contributions") and ὁ ἐλεῶν ("the one who does acts of mercy") speaks in favor of the latter rendering ("one who gives aid"). Such a person is to act ἐν σπουδῇ ("with diligence" or "attentively"). Finally, Paul lists the person who is ὁ ἐλεῶν ("the who does acts of mercy"); such acts are to be done ἐν ἱλαρότητι ("with cheerfulness"; the noun used, ἱλαρότης, appears only here in the NT).

In each case where a gift is listed, Paul adds a notation about making use of it for the sake of others. Common to all is that they are gifts given according to the "grace" (χάρις) bestowed. The gifts may well be correlated with human abilities and temperaments that people have, based on creation ("natural endowments"), but not in every case (e.g., prophecy). Nevertheless, in all cases they are finally "gifts" (χαρίσματα) of God's "grace" (χάρις as empowerment), for God's grace transforms those abilities considered to be natural and supplements them with new powers. The gifts are enlivened by the Spirit within the body of Christ. Paul's primary interest in discussing the gifts, however, is not to be exhaustive

---

42. BDAG 766 (παράκλησις, 1, 3).
43. Cf. KJV: "with simplicity." BDAG 104 (ἁπλότης) suggests "sincere concern, simple goodness," opposing "with generosity" (NRSV).
44. BDAG 870 (προΐστημι).

concerning them (for other gifts could be listed as well) but to speak of their use in order that the body of Christ might carry out the work of Christ in the world through both word and deed. One need not conclude that Paul has to convince the believers in Rome to use their gifts, for their faith and life are exemplary (1:8; 15:14). In preparation for his arrival, however, he acknowledges the manifold gifts that he can expect to find there and can encourage.

BIBLIOGRAPHY

Aune, David. *Prophecy in Early Christianity and the Ancient Mediterranean World.* Grand Rapids: Wm. B. Eerdmans, 1983.

Baumert, Norbert. "Charisma und Amt bei Paulus." In *L'Apôtre Paul: Personnalité, style et conception du ministère,* 203-28. Ed. Albert Vanhoye. BETL 73. Louvain: Leuven University, 1986.

Berding, Kenneth. "Romans 12.4-8: One Sentence or Two?" *NTS* 52 (2006): 433-39.

Birdsall, J. Neville. "ΕΜΕΤΡΗΣΕΝ in Rom. 12.3." *JTS* 14 (1963): 103-4.

Cranfield, C. E. B. "Μέτρον πίστεως in Romans 12:3." *NTS* 8 (1961-62): 345-51; reprinted in his *The Bible and Christian Life: A Collection of Essays,* 203-14. Edinburgh: T&T Clark, 1985.

Ellis, E. Earle. "'Spiritual' Gifts in the Pauline Community." *NTS* 20 (1973-74): 128-44.

Gundry, Robert H. *Sōma in Biblical Theology: With Emphasis on Pauline Anthropology.* SNTSMS 29. Cambridge: Cambridge University Press, 1976.

Moxnes, Halvor. "The Quest for Honor and the Unity of the Community in Romans 12 and the Orations of Dio Chrysostom." In *Paul in His Hellenistic Context,* 203-30. Ed. Troels Engberg-Pedersen. Minneapolis: Fortress Press, 1995.

Schürmann, Heinz. "Die geistlichen Gnadegaben in den paulinischen Gemeinden." In *Ursprung und Gestalt: Erörterungen und Besinnungen zum Neuen Testament,* 236-67. Düsseldorf: Patmos Verlag, 1970.

Schulz, Siegfried. "Die Charismenlehre des Paulus: Bilanz der Probleme und Ergebnisse." In *Rechtfertigung: Festschrift für Ernst Käsemann,* 443-60. Ed. Johannes Friedrich et al. Tübingen: J. C. B. Mohr (Paul Siebeck), 1976.

Unnik, Willem C. van. "The Interpretation of Romans 12:8: *ho metadidous en haplotēti.*" In *On Language, Culture, and Religion: In Honor of Eugene A. Nida,* 169-83. Ed. Matthew Black and W. A. Smalley. Paris: Mouton, 1974.

6.3. Exhortation to Love and Harmony, 12:9-21

9*Let love be without hypocrisy. Hate what is evil; cling to what is good;* 10*show love for one another with mutual affection; outdo one another in showing honor.* 11*Do not lag in zeal; be aglow with the Spirit, serve the Lord.* 12*Rejoice in hope, endure suffering, persist in prayer,* 13*share in the needs of the saints, provide hospitality.*

14*Bless those who persecute you; bless and do not curse them.* 15*Rejoice with those who rejoice; weep with those who weep.* 16*Be intent on having the same mind toward one another, not being haughty, but associating with the lowly. Do not be wise in your own estimation.*

17*Do not render evil for evil to anyone; take thought for what is good in the sight of all people.* 18*If possible, as far as it depends on you, be at peace with all people.* 19*Do not avenge yourselves, beloved, but give place for God's wrath, for it is written, "Vengeance is mine; I will repay," says the Lord.* 20*Instead, "if your enemy is hungry, feed him; if he thirsts, give him something to drink. For by doing this you will be heaping burning coals on his head."* 21*Do not be overcome by evil, but overcome evil with good.*

Notes on the Text and Translation

12:9 The first three Greek words (ἡ ἀγάπη ἀνυπόκριτος) constitute a clause, but a verb is lacking. The verb that is implied is ἔστω ("let . . . be").[45]

12:11 Some texts (primarily Western, such as D, F, and G) read τῷ καιρῷ δουλεύοντες ("serving the time") instead of τῷ κυρίῳ δουλεύοντες ("serving the Lord"), which is much more widely attested. The first of these can be attributed to a scribal error.[46]

12:14 It is difficult to know whether the plural "you" (ὑμᾶς) should be included in the Greek text. It is not present in some important witnesses (such as 𝔓[46] and B) but is present in others (such as ℵ and A), including the Majority Text. It is possible that it was added in order to conform the saying to similar sayings in Matthew 5:44 and Luke 6:28,[47] although the wording is not actually parallel. It is more likely that the word was added than omitted. In any case, its presence (for translation purposes) is implied.

General Comment

In this section of the letter Paul describes the life of the person who is in Christ, drawing upon common ethical traditions of the early church, including teachings from the wisdom tradition and Jesus. Most of the teachings are familiar from other literary contexts, including Jewish traditions preserved outside the

---

45. Cf. J. Fitzmyer, *Romans*, 653; E. Lohse, *Römer*, 345.
46. B. Metzger, *TCGNT* 466. The Western reading is favored by B. Byrne, *Romans*, 379.
47. B. Metzger, *TCGNT* 466, calls the evidence for each "fairly evenly supported." The word is rejected by C. Cranfield, *Romans*, 640; B. Byrne, *Romans*, 380; and R. Jewett, *Romans*, 755.

OT and Christian teaching elsewhere in the NT itself. Moreover, with the exception of the enigmatic statement in 12:20b, all can be understood easily. The entire section is in some respects like a brief catechism on the Christian life: Practice love for one another, honor one another, serve Christ, pray, be generous, be hospitable, live at peace with others, and avoid revenge. The sheer number of admonitions collected here in one place should caution one against concluding that Paul is addressing specific problems in Rome. The admonitions are general maxims that any Christian community might consider its own guides for thought and conduct.

The passage is filled with hortatory terminology, expressed in various ways in Greek: nine imperatives,[48] seventeen participles,[49] two infinitives,[50] two verbal adjectives,[51] and one implied imperative.[52] Some English versions, such as the RSV and NRSV, render them all as imperatives, numbering 31 in all. The NIV has 30 (one less in 12:11). Whereas the NRSV has three imperatives in that verse ("Do not lag in zeal, be ardent in spirit, serve the Lord"), the NIV has two ("Never be lacking in zeal, but keep your spiritual fervor, serving the Lord").

Both in Greek and in English the impression can be created that all of the hortatory terms are an undifferentiated staccato. But there is a priority — the priority of love — as indicated below.

Detailed Comment

12:9-10 Up to this point in his letter Paul has spoken of love in a theological sense, i.e., God's love for those whom he has redeemed (5:5, 8; 8:39), Christ's love for them (8:35), and their love for God (8:28). He will also speak of the love of the Spirit (15:30) near the end of the letter. Here for the first time he speaks of love in an ethical sense, and that will continue later (13:8-10; 14:15).

The love of which he speaks is ἀγάπη *(agapē),* a self-giving love that is modeled on divine love, the love of God shown forth in his sending of his Son: "God demonstrates his love for us in that while we were still sinners, Christ

---

48. Rom 12:14 (three), 16, 19, 20 (two), 21 (two).

49. Rom 12:9 (two), 10, 11 (two), 12 (three), 13 (two), 16 (three), 17 (two), 18, 19. On the use of participles for imperatives, cf. BDF 245 (§468, 2), C. F. D. Moule, *An Idiom-Book of New Testament Greek,* 179-80, and P. Kanjuparambil, "Imperatival Participles in Rom 12:9-21," 285-88. A. Salom, "The Imperatival Use of the Participle in the New Testament," 41-49, provides illustrations from papyri and other sources.

50. Both in Rom 12:15. On this usage, cf. BDF 196-97 (§389); C. F. D. Moule, *An Idiom-Book of New Testament Greek,* 126-27.

51. Rom 12:10 (φιλόστοργοι), 11 (ὀκνηροί).

52. Rom 12:9; the imperative verb ἔστω is implied.

died for us" (Rom 5:8). When Paul speaks of love in the ethical sense along with other virtues or fruits of the Spirit, especially in lists (2 Cor 6:5-8; Gal 5:22; Phil 2:1-2), one can get the impression that it is but one virtue among others. But in fact Paul stresses the priority of love over all, especially in 1 Corinthians 13:1-13, but also in other passages (Gal 5:6; Phil 1:9).[53] The same can be said for the present passage. All of the admonitions that follow can be regarded as ways in which love is expressed.[54] To be sure, they are not equivalencies of love, but they are inspired by it.

Love, Paul says, must be ἀνυπόκριτος, which can be translated literally as "unhypocritical" or "without hypocrisy" (as in the ASV and NET), although most modern versions have "genuine" (RSV, NRSV, ESV) or "sincere" (NIV). The word is related to the classical Greek word ὑποκριτής, which means "an actor" or "one who plays a part on the stage."[55] The term is used 18 times in the gospels, particularly in the Gospel of Matthew (6:2, 5, 16, etc.), to designate a person who is a "pretender" to righteousness,[56] giving a false appearance; it is rendered as a loan word ("hypocrite") in English versions. The term "love without hypocrisy" is used by Paul elsewhere (2 Cor 6:6), suggesting that he was aware of love's possible corruption.

Hating what is evil and holding on to the good are related to the practice of love without hypocrisy, but they are surely not its definition. There is wisdom in placing a period after 12:9a, as in the Nestle-Aland Greek text (27th ed.) and in some English versions (KJV, ASV, NIV, ESV, and NET), but not all (RSV and NRSV have semicolons). Paul's contrast between the evil (τὸ πονηρός) and the good (τὸ ἀγαθός) is more closely related to the specifics that follow in subsequent verses. The contrast made by Paul is traditional, having its formulation already at Amos 5:15: "Hate evil and love good"; in the LXX the nouns are the same, although different verbs are used.

When Paul speaks of showing "love for one another with mutual affection," he does not continue using the noun ἀγάπη but rather uses the noun φιλαδελφία, translated as "brotherly love" (KJV, NIV), "brotherly affection" (RSV), or "mutual affection" (NRSV). The term is used in Greek literature elsewhere in a literal manner to speak of affection between actual siblings ("blood brothers"), but in the NT it is used figuratively to refer to the affection between

---

53. A. Nygren, *Romans*, 425; Gerhard Schneider, "ἀγάπη," *EDNT* 1:10.

54. Cf. W. Sanday and A. Headlam, *Romans*, 360; C. H. Dodd, *Romans*, 198; A. Nygren, *Romans*, 425; J. G. D. Dunn, *Romans*, 739; J. Fitzmyer, *Romans*, 651-52; R. Harrisville, *Romans*, 197; J. Ziesler, *Romans*, 301; D. Moo, *Romans*, 773; L. Keck, *Romans*, 303; R. Jewett, *Romans*, 756, 758. Contra E. Käsemann, *Romans*, 343, who declares: "[Love] is simply one mode of behavior among others, not the criterion and true modality of all the rest."

55. LSJ 1886 (ὑποκριτής).

56. BDAG 1038 (ὑποκριτής).

Christians united together as children of God (Rom 12:10; 1 Thess 4:9; Heb 13:1; 1 Pet 1:22; 2 Pet 1:7).[57] Combined with the verbal adjective φιλόστοργος ("showing love," used only here in the NT) and the phrase εἰς ἀλλήλους ("for one another"), the expression speaks of "the intimate, tender love of a family."[58]

The next clause (12:10b) is translated variously, depending on how one understands the participle (προηγούμενοι), derived from the verb προηγέομαι, which in its basic etymological sense can mean to "go first and lead the way" or the like.[59] In the present context, in connection with showing honor to others, it could be rendered to say that one should lead the way in showing such honor, which is the simplest rendering and functions well contextually. With that as a basis for a translation, the familiar "outdo one another in showing honor" (RSV, NRSV) works well.[60] Other renderings, which speak of preferring the other person above oneself (cf. NIV: "honor one another above yourselves"),[61] demand a translation of the verb that must be idiosyncratic.

12:11-12 The series of admonitions that follows has to do with both spiritual and practical dimensions of the believer's life. The first is "Do not lag in zeal" (or, more literally, "Do not be indolent in diligence"), signifying an eagerness to show works of love and service. The admonition τῷ πνεύματι ζέοντες can be translated either as to be "aglow with the Spirit" (as in RSV), referring to the Holy Spirit,[62] or to be "ardent in spirit" (as in NRSV), referring to the human spirit.[63] The former is probably to be preferred (in spite of a similar phrase in Acts 18:25, which can be taken in the latter sense). The participle ζέοντες (from ζέω, meaning "to be stirred up emotionally" or "to boil, bubble up")[64] implies that believers are stirred up by the life-giving Spirit. The Spirit energizes the life of the believer. The third admonition in the series ("serve the Lord") is a generalization in which the term "Lord" refers to Christ (not God the Father), and serving him implies obedience (Rom 6:16; 16:19; 2 Cor 9:13).

---

57. Eckhard Plümacher, "φιλαδελφία," *EDNT* 3:424; cf. Hans F. von Soden, "φιλαδελφία," *TDNT* 1:146: "There are no examples of this more general use of φιλαδελφία and φιλάδελφος outside Christian writings."

58. M. Black, *Romans*, 173.

59. LSJ 1480 (προηγέομαι).

60. So also J. Fitzmyer, *Romans*, 654; P. Stuhlmacher, *Romans*, 195; R. Jewett, *Romans*, 761. The NET has, "showing eagerness in honoring one another."

61. BDAG 869 (προηγέομαι, 3) offers another possibility: "as far as honor is concerned, let each one esteem the other more highly (than oneself)." BDF 84 (§150) prescribes "'preferring' (not 'outdoing')." Cf. also C. Cranfield, *Romans*, 632-33.

62. So also C. Cranfield, *Romans*, 633-34; E. Käsemann, *Romans*, 346; J. Dunn, *Romans*, 742; B. Byrne, *Romans*, 376; D. Moo, *Romans*, 778; E. Lohse, *Römer*, 346; R. Jewett, *Romans*, 755, 763.

63. U. Wilckens, *Römer*, 3:21; J. Fitzmyer, *Romans*, 654.

64. BDAG 426 (ζέω); LSJ 755 (ζέω).

The next three admonitions characterize the life of the believer who has been shaped by faith and baptism. To "rejoice in hope" is possible on the basis of having been justified and reconciled. As Paul has declared earlier (5:2), believers can "rejoice on the basis of [their] hope of sharing the glory of God" (God's eternal presence). But, as also emphasized earlier in the letter, although the believer is justified and reconciled to God, he or she is not exempt from suffering, so one is to "endure suffering." The admonition to "persist in prayer" stands out from the previous ones in the series, since it (like those following) speaks of an activity. It is by no means an unusual admonition, for Paul calls upon his readers elsewhere to "pray without ceasing" (1 Thess 5:17; cf. 1 Cor 7:5; Phil 4:6).

12:13 In the phrase ταῖς χρείαις τῶν ἁγίων κοινωνοῦντες ("share in the needs of the saints") Paul uses the verb form (a participle of κοινωνέω) to express participation, taking an interest in, the needs of others.[65] He is not likely to be referring here to the collection for the saints in Jerusalem, to which he refers in 15:25-28, since the Roman community was not asked to make a contribution. Paul expects that by the time he arrives in Rome, he will have delivered the collection. In this verse, then, the admonition is a general one, in which believers in Christ share in the sufferings and needs of one another (cf. Rom 12:15; Gal 6:2). The admonition does not, strictly speaking, include care for those outside the Christian community.

The admonition to practice hospitality can hardly be underestimated in its importance for the mission of the church in the first (and subsequent) centuries.[66] The journeys of Jesus and Paul are well attested in the gospels and Acts. But travel is mentioned incidentally at many other places in the NT (Rom 16:1-2; 2 Cor 8:19; 11:25; Eph 6:21; Phil 2:25-29; 4:18; Col 1:2; 4:12), and the sheer amount of travel implied is remarkable. Since travel and staying at inns were both difficult and dangerous,[67] hospitality within Christian homes was important for reasons of safety. Christians in Rome were especially in a position to offer hospitality to other Christians coming there. It is particularly of interest to observe that it is especially in letters having an association with the Roman community that hospitality is spoken of as an obligation (Rom 12:13; 16:1-2; 1 Pet 4:9; and Heb 13:2); in addition, being hospitable is an expectation for church leaders (1 Tim 3:2; Titus 1:8). Hospitality for travelers made Christian mission possible in the ancient cities of the world; without it, travel would have been so much more difficult and perilous.[68]

---

65. BDAG 552 (κοινωνέω, 1, b, γ); J. Campbell, "KOINΩNIA," 368: "making common cause with the needs of the saints" through practical helpfulness.

66. D. Riddle, "Early Christian Hospitality," 141-54.

67. S. Vernon McCasland, "Travel and Communication in the NT," *IDB* 4:690-93.

68. J. Koenig, *New Testament Hospitality, passim.*

12:14 Beginning with 12:14 the admonitions are all drawn from traditions that can be located in the OT or the teachings of Jesus, even if they are derived indirectly, rather than directly, from them in some cases. Moreover, although the admonitions in 12:9-13 can be taken to speak of the internal life of the Christian community (i.e., behavior among believers), most of those in 12:14-21 (a possible exception being 12:16a, "Be intent on having the same mind toward one another") are applicable to life within the broader society.

The admonition, "Bless those who persecute you; bless and do not curse them" (12:14), is similar to (but not exactly like) sayings of Jesus (Matt 5:44: "Pray for those who persecute you"; and Luke 6:28: "Bless those who curse you, pray for those who abuse you"). One can only wonder whether Paul is quoting directly from a tradition from Jesus, even if it is not attested in the gospels; and if he is, whether he is aware of it. It is possible that a teaching of Jesus on love for one's enemies could itself have been expressed in various ways, and in any case formulated later with variations. Paul's saying, "Bless those who persecute you," is, in substance, remarkably similar to Jesus' saying in Luke, "Bless those who curse you."[69] It seems likely that Paul would have been aware of his saying as having its origins in some fashion with Jesus,[70] although one can not claim certainty.

12:15 "Rejoice with those who rejoice; weep with those who weep." The saying is similar to the one from Israel's wisdom tradition: "Do not avoid those who weep, but mourn with those who mourn" (Sir 7:34). John Chrysostom was insightful about this passage when he said that rejoicing with those who rejoice (because of their good fortune) is actually more noble than weeping with those who weep (because of their misfortune):

> [Rejoicing with those who rejoice] requires more of a high Christian temper . . . than to weep with them that weep. For . . . there is none so half-hearted as not to weep over him that is in calamity: but the other requires a very noble soul, so as not only to keep from envying, but even to feel pleasure with the person who is in esteem.[71]

---

69. According to L. Schottroff, "Non-violence and the Love of Enemies," 22, Paul's parallel saying demonstrates that the saying attributed to Jesus in Luke existed at a very early stratum of the Jesus tradition. J. Sauer, "Traditionsgeschichtliche Erwägungen zu den synoptischen und paulinischen Aussagen," 1-28, has sought to reconstruct the history of this and other sayings in 12:9-21 in terms of their Synoptic and Pauline backgrounds. D. Wenham, "Paul's Use of the Jesus Tradition," 17-24, maintains that the traditions in the Synoptics are primitive, known already to Paul.

70. That Paul is quoting from Jesus is affirmed by T. Holtz, "Paul and the Oral Gospel Tradition," 391-92; V. Furnish, *The Love Command in the New Testament,* 61-62, 106; J. Dunn, *Romans,* 745; and D. Allison, "The Pauline Epistles and the Synoptic Gospels," 11-12.

71. John Chrysostom, *Homilies on Romans* 22; quoted from the translation by J. B. Morris and W. H. Simcox in *NPNF* 11:507. The Greek text is in *PG* 60:610.

12:16 The expression "Be intent on having the same mind toward one another" (τὸ αὐτὸ εἰς ἀλλήλους φρονοῦντες) is similar to other expressions in Paul's letters (2 Cor 13:11 Phil 2:2; 4:2) and is very much like his exhortation in 15:5 (τὸ αὐτὸ φρονεῖν ἐν ἀλλήλοις, "be of the same mind with one another"). The admonition concerns relationships within the community of believers; mutual respect and regard are to be expected, and the next three clauses make clear that, in order to achieve that, there is to be no haughtiness, intentional association with those considered "lowly," and refraining from being wise in one's own estimation. The threefold use of words having to do with being wise in this verse (φρονοῦντες in both 12:16a and 12:16b; and φρόνιμοι in 12:16c) highlights the importance of giving thought to finding one's place within the company of saints in such a way that mutual acceptance and mutual regard can flourish. There is no room for arrogance or lording over others on the basis of supposed superiority. The admonitions are elaborations of what is found in the wisdom tradition, such as the saying in Proverbs: "Do not be wise in your own estimation; fear God, and turn away from evil" (3:7).

Two phrases within this verse are particularly difficult to interpret. The first is μὴ τὰ ὑψηλὰ φρονοῦντες, translated above as "not being haughty" (as similarly in RSV, NIV, NRSV, ESV, and NET). This is favored over "not setting your mind on high things" (cf. ASV: "Set not your mind on high things"). The phrase can hardly mean that one should not have lofty thoughts in general (which is commended, using different terminology, at Phil 4:8-9; cf. 3:19-20; Col 3:2); rather, in this context it can only mean to think in a haughty manner (τὰ ὑψηλα being adverbial), as also at 11:20. The second difficult phrase in this verse is τοῖς ταπεινοῖς συναπαγόμενοι, translated above as "associate with the lowly" (as in RSV, NRSV, NET, ESV; cf. NIV: "associate with people of low position"). The words τοῖς ταπεινοῖς are taken in this case to refer to persons. But the term could be neuter, referring to "lowly things" (cf. ASV: "condescend to things that are lowly"). It is more likely, however, that a reference to persons is meant, since its context is social.[72]

12:17-18 The command not to take revenge is familiar from the wisdom tradition of the OT (Prov 17:13; 20:22; 24:29), pseudepigrapha,[73] the Qumran scrolls,[74] the gospels (Matt 5:38-39, 44; Luke 6:29, 35), and other parts of the NT (1 Thess 5:15; 1 Pet 3:9). To "take thought for what is good in the sight of all people" concerns the public witness of believers within the wider society. It, too, is familiar from the wisdom tradition, containing wording similar to the LXX version of Proverbs (3:4: "Take thought of the good in the sight of the Lord and

---

72. Heinz Giesen, "ταπεινός," *TDNT* 3:333: "The believers are urged not to be conceited but to turn their attention to the insignificant ones in the church."

73. *T. Gad* 6.1-3; *T. Jos.* 18.2; *T. Ben.* 4.2-3.

74. 1QS 10.17-18. H.-W. Kuhn, "Qumran und Paulus," 233-34, detects six expressions within 1QS 10.17-21 that are similar to those in Rom 12:17-20, although not in the same sequence.

humanity"; cf. also 2 Cor 8:21).[75] The public face of the believing community is also to be evident in its being able to "be at peace with all people" (12:18), a teaching that became increasingly important in the apostolic church with the passing of time (cf. 1 Tim 2:1-2; Titus 3:2; Heb 12:14).

12:19 The exhortation not to avenge oneself echoes what has been said in 12:17. But here Paul gives a reason for the restraint being urged, which is that God will exercise judgment, and that that judgment will be just. By writing "for it is written," Paul seems to quoting from the OT (Deut 32:35): "Vengeance is mine; I will repay." But what he writes differs greatly from what is presented in the LXX:

Deut 32:35:
ἐν ἡμέρᾳ ἐκδικήσεως ἀνταποδώσω.

In the day of vengeance I will repay.

Rom 12:19:
ἐμοὶ ἐκδίκησις, ἐγὼ ἀνταποδώσω

Vengeance is mine; I will repay.

The wording that Paul provides appears also in Hebrews 10:30. It appears that the two authors, presumably independent of one another, made use of a Greek text that differs from the LXX.[76] The wording of Paul (and Heb 10:30) is closer to the Hebrew text in its opening phrase (לִי נָקָם, "Vengeance is mine") and identical to the LXX at the end (ἀνταποδώσω, "I will repay"), to which the emphatic ἐγώ ("I") is added.

12:20 Paul quotes from Proverbs 25:21-22a. His wording is that of the LXX, with one possible exception at the outset. Paul writes, ἐὰν πεινᾷ ὁ ἐχθρός σου, ψώμιζε αὐτόν ("if your enemy is hungry, feed him"). The verb he uses (ψώμιζε, "feed") is the reading of the B version of the LXX, but others (including ℵ and A) use the synonymous and more common τρέφε. It is possible that the B reading is due to a harmonization with Paul's text.[77] In any case, the verse continues the emphasis on love of one's enemies (12:14, 17).

The remaining portion of the verse has been an exegetical puzzle from the beginning.[78] Paul continues to quote from Proverbs (25:22a), and his word-

---

75. Rom 12:17, προνοούμενοι καλὰ ἐνώπιον πάντων ἀνθρώπων; Prov 3:4, προνοοῦ καλὰ ἐνώπιον κυρίου καὶ ἀνθρώπων.

76. H. Attridge, *Hebrews*, 295; T. Lim, *Holy Scripture in the Qumran Commentaries and Pauline Letters*, 147.

77. J. Dunn, *Romans*, 750; J. Fitzmyer, *Romans*, 657; D. Moo, *Romans*, 787 (n. 96).

78. For brief surveys of interpretations, cf. S. Segert, "Live Coals Heaped on the Head," 159-64, and J. Fitzmyer, *Romans*, 657-58.

ing is exactly like that found in the LXX: τοῦτο γὰρ ποιῶν ἄνθρακας πυρὸς σωρεύσεις ἐπὶ τὴν κεφαλὴν αὐτοῦ ("For by doing this you will be heaping burning coals on his head"). Whatever the meaning of the verse in the OT, the context in Romans requires that it have to do with causing a transformation of the attitudes and behavior of one's enemy. That basic idea permeates interpretation in the history of exegesis, even if the exact meaning of the imagery is not understood. According to Origen, an enemy can be moved by kindness; being struck by it, he "will swear that as his conscience torments him for the wrong which he has done, it is as if a fire were enveloping him."[79] According to Augustine, "the coals of fire serve to burn, i.e., to bring anguish" to the soul of one's enemy so that "all malice is burnt out when one is changed for the better through repentance."[80] Similarly, Jerome wrote: "If someone does you a wrong and in return you do him good, you will be heaping coals of fire on his head." Moreover, then "you are curing him of his vices and burning out his malice, in order to bring him to repentance."[81] While commenting on this passage, Martin Luther concluded that it has to do with converting the other person through love and kindness, saying that "he who is converted by love is completely burned up against himself. For love teaches him all things; and when he has been touched by love, he will exhaust himself in seeking out the person whom he has offended."[82]

It is unknown for certain what custom is being alluded to in the passage from Proverbs. A good possibility, favored by various interpreters,[83] is that the imagery portrays an Egyptian penitential rite in which a person carries a dish of burning charcoal on his head as a sign of repentance and self-punishment. Whether either Proverbs or Paul actually presupposes that rite,[84] its symbolism fits the sense of what Paul is clearly getting at: By doing good to one's enemy, a person may cause him or her to repent and have a sense of remorse for an of-

---

79. Origen, *Commentarii in Epistulam ad Romanos* 12.20, ed. Theresia Heither, 5 vols. (Freiburg im Breslau: Herder, 1990-95), 5:86; ET quoted from *Romans*, ed. Gerald Bray, ACCS.NT (Downers Grove: InterVarsity Press, 1998), 6:321.

80. Augustine, *Unfinished Commentary on the Epistle to the Romans* 71.4. Quoted from Paula Fredriksen Landes, *Augustine on Romans: Propositions from the Epistle to the Romans, Unfinished Commentary on the Epistle to the Romans*, SBL.TT 23, ECLS 6 (Chico: Scholars Press, 1982), 71.

81. Jerome, *Homilies on the Psalms* 41; quoted from *The Homilies of Saint Jerome*, trans. Marie L. Ewald, 2 vols., FC 48 (Washington, D.C.: Catholic University of America, 1964), 1:313.

82. M. Luther, *Romans*, 466.

83. S. Morenz, "Feurige Kohlen auf dem Haupt," 187-92; W. Klassen, "Coals of Fire," 337-50; U. Wilckens, *Römer*, 3:26; E. Käsemann, *Romans*, 349; C. Cranfield, *Romans*, 650; Horst Balz, "ἄνθραξ," *EDNT* 1:99-100; P. Stuhlmacher, *Romans*, 198; N. T. Wright, *NIB (Romans)*, 10:715; E. Lohse, *Römer*, 349; R. Jewett, *Romans*, 777.

84. Cautions are expressed by J. Ziesler, *Romans*, 306, and L. Keck, *Romans*, 309.

fense committed. Although Paul may not have known the origins of the saying in Proverbs itself, and although he could hardly have expected his readers to know it, he was clearly informed about its significance at the textual level in the OT. The preceding verse in Proverbs (25:21) speaks of doing good to one's enemy, and that provides a context for 25:22 in such a way that the latter can only be understood as an act that transforms one's enemy, causing that person to put away any animosity. The view that heaping burning coals on the head of one's enemy is a sign of judgment against that person does not fit the context of this part of the letter,[85] in which love for the enemy is being taught.

12:21 The closing comment in this section of the letter ("Do not be overcome by evil, but overcome evil with good") confirms that the verse from Proverbs does not imply an expression of revenge or judgment, but points toward possible reconciliation. The verse reiterates what was said in 12:14 (blessing the persecutor) and 12:17 (not repaying evil for evil) and serves as a conclusion to the whole section (12:9-21).

BIBLIOGRAPHY

Allison, Dale C., Jr. "The Pauline Epistles and the Synoptic Gospels: The Pattern of the Parallels." *NTS* 28 (1982): 1-32.

Ashe, R. P. "Romans xii.13, 14." *ExpTim* 39 (1927-28): 46.

Attridge, Harold W. *The Epistle to the Hebrews: A Commentary on the Epistle to the Hebrews.* Hermeneia. Philadelphia: Fortress Press, 1989.

Barrett, C. K. "The Imperatival Participle." *ExpTim* 59 (1947-48): 165-66.

Black, David A. "The Pauline Love Command: Structure, Style, and Ethics in Romans 12:9-21." *FilNeot* 2 (1989): 3-22.

Braaten, Carl E. "Romans 12:14-21." *Int* 38 (1984): 291-95.

Campbell, J. Y. "KOINΩNIA and Its Cognates in the New Testament." *JBL* 51 (1932): 352-80.

Dahood, Mitchell J. "Two Pauline Quotations from the Old Testament." *CBQ* 17 (1955): 19-24.

Dunn, James D. G. "Paul's Knowledge of the Jesus Tradition: The Evidence of Romans." In *Christus Bezeugen: Festschrift für Wolfgang Trilling zum 65. Geburtstag,* 193-207. Ed. Karl Kertelge et al. ETS 59. Leipzig: St. Benno, 1989.

Esler, Philip F. "Paul and Stoicism: Romans 12 as a Test Case." *NTS* 50 (2004): 106-24.

Fitzmyer, Joseph A. "Paul and the Dead Sea Scrolls." In *The Dead Sea Scrolls after Fifty Years: A Comprehensive Assessment,* 2:599-621. Ed. Peter W. Flint and James C. VanderKam. 2 vols. Boston: E. J. Brill, 1998-99.

Furnish, Victor Paul. *The Love Command in the New Testament.* Nashville: Abingdon Press, 1972.

---

85. Contra K. Stendahl, "Hate, Non-Retaliation, and Love," 348, and J. Piper, *"Love Your Enemies,"* 114-19.

Gräbe, Petrus J. *The Power of God in Paul's Letters.* 2d ed. WUNT 2/123. Tübingen: Mohr Siebeck, 2008.

Holtz, Traugott. "Paul and the Oral Gospel Tradition." In *Jesus and the Oral Tradition,* 380-93. Ed. Henry Wansbrough. JSNTSup 64. Sheffield: JSOT Press, 1991.

Kanjuparambil, Philip. "Imperatival Participles in Rom 12:9-21." *JBL* 102 (1983): 285-88.

Keesmaat, Sylvia C. "If Your Enemy Is Hungry: Love and Subversive Politics in Romans 12–13." In *Character Ethics and the New Testament: Moral Dimensions of Scripture,* 141-58. Ed. Robert Brawley. Louisville: Westminster John Knox, 2007.

Klassen, William. "Coals of Fire: Sign of Repentance or Revenge?" *NTS* 9 (1962-63): 337-50.

Koenig, John. *New Testament Hospitality: Partnership with Strangers as Promise and Mission.* Philadelphia: Fortress Press, 1985.

Kuhn, Heinz-Wolfgang. "The Impact of the Qumran Scrolls on the Understanding of Paul." In *The Dead Sea Scrolls: Forty Years of Research,* 327-39. Ed. Devorah Dimant and Uriel Rappaport. STDJ 10. New York: E. J. Brill, 1992.

——. "Qumran und Paulus: Unter traditionsgeschichtlichem Aspekt ausgewählte Parallelen." In *Das Urchristentum in seiner literarischen Geschichte: Festschrift für Jürgen Becker zum 65. Geburtstag,* 227-46. Ed. Ulrich Mell and Ulrich B. Müller. BZNW 100. Berlin: Walter de Gruyter, 1999.

Légasse, Simon. "Vengeance humaine et vengeance divine en Romains 12,14-21." In *La Vie de la parole: De l'Ancien au Nouveau Testament: Études d'exégèse et d'herméneutique bibliques offertes à Pierre Grelot,* 36-47. Paris: Desclée de Brouwer, 1987.

Longsworth, W. M. "Ethics in Paul: The Shape of Christian Life and a Method of Moral Reasoning." In *Annual of the Society of Christian Ethics,* 29-56. Ed. Thomas Ogletree. Dallas: Society of Christian Ethics, 1981.

Meecham, H. G. "The Use of the Participle for the Imperative in the New Testament." *ExpTim* 58 (1946-47): 207-8.

Morenz, Siegfried. "Feurige Kohlen auf dem Haupt." *TLZ* 78 (1953): 187-92.

Moule, C. F. D. *An Idiom-Book of New Testament Greek.* 2d ed. Cambridge: Cambridge University Press, 1960.

Moxnes, Halvor. "The Quest for Honor and the Unity of the Community in Romans 12 and the Orations of Dio Chrysostom." In *Paul in His Hellenistic Context,* 203-30. Ed. Troels Engberg-Pedersen. Minneapolis: Fortress Press, 1995.

Nestle, E. "A Parallel to Rom. xii.11." *ExpTim* 10 (1898-99): 284.

Neirynck, Frans. "Paul and the Sayings of Jesus." In In *L'Apôtre Paul: Personnalité, style et conception du ministère,* 265-321. Ed. Albert Vanhoye. BETL 73. Louvain: Leuven University, 1986.

Perkins, Pheme. *Love Commands in the New Testament.* New York: Paulist Press, 1982.

Piper, John. *"Love Your Enemies": Jesus' Love Command in the Synoptic Gospels and the Early Christian Paraenesis: A History of the Tradition and Interpretation of Its Uses.* SNTSMS 38. Cambridge: Cambridge University Press, 1979.

Riddle, Donald W. "Early Christian Hospitality: A Factor in the Gospel Transmission." *JBL* 57 (1938): 141-54.

Robertson, S. "A Note on Romans xii.21: μὴ νικῶ ὑπὸ τοῦ κακοῦ." *ExpTim* 60 (1948-49): 322.

Salom, A. P. "The Imperatival Use of the Participle in the New Testament." *AusBR* 11 (1963): 41-49.

Sauer, Jürgen. "Traditionsgeschichtliche Erwägungen zu den synoptischen und paulinischen Aussagen über Feindesliebe und Wiedervergeltungsverzicht." *ZNW* 76 (1985): 1-28.

Schottroff, Luise. "Non-violence and the Love of Enemies." In her *Essays on the Love Commandment,* 9-39. Philadelphia: Fortress Press, 1978.

Segert, Stanislav. "'Live Coals Heaped on the Head.'" In *Love and Death in the Ancient Near East: Essays in Honor of Marvin H. Pope,* 159-64. Ed. J. H. Marks and R. M. Good. Guilford: Four Quarters, 1987.

Smothers, Edgar R. "Give Place to the Wrath (Rom. 12:19): An Essay in Verbal Exegesis." *CBQ* 6 (1944): 205-15.

Stendahl, Krister. "Hate, Non-Retaliation, and Love: 1QS x.17-20 and Rom. 12:19-21." *HTR* 55 (1962): 343-55; reprinted in his *Meanings: The Bible as Document and as Guide,* 137-49. Philadelphia: Fortress Press, 1984.

Stuhlmacher, Peter. "Jesustradition im Römerbrief? Eine Skizze." *TBei* 14 (1983): 140-50.

Talbert, Charles H. "The Pauline Love Command: Structure, Style, and Ethics in Romans 12.9-21." *FilNeot* 2 (1989): 3-22.

———. "Tradition and Redaction in Romans xii.9-21." *NTS* 16 (1969-70): 83-93.

Thorsteinsson, Runar M. "Paul and Roman Stoicism: Romans 12 and Contemporary Stoic Ethics." *JSNT* 29 (2006): 139-61.

Walter, Nikolaus. "Paulus und die urchristliche Jesustradition." *NTS* 31 (1985): 498-522.

Wenham, David. "Paul's Use of the Jesus Tradition: Three Samples." In *The Jesus Tradition outside the Gospels,* 7-37. Ed. David Wenham. GP 5. Sheffield: JSOT Press, 1985.

Wilson, Walter T. *Love without Pretense: Romans 12:9-12 and Hellenistic-Jewish Wisdom Literature.* WUNT 2/46. Tübingen: J. C. B. Mohr (Paul Siebeck), 1991.

Wong, Eric K. C. "The De-radicalization of Jesus' Ethical Sayings in Romans." *NovT* 43 (2001): 245-63.

Yinger, Kent L. "Romans 12:14-21 and Nonretaliation in Second Temple Judaism: Addressing Persecution within the Community." *CBQ* 60 (1998): 74-96.

CHAPTER 7

On Governing Authorities, Love, and Conduct, 13:1-14

Chapter 13 of Romans is best known for its hortatory verses on being subject to the governing authorities (13:1-7). That is not surprising for a couple of reasons. First, it is a relatively long section on a particular topic, on which Paul has obviously given considerable reflection. Second, it is a text that has been used in the history of the Christian church as a basis for, or at least a major ingredient in, its doctrinal teaching concerning civil government and the place of persons (whether Christian or not) within it.

But that concern does not exhaust the chapter. The chapter also contains two other sections of importance. The first of them (13:8-10) is of interest for its recital of the love commandment, which is in the Torah (Lev 19:18) and in the teaching tradition of Jesus (Matt 22:39//Mark 12:31//Luke 10:27-28). Moreover, Paul cites that commandment as a summary of the essential teaching of the Decalogue (Exod 20:13-17; Deut 5:17-21) after the manner of Jesus.

The other section of the chapter (13:11-14) is of interest because of its importance for any discussion of the eschatology of Paul and its relationship to his ethical teaching. The way the two are related is that, for Paul, the return of Christ in glory is imminent, and since that is so, it is imperative for those who belong to him in faith to "put on the armor of light" and live the new life in Christ expectantly and morally.

7.1. Submission to Governing Authorities, 13:1-7

1Let every person be subject to the governing authorities; for there is no authority except from God, and those that exist have been instituted by God. 2Whoever, therefore, opposes authority resists what has been established by God, and those who resist incur judgment upon themselves. 3For rulers are not a threat to good conduct but to bad. And do you not want to fear authority? Do good, and you will receive praise from it. 4For it is God's servant for your good. But if you do evil, be afraid. For it does not bear the sword in vain; it is God's agent of punishment on the one who does evil. 5Therefore one must be subject, not only because of wrath but also on account of one's conscience. 6Therefore you also pay taxes; for the authorities are God's ministers attending to this very thing. 7Render to everyone what you owe: tax to whom tax is due, revenue to whom revenue is due, respect to whom respect is due, honor to whom honor is due.

Notes on the Text and Translation

13:1 In some ancient witnesses (including 𝔓⁴⁶ and various Western texts) the sentence begins with πάσαις ἐξουσίαις ὑπερεχούσαις ὑποτάσσεσθε. In that case the main verb (ὑποτάσσεσθε) is a second person plural imperative, "be subject to the governing authorities." In spite of the importance of those witnesses, other major witnesses (including ℵ and B, Old Latin, and Syriac versions) have the third person singular imperative (ὑποτασσέσθω), so that the clause should be rendered as "let every person be subject."

13:3-4 The discussion about authority seems abstract. The RSV seeks to remedy that by translating: "Would you have no fear of him who is in authority? Then do what is good, and you will receive his approval, for he is God's servant for your good. But if you do wrong, be afraid, for he does not bear the sword in vain; he is the servant of God to execute his wrath on the wrongdoer." Yet the Greek keeps all on an abstract level. For example, at the end of 13:3 the antecedent for the noun in the phrase ἐξ αὐτῆς (with the feminine pronoun) is ἐξουσία ("authority"), and so "from it" is more appropriate than "from him."

General Comment

In this section Paul exhorts his readers to be subject to the governing authorities, affirms that authority is divinely instituted, claims that rulers reward good and punish evil, and calls upon the Roman Christians to be subject to the authorities for the sake of conscience. Few NT passages have been more controversial in modern times. Reinhold Niebuhr, for example, wrote that the passage gives an "unqualified endorsement of government," is mistaken in its assumption that "government is no peril to virtue but only to vice," and has become "a vehicle for a too uncritical devotion to government."[1]

---

1. R. Niebuhr, *The Nature and Destiny of Man*, 2:270-71; cf., similarly, W. Pilgrim, *Uneasy Neighbors*, 27.

But when the passage is set within its literary and historical contexts, it takes on a different tone. Within its literary context, the passage belongs to a lengthy paraenetic section of the letter (Rom 12:1–15:13), and just prior to it Paul has spoken of the need to be patient in tribulation (12:12), to live in harmony (12:16), and to live peaceably with all (12:18). Paraenesis continues within this passage itself (13:1, 5). That means that the passage should not be singled out as a brief essay by Paul on the Christian "doctrine of the state" or "Paul's theory of civil government,"[2] as often assumed. Least of all can the passage be considered Paul's "Christological grounding of the state,"[3] for there is no mention at all of Christ in the entire passage. Paul's concern here is not with the state or civil government per se, but with the life of the believer that takes place in the world and within its civic life.

Concerning the historical context of the passage, two matters are important to consider. First, for some time both prior to Paul and after him, some Jewish traditions regarded political authority as given to rulers by God. That view appears in the OT (Isa 45:1-3; Jer 27:1-7; Prov 8:15-16; 24:21; Dan 2:21, 36-38; 4:17; cf. Wis 6:3-4; Sir 10:14; 17:17) and then later in the first century A.D. According to Josephus, "no ruler attains his office save by the will of God."[4] Moreover, the emphasis on loyalty to the governing authorities, even when they were foreign, has a basis in the OT, as at Jeremiah 29:7: "But seek the welfare of the city where I have sent you into exile, and pray to the LORD on its behalf, for in its welfare you will find your welfare" (cf. Bar 1:11). In addition to other Jewish texts and traditions,[5] various Gentile Hellenistic traditions expressed essentially what Paul says in these verses concerning the state and one's duty of loyalty to it.[6] It is striking also to find a similar passage in 1 Peter 2:13-17. Although neither author is likely to be dependent directly on the teachings of Jesus, the gospels portray Jesus as endorsing respect for the emperor and the paying of taxes (Matt 22:21//Mark 12:17//Luke 20:25).

The other matter of importance here is the question whether Paul speaks in this passage about a live issue among the Christians at Rome. In terms of

2. C. H. Dodd, *Romans*, 204, calls it "Paul's theory of civil government"; J. Dunn, *Romans*, 771, speaks of 13:2-5 as setting forth "a theology of the orderly state, of good government." Cf. similar statements on pp. 768, 773.

3. O. Cullmann, *The State in the New Testament*, 66; cf. C. Cranfield, *Romans*, 654: a "christological understanding of the state."

4. Josephus, *J. W.* 2.8.7 §140; quoted from the translation by H. St.-J. Thackeray, *Josephus*, 10 vols., LCL (Cambridge: Harvard University Press, 1956-65), 2:376-77.

5. Philo, *Legat.* 21.140; *Let. Arist.* 19-21; Josephus, *Ant.* 15.374; *m. Abot* 3.2.

6. E.g., Plutarch, *Mor.* 780d; Epictetus, *Dis.* 1.12.7; 2.10.5; 3.7.27-28; Dio Chrysostom, *Orations* 3.55. Cf. A. Strobel, "Furch, wem Furcht gebuhrt," 59; R. Heiligenthal, "Strategien conformer Ethik im Neuen Testament," 55-61; B. Blumenfeld, *The Political Paul*, 244. Various texts are cited by Gerhard Delling, "ὑποτάσσω," *TDNT* 8:39-40.

general knowledge of the Roman situation, Paul would have been aware of the recent expulsion of Jews and Jewish Christians under the emperor Claudius in A.D. 49,[7] followed by their return after the death of Claudius in A.D. 54. But how much more he would have known is less clear, and the degree to which whatever else he knew prompted his writing of 13:1-7 is uncertain. Various suggestions have been made, such as the following: (1) Paul feared an outbreak once again of the controversy between Christian Jews and other Jews that led to the earlier expulsion.[8] (2) The newly returned Jewish Christians were sympathetic (along with the wider Jewish community there) with the Jewish nationalist struggle against Rome in Judea, and Paul sought to curb those sympathies.[9] (3) The Christians at Rome, like others there, were obligated to pay extremely heavy taxes, which finally led to civil unrest in Rome in A.D. 57-58, and Paul seeks to quell the developing unrest.[10] (4) The Christians at Rome may have been refusing to pay taxes.[11] (5) The Christians at Rome tended to reject political authority in general.[12] (6) Paul sought to keep members of the Roman church "from making trouble in the streets."[13] (7) The Christians at Rome had been exhibiting tendencies toward "enthusiasm" and were indifferent to the world and its powers.[14] (8) There was sharp division among the Christians at Rome, whereby Gentile Christians considered themselves emancipated from the usual religious and moral restraints and ridiculed Jewish Christians for not being "liberated" as they had been.[15] (9) Paul wrote the section to head off any suspicions that he might be disloyal to Rome.[16] (10) One of the least convincing proposals is that, by means of this passage, Paul urged Christians to be subject not to the Roman authorities but to authorities within the synagogues.[17] The proposal has been criticized for various reasons, not

---

7. Cf. Acts 18:2-3; Suetonius, *Claudius* 25.15; for discussion, see the Introduction, pp. 3-4.

8. W. Sanday and A. Headlam, *Romans*, 370; C. H. Dodd, *Romans*, 202; E. Bammel, "Romans 13," 365-83; C. Talbert, *Romans*, 296.

9. M. Borg, "A New Context for Romans XIII," 205-18.

10. J. Friedrich, W. Pöhlmann, and P. Stuhlmacher, "Zu historischen Situation und Intention von Röm 13,1-7," 131-66; J. Dunn, *Romans*, 766; B. Byrne, *Romans*, 386; P. Stuhlmacher, *Romans*, 200-201; T. Tobin, *Paul's Rhetoric in Its Contexts*, 399-400; N. Elliott, *The Arrogance of Nations*, 154. The tax situation in Rome is spoken of by Tacitus, *Ann.* 13.50-51, and Suetonius, *Nero* 10.1.

11. M. Black, *Romans*, 159.

12. G. Bornkamm, *Paul*, 213; U. Schnelle, *Apostle Paul*, 356.

13. N. Elliott, *Liberating Paul*, 223.

14. E. Käsemann, *Romans*, 357-59.

15. P. Minear, *The Obedience of Faith*, 10-12, 89.

16. K. Wengst, *Pax Romana*, 82-83.

17. M. Nanos, *The Mystery of Romans*, 289-336.

least of all because the vocabulary within the passage has to do with civil authorities and civic life.[18]

None of these views can be adopted with certainty. The admonition is in fact so general, and so much in keeping with both Jewish and Gentile Hellenistic traditions, that it is not clear that Paul has any particular problem at Rome in view at all.[19] Given the experience of the Roman Christians in years gone by so recently, it is not likely that Paul would have much to teach them concerning the power of the governing authorities. On the contrary, this is a case where the apostle may just as well be seeking common ground with his readers, which is regularly done by using paraenetic style.[20] That view can be confirmed by looking back at exhortations made prior to this passage. When Paul speaks of hating evil and loving the good (12:9, 21), living in harmony with one another (12:16), and refraining from seeking revenge (12:19), it is not necessary to conclude that the Christians at Rome love evil, hate the good, have no harmony among themselves, and are vengeful. Just so, it is not necessary to conclude that they are prone to civil disobedience.

But Paul has good reason to write what he does in 13:1-7. The fact that he had suffered under both Jewish religious authorities and Gentile civil authorities (2 Cor 11:24-27; Acts 14:19; 16:19-24) would have been known among the Roman Christians. In the case of the former, his suffering was due to his preaching Christ within Jewish communities,[21] and the preaching of Christ had apparently also been the cause of the civil disturbances in Rome prior to the expulsion of Jews and Jewish Christians by Claudius. Moreover, Paul's views concerning the life in Christ as free from the law of Moses could be considered potentially divisive among the Christians at Rome. In order to head off any concerns about his precipitating another civil disturbance upon his arrival in Rome, Paul stresses the importance of civil order and implicitly pledges to refrain from stirring up old issues among persons who are now living at peace with one another within the Christian community itself and with the Jewish community at Rome.

Although Paul maintains in this passage that authority has been given by God to the governing authorities, he does not thereby endorse supreme authority of the state. In fact he relativizes those in authority. Over against the view that

18. B. Witherington, *Romans*, 310.

19. Cf. J. Fitzmyer, *Romans*, 664; D. Moo, *Romans*, 792-94.

20. L. Perdue, "The Social Character of Paraenesis," 23; Benjamin Fiore, "Parenesis and Protreptic," *ABD* 5:164, who says concerning paraenesis in general: "what Paul writes is not new but is a reminder of what his correspondents already know, so that they might continue along their chosen path." Cf. also S. Stowers, *Letter Writing in Greco-Roman Writing*, 92: paraenesis can be "advice and exhortation to continue in a certain way of life."

21. 2 Cor 11:24-26; 12:10; Gal 5:11; 6:12; cf. Acts 17:1-9.

the emperor is divine, Paul grants only that the emperor and all others are servants of God (13:4); they are not themselves divine. Nor does Paul take up the
matter of civil disobedience. At that time there had been no state-sponsored persecutions of Christians, and although he had experienced beatings from Roman
authorities (2 Cor 11:25; cf. Acts 16:19-24), those would have been punishments
for creating civil disturbances, not for doing deliberate acts of civil disobedience
per se. It appears from his own life that Paul contemplated disobedience at one
point only, and that was at the point of refusing to renounce the confession of
Christ as Lord. Disobedience there would have been in keeping with the traditional apostolic dictum: "We must obey God rather than any human authority"
(Acts 5:29). Paul's death by execution under Roman authority most likely testifies to his civil disobedience at that point. He would have been found guilty of
maiestas (treason), a capital crime. As a citizen he would not be crucified,
burned alive, or thrown to the beasts, but decapitated by the sword.[22]

Some interpreters have regarded the passage as "a foreign body" incorporated into the letter or even a post-Pauline interpolation.[23] That the passage is an
interpolation is unlikely on both internal and external grounds. There are no
known ancient Greek texts that lack the passage, and it is cited already in the late
second century in patristic sources.[24] Nor need the passage be considered alien to
the text.[25] The passage is a paraenetic one, by which Paul seeks to gain a common
understanding and trust with his readers. Moreover, there are conceptual and terminological similarities between this section and what has gone before or follows
immediately: references to "wrath" (ὀργή) in 13:4-5 and 12:19; to "repay" or "render" (ἀποδίδωμι) in 13:7 and 12:17; to "execute" or "avenge" (ἔκδικος/ἐκδικέω) in
13:4 and 12:19; and "what is due" and to "owe" (ὀφειλή/ὀφείλω) in 13:7 and 13:8.[26]

One of the more striking things about the passage is that it is heavily
loaded with conjunctions,[27] and that makes following the argument somewhat
complicated. Nevertheless, an essential framework is evident. The section be-

---

22. H. Tajra, *The Martyrdom of St. Paul,* 22, 200.

23. The passage is considered "eine selbstständige Einlage" ("an independent insertion")
by O. Michel, *Römer,* 312, and "a foreign body" by E. Käsemann, "Principles of the Interpretation
of Romans 13," 198; idem, *Romans,* 352. E. Bammel, "Romans 13," 381, speaks of it as "a side aisle"
discussion. The passage is considered an interpolation by J. O'Neill, *Romans,* 15, 207-9;
E. Barnikol, "Römer 13," 65-133; J. Kallas, "Romans xiii. 1-7," 365-74; W. Munro, "Romans 13:1-7,"
161-68; and W. Schmithals, *Der Römerbrief als historisches Problem,* 185-97.

24. Irenaeus, *Against the Heresies* 24.1.

25. The arguments for the integrity of the passage are well presented by F. F. Bruce, "Paul
and 'the Powers That Be,'" 78-96; against interpolation, cf. R. Jewett, *Romans,* 782-84.

26. U. Wilckens, *Römer,* 3:30-31; E. Lohse, *Römer,* 352.

27. These include γάρ ("for") at 13:1b, 3, 4a, 4b, 4c, 6b; δέ ("and" or "but") at 13:1c, 2b, 3b,
4b; ἀλλά at 13:5b; καί ("and") at 13:3b; ὥστε ("so that" or "therefore") at 13:2; διό ("therefore") at
13:5; and διὰ τοῦτο ("therefore") at 13:6.

gins with an exhortation in 13:1a, and it is recapitulated in 13:5. Between these two poles Paul gives the basis for the exhortation. That is that authority is divinely established (13:1b-2), and that rulers, as servants of God, reward good conduct and punish evil conduct (13:3-4).

Detailed Comment

13:1-2 Paul calls upon "every person" (πᾶσα ψυχή, literally, "every soul") to be subject to the governing authorities. The plural "authorities" (ἐξουσίαι) soon gives way to the singular "authority" (ἐξουσία) in the same verse and those following (13:2, 3).[28] The combination helps to interpret the entire passage. Paul is not talking about supernatural forces in this passage, as in 1 Corinthians 15:24,[29] but of temporal authority and temporal authorities in this world.[30] He speaks of "authorities" (actual persons) in 13:1a and of "authority" (as both person and political agency) in 13:1b and following.

The verb Paul uses (ὑποτασσέσθω) is usually translated "be subject [to]," and need not have the meaning of being submissive (contra NIV, "everyone must submit himself").[31] The latter carries the sense of a servile behavior that need not be intended. Paul sketches out what it means later in the passage, and that is doing good in society (13:3), paying taxes, and showing respect and honor to whom these are due (13:7). One attends to these, wrote Augustine, "for the sake of everyday social order," but one "should not submit to any man desiring to destroy that very thing in us through which God deigned to give us eternal life,"[32] referring to faith in Christ. The main thing is that a person recognize the legitimacy of the governing authorities.

28. Although the plural "authorities" is used in 13:6 in various English versions (RSV, NIV, NRSV, ESV, and NET) for the sake of ease of reading, the corresponding word is not found in the Greek text (nor in the KJV and ASV).

29. Contra O. Cullmann, *The State in the New Testament,* 191-210; M. Black, *Romans,* 159; C. Morrison, *The Powers,* 98-101. The term is used more frequently in that sense within the Deutero-Pauline letters (Eph 1:21; 3:10; 6:12; Col. 1:16; 2:10, 25) and at 1 Pet 3:22. For an extensive discussion, cf. C. Cranfield, *Romans,* 657-59, and for a critique and rejection of the view, cf. W. Carr, *Angels and Principalities,* 115-18.

30. So various commentaries, e.g., E. Käsemann, *Romans,* 353; J. Fitzmyer, *Romans,* 666; J. Ziesler, *Romans,* 311; J. Dunn, *Romans,* 760. Cf. also A. Strobel, "Zum Verständnis von Röm 13," 79; R. Barraclough, "Romans 13:1-7," 16-21. W. Wink, *Naming the Powers,* 45-47, concludes that Paul would have affirmed the existence of such powers, but is here concerned about practical and mundane issues facing the church.

31. Cf. BDAG 1042 (ὑποτάσσω, 1, b, β).

32. Augustine, *Propositions from the Epistle to the Romans* 72.2-5. Quoted from *Augustine on Romans: Propositions from the Epistle to the Romans; Unfinished Commentary on the Epistle to the Romans,* ed. Paula Fredriksen Landes, SBL.TT 23 (Chico: Scholars Press, 1982), 41-43.

That also means, however, that one cannot lift 13:1b out of its ancient context and say that, for Paul, only that which modern people call "legitimate authority" is valid; that is, that one should obey only those authorities that are lawful and serve the public good. As important as that is for modern consciousness, Paul accepts the view that governing authorities have legitimate authority because they have been instituted by God. That becomes obvious in 13:2; resistance to the authorities is to be avoided, for whoever resists the civil authorities resists those whom God has appointed. As indicated previously, however, that does not mean that Paul provides here a theory of the state. He is more concerned about the life of the believer within the civil sphere than about the nature of the state itself.

13:3-4 Paul seems naïve in these verses. He says that rulers reward good conduct and punish evildoers. If Paul means that personal goodness is rewarded and bad personal behavior is punished in all times and places, that could be true only in an ideal world. Life is not so simple. Too often the humble are taken advantage of and the arrogant flourish within political systems. Paul must therefore have something else in mind, namely, that, in the face of the political realities of his day, persons who practice civil virtues gain approval. It is possible that Paul has in mind the usual custom that officials praise and formally honor those who provide civil service or benevolences.[33] The verses are descriptive, not prescriptive, although with overtones of the latter.

There is a bit of irony in 13:4. Paul says twice that the one in authority is God's "servant" (διάκονος). To the modern ear the term carries with it only one nuance of the metaphor, and that is that such a person carries out God's purposes. But going beyond that, taking it within its ancient context, the term means that the one in authority is not divine, but subject to God. The term relativizes the standing of persons in authority.

13:5 Paul repeats the theme of being subject to authority. This time, however, it is not a matter simply of doing that which is in accord with God's will, but also for the sake of "conscience." The expression "for the sake of conscience" (διὰ τὴν συνείδησιν) is used by Paul elsewhere (1 Cor 10:25, 27, 28). The term "conscience" (συνείδησις), familiar in Hellenistic writings in general, particularly those of the Stoics,[34] is also used in Hellenistic Judaism prior to Paul.[35] Of its 30 appearances within the NT, 14 are in the letters of Paul.[36] It signifies a moral awareness that is presumptively common to all people,[37] and therefore

---

33. B. Winter, "Roman Law and Society in Romans 12–15," 82.

34. For a survey of the use of the term in secular Greek, cf. Christian Maurer, "σύνοιδα, συνείδησις," *TDNT* 7:899-907.

35. Eccl 10:20; Wis 17:10; Josephus, *Ant.* 16.108; *T. Reuben* 4.3.

36. Rom 2:15; 9:1; 13:5; 1 Cor 8:7, 10, 12; 10:26, 27, 28, 29 (twice); 2 Cor 1:12; 4:2; 5:11.

37. Cf. Gerd Lüdemann, "συνείδησις," *EDNT* 3:302.

apart from revelation. To be subject to the governing authorities "for the sake of conscience" places the Christian community within the larger sphere of humanity and grants that one can know what ought to be done in the civil sphere.[38] To be subject to the governing powers or not is not something peculiar to Paul's gospel, but is based within common human sensitivity of the need for good order. Nevertheless, the conscience of the Christian is aroused by the "renewal of the mind" that discerns the will of God — "that which is good, pleasing, and perfect" (12:2). The gospel does not call common, civic values into question insofar as they conform to the life based on grace.

Here the view that Paul counsels withdrawal from society, as has been claimed,[39] is incorrect. In fact Paul calls for the integration of Christians into the existing social and political order. To be sure, he does not call for engaging in social and political change — and it would be virtually meaningless for him to do so — but he does expect that believers in Christ will understand themselves as persons who are incorporated into the larger social setting.

13:6 The Roman Christians pay "taxes" (φόροι), clearly meaning in this context civil taxes imposed by Roman rulers.[40] Doing so testifies to their respect for the governing authorities. The authorities are God's "servants" or "ministers" (λειτουργοί). The designation is an old one, composed from an Ionic word λεῖτος, meaning "people," and ἔργον, meaning "work."[41] It was used in both pre-Christian secular Greek literature and in the LXX for civil authorities, persons who perform a public service for the people.[42] Later on in the letter Paul uses a verb form of the term in its religious (cultic) meaning concerning himself (Rom 15:16). But in the present case the term is used for officials in the secular sense; Paul does not suggest that they serve a religious function in the state cultus, as though that would give them greater authority. In reference to the civil officials previously, Paul had used the term "authority" (singular) and "God's servant" (15:4); now he calls them "God's ministers." In neither case does Paul assume that rulers are divine. As "God's ministers" (λειτουργοὶ θεοῦ), they are subject to God for the sake of the people.

Paul goes on to say that the authorities are God's ministers, "attending to this very thing." The antecedent is unclear. Does it include all that has been said

---

38. M. Thrall, "The Pauline Use of συνείδησις," 118-25; T. Engberg-Pedersen, *Paul and the Stoics*, 271-72.

39. H. von Campenhausen, "The Christian and Social Life according to the New Testament," 147, has written that Paul is "wholly defensive," avoiding "social integration" of Christians within society.

40. LSJ 1951 (φόρος); cf. also Daniel C. Snell, "Taxes and Taxation," *ABD* 6:338-40.

41. Hermann Strathmann, "λειτουργέω," *TDNT* 4:216.

42. Plutarch, *Rom.* 26.3; 2 Sam 13:18; 3 Kgdms 10:5; 3 Macc 5:5; Sir 10:2. Cf. H. Strathmann, "λειτουργός," *TDNT* 4:229-31; A. Strobel, "Zum Verständnis von Röm 13," 86-87.

about the duties of the authorities in 13:3-4,[43] or does it refer simply to the collecting of taxes (13:6a)?[44] Although one can hardly be certain, it appears that the more limited range is more likely. The Roman Christians pay taxes, and the authorities serve the public. That service includes gaining the support needed through the collection of taxes. It is a service that is necessary in order to contribute to the welfare of all.

13:7 The section ends with a general admonition followed by a rhetorical flourish in four lines of equal length. Each line has five words in Greek; six in English versions:

> Render to everyone what you owe:
>> tax to whom tax is due,
>> revenue to whom revenue is due,
>> respect to whom respect is due,
>> honor to whom honor is due.

That covers most contingencies in the civil sphere. The duties enumerated fall into two groups of two: first, "tax" and "revenue"; and second, "respect" and "honor." There are different degrees of gravity in each of the two cases, but the main thing is the rhetorical effect, by which Paul covers the field from the greater to the lesser in each case. The "tax" (φόρος) of which he speaks is the "tribute" owed directly to the Roman government, while the "revenue" (τέλος) mentioned would be lesser, specific taxes ("duties" or "levies,"[45] corresponding largely to "user fees" in modern times). "Respect" (φόβος, translated as "fear" in KJV) and "honor" (τιμή) are virtually the same, but they must be distinguished in some way, however slight. It is possible that the first applies to that deference and reverence that one gives to a high official,[46] since the word is used also to express that level of reverence that is due to God (cf. Rom 3:18; 2 Cor 5:11; 7:11; 1 Pet 2:17), while "honor" could mean the regard that one would give to lesser officials, since it is also to be rendered to other persons (cf. Rom 12:10: "outdo one another in showing honor").

It has been said that there is nothing particularly "Christian" about 13:1-7, for there is no reference to Christ within the passage.[47] Nevertheless, the passage speaks indirectly of the life of the believer shaped by grace. As indicated

---

43. C. K. Barrett, *Romans*, 227.

44. J. Fitzmyer, *Romans*, 669.

45. LSJ 1951 (φόρος) and 1773 (τέλος, 8)

46. Horst Balz, "φόβος," *TDNT* 9:214-15. The claim that "respect (φόβος) to whom respect is due" in 13:7 refers to God alone (cf. 1 Pet 2:17) has been made by U. Wilckens, *Römer,* 3:38; C. Cranfield, *Romans*, 669-73, considers it as a possibility.

47. O. Michel, *Römer,* 289; G. Bornkamm, *Paul,* 210; E. Käsemann, *Romans,* 351.

earlier, the passage is not about the authority of the state per se, nor does it set forth a "doctrine of the state." Instead it speaks of the life of the believer in the world, which is the place where discipleship actually takes place. The new life in Christ does not exempt one from civic obligations. In each era of history, and in each location around the globe, those who live in Christ will have to discern the particular form that must take. In many places where democratic structures exist, terms such as "participation" and "responsibility" are at hand to bring out contemporary applications of the passage.[48] In any case, underlying the passage is the common conviction that the primary function of the state is to promote the general welfare (which, however, is understood differently across time and cultures) and to hold the powers of evil in check.

BIBLIOGRAPHY

Aalders H. W., J. D. Gerhard, and Lukas de Blois. "Plutarch und die politische Philosophie der Griechen." *ANRW* II.36.5 (1992): 3384-3404.
Aland, Kurt. "Das Verhältnis von Kirche und Staat in der Frühzeit." *ANRW* II.23.1 (1979): 60-246.
Amiet, Peter. "*Exousia* im NT." *IKZ* 61 (1971): 233-42.
André, Jean-Marie. "La conception de l'État et de l'Empire dans la pensée gréco-romaine des deux premiers siècles de notre ère." *ANRW* II.30.1 (1982): 3-73.
Arzt, Peter. "Über die Macht des Staates nach Röm 13,1-7." *SNTU* 18 (1993): 163-81.
Bailey, Jon N. "Paul's Political Paraenesis in Romans 13:1-7." *ResQ* 46 (2004): 11-28.
Bammel, Ernst. "Romans 13." In *Jesus and the Politics of His Day*, 365-83. Ed. Ernst Bammel and C. F. D. Moule. Cambridge: Cambridge University Press, 1984.
Barnikol, Ernst. "Römer 13: Der nichtpaulinische Ursprung der absoluten Obrigkeitsbejahung von Römer 13,1-7." In *Studien zum Neuen Testament und zur Patristik: Erich Klostermann zum 90. Geburtstag dargebracht*, 65-133. Ed. Jürgen Dummer et al. TUGAL 77. Berlin: Akademie Verlag, 1961.
Barraclough, Ray. "Philo's Politics: Roman Rule and Hellenistic Judaism." *ANRW* II.21.1 (1984): 417-553.
———. "Romans 13:1-7: Application in Context." *Colloq* 17 (1985): 16-21.
Barrett, C. K. "The New Testament Doctrine of Church and State." In his *New Testament Essays*, 1-19. London: SPCK, 1972.
Bauer, Walter. "'Jedermann sei untertan der Obrigkeit.'" In *Walter Bauer: Aufsätze und*

---

48. The terms are taken from J. Bennett, *The Christian as Citizen*, 46-53; idem, *Christians and the State*, 27-35. Speaking comprehensively about church and state in the NT, W. Pilgrim, *Uneasy Neighbors*, 192, writes that there are three principal stances for the church to make toward governments: (1) a critical-constuctive stance is appropriate when the powers that be are attempting to achieve justice; (2) a critical-transformative stance when authority errs but can be realistically moved to salutary change; and (3) a critically resistive stance when the powers are responsible for demonic injustice or idolatry and refuse to be responsible to change.

kleine Schriften, 263-84. Ed. Georg Strecker. Tübingen: J. C. B. Mohr (Paul Siebeck), 1967.

Bauman, Richard A. *Crime and Punishment in Ancient Rome.* New York: Routledge, 1996.

Beck, Norman A. *Anti-Roman Cryptograms in the New Testament: Hidden Transcripts of Hope and Liberation.* Rev. ed. SBL 127. New York: Peter Lang, 2010.

Bennett, John C. *The Christian as Citizen.* New York: Association Press, 1955.

————. *Christians and the State.* New York: Charles Scribner's Sons, 1958.

Bergmeier, Roland. "Die Loyalitätsparänese Röm 13:1-7 im Rahmen von Römer 12 und 13." *TBei* 27 (1996): 341-57.

Blumenfeld, Bruno, ed. *The Political Paul: Justice, Democracy and Kingship in a Hellenistic Framework.* JSNTSup 210. Sheffield: Sheffield Academic Press, 2001.

Borg, Marcus. "A New Context for Romans XIII." *NTS* 19 (1972/73): 205-18.

Bornkamm, Günther. *Paul.* New York: Harper & Row, 1971; reprinted, Minneapolis: Fortress Press, 1994.

Botha, Jan. "Creation of New Meaning: Rhetorical Situations and the Reception of Romans 13:1-7." *JTSA* (1992): 24-37.

————. "Social Values in the Rhetoric of Pauline Paraenetic Literature." *Neot* 28 (1994): 109-26.

————. *Subject to Whose Authority? Multiple Readings of Romans 13.* ESEC 4. Atlanta: Scholars Press, 1994.

Boyer, Susan. "Exegesis of Romans 13:1-7." *BLT* 32 (1987): 208-16.

Bruce, Frederick F. "Paul and 'The Powers That Be.'" *BJRL* 66 (1983-84): 78-96.

Campenhausen, Hans von. "Zur Auslegung von Röm. 13: Die dämonische Deutung des *exousia*-Begriffs." In his *Aus der Frühzeit des Christentums*, 81-101. Tübingen: J. C. B. Mohr (Paul Siebeck), 1963.

————. "The Christian and Social Life according to the New Testament." In his *Tradition and Life in the Church: Essays and Lectures in Church History*, 141-59. Philadelphia: Fortress Press, 1968.

Carr, Wesley. *Angels and Principalities: The Background, Meaning and Development of the Pauline Phrase* hai archai kai hai exousiai. SNTSMS 42. Cambridge: Cambridge University Press, 1981.

Carter, Timothy L. "The Irony of Romans 13." *NovT* 46 (2004): 209-28.

Carter, Warren. *The Roman Empire and the New Testament: An Essential Guide.* Nashville: Abingdon Press, 2006.

Cassidy, Richard J. *Christians and Roman Rule in the New Testament.* New York: Crossroads Publishing Company, 2001.

————. *Paul in Chains: Roman Imprisonment and the Letters of Paul.* Crossroads Publishing Company, 2001.

Coleman, Thomas M. "Binding Obligations in Romans 13:7: A Semantic Field and Social Context." *TynB* 48 (1997): 307-27.

Collins, J. H. "Caesar as Political Propagandist." *ANRW* I.1 (1972): 922-66.

Cranfield, C. E. B. "Some Observations on Romans 13:1-7." *NTS* 6 (1959-60): 241-49.

Cullmann, Oscar. *The State in the New Testament.* New York: Charles Scribner's Sons, 1956.

Delling, Gerhard. *Römer 13,1-7 innerhalb der Briefe des Neuen Testaments*. Berlin: Evangelische Verlagsanstalt, 1962.

Denova, Rebecca. "Paul's Letter to the Romans, 13:1-7: The Gentile Response to Civil Authority." *Encounter* 53 (1992): 201-29.

Draper, Jonathan A. "'Humble Submission to Almighty God' and Its Biblical Foundation." *JTSA* (1988): 30-38.

Dunn, James D. G. "Romans 13:1-7 — A Charter for Christian Quietism?" *ExAud* 2 (1986): 55-68.

Elliott, Neil. *The Arrogance of Nations: Reading Romans in the Shadow of Empire*. PCC. Minneapolis: Fortress Press, 2008.

———. *Liberating Paul: The Justice of God and the Politics of the Apostle*. Maryknoll: Orbis Books, 1994.

———. "Political Formation in the Letter to the Romans." In *Character Ethics and the New Testament: Moral Dimensions of Scripture*, 179-90. Ed. Robert Brawley. Louisville: Westminster John Knox, 2007.

———. "Romans 13:1-7 in the Context of Imperial Propaganda." In *Paul and Empire: Religion and Power in Roman Imperial Society*, 184-204. Ed. Richard A. Horsley. Harrisburg: Trinity Press International, 1997.

Engberg-Pedersen, Troels. *Paul and the Stoics*. Louisville: Westminster John Knox, 2000.

———. "Paul's Stoicizing Politics in Romans 12–13: The Role of 13.1-10 in the Argument." *JSNT* 29 (2006): 163-72.

Friedrich, Johannes, Wolfgang Pöhlmann, and Peter Stuhlmacher. "Zu historischen Situation und Intention von Röm 13,1-7." *ZTK* 73 (1976): 131-66.

Furnish, Victor Paul. *The Moral Teaching of Paul: Selected Issues*. 3d ed. Nashville: Abingdon Press, 2009.

Gale, Herbert M. "Paul's View of the State: A Discussion of the Problem in Romans 13:1-7." *Int* 6 (1952): 409-14.

Gaugusch, L. "Die Staatslehre des Apostels Paulus nach Rom. 13." *TGl* 26 (1934): 529-50.

Goppelt, Leonhard. "Der Staat in der Sicht des Neuen Testaments." In his *Christologie und Ethik: Aufsätze zum Neuen Testament*, 190-207. Göttingen: Vandenhoeck & Ruprecht, 1968.

Heiligenthal, Roman. "Strategien konformer Ethik im Neuen Testament am Beispiel von Röm 13,1-7." *NTS* 29 (1983): 55-61.

Herz, Peter. "Bibliographie zum römischen Kaiserkult (1955-1975)." *ANRW* II.16.2 (1978): 833-910.

———. "Kaiserfeste der Prinzipatszeit." *ANRW* II.16.2 (1978): 1135-1200.

Hillerdal, Gunnar. "Romans 13 and Luther's Doctrine of the 'Two Kingdoms.'" *LW* 7 (1960): 10-23.

Hollingshead, James R. *The Household of Caesar and the Body of Christ: A Political Interpretation of the Letters of Paul*. Lanham: University Press of America, 1998.

Horsley, Richard A., ed. *Paul and the Roman Imperial Order*. Harrisburg: Trinity Press International, 2004.

Hultgren, Arland J. "Reflections on Romans 13:1-7: On Submission to Governing Authorities." *Dialog* 15 (1976): 263-69.

Huzar, Eleanor Goltz. "Claudius — the Erudite Emperor." *ANRW* II.32.1 (1984): 611-50.

Jeffers, James S. *Conflict at Rome: Social Order and Hierarchy in Early Christianity.* Minneapolis: Fortress Press, 1991.

Jones, Donald L. "Christianity and the Roman Imperial Cult." *ANRW* II.23.2 (1980): 1023-54.

Käsemann, Ernst. "Principles of the Interpretation of Romans 13." In his *New Testament Questions of Today,* 196-216. London: SCM Press, 1969.

Kallas, James. "Romans xiii.1-7: An Interpolation." *NTS* 11 (1964-65): 365-74.

Keresztes, Paul. "The Imperial Roman Government and the Christian Church, 1: From Nero to the Severi." *ANRW* II.23.1 (1979): 247-315.

Kim, Seyoon. *Christ and Caesar: The Gospel and the Roman Empire in the Writings of Paul and Luke.* Grand Rapids: Wm. B. Eerdmans, 2008.

Koch-Mehrin, J. "Die Stellung des Christen zum Staat nach Röm. 13 und Apok. 13." *EvT* 7 (1947-48): 378-401.

Krauter, Stefan. *Studien zu Röm 13,1-7: Paulus und der politische Diskurs der neronischen Zeit.* WUNT 2/243. Tübingen: Mohr Siebeck, 2009.

Krodel, Gerhard. "Church and State in the New Testament." *Dialog* 15 (1976): 21-28.

Kroger, Daniel. "Paul and the Civil Authorities: An Exegesis of Romans 13:1-7." *AJT* 7 (1993): 344-66.

Kuss, Otto. "Paulus über die staatliche Gewalt." *TGl* 45 (1955): 321-34; reprinted in his *Auslegung und Verkündigung,* 1:246-59. 3 vols. Regensburg: Pustet Verlag, 1963-71.

Légasse, Simon. "Paul et César: Romains 13,1-7: Essai de synthèse." *RB* 101 (1994): 516-32.

Lichtenberger, Hermann. "Jews and Christians in Rome in the Time of Nero: Josephus and Paul in Rome." *ANRW* II.26.3 (1996): 2142-76.

Lorimer, W. L. "Romans xiii.3." *NTS* 12 (1965-66): 389-90.

McDonald, James I. H. "Romans 13:1-7: A Test Case for New Testament Interpretation." *NTS* 35 (1989): 540-49.

Merklein, Helmut. "Sinn und Zweck von Röm. 13,1-7: Zur semantischen und pragmatischen Struktur eines umstrittenen Textes." In *Neues Testament und Ethik: Für Rudolf Schnackenburg,* 238-70. Ed. Helmut Merklein. Freiburg im Breisgau: Herder, 1989; reprinted in his *Studien zu Jesus und Paulus,* 2:405-37. 2 vols. WUNT 43, 105. Tübingen: J. C. B. Mohr (Paul Siebeck), 1987.

Minear, Paul S. *The Obedience of Faith: The Purposes of Paul in the Epistle to the Romans.* SBT 2/19. Naperville: Alec R. Allenson, 1971.

Miyata, Mitsuo. *Authority and Obedience: Romans 13:1-7 in Modern Japan.* TR 294. New York: Peter Lang, 2009.

Morrison, Clinton. *The Powers That Be: Earthly Rulers and Demonic Powers in Romans 13:1-7.* SBT 29. Naperville: Alec R. Allenson, 1960.

Moulder, James. "Romans 13 and Conscientious Disobedience." *JTSA* 21 (1977): 13-23.

Munro, Winsome. *Authority in Paul and Peter.* SNTSMS 45. Cambridge: Cambridge University Press, 1983.

————. "Romans 13:1-7: Apartheid's Last Biblical Refuge." *BTB* 20 (1990): 161-68.

Nanos, Mark. *The Mystery of Romans: The Jewish Context of Paul's Letter.* Minneapolis: Fortress Press, 1996.

Neufeld, Karl H. "Das Gewissen: Ein Deutungsversuch im Anschluss an Röm 13,1-7." *BibLeb* 12 (1971): 32-45.

Neugebauer, Fritz. "Zur Auslegung von Röm 13,1-7." *KuD* 8 (1962): 151-72.

Niebuhr, Reinhold. *The Nature and Destiny of Man*. 2 vols. New York: Charles Scribner's Sons, 1941.

Oakes, Peter. "Christian Attitudes to Rome at the Time of Paul's Letter." *RevExp* 100 (2003): 103-11.

Perdue, Leo G. "The Social Character of Paraenesis and Paraenetic Literature." In *Paraenesis: Act and Form*, 5-39. Semeia 50. Atlanta: Scholars Press, 1990.

Pierce, Claude A. *Conscience in the New Testament*. SBT 15. London: SCM, 1955.

Pilgrim, Walter E. *Uneasy Neighbors: Church and State in the New Testament*. Overtures to Biblical Theology. Minneapolis: Fortress Press, 1999.

Pohle, Lutz. *Die Christen und der Staat nach Römer 13: Eine typologische Untersuchung der neueren deutschsprächigen Schriftauslegung*. Mainz: Grünwald, 1984.

Porter, Stanley E. "Romans 13:1-7 as Pauline Political Rhetoric." *FilNeot* 3 (1990): 115-39.

Reasoner, Mark. "Ancient and Modern Exegesis of Romans 13 under Unfriendly Governments." In *Society of Biblical Literature 1999 Seminar Papers*, 359-74. Ed. Kent H. Richards. SBLSP 38. Atlanta: Society of Biblical Literature, 1999.

Reese, Thomas J. "Pauline Politics: Rom 13:1-7." *BTB* 3 (1973): 323-31.

Riekkinen, Vilho. *Römer 13: Auszeichnung und weiterführung der exegetischen Diskussion*. AASF 23. Helsinki: Suomalainen Tiedeakatemia, 1980.

Røsaeg, Nils A. "Rom 13.1-7 i sosialpolitisk kontekst: Ny forskning — en oversikt og vurdering." *NTT* 94 (1993): 35-54.

Schlier, Heinrich. *Principalities and Powers in the New Testament*. New York: Herder and Herder, 1961.

———. "The State according to the New Testament." In his *The Relevance of the New Testament*, 215-38. New York: Herder and Herder, 1968.

Schmithals, Walter. *Der Römerbrief als historisches Problem*. SNT 9. Gütersloh: Gütersloher Verlagshaus Gerd Mohn, 1975.

Schnelle, Udo. *Apostle Paul: His Life and Theology*. Grand Rapids: Baker Academic, 2005.

Schrage, Wolfgang. "Römer 13." In his *Die Christen und der Staat nach dem Neuen Testament*, 50-62. Gütersloh: Gütersloher Verlagshaus Gerd Mohn, 1971.

Stein, Robert H. "The Argument of Romans 13:1-7." *NovT* 31 (1989): 325-43.

Steinmetz, David C. "Calvin and Melanchthon on Romans 13:1-7." *ExAud* 2 (1986): 74-81.

Strobel, August. "Furcht, wem Furcht gebuhrt, zum profangriechischen Hintergrund von Rm 13:7." *ZNW* 55 (1964): 58-62.

———. "Zum Verständnis von Röm 13." *ZNW* 47 (1956): 67-93.

Stowers, Stanley K. *Letter Writing in Greco-Roman Antiquity*. LEC 5. Philadelphia: Westminster Press, 1986.

Tajra, Harry W. *The Martyrdom of St. Paul: Historical and Judicial Context, Traditions, and Legends*. WUNT 2/67. Tübingen: J. C. B. Mohr (Paul Siebeck), 1994.

Tellbe, Mikael. *Paul between Synagogue and State: Christians, Jews, and Civic Authorities in 1 Thessalonians, Romans, and Philippians*. ConBNT 34. Stockholm: Almqvist & Wiksell, 2001.

Thrall, Margaret. "The Pauline Use of συνείδησις." *NTS* 14 (1967-68): 118-25.

Towner, Philip H. "Romans 13:1-13 and Paul's Missiological Perspective: A Call to Political Quietism or Transformation?" In *Romans and the People of God: Essays in Honor of Gordon D. Fee on the Occasion of His 65th Birthday*, 149-69. Ed. Sven K. Soderlund and N. T. Wright. Grand Rapids: Wm. B. Eerdmans, 1999.

Unnik, Willem C. van. "Lob und Strafe durch die Obrigkeit: Hellenistisches zu Röm 13,3-4." In *Jesus und Paulus: Festschrift für Werner Georg Kümmel zum 70. Geburtstag*, 334-43. Ed. E. Earle Ellis and Erich Grässer. Göttingen: Vandenhoeck & Ruprecht, 1975.

Walker, Rolf. *Studie zu Römer 13:1-7.* TEH 132. Munich: Kaiser Verlag, 1966.

Webster, Alexander F. C. "St. Paul's Political Advice to the Haughty Gentile Christians in Rome: An Exegesis of Romans 13:1-7." *SVTQ* 28 (1981): 259-82.

Wengst, Klaus. *Pax Romana and the Peace of Jesus Christ.* Philadelphia: Fortress Press, 1987.

Wink, Walter. *Naming the Powers: The Language of Power in the New Testament.* Philadelphia: Fortress Press, 1984.

Winter, Bruce W. "The Public Honoring of Christian Benefactors: Romans 13:3-4 and 1 Peter 2:14-15." *JSNT* 34 (1988): 87-103.

———. "Roman Law and Society in Romans 12–15." In *Rome in the Bible and the Early Church*, 67-102. Ed. Peter Oakes. Grand Rapids: Baker Academic, 2002.

———. *Seek the Welfare of the City: Christians as Benefactors and Citizens. First-Century Christians in the Graeco-Roman World.* Grand Rapids: Wm. B. Eerdmans, 1994.

Wright, N. T. "The New Testament and the 'State.'" *Themelios* 16 (1990): 11-17.

7.2. Love as Fulfillment of the Law, 13:8-10

8*Owe nothing to anyone, except to love one another. For the person who loves another has fulfilled the law. 9For the commandments — "You shall not commit adultery," "You shall not murder," "You shall not steal," "You shall not covet," and if there is any other commandment — are summed up in this statement: "You shall love your neighbor as yourself." 10Love does no wrong to a neighbor; for love is the fulfillment of the law.*

Notes on the Text and Translation

13:9a Some ancient witnesses (including ℵ, P, Old Latin, and others) include οὐ ψευδομαρτυρήσεις ("You shall not bear false witness") as the third commandment listed (located after "You shall not steal"). The commandment is not included in other witnesses (including 𝔓⁴⁶, A, B, D, and others). Although the external evidence is nearly balanced, the evidence for the reading that omits the phrase can be considered slightly stronger. The fact that Paul is being more il-lustrative than complete in his citing of the commandments may favor brevity. In any case, the shorter reading is to be preferred.

13:9b Significant witnesses (including B and apparently 𝔓⁴⁶) omit the Greek expression ἐν τῷ that appears redundant in light of ἐν τῷ λόγῳ τούτῳ ("in this statement"); while it means, literally, "in this," it can be translated "namely." The expression is present in other major witnesses (including ℵ, A, D, Ψ, the Majority Text, and others) and (again, redundantly) at Galatians 5:14. On the basis of the external evidence, the expression should be included, but it need not be represented in an English translation.

General Comment

In these three verses Paul sums up his ethical teachings, drawing upon tradi-tions from both the OT and the teachings of Jesus in the gospels. His exhorta-tion to practice love for one another, and indeed for all of humankind, refers to the central moral teaching of the OT and Jewish heritage (the Decalogue, Exod 20:1-17; Deut 5:6-21), and concludes with a pronouncement from Leviticus 19:18 as a summary of the law.

Because of his background in Judaism, Paul's ethics is naturally rooted in the moral teaching of the OT, of which the Decalogue is central and crucial. But OT teachings alone do not account for its breadth, language, and norms. One need only look to Philippians 4:8-9 to discover that Paul draws on common Hellenistic moral traditions. Indeed, even the concept of being indebted to oth-ers in a moral (rather than a financial) sense, as in the present passage (13:8), has antecedents in pagan Hellenism.[49] In addition, the teachings of Jesus are a source, as seen in this passage. Whatever moral teaching coheres with the life in Christ, regardless of its source, is taken over by Paul and put to use.

Detailed Comment

13:8 "Owe nothing to anyone, except to love one another." Here the imperative verb ὀφείλετε ("owe") is a catchword, the verbal form of the noun ὀφειλή in the preceding verse (13:7), and what is owed is love for one another. Although it would seem that love cannot be owed to another in the sense of an obligatory debt to be paid,[50] the metaphorical use of obligation is effective in an exhorta-

---

49. Homer, *Iliad* 19.200; Sophocles, *Ajax* 590; Herodotus, *Hist.* 1.41.
50. Cf. J. Fitzmyer, *Romans,* 677, who calls love as a debt an "oxymoron."

tion.[51] It is another way of expressing the love command, a variation within a constellation of exhortations in the NT to love other persons (John 13:34; 15:12; Rom 12:9-10; Gal 5:13; Eph 4:2; 1 Thess 3:12; 4:9; Heb 10:24; 1 Pet 1:22; 3:8; 4:8; 1 John 3:14; 4:7, 11); one is obligated to love. Here it is important to bear in mind that the verb ἀγαπάω ("to love") does not mean simply to have affection for others, a matter of the heart alone, but also to hold the other person in high regard, caring for his or her interests.[52] It is a matter of the will as much as the heart, transformed by the joy and gratitude of knowing the love of God. As the statement stands, it is an exhortation to mutual love within the community of believers ("love one another"). But that is not the end of the matter, for Paul goes on very soon to speak of loving the "neighbor" (13:9), which directs one's love outward beyond the community.

What follows in 13:8b is quite astonishing. Paul says that "the person who loves another has fulfilled the law." On one reading that could mean that the person who exercises love fulfills the entire Torah; there is nothing more one need be concerned about. But that cannot be, since the statement is qualified by what follows. Paul goes on in 13:9 to quote and endorse commandments having to do with human relationships. The interpretive key to the statement is the meaning of the verb πεπλήρωκεν (perfect tense of πληρόω, "to fulfill"). The tense of the verb is important. The person who practices love "has fulfilled" the Torah, for such a person has been shaped, formed, to do the will of God, which is expressed in the commandments. Paul does not mean that such a person does God's will perfectly any more than one can keep all the commandments perfectly. But the commandments of the Torah were intended to train the people of Israel in righteousness; they have functioned in the manner of a disciplinarian (Gal 3:24). Anyone who exercises love has met the requirements of the Torah and so "has fulfilled" the Torah. Paul can make such a statement because, for him, the commandment to love one's neighbor summarizes all others (13:9; Gal 5:14).

13:9 Paul cites four commandments from the Decalogue. They consist of prohibitions against deeds and attitudes that destroy human relationships: adultery, murder, stealing, and covetousness. The wording of the individual commandments corresponds to that of the LXX at both Exodus 20:13-17 and Deuteronomy 5:17-21, but their sequence is another matter. Paul's order does not correspond to that of the Hebrew text (MT) nor to that of the LXX text of Exodus. It corresponds only to the LXX version of Deuteronomy (B, but not A and others), which also has the prohibition against adultery first. The sequence must have been common within Hellenistic Judaism, for it appears in the writ-

---

51. Cf. C. F. D. Moule, "Obligation in the Ethic of Paul," 389-406.

52. BDAG (ἀγαπάω, 1, a, α): "to have a warm regard for and interest in another, cherish, have affection for, love."

ings of Philo,[53] who says that the prohibition against adultery is the "first com-mandment" on the second table of the Law.[54] It stands first also at Luke 18:20 and James 2:11.

In addition to the four commandments cited, Paul adds, literally, "and if there is any other commandment." Of course there are others. There are six oth-ers in the Decalogue itself and hundreds of others elsewhere in the Torah (esti-mated to be 613 in a computation by Rabbi Simlai, early third century).[55] There are moral, cultic, and dietary commandments, and in Jewish tradition they are indivisible, although some commandments are more weighty than others.[56] Clearly in the present context Paul has moral commandments alone in mind, not the others.[57]

Paul quotes a portion of Leviticus 19:8 as a summation of all the com-mandments. The verse in its entirety reads: "You shall not take vengeance or bear a grudge against any of your people, but you shall love your neighbor as yourself (καὶ ἀγαπήσεις τὸν πλησίον σου ὡς σεαυτόν): I am the LORD." Within this particular verse the term "neighbor" of 19:8b refers to "any of your people" of 19:8a, i.e., the people of Israel. But the commandment did not need to be re-stricted to that meaning, and it would be incorrect to conclude that that was done in Jewish tradition generally. Leviticus 19:34 ("you shall love the alien as yourself") provides evidence that love for the other was to be extended beyond the circle of one's own people.[58] The love commandment appears seven times in the NT (Mark 12:31//Matt 22:39; Matt 19:19; Luke 10:27; Rom 13:9; Gal 5:14; Jas 2:8), and at James 2:8 it is called the "royal law." Its multiple attestation in the Synoptic tradition, to say nothing of the other instances of its use, attests to its origins in the teachings of Jesus and, consequently, its transmission in the com-mon tradition of early Christianity. The use of it in connection with the Parable

---

53. Philo, *Decal.* 1.36, 51.

54. Philo, *Spec. Leg.* 3.8.

55. Abraham H. Rabinowitz, "Commandments, The 613," *EncJud* 5:73-85, citing sources.

56. Cf. *m. Aboth* 2.1; *m. Yoma* 8.6. The matter is presupposed in the discussion of Matt 23:23.

57. C. K. Barrett, *Romans,* 231; E. Käsemann, *Romans,* 361; J. Dunn, *Romans,* 778, 782; D. Moo, *Romans,* 815; H. Hübner, *Law in Paul's Thought,* 83-85; B. Martin, *Christ and the Law in Paul,* 151; contra W. Sanday and A. Headlam, *Romans,* 374 (that Paul does not refer to any law at all beyond those illustrated). J. Fitzmyer, *Romans,* 679, and R. Jewett, *Romans,* 812, conclude that the phrase can encompass law not only beyond the Decalogue but law in any legal system (Fitzmyer) or law in general (Jewett). But in context it would seem that Paul is referring to moral commandments within the Jewish tradition.

58. The love command is applied to humanity in general at the end of the discussion in *Sifra,* Qedoshim Pereq 4. For text, cf. Jacob Neusner, *Sifra: An Analytical Translation,* BJS 138-40, 3 vols. (Atlanta: Scholars Press, 1988), 3:108-9. Love for humankind is taught in sayings of R. Hillel and R. Meir, *m. Aboth* 1.12; 6.1.

of the Good Samaritan (Luke 10:25-37) indicates that it was understood by Jesus to command love for all persons. The lawyer's question, "Who is my neighbor?" is disingenuous. Behind it lurks the question, "Who is not my neighbor?" Jesus tells the parable to show that love for one's neighbor exceeds all boundaries that humans seek to construct.[59] Far from being a command to love oneself first, prior to loving the other, the command to love one's neighbor as oneself means to have regard for the other to the same degree as one would want for oneself.

The summing up of the law by means of a single principle is not unusual. Already in Deuteronomy, after he had spoken the commandments to Israel, Moses provided a brief declaration of what the Lord required (Deut 10:12-13), and prophets summarized what was central and essential to a life in covenant with God (Mic 6:8; Amos 5:24). Yet, allowing for that, it was assumed that the commandments are to be kept, as expressed above all in the passage from Deuteronomy (cf. Josh 22:5):

> So now, O Israel, what does the LORD your God require of you? Only to fear the LORD your God, to walk in all his ways, to love him, to serve the LORD your God with all your heart and with all your soul, 13and to keep the commandments of the LORD your God and his decrees that I am commanding you today, for your own well-being.

The same would prevail in later Jewish tradition. Paul's contemporary Hillel is known to have summarized the Torah by means of the "negative golden rule": "What is hateful to you, do not to your neighbor: that is the whole Torah, while the rest is the commentary thereof; go and learn it."[60] In his view the Torah in its details is commentary on the golden rule, and the antecedent of "go and learn it" refers to the Torah.

Prior to Paul, Jesus summed up the commandments with the double commandment of love, derived from Deuteronomy 6:5 and Leviticus 19:18 (Mark 12:29-31; Matt 22:37-39), concluding that these are the foremost (Mark 12:31) or that all the commandments depend upon them (Matt 22:40). The linking of the two commandments is doubly attested in the Synoptic tradition,[61] and can therefore most likely be attributed to Jesus, although there are close parallels in other Jewish sources, so the tradition of linking might antedate him.[62] Moreover,

---

59. For discussion, cf. A. Hultgren, *The Parables of Jesus*, 93-103.

60. *B. Shab.* 31a; quoted from *BabT (Shab.)* 140.

61. The Matthean passage is not dependent upon Mark's Gospel at this point; so there is multiple attestation (Mark and M) of the tradition. Cf. A. Hultgren, "The Double Commandment of Love in Matthew 22:34-40," 373-78.

62. *T. Iss.* 5.2: "Love the Lord and your neighbor"; *T. Dan* 5.3: "Throughout all your life love the Lord, and one another with a true heart" (quoted from *OTP* 1:803 and 809, respectively).

according to the Gospel of Matthew, Jesus declared that the (positive) golden rule is the summation of the law and the prophets (7:12). It is probable that Paul's own summarizing of the commandments by means of the love commandment is dependent upon the Jesus tradition.

By saying that the commandments are "summed up" (from the verb ἀνακεφαλαιόω, "to sum up," "recapitulate")[63] in the commandment to love one's neighbor, Paul says that the love commandment gives expression to the will of God as revealed in the Torah. Every person of Jewish heritage would agree that the will of God is revealed in the Torah. The question that is ever present is how the words of the Torah are to be interpreted. For Paul the "Ten Words" (the Decalogue) — and "if there is any other commandment" — are summed up, or recapitulated, in the commandment to love one's neighbor as oneself. If that is so, one does not dispense with the commandments, but one's focus is now on the love commandment. It is not a substitute for the commandments but a final and full articulation (as in a summary) of what the commandments teach. The reasoning is: "If you practice love for the neighbor to the degree that you love yourself (and so a particular quality of love is presumed), you will be doing what the commandments teach you to do."

13:10 That love does no wrong to the neighbor is similar in content to the "negative golden rule." While the statement is hardly necessary, it prepares the way for a recapitulation of what has been said. In 13:8 Paul said that "the person who loves another has fulfilled the law," referring to the human subject and using the verb "to fulfill" (πληρόω). Now, however, he refers to love itself and uses the noun "fulfillment" (πλήρωμα), saying that "love is the fulfillment of the law."[64] The shift is subtle. In a hortatory passage such as this, one can expect that the focus will be on the human subject, as it is at the outset, but the epigrammatic saying in 13:9 — with love as the subject — forms a fitting *inclusio.*

BIBLIOGRAPHY

Bencze, Anselm L. "An Analysis of 'Romans xiii.8-10.'" *NTS* 20 (1973-74): 90-92.
Berger, Klaus. *Die Gesetzesauslegung Jesu: Ihr historischer Hintergrund im Judentum und im Alten Testament.* WMANT 40. Neukirchen-Vluyn: Neukirchener Verlag, 1971.

63. BDAG 65 (ἀνακεφαλαιόω, 1); Helmut Merklein, "ἀνακεφαλαιόω," *EDNT* 1:82-83. LSJ 108 (ἀνακεφαλαιόομαι): "to sum up an argument."
64. According to R. Jewett, "Are There Allusions to the Love Feast?" 265-78, and *Romans,* 813-15, Paul refers in 13:10 to the agape feast ("the love feast, the common meal shared by most sectors of the early church in connection with the Lord's Supper," p. 814). Much of his argument rests on Paul's use of the definite article ἡ ("the") prior to ἀγάπη *(agapē).* But the article is regularly used prior to an abstract noun. Cf. BDAG 686 (ὁ, ἡ, τό, 2, a, ‭א‬): the article is used with "virtues, vices, etc." So Paul uses the definite article with the noun (ἡ ἀγάπη) regularly when speaking of love in the abstract (Rom 12:9; 13:10a; 1 Cor 8:1; 13:8, 13; 14:1; Gal 5:13; 1 Thess 3:12; Phlm 9).

Furnish, Victor Paul. *The Love Command in the New Testament.* Nashville: Abingdon Press, 1972.

Giesen, Heinz. "Nächstenliebe und Heilsvollendung: Zu Röm 13,8-14." *SNTU* 33 (2008): 67-97.

Gorman, Michael J. "Romans 13:8-14." *Int* 62 (2008): 170-72.

Hübner, Hans. *Law in Paul's Thought.* Edinburgh: T&T Clark, 1984.

Hultgren, Arland J. "The Double Commandment of Love in Matthew 22:34-40: Its Sources and Composition," *CBQ* 36 (1975): 373-78.

————. *The Parables of Jesus: A Commentary.* Grand Rapids: Wm. B. Eerdmans, 2000.

Jewett, Robert. "Are There Allusions to the Love Feast in Romans 13:8-10?" In *Common Life in the Early Church: Essays Honoring Graydon F. Snyder,* 265-78. Ed. Julian Hills et al. Harrisburg: Trinity Press International, 1998.

Martin, Brice L. *Christ and the Law in Paul.* NovTSup 62. Leiden: E. J. Brill, 1989.

Marxsen, Willi. "Der ἕτερος νόμος Röm. 13,8." *TZ* 11 (1955): 230-37.

Moule, C. F. D. "Obligation in the Ethic of Paul." In *Christian History and Interpretation: Studies Presented to John Knox,* 389-406. Ed. Willam Farmer et al. Cambridge: Cambridge University Press, 1967.

Neirynck, Frans. "Paul and the Sayings of Jesus." In *L'Apôtre Paul: Personnalité, style et conception du ministère,* 265-321. Ed. Albert Vanhoye. Leuven: Uitgeverij Peeters, 1986.

Nissen, Andreas. *Gott und der Nächste im antiken Judentum: Untersuchungen zum Dopplegebot der Liebe.* WUNT 15. Tübingen: J. C. B. Mohr (Paul Siebeck), 1974.

Perkins, Pheme. *Love Commands in the New Testament.* New York: Paulist Press, 1982.

Piper, John. *"Love Your Enemies": Jesus' Love Command in the Synoptic Gospels and the Early Christian Paraenesis.* SNTSMS 38. Cambridge: Cambridge University Press, 1979.

Räisänen, Heikki. *Paul and the Law.* Philadelphia: Fortress Press, 1983.

Sanders, E. P. *Jewish Law from Jesus to the Mishnah: Five Studies.* Philadelphia: Trinity Press International, 1990.

————. *Paul, the Law, and the Jewish People.* Philadelphia: Fortress Press, 1983.

Schreiner, Thomas R. "The Abolition and Fulfillment of the Law in Paul." *JSNT* 35 (1989): 47-74.

Smith, D. Moody. "The Love Command: John and Paul?" In *Theology and Ethics in Paul and His Interpreters: Essays in Honor of Victor Paul Furnish,* 207-17. Ed. Eugene H. Lovering Jr. and Jerry L. Sumney. Nashville: Abingdon Press, 1996.

Taylor, Walter F. "Obligation: Paul's Foundation for Ethics." *TSR* 19 (1997): 91-112.

Wischmeyer, Oda. "Das Gebot der Nächstenliebe bei Paulus: Eine traditionsgeschichtliche Untersuchung." *BZ* 30 (1986): 161-87.

7.3. Living the New Life in a New Day, 13:11-14

11*And be sure to attend to this, since you know the time. The hour is already here for you to awake from sleep, for our salvation is nearer now than when we* *came to believe.* 12*The night is far gone, and the day is at hand. Let us therefore cast off the works of darkness, and let us put on the weapons of light.* 13*Let us walk decently, as in the day, not in reveling and drunkenness, not in sexual immorality and licentiousness, not in quarreling and jealousy,* 14*but clothe yourselves with the Lord Jesus Christ, and make no provision for the flesh to arouse its desires.*

Notes on the Text and Translation

13:11 The verse begins with καὶ τοῦτο (literally, "and this"), which has been translated rather freely here as, "and be sure to attend to this." The expression appears also at 1 Corinthians 6:6, 8. In each case it marks an important item to follow and has the sense of "and at that" or "and especially,"[65] but it also refers back to what has just been said, which in this case is a series of exhortations beginning at 12:1. The expression therefore presupposes the exhortations and then alerts the reader to pay particular attention to what is coming.

The textual evidence is quite evenly divided between ὑμᾶς ("you," plural), so that the verse reads "the hour for *you* to awake from sleep," and ἡμᾶς ("us"), "the hour for *us* to awake from sleep." The former can be preferred, however, on the grounds that it is more likely that ὑμᾶς was altered to ἡμᾶς, so that it corresponds to ἡμῶν ("our") in the next clause than vice versa.[66] The Westcott-Hort and Nestle-Aland texts have ὑμᾶς ("you") at this place. Major English versions follow that reading with "you" (ASV, RSV, NIV, NRSV, ESV), although the KJV has neither, and the NET has "us."

13:12 Some major majuscules (including 𝔓⁴⁶) read ἀποβαλώμεθα instead of ἀποθώμεθα. The two words are virtual synonyms (meaning "to cast off" or "reject"). The latter term, however, has major support (including ℵ, A, B, C, D, et al.) and should be preferred. Moreover, the former term is not found elsewhere in the undisputed letters of Paul.

General Comment

Paul's hortatory statements since 12:1, in which he has put forth moral teachings of various kinds, have consisted of generalized maxims and instructions. But now in 13:11-14 Paul sets his exhortations within an eschatological framework. The present era, under the power of sin, is about to end. The new era of life in God's eternal kingdom has already begun through the resurrection of Jesus

---

65. BDAG 741 (οὗτος, 1, b, γ); BDF 151 (§290, 5); 229 (§442, 9); 254 (§480, 5).
66. Cf. B. Metzger, *TCGNT* 467.

from the dead, and it is about to come in its fullness. In light of that, those who are in Christ will shed the ways of the old era and lean into the new, anticipating the parousia of Christ and the renewal of all things.

It has been suggested that Paul cites a traditional "eschatological call to wakefulness" within 13:11a and 13:12 (omitting 13:11b),[67] which would read as follows:

> The hour is already here for you to awake from sleep.
> The night is far gone, and the day is at hand.
> Let us therefore cast off the works of darkness.
> And let us put on the weapons of light.

According to this proposal, the apostle would have inserted the clause of 13:11b, "for our salvation is nearer now than when we came to believe." It is argued that the four lines cited presuppose an imminent eschatology, but 13:11b reflects a moment of salvation further off into the future. Yet it is not clear that there is such a contrast. The line in 13:11b need not be interpreted as viewing salvation to be off in the future. It speaks of coming to faith as past, but the time of salvation can be understood as imminent; it is nearer now than ever.

Another proposal is that 13:11-14 is a fragment from a baptismal homily, an exhortation to a person who is about to be baptized.[68] The reasons for that view are that there are exhortations to leave a former life behind and to "clothe yourselves with Christ." These are elements that can be attributed to baptismal exhortations (see comments below). But whether one can consider the passage as a portion of a baptismal homily is uncertain. What is more certain is that Paul uses expressions and metaphors that are associated with baptism. He writes to persons already baptized within the Roman community, persons already "in the know" about the eschatological basis for the moral life (cf. 13:11). They are believers, and they have already clothed themselves with Christ in baptism. Writing to them at this critical juncture of the letter, Paul recalls traditional baptismal terms, reminding his readers to return to their baptisms, ever reestablishing the communion they have with Christ.

The passage is loaded with imagery compacted in tight succession. The

---

67. O. Michel, *Römer*, 328; H. Schlier, *Römer*, 395-96; U. Wilckens, *Römer*, 3:75; B. Byrne, *Romans*, 398; E. Löhse, *Römer*, 363 (n. 1). That Paul draws upon a fixed tradition in any case, even apart from the specifics suggested, is maintained by A. Grabner-Haider, *Paraklese und Eschatologie bei Paulus*, 84; J. Baumgarten, *Paulus und die Apokalyptik*, 209-10; E. Käsemann, *Romans*, 362.

68. E. Lövestam, *Spiritual Wakefulness*, 41; E. Käsemann, *Romans*, 362; J. Fitzmyer, *Romans*, 683-84; P. Stuhlmacher, *Romans*, 212; J. Kim, *The Significance of Clothing Imagery*, 136-39. Reservations (but not an outright rejection) are expressed by J. Dunn, *Romans*, 793. R. Jewett, *Romans*, 817-18, maintains that the passage is based on a hymn used within an agape meal.

imagery is set in a series of three antitheses: asleep/awake, night/day, and darkness/light (13:11-12). In each case the first metaphor is a negative one, and the second is a positive. The succession of antithetical metaphors is then followed by a call to living honorably, which means avoiding those things enumerated in a list of six vices (13:13). This is followed by the more specific exhortation to "clothe yourselves with the Lord Jesus Christ" (13:14).

Detailed Comment

13:11 On the basis of what has been said since 12:1, Paul now treats the motivation for the conduct of a person who is in Christ. The καιρός ("time") is drawing nigh for making an account of one's life. By using that term, which typically connotes a moment or a period of time characterized by some particular crisis in the flow of history,[69] Paul prepares his readers for what is to come in the rest of the verse. He speaks of the present "hour" (ὥρα) as a moment of crisis; it is a time to wake from sleep. The term "hour" is used by Paul elsewhere,[70] but only here to designate a critical moment of eschatological significance (cf. John 5:25; 1 John 2:18). Now, Paul says, is the time to "awake from sleep." The concept of being asleep in this world and the need, therefore, to be awakened is present in various religious traditions (particularly in Gnosticism),[71] including the OT (Isa 29:10; Prov 6:9) and postcanonical Jewish literature.[72] Sleep as a metaphor implies a spiritual stupor from which one must be awakened. NT texts use the imagery as well (Matt 24:43//Luke 12:39; Mark 13:35-36; 1 Thess 5:6-10; Eph 5:14), signifying a spiritual stupor possessed by persons who are devoted to the ways of the present age or, as Paul has put it earlier, people who are "conformed to this age" (12:2). Becoming or being awake and vigilant is the antithesis, signifying the life that is attentive to God's will and purposes. In calling upon his readers to "awake from sleep," Paul thereby alerts and reminds them that they are not to be conformed to this world and its values but transformed by the renewal of their minds for lives given in obedience to Christ (12:20).

The exhortation raises the question whether Paul is addressing a particular issue at this place. Could it be that, for Paul, the Roman community of believers must be considered asleep spiritually and in need of being awakened? There is much in the letter to conclude the contrary, as when Paul commends the members of the community for their faith (1:8) and their sound faith and

---

69. BDAG 498 (καιρός, 3, a).

70. 1 Cor 4:11; 15:30; 2 Cor 7:8; Gal 2:5; 1 Thess 2:17; Phlm 16.

71. Samaritan, Jewish, and Gnostic texts are cited by E. Lövestam, *Spiritual Wakefulness,* 36-40.

72. Sir 22:10; 4 Macc 5.11; *T. Reuben* 3.1, 7; *Pss. Sol.* 16.1-4; Philo, *Somn.* 1.121; 2.160-62.

teaching (1:12; 15:14). In light of that, it appears that Paul uses paraenesis here and elsewhere to affirm values and ways of life that are held in common between him and his readers (cf. Rom 15:30-33; 1 Thess 4:1-12; Phil 1:27-30), as is the case with other NT writers (cf. Eph 5:6-20; 1 Pet 4:1-11). Paraenesis in the NT is not always a summons to persons who need a new perspective and who are at odds with the writer. In some cases it is a means for the author of a letter to state a point of view that is shared between him and his readers, just as sermons often are in modern times.[73]

Paul declares that "salvation is nearer now than when we came to believe." In doing so, he speaks of the final salvation that is to come with the parousia of Christ. Paul can speak of salvation in the past tense (Rom 8:24), as a process in the present (Rom 1:16; 1 Cor 1:18; 2 Cor 2:15; 6:2), and as a reality in the future, as here (cf. also Rom 5:9-10; 10:9; 1 Cor 5:5; 1 Thess 5:9). From what he has written, it appears that for Paul salvation is essentially future, but whoever is in union with Christ in this life has salvation already — at least in part. Salvation consists of being set free from the divine wrath on the day of judgment (Rom 5:9; 1 Thess 1:10; 5:9). It is for something in both the present and the future: being reconciled to God (Rom 5:10-11), becoming an adopted and redeemed child of God (Rom 8:23-24), living already in the new age (Rom 5:17; 2 Cor 5:17), and being conformed to the image of God's Son (Rom 8:29; Phil 3:20-21).

The verse does not, standing by itself, determine whether Paul expresses here an expectation that the parousia would occur in his lifetime (as at 1 Thess 4:13-18) or beyond (as at Phil 1:20-26). But within its context, where Paul speaks of the passing of the night and the dawning of a new day, it speaks of an imminent parousia when salvation will be complete. This salvation to come is nearer now than "when we came to believe." The verb ἐπιστεύσαμεν is aorist and can be considered "ingressive" or "inceptive," i.e., a verb that denotes the starting point of an action that continues,[74] and so can be understood in this case as "we came to believe" (not simply "we believed," as though such believing was in the past but not in the present).

13:12 When Paul writes that "the night is far gone, and the day is at hand," he implies that the "night," while far advanced,[75] is still present. The new "day,"

---

73. L. Perdue, "The Social Character of Paraenesis," 23; S. Stowers, *Letter Writing in Greco-Roman Writing,* 92: "advice and exhortation to continue in a certain way of life"; Benjamin Fiore, "Parenesis and Protreptic," *ABD* 5:164: "what Paul writes is not new but is a reminder of what his correspondents already know, so that they might continue along their chosen path."

74. C. F. D. Moule, *An Idiom-Book of New Testament Greek,* 10-11; cf. BDF 166 (§318, 1); 171 (§331).

75. The verb προκόπτω means to move toward a final stage; it does not signify completion. Cf. BDAG 871 (προκόπτω, 1).

drawing near,[76] is dawning, but it is not yet present in its fullness. The new day that is dawning was inaugurated by God in raising Jesus from the dead, the first fruits of the dead (1 Cor 15:20-23). The "already" of the new age has happened in the event of Easter. All who belong to Christ share his destiny; they belong already to the new age that is dawning. At the same time, the "not yet" of existence in the present age is very real. Temptations to fall back, away from life in its newness, is always a possibility. And so Paul calls upon his readers to persevere.

The "works of darkness" mentioned by Paul would be those things that are done in the "night," which is passing away. Believers in Christ, Paul declares, "are not in darkness" but are "children of the light and children of the day" (1 Thess 5:4-5). But it is possible for believers to forget who they are and follow the ways of darkness, the powers of evil.

Putting on the "armor of light" (τὰ ὅπλα τοῦ φωτός) recalls the imagery of putting on weaponry at Isaiah 59:17, although the particulars of that verse are not quoted here. Paul himself speaks of spiritual armor also at 1 Thessalonians 5:8: "Since we belong to the day, let us put on the breastplate of faith and love (θώρακα πίστεως καὶ ἀγάπης), and for a helmet the hope of salvation." The use of "armor" imagery suggests a more defensive than offensive strategy. In context, however, the imagery of putting on the "armor of light" stands in antithesis to living a life in darkness. It is an action that involves a discipline to set one's mind, indeed one's entire being, within the realm of the divine light that comes from the risen Christ (2 Cor 4:6; 6:14): "for you are all children of light and children of the day; we are not of the night or of darkness" (1 Thess 5:5). Walking by the Spirit, those who live in Christ put off the ways of the present age and take up the ways of the new era that has dawned since the resurrection of Jesus from the dead.

13:13 Having laid aside the "works of darkness," Paul says, those who live in Christ are to live decently "as if" the full day is already present. He lists six vices (in three pairs) that are familiar in his writings elsewhere.[77] To be sure, the term used for "sexual immorality" (κοίτη) does not appear as such in his vice lists,[78] but he uses a virtual synonym for it elsewhere (πορνεία, meaning either "sexual immorality" or "fornication," depending on its context, 1 Cor 5:1; 6:13, 18; 7:2; 2 Cor 12:21; Gal 5:19). Four of the vices listed appear also in the list of 15 that Paul calls "works of the flesh" in Galatians 5:19-21 (reveling, drunkenness, licentiousness, and jealousy). All of these behaviors are antithetical to living "decently, as in the day." The life of the believer in Christ is life in the Spirit and

76. BDAG 270 (ἐγγίζω, 2): "to draw near in a temporal sense."

77. Five of the terms appear elsewhere as follows: "reveling" (κῶμος, Gal 5:21); "drunkenness" (μέθη, Gal 5:21), "licentiousness" (ἀσέλγεια, 2 Cor 12:21; Gal 5:19), "quarreling" (ἔρις, Rom 1:29), and "jealousy" (ζῆλος, 1 Cor 3:3; 2 Cor 12:20; Gal 5:20).

78. Paul uses the term κοίτη also at Rom 9:10, but not in the sense of an immoral act.

life in the new age. It is conditioned, to be sure, by the realities of the old age, but it is a life lived "as though" one no longer has dealings with the present age (cf. 1 Cor 7:29-31) but is within the new.

This verse has had an inestimable importance in the history of the Western church. It is mentioned by Augustine (*Confessions* 8.29) as decisive in his conversion from Manichaeism to Christianity while he was a teacher of rhetoric in Milan. He recounts the following event that took place while he was sitting under a fig tree in a garden not far from a friend by the name of Alypius (ca. A.D. 386):

> I heard from a nearby house, a voice like that of a boy or a girl, I know not which, chanting and repeating over and over, "Take up and read. Take up and read." . . . I interpreted this solely as a command given to me by God to open the book and read the first chapter I should come upon. . . . So I hurried back to the spot where Alypius was sitting, for I had put there the volume of the apostle when I got up and left him. I snatched it up, opened it, and read in silence the chapter on which my eyes first fell: "Not in rioting and drunkenness, not in chambering and impurities, not in strife and envying; but put you on the Lord Jesus Christ, and make not provision for the flesh in its concupiscences." No further wished I to read, nor was there need to do so. Instantly, in truth, at the end of this sentence, as if before a peaceful light streaming into my heart, all the dark shadows of doubt fled away.[79]

Why these particular verses, rather than others in Paul's great epistle, should have struck Augustine's conscience so dramatically remains a personal matter with him. But the result was the conversion to Christian faith of one of the major figures in Western theology.

Not to be missed in 13:13 is Paul's use of the verb περιπατέω ("to walk"), once more in reference to ethical conduct (as in 6:4; 8:4, and then again in 14:15), and the adverb εὐσχημόνως ("decently"). He combines the two at another place where he speaks of the behavior of believers in the public sphere (1 Thess 4:12). The adverb εὐσχημόνως means to have a "good external appearance" and is used by Hellenistic writers across the centuries concerning conduct.[80] Much more widely used within the NT, however, is the verb περιπατέω, a term that Paul uses 15 additional times to speak of the way of life expected of the believer.[81] The way of life is one of "walking," a habit of speech that Paul re-

79. Quoted from *The Confessions of St. Augustine,* trans. John K. Ryan (Garden City: Doubleday, 1960), 202.

80. Heinrich Greeven, "εὐσχημων," *TDNT* 2:771.

81. Rom 6:4; 8:4; 14:15; 1 Cor 3:3; 7:17; 2 Cor 4:2; 5:7; 10:3; 12:18; Gal 5:16; Phil 3:17, 18; 1 Thess 2:12; 4:1, 12.

tains from his Jewish heritage, in which one's "walking" is guided by precepts of the Torah (the *halakhot,* derived from the verb "to walk"). But believers in Christ "walk" in "newness of life" (Rom 6:4), "by the Spirit" (Rom 8:4; Gal 5:16), and "in love" (Rom 14:15). For more on the verb, see the exegesis of 6:4.

13:14 The verse is hortatory, containing two imperatives (ἐνδύσασθε, "clothe yourselves," and μὴ ποιεῖσθε, "do not make"). The use of the metaphor of putting on clothing to speak of making a spiritual transformation has a long and varied history in ancient religions,[82] but in this particular case it is derived most immediately from baptism, since Paul himself speaks of baptism with the metaphor elsewhere: "As many of you as were baptized into Christ have clothed yourselves (ἐνεδύσασθε) with Christ" (Gal 3:27).[83] Paul calls upon his readers to recall their baptisms and confirm once more what happened then and has ongoing importance for their lives. Moreover, baptism is not the end of the struggle with sin. Therefore, Paul says, the baptized must make "no provision for the flesh to arouse its desires." Once again the apostle makes use of the concept of "the flesh" (σάρξ) to speak of that realm of human life that is hospitable to desires that lead one away from the life expected of a person who is "in Christ." For more on the concept, see the exegesis of 6:19.

SELECT BIBLIOGRAPHY

Barr, James. *Biblical Words for Time.* SBT 33. Naperville: Alec R. Allenson, 1962.

Baumgarten, Jörg. *Paulus und die Apokalyptik: Die Auslegung apokalyptischer Überliefe- rungen in den echten Paulusbriefen.* WMANT 44. Neukirchen-Vluyn: Neukirchener Verlag, 1975.

Bjerkelund, Carl J. *Parakalô: Form, Funktion und Sinn der parakalô-Sätze in den pauli- nischen Briefen.* BTN 1. Oslo: Universitetsforlaget, 1967.

Dautzenberg, Gerhard. "Was bleibt von der Naherwartung? Zu Röm 13,11-14." In *Biblische Randbemerkungen: Schülerfestschrift für Rudolf Schnackenburg zum 60. Geburtstag,* 361-74. Ed. Helmut Merklein and Joachim Lange. 2d ed. Würzburg: Echter-Verlag, 1974.

Grabner-Haider, Anton. *Paraklese und Eschatologie bei Paulus: Mensch und Welt im Anspruch der Zukunft Gottes.* NTAbh 4. Münster: Aschendorff, 1968.

Kim, Jung Hoon. *The Significance of Clothing Imagery in the Pauline Corpus.* JSNT 268. London: T&T Clark, 2004.

Lafont, Ghislain. "Le Temps du salut: Rm 13,11-14." *ASeign* 5 (1969): 12-16.

82. The backgrounds are surveyed by J. Kim, *The Significance of Clothing Imagery,* 8-103. Objections to Paul's dependence on any of them is well documented by M. Thompson, *Clothed with Christ,* 151 (n. 2).

83. Actual accounts of baptismal practices that included the putting on of new garments are from the second and subsequent centuries A.D. Cf. J. Kim, *The Significance of Clothing Imag- ery,* 98-101.

Lövestam, Evald. *Spiritual Wakefulness in the New Testament.* LUÅ 55.3. Lund: G. W. K. Gleerup, 1963.

Moule, C. F. D. *An Idiom-Book of New Testament Greek.* 2d ed. Cambridge: Cambridge University Press, 1960.

Perdue, Leo G. "The Social Character of Paraenesis and Paraenetic Literature." In *Paraenesis: Act and Form,* 5-39. Semeia 50. Atlanta: Scholars Press, 1990.

Stowers, Stanley K. *Letter Writing in Greco-Roman Antiquity.* LEC 5. Philadelphia: Westminster Press, 1986.

Thompson, Michael B. *Clothed with Christ: The Example and Teaching of Jesus in Romans 12.1–15.13.* JSNTSup 59. Sheffield: JSOT Press, 1991.

Vögtle, Anton. "Röm 13,11-14 und die 'Nah'-Erwartung." In *Rechtfertigung: Festschrift für Ernst Käsemann zum 70. Geburtstag,* 191-204. Ed. Johannes Friedrich et al. Tübingen: J. C. B. Mohr (Paul Siebeck), 1976.

CHAPTER 8

The Weak and the Strong, 14:1–15:13

The discussion of "the weak and the strong" (14:1–15:13) is lengthy (36 verses), and for that and other reasons it is of major importance for the letter as a whole. It also marks a major transition in the letter. In chapters 12 and 13 Paul's hortatory statements tend to be brief and general, except for 13:1-7 on the Christian in the civil sphere. Within 14:1–15:13 the hortatory statements of Paul are more fully developed, and they are bound up not only with descriptions concerning the weak and the strong (14:2, 5-6), but also with homiletical statements (14:7-9, 17) and OT quotations (14:11; 15:3, 9-12). After this section of the letter is concluded, Paul goes on to tell of his travel plans (15:14-33) and sends his greetings to the Christians at Rome (16:1-23). The exhortations concerning the weak and the strong thus close the paraenetic section of Romans running from 12:1 through 15:13. Its length and its placement at the close of the paraenetic section, plus its relatively lengthy development of a topic, indicate its importance.

What Paul has written in 14:1–15:13 presents the interpreter with challenges on several fronts. One of the major questions is the identity of the persons designated by the terms "weak" and "strong," and closely associated with that the question why Paul feels compelled to speak about them and to them. Various proposals have been made,[1] among which the following appear to have most support:[2]

---

1. For additional surveys and assessments, cf. C. Cranfield, *Romans*, 690-98; M. Reasoner, *The Strong and the Weak*, 1-23; and V. Gäckle, *Die Starken und die Schwachen in Korinth und Rom*, 22-35.

2. In addition to these, two other specific proposals have been made. According to M. Nanos, *The Mystery of Romans*, 143-44, 154, the "weak" were non-Christian Jews of Rome; the "strong" were Christians (mostly Gentile, but some Jewish). Paul hoped that the non-Christian Jews would become Christians, and that they would continue practicing the law and Jewish customs without ridicule by those known already to be "strong." But this proposal is in-

1. The "weak" consisted of a core of Jewish Christians who preserved traditions regarding cultic and dietary matters, and perhaps some Gentiles who adopted them, and the "strong" were Gentile Christians and others of Jewish heritage, like Paul himself (15:1), who did not. Actually there is a wide spectrum here among interpreters. Some would say that both groups could have been mixed in terms of actual ethnicity and religious backgrounds, but that they can be divided nonetheless into two camps; the one reflected Jewish traditionalism, and the other rejected it.[3]

2. The "weak" were Jewish Christians (or perhaps a mixed group of pious Jewish and Gentile Christians) who were vegetarians because they feared that any meat they might eat could have been offered previously to idols. The "strong" had no such scruples.[4]

---

adequate, for in 15:5 and 15:7 Paul, while speaking to both the weak and the strong, appeals to their faith in Christ. If the "weak" are non-Christian Jews, that appeal would carry no weight. Moreover, in 14:18 Paul, when referring to the "weak," speaks of their service to Christ. According to M. Reasoner, *The Strong and the Weak*, 58-62, 202, 210-19, the terms "weak" and "strong" designated a person's social status. The "strong" were believers who had a higher status than the "weak." Most would have been Roman citizens, wealthy, and leading persons in the community. The "weak" had a lower status, kept Jewish dietary laws, and observed the Sabbath and possibly other fast days. For a brief response to this proposal, cf. A. Pitta, "The Strong, the Weak and the Mosaic Law," 94.

   3. Origen, *Commentary on the Epistle to the Romans* 9.35; text in Origen, *Commentary on the Epistle to the Romans, Books 6-10*, trans. Thomas P. Scheck, FC 104 (Washington, D.C.: Catholic University of America Press, 2002), 233-34; John Chrysostom, "Homilies on Romans: Homily 25"; text in *NPNF* 11:522-23; Theodoret of Cyrrhus, *Interpretatio epistolae ad Romanos*, 141; text in *PG* 82:200; O. Michel, *Römer*, 334; E. Käsemann, *Romans*, 368-69; U. Wilckens, *Römer*, 3:109-15; E. Best, *Romans*, 155; C. Cranfield, *Romans*, 694-97; P. Minear, *The Obedience of Faith*, 8-17 (in general, but proposing five groups); F. Watson, "The Two Roman Congregations," 203-7; idem, *Paul, Judaism, and the Gentiles*, 175-82; J. Fitzmyer, *Romans*, 687-88; J. Dunn, *Romans*, 795, 811; A. Segal, *Paul the Convert*, 234-36; J. Barclay, "Do We Undermine the Law?" 288-93; W. Lane, "Social Perspectives on Roman Christianity," 198-202; S. Gathercole, "Romans 1–5 and the 'Weak' and the 'Strong,'" 35-51; D. Moo, *Romans*, 829; N. T. Wright, *NIB (Romans)*, 10:731; Josef Zmijewski, "ἀσθενέω," *EDNT* 1:171; P. Stuhlmacher, *Romans*, 219-21; P. Lampe, *From Paul to Valentinus*, 72-74; W. Campbell, "The Rule of Faith in Romans 12:1–15:13," 275; P. Esler, *Romans*, 343-44; T. Tobin, *Paul's Rhetoric in Contexts*, 404-16; C. Talbert, *Romans*, 313-15; B. Witherington, *Romans*, 327; U. Schnelle, *Apostle Paul*, 298, 304; K. Ehrensperger, *That We May Be Mutually Encouraged*, 181-82; L. Keck, *Romans*, 336-38; R. Jewett, *Romans*, 71 (the strong: Gentiles and "Jewish liberals"; the weak: Jewish adherents plus some Gentiles "close to synagogues before becoming believers"), 838; V. Gäckle, *Die Starken und die Schwachen in Korinth und in Rom*, 361-86; D. Bolton, "Who Are You Calling 'Weak'?" 621 (division between Torah-observant traditionalists and Torah-observant ultratraditionalists); F. Matera, *Romans*, 305-9.

   4. Augustine, *Propositions from the Epistle to the Romans* 78; text in *Augustine on Romans: Propositions from the Epistle to the Romans; Unfinished Commentary on the Epistle to the Romans*, ed. Paula Fredriksen Landes, SBL.TT 23 (Chico: Scholars Press, 1982), 45; H.-W. Bartsch, "Die antisemitischen Gegner des Paulus im Römerbrief," 33; J. Ziesler, *Romans*, 324-26.

3. The Letter to the Romans was addressed to Gentile Christians (the implied readers) and to the "strong" in particular.[5] The "strong" were therefore Gentiles (although Paul includes himself among them, 15:1), but the identity of the "weak" is less certain. They could have been of Gentile origin also,[6] or possibly of Jewish background.[7] But they adopted their attitudes from Jewish tradition,[8] some non-Jewish Hellenistic tradition,[9] or both.[10]

4. Paul does not address any specific, actual problem at Rome but uses the argument concerning how the strong should deal with the weak, modeled on his exhortation to the Christians at Corinth (1 Cor 8:1–10:32), for a more general purpose, i.e., that persons should bear with one another in spite of differences of opinion and conviction.[11] One of the major proponents of this view is Robert Karris, who says, "Romans 14:1–15:13 is better explained as general Pauline paraenesis, which is adapted and generalized especially from Paul's discussion in 1 Corinthians 8–10 and is addressed to a problem that may arise in any community. Any problem with regard to indifferent things, such as eating or not eating certain foods, should be solved in faith, with love, in the interests of edification."[12]

In the attempt to resolve the issues regarding the weak and the strong, the following points need to be considered.

1. The Relationship of Romans 14:1–15:13 to 1 Corinthians 8:1–10:33. There are similarities in language and point of view between the two passages,[13] but there are differences as well. In 1 Corinthians 8:1–10:33 Paul takes up the question whether it is permissible for believers at Corinth to eat meat that remains after sacrifices have been made in pagan temples. Those who refuse to eat such meat consider it a matter of conscience. Essentially Paul argues that, since idols

---

5. N. Elliott, *The Rhetoric of Romans,* 56-59, 96, 293-95; S. Stowers, *A Rereading of Romans,* 45, 320-23, 326; A. Das, *Solving the Romans Debate,* 109-14, 123; T. Engberg-Pedersen, "'Everything Is Clean,'" 29-34.

6. A. Das, *Solving the Romans Debate,* 123. Cf. B. Byrne, *Romans,* 12 (both weak and strong were Gentiles), but on p. 406 he says that the "weak" could be Jewish or Gentile believers.

7. N. Elliott, *The Rhetoric of Romans,* 252.

8. A. Das, *Solving the Romans Debate,* 109-14, 123.

9. M. Rauer, *Die "Schwachen" in Korinth und Rom,* 164-68.

10. C. K. Barrett, *Romans,* 237: "There are traces of both Judaism and Gnosticism in their practices and beliefs."

11. W. Sanday and A. Headlam, *Romans,* 399-403; R. Karris, "Romans 14.1–15:13," 65-84 (especially p. 77); idem, *Galatians and Romans,* 90; W. Meeks, "Judgment and the Brother: Romans 14:1–15:13," 292-93; J. P. Sampley, "The Weak and the Strong," 40-52.

12. R. Karris, "Romans 14:1–15:13," 84.

13. For various comparisons, cf. U. Wilckens, *Römer,* 3:115; C. Cranfield, *Romans,* 691-92; R. Karris, "Romans 14:1–15:13," 73-75; C. Talbert, *Romans,* 311; A. Pitta, "The Strong, the Weak and the Mosaic Law," 91-93; V. Gäckle, *Die Starken und die Schwachen in Korinth und in Rom,* 438-44.

have no real existence (as actual gods), one has freedom in regard to this question (8:4, 8; 10:23, 25-27). But nevertheless, out of love and regard for the other person, the one who claims such freedom should be willing to relinquish it (8:9-13; 10:23, 28-29).

Similarities in vocabulary between the texts in Romans and 1 Corinthians include words for "the weak" (ἀσθενής, ἀσθενέω, and ἀσθένημα in Rom 14:1-2; 15:1 and in 1 Cor 8:7, 9-12; 9:2); some nouns, such as "hindrance" (πρόσκομμα in Rom 14:13 and in 1 Cor 8:9), "meat" (κρέα in Rom 14:21 and in 1 Cor 8:13), and "food" (βρῶμα in Rom 14:15, 20 and in 1 Cor 8:8, 13); and verbs very important to the argument in both cases, such as "to eat" (ἐσθίω in Rom 14:2-3, 6, 15, 20-21, 23 and in 1 Cor 8:7-8, 13, 18, 26-28, 31), "to please" (ἀρέσκω in Rom 15:1-2 and in 1 Cor 10:33), and "to destroy" (ἀπόλλυμι in Rom 14:15 and in 1 Cor 8:11; cf. καταλύω at Rom 14:20).

Similarities in point of view include the claim that one's standing before God does not depend on eating or not eating certain foods (Rom 14:17 and 1 Cor 8:8). But along with that there is a concern not to let what a person eats destroy another person (Rom 14:15 and 1 Cor 8:11). A definite principle is stated, which is that one ought not eat certain foods if that causes another person to stumble (Rom 14:21 and 1 Cor 8:13).

One cannot conclude, however, that the passages in the two letters are about the same thing or that the passage in Romans repeats what is said in 1 Corinthians. Although the eating of certain foods is an issue in both cases, nothing in Romans suggests explicitly that the question is about "food sacrificed to idols" (τὸ εἰδωλόθυτον, 1 Cor 8:1, 4, 7, 10, 19, 28); the term in Romans is simply the generic word for "meat" (κρέα, 14:21), and "the weak" are simply vegetarians (Rom 14:2). The nouns "knowledge" (γνῶσις, 1 Cor 8:1, 7, 10-11), "freedom" (ἐλευθερία, 1 Cor 10:29), "idols" (τὰ εἴδωλα, 1 Cor 8:4, 7; 10:19), and "conscience" (συνείδησις, 1 Cor 8:7, 10, 12; 10:25, 27-29) appear in 1 Corinthians 8–10, but not in Romans 14:1–15:13.

2. Foods and Days. The reason why "the weak" abstain from certain foods and observe certain days is a vexing problem. It is often assumed that, because of what is said at 14:17, 21, "the weak" also abstain from wine.[14] But that is not clear.[15] In the first of these two verses, Paul does not actually mention wine and appears to be quoting a general maxim concerning the kingdom of God ("For

---

14. C. K. Barrett, *Romans*, 237; E. Käsemann, *Romans*, 367; F. Watson, "The Two Roman Congregations," 204; B. Byrne, *Romans*, 404; E. Lohse, *Römer*, 372.

15. That the passage does not suggest that "the weak" drink no wine is held by C. Cranfield, *Romans*, 725; and R. Karris, "Romans 14:1–15:13," 69 (n. 27), 77 (n. 61), who cites M. Rauer, *Die "Schwachen" in Korinth und Rom*, 97-100; V. Gäckle, *Die Starken und die Schwachen in Korinth und in Rom*, 404, maintains that βρῶσις καὶ πόσις ("food and drink") in 14:17 is a festive formula, and so we may have here a hypothetical case.

the kingdom of God is not food and drink but righteousness and peace and joy in the Holy Spirit"). In regard to the second of these verses, Paul puts forth a general principle for conduct relating to not causing someone else to stumble ("it is good not to eat meat or drink wine or do anything that makes your brother or sister stumble"); the "or do anything" in the list assures a generalization. The reference to wine in the list may have been suggested by the reference to drink in 14:17.

The issues that Paul takes up have to do, then, explicitly only with vegetarianism and the observing of certain days. But Paul writes also of the distinction some would make between "clean" (καθαρός, 14:20) and "unclean" (κοινός, 14:14) foods, a distinction nullified elsewhere in the NT (Mark 7:19; Acts 10:15). One could draw the implication from this that such a distinction is being made at Rome, and that "the weak" are making it. If so, it would appear that "the weak" must be Jewish Christians, for whom such a distinction would be traditional and familiar (cf. Lev 11:1-47). Although certain non-Jewish groups in antiquity were vegetarians (e.g., Orphics and Pythagoreans),[16] the clean/unclean dichotomy does not point in those directions concerning "the weak."

The main characteristic of "the weak" is that they are vegetarians and observe certain days. In regard to vegetarianism, there are no commands in the Torah that anyone should abstain from consuming meat, as long as it is classified as "clean." To be sure, there are instances where persons in Jewish tradition refrain from eating meat. That is particularly the case where persons are living in pagan environments (cf. Tob 1:11; 2 Macc 5:27). Daniel eats no meat and drinks no wine of the king while in Babylon (Dan 1:8-16; 10:3). Judith abstained from food and wine offered to her by the Assyrian officer Holofernes (Jdt 12:1-2). Esther prided herself in never having eaten at Haman's table, and she refused wine that may have been used in libations (LXX Esth 14:17). In the pseudepigraphal *Testament of Reuben,* Reuben declares that at one time he repented for seven years, and during that time he refrained from drinking wine and eating meat, concluding with the words: "Never had anything like it been done in Israel."[17] Philo recounted how the sect of the Therapeutai in Egypt limited themselves to eating bread and drinking water.[18] Within early Christianity, there is at least one instance where vegetarianism was practiced. According to Eusebius, quoting from Hegesippus (ca. A.D. 110-80), James the brother of Jesus, residing in Jerusalem, was known to refrain from drinking wine and eating

16. On Pythagorean and Orphic vegetarianism, respectively, cf. Diogenes Laertius, *Lives* 8.13, 19 and Plato, *Leg.* 782.

17. *T. Reuben* 1.9-10; quotation from the translation of Howard C. Kee in *OTP* 1:782.

18. Philo, *Cont.* 4.37.

meat.[19] In addition, the writer of Colossians speaks about persons who are discriminating "in matters of food and drink" (2:16).

Observing certain days is a practice that is much more familiar than vegetarianism in Jewish tradition, and there are references to it in early Christian texts. The Jewish observance of the Sabbath and festival days was common enough to receive notice by various Latin writers.[20] Moreover, while the Sabbath was ordinarily considered a day of rejoicing and feasting, Jews in Rome appear to have kept it as a day of fasting.[21] The reason for that is that in both 63 and 37 B.C. "it was on the Sabbath that Jerusalem fell to the Romans and its defenders were taken into captivity."[22]

It is possible that some Christians in Rome observed the Sabbath in keeping with Jewish traditions. In any case, they observed whatever day is being referred to "in honor of the Lord" (RSV and NRSV; literally, "to the Lord"), meaning Christ.[23] But whether the Sabbath is being referred to is not certain. Among early Christians elsewhere there are indications that some observed certain days as special, such as the Christians in Galatia (Gal 4:10, "You are observing special days, and months, and seasons, and years") and Colossae (Col 2:16, "Therefore do not let anyone condemn you in matters of food and drink or of observing festivals, new moons, or Sabbaths"). Moreover, by the end of the first century some Christians fasted on Wednesdays and Fridays; Wednesdays because that was the day on which the betrayal of Jesus was arranged, and Fridays because that was the day of his crucifixion.[24] The practice of fasting on Fridays is alluded to already in the gospels (Mark 2:20//Matt 9:15//Luke 5:33).[25] Fasting by Christians on certain occasions is taken for granted also in the time and place of the composition of the Gospel of Matthew (cf. Matt 6:16-18). The relevance of these passages for Romans 14:1–15:13 is that it may be too simplistic to conclude that Paul is referring to the observance of Jewish traditions by Christians at Rome. It is just as possible that he refers to fasting on Fridays. He speaks only of a singular day ("the day," 14:6). In light of the various possibilities, it is possible that Paul is not re-

---

19. Eusebius, *Ecclesiastical History* 2.23.4-5.

20. Horace, *Sermones* 1.9.69; Ovid, *Ars Amatoria* 1.76; Petronius, *Fragmenta* 37.6. These and other references are provided by M. Williams, "Being a Jew in Rome," 9.

21. Josephus, *Ant.* 14.66-68; 14.487-88; Strabo, *Geogr.* 16.2.40; Cassius Dio, *Rom. Hist.* 37.16.4; 49.22.4. Texts cited and provided by M. Williams, "Being a Jew in Rome," 12-15.

22. M. Williams, "Being a Jew in Rome," 16.

23. See the exegesis of 14:6.

24. *Didache* 8.2; *Apostolic Constitutions* 7.23.1. The provenance and dating of the *Didache* are notoriously difficult to establish, but it could contain traditions from the first century. On the range of dating, cf. Robert A. Kraft, "Didache," *ABD* 2:197-98.

25. For discussion of this claim, cf. A. Hultgren, *Jesus and His Adversaries*, 78-82.

ferring to any particular day, but to any day that would be of such importance to anyone that it would be "the day" for observance.

Whatever the evidence outside of Romans 14:1–15:13, the implied view of "the weak" is that they are vegetarians and persons who observe either a particular day or certain days, which could include (but need not be limited to) the Sabbath, Friday, or some other day that is held worthy of observance.

3. It is helpful to ask the question: To whom does Paul speak in 14:1–15:13, and how does he do it? A survey of those addressed yields the following results:[26]

A. Paul addresses the Roman Christians as a whole, using *second person plural* verbs:

14:1, προσλαμβάνεσθε: second person, plural, imperative, "welcome."

14:13, κρίνατε: second person, plural, imperative, "decide."

15:6, δοξάζητε: second person, plural, subjunctive, "glorify."

15:7, προσλαμβάνεσθε: second person, plural, imperative, "welcome."

B. Paul addresses the Roman Christians as a whole, using *first person plural* verbs to include himself:

14:13, μηκέτι . . . κρίνωμεν: first person, plural, subjunctive, "no longer . . . let us judge."

14:19, διώκωμεν: first person, plural, subjunctive, "let us pursue."

15:1, ὀφείλομεν: first person, plural, indicative, "we ought."

C. Paul addresses the Roman Christians as a whole, using a *third person singular* verb:

14:5, πληροφορείσθω: third person, singular, imperative, "let [each person] be fully convinced."

D. Paul addresses "the strong," using *singular* verbs:

14:3, μὴ ἐξουθενείτω: third person, singular, imperative, "let [him] not despise."

14:4, εἶ: second person, singular, indicative, "you are."

14:10b, ἐξουθενεῖς: second person, singular, indicative, "you despise."

14:15a, περιπατεῖς: second person, singular, indicative, "you are walking."

14:15b, μὴ . . . ἀπόλλυε: second person, singular, imperative, "do not . . . cause ruin."

14:16, μὴ βλασφημείσθω: third person, singular, imperative, "let [it] not be defamed."

14:20, μὴ . . . κατάλυε: second person, singular, imperative, "do not . . . destroy."

14:22, ἔχεις: second person, singular, indicative, "you have."

---

26. For a different, but methodologically related, approach, cf. R. Karris, "Romans 14:1–15:13," 72.

14:22, ἔχε: second person, singular, imperative, "keep."

15:2, ἀρεσκέτω: third person, singular, imperative, "let [each] please."

E. Paul addresses "the weak," using *singular* verbs:

14:3, μὴ κρινέτω: third person, singular, imperative, "let [him] not judge."

14:10a, κρίνεις: second person, singular, indicative, "you judge."

The passage contains (1) eleven imperatives (14:1, 3 [twice], 5, 13, 15, 16, 20, 22; 15:2, 7), of which three are second person plural (14:1, 13; 15:7), (2) two hortatory subjunctives (14:13, 19), and (3) one plural verb expressing obligation (15:1, ὀφείλομεν, "we ought"). The plural imperatives are addressed to the Roman Christians as a whole. The two hortatory subjunctives, which express an obligation, and the verb expressing obligation at 15:1, are also addressed to the Roman Christians in general. The remaining eight imperatives, all singular, are addressed to either "the weak" or "the strong." By far the most of what Paul has to say is directed toward "the strong," but it would not be correct to say that Paul addresses them alone.[27]

It is odd that, when speaking to either "the weak" or "the strong," Paul does not address them in the plural (that is clear from the Greek, but not in English versions).[28] Paul uses the singular in every case while making any complaint he might possibly have, which differs from his use of the plural in 1 Corinthians (8:9; 10:25, 27-28, 31-32). Why, for example, does he not address "the strong" in the plural when he exhorts them not to let what they eat "cause the ruin of one for whom Christ died" (Rom 14:15)? These observations prompt the question whether Paul addresses any groups at all. When Paul uses the plural verbs, he is much more general and usually positive. The imperative "welcome" (προσλαμβάνεσθε), used twice (14:1; 15:7), is the most direct command, and that is not an admonition against any kind of behavior that requires apostolic intervention. It is basic for building up the community; it does not specify a particular fault within it. The other plural imperative (14:13, ἀλλὰ . . . κρίνατε μᾶλλον, "but decide rather") does not have to do with any overt behavior that needs correction. The use of the singular verbs for "the weak" and "the strong," on the other hand, is particularly effective if Paul is actually expressing diatribe within the framework of paraenesis. Indeed, that appears to be the case. He addresses a concept, not a group of persons.

In light of these concerns having to do with (1) the relationship between Romans 14:1–15:13 and 1 Corinthians 8–10, (2) the inconclusive results concern-

27. Contra J. O'Neill, *Romans,* 221; B. Malina and J. Pilch, *Social-Science Commentary on the Letters of Paul,* 283.

28. In the NRSV one might assume, right from the outset of 14:1–15:13, that plurals are used all the way through. At 14:3 the singular is used in Greek (literally, "let the one who eats" and "let the one who abstains"), but the NRSV has "those who" in each case.

ing foods and days, and (3) the way that Paul addresses his readers in this passage, the question has to be raised whether Paul is actually addressing a live issue among contending parties at Rome. Is the "problem" at Rome, or is it with Paul? It is possible that, instead of apostolic intervention, the passage is one of apostolic introduction for the apostle, who has dealt with matters of food at Corinth and of days at Galatia. These matters of concern would be known at Rome through persons who had been with Paul in Ephesus, from whence he wrote 1 Corinthians and possibly Galatians.[29] Those persons would have included Prisca and Aquila, who were present with Paul and sent greetings when he wrote to the church at Corinth (1 Cor 16:19). The fact that 14:1–15:13 is a paraenetic section and that Paul uses imperative verbs need not indicate that he is at odds with his readers. This can be a case once more (as in 13:1-7) where Paul uses paraenesis to affirm values and ways of living held by both his readers and himself.[30] He can draw on past experiences, such as those at Corinth and in Galatia, for some of his language and thinking. As he writes Romans, introducing himself and his theology, Paul might reasonably wonder whether the Christians at Rome had worries about his coming, for he was known to be an apostle with strongly held views (2 Cor 10:10). What would his coming mean for relationships between persons with differing opinions? Resorting to the form of a diatribe, but one clothed in paraenesis, Paul can set up a scenario of a possible conflict concerning "the weak" and "the strong." Then he can say what he thinks the Christians at Rome would want to hear from him. The goal is to establish commonality or "communion" with his readers. Within epideictic discourse, which Romans can be considered, "every device of literary art is appropriate, for it is a matter of combining all the factors that can promote this communion of the audience."[31]

A final matter concerning this section is that Paul's use of the terms "the weak" and "the strong" appears in a letter addressed to a community of Chris-

---

29. The location for the writing of 1 Corinthians appears settled (Ephesus); cf. W. Kümmel, *Introduction*, 279, and R. Brown, *Introduction*, 512. The provenance for Galatians (Ephesus or Macedonia?) is not settled, but Ephesus is favored by R. Brown, *Introduction*, 468; Macedonia or Achaia by J. L. Martyn, *Galatians*, 19; Ephesus or Macedonia by W. Kümmel, *Introduction*, 304; and Ephesus, Macedonia, or Corinth by H. Betz, *Galatians*, 12.

30. That is typical of paraenesis. Cf. L. Perdue, "The Social Character of Paraenesis," 23. S. Stowers, *Letter Writing in Greco-Roman Antiquity*, 92, speaks of paraenesis as "advice and exhortation to continue in a certain way of life"; Benjamin Fiore, "Parenesis and Protreptic," *ABD* 5:164: "what Paul writes is not new but is a reminder of what his correspondents already know, so that they might continue along their chosen path." Cf. C. Bjerkelund, *Parakalô*, 173, 188, and the statement concerning paraclesis by Johannes Thomas, "παρακαλέω," *EDNT* 3:25: it "(almost) always assumes a believing or assenting response."

31. C. Perelman and L. Olbrechts-Tyteca, *New Rhetoric*, 51, quoted by W. Wuellner, "Paul's Rhetoric of Argumentation," 140.

tians that he has neither founded nor visited previously. To call some within that community "the weak" would seem to be counterproductive to any apostolic intervention within an actual controversy.[32] But one is free in diatribe to create the cast of characters desired to carry on an argument. That seems to be what Paul does in this section of the letter. He demonstrates to his readers that, although he is strong in his convictions concerning freedom in Christ (15:1), he knows and accepts the point that one must accommodate the sensibilities of others on issues that arise.[33] The Christians in Rome have no need to be concerned.

BIBLIOGRAPHY

Allison, Dale C., Jr. "The Pauline Epistles and the Synoptic Gospels: The Pattern of the Parallels." *NTS* 28 (1982): 1-32.

Barclay, John M. G. "'Do We Undermine the Law?': A Study of Romans 14.1–15.13." In *Paul and the Mosaic Law*, 287-308. Ed. James D. G. Dunn. Grand Rapids: Wm. B. Eerdmans, 2001.

Bartsch, Hans-Werner. "Die antisemitischen Gegner des Paulus im Römerbrief." In *Antijudaismus im Neuen Testament? Exegetische und systematische Beiträge*, 27-43. Ed. Willehad P. Eckert et al. AbCJD 2. Munich: Kaiser Verlag, 1967.

Betz, Hans D. *Galatians*. Hermeneia. Philadelphia: Fortress Press, 1979.

Bjerkelund, Carl J. *Parakalô: Form, Funktion und Sinn der parakalô-Sätze in den paulinischen Briefen*. BTN 1. Oslo: Universitetsforlaget, 1967.

Black, David Alan. "A Note on 'the Weak' in 1 Corinthians 9,22." *Bib* 64 (1983): 240-42.

―――. *Paul, Apostle of Weakness: Astheneia and Its Cognates in the Pauline Literature*. American University Studies 7. New York: Peter Lang, 1984.

Bolton, David L. "Who Are You Calling 'Weak'? A Short Critique on James Dunn's Reading of Rom 14,1–15,6." In *The Letter to the Romans*, 617-29. BETL 226. Ed. Udo Schnelle. Walpole: Peeters, 2009.

Campbell, William S. "The Rule of Faith in Romans 12:1–15:13: The Obligation of Humble Obedience to Christ as the Only Adequate Response to the Mercies of God." In *Pauline Theology*, vol. 3, *Romans*, 259-86. Ed. David M. Hay and E. Elizabeth Johnson. Minneapolis: Fortress Press, 1991.

Cambier, Jules. "La liberté chrétienne est et personnelle et communautaire (Rom 14–15:13)." In *Freedom and Love: The Guide for Christian Life (1 Cor 8–10; Rom 14–15)*, 57-84. Ed. Lorenzo de Lorenzi. Rome: St. Paul's Abbey, 1981.

Cranfield, C. E. B. "Some Observations on the Interpretation of Romans 14.1–15.3." *CV* 17 (1974): 193-204.

Das, A. Andrew. *Solving the Romans Debate*. Minneapolis: Fortress Press, 2007.

Dederen, Raoul. "On Esteeming One Day Better than Another." *AUSS* 9 (1971): 16-35.

---

32. Cf. B. Byrne, *Romans*, 405.
33. Cf. K. Ehrensperger, *That We May Be Mutually Encouraged*, 199-200.

Ehrensperger, Kathy. *That We May Be Mutually Encouraged: Feminism and the New Perspective in Pauline Studies.* Edinburgh: T&T Clark, 2004.

Elliott, Neil. "Asceticism among the 'Weak' and 'Strong' in Romans 14–15." In *Asceticism and the New Testament,* 231-51. Ed. Leif E. Vaage and Vincent L. Wimbush. New York: Routledge, 1999.

———. *The Rhetoric of Romans: Argumentative Constraint and Strategy and Paul's Dialogue with Judaism.* JSNTSup 45. Sheffield: JSOT Press, 1990.

Engberg-Pedersen, Troels. "'Everything Is Clean' and 'Everything That Is Not of Faith Is Sin': The Logic of Pauline Casuistry in Romans 14.1–15.13." In *Paul, Grace and Freedom: Essays in Honour of John K. Riches,* 22-38. Ed. Paul Middleton, Angus Paddison, and Karen Wenell. New York: T&T Clark, 2009.

Gäckel, Volker. *Die Starken und die Schwachen in Korinth und in Rom: Zur Herkunft und Funktion der Antithese in 1 Kor 8,1–11,1 und Röm 14,1–15,13.* WUNT 2/200. Tübingen: Mohr Siebeck, 2004.

Gathercole, Simon. "Romans 1–5 and the 'Weak' and the 'Strong': Pauline Theology, Pastoral Rhetoric, and the Purpose of Romans." *RevExp* 100 (2003): 35-51.

Gagnon, Robert A. J. "Why the 'Weak' at Rome Cannot Be Non-Christian Jews." *CBQ* 62 (2000): 64-82.

Giblin, Charles H. "The 'Strong' and the 'Weak.'" In his *In Hope of God's Glory,* 231-36. New York: Herder and Herder, 1970.

Goldenberg, Robert. "The Jewish Sabbath in the Roman World up to the Time of Constantine the Great." *ANRW* II.19.1 (1979): 414-47.

Gooch, Paul W. "St. Paul on the Strong and the Weak: A Study in the Resolution of Conflict." *Crux* 13 (1975-76): 10-20.

Grant, Robert M. "Dietary Laws among Pythagoreans, Jews, and Christians." *HTR* 73 (1980): 299-310.

Ehrensperger, Kathy. *That We May Be Mutually Encouraged: Feminism and the New Perspective in Pauline Studies.* Edinburgh: T&T Clark, 2004.

Haussleiter, Johannes. *Der Vegetarismus in Antike.* RVV 24. Berlin: Alfred Töpelmann, 1935.

Hultgren, Arland J. *Jesus and His Adversaries: The Form and Function of the Conflict Stories in the Synoptic Tradition.* Minneapolis: Augsburg Publishing House, 1979.

Jewett, Robert. *Christian Tolerance: Paul's Message to the Modern Church.* Philadelphia: Westminster Press, 1982.

———. "Form and Function of the Homiletic Benediction." *ATR* 51 (1969): 18-34.

Karris, Robert J. *Galatians and Romans.* NCBC. Collegeville: Liturgical Press, 2005.

———. "Romans 14:1–15:13 and the Occasion of Romans." In *The Romans Debate,* 65-84. Rev. ed. Ed. Karl P. Donfried. Peabody: Hendrickson Publishers, 1991.

Kromminga, Carl G. "Christian Love and Offending the 'Weak': A Review Article." *CTJ* 28 (1993): 155-65.

Lampe, Peter. *From Paul to Valentinus: Christians at Rome in the First Two Centuries.* Minneapolis: Fortress Press, 2003.

Lane, William L. "Social Perspectives on Roman Christianity during the Formative Years from Nero to Nerva: Romans, Hebrews, *1 Clement.*" In *Judaism and Christianity in*

First-Century Rome, 196-244. Ed. Karl P. Donfried and Peter Richardson. Grand Rapids: Wm. B. Eerdmans, 1998.

Malina, Bruce J., and John J. Pilch. *Social-Science Commentary on the Letters of Paul*. Minneapolis: Fortress Press, 2006.

Martyn, J. Louis. *Galatians*. AB 33A. New York: Doubleday, 1997.

McCruden, Kevin B. "Judgment and Life for the Lord: Occasion and Theology of Romans 14,1–15,13." *Bib* 86 (2005): 229-44.

Meeks, Wayne A. "Judgment and the Brother: Romans 14:1–15:13." In *Tradition and Interpretation in the New Testament: Essays in Honor of E. Earle Ellis*, 290-300. Ed. Gerald F. Hawthorne with Otto Betz. Grand Rapids: Wm. B. Eerdmans, 1987.

Minear, Paul S. *The Obedience of Faith: The Purpose of Paul in the Epistle to the Romans*. SBT 2/19. Naperville: Alec R. Allenson, 1971.

Murray, John. "The Weak and the Strong." *WTJ* 12 (1949-50): 136-53.

Nanos, Mark. *The Mystery of Romans: The Jewish Context of Paul's Letter*. Minneapolis: Fortress Press, 1996.

Palmer, R. E. A. "Severan Ruler-Cult and the Moon in the City of Rome." *ANRW* II.16.2 (1978): 1085-1120.

Perdue, Leo G. "The Social Character of Paraenesis and Paraenetic Literature." In *Paraenesis: Act and Form*, 5-39. Semeia 50. Atlanta: Scholars Press, 1990.

Perelman, Chaim, and L. Olbrechts-Tyteca. *The New Rhetoric: A Treatise on Argumentation*. Notre Dame: University of Notre Dame, 1971.

Phua, Richard Liong-Seng. *Idolatry and Authority: A Study of 1 Corinthians 8.1–11.1 in the Light of the Jewish Diaspora*. London: T&T Clark, 2005.

Pitta, Antonio. "The Strong, the Weak and the Mosaic Law in the Christian Communities of Rome (Rom. 14.1–15.13)." In *Christians as a Religious Minority in a Multicultural City: Modes of Interaction and Identity Formation in Early Imperial Rome*, 90-102. Ed. Jürgen Zangenberg and Michael Labahn. JSNTSup 243. London: T&T Clark, 2004.

Rauer, Max. *Die "Schwachen" in Korinth und Rom nach den Paulusbriefen*. BibSF 21.2-3. Freiburg im Breisgau: Herder, 1923.

Reasoner, Mark. *The Strong and the Weak: Romans 14:1–15:13 in Context*. SNTSMS 103. Cambridge: Cambridge University Press, 1999.

———. "The Theology of Romans 12:1–15:13." In *Pauline Theology*, vol. 3, *Romans*, 287-99. Ed. David M. Hay and E. Elizabeth Johnson. Minneapolis: Fortress Press, 1991.

Sampley, J. Paul. "The Weak and the Strong: Paul's Careful and Crafty Rhetorical Strategy in Romans 14:1–15:13." In *The Social World of the First Christians: Studies in Honor of Wayne A. Meeks*, 40-52. Ed. L. Michael White and O. Larry Yarbrough. Minneapolis: Fortress Press, 1994.

Schmithals, Walter. "Die Starken und die Schwachen in Rom 14:1–15:6." In his *Der Römerbrief als historisches Problem*, 95-107. Gütersloh: Gerd Mohn, 1975.

Schnelle, Udo. *Apostle Paul: His Life and Theology*. Grand Rapids: Baker Academic, 2005.

Segal, Alan F. *Paul the Convert: The Apostolate and Apostasy of Saul the Pharisee*. New Haven: Yale University Press, 1990.

Smallwood, E. Mary. *The Jews under Roman Rule from Pompey to Diocletian.* SJLA 20. Leiden: E. J. Brill, 1976.

Stern, Menachem. *Greek and Latin Authors on Jews and Judaism.* 3 vols. Jerusalem: Israel Academy of Sciences and Humanities, 1974-84.

Stowers, Stanley K. *Letter Writing in Greco-Roman Antiquity.* LEC 5. Philadelphia: Westminster Press, 1986.

————. *A Rereading of Romans: Justice, Jews and Gentiles.* New Haven: Yale University Press, 1994.

Tan, Yak-Hwee. "Judging and Community in Romans: An Action within the Boundaries." In *Society of Biblical Literature 2000 Seminar Papers,* 559-82. SBLSPS 38. Atlanta: Society of Biblical Literature, 2000.

Theissen, Gerd. "The Strong and the Weak in Corinth: A Sociological Analysis of a Theological Quarrel." In *Understanding Paul's Ethics: Twentieth-Century Approaches,* ed. Brian S. Rosner, 107-28. Grand Rapids: Wm. B. Eerdmans, 1995; reprinted from his *The Social Setting of Pauline Christianity: Essays on Corinth,* 121-43. Philadelphia: Fortress Press, 1982.

Tobin, Thomas H. *Paul's Rhetoric in Its Contexts: The Argument of Romans.* Peabody: Hendrickson Publishers, 2004.

Tomson, Peter J. *Paul and the Jewish Law: Halakah in the Letters of the Apostle to the Gentiles.* Minneapolis: Fortress Press, 1991.

Toney, Carl N. *Paul's Inclusive Ethic: Resolving Community Conflicts and Promoting Mission in Romans 14–15.* WUNT 2/252. J. C. B. Mohr (Paul Siebeck), 2008.

Watson, Francis. *Paul, Judaism and the Gentiles: Beyond the New Perspective.* Rev. ed. Grand Rapids: Wm. B. Eerdmans, 2007.

————. "The Two Roman Congregations: Romans 14:1–15:13." In *The Romans Debate,* 203-15. Ed. Karl P. Donfried. Rev. ed. Peabody: Hendrickson Publishers, 1991.

Weiss, Herold. "Paul and the Judging of Days." *ZNW* 86 (1995): 137-53.

Williams, Margaret. "Being a Jew in Rome: Sabbath Fasting as an Expression of Romano-Jewish Identity." In *Negotiating Diaspora: Jewish Strategies in the Roman Empire,* 8-18. Ed. John M. G. Barclay. LSTS 45. New York: T&T Clark, 2004.

Willis, Wendell L. *Idol Meat in Corinth: The Pauline Argument in 1 Corinthians 8 and 10.* SBLDS 68. Chico: Scholars Press, 1985.

Wuellner, Wilhelm. "Paul's Rhetoric of Argumentation in Romans: An Alternative to the Donfried-Karris Debate over Romans." In *The Romans Debate,* 128-46. Ed. Karl P. Donfried. Rev. ed. Peabody: Hendrickson Publishers, 1991.

Zimmerman, Theodore I. "The Weak and the Strong: A Study of Romans 14:1–15:13." Th.D. diss. Luther Seminary, St. Paul, Minnesota, 1993.

8.1. Restraining Judgment, 14:1-12

1*Welcome the person who is weak in faith, but not for the purpose of quarreling over opinions.* 2*One person believes in eating anything, but the weak person*

eats only vegetables. ₃Let not the one who eats anything despise the one who ab-
stains, and let not the one who abstains condemn the one who eats, for God has
accepted him. ₄Who are you that you pass judgment on the servant of another? It
is before his own master that he stands or falls. And he will be upheld, for the Lord
is able to make him stand.

₅One person regards one day as better than another, but another esteems all
days alike. Let each person be fully convinced in his own mind. ₆The one who ob-
serves the day does so for the Lord. And the one who eats does so unto the Lord,
for he gives thanks to God. And the one who abstains from eating abstains unto
the Lord and gives thanks to God. ₇For none of us lives for himself, and no one dies
for himself. ₈If we live, we live to the Lord, and if we die, we die to the Lord; so
then, whether we live or whether we die, we are the Lord's. ₉For unto this end
Christ died and lived again, in order that he might be Lord of both the dead and
the living.

₁₀You then, why do you pass judgment on your brother? Or you, why do you
despise your brother? For we shall all stand before the judgment seat of God; ₁₁for
it is written,

> *"As I live, says the Lord, every knee shall bow to me, and every*
> *tongue shall confess to God."*

₁₂So, therefore, each of us shall give account of himself to God.

Notes on the Text and Translation

14:4 Some ancient witnesses have ὁ θεός ("God") instead of ὁ κύριος ("the
Lord") in the final clause. These include various Western and Byzantine texts,
and they are followed by the reading in the KJV. But superior texts (including
𝔓⁴⁶, ℵ, and B) read ὁ κύριος, which modern versions (e.g., RSV, NIV, and
NRSV) follow. The NIV and NRSV have "the Lord," while the RSV has "the
Master."

14:6 Based on later witnesses, the Majority Text has an additional sentence between the two provided above, which reads: καὶ ὁ μὴ φρονῶν τὴν
ἡμέραν κυρίῳ οὐ φρονεῖ ("And the one who does not observe the day does so
for the Lord"). This accounts for the additional sentence in the KJV. It is not in
superior texts (including ℵ and B) and can be regarded as "a typical Byzantine
gloss, prompted by the desire to provide a balanced statement after the model
of the clause καὶ ὁ μὴ ἐσθίων ["the one who abstains from eating"] later in the
verse."[34]

---

34. B. Metzger, *TCGNT* 468.

14:12 Some important witnesses (including B, F, and G) lack τῷ θεῷ ("to God") at the end of the verse. It is possible that scribes added those two words to fill out the meaning, conforming the verse (in meaning) to 3:19. On the other hand, other significant witnesses, both Greek (‭א‬, A, C, D) and other early versions (Latin, Syriac, and Coptic), include the words. The evidence is slightly stronger for inclusion than exclusion.[35]

General Comment

Romans 14:1–15:13, concerning "the weak and the strong," concludes the collection of hortatory materials so prominent in 12:1–15:13. It marks a turning point in that, while in the immediately previous sections (12:14–13:14) Paul's exhortations generally — but not exclusively — have to do with the life of the believer in the public arena, now they turn toward life within the community of believers. He exhorts them to mutual care as an extension of what he has said earlier about the practice of love (12:9-10; 13:8) and about not being haughty (12:16).

The section is directed not only toward life together in community, but also toward what is endemic within Christian communities. Differences exist between persons or even factions about issues that affect a particular community. To some, those issues are a matter of conscience, having to do with core beliefs, while for others they are not. In the present passage Paul presents an issue to consider, describing two possible positions on it, and then begins his own analysis without immediately stating his own view. He does, however, make an emphatic point, and that is that passing judgments and despising one another have no place in the household of God, before whom each person is finally accountable (14:12).

Issues concerning the identity of the weak and the strong are dealt with in "8. The Weak and the Strong," and the conclusions drawn from that discussion are presupposed here.

Detailed Comment

14:1-2 The NRSV opens with the words, "Welcome those who are weak in faith," using the plural "those." The Greek text, however, has a singular referent (τὸν ἀσθενοῦντα τῇ πίστει), and that is followed by most modern versions, such as the RSV, which has, "As for the man who is weak in faith" or, as here, "Welcome the person who is weak in faith."

---

35. B. Metzger, *TCGNT* 469.

An alternative translation to "weak in faith" is "weak in *the* faith." The former (or something like it) appears in the most widely used English versions (RSV, NRSV; the NIV has, "him whose faith is weak"). The latter ("weak in *the* faith") appears in other versions (KJV and NET). In spite of the linguistic possibility, the former is to be preferred.[36] Paul is not speaking here of "*the* faith," as though there was a prescribed formulation of faith, but of "faith" in God, as said specifically in 14:22-23. The presence of the article τῇ ("the") is not unusual; it appears elsewhere when Paul is clearly speaking of "faith" as an abstract noun (Rom 4:19-20; 11:20; 2 Cor 1:24; Phil 3:9). A similar expression is used regarding Abraham: μὴ ἀσθενήσας τῇ πίστει (4:19, "he did not weaken in faith") where "faith," not "the faith," is clearly meant.

The person who is "weak in faith" abstains from eating meat and observes some particular day or days (14:1-2, 5, 21); the person who is counted as "the strong" does not, and Paul counts himself among the strong (14:2-5; 15:1). Although it might appear that the person who is "weak in faith" also drinks no wine (14:17, 21), that is not certain due to the character of the verses in question. In the first of them (14:17, "For the kingdom of God is not food and drink but righteousness and peace and joy in the Holy Spirit") Paul does not mention wine explicitly and seems to be quoting a familiar maxim concerning the kingdom of God (cf. 1 Cor 4:20 for another), and in the second (14:21, "it is good not to eat meat or drink wine or do anything that makes your brother or sister stumble") Paul provides a general principle regarding conduct; the reference to wine may have been suggested by the word "drink" in 14:17. The person who abstains from meat and observes some particular day or days does all this in honor of the Lord (14:6), meaning Christ, and the same can be said of the person who does not (14:6).

The question whether Paul takes up a live issue here among Roman Christians, as well as the question of the identity of "the weak" and "the strong," is discussed in the previous section ("8. The Weak and the Strong"). There we concluded that it is impossible to identify two groups of people at Rome that can be referred to by these terms with sufficient certainty. The problem is not simply the lack of historical material by which to illumine the situation, but the kind of language used as well. Although the section consists formally of paraenesis, there is extensive diatribe within it. Paul is able thereby to construct imaginary opponents, "the weak" and "the strong," to make a case study of persons in conflict that has implications for any community that is divided over matters that some consider important and others consider indifferent.

The section begins with an exhortation to "welcome" the person who is

---

36. Cf. also L. Keck, *Romans,* 336, who takes the last two words to be a dative of respect: "the weak with respect to faith."

"weak in faith." The verb form used (προσλαμβάνεσθε) is an imperative in second person plural, and it appears again at 15:7: "welcome one another." In the latter case Paul provides a theological basis for extending a welcome. Using the same verb, but in the indicative, he bases mutual welcome on the fact that Christ has already welcomed (προσελάβετο) all (15:7). At 14:3, using the same verb, Paul says that God has welcomed (προσελάβετο) "the strong."

When the welcome is extended, however, that is not for setting a trap. Extend a welcome, says Paul, "but not for the purpose of quarreling over opinions." The word for "opinion" (διαλογισμός) can also be translated as "thought" or "reasoning."[37] Within its context "opinion" is suitable (RSV, NRSV, NET) or "disputable matters" (NIV). Paul could not mean nonnegotiable "convictions" in this case. But in these matters what might be an "opinion" to one person might be a "conviction" for another. Clearly Paul writes from the perspective of "the strong," for whom some matters are indifferent (or adiaphora). But as the discussion unfolds, Paul is aware that for "the weak" they are much more serious. The one who is "weak in faith" from the standpoint of "the strong" practices what he or she does "for the Lord" (14:6) and as a matter of "faith" (14:22-23).

14:3-4 Paul continues with the use of the singular (as in the RSV, NIV, and NET; the NRSV has plural pronouns). The temptation of "the strong" is to "despise" or regard as nothing (ἐξουθενέω) "the weak." The verb used means to show by one's attitude or manner of treatment that someone has no merit or worth.[38] Here it is a matter of regarding a person who is scrupulous in some matters of personal piety as not worthy of one's respect. On the other hand, the temptation of "the weak" is to judge or condemn (κρίνω) "the strong." It is easy to fall into the habit of thinking that the person who does not act in a certain manner obviously has no regard for the norms that are to guide the new life in Christ. Such a person is not worthy of being considered a believer.

Paul insists, however, that the attitudes mentioned are to be set aside. Although for most of 14:1–15:13 Paul has a special regard for and defends "the weak," here at the outset it is to the latter that most of what he has to say is directed.[39] The person designated "weak" must refrain from condemning the other, for God has already welcomed that person into the community of Christ. The person, as a believer, has been bought with a price (1 Cor 6:20; 7:23) and belongs to Christ (Rom 1:6; 7:4). Paul compares such a person to a domestic servant (οἰκέτης) who be-

---

37. BDAG 232-33 (διαλογισμός, 2).

38. BDAG 352 (ἐξουθενέω, 1).

39. So most interpreters seem to think — e.g., W. Sanday and A. Headlam, *Romans*, 385; C. K. Barrett, *Romans*, 238; C. Cranfield, *Romans*, 702-3; J. Dunn, *Romans*, 803; J. Fitzmyer, *Romans*, 689; J. Zeisler, *Romans*, 328; D. Moo, *Romans*, 839; and L. Keck, *Romans*, 339. That Paul addresses "the strong" is held by P. Stuhlmacher, *Romans*, 223; that he addresses both is held by B. Byrne, *Romans*, 412, and R. Jewett, *Romans*, 838-41.

longs to an earthly master. No one has the right to judge that servant and his conduct except the master himself, before whom the servant will stand or fall. Likewise, "the strong" will stand in the final judgment, for the Lord is able to make that person stand. The possibility that "the strong" might fall is not even contemplated. That is not because of any inner strength or virtue, but because of the gracious power of Christ, the Lord, to whom the person belongs.

14:5-6 On the identity of the person who "regards one day better than another," see the discussion in "8. The Weak and the Strong." According to what Paul says, it appears that a particular day is in question, since it is called "the day" (singular) in 14:6. If only one day is in question, and if Paul is aware of the observance of a particular day, two possibilities present themselves. One possibility is that "the day" is the Sabbath, which Jews of Rome observed not with joy and feasting — the usual manner — but with fasting.[40] Whether there were Christians at Rome who practiced Sabbath fasting, however, is not supported in known sources. The other possibility is that "the day" is Friday, and that it was commemorated as the day on which Jesus was crucified. That practice is attested in early sources,[41] and it is alluded to already in the gospels (Mark 2:20// Matt 9:15//Luke 5:33).[42] But whether it was practiced at Rome by the time Paul wrote Romans cannot be known. One must finally conclude that Paul may be constructing here an imaginary potential problem by analogy to his knowledge of the observing of certain "days" by the Christians in Galatia (Gal 4:10, "You are observing special days, and months, and seasons, and years"). There is evidence that Christians elsewhere observed certain days as well (Matt 6:16-18; Col 2:16). Speaking first of no particular day (14:5, literally, "a day") that is judged better than any other, and then of observing that day as special ("the day," 14:6), it is possible that Paul does not have any specific day in mind, but refers to any day that is of importance to anyone.

Each person, the strong or the weak, is to be "fully convinced" (πληρο-φορέω) in his or her mind about these matters of foods and days. When that is the case, what a person does is no longer simply a matter of indifference. The "strong" might consider the practices of the "weak" as indifferent. But when those practices are seen from the viewpoint of the latter, and when the latter is "fully convinced" about them, that is not the case. For that person, convictions are at stake. Likewise, the "weak" might consider the apparent indifference of the "strong" as a blatant disregard for matters of importance. But when the latter

---

40. The practice is referred to in the writings of several writers of antiquity (including Josephus, Strabo, and Cassius Dio), as surveyed by M. Williams, "Being a Jew in Rome," 9-10; for references see n. 21 in section "8. The Weak and the Strong."

41. *Didache* 8.2; *Apostolic Constitutions* 7.23.1. On the range of dating, cf. Robert A. Kraft, "Didache," *ABD* 2:197-98.

42. For discussion of this claim, cf. A. Hultgren, *Jesus and His Adversaries*, 78-82.

person is fully convinced that the observances are not important for salvation, but simply indifferent, that, too, is a matter of conviction. Paul lists three cases where either doing or not doing something is done or not done "to the Lord" (RSV and NRSV: "in honor of the Lord"): (1) observing "the day"; (2) eating meat; (3) abstaining from eating meat. He does not mention the fourth possibility: not observing "the day," although that is implicit from 14:5. When using the term "Lord," Paul is referring to Christ.[43] He uses the phrase "to the Lord" three times over in the verse, and it is differentiated from "God" at the end. Then he speaks of the believers' belonging to the Lord, whether alive or dead. That is followed by saying that Christ is Lord of both the dead and the living (14:9), which sums up the meaning of "the Lord" in 14:6-9.

Whatever one does (eat meat, abstain from meat, observe a particular day, or not observe one), it is done out of devotion to the Lord. In regard to eating or not eating meat, Paul can add an additional item. In each case the person gives thanks to God (14:6). What is to be learned from all this is that each person who is a believer should have an imagination that allows for a variety of religious habits. No one should be asked to change practices that are done for the Lord.

14:7-9 These verses have been considered a doctrinal affirmation that Paul composed independently of his writing of the letter, and which he has incorporated into it.[44] That is plausible, since the verses comprise a liturgical unit that would fit many occasions. Here it appears that the liturgical association is in the expression "to the Lord" (τῷ κυρίῳ). In 14:6 Paul has said that a person observes, eats, or abstains "to the Lord" (κυρίῳ). Picking up on the idea that all do whatever they do "to the Lord," Paul continues with the liturgical phrases in 14:7-8. These contain a contrast that works particularly well within the context: no one lives or dies "to himself" (ἑαυτῷ), for if we live, we live "to the Lord" (τῷ κυρίῳ), and if we die, we die "to the Lord" (τῷ κυρίῳ). In either case, "we are the Lord's." It is not religious practices that certify one's relationship to God. All members of the body of Christ, regardless of their particular practices or lack thereof, belong to Christ through their common confession, not their habits.

Paul continues with another liturgical expression (14:9). It appears to have been prompted by Paul's reference to living and dying — and belonging to Christ in either case. The expression is Christological, speaking of the lordship of Christ over both the dead and the living.[45] It expresses the purpose of his

---

43. Interpreters are divided on this. Among those who take "Lord" as a designation for Christ are C. H. Dodd, *Romans*, 215; E. Käsemann, *Romans*, 370-71; C. Cranfield, *Romans*, 707; J. Dunn, *Romans*, 806; J. Ziesler, *Romans*, 330; B. Byrne, *Romans*, 409; D. Moo, *Romans*, 843 (n. 78); R. Jewett, *Romans*, 847. An exception is J. Fitzmyer, *Romans*, 690.

44. M. Theobald, "Der Einsamkeit des Selbst entnommen," 144, 158.

45. V. Neufeld, *The Earliest Christian Confessions*, 47; K. Wengst, *Christologische Formeln und Lieder des Urchristentums*, 45-46; J. Lambrecht, "'It Is for the Lord,'" 143-54.

death and resurrection ("for unto this end . . . in order that"). The purpose is not simply that he might be Lord, although that is certainly expressed, but that he might be Lord for both the dead and the living. As their Lord, he is able to save and sustain all in life and in death.

14:10-12 Paul resumes his discussion of the weak and the strong. He returns to the language of passing judgment and despising another person, applied earlier to the attitudes of, respectively, the weak about the strong and the strong about the weak (14:3-4). In each case Paul indicates that the other person is a "brother" (ἀδελφός, used twice) or sibling. He goes on to use that term three more times in close proximity (14:13, 15, 21). The implication is that Christians should give persons with whom they disagree the kind of consideration and respect that one would give to siblings within one's own family.[46] In the end, believers are not to judge one another in these matters, for at the last judgment each person will have to stand before God at his judgment seat, who is the only judge that matters. The term used for "judgment seat" (βῆμα) is a platform upon which a civic officer was seated. The structure was familiar to Paul, since it was at the base of the βῆμα at Corinth that Paul appeared before the proconsul Gallio (Acts 18:12-17), and the βῆμα is still visible at the ancient site today.[47] The term is used in Jewish texts prior to Paul in reference to God's judgment seat.[48] Paul himself uses it again to speak of "the judgment seat of Christ" (τὸ βῆμα τοῦ Χριστοῦ, 2 Cor 5:10).

At 14:11 Paul quotes from Isaiah 45:23. The wording of the quotation is almost identical to that of the LXX, except that Paul has "every tongue" (πᾶσα γλῶσσα) prior to the verb in the second of the two clauses:

> Isaiah 45:23: ὅτι ἐμοὶ κάμψει πᾶν γόνυ καὶ ἐξομολογήσεται πᾶσα γλῶσσα τῷ θεῷ.
>
> Romans 14:11: ὅτι ἐμοὶ κάμψει πᾶν γόνυ καὶ πᾶσα γλῶσσα ἐξομολογήσεται τῷ θεῷ.
>
> For every knee shall bow to me, and every tongue shall confess to God.

Paul quotes the same passage within a longer sentence at Philippians 2:10-11, although again with slight variations in word order from the LXX.[49] There the

---

46. A. Hultgren, "The Self-Definition of Paul and His Communities," 93-94. Cf. D. Horrell, "From ἀδελφοί to οἶκος θεοῦ," 300; S. Bartchy, "Undermining Ancient Patriarchy," 77.

47. A photo is provided in the photo collection between p. 192 and p. 193 of F. F. Bruce, *Paul.* An illustration of the city plan of ancient Corinth is presented by Jerome Murphy-O'Connor, "Corinth," *ABD* 1:1137.

48. *Sib. Or.* 2.218; 8.222, 242.

49. The verbs are placed last in both clauses: πᾶν γόνυ κάμψῃ . . . καὶ πᾶσα γλῶσσα ἐξομολογήσηται.

bowing and confessing are in respect to Christ as cosmic Lord. But here in Romans the reverence is in respect to God.

14:12 The section closes with the declaration that each person must give a final account before God. The word for "account" is λόγος, one of the most comprehensive words in the Greek language. It is used elsewhere to speak of managing accounts (Luke 16:2) and being able to give an account of behavior (Acts 19:40). But it is also used for a final "account" to be made at the last judgment before God (Matt 12:36; Heb 4:13; 13:17) or before Christ (1 Pet 4:5). Here the passage points to the final judgment before God. The whole world is accountable before God (3:19), and that includes the believer as well.

BIBLIOGRAPHY

Bartchy, Scott. "Undermining Ancient Patriarchy: The Apostle Paul's Vision of a Society of Siblings." *BTB* 29 (1999): 68-78.

Bruce, F. F. *Paul: Apostle of the Heart Set Free.* Grand Rapids: Wm. B. Eerdmans, 1977.

Horrell, David G. "From ἀδελφοί to οἶκος θεοῦ: Social Transformation in Pauline Christianity." *JBL* 120 (2001): 293-311.

Hultgren, Arland J. *Jesus and His Adversaries: The Form and Function of the Conflict Stories in the Synoptic Tradition.* Minneapolis: Augsburg Publishing House, 1979.

———. "The Self-Definition of Paul and His Communities." *SEÅ* 56 (1991): 78-100.

Lambrecht, Jan. "'It Is for the Lord That We Live and Die': A Theological Reflection on Romans 14:7-9." *LS* 28 (2003): 143-54.

Neufeld, Vernon. *The Earliest Christian Confessions.* NTTS 5. Grand Rapids: Wm. B. Eerdmans, 1963.

Theobald, Michael. "Der Einsamkeit des Selbst entnommen — dem Herrn gehörig: Ein christologisches Lehrstück des Paulus (Röm 14,7-9)." In his *Studien zum Römerbrief,* 142-61. WUNT 136. Tübingen: J. C. B. Mohr (Paul Siebeck), 2001.

Weiss, Herold. "Paul and the Judging of Days." *ZNW* 86 (1995): 137-53.

Wengst, Klaus. *Christologische Formeln und Lieder des Urchristentums.* SNT 7. Gütersloh: Gütersloher Verlagshaus Gerd Mohn, 1972.

Williams, Margaret. "Being a Jew in Rome: Sabbath Fasting as an Expression of Romano-Jewish Identity." In *Negotiating Diaspora: Jewish Strategies in the Roman Empire,* 8-18. Ed. John M. G. Barclay. New York: T&T Clark, 2004.

8.2. Pursuing Peace and Mutual Upbuilding, 14:13-23

13*Let us therefore not make judgments about one another, but decide rather never to put a stumbling block or hindrance in the way of a brother.* 14*I know and am persuaded in the Lord Jesus that nothing is unclean in itself; but it is unclean for anyone who thinks it unclean.* 15*For if your brother is being injured by what* *you eat, you are no longer walking in love. Do not let what you eat destroy one for whom Christ died. 16Therefore, do not let what you consider good be spoken of as evil. 17For the kingdom of God does not consist of food and drink, but righteousness, peace, and joy in the Holy Spirit. 18For whoever serves Christ in this manner is acceptable to God and has human approval. 19Let us then pursue what makes for peace and for mutual upbuilding. 20Do not, for the sake of food, destroy the work of God. All things are clean, but it is wrong for anyone to make others fall by what he eats. 21It is good not to eat meat or drink wine or do anything that makes your brother stumble. 22The faith that you have, keep between yourself and God. Blessed is the person who has no reason to judge himself for what he approves. 23But whoever has doubts is condemned, if he eats, because he does not act from faith; and whatever does not proceed from faith is sin.*

Notes on the Text and Translation

14:14 The Greek expression εἰ μή is usually translated "except," but in the present instance is better translated simply as "but," as in various versions (KJV, RSV, NIV, and NRSV; NET: "still").

14:16 One should expect the singular σου ("your") at this place rather than the plural ὑμῶν ("your"). This may be an indication that Paul is using a familiar saying that contains the plural term. Some ancient texts (D, F, G, and ψ) read ἡμῶν ("our").

14:23 Some ancient textual witnesses include a doxology here, following the ending of the verse as printed above. The wording is identical to that which appears at 16:25-27. In more important texts ($\mathfrak{P}^{61}$ [apparently], ℵ, B, C, and D), however, the doxology appears only after 16:23, not here.[50] The latter reading has been adopted by the Nestle-Aland Greek NT, 27th edition, and most current English versions, as well as here. Most Old Latin and Vulgate manuscripts are of particular interest here. After 14:23 they include what is 16:24 in some texts and then close with the doxology. Chapters 15 and 16 (except for 16:24) are not included.[51]

General Comment

At 14:4 Paul asked the question, "Who are you that you pass judgment on the servant of another?" Now he lifts up that concern and continues a discussion of its

---

50. For a discussion of six possible locations of the doxology in ancient manuscripts of Romans, cf. B. Metzger, *TCGNT* 470-73, who provides references to other studies.

51. On the various endings to the letter in texts, see the list by K. Aland, "Der Schluss," 286-90.

dynamics and its consequences. Essentially what he goes on to say is that when a person judges another, and particularly when the latter is sensitive to the opinions of others, it can be devastating. That is especially the case when the judging is accompanied by actions that are offensive to the conscience of the person being judged. Paul seems to be envisioning cases where ridicule and/or taunting would accompany what is said, and that could lead the person being offended into compromises in order to please the one who does the judging.

Paul commends instead an attitude and way of life in which it is recognized that all who belong to Christ are held together in a community; none is to be injured or destroyed (14:15). The way to honor the community is to walk in love, pursue peace, and build one another up rather than to tear one another down.

Detailed Comment

14:13 Paul resumes the theme of not judging one another, which had been spoken of explicitly in the foregoing (14:3-4, 10) and implicitly in the entire section (14:1-12). For Paul, the very act of judging can lead the other person to react or respond in a way that goes against his or her conscience. It is far better, then, to decide not to do so, and thereby not place an impediment in the course of the other's spiritual life. Once again, as in 14:10, Paul uses the language of sibling relationships (ἀδελφός, literally, "brother"), which he shall do again at 14:15 and 14:21. Believers are thereby expected to give persons with whom they disagree the respect they give to siblings within their own family. See the exegesis of 14:10.

14:14 Paul uses the term "unclean" (κοινός, literally "common") in this verse and "clean" (καθαρός) in 14:20. The distinction is traditional in Judaism, expressed in the Torah (Lev 20:25):

> You shall therefore make a distinction between the clean (LXX: καθαρός) animal and the unclean (ἀκάθαρτος), and between the unclean (ἀκάθαρτος) bird and the clean (καθαρός); you shall not bring abomination on yourselves by animal or by bird or by anything with which the ground teems, which I have set apart for you to hold unclean (ἐν ἀκαθαρσίᾳ).

The adjective that Paul uses for "unclean" is κοινός, rather than the more fitting word ἀκάθαρτος used in Leviticus (LXX; also at Hos 9:3), but this usage in regard to foods is well attested in Hellenistic Judaism (1 Macc 1:47, 62; cf. also the verb form κοινόω, "to make unclean" or "to defile" at Matt 15:11). Both adjectives are used together at Acts 10:14, "common or unclean" (κοινὸς ἢ ἀκάθαρτος).

For Paul, the traditional distinction of "clean" and "unclean" foods does not exist (cf. 1 Cor 10:25-27). That is in keeping with the tradition from Jesus (Mark 7:19) and within major streams of early Christian teaching (Acts 10:15; 1 Tim 4:3-4; Titus 1:15). And yet in some cases it is possible that a person, on the basis of conscience, might think of some foods as unclean, and that conviction is to be respected. Whether that is actually happening among Christians at Rome is not certain, since Paul is stating a principle here, not necessarily addressing an actual situation.

14:15 As in the case of Corinth, where Paul says that one should not use one's freedom to cause another to fall (1 Cor 8:9, 13), so similar considerations are to be held and lived by here. One who is considered to be among the "strong" is not to cause injury to a sibling by what he or she eats. Here and in what follows Paul uses a series of maxims to highlight basic principles (14:15, 16, 20).[52] They are negative commands in each case, expressed in singular imperative verb forms. It is unlikely, therefore, that Paul is addressing an actual group of persons who can be considered "the strong." The wording is that of diatribe, in which an imaginary opponent is constructed and addressed. The main point is that one is not to act in such a way that one destroys another person, a person "for whom Christ died" (ὑπὲρ οὗ Χριστὸς ἀπέθανεν). The clause speaks of the saving work of Christ and makes use of the kerygmatic ὑπέρ-formula so familiar in the writings of Paul.[53] (For more on the formula, see the exegesis of 5:6.) But in this case Paul is not so much proclaiming as he is giving attention to the value of the person designated "weak in faith." That person is one for whom Christ spent his life unto death.

"Walking in love" is central to Paul's ethical teaching in two respects. First, in his use of the term περιπατέω ("to walk"), he makes use once more (as in 6:4; 8:4; and 13:13) of his major metaphor for conduct,[54] a term derived from his background in Hellenistic Judaism where conduct is a matter of "walking" according to precepts in the Torah (the *halakhot* [הֲלָכוֹת], derived from the verb הָלַךְ [*halak*], "to walk").[55] For more on that verb, see the exegesis of 6:4. The expression "walking in love" is central to Paul's ethical teaching in another respect, and that is that love is the fulfilling of the law (Rom 13:10; Gal 5:14) and the first of the "fruits of the Spirit" that he mentions (Gal 5:22).

14:16 In the maxim expressed here, Paul takes action against the view that a person is free to criticize another on the basis of his or her own convic-

---

52. P. Holloway, "The Enthymeme," 337-38.

53. K. Wengst, *Christologische Formeln und Lieder des Urchristentums*, 78-80.

54. In addition to his use of the term in Romans, Paul also uses it at 1 Cor 3:3; 7:17; 2 Cor 4:2; 5:7; 10:3; 12:18; Gal 5:16; Phil 3:17, 18; 1 Thess 2:12; 4:1, 12.

55. Cf. LXX Prov 8:20: ἐν ὁδοῖς δικαιοσύνης περιπατῶ ("I walk in the ways of righteousness").

tions. The person who considers himself "strong," in spite of "good" convictions, should not act in such a way toward others that those convictions can be spoken of as evil. By causing harm to another, even while doing so out of conviction, a person can rightly be accused of being evil to that person.

14:17 This is one of those rare places — one of six — where Paul uses the phrase "the kingdom of God" (ἡ βασιλεία τοῦ θεοῦ). The phrase appears only here in Romans, and it appears only five more times in Paul's other letters (1 Cor 4:20; 6:9-10; 15:50; Gal 5:21). By way of contrast, the phrase appears 51 times in the Synoptic Gospels,[56] twice in the Gospel of John (3:3, 5), and six times in Acts (1:3; 8:12; 14:22; 19:8; 28:23, 31). Except for a half dozen instances in the Synoptic Gospels, all the uses of the phrase are in sayings of Jesus.[57] That the phrase is so rare in the letters of Paul is due to the fact that Paul speaks about Christ and what God has done in Jesus' death and resurrection; rarely does he repeat the preaching or teaching of Jesus (exceptions are at 1 Cor 7:10-11; 9:14; 11:23-26). But Paul most likely heard the phrase in early Christian preaching, and the connection between the kingdom and righteousness can be traced back to the Jesus tradition (Matt 6:33).

The saying here concerning the kingdom has been called an "antithetical definition formula,"[58] telling what the kingdom is not — and then what it is (similarly, the saying at 1 Cor 4:20). It has been shaped by Christian proclamation, since the kingdom of God is said to consist of righteousness, peace, and joy "in the Holy Spirit." It is possible that the saying originated in early baptismal catechesis, where the antithetical principle of the saying is most applicable.[59] Paul would then have made use of the saying within communities of believers to remind them of their baptismal identity (or at least their obligation as Christians). When writing to the Thessalonians, for instance, Paul speaks of his preaching at Thessalonica. He says that, while there, he was urging and encouraging the Thessalonians to "lead a life worthy of God," who calls them "into his own kingdom (βασιλεία) and glory" (1 Thess 2:12).

In saying that the kingdom of God "does not consist of food and drink,"

---

56. In addition, the equivalent phrase "kingdom of heaven" appears 32 times in the Gospel of Matthew. The phrase "kingdom of God" appears 5 times in Matthew, 14 times in Mark, and 32 times in Luke, leaving aside the textually uncertain cases of Mark 1:14; Luke 12:31. These statistics do not account for other equivalent expressions or where the full phrase is implied, such as "gospel of the kingdom" (Matt 24:14), "my Father's kingdom" (Matt 26:29), "your kingdom come" (Matt 6:10//Luke 11:2), and others. The statistics are taken from J. Kohlenberger, *The Greek-English Concordance to the New Testament*, 107.

57. The exceptions are at Matt 3:2; 18:1; Mark 15:43; Luke 17:20a; 19:11; 23:51.

58. G. Haufe, "Reich Gottes bei Paulus und in der Jesustradition," 469 (*"ein antithetischer Definitionssatz"*).

59. G. Haufe, "Reich Gottes bei Paulus und in der Jesustradition," 470.

Paul relativizes human activities that can be taken by some as matters of importance for their lives in faith. The words "food and drink" (βρῶσις καὶ πόσις) can be considered a general reference to human activities (cf. Matt 6:25; 11:18-19; 1 Cor 9:4; 10:7, 31; 11:22; Col 2:16, classical, and other sources),[60] but in this case they are activities that are of no consequence to faith (adiaphora). Paul's own attitude is expressed in the words: "whether you eat or drink, or whatever you do, do everything for the glory of God" (1 Cor 10:31).

14:18 Although the saying about serving Christ is brief, it is central to what is being said and sums up much of what is said up to this point in this section of the letter. Serving Christ enables a nexus of unity in two respects: unity of the self with God, and unity of the self with other believers. The person who serves Christ is "acceptable (εὐάρεστος) to God." To be acceptable to God, or to act in ways that are acceptable to God, is stressed by Paul elsewhere (Rom 12:1-2; 2 Cor 5:9; Phil 4:18). The concept appears also in Jewish traditions before Paul and in his era.[61] For Paul, it is equivalent to doing the will of God (Rom 12:2). But the passage is not simply about service in a general sense. It is quite specific in the present instance, for Paul speaks about serving Christ "in this way" (ἐν τούτῳ). The significance of the phrase is almost lost with the bland translation "thus" in the RSV and NRSV. The NIV and NET do better by rendering it as "in this way." The phrase refers to all that has gone before it concerning respect for the views of others, not injuring them. The service spoken of is, therefore, not for winning God's favor in the final judgment, but for service that pleases God in the present.

The person who serves Christ also has "human approval" (δόκιμος τοῖς ἀνθρώποις; literally, the person "is approved by people"). That is to say, the person is found to be trustworthy (δόκιμος means being "tried and true")[62] and of a generous spirit, respecting the rights of those with whom one disagrees. This is different from trying to please others for one's own advantage (cf. Gal 1:10).

14:19-21 Paul resumes with exhortation and a conclusion: "Let us then pursue what makes for peace and for mutual upbuilding." Controversy over matters of food and drink is not acceptable for the person who seeks to please God and foster community. Although all foods can be considered "clean" (καθαρός), one can refrain from eating them if it causes another person to join in and go against his or her conscience. That is the way of love (14:15). It is also the way of "peace" and "mutual upbuilding." Paul speaks often in his letters about peace among believers, and exhorts them to live together in peace (Rom 14:17; 1 Cor

---

60. Homer, *Od.* 1.191; 15.490; Plato, *Leg.* 783c; Xenophon, *Mem.* 1.3.15; Philo, *Mos.* 1.184; idem, *Jos.* 20.154; Plutarch, *Mor.* 126; *b. Ber.* 17a.

61. Wis 4:10; Philo, *Spec. Leg.* 1.37.201; *Virt.* 11.67; *T. Dan* 1.3.

62. BDAG 256 (δόκιμος, 1).

7:15; 14:33; 2 Cor 13:11; Gal 5:22; 1 Thess 5:13; cf. also 1 Pet 3:10-11). He is also a strong proponent of mutual upbuilding (edification) as a prime value within Christian communities (15:2; 1 Cor 10:23; 14:3, 26; 2 Cor 12:19; 1 Thess 5:11).

Abstaining from foods that the "weak" person considers unclean, but are matters of indifference to the "strong," is more than a simple courtesy. It is faith active in love (cf. Gal 5:6). It is also an act of evangelical freedom, i.e., freedom that is inspired and allowed by the gospel. The person who abstains loses nothing, not even the freedom that being strong implies. On the contrary, that person uses that very freedom in love and thereby affirms the reality of the new life in Christ.[63]

14:22-23 The "faith" (πίστις) spoken of in both 14:22 and 23 is probably not simply faith in the sense of "trust" but has the connotation of one's "conviction."[64] The "strong" may indeed have a strong "faith" in contrast to the one who is "weak in faith" (14:1). But to impose it upon another or to despise another whose faith does not match one's own (14:3, 10) is unacceptable. Such faith is admirable, but it is between the believer and God.

Paul utters an expression reminiscent of the Beatitudes, using the word μακάριος ("blessed" in NIV and NRSV; "happy" in KJV and RSV) at the beginning of a sentence. Within the Beatitudes of the gospels, the word connotes divine favor at the final judgment, which Jesus bestows proleptically (Matt 5:3-12// Luke 6:20-23).[65] Here, however, the term signifies the good fortune that has come upon a person who refrains from judging and despising another person. The person is "blessed" because, not worrying about eating foods or abstaining from them, he need not judge or condemn himself.

On the other hand, the person who has doubts (or continues to make distinctions between foods) is in a sorry state if he eats foods that he considers unclean. In fact, that person is in the state of having been "condemned," for Paul's use of the perfect tense (κατακέκριται, literally "has been condemned") means that the judgment has taken place already (not simply anticipated at the last judgment). The person does not act from faith (or conviction), but against it. And to act against one's conviction is sin, i.e., sinful behavior.[66]

The view that to act contrary to convictions is sinful behavior appears at first sight not in keeping with the view of Paul, for whom sin is first of all a

---

63. Cf. V. Furnish, *The Love Command in the New Testament*, 118.

64. BDAG 820 (πίστις, 2, d, ε); cf. similar proposals by H. Schlier, *Römer*, 418; C. Cranfield, *Romans*, 697; J. Fitzmyer, *Romans*, 698; K. Haacker, *Römer*, 280, 290; D. Moo, *Romans*, 861; E. Lohse, *Römer*, 381; L. Keck, *Romans*, 347; V. Gäckel, *Die Starken und die Schwachen in Korinth und Rom*, 422-24. Cf. also the NRSV: "The faith that you have, have as your own conviction before God."

65. BDAG 611 (μακάριος, 2, a).

66. Cf. Jas 4:17: "Whoever knows what is right to do and fails to do it, for him it is sin."

power and can be described existentially as alienation from God.[67] Sin as activity is a matter of disobedience against the express will of God and obedience to one's passions (Rom 5:12-21; 6:12-14; 7:15-17). But here Paul says that acting against one's convictions is sin, as though convictions are a true measure of God's will. One can rightly ask whether convictions are an adequate measure.

That, however, is not the only interpretive path to pursue. More likely, Paul is saying that acting against one's convictions can be so severe that it destroys a person's relationship to God. A sense of guilt can drive one away from intimate communion with God. That would be the case especially for the person known to be "weak in faith," the one who abstains in honor of the Lord (14:6), believing that abstaining from "unclean" foods is necessary, and considering any compromise to be a breach of faith. "That person transgresses what is deemed by him or her to be the valid will of God, and this is precisely what constitutes sin."[68]

BIBLIOGRAPHY

Aland, Kurt. "Der Schluss und die ursprüngliche Gestalt des Römerbriefes." In his *Neutestamentliche Entwürfe*, 284-301. TBü 63. Munich: Chr. Kaiser Verlag, 1979.

Donfried, Karl P. "The Kingdom of God in Paul." In *The Kingdom of God in Twentieth-Century Interpretation*, 175-90. Ed. W. Willis. Peabody: Hendrickson Publishers, 1987.

Furnish, Victor Paul. *The Love Command in the New Testament*. Nashville: Abingdon Press, 1972.

Gäckel, Volker. *Die Starken und die Schwachen in Korinth und in Rom: Zur Herkunft und Funktion der Antithese in 1 Kor 8,1–11,1 und Röm 14,1–15,13*. WUNT 2/200. Tübingen: Mohr Siebeck, 2004.

Gagnon, Robert A. J. "The Meaning of ὑμῶν τὸ ἀγαθόν in Romans 14:16." *JBL* 117 (1998): 675-89.

Haufe, Günter. "Reich Gottes bei Paulus und in der Jesustradition." *NTS* 31 (1985): 467-72.

Holloway, Paul A. "The Enthymeme as an Element of Style in Paul." *JBL* 120 (2001): 329-39.

Hübner, Hans. "Unclean and Clean: New Testament." *ABD* 6:741-45.

Johnston, George. "'Kingdom of God' Sayings in Paul's Letters." In *From Jesus to Paul: Studies in Honour of Francis Wright Beare*, 143-56. Ed. Peter Richardson and John C. Hurd. Waterloo: Wilfrid Laurier University, 1984.

Kohlenberger, John R., et al., *The Greek-English Concordance to the New Testament*. Grand Rapids: Zondervan, 1997.

Lewis, Jack P. "'The Kingdom of God . . . Is Righteousness, Peace, and Joy in the Holy Spirit' (Rom 14:17): A Survey of Interpretation." *ResQ* 40 (1998): 53-68.

---

67. E. P. Sanders, "Sin, Sinners: New Testament," *ABD* 6:43-46.
68. P. Stuhlmacher, *Romans*, 229.

Neirynck, Frans. "Paul and the Sayings of Jesus." In *L'Apôtre Paul: Personnalité, style et conception du ministère*, 265-321. Ed. Albert Vanhoye. Leuven: Uitgeverij Peeters, 1986.

Shogren, Gary S. "'Is the Kingdom of God about Eating and Drinking or Isn't It?' (Romans 14:17)." *NovT* 42 (2000): 238-56.

Smit, Peter-Ben. "A Symposium in Romans 14:7? A Note on Paul's Terminology." *NovT* 49 (2007): 40-53.

Wengst, Klaus. *Christologische Formeln und Lieder des Urchristentums*. SNT 7. Gütersloh: Gütersloher Verlagshaus Gerd Mohn, 1972.

8.3. Harmony in Christ, 15:1-6

1*But we who are strong ought to accommodate the failings of the weak, and not to please ourselves.* 2*Let each of us please his neighbor for his good to build him up.* 3*For even Christ did not please himself but, as it is written:*

"The insults of those who insult you have fallen on me."

4*For whatever was written formerly was written for our instruction, in order that through perseverance and through the encouragement of the scriptures we might have hope.* 5*May the God of perseverance and encouragement grant you to be of the same mind with one another in accord with Christ Jesus,* 6*in order that together with one voice you may glorify the God and Father of our Lord Jesus Christ.*

Notes on the Text and Translation

15:2 Some important witnesses (including D¹ [first corrector], F, G, and Old Latin) support the reading "let each of you" (ὑμῶν), but the superior witnesses (including ℵ, A, B, D* [original reading], and many others) have "each of us" (ἡμῶν). The latter is to be preferred. The alternative appears to be an attempt to make Paul an exhorter of others, not one to include himself.

15:6 The word ὁμοθυμαδόν is translated variously as "with one mind" (KJV), "with one accord" (ASV), "together" (RSV, NRSV, and NET), and "with one heart" (NIV). It is a compound word made up of ὁμο ("same") and θυμός ("passion," "desire," "longing"), so "to be of the same mind" or "of the same persuasion." The entry in BDAG has: "with one mind/purpose/impulse," "unanimously," or (in a weakened sense) "together."[69] In 15:6 the word is followed immediately by "with one voice," which also stresses unity. In order to avoid using "one" in two adverbial phrases in succession (e.g., "with one purpose, with one voice"), the reading of the NRSV ("together") seems apt ("together with one voice").

69. BDAG 706 (ὁμοθυμαδόν).

General Comment

In the previous chapter Paul describes the issues between the weak and the strong. Those issues are no longer discussed in the rest of the section (15:7-13). In 15:1-6 Paul begins to use a different tone and a different approach. His tone is softer, and he is less direct in addressing the reader than he was in previous paragraphs. He turns their attention to look upon Jesus as a model of behavior.

As elsewhere in his letters (see below), Paul speaks of mutual encouragement and building one another up within the community of believers. As Christ did not look to his own interests, but served those of others, so believers are to seek the good of others.

Paul identifies himself as among the "strong" but does not take up the cause of the strong over against the one who is "weak." Since all are one in Christ, all can be of the same mind concerning essentials and glorify God with one voice.

Detailed Comment

15:1-2 Paul describes himself as one of "the strong," i.e., those who are strong in faith (i.e., conviction), and he implies with the first person plural ("we") that there are others who can be counted among the strong as well. By contrast, when he mentions "the weak in faith," he consistently uses the singular pronoun or verb form (14:1-3, 5-6, 10, 14-15, 20-21, 24). As indicated previously, it is therefore unlikely that Paul addresses groups of actual persons with the terms "weak in faith" and "the strong." Rhetorically, all readers of the letter would normally think of themselves as being addressed as "the strong." (For additional discussion on this and related matters, see "8. The Weak and the Strong.")

The one who is strong ought to accommodate the failings of the weak. The verb used by Paul (βαστάζω) is usually translated "bear" (KJV), "bear with" (RSV, NIV, NET), or "put up with" (NRSV), so one is to "bear with" or "put up with the failings of the weak." Other translations of the verb have been suggested, such as "endure,"[70] "tolerate,"[71] "support,"[72] and "carry."[73] These are all plausible renderings of the verb.[74] But since that which is to be borne is not per-

---

70. C. K. Barrett, *Romans*, 247.

71. L. Morris, *Romans*, 497.

72. J. Dunn, *Romans*, 835; N. T. Wright, *NIB (Romans)*, 10:745. Cf. "help" in T. Schreiner, *Romans*, 746.

73. C. Cranfield, *Romans*, 730; B. Byrne, *Romans*, 424; R. Jewett, *Romans*, 877. Cf. the use of the verb "tragen" by U. Wilckens, *Römer*, 3:100-101; E. Lohse, *Römer*, 382-83.

74. BDAG 171 (βαστάζω); cf. LSJ 310 (βαστάζω).

sons, but the failings of persons, it would seem that one does not simply "tolerate" or "endure" them, nor does one only "support" or "carry" them. One accommodates them, i.e., makes room for them, within the Christian community.[75] That opens the door for respect for the one with whom one disagrees. It is also consistent with the concept of "walking in love" (14:15), pursuing peace, and building one another up within the community (14:19).

The exhortation not to please oneself but to please one's neighbor, seeking that person's good, and building that person up picks up a cluster of familiar terms in Paul's paraenesis. To be sure, pleasing others can be thought of negatively, as in flattery (Gal 1:10; 1 Thess 2:4), but here it is for the neighbor's "good." It is also for that person's edification ("to build him up"). Once again, for Paul, mutual edification is a prime value within the Christian community (cf. 14:19; 1 Cor 10:23; 14:3, 26; 2 Cor 12:19; 1 Thess 5:11).

15:3 The model of behavior is Christ. Using the same verb as used twice in 15:1-2 (ἀρέσκω, "to please"), Paul says that "Christ did not please himself." As an illustration of that, Paul quotes a portion of Psalm 69:9 (LXX 68:10), replicating the wording of the LXX exactly: οἱ ὀνειδισμοὶ τῶν ὀνειδιζόντων σε ἐπέπεσαν ἐπ' ἐμέ ("The insults of those who insult you have fallen on me").

Within its OT context the psalm is addressed to God. The one who prays the psalm there refers to God as the one to whom insults are normally directed, but now they are directed at the psalmist, who evidently is receiving abuse unjustly from enemies and perhaps even from his own people. It is possible that Paul knew the portion that he quotes as a reference to the suffering and death of Jesus.[76] In any case, the apostle quotes from the psalm as though it is Jesus who is speaking. The abuse which God has received from disobedient humanity has now fallen upon Jesus himself (cf. Mark 15:32).

Paul does not, however, use the line from the psalm here for an explicitly Christological purpose or to speak of the atoning effects of Jesus' suffering and death. He uses it rather to illustrate how Jesus "did not please himself" and bore with the failings of others, which is an example for others to follow. The use of the imagery is similar to that employed in connection with the Philippian hymn (Phil 2:6-11). There Paul calls upon his readers to have the same attitude toward one another that Jesus did, giving himself through suffering and death for the good of others (cf. 2 Cor 8:9).

15:4 It has been suggested that this verse is a post-Pauline interpolation into the letter. The basis for that suggestion is that the verse is exceedingly

---

75. That would mean going even further than the admonition in Gal 6:2 to "bear one another's burdens," where Paul uses the same verb (βαστάζω).

76. There seems to be an allusion to Heb 11:26, referring to the suffering of Moses on behalf of (the anticipated) Christ. The first line of the verse (not repeated by Paul) is quoted in John 2:17.

sweeping ("whatever was written"), whereas Paul's usual way of quoting the OT is more limited to the matter at hand.[77] But the suggestion is not finally convincing. Granted its sweep, the wording is otherwise comparable to what Paul has written at 4:23-24 and elsewhere (1 Cor 9:10; 10:11). Moreover, the verse continues the discussion at hand. Paul has said that each person should seek to please others (Rom 15:2). He quotes from the psalm, impersonating Jesus as a model of one who sought not to please himself, but who suffered even when he was maligned (15:3). And that utterance, Paul says, "was written for our instruction" (15:4). In other words, the words of Jesus in the psalm are a model for believers. There in "the scriptures" believers in Christ have encouragement, since bearing with the failures of others, pleasing them, and building them up is doing the will of God, as modeled by Jesus himself.

The "encouragement of the scriptures" leads to "hope" (ἐλπίς). Here, as so many times in his writings, Paul speaks of the hope that the believer has in the redemptive work of God in Christ. Being united with Christ in faith and baptism, and encouraged by the Scriptures in perseverance, one can live in hope for final salvation.

15:5-6 The two verses make up one long sentence. The main verb δῴη ("may [God] grant") is an aorist optative from the verb δίδωμι ("to give," "grant"), which grammatically expresses a wish.[78] In this particular case Paul expresses what is conventionally called a "prayer wish."[79] But the words also have the sound of a liturgical line from a blessing or benediction.[80] Since that is so, the verses, when read aloud to a gathered community, convey an apostolic blessing from Paul to those who hear him. The apostle is heard as saying that he is calling upon God to grant that for which he prays.

The expression "the God of perseverance and encouragement," based on words in the previous verse, is rendered in the NIV as "the God who gives en-

---

77. L. Keck, "Romans 15:4," 129; cf. idem, *Romans,* 351. For a response, cf. R. Hays, "Christ Prays the Psalms," 122-36. J. Ziesler, *Romans,* 338, speaks of the verse as an "explanatory digression" by which Paul justifies his use of the psalm.

78. BDF 194 (§384).

79. C. Cranfield, *Romans,* 736; E. Käsemann, *Romans,* 383; J. Dunn, *Romans,* 840; G. Wiles, "Two Related Wish-Prayers — Rom 15:5f and 15:13," 79; B. Byrne, *Romans,* 427; P. Stuhlmacher, *Romans,* 231; D. Moo, *Romans,* 871. "Gebetswunsch" is the term used by O. Michel, *Römer,* 357; E. Lohse, *Römer,* 385; and V. Gäckel, *Die Starken und die Schwachen in Korinth und in Rom,* 426. R. Jewett, *Romans,* 883, prefers to call it a "homiletic benediction."

80. The ambiguity is shown in the commentaries by U. Wilckens, *Römer,* 3:102 ("Fürbitte-Segen," intercession-blessing) and P. Stuhlmacher, *Romans,* 229 and 231. At the former Stuhlmacher calls the verses a "benediction," and at the latter a "prayerful wish." Cf. also R. Jewett, "The Form and Function of the Homiletic Benediction," 18-34, who points out that benedictions are often expressed by the use of δέ and an optative verb; cf. also idem, *Romans,* 883. But the optative can also be used in the language of prayer; cf. E. Käsemann, *Romans,* 383.

durance and encouragement." By so doing the NIV renders the Greek genitive as a genitive of origin, so that already in this phrase "endurance and encouragement" are said to be given by God to believers.[81] More likely, however, these are to be understood primarily as genitives that speak of the character of God, and it is common to do so in the language of praise.[82] Since God is indeed "the God of perseverance and encouragement," he is able and willing to grant the believers at Rome "to be of the same mind with one another in accord with Christ Jesus."

Paul's prayer and expectation is that believers may all live in harmony with one another and glorify God "together . . . with one voice." The word ὁμοθυμαδόν (translated "together" here) "denotes the inner unity of a group of people engaged in an externally similar action."[83] Within the OT (LXX) the classic text that uses the term is Exodus 19:8. There the people of Israel have reached the wilderness of Sinai, and they respond to the words of Moses. Moses had already gone up the mountain, and God had told him that if the people of Israel obeyed his voice, they would be God's own possession from among all the peoples of the earth. Moses reports this to the people and, "The people all answered as one (ὁμοθυμαδόν): 'Everything that the LORD has spoken we will do.'" Within the deuterocanonical/apocryphal books of the OT it is used particularly in reference to the people at worship, praying together with one voice (Jdt 9:12; 7:29; 13:17) and praising God together (Wis 10:20). The word is used in Acts to portray the unity of the earliest church in fellowship (1:14), common meals (2:46), and prayer (4:24). Paul, therefore, uses an expression that has liturgical and communal associations within the long sweep of the history of the people of God. It recalls the origins of both Israel and the church where the people are together in their commitment to God and then, with his coming, to his Christ.

The question can hardly be evaded concerning the kind and degree of oneness of mind and heart that Paul speaks of in these verses. On the basis of what has been said from 14:1 through to this point, what emerges is that the oneness spoken of is twofold. First, it is oneness in commitment to Christ. Like spokes in a wheel, the closer the members are to the center, the closer they are to one another. Second, it is oneness expressed in behavior. Differences and disagreements are inevitable. But these can and must be accommodated, leading to mutual respect and, from there, mutual upbuilding in love and peace. That way of being in the world comes about not simply by human effort, but with the help of God.

81. That is also the interpretation of E. Käsemann, *Romans*, 383; U. Wilckens, *Römer*, 3:102; J. Fitzmyer, *Romans*, 703; B. Byrne, *Romans*, 427; P. Stuhlmacher, *Romans*, 231; E. Lohse, *Römer*, 385.

82. O. Michel, *Römer*, 357; G. Delling, "Die Bezeichnung 'Gott des Friedens,'" 82-83; C. Cranfield, *Romans*, 736.

83. Hans W. Heidland, "ὁμοθυμαδόν," *TDNT* 5:185.

BIBLIOGRAPHY

Delling, Gerhard. "Die Bezeichnung 'Gott des Friedens' und ähnliche Wendungen in den Paulusbriefen." In *Jesus und Paulus: Festschrift für Werner Georg Kümmel zum 70. Geburtstag*, 76-84. Ed. E. Earle Ellis and Erich Grässer. Göttingen: Vandenhoeck & Ruprecht, 1975.

Fredrickson, David E. "A Piece of Scripture on Part of the Bible: Listening to Romans 15:1-6." *WW* 26 (2006): 412-18.

Gäckel, Volker. *Die Starken und die Schwachen in Korinth und in Rom: Zur Herkunft und Funktion der Antithese in 1 Kor 8,1–11,1 und Röm 14,1–15,13.* WUNT 2/200. Tübingen: Mohr Siebeck, 2004.

Hays, Richard B. "Christ Prays the Psalms: Paul's Use of an Early Christian Exegetical Convention." In *The Future of Christology: Essays in Honor of Leander E. Keck*, 122-36. Ed. Abraham J. Malherbe and Wayne A. Meeks. Minneapolis: Fortress Press, 1993; reprinted as "Christ Prays the Psalms: Israel's Psalter as Matrix of Early Christology," in his *The Conversion of the Imagination: Paul as an Interpreter of Israel's Scripture*, 101-18. Grand Rapids: Wm. B. Eerdmans, 2005.

Jewett, Robert. "The Form and Function of the Homiletic Benediction." *ATR* 51 (1969): 18-34.

Keck, Leander E. "Romans 15:4 — An Interpolation?" In *Faith and History: Essays in Honor of Paul W. Meyer*, 125-36. Ed. John T. Carroll et al. Atlanta: Scholars Press, 1991.

Schweizer, Eduard. "Röm 15,1-13." In his *Neues Testament und heutige Verkündigung*, 81-86. BSt 56. Neukirchen-Vluyn: Neukirchener Verlag, 1969.

Wiles, Gordon P. "Two Related Wish-Prayers — Rom 15:5f and 15:13." In his *Paul's Intercessory Prayers: The Significance of the Intercessory Prayer Passages in the Letters of Saint Paul*, 77-90. SNTSMS 24. Cambridge: Cambridge University Press, 1974.

8.4. Mutual Acceptance Based on Christ's Welcome, 15:7-13

7 *Welcome one another, therefore, just as Christ has welcomed you, for the glory of God.* 8*For I declare that Christ has become a servant of the circumcised on behalf of God's truth in order to confirm the promises made to the patriarchs,* 9*and that the Gentiles might glorify God for his mercy. As it is written,*

> *"Therefore I will confess you among the Gentiles, and I will sing praises to your name."*

10*And again it says,*

> *"Rejoice, O Gentiles, with his people";*

11*and again,*

> *"Praise the Lord, all Gentiles, and let all the peoples praise him";*

12*and again Isaiah says,*

> *"The root of Jesse shall come, even he who rises to rule the nations;*
> *in him shall the Gentiles hope."*

13*May the God of hope fill you with all joy and peace in believing, in order that you may abound in hope by the power of the Holy Spirit.*

Notes on the Text and Translation

15:7 Several ancient witnesses (including B, D [original hand], and P) have ἡμᾶς ("us") rather than ὑμᾶς (plural, "you"). That is followed by earlier versions of the Nestle-Aland Greek NT (25th ed.), which, along with the KJV, have "us." The result is "just as Christ has welcomed us." But other major witnesses have ὑμᾶς (including ℵ, A, C, and others), as does the 27th edition of the Nestle-Aland Greek text. Contextually that is more fitting, paralleling other second person plural designations.

15:12 Modern versions typically translate the words ἄρχειν ἐθνῶν as "to rule the Gentiles" (KJV, RSV, NRSV). The exception is the NIV, which has "to rule over the nations." Contextually "nations" is more appropriate at this place for ἔθνη in spite of the emphasis on "Gentiles" in the second half of the verse (and 15:9-11).

General Comment

Paul resumes the exhortation to welcome others that he began at 14:1, the very beginning of the section on "the weak and the strong." He uses the same verb form (προσλαμβάνεσθε), which is an imperative in second person plural. At 14:1 the welcome was to be extended to the person who is "weak in faith." Now the welcome is generalized; it is to be extended to all. Further, Paul expresses the basis for mutual welcome among believers. It is expected because Christ has already welcomed (προσελάβετο) all believers first. Whoever has been welcomed by Christ should be welcomed by all.

In its first-century setting everywhere the Christian movement was made up of persons of different opinions. What is essential to the Christian life, and what is a matter of indifference? Paul's way of reasoning is that the Christian life is, first of all, a life given to serve others in love and upbuilding (15:15, 19). Moreover, one is to regard the other no longer "from a human point of view" (2 Cor 5:16) but as one for whom Christ has died (14:15) and a new creation (2 Cor 5:17). That means putting away secular standards of judgment and looking at others through the prism of divine love. One should not regard human opinions among persons in Christ as positions that are walled in by barriers that reach to heaven.

Detailed Comment

15:7 Believers in Christ, including the readers of the letter, are to welcome one another, just as Christ has welcomed them. That much of the opening sentence is clear. But in terms of the syntax of the rest of the sentence, it is possible to construe what Paul says in either of two ways: (1) Christ's act of welcoming the readers was "for the glory of God" or (2) the readers' act of welcoming one another is to be done "for the glory of God." Although the first of these interpretations has been favored by some interpreters,[84] it can be set aside. The phrase should more likely be connected to the act of believers in welcoming one another.[85] Extending a welcome to one another within the community of faith is an act that in itself glorifies God. Within the prior verse (15:6) Paul has already called upon his readers to glorify God together with one voice. Welcoming one another, as Christ has welcomed all, is an outward, bodily expression of the same.[86]

15:8-9 Paul begins with the words, "for I declare,"[87] which anticipates a solemn pronouncement (cf. Rom 12:3). The translation "for I tell you" in various modern English versions (RSV, NIV, NET, NRSV, ESV) is too weak, and the plural pronoun "you" (ὑμῖν) is not in the Greek text. His declaration is about Christ, stressing that in his own life Christ confirmed the promises made by God to the patriarchs, thereby also establishing the truthfulness of God (ὑπὲρ ἀληθείας θεοῦ; cf. 3:3-4, 7 [ἡ ἀλήθεια τοῦ θεοῦ]); God is a God who keeps his promises (9:4; 11:28-29).[88] In speaking of Christ as servant of the circumcised, Paul emphasizes once again the priority of the Jewish people in the history of salvation for the sake of the world (cf. 1:16; 2:10; 3:1-4; 9:4-5; 11:13-24). The use of

---

84. W. Sanday and A. Headlam, *Romans*, 397; O. Michel, *Römer*, 358; J. Murray, *Romans*, 2:204; E. Käsemann, *Romans*, 385.

85. C. Cranfield, *Romans*, 739; U. Wilckens, *Römer*, 3:105; P. Stuhlmacher, *Romans*, 232; D. Moo, *Romans*, 873-74; E. Lohse, *Römer*, 387; L. Keck, *Romans*, 354; R. Jewett, *Romans*, 889; V. Gäckel, *Die Starken und die Schwachen in Korinth und in Rom*, 395-97, 427.

86. Some prefer to have the phrase connected to the welcome extended by both Christ and believers, including C. K. Barrett, *Romans*, 248; J. Dunn, *Romans*, 846; J. Fitzmyer, *Romans*, 706.

87. Cf. BDAG 590 (λέγω, 2, e): "*maintain, declare, proclaim* as teaching, w. direct discourse foll.," citing Rom 15:8; 1 Cor 15:12; Gal 4:1 within the Pauline letters.

88. References to the promises to the patriarchs are also made at Mic 7:20; Sir 36:20; Acts 3:25.

the term "servant" (διάκονος) in reference to Christ raises the question whether Paul is not only recalling the tradition of Jesus as one who came to serve and to give his life (Mark 10:45), which is surely plausible, but also whether he is using a Christological title related to the "suffering servant" of Isaiah. Some interpreters have concluded that that is so.[89] That view, however, is difficult to sustain.[90] The word used for the "servant" in LXX Isaiah is παῖς (42:1; 49:6; 52:13), not διάκονος. Furthermore, the verb in Paul's declaration (γεγενῆσθαι) is in the perfect tense, implying duration. That indicates that Christ not only became a servant of the Jewish people in his earthly life, but continues to be such in his heavenly reign. His role of servant was not limited to his passion and death. The fact that he continues to be a servant of the Jewish people is confirmed by his calling of Jewish persons, like Paul himself, into the company of believers (11:1; 2 Cor 11:22-23; Phil 3:4-8).

The promises to the patriarchs include, above all, the promise to Abraham that he would be the "father of the circumcised" (πατὴρ περιτομῆς) with many descendants (Rom 4:12-13; Gen 12:2; 13:16; 15:5; 18:18; 22:16-18). It is among those descendants that Christ carried on his earthly ministry (cf. Matt 15:24). For that reason Paul can say that Christ became "servant of the circumcised" (διάκονος περιτομῆς), and as exalted Lord he remains their servant.

The promise that Abraham would be father of the circumcised, however, does not exhaust the promises. For it was promised to him also that he would be the father of all who believe (Rom 4:11, 16-18). That promise has been realized in the glorifying of God for his mercy among the Gentiles who have come to faith in Jesus Christ. Paul says, in effect, that Christ's having become a servant of the Jews has had twin purposes:[91] (1) to confirm the promises made to the patriarchs and (2) to bring about the praise of God for his mercy among the Gentiles.[92] On the latter point, it is purely by the mercy of God that the gospel has been extended to the Gentiles (11:31-32).

Admittedly the Greek syntax of 15:8-9a is difficult to unravel, and any attempt will have consequences for translation and interpretation.[93] There are those, for example, who see three purposes expressed in the passage,[94] and

---

89. O. Michel, Römer, 359; C. Cranfield, Romans, 741.

90. Cf. B. Schaller, "Christus, 'der Diener der Beschneidung,'" 268-69.

91. That two purposes are in view (and in parallel), cf. J. Dunn, Romans, 847-48; J. Ziesler, Romans, 339; P. Stuhlmacher, Romans, 232-33; R. Jewett, Romans, 892.

92. In order to make the latter clearly a purpose clause, the RSV and NRSV read: "and in order that the Gentiles might glorify God for his mercy."

93. Six different interpretations of 15:9a are provided and discussed by C. Cranfield, Romans, 742-44. He considers the clause to be directly dependent on "I declare," so "I declare that . . . but that the Gentiles are glorifying."

94. J. Fitzmyer, Romans, 706.

those who assume that there are ellipses that, once filled in, make the passage read better.[95] But in spite of the difficulties, it is not impossible to read the passage as having a twofold purpose. Paul often expresses purpose with εἰς τό followed by an infinitive. Fifteen such expressions appear in Romans alone.[96] In the present verse the two purposes are expressed by Paul's use of εἰς τό followed by the two infinitives βεβαιῶσαι ("to confirm") and δοξάσαι ("to glorify").

Paul cites Psalm 18:49 (LXX 17:50; cf. 2 Sam 22:50), quoting it exactly as it is in the LXX, except that he leaves out the word "Lord" (κύριε, a vocative required in the psalm but not in Paul's case). It has been suggested that, for Paul, the person speaking the verse from the psalm ("Therefore I will confess you among the Gentiles, and I will sing praises to your name") impersonates Paul himself,[97] David,[98] or even Jesus (speaking through a psalm, as at 15:3).[99] If the latter is to be accepted, that would account for Paul's omission of the address, "Lord." But it should be noticed that the term "Gentiles," spoken by Paul in 15:9a, is repeated in each of the four OT quotations that follow. It is the catchword that binds the verses together and accounts for their presence. In light of that, it is doubtful that one can be so highly specific in identifying the one who is speaking as either Paul, David, or Jesus. It is better to interpret the verse more broadly, and that is that, for Paul, the Scriptures are being fulfilled. He introduces the quotation from the psalm with the words "as it is written." That is to say, says Paul, that the Gentile mission is being fulfilled in accord with what is prefigured in the psalm.[100] The text of the psalm speaks immediately to the present situation.

15:10-12   The next three OT quotations serve to underscore the advent of the mission to the Gentiles (or to the Gentile "nations") in the days of the Messiah. For more on that theme in general, see the exegesis of the next section of the letter (15:14-21). The passages quoted are from major sections and books of the OT: the Torah, the Psalms, and the prophets. The first of the quotations (Deut 32:43 at 15:10) corresponds to the wording of the LXX, in which the verse is considerably longer than it is in the Hebrew OT (and English versions). The second (Ps 117:1; LXX Ps 116:1 at 15:11) differs considerably. The LXX reads:

95. J. Wagner, "The Christ, Servant of Jew and Gentile," 481-82; L. Keck, *Romans*, 355-56.

96. Rom 1:11, 20; 3:25; 4:11, 16, 18; 6:12; 7:4, 5; 8:29; 11:11; 12:2, 3; 15:8, 13.

97. E. Käsemann, *Romans*, 386; G. Sass, "Röm 15,7-13," 524; R. Jewett, *Romans*, 894.

98. J. Dunn, *Romans*, 849.

99. W. Sanday and A. Headlam, *Romans*, 398; C. Cranfield, *Romans*, 745-46; L. Keck, "Christology, Soteriology, and the Praise of God," 93; idem, *Romans*, 357; R. Hays, "Christ Prays the Psalms," 136; J. Wagner, "The Christ, Servant of Jew and Gentile," 475-76; D. Moo, *Romans*, 878-79.

100. Cf. B. Frid, "Jesaja und Paulus in Röm 15:12," 237-41; E. Lohse, *Römer*, 388; V. Gäckel, *Die Starken und die Schwachen in Korinth und in Rom*, 430.

αἰνεῖτε τὸν κύριον πάντα τὰ ἔθνη ἐπαινέσατε αὐτὸν πάντες οἱ λαοί ("Praise the Lord, all you Gentiles; all you peoples, praise him"). The third quotation (Isa 11:10 at 15:12) is almost identical to the reading in the LXX, except that the latter contains "on that day" (ἐν τῇ ἡμέρᾳ ἐκείνῃ) as well, following the Hebrew OT (MT).[101] The "root of Jesse" (i.e., a descendant of Jesse, David's father) is a metaphor for the Messiah (cf. Sir 47:22; Rev 5:5; 22:16), and he shall rule the nations. "From the pitiable remnant of the house of Jesse there will come forth, as from the remaining stump of a tree, a new shoot which will establish the coming kingdom of peace and righteousness."[102]

The four OT texts quoted anticipate universal praise of the God of Israel by the Gentiles, or the (Gentile) nations (15:12), in concert with the Jewish people as an eschatological hope. That time has now come, and Paul goes on to speak of it more fully in 15:14-21.

15:13 Paul closes this lengthy section (14:1–15:13) with a flourish. What he says recalls the formulation of 15:5-6, where he used an aorist optative verb (δῴη, "may [God] grant") to express a prayer wish that serves as a blessing or benediction. Here the main verb, πληρώσαι ("may [God] fill you"), is an aorist optative — from the verb, πληρόω ("to fill") — which expresses likewise both a prayer wish and a blessing. For more on the usage, see the exegesis of 15:5-6. Paul conveys an apostolic blessing to his readers, letting them know that he is calling upon God to grant that for which he prays.

It has been suggested that 15:13 marks the end of the body of the letter.[103] But that cannot be, for the body of a Pauline letter is customarily followed by greetings and a doxology and/or benediction.[104] More to the point is that with 15:13 Paul not only brings the discussion of the weak and the strong to an end but affirms once again, as from the beginning of the letter, the unity of Jew and Gentile in Christ.[105] Paul goes on in 15:14-32 to speak of his plans. That section can be considered a portion of the body itself, since within it Paul is providing important information about himself, including previous activities and future plans.

---

101. B. Frid, "Jesiah und Paulus in Röm 15:12," 237-41. According to S.-L. Shum, *Paul's Use of Isaiah in Romans*, 253, the omission of the prepositional phrase may be due to Paul's conviction that the "day" has already arrived. But the phrase stands at the beginning of the sentence, and its absence can more likely be accounted for because it is superfluous for Paul's context.

102. Christian Maurer, "ῥίζα," *TDNT* 6:986; cf. M. Novenson, "The Jewish Messiahs, the Pauline Christ, and the Gentile Question," 357-73.

103. D. Starnitzke, *Die Struktur paulinischen Denkens im Römerbrief*, 21.

104. Cf. H.-J. Klauck, *Ancient Letters and the New Testament*, 24-25, 302.

105. B. Schaller, "Christus, 'der Diener der Beschneidung,'" 261-85.

BIBLIOGRAPHY

Black, Matthew. "The Christological Use of the Old Testament in the New Testament." *NTS* 18 (1971-72): 1-14.

Frid, Bo. "Jesaja und Paulus in Röm 15:12." *BZ* 27 (1983): 237-41.

Gäckel, Volker. *Die Starken und die Schwachen in Korinth und in Rom: Zur Herkunft und Funktion der Antithese in 1 Kor 8,1–11,1 und Röm 14,1–15,13.* WUNT 2/200. Tübingen: Mohr Siebeck, 2004.

Grieb, A. Katherine. "The Root of Jesse Who Rises to Rule the Gentiles: Paul's Use of the Story of Jesus in Romans 15:7-13." *Proceedings: Eastern Great Lakes and Midwest Biblical Societies* 13 (1993): 71-88.

Hafemann, Scott. "Eschatology and Ethics: The Future of Israel and the Nations in Romans 15:1-13." *TynB* 51 (2000): 161-92.

Hays, Richard B. "Christ Prays the Psalms: Paul's Use of an Early Christian Exegetical Convention." In *The Future of Christology: Essays in Honor of Leander E. Keck,* 122-36. Ed. Abraham J. Malherbe and Wayne A. Meeks. Minneapolis: Fortress Press, 1993.

Keck, Leander E. "Christology, Soteriology, and the Praise of God in Romans (15:7-13)." In *The Conversation Continues: Studies in Paul and John: In Honor of J. Louis Martyn,* 85-97. Ed. Robert T. Fortna and Beverly R. Gaventa. Nashville: Abingdon Press, 1990.

Klauck, Hans-Josef. *Ancient Letters and the New Testament: A Guide to Context and Exegesis.* Waco: Baylor University Press, 2006.

Lambrecht, Jan. "The Confirmation of the Promises: A Critical Note on Romans 15,8." *ETL* 78 (2002): 156-60.

———. "Syntactical and Logical Remarks on Romans 15:8-9a." *NovT* 42 (2000): 257-61.

Novenson, Matthew V. "The Jewish Messiahs, the Pauline Christ, and the Gentile Question." *JBL* 128 (2009): 357-73.

Sass, Gerhard. "Röm 15,7-13 als Summe des Römerbriefs gelesen." *EvT* 53 (1993): 510-27.

Schaller, Berndt. "Christus, 'der Diener der Beschneidung . . . , auf ihn werden die Völker hoffen': Zu Charakter und Funktion der Schriftzitate in Röm 15,7-13." In *Das Gesetz im frühen Judentum und im Neuen Testament: Festschrift für Christoph Burchard zum 75. Geburtstag,* 261-85. Ed. Dieter Sänger and Matthias Konradt. NTOA 57. Göttingen: Vandenhoeck & Ruprecht, 2006.

Shum, Shiu-Lun. *Paul's Use of Isaiah in Romans: A Comparative Study of Paul's Letter to the Romans and the Sibylline and Qumran Sectarian Texts.* WUNT 2/156. Tübingen: J. C. B. Mohr (Paul Siebeck), 2002.

Söding, Thomas. "Verheissung und Erfüllung im Lichte paulinischer Theologie." *NTS* 47 (2001): 146-70.

Starnitzke, Dierk. *Die Struktur paulinischen Denkens im Römerbrief: Eine linguistische-logische Untersuchung.* BWANT 8/3. Stuttgart: W. Kohlhammer, 2004.

Wagner, J. Ross. "The Christ, Servant of Jew and Gentile: A Fresh Approach to Romans 15:8-9." *JBL* 116 (1997): 473-85.

Wiles, Gordon P. "Two Related Wish-Prayers — Rom 15:5f and 15:13." In his *Paul's Intercessory Prayers: The Significance of the Intercessory Prayer Passages in the Letters of Saint Paul,* 77-90. Cambridge: Cambridge University Press, 1974.

CHAPTER 9

Paul's Plans, 15:14-33

Paul makes an abrupt shift at 15:14. He has just completed a long (36-verse) section on "the weak and the strong," the closing section of what is typically called the "hortatory" portion of the letter (12:1–15:13), in which Paul uses a hortatory mode of speech to sketch out the shape of the Christian life.

The section that follows here is not the closing of the entire letter,[1] since Paul goes on to speak of various matters of importance concerning his work as it relates to the Roman community, but it has been called a "body-closing unit" that appears also in other letters of Paul, as well as in other Greco-Roman letters. Typically the unit contains three elements, in which the author (1) expresses the motivation for writing the letter; (2) affirms confidence in an appropriate response from his readers; and (3) discloses his intention or hope to pay a visit himself or to send an emissary.[2]

Within the section Paul accomplishes these things in elaborate detail. He expresses once again (as in 1:8-15) his high regard for the believers in Rome, tells of his principles and strategies for mission, repeats his desire to arrive in due course at Rome (as in 1:10-15), projects his immediate plans to go to Jerusalem with a collection that he has raised in his churches, and announces for the first time his intention to go on from Rome to Spain, making Rome not a final destination so much as a base for further mission.

Less helpfully, instead of designating Romans 15:14-33 a "body-closing unit," it has been called an instance of "apostolic parousia," in which Paul dis-

---

1. Not all interpreters agree on this; they say that the letter's "closing" or "conclusion" begins at 15:14. Among them are C. Cranfield, *Romans*, 29, 749; J. Dunn, *Romans*, 855; D. Moo, *Romans*, 884; H.-J. Klauck, *Ancient Letters and the New Testament*, 302; and R. Jewett, *Romans*, ix, 903, who calls 15:14–16:24 the letter's *peroration* (conclusion).

2. J. White, *The Form and Function of the Body of the Greek Letter*, 98-111.

closes his forthcoming visit to Rome.[3] In that case the term "parousia" (Greek παρουσία) means "presence,"[4] and an apostolic parousia designates a means by which an apostle is present (personally, by an emissary, or through a letter). But the section contains considerably more concerns than that.

BIBLIOGRAPHY

Funk, Robert W. "The Apostolic *Parousia*: Form and Significance." In *Christian History and Interpretation: Studies Presented to John Knox*, 249-68. Ed. William R. Farmer et al. Cambridge: Cambridge University Press, 1967.

Klauck, Hans-Josef. *Ancient Letters and the New Testament: A Guide to Context and Exegesis*. Waco: Baylor University Press, 2006.

Knox, John. "Romans 15.14-33 and Paul's Conception of His Apostolic Mission." *JBL* 83 (1964): 1-11.

Müller, Peter. "Grundlinien paulinischer Theologie (Röm 15,14-33)." *KuD* 35 (1989): 212-35.

White, John L. *The Form and Function of the Body of the Greek Letter: A Study of the Letter-Body in the Nonliterary Papyri and in Paul the Apostle*. SBLDS 2. Missoula: Scholars Press, 1972.

9.1. Mission Strategy Past and Present, 15:14-21

14*But I myself am fully convinced about you, my brothers and sisters, that you yourselves are full of goodness, filled with all knowledge, and able to admonish one another.* 15*But on some points I have written to you rather boldly so as to remind you, because of the grace given to me by God* 16*to be a minister of Christ Jesus to the nations, serving as a priest of the gospel of God, in order that the offering of the nations may be acceptable, sanctified by the Holy Spirit.* 17*In Christ Jesus, then, I have reason to boast of my work for God.* 18*For I will not dare to speak of anything except what Christ has accomplished through me in order to bring about the obedience of the nations, by word and deed,* 19*by the power of signs and wonders, by the power of the Spirit of God, so that from Jerusalem and as far around as Illyricum I have fully proclaimed the good news of Christ.* 20*And thus making it my ambition to preach the gospel, not where Christ has already been named, lest I build upon another person's foundation,* 21*but as it is written:*

> *"Those to whom nothing about him was reported will see, and those who have not heard will understand."*

---

3. R. Funk, "The Apostolic *Parousia*," 249-68.
4. BDAG 780 (παρουσία, 1).

Notes on the Text and Translation

15:15 Some ancient Greek witnesses (including 𝔓⁴⁶, D, F, and others) have the word ἀδελφοί after the fourth Greek word in this verse, so as to read: τολμηρότερον δὲ ἔγραψα ὑμῖν, ἀδελφοί ("But I have written to you rather boldly, brothers and sisters"). That is followed by the Majority Text and represented by the KJV reading: "Nevertheless, brethren, I have written the more boldly." The word is not present in ℵ* (original hand), B, and others. The word is more likely to have been added than omitted and should probably be excluded. It is not in the Greek texts of Westcott-Hort and Nestle-Aland (27th edition) nor in various modern versions (RSV, NIV, NRSV, NET, and ESV).

15:19 The major textual question is whether the word πνεύματος (genitive of πνεῦμα, "Spirit") should stand alone (as in B, followed by the NIV and NAS) or whether it should be supplemented by other words so as to read πνεύματος ἁγίου ("Holy Spirit," as in A, D, and other texts, followed by the RSV) or πνεύματος θεοῦ ("Spirit of God," as in 𝔓⁴⁶, ℵ, and the Majority Text, followed by the KJV, NET, and NRSV). All three expressions ("Spirit," "Holy Spirit," and "Spirit of God") appear in Paul's letters. It is possible that Paul simply spoke here of the "Spirit" and that later scribes made the additions. But that would mean that one solitary text (B) has to be favored over so many others. Perhaps "Spirit of God" should be adopted. In any case, any of the three terms chosen does not affect the meaning of the passage.[5]

15:21 Paul quotes a portion of Isaiah 52:15. According to most ancient Greek texts (including 𝔓⁴⁶, ℵ, A, and the Majority Text), his wording is exactly like that in the LXX. But there is one major variant in some witnesses (B, plus others) in which the verb ὄψονται ("[they] will see") is placed prior to the relative pronoun οἷς ("to whom"). That is probably the original reading, but scribes probably altered Paul's text to conform it to the LXX.[6] Adopting the reading of B, however, would not change one's translation or interpretation.

General Comment

What follows marks an abrupt shift in the letter. The hortatory section of the letter was concluded at 15:13, and now Paul turns to take up matters concerning his apostleship as it relates to the mission he has accomplished up to the present moment and as it concerns his forthcoming visit to Rome.

In 14:1–15:13 he has carried on a serious discussion concerning the accom-

---

5. For further discussion, cf. B. Metzger, *TCGNT* 473.
6. C. Cranfield, *Romans,* 765; J. Dunn, *Romans,* 856; R. Jewett, *Romans,* 902.

modation of various views within communities of believers. As if he might be misunderstood concerning the composition and life of the community at Rome, he seems to pull back at 15:14, go out of his way to commend those to whom he writes, and say that what he has written is but a reminder of what they know and believe already.

Although he does not say in this section of the letter that he plans to come to Rome, he has spoken already of his desire to do so (1:11-15), and will speak of it directly in the next section (15:22-24). But before speaking of his visit there directly, he declares that his missionary work has always been to places previously unevangelized and that he does not "build upon another person's foundation." That means that he will not start a distinct "Pauline" mission in Rome in competition to the existing Roman community of faith or seek to refashion it so that it reflects his emphases.

Detailed Comment

15:14-15 If Paul intended to intervene in the life of the Christian community at Rome, thereby taking up problems and directing the believers toward a solution, he does not indicate so in these verses. On the contrary, he expresses his profound admiration for the community, mentioning three things in particular: their inherent goodness, their substantial knowledge, and their ability to admonish one another. The verb νουθετέω, translated as "admonish" here (and in the KJV and NASV), can also mean "to instruct" (cf. RSV, NIV, and NRSV), but it has the sense of counseling persons concerning conduct,[7] and in the present context that seems fitting, so "to admonish" is more appropriate.

Since the Roman community is in good order, Paul does not need to exercise apostolic intervention, but he nevertheless alludes to his apostolic authority by mentioning the special gift of grace that has been given to him. He admits that he has written "rather boldly" regarding some matters. That comes as an apologetic remark in light of what he had said at the outset of the letter. There he had stated that he expected that both he and his readers would be mutually encouraged (1:12). But in the meantime he has written this letter at length concerning matters that are of mutual importance to both them and himself. All of that which he has written he now speaks of as things that are intended as reminders. In the case of persons known to him personally at Rome, the statement could be taken literally, reminding them of things he has taught and proclaimed in their presence previously. But the statement can also have a more general applicability: What he sets forth in this letter is

---

7. BDAG 679 (νουθετέω).

the tradition known to both them and himself. He has not introduced anything new or novel.[8]

Here and at 15:30 Paul refers to his readers as "brothers and sisters." On
"brothers and sisters," see the comment on 1:13.

15:16-19 Paul calls himself a "minister (λειτουργός) of Christ Jesus to the
nations (εἰς τὰ ἔθνη), serving as a priest (ἱερουργοῦντα) of the gospel of God,
in order that the offering of the nations (ἡ προσφορὰ τῶν ἐθνῶν) may be acceptable, sanctified by the Holy Spirit."[9] Using cultic language, he speaks of
himself as making an offering to God.[10] The offering that he presents is the "offering of the nations," and that is to be understood not as an offering "from"
(subjective genitive) the nations (i.e., not the collection "from" his Gentile
churches that he mentions in 15:28), but an offering of the nations themselves
(an objective genitive; more precisely a genitive of apposition) — "the offering
that consists of the nations."[11] That view was adopted by Augustine, who wrote:
"Thus the Gentiles are offered to God as an acceptable sacrifice when, believing
in Christ, they are sanctified through the Gospel."[12]

The imagery recalls that of Sirach 50:12-14 (LXX), in which the writer describes the cultic activity of Simon as high priest (ca. 219-196 B.C.). In that scene
priests from all around (κυκλόθεν) surround (κυκλόω) the high priest. Together they present an offering (προσφορά) before the congregation (Israel) as
an act of priestly service (λειτουργέω)[13] for the Most High, the Almighty (ὁ
παντοκράτωρ). That Paul was familiar with Sirach is beyond dispute, since his
letters contain allusions to it elsewhere.[14] Paul had used the noun λειτουργοί

8. O. Michel, *Römer*, 456; J. Fitzmyer, *Romans*, 711.

9. Portions of the discussion here are adapted from A. Hultgren, "The Scriptural Foundations for Paul's Mission to the Gentiles," 32-34.

10. According to C. Cranfield, *Romans*, 756, the term ἱερουργέω "occurs frequently in
Philo and Josephus but always in the sense of offering (a sacrifice)." Cf. BDAG 471 (ἱερουργέω).

11. The objective genitive has very wide support; cf. BDAG 887 (προσφορά, 2); Str-B 3:153;
C. K. Barrett, *Romans*, 252; O. Michel, *Römer*, 365; E. Käsemann, *Romans*, 393; C. Cranfield,
Romans, 756-57; J. Dunn, *Romans*, 860; U. Wilckens, *Römer*, 3:118; J. Fitzmyer, *Romans*, 712;
P. Stuhlmacher, *Romans*, 237-38; T. Schreiner, *Romans*, 767; D. Moo, *Romans*, 890; E. Lohse,
Römer, 394; R. Jewett, *Romans*, 907; R. Riesner, *Paul's Early Period*, 247; F. Horn, "Paulus und
der Herodianische Tempel," 201. The subjective genitive is favored by A.-M. Denis, "La fonction
apostolique et la liturgie nouvelle en esprit," 405-7; D. J. Downs, "'The Offering of the Gentiles,'"
173-86; and idem, *The Offering of the Gentiles*.

12. Augustine, *Propositions from the Epistle to the Romans*, 83. Quoted from *Augustine on
Romans: Propositions from the Epistle to the Romans; Unfinished Commentary on the Epistle to
the Romans*, ed. Paula Fredriksen Landes, SBL.TT 23 (Chico: Scholars Press, 1982), 49. Cf. also
M. Luther, *Romans*, 123.

13. On the use of the verb in cultic settings, cf. Exod 28:35, 43; 29:30; Num 18:2; Sir 4:14;
45:15; Jdt 4:14; 1 Macc 10:42; Philo, *Mos.* 2.153; Josephus, *J.W.* 2.409; *Ant.* 20.218.

14. The appendix to the Nestle-Aland text (27th ed.) lists some 22 allusions to Sirach in

previously to speak of civil officials as God's "servants" or "ministers" (13:6), persons who perform public service for the people.[15] Here, however, Paul uses the word in its religious (cultic) meaning, which is attested concerning the work of priests in the OT and Jewish sources.[16]

Paul speaks of himself as carrying out the priestly work of presenting the Gentile nations themselves from the regions of his missionary work, which extends in the arc (κύκλῳ, 15:19) from Jerusalem to Illyricum (located on the Balkan peninsula northwest of Macedonia along the east coast of the Adriatic Sea; although its limits were variable, it corresponded roughly to modern Albania[17]). The statement does not imply that Paul had actually carried on an apostolic mission in Illyricum, since the preposition μέχρι implies only that he would have gone up to the area ("as far as"[18]), not necessarily within it. And although he declares that he has "fully proclaimed the good news of Christ" within that arc, that does not mean that he claims to have covered every conceivable area within it. Instead, he has evangelized within major population centers, expecting that the gospel would go from there into the larger territories in which they were located. As Günther Bornkamm has put it:

> [Paul's] thought always extends beyond the individual community to countries and districts. Each of the churches founded, but no more than founded, by Paul stands for a whole district: Philippi for Macedonia (Phil. 4:15), Thessalonica for Macedonia and Achaia (1 Thess. 1:7f.), Corinth for Achaia (1 Cor. 16:15; 2 Cor. 1:1), and Ephesus for Asia (Rom. 16:5; 1 Cor. 16:19; 2 Cor. 1:8). Romans 15:19 is therefore anything but adventitious and exaggerated. Instead, it expresses the apostle's amazing confidence that the gospel needed only to be preached for it to spread automatically: starting from the various cities, it would reach out to the whole of the country round about and pervade it.[19]

---

the seven undisputed letters of Paul. For illustrations, see E. Ellis, *Paul's Use of the Old Testament*, 59, 76, 153.

15. On the etymology and usage of the word λειτουργός, see the notations to 13:6. R. Jewett, *Romans*, 906-7, claims that the term has a similar, noncultic role at 15:16, i.e., that Paul has an "ambassadorial role." But the term is used within a passage filled with cultic associations.

16. Neh 10:40; Isa 61:6; Sir 7:30; *Let. Aris.* 95; cf. Hermann Strathmann, "λειτουργός," *TDNT* 4:230.

17. Jack Finegan, "Illyricum," *IDB* 2:681.

18. BDAG 644 (μέχρι, 1). Cf. E. Käsemann, *Romans*, 394-95; J. Dunn, *Romans*, 864; U. Wilckens, *Römer*, 3:119 (n. 583); P. Stuhlmacher, *Romans*, 238; C. Talbert, *Romans*, 329; E. Lohse, *Römer*, 396. On the other hand, C. Cranfield, *Romans*, 761-62, and D. Moo, *Romans*, 894 (n. 64), conjecture that Paul may have actually passed over the border into Illyricum; R. Jewett, *Romans*, 913-14, speaks of a ministry in Illyricum and even of a "founding visit" there.

19. G. Bornkamm, *Paul*, 53-54. Cf. W.-H. Ollrog, *Paulus und seine Mitarbeiter*, 234;

Since he has evangelized in Philippi and Thessalonica, major cities of Macedonia, he can claim that he has worked "as far as" (not necessarily within) Illyricum. He plans to go on to Spain, and so continue the arc (traveling κύκλῳ, "in an arc"[20]), as he goes on to say in 15:24.

The offering that Paul makes consists of the ἔθνη, a term that can be translated either as "Gentiles" or as "nations" (the latter meaning Gentile nations). At this place in his letter, recalling the sweeping arc that he has made from Jerusalem to Illyricum, Paul would be thinking not simply of an offering of "the Gentiles" (RSV, NIV, and NRSV) — there were plenty of Gentiles in Syria and Palestine — but of the Gentile "nations" located within the arc.

The phrase "offering of the nations" recalls the closing words of Isaiah that envision the end times: God will come and "gather all the nations and tongues; and they shall come and shall see my glory" (66:18). God will send his witnesses to declare his glory "among the nations" (66:19). "They shall bring all your kindred from all the nations as an offering to the Lord" (LXX, ἐκ πάντων τῶν ἐθνῶν δῶρον κυρίῳ, 66:20)."[21] In spite of the terminological difference between δῶρον ("gift," Isa 66:20) and προσφορά ("offering," Rom 15:16), the concept of the "offering of the nations" to the Lord in Isaiah can be considered the background for the apostle's own expression in Romans.[22] A similar expression appears at Philippians 2:17, where Paul speaks of the faith of the Philippians as an "offering and service," using still other terms (θυσία καὶ λειτουργία).

Questions can be raised concerning the texts at the end of Isaiah — as well as other OT texts[23] — as to whether they actually speak of the ingathering of the nations. Some interpreters speak of a "universalism" in Isaiah, asserting that the texts envision the inclusion of "the nations" within God's redemptive plan.[24]

U. Wilckens, *Römer*, 3:122; D. Senior and C. Stuhlmueller, *Biblical Foundations*, 184; J. Nissen, *New Testament and Mission*, 110; T. Schreiner, *Romans*, 770; E. Käsemann, *Romans*, 395, calls Rom 15:19 "an enormous exaggeration."

20. BDAG 574 (κύκλῳ, 3).

21. In Isa 66:20 the reference is to Jews of the Diaspora who will come from the nations, but in Rom 15:16 it is the nations themselves that are in view. For further discussion, see the following paragraph.

22. Cf. J. Murray, *Romans*, 2:210; O. Michel, *Römer*, 365; M. Black, *Romans*, 175; K. Weiss, "Paulus — Priester der christlichen Kultgemeinde," 355-63; G. Wiles, *Paul's Intercessory Prayers*, 85 (n. 5); R. Riesner, *Paul's Early Period*, 245 (n. 57). On the significance of Deutero-Isaiah for Paul's understanding of his apostleship, see T. Holtz, "Zum Selbstverständnis des Apostels Paulus," 321-30.

23. Isa 2:2-4; 12:4; 25:6-8; 51:4-5; 60:3; Jer 16:19; Mic 4:1-3; Zech 8:20-23; Pss 22:27; 86:9; Tob 13:11; 14:6; Wis 8:14; Sir 39:10.

24. P. Hanson, *Isaiah 40–66*, 130; K. Baltzer, *Deutero-Isaiah*, 43: "His theology embraces the world and the nations." J. Blenkinsopp, *Isaiah 56–66*, 84, speaks of "a remarkable open and generous attitude to outsiders," but refrains from using the term "universalism."

Others have concluded that the various texts in Isaiah speak only of the restoration of Israel, the ingathering of the people of Israel from the Diaspora, but not an ingathering of the Gentile nations.[25] It has also been said that there is, paradoxically, a universalism within the texts (particularly in Isa 40–55) that stands in tension with the particularism.[26] Strictly speaking, Isaiah 66:20 refers to the ingathering of Jews of the Diaspora from among the Gentile nations, but for Paul it is the ingathering of the Gentile nations themselves that is in view. By transforming the sense of the passage in this way, Paul makes an interpretive *tour de force*. "In presenting the Gentiles as an offering Paul has created a new idea."[27] From his own vantage point and in light of his commission as "apostle to the Gentiles" or "nations" (Rom 11:13; cf. 15:16), he finds a meaning in the texts that is provocative and plausible in light of the preceding verse, Isaiah 66:18, which speaks of the gathering of "all nations and tongues." In his own understanding, the passages anticipate the eschatological ingathering of the nations, which he sees being fulfilled in his own time and ministry.[28]

The "offering" of which Paul speaks (Rom 15:16) is presumably not "the Gentile world itself,"[29] except in a representative sense, for the offering is one that has been "sanctified by the Holy Spirit." That would include Christians alone (cf. 1 Cor 1:2; 6:11, where the term "sanctified" applies to Christians).[30] But an offering in Jewish tradition represents the whole. Elsewhere Paul uses the cultic language of "first fruits" (ἀπαρχή) offered to God to speak of his first converts of Asia (Rom 16:5) and Achaia (1 Cor 16:15), and he speaks of Christians generally as those who have the "first fruits (ἀπαρχή) of the Spirit" (Rom 8:23).[31] On one occasion he speaks of Jewish Christians as "first fruits" (ἀπαρχή) offered to God (Rom 11:16).

For Paul, then, the church is the "first fruits" of the Spirit offered to God

25. H. Orlinsky, "The So-Called 'Servant of the Lord' and 'Suffering Servant' in Second Isaiah," 97-117, and N. Snaith, "Isaiah 40–66: A Study of the Teaching of Second Isaiah and Its Consequences," 154-65; C. Stuhlmueller, *Creative Redemption in Deutero-Isaiah*, 129-31.

26. R. Davidson, "Universalism in Second Isaiah," 166-85.

27. L. Peerbolte, *Paul the Missionary*, 248. Cf. F. Horn, "Paulus und der Herodianische Tempel," 201-2.

28. According to L. Peerbolte, *Paul the Missionary*, 246-48, Paul fused the concept of the ingathering of the Israelites of the Diaspora with the eschatological conversion of the Gentiles that is envisioned in *Pss. Sol.* 17. Cf. also J. Bieder, *Gottes Sendung*, 39; J. Nissen, *New Testament and Mission*, 113.

29. E. Käsemann, *Romans*, 393.

30. Cf. A. Schlatter, *Romans*, 265; O. Michel, *Römer*, 365; U. Luz, *Das Geschichtsverständnis des Paulus*, 392; C. Cranfield, *Romans*, 757; U. Wilckens, *Römer*, 3:118; and Martin Hengel, "The Origins of the Christian Mission," 51.

31. Cf. Gerhard Delling, "ἀπαρχή," *TDNT* 1:484-86. Cf. also 2 Cor 5:5, where Paul uses the synonym ἀρραβών ("first installment") of the Spirit.

(cf. also 2 Thess 2:13; Jas 1:18; Rev 14:4; *1 Clement* 42.4).[32] The "offering of the nations . . . sanctified by the Holy Spirit" (Rom 15:16) — an offering prepared through his priestly service of the gospel — is the "first fruits" of redeemed humanity. The imagery of "first fruits" is based on OT cultic festivals at which the first fruits were given to the Lord (Exod 23:16; 34:26; Num 28:26; Deut 26:1-11). Through this act God is acknowledged to be the actual owner of all things; the remaining crop is sanctified, and it therefore shares in the divine blessing.[33] The first fruits "represent the whole."[34] In his apostolic work the apostle Paul intended to gather from the nations an offering acceptable to God — sanctified by the Spirit — by which the divine blessing extends to all the nations. For God possesses all the nations — the God who is God of both Jews and Gentiles (Rom 3:29). Through his proclamation of the gospel from Jerusalem to Illyricum, which was to be extended to Spain and perhaps beyond, Paul made a circuit (15:19) among the nations to render to the Lord the "offering of the nations" in terms of the eschatological expectation expressed in Isaiah 66.

Paul says in 15:17 that he has reason to boast of his work for God. The basis for his boasting is, he says, "what Christ has accomplished through me in order to bring about the obedience of the nations, by word and deed, by the power of signs and wonders, by the power of the Spirit of God" (15:18-19). Paul lists three things that have characterized him and his work, ranging from the most basic of human activities to the highest of divine actions. The first is a set of terms — "by word and deed" — that is somewhat traditional in Jewish and early Christian speech to speak of a trustworthy unity of speech and activity (Sir 3:8; 4 Macc 16:14; Luke 24:2; Col 3:17). When one's deeds do not match one's words, there is insincerity (3 Macc 3:17). Jesus himself was a model of that unity (Luke 24:2), and it is expected of believers (cf. Col 3:17).

The second set of terms — "by the power of signs and wonders" — is

32. In spite of differences in terminology between "offering" (προσφορά) in Rom 15:16 and "first fruits" (ἀπαρχή) elsewhere in Paul's writings, the two terms are associated in early Christian literature, as witnessed by the fact that the writer of the *Apostolic Constitutions* speaks of Christians as "first fruits" (ἀπαρχή) and "offerings" (προσφοραί) offered (προσφερόμεναι) to God (2.26.2). Already in the OT ἀπαρχή is used beyond the meaning of "first fruits" to include regular offerings brought to the Temple or to the priests; cf. G. Delling, "ἀπαρχή," *TDNT* 1:485. The verb "to offer" (προσφέρω) takes "first fruits" (ἀπαρχή) as its direct object (Lev 2:12: Num 5:9); and within a single chapter of Sirach various terms concerning offerings are used in parallel: 35:5, προσφορά; 35:6, θυσία; and 35:7, ἀπαρχή. Furthermore, there is a linkage in terminology even in Paul's own writings in that the "offering" (προσφορά) is "sanctified by the Holy Spirit" (Rom 15:16), and Christians as "first fruits" (ἀπαρχή) are such because of the work of the Spirit in them (Rom 8:23).

33. W. Eichrodt, *Theology of the Old Testament*, 1:152; G. von Rad, *Old Testament Theology*, 1:254.

34. J. Pedersen, *Israel*, 2:301.

more specific to apostolic ministry. Paul uses the same set of characteristics to speak of the work of a true apostle (2 Cor 12:12). The combination of the words "signs and wonders" recalls those places in the OT where God had performed miraculous deeds through Moses against Pharaoh in Egypt. Stephen, in his speech at the time of martyrdom, sums up the matter concerning Moses and the people of Israel: "He led them out, having performed wonders and signs in Egypt, at the Red Sea, and in the wilderness for forty years" (Acts 7:36). Various OT passages, widely scattered across the texts, speak of the "signs and wonders" of God at the time of the exodus from Egypt (Exod 7:3; Deut 6:22; 7:19; 26:8; 34:11; Jer 32:20-21; Bar 2:11). Peter speaks of Jesus as having performed "signs and wonders" (Acts 2:22), and "signs and wonders" are attributed to the apostles (Acts 2:43; 4:30; 5:12; 6:8), including Paul (Acts 14:3; 15:12). And just as Paul says that "signs and wonders" were done through him to win the obedience of the Gentiles to the gospel (15:18-19), so in Acts it is said that Paul and Barnabas testified at the Jerusalem assembly to "the signs and wonders that God had done through them among the Gentiles" (Acts 15:12). In all of this Paul is declaring that there is a similarity between what transpired at the exodus — and implicitly in the ministries of Jesus and other apostles — and in his own ministry as an apostle. The history of God's saving activity is being carried out as Gentile peoples are being incorporated into the people of the God of Israel, the God of the whole world.

Finally, Paul declares that his ministry to bring the nations into obedience has been carried out "by the power of the Spirit of God." Here is the crescendo of the series of characteristics concerning his ministry. He speaks of God's power at work at the close of the age. The eschatological gift of the Spirit is being poured out, which empowers Paul's own ministry and brings about the response of faith among the nations (1 Cor 12:3; cf. 12:9; Gal 5:5). The phrase εἰς ὑπακοὴν ἐθνῶν ("unto the obedience of the nations") recalls the phrase εἰς ὑπακοὴν πίστεως ἐν πᾶσιν τοῖς ἔθνεσιν ("unto the obedience of faith among all the nations") at 1:5. In the present context the phrase means the conversion of the Gentile peoples through the proclamation of the gospel.[35]

15:20 Paul states his apostolic and missionary principle, i.e., that he had sought to proclaim the gospel where it had not yet been heard (cf. 2 Cor 10:15-16). That statement does not stand in conflict with what he had said at the outset of the letter (1:11-15). Although he had said there that in coming to Rome he would "reap some fruit" among those at Rome and "proclaim the gospel" there

---

35. Cf. C. K. Barrett, *Romans*, 253; O. Michel, *Römer*, 459; E. Käsemann, *Romans*, 393-94; J. Dunn, *Romans*, 862; P. Stuhlmacher, *Romans*, 238; D. Moo, *Romans*, 892; R. Jewett, *Romans*, 910; E. Lohse, *Römer*, 395. According to D. Garlington, *Faith, Obedience and Perseverance*, 25, and others whom he cites, the phrase means "obedience which proceeds from faith,"

(1:13, 15), his intent was not to start a new mission in Rome nor to transform the church into a "Pauline" church.[36] In those verses he also speaks of the mutual enrichment that he anticipates while he is among the believers at Rome (1:12). His plan was not to become a resident and leader there but to be a visitor who, after a time of mutual encouragement and refreshment, would be sent on by that community to Spain, which he explains at 15:24, 28. He has already said explicitly that he is convinced about the sound faith and knowledge of the Roman community (15:14; cf. 1:8).

15:21 Paul quotes a portion of Isaiah 52:15 in wording that is almost exactly that of the LXX (see the text-critical notation above), which reads:

οἷς οὐκ ἀνηγγέλη περὶ αὐτοῦ ὄψονται καὶ οἳ οὐκ ἀκηκόασιν συνήσουσιν.

Those to whom nothing about him was reported will see, and those who have not heard will understand.

In its entirety the passage in Isaiah concerns the Suffering Servant. According to that passage, "kings shall shut their mouths because of him," and those "kings" are the antecedents of the pronoun "those" within the portion quoted. But Paul's interest in the verse is on the latter part only.[37] That is that persons who have not heard the gospel will have opportunities to do so.[38] Looking toward his mission in Spain and perhaps beyond, Paul sees the passage being fulfilled in his own time, and he sees his own apostolic mission as having a role in it.

BIBLIOGRAPHY

Ådna, Jostein, and Hans Kvalbein, eds. *The Mission of the Early Church to Jews and Gentiles*. WUNT 127. Tübingen: J. C. B. Mohr (Paul Siebeck), 2000.

Baird, William. *Paul's Message and Mission*. Nashville: Abingdon Press, 1960.

Baltzer, Klaus. *Deutero-Isaiah*. Hermeneia. Minneapolis: Fortress Press, 2001.

Barram, Michael. *Mission and Moral Reflection in Paul*. StudBL 75. New York: Peter Lang, 2006.

36. Contra A. Reichert, *Der Römerbrief als Gratwanderung*, 96-97. Nor does Paul regard the Roman community as lacking an "apostolic foundation" or the "fundamental kerygma," as suggested by G. Klein, "Paul's Purpose in Writing the Epistle to the Romans," 29-43 (see esp. pp. 39, 42).

37. According to D. Moo, *Romans*, 897-98, Paul understands the psalm as referring to the Suffering Servant; he holds that the latter is Jesus, and that Gentiles can now "come to see and understand the message about the Servant of the Lord." C. Cranfield, *Romans*, 765, and R. Jewett, *Romans*, 917, also claim that Paul's message includes knowledge of Jesus as the Servant. But that is not clear, and Paul's interest in using the verse is to highlight the fulfillment of Scripture in the mission to those who have not heard the gospel.

38. S.-L. Shum, *Paul's Use of Isaiah in Romans*, 257.

Barnett, Paul. *Paul: Missionary of Jesus.* Grand Rapids: Wm. B. Eerdmans, 2008.

Barrett, C. K. "Paul: Missionary and Theologian." In his *Jesus and the Word and Other Essays,* 149-62. PTMS 41. Allison Park: Pickwick Publications, 1995.

———. "The Gentile Mission as an Eschatological Phenomenon." In his *Jesus and the Word and Other Essays,* 185-94. PTMS 41. Allison Park: Pickwick Publications, 1995.

Bauckham, Richard. *Bible and Mission: Christian Witness in a Postmodern World.* Grand Rapids: Baker Book House, 2003.

Berger, Klaus. "Almösen für Israel: Zum historischen Kontext der paulinischen Kollekte." *NTS* 23 (1976-77): 180-204.

Bieder, Werner. *Gottes Sendung und der missionarische Auftrag der Kirche nach Matthäus, Lukas, Paulus und Johannes.* Theologische Studien 82. Zurich: EVZ-Verlag, 1965.

Bjerkelund, Carl. "'Vergeblich' als Missionsergebnis bei Paulus." In *God's Christ and His People: Studies in Honour of Nils Alstrup Dahl,* 175-91. Ed. Jacob Jervell and Wayne A. Meeks. Oslo: Universitetsforlaget, 1977.

Blenkinsopp, Joseph. *Isaiah 56–66.* AB 19B. New York: Doubleday, 2003.

Bolt, Peter, and Mark Thompson, eds. *The Gospel to the Nations: Perspectives on Paul's Mission.* Downers Grove: InterVarsity, 2000.

Bornkamm, Günther. *Paul.* New York: Harper & Row, 1971; reprinted, Minneapolis: Fortress Press, 1995.

Bowers, W. Paul. "Church and Mission in Paul." *JSNT* 44 (1991): 89-111.

———. "Fulfilling the Gospel: The Scope of the Pauline Mission." *JETS* 30 (1987): 185-98.

———. "Paul and Religious Propaganda in the First Century." *NovT* 22 (1980): 316-23.

Campbell, Thomas H. "Paul's 'Missionary Journeys' as Reflected in His Letters." *JBL* 74 (1955): 80-92.

Campbell, William S. "Divergent Views of Paul and His Mission." In *Reading Israel in Romans: Legitimacy and Plausibility of Divergent Interpretations,* 187-211. Ed. Cristina Grenholm and Daniel Patte. RHCS 1. Harrisburg: Trinity Press International, 2000.

———. "Paul's Missionary Practice and Policy in Romans." *IBS* 12 (1990): 2-25.

Dabelstein, Rolf. *Die Beurteilung der 'Heiden' bei Paulus.* BET 14. Frankfurt: Lang, 1981.

Dahl, Nils A. "The Missionary Theology in the Epistle to the Romans." In his *Studies in Paul,* 70-94. Minneapolis: Augsburg Publishing House, 1977.

Davies, Paul E. "Paul's Missionary Message." *JBR* 16 (1948): 205-11.

Denis, Albert-Marie. "La fonction apostolique et la liturgie nouvelle en esprit: Étude thématique des metaphors pauliniennes du culte nouveau." *RSPT* 42 (1958): 405-7.

Dickson, John P. *Mission-Commitment in Ancient Judaism and in the Pauline Communities.* WUNT 2/159. Tübingen: J. C. B. Mohr (Paul Siebeck), 2003.

Dillon, Richard J. "The 'Priesthood' of St. Paul, Romans 15:15-16." *Worship* 74 (2000): 156-68.

Donaldson, Terence L. *Paul and the Gentiles: Remapping the Apostle's Convictional World.* Minneapolis: Fortress Press, 1997.

Downs, David J. *The Offering of the Gentiles: Paul's Collection for Jerusalem in Its Chronological, Cultural, and Cultic Contexts.* WUNT 2/248. Tübingen: Mohr-Siebeck, 2008.

———. "'The Offering of the Gentiles' in Romans 15:16." *JSNT* 29 (2006): 173-86.

Eichrodt, Walther. *Theology of the Old Testament*. 2 vols. Philadelphia: Westminster Press, 1961-67.

Ellis, E. Earle. *Paul's Use of the Old Testament*. Edinburgh: Oliver & Boyd, 1957.

Garlington, Don B. *Faith, Obedience, and Perseverance: Aspects of Paul's Letter to the Romans*. WUNT 79. Tübingen: J. C. B. Mohr (Paul Siebeck), 1994.

———. *'The Obedience of Faith' — A Pauline Phrase in Historical Context*. WUNT 2/38. Tübingen: J. C. B. Mohr (Paul Siebeck), 1991.

Gaston, Lloyd. "Paul and Jerusalem." In *From Jesus to Paul: Studies in Honour of Francis Wright Beare*, 61-72. Ed. Peter Richardson and John C. Hurd. Waterloo: Wilfrid Laurier Press, 1984.

Geyser, Albert S. "Une Essai d'explication de Rom. xv.19." *NTS* 6 (1959-60): 156-59.

Gilliland, Dean S. *Pauline Theology and Mission Practice*. Grand Rapids: Baker Book House, 1983.

Goulder, Michael D. "The Jewish-Christian Mission, 30-130." *ANRW* II.26.3 (1996): 1979-2037.

Haas, Odo. *Paulus der Missionar: Ziel, Grundsätze und Methoden der Missionstätigkeit des Apostels Paulus nach seinen eigenen Aussagen*. Münsterschwarzach: Vier-Tüme-Verlag, 1971.

Hanson, Paul D. *Isaiah 40–66*. A Bible Commentary for Teaching and Preaching. Louisville: John Knox Press, 1995.

Hengel, Martin. "The Origins of the Christian Mission." In his *Between Jesus and Paul: Studies in the Earliest History of Christianity*, 48-64. Philadelphia: Fortress Press, 1983.

Hofius, Otfried. "Paulus-Missionar und Theologe." In *Evangelium, Schriftauslegung, Kirche: Festschrift für Peter Stuhlmacher zum 65. Geburtstag*, 224-37. Ed. Jostein Ådna et al. Göttingen: Vandenhoeck & Ruprecht, 1997.

Holtz, Traugott. "Zum Selbstverständnis des Apostels Paulus." *TLZ* 91 (1966): 321-30.

Horn, Friedrich W. "Paulus und der Herodianische Tempel." *NTS* 53 (2007): 184-203.

Hultgren, Arland J. "The Scriptural Foundations for Paul's Mission to the Gentiles." In *Paul and His Theology*, 21-44. PAST 3. Ed. Stanley E. Porter. Boston: E. J. Brill, 2006.

Jewett, Robert. "Ecumenical Theology for the Sake of Mission: Romans 1:1-17 + 15:14–16:24." In *Pauline Theology*, vol. 3, *Romans*, 89-108. Ed. David M. Hay and E. Elizabeth Johnson. Minneapolis: Fortress Press, 1995.

Kaiser, Walter C. *Mission in the Old Testament: Israel as a Light to the Nations*. Grand Rapids: Baker Book House, 2000.

Kasting, Heinrich. *Die Anfänge der urchristlichen Mission: Eine historische Untersuchung*. BEvT 55. Munich: Kaiser Verlag, 1969.

Keathley, Naymond H. *The Church's Mission to the Gentiles: Acts of the Apostles, Epistles of Paul*. Macon: Smyth & Helwys, 1999.

Kertelge, Karl. "Paul the Apostle as Missionary." In *Dictionary of Mission: Theology, History, Perspectives*, 343-48. Ed. Karl Müller et al. Maryknoll: Orbis, 1997.

Klauck, Hans-Josef. "Kultische Symbolsprache bei Paulus." In *Freude am Gottesdienst: Aspekte ursprünglicher Liturgie*, 107-18. Ed. Heinrich Riehm. Heidelberg: H. Riehm, 1988.

Klein, Günter. "Paul's Purpose in Writing the Epistle to the Romans." In *The Romans Debate*, 29-43. Rev. ed. Ed. Karl P. Donfried. Peabody: Hendrickson Publishers, 1991.

Knox, John. "Romans 15.14-33 and Paul's Conception of His Apostolic Mission." *JBL* 83 (1964): 1-11.

Koch, Stefan. "'Wenn ich nach Spanien reise' (Rom 15,24): Hinweise zu Hintergründ und Bedeutung der Reisepläne des Paulus." In *The Letter to the Romans*, 699-712. BETL 226. Ed. Udo Schnelle. Walpole: Peeters, 2009.

Lindemann, Andreas. "Pauline Mission and Religious Pluralism." In *Theology and Ethics in Paul and His Interpreters: Essays in Honor of Victor Paul Furnish*, 275-88. Ed. Eugene H. Lovering Jr. and Jerry L. Sumney. Nashville: Abingdon Press, 1996.

Lopez, Davina C. *Apostle to the Conquered: Reimagining Paul's Mission.* PCC. Minneapolis: Augsburg Fortress, 2008.

Luz, Ulrich. *Das Geschichtsverständnis des Paulus.* BEvT 49. Munich: Kaiser Verlag, 1968.

Madvig, Donald H. "The Missionary Preaching of Paul: A Problem in New Testament Theology." *JETS* 20 (1977): 147-55.

Magda, Ksenija. *Paul's Territoriality and Mission Strategy: Searching for the Geographical Awareness Paradigm behind Romans.* WUNT 2/266. Tübingen: Mohr Siebeck, 2009.

Meyer, Ben F. "The World Mission and the Emergent Realization of Christian Identity." In *Jesus, the Gospels and the Church*, 243-63. Ed. E. P. Sanders. Macon: Mercer University Press, 1987.

Minear, Paul S. "Paul's Missionary Dynamic." In his *The Obedience of Faith: The Purpose of Paul in the Epistle to the Romans*, 91-101. SBT 2/19. Naperville: Alec R. Allenson, 1971.

Müller, Peter. "Grundlinien paulinischer Theologie (Röm 15,14-33)." *KuD* 35 (1989): 212-35.

Munck, Johannes. *Paul and the Salvation of Mankind.* Richmond: John Knox Press, 1959.

Nissen, Johannes. *New Testament and Mission: Historical and Hermeneutical Perspectives.* 2d ed. New York: Peter Lang, 2002.

Ollrog, Wolf-Henning. *Paulus und seine Mitarbeiter: Untersuchungen zu Theorie und Praxis der paulinischen Mission.* WMANT 50. Neukirchen-Vluyn: Neukirchener Verlag, 1979.

Olson, Stanley N. "Epistolary Uses of Expressions of Self-Confidence." *JBL* 103 (1984): 585-97.

———. "Pauline Expressions of Confidence in His Addressees." *CBQ* 47 (1985): 282-95.

O'Neill, John C. "Paul's Missionary Strategy." *IBS* 19 (1997): 174-90.

Orlinsky, Harry M. "The So-Called 'Servant of the Lord' and 'Suffering Servant' in Second Isaiah." In *Studies in the Second Part of the Book of Isaiah*, 97-117. Ed. G. W. Anderson et al. VTSup 14. Leiden: E. J. Brill, 1967.

Pedersen, Johannes. *Israel: Its Life and Culture.* 2 vols. London: Oxford University Press, 1926-40.

Peerbolte, L. J. Lietaert. *Paul the Missionary.* CBET 34. Louvain: Peeters, 2003.

Pesch, Rudolf. "Voraussetzungen und Anfänge der urchristlichen Mission." In *Mission im Neuen Testament*, 11-70. Ed. Karl Kertelge. Freiburg: Herder, 1982.

Ponthot, Joseph. "L'Expression culturelle du ministère paulinien selon Rom 15,16." In

L'Apôtre Paul: Personnalité, style et conception du ministère, 254-62. BETL 73. Ed. Albert Vanhoye. Louvain: Leuven University Press, 1986.

Rad, Gerhard von. *Old Testament Theology.* 2 vols. New York: Harper & Row, 1962-65.

Reichert, Angelika. *Der Römerbrief als Gratwanderung: Eine Untersuchung zur Abfassungsproblematik.* FRLANT 194. Göttingen: Vandenhoeck & Ruprecht, 2001.

Riesner, Rainer. *Paul's Early Period: Chronology, Mission Strategy, Theology.* Grand Rapids: Wm. B. Eerdmans, 1998.

Robinson, D. W. B. "The Priesthood of Paul in the Gospel of Hope." In *Reconciliation and Hope: New Testament Essays on Atonement and Eschatology Presented to L. L. Morris on His 60th Birthday,* 231-45. Ed. Robert Banks. Grand Rapids: Wm. B. Eerdmans, 1974.

Schelkle, Karl-Hermann. "Der Apostel als Priester." *TQ* 136 (1956): 257-83.

Schlier, Heinrich. "Die 'Liturgie' des apostolischen Evangeliums (Römer 15,14-21)." In his *Das Ende der Zeit: Exegetische Aufsätze und Vorträge 3,* 169-83. Freiburg: Herder, 1971.

Schnabel, Eckhard J. *Early Christian Mission.* 2 vols. Downers Grove: InterVarsity Press, 2004.

————. *Paul the Missionary: Realities, Strategies and Methods.* Downers Grove: InterVarsity Press, 2008.

Scott, James M. *Paul and the Nations: The Old Testament and Jewish Background of Paul's Mission to the Nations with Special Reference to the Destination of Galatians.* WUNT 84. Tübingen: J. C. B. Mohr (Paul Siebeck), 1995.

Senior, Donald, and Carroll Stuhlmueller. *The Biblical Foundation for Missions.* New York: Orbis Books, 1983.

Shum, Shiu-Lun. *Paul's Use of Isaiah in Romans: A Comparative Study of Paul's Letter to the Romans and the Sibylline and Qumran Sectarian Texts.* WUNT 2/156. Tübingen: J. C. B. Mohr (Paul Siebeck), 2002.

Snaith, Norman H. "Isaiah 40–66: A Study of the Teaching of Second Isaiah and Its Consequences." In *Studies in the Second Part of the Book of Isaiah,* 154-65. Ed. G. W. Anderson. VTSup 14. Leiden: E. J. Brill, 1967.

Stuhlmueller, Carroll. *Creative Redemption in Deutero-Isaiah.* AnBib 43. Rome: Biblical Institute Press, 1970.

Thornton, T. C. G. "St Paul's Missionary Intentions in Spain." *ExpTim* 86 (1974-75): 120.

Trocmé, Étienne. "L'Épître aux Romains et la méthode missionaire de l'apôtre Paul." *NTS* 7 (1960-61): 148-53.

Wagner, J. Ross. *Heralds of the Good News: Isaiah and Paul "in Concert" in the Letter to the Romans.* NovTSup 101. Boston: E. J. Brill, 2002.

————. "The Heralds of Isaiah and the Mission of Paul: An Investigation of Paul's Use of Isaiah 51–55 in Romans." In *Jesus and the Suffering Servant: Isaiah 53 and Christian Origins,* 193-222. Ed. William H. Bellinger Jr. and William R. Farmer. Harrisburg: Trinity Press International, 1998.

Weiss, Konrad. "Paulus — Priester der christlichen Kultgemeinde," *TLZ* 79 (1954): 355-63.

Wiles, Gordon P. *Paul's Intercessory Prayers,* SNTSMS 24. Cambridge: Cambridge University Press, 1974.

Wernle, Paul. *Paulus als Heidenmissionar.* Freiburg: J. C. B. Mohr (Paul Siebeck), 1899.

Wiéner, Claude. "Ἱερουργεῖν (Rm 15,16)." In *Studiorum paulinorum congressus internationalis catholicus, 1961,* 2:399-404. 2 vols. AnBib 17-18. Rome: Pontifical Biblical Institute Press, 1963.

Zeller, Dieter. "Theologie der Mission bei Paulus." In *Mission im Neuen Testament,* 164-89. Ed. Karl Kertelge. Freiburg: Herder, 1982.

9.2. The Visit to Rome, 15:22-24

22*This explains why I have been prevented many times from coming to you.* 23*But now, since I have no longer any room in these regions, and since for many years I have had a desire to come to you* 24 *as I proceed to Spain, I hope to see you as I pass through and to be assisted by you in my journey there, if first I may enjoy your company for a while.*

Notes on the Text and Translation

15:22 The sentence begins simply with διό, which has been called an "inferential conjunction" and means "therefore" or "for this reason."[39] That has been expanded here to "this explains why" in order to make it clear that Paul is drawing out an inference for his readers.

15:24 The syntax of 15:23-24 is extremely awkward. In order to complete the thought, some scribes added ἐλεύσομαι πρὸς ὑμᾶς ("I shall come to you") after the word for Spain. That addition stands in the Majority Text and is reflected in the KJV. But the shorter reading is found in 𝔓[46], ℵ, A, B, and other important witnesses and is to be preferred.[40]

General Comment

Continuing his discussion of his travel plans, Paul now picks up where he left off at 1:10-15. There he had announced his desire to travel to Rome and anticipated his visit there. He now makes the astonishing claim that he has no more work to do in the eastern regions of the Mediterranean world. Obviously he has not reached many of the millions of persons there with the gospel of Christ. At most he has preached the gospel in strategic places, from which it will reach further through the work of others.

39. BDAG 250 (διό); BDF 235 (§451, 5).
40. B. Metzger, *TCGNT* 474.

In this section Paul makes what must have been an astonishing and surprising announcement to his readers. That is that Rome is not his final destination in the West. Once he has enjoyed the company of the believers in Rome "for a while," he plans to go on to Spain. He had not said anything about a journey to Spain in the opening part of the letter (1:10-15), but he now unveils a much larger panorama. Moreover, he asks for their assistance to make that journey possible.

Detailed Comment

15:22-23 Paul claims to have been prevented from getting to Rome because of his need first to evangelize in the eastern territories between Jerusalem and Illyricum. But he says that he had been wanting to get to Rome and on to Spain for "many years." One cannot help but wonder whether Paul is simply being diplomatic. Yet he had known some of the persons located in Rome for many years, such as Prisca and Aquila, Epaenetus, Andronicus and Junia, and others (16:3-7). It is certainly possible that they had sought to prevail upon him to come to Rome either in personal conversations on occasions when they were together or in correspondence prior to Paul's writing his letter to Rome. Paul's wish to travel to Rome was fulfilled only in part. He expected to travel there as a free man, but he arrived as a prisoner (Acts 28:14). On Paul's not having any more room in the regions of the east, see the commentary on 15:16-19.

15:24 Paul's goal is to travel to Spain and carry out his apostolic ministry there. Spain was obviously a Gentile area. Whether there were any Jewish communities there in which Paul might find "God-fearers" as an entrée to Gentiles is an open question.[41] Some interpreters have assumed that Paul would have found synagogues there,[42] and some historians have claimed that Jewish communities did in fact exist within Spain in Paul's day.[43] But that is not certain.

---

41. For more on the view that Paul, as an apostle to the Gentiles, sought to find them at synagogues among the God-fearers, see A. Hultgren, "The Scriptural Foundations for Paul's Mission to the Gentiles," 36-43. Cf. also A. D. Nock, *Conversion*, 191-92; H. Gülzow, "Soziale Gegebenheiten der altkirchlichen Mission," 189-226; and A. Malherbe, *Social Aspects of Early Christianity*, 64.

42. O. Michel, *Römer*, 463 (n. 3); E. Käsemann, *Romans*, 398; C. Cranfield, *Romans*, 769; J. Dunn, *Romans*, 872.

43. S. Baron, *A Social and Religious History of the Jews*, 1:170; 3:33-34; Y. Baer, *A History of the Jews in Christian Spain*, 1:15-16; M. Stern, "The Jewish Diaspora," 1:169-70; E. Smallwood, *The Jews under Roman Rule*, 122; and A. Rabello, "The Situation of the Jews in Roman Spain," 161. These persons base their claims solely on Rom 15:24, 28, assuming that Paul's reason for wanting to go to Spain was to evangelize Jews there.

Neither archaeological nor literary evidence for the existence of Jewish communities in Spain that early has been attested with confidence.[44] What Paul would have known, and not known, about the demographics of Spain can hardly be discerned. He must have been aware of linguistic barriers, although that would be nothing new, and it should not be pressed too far. There would have been some persons there who could converse in Greek, since Greek traders had carried on business in ports of Spain from as early as the sixth century B.C.[45] In any case, Paul had confidence that he could evangelize both "Greeks and barbarians," and must do so (1:14).

Paul speaks of being assisted by the Roman community for his voyage to Spain. The verb used for being assisted (προπέμπω, literally, "to send forth") is hardly subtle. Paul is explicit, asking the community in Rome to outfit him for the journey in whatever way possible with things that would be needed, such as companions, food, money, and perhaps a means for travel by sea from Rome to the Iberian peninsul. [46]

Whether Paul would have considered Spain the terminus of his work is open to question.[47] It is possible that he envisioned the continuation of his ap-

44. Cf. W. Bowers, "Jewish Communities in Spain in the Time of Paul the Apostle," 395-402; and B. Wander, "Warum wollte Paulus nach Spanien?" 175-95. It is generally conceded that "Sepharad" (the name for Spain in Hebrew) at Obad 20 is not likely to be a reference to Spain (as claimed in some postbiblical traditions) but applicable to an ancient city called Saparda in western Media or to Sardis in Asia Minor. For a review of the literature and discussion, cf. P. Raabe, *Obadiah,* 266-68.

45. M. Rostovtzeff, *Greece,* 70, 146, 202, 214; Simon J. Keay, "Spain," *OCD* 1429.

46. BDAG 873 (προπέμπω, 2). Cf. A. Malherbe, *Social Aspects of Early Christianity,* 96 (n. 11): "*Propempō* is used in the New Testament only for sending a departing traveler on his way. It could mean accompanying him for a short distance (Acts 20:38; 21:5) or simply sending him on a mission (Acts 15:3), but more generally it means to equip him with all things necessary for the journey (Tit. 3:13; cf. Rom. 15:24; I Cor. 16:6, 11; II Cor. 1:16; III John 6; Polycarp, *Philippians* 1:1)."

47. According to R. Aus, "Paul's Travel Plans to Spain," 234, 260, Spain (which he takes to be the Tarshish of Isa 66:19, pp. 242-46) was the final goal of Paul's travels, since from there he would gain the last of his converts to accompany him to Jerusalem as representatives of "the full number of the Gentiles" (11:25). Cf. also R. Jewett, *Romans,* 924. But this is to fuse together the purpose of the collection (aid for the poor among the saints in Jerusalem) and the eschatological ingathering of the nations through the proclamation of the gospel. Moreover, it is far from clear that Paul would have understood the reference to Tarshish in Isa 66:19 as Spain. The location of Tarshish has been proposed for many places from Rhodes to Carthage; cf. David W. Baker, "Tarshish," *ABD* 6:331-33, and A. Das, "Paul of Tarshish," 60-73 (and literature cited). The only ancient writer to propose a place for Tarshish was Josephus, who identified it with Tarsus (*Ant.* 9.10.2 §§208-9); cf. discussion in R. Riesner, *Paul's Early Period,* 250-53. It is not likely, however, that Paul would have made the same identification (biblical Tarshish would have been a far-off place for him, not his hometown). In the final analysis, whether a single verse from Isaiah could have actually functioned as an itinerary for Paul seems to load it with more significance than is warranted.

ostolic mission well beyond Spain. It has been conjectured that he might have thought of going on to Gaul and Britain.[48] More sweeping is the proposal that Paul would have continued the arc (or circle) around the Mediterranean Sea, making a complete circuit of the nations both north and south of the sea, completing "one great journey beginning and ending in Jerusalem, but encompassing the whole Mediterranean world in its scope."[49]

Of these two proposals, the latter has a stronger base of support, and that is so for a couple of reasons. The first concerns Paul's use of the word κύκλῳ (15:19). Within the LXX the word κύκλῳ is used by various writers in reference to peoples and nations surrounding Jerusalem,[50] the "navel" of the world (Ezek 38:12). Moreover, according to Ezekiel, the Lord has set Jerusalem "in the midst of the nations (ἐν μέσῳ τῶν ἐθνῶν) and [has set] the countries in a circle (κύκλῳ) around her" (Ezek 5:5).[51]

The second reason why Paul could have planned to go from Spain to northern Africa is that both literary and archaeological evidence attests the existence of Jewish communities there. Paul could have considered their synagogues as bases of evangelization among the Gentile "God-fearers." Literary evidence indicates the presence of Jewish communities in Libya and Egypt,[52] particularly at Alexandria, where Philo estimated that a million Jews lived in the first century A.D.[53] Gustav Adolf Deissmann has mapped out the existence of 143 Jewish communities outside Palestine encircling the Mediterranean basin, based on archaeological as well as literary evidence, and many of these dot his map across northern Africa.[54]

Finally, however, it needs to be emphasized that any projections that interpreters might make for Paul's work beyond Spain, including this one, remain highly speculative. They are hypotheses at most. All that is certain is that Paul intended to go to Spain, and even that plan was not likely ever to have been realized. The only basis for claiming that he did get to Spain is an oblique statement in *1 Clement*, written in Rome near the close of the first century.[55] The author says that "when [Paul] had reached the limits of the west (τὸ τέρμα τῆς

48. J. Munck, *Paul and the Salvation of Mankind*, 52.

49. J. Knox, "Romans 15:14-33," 11; discussed further in A. Hultgren, *Paul's Gospel and Mission*, 132-37; cf. J. Wagner, *Heralds of the Good News*, 331.

50. Ps 78:3-4; Isa 49:18; 60:4; Jer 39:44; 40:13; Ezek 5:5; cf. Bar 2:4; 2 Macc 4:32.

51. Cf. J. Scott, *Paul and the Nations*, 138-39, 179, 217.

52. On Libya, cf. Acts 2:10; on Egypt, cf. Philo, *Legat.* 6.36; also the Elephantine Papyri from upper Egypt are evidence.

53. Philo, *Flacc.* 6.8.

54. G. Deissmann, *St. Paul*, 41 (n. 1), 88 (n. 3), and the map on the jacket of his book, "The World as Known to Paul."

55. Laurence L. Welborn, "Clement, First Epistle of," *ABD* 1:1055-60.

δύσεως) he gave his testimony before the rulers" (5.7).[56] The phrase "limits of the west" has been interpreted to mean Spain and considered reliable by very few interpreters.[57] But the reference is possibly a reference not to Spain, but to Rome itself, the place at which Paul bore "testimony before the rulers." If it is indeed a reference to Spain, the evidence is still not conclusive. It is possible that the only source the author of *1 Clement* had was what Paul wrote in 15:24-28. From that he may have assumed that Paul's hope was fulfilled, and that he understood the phrase to mean Spain.[58]

BIBLIOGRAPHY

Aus, Roger D. "Paul's Travel Plans to Spain and the 'Full Number of the Gentiles' of Rom. xi 25." *NovT* 21 (1979): 232-62.

Baer, Yitzhak. *A History of the Jews in Christian Spain.* 2 vols. Philadelphia: Jewish Publication Society of America, 1966.

Barnikol, Ernst. *Spanienreise und Römerbrief.* Halle an der Saale: Akademischer Verlag, 1934.

Baron, Salo W. *A Social and Religious History of the Jews.* 2d ed. 18 vols. New York: Columbia University Press, 1952-83.

Bornkamm, Günther. *Paul.* New York: Harper & Row, 1971; reprinted, Minneapolis: Fortress Press, 1995.

Bowers, W. Paul. "Church and Mission in Paul." *JSNT* 44 (1991): 89-111.

———. "Fulfilling the Gospel: The Scope of the Pauline Mission." *JETS* 30 (1987): 185-98.

———. "Jewish Communities in Spain in the Time of Paul the Apostle." *JTS* 26 (1975): 395-402.

———. "Paul and Religious Propaganda in the First Century." *NovT* 22 (1980): 316-23.

Das, A. Andrew. "Paul of Tarshish: Isaiah 66.19 and the Spanish Mission of Romans 15.24, 28." *NTS* 54 (2008): 60-73.

Deissmann, Gustav Adolf. *St. Paul: A Study in Social and Religious History.* London: Hodder & Stoughton, 1912.

Dewey, Arthur J. "Εἰς τὴν Σπανίαν: The Future and Paul." In *Religious Propaganda and Missionary Competition in the New Testament World: Essays Honoring Dieter Georgi,* 321-49. Ed. Lukas Bormann et al. Leiden: E. J. Brill, 1994.

———. "Social-Historical Observations on Romans (15:23-24)." *EGLBMSP* 7 (1987): 49-57.

Güzlow, Henneke. "Soziale Gegebenheiten der altkirchlichen Mission." In *Die alte Kirche,* 189-226. Ed. Heinzgütner Frohnes and Uwe W. Knorr. KGMG 1. Munich: Kaiser Verlag, 1974.

56. Quoted from *The Apostolic Fathers,* trans. Kirsopp Lake, LCL, 2 vols. (New York: G. P. Putnam's Sons, 1912-13), 1:16-17.

57. C. Cranfield, *Romans,* 768.

58. Cf. A. D. Nock, *St. Paul,* 143; G. Bornkamm, *Paul,* 106.

Hultgren, Arland J. *Paul's Gospel and Mission: The Outlook from His Letter to the Romans.* Philadelphia: Fortress Press, 1985.

———. "The Scriptural Foundations for Paul's Mission to the Gentiles." In *Paul and His Theology,* 21-44. PAST 3. Ed. Stanley E. Porter. Boston: E. J. Brill, 2006.

Jewett, Robert. "Paul, Phoebe, and the Spanish Mission." In *The Social World of Formative Christianity and Judaism: Essays in Tribute to Howard Clark Kee,* 142-61. Ed. Jacob Neusner et al. Philadelpha: Fortress Press, 1988.

Knox, John. "Romans 15.14-33 and Paul's Conception of His Apostolic Mission." *JBL* 83 (1964): 1-11.

Kraabel, A. Thomas. "The Diaspora Synagogue: Archaeological and Epigraphic Evidence since Sukenik." *ANRW* II.19.1 (1979): 477-510.

Malherbe, Abraham J. *Social Aspects of Early Christianity.* 2d ed. Philadelphia: Fortress Press, 1983.

Meinardus, Otto F. A. "Paul's Missionary Journey to Spain: Tradition and Folklore." *BA* 41 (1978): 61-63.

Munck, Johannes. *Paul and the Salvation of Mankind.* Richmond: John Knox Press, 1959.

Nock, Arthur D. *Conversion: The Old and the New in Religion from Alexander the Great to Augustine of Hippo.* Oxford: Clarendon Press, 1933.

Nock, Arthur D. *St. Paul.* New York: Harper & Row, 1938.

Raabe, Paul R. *Obadiah.* AB 24D. New York: Doubleday, 1996.

Rabello, Alfredo M. "The Situation of the Jews in Roman Spain." In his *The Jews in the Roman Empire: Legal Problems, from Herod to Justinian,* 159-90. Burlington: Ashgate Publishing Company, 2000.

Riesner, Rainer. *Paul's Early Period: Chronology, Mission Strategy, Theology.* Grand Rapids: Wm. B. Eerdmans, 1998.

Rostovtzeff, Michael I. *Greece.* New York: Oxford University Press, 1963.

Scott, James M. *Paul and the Nations: The Old Testament and Jewish Background of Paul's Mission to the Nations with Special Reference to the Destination of Galatians.* WUNT 84. Tübingen: J. C. B. Mohr (Paul Siebeck), 1995.

Smallwood, E. Mary. *The Jews under Roman Rule from Pompey to Diocletian: A Study in Political Relations.* Leiden: E. J. Brill, 2001.

Stern, Menachem. "The Jewish Diaspora." In *The Jewish People in the First Century: Historical Geography, Political History, Social, Cultural and Religious Life and Institutions,* 1:117-83. Ed. Shemuel Safrai and Menachem Stern. CRINT 1. 2 vols. Philadelphia: Fortress Press, 1974-76.

Thornton, T. C. G. "St Paul's Missionary Intentions in Spain." *ExpTim* 86 (1974-75): 120.

Trocmé, Étienne. "L'Épître aux Romains et la méthode missionaire de l'apôtre Paul." *NTS* 7 (1960-61): 148-53.

Wagner, J. Ross. *Heralds of the Good News: Isaiah and Paul "in Concert" in the Letter to the Romans.* NovTSup 101. Boston: E. J. Brill, 2002.

Wander, Bernd. "Warum wollte Paulus nach Spanien? Ein Forschungs- und motivgeschichtlicher Überblick." In *Das Ende des Paulus: Historische, theologische und literaturgeschichtliche Aspekte,* 175-95. Ed. Friedrich W. Horn. BZNW 106. Berlin: Walter de Gruyter, 2001.

9.3. The Intervening Visit to Jerusalem, 15:25-33

25But now I am going to Jerusalem to provide aid for the saints; 26for Macedonia and Achaia have been pleased to make a contribution for the poor among the saints in Jerusalem. 27Indeed, they were pleased to do this, and they are indebted to them; for if the Gentiles have shared in their spiritual things, they are obligated also to render service to them in material things. 28Then, after I have completed this, and have made sure that they have received what has been raised, I shall go on by way of you to Spain; 29and I know that when I come to you I shall come in the fullness of the blessing of Christ.

30Now I urge you, brothers and sisters, through our Lord Jesus Christ and through the love of the Spirit, to strive earnestly with me in prayer to God on my behalf 31that I may be rescued from the unbelievers in Judea, and that my ministry to Jerusalem may be acceptable to the saints, 32so that by the will of God I may come to you in joy and be refreshed in your company.

33The God of peace be with you all. Amen.

Notes on the Text and Translation

15:27 The γάρ in this verse, otherwise usually translated as "for," can better be translated as "indeed" or "in fact," marking an inference.[59]

15:31 Instead of reading "my ministry (διακονία) to Jerusalem," some major texts (B, D, and others) read "my bringing of gifts (δωροφορία) to Jerusalem." The former appears, however, in other major texts (including $\mathfrak{P}^{46}$, ℵ, A, and the Majority Text) and is to be preferred. The alternative is otherwise never found in Paul's letters (nor elsewhere in the NT) and may be due to some scribal desire to avoid the idea that Paul would carry on a ministry of preaching in Jerusalem. He had used the verbal expression διακονέω ("to minister," "to give aid") at 15:25, but the context is clearly relief work.

15:32 The expression "the will of God (θεοῦ)" is attested in $\mathfrak{P}^{46}$, A, and the Majority Text, and supported by Vulgate and Syriac readings. Curiously, ℵ has "the will of Jesus Christ," and B has "the will of the Lord Jesus." But elsewhere Paul always uses the former phrase, never the latter two.

The verb συναναπαύομαι appears only here in the NT. It is omitted altogether in $\mathfrak{P}^{46}$ and B and replaced by other verbs in other texts. But the expression συναναπαύσωμαι ὑμῖν ("I may be refreshed in your company") has support in ℵ, A, and other texts; and its inclusion preceded by καί ("and") is supported by additional texts (including the Majority Text). The basis for its inclusion is therefore somewhat tenuous, but stronger than the alternatives.

59. BDAG 190 (γάρ, 3).

15:33 The word ἀμήν ("amen") appears in several major textual witnesses, including ℵ, B, C, D, and others (including the Majority Text), and is supported by Old Latin, Syriac, and Coptic witnesses. It is lacking in 𝔓⁴⁶, probably because that text has a doxology here, followed by the word itself.[60] It has sufficient support for its inclusion.

General Comment

After letting the members of the community at Rome know that he plans to come there and go on to Spain, Paul informs them that the visit cannot be at once. Instead of coming there directly and soon, he must go to Jerusalem to deliver a collection from churches that he had founded to "the saints" in the city where the Christian movement had its origins.

Reflecting back, he speaks of the generosity of the churches that had made contributions. But thinking of the future, he expresses some concern about his reception in Jerusalem, for which he wants the prayers of the believers in Rome. Nevertheless, in spite of the foreboding, at this point in his career he continues to anticipate a journey to Rome as a free man and as an apostle, from where he will proceed to Spain.

Detailed Comment

15:25-27 In calling the believers of Jerusalem "the saints" (as he does at 1 Cor 16:1 also), Paul is not giving them special deference or status, for that is the same term that he has used for the Roman Christians already (1:7) and has used often as a general designation for believers in his letters (e.g., Rom 8:27; 12:13; 1 Cor 1:2; 6:1-3; Phil 1:1; 1 Thess 3:13).

Macedonia and Achaea are mentioned as places from which the aid for the saints has come. The background to the comments made by Paul is the conclusion of the Jerusalem assembly attended by Paul in the presence of Peter, James, and John (Gal 2:1-10; Acts 15:1-29). At the conclusion of that event, and as Paul departed on his mission among the Gentiles, the leaders of the church at Jerusalem asked Paul to "remember the poor," which very thing Paul resolved to do (Gal 2:10).

"Macedonia" would include both Philippi and Thessalonica. While writing to the Corinthians, Paul mentions the generosity of the Macedonian churches as an example for them (2 Cor 8:1-6). "Achaea" would include Corinth,

---

60. B. Metzger, *TCGNT* 475.

to whom Paul wrote explicit directions concerning their raising funds for the collection (1 Cor 16:1-4; 2 Cor 8:7–9:15), and from where he was writing his letter to Rome (see Introduction, pp. 2-3). Paul does not mention here the churches of Galatia and Ephesus as sources for funds. He apparently mentions Macedonia and Achaea because he had only recently been in Macedonia (cf. Acts 20:1-3) and was writing from Corinth (Achaea). But one should not conclude that the churches of Galatia and Ephesus were not asked to contribute. In writing to the Corinthians Paul had mentioned that he had given directions to the churches of Galatia for their participation (1 Cor 16:1), and one can surely expect that Paul urged the participation of the church at Ephesus. In light of the strained relations he had with the churches of Galatia subsequent to his departure, it is possible that the churches there refused to participate.[61] On the other hand, it is possible that at the time of writing Romans the representatives of Galatia had not yet arrived or had not made a final commitment.[62] We cannot know. Ephesus was a different matter. According to Luke, the church at Ephesus was represented by Tychicus and Trophimus among the delegation to Jerusalem (Acts 20:4).

Paul says now in his letter to Rome that he is taking the collection from the Pauline churches to Jerusalem. It is designated not for the church in general but specifically "for the poor among the saints in Jerusalem." There can be little doubt but what the collection for Jerusalem was a symbolic gesture that, for Paul, signaled the unity between his Gentile churches and the church at Jerusalem.[63] But at the time of writing Romans Paul picks up once again the language of his resolve in Jerusalem. The collection was for "the poor," those who were impoverished in a material sense. There were good reasons for such an act of relief, for there is evidence of famine in Palestine during the reign of Claudius, probably about A.D. 46-48, prior to the meeting of Paul with the apostles in Jerusalem.[64] But of course the entire church in Judea would benefit, since any relief given to the poor would lessen the load of any others in that area who would be giving aid to their co-believers. That Paul considered the collection and its delivery a high priority is evident from his references to it in Romans and the Corinthian corre-

61. J. L. Martyn, *Galatians,* 227 (n. 81).

62. D. Georgi, *Remembering the Poor,* 123.

63. C. K. Barrett, *Romans,* 255; J. Munck, *Paul and the Salvation of Mankind,* 301-2; C. Cranfield, *Romans,* 770; U. Wilckens, *Römer,* 3:125; B. Holmberg, *Paul and Power,* 38; J. Dunn, *Romans,* 873; K. Nickle, *The Collection,* 111-28; D. Georgi, *Remembering the Poor,* 113-17; P. Stuhlmacher, *Romans,* 242; Josef Hainz, "κοινωνία," *EDNT* 2:304; S. Joubert, *Paul as Benefactor,* 207-8; J. L. Martyn, *Galatians,* 227-28; E. Lohse, *Römer,* 400-401.

64. Acts 11:27-30; Josephus, *Ant.* 20.5.2 (§101); cf. 3.15.3 (§320-21). Other references to famines during the reign of Claudius (A.D. 41-54) are in Suetonius, *Claudius* 18; Tacitus, *Ann.* 12.43. For discussion, cf. J. Jeremias, *Jerusalem in the Time of Jesus,* 141-43; L. Johnson, *The Acts of the Apostles,* 205-6; J. Fitzmyer, *The Acts of the Apostles,* 482 (with literature); S. Joubert, *Paul as Benefactor,* 108-10.

spondence. Moreover, in regard to the delivery of the collection, he planned to be accompanied by members of his churches (1 Cor 16:3; 2 Cor 8:19) as their representatives, further providing evidence of the work of the Spirit through his own proclamation among the Gentiles, who are turning to God. According to Luke (Acts 20:4), Paul was accompanied on the journey to Jerusalem by several persons (he names seven) from cities in Macedonia (Beroea and Thessalonica) and Asia Minor (Derbe and simply "Asia"). The list is probably incomplete,[65] since he makes no mention of representatives from Philippi and Corinth.

Some interpreters have concluded that the "poor" at this place is a self-designation of the church at Jerusalem. In this case the genitival construction within the phrase τοὺς πτωχοὺς τῶν ἁγίων τῶν ἐν Ἰερουσαλήμ is taken to be an epexegetical one (also called the genitive of apposition[66]), meaning "the poor [that consists] of the saints of Jerusalem."[67] That interpretation is influenced in part by the fact that the sect known as the Ebionites (Ἐβιωναῖοι, from אֶבְיוֹנִים), meaning "the poor" as a self-designation, may have had its origins in Jerusalem.[68] According to Epiphanius, the Ebionites traced their lineage back to the church there. But Epiphanius does not attribute the origins of the Ebionites to the earliest community; instead, he says that they originated after the fall of Jerusalem (A.D. 70).[69] The first reference to the Ebionites is in the writings of Irenaeus toward the end of the second century.[70] It is possible that those who designated themselves as Ebionites took their name after the destruction of Jerusalem due to the devastation and destitution that they had suffered.[71] But they were nevertheless a heterodox sect of the second and later centuries and should not be confused with the heirs of the early, Aramaic-speaking Christians generally.[72] There is no warrant for thinking that the early community used "the poor" as a self-designation. Moreover, the genitival construction

65. J. Munck, *Paul and the Salvation of Mankind*, 303; D. Georgi, *Remembering the Poor*, 122-23; S. Joubert, *Paul as Benefactor*, 205.

66. For illustrations of this genitive, cf. BDF 92 (§167); C. F. D. Moule, *An Idiom-Book of New Testament Greek*, 38.

67. K. Holl, "Der Kirchenbegriff des Paulus in seinem Verhältnis zu dem der Urgemeinde," 2:58; H. Lietzmann, *Römer*, 122; Ernst Bammel, "πτωχός," *TDNT* 6:909; F. Hahn, *Mission in the New Testament*, 108-9. D. Georgi, *Remembering the Poor*, 114, and B. Byrne, *Romans*, 444, regard "the poor" as a self-designation of the Jerusalem church at Gal 2:10, but no longer at Rom 15:26, where they agree that a partitive genitive is used.

68. Cf. E. Bammel, "πτωχός," *TDNT* 6:909.

69. Epiphanius, *Panarion* 30.2.7. For this and other ancient texts on the Ebionites, cf. *The Earliest Christian Heretics*, ed. A. Hultgren and S. Haggmark, 116-22.

70. Irenaeus, *Against Heresies* 1.26.2.

71. J. Fitzmyer, "The Qumran Scrolls, the Ebionites and Their Literature," 439-40.

72. J. Daniélou, *The Theology of Jewish Christianity*, 55-56; J. Fitzmyer, "The Qumran Scrolls, the Ebionites and Their Literature," 439-40;

within the phrase τοὺς πτωχοὺς τῶν ἁγίων τῶν ἐν Ἰερουσαλήμ should be interpreted in its most natural sense, i.e., as a partitive genitive,[73] meaning "the poor who are among the saints in Jerusalem."[74]

That the collection and its delivery was a symbolic gesture concerning the unity of Jews and Gentiles in the church is well founded. But is there more? Some interpreters have maintained that, for Paul, the collection was a fulfillment of the eschatological expectation that the Gentiles would bring their wealth to Jerusalem in the last days (Isa 2:2-3; 45:14; 60:5-17; 61:6; Mic 4:1-2, 13; Tob 13:11; 1QM 12.13-15).[75] But neither the original request at Jerusalem nor statements concerning the collection in Paul's letters support that view. The original resolve of Paul was "to remember the poor" of Jerusalem (Gal 2:10), and in Romans 15:25-27 Paul says that his ministry is for the poor among the saints in Jerusalem; furthermore, he says that his churches were pleased to participate in that ministry.[76] It is difficult to imagine that Paul would have sought to gather a collection, and be able to promote it among the donors, for any purpose other than that which he had stated.

The symbolic nature of the collection and its delivery can be explored along different lines. The mission to the Gentiles was itself understood as an eschatological ingathering, culminating the long history of Israel and God's salvation of the world through Israel. The Gentiles, Paul says, have come to share in (ἐκοινώνησαν) the spiritual blessings enjoyed by the Jerusalem church (15:27). Here Paul uses the aorist form of the verb κοινωνέω, which means essentially to have fellowship with another and to have something in common.[77] Therefore the unity of Paul's churches with the Jerusalem church should be self-evident. It is on that basis that Paul says that the Gentile churches are under obligation to render service (λειτουργέω) to the poor in Jerusalem with material things. The verb λειτουργέω, like the noun related to it (λειτουργός), can have either a secular meaning or a religious one.[78] But if it has a purely secular meaning ("to

---

73. C. Moule, *An Idiom-Book of New Testament Greek,* 43, referring to Rom 15:26; cf. BDF 90-91 (§164).

74. This interpretation, based on Paul's use of a partitive genitive, is widely held, e.g., by E. Käsemann, *Romans,* 401; C. Cranfield, *Romans,* 772; U. Wilckens, *Römer,* 3:125; J. Fitzmyer, *Romans,* 722; D. Georgi, *Remembering the Poor,* 114; and B. Byrne, *Romans,* 444 (both making a distinction between the poor in Rom 15:26 and those of Gal 2:10); D. Moo, *Romans,* 903-4; E. Lohse, *Römer,* 400.

75. J. Munck, *Paul and the Salvation of Mankind,* 303-4; J. Dunn, *Romans,* 874; D. Georgi, *Remembering the Poor,* 119; R. Aus, "Paul's Travel Plans to Spain and the 'Full Number of the Gentiles' of Rom. xi 25," 235-37; P. Stuhlmacher, *Romans,* 242; T. Schreiner, *Romans,* 776.

76. Cf. C. Talbert, *Romans,* 330.

77. J. Hainz, "κοινωνία," 2:303-5; J. Campbell, "ΚΟΙΝΩΝΙΑ," 372-73.

78. The noun λειτουργός ("servant," "minister") has been used previously to speak of either secular (13:6) or cultic service (15:16).

serve" a community), that would be exceptional in the NT.[79] In choosing the term Paul conveys to the reader a religious connotation.[80] By means of the collection Paul and his churches are doing spiritual service. In that effort Paul speaks of serving (διακονέω, 15:25, "to provide aid")[81] and sharing (κοινωνίαν . . . ποιήσασθαι, literally, "do an act of sharing," 15:26). It is possible that Paul thought along these lines after meeting with the leaders of the church in Jerusalem (Gal 2:1-10). Their request to Paul — and through Paul to his churches — to remember the poor was no doubt primarily a financial matter for them. But it could prompt Paul to think of the need for solidarity between his churches and the church at Jerusalem. There can hardly be a more tangible means of providing evidence for that than the collecting and delivering of funds for relief.

According to the language used, the collection for Jerusalem was a voluntary act of charity, for twice in this passage he says that those who contributed "were pleased" to do what they did (15:26-27). The verb εὐδοκέω ("to be pleased") indicates that they considered their action as something that they wanted to do, something that is good.[82] There is no basis for considering the collection as having been derived from a "ruling of the Apostolic Council."[83]

15:28 Jerusalem (by implication), Rome (by implication), and Spain are all mentioned in this brief verse, an itinerary in broad outline. Looking ahead to his visit to Jerusalem, Paul wants to complete what he has been working on for a half-dozen years, getting the collection delivered. The delivery will not be casual but formal. He envisions an occasion where a formal transfer of the funds will take place, using the verb σφραγίζω, which literally means "to seal something for delivery." It may be derived from the practice of sealing sacks of grain for delivery, thus making the transfer certain.[84] In the present case it would mean that Paul wants to make certain that the collection is placed safely into the hands of the church at Jerusalem. Once that is done, he expects that he will depart from Jerusalem, go to Rome, and get on his way to Spain.

15:29 Paul expresses confidence in his being welcomed at Rome. He uses an expression here that he does not use elsewhere. He will come "in the fullness

---

79. Cf. the entries in BDAG 590-91 (λειτουργέω).

80. Horst Balz, "λειτουργία," *EDNT* 2:347-49. On the other hand, T. Schreiner, *Romans,* 777, says that "a cultic nuance is improbable," and R. Jewett, *Romans,* 931, affirms a "secular sense" only. Better is the view of J. Dunn, *Romans,* 876: "the boundary between cultic and profane" is broken down.

81. Paul uses a participle to express purpose; cf. J. O'Rourke, "The Participle in Rom 15,25," 116-18; U. Wilckens, *Römer,* 3:124.

82. BDAG 404 (εὐδοκέω, 1).

83. E. Käsemann, *Romans,* 399. Cf. E. Bammel, "πτωχός," 6:909. For a survey of this and similar theories, cf. K. Nickle, *The Collection,* 74-93.

84. BDAG 980 (σφραγίζω, 5). L. Radermacher, "σφραγίζεσθαι," 87-89. C. Cranfield, *Romans,* 774-75, cites other possible meanings.

of the blessing of Christ." Does that mean that he will bring the fullness of Christ's blessing with him as he comes?[85] Or does he mean that he will be welcomed with the fullness of Christ's blessing being bestowed on him by the community at Rome? Is it something he possesses, or is it something the Roman believers have to give? An either/or is not required in this case. Surely it is going too far to say that "the apostle . . . believes that he can come to Rome with all the power he has been given."[86] Rather than that, it is likely that Paul expects to be received by and to share in the fullness of Christ's blessing.[87] The expression resonates with what Paul has said in 1:11-12: he will indeed share "some spiritual gift to strengthen" the community, but he will also experience mutual encouragement.[88] It also anticipates Paul's wish to be refreshed in the company of the Roman believers (15:32).

15:30-32 But there is some serious foreboding. Paul requests prayers for two things: (1) that he may have safe passage to Jerusalem while in Judea and (2) that his collection will be received. Concerning the first point, Paul wishes to be "delivered" or "rescued" from "the unbelievers in Judea." The term used for "the unbelievers" (οἱ ἀπειθοῦντες) can just as well be translated "the disobedient,"[89] and here it signifies Jewish persons who had not accepted the gospel (cf. Rom 10:16, 21; 11:31; 2 Cor 4:4). Paul's fear of being seized by such persons and being treated severely, perhaps even killed, was well founded. Prior to his call as an apostle, Paul himself had been involved in the persecution of Christians in Judea (Gal 1:13, 22-23),[90] and he would not necessarily be the only one to do so. Furthermore, according to what he had written prior to his letter to the Romans, he had received floggings (the 39 lashes) five times from Jewish officials (2 Cor 11:24),[91] which could be lethal, and he claimed to have experienced "danger from [his] own people" (2 Cor 11:26).[92]

The second concern expresses a foreboding in reference to persons on a

---

85. So W. Sanday and A. Headlam, *Romans,* 414; E. Käsemann, *Romans,* 402; U. Wilckens, *Römer,* 3:128; J. Fitzmyer, *Romans,* 723; E. Lohse, *Römer,* 401; R. Jewett, *Romans,* 932.

86. E. Käsemann, *Romans,* 402.

87. C. K. Barrett, *Romans,* 255-56; J. Dunn, *Romans,* 877.

88. According to K. Nickle, *The Collection,* 122 (n. 188), Paul considered the blessing incomplete at the time of writing, since he was awaiting the outcome of his visit to Jerusalem. But the expectation is that it will be full when he arrives in Rome. It seems more likely, however, that Paul is simply being effusive in his piling up of terms ("the fullness of the blessing of Christ").

89. Cf. BDAG 99 (ἀπειθέω).

90. For discussion, cf. A. Hultgren, "Paul's Pre-Christian Persecutions of the Church," 97-111.

91. On flogging, reasons for it (primarily disciplinary), and its administration, cf. Haim H. Cohn, "Bet Din and Judges," *EncJud* 4:720-21.

92. Cf. also 1 Thess 2:14-15, which speaks of Jewish persecution of Christians in Judea, but various interpreters have maintained that the passage is a post-Pauline interpolation.

different front. Paul is uncertain whether his collection for the poor will be received by "the saints" (apparently not only the leaders of the church) in Jerusalem. Whether or not it was received, we cannot be certain. The Acts of the Apostles is silent on the matter, except for a possible passing reference at 24:17. This has led various interpreters to conclude that Paul's collection was either not received at all or not well received.[93] Others have maintained that the collection was probably received, even if we know little about why or how.[94] In a more extensive and plausible construction, it has been suggested that, on the basis of Acts, one can say that Paul and James (the undisputed leader of the church at Jerusalem at the time, Acts 21:18) made a compromise. Paul paid for the release of four destitute Nazirites and joined them in purification rites at the Temple (21:17-26). He would have used a portion of the collection for those acts, and the rest would have been turned over to the leaders of the church for the poor.[95] The suggestion is possible, even if not certain. It depends on the certainty that Acts 24:17 refers to Paul's collection, but that is highly speculative and has been called into serious question.[96] The end result is that we do not know whether or, if so, how the collection was received. In any case, setting that issue aside, we can be on firmer ground concerning Luke's account of Paul's fate in Jerusalem. According to him, after a purification rite at the Temple, events unfold in a disastrous way. Paul was nearly lynched by the people of Jerusalem (21:30-31, corresponding to "the unbelievers in Judea" that Paul speaks of with ominous apprehension in Rom 15:31), is "rescued" by the Roman guard, and is subsequently sent to Rome as a prisoner.

The concern expressed in 15:31b concerning Paul's relationship to the church at Jerusalem is crucial for understanding the purpose of his letter to Rome. Although it has been suggested that Paul was seeking to obtain intervention by the Roman Christians on his behalf in Jerusalem,[97] that does not seem likely, since Paul wrote his letter on the eve of his departure for the holy city. It is more likely that Paul, concerned about whether he (and his collection) would be accepted in Jerusalem, wrote the letter to prepare for his visit to Rome. If he (and his collection) should somehow be rejected in Jerusalem, his support from Rome for his mission to Spain would come to naught. By writing his letter to Rome, however, Paul was able to share with them his gospel, thereby persuad-

---

93. J. Dunn, *Romans*, 880; J. Ziesler, *Romans*, 347; B. Byrne, *Romans*, 445; L. Keck, *Romans*, 367.

94. K. Nickle, *The Collection*, 70-72; J. Fitzmyer, *Romans*, 726.

95. D. Georgi, *Remembering the Poor*, 122-27; S. Joubert, *Paul as Benefactor*, 213-15; R. Jewett, *Romans*, 937.

96. For survey and discussion, cf. D. Downs, "Paul's Collection and the Book of Acts Revisited," 62-70.

97. E. Käsemann, *Romans*, 405; P. Stuhlmacher, *Romans*, 244.

ing the believers there of his gospel's veracity and gaining their support for his mission to Spain.

15:33   Paul closes this section with a blessing.[98] The expression "God of peace" appears elsewhere in Paul's letters (Rom 16:20; Phil 4:9; 1 Thess 5:23; cf. 1 Cor 14:33), has a background already in Judaism,[99] and can be considered a liturgical expression. Paul pronounces this blessing upon the community of believers at Rome, as he does to the Philippians (Phil 4:9). It is a gesture fitting for the close of a letter that speaks of an ominous future. Whatever is to happen during his travels to Jerusalem or in the city itself, Paul extends a blessing to his readers, granting his desire that the "God of peace," who is the source of peace, will keep the hearts and minds of his readers at peace. The apostle is heard at Rome as desiring that which only God can finally grant. It is characteristic of blessings to express the audacity of one who believes firmly in the power of God to grant all good things.

Formally, this verse marks the end of the body of the letter.[100] In chapter 16 Paul goes on to send greetings.

BIBLIOGRAPHY

Aus, Roger D. "Paul's Travel Plans to Spain and the 'Full Number of the Gentiles' of Rom. xi 25." *NovT* 21 (1979): 232-62.

Bartsch, Hans-Werner. ". . . wenn ich ihnen diese Frucht versiegelt habe. Röm 15.28: Ein Beitrag zum Verständnis der paulinischen Mission." *ZNW* 63 (1972): 95-107.

Berger, Klaus. "Almösen für Israel: Zum historischen Kontext der paulinischen Kollekte." *NTS* 23 (1976-77): 180-204.

Beckheuer, Burkhard. *Paulus und Jerusalem: Kollekte und Mission im theologischen Denken des Heidenapostels.* EHS.T 23/611. Frankfurt am Main: Peter Lang, 1997.

Bowen, Clayton R. "Paul's Collection and the Book of Acts." *JBL* 42 (1923): 49-58.

Campbell, J. Y. "KOINΩNIA and Its Cognates in the New Testament." *JBL* 51 (1932): 352-80.

Daniélou, Jean. *The Theology of Jewish Christianity.* Chicago: Henry Regnery Company, 1964.

Delling, Gerhard. "Die Bezeichnung 'Gott des Friedens' und ähnliche Wendungen in den Paulusbriefen." In *Jesus und Paulus: Festschrift für Werner Georg Kümmel zum 70.*

---

98. The expression is variously considered. It is a blessing or benediction according to E. Käsemann, *Romans*, 408; U. Wilckens, *Römer*, 3:130; J. Fitzmyer, *Romans*, 746; P. Stuhlmacher, *Romans*, 244; E. Lohse, *Römer*, 402; R. Jewett, *Romans*, 938; but it is a prayer or prayer wish according to W. Sanday and A. Headlam, *Romans*, 416; C. H. Dodd, *Romans*, 233; C. K. Barrett, *Romans*, 256; C. Cranfield, *Romans*, 779; J. Dunn, *Romans*, 880; B. Byrne, *Romans*, 445.

99. Cf. its use in *T. Dan* 5.2; Heb 13:20.

100. J. White, *The Form and Function of the Body of the Greek Letter*, 98.

Geburtstag, 76-84. Ed. E. Earle Ellis and Erich Grässer. Göttingen: Vandenhoeck & Ruprecht, 1975.

Downs, David J. "Paul's Collection and the Book of Acts Revisited." *NTS* 52 (2006): 50-70.

————. *The Offering of the Gentiles: Paul's Collection for Jerusalem in Its Chronological, Cultural, and Cultic Contexts.* WUNT 2/248. Tübingen: Mohr-Siebeck, 2008.

Fitzmyer, Joseph. *The Acts of the Apostles.* AB 31. New York: Doubleday, 1998.

————. "The Qumran Scrolls, the Ebionites and Their Literature." In his *Essays on the Semitic Background of the New Testament*, 435-80. SBLSBS. London: Geoffrey Chapman, 1974.

Gaston, Lloyd. "Paul and Jerusalem." In *From Jesus to Paul: Studies in Honour of Francis Wright Beare*, 61-72. Ed. Peter Richardson and John C. Hurd. Waterloo: Wilfrid Laurier Press, 1984.

Georgi, Dieter. *Remembering the Poor: The History of Paul's Collection for Jerusalem.* Nashville: Abingdon Press, 1992.

Hahn, Ferdinand. *Mission in the New Testament.* SBT 47. Naperville: Alec R. Allenson, 1965.

Heckel, Ulrich. *Der Segen im Neuen Testament: Begriff, Formeln, Gesten: Mit einem präktische-theologischen Ausblick.* WUNT 150. Tübingen: J. C. B. Mohr (Paul Siebeck), 2002.

Holl, Karl. "Der Kirchenbegriff des Paulus in seinem Verhältnis zu dem der Urgemeinde." In his *Gesammelte Aufsätze zur Kirchengeschichte*, 2:44-67. 3 vols. Tübingen: J. C. B. Mohr (Paul Siebeck), 1928-48.

Holmberg, Bengt. *Paul and Power: The Structure of Authority in the Primitive Church as Reflected in the Pauline Epistles.* ConBNT 11. Lund: C. W. K. Gleerup, 1978.

Hultgren, Arland J. "Paul's Pre-Christian Persecutions of the Church: Their Purpose, Locale, and Nature." *JBL* 95 (1976): 97-111.

————. "The Scriptural Foundations for Paul's Mission to the Gentiles." In *Paul and His Theology*, 21-44. PAST 3. Ed. Stanley E. Porter. Boston: E. J. Brill, 2006.

Hultgren, Arland J., and Steven A. Haggmark, eds. *The Earliest Christian Heretics: Readings from Their Opponents.* Minneapolis: Fortress Press, 1996.

Hurtado, Larry W. "The Jerusalem Collection and the Book of Galatians." *JSNT* 5 (1979): 46-62.

Jeremias, Joachim. *Jerusalem in the Time of Jesus: An Investigation into Economic and Social Conditions during the New Testament Period.* Philadelphia: Fortress Press, 1969.

Jewett, Robert. "The God of Peace in Romans: Reflections on Crucial Lutheran Texts." *CurTM* 25/3 (1998): 186-94.

————. "Paul, Phoebe, and the Spanish Mission." In *The Social World of Formative Christianity and Judaism: Essays in Tribute to Howard Clark Kee*, 142-61. Ed. Jacob Neusner, Peder Borgen, Ernest S. Frerichs, and Richard Horsley. Philadelpha: Fortress Press, 1988.

Johnson, Luke T. *The Acts of the Apostles.* SP 5. Collegeville: Liturgical Press, 1992.

Joubert, Stephan. *Paul as Benefactor: Reciprocity, Strategy, and Theological Reflection in Paul's Collection.* WUNT 2/1124. Tübingen: J. C. B. Mohr (Paul Siebeck), 2000.

Keck, Leander E. "The Poor among the Saints in the New Testament." *ZNW* 56 (1965): 100-129.

Meinardus, Otto F. A. "Paul's Missionary Journey to Spain: Tradition and Folklore." *BA* 41 (1978): 61-63.

Martyn, J. Louis. *Galatians.* AB 33A. New York: Doubleday, 1997.

Moule, C. F. D. *An Idiom-Book of New Testament Greek.* 2d ed. Cambridge: Cambridge University Press, 1960.

Munck, Johannes. *Paul and the Salvation of Mankind.* Richmond: John Knox Press, 1959.

Nickle, Keith F. *The Collection: A Study in Paul's Strategy.* SBT 48. Naperville: Alec R. Allenson, 1966.

O'Rourke, John J. "The Participle in Rom 15,25." *CBQ* 29 (1967): 116-18.

Peterman, Gerald W. "Romans 15:26: Make a Contribution or Establish Fellowship?" *NTS* 40 (1994): 457-63.

Radermacher, Ludwig. "σφραγίζεσθαι: Röm 15:28." *ZNW* 32 (1933): 87-89.

Scott, James M. *Paul and the Nations: The Old Testament and Jewish Background of Paul's Mission to the Nations with Special Reference to the Destination of Galatians.* WUNT 84. J. C. B. Mohr (Paul Siebeck), 1995.

Thornton, T. C. G. "St Paul's Missionary Intentions in Spain." *ExpTim* 86 (1974-75): 120.

Wedderburn, A. J. M. "Paul's Collection: Chronology and History." *NTS* 48 (2002): 95-110.

White, John L. *The Form and Function of the Body of the Greek Letter: A Study of the Letter-Body in the Nonliterary Papyri and in Paul the Apostle.* 2d ed. SBLDS 2. Missoula: Scholars Press, 1972.

CHAPTER 10

Greetings and Closure, 16:1-27

Letters of the Greco-Roman world ended with a greeting, and other variable elements were often added, such as a peace wish, a wish for health, a farewell (forms of the verb ἐρρῶσθαι), and perhaps the date of the letter's composition.[1] In many letters from antiquity, as illustrated in papyri, the closing contains, among other things, the simple phrase, ἐπιμέλου δὲ σεαυτοῦ ἵν᾽ ὑγιαίνῃς ("Take care of yourself in order that you may be well").[2]

The closings of Paul's letters are "less bound to the closing conventions of the Hellenistic letters than to any other formulaic portion."[3] They lack, for instance, the wish for health and the usual word for "farewell" (forms of ἐρρῶσθαι). Instead all of his undisputed letters close with a benediction near the end (Rom 16:20; 1 Cor 16:23; 2 Cor 13:14; Gal 6:18; Phil 4:23; 1 Thess 5:28; Phlm 25). In the case of Romans, the wording is ἡ χάρις τοῦ κυρίου ἡμῶν Ἰησοῦ μεθ᾽ ὑμῶν ("The grace of our Lord Jesus be with you"), and the same or similar expressions are found in the others. Beyond that, there are a few variables. These may include a peace wish (Rom 15:33; 2 Cor 13:11b; Gal 6:16; Phil 4:7-9; 1 Thess 5:23-24), greetings (Rom 16:1-15; 1 Cor 16:19-20a; 2 Cor 13:13; Phil 4:21-22), the request for a holy kiss among his addressees (1 Cor 16:20b; 2 Cor 13:12; 1 Thess 5:26), or some form of apostolic command (1 Cor 16:22; 1 Thess 5:27).[4]

The Letter to the Romans has an extraordinarily long closure. Most of that can be accounted for by the long list of greetings that are sent. That very length has caused some interpreters to wonder whether the chapter can in fact have been integral to the Letter to the Romans, since Paul had never been in

1. H.-J. Klauck, *Ancient Letters and the New Testament*, 24-25.
2. Many illustrations are presented in F. Exler, *The Form of the Ancient Greek Letter*, 113-16.
3. W. Doty, *Letters in Primitive Christianity*, 39.
4. Altered slightly from C. Roetzel, *The Letters of Paul*, 61-66. The range of variations is discussed by W. Doty, *Letters in Primitive Christianity*, 39-42.

Rome prior to sending the letter. Is it possible that he could have known that many persons there? The matter is dealt with in the Introduction, section 3, "Romans 16 in Light of Textual and Historical Criticism."

The length of the closure is also due in part to the likelihood that some of the material in chapter 16 has been interpolated into the letter, such as 16:24-27 (discussed also in the previously mentioned section of the Introduction).

The closing section of the letter provides a glimpse of Paul that is not otherwise well known. He expresses a deep affection for persons named. Moreover, the section provides considerable information about the house churches and their leaders in the city of Rome.

BIBLIOGRAPHY

Aune, David E. "Letters." In *The Westminster Dictionary of New Testament and Early Christian Literature and Rhetoric.* Louisville: Westminster John Knox, 2003.

Doty, William G. *Letters in Primitive Christianity.* Philadelphia: Fortress Press, 1973.

Exler, Francis X. J. *The Form of the Ancient Greek Letter of the Epistolary Papyri (3rd c. B.C.– 3rd c. A.D.).* Chicago: Ares Publishers, 1976.

Klauck, Hans-Josef. *Ancient Letters and the New Testament: A Guide to Context and Exegesis.* Waco: Baylor University Press, 2006.

Roetzel, Calvin J. *The Letters of Paul.* 5th ed. Louisville: Westminster John Knox Press, 2009.

Stowers, Stanley K. *Letter Writing in Greco-Roman Antiquity.* LEC 5. Philadelphia: Westminster Press, 1986.

White, John L. *The Form and Function of the Body of the Greek Letter: A Study of the Letter-Body in the Nonliterary Papyri and in Paul the Apostle.* SBLDS 2. Missoula: Scholars Press, 1972.

10.1. A Recommendation of Phoebe, 16:1-2

1I commend to you our sister Phoebe, deacon of the church at Cenchreae, 2that you may receive her in the Lord in a manner worthy of the saints and help her in whatever she might need of you; for she has also become a benefactor of many and also of me.

General Comment

These verses stand at the outset of closing remarks and greetings that are quite revealing of the Christian community at Rome and persons within it. But first there is a recommendation of Phoebe of Cenchreae, the eastern port of Corinth, who had an important role not only in her home community but also in the career and ongoing existence of the Letter to the Romans itself. Without Phoebe's activity and her care for the actual letter itself, for Paul as its sender, and for its recipients, the letter may not have survived.

That viewpoint presupposes that Romans 16 is integral to Paul's Letter to the Romans. For discussion of that question, see the Introduction to Romans, pp. 20-23.

Paul's commendation has a fourfold structure, in which he (1) identifies Phoebe by name; (2) mentions her credentials (a sister and deacon); (3) expresses a desired action from his readers (to receive her and to assist her); and (4) adds further credentials (calling her a benefactor of many and of Paul). Typically the first three items (identification, credentials, and desired action) appear in Pauline commendations.[5] But in this case Paul adds an additional statement concerning Phoebe's credentials. That is especially appropriate in this instance, since it sets up a reciprocity. Paul asks that the Roman Christians receive Phoebe and assist her, for she has assisted others, including Paul himself.

Phoebe would have had a role to play at Rome that is not mentioned explicitly, but which is implied. As the one person entrusted with the letter to Rome, she was also entrusted by Paul to comment on anything in the letter that would not have been understood, making her the first commentator on and exegete of the letter.[6] In addition, she could supplement the actual contents of the letter, filling in any gaps and informing the Christian house churches at Rome as needed concerning Paul's views and plans in more detail.

Detailed Comment

16:1 Phoebe is mentioned only here in the NT. She was probably of Gentile background since she bore a name from Greek mythology.[7] It is all but certain that she was the bearer of the letter from Paul to the Christians at Rome, as attested in early sources[8] and widely affirmed in modern scholarship.[9]

---

5. E. Agosto, "Paul and Commendation," 111, 122-23.

6. That letter carriers in antiquity were typically depended on to provide further explanations of letters has been illustrated by P. Head, "Named Letter-Carriers among the Oxyrhynchus Papyri," 279-99.

7. BDAG 1062 (Φοίβη). The name Φοίβη appears among inscriptions on the island of Cos published in William R. Paton and Edward L. Hicks, *The Inscriptions of Cos* (Oxford: Clarendon Press, 1891), 132 (inscription #94).

8. Pseudo-Constantius, *The Holy Letter of St. Paul to the Romans* (on 16:1); text in *Ein neuer Paulustext und Kommentar*, ed. Hermann J. Frede (Freiburg im Breisgau: Herder, 1974), 91, dated ca. A.D. 405; cf. also the various subscriptions to Romans in the Nestle-Aland Greek NT (27th ed.). According to the Majority Text, the letter was written "through Phoebe."

9. M. Gibson, "Phoebe," 281 (already in an essay published in 1911-12); C. Cranfield,

There are good reasons for adopting that view. As a formality, it was common in the first century for authors to recommend letter-bearers, asking that they be received (using forms of the verb δέχομαι, as in 16:2) in place of the authors themselves.[10] Moreover, Paul's commending her to the Christians at Rome indicates that she is expected by Paul to arrive either at the same time that the letter does or shortly thereafter. Just why Paul would have enlisted Phoebe to be his emissary at Rome is a matter of conjecture, but several things would have commended her. Not only was she a leader in the early Christian movement at Cenchreae, the port of Corinth, but she was clearly an acquaintance of Paul and implicitly trusted by him. Furthermore, she almost certainly would have known Prisca and Aquila personally, since they had lived in Corinth and, according to Acts 18:18-19, departed for Ephesus with Paul from Cenchreae. It has been suggested that Paul sent her to Rome for the purpose of creating a "logistical base for the Spanish mission,"[11] and that he considered her to be his patroness for that, expecting that she would enlist additional support from the Christians in Rome for his mission to Spain. Although that is a possibility, the most one can say with a high level of certainty is that he expected her to meet leaders of the house churches in Rome, fill them in on Paul's plans, secure arrangements for his arrival, alleviate any concerns they might have about his coming and being with them, and, above all, interpret the Letter to the Romans among its recipients prior to Paul's arrival.

Besides being called a "sister," Phoebe is called a "deacon of the church at Cenchreae" (16:1) and a "benefactor" (16:2). The term "deacon" (διάκονος, "deaconess" in RSV, "servant" in KJV, ASV, NIV, and NET, but "deacon" in the NRSV) has been understood from ancient times to be the title for an office in the church (including those instances where the person having the title was a woman),[12] and women in that office were known to conduct baptisms for women and to preach the Word of God.[13] The degree to which the term designated an actual office at the time Paul wrote Romans is not so clear. But the fact

---

Romans, 780; J. Fitzmyer, *Romans,* 729; E. Schüssler-Fiorenza, "Missionaries, Apostles, Co-workers," 424; P. Stuhlmacher, *Romans,* 246; J. Dunn, *Romans,* 886; B. Byrne, *Romans,* 447; Florence M. Gillman, "Phoebe," *ABD* 5:348.

10. C.-H. Kim, *Form and Structure of the Familiar Greek Letter of Recommendation,* 50-60; A. Malherbe, *Social Aspects of Early Christianity,* 101-03.

11. R. Jewett, "Paul, Phoebe, and the Spanish Mission," 151.

12. Origen, *Ad Romanos* (on 16:1); text in *Commentarii in Epistulam ad Romanos,* ed. Theresia Heither, 5 vols. (Freiburg im Breslau: Herder, 1990-95), 5:244; Pelagius, *Commentary on Romans* (on 16:1); text in *Pelagius' Commentary on St. Paul's Epistle to the Romans,* trans. Theodore S. de Bruyn (Oxford: Oxford University Press, 1993), 150-51.

13. Pelagius, *Commentary on Romans* (on 16:1).

that Paul uses the term also at Philippians 1:1 (along with "bishops") indicates that it has begun to take on an official meaning. Although the term can be translated simply as "servant," as in some versions of the English Bible, suspicion arises that the translators of those versions could not come to terms with the idea that a woman could possess a title or office comparable to that held elsewhere by persons who were male. The term (plural form) is translated as "deacons" at Philippians 1:1 by the KJV, ASV, RSV, NIV and NRSV, and the term is applied to co-workers such as Apollos (1 Cor 3:5) and Timothy (1 Thess 3:2); in fact, Paul applies the term to himself as well (1 Cor 3:5; 2 Cor 3:6; 6:4; 11:23). That being the case, one can conclude that Phoebe had a recognized, continuing ministerial role at the church in Cenchreae, even if we cannot produce a list of duties that flow from that. In any case, to translate the word here as "deaconess" implies a distinction from that of a (male) "deacon." But since a distinction need not be made in terms of gender, the term should be translated as "deacon" here as elsewhere.[14]

16:2 The other term used of Phoebe is "benefactor (προστάτις) of many and also of me." The word appears only here in the NT. The masculine form of the noun is προστάτης, which does not appear in the NT at all (but it does appear in the LXX at 2 Chr 24:11; 2 Macc 3:4). In Greek texts it has the meaning of "one who stands before" and so a "leader," "president," or "ruler."[15] The noun forms are related to the verb προΐστημι, which has the meaning of "to stand before" others, and appears twice in Paul's letters (Rom 12:8; 1 Thess 5:12) and four times in the deutero-Pauline Pastoral Epistles (1 Tim 3:4, 12; Titus 3:8, 14). In its active sense it can have the meaning of "to place something before" another; and in its passive sense "to be at the head of" or to preside. Whether the term προστάτις at 16:2 can function as a term specifically for presiding at worship in this particular case is unlikely because of the genitives that follow: "of many and also of me." In context it appears to indicate that it means "benefactor" (NRSV) or "patron."[16] Other terms exist in modern versions, such as "helper" (ASV, RSV) or "a great help" (NIV). Since she had that role, one can expect that Phoebe welcomed others into her home, a house church, at Cenchreae. Such a house would have to be of sufficient size for a gathering of people for worship, which implies that she was a woman of means. That would also have made it

---

14. M. Gibson, "Phoebe," 281; D. Arichea, "Who Was Phoebe?" 401-9. Contra the conclusions of R. Myerscough, "Exegesis 21: Was Phoebe Really a Deacon?" 24-26, and K. Romaniuk, "Was Phoebe in Romans 16,1 a Deaconness?" 132-34, who suggests that the use of the term here is "courteous" or a "pleasant exaggeration" (p. 133).

15. For entries, cf. LSJ 1526-27.

16. BDAG 885 (προστάτις); A. Malherbe, *Social Aspects of Early Christianity,* 97-98; E. Schüssler Fiorenza, "Missionaries, Apostles, Coworkers," 426; R. Kearsley, "Women in Public Life," 202; C. Osiek et al., *A Woman's Place,* 228.

possible for her to assist Paul and others in financial support. Although Paul made his living in Corinth as a tentmaker (Acts 18:3), he must have enlisted Phoebe's support as well. Whether she would have presided at worship in her home can hardly be determined, but it cannot be ruled out. Paul refers to her first as a "deacon," which would have been her public role within the church of Cenchreae, and then as a "benefactor," a term that applies to her activities in reference to certain persons ("of many and also of me"). Both terms are important, but the combination of them, and the fact that Paul speaks of her first of all as a "deacon," points toward a leadership role in worship within her own home.[17]

Paul calls upon the Christians in Rome to receive Phoebe "in a manner worthy of the saints." The Greek expression ἀξίως τῶν ἁγίων (more literally, "worthily of the saints") could mean that she is to be received in the way that a saint should be received, and being a traveling emissary from Paul would warrant such. But more likely the expression means that the Christians at Rome are to act in the way one would expect of saints. The words "saints" here recalls Paul's use of it in 1:7 when he addresses the Roman community ("called to be saints"). Hospitality for traveling missionaries and apostles was extremely important in the first century. To be sure, some of those who traveled about took advantage of hospitality, and therefore those who offered it had to be cautious (cf. 2 John 10; *Didache* 11–12). Paul's recommendation of Phoebe was therefore extremely important. Paul assumes, however, that the Christians at Rome would welcome Phoebe, as saints ought to do, and help her in whatever needs she had. The practice of hospitality in a world where inns were dangerous and strangers often a threat was one of the major means of carrying on the Christian mission.[18]

BIBLIOGRAPHY

Agosto, Efrain. "Paul and Commendation." In *Paul in the Greco-Roman World: A Handbook*, 101-33. Ed. J. Paul Sampley. Harrisburg: Trinity Press International, 2003.
Arichea, Daniel C. "Who Was Phoebe? Translating *Diakonos* in Rom. 16.1." *BT* 39 (1988): 401-09.
Barr, George K. "Romans 16 and the Tentmakers." *IBS* 20 (1998): 97-113.
Blum, Georg G. "Das Amt der Frau im Neuen Testament." *NovT* 7 (1964): 142-61.
Collins, John N. *Diakonia: Reinterpreting the Ancient Sources*. New York: Oxford University Press, 1990.

17. That she was not the leader of a congregation, but provided hospitality and practical help to Paul and others in her home, is maintained by E. Ng, "Phoebe as *Prostatis*," 4-13.
18. On "house church hospitality," as gleaned from Paul's letters, cf. J. Koenig, *New Testament Hospitality*, 61-65.

Cotter, Wendy. "Women's Authority Roles in Paul's Churches: Countercultural or Conventional?" *NovT* 36 (1994): 350-72.

Danker, Frederick W. *Benefactor: Epigraphic Study of a Graeco-Roman and New Testament Semantic Field.* St. Louis: Clayton, 1982.

Gibson, Margaret D. "Phoebe." *ExpTim* 23 (1911-12): 281.

Gillman, Florence M. *Women Who Knew Paul.* Wilmington: Michael Glazier, 1989.

Goodspeed, Edgar J. "Phoebe's Letter of Introduction." *HTR* 44 (1951): 55-57.

Head, Peter M. "Named Letter-Carriers among the Oxyrhynchus Papyri." *JSNT* 31 (2009): 279-99.

Jewett, Robert. "Paul, Phoebe and the Spanish Mission." In *The Social World of Formative Christianity and Judaism: Essays in Tribute to Howard Clark Kee,* 142-61. Ed. Jacob Neusner et al. Philadelphia: Fortress Press, 1988.

Kearsley, R. A. "Women in Public Life in the Roman East: Iunia Theodora, Claudia Metrodora and Phoebe, Benefactress of Paul." *TynB* 50 (1999): 189-211.

Kim, Chan-Hie. *Form and Structure of the Familiar Greek Letter of Recommendation.* SBLDS 4. Missoula: Society of Biblical Literature, 1972.

Koenig, John. *New Testament Hospitality: Partnership with Strangers as Promise and Mission.* Philadelphia: Fortress Press, 1985.

Malherbe, Abraham J. *Social Aspects of Early Christianity.* 2d ed. Philadelphia: Fortress Press, 1983.

Myerscough, Richard. "Exegesis 21: Was Phoebe Really a Deacon?" *Foundations* 36 (1996): 24-26.

Ng, Esther Y. L. "Phoebe as *Prostatis.*" *TJ* 25 (2004): 3-13.

Økland, Jorunn. *Women in Their Place: Paul and the Corinthian Discourse of Gender and Sanctuary Space.* JSNTSup 269. New York: T&T Clark, 2004.

Osiek, Carolyn. "Women in the Ancient Roman World." *BR* 39 (1994): 57-61.

————, Margaret Y. MacDonald, with Janet H. Tulloch. *A Woman's Place: House Churches in Earliest Christianity.* Minneapolis: Fortress Press, 2006.

Romaniuk, Kazimierz. "Was Phoebe in Romans 16,1 a Deaconess?" *ZNW* 81 (1990): 132-34.

Schüssler Fiorenza, Elisabeth. "Missionaries, Apostles, Coworkers: Romans 16 and the Reconstruction of Women's Early Christian History." *WW* 6 (1986): 420-33.

Schulz, Ray R. "A Case for 'President': Phoebe in Romans 16:2." *LTJ* 24 (1990): 124-27.

Sema, Aheto. "Phoebe: Deacon or Deaconness?" *BT* 60 (2009): 106-11.

Whelan, Caroline F. "Amica Pauli: The Role of Phoebe in the Early Church." *JSNT* 49 (1993): 67-85.

10.2. Greetings to Recipients in Rome, 16:3-16

3*Greet Prisca and Aquila, my coworkers in Christ Jesus,* 4*who put their necks at risk for my life, to whom not only I give thanks but also all the churches of the Gentiles,* 5*and greet the church in their house. Greet my beloved Epaenetus,* *who is the first convert for Christ in Asia. 6Greet Mary, who has worked hard for you. 7Greet Andronicus and Junia my kindred, who were imprisoned with me, who are prominent among the apostles, and who were in Christ before I was. 8Greet Ampliatus, my beloved in the Lord. 9Greet Urbanus, our coworker in Christ, and my beloved Stachys. 10Greet Apelles, who is approved in Christ. Greet those who belong to the household of Aristobulus. 11Greet Herodion, my kinsman. Greet those in the Lord who belong to the household of Narcissus. 12Greet Tryphaena and Tryphosa, workers in the Lord. Greet the beloved Persis, who has worked hard in the Lord. 13Greet Rufus, chosen in the Lord, and his mother and mine. 14Greet Asyncritus, Phlegon, Hermes, Patrobas, Hermas, and the brothers and sisters with them. 15Greet Philologus, Julia, Nereus and his sister, Olympas, and all the saints with them. 16Greet one another with a holy kiss. All the churches of Christ greet you.*

Notes on the Text and Translation

16:6 The Majority Text reads that Mary has worked hard εἰς ἡμᾶς ("for us"), which is represented by the KJV. But the phrase εἰς ὑμᾶς ("for you") has far greater support among the early Alexandrian ($\mathfrak{P}^{46}$, ℵ, B) and other texts, and it is adopted in more recent modern versions in general (RSV, NIV, NRSV, etc.).

16:7 The name translated here as "Junia" in its unaccented form in Greek is Ἰουνιαν. How it should be accented is left to the modern text critic, since the oldest uncial manuscripts do not contain accents. The question is whether it should be accented as Ἰουνίαν or as Ἰουνιᾶν. The former would be correct if the name is (feminine) "Junia" (Ἰουνία in nominative form). The latter would be the way to accent the name if it is (masculine) "Junias" (Ἰουνιᾶς in nominative form).[19] Of importance here, however, is that the "correctors" (later scribes) of some of the earliest manuscripts have supplied accents, and the name is then "Junia" (feminine form). That is so with the correctors of some major uncials (the corrector of B in the sixth or seventh century; and that of D in the ninth century), and the corrector the "queen of the minuscules" (#33, ninth century).[20] In addition, "from the time accents were added to the text until the early part of the twentieth century, editions of the Greek NT printed the feminine acute accent and not the masculine circumflex," and that is so from the texts of Erasmus (1516-35) to that of Westcott and Hort (1881: Ἰουνίαν).[21]

---

19. BDF 68 (§125, 2).

20. U.-K. Plisch, "Die Apostolin Junia," 477-78, who adds that the Sahidic version requires a feminine reading. Cf. for further textual evidence, J. Thorley, "Junia, a Woman Apostle," 18-29.

21. L. Belleville, "Ἰουνιαν . . . ἐπίσημοι ἐν τοῖς ἀποστόλοις," 238.

Moreover, there is no known evidence for the existence of the masculine name "Junias," whereas the feminine name "Junia" has been found over 250 times in ancient Roman inscriptions.[22] Another important point is that some 16 commentators of the first Christian millennium understood the name to be "Junia."[23] In light of the overwhelming evidence, the person must be understood to be "Junia," and she and Andronicus can be considered a married couple.[24] See further discussion below. "Junia" is the reading favored in the KJV (1611) and most recent English versions (ESV, NAB, REB, NKJV, ESV, NRSV). The RSV and NIV have "Junias."

The alternative to Ιουνιαν ("Junia") in 𝔓[46] (and 6, an eighth-century minuscule) is Ιουλιαν ("Julia"), which is followed in respective translations by the Vulgate and Bohairic texts. All the other Greek evidence favors "Junia." A "Julia" appears in 16:15, and most likely some scribes transferred it to 16:7 by an eye skip. Both names are preceded by καί ("and") and have similar appearance otherwise, except for the letters ν and λ in the center.

The term συγγενεῖς (συγγενής in singular) is translated variously in modern English versions as "kinsmen" (KJV, ASV, RSV, NASV), "relatives" (NIV, NAB, NRSV), or "fellow-countrymen" (NEB). The term need not mean "relatives" in the usual sense (siblings, cousins, etc.). As in Romans 9:3, where Paul speaks of the Jewish people as a whole as his συγγενεῖς, it signifies that Andronicus and Junia are of the same ethnic group as Paul (i.e., Jews). The same term is used in regard to Herodion (16:11) and Jason and Sosipater (16:21). The term "kinsmen" has been chosen here to represent that.

General Comment

The chapter consists primarily of greetings both to the community of Christians at Rome as a whole (16:16) and to individuals. Those mentioned by name are 26 persons, of whom 19 are men and 7 are women. In addition, two other

---

22. P. Lampe, *From Paul to Valentinus,* 169, 176. The masculine name "Junianus," however, appears 21 times. Cf. also inscription #206 from Cos with the name Ἰουνία, published in William R. Paton and Edward L. Hicks, *The Inscriptions of Cos* (Oxford: Clarendon Press, 1891), 180. For a survey of how Latin names were transcribed into Greek, and therefore supporting a feminine name here, cf. R. Cervin, "A Note regarding the Name Junia(s) in Romans 16.7," 464-70.

23. These are listed by J. Fitzmyer, *Romans,* 737-38; E. Epp, "Text-Critical, Exegetical and Socio-Cultural Factors Affecting the Junia/Junias Variation in Romans 16,7," 251-52; and L. Belleville, "Ἰουνιαν . . . ἐπίσημοι ἐν τοῖς ἀποστόλοις," 232 (n. 1), 234-36.

24. The proposal of A. Wolters, "IOUNIAN (Romans 16:7)," 397-408, that the person addressed could have been a man named Ἰουνίας (Hellenized for a Hebrew name *Yĕḥunnī*) — so "Junias" in English — is much less likely. It is not otherwise attested, and the coupling of "Andronicus and Junia" as a married couple is more likely than a combination of "Andronicus and Junias."

women are mentioned to receive greetings; these are the mother of Rufus (16:13) and the sister of Nereus (16:15), which means that actually nine women are to be greeted on behalf of Paul (Prisca, Mary, Junia, Tryphaena, Tryphosa, Persis, Julia, the mother of Rufus, and the sister of Nereus), and in fact 28 persons are referred to, if not always by name. In addition, greetings are to be sent in some cases to "brothers and sisters" (16:14), the "household" of certain persons (twice, 16:10, 11), and the "saints" associated with others who are named (16:15). Some persons mentioned are linked with house churches or associations in Rome (16:5, 10, 11, 14, 15), of which there were at least three and, more likely, five or even seven of which Paul was aware.[25]

The reason for mentioning so many recipients by name begs for an explanation. The most obvious is that Paul seeks here to establish a bond between himself and the Christians at Rome in general. By calling upon them to greet certain individuals, he expects that the latter will, in effect, provide references for him. He shows that he and the Roman community addressed are already bound together because of those persons at Rome who know him personally — and are known by others there.[26] Another likely reason for greeting so many is that the community of Christians at Rome would have been scattered about in the city, and Paul indicated by greeting people by name that his letter was to be circulated. At least all who are named were expected to receive it.

An analysis of the names of those to be greeted is instructive concerning the composition of the Christian community of Rome.

1. Although Aristobulus and Narcissus obviously had Christians in their households, and may well have offered them accommodations for worship and other gatherings, it is not likely that they themselves were Christians. The reasons for that are: (1) they are not actually greeted, but people in their households are; (2) only a portion of their households are greeted (τοὺς ἐκ τῶν Ἀριστοβούλου and τοὺς ἐκ τῶν Ναρκίσσου, meaning "those from the household of Aristobulus/Narcissus," rather than simply τοὺς Ἀριστοβούλου and τοὺς Ναρκίσσου, 16:10, 11); and (3) in the case of Narcissus those greeted are explicitly "those who belong in the Lord" (16:11).[27] When this is taken into ac-

---

25. W. Sanday and A. Headlam, *Romans*, 421; E. A. Judge, *Social Pattern of the Christian Groups in the First Century*, 36; and A. Malherbe, *Social Aspects of Early Christianity*, 70, 100, identify three, based on 16:5, 14, 15. P. Lampe, *From Paul to Valentinus*, 359, identifies seven at the time Paul wrote the letter, based on 16:5, 10, 11, 14, 15 (estimating that 14 persons mentioned with reference to specific house churches would be in two more associations). R. Gehring, *House Church and Mission*, 145-46, speaks of seven different groups. L. White, "House Churches," 119, concludes that Paul addresses "eight distinct cells in Rome."

26. P. Lampe, *From Paul to Valentinus*, 156.

27. H.-J. Klauck, *Hausgemeinde und Hauskirche*, 69-70; P. Lampe, *From Paul to Valentinus*, 164-65; R. Gehring, *House Church and Mission*, 145.

count, the number of individual Christians named or referred to in 16:3-16 drops from 28 to 26.

2. Those known to Paul personally, stated explicitly, include: Prisca and Aquila (16:3, "my coworkers"; cf. Acts 18:2), Epaenetus (16:5, Paul's "first convert in Asia"), Andronicus and Junia (16:7, imprisoned with Paul), Ampliatus (16:8, "my beloved"), Urbanus (16:9, "coworker"), Stachys (16:9, "my beloved"), and Rufus and his mother (16:13, "his mother and mine"). To this list should probably be added Apelles (16:10, known by Paul as "approved in Christ") and Persis (16:12, called simply "beloved," but also known to Paul as having "worked hard in the Lord"). Other persons to whom Paul sends greetings may also have been known to him. But these twelve would have been persons who could speak on behalf of Paul among the Christian house churches in Rome.

3. Those who can be identified explicitly as Jewish Christians are: Aquila (identified as "a Jew" at Acts 18:2), possibly his wife Prisca (or Priscilla, as in Acts 18:2, 18, 26), Andronicus and Junia (16:7, "my kindred"), and Herodion (16:11, "my kinsman"). Others named could have been Jewish Christians as well, but actually only four (Aquila, Andronicus, Junia, and Herodion) are named as such in the New Testament. If Prisca can be included, there are five. If Mary (16:6) — a common Jewish name — can be included, there would be six. But we can be certain of neither of these, and they should probably not be included. The name Prisca/Priscilla is found among Gentiles, such as in the case of a priestess of Zeus.[28] Moreover, the name appears frequently in Latin inscriptions, of which a good number are former female slaves.[29] The name Mary appears frequently in Latin inscriptions as the feminine form of the pagan name Marius, and if that is so here, she would probably be a Gentile.[30] The entire picture at Rome is blurred by the fact that "according to epigraphic evidence, the Jews of Rome had Latin names more often than Greek ones, and Greek ones more often than Semitic ones. Semitic names occur in 13.1% of the epitaphs."[31]

4. Those who are commended for having special roles in Christian communities or having special relationships to Paul are: Prisca and Aquila (16:3-4, "my coworkers"), Mary (16:6, "who has worked hard" in Rome), Andronicus and Junia (16:7, "outstanding among the apostles"); Urbanus (16:9, "our coworker"), Apelles (16:10, "approved in Christ"), Tryphaena and Tryphosa (16:12, "workers in the Lord"), Persis (16:12, "who has worked hard"), Rufus (16:13,

28. For evidence, cf. BDAG 863 (Πρίσκα).

29. P. Lampe, *From Paul to Valentinus*, 18: the name appears over 200 times; 31 (16%) are freed female slaves.

30. P. Lampe, *From Paul to Valentinus*, 175-76. Cf. also inscription #165 from Cos with the name Μαρία, published in W. Paton and E. Hicks, *The Inscriptions of Cos*, 170.

31. D. Noy, *Foreigners at Rome*, 262.

"chosen in the Lord"), and the mother of Rufus (16:13, "his mother and mine"). Of these twelve persons, seven are women. These women make up a disproportionate amount of persons who are distinguished for their service in early Christian communities or in association with Paul. While about 35 percent of those named or referred to in 16:3-16 are women (9 of 26, not counting Aristobulus and Narcissus, who are not Christians, among the 26), no less than 58 percent of those singled out for having had special roles are women (7 of 12). Of the women, only Julia and the sister of Nereus (16:15) do not have words or phrases attached to their names. In contrast, there are twelve men who have no terms or phrases accompanying their names to indicate significant roles. To be sure, that fact does not necessarily mean that those men are less distinguished in service; after all, Paul's mentioning them by name can be taken as significant in itself. But the remarks about the service of women stand out nevertheless.

5. Those who are leaders of house churches, associated with specific groups, or make accommodations for them are: Prisca and Aquila (16:5, "the church in their house"), Aristobulus (16:10, his "household"), Narcissus (16:11, his "household"), Asyncritus, Phlegon, Hermes, Patrobas, Hermas (16:14, "and the brothers and sisters with them"), and Philologus, Julia, Nereus and his sister, and Olympas (16:15, "and all the saints with them"). These thirteen persons are mentioned as belonging to five specific communities. They account for nearly half of those named.

6. Others not associated with specific communities are Epaenetus, Mary, Andronicus, Junia, Ampliatus, Urbanus, Stachys, Apelles, Herodion, Tryphaena, Tryphosa, Persis, Rufus, and his mother. It is possible that these fourteen persons belonged to other house churches or associations.[32] If so, it is not likely that any of them hosted house churches, at least not any known to Paul, since he does not ask that greetings be extended to churches in the homes of any. But they may not have belonged to communities other than those already mentioned. What is unusual about the list is that Paul adds a commendation, a reference to their significance to him or to the churches in Rome, or a term of endearment for each person. It is possible, therefore, that they are persons whom he singles out for special greetings.

Beyond this, not much more can be said with certainty about those named in Romans 16. The work of Peter Lampe is highly important, however, for he makes comparisons between the names listed and those appearing in collections of inscriptions. His study reveals that fourteen of the persons listed may have been immigrants, and nine others could have been slaves or

---

32. P. Lampe, *From Paul to Valentinus*, 359, says that the 14 would have made up at least two additional groups; similarly, R. Gehring, *House Church and Mission*, 146; L. White, "House Churches," 119, concludes that Paul addresses "eight distinct cells in Rome."

freedmen and freedwomen.[33] To the former group (immigrants) belong: Andronicus, Apelles, Aquila, Asyncritus, Epaenetus, Hermas, Herodion, Junia, Olympas, Patrobas, Persis, Philologus, Phlegon, and Stachys. To the latter group (slaves/freed persons) belong: Ampliatus, Hermes, Herodion, Julia, Junia, Nereus, Persis, Tryphaena, and Tryphosa; perhaps Mary also. Because one cannot know which persons belonged to which house churches, aside from those listed in 16:14 and 16:15, it is impossible to know how mixed a given house church was in terms of ethnicity (Jewish or Gentile), class (slave, freeborn, freed), and place of origin (Rome or elsewhere). Were the house churches homogeneous or diverse? Going with what we have, it appears that the five persons mentioned in 16:14 and the four in 16:15 were Gentiles. Beyond that, within the group of five in 16:14, it appears that three or four were immigrants, Hermes being the possible exception. Within the group of four in 16:15, Julia and Nereus may have been natives of Rome. Several names in both groups indicate slave or freedperson status. There are hints of social and economic diversity, but the samples are so small that any generalities made about the composition of any of the house churches have meager support. But it appears that the persons named would have known one another, which is established by Paul's admonition to greet one another with a holy kiss (16:16). That act would relativize any distinctions of class, gender, and ethnicity throughout the Roman community of believers, expressing their oneness in Christ despite the distinctions that existed in the Roman world. It would also shape the ethos of the various house churches to be hospitable to all.

Detailed Comment

Forms of the verb "to greet" someone (ἀσπάζομαι) appear in chapter 16 no fewer than 21 times (16 times from Paul in 16:3-16a; five times from others in 16:16b, 21-23). In verses 16:3-16a the verb form is ἀσπάσασθε (second person, plural, aorist, imperative, middle) and can be translated simply by the English imperative "greet." When the verb is translated that way, it appears at first glance that Paul himself is not doing the greeting, but is calling upon the community to greet certain persons. But the imperative can also be translated as "greetings to (someone)" or "remember me to (someone)."[34] One can think here of modern usage. A person might say at the conclusion of a conversation, or in a letter, "be sure to

---

33. P. Lampe, *From Paul to Valentinus,* 170, 183.

34. BDAG 144 (ἀσπάζομαι), who cites not only the passages in Rom 16, but also 1 Cor 16:19-20; 2 Cor 13:12; Phil 4:21-22; Col 4:10, 12, 14-15; 2 Tim 4:19, 21; Titus 3:15; Phlm 23; Heb 13:24; 1 Pet 5:13-14; 2 John 13; 3 John 15; Ignatius, *Magn.* 15; *Trall.* 12.1; 13.1; *Rom.* 9.3; *Phld.* 11.2; *Smyrn.* 11.1; 12.1-2; 13.1-2; *Pol.* 8.2-3; and other sources.

greet" so-and-so, whereby it is understood that the greetings being conveyed are those of the sender. It is possible that those to whom greetings are to be conveyed are not expected by Paul to be actual readers of the letter,[35] but they could certainly be among the hearers when it would be read aloud.

16:3-5a Paul sends greetings first of all to a couple of long acquaintance and association, Prisca and Aquila. Prisca (also mentioned at 1 Cor 16:19; 2 Tim 4:19) is known in Acts with the diminutive form of the name, Priscilla (18:2, 18, 26). According to Luke, both she and her husband were tentmakers by trade, as was Paul himself (Acts 18:3). The fact that she is mentioned first (rather than Aquila; she is also mentioned first at Acts 18:18, 26 and 2 Tim 4:19, but not at 1 Cor 16:19) indicates that she was more prominent in the community than her husband.[36]

According to Acts 18:2, Aquila was a Jewish Christian who had originated in Pontus, a Roman province in Asia Minor along the south shore of the Black Sea, and then settled in Rome. He and Prisca were among those Jews (including Jewish Christians) evicted by Emperor Claudius in A.D. 49 over the controversy concerning Christ, as attested by Suetonius: "He expelled the Jews from Rome because they constantly made disturbances at the instigation of Chrestus."[37] According to Luke, the couple came to Corinth because of the expulsion, Paul met them there, resided with them, and joined them in making tents (Acts 18:1-3). After a year and a half (18:11) Paul, Aquila, and Prisca left Corinth. Paul went by way of Ephesus to Syria, but the couple remained in Ephesus (18:18-19). There they met and instructed Apollos (18:24-26) and had a house church (1 Cor 16:19). After the death of Claudius (A.D. 54), Prisca and Aquila returned to Rome and had a house church there (Rom. 16:5). The move might have been strategic, for it would prepare the way for Paul's arrival later and may explain why they were the first to be greeted by Paul in his letter.[38] The couple is commemorated in the deutero-Pauline Pastoral Epistles (2 Tim 4:19). Concerning house churches, see the appendix, "House Churches and Communities in Rome."

Paul speaks of Prisca and Aquila as coworkers, "who put their necks at risk" for his life. Where would that have been? One can only conjecture. The most likely answer is that while he was in Ephesus, Paul was arrested and endured some hardships (1 Cor 15:32; 2 Cor 1:8), and somehow Prisca and Aquila were able to in-

---

35. T. Mullins, "Greeting as a New Testament Form," 426.

36. Cf. BDAG 863 (Πρίσκα), citing a text where a first-century woman is named prior to her husband because of her higher social rank. Cf. also the discussion of D. Kurek-Chomycz, "Is There an 'Anti-Priscan' Tendency?" 114 (n. 18); and M. Flory, "Where Women Precede Men," 216-24.

37. Suetonius, *Claudius* 25.15: "Iudaeos impulsore Chresto assidue tumultuantes Roma expulit."

38. Peter Lampe, "Aquila," *ABD* 1:320.

tervene in some way.[39] In any case, their heroism was well known since, Paul says, both he and "all the churches of the Gentiles" give thanks to them.

16:5b-6 Concerning Epaenetus and Mary, nothing more is known than what is said here. Epaenetus was Paul's "first convert in Asia," probably meaning Ephesus. If so, he may have known Prisca and Aquila already in Ephesus, since they had been in Ephesus prior to their return to Rome. The woman named Mary is not to be confused with the others who bear that name: (1) Mary the mother of Jesus, (2) Mary Magdalene, (3) Mary the mother of James and Joses (Mark 15:40), (4) Mary the wife of Clopas (John 19:25), (5) Mary the sister of Martha (Luke 10:39, 42), and (6) Mary the mother of John Mark (Acts 12:12). Whether Paul knew her personally or not, she has worked hard in the Roman community, and Paul is aware of that. Both here and at 16:12 Paul employs a form of the verb κοπιάω ("to work"). The fact that Paul uses the term elsewhere in reference to church leadership that is recognized by the community (1 Cor 16:15-18; 1 Thess 5:12-13) implies that it be understood that way here, too. Mary "has worked hard for you" implies, then, that she had a recognized leadership role in the Christian community at Rome.[40]

16:7 The combination of Andronicus and Junia suggests that they, like Prisca and Aquila, were a married couple. They are identified here as Jewish Christians, and Paul says that they were Christians prior to his being one. If the so-called "conversion" (more properly, the "call") of Paul is placed no later than A.D. 32, or possibly 33 at the latest, that means that they became Christians within the first few years after the death and resurrection of Jesus. Paul indicates, too, that they had been in prison with him at one time.

The NRSV departs, rightly, from other modern versions (ASV, RSV, NIV) by having the name of the second person mentioned as the feminine "Junia" (as in the KJV), rather than the masculine "Junias." Early Christian writers, such as Origen (A.D. 185-254), Chrysostom (A.D. 347-407), and Theodoret of Cyrrhus (A.D. 393-466), wrote without hesitation that at this place Paul refers to a woman named Junia,[41] and Chrysostom considered her an apostle: "Think how great the devotion of this woman Junia must have been, that she should be worthy to be called an apostle!"[42]

39. W.-H. Ollrog, *Paulus und seine Mitarbeiter*, 27.

40. S. Schreiber, "Arbeit mit der Gemeinde," 204-26.

41. Origen, *Comment. in Epist. ad Rom.* 10.26, *PG* 14:1281B; 10.39, *PG* 14:1289A; Chrysostom, *In Epist. ad Rom.* 31.2, *PG* 60:669-70; Theodoret of Cyrrhus, *Interpretatio Epist. ad Rom.*, *PG* 82:220. These references are taken from B. Brooten, "Junia," 141-44. For an extensive survey of both Greek and Latin writers, cf. L. Belleville, "Ἰουνιαν . . . ἐπίσημοι ἐν τοῖς ἀποστόλοις," 234-36.

42. Chrysostom, "Homily 31," *The Epistle to the Romans* (on 16:7); quoted from *NPNF* (series 1) 11:554-55.

But when Paul says that Andronicus and Junia are "prominent among the apostles," there are two possible meanings. One is that they are prominent within the circle of apostles, of which they are a part (the inclusivist view). The other is that they are highly esteemed by the apostles, but that they are not themselves to be counted among them (the exclusivist view). The word translated here as "prominent" is ἐπίσημος, which appears only one other place in the NT (Matt 27:16), meaning "notorious" (modifying "prisoner" and applied to Barabbas).

There are good reasons for affirming that Andronicus and Junia are to be included within the circle of "the apostles" (the inclusivist view).[43] First, that there were persons designated as "apostles" beyond the circle of the Twelve — Paul himself being one of them, as well as James the brother of the Lord (Gal 1:19) and Barnabas (1 Cor 9:5-6; Acts 14:14) — is indisputable, based on evidence from elsewhere (cf. also 1 Cor 15:5, 7; cf. 4:9; 9:5; 12:28; 2 Cor 8:23; Eph 4:11). In that light, it is not surprising that Andronicus, Junia, and several or even many other persons could have been considered apostles. Second, the fact that Andronicus and Junia were of Jewish background and were "in Christ" (Paul's familiar designation for Christians; cf. Rom 8:1; 16:7; 1 Cor 3:1; 2 Cor 5:17; 12:2; Phil 3:8-9) even before Paul's own call to apostleship speaks in favor of their being among the originating circle of apostles that Paul refers to in his list of those to whom the risen Christ appeared, and whom he calls "all the apostles" prior to his own call as an apostle (1 Cor 15:7-8). Since Paul seems to have considered himself to have been the last apostle commissioned by the risen Christ (1 Cor 15:8), Andronicus and Junia would certainly qualify within the time allotted, in Paul's view, for the commissioning of apostles. Third, the phrase was understood in the inclusivist sense in patristic commentaries (see below). Fourth, if the term is used in this case as a reference to a nameless third party ("the apostles") in the exclusivist sense, it would appear that Paul is thereby excluding himself also from that same circle of apostles, which very thing he would never do. But if he means to include Andronicus and Junia as prominent within that circle, of which he himself is a part, he would be complimenting them as "insiders" from one who is an "insider" himself. Fifth, the best explanation for Paul's mentioning that they are "prominent among the apostles" is that they are apostles themselves. Why would Paul otherwise refer to their prominence? There seem to be two possibilities, but neither is satisfactory. One possibility would be that Paul is telling his readers here, in so many words, that Andronicus and Junia were highly regarded by "the apostles" and could

---

43. Karl H. Rengstorf, "ἐπίσημος," *TDNT* 7:268 (n. 1), favors this view, but allows for the possibility of the other. But the work of L. Belleville, "᾿Ιουνιαν . . . ἐπίσημοι ἐν τοῖς ἀποστόλοις," 242-48, is decisive for the inclusivist view.

therefore be trustworthy references for him, if anyone should need their evaluation regarding him. Yet that is not a likely reason for the comment concerning them. He has already spoken of them as having been imprisoned along with him. Being personally known to this couple would be of more value as a reference for him than would their standing among "the apostles." And in the wake of the incident at Antioch (Gal 2:11-21), it is questionable whether Paul would want to defer to the opinions of such persons as Peter, James, and John (if they are counted among "the apostles") regarding the couple. The other possibility is that Paul is simply being complimentary concerning Andronicus and Junia; they are highly regarded by "the apostles." In favor of this, they could have been residents of Jerusalem at the time of their conversions, and were perhaps even converted through the preaching of "the apostles" there. They could thereafter have been commissioned as missionaries to Rome, or perhaps they could have become missionaries on their own initiative. Or, again, it is possible that Andronicus and Junia were simply known to "the apostles," had captured their attention as outstanding, and were thus regarded highly by them. Although a compliment along these lines cannot be excluded as a possibility, other considerations mentioned already weigh heavily in favor of Paul's inclusion of them among the circle of apostles, which is a view expressed already in the first half of the twentieth century by various interpreters,[44] and has been shared widely among others since the latter part of the twentieth century.[45]

As an aside to this discussion, it is instructive (and surely interesting) to notice that when the person named here as "Junia" was named "Junias" and was previously considered a man by major interpreters in their commentaries, there was no hesitation to speak of both Andronicus and "Junias" as within the circle of apostles.[46] Viewpoints should not be changed when it is realized that the person in question is a woman.

Moreover, there is no reason to insist that Andronicus and Junia belonged to a broader circle of persons called (in a loose way) "apostles," consist-

44. See notations by Karl H. Rengstorf, "ἐπίσημος," *TDNT* 7:268.

45. U. Wilckens, *Römer*, 3:135; E. Schüssler Fiorenza, *In Memory of Her*, 172; C. Cranfield, *Romans*, 789; J. Dunn, *Romans*, 894-95; J. Fitzmyer, *Romans*, 739; B. Byrne, *Romans*, 453; P. Stuhlmacher, *Romans*, 249; B. Witherington, *Romans*, 390; E. Lohse, *Römer*, 408; C. Talbert, *Romans*, 335; R. Jewett, *Romans*, 963; C. Keener, *Romans*, 186-87; R. Cervin, "A Note regarding the Name Junia(s) in Romans 16.7," 470; F. Gillman, "The Ministry of Women in the Early Church," 89-94; E. Epp, "Text-Critical, Exegetical and Socio-Cultural Factors Affecting the Junia/Junias Variation in Romans 16,7," 227-91; idem, *Junia*, 69-78; L. Belleville, "Ἰουνιαν . . . ἐπίσημοι ἐν τοῖς ἀποστόλοις," 231-49. For a brief history of interpretation, cf. B. Brooten, "Junia," 141-44.

46. F. Godet, *Commentary on St. Paul's Epistle to the Romans*, 2:343; W. Sanday and A. Headlam, *Romans*, 422-23; A. Schlatter, *Romans*, 274 (German ed., 1935); O. Michel, *Römer*, 379-80.

ing of traveling missionaries who did not belong to the circle of the apostles in the strict sense.[47] The fact that Paul himself took the term seriously in reference to himself speaks in favor of his recognition of others as apostles only when he understood them to have been commissioned by the risen Lord.[48] Moreover, when Paul refers to persons as apostles in the broader sense, he refers to them as "apostles of the churches" (2 Cor 8:23; RSV and NRSV translate ἀπόστολοι here as "messengers") or "your apostle" (Phil 2:25; RSV and NRSV have "your messenger").

Not all interpreters, however, agree with the inclusivist view. The exclusivist view (that Paul means that the couple were esteemed by the apostles, of which they were not to be counted) has been argued vigorously on the grounds of syntax by Michael Burer and Daniel Wallace.[49] According to them, when ἐπίσημος is used to include persons, it is normally followed by genitive nouns. That is the case, for example, at 3 Maccabees 6:1: Ελεαζαρος . . . ἐπίσημος τῶν ἀπὸ τῆς χώρας ἱερέων ("Eleazar . . . prominent among the priests of the country"). On the other hand, when Greek writers intend to exclude the subject from the group, it is customary to use ἐπίσημος followed by the preposition ἐν and a dative noun (as at Rom 16:7). This appears, for example, at *Psalms of Solomon* 2.6: ἐπισήμῳ ἐν τοῖς ἔθνεσιν ("a spectacle among the Gentiles"). But the argument from syntax does not actually hold up. There are several passages, illustrated by Burer and Wallace themselves, that have the ἐν plus dative noun construction and are inclusive.[50] Moreover, the fact that patristic writers whose working language was Greek understood Paul's reference to Andronicus and Junia in the inclusivist manner speaks against the syntactical argument put forth.[51]

47. Contra E. E. Ellis, "Coworkers," 186; D. Moo, *Romans,* 923-24; E. Lohse, *Römer,* 408.

48. B. Brooten, "Junia," 143.

49. M. Burer and D. Wallace, "Was Junia Really an Apostle?" 76-91.

50. The passages include Add Esth 16:22 (ἐν ταῖς ἑορταῖς ἐπίσημμον ἡμέραν, "a notable day among the festivals"); Josephus, *J. W.* 2.418 (ἐν οἷς ἦσαν ἐπίσημοι Σαῦλός τε καὶ Ἀντίπας καὶ Κοστόβαρος, "among whom were eminent persons, Saul, Antipas, and Costobar"); Philo, *Fug.* 2.10 (ἐπίσημον . . . ἐν μὲν τοῖς ὅλοις, "prominence within the universe"); Lucian, *Merc. cond.* 28.5 (not 2.8, as the authors have on p. 89, n. 64: ἐπίσημος . . . ἐν τοῖς ἐπαινοῦσι, "prominent among those who express praise"). The authors' claim that these passages can be considered irrelevant to the discussion, since the preposition ἐν is followed in each case by "impersonal nouns" (p. 86) rather than by personal nouns, or is located within a "relative clause" (p. 89), is irrelevant. Another text in Lucian, using ἐν plus dative and clearly in an inclusive sense, appears at *Dial. mort.* 22.2.2 (§438): καὶ ἄλλοι μὲν πολλοὶ συγκατέβαινον ἡμῖν, ἐν αὐτοῖς δὲ ἐπίσημοι Ἰσμηνώδρος, κτλ. ("and many others accompanied us, and among them prominent [persons], Ismenodorus," etc.). Additional data are offered by L. Belleville, "Ἰουνιαν . . . ἐπίσημοι ἐν τοῖς ἀποστόλοις," 242-48.

51. For further critique, cf. R. Bauckham, *Gospel Women,* 172-80; and E. Epp, "Text-Critical, Exegetical and Socio-Cultural Factors Affecting the Junia/Junias Variation in Romans 16,7," 285-90.

Since Andronicus and Junia had become Christians very early on in the first decade of the Christian movement, and since they were regarded as apostles, they may have been among the founders of the church in Rome.[52] Paul says that they had been imprisoned with him. There is no direct evidence for this outside of this one statement, and the grounds and place for imprisonment are therefore unknown. At 2 Corinthians 11:23-24 Paul says that he had been imprisoned several times "with countless floggings," and that may have been due to his preaching Jesus as the Christ in synagogues. Perhaps Andronicus and Junia were involved with him on some such occasion, but one cannot be certain.

16:8-10 The four persons named and to whom greetings are sent (Ampliatus, Urbanus, Stachys, and Apelles) are among those persons listed as known by Paul. A phrase is attached to each. Ampliatus and Stachys are called "my beloved"; Urbanus is "our coworker in Christ"; and Apelles is one known to Paul as "approved in Christ." The names of each are commonly known from inscriptions, and often they are names borne by slaves or former slaves.[53] There are no other references to these persons in early Christian literature.

Paul sends greetings to "those who belong to the household of Aristobulus." He does not greet Aristobulus himself, who is probably therefore not a Christian, and the fact that he does not refer to the entire household (which in Greek would normally be written τοὺς Ἀριστοβούλου, literally, "those of [= "those who belong to"] Aristobulus"), but only a portion (τοὺς ἐκ τῶν Ἀριστοβούλου, literally, "those from among those of [= "those who belong to"] Aristobulus"), indicates that not all within the household were Christians.

Aristobulus (meaning "best counselor") was a common name,[54] but there is a possibility that this person can be identified further as the Aristobulus who was a grandson of Herod the Great (ca. 70–4 B.C.) and brother to Herod Agrippa I (10 B.C.–A.D. 44). Herod Agrippa I lived for many years in Rome and was a friend of the emperor Claudius.[55] It is plausible that Aristobulus resided in Rome as well, and that some within his extended household were Christians.[56] The date of his death is unknown, but even if he had died by the time

---

52. R. Bauckham, *Gospel Women*, 181 (they may have been founders), 215; F. Watson, *Paul, Judaism and the Gentiles*, 185 (it is "plausible that Paul regards Andronicus and Junia as founders of the original Jewish Christian congregation in Rome"). Cf. also B. Byrne, *Romans*, 451.

53. References to inscriptions and other sources are provided in BDAG 55 (Ἀμπλιᾶτος), 101 (Ἀπελλῆς), 739 (Οὐρβάνος), and 942 (Στάχυς), and in P. Lampe, *From Paul to Valentinus*, 173, 179, 180-81 (referring to inscriptions of slave or former slave names in all four cases).

54. Cf. Scott T. Carroll, "Aristobulus," *ABD* 1:382-83.

55. Josephus, *J.W.* 2.221-22; *Ant.* 18.273-76; 20.13. Cf. David C. Braund, "Herodian Dynasty," *ABD* 3:173-74.

56. C. Cranfield, *Romans*, 791; P. Lampe, *From Paul to Valentinus*, 165; J. Dunn, *Romans*, 896; J. Fitzmyer, *Romans*, 740.

that Paul wrote his letter, the persons of his household would have retained their identity.

16:11 If there was a connection between Aristobulus and the Herodian dynasty, it is not particularly surprising that, if he is to be greeted at all, the next person to be greeted is Herodion. The name has not been attested in Latin literature or inscriptions at Rome, although "Herodianus" has.[57] The form of the name (with its "-on" ending) appears to have been Greek in origin and most likely was applied to the man while he was a slave of Herod the Great.[58] At this point he must be a freedman, and he is designated as a Jewish Christian.

Greetings are sent once again to persons within a household of one who is not himself a Christian, nor are many (most?) within that household. The greetings are sent specifically and explicitly to "those in the Lord" (τοὺς ὄντας ἐν κυρίῳ) of the household of Narcissus. "The name [Narcissus] is found as a slave's name about 50 times in Rome,"[59] although as a householder having a home large enough for gatherings for Christian worship, he is probably to be considered a freedman. Whether he was still alive when Paul wrote his letter is uncertain, for even if he had died, his household would still have maintained their identification with him. Attempts have been made to identify this particular person further. A freedman by that name had been a slave to the emperor Claudius, but became a freedman.[60] Shortly after Nero became emperor (A.D. 54), he was forced to commit suicide.[61] Although it is possible that the Narcissus mentioned by Paul can be identified with this person,[62] it is not certain.

16:12 As in the case of Mary (16:6), Tryphaena and Tryphosa are "workers in the Lord." A form of the verb κοπιάω ("to work") is used again in reference to two persons who must have had a leadership function. See the comments on 16:2.

16:13 Rufus is greeted. Although Rufus was a common name,[63] could this be the Rufus mentioned in Mark 15:21: "They compelled a passerby, who was coming in from the country, to carry his cross; it was Simon of Cyrene, the father of Alexander and Rufus"? The event referred to by Mark would have occurred ca. A.D. 30 within Jerusalem. When Paul writes Romans, an entire generation (timewise) has passed. It is certainly possible that the same Rufus was in Rome when

---

57. P. Lampe, *From Paul to Valentinus*, 169, 177.

58. P. Lampe, *From Paul to Valentinus*, 178; idem, "Herodion," *ABD* 3:176.

59. P. Lampe, *From Paul to Valentinus*, 165.

60. Juvenal, *Sat.* 14.329-31.

61. Tacitus, *Ann.* 31.1; Cassius Dio, *Rom. Hist.* 60.34.

62. W. Sanday and A. Headlam, *Romans*, 423-24; C. Cranfield, *Romans*, 792-94; J. Dunn, *Romans*, 896; J. Fitzmyer, *Romans*, 741.

63. BDAG 907 (῾Ροῦφος); no fewer than 16 entries with that name are provided in W. Paton and E. Hicks, *The Inscriptions of Cos* (see index, p. 385).

Paul wrote his letter.[64] Moreover, the traditional venue for the writing of the Gospel of Mark is Rome. The writer of that gospel could be referring to the sons of Simon some ten to fifteen years after Paul wrote Romans, taking for granted that the Christian community there knew Alexander and Rufus. They could still have been alive, and, if not, they could nevertheless still be remembered there. In any case, when Paul sends greetings, he calls Rufus a person "chosen in the Lord," an honorific title of one who has a long and tested record of discipleship. Paul knows and greets the mother of Rufus as well, and calls her his own mother. The relationship between Paul and the mother of Rufus recalls the words of Jesus: "Whoever does the will of God is my brother and sister and mother" (Mark 3:35).

16:14-15 Greetings are sent to a number of persons, both by name and by association with those named. There are two groups of persons. The first group consists of five named persons — Asyncritus, Phlegon, Hermes, Patrobas, Hermas — and "the brothers and sisters with them." Paul apparently thinks that these persons make up a house church in Rome. The second group consists of four named persons — Philologus, Julia, Nereus, and Olympas — and "all the saints with them." This would be another house church. As indicated above, three of the persons named (Hermes, Julia, and Nereus) may have had slave origins, and the rest may have been immigrants to Rome. None of the nine persons named in the two groups is otherwise mentioned in the NT.

16:16 Whether the "holy kiss" (φίλημα ἅγιον) was a common gesture in the worship of the churches known to Paul is not clear; in any case, it is not mentioned. A kiss at eucharistic worship is attested for the first time in the writings of Justin Martyr in the second century.[65] References to the "holy kiss" within the NT appear always within the context of sending greetings (1 Cor 16:20; 2 Cor 13:12; 1 Thess 5:26; cf. 1 Pet 5:14). Such a gesture helps to make certain that the greetings will not be neglected.[66] As "holy" or "sacred," it is not meant to be erotic; according to 1 Peter, it is a "kiss of love" (φίλημα ἀγάπης, 5:14). As such, it is a sign of affection and welcome among members of the churches. Since kissing was normally restricted to family members in most Mediterranean cultures of antiquity, the holy kiss alters boundaries in such a way that persons who are otherwise unrelated become brothers and sisters within the one body.[67]

Paul ends this portion of the letter with what has appropriately been

---

64. W. Sanday and A. C. Headlam, *Romans*, 426; J. Dunn, *Romans*, 897; B. Byrne, *Romans*, 454. But making the connection is called a "pious speculation" by E. Käsemann, *Romans*, 414. J. Fitzmyer, *Romans*, 741, says that making the connection "may be sheer speculation"; L. Keck, *Romans*, 374, considers it unlikely; and for E. Lohse, *Römer*, 410, the connection is uncertain.

65. Justin, *1 Apology* 65.

66. William Klassen, "Kiss," *ABD* 4:92.

67. L. Edward Phillips, "Kiss, Ritual," *The New Westminster Dictionary of Liturgy and Worship*, ed. Paul Bradshaw (Louisville: Westminster John Knox Press, 2002), 267.

called "an ecumenical greeting,"[68] a greeting from all the churches known to him: "All the churches of Christ greet you." Paul had been planning to travel to Rome for many years (1:13; 15:22-23), and while making plans, he would have had opportunity to speak of them with his congregations in Galatia, Ephesus, Philippi, Thessalonica, and Corinth. As their apostle, he sends greetings on their behalf. It is not likely that he could speak on behalf of the churches in Palestine, Syria, and other parts of Asia Minor.[69] The greeting is an epistolary flourish; it need not be taken to refer to every single congregation, for he had not participated in the life of every one.

BIBLIOGRAPHY

Banks, Robert J. *Paul's Idea of Community: The Early House Churches in Their Historical Setting.* Grand Rapids: Wm. B. Eerdmans, 1980.
Bauckham, Richard. *Gospel Women: Studies of the Named Women in the Gospels.* Grand Rapids: Wm. B. Eerdmans, 2002.
Belleville, Linda. "Ἰουνιαν . . . ἐπίσημοι ἐν τοῖς ἀποστόλοις: A Re-examination of Romans 16.7 in Light of Primary Source Materials." *NTS* 51 (2005): 231-49.
Benko, Stephen. "The Kiss." In his *Pagan Rome and the Early Christians,* 79-102. Bloomington: Indiana University Press, 1984.
Brooten, Bernadette. "'Junia . . . Outstanding among the Apostles' (Romans 16.7)." In *Women Priests: A Catholic Commentary on the Vatican Declaration,* 141-44. Ed. Leonard Swidler and Arlene Swidler. New York: Paulist Press, 1977.
————. *Women Leaders in Ancient Synagogues.* BJS 36. Chico: Scholars Press, 1982.
Burer, Michael H., and Daniel B. Wallace, "Was Junia Really an Apostle? A Reexamination of Rom 16.7." *NTS* 47 (2001): 76-91.
Cervin, Richard S. "A Note regarding the Name Junia(s) in Romans 16.7." *NTS* 40 (1994): 464-70.
Clarke, John R. *The Houses of Roman Italy, 100 B.C.–A.D. 250: Ritual, Space, and Decoration.* Berkeley: University of California Press, 1991.
Ellis, E. Earle, "Coworkers, Paul and His." In *Dictionary of Paul and His Letters,* 183-89. Ed. Gerald F. Hawthorne et al. Downers Grove: InterVarsity Press, 1993.
Epp, Eldon J. *Junia — The First Woman Apostle.* Minneapolis: Fortress Press, 2005.
————. "Text-Critical, Exegetical and Socio-Cultural Factors Affecting the Junia/Junias Variation in Romans 16,7." In *New Testament Textual Criticism and Exegesis: Festschrift J. Delobel,* 227-92. Ed. Adelbert Denaux. BETL 161. Leuven: Peeters, 2002.
Filson, Floyd. "The Significance of the Early House Churches." *JBL* 58 (1939): 105-12.
Flory, Marleen Boudreau. "Where Women Precede Men: Factors Influencing the Placement of Names in Roman Epitaphs." *CJ* 79 (1983-84): 216-24.

68. H.-J. Klauck, *Ancient Letters and the New Testament,* 302.

69. It is not likely that Paul could send greetings on behalf of non-Pauline churches in "Syria and elsewhere in the eastern part of the empire," as suggested by J. Weima, *Neglected Endings,* 277; and R. Jewett, *Romans,* 977.

Gehring, Roger W. *House Church and Mission: The Importance of Household Structures in Early Christianity.* Peabody: Hendrickson Publishers, 2004.

Gielen, Marlis. "Zur Interpretation der paulinischen Formel ἡ κατ᾽ οἶκον ἐκκλησία." *ZNW* 77 (1986): 109-25.

Gillman, Florence M. "The Ministry of Women in the Early Church." *NTR* 6/2 (1993): 89-94.

Godet, Frédéric L. *Commentary on St. Paul's Epistle to the Romans.* 2 vols. Edinburgh: T&T Clark, 1880-81.

Judge, Edwin A. "The Roman Base for Paul's Mission." *TynB* 56 (2005): 103-17.

————. *Social Pattern of the Christian Groups in the First Century.* London: Tyndale Press, 1960.

Klauck, Hans-Josef. *Ancient Letters and the New Testament: A Guide to Context and Exegesis.* Waco: Baylor University Press, 2006.

Kunst, Christiane. "Wohnen in der antiken Grosstadt: Zur sozialen Topographie Roms in der frühen Kaiserzeit." In *Christians as a Religious Minority in a Multicultural City: Modes of Interaction and Identity Formation in Early Imperial Rome,* 2-19. Ed. Jürgen Zangenberg and Michael Labahn. JSNTSup 243. London: T&T Clark, 2004.

Kurek-Chomycz, Dominika. "Is There an 'Anti-Priscan' Tendency in the Manuscripts? Some Textual Problems with Prisca and Aquila." *JBL* 125 (2006): 107-28.

Lampe, Peter. "Early Christians in the City of Rome: Topographical and Social Historical Aspects of the First Three Centuries." In *Christians as a Religious Minority in a Multicultural City: Modes of Interaction and Identity Formation in Early Imperial Rome,* 20-32. Ed. Jürgen Zangenberg and Michael Labahn. JSNTSup 243. London: T&T Clark, 2004.

———— *From Paul to Valentinus: Christians at Rome in the First Two Centuries.* Minneapolis: Fortress Press, 2003.

————. "Iunia/Iunias: Sklavenherkunft im Kreise der vorpaulinischen Apostel (Rom 16,7)." *ZNW* 76 (1985): 132-34.

————. "The Roman Christians of Romans 16." In *The Romans Debate,* 216-30. Ed. Karl P. Donfried. Rev. ed. Peabody: Hendrickson Publishers, 1991.

————. "Zur Textgeschichte des Römerbriefes." *NovT* 27 (1985): 273-77.

Linss, Wilhelm C. "St Paul and Women." *Dialog* 24 (1985): 36-40.

Malherbe, Abraham J. *Social Aspects of Early Christianity.* 2d ed. Philadelphia: Fortress Press, 1983.

Mullins, Terence Y. "Greeting as a New Testament Form." *JBL* 87 (1968): 418-26.

Noy, David. *Foreigners at Rome: Citizens and Strangers.* London: Gerald Duckworth & Company, 2000.

Ollrog, Wolf-Henning. *Paulus und seine Mitarbeiter: Untersuchungen zu Theorie und Praxis der paulinischen Mission.* WMANT 50. Neukirchen: Neukirchener Verlag, 1979.

Osiek, Carolyn A., and David L. Balch. *Families in the New Testament World: Households and House Churches.* Louisville: Westminster John Knox Press, 1997.

————, Margaret Y. MacDonald, with Janet H. Tulloch. *A Woman's Place: House Churches in Earliest Christianity.* Minneapolis: Fortress Press, 2006.

Oster, Richard E. "'Congregations of the Gentiles' (Rom 16:4): A Culture-based Ecclesiology in the Letters of Paul." *ResQ* 40 (1998): 39-52.

Petersen, Joan M. "House Churches in Rome." *VC* 23 (1969): 264-72.

Plisch, Uwe-Karsten. "Die Apostolin Junia: Das exegetische Problem in Röm 16,7 im Licht von Nestle-Aland 27 und der sahidischen Überlieferung." *NTS* 42 (1996): 477-78.

Schreiber, Stefan. "Arbeit mit der Gemeinde (Röm 16.6, 12): Zur versunkenen Möglichkeit der Gemeindeleitung durch Frauen." *NTS* 46 (2000): 204-26.

Schüssler Fiorenza, Elisabeth. "The Apostleship of Women in Early Christianity." In *Women Priests: A Catholic Commentary on the Vatican Declaration*, 135-40. Ed. L. Swidler and A. Swidler. New York: Paulist Press, 1977.

———. *In Memory of Her: A Feminist Theological Reconstruction of Christian Origins*. New York: Crossroad Publishing Company, 1983.

———. "Missionaries, Apostles, Coworkers: Romans 16 and the Reconstruction of Women's Early Christian History." *WW* 6 (1986): 420-33.

Schulz, Ray R. "Romans 16:7: Junia or Junias?" *ExpTim* 98 (1987): 108-10.

———. "Die Rolle der Frau, in der urchristlichen Bewegung." *Konzilium* 12 (1976): 3-9.

Thorley, John. "Junia, a Woman Apostle." *NovT* 38 (1996): 18-29.

Watson, Francis. *Paul, Judaism, and the Gentiles: Beyond the New Perspective*. Rev. ed. Grand Rapids: Wm. B. Eerdmans, 2007.

Weima, Jeffrey A. D. *Neglected Endings: The Significance of the Pauline Letter Closings*. JSNTSup 101. Sheffield: JSOT Press, 1994.

White, L. Michael. "House Churches," *OEANE* 3:118-21.

Wolters, Al. "IOYNIAN (Romans 16:7) and the Hebrew Name *Yĕḥunnī*." *JBL* 127 (2008): 397-408.

10.3. A Warning against Contentious Persons, 16:17-20

17*But I appeal to you, brothers and sisters, to keep an eye on those who create dissensions and offenses contrary to the teaching that you have learned, and avoid them.* 18*For their kind do not serve our Lord Christ but their own appetites, and they deceive the hearts of the innocent through their smooth talk and flattery.* 19*For your obedience is known among all; therefore, I rejoice over you, and I want you to be wise regarding the good, but without guile as far as evil is concerned.* 20*The God of peace will crush Satan under your feet soon. The grace of our Lord Jesus be with you.*

Notes on the Text and Translation

16:17 Some manuscripts (including $\mathfrak{P}^{46}$ and D) add λέγοντας ἤ prior to ποιοῦντας, resulting in the reading: "keep an eye on those who speak or create dissensions." The additional words are not in other major witnesses (𝕬, A, B, etc.) and should not be included. Apparently the intent of this addition would have been to include speaking in connection with uttering things contrary to sound teaching.

16:20b The last sentence ("The grace of our Lord Jesus be with you") is missing in some important Western texts (D and Vulgate mss), but it is present in important Alexandrians (𝔓⁴⁶, 𝕬, B). Its omission in those texts mentioned is probably due to their inclusion of 16:24 ("The grace of our Lord Jesus Christ be with you all"), which would be redundant if 16:20b is included. Those texts that include 16:20b omit 16:24. The Majority Text includes the sentence (and so consequently the KJV and ASV), but it has "Lord Jesus Christ" instead of simply "Lord Jesus." The Majority Text can be explained as having been conformed to the reading in 1 Thessalonians 5:28.

General Comment

The verses consist of an admonition of Paul to the Christians at Rome. That he would admonish persons other than his own converts to avoid false teachers has caused some interpreters to question whether the verses are integral to the letter, and to suggest that they may be an interpolation.[70] The similarity of the warnings in these verses to those in the deutero-Pauline Pastoral Epistles (1 Tim 4:7; 6:3-5; 2 Tim 2:14-19; 3:1-5; Titus 3:10) is striking and gives some support to such a view. But that is not decisive. Paul does, after all, admonish readers in his own letters, warning them against false teachers (Gal 6:12-15; Phil 3:2, 17-19) as well, and he inserts sharp admonitory comments near the close of other letters too (cf. 1 Cor 16:22; 2 Cor 13:3; 1 Thess 5:22). As indicated by others, it is possible that Paul added these verses as a personal postscript in his own hand (cf. Gal 6:11-18; 1 Cor 16:21-24).[71]

What is distinctive about the admonition here is that, although Paul calls

---

70. J. Knox, *IB (Romans)*, 9:664; W. Schmithals, "The False Teachers of Romans 16:17-20," 219-38; J. O'Neill, *Romans*, 252, 248; W.-H. Ollrog, "Die Abfassungsverhältnisse von Röm 16," 232-34; B. Byrne, *Romans*, 446-47, 455-56; V. Mora, "Romains 16,17-20," 541-47; L. Keck, *Romans*, 27-28, 377-78; R. Jewett, "Ecumenical Theology for the Sake of Mission," 90, 105-8; idem, *Romans*, 986-88. For a rejoinder to Jewett, cf. J. Sampley, "Romans in a Different Light," 127-28. That the passage is not an interpolation, cf. U. Wilckens, *Römer*, 3:140; H. Gamble, *Textual History*, 42 52-53, 94; J. G. D. Dunn, *Romans*, 901-2; J. Fitzmyer, *Romans*, 745; D. Moo, *Romans*, 928; E. Lohse, *Römer*, 411-12. According to M.-É. Boismard, "Rm 16,17-20," 548-57, the passage was originally located in Ephesians (between 6:20 and 6:21).

71. J. Dunn, *Romans*, 901-2; J. Fitzmyer, *Romans*, 745; E. Lohse, *Römer*, 412. H. Gamble, *Textual History*, 94, contends that all of Rom 16:1-20 would have been written by Paul in his own hand.

upon his readers to avoid those who create dissensions and offenses, he does not refer to opponents who would seek to undermine his own teaching, but rather "the teaching . . . learned" from teachers other than himself. After all, Paul was quite satisfied with the faith and life of the Christians at Rome (Rom 1:8; 15:14). Moreover, one need not assume that those to be avoided are currently at Rome and known by Paul to be there. Paul's experiences elsewhere had taught him that wherever he planted a church it was only a matter of time before dissension would arise due to persons who opposed him either from outside or from within. Although he had not been to Rome previously, Paul could assume that what had happened in his churches could happen anywhere, even ultimately at Rome (and it certainly did with the passing of time and the rise of the Valentinian Gnostics and Marcion in the second century), and the Roman Christians themselves could well have thought along the same lines. In any case, the admonition is general enough and could be taken by the readers at Rome as an admonition that could be expected from the apostle Paul.

Detailed Comment

16:17 This small unit begins with an appeal by Paul to his readers. The expression "I appeal to you" (παρακαλῶ ὑμᾶς) appears elsewhere in Paul's letters at those places where he is making a particularly important admonition (Rom 12:1; 15:30; 1 Cor 1:10; 4:16; 16:15; 2 Cor 2:8; 10:1). For further discussion of this formula, see the comments on 12:1. Again Paul addresses his readers as "brothers and sisters" (ἀδελφοί), as many times elsewhere, to express affection, mutual responsibility, and reciprocity. For more on the term, see the comments on 1:13.

Who are the persons who would "create dissensions and offenses contrary to the teaching" that the Roman Christians had learned? It is not likely that he refers either to "the weak" or to "the strong" of 14:1–15:13. If he were referring to "the weak," he would be undercutting all that he tried to do in that section. And he could hardly be referring to "the strong," since he considered himself to be among "the strong" (Rom 15:1). It has been suggested that Paul is referring to Jewish Christian Gnostics, and that they are present in Rome.[72] But there is no evidence elsewhere that any form of Christian Gnosticism existed in Rome when Paul wrote this letter. In any case, neither in this verse nor in the following verses is enough said concerning the content of any possible opponents' teaching to identify them as Gnostics. The "teaching" (διδαχή) that the Roman Christians had been taught can be considered the common Chris-

---

72. W. Schmithals, "The False Teachers of Romans 16:17-20," 219-38.

tian tradition that they had received from early proclamation and catechesis in that city.

The admonition to "avoid" persons who cause dissensions or misbehave in other ways, rather than to confront them, is a familiar theme in the Pauline corpus (1 Cor 5:9-11; 2 Thess 3:6, 14; 2 Tim 3:5; Titus 3:10-11). The reason for avoiding such persons is not spelled out. Perhaps the simplest explanation is that to engage them in any way serves to honor their point of view or behavior, and that can open the door to possible compromises with them.

16:18 Those to be avoided serve their own appetites. The term translated "appetites" is κοιλία ("stomach"). The verse can be rendered more literally, then, to read that such persons are "slaves to their own stomach." The metaphor of slavery to one's stomach is used by Paul also at Philippians 3:19 ("their god is the belly"). Whatever the phrase may mean in that letter, at this place in Romans the term does not refer simply to gluttony but to something that is contrary to serving Christ. For Paul an either/or is at stake when he uses the verb "to serve" (δουλεύω; cf. Rom 6:6; 7:25; 12:11; 14:18; Gal 4:8-9; 1 Thess 1:9). The metaphor is used in other writings to mean apostasy,[73] and that is what it could mean here.[74] Its obvious meaning (both here and at Phil 3:19) is having a life oriented toward luxury and the fulfilling of one's desires. Whether that can be branded as apostasy or not (i.e., the outright rejection of the confession of Jesus as Lord), it does mean abandoning one's service of Christ. Such a life, described by Paul as a life "according to the flesh" (κατὰ σάρκα), is in opposition to a life under the lordship of Christ and the Spirit's leading (Rom 8:4-5, 12-13).

The persons to be avoided deceive by means of "smooth talk and flattery." The term translated "smooth talk" (χρηστολογία) is found only here in the NT and normally refers to the speech of a good person in Hellenistic texts,[75] but it is used here for the fine speech of a deceitful person.[76] Persons of that kind deceive "the hearts of the innocent." The term "innocent" (ἄκακος), as in the ASV and NAB, has been translated also as "simple" (KJV), "simple-minded" (RSV, NRSV), and "naïve" (NIV). But since its opposite would be an "evil" (κακός) person, it has to have the connotation of being disposed to good, not just being

---

73. *3 Macc.* 7:11; Philo, *Virt.* 34.182; *T. Moses* 7.4.

74. K. O. Sandnes, *Belly and Body in the Pauline Epistles*, 165-80.

75. Konrad Weiss, "χρηστολογία," *TDNT* 9:492.

76. J. North, "'Good Wordes and Faire Speeches,'" 600-614, contends that the term is related to χρηστόν ("wild endive") and means "endive-pickers," referring back then to the vegetarians in 14:2. The etymological connection proposed seems unlikely; the word χρηστόν would have been so rare that it does not even appear in the LSJ lexicon. The term more likely is coined from the common word χρηστός ("useful," "good," "mild," etc.). The use of the term by Greek-speaking patristic writers confirms the sense of "smooth talk" or "fair speaking"; for references, cf. *PGL* 1528 (χρηστολογία).

simple. The term "innocent" can carry both nuances. Those who would seek to create dissension are most likely to approach those who are unsuspecting and disposed to hear them out due to their inherent readiness to think that they mean well.

16:19 The term "obedience" (ὑπακοή), as in an *inclusio,* is picked up from 1:5. There Paul refers to his ministry as one that seeks to bring about the "obedience of faith" among the Gentile nations (cf. also 16:26). Here Paul declares that such obedience exists among the Roman Christians and that it is "known among all," presumably among all Christian communities of the time. Although there may be hyperbole in such a statement, it coheres with what Paul has said earlier about the faith of the Roman Christians (1:8; 15:14). See the comments on 1:8. His wish is that they may be wise (σοφός) in regard to good but without guile (ἀκέραιος) in terms of evil. The contrast recalls a similar saying of Jesus at the sending out of his disciples in which he says that they should be "wise (φρόνιμος) as serpents and innocent (ἀκέραιος) as doves" (Matt 10:16). Paul makes a contrast elsewhere between doing evil, on the one hand, and thinking as mature persons on the other, which apparently leads to good behavior: "Brothers and sisters, do not be children in your thinking; rather, be infants in evil, but in thinking be adults" (1 Cor 14:20).

16:20 The phrase "the God of peace" is a Pauline expression (Rom 15:33; Phil 4:9; 1 Thess 5:23; cf. 1 Cor 14:33; 2 Cor 13:11). See the the comments at 15:33. The promise is made that God will "crush" or "annihilate" (συντρίψει) Satan. The verb is in the future tense, resulting in an apocalyptic saying concerning the work of God over against Satan. Here Paul shares the view of other NT writers concerning the victory of God over Satan (Luke 10:18; 1 John 3:8; Rev 12:7-9; 20:10). It is possible that an allusion is being made here to Genesis 3:15 (concerning the crushing of the serpent's head underfoot), although the terminology is different, and the verb used appears elsewhere in reference to subduing enemies generally (1 Macc 3:22; *Ps. Sol.* 17.24; cf. Rev 2:26-27).

The word "Satan" (ὁ σατανᾶς, a transliteration of the Hebrew שָׂטָן) appears 36 times in the NT, of which seven instances are in the undisputed letters of Paul (Rom 16:20; 1 Cor 5:5; 7:5; 2 Cor 2:11; 11:14; 12:7; 1 Thess 2:18).[77] In every case except one (2 Cor 12:7) the article ὁ ("the," which need not be included in translation) is present. For Paul, Satan is a deceiver (1 Cor 2:11, 14), a tempter (1 Cor 7:5), and a power that torments him (2 Cor 12:7) and hinders him in his work (1 Thess 2:18). Other terms used in the NT include "the devil" (ὁ διάβολος), which appears 34 times, but never in the undisputed letters of Paul. Besides referring to him as "Satan," Paul speaks of the evil one as "the

---

77. The form σατάν appears twice in one verse of the LXX (3 Kgdms 11:14), but never in the NT.

god of this world" (2 Cor 4:4), "Beliar" (2 Cor 6:15), and "the tempter" (ὁ πειράζων, 1 Thess 3:5; cf. 1 Cor 7:5).[78]

By saying that God will crush Satan "under your feet soon," Paul could be speaking of the resolution of some specific problem among his Roman readers. It has been suggested, for example, that he is speaking of their overcoming those persons mentioned in 16:17 (who are thus under the power of Satan).[79] Yet, more likely, the reference is more general, possibly recalling the imagery of the wily serpent of Genesis 3:14-15, understood as Satan, whom God will crush. In any case, the apocalyptic language used refers to the eschatological victory of God over Satan, which Paul expects soon, and which will result in the triumph of the saints as well, for the phrase "under your feet" (cf. Ps 8:6; Mal 4:3) implies victory for them as well.[80]

The blessing in 16:20b ("The grace of our Lord Jesus be with you") is similar to those at the ends of other letters (1 Cor 16:23; Gal 6:18; 1 Thess 5:28; Phlm 25; cf. 2 Thess 3;18). Whether in spoken or written discourse, it is a performative utterance of the apostle, by which he exercises the authority to extend the grace (or favor) of Christ to his hearers or readers. The favor of Jesus Christ rests upon them — persons who are already "in Christ" — and they are empowered to live in obedience to him.

BIBLIOGRAPHY

Boismard, Marie-Émile. "Rm 16,17-20: Vocabulaire et style." *RB* 107 (2000): 548-57.

Gamble, Harry, Jr. *The Textual History of the Letter to the Romans: A Study in Textual and Literary Criticism.* SD. Grand Rapids: Wm. B. Eerdmans, 1977.

Hassold, William J. "'Avoid Them': Another Look at Romans 16:17-20." *CurTM* 27 (2000): 196-208.

Jewett, Robert. "Ecumenical Theology for the Sake of Mission: Romans 1:1-17 + 15:14–16:24." In *Pauline Theology*, vol. 3, *Romans*, 89-108. Ed. David M. Hay and E. Elizabeth Johnson. Minneapolis: Fortress Press, 1995.

Mora, Vincent. "Romains 16,17-20 et la letter aux Éphésiens." *RB* 107 (2000): 541-47.

North, J. Lionel. "'Good Wordes and Faire Speeches' (Rom 16.18 AV): More Materials and a Pauline Pun." *NTS* 42 (1996): 600-614.

Ollrog, Wolf-Henning. "Die Abfassungsverhältnisse von Röm 16." In *Kirche: Festschrift für Günther Bornkamm zum 75. Geburtstag*, 221-44. Ed. Dieter Lührmann and Georg Strecker. Tübingen: J. C. B. Mohr (Paul Siebeck), 1980.

---

78. On "Satan" in the NT, cf. Otto Böcher, "σατανᾶς," *EDNT* 3:234; Victor P. Hamilton, "Satan," *ABD* 5:985-89.

79. Georg Bertram, "συντρίβω," *TDNT* 7:924; J. Fitzmyer, *Romans*, 746-47.

80. C. Cranfield, *Romans*, 803 (although he asserts that Paul does not imply an imminent parousia here); J. Dunn, *Romans*, 905.

Sampley, J. Paul. "Romans in a Different Light: A Response to Robert Jewett." In *Pauline Theology*, vol. 3, *Romans*, 109-29. Ed. David M. Hay and E. Elizabeth Johnson. Minneapolis: Fortress Press, 1995.

Sandnes, Karl O. *Belly and Body in the Pauline Epistles*. SNTSMS 120. New York: Cambridge University Press, 2002.

Schmithals, Walter. "The False Teachers of Romans 16:17-20." In his *Paul and the Gnostics*, 219-38. Nashville: Abingdon Press, 1972.

10.4. Greetings from Paul's Coworkers, 16:21-23

21*Timothy, my coworker, greets you as do Lucius, Jason, and Sosipater, my kinsmen.* 22*I, Tertius, the writer of this letter, greet you in the Lord.* 23*Gaius, host to me and the whole church, greets you. Erastus, the city treasurer, greets you; so does our brother Quartus.*

Notes on the Text and Translation

16:21 Some Greek texts (including the Majority Text) have the verb ἀσπάζον-ται (third person plural, "[they] greet you") instead of ἀσπάζεται (third person singular, "he" or "she greets you") at the beginning of the verse. Since Paul sends greetings from several persons, one is inclined to expect the plural form. But the singular is better attested ($\mathfrak{P}^{46}$, ℵ, A, B, etc.), and it is grammatically acceptable when the verb stands before a singular form of the subject followed by καί and another noun as subject, as here.[81]

16:24 Concerning this verse (lacking in modern versions), see the discussion in the Introduction (Section 3, "Romans 16 in Light of Textual and Historical Criticism").

General Comment

It is not uncommon for Paul to add greetings from coworkers at the ends of his letters (1 Cor 16:19-20; Phil 4:21-22; Phlm 23-24). Writing from Corinth, where he has stayed for three months (Acts 20:3), presumably at the home of Gaius (16:23), he is able to send greetings from several persons. Paul sends greetings from eight people, all men, to the Christians at Rome.

---

81. BDF 74 (§135).

Detailed Comment

16:21 The first of those sending greetings is Timothy, a traveling companion and "coworker" (συνεργός) with Paul. Paul met him at Lystra and circumcised him (Acts 16:1-3). Timothy accompanied Paul on various journeys, was present with him in Macedonia and Corinth (2 Cor 1:19; Acts 17:14-15; 18:5; cf. 1 Cor 16:10), and is identified as a coauthor of four of Paul's undisputed letters (2 Cor 1:1; Phil 1:1; 1 Thess 1:1; Phlm 1). He is now at Corinth with Paul. Among those at Rome to whom Timothy would certainly have sent greetings are Prisca and Aquila, since they had been in Corinth a few years earlier while Timothy was there (Acts 18:1-5).

Of Lucius, Jason, and Sosipater not much more can be known beyond the fact that they are with Paul in Corinth at the time of writing the letter. Paul identifies them as Jewish Christians (οἱ συγγενεῖς μου, "my kinsmen"). Lucius (Λούκιος) is a common name, and therefore any further attempt to identify this man gets speculative. Some interpreters have surmised that the person named is Luke (Λουκᾶς), the author of Luke-Acts,[82] for there is evidence that the names were interchangeable.[83] While that is not impossible, it is only a guess. Since Paul refers to Luke as "Luke" (Λουκᾶς) elsewhere (Phlm 24), the likelihood diminishes. There is also a Lucius of Cyrene who is named among the "prophets and teachers" at Antioch of Syria (Acts 13:1). If that is the same Lucius, he would have moved from Antioch to Corinth. But once again there can be no certainty that he is the person mentioned by Paul, although that has been suggested.[84]

Jason ('Ιάσων) was also a common name, and Jews sometimes took it as a substitute for the name Jesus ('Ιησοῦς).[85] Luke writes concerning a Jason of Thessalonica who became a convert to the faith through the preaching of Paul (Acts 17:5-9). Whether this could be the same person will be taken up momentarily. Sosipater (Σωσίπατρος) bears a more unusual name and could conceivably be the person known as Sopater (Σώπατρος) of Beroea (Acts 20:4).

Names in Romans 16:21 and 23 appear also at Acts 20:4-6, in the scene following the three months' stay of Paul in Corinth when he wrote his letter to the Romans. As Paul left Corinth, says Luke, he was accompanied to Macedonia by several persons, including "Sopater of Beroea," "Gaius of Derbe," "Timothy," and others, including some "Thessalonians" (Aristarchus and Secundus are named). The person named Timothy must surely be the same person in both texts. If Sosipater in Romans (16:21) can be identified with Sopater of Acts

---

82. Origen, *Rom. Comm.* 10.39; A. Deissmann, "Loukios-Lukas," 117-20.
83. BDAG 603 (Λουκᾶς).
84. W. Sanday and A. Headlam, *Romans*, 432.
85. Cf. BDAG 453 ('Ιάσων).

(20:4), and Gaius of Romans (16:23) with Gaius of Derbe in Acts (20:4; see below), it is also possible that Jason of Romans (16:21) would be the Jason of Thessalonica (Acts 17:5-9), who is unnamed in Acts 20:4-6 but can be included among the "Thessalonians" who left Corinth with Paul and the others.[86]

16:22 Tertius (Τέρτιος) sends his own greeting, identifying himself as "the writer" (ὁ γράψας) of the letter. As such, he would have been Paul's amanuensis. There is no reason to consider him a joint author. It may seem impertinent for him to have added his own greeting, but it is surely a delight that he did. Elsewhere in his letters it is evident that Paul had an amanuensis to write his letters in final form prior to sending them (1 Cor 16:21; Gal 6:11-18; Phlm 19). It can never be known whether Paul dictated Romans in its entirety to Tertius, or whether he put ink to paper himself (at least as notations) in places where he carried on detailed discussion and then turned the composition over to Tertius.[87] An example of where Paul might have worked at a desk with pen and ink would be chapters 9–11, where the argument is very intricate, drawing upon extensive OT material. Since Tertius sends greetings "in the Lord," he is a Christian. Like others listed here, he probably knows some of the Roman Christians personally — almost certainly Prisca and Aquila — although that is not imperative for the sending of greetings. It has even been suggested that Tertius was a Roman Christian living for a while in Corinth, and that Paul enlisted him to be his amanuensis for the writing of this letter.[88] But that is not certain or necessary, and his greeting appears more as a friendly outburst than a calculated gesture. Having heard from Paul the roll call of names in this chapter, he could have been moved to join the apostle in sending greetings to them all.

16:23 Gaius is Paul's host at Corinth as the apostle writes his letter, but he is also the host (ξένος) of a church in his house. Paul had baptized him while in Corinth at an earlier time (1 Cor 1:14). Gaius would have to have been a person of sufficient means to provide a place for "the whole church" of Corinth to meet for worship and other occasions,[89] which Paul implies by calling him "host" of the "whole church" there. How many he had to accommodate can never be known, but the fact that Paul refers to "the whole church" rather than simply "the

---

86. The possibility is held by C. Cranfield, *Romans*, 805-6; J. Dunn, *Romans*, 909; J. Fitzmyer, *Romans*, 749, 934; D. Moo, *Romans*, and F. Gillman, "Jason of Thessalonica (Acts 17,5-9)," 39-49 (esp. on p. 40).

87. G. Bahr, "Subscriptions," 38-40, maintains that Paul began writing (with his own hand) at Rom 12:1. That seems rather soon.

88. G. Edmundson, *The Church in Rome*, 22. Edmundson indicates that a Tertius is mentioned in a Greek inscription in a Roman cemetery, and while he suggests that that person could be the same person who sends greetings, he does not press it.

89. A. Malherbe, *Social Aspects of Early Christianity*, 97. The view that "the whole church" "has to mean the universal church," as maintained by E. Käsemann, *Romans*, 421, is unnecessary.

church" implies that the house must have been rather impressive in its size, being able to accommodate persons from various house churches in the city.[90] The name Gaius appears in other NT texts (Acts 19:29; 20:4; 3 John 1) in addition to these two instances in the letters of Paul. As indicated above, the Gaius mentioned by Paul could well be the Gaius of Derbe mentioned by Luke (Acts 20:4).

Erastus, another Christian, is identified as "the city treasurer" (ὁ οἰκονόμος τῆς πόλεως) of Corinth. Whether he is the same person as the Erastus mentioned in Acts 19:22, who traveled with Paul, and/or the Erastus at 2 Timothy 4:20 (who "remained at Corinth") is inconclusive. The name was common. Considerable debate has centered around the question whether the Erastus mentioned here by Paul is a man by that name mentioned in a Latin inscription. The inscription, dated to the middle of the first century, was discovered in 1929. It was located between the north market and the theater in Corinth, reading: "Erastus in return for his aedileship paved [this area] at his own expense."[91] Could this be the person mentioned by Paul? Once again, there is no certainty. In the inscription the status of Erastus is that of an *aedilis*, i.e., a Roman magistrate charged with the supervision of public buildings, games, and markets.[92] The usual Greek equivalent for the Latin term *aedilis*, however, is ἀγορανόμος (rather than οἰκονόμος).[93] Moreover, it has been argued that the Latin equivalent for οἰκονόμος would more likely be *quaestor* (a chief financial magistrate of a city), not *aedilis*.[94] There is merit in the suggestion that the person in the inscription could either (1) have had the title *aedilis*, and one of his functions was to be the city treasurer (οἰκονόμος) when Paul met him, or (2) that Erastus rose from the office of οἰκονόμος in Paul's day to the position of *aedilis* subsequently.[95]

Quartus, the third person mentioned in this verse, is otherwise unknown. All three of these persons were, presumably, Gentiles, in contrast to the three mentioned in 16:21 who were Jewish.

BIBLIOGRAPHY

Bahr, Gordon J. "The Subscriptions in the Pauline Letters." *JBL* 87 (1968): 27-41.

Cadbury, Henry J. "Erastus of Corinth." *JBL* 50 (1931): 42-58.

90. J. Murphy-O'Connor, *Paul*, 267.

91. J. Kent, *Corinth VIII/3*, 99; J. Murphy-O'Connor, *St. Paul's Corinth*, 34-35.

92. *Oxford Latin Dictionary*, ed. P. G. W. Glare (New York: Oxford University Press, 1982), 61.

93. LSJ 13 (ἀγορανόμος).

94. G. Theissen, *The Social Setting of Pauline Christianity*, 83; J. Goodrich, "Erastus, Quaestor of Corinth," 90-115.

95. G. Theissen, *The Social Setting of Pauline Christianity*, 83; J. Murphy-O'Connor, *Paul*, 269.

Clarke, Andrew D. "Another Corinthian Erastus Inscription." *TynB* 42 (1991): 146-51.

Deissmann, Adolf. "Loukios-Lukas." In *Festgabe von Fachgenossen und Freunden von A. von Harnack zum siebzigsten Geburtstagdargebracht*, 117-20. Ed. Karl Holl et al. Tübingen: J. C. B. Mohr, 1921.

Edmundson, George. *The Church in Rome in the First Century*. New York: Longmans, Green, 1913.

Ellis, E. Earle. "Paul and His Co-Workers." *NTS* 17 (1970-71): 437-52.

Gill, David W. J. "Erastus the Aedile." *TynB* 40 (1989): 293-301.

Gillman, Florence M. "Jason of Thessalonica (Acts 17,5-9)." In *The Thessalonian Correspondence*, 39-49. Ed. Raymond E. Collins. BETL 87. Louvain: Leuven University Press, 1990.

Goodrich, John K. "Erastus, Quaestor of Corinth: The Administrative Rank of ὁ οἰκονόμος τῆς πόλεως (Roman 16.23) in an Achaean Colony." *NTS* 56 (2010): 90-115.

Goodspeed, Edgar J. "Gaius Titius Justus." *JBL* 69 (1950): 382-83.

Harrison, P. N. "Erastus and His Pavement." In his *Paulines and Pastorals*, 100-105. London: Villiers, 1964.

Kent, John H. *Corinth VIII/3: The Inscriptions 1926-1950*. Princeton: American School of Classical Studies at Athens, 1966.

Longenecker, Richard N. "Ancient Amanuenses and the Pauline Epistles." In *New Dimensions in New Testament Study*, 281-97. Ed. R. N. Longenecker and Merrill C. Tenney. Grand Rapids: Zondervan, 1974.

Malherbe, Abraham J. *Social Aspects of Early Christianity*. 2d ed. Philadelphia: Fortress Press, 1983.

Meggitt, Justin J. "The Social Status of Erastus (Rom. 16:23)." *NovT* 38 (1996): 218-23.

Murphy-O'Connor, Jerome. *Paul: A Critical Life*. New York: Oxford University Press, 2002.

———. *St. Paul's Corinth: Texts and Archaeology*. 3d ed. Wilmington: Michael Glazier, 2002.

Redlich, E. Basil. *St. Paul and His Companions*. London: Macmillan, 1913.

Richards, E. Randolph. *The Secretary in the Letters of Paul*. WUNT 2/42. Tübingen: J. C. B. Mohr (Paul Siebeck), 1991.

Theissen, Gerd. *The Social Setting of Pauline Christianity: Essays on Corinth*. Philadelphia: Fortress Press, 1982.

10.5. Concluding Doxology, 16:25-27

25*And to the one who is able to strengthen you according to my gospel and the proclamation of Jesus Christ, according to the revelation of the mystery kept secret for an eternal time,* 26*but now made manifest and through the prophetic writings made known to all the nations according to the command of the eternal God for the obedience of faith,* 27*to the only wise God be glory forever through Jesus Christ. Amen.*

General Comment

This unit can be considered a deutero-Pauline addition to the Letter to the Romans. That judgment rests in part on text-critical issues, which are discussed in the Introduction (Section 3, "Romans 16 in Light of Textual and Historical Criticism"). But vocabulary and style are also a consideration. In regard to the vocabulary of the unit, there actually are no *hapax legomena*, but what is unusual is the way that the words are assembled. These three verses, which compose one long sentence of 53 words in the Greek NT (as printed by Nestle-Aland, 27th ed.), contain phrases not found elsewhere in the undisputed letters of Paul. The phrases that stand out are: "according to the revelation of the mystery kept secret for an eternal time" (κατὰ ἀποκάλυψιν μυστηρίου χρόνοις αἰωνίοις σεσιγημένου), "according to the command of the eternal God" (κατ' ἐπιταγὴν τοῦ αἰωνίου θεοῦ), and "the only wise God" (μόνος σοφὸς θεός). As often said, the doxology is written in the style of Ephesians and the Pastoral Epistles, and it is likely that a post-Pauline editor of Paul's letters is the author of this unit as well.[96]

The subject of this long sentence is the noun "glory" near the end. "Glory" is thereby given to God, bringing the letter to a close. To have a doxology at the end of a letter by Paul is unusual, for although doxologies appear *within* Paul's undisputed letters (e.g., at Rom 11:36; Gal 1:5; Phil 4:20), they do not occur at the *end* of any of them. Instead they end with a benediction (1 Cor 16:23; 2 Cor 13:14; Gal 6:18; Phil 4:23; 1 Thess 5:28; Phlm 25).[97]

Detailed Comment

16:25 The verse begins exactly in the same way as Ephesians 3:20 and Jude 24 (τῷ δὲ δυναμένῳ). God is the one who gives strength and is therefore worthy of

---

96. For a detailed study of the particulars, cf. J. K. Elliott, "The Language and Style of the Concluding Doxology to the Epistle to the Romans," 124-30. The deutero-Pauline character of the passages is affirmed (at least as probable), among others, by C. Cranfield, *Romans*, 809; E. Käsemann, *Romans*, 422-28; U. Wilckens, *Römer*, 1:22-24; 3:147; J. Dunn, *Romans*, 913; J. Fitzmyer, *Romans*, 753; B. Byrne, *Romans*, 461-62; R. Collins, "The Case of a Wandering Doxology," 293-303; W. Walker, "Interpolations," 235; H.-J. Klauck, *Ancient Letters*, 462; R. Jewett, *Romans*, 998-1002; E. Lohse, *Römer*, 417. Cf. also the same conclusion via another route by S. Hultgren, "2 Cor 6.14–7.1 and Rev 21.3-8," 54. For the view that the verses are truly Pauline (but moved from their original place after 14:23), cf. U. Borse, "Das Schlusswort des Römerbriefes," 173-92. Others who maintain Pauline authorship include L. Johnson, *Romans*, 221-23; D. Moo, *Romans*, 936-37 (n. 2); T. Schreiner, *Romans*, 810-11; and I. H. Marshall, "Romans 16:25-27," 170-84. D. Garlington, *'The Obedience of Faith'*, 1 (n. 1), seems to be ambivalent.

97. W. Walker, *Interpolations in the Pauline Letters*, 194-95.

praise (δόξα). Elsewhere Paul speaks of the strength that Christ gives to the hearts of those who await his coming (1 Thess 3:13). The term "my gospel" is used by Paul earlier in this letter (2:16), and it appears in (deutero-Pauline) 2 Timothy 2:8. The phrase "the proclamation of Jesus Christ" (τὸ κήρυγμα Ἰησοῦ Χριστοῦ) can be taken in two ways: (1) Jesus' own proclamation (transmitted in the gospel tradition) or (2) early Christian proclamation concerning Jesus. When Paul uses the term "proclamation" (κήρυγμα) elsewhere, it refers to Christian proclamation (1 Cor 2:4; 15:14). In light of that, and since the phrase used here is preceded by "my gospel" and followed by references to revelation, the usual Pauline sense is quite certainly meant.[98]

The "revelation of the mystery kept secret for an eternal time" refers to the proclamation of the gospel in the present, the unveiling of what has been hidden from eternity. The term "mystery" (μυστήριον) designates a "divine secret," and the idea that God has kept secrets from the past until the present moment of revelation is attested in other sources. According to them, the prophets of Israel, who had access to the counsel of God, knew that God had secrets yet to be disclosed, and that those secrets would be revealed in God's good time.[99] The mystery has been kept secret (literally, "kept silent") by God — and so the divine silence has been maintained — for all time up to the present, but now it has been revealed in the saving work of God in Christ, which is proclaimed in the gospel. Similar expressions occur elsewhere in Paul's own letters (Rom 11:25; 1 Cor 2:7, 10), but above all in the deutero-Pauline letters (Eph 3:3-6 and Col 1:26-27; 2 Tim 1:9-10). That which was in the beginning, but long hidden, is now being made visible.[100]

16:26 The "mystery" is now being "made manifest," and so the silence is over. The verse contains two Greek participles, both genitives in the passive voice (φανερωθέντος, "made manifest," and γνωρισθέντος, "made known"). In both cases it is the "mystery" that is "made manifest" and "made known." There is a slight nuance here of importance due to the inclusion of a little easy-to-miss conjunction τε ("and"). In the first case the mystery has been "made manifest" in the present (νῦν) through proclamation. In the second instance the mystery has been "made known" through the "prophetic writings" of the past. Just how the "prophetic writings" could have made the mystery known "to all the nations" is a puzzle, if it is the case that the mystery is only "now" being revealed. But within the writings of certain OT prophets there is an eschatological expectation of the coming of the nations to faith (e.g., Isa 2:2-4; 60:3; Jer 16:19; Mic

---

98. Cf. W. Sanday and A. Headlam, *Romans*, 433; R. Brown, *Semitic Background*, 51; C. Cranfield, *Romans*, 810; J. Dunn, *Romans*, 914.

99. 2 Esdr 14:5; 12:36-37; *1 Enoch* 104.10-12; 1QpHab 7.1-5. Cf. R. Brown, *Semitic Background*, 52.

100. K. Wengst, *Christologische Formeln und Lieder des Urchristentums*, 164.

4:1-3; Zech 8:20-23), which is only now being accomplished.[101] As the gospel is proclaimed to the nations of the world, in accord with the message of the prophets and the divine command, the mystery is being made manifest. The expression "through the prophetic writings" (διά τε γραφῶν προφητικῶν) recalls an expression of Paul in 1:2. But it differs somewhat. At 1:2 Paul speaks not simply of the message of the Scriptures, but of the message of the prophets themselves that is set forth in the Scriptures: "through his prophets in the holy scriptures" (διὰ τῶν προφητῶν αὐτοῦ ἐν γραφαῖς ἁγίαις). In the latter case, Paul declares that the prophets uttered the divine promise, as recorded in the Scriptures, whereas at 16:26 the Scriptures are a deposit of the divine revelation.

The phrase "according to the command of the eternal God" (κατ᾽ ἐπιταγὴν τοῦ αἰωνίου θεοῦ) is similar to "according to the command of God our Savior" (κατ᾽ ἐπιταγὴν τοῦ σωτῆρος ἡμῶν θεοῦ) in Titus 1:3. But ὑπακοὴ πίστεως ("obedience of faith") is familiar from Romans 1:5. For comments on the phrase, see the exegesis there. Cf. also ὑπακοὴ ἐθνῶν ("obedience of the nations") at 15:18.

16:27 The subject of the sentence is now finally given, "glory" (δόξα). Glory is given to God, who provides strength to those who are faithful. To ascribe glory to God by means of doxologies is to recognize the splendor and power of God, which has been made evident through revelation (Luke 2:14; 19:38; Rom 11:36; Eph 3:21; Phil 4:20; 1 Tim 1:17; Rev 4:9; 7:12).[102] Here God is called the "only wise God," a phrase found nowhere else in the NT. The last phrase, "to whom be glory for ever. Amen" (ᾧ ἡ δόξα εἰς τοὺς αἰῶνας, ἀμήν), is Pauline, appearing three other times in the undisputed Pauline letters (Rom 11:36; Gal 1:5; Phil 4:20) and with a slight variation in two additional cases ("forever and ever," τοὺς αἰῶνας τῶν αἰώνων; Gal 1:5; Phil 4:29). The longer phrase appears also in the Pastoral Epistles (1 Tim 1:17; 2 Tim 4:18).

BIBLIOGRAPHY

Bacon, Benjamin W. "The Doxology at the End of Romans." *JBL* 18 (1899): 167-76.

Bockmuehl, Markus N. A. *Revelation and Mystery in Ancient Judaism and Pauline Christianity.* WUNT 2/36. Tübingen: J. C. B. Mohr (Paul Siebeck), 1990.

Borse, Udo. "Das Schlusswort des Römerbriefes: Segensgruss (16,24) statt Doxologie (VV. 25-27)." *SNTU* 19 (1994): 173-92.

Brown, Raymond E. *The Semitic Background of the Term "Mystery" in the New Testament.* FBBS 21. Philadelphia: Fortress Press, 1968.

Collins, Raymond F. "The Case of a Wandering Doxology: Rom 16,25-27." In *New Testa-*

---

101. For discussion, cf. A. Hultgren, "The Scriptural Foundations for Paul's Mission to the Gentiles," 21-44.

102. Gerhard Kittel, "δόξα," *TDNT* 2:247-48.

ment Textual Criticism and Exegesis: Festschrift J. Delobel, 293-303. Ed. Adelbert Denaux. BETL 161. Leuven: Peeters, 2002.

Dewailly, Louis M. "Mystère et silence dans Rom. xvi.25." *NTS* 14 (1967-68): 111-18.

Elliott, James K. "The Language and Style of the Concluding Doxology to the Epistle to the Romans." *ZNW* 72 (1981): 124-30.

Fahy, Thomas. "Epistle to the Romans 16:25-27." *ITQ* 28 (1961): 238-41.

Fitzmyer, Joseph A. "Paul and the Dead Sea Scrolls." In *The Dead Sea Scrolls after Fifty Years: A Comprehensive Assessment*, 2:599-621. Ed. Peter W. Flint and James C. VanderKam. 2 vols. Boston: E. J. Brill, 1998-99.

Garlington, Don B. *Faith, Obedience, and Perseverance: Aspects of Paul's Letter to the Romans*. WUNT 79. Tübingen: J. C. B. Mohr (Paul Siebeck), 1994.

————. *'The Obedience of Faith' — A Pauline Phrase in Historical Context*. WUNT 2/38. Tübingen: J. C. B. Mohr (Paul Siebeck), 1991.

————. "The Obedience of Faith in the Letter to the Romans, Part I: The Meaning of ὑπακοὴ πίστεως (Rom 1:5; 16:26)." *WTJ* 52 (1990): 201-24.

Hultgren, Arland J. "The Scriptural Foundations for Paul's Mission to the Gentiles." In *Paul and His Theology*, 21-44. Ed. Stanley E. Porter. PAST 3. Boston: E. J. Brill, 2006.

Hultgren, Stephen J. "2 Cor 6.14–7.1 and Rev 21.3-8: Evidence for the Ephesian Redaction of 2 Corinthians." *NTS* 49 (2003): 39-56.

Hurtado, Larry W. "The Doxology at the End of Romans." In *New Testament Textual Criticism: Its Significance for Exegesis: Essays in Honour of Bruce M. Metzger*, 185-99. Ed. Eldon J. Epp and Gordon D. Fee. New York: Oxford University Press, 1981.

Kamlah, Erhard. "Traditionsgeschichtliche Untersuchungen zur Schlussdoxologie des Römerbriefes." Unpublished doctoral diss., University of Tübingen, 1955.

Marshall, I. Howard. "Romans 16:25-27 — An Apt Conclusion." In *Romans and the People of God: Essays in Honor of Gordon D. Fee on the Occasion of His 65th Birthday*, 170-84. Ed. S. K. Soderlund and N. T. Wright. Grand Rapids: Wm. B. Eerdmans, 1999.

Schmithals, Walter. "Die Doxologie: 16.25-27." In his *Der Römerbrief als historisches Problem*, 108-24. Gütersloh: Gerd Mohn, 1975.

Walker, William O., Jr. *Interpolations in the Pauline Letters*. JSNTSup 213. Sheffield: Sheffield Academic Press, 2001.

————. "Interpolations in the Pauline Letters." In *The Pauline Canon*, 189-235. Ed. Stanley E. Porter. PAST 1. Boston: E. J. Brill, 2004.

Weima, Jeffrey A. D. *Neglected Endings: The Significance of the Pauline Letter Closings*. JSNTSup 101. Sheffield: JSOT Press, 1994.

————. "The Pauline Letter Closings: Analysis and Hermeneutical Significance." *BBR* 5 (1995): 177-97.

Wengst, Klaus. *Christologische Formeln und Lieder des Urchristentums*. SNT 7. Gütersloh: Gütersloher Verlagshaus Gerd Mohn, 1972.

Wiens, Devon H. "Mystery Concepts in Primitive Christianity and in Its Environment." *ANRW* II.23.2 (1980): 1248-84.

The "Righteousness of God" in Paul

The phrase "righteousness of God" (δικαιοσύνη θεοῦ or slight variations) appears several times in Paul's letters. The exact phrase δικαιοσύνη θεοῦ appears at Romans 1:17; 3:5, 21, 22; 10:3 (twice); and 2 Corinthians 5:21. In most of those cases the usage is anarthrous. Two exceptions occur where the full phrase "the righteousness of God" (ἡ δικαιοσύνη τοῦ θεοῦ) is employed (Rom 10:3). Once Paul writes concerning "his" (= God's) righteousness (ἡ δικαιοσύνη αὐτοῦ, Rom 3:26), and on another occasion he uses the expression "the righteousness from God" (ἡ ἐκ θεοῦ δικαιοσύνην, Phil 3:9). The phrase expresses a major theme in Paul's letters, having significance for interpreting other aspects of his theology, and interpreters have disagreed concerning its meaning. Other NT writings that make use of the term in reference to God are James (1:20), 2 Peter (1:1), and the Gospel of Matthew ("his righteousness," 6:33).

1.1. Points of View among Interpreters

Disagreement among interpreters revolves around a grammatical distinction. The phrase in question contains a term in the genitive case (θεοῦ, "of God"), but the kind of genitive it is has been a matter of disagreement.[1] One could say, for example, that the phrase contains a possessive genitive. If so, the phrase speaks of the righteousness that God has — presumably a righteousness that exceeds normal human righteousness (as in Matt 6:33). That tendency is reflected in the Vulgate, which translates the term as *iustitia Dei*, which can in

---

1. For helpful surveys, see K. Kertelge, *Rechtfertigung bei Paulus*, 6-14; J. Reumann, *Righteousness*, 66; idem, "Righteousness (NT)," 5:758; M. Brauch, "Perspectives on 'God's Righteousness' in Recent German Discussion," 523-42; J. Fitzmyer, *Romans*, 257-63.

turn be translated into English as the "justice of God." That God is just or righteous in an absolute sense is affirmed elsewhere in Scripture (e.g., Pss 7:9; 111:7; 145:17; Isa 24:16; Jer 12:1; Ezek 18:25), and certainly by Paul himself (Rom 2:5, 11; 3:4, 26). But that is only the beginning of the matter. With one exception (Rom 3:5) Paul does not use the phrase to speak of God's righteousness as a divine possession or attribute in comparison or contrast to human righteousness. What is characteristic of Paul, rather, is that when he speaks of the righteousness of God, he uses relational language. God is righteous because of some factor in the divine-human relationship. In light of that, there are two main viewpoints concerning the meaning of the phrase.

According to one major point of view, the phrase should be read as employing a "genitive of origin" (or *genitivus auctoris*). In this case the righteousness of God is a gift that proceeds from God, as works come from an author (such as the works of Shakespeare). The righteousness of God is the righteousness that God bestows upon the believer. It proceeds from God to the believer, who is thereby seen as righteous (is justified). The focus is anthropological and forensic.[2] That is to say, the focus is primarily on the person who stands before God, and that person is declared righteous, or acquitted, as in a law court (Latin *forum*). Rudolf Bultmann, for example, has written that righteousness is something that a person "has in the verdict of the 'forum' (law court — the sense of 'forum' from which 'forensic' as here used is derived) to which he is accountable."[3] "He is 'righteous' not to the extent that he may *be* innocent, but to the extent that he is *acknowledged* innocent."[4] Anders Nygren has written that the righteousness of God is a "righteousness originating in God, purposed by God, revealed in the gospel and therein offered to us."[5] Hans Conzelmann has asserted that the concept is "anthropological" and is an "alien righteousness" bestowed on the believer.[6] Herman Ridderbos says that the "righteousness of God" is the righteousness granted to the believer which is required for the latter "to go free in the divine judgment."[7] This viewpoint, if not the same terminol-

---

2. With variations in terminology and emphases, the following (among others) represent this viewpoint: BDAG 247 (δικαιοσύνη, 2); R. Bultmann, *Theology of the New Testament*, 1:270-85; idem, "ΔΙΚΑΙΟΣΥΝΗ ΘΕΟΥ," 12-16; A. Nygren, *Romans*, 175-77; J. Murray, *Romans*, 1:30-31; H. Conzelmann, *An Outline of the Theology of the New Testament*, 214-20; E. Lohse, "Gerechtigkeit Gottes," 223; idem, *Grundriss der neutestamentlichen Theologie*, 86; idem, *Römer*, 78-81; G. Klein, "Righteousness," 750-52; C. Cranfield, *Romans*, 1:91-100; H. Ridderbos, *Paul*, 163-64; G. Bornkamm, *Paul*, 136-38.

3. R. Bultmann, *Theology of the New Testament*, 1:272.

4. R. Bultmann, *Theology of the New Testament*, 1:272. The emphases appear in the English text.

5. A. Nygren, *Romans*, 76.

6. H. Conzelmann, *An Outline of the Theology of the New Testament*, 220.

7. H. Ridderbos, *Paul*, 163.

ogy, was expressed by Martin Luther in the Reformation era,[8] and it has been the prevailing one in Protestant theology.[9] The "righteousness of God" is that righteousness that is necessary for humanity in the final judgment, and which is granted to the believer.

According to the other major point of view, a "subjective genitive" is operative here. In this case the righteousness of God is an attribute of God, to be sure, just as the wrath of God is (Rom 1:18), but there is more. The righteousness of God is, first of all, a "relational concept" rather than an objective standard.[10] It signifies God's action to save, his own act of "right-wising" the believer. The focus is theological and eschatological.[11] That is to say, the focus is on the activity of God in the cross and resurrection of Christ and an act by which the judgment of God, anticipated at the end of human history, is exercised in the present. Ernst Käsemann, for example, has written that by means of the expression, Paul declares that God's righteousness is "a power which brings salvation to pass."[12] It is for Paul "God's sovereignty over the world revealing itself eschatologically in Jesus."[13] Peter Stuhlmacher has written that, for Paul, "this righteousness of God is already being revealed before the beginning of the day of judgment and made possible for those who believe."[14]

With either understanding of the phrase, to be sure, the believer is justified

---

8. Martin Luther, "Preface to Latin Writings," in *Luther's Works,* ed. Jaroslav Pelikan and Helmut T. Lehmann, 55 vols. (St. Louis: Concordia Publishing House; Philadelphia: Fortress Press, 1955-76), 34:336-37.

9. This can be illustrated by reference to, among others, Lutheran and Reformed texts. Cf. passages in the *Apology of the Augsburg Confession* (4.73, 252) and the *Formula of Concord* (Epitome 3.4; Solid Declaration 3.9) in *The Book of Concord,* ed. Robert Kolb and Timothy J. Wengert (Minneapolis: Fortress Press, 2000), 132, 159, 495, 563; and in the *Institutes* of John Calvin (3.11.23); text in John Calvin, *Institutes of the Christian Religion,* ed. John T. McNeill, LCC (Philadelphia: Westminster Press, 1960), 1:753.

10. H. Cremer, *Biblio-Theological Lexicon of New Testament Greek,* 193; idem, *Die paulinische Rechtfertigungslehre,* 33-34.

11. With variations in terminology and emphases, the following (among others) represent this viewpoint: J. Ropes, "Righteousness," 211-27; C. H. Dodd, *Romans,* 9-13; A. Schlatter, *Romans,* 21-22; Gottlob Schrenk, "δικαιοσύνη," *TDNT* 2:203; E. Käsemann, "'The Righteousness of God' in Paul," 168-82; idem, *Romans,* 24-30; W. Kümmel, *The Theology of the New Testament,* 196-98; P. Stuhlmacher, *Gerechtigkeit Gottes* (esp. 217-36); idem, *Romans,* 29-32; K. Kertelge, *Rechtfertigung bei Paulus* (esp. 286-304); idem, "δικαιοσύνη," *EDNT* 1:327-28; J. Ziesler, *The Meaning of Righteousness in Paul,* 186-91 (with reservations, allowing for multiple meanings); idem, *Romans,* 70-71 (on Rom 1:17 and elsewhere); V. Furnish, *Theology and Ethics in Paul,* 143-46; U. Wilckens, *Römer,* 1:202-33 (esp. 220-22); P. Achtemeier, *Romans,* 61-66; J. C. Beker, *Paul the Apostle,* 262-64; K. Haacker, *Römer,* 39-42; R. Moore, *Rectification,* 1:252-61; J. Flebbe, *Solus Deus,* 71-77.

12. E. Käsemann, "'The Righteousness of God' in Paul," 181.

13. E. Käsemann, "'The Righteousness of God' in Paul," 180.

14. P. Stuhlmacher, *Romans,* 31.

(right-wised) apart from the law. That is not at issue. But there are nuances that have far-reaching effects on how one understands the justifying work of God in Christ. If Paul employs the "genitive of origin," the righteousness of God is bestowed upon the believer as an "alien righteousness." The believer is thereupon acquitted, declared innocent, justified. If, on the other hand, Paul employs the "subjective genitive," the righteousness of God — like the grace of God, the love of God, the mercy of God, or the wrath of God — stands behind the activity of God. It is revealed in the gospel (Rom 1:17) and manifested in God's saving activity in Christ (Rom 3:21). The righteousness of God is, in short, that attribute that expresses itself in God's saving activity, restoring the world unto himself. It has been manifested already in history, as the OT reveals (Rom 3:21b), and now has been manifested in God's saving activity in Christ (Rom 3:21a).

In discerning the meaning (or meanings) of the phrase in question, it is both necessary and helpful to explore its background in the OT and other Jewish literature. It is less helpful, finally, to look upon the law court (the forum) as background. It is understandable that interpreters have looked to the law court in their search for meaning, for it shares the same terms ("righteousness," "justice," "acquittal"), but it is unlikely that Paul did. Paul himself would have gained the terms and their meanings from his OT and Jewish tradition.

1.2. The Background to Paul's Concept of the "Righteousness of God"

Strictly speaking, the term "righteousness of God" (צִדְקַת אֱלֹהִים) does not appear in the Hebrew OT, nor does its Greek translation (δικαιοσύνη θεοῦ) appear in the LXX. Deuteronomy 33:21 is often referred to in discussions of the background of the term, but it actually speaks of the "righteousness of the Lord" (צִדְקַת יְהוָה; the LXX has δικαιοσύνην κύριος ἐποίησεν). Similarly, at LXX 1 Samuel 12:7 and Micah 6:5 the phrase ἡ δικαιοσύνη τοῦ κυρίου ("the righteousness of the Lord") appears, referring to a "saving deed" of the Lord in each case.

The Greek phrase δικαιοσύνη θεοῦ has no clear attestation in other Hellenistic Jewish sources (including Philo and Josephus). Some textual witnesses to the pseudepigraphal *Testament of Dan* 6.10 contain the phrase ("Forsake all unrighteousness and cling to the righteousness of God [τῇ δικαιοσύνῃ τοῦ θεοῦ]"), but other witnesses refer here to the law of God ("Forsake all unrighteousness and cling to the righteousness of the Law of God [τῇ δικαιοσύνῃ τοῦ νόμου τοῦ θεοῦ]"), which is actually better attested.[15] The Hebrew term appears in the *Rule*

---

15. Cf. Robert H. Charles, *The Greek Versions of the Testaments of the Twelve Patriarchs* (Oxford: Clarendon Press, 1908), 142. The longer text is preferred by Marinus de Jonge,

of the Community from Qumran ("When I stumble over fleshly iniquity, my judgment (is) by God's righteousness [צדקת אל]," 1QS 11.12)[16] and in the *War Scroll* (צדק אל, 1QM 4.6). Other Qumran passages speak of "righteousness" in reference to God's saving work, mercy, and goodness.[17]

Although the phrase "righteousness of God" does not appear in the OT, the OT speaks frequently about "his [= God's] righteousness," "your [= God's] righteousness," etc. Concerning such usage, Gerhard von Rad has written that two concepts are excluded from the term: (1) that it refers to an absolute norm, established by God, by which humanity is measured; and (2) that it carries a punitive meaning.[18] On the contrary, the term refers to God's saving acts in history, and it can be a synonym for salvation.[19] That can be confirmed by reference to many texts, but it is particularly evident in cases of synonymous parallelism where the word "righteousness" (צְדָקָה, δικαιοσύνη) refers to God's saving acts and is a synonym for "salvation" (יְשׁוּעָה, σωτήριον). A passage that illustrates this particularly well is Psalm 98:2 (LXX 97:2):

> The LORD has made known his *salvation* (יְשׁוּעָה, σωτήριον; NRSV: "victory");
>
> he has revealed his *righteousness* (צְדָקָה, δικαιοσύνη; NRSV: "vindication") before the nations.

Other texts that contain the explicit parallel, where "righteousness" and "salvation" are set in parallel, include Psalm 40:10 (LXX 39:11); 51:14 (LXX 50:16); Isaiah 46:13; 51:5-6; 61:10; 62:1.

There are several passages in the LXX that speak of the manifestation of righteousness (δικαιοσύνη) in the future, and which Paul would associate with the coming of the Messiah. Here are only two, translated from the LXX:

Jeremiah 23:5-6:
Behold, the days are coming, says the Lord,

Testamentum XII Patriarchum, PVTG 1 (Leiden: E. J. Brill, 1964), 51, and is adopted in the translation by Howard C. Kee, "Testaments of the Twelve Patriarchs," *OTP* 1:810.

16. Quoted from *The Dead Sea Scrolls: Hebrew, Aramaic, and Greek Texts with English Translation*, vol. 1, *Rule of the Community and Related Documents*, ed. James H. Charlesworth (Louisville: Westminster John Knox Press, 1994), 48-49.

17. Cf. especially the *Thanksgiving Hymns* (1QH 4.30; 14:16), the *Damascus Document* (CD 20.20); and 4Q504.1-2.6.3. Within these passages the manifestation of the righteousness of God is an eschatological hope, whereas for Paul it has appeared already. Cf. H.-W. Kuhn, "The Impact of the Qumran Scrolls on the Understanding of Paul," 332-33.

18. G. von Rad, *Old Testament Theology*, 1:370-71, 377; cf. also Elizabeth R. Achtemeier, "Righteousness in the Old Testament," *IDB* 4:80-85; and Klaus Koch, "צדק," *TLOT* 2:1053.

19. G. von Rad, *Old Testament Theology*, 1:372, 377.

and I shall raise up for David a righteous offspring (ἀνατολὴν δικαίαν,
NRSV: "righteous Branch"),
And as a king he shall reign and understand
and do justice and righteousness (δικαιοσύνην) upon the earth.
In his days Judah will be saved, and Israel will dwell securely.
And this is the name which will be given to him,
Lord of righteousness (κύριος Ιωσεδεκ).

Isaiah 11:1-2, 5:
A shoot shall come forth from the stump of Jesse
and a branch shall rise up from the stump.
And the spirit of God shall rest upon him. . . .
And he shall be girded about his loins with righteousness (δικαιοσύνη)
and his sides with truth.

Additional passages can be added (Pss 9:7 [LXX 9:6]; 72:1-4, 7 [LXX 71:1-4, 7];
96:13 [LXX 95:13]; Isa 9:7 [LXX 9:6]; 53:10b-11; Mal 4:2 [LXX 3:20]; Hebrew Jer
33:14-16) that associate the manifestation of righteousness with the coming one,
the Messiah in Pauline and other Christian traditions.

In addition to these passages, which are more explicit, others speak of the
future coming manifestation of the righteousness of God in a more general
sense, which for Paul could be fulfilled with the coming of the Messiah:

Isaiah 61:11:
And as the earth brings forth its flower
and as a garden [brings forth] its seeds,
so the LORD will cause righteousness (δικαιοσύνην) and gladness to
spring up before all the nations (ἐναντίον πάντων τῶν ἐθνῶν).

Isaiah 62:1-2:
For Zion's sake I shall not be silent,
and for Jerusalem's sake I shall not rest
until my righteousness (δικαιοσύνη) goes forth as light
and my salvation (σωτήριον) burns as a torch.
And nations (ἔθνη) shall see your righteousness (δικαιοσύνην)
and kings your glory.

Once again, additional passages can be added from the OT (Pss 85:11-13 [LXX
84:12-14]; 98:2, 9 [LXX 97:2, 9]; Isa 45:8, 22-25; 51:5-6) and apocryphal/deutero-
canonical works (Bar 5:9; Wis 5:18) that speak of God's saving righteousness as a
future expectation to be fulfilled — an eschatological hope — which for Paul
would be fulfilled with the coming of the Messiah.

Beyond the OT additional passages and traditions in Jewish literature speak of righteousness in connection with the Messiah or messianic age. In the *Psalms of Solomon,* produced in Pharisaic circles during the second half of the first century B.C.[20] — and as Pharisaic, they stand in the same spiritual and intellectual tradition as Paul — there are several references to the Messiah and his righteousness. It is said that the Messiah will be a "righteous king" (17.31); "he will gather a holy people whom he will lead in righteousness" (17.26); he will be endowed with "strength and righteousness" (17.37), and he "will judge peoples and nations in the wisdom of his righteousness" (17.29).[21] Other pseudepigraphal books convey traditions that link righteousness with the coming of the Messiah (or a messianic figure) as well, but it is not clear whether the passages in question are pre-Christian or Christian interpolations. These include the *Testament of Judah* (contained within the *Testaments of the Twelve Patriarchs*), in which the Messiah will walk in righteousness (24.1), judge, and save all who call upon the name of the Lord (24.6).[22] In addition, the *Similitudes of Enoch* (chapters 37–71 of *Ethiopian Enoch*) — judged even more often than the *Testaments of the Twelve Patriarchs* to have been composed by Christians, and therefore of less weight in our discussion — have much to say about a messianic figure (usually the Son of man) who will be righteous and who will judge and lead people in righteousness (38.2; 39.6-7; 46.3; 53.6; 71.14-15).[23] Even if the passages in question are of Christian origin, they witness to the connection between the manifestation of divine righteousness and the coming of the Messiah.

That connection appears explicitly in the NT at various places. The Messiah is a figure endowed with or acting with "righteousness" in various strands of tradition (Matt 3:15; John 5:30; Acts 17:31; Heb 1:9; 7:2-3; 1 John 2:28-29; 3:7; 2 Pet 1:1; Rev 19:11; cf. also 2 Pet 3:13) in addition to passages in the letters of Paul (Rom 5:18; 1 Cor 1:30). At other places the Messiah Jesus is called "righteous" (1 Pet 3:18; 1 John 2:1, 29; 3:7; Rev 15:3; cf. Luke 23:47; 1 John 1:9).

Later Jewish traditions continue to speak of the Messiah as righteous. In *Pesikta Rabbati* 37.2 it is said that "when the Messiah appears, He will be clothed in righteousness, as is said, 'And he put on righteousness as a coat of mail' (Isa

---

20. R. B. Wright, "Psalms of Solomon," *OTP* 2:640-41; L. Rost, *Jewish Literature outside the Hebrew Canon,* 119; G. Nickelsburg, *Jewish Literature between the Bible and the Mishnah,* 203-4.

21. Quotations from *OTP* 2:667-68.

22. For texts, cf. *OTP* 1:801. According to H. C. Kee, "Testaments of the Twelve Patriarchs," *OTP* 1:777-78, the books in question originated in pre-Christian times but contain later Christian interpolations.

23. For texts, cf. *OTP* 1:29-50. E. Isaac, "1 (Ethiopic Apocalypse) of Enoch," *OTP* 1:7, considers the *Similitudes* a Christian composition from the first century A.D.

59:17)."[24] In the *Midrash on Psalms* the Messiah is designated as bearing righteousness (21.2; 72:5).[25] The term "Messiah of righteousness" appears in the *Targum on Jeremiah* (23.6), and it is said that he will "perform . . . righteousness in the land."[26] Sigmund Mowinckel has offered still further references in the rabbinic material and says that the Messiah's righteousness implies his just government and judgment of his people, but "as a rule" the term is "closely associated with salvation. . . . The righteousness of the Messiah consists of his saving his people: righteousness and salvation are identical."[27]

1.3. The Pauline Synthesis

In light of the background that exists, in which the term "righteousness" is used in association with pronouns for God, it is clear that the concept of the righteousness of God, if not the exact phrase, was close at hand for Paul and other NT writers. Whether the phrase was pre-Pauline, as suggested by its use outside of Paul's own writings and the use of it in what might be a pre-Pauline tradition (Rom 3:25-26),[28] or whether it was coined by Paul himself, the Pauline usage has its own distinctive meaning. At Romans 3:21 Paul indicates in a creative manner that the righteousness of God is evident from a reading of the OT ("the law and the prophets"), in which the "righteousness of God . . . is attested" (Rom 3:21). In response to the question of where that might be, it is attested frequently in those passages that speak of the revelation of God's righteousness as an eschatological act, including those that speak of an expected messianic age or messianic figure as manifesting the righteousness of God. Most of those texts appear in the Psalms, Isaiah, and Jeremiah. They are texts that Paul would have encountered while searching the Scriptures in light of the cross and resurrection of Jesus as the Christ. For Paul, God's sending his Son was the supreme moment of the manifestation of his righteousness (Rom 3:21-22), and the gospel is the means by which the righteousness of God is revealed (Rom 1:17). In this

---

24. Quoted from *Pesikta Rabbati*, trans. William C. Braude, 2 vols. (New Haven: Yale University Press, 1968), 2:689.

25. *The Midrash on Psalms,* trans. William C. Braude, 2 vols. (New Haven: Yale University Press, 1959), 1:294, 562.

26. *The Targum of Jeremiah,* trans. Robert Hayward, The Aramaic Bible 12 (Wilmington: Michael Glazier, 1987), 110-11.

27. S. Mowinckel, *He That Cometh,* 308-9.

28. Such is the view of E. Käsemann, "'The Righteousness of God' in Paul," 172; H. Conzelmann, *An Outline of the Theology of the New Testament,* 219; E. Lohse, *Gerechtigkeit Gottes,* 220; idem, *Grundriss der neutestamentlichen Theologie,* 85-86; and K. Kertelge, "δικαιοσύνη," 1:328.

regard, Paul alludes to Psalm 98:2 (LXX 97:2) — that God "has revealed his righteousness" — at Romans 1:17 when he writes that the righteousness of God has been revealed in the present by means of the gospel.

The discussion to this point confirms that the reading of the "righteousness of God" as a subjective genitive is warranted in light of the OT and other traditions previous to and contemporary with the apostle Paul. But must that always be the case in Paul's letters? The debate over the type of genitive being used by Paul has tended to assign only one meaning to all passages in which the expression appears. But it is certainly possible that Paul uses both kinds of genitives, depending on context. The subjective genitive reading can be seen to apply particularly to Romans 1:17; 3:5, 21, 26; 10:3.[29] But that need not exclude the possibility of its use as a genitive of origin elsewhere, particularly at 2 Corinthians 5:21 ("so that in [Christ] we might become the righteousness of God," a people who are beneficiaries) and Philippians 3:9 ("the righteousness from God," ἡ ἐκ θεοῦ δικαιοσύνη). Similarly, as confirmation that Paul can speak of righteousness as an endowment bestowed as a consequence of God's action in Christ, he speaks elsewhere of "the free gift (δωρεά) of righteousness (δικαιοσύνη)" (Rom 5:17).

What is at stake, finally, is how one begins to speak of the "righteousness of God" in Paul. If one starts with reference to the righteousness required of a person in the final judgment, which is bestowed upon the believer as an "alien righteousness," and if one then goes to the law court (forum) as a model, one misses the dynamic of Paul's concept. Theological priority must be given not to the human plight before God (the "anthropological" approach) but to God, a God who seeks to restore a relationship with rebellious humanity (the "theological" approach). The gospel reveals the "righteousness of God" that has been manifested, even exercised, by God in Christ. That righteousness had been manifested in the prior saving acts of God, as the OT gives witness, but now it has been manifested even more fully in Christ. Furthermore, it has been manifested not only for the sake of Israel, but for the sake of the entire world. To be sure, it will be manifested again at the last judgment. But it has been made manifest already, proleptically, in God's saving action in Christ, and it is effective in the present for those who believe. It is on that basis that one can speak of being justified freely as a gift from God.

BIBLIOGRAPHY

Beker, J. Christiaan. *Paul the Apostle: The Triumph of God in Life and Thought.* Philadelphia: Fortress Press, 1980.

---

29. Although an opponent of the subjective genitive reading in Paul, R. Bultmann, "ΔΙΚΑΙΟΣΥΝΗ ΘΕΟΥ," 12, accepts Rom 3:5, 25 as such.

Berger, Klaus. "Neues Material zur 'Gerechtigkeit Gottes.'" *ZNW* 68 (1977): 266-75.

Bird, Michael F. *The Saving Righteousness of God: Studies on Paul, Justification and the New Perspective.* PBM. Colorado Springs: Paternoster, 2006.

Brauch, Manfred T. "Perspectives on 'God's Righteousness' in Recent German Discussion." In E. P. Sanders, *Paul and Palestinian Judaism: A Comparison of Patterns of Religion,* 523-42. Philadelphia: Fortress Press, 1977.

Bultmann, Rudolf. "ΔΙΚΑΙΟΣΥΝΗ ΘΕΟΥ." *JBL* 83 (1964): 12-16; reprinted in his *Exegetica,* 470-75. Tübingen: J. C. B. Mohr (Paul Siebeck), 1967.

————. *Theology of the New Testament.* 2 vols. New York: Charles Scribner's Sons, 1951-55.

Campbell, Douglas A. "The Meaning of δικαιοσύνη θεοῦ in Romans: An Intertextual Suggestion." In *As It Is Written: Studying Paul's Use of Scripture,* 189-212. Ed. Stanley E. Porter and Christopher D. Stanley. SBLSymS 50. Atlanta: Society of Biblical Literature, 2008.

Conzelmann, Hans. *An Outline of the Theology of the New Testament.* New York: Harper & Row, 1969.

Cremer, Herman. *Biblio-Theological Lexicon of New Testament Greek.* 3d ed. Edinburgh: T&T Clark, 1886.

————. *Die paulinische Rechtfertigungslehre im Zusammenhang ihrer geschichtlichen Voraussetzungen.* 2d ed. Gütersloh: G. Bertelsmann, 1900.

Fiedler, Martin J. "Δικαιοσύνη in der diaspora-jüdischen und intertestamentarischen Literatur." *JSJ* 1 (1970): 120-43.

Flebbe, Jochen. *Solus Deus: Untersuchungen zur Rede von Gott im Brief des Paulus an die Römer.* BZNW 158. Berlin: de Gruyter, 2008.

Furnish, Victor Paul. *Theology and Ethics in Paul.* Nashville: Abingdon Press, 1968; new ed. NTL. Louisville: Westminster John Knox, 2009.

Gyllenberg, Rafael. "Die paulinische Rechtfertigungslehre und das Alte Testament." *ST* 1 (1935): 35-52.

Herold, Gerhart. *Zorn und Gerechtigkeit Gottes bei Paulus: Eine Untersuchung zu Röm. 1,16-18.* Europäische Hochschulschriften 23.14. Bern: Herbert Lang, 1973.

Käsemann, Ernst. "'The Righteousness of God' in Paul." In his *New Testament Questions of Today,* 168-82. Philadelphia: Fortress Press, 1969.

Kertelge, Karl. "δικαιοσύνη." *EDNT* 1:325-30.

————. *"Rechtfertigung" bei Paulus: Studien zur Struktur und zum Bedeutungsgehalt des paulinischen Rechtfertigungsbegriffs.* NTAbh 3. 2d ed. Munster: Aschendorff, 1971.

Klaiber, Walter. "Rechtfertigung II: Neues Testament." In *RGG*[4] 7:98-103.

Klein, Günter. "Gottes Gerechtigkeit als Thema der neuesten Paulus-Forschung." In *Rekonstruktion und Interpretation,* 225-36. Munich: Kaiser Verlag, 1969.

————. "Rechtfertigung I." In *RGG*[3] 5:825-28.

————. "Righteousness." *IDBSup* 750-52.

Kuhn, Heinz-Wolfgang. "The Impact of the Qumran Scrolls on the Understanding of Paul." In *The Dead Sea Scrolls: Forty Years of Research,* 327-39. Ed. Devorah Dimant and Uriel Rappaport. STDJ 10. New York: E. J. Brill, 1992.

Kümmel, Werner G. *The Theology of the New Testament according to Its Main Witnesses: Jesus — Paul — John.* Nashville: Abingdon Press, 1973.

Lohse, Eduard. "Die Gerechtigkeit Gottes in der paulinischen Theologie." In his *Die Einheit des Neuen Testaments*, 209-27. Göttingen: Vandenhoeck & Ruprecht, 1973.

————. *Grundriss der neutestamentlichen Theologie*. TW 5. Stuttgart: W. Kohlhammer, 1974.

McGrath, Alister E. *Iustitia Dei: A History of the Christian Doctrine of Justification*. 2 vols. Cambridge: Cambridge University Press, 1986.

————. "The Righteousness of God from Augustine to Luther." *ST* 36 (1982): 63-78.

Moore, Richard K. "Issues Involved in the Interpretation of *Dikaiosunē Theou* in the Pauline Corpus." *Coll* 23 (1991): 59-70.

————. *Rectification ("Justification") in Paul, in Historical Perspective, and in the English Bible*. SBEC 50. 3 vols. Lewiston: Edwin Mellen Press, 2002.

Mowinckel, Sigmund. *He That Cometh*. Nashville: Abingdon Press, 1954.

Müller, Christian. *Gottes Gerechtigkeit und Gottes Volk: Eine Untersuchung zu Römer 9–11*. FRLANT 86. Göttingen: Vandenhoeck & Ruprecht, 1964.

Nickelsburg, George W. E. *Jewish Literature between the Bible and the Mishnah*. Philadelphia: Fortress Press, 1981.

Olley, John W. *"Righteousness" in the Septuagint of Isaiah: A Contextual Study*. SBLSCS 8. Missoula: Scholars Press, 1979.

Plutta-Messerschmidt, Elke. *Gerechtigkeit Gottes bei Paulus*. HUTh 14. Tübingen: J. C. B. Mohr (Paul Siebeck), 1973.

Rad, Gerhard von. *Old Testament Theology*. 2 vols. New York: Harper & Row, 1962-65.

Reumann, John, *"Righteousness" in the New Testament: "Justification" in the United States Lutheran-Roman Catholic Dialogue*. Philadelphia: Fortress Press, 1982.

————. "Righteousness (NT)." *ABD* 5:745-73.

Ropes, James Hardy. "Righteousness in the Old Testament and in St. Paul." *JBL* 22 (1903): 211-27.

Rost, Leonhard. *Jewish Literature outside the Hebrew Canon: An Introduction to the Documents*. Nashville: Abingdon Press, 1976.

Schmid, Hans H. "Rechtfertigung als Schöpfungsgeschehen: Notizen zur alttestamentlichen Vorgeschichte eines neutestamentlichen Themas." In *Rechtfertigung: Festschrift für Ernst Käsemann zum 70. Geburtstag*, 403-14. Ed. Johannes Friedrich et al. Tübingen: J. C. B. Mohr (Paul Siebeck), 1976.

Schulz, Siegfried, "Zur Rechtfertigung aus Gnaden in Qumran und bei Paulus," *ZTK* 56 (1959): 155-85.

Soards, Marion L. "The Righteousness of God in the Writings of the Apostle Paul." *BTB* 15 (1985): 104-9.

Stuhlmacher, Peter. *Gerechtigkeit Gottes bei Paulus*. FRLANT 87. Göttingen: Vandenhoeck & Ruprecht, 1965.

Westerholm, Stephen. "The Righteousness of the Law and the Righteousness of Faith in Romans." *Int* 58 (2004): 253-64.

Williams, Sam. "The 'Righteousness of God' in Romans." *JBL* 99 (1980): 241-90.

Zänker, Otto. *"Dikaiosunē Theou* bei Paulus." *ZST* 9 (1931-32): 398-420.

Ziesler, John A. *The Meaning of Righteousness in Paul: A Linguistic and Theological Inquiry*. SNTSMS 29. Cambridge: Cambridge University Press, 1972.

APPENDIX 2

Romans 1:26-27 and Homosexuality

These verses belong within a lengthy portion of Paul's Letter to the Romans ex-tending from Romans 1:18 to 3:20. At the outset of that section Paul speaks of the revelation of the wrath of God against the world (1:18). Then at 3:21, after concluding the section on the wrath of God, he makes a complete turnabout to declare that "but now" the "righteousness of God" has been revealed in the death and resurrection of Christ, by means of which God justifies the ungodly. The two verses under discussion here should be read within the context of 1:18–3:20, and more specifically within 1:18-32. The comments that follow pertain to the latter portion in particular and presuppose the exegetical work on it.

1. The section where these verses appear has to do with the Gentile world,[1] since it is preceded by verses that speak of idolatry (1:23, 25). Paul turns to Jewish accountability before God in 2:17–3:8.

2. The idolatry of the Gentile world has provoked the divine wrath, which expresses itself in God's delivering that world to its own abusive, destructive be-

---

1. That Rom 1:18-32 is a critique of Gentiles is held explicitly by interpreters across the spectrum. This includes major commentaries: W. Sanday and A. Headlam, *Romans,* 39-52; C. Cranfield, *Romans,* 105 ("primarily the Gentiles"); E. Käsemann, *Romans,* 33; H. Schlier, *Römer,* 47-48; U. Wilckens, *Römer,* 1:93; J. Dunn, *Romans,* 51; J. Fitzmyer, *Romans,* 270; P. Stuhl-macher, *Romans,* 33-38; D. Moo, *Romans,* 97 ("reference mainly to Gentiles"); L. Keck, *Romans,* 56-57, 60-73. Cf. also F. Flückiger, "Zur Unterscheidung," 158; V. Furnish, *The Moral Teaching of Paul,* 85; H. Moxnes, *Theology in Conflict,* 35; E. P. Sanders, *Paul, the Law, and the Jewish People,* 123; H. Räisänen, *Paul and the Law,* 97; K. Yinger, *Paul, Judaism and Judgment according to Deeds,* 148; M. Nissinen, *Homoeroticism,* 104; R. Brown, *Introduction,* 566; E. Kalin, "Romans 1:26-27 and Homosexuality," 426; and R. Gagnon, *The Bible and Homosexual Practice,* 246. Not all interpreters agree. For the view that the section speaks about all of humanity (or the human condition in general), not simply the Gentiles, cf. J. Bassler, *Divine Impartiality,* 121-37; B. Brooten, *Love between Women,* 203-14; R. Hays, *The Moral Vision of the New Testament,* 385; G. Davies, *Faith and Obedience in Romans,* 47-49; F. Matera, *Romans,* 43-56.

havior. The threefold pairing of the verbs "exchanged" and "gave [them] over" (NRSV) in 1:23-24, 1:25-26a, and 1:26b-28 should be taken as one dynamic, expressed in three different ways rather than as a sequence of three occasions.

3. The consequences of the idolatry of the Gentiles — and their being delivered to their own devices — include foolish thinking, destructive behavior, and abuse. That larger context of this section has implications for the interpretation of 1:26-27. It favors the view that even in those verses reference is being made to destructive and/or abusive behavior.

4. In order to make the point that the Gentiles stand before God as condemned because of their idolatry, Paul paints not only with a broad brush but also with extremely dark, vivid colors. The behavior of which he speaks in 1:18-32, including 1:26-27, appears to apply to the Gentiles as a whole and as something typical of them. That does not mean that every single Gentile indulges in any one item listed, but it means that Paul is being indiscriminate in describing how the Gentiles tend to be: idolatrous and abusive.

5. Throughout 1:19b-27 the indicative verbs in Greek are in the aorist (simple past) tense. The effect is that Paul carries on his discourse as though he is talking about something that happened at some point in the past (*in illo tempore*, "in that time" of mythical origins) that explains the present. In effect, he is saying that the way to account for Gentile misbehavior in the present is that "ever since the creation of the world" (1:20) the Gentiles have had the opportunity to worship God, but instead they have been idolatrous; and their misbehavior flows from that.

Once these observations have been made, a host of interpretive issues arise. Some of the most important are historical and philological questions.

In order for Paul to portray the Gentile world the way he does, it is convenient and not particularly surprising that he would pick up and use a familiar "topos" in Hellenistic Jewish tradition.[2] A familiar topos in that tradition is that, when a writer wants to make a sweeping, negative statement about the Gentiles, he calls them idolaters and sexual deviants.[3] Common criticisms of the Gentiles

---

2. A "topos" (directly from the Greek word τόπος) is a common theme or commonplace in speeches and letters. Cf. D. Aune, *The New Testament in Its Literary Environment*, 172-74, 189. Within the larger Greco-Roman tradition Aristotle, *Rhet.* 2.23.1–2.23.30, lists 28 "topoi" and discusses them briefly. Of these 28, one consists of making use of errors committed by another party for purposes of accusation (2.23.28). No similar discussion can be found within Hellenistic Jewish sources, but it is exhibited in sources cited in subsequent notations.

3. Cf. the statement of M. Nissinen, *Homoeroticism*, 112: "Paul's thoughts have a background in Hellenistic Jewish tradition and language. . . . In his criticism of homoeroticism as such, he does not present any independent ideas." For a collection of texts and references in Jewish literature to Gentiles as immoral, cf. C. Hayes, *Gentile Impurities and Jewish Identifiers*, 54-58.

are that they have tendencies toward adultery[4] and that they indulge in same-gender sexual activities, for nearly all of the known Hellenistic Jewish texts that speak of and condemn same-gender sexual activities are directed against Gentiles.[5] (Exceptions are texts that refer to OT passages.)[6] In fact, such activities were often considered a Gentile vice.[7] Moreover, instances in intertestamental and later Jewish literature where idolatry and sexual misbehavior are linked together specifically are cases where pederasty is being condemned.[8] (Pederasty is an ongoing relationship between an adult man and a boy, in which the elder assumes the active role, and the latter — typically aged about 12 to 15 — the passive, in sexual relationships; the relationship typically ceased when the boy entered puberty.)[9] While pederasty was not the only form of same-gender sexual activity that the Hellenistic Jewish writers criticized, it was the most obvious, most prominent, and one of the most appalling forms.[10] The most public and most severely criticized same-gender sexual activities were not between persons of the same age and class; in fact, same-gender sexual activities between persons of the same age and class are virtually unknown in the sources (exceptions being adult male prostitution).[11]

4. Wis 14:22-29; Philo, *Abr.* 135.

5. *Ep. Arist.* 152; Philo, *Cont.* 7.59-62; *Spec. Leg.* 3.37-42; Josephus, *Ag. Ap.* 2.199; 2.273-75; *Ant.* 15.28-29; *T. Naph.* 3.3-4; *Sib. Or.* 3.596; 5.166.

6. Examples are passages that refer to the Sodom and Gomorrah narrative (Gen 19:1-11) and Lev 18:22 and 20:13, such as Philo, *Abr.* 135-36; Josephus, *Ant.* 1.200; and other texts. The Mishnah text *Sanhedrin* 7.4 picks up the legislation of Lev 20:13 but would have been written down later (ca. A.D. 200) than the books of the NT.

7. Josephus, *Ag. Ap.* 2.199; *Ant.* 15.28-29; *Ep. Arist.* 152; Philo, *Cont.* 7.59-62.

8. These are in the *T. Levi* 17.11 and in the *Sib. Or.* 3.586-600. Both documents are commonly thought to have been composed in the second century B.C. In the latter text there is a list of national groups that are said to practice pederasty: the Phoenicians, Egyptians, Romans, Greeks, Persians, Galatians, and all the people of Asia Minor! A text commonly regarded as from late in the first century A.D. that connects idolatry and pederasty (or perhaps the rape of a child) is 2 Enoch 10.4. For texts, see *OTP* 1:794, 1:375, and 1:118, respectively.

9. Loving a boy (pederasty) is considered superior to loving a woman, according to Pausanias in Plato, *Symp.* 181b, c. The relationship was usually terminated by the adult male when the youth showed signs of reaching adulthood, particularly the onset of a beard. According to Strato of Sardis, *Mus.* 12.4, the ideal age of the boy was 12 to 15; text in *The Greek Anthology*, trans. W. R. Paton, 5 vols. (Cambridge: Harvard University Press, 1918), 4:285. For a discussion of pederastic relationships, cf. D. Halperin, *One Hundred Years*, 88.

10. R. Scroggs, *The New Testament and Homosexuality*, 126, *et passim*; M. Nissinen, *Homoeroticism*, 96-97; R. Gagnon, *The Bible and Homosexual Practice*, 162.

11. K. Dover, *Greek Homosexuality*, 16, 202-3; A. Karlen, "Homosexuality in History," 79; D. Halperin, *One Hundred Years*, 21 ("reciprocal erotic desire among males is unknown"); and R. Scroggs, *The New Testament and Homosexuality*, 35. Dover writes: "On growing up, in any Greek community, the *eromenos* [the boy in a pederastic situation] graduated from pupil to friend, and the continuance of an erotic relationship was disapproved, as was such a relationship between coevals" (pp. 202-3).

Since Paul picks up and uses a "topos" at Romans 1:26-27 to build a case for a sweeping indictment of the Gentiles as a whole, he is not responding to known situations at Rome. Moreover, it is not therefore likely that he is directing his comments to a small minority of the population at Rome (or even elsewhere) who could be regarded as "homosexuals" today (a term not current in Paul's day); rather, he has the whole Gentile world in mind. There is plenty of evidence in the sources to indicate that various forms of same-gender sexual activity were practiced and tolerated widely among Gentiles — from abusive to nonabusive, one can assume. Paul includes all forms of those activities in one category.

In the discussion of Romans 1:26-27 and homosexuality, it is important to ask whether there is symmetry between what Paul knows, envisions, or imagines as same-gender sexual behavior in those verses and what the church and society face in modern times. A new reality has come on the scene for the church, in which persons of the same gender claim to be Christians (not idolaters), know themselves to be homosexual (not heterosexual deviants), pledge themselves to lives of fidelity (rejecting promiscuity), and want their relationship public (not hidden away).

The degree to which all this is new can be seen by examining ancient texts. Primary texts from the seventh century B.C. into the fourth century A.D. have been collected by Thomas Hubbard.[12] A reading of those 447 texts is revealing about same-gender sexual activity in the ancient world. A wide variety of activities is portrayed and discussed. The most prevalent activity referred to by far is pederasty, but there are other things in these texts as well. Some texts make it clear that certain men were publicly known for their love of boys and other men. Most texts, however, are not about persons known to have same-gender attractions as something distinctive about them, but are about men who have both boys and women (presumably their wives in most cases) as lovers. Those men appear to be persons that would be called heterosexuals (and perhaps bisexuals in some cases) in modern times.

The texts speak of same-gender sexual activities of all kinds. The activities run the whole gamut: pederasty, promiscuity, prostitution, drunken orgies, sexual abuse of slaves, rape of boys and men, bawdy role play in the theater, charges of indecency at trials in court, and more.

Out of all those hundreds of texts there are a half-dozen that speak of the "marriage" of persons of the same gender. But two of those cases involve pederastic relationships (and the prior castration of the boy in one of them), ridicule in another case, an imaginary marriage between two men on the moon, deception in which a man is passed off as a bride, and a lesbian relation-

---

12. T. K. Hubbard, ed., *Homosexuality in Greece and Rome.*

ship without fidelity.[13] In no case does one find references to or hints of committed same-gender relationships entered into by adults who pledge lifelong fidelity. On the contrary, there is plenty of evidence for promiscuity and abuse.

The modern discussion of homosexuality in the church and society needs to be informed about the conceptual differences between ancient and modern understandings. The long-standing view that same-gender attraction and sexual activities are due to moral perversion is no longer the only view to hold. The concept of sexual orientation has become well established in modern scientific understanding,[14] and the term "homosexual," coined late in the nineteenth century,[15] is familiar in the vocabulary of modern times to speak of persons with a sexual orientation toward persons of their own gender. As soon as the concept of sexual orientation is brought into the discussion and the words "heterosexual" and "homosexual" exist and can be used, the judgments made concerning persons must be changed significantly. There can be no virtue in perpetuating an error in judgment, even if it is traditional and is, according to a traditional reading, thought to be expressed in Scripture itself. Although the Bible knows about same-gender relationships, it knows nothing of sexual orientation, and therefore it knows nothing of "homosexuality" or "heterosexuality" as descriptors of conditions or behaviors.

BIBLIOGRAPHY

Aune, David E. *The New Testament in Its Literary Environment.* Philadelphia: Westminster Press, 1987.

13. Cicero, *Philippics* 2.44-45, writes concerning the marriage between Mark Anthony and Curio; the former had been a prostitute as a boy, and Curio (a customer) took him as his partner. Suetonius, *Nero* 28–29, writes about the marriage of Nero to Sporus, a boy, after castrating him. Juvenal, *Sat.* 2.129-30, refers to same-sex marriage in a joking manner. Lucian, *Ver. hist.* 1.22, relates an imaginary voyage to the moon where men marry men. Aelius Lampridius, *Elag.* 10.5, says that Elagabalus was given away in marriage as a woman. Lucian, *Dial. meretr.* 5, provides an account in which a woman claims to be married to another woman, but the account makes it clear that there is no sexual fidelity between them. These texts are printed in T. Hubbard, *Homosexuality in Greece and Rome,* 341-42, 391, 435-36, 471-72, 496-97, and 468-69, respectively. To this collection should be added the story of Hadrian and Antinous, as recorded in Dio Cassius, *Rom. hist.* 69.11. According to that account, Hadrian met Antinous, a youth, during his travels and took him along with him as a companion ("a favorite"). When the latter was 20 years old, he either drowned in the Nile River or was offered up as a sacrifice by Hadrian; Hadrian was 34 years older.

14. J. Marmor, "Homosexuality," 5:409; W. Gadpaille, "Homosexuality and Homosexual Activity," 1:1321-33 (esp. 1:1321, 1332-33).

15. It is commonly thought that the term "homosexuality" appeared for the first time in the writings of Károly Mária Benkert (whose pseudonym was "Kertbeny") of Vienna in 1869. Cf. Wayne R. Dynes and Warren Johansson, "Homosexual (Term)," 1:555. The earliest entries for both "homosexuality" and "homosexual" in English are from 1892 in the *OED* 7:345.

Balch, David L. "Romans 1:24-27, Science, and Homosexuality." *CurTM* 25 (1998): 433-40.

Bassler, Jouette M. *Divine Impartiality: Paul and a Theological Axiom.* SBLDS 59. Chico: Scholars Press, 1982.

Boswell, John. *Christianity, Social Tolerance, and Homosexuality: Gay People in Western Europe from the Beginning of the Christian Era to the Fourteenth Century.* Chicago: University of Chicago Press, 1980.

Bradley, David G. "The *Topos* as Form in the Pauline Paraenesis." *JBL* 72 (1953): 238-46.

Brooten, Bernadette J. *Love between Women: Early Christian Responses to Female Homoeroticism.* Chicago: University of Chicago Press, 1996.

Davies, Glenn N. *Faith and Obedience in Romans: A Study in Romans 1–4.* JSNTSup 39. Sheffield: JSOT Press, 1990.

Davies, Margaret. "New Testament Ethics and Ours: Homosexuality and Sexuality in Romans 1:26-27." *BibInt* 3 (1995): 315-31.

Dover, Kenneth J. *Greek Homosexuality.* Cambridge: Harvard University Press, 1978.

Dynes, Wayne R., and Warren Johansson, "Homosexual (Term)." In *Encyclopedia of Homosexuality,* 1:555-56. Ed. Wayne R. Dynes. 2 vols. New York: Garland Publishing Company, 1990.

Flückiger, Felix. "Zur Unterscheidung von Heiden und Juden in Röm. 1,18–2,3." *TZ* 10 (1954): 154-58.

Fredrickson, David E. "Natural and Unnatural Use in Romans 1:24-27: Paul and the Philosophic Critique of Eros." In *Homosexuality, Science, and the "Plain Sense" of Scripture,* 197-222. Ed. David L. Balch. Grand Rapids: Wm. B. Eerdmans, 2000.

Furnish, Victor P. *The Moral Teaching of Paul: Selected Issues.* 3d ed. Nashville: Abingdon Press, 2009.

Gadpaille, Warren J. "Homosexuality and Homosexual Activity." In *Comprehensive Textbook of Psychiatry,* 1:1321-33. Ed. Harold I. Kaplan and Benjamin J. Sadok. 2 vols. 6th ed. Baltimore: Williams & Wilkins, 1995.

Gagnon, Robert A. J. *The Bible and Homosexual Practice: Texts and Hermeneutics.* Nashville: Abingdon Press, 2001.

Halperin, David M. *One Hundred Years of Homosexuality and Other Essays on Greek Love.* New York: Routledge, 1990.

Hayes, Christine E. *Gentile Impurities and Jewish Identifiers: Intermarriage and Conversion from the Bible to the Talmud.* New York: Oxford University Press, 2002.

Hays, Richard B. "Awaiting the Redemption of Our Bodies: Drawing on Scripture and Tradition in the Church Debate on Homosexuality." *Sojourners* 20 (1991): 17-21.

———. *The Moral Vision of the New Testament: Community, Cross, New Creation: A Contemporary Introduction to New Testament Ethics.* San Francisco: HarperSanFrancisco, 1996.

———. "Relations Natural and Unnatural: A Response to John Boswell's Exegesis of Romans 1." *JCE* 14 (1986): 184-215.

Hubbard, Thomas K., ed. *Homosexuality in Greece and Rome: A Sourcebook of Basic Documents.* Berkeley: University of California Press, 2003.

Hultgren, Arland J. "Being Faithful to the Scriptures: Romans 1:26-27 as a Case in Point." *WW* 14 (1994): 315-25.

Jewett, Robert. "The Social Context and Implications of Homoerotic References in Romans 1:24-27." In *Homosexuality, Science, and the "Plain Sense" of Scripture*, 223-41. Ed. David L. Balch. Grand Rapids: Wm. B. Eerdmans, 2000.

Kalin, Everett R. "Romans 1:26-27 and Homosexuality." *CurTM* 33 (2006): 423-32.

Karlen, Arno. "Homosexuality in History." In *Homosexual Behavior: A Modern Reappraisal*, 75-99. Ed. Judd Marmor. New York: Basic Books, 1980.

Keck, Leander E. "Romans 1:18-23." *Int* 40 (1986): 402-6.

Kuhn, Karl A. "Natural and Unnatural Relations between Text and Context: A Canonical Reading of Romans 1:26-27." *CurTM* 33 (2006): 313-29.

Lilja, Saara. *Homosexuality in Republican and Augustan Rome*. Commentationes humanarum litterarum 74. Helsinki: Societas Scientiarum Fennica, 1983.

———. *The Roman Elegists' Attitude to Women*. Suomalaisen Tiedeakatemian Toimituksia B/135/1. New York: Garland Publications, 1978.

Marmor, Judd. "Homosexuality: An Overview." In *International Encyclopedia of Psychiatry, Psychology, Psychoanalysis, and Neurology*, 5:407-10. Ed. Benjamin B. Wolman. 12 vols. New York: Van Nostrand Reinhold, 1977.

Martin, Dale B. "*Arsenokoitēs* and *Malakos*: Meanings and Consequences." In *Biblical Ethics and Homosexuality: Listening to Scripture*, 117-36. Ed. Robert L. Brawley. Louisville: Westminster John Knox, 1996.

———. "Heterosexism and the Interpretation of Romans 1:18-32." *BibInt* 3 (1995): 332-55.

Monti, Joseph. *Arguing about Sex: The Rhetoric of Christian Sexual Morality*. Albany: State University of New York Press, 1995.

Moxnes, Halvor. *Theology in Conflict: Studies in Paul's Understanding of God in Romans*. NovTSup 53. Leiden: E. J. Brill, 1980.

Mullins, Terence Y. "*Topos* as a New Testament Form." *JBL* 99 (1980): 541-47.

Nissinen, Martti. *Homoeroticism in the Biblical World: A Historical Perspective*. Minneapolis: Fortress Press, 1998.

Nolland, John. "Romans 1:26-27 and the Homosexuality Debate." *HBT* 22 (2000): 32-57.

Phipps, William E. "Paul on 'Unnatural' Sex." *CurTM* 29 (2002): 128-31.

Räisänen, Heikki. *Paul and the Law*. Philadelphia: Fortress Press, 1986.

Sanders, E. P. *Paul, the Law and the Jewish People*. Minneapolis: Fortress Press, 1983.

Scroggs, Robin. *The New Testament and Homosexuality: Contextual Background for Contemporary Debate*. Philadelphia: Fortress Press, 1983.

Smith, Abraham. "The New Testament and Homosexuality." *QR* 11 (1991): 18-32.

Smith, Mark D. "Ancient Bisexuality and the Interpretation of Romans 1:26-27." *JAAR* 64 (1996): 223-56.

Thielicke, Helmut. *The Ethics of Sex*. New York: Harper & Row, 1964.

White, Leland J. "Does the Bible Speak about Gays or Same-Sex Orientation? A Test Case in Biblical Ethics." *BTB* 25 (1995): 14-23.

Wischmeyer, Oda. "ΦΥΣΙΣ und ΚΤΙΣΙΣ bei Paulus: Die paulinische Rede von Schöpfung und Natur." *ZTK* 93 (1996): 352-75.

Yinger, Kent L. *Paul, Judaism and Judgment according to Deeds*. SNTSMS 105. Cambridge: Cambridge University Press, 1999.

APPENDIX 3

Pistis Christou: *Faith in or of Christ?*

Within his undisputed letters the apostle Paul uses the term πίστις ("faith") followed by the genitive form of Jesus, a Christological title, or both on seven occasions.[1] The specific cases are as follows, quoting the NRSV text and inserting the Greek phrases:

Romans 3:22, "But now . . . the righteousness of God has been disclosed, . . . the righteousness of God through faith in Jesus Christ (διὰ πίστεως Ἰησοῦ Χριστοῦ) for all who believe."

Romans 3:26, "It was to prove . . . that [God] justifies the one who has faith in Jesus (τὸν ἐκ πίστεως Ἰησοῦ)."

Galatians 2:16a, "We know that a person is justified not by the works of the law but through faith in Jesus Christ (διὰ πίστεως Ἰησοῦ Χριστοῦ)."

Galatians 2:16b, ". . . that we might be justified by faith in Christ (ἐκ πίστεως Χριστοῦ)."

Galatians 2:20, "And the life I now live in the flesh I live by faith in the Son of God (ἐν πίστει ζῶ τῇ τοῦ υἱοῦ τοῦ θεου)."

Galatians 3:22, "So that what was promised through faith in Jesus Christ (ἐκ πίστεως Ἰησοῦ Χριστοῦ) might be given to those who believe."

Philippians 3:9, ". . . being found in [Christ], not having a righteousness of my own that comes from the law, but one that comes through faith in Christ (διὰ πίστεως Χριστοῦ)."

1. K. Ulrichs, *Christusglaube*, 71-93, includes 1 Thess 1:3 in the discussion, suggesting that the connection between πίστις and Χριστοῦ can be seen there already. But it is not clear whether the phrase "in our Lord Jesus Christ" should be taken with "work of faith" and "labor of love" or only with "steadfastness of hope." The phrase "work of faith" is rather remote from "our Lord Jesus Christ."

In each case the phrase in question has been translated as though Paul has used an objective genitive ("faith in Christ," etc.). As footnotes in the NRSV to these seven texts indicate, however, it is grammatically possible to translate the phrase as though Paul has used a subjective genitive ("faith of Christ" or "faithfulness of Christ"). The difference reflects a scholarly debate, generally called the "Pistis Christou Debate," using a brief expression in Greek (πίστις Χριστοῦ) as a convenient shorthand for all the expressions used above that enter into the discussion.

Before we proceed further, I should emphasize two things. First, not all scholars have been willing to take either of the two positions. They have proposed alternatives, but in the final analysis they give priority to the faithfulness or faith of Christ (subjective genitive) as that which calls forth the participating faith of the believer.[2]

The second point to make at the outset is that interpreters on all sides of the debate agree that Paul had a powerful sense of the faithfulness of God (Rom 3:3) and of the faithfulness of Christ manifested in his obedience to God, even unto death on the cross (Rom 5:6-8; 5:18-19; Phil 2:5-11).[3] That is not in dispute. Indeed, the faithfulness of the Son to the Father is the basis for God's justifying and saving work in him.[4] Having said that, the essential and basic question to be faced is whether in those passages quoted above Paul has the faith of Christ or the faith of the believer in view. The view expressed here, as in earlier work,[5] is that Paul is referring to the faith of believers in Christ. But that view cannot simply be asserted. It needs to be justified, for there are interpreters who claim that the matter is now settled in favor of the opposing view,[6] and there are several interpreters who have adopted it.

The discussion that follows is divided into three main parts. The first takes up matters of syntax; the second gives attention to certain key texts; and

---

2. Three examples are M. Hooker, "ΠΙΣΤΙΣ ΧΡΙΣΤΟΥ," 184-86: the believer participates, shares in the faith of Christ; and D. Rusam, "Was Versteht Paulus?" 70: Paul uses the *genitivus auctoris* (or genitive of origin), and so the expression means the faith that comes from Christ, i.e., faith created by divine action in the believer. Similarly, B. Schliesser, *Abraham's Faith in Romans 4,* 277, uses the term "Christ-faith" and suggests that the expression could be described as a *genitivus relationis;* the expression "describes not only Christ's bringing about faith in his coming, but also the resultant state of those who receive that faith and are called 'believers.'"

3. Even before the rise of Christianity, Jewish messianism held that the Messiah would act "in faithfulness and righteousness" (ἐν πίστει καὶ δικαιοσύνῃ, *Pss. Sol.* 17.40).

4. A. Hultgren, "The *Pistis Christou* Formulation in Paul," 252-53; L. T. Johnson, "Romans 3:21-26," 79; S. Williams, "The 'Righteousness of God' in Romans," 275; idem, "Again *Pistis Christou*," 438; R. Hays, "ΠΙΣΤΙΣ and Pauline Christology," 274-75; M. Hooker, "ΠΙΣΤΙΣ ΧΡΙΣΤΟΥ," 181-82; J. L. Martyn, *Galatians,* 251, 270-71.

5. A. Hultgren, "The *Pistis Christou* Formulation in Paul," 248-63.

6. L. Gaston, *Paul and the Torah,* 12; S. Stowers, "ἐκ πίστεως," 667.

the third deals with theological and related concerns. Such a division is of course artificial. Matters of syntax, for example, are related to the other two areas, and texts are dealt with all the way through. Yet there are advantages to dividing the discussion into discrete areas to avoid repetition.

3.1. Matters of Syntax

When the two words πίστις Χριστοῦ appear on the page, the most natural way to render them is "faith of Christ" (or "Christ's faith"). Since the word πίστις can also be translated as "faithfulness" (as at Rom 3:3), the phrase can be rendered as (the) "faithfulness of Christ" (or "Christ's faithfulness"). This uncomplicated rendering is fundamental to the debate. Any alternative rendering, such as "faith in Christ" appears awkward and to be forcing an interpretation that is not warranted. On the other hand, whenever Paul uses the formulation, it always lacks the definite article (ἡ in Greek, "the" in English) prior to the word "faith" (πίστις).[7] If Paul is clearly speaking of "the faith of Christ" (subjective genitive), why does he not write out ἡ πίστις τοῦ Χριστοῦ (or ἡ πίστις Χριστοῦ)?[8] He never does. The question can be raised whether there is any syntactical significance to the manner in which Paul expresses himself.

3.1.1. *The Objective Genitive in General*

In order to translate the phrase as "faith in Christ," one has to argue that Paul used an objective genitive construction. Characteristic of objective genitive expressions is that they are "transitive," having an object in view of an action expressed in the first of the two nouns.[9] Such nouns express, for example, a "desire for," "love (or affection) for," "hope for," "knowledge of," or "fear of" something or someone; consequently, they have an object.[10] Examples of the use of nouns of this kind in objective genitive constructions are abundant in the NT, including the writings of Paul. On the one hand, familiar phrases such as

7. Paul's expression also lacks the definite article (τοῦ) prior to "Christ" (Χριστοῦ). It is present, however, in Gal 2:20, where (in our view) the object of faith is the Son of God (ἐν πίστει ζῶ τῇ τοῦ υἱοῦ τοῦ θεοῦ, "I live by faith [which is] in the Son of God").

8. According to the canon of Apollonius, an article must appear before the genitive (governed noun) if one appears prior to the governing noun; a writer must have "both or neither." Cf. N. Turner, *Syntax*, 3.180; cf. also C. F. D. Moule, *An Idiom-Book of New Testament Greek*, 114-15. Paul himself, however, does not abide by that canon strictly. Cf. Phil 3:8, ἡ γνῶσις Χριστοῦ Ἰησοῦ.

9. BDF 90 (§163); H. Smyth, *Greek Grammar*, 318.

10. Concerning "desire," H. Smyth, *Greek Grammar*, 318, provides an example from Thucydides (2.52): τοῦ ὕδατος ἐπιθυμία ("desire for water").

"the love of God" (ἡ ἀγάπη τοῦ θεοῦ, Rom 5:5; 8:39) or "the love of Christ" (ἡ ἀγάπη τοῦ Χριστοῦ, Rom 8:35; Eph 3:19) often denote the love of God or of Christ for humanity and so can be considered subjective genitives. On the other hand, writers can make use of ἀγάπη ("love") followed by what is clearly an objective genitive to speak of one's own love *for* God (ἡ ἀγάπη τοῦ θεοῦ, Luke 11:42); other expressions of love using the objective genitive include ἡ ἀγάπη ... πάντων ("love for all," 2 Thess 1:3) and ἡ ἀγάπη τῆς ἀληθείας ("love for the truth," 2 Thess 2:10).[11] The word for "knowledge" (γνῶσις) is frequently followed by an objective genitive, as in ἡ γνῶσις τοῦ θεοῦ ("the knowledge of God," 2 Cor 10:5; cf. 4:6), meaning human knowledge of God, and ἡ γνῶσις Χριστοῦ Ἰησοῦ ("the knowledge of Christ Jesus," Phil 3:8), referring to Paul's own knowledge concerning Christ.[12] Hope (ἐλπίς) is often expressed by the noun followed by another noun in the genitive, as in ἡ ἐλπὶς τοῦ κυρίου ἡμῶν Ἰησοῦ Χριστοῦ ("hope in our Lord Jesus Christ," 1 Thess 1:3) and ἐλπὶς ζωῆς αἰωνίου ("hope of eternal life," Titus 1:2; 3:7).[13] Fear is frequently expressed with the same kind of expression, as in ὁ φόβος τοῦ κυρίου ("the fear of the Lord," Acts 9:31; 2 Cor 5:11), φόβος θεοῦ ("fear of God," Rom 3:18; 2 Cor 7:1), and φόβος Χριστοῦ (literally, "fear of Christ," Eph 5:21).[14] It is not uncommon for the word rendered "revelation" to be followed by the objective genitive, as in ἀποκαλύψις δικαιοκρισίας τοῦ θεοῦ ("revelation of the righteous judgment of God," Rom 2:5) and ἡ ἀποκάλυψις τοῦ κυρίου ἡμῶν Ἰησοῦ Χριστοῦ ("the revelation of our Lord Jesus Christ," 1 Cor 1:7; Gal 1:12; 1 Pet 1:7, 13).[15] Other well-known expressions of the objective genitive in the letters of Paul include ζῆλος θεοῦ ("zeal for God," Rom 10:2), ἡ ὑπακοὴ τοῦ Χριστοῦ ("the obedience of Christ," 2 Cor 10:5), and ἔπαινος θεοῦ ("praise of God," Phil 1:11).[16]

3.1.2. *The Noun* πίστις *in Objective Genitive Constructions Aside from the Disputed Cases*

In light of this common use of the objective genitive with "transitive" nouns, the possibility of a similar use with πίστις has to be considered. Here it must be

---

11. In some cases there is ambiguity as to whether the writer means love for God or God's love (John 5:42), love for the Spirit or the Spirit's love (Rom 15:30), and love for Christ or Christ's love (2 Cor 5:14).

12. For other examples, cf. Luke 1:77; 2 Cor 2:14; 4:6; 2 Pet 3:18.

13. For other examples, cf. Acts 16:19; 26:6; Rom 5:2; Gal 5:5; Col 1:27; 1 Thess 5:8.

14. For other examples, cf. Matt 28:4; John 7:13; 19:38; 20:19; Heb 2:15; Rev 18:10, 15.

15. For other examples, cf. Rom 8:19; 16:25; 2 Cor 12:1; 2 Thess 1:7; 1 Pet 4:13; Rev 1:1.

16. Additional illustrations of the objective genitive are provided by N. Turner, *Syntax*, 3:211-12.

said that, if πίστις never has a transitive meaning, it might be excluded from further consideration as capable of expressing the objective genitive.[17] Clearly, however, this noun does have a "transitive" sense — and appears in objective genitive constructions — in the works of Josephus,[18] the NT, other early Christian literature,[19] and Hellenistic Greek authors of that era.[20] Leaving aside the passages that are in dispute, some unambiguous examples from the NT are as follows: Mark 11:22, ἔχετε πίστιν θεοῦ ("Have faith in God"); Acts 3:16, ἐπὶ τῇ πίστει τοῦ ὀνόματος αὐτοῦ ("by faith in his name"); and 2 Thessalonians 2:13, πίστει ἀληθείας ("by faith in the truth").

Other examples may also qualify, but they are contested.[21] These include Colossians 2:12, διὰ τῆς πίστεως τῆς ἐνεργείας τοῦ θεοῦ ("through faith in the working of God"),[22] and James 2:1, ἡ πίστις τοῦ κυρίου ἡμῶν Ἰησοῦ Χριστοῦ τῆς δόξης ("faith in our glorious Lord Jesus Christ").[23] But alternatives have been posed to both of these: "through the faithfulness of the working of God" (Col 2:12)[24] and "the faithfulness of our glorious Lord Jesus Christ" (Jas 2:1).[25] When Paul writes the phrase τῇ πίστει τοῦ εὐαγγελίου (Phil 1:27), it is usually translated "by faith in the gospel" (objective genitive); yet "by the faith of the gospel" is possible. The writer of Ephesians employs the phrase διὰ τῆς πίστεως αὐτοῦ (3:12), which is usually translated "through faith in him [= Christ]";[26] but "through his [= Christ's] faith" is linguistically possible.[27]

---

17. P. Meyer, "Pauline Theology," 115 (n. 82), is mistaken when he says that, since the verb πιστεύειν does not have a transitive usage with the meaning "to trust, believe" (but only when it has prepositions following it — presumably such as εἰς, as frequently in the NT), the noun πίστις cannot have a transitive sense either. But the verb is transitive (and not followed by a preposition) at John 11:26; Acts 13:41; 1 Cor 13:7; and 1 John 4:16.

18. Josephus, *Ant.* 19.16: πίστιν τοῦ θεοῦ.

19. *Epistle of Diognetus* 11.6: εὐαγγελίων πίστις.

20. R. B. Matlock, "Detheologizing the ΠΙΣΤΙΣ ΧΡΙΣΤΟΥ Debate," 19 (n. 59), and "'Even the Demons Believe,'" 304 (nn. 23-24). In the latter essay Matlock lists many examples, including 13 instances in the writings of Plutarch.

21. We leave aside Rev 2:13 (τὴν πίστιν μου); 14:12 (τὴν πίστιν Ἰησοῦ). While they may express faith in Christ, they may simply mean *the* (Christian) faith.

22. Cf. E. Lohse, *Colossians and Philemon*, 105-6.

23. Cf. M. Dibelius and H. Greeven, *James*, 128. The context militates against "the faith of our glorious Lord Jesus Christ."

24. G. Hebert, "'Faithfulness' and 'Faith,'" 377.

25. I. Wallis, *The Faith of Jesus Christ*, 175.

26. The objective genitive is represented in the ASV, RSV, NIV, and NRSV and favored by J. Muddiman, *A Commentary on the Epistle to the Ephesians*, 163, and A. Lincoln, *Ephesians*, 189-90.

27. The subjective genitive is represented in the NET and favored by M. Barth, *Ephesians*, 1:347; I. Wallis, *The Faith of Jesus Christ*, 128-34; D. Campbell, *The Rhetoric of Righteousness*, 215; and P. Foster, "The First Contribution," 75-96. The fact that a definite article appears between

In spite of the ambiguities in some cases, it is clear that the term πίστις can be followed by an objective genitive elsewhere in the NT and in other contemporary sources. It is surely possible that the same construction is being used in the πίστις Χριστοῦ formulation.

3.1.3. The Subjective Genitive in Paul's Letters

When Paul speaks of an attribute of Christ (so a subjective genitive), it is typical for him to make use of the definite article prior to the noun that attributes a quality to Christ.[28] Thus he includes the article when he writes of "the love of Christ" (ἡ ἀγάπη τοῦ Χριστοῦ, Rom 8:35; 2 Cor 5:14), "the grace of Christ" (ἡ χάρις τοῦ Χριστοῦ, 2 Cor 8:9; Gal 6:18; Phil 4:23; 1 Thess 5:26; Phlm 25), and "the meekness and gentleness of Christ" (ἡ πραΰτης καὶ ἐπιείκεια τοῦ Χριστοῦ, 2 Cor 10:1). But that is not always the case. Exceptions occur when Paul writes about his longing for his readers "with the compassion of Christ" (ἐν σπλάγχνοις Χριστοῦ, Phil 1:8) and once when he refers to his readers as persons whom he had called "in the grace of Christ" (ἐν χάριτι Χριστοῦ, Gal 1:6). These cases might not be true exceptions, since they are found within statements of Paul concerning himself and his ministry and are only secondarily about the attributes of Christ. In any case, one cannot rule out the subjective genitive strictly because he does not make use of the definite article.

3.1.4. The Noun πίστις in Subjective Genitive Constructions aside from the Disputed Cases

In regard to πίστις in cases where the subjective genitive is clearly intended, there is little to rely on. In his survey of the NT evidence as a whole regarding the use of πίστις accompanied by the subjective genitive (other than πίστις Χριστοῦ), Ernest D. Burton has written that "the article is . . . almost invariably present."[29] The statement is based almost entirely, however, on cases in the NT where the subsequent word in the subjective genitive is actually a personal pronoun ("your," "his," etc.) — cases where the latter can actually be considered possessive genitives.[30] There is actually only one passage cited by Burton

---

the preposition and the noun πίστις makes the expression different from the anarthrous πίστις in the undisputed letters of Paul.

28. Similarly concerning God, e.g., "the peace of God" (Phil 4:7).

29. E. Burton, *Galatians*, 482.

30. In "The *Pistis Christou* Formulation in Paul," 253, I followed Burton's lead uncritically and listed a number of such passages with personal pronouns for support of the presence of the

in which the noun πίστις is accompanied by a noun in the genitive case, thereby supporting his statement, and that is at Revelation 13:10, ἡ πίστις τῶν ἁγίων ("the faith of the saints"). To this should be added Romans 3:3, ἡ πίστις τοῦ θεοῦ ("the faithfulness of God"). Going beyond the NT (which Burton does not do), one can add a case from the writings of Josephus, ἡ . . . τοῦ πλήθους τῶν Γαλιλαίων . . . πίστις ("the faith of the multitude of the Galileans"),[31] and another from the LXX, ἡ πίστις τοῦ Σίμωνος ("the faith of Simon," 1 Macc 14:35). Although the article is present in each of the cases cited, there is one case where the subjective genitive is anarthrous, and that is at (deutero-Pauline) Titus 1:1, κατὰ πίστιν ἐκλεκτῶν θεοῦ ("according to the faith of the elect of God").

There is only one passage in which Paul speaks unambiguously of the faith of a specific person that can serve as an expression of the subjective genitive, and there he makes use of the definite article. That is in regard to the faith of Abraham, specifically, in the phrase τοῖς στοιχοῦσιν τοῖς ἴχνεσιν τῆς . . . πίστεως τοῦ πατρὸς ἡμῶν Ἀβραάμ ("to those who follow the example of the faith of our ancestor Abraham," Rom 4:12). In this case Paul follows the usual convention of using the definite article for "the" twice (τῆς and τοῦ). By analogy, then, if Paul were speaking of "the faith of Christ" (subjective genitive) in the passages under question, one would expect the same syntax, i.e., ἡ πίστις τοῦ Χριστοῦ. But that is precisely what he does not do. The πίστις Χριστοῦ formulation lacks the article consistently.

The observation is important, but it is not decisive. As others have shown,[32] there are places where Paul uses expressions that may or may not include the definite article when the subjective genitive is being used. So he can write both ways concerning "the righteousness of God" (so ἡ δικαιοσύνη τοῦ θεοῦ at Rom 10:3, but simply δικαιοσύνη θεοῦ at Rom 1:17; 3:5, 21, 22), "the law of God" (ὁ νόμος τοῦ θεοῦ at Rom 7:22, but νόμος θεοῦ at Rom 7:25), and "the law of sin" (ὁ νόμος τῆς ἁμαρτίας at Rom 7:23, but νόμος ἁμαρτίας at Rom 7:25). But the argument can go both ways. If Paul can make use of, or dispense with, the definite article in subjective genitive constructions, why is it that the definite article *never* appears before πίστις in the seven instances under discussion?

The upshot is that the evidence is mixed on this point. What is more likely is that, since Paul is consistent in his use of πίστις Χριστοῦ and similar formulations as a kind of shorthand without the use of a definite article, the for-

---

article when a subjective genitive is meant. S. Williams, "Again *Pistis Christou*," 432, zeroed in on that as lacking evidential value — and rightly so.

31. Josephus, *Life* 1.84.

32. G. Howard, "Faith of Jesus," 2:759; P. Pollard, "The 'Faith of Christ' in Current Discussion," 224.

mulation must have become set and familiar for Paul and his readers,[33] "a regular pattern of speech."[34]

3.1.5. The Noun πίστις and Subsequent Prepositions

One way for NT writers to express faith in Christ or God is to write the noun πίστις followed by a prepositional phrase introduced by a word that can be translated as "in" or "toward" (ἐν, εἰς, ἐπί, or πρός). There are several examples of this: (1) πίστις ἐν Χριστῷ ("faith in Christ") or πίστις ἐν τῷ κυρίῳ ("faith in the Lord") appears several times (Eph 1:15; Col 1:4; 1 Tim 3:13; and 2 Tim 3:15); (2) πίστις εἰς Χριστόν ("faith in Christ"), πίστις εἰς τὸν κύριον ("faith in the Lord"), and πίστις εἰς θεόν ("faith in God") is attested frequently (Acts 20:21; 24:24; 26:18; Col 2:5; and 1 Pet 1:21); and (3) πίστις ἐπὶ Θεόν ("faith in God") appears once (Heb 6:1). The phrases πίστις πρὸς θεόν and πίστις πρὸς τὸν θεόν ("faith toward/in reference to [or simply "in"] God") appear in 4 Maccabees 15:24 and 16:22.

Some interpreters have asserted that these formulations are equivalent to the πίστις Χριστοῦ formulation as "faith in Christ" (objective genitive).[35] But actually, if those formulations were typical ways for Paul to express faith in Christ — and were therefore ready at hand — one could argue that he should have used them.[36] It can be argued further, then, that, whenever Paul used the πίστις Χριστοῦ formulation, he employed the subjective genitive. None of the passages listed, however, is from the undisputed letters of Paul. One searches in vain to find an instance where the noun πίστις is followed by a preposition and has Christ or God as an object (unless Gal 3:26 is so taken; see below).[37] To be

---

33. It appears also to have become a shorthand for the Christian faith for Ignatius, who addresses his readers ἐν πίστει Ἰησοῦ Χριστοῦ (*Magn.* 1.1), signifying the faith of believers.

34. J. Dunn, "Once More," 253.

35. W. Hatch, *The Pauline Idea of Faith*, 46; Rudolf Bultmann, "πιστεύω," *TDNT* 6:204; idem, *Theology of the New Testament*, 1:317-18; BDF 90 (§163); Gerhard Barth, "πίστις," *EDNT* 3:93; cf. E. Burton, *Galatians*, 482.

36. I. Wallis, *The Faith of Jesus Christ*, 70. According to S. Williams, "Again *Pistis Christou*," 434, the answer to this lack of usage is simple: "Paul was not accustomed to thinking of Christ as the 'object' of faith." And he goes on to say that "the person of Christ is not faith's object. *God* is." But Christ is faith's object in Gal 2:16 and Phil 1:29.

37. D. Campbell, *The Rhetoric of Righteousness*, 216, has written (erroneously) that in my essay on "The *Pistis Christou* Formulation," 254, I claimed that "πίστις ἐν 'is not a Pauline idiom.'" Then he goes on to cite various passages (1 Cor 2:5; 1 Thess 1:18; Phlm 5) to refute the claim. The passages he cites, however, are in my article, making the same point as made in the paragraph above. His quotation is incorrect, since what I wrote is that πίστις ἐν Χριστῷ (having Χριστῷ as the object of the preposition) "is not a Pauline idiom." I wrote in addition that

sure, Paul does make use of πίστις ἐν plus the dative at 1 Corinthians 2:5; and at 1 Thessalonians 1:8 and Philemon 5 he uses πίστις πρός plus an accusative noun. None of these, however, is equivalent to πίστις Χριστοῦ. In the first of these the apostle writes to his readers about the manner of his apostolic ministry as being carried on "in order that your faith may not be in human wisdom, but in the power of God" (ἵνα ἡ πίστις ὑμῶν μὴ ᾖ ἐν σοφίᾳ ἀνθρώπων ἀλλ᾽ ἐν δυνάμει θεοῦ). Here the prepositional phrases following the verb ᾖ ("may be"), and so in the predicate position, express two possible ways for faith to be directed; they are not formulaic in the sense that πίστις ἐν Χριστῷ is in the other passages mentioned. In the other two passages, in which he speaks of the exemplary faith of his readers, Paul uses constructions that are more complex, including both possessive and relative pronouns in both cases prior to the prepositional phrases employed (ἡ πίστις ὑμῶν ἡ πρὸς τὸν θεόν ["your faith that is in God"], 1 Thess 1:8; ἀκούων σου τὴν ἀγάπην, καὶ τὴν πίστιν ἣν ἔχεις πρὸς τὸν κύριον Ἰησοῦν καὶ εἰς πάντας τοὺς ἁγίους ["hearing of your love and your faith, which you have for the Lord Jesus and for all the saints"], Phlm 5). Moreover, in these cases Paul is not calling for faith in the saving work of Christ (nor is he proclaiming the fidelity of Christ), but he is praising the widely known quality of the faith that his readers display in each case. Those spoken to are models of faith for others. The πίστις acclaimed in these passages is more a matter of faith as a condition and a vitality than faith as a response to God, Christ, or the gospel.[38]

The statement of Paul in Galatians 3:26 (πάντες γὰρ υἱοὶ θεοῦ ἐστε διὰ τῆς πίστεως ἐν Χριστῷ Ἰησοῦ) is not an exception to the claim that Paul does not make use of πίστις ἐν Χριστῷ as a way of expressing faith in Christ.[39] Although it is possible to translate the sentence as "for you all are children of God through faith in Christ Jesus," so that Christ is the object of faith here,[40] it is

---

"Within Paul's own writings . . . such constructions — *having Christ or God as object of a preposition* — do not exist" (emphasis added here).

38. For this and other distinctions of meanings of the term, cf. R. Bultmann, "πιστεύω," *TDNT* 6:217-19; G. Barth, "πίστις," *EDNT* 3:93-94.

39. D. Campbell, *The Rhetoric of Righteousness*, 216, contends that "Gal. 3.26 (perhaps supported by 2.20) and Rom. 4.12 are clear refutations of [the] entire contention" that "πίστις ἐν is not Pauline." He goes on to suggest that "these are references to the faithfulness of Christ" and that they are "expressed in genitive ἐν constructions" (actually Rom 4:12 has to do with Abraham, and the object of the preposition is not Christ, but ἀκροβυστία, "uncircumcision"). Staying with the subjective genitive rendering (Campbell's position), that means that διὰ τῆς πίστεως ἐν Χριστῷ Ἰησοῦ would have to be translated as "through the faithfulness [that is] in Christ Jesus." If that is so, it does not undermine my earlier contention, "The *Pistis Christou* Formulation," 254, that πίστις ἐν Χριστῷ is not a Pauline expression for the *believer's* faith.

40. Cf. the NIV rendering: "You are all sons of God through faith in Christ Jesus." Cf. also KJV, "by faith in Christ Jesus." On the other hand, J. L. Martyn, *Galatians*, 373, 375, adopting the

more likely that the two prepositional phrases are to be divided so that the verse can be translated as "for you are all children of God in Christ Jesus through faith."[41] Paul has been maintaining within this chapter that (1) the blessing of Abraham comes to the Gentiles "in Christ Jesus," Abraham's offspring (3:14, 16), and (2) the Gentiles are children of God by faith in the promises of God that they have heard in the gospel message, not by works of the law (3:2-3, 5, 8-9). And so, by way of summary, Paul declares that his Gentile readers are children of God, and therefore heirs of the promises, by virtue of their being "in Christ Jesus (ἐν Χριστῷ Ἰησοῦ)" and believing in the promises of God, rather than by seeking righteousness through works of the law. By means of their baptism, he says, they have put on Christ; they are "in Christ Jesus (ἐν Χριστῷ Ἰησοῦ)," belong to Christ, and consequently are Abraham's children and heirs (3:27-29). It must be said parenthetically that both sides of the πίστις Χριστοῦ debate tend to gain from separating the two prepositional phrases. For those contending for the subjective genitive in Paul's letters, the passage then provides no support for reading "faith in Christ" in this key text. On the other hand, for those contending for the objective genitive, the passage cannot be taken as evidence that πίστις ἐν Χριστῷ is a Pauline expression ready at hand, which would open the possibility that πίστις Χριστοῦ is more likely a subjective genitive.[42]

There is another matter concerning this verse, however, that is of interest for our discussion. The wording for the verse provided above corresponds to what is printed in the Nestle-Aland text (27th edition), and that need not be contested. But there is a significant variant, and that is the wording of 𝔓⁴⁶, an early Alexandrian text type from ca. A.D. 200. The reading there omits two words (τῆς and ἐν) and changes the case of Christ Jesus from the dative (Χριστῷ Ἰησοῦ) to the genitive (Χριστοῦ Ἰησοῦ). The resulting reading contains the familiar πίστις Χριστοῦ formulation! It reads as follows: πάντες γὰρ υἱοὶ Θεοῦ ἐστε διὰ πίστεως Χριστοῦ Ἰησοῦ, and it can then be rendered "for you are all children of God through faith in Christ Jesus." While this alternative reading is not to be preferred in light of other textual witnesses, it is significant

---

subjective genitive rendering, translates the text to read: "For you are — all of you — sons of God through the faith that is in Christ Jesus" and says that the Galatians "were taken into the realm of the Christ whose faith had elicited their own faith."

41. Cf. E. Burton, *Galatians*, 202-3; F. Matera, *Galatians*, 141-42; and R. Hays, *The Faith of Jesus Christ*, 155-56, who cites H. Schlier, *Galater*, 156. R. Longenecker, *Galatians*, 150-54, separates the "in Christ" formula from "through faith" in his discussion, if not in his translation. Cf. also the NRS, "for in Christ Jesus you are all children of God through faith," and the separation of the two prepositional phrases in the RSV, NEB, and NET.

42. Romans 3:25 (διὰ πίστεως ἐν τῷ αὐτοῦ αἵματι) is another case where πίστις is followed — on the page — by the preposition ἐν, but the prepositional phrase should be linked to the noun ἱλαστήριον, not to πίστις. See the discussion at 3:25.

in terms of the interpretation of the πίστις Χριστοῦ formula. It appears that the scribe who produced 𝔓⁴⁶ understood the verse to speak of faith in Christ and has conformed the verse to reflect what he knew as a Pauline expression from elsewhere. In order to express "faith in Christ," the scribe has "improved" the text by replacing διὰ τῆς πίστεως ἐν Χριστῷ Ἰησοῦ with the more familiar διὰ πίστεως Χριστοῦ Ἰησοῦ.⁴³ That being the case, it provides confirmation that for that particular (presumably Greek-speaking) scribe, the πίστις Χριστοῦ formulation expressed an objective genitive. The subjective genitive rendering ("for you are all children of God through [the] faith [or "faithfulness"] of Christ Jesus") would be possible only if that same scribe was insistent that the other reading — clearly specifying faith in Christ (διὰ τῆς πίστεως ἐν Χριστῷ) *in his (erroneous) reading of it* — needs to be changed radically to speak of becoming children of God through Christ's own faith. If that had been so, it seems odd that he eliminated the definite article (τῆς, "the"), since its presence would specify that it is "the faith of Christ" that is meant, thereby emphasizing his point — but of course he did not do that.

3.1.6. The Noun πίστις within Prepositional Phrases

In each of the passages making use of the πίστις Χριστοῦ formulation a preposition (διά, ἐκ, or ἐν) precedes a form (genitive or dative) of πίστις, so there is (1) a preposition (e.g., διά), (2) a form of πίστις (e.g., πίστεως), and (3) Χριστοῦ (or other term in the genitive). The question can be raised whether there are analogies elsewhere in Paul's writings.

First, are there cases within the letters of Paul where there is a prepositional phrase with a noun other than a form of πίστις as the middle term, followed by Χριστοῦ, and, if so, do those analogies support either an objective or subjective reading in our controverted phrase? There are five such instances, and in three of them the pattern represents a subjective genitive: (1) 2 Corinthians 2:10 (ἐν προσώπῳ Χριστοῦ, "in the presence of Christ" [NRSV]); (2) 4:6 (ἐν προσώπῳ Χριστοῦ, "in the face of Christ" [NRSV]); and (3) Galatians 1:6 (ἐν χάριτι Χριστοῦ, "in the grace of Christ"). But there are two other instances

---

43. F. Matera, *Galatians*, 142, maintains that the variant διὰ πίστεως Χριστοῦ can be translated here as either an objective or a subjective genitive. For the view that it is an objective genitive, cf. H. Betz, *Galatians*, 181-86; R. B. Matlock, "PISTIS in Galatians 3.26," 433-39. Among other things, Matlock points out that the variant is conformed to Paul's syntax in Gal 2:16 (διὰ πίστεως Ἰησοῦ Χριστοῦ), except for its following the word order of 3:26 ("Christ Jesus"), and that the variant could not consist of a *subjective* genitive as a substitution for the (prior) textual reading, which could only be read as an *objective* genitive, if the two prepositional phrases are taken together ("through faith in Christ Jesus").

where the objective genitive is used: (1) Romans 10:17 (διὰ ῥήματος Χριστοῦ, "through the preaching of Christ")[44] and (2) Galatians 1:12 (δι᾽ ἀποκαλύψεως Ἰησοῦ Χριστοῦ, "through a revelation of Jesus Christ"). The result is that both objective and subjective genitives are employed when a noun other than πίστις is the middle term of analogous phrases.

Second, are there cases where there is a prepositional phrase employing a form of πίστις as the middle term and a noun other than Χριστοῦ as the end term, and, if so, do those analogies support either reading? There is one such phrase at Romans 4:16 (ἐκ πίστεως Ἀβραάμ), but that is exceptionally complex and highly debatable as to its meaning in context, and it will be taken up below as a special case. Other than that, there are no other analogous phrases. There are two instances where pronouns, rather than nouns, are used: Romans 1:12 (διὰ τῆς ἐν ἀλλήλοις πίστεως ὑμῶν τε καὶ ἐμοῦ, "through our mutual faith, both yours and mine") and 1 Thessalonians 3:7 (διὰ τῆς ὑμῶν πίστεως, "through your faith"). Otherwise whenever Paul uses the prepositional phrases διὰ πίστεως (Rom 3:25, 30, 31; 2 Cor 5:7; Gal 3:14, 26), ἐκ πίστεως (Rom 1:17; 3:30; 4:16a; 5:1; 9:30, 32; 10:6; 14:23; Gal 3:7, 8, 9, 11, 12, 24; 5:5), or ἐν πίστει (1 Cor 16:13; 2 Cor 13:5), the word πίστις appears in the genitive or dative without an additional noun in the genitive following it (the problematical Rom 4:16b being the exception). Furthermore, when Paul uses any of the three prepositional phrases without further modification, he speaks of the faith of the believer. The implications of this, however, are debated. It could be argued that when Paul uses the prepositional phrase ending with Χριστοῦ, the same pattern is operative in those instances; he is speaking of the faith of the believer, which is in Christ.[45] But it is plausible that the opposite is the case. The addition of Χριστοῦ, it can be argued, changes everything so that Paul is speaking of something other than the believer's faith, i.e., the faith/faithfulness of Christ.[46]

3.1.7. *The Noun* πίστις *and the Verb* πιστεύειν

According to various interpreters, the πίστις Χριστοῦ formulation can be considered equivalent to the Pauline phrase πιστεύειν εἰς Χριστόν ("to believe in

44. Admittedly this phrase is ambiguous. For some interpreters, the "preaching of Christ" is primarily the message about him; so W. Sanday and A. Headlam, *Romans*, 298; J. Fitzmyer, *Romans*, 598; K. Haacker, *Römer*, 215; D. Moo, *Romans*, 666. For others, the phrase includes that, but also the idea that the risen Christ speaks through his messengers; so U. Wilckens, *Römer*, 2:229; C. Cranfield, *Romans*, 537; J. Dunn, *Romans*, 623.

45. A. Hultgren, "The *Pistis Christou* Formulation," 255-56.

46. S. Williams, *Galatians*, 68.

Christ") or similar expressions that appear in the undisputed letters of Paul.[47] But here there is little to go on. There is only one instance where that phrase is used explicitly (Gal 2:16), and only one other that is similar ("to believe in him [= Christ]," Phil 1:29).[48] The former of these is considered by many to confirm an objective genitive reading of the entire passage, but others see the matter entirely differently. The issue will be taken up below in the section entitled "Redundancy or Emphasis (Rom 3:22; Gal 2:16; 3:22; Phil 3:9)?"

3.2. Some Key Texts

The question of whether Paul uses the objective or subjective genitive in the passages under discussion cannot be settled on the basis of syntax alone. Exegetical and contextual issues have to be taken into consideration. There are three passages and sets of passages that need particular attention.

3.2.1. Romans 4:16

Although Romans 4:16 is not one of the seven texts using the formulation, it has been important for the discussion, since it contains two words, "faith" and "Abraham," in a construction appearing to have a direct bearing on the formulation. In that verse Paul writes concerning the promise of God, saying that the promise extended through Abraham has been given not only "to the adherent of the law" (τῷ ἐκ τοῦ νόμου) but also "to the one who is an adherent of the faith of Abraham" (τῷ ἐκ πίστεως Ἀβραάμ). This expression — with a definite article, followed by ἐκ πίστεως, and then a proper name — is similar to the phrase τὸν ἐκ πίστεως Ἰησοῦ (Rom 3:26) and is said to be "a fatal embarrassment for all interpreters who seek to treat Ἰησοῦ as an objective genitive."[49] The implication is that at Romans 3:26 Paul is speaking of the "faith" or "faithfulness" of Jesus, and what is said by Paul there can be applied elsewhere.

On closer examination, however, it can be seen that the view that Paul is speaking of the (personal) faith of Abraham in Romans 4:16 and therefore, by analogy, of the (personal) faith or faithfulness of Jesus in Romans 3:26 does not hold up. In Romans 4:16 Paul does not write specifically concerning the personal faith of Abraham the man (in contrast to 4:12 — where he refers to Abra-

---

47. R. Bultmann, "πιστεύω," *TDNT* 6:204; idem, *Theology of the New Testament*, 1:317-18; BDF 90 (§163); H. Ridderbos, *Paul*, 239 (n. 70); K. Kertelge, *"Rechtfertigung" bei Paulus*, 172.

48. Romans 10:14 speaks of believing in "one" (the Lord), but it is not clear that that is belief in Christ.

49. R. Hays, "ΠΙΣΤΙΣ and Pauline Christology," 284.

ham's faith by twice using the definite article, τῆς . . . πίστεως τοῦ . . . Ἀβραάμ, "of the faith of Abraham").[50] Instead he is referring to the faith of the (spiritual) descendants of the patriarch Abraham. Here, as elsewhere, he uses a definite article followed by ἐκ to speak of a person's identity (a sect or a persuasion).[51] Instances of similar usage appear at Romans 4:14 (οἱ ἐκ νόμου, "those of the law" or "the adherents of the law"); 4:16 (τῷ ἐκ τοῦ νόμου, "the adherent of the law"); 1 Corinthians 15:23 (οἱ τοῦ Χριστοῦ, "those of Christ" or "those who belong to Christ"); Galatians 2:12 (τοὺς ἐκ περιτομῆς, "those of the circumcision"); 3:7 and 3:9 (οἱ ἐκ πίστεως, "the people of faith," "those who believe," i.e., believers in Christ).[52] Accordingly, the verse under discussion can be translated to read: "Therefore, it [= the promise to the descendants of Abraham that they would be his heirs] is a matter of faith — that it might be due to grace — in order that the promise might be confirmed to every descendant, not only to the one who adheres to the law, but also to the one who adheres to [or "is of"] the faith of Abraham [= "the Abrahamic faith" or "the Abrahamic tradition," which can now include Gentile believers] — who is the father of us all." The verse concerns the faith of the believer whose identity is marked by faith in the promises of God given to Abraham and (through him) to his descendants, a faith that had its first expression in Abraham their ancestor even before he was circumcised (4:10-12). The proper way for Paul to refer to a true (spiritual) descendant of Abraham is to speak of that person as ὁ ἐκ πίστεως Ἀβραάμ, a person who belongs to the Abrahamic tradition, and that is precisely what he does in this verse. For Paul, those who are believers in Christ are the true descendants of Abraham (Rom 4:11-13; Gal 3:6-9, 14).

The implications of this can be applied to Romans 3:26, which is customarily translated (as in the NRSV): "[God] justifies the one who has faith in Jesus (δικαιοῦντα τὸν ἐκ πίστεως Ἰησοῦ)." While that translation may be satisfactory, it can more properly be translated by analogy to 4:16 (as well as to Rom 4:14; 1 Cor 15:23; Gal 3:7, 9) as "[God] justifies the one who adheres to [or "is of"] the faith of Jesus [= "the Jesuanic faith" or "the Jesus-faith"]," thereby iden-

---

50. Contra J. Dunn, "Once More," 254, who refers to this verse as "a genuine exception" to the rule that Paul uses the definite article before "faith" when he makes use of the subjective genitive.

51. Cf. N. Turner, *Grammar*, 3.15, 260.

52. According to R. Hays, "ΠΙΣΤΙΣ and Pauline Christology," 296, the term "those of faith" must "like Abraham, be those who believe in *God*. Nothing is said in 3:7-9 . . . about 'faith in Christ.'" But the passage speaks eloquently of the Gentiles as believers in the gospel, which was preached to them; i.e., they became believers from hearing the gospel concerning Christ's redemptive work for them. Cf. J. Dunn, *Galatians*, 163; R. Longenecker, *Galatians*, 114; and J. L. Martyn, *Galatians*, 299. F. Matera, *Galatians*, 118, has written that "*hoi ek pisteōs* are the ones from Christ-faith."

tifying a person by his or her "sect or persuasion."[53] God, therefore, justifies the person who is an adherent of the "Jesus-faith," i.e., the one who is a believer in Jesus.

3.2.2. *Romans 3:22 and 26 in Context*

To interpret Romans 3:22 and 26 as subjective genitives is possible only by avoiding their larger context. Within 3:21-26 Paul declares that justification is granted freely apart from the law by God's redemptive work in Christ. There can be little doubt but that justification is effective for the believer; all interpreters can agree on that, for the verses say so explicitly. But is the faith spoken of in 3:22 and 3:26 that of the believer or that of Christ? Too often attention to those two verses is limited to a consideration of other πίστις Χριστοῦ parallels within the letters of Paul. But they need to be interpreted contextually in light of what follows in chapter 4 of the letter. There Abraham is used as an illustration of justification by faith. He believed in the promises of God and so was justified (4:3, 11, 22; cf. Gal 3:9). According to Paul, the story of Abraham provides a lesson for succeeding generations. That is that justification is a gift to believers (4:11). Or to put it another way, those who believe in God, "who raised Jesus our Lord from the dead," are justified (4:24-25). Although there is no explicit statement about faith in Christ in this chapter, the point is that the "faith" (or the act of believing) spoken of in it is that of the believer. And that — as a proof from Scripture — confirms what is claimed in the previous chapter (3:22, 26). Christian faith is seen to be equivalent to that of Abraham, for it is faith in a God who brings life out of death and who justifies the ungodly (4:5). Justification is based on the righteousness of God, which is for all believers, Jew and Gentile alike.

3.2.3. *Redundancy or Emphasis (Rom 3:22; Gal 2:16; 3:22; Phil 3:9)?*

One of the arguments for the subjective genitive maintained with a lot of energy is that in some passages one would have redundancy if the objective genitive is meant. One such passage is Galatians 2:15-16. The passage reads as follows (and with portions placed in separate lines to aid discussion):

Line 1: ἡμεῖς φύσει Ἰουδαῖοι καὶ οὐκ ἐξ ἐθνῶν ἁμαρτολοί,
Line 2: εἰδότες δὲ ὅτι οὐ δικαιοῦται ἄνθρωπος ἐξ ἔργων νόμου ἐὰν μὴ διὰ πίστεως Ἰησοῦ Χριστοῦ,

53. N. Turner, *Grammar*, 3.15, 260.

Line 3: καὶ ἡμεῖς εἰς Χριστὸν Ἰησοῦν ἐπιστεύσαμεν,
Line 4: ἵνα δικαιωθῶμεν ἐκ πίστεως Χριστοῦ καὶ οὐκ ἐξ ἔργων νόμου,
Line 5: ὅτι ἐξ ἔργων νόμου οὐ δικαιωθήσεται πᾶσα σάρξ.

The lines can be translated as follows, employing both the objective and subjective genitives, placing the latter in parentheses:

Line 1: We who are Jews by nature and not Gentile sinners;
Line 2: and having come to know that a person is not justified by works of the law but rather through faith in Jesus Christ ([or] through [the] faithfulness of Jesus Christ),
Line 3: even we have come to believe in Christ Jesus,
Line 4: in order that we might be justified by faith in Christ ([or] by [the] faithfulness of Christ) and not by works of the law,
Line 5: for from works of the law shall no one be justified.

It has been claimed that if an objective genitive is operative here, we have an extreme case of redundancy.[54] It would be needless repetition for Paul to say that we are justified by faith in Christ in line 2, that we believe in Christ in line 3, and that all this is for the sake of being justified by faith in line 5. The way to avoid the redundancy is to read it in such a way that Paul says that we are justified by the faith or faithfulness of Jesus, that we have believed in him, in order that we might be justified by the faithfulness of Christ.

The question for interpreters here is whether the Greek phrase means "through faith in Jesus Christ"[55] or "through [the] faith of Jesus Christ."[56] The most plausible reading is "through faith in Jesus Christ." There are three major reasons for saying so. First, the syntactical observation above applies here. If the apostle intended the subjective genitive, it would have been normal syntax — even if not absolutely necessary — for him to use the definite article and write διὰ τῆς πίστεως τοῦ Ἰησοῦ Χριστοῦ ("through the faith of Jesus Christ") in line

---

54. M. Barth, "The Faith of the Messiah," 368; G. Howard, "Faith of Christ," 2:758; R. Hays, *The Faith of Jesus Christ,* 142, 153; L. T. Johnson, "Romans 3:21-26," 79, 83; M. Hooker, "ΠΙΣΤΙΣ ΧΡΙΣΤΟΥ," 180; L. Keck, "'Jesus' in Romans," 456; D. Campbell, *The Rhetoric of Romans,* 62-63, 216 (who says that the objective genitive would mean a "triple redundancy"); S. Williams, "The 'Righteousness of God' in Romans," 274 (who speaks of "to those who believe" in Gal 3:22 as "superfluous"); idem, *Galatians,* 68 ("the phrase is redundant"); F. Matera, *Galatians,* 100; I. Wallis, *The Faith of Jesus Christ,* 71, 75. Cf. also G. Davies, *Faith and Obedience in Romans,* 107.

55. H. Betz, *Galatians,* 113, 117; K. Ulrichs, *Christusglaube,* 118-20; 131-32; G. Fee, *Pauline Christology,* 224.

56. J. L. Martyn, *Galatians,* 246.

2 and ἐκ τῆς πίστεως τοῦ Χριστοῦ ("by the faith of Christ") in line 4. Paul is making an emphatic contrast, and if he meant to set the faith of Jesus as the (only) means of justification over against all attempts at justification through works of the law, it seems that he would have specified the faith or faithfulness of Jesus by use of the definite article.

Second, any ambiguity about the Greek prepositional phrases in lines 2 and 4 is cleared up by the verb and prepositional phrase in line 3. This can be seen when the lines are arranged in the following way:

What we know: A person is justified διὰ πίστεως Ἰησοῦ Χριστοῦ (line 2).
What we have sought: To be justified ἐκ πίστεως Χριστοῦ (line 4).
What we have done: We have believed in Christ Jesus (line 3).

The act of believing in Christ (line 3) makes sense only if the expressions of lines 2 and 4 are objective genitive formulations. Otherwise, what function does line 3 have within the verse?

The third reason for favoring the objective genitive here is that Paul makes a sharp contrast between two ways of thinking about justification. Clearly for Paul, no person can be justified by works of the law. A person is justified only διὰ πίστεως Ἰησοῦ Χριστοῦ. But what does that mean? The usual interpretation is that Paul contrasts the impossibility of justification "through works of the law" with justification "through faith in Jesus Christ."[57] It has been proposed more recently, however, that the contrast Paul sets over against justification by means of the law is justification "by the deed of God in Christ," so that "pistis Christou is an expression by which Paul speaks of Christ's atoning faithfulness, as, on the cross, he died faithfully for human beings while looking faithfully to God."[58] In that reading the contrast is then between human works and God's work in Christ.[59] While such a contrast is appealing on theological grounds, it does not do justice to the actual passage in question. The statement about having come to believe in Christ and the purpose clause following it (lines 3 and 4 above) remain as a testimony, once again, to justification by faith

---

57. The sharpness of the contrast is highlighted when the Greek conjunction ἐὰν μή ("except," "unless," "but rather") in 2:16 is understood to refer to the words "a person is not justified." Cf. W. Walker, "Translation and Interpretation of ἐὰν μή in Galatians 2:16," 516-17: "Paul is *not* saying that 'a person is not justified by works of law except through faith in Christ Jesus'; rather, he is saying (in this part of the verse) that 'a person is not justified except through faith in Jesus Christ.'" Cf. also A. Das, "Another Look at ἐὰν μή in Galatians 2:16," 529-39; K. Ulrichs, *Christusglaube,* 121-22.

58. J. L. Martyn, *Galatians,* 271. Cf. S. Williams, "The 'Righteousness of God' in Romans," 276.

59. J. L. Martyn, *Galatians,* 271; R. Hays, *The Faith of Jesus Christ,* xlvii.

in Christ. According to Paul, there are two ways of thinking about justification. The one is by doing works of the law, which is a dead end. The other is by trusting in Christ as the divinely given means of justification through his death and resurrection. As true as it is that Christ's own faithfulness to God must be considered a basis for justification, and prior to a believer's faith, it is most certainly the believer's faith, not Christ's faithfulness, that is being spoken of by Paul.

There are two other passages in which the πίστις Χριστοῦ formulation and the verb to believe (πιστεύειν) are associated, and those who favor the subjective genitive think that they contain redundancies if the objective genitive is being used.[60] The one is at Romans 3:22, and the other is at Galatians 3:22. In the first of these Paul declares that the "righteousness of God" has been made manifest in the Christ event, δικαιοσύνη δὲ θεοῦ διὰ πίστεως Ἰησοῦ Χριστοῦ εἰς πάντας τοὺς πιστεύοντας, which can be translated as "God's righteousness through faith in Jesus Christ for all who believe." Why repeat "all who believe" if they are included in the first part of the sentence as believers? The subjective reading would render the phrase in question as "God's righteousness through [the] faith of Jesus Christ for all who believe." Now there is no redundancy.

The same applies to Galatians 3:22. The redundancy is removed with the subjective genitive reading: "So that what was promised through [the] faith of Jesus Christ might be given to those who believe."

Aside from the possibility, even likelihood, that "Paul is perfectly capable of using redundant phrases,"[61] there is another way to read these passages. In the case of Romans 3:22 and Galatians 3:22, the participial phrase exists for the sake of emphasis upon universality, as indicated by the "all" of Romans 3:22,[62] bringing out the pragmatic and ecclesiological function of the disclosure and gift of God's righteousness through faith.[63] The righteousness of God, received by faith in Christ, is extended to *all* who believe, including Gentiles. That is so because the righteousness of God has been made manifest and is effective for believers "*apart* from the law" (3:21). Likewise, the statement in Galatians 3:22 is a sweeping one in which the apostle has all believers in view.

Less often brought into the debate is Philippians 3:9 ("not having a righteousness of my own that comes from the law, but one that comes through faith

---

60. S. Williams, "The 'Righteousness of God' in Romans," 274; idem, "Again *Pistis Christou*, 436 (n. 19); R. Hays, *The Faith of Jesus Christ*, 142, 158; L. Keck, "'Jesus' in Romans," 454-56. Cf. also L. T. Johnson, "Romans 3:21-26," 79, 83; M. Hooker, "ΠΙΣΤΙΣ ΧΡΙΣΤΟΥ," 166; N. T. Wright, *NIB (Romans)*, 10:470.

61. M. Hooker, "ΠΙΣΤΙΣ ΧΡΙΣΤΟΥ," 173. Cf. P. Achtemeier, "Apropos the Faith of/in Christ," 84, who cites Rom 5:18-19 and 2 Cor 5:18-19 as examples of redundancy. To these can be added 1 Thess 1:7-8 and Rom 3:24 (where Paul says that God justifies "freely by his grace").

62. Cf. J. Dunn, "Once More," 264; C. Cranfield, "On the Πίστις Χριστοῦ Question," 87.

63. K. Ulrichs, *Christusglaube*, 176.

in Christ [τὴν διὰ πίστεως Χριστοῦ], the righteousness from God based on faith [ἐπὶ τῇ πίστει]"). But there, too, the claim has been made that, if the objective genitive is being used, a redundancy follows. If Paul speaks of the believer's faith in Christ in the first of the prepositional phrases, the second phrase — clearly referring to the believer's faith — is redundant. On the other hand, if Paul is using the subjective genitive ("through the faithfulness of Christ"), there is no redundancy.[64]

While it is possible that the second preposition is redundant, nevertheless, it also functions as a clarifying one. That becomes more clear when the passage is written out in phrases in this manner:

μὴ ἔχων ἐμὴν δικαιοσύνην
τὴν ἐκ νόμου
ἀλλὰ
τὴν διὰ πίστεως Χριστοῦ,
τὴν ἐκ θεοῦ δικαιοσύνην ἐπὶ τῇ πίστει.

Not having my righteousness,
the [righteousness] from the law,
but
the [righteousness] through faith in Christ,
the righteousness from God by faith.

The threefold use of the definite article (τήν) is attributive, modifying the word δικαιοσύνη, a syntactical usage from classical times into the NT.[65] That explains why the word δικαιοσύνη need not be repeated between the first and last lines. Moreover, the article is used in particular to imply contrast or to avoid ambiguity.[66] The last line picks up the term once more, and it does so to make a stark contrast between one's own righteousness and that which is from God, received by faith. For the line prior to it to refer to the faithfulness (or faith) of Christ would destroy the parallelism and its clarifying function.[67]

In the final analysis, the charge of redundancy is a weak argument against the objective genitive. It is generally agreed that Paul dictated his letters. Redundancy for the sake of emphasis is more likely to take place in oral dictation than in written composition, particularly when the author is trying to make a

---

64. M. Hooker, *The Letter to the Philippians*, 528; M. Bockmuehl, *The Epistle to the Philippians*, 208-13.

65. H. Smyth, *Greek Grammar*, 293 (§1158); BDF 140 (§269).

66. BDF 140-41 (§269, 1).

67. For additional approaches against the view that the objective genitive causes a redundancy, cf. R. B. Matlock, "The Rhetoric of πίστις in Paul," 177-84; T. Tobin, *Paul's Rhetoric in Its Contexts*, 133-34; and J. Reumann, *Philippians*, 494-96, 521-22.

point with extra strength. Moreover, when the letters of Paul are heard with the ear rather than seen with the eye on a page, the so-called redundancy fades.

3.3. Attendant Interpretive and Theological Issues

3.3.1. Narrative Approaches and the Phrase

The rise of "narrative" approaches to the letters and theology of Paul has had an important part in the πίστις Χριστοῦ debate. According to those analyses, the letters of Paul reveal a narrative framework that the interpreter can and should attend to in exegetical work. The letters do not simply set forth theological truths in abstraction, but rehearse a narrative about God's saving involvement in the world. Ingredients in that narrative inform and influence Paul's theological claims at any given point in his letters.[68] The telling of what that narrative entailed, however, differs among those who take this approach. For some it includes the whole sweep of the story of Israel culminating in Christ's parousia,[69] while for others it is primarily the story of what God has done in Jesus as the Christ for Israel and the Gentile world.[70]

It is commonly held by those who contend for a "narrative" reading of Paul's letters that when the phrase is understood to be a subjective genitive, it fits well within the narrative sequence and content of Paul's theology; but it does not fit well when it is taken to be an objective genitive. Richard Hays, for example, has stated the connection between the narrative and the phrase this way:

> The narrative structure of the gospel story depicts Jesus as the divinely commissioned protagonist who gives himself up to death on a cross in order to liberate humanity from bondage (Gal 1:4; 2:20; 3:13-14; 4:4-7). His death, in obedience to the will of God, is simultaneously a loving act of faithfulness (πίστις) to God and the decisive manifestation of God's faithfulness to his covenant promise to Abraham. Paul's uses of πίστις Ἰησοῦ Χριστοῦ and similar phrases should be understood as summary allusions to this story.[71]

---

68. Cf. B. Longenecker, "Narrative Interest in the Study of Paul," 3-4.

69. N. T. Wright, *The New Testament and the People of God*, 79; B. Witherington, *Paul's Narrative Thought World*, 5; and J. Dunn, *The Theology of Paul the Apostle*, 18.

70. R. Hays, *The Faith of Jesus Christ*, xxiv-xxvi, 9, 27, 30, 209, 274 (but on pp. xxv-xxxviii Hays indicates that, if he were to revise his work, the story of Jesus should be located within the broader story of Israel); A. K. Grieb, *The Story of Romans*, xxiii-xxiv.

71. R. Hays, "ΠΙΣΤΙΣ and Pauline Christology," 274-75.

Furthermore, Hays says that those who stress syntactical and semantic studies of the phrase, and on that basis opt for the objective genitive, fail to give attention to the larger context of the phrase within the narrative.[72] Likewise, Katherine Grieb has written that the subjective genitive reading is the most "straightforward" one at Romans 3:25-26, since "Jesus Christ is God's own covenant righteousness shown in his faithful obedience to death on behalf of the lost world."[73]

Nevertheless, the question is not whether Paul affirms the faithfulness of Jesus, for that is established without doubt. The question is the meaning of the πίστις Χριστοῦ phrase in its various contexts.

3.3.2. Christology: The Faithfulness of Christ

Those who favor the subjective genitive rendering stress the faithfulness of Christ as a Pauline theme. Leander Keck, for example, has written: "It is Christ's faithfulness that makes possible the redemption through which persons who believe the gospel are made right with God."[74] Such a statement is beyond dispute for those who favor the objective genitive reading every bit as much as for those who favor the alternative. The humanity and obedience of Jesus — and therefore his implied faithfulness — remain in place in Paul's letters, as other passages (cf. Rom 5:19; Phil 2:6-8) show.

But having said that, it is striking that Paul does not draw attention otherwise to the faithfulness of Christ as a discernible theme, even if one claims that he does so in the seven disputed passages.[75] The specific term πίστος ("faithful") is applied to God on four occasions (1 Cor 1:9; 10:13; 2 Cor 1:18; 1 Thess 5:24), and twice to persons (1 Cor 4:2; 7:25), but never to Christ. The term πίστις itself is used abundantly in Paul's writings for the faith of believers. And although Christ is on two occasions the object of the verb πιστεύω ("to believe," Gal 2:16; Phil 1:29),[76] he is never the subject of it. "The verb πιστεύω appears 42

72. R. Hays, "ΠΙΣΤΙΣ and Pauline Christology," xlvii, 276-77.

73. K. Grieb, The Story of Romans, 37-38.

74. L. Keck, "'Jesus' in Romans," 457; cf. N. T. Wright, Paul, 47.

75. Cf. J. Dunn, Romans, 166; J. Fitzmyer, Romans, 345; C. Cranfield, "On the Πίστις Χριστοῦ Question," 82-84; G. Fee, Pauline Christology, 225.

76. Contra the astonishing statement of S. Williams, "Again Pistis Christou," 434: "Paul was not accustomed to thinking of Christ as the 'object' of faith." In his Galatians, 70, Williams is more precise: Paul never uses the Greek prepositional phrase πίστις ἐν Χριστῷ ("faith in Christ," emphasis mine). But of course Paul uses the verb (πιστεύω) followed by "in Christ (εἰς Χριστόν)" at Gal 2:16. On this Williams concludes that "Christ-faith is believing 'unto Christ.'" Yet Williams insists that "insofar as one can speak of the 'object' toward which faith is directed, for Paul that 'object' is God" (emphasis his).

times in Paul's letters. Not once is 'Jesus Christ' or its equivalent the subject of the verb."[77] In each instance where the noun "faith" or the verb "believe" is used, the faith of the believer is being spoken of. If in fact the faith or faithfulness of Christ is spoken of in the seven cases discussed here, it is necessary to conclude that they are exceptions. Although Paul would have had occasion to speak of Christ as being faithful to God in soteriological contexts within his letters, he tends to accent the divine initiative more than the responsiveness of Christ to the divine purpose. For Paul, Christ (or the Son) is the manifestation of the saving work and righteousness of God. Paul's theology is primarily theocentric, even theopractic.[78] That is to say, although Christ is the agent of redemption, the major actor in redemption is God, who has sent forth his Son for a redemptive purpose (Rom 3:25; 8:3, 32; Gal 4:4-5) and through him has reconciled the world to himself (2 Cor 5:19).

3.3.3. *Faith as a Good Work?*

Various interpreters have claimed that the objective genitive interpretation runs the danger of making faith itself into a good work.[79] Douglas Campbell, for example, has written that the objective genitive expresses "what *the individual* must do in order to be saved, denoting activity by the Christian."[80] Ian Wallis has concluded that "it seems theologically incoherent for Paul to maintain that the efficacy of Christ's sacrificial death is dependent upon human faith."[81] And Richard Hays has written that the danger of the objective genitive reading is that "with its emphasis on the salvific efficacy of individual faith, is its tendency to . . . turn faith into a bizarre sort of work."[82] The advantage of the subjective genitive reading is that justification is left solely to the work of God in Christ; faith cannot be construed in any way as a good work. This is illustrated by exegesis of passages which have to do with "works of the law" and "faith," such as Romans 3:20-22 and Galatians 2:16. Traditional interpretation considers these as two pathways for a

---

77. T. Tobin, *Paul's Rhetoric in Its Contexts*, 132.

78. For a discussion of the term "theopractic" and of Paul's redemptive Christology, cf. A. Hultgren, *Christ and His Benefits*, 42, 47-67.

79. Cf. M. Barth, "The Faith of the Messiah," 363, 368-69; J. Bligh, *Galatians*, 204; R. Hays, *The Faith of Jesus Christ*, 120; L. Keck, "'Jesus' in Romans," 454, 459; cf. idem, *Romans*, 105, and others noted in subsequent notes. On the other hand, L. T. Johnson, "Romans 3:21-26," 80, suggests that a "fear of a notion of faith as a sort of 'work'" may prevent some interpreters from applying it to Jesus.

80. D. Campbell, "The Story of Jesus in Romans and Galatians," 120.

81. I. Wallis, *The Faith of Jesus Christ*, 82-83. Cf. similar views on pp. 75, 105, and 120.

82. R. Hays, "ΠΙΣΤΙΣ and Pauline Christology," 293.

person to take: works or faith. But those who favor the subjective genitive maintain that in these instances Paul does not distinguish between two possibilities for humans. Instead he speaks in the first instance of human activity (observance of the law) and in the second of divine activity (the faithfulness of Christ).[83] The latter does not refer to human faith at all.

There are problems with this approach. The antithesis between faith and works appears in other contexts as well. At Galatians 3:2 and 3:5 Paul contrasts the hearing of faith (clearly that of believers) over against works of the law. The post-Pauline authors of Ephesians and Hebrews contrast faith and works (Eph 2:8-9; Heb 6:1), and in each case the "faith" is that of believers.[84] And the author of James asserts the importance of works over against faith time and again (2:14-26). Unless he totally misunderstood Paul, he stands as a clear witness to faith and works as two different human pathways.

The view that faith can be made into, or understood to be, one more good work or a precondition of justification or salvation has been recognized by interpreters of Paul's letters for a long time.[85] Yet it has to be said that persons on the objective genitive side of the debate are in total agreement with those on the other that, for Paul, justification is due solely to the initiative and work of God in Christ. Through the death and resurrection of his Son, God has done, once and for all, the decisive deed of reconciling the world to himself. Wherever the gospel is heard and believed, that which God has done for the world is realized proleptically in that person's life. The believer does not put faith in his or her own faith, but on the contrary, abandoning any trust in the self or one's own potential whatsoever, places all trust in what God has done, announced in the gospel.

In the final analysis the subjective genitive reading actually has more potential for construing faith as a good work than the other. In one instance those who accept the subjective genitive reading, perhaps unwittingly, make the faith of the believer a main point, and that is at Romans 3:26, as seen quite blatantly in the alternative reading of the NRSV footnote: "[God justifies the one] who has the faith of Jesus." Other renderings have been proposed, such as "[God] justifies the one who lives by the faithfulness of Jesus"[86] or ". . . the one participating in Jesus' faith."[87] But one must ask: What does it mean that God justifies the one who "lives by the faithfulness of Jesus" or is "participating in Jesus'

83. S. Williams, "'Righteousness' in Romans," 276; L. Keck, "'Jesus' in Romans," 454; F. Matera, *Galatians*, 100; J. L. Martyn, *Galatians*, 271.

84. Contra M. Barth, *Ephesians*, 224-25; for critique, cf. E. Best, *Ephesians*, 226.

85. One of the most eloquent statements that unmasks the possibility of faith as a good work is that of A. Nygren, *Romans*, 67-71.

86. L. Keck, "'Jesus' in Romans," 456. The phrase is altered slightly in L. Keck, *Romans*, 111: "the one who lives out of the faithfulness of Jesus."

87. I. Wallis, *The Faith of Jesus Christ*, 72.

faith"? Either reading sets forth a condition for justification.[88] One has to live or participate in a particular way, as becomes obvious in the statement: "Paul balances out nicely the objective basis for Christian faith ('the faith/faithfulness of Jesus Christ') and mankind's *necessary* subjective response ('by faith')."[89] Moreover, if one accepts that condition, how does one ever know that he or she is fulfilling it adequately? C. E. B. Cranfield has stated the issue in as crisp a manner as may be possible:

> If God's justification is only for those who live from Jesus' faith or actually participate in it, is this not justification by works with a vengeance? For to say that someone 'lives from Jesus' faith' or participates in Jesus' faith is surely to say much more than to say that someone believes in, trusts, Jesus Christ.[90]

3.3.4. Justification by Christ's Faithfulness — But the Believer's Participation?

Richard Hays asks, "What is at stake?" theologically in the debate.[91] No doubt he speaks not only for himself but for many others in the debate when he indicates that one of the major issues has to do with the desire to understand how, for Paul, the death of Jesus has soteriological significance. After dismissing what he calls the "Lutheran-Reformation accounts of justification by faith," he seeks to make a constructive statement, quoting from an essay by Sam K. Williams:

> Christians are justified by that faith which derives its very character from [Jesus'] self-giving obedience, that faith which was first his and has now becomes theirs.[92]

After going on to say that "we are saved by Jesus' faithfulness, not by our own cognitive disposition or confessional orthodoxy," Hays adds:

> The particular interpretation of "the faith of Jesus Christ" that I have promulgated has the effect of stressing the pattern of correspondence between

---

88. Cf. also L. T. Johnson, "Romans 3:21-26," 80: God justifies the "one who has faith as Jesus had faith" and S. Williams, "Again *Pistis Christou*," 447 (n. 48): "one who has faith *like* the faith of Jesus."

89. R. Longenecker, *Galatians*, 87 (emphasis added).

90. C. Cranfield, "On the Πίστις Χριστοῦ Question," 90.

91. R. Hays, "ΠΙΣΤΙΣ and Pauline Christology," 292-94.

92. R. Hays, "ΠΙΣΤΙΣ and Pauline Christology," 293, quoting from S. Williams, "Again *Pistis Christou*," 444.

Jesus and the believing community: those who are in Christ are called to live the same sort of faith-obedience that he revealed.[93]

But one has to ask, in light of that statement, how one becomes a person "in Christ" to make the "pattern of correspondence" possible in the first place. Hays contends that there is a "metaphorical correspondence" between the life-pattern defined by Christ's death and the suffering experienced by those who are in Christ:

> The relation between our faith and the faith of Christ is similarly meta-phorical: our faith answers and reflects his — indeed, *participates in* his — because according to Paul it is God's design for us "to be conformed to the image of his Son" (Rom 8:29).[94]

The noun "participation" (on the part of the believer) or the verb "partici-pate" appears in discussions of the πίστις Χριστοῦ formulation by others who maintain the subjective genitive reading. They speak of the faithfulness of Christ and the "participation" of the believer "in" him. And so Ian Wallis, when commenting on Galatians 3:27, writes:

> for Paul the promise is not simply appropriated by faith (τοῖς πιστεύουσιν, 3.22), but by participating — through faith — in Jesus Christ, who inherited the promise through faith (ἐκ πίστεως Ἰησοῦ Χριστοῦ). In consequence, the faith of believers can never be dissociated from the faith of Christ. It is his faith which makes the faith of others possible and enables them to par-ticipate in its inheritance.[95]

Elsewhere he says that, for Paul, "the relationship between the faith of Christ and believers can be described as participatory" and that "faith is possible be-cause all may participate in a dispensation of faith established by Christ's faith." Moreover, faith is a matter of "finding oneself in the faith of Christ."[96]

Morna Hooker, who speaks of the Christian life as one of "participation" and grants that the πίστις Χριστοῦ formulation refers not only to Christ's faith-fulness but also to the faith of the Christian,[97] has written:

> Our study has driven us to the conclusion that the phrase πίστις Χριστοῦ must contain *some* reference to the faith of Christ himself. I suggest that we

---

93. R. Hays, "ΠΙΣΤΙΣ and Pauline Christology," 294.

94. R. Hays, "ΠΙΣΤΙΣ and Pauline Christology," 297 (emphasis in the text); cf. also pp. 166, 203.

95. I. Wallis, *The Faith of Jesus Christ,* 117.

96. I. Wallis, *The Faith of Jesus Christ,* 126, 217.

97. M. Hooker, "ΠΙΣΤΙΣ ΧΡΙΣΤΟΥ," 167, 183, 185-86.

should think of it not as a polarized expression, which suggests antithesis, but as a *concentric* expression, which begins, always, from the faith of Christ himself, but which includes, necessarily, the answering faith of believers, who claim that faith as their own. . . . Paul understands the whole of Christian existence . . . in terms of participation in Christ: to believe is to share in the faith of Christ himself.[98]

Luke Timothy Johnson (though not using the word "participation" per se) writes that:

the faith of Jesus, understood as obedience, is soteriologically significant. It provides the basis for the faith response of others. . . . The point is (and I believe it is Paul's point) that by virtue of the gift of the Spirit the faith of Christians might become like that of Jesus.[99]

One of the most tightly woven presentations on the connection between the faithfulness of Christ and the faith of the believer has been that of Sam Williams. In a survey of the various passages under discussion, Williams uses the following expressions: Christ's own faith is a "prototype" for others; it is an "eschatological faith . . . introduced into the world by Christ as a new possibility of human existence"; and it is "the means through which God can and does manifest his righteousness to all persons who make Christ's stance their own and thus participate in the consummation of God's historical purpose." "To adopt this stance is to trust and obey Him who raised Jesus from the dead, to believe *like* Christ, and thereby to stand *with* Christ in that domain."[100] He says that when Paul speaks of πίστις Χριστοῦ, "he has in mind that faith which is given its distinctive character by the absolute trust and unwavering obedience of Jesus, who created . . . this mode of being human in the world." Christ is not the "object" of Christian faith, but its "supreme exemplar — indeed, its creator." He concludes:

For the Apostle Paul, faith is that way of responding to God which is now a reality because at a particular moment in the fullness of time Jesus trusted and obeyed. When Paul wishes to direct focal attention to the source, the actualizer, of this faith, he uses the phrase *pistis Christou*. When he wishes to emphasize the commitment of persons who have shared Christ's death and now live "in Christ," he can use the noun *pistis* absolutely. Yet the *pistis* of believers . . . is always nothing else than that way which Christ created, just as *pistis Christou* . . . is always that way which believers have taken as

---

98. M. Hooker, "ΠΙΣΤΙΣ ΧΡΙΣΤΟΥ," 184-86.
99. L. T. Johnson, "Romans 3:21-26," 89.
100. S. Williams, "Again *Pistis Christou*," 442-47 (emphases in the text).

their own. In other words, Paul's phrase focuses attention on the pioneering faith of Christ, but *his* faith now marks the life of every person who lives in him. Thus, in its fundamental character, *pistis Christou* is identical with *pistis*. It is from this perspective, I think, that we can see how Paul sometimes distinguishes between *pistis* and *pistis Christou* while at other times he uses the two as virtual equivalents.[101]

The move to the language of "participation" is easy to understand. If all seven of the passages under discussion have to do with the faithfulness of Christ, one has to deal with the obvious problem that remains: How can the faithfulness of Christ (unto death on the cross) have saving significance for anyone? Surely there has to be a response of some kind, it is said,[102] or else the saving work of God in Christ is a drama that goes on within the life of God (even if it takes place on the stage of history), but does not involve a relationship with humanity. The language of participation is brought in to fill the gap.

But a series of issues needs to be raised. First, whatever is offered by the proponents of the subjective genitive reading with one hand to emphasize the divine work and grace alone apart from any human agency (e.g., "the emphasis in Paul's theology lies less on the question of how we should dispose ourselves towards God than on the question of how God has acted in Christ to effect our deliverance")[103] is taken away by the other. The proponents finally come around to speaking of the faith (or participation) of the believer as necessary to close the soteriological gap. That is true, in one form or another, in each of the statements recorded above.[104] The faithfulness of Christ in the seven passages under discussion then becomes a model of faith for others, as in the alternative translation of Romans 3:26 in the NRSV: "[God] justifies the one who has the faith of Jesus." But Paul does not commend Christ's faith (or faithfulness) elsewhere as a model for persons in Christ to emulate. Alternatively, it has been proposed that the passage can be translated to read that God justifies "the one who lives by the faithfulness of Jesus."[105] That, however, leaves the reader with a puzzle: How does one

101. S. Williams, "Again *Pistis Christou*," 447.

102. Terms used include "answering faith," M. Hooker, "ΠΙΣΤΙΣ ΧΡΙΣΤΟΥ," 185; "answering response," R. Hays, "ΠΙΣΤΙΣ and Pauline Christology," 292; "to stand with Christ," S. Williams, "Again *Pistis Christou*," 443; "mankind's necessary subjective response," R. Longenecker, *Galatians*, 87; and "faith response," L. T. Johnson, "Romans 3:21-26," 89.

103. R. Hays, "ΠΙΣΤΙΣ and Pauline Christology," 275.

104. R. Hays: "those who are in Christ are called to live the same sort of faith-obedience that he revealed," and "our faith answers and reflects his"; I. Wallis: "the faith of believers can never be dissociated from the faith of Christ"; M. Hooker: "the answering faith of believers, who claim that faith as their own"; L. T. Johnson: "the faith of Christians might become like that of Jesus"; and S. Williams: "*his* [= Christ's] faith now marks the life of every person who lives in him."

105. L. Keck, "'Jesus' in Romans," 456.

live by the faithfulness of Jesus? Is it a matter of having faith in Jesus' faithfulness? Or, again, is the faithfulness of Jesus a model for the believer?

Second, the term "participation" is itself a problem. From where is it derived, and in what does the believer participate? It should be noticed that what appears in most of the statements above (L. T. Johnson being the exception) is not that the believer participates *in Christ,* but that he or she participates *in Christ's faith or faithfulness:* "our faith . . . *participates in* his" (R. Hays — emphasis by Hays); believers "claim" Christ's faith "as their own" and "share in the faith of Christ himself" (M. Hooker); they "have taken" it "as their own" (S. Williams); it is a matter of "finding oneself in the faith of Christ" (I. Wallis). But is this the way that Paul thinks? Participation in the faith or faithfulness of Christ by means of one's own faith involves a synergy that, if it is in the letters of Paul elsewhere (aside from the claim that it is in the passages under discussion), needs to be demonstrated. Furthermore, how can the faith of the believer be like that of Jesus?

One might argue that the key to "participation" is Paul's concept of the believer as being "in Christ." In some passages Paul uses that phrase to speak of the believer as so identified with Christ that the eschatological benefits of Christ are applicable to the believer in the present. And so — already — for those who are "in Christ" there is righteousness (Phil 3:9), a new creation (2 Cor 5:17), and no condemnation (Rom 8:1). Consequently, could it not be that, for Paul, whoever is "in Christ" has "the faith [or faithfulness] of Christ" by virtue of being "in" him? If that is so, it would nevertheless remain that the faith spoken of in the passages under discussion is the faith of the believer.

An approach by way of the "in Christ" formulation has been taken most forcefully by Sam Williams. He has written that the πίστις Χριστοῦ formulation designates something "prior to" and "distinguishable from the believer's faith," but for those baptized "into Christ," it can become their own.[106] According to Williams, Christ is for Paul both the "exemplar" and "creator" of faith, and faith is a "life-stance" that is "available as a real human possibility in the last days." "Christians are those persons who exploit this possibility by living 'in Christ,' joining him, as it were, and adopting his life-stance as their own."[107] But if faith is a "possibility" that is available, rather than a present reality, for those "in Christ," the charge of faith as a good work applies. It is something that one must obtain. Moreover, following the line of reasoning proposed, it would finally be the faith of the believer — or the quality of it — that is referred to in the passages being discussed. That becomes all the more apparent when Williams writes: "*Pistis Christou* is that faith which is characteristic of believers because

---

106. S. Williams, "Again *Pistis Christou,* 443.
107. S. Williams, "Again *Pistis Christou,* 447.

they are 'in Christ.'"[108] It is finally, then, the believer's faith that Paul speaks about in the contested passages.

Third, if the faith of the believer corresponds to that of Christ's own, or becomes like his, what ongoing significance does Christ himself have beyond his death upon the cross, his ultimate act of faithfulness? Does he not become a "transitory figure, no longer needed once we too have achieved such a 'faith'"?[109] For Paul that would be impossible. According to him, Christ is the risen and living Lord, whose presence in the Spirit continues (2 Cor 3:17-18; cf. Rom 8:9; Phil 1:19), who intercedes for us (Rom 8:34), and in whom believers place their trust for salvation. While it may be true that, for Paul, faith is to be directed primarily to God,[110] he can speak of faith not only in God (Rom 4:24; 1 Thess 1:8), but also in Christ (Gal 2:16; Phil 1:29), or in the gospel (Rom 10:9; 1 Cor 15:14; Gal 3:2, 5; 1 Thess 4:14). Faith is in God, who redeems in Christ, as announced by the gospel. To believe is to trust in God, Christ, and the gospel.

Fourth, a threefold *ordo salutis* is implied in the participationist proposal that needs testing: (1) justification is a gift given on the basis of the faithfulness of Christ; (2) believers participate in Christ's faithfulness by their "answering faith" (M. Hooker), having a faith like his; and (3) salvation is the outcome. Such a scheme does not appear elsewhere in the writings of Paul. Paul seems to think in terms of "antinomies" or black-and-white. Either a person is "in" or "out" in terms of justification and salvation. One is justified and has salvation in the hearing of the gospel in faith.

Finally, one must ask how much the seven πίστις Χριστοῦ statements of Paul can bear. If it is granted that in each case Paul writes concerning the faithfulness of Christ in the work of redemption, and if that faithfulness is effective and available for the salvation of those who will participate in it, why the silence of Paul about participation? How could Paul's readers have caught all that is involved in the dynamic of salvation without some explanation — or at least some exhortation to participate in "the faith/faithfulness of Christ"?[111]

3.3.5. Faith and Justification in Other Contexts

The larger context of each of the seven uses of πίστις Χριστοῦ is justification; either the noun δικαιοσύνη or a form of the verb δικαιόω is found within the con-

---

108. S. Williams, *Galatians*, 69.

109. P. Achtemeier, "Apropos the Faith of/in Christ," 91.

110. L. T. Johnson, "Romans 3:21-26," 84; S. Williams, "Again *Pistis Christou*," 434.

111. This reserve is not shared by D. Stubbs, "The Shape of Soteriology and the *Pistis Christou* Debate," 155, who declares that combining the subjective genitive with "participation in Christ" brings "coherence to the full range of [Paul's] writings."

text. When one looks elsewhere in the letters of Paul for statements about justification apart from the disputed verses, it is clearly the faith of the believer — not the faithfulness of Christ — that is the means by which justification is appropriated. There are five things to observe. (1) Paul links the justification of the believer with the latter's faith, using either the noun πίστις (Rom 1:17; 3:28, 30; 4:5, 9, 11, 13; 5:1; 9:30-33; 10:6; Gal 3:8, 11, 24; cf. Gal 5:5; Phil 3:9b) or forms of the verb πιστεύω (Rom 10:4, 10).[112] (2) He uses ἐκ πίστεως with forms of the verb δικαιόω in contexts — once again, apart from the disputed verses — where he speaks of the faith of the believer (Rom 3:30; 5:1; Gal 3:8, 24) in justification. (3) He speaks of hearing and trusting the gospel as the saving event (Rom 1:16; 10:9-17; 1 Cor 1:18-21; 1 Thess 2:4). (4) He uses Abraham as an example and precedent of one who was justified (reckoned as righteous) by faith (Rom 4:3, 11, 22; Gal 3:9). (5) He quotes Habakkuk 2:4 in two of his letters to establish that justification is by faith (Rom 1:17; Gal 3:11).

To be sure, the last point is contested by some who favor the subjective genitive reading. They contend that Paul understands Habakkuk 2:4 in those two letters as messianic and consequently interpret the term ὁ δίκαιος as referring to Christ rather than to the believer.[113] In addition, the phrase ἐκ πίστεως in Romans 1:17 is then regarded as referring to the faithfulness of Christ.[114] But the messianic interpretation is unconvincing. The Greek phrase ἐκ πίστεως is used frequently by Paul, and leaving aside the contested passages (Rom 1:17; 3:26; 4:16; Gal 2:16; 3:11, 22), it is most often used in passages concerning justification, and in those it refers consistently to the faith of the believer (Rom 3:30; 5:1; 9:30, 32; 10:6; Gal 3:8, 24) — which is also true of other passages where justification is not being discussed (Rom 14:23; Gal 3:12; 5:5). Moreover, at Romans 1:16-17 Paul declares that the gospel is the power of God for salvation to everyone who has faith, and he uses the Habakkuk quotation as a scriptural proof that life (synonymous here with salvation) is a gift given to the person of faith, and at Galatians 3:11 he asserts that no one is justified by observing the law; and the reason for that is stated clearly in the quotation from Habakkuk: life comes to the person who is righteous through faith.[115] A major Christological prob-

---

112. H.-S. Choi, "ΠΙΣΤΙΣ in Galatians 5:5-6," 467-90, seeks to maintain that the word πίστις in Gal 5:5-6 refers to the "faithfulness of Christ." But to arrive there he has to assert that Χριστοῦ is implied after πίστις (and as a subjective genitive), that Paul abbreviates often after his use of the latter word (n. 2, p. 467), and to oppose "nearly all commentators" on 5:5 and "virtually all commentators" on 5:6 (p. 470).

113. L. T. Johnson, "Romans 3:21-26," 90; R. Hays, *The Faith of Jesus Christ*, 132-41, 279-81, *et passim*; I. Wallis, *The Faith of Jesus Christ*, 111; and D. Campbell, "Romans 1:17," 280-85.

114. D. Campbell, "Romans 1:17," 267, 280-81.

115. For critique of the messianic interpretation on other grounds, cf. John W. Taylor, "From Faith to Faith," 337-41.

lem with adopting the messianic interpretation is that one must also ask whether it would have been likely for Paul to be saying by means of the scriptural quotation that Jesus was or became righteous on the basis of his faith (i.e., that, like Abraham, Christ believed God, and it was reckoned to him as righteousness).[116] In order to avoid that, but to maintain the Christological interpretation, one has to opt for the translation "the Righteous One through faithfulness [unto death] shall live"[117] (or something similar). But a translation along those lines (with "through faithfulness" modifying "shall live") is not self-evident; on this, see our exegesis of Romans 1:17 (concluding that the verse should be translated: "The one who is righteous by faith will live").[118] In any case, in light of the passages cited here having to do with justification by faith, in which the faith language concerns the faith of the believer, it is difficult to conclude that the seven passages under discussion — also having to do with faith and justification — refer to the faithfulness of Jesus rather than that of the believer.

3.3.6. The Earliest Interpreters of Paul

The way that Paul was understood by his earliest interpreters is important for the discussion, and those understandings support the objective genitive interpretation. The author of Ephesians, echoing Paul, writes: "For by grace you have been saved through faith (διὰ πίστεως), and this is not your own doing; it is the gift of God — not the result of works, so that no one may boast" (2:8-9). It is not likely that the term πίστις in this instance refers to the "faithfulness" of Christ; it is much more likely to refer to the "faith" of the believer. Moreover, the statement that all is "the gift of God" "corrects a possible misunderstanding of 'faith' as the meritorious virtue of faithfulness."[119]

Another early interpreter of Paul is the author of the Letter of James. The author asserts that "faith by itself, if it has no works, is dead" (2:17; cf. 2:36). He goes on to make his point, speaking of the importance of good works, and con-

---

116. As J. L. Martyn, *Galatians*, 313, has put it: "It seems unlikely that Paul speaks here of the rectification of Christ himself." Cf. also B. Byrne, *Romans*, 61.

117. D. Campbell, "False Presuppositions," 714. Cf. L. T. Johnson, "Romans 3:21-26," 90.

118. Interpreters disagree on this matter. The phrase ἐκ πίστεως modifies ὁ δίκαιος, according to C. Cranfield, *Romans*, 87, 102, and J. L. Martyn, *Galatians*, 307, 313; it modifies the verb ζήσεται according to J. Fitzmyer, *Romans*, 265, and R. Hays, *The Faith of Jesus Christ*, 134. J. Dunn, *Romans*, 45-46, 48, contends for deliberate ambiguity on Paul's part, but in his translation (p. 37) the phrase modifies ὁ δίκαιος.

119. J. Muddiman, *Ephesians*, 111; cf. also M. Barth, *Ephesians*, 1:224-25; and A. Lincoln, *Ephesians*, 111.

cludes with the affirmation that "a person is justified by works and not by faith alone" (2:24). The author opposes an interpretation of Paul, not necessarily with the letters of Paul at hand,[120] and it is clear that, for him, the Pauline tradition spoke of justification by faith on the part of the believer, not justification by the faithfulness of Christ.

3.3.7. Greek Patristic Writers

The question has been raised how other early Christian interpreters, especially those whose primary language was Greek, interpreted the πίστις Χριστοῦ phrase. Reference has been made already to the interpretation of Galatians 3:26 by a scribe responsible for 𝔓⁴⁶, who rendered the verse in such a way that the objective genitive is most likely meant. When the exegetical works of early Greek-speaking writers are surveyed, the evidence points primarily (but not exclusively) in one direction, and that is that writers routinely understood the formulation as an objective genitive.[121] That is true in commentaries by Origen (d. A.D. 254),[122] Apollinaris of Laodicea (A.D. 310-92),[123] and Gennadius of Constantinople (d. A.D. 471) on Romans,[124] a commentary by Chrysostom (d. A.D. 407) on Galatians,[125] and other writings.[126] There are, however, two no-

---

120. M. Dibelius and H. Greeven, *James,* 174-80.

121. Cf. the essay by R. Harrisville, "ΠΙΣΤΙΣ ΧΡΙΣΤΟΥ," 233-41, from which some of the texts cited here are taken. R. Hays, *The Faith of Jesus Christ,* il, contests three of the texts cited by Harrisville (not effectively, however), but grants that other texts cited support the objective genitive. Although I. Wallis, *The Faith of Jesus Christ,* 175-212, surveys patristic texts relevant for his thesis, he does not deal with patristic exegesis of the biblical texts, and some of the texts cited (pp. 187, 188, 190, 191, 192) actually appear to support the objective genitive rendering.

122. Origen, *Comm. Rom* (on Rom 3:21-26), *PG* 14:941.

123. Greek text in *Pauluskommentare aus der griechischen Kirche: Aus Katenenhandschriften gesammelt und herausgegeben,* ed. Karl Staab, 2d ed. (NTAbh 15. Münster: Aschendorff, 1984), 61.

124. Greek text in *Pauluskommentare aus der griechischen Kirche: Aus Katenenhandschriften gesammelt und herausgegeben,* 362.

125. John Chrysostom, *Comm. Gal* (on Gal 3:26), *PG* 61:656.

126. John Chrysostom, *Comm. Phil* (on Phil 3:9), *PG* 62:266; idem, *De incomprehensibilite dei natura,* Homily 2 (l. 419); text in Jean Chrysostome, *Sur l'incompréhensibilité de dieu,* SC 28, 2d ed., ed. Robert Flacelière (Paris: Editions du Cerf, 1970), 162; *Acts of Peter* 30.1; text in *Les Actes de Pierre,* ed. Leon Vouaux (Paris: Librairie Letouzey & Ané, 1913), 398; Origen, *Selecta in Psalmos* (on Ps 17:24), *PG* 12:1233; idem (on Ps 39), *PG* 12:1409; additional texts in Origen from *TLG* include *Commentarii in evangelium Joannis* 2.16.115.3 and *Canticum canticorum* 193.28. Latin authors who affirm the objective genitive when commenting on Rom 3:21-26 include Ambrosiaster (Rome, writing between 366 and 384), *Commentary on Paul's Epistles* on Rom 3:22 and 26; quoted in Ambrosiaster, *Ambrosiastri Qui Dicitur Commentarius in Epistulas*

table exceptions. Once, among the Apostolic Fathers, Ignatius (d. ca. A.D. 117) uses the expression ἐν τῇ αὐτοῦ πίστει ("in his faith"), referring to the faith of Jesus,[127] and on one occasion Hippolytus (ca. A.D. 170-236) uses the subjective genitive ('Ἰησοῦ Χριστοῦ πίστιν, "[the] faith of Jesus Christ").[128] But the objective genitive usage is more common. It is simply not accurate to say that the objective genitive reading is an innovation from the Reformation era.[129]

The point has sometimes been made in favor of the subjective genitive reading that other ancient versions (Syriac, Latin, and Coptic) render the passages under consideration in such a way that they mean "the faith" or "faithfulness of Christ."[130] Yet it must be said that the evidence is not conclusive, since the translators may have rendered the phrase in a wooden, literal manner without thereby giving it an interpretation either way.[131] Moreover, since the Latin translations of the various forms of *fides Christi* use neither definite nor indefinite articles, the ambiguity is greater than that of their equivalents in Greek. The same could have been true of the translators of the KJV. Except for their translation of Romans 3:26 ("him which believeth in Jesus"), they use the preposition "of" in the other passages at stake. But that preposition has served to express an objective genitive in the history of the English language,[132] which can be demonstrated within the KJV itself. Examples include Romans 10:2, where ζῆλον θεοῦ (meaning "zeal for God") is translated as "zeal of God"; Colossians 2:12, where διὰ τῆς πίστεως τῆς ἐνεργείας τοῦ θεοῦ (meaning "through faith in the working of God") is translated as "through the faith of the operation of God"; and 2 Thessalonians 2:13, where πίστει ἀληθείας (meaning "by belief in the truth") is translated "through belief of the truth."

Paulinas, ed. Heinrich J. Vogels (CSEL 18.1; Vienna: Hoelder-Pichler-Tempsky, 1966), 81; and Pelagius, *Commentary on Romans* on Rom 3:22, 25, 26; text in *Pelagius's Commentary on St. Paul's Epistle to the Romans,* trans. Theodore de Bruyn (Oxford: Oxford University Press, 1993), 81-83. R. Harrisville, "ΠΙΣΤΙΣ ΧΡΙΣΤΟΥ," 240, cites two passages from Augustine, *De spiritu et littera* 9 and 32, in which the latter specifically rejects a subjective interpretation.

127. Ignatius, *Eph.* 20.1.

128. M. Bird and M. Whitenton, "The Faithfulness of Jesus Christ," 552-62, citing the text on p. 559. They cite other texts in the Apostolic Fathers on p. 555, but they say that their meaning is ambiguous. Actually they refer to the Christian faith, not to the faith or faithfulness of Jesus.

129. G. Howard, "Faith of Christ," 2:759, says that Martin Luther was the first translator "to render *pistis Christou* as an objective genitive"; R. Hays, *The Faith of Jesus Christ,* lii, says that the objective genitive "may be . . . a modern, or at least post-Reformation, innovation." Cf. also his phrases on p. xlvii, "commentators since the Reformation," and on p. 273 (n. 4), "the 'traditional' (since Luther) objective genitive interpretation."

130. G. Howard, "The 'Faith of Christ,'" 213; idem, "Faith of Christ," 2:759.

131. Cf. M. Hooker, "ΠΙΣΤΙΣ ΧΡΙΣΤΟΥ," 166 (n. 4); P. Pollard, "The 'Faith of Christ' in Current Discussion," 214; and R. B. Matlock, "'Even the Demons Believe,'" 305.

132. Cf. *OED* 10:714.

3.3.8. *The Dynamics of Faith*

The advocates for the subjective genitive reading of the πίστις Χριστοῦ formulation stress two points consistently: (1) that, for Paul, Christ (in his obedience) exemplified faith or faithfulness to God in his ministry and death on the cross; and (2) that, for Paul, Christians are to emulate Christ's faith and, in some way, participate in it. The problem with these twin assertions is that one looks in vain for their support once the disputed verses are set aside. There are no places where Paul speaks of Jesus as the subject of the act of believing.[133] The model of faith is Abraham (Rom 4:12, 24; Gal 3:6-9), and the model of faithfulness is God (Rom 3:3). Furthermore, "in no passage does Paul directly state that Christians should have a faith comparable or akin to the faith that Jesus possessed."[134]

3.4. Concluding Comment

Reading the πίστις Χριστοῦ passages as expressions of Paul's use of a subjective genitive has earned its place in the scholarly literature, and the force of that view is evident in the alternative readings provided in the NRSV. Debate over the formulation involves syntactical considerations, exegetical conclusions, and theological issues. The question continues to be posed whether those passages speak of Christ as the subject of faith/faithfulness and God as the object; or whether they speak of the believer as the subject of faith and Christ as the object.

The subjective genitive reading leads the reader in a direction that is appealing theologically. It underscores the humanity of Jesus as a believer; it coincides with Paul's emphasis on his obedience; it highlights the God of Israel (to whom Christ is obedient) as the major actor in redemption; and it undercuts any notion that the faith of the believer, rather than God's act in Christ, is the basis for justification.

Having said that, however, the question is the meaning of the specific passages under discussion that make use of the πίστις Χριστοῦ formulation. It can

---

133. Cf. the discussion of V. Koperski, "Meaning of *Pistis Christou*," 198-216. K. Schenck, "2 Corinthians and the Πίστις Χριστοῦ Debate," 524-37, suggests that at 2 Cor 4:13 Paul understands Jesus to be speaking in the psalm quoted ("I believed, and so I spoke," Ps 115:1 LXX), that the verse therefore speaks of the faith of Jesus, and that Paul identifies with the faith of Jesus; similarly, D. Campbell, "2 Corinthians 4:13: Evidence in Paul That Christ Believes," 337-56. Yet the emphasis is on Paul's own faith, which accords, he says, with Scripture. Cf. M. Thrall, *Second Epistle to the Corinthians*, 1:340: the quotation provides "scriptural warrant for Paul's assertion that because he believes the gospel he proclaims it." No reference to Jesus as speaker is detected either by M. Harris, *Second Epistle to the Corinthians*, 351-52.

134. D. Hay, "*Pistis* as 'Ground for Faith,'" 475.

be said in conclusion that in none of them is there a reference to God as the object of Jesus' faith. In order to adopt the subjective genitive view, one has to fill in the blank with a reference to God. Then one has to explain the relationship between Jesus' faith/faithfulness, his saving work, and the faith of the believer. Being a believer in Christ, or in the gospel, is finally insufficient, since some form of "participation" in Christ's own faith is necessary, so that one becomes like him in faith or faithfulness, for salvation. Some find that way of thinking to have been possible and present for Paul and his readers. But the discussion here leads to a different conclusion. To be sure, the objective genitive reading poses problems — otherwise there would be no debate — but it is syntactically possible and, in light of what is argued here, exegetically more adequate in discerning the theology of the letters of Paul.

BIBLIOGRAPHY

Achtemeier, Paul J. "Apropos the Faith of/in Christ: A Response to Hays and Dunn." In *Pauline Theology*, vol. 4, *Looking Back, Pressing On*, 82-92. Ed. E. Elizabeth Johnson and David M. Hay. SBLSS 4. Atlanta: Scholars Press, 1997.

Barth, Marcus. *Ephesians*. AB 34. 2 vols. Garden City: Doubleday, 1974.

————. "The Faith of the Messiah." *HeyJ* 10 (1969): 363-70.

Best, Ernest. *A Critical and Exegetical Commentary on Ephesians*. ICC. Edinburgh: T&T Clark, 1998.

Betz, Hans Dieter. *Galatians*. Hermeneia. Philadelphia: Fortress Press, 1979.

Bird, Michael F., and Preston M. Sprinkle, eds. *The Faith of Jesus Christ: Exegetical, Biblical, and Theological Studies*. Peabody: Hendrickson Publishers, 2010.

————, and Michael R. Whitenton. "The Faithfulness of Jesus Christ in Hippolytus's *De Christo et Antichristo*: Overlooked Evidence in the Πίστις Χριστοῦ Debate." *NTS* 55 (2009): 552-62.

Bockmuehl, Markus N. A. *The Epistle to the Philippians*. BNTC. Peabody: Hendrickson Publishers, 1998.

Bultmann, Rudolf. *Theology of the New Testament*. 2 vols. New York: Charles Scribner's Sons, 1951-55.

Burton, Ernest D. *A Critical and Exegetical Commentary on the Epistle to the Galatians*. ICC. Edinburgh: T&T Clark, 1921.

Campbell, Douglas A. "2 Corinthians 4:13: Evidence in Paul That Christ Believes." *JBL* 128 (2009): 337-56.

————. "False Presuppositions in the ΠΙΣΤΙΣ ΧΡΙΣΤΟΥ Debate: A Response to Brian Dodd." *JBL* 116 (1997): 713-19.

————. *The Rhetoric of Righteousness in Romans 3.21-26*. JSNTSup 65. Sheffield: Sheffield Academic Press, 1992.

————. "Romans 1:17 — A *Crux Interpretum* for the Πίστις Χριστοῦ Debate." *JBL* 113 (1994): 265-85.

————. "The Story of Jesus in Romans and Galatians." In *Narrative Dynamics in Paul: A Critical Assessment,* 97-124. Ed. Bruce W. Longenecker. Louisville: Westminster John Knox Press, 2002.

Choi, Hung-Sik. "ΠΙΣΤΙΣ in Galatians 5:5-6: Neglected Evidence for the Faithfulness of Christ." *JBL* 124 (2005): 467-90.

Cranfield, C. E. B. "On the Πίστις Χριστοῦ Question." In his *On Romans and Other New Testament Essays,* 81-97. Edinburgh: T&T Clark, 1998.

Das, A. Andrew. "Another Look at ἐὰν μή in Galatians 2:16." *JBL* 119 (2000): 529-39.

Davies, Glenn N. *Faith and Obedience in Romans: A Study in Romans 1–4.* JSNTSup 39. Sheffield: JSOT Press, 1990.

De Roo, Jacqueline C. R. "πίστις Χριστοῦ." In her *"Works of the Law" at Qumran and in Paul,* 234-45. Sheffield: Sheffield Phoenix Press, 2007.

Dibelius, Martin, and Heinrich Greeven. *James.* Hermeneia. Philadelphia: Fortress Press, 1976.

Dodd, Brian J. "Romans 1:17 — A *Crux Interpretum* for the Πίστις Χριστοῦ Debate?" *JBL* 114 (1995): 470-73.

Dognin, Paul-Dominique. "La foi du Christ dans la théologie de saint Paul." *RSPT* 89 (2005): 713-28.

Dunn, James D. G. *A Commentary on the Epistle to the Galatians.* BNTC. London: A. & C. Black, 1993.

————. "Once More, ΠΙΣΤΙΣ ΧΡΙΣΤΟΥ." In *Society of Biblical Literature 1991 Seminar Papers,* 730-44. Ed. Eugene H. Lovering. SBLSP 30. Atlanta: Scholars Press, 1991; reprinted in Richard B. Hays, *The Faith of Jesus Christ: The Narrative Substructure of Galatians 3:1–4:11,* 249-71. 2d ed. Grand Rapids: Wm. B. Eerdmans, 2002. Since the author has added an "Additional Note" to the essay in the latter volume, references in this essay are to page numbers there.

————. *The Theology of Paul the Apostle.* Grand Rapids: Wm. B. Eerdmans, 1998.

Dunnill, John. "Saved by Whose Faith? The Function of Πίστις Χριστοῦ in Pauline Theology." *Coll* 30 (1998): 3-25.

Fee, Gordon D. *Pauline Christology: An Exegetical-Theological Study.* Peabody: Hendrickson Publishers, 2007.

Foster, Paul. "The First Contribution to the πίστις Χριστοῦ Debate: A Study of Ephesians 3:12." *JSNT* 85 (2002): 75-96.

Garlington, Don. "Paul's 'Partisan ἐκ' and the Question of Justification in Galatians." *JBL* 127 (2008): 567-89.

Gaston, Lloyd. *Paul and the Torah.* Vancouver: University of British Columbia Press, 1987.

Goetchius, Eugene Van Ness. "*Pistis Iesou Christou.*" In *Lux in Lumine: Essays in Honor of W. Norman Pittenger,* 35-45. Ed. Richard A. Norris Jr. New York: Seabury Press, 1966.

Grieb, A. Katherine. *The Story of Romans: A Narrative Defense of God's Righteousness.* Louisville: Westminster John Knox, 2002.

Harris, Murray J. *The Second Epistle to the Corinthians: A Commentary on the Greek Text.* NIGTC. Grand Rapids: Wm. B. Eerdmans, 2005.

Harrisville, Roy A., III. "Before ΠΙΣΤΙΣ ΧΡΙΣΤΟΥ: The Objective Genitive as Good Greek." *NovT* 48 (2006): 353-58.

———. "ΠΙΣΤΙΣ ΧΡΙΣΤΟΥ: Witness of the Fathers." *NovT* 36 (1994): 233-41.

Hatch, W. H. P. *The Pauline Idea of Faith*. Cambridge: Harvard University Press, 1917.

Haussleiter, Johannes. "Der Glaube Jesu Christi und der christliche Glaube: Ein Beitrag zur Erklärung des Römerbriefes." *NKZ* 2 (1891): 109-45, 205-30.

Hay, David M. "Paul's Understanding of Faith as Participation." In *Paul and His Theology*, 45-76. PAST 3. Ed. Stanley E. Porter. Boston: E. J. Brill, 2006.

———. "*Pistis* as 'Ground for Faith' in Hellenized Judaism and Paul." *JBL* 108 (1989): 461-76.

Hays, Richard B. *The Faith of Jesus Christ: An Investigation of the Narrative Substructure of Galatians 3:1–4:11*. 2d ed. Grand Rapids: Wm. B. Eerdmans, 2002.

———. "ΠΙΣΤΙΣ and Pauline Theology: What Is at Stake?" In *Society of Biblical Literature 1991 Seminar Papers*, 714-29. Ed. Eugene H. Lovering. SBLSP 30. Atlanta: Scholars Press, 1991; reprinted in his *The Faith of Jesus Christ: The Narrative Substructure of Galatians 3:1–4:11*, 272-97. 2d ed. Grand Rapids: Wm. B. Eerdmans, 2002. References to this essay are to page numbers in the latter volume.

Hebert, Gabriel. "'Faithfulness' and 'Faith.'" *Theology* 58 (1955): 373-79.

Hooker, Morna D. *The Letter to the Philippians*. In *The New Interpreter's Bible*, 11:466-549. Ed. Leander E. Keck. 12 vols. Nashville: Abingdon Press, 1994-2004.

———. "ΠΙΣΤΙΣ ΧΡΙΣΤΟΥ." *NTS* 35 (1989): 321-42; reprinted in her *From Adam to Christ: Essays on Paul*, 165-86. Cambridge: Cambridge University Press, 1990. References to this essay are to page numbers in the latter volume.

Howard, George. "Faith of Christ." *ABD* 2:758-60.

———. "On the Faith of Christ." *HTR* 60 (1967): 459-65.

———. "The 'Faith of Christ.'" *ExpTim* 85 (1973/74): 212-15.

Hultgren, Arland J. *Christ and His Benefits: Christology and Redemption in the New Testament*. Philadelphia: Fortress Press, 1987.

———. "The *Pistis Christou* Formulation in Paul." *NovT* 22 (1980): 248-63.

Hunn, Debbie. "'Ἐὰν μή in Galatians 2:16: A Look at Greek Literature." *NovT* 49 (2007): 281-90.

———. "ΠΙΣΤΙΣ ΧΡΙΣΤΟΥ in Galatians 2:16: Clarification from 3:1-6." *TynB* 57 (2006): 23-33.

Johnson, Luke Timothy. "Romans 3:21-26 and the Faith of Jesus." *CBQ* 44 (1982): 77-90.

Keck, Leander E. "'Jesus' in Romans." *JBL* 108 (1989): 443-60.

———. "The Rhetoric of Righteousness in Romans 3:21-26." *JBL* 112 (1993): 717-18.

Kertelge, Karl. *"Rechtfertigung" bei Paulus*. 2d ed. Munster: Aschendorff, 1971.

Kittel, Gerhard. "πίστις Ἰησοῦ Χριστοῦ bei Paulus." *TSK* 79 (1906): 419-36.

Koperski, Veronica. "The Meaning of *Pistis Christou* in Philippians 3:9." *LS* 18 (1993): 198-216.

Lincoln, Andrew T. *Ephesians*. WBC 43. Dallas: Word Books, 1990.

Ljungman, Henrik. *Pistis: A Study of Its Presuppositions and Its Meaning in Pauline Use*. SHLL 64. Lund: Gleerup, 1964.

Lohse, Eduard Lohse. *Colossians and Philemon.* Hermeneia. Philadelphia: Fortress Press, 1971.

Longenecker, Bruce W. "Narrative Interest in the Study of Paul: Retrospective and Prospective." In *Narrative Dynamics in Paul: A Critical Assessment,* 3-16. Ed. B. W. Longenecker. Louisville: Westminster John Knox Press, 2002.

———. "Πίστις in Romans 3.25: Neglected Evidence for the 'Faithfulness of Christ'?" *NTS* 39 (1993): 478-80.

Longenecker, Richard N. *Galatians.* WBC 41. Dallas: Word Books, 1990.

Matera, Frank J. *Galatians.* SPS 9. Collegeville: Liturgical Press, 1992.

Martyn, J. Louis. *Galatians.* AB 33A. New York: Doubleday, 1997.

Matlock, R. Barry. "Detheologizing the ΠΙΣΤΙΣ ΧΡΙΣΤΟΥ Debate: Cautionary Remarks from a Lexical Semantic Perspective." *NovT* 42 (2000): 1-23.

———. "'Even the Demons Believe': Paul and Πίστις Χριστοῦ." *CBQ* 64 (2002): 300-318.

———. "PISTIS in Galatians 3.26: Neglected Evidence for 'Faith in Christ'?" *NTS* 49 (2003): 433-39.

———. "The Rhetoric of πίστις in Paul: Galatians 2.16, 3.22, Romans 3.22, and Philippians 3.9." *JSNT* 30 (2007): 173-203.

Meyer, Paul W. "Pauline Theology: A Proposal for a Pause in Its Pursuit." In his *The Word in This World: Essays in New Testament Exegesis and Theology,* 95-116. Louisville: Westminster John Knox Press, 2004.

Moule, C. F. D. "The Biblical Concept of 'Faith.'" *ExpTim* 68 (1957): 157.

———. *An Idiom-Book of New Testament Greek.* 2d ed. Cambridge: Cambridge University Press, 1959.

Muddiman, John. *A Commentary on the Epistle to the Ephesians.* BNTC. New York: Continuum, 2001.

O'Rourke, J. J. "*Pistis* in Romans." *CBQ* 35 (1973): 188-94.

Peterman, G. W. "Δικαιωθῆναι διὰ τῆς ἐκ Χριστοῦ πίστεως: Notes on a Neglected Greek Construction." NTS 56 (2010): 163-68.

Pollard, Paul. "The 'Faith of Christ' in Current Discussion." *ConJ* 23 (1997): 213-28.

Reumann, John H. P. *Philippians,* AYB 33B. New Haven: Yale University Press, 2008.

———. *"Righteousness" in the New Testament: "Justification" in the United States Lutheran–Roman Catholic Dialogue.* Philadelphia: Fortress Press, 1982.

Ridderbos, Herman. *Paul: An Outline of His Theology.* Grand Rapids: Wm. B. Eerdmans, 1975.

Robinson, D. W. B. "'Faith of Jesus Christ' — A New Testament Debate." *RTR* 29 (1970): 71-81.

Rusam, Dietrich. "Was Versteht Paulus unter der πίστις ('Ιησοῦ) Χριστοῦ (Röm 3,22.26; Gal 2,16.20; 3,22; Phil 3,9)?" *ProtoBib* 11 (2002): 47-70.

Schenck, Kenneth. "2 Corinthians and the Πίστις Χριστοῦ Debate." *CBQ* 70 (2008): 524-37.

Schlier, Heinrich. *Der Brief an die Galater.* KEKNT 7. 4th ed. Göttingen: Vandenhoeck & Ruprecht, 1965.

Schliesser, Benjamin. *Abraham's Faith in Romans 4: Paul's Concept of Faith in Light of the History of Reception of Genesis 15:6.* WUNT 2/224. Tübingen: Verlag Mohr Siebeck, 2007.

Scott, Ian W. "Common Ground? The Role of Galatians 2.16 in Paul's Argument." *NTS* 53 (2007): 425-35.

Seeley, David. "The Rhetoric of Righteousness in Romans 3:21-26." *CBQ* 55 (1993): 572-73.

Shauf, Scott. "Galatians 2.20 in Context." *NTS* 52 (2006): 86-101.

Smyth, Herbert W. *Greek Grammar.* Cambridge: Harvard University Press, 1920.

Stowers, Stanley K. "ἐκ πίστεως and διὰ τῆς πίστεως in Romans 3.30." *JBL* 108 (1989): 665-74.

Stubbs, David L. "The Shape of Soteriology and the *Pistis Christou* Debate." *SJT* 61 (2008): 137-57.

Taylor, Greer. "The Function of ΠΙΣΤΙΣ ΧΡΙΣΤΟΥ in Galatians." *JBL* 85 (1966): 58-76.

Taylor, John W. "From Faith to Faith: Romans 1:17 in the Light of Greek Idiom." *NTS* 50 (2004): 337-48.

Thrall, Margaret E. *A Critical and Exegetical Commentary on the Second Epistle to the Corinthians.* 2 vols. ICC. Edinburgh: T&T Clark, 1994-2000.

Tobin, Thomas H. *Paul's Rhetoric in Its Contexts: The Argument of Romans.* Peabody: Hendrickson Publishers, 2004.

Tonstad, Sigve. "Πίστις Χριστοῦ: Reading Paul in a New Paradigm." *AUSS* 40 (2002): 37-59.

Turner, Nigel. *Syntax.* Vol. 3 of *A Grammar of New Testament Greek* by James H. Moulton. 3 vols. Edinburgh: T&T Clark, 1908-63.

Ulrichs, Karl F. *Christusglaube: Studien zum Syntagma πίστις Χριστοῦ und zum paulinischen Verständnis von Glaube und Rechtfertigung.* WUNT 2/227. Tübingen: Mohr Siebeck, 2007.

Vanhoye, Albert. "Πίστις Χριστοῦ: Fede in Cristo o affidabilità di Cristo?" *Bib* 80 (1999): 1-21.

Wagner, Guy. "La foi de Jésus-Christ." *ETR* 59 (1984): 41-52.

Walker, William O. "Translation and Interpretation of ἐὰν μή in Galatians 2:16." *JBL* 116 (1997): 515-20.

Wallis, Ian G. *The Faith of Jesus Christ in Early Christian Traditions.* SNTSMS 84. Cambridge: Cambridge University Press, 1995.

Williams, Sam K. "Again *Pistis Christou.*" *CBQ* 49 (1987): 431-47.

————. "The 'Righteousness of God' in Romans." *JBL* 99 (1980): 241-90.

Witherington, Ben, III. *Paul's Narrative Thought World: The Tapestry of Tragedy and Triumph.* Louisville: Westminster John Knox Press, 1994.

Wright, N. T. *The New Testament and the People of God.* London: SPCK, 1992.

————. *Paul: In Fresh Perspective.* Minneapolis: Fortress Press, 2005.

Yeung, Maureen W. *Faith in Jesus and Paul.* WUNT 2/147. Tübingen: J. C. B. Mohr (Paul Siebeck), 2002.

The Imagery of Romans 3:25

At Romans 3:25 Paul writes of Christ as the one "whom God put forth as a ἱλαστήριον by his blood, to be received by faith." The meaning of the term ἱλαστήριον (*hilastērion*) is disputed. It has been translated variously, as follows:

Vulgate (fifth century): *propitiationem* (propitiation)
Luther's German New Testament (1522): *Gnadenstuhl* (mercy seat)
Tyndale (1534): "seate of mercy"
KJV (1611): "a propitiation"
ASV (1901): "a propitiation"
RSV (1946): "an expiation"
NEB (1961): "a means of expiating sin"
JB (1966): using a circumlocution, "to sacrifice his life so as to win reconciliation"
TEV (1966): "a means by which men's sins are forgiven"
NAB (1970): "a means of expiation"
NIV (1973): "a sacrifice of atonement"
NASV (1977): "a propitiation"
NKJV (1982): "a propitiation"
NRSV (1989): "a sacrifice of atonement"
REB (1989): "a means of expiation"
ESV (2001): "a propitiation"
NET (2005): "mercy seat"

4.1. Proposed Meanings

In spite of differences in wordings in this list, there are essentially three proposed meanings in the history of translation (and underlying interpretations) of major versions. These are "propitiation" (appeasing the wrath of God: Vulgate, KJV, ASV, JB, NASV, NKJV, and ESV), "expiation" (removing the offense of sin before God: RSV, NEB, NAB, and REB), and "mercy seat" (a place of atonement: Luther, Tyndale, and NET). The phrase "a sacrifice of atonement" (NIV and NRSV) leaves the matter somewhat ambiguous, but it reflects ideas of both "propitiation" and "expiation" without leaning in one way or the other. It conveys the idea that the death of Jesus was a "sacrifice" for sin (as in propitiation), but the modifier "of atonement" (or reconciliation) need not mean an appeasement.

The term ἱλαστήριον appears at only one other place in the NT (Heb 9:5). At that place it is typically translated "mercy seat," a clear allusion to the mercy seat (כַּפֹּרֶת, kappōreth) of the OT (Exod 25:17-22; Lev 16:11-17). It appears 28 times in the LXX, of which 21 instances are also references to the mercy seat (כַּפֹּרֶת, kappōreth),[1] the lid (or cover) over the ark of the covenant, which was sprinkled with blood for the sin offering on the Day of Atonement. In six of the remaining cases within the LXX the word is used to translate two other Hebrew terms: כַּפְתּוֹר (kaptôr, a "capital" on top of a pillar) at Amos 9:1 and עֲזָרָה ('ăzārâ, a "ledge") at Ezekiel 43:14 (3 times), 17, 20. One case remains in the LXX where the word occurs in a passage praising the seven brothers who died as martyrs during the persecutions of Antiochus IV Epiphanes. It is said that they became "a ransom (ἀντίψυχον) for the sin of our nation," and that God preserved Israel "through the propitiation of their death" (διὰ . . . τοῦ ἱλαστηρίου θανάτου αὐτῶν, 4 Macc 17:22).[2] Although some scholars regard this passage as most significant as background to Paul's imagery, that document originated late — perhaps not until the first century A.D. — and its influence on Paul's own thinking therefore remains questionable.[3] Moreover, the term ἱλαστήριον has to be understood in this instance as a "propitiation" or "atoning sacrifice,"[4] an

1. Exod 25:17, 18, 19, 20 (twice), 21, 22; 31:7; 35:12; 38:5, 7 (twice), 8; Lev 16:2 (twice) 13, 14 (twice), 15 (twice); Num 7:89.

2. The reading is that of Alexandrinus, and ἱλαστήριον is taken as adjectival. Sinaiticus reads τοῦ ἱλαστηρίου τοῦ θανάτου αὐτῶν (including τοῦ as a third word, which is absent in Alexandrinus), by which ἱλαστήριον is definitely a noun (so "through the expiation of their death"). The *lectio brevior* of Alexandrinus is to be preferred. Cf. Henry B. Swete, *The Old Testament in Greek according to the Septuagint*, 2 vols. (Cambridge: Cambridge University Press, 1930), 2:760; Friedrich Büchsel, "ἱλαστήριον," TDNT 3:319 (n. 7); and J. van Henten, *Maccabean Martyrs*, 152 (n. 111).

3. H. Anderson, "4 Maccabees," OTP 2:533-34, remains rather inconclusive but cites scholars who place it in the first century A.D.; G. Nickelsburg, *Jewish Literature between the Bible and the Mishnah*, 226, maintains A.D. 20-54 as the outer limits, but more likely 40-54, composed at Antioch of Syria.

4. The translation of ἱλαστήριον as "propitiation" is that of H. Anderson, "4 Maccabees," 2:563; the NRSV renders it as "atoning sacrifice."

offering to which God responds by delivering his people, rather than that which God himself accomplishes.[5]

Beyond the LXX,[6] the word appears six times in the writings of Philo, referring to the "mercy seat,"[7] and once in the writings of Josephus, where it is not clear whether it is a noun or an adjective, leaving its meaning unclear.[8] Finally, the word appears a few times in nonbiblical Greek sources. It appears in inscriptions on monuments denoting honor to the emperor or to deities (Athena and Zeus),[9] and once in a papyrus fragment probably meaning an "atoning sacrifice" (εἰλαστη[ρίο]υς θυσίας).[10]

Related terms within the NT include the verb ἱλάσκομαι ("to have mercy," Luke 18:13; "to atone for" or "to expiate," Heb 2:17) and ἱλασμός ("atonement" or "expiation," 1 John 2:2; 4:10). Clearly, these terms carry similar problems of translation.

Early Christian writers interpreted Romans 3:25 using typological exegesis, i.e., the method that discerns events or institutions in the OT as foreshadowing or prefiguring events or meanings in reference to Christ and his redemptive work. OT events or institutions are considered to be "types," "prototypes," or illustrations of what is to be fulfilled in Christ, and the latter events or meanings are the "antitypes."[11]

In the case of Romans 3:25 the term ἱλαστήριον is seen in typological exe-

---

5. K. Kertelge, *"Rechtfertigung" bei Paulus,* 57-58; J. Dunn, *Romans,* 171; J. van Henten, "Jewish Martyrdom and Jesus' Death," 153.

6. The term appears once more in the Greek translation of the OT by Symmachus (late second century A.D.) for the "ark" of Noah (Gen 6:16). It also appears in the works of patristic Greek authors when commenting on biblical texts, as indicated later in this essay.

7. Philo, *Cher.* 8.25; *Fug.* 19.100, 101; *Her.* 34.166; *Mos.* 2.20.95, 97.

8. Josephus, *Ant.* 16.182. The phrase containing the word is τοῦ δέους ἱλαστήριον μνῆμα λευκῆς πέτρας . . . κατεσκευάσατο. The term is regarded as an adjective in the following translation, in which it is said that King Herod "built a propitiatory monument (ἱλαστήριον μνῆμα) of that fright he had been in; and this of white stone"; and as a noun in the following: "and as a propitiation (ἱλαστήριον) of the terror he built . . . a memorial (μνῆμα) of white marble." The first is the translation of William Whiston, *Josephus: Complete Works* (Grand Rapids: Kregel Publications, 1960), 345; the second is the translation of Ralph Marcus, *Josephus,* 10 vols., LCL (Cambridge: Harvard University Press, 1926-65), 8:281.

9. Dio Chrysostom, *Discourses* 11.121 (honoring Athena); two inscriptions from Cos published in William R. Paton and Edward L. Hicks, *The Inscriptions of Cos* (Oxford: Clarendon Press, 1891), 126 (#81, honoring the emperor), 225-26 (#347, honoring Zeus).

10. Fayûm Papyrus 337. Text in Bernhard P. Grenfell and Arthur S. Hunt, *Fayûm Towns and Their Papyri* (London: Egypt Exploration Fund, 1900), 313.

11. For a discussion of typology, see G. von Rad, "Typological Interpretation of the Old Testament," 17-39; idem, *Old Testament Theology,* 2:319-429 (esp. pp. 329-35, 364-71); G. W. H. Lampe and K. J. Woolcombe, *Essays on Typology;* and L. Goppelt, *The Typological Interpretation of the Old Testament in the New.*

gesis to have been derived from those passages in the LXX that speak of the "mercy seat." According to the instructions given, the "mercy seat" (כַּפֹּרֶת, ἱλαστήριον) was to be made of pure gold and in the shape of a flat slab two and a half cubits long, one and a half cubits wide, and with two golden cherubim mounted upon it — one on each end (Exod 25:17-22). It was placed over the ark itself, and it was considered to be the place at which the Lord would meet the priestly representatives of the people; it was in effect the throne of the invisible God (Exod 25:22; Lev 16:2; Num 7:89).[12] It was to be located in the "most holy place" of the tabernacle (Exod 26:34). Later, after the construction of the Jerusalem Temple, the ark of the covenant (with the כַּפֹּרֶת) was placed in the "most holy place" (or "holy of holies") of the Temple (1 Kgs 8:6; 2 Chr 5:7). The typological significance of the כַּפֹּרֶת/ἱλαστήριον centers in its function within the cultus of Israel on the Day of Atonement, as prescribed in Leviticus 16. On that day the high priest is to enter into the Holy of Holies to make atonement for sins. Among his duties is that of sprinkling blood from a slain bull on the front of the כַּפֹּרֶת/ἱλαστήριον and seven times before it (16:14). Then he is to sprinkle the blood of a slain goat upon and before it (16:15). These rites, together with the sin offerings (16:11, 15), are performed to make atonement for the priest himself (16:6, 11, 17, 24), the community (16:10, 17, 24), and the Holy Place itself (16:20).[13]

According to a typological interpretation of Romans 3:25, the crucified Christ is the ἱλαστήριον "by his blood" (= his death) — the "antitype" of the OT "type" (the mercy seat on which blood is sprinkled). God has now set forth (προέθετο) this "mercy seat" publicly, visibly, and out in the open at the cross. According to the OT regulations, the mercy seat was to be located in the Holy of Holies, where no one could enter except the high priest once a year on the Day of Atonement. But according to the typological interpretation, in Christ crucified the place of atonement is brought into the midst of his people, and atonement is made once and for all.

The typological interpretation of Romans 3:25 appears widely in the works of early Greek-speaking Christian writers. These writers include Origen (A.D. 182-251), whose commentary on Romans actually exists only in Latin translation made from an earlier Greek version. In the surviving text Origen says that the background of Romans 3:25 is the OT account in which Moses is directed by God to make a *propitiatorium* (Exod 25:10-22). The term *propitiatorium* means "propitiatory" or "place of propitiation" and is used in Latin versions of the OT, including the Vulgate, to translate כַּפֹּרֶת (LXX, ἱλαστήριον).

12. Cf. M. Noth, *Exodus*, 205, and H. Gese, "The Atonement," 112-13.

13. G. von Rad, *Old Testament Theology*, 1:272, writes that the ritual in Lev 16 "shows a vast accumulation of expiatory rites." Leviticus 16 (priestly material) gives us a final form of the accumulation. The origins of the various rites connected with the Day of Atonement, however, may be very ancient. Cf. H. Ringgren, *Israelite Religion*, 173-74.

Origen called the *propitiatorium* of the OT cultus a *figura* ("figure" or "type," the term used in typological correlations within Latin texts) of what was to come, and by implication Christ is then the "antitype."[14] Besides Origen, other interpreters saw a typological correlation as well. Eusebius of Caesarea (A.D. 260-339) wrote concerning Romans 3:25 that the whole human race was in need of a "living and true expiation, of which the mercy seat (ἱλαστήριον) constructed by Moses produced a type (τύπος), and this was our Savior and Lord, the Lamb of God."[15] Theodoret (ca. A.D. 393-466) wrote concerning Romans 3:25 that "the true mercy seat (ἱλαστήριον) . . . is Christ. For he fulfills the old as a type (τύπος)."[16] And John of Damascus (ca. A.D. 700-753), when commenting on the verse, wrote, "See how [Paul] recalls things in the Old [Testament]; . . . there was, as the type (τύπος), the mercy seat (ἱλαστήριον)."[17]

The Vulgate breaks rank with the typological correlation at Romans 3:25. On the one hand, wherever כַּפֹּרֶת/ἱλαστήριον occurs in the OT for the mercy seat, the term is rendered *propitiatorium* ("propitiatory" or "place of propitiation," Exod 25:17-22; 31:7; 35:12; 37:6-9; Lev 16:2, 14-15; Num 7:89), and the same term is used at Hebrews 9:5. But at Romans 3:25 ἱλαστήριον is translated *propitiationem* ("propitiation"). Here the typological correlation has given way to the view that Christ is the one "whom God put forth as a propitiation . . . for a display of his justice" (*quem proposuit Deus propitiationem per fidem in sanguine ipsius ad ostensionem iustitiae suae*).[18]

During the Reformation era the typological interpretation was revived. Already in his lectures on Romans in 1515 Martin Luther favored *propitatorium* (instead of the Vulgate's *propitiationem*) at Romans 3:25.[19] In his translation of the NT (1522) Luther translated the term ἱλαστήριον at both Romans 3:25 and Hebrews 9:5 as *gnade stuel* (subsequently, *Gnadenstuhl*, "mercy seat").[20] In his later translation of the entire Bible (1534) Luther continued this usage and used the same term in the OT passages (Exodus, Leviticus, and Numbers). Whether Luther had knowledge of the early Christian interpreters at this point, or whether he rediscovered the linguistic and typological connections himself, is not clear. In any case, he perceived the typological correlation and translated accordingly.[21]

---

14. Origen, *Commentaria in Epistolam B. Pauli ad Romanos*, PG 14:946A-47B.

15. Eusebius, *De demonstratione evangelica* 8.2, PG 22:601D.

16. Theodoret, *Interpretatio Epistolae ad Romanos*, PG 82:84.

17. John of Damascus, *In Epistolam ad Romanos*, PG 95:465A.

18. Quoted from *Biblia Sacra: Iuxta Vulgatam Versionem*, ed. B. Fischer et al., 2 vols. (Stuttgart: Württembergische Bibelanstalt, 1969), 2:1753.

19. M. Luther, *Romans*, 32. For discussion, cf. H. Bluhm, *Luther Translator of Paul*, 100-101.

20. H. Bluhm, *Luther Translator of Paul*, 100.

21. Luther also speaks of Christ as the "mercy seat" (apparently alluding to Rom 3:25 and

Likewise, John Calvin, in his commentary on Romans (1539), allows the possibility of typology here in Paul: "There seems to be an allusion in the word ἱλαστήριον . . . to the ancient propitiatory; for he teaches us that the same thing was really exhibited in Christ, which had been previously typified."[22] Yet Calvin does not finally decide the issue, for he allows that appeasement of the Father may be the meaning (by implication, Christ would then be the "propitiation"). Finally, William Tyndale, who resided in Germany and became acquainted with Luther,[23] translated ἱλαστήριον as "seate of grace" at Romans 3:25 in his English translation of the NT in 1525. In his translation of the OT (1530) he rendered כַּפֹּרֶת as "merci seate." And in his revised translation of the NT (1534) he rendered ἱλαστήριον at Romans 3:25 as "seate of mercy."[24] But the translators of the KJV (1611) did not follow Tyndale. While they used the term "mercy seat" for the OT passages and at Hebrews 9:5, they chose "propitiation" at Romans 3:25. That is what had been provided in the Vulgate earlier (i.e., *propitiationem*). In both instances a break has been made so that the imagery is no longer that of a place of atonement but rather that of its victim.

In modern times interpreters have varied widely concerning the meaning of ἱλαστήριον at Romans 3:25. The term "mercy seat" continues in favor with some;[25] "propitiation" (or a similar concept) is preferred by others;[26] and "expi-

---

Heb 4:16; 9:5) in his Large Catechism; see *The Book of Concord*, ed. Robert Kolb and Timothy J. Wengert (Minneapolis: Fortress Press, 2000), 466.86.

22. Quoted from John Calvin, *Commentaries on the Epistle of Paul the Apostle to the Romans*, trans. and ed. John Owen (Edinburgh: Calvin Translation Society, 1849), 142.

23. H. Bluhm, *Luther Translator of Paul*, 155, has written: "The general view is that the English Protestant martyr translated directly from the Greek original and not from the Vulgate as Wicliffe and his followers had done. It is also widely held that Tyndale either was in Wittenberg himself or at least had a copy of one of Luther's earlier renderings of the NT into German before him when he worked on his translation into English."

24. *The New Testament*, trans. William Tyndale, ed. N. Hardy Wallis (Cambridge: Cambridge University Press, 1938), 323. This is the edition of 1534.

25. A. Ritschl, *Die christliche Lehre von der Rechtfertigung und Versöhnung*, 2:168-74; H. Cremer, *Biblico-Theological Lexicon of New Testament Greek*, 305-6; J. Bengel, *Gnomon of the New Testament*, 2:48-49; H. Liddon, *Romans*, 75; T. W. Manson, "ἱλαστήριον," 1-10 (esp. p. 6); F. Büchsel, "ἱλαστήριον," 3:320-23; A. Nygren, *Romans*, 156; U. Wilckens, *Römer*, 1:190-96; M. Hengel, *The Atonement*, 45; L. Goppelt, *Theology of the New Testament*, 2:95-97; B. Meyer, "The Pre-Pauline Formula," 198-208; A. Hultgren, *Paul's Gospel and Mission*, 47-80; J. Fitzmyer, *Romans*, 349-50; P. Stuhlmacher, "Recent Exegesis of Romans 3:24-26," 94-109; idem, *Romans*, 60; Jürgen Roloff, "ἱλαστήριον," *EDNT* 2:185-86; O. Hofius, "Sühne und Versöhnung," 38 (n. 18); J. Gundry Volf, "Expiation, Propitiation, Mercy Seat," 283; N. Fryer, "The Meaning and Translation of *Hilastērion*," 99-116; B. Byrne, *Romans*, 126-27, 132-33 (but he translates the term "a means of expiation"); F. Matera, *New Testament Christology*, 116; N. T. Wright, *NIB (Romans)*, 10:474-76; D. Bailey, "Jesus as the Mercy Seat" (dissertation and article); C. Talbert, *Romans*, 110-15; F. Matera, *Romans*, 94, 98-99; M. Vahrenhorst, *Kultische Sprache in den Paulusbriefen*, 321.

26. Philip Melanchthon, *Commentary on Romans* (St. Louis: Concordia Publishing

ation" (or a similar concept) is the choice of still others.[27] Of these, "propitiation" is the least satisfactory. The syntax of the clause itself speaks against it. Paul writes that God has put forth Christ as a ἱλαστήριον to *demonstrate* his righteousness, not to placate it. The clause speaks of (1) God as subject, (2) Christ as object, and (3) a divine action, and the action is expressed by an aorist verb stating that God has put forth his Son for a redemptive purpose (cf. similar forms of expression at Rom 8:3; 8:32; and Gal 4:4). Thus the emphasis is totally on divine action. There are not two stages — in which (1) God puts forth Christ, and then (2) Christ offers his life as a sacrifice — but a singular action of God. In addition to the syntactical form of expression, the concept of propitiation (appeasing God by sacrifice) is entirely foreign to the theology of Paul. When Paul refers to redemptive activity, he refers to the work of God through Christ, not to the work of Christ himself, as though the Son must prevail upon the Father for mercy. That is abundantly clear in such passages as Romans 8:3; 8:32; 2 Corinthians 5:19; and Galatians 4:4.

The substitution of "expiation" (or related concepts) for "propitiation" is an improvement, but it carries problems with it, too. There is a specificity in the language of Paul that is missing in the more abstract word "expiation," a theological construct signifying a process (as in any English word, derived from Latin, ending in "-tion"). When Paul uses the term ἱλαστήριον in this place, it is part of a double accusative construction, parallel to "whom" (ὅν), the antecedent of which is "Christ Jesus." While Paul is capable of speaking of Christ in abstract terms (1 Cor 5:7; 2 Cor 5:21), in this case he uses additional imagery associated with the mercy seat in the OT, including the reference to blood ("by his blood"), and he uses a verb (προέθετο, "set forth") that is typically used in cultic actions, in which a presentation is made before God and/or the people (Exod

---

House, 1992), 100 ("propitiator"); W. Sanday and A. Headlam, *Romans*, 88; L. Morris, "The Meaning of ἹΛΑΣΤΗΡΙΟΝ in Romans III.25," 33-43 (esp. p. 40); idem, *The Apostolic Preaching*, 167-74, and *The Cross in the New Testament*, 225-26; J. Murray, *Romans*, 1:116-17; C. Cranfield, *Romans*, 214-18; B. Witherington, *Romans*, 108-9 ("means of propitiation").

27. C. H. Dodd, "Atonement," 82-95; idem, *Romans*, 54-55; O. Michel, *Römer*, 92-93; C. K. Barrett, *Romans*, 73-74 (rejecting "propitiation," but allowing for "mercy seat"); E. Best, *Romans*, 43; W. Kümmel, *"Paresis* und *Endeixis,"* 160 ("Sühnemittel," "means of expiation"); E. Käsemann, *Romans*, 97; S. Williams, "The Meaning of Jesus' Death in Romans 3:24-26," 39; C. Breytenbach, *Versöhnung*, 166-68; G. Friedrich, *Die Verkündigung*, 60-67; J. Dunn, *Romans*, 171; N. Young, "'Hilaskesthai' and Related Words," 169-76; D. Moo, *Romans*, 231-36; K. Haacker, *Römer*, 85, 90-91 ("Sühnemittel"); W. Kraus, *Der Tod Jesu als Heiligtumsweihe*, 159, 190, 260 ("Sühneort," "place of expiation," but an eschatological sanctuary, not the mercy seat of the OT); E. Lohse, *Römer*, 135 ("Sühnopfer," "expiatory sacrifice"); C. VanLandingham, *Judgment and Justification in Early Judaism and the Apostle Paul*, 322; T. Do, "The LXX Background of ἱλαστήριον in Rom 3,25," 657 ("a means of expiating sin"). J. Ziesler, *Romans*, 112-14, favors "expiation" but allows for "mercy seat" as a possibility.

29:23; 40:23; Lev 24:8; 1 Chr 29:6, 9, 17; 2 Macc 1:8). Moreover, the term "expiation" implies that the crucified Christ is the *means* of expiating sin, but the verb used by Paul implies that the crucified Christ is the *place* at which, or the one in whom, sin is dealt with effectively by God.

The typological view is the most satisfactory. Paul says, in effect, that the crucified Christ is the one whom God has put forth to show his righteousness once and for all, and whose death was prefigured in the OT ritual at the mercy seat on the Day of Atonement. By this means God has shown forth his righteousness "at the present time" (ἐν τῷ νῦν καιρῷ, Rom 3:26). But there are objections to the typological interpretation, and these need to be discussed.

4.2. Issues concerning the Typological Interpretation

1. A major objection to the typological view is that, in the words of William Sanday and Arthur Headlam, "There is great harshness, not to say confusion, in making Christ at once priest and victim and place of sprinkling. . . . The Christian ἱλαστήριον . . . is rather the Cross."[28] Similarly, Ernst Käsemann has written that "Jesus could not easily be simultaneously the site of the offering and the sacrifice itself."[29] But this objection does not take into consideration that the subject of the sentence is God. Christ is not portrayed as a priest making a sacrifice, nor does Paul stress here the ritual of atonement and its sacrificial victim per se. His emphasis is rather upon the crucified Christ as the one in whom atonement is made, the antitype and fulfillment of the place of atonement in the OT. In the crucified Christ atonement has been made.

2. Another objection is that, according to some, the term ἱλαστήριον is actually an adjective, not a noun.[30] The first time that it appears in the OT, for example, is within a sentence reading "you shall make a mercy seat of pure gold" (ποιήσεις ἱλαστήριον ἐπίθεμα χρυσίου καθαροῦ, Exod 25:17), in which ἱλαστήριον is taken to be an adjective modifying ἐπίθεμα (*epithema*, "cover"). But this objection can be met in a couple of ways. First, in all other cases within the LXX where ἱλαστήριον is used, it stands alone. Second, it is certainly possible that, since the word ἱλαστήριον is otherwise rare, the translators of the LXX inserted the word ἐπίθεμα as an explanation for the first use of the term ἱλαστήριον, i.e., that the ἱλαστήριον was a cover or lid over the ark of the covenant.[31] Other

---

28. W. Sanday and A. Headlam, *Romans*, 88; similarly E. Lohse, *Römer*, 135; T. Söding, "Sühne durch Stellvertretung," 379-81.

29. E. Käsemann, *Romans*, 97.

30. G. Deissmann, *Bible Studies*, 125-27; W. Sanday and A. Headlam, *Romans*, 88.

31. Another possibility is that the word ἐπίθεμα was originally a marginal gloss explaining the term ἱλαστήριον, and that later on it was moved into the text of the LXX. This has been

writers (Philo and the author of Hebrews) use the term ἱλαστήριον as though it was clearly understood by their readers to refer to the mercy seat.

3. It is sometimes objected that whenever the term ἱλαστήριον appears in the OT for the mercy seat — with one exception (Exod 25:17) — it is preceded by the definite article τό ("the"), but the article is lacking in Romans 3:25.[32] But that is hardly a valid objection. Philo, for example, leaves the article out in three cases where he is speaking of the OT mercy seat, and where one might expect the article to exist: "and he [Moses] calls it the mercy seat" (καλεῖ δὲ αὐτὸ ἱλαστήριον); "on which (the ark of the covenant) there was a covering, like a lid, which is called in the sacred books the mercy seat" (ἧς ἐπίθεμα ὡσανεὶ πῶμα τὸ λεγόμενον ἐν ἱεραῖς βίβλιοις ἱλαστήριον); "and the covering (of the ark), which is called the mercy seat" (τὸ δ' ἐπίθεμα τὸ προσαγορευόμενον ἱλαστήριον).[33]

4. Some interpreters hold that the first-century readers of Romans, primarily Gentiles, would not have understood ἱλαστήριον as an allusion to the OT mercy seat.[34] Not only would the word have been obscure, but the ἱλαστήριον/ כַּפֹּרֶת — along with the rest of the ark of the covenant — was no longer to be found in the Second Temple.[35] Indeed, the suggestion has been made that the term was drawn from "everyday language."[36] But evidence that the term existed in everyday language is lacking.[37] On the contrary, the OT imagery is the most likely understanding that readers would have had, for even though the ark of the

---

suggested by T. W. Manson, "ἱλαστήριον," 3, and taken up by W. D. Davies, *Paul and Rabbinic Judaism,* 240.

32. L. Morris, "The Meaning of ἹΛΑΣΤΗΡΙΟΝ in Romans III.25," 35; E. Lohse, *Märtyer und Gottesknecht,* 151; idem, *Römer,* 134.

33. Philo, *Fug.* 19.100; *Mos.* 2.20.95, 97, respectively. The article appears when Philo is quoting a passage from the OT where it is included already (at least in the LXX, Exod 25:22), *Her.* 34.166; *Fug.* 19.101. Cf. also *Cher.* 8.25, where the article exists independently of an OT quotation.

34. G. Deissmann, *Bible Studies,* 129; W. Sanday and A. Headlam, *Romans,* 87; L. Morris, "The Meaning of ἹΛΑΣΤΗΡΙΟΝ in Romans III.25," 40-41; and C. Cranfield, *Romans,* 215.

35. S. Stowers, *A Rereading of Romans,* 210. On the disappearance of the ark of the covenant, cf. C. L. Seow, "Ark of the Covenant," *ABD* 1:390-91. Ancient Jewish literature, though post-70, contains details about the Temple and its furnishings, worship, and rites of purification that reflect pre-70 traditions. These demonstrate a familiarity with the Temple and its furnishings in the Diaspora. Cf. S. Fraade, "The Temple as a Marker of Jewish Identity before and after 70 C.E.," 237-65.

36. S. Stowers, *A Rereading of Romans,* 210 (and nn. 35 and 36 on pp. 354-55).

37. As evidence for use in "everyday language," S. Stowers (see previous note) cites the work of G. H. R. Horsley, *New Documents Illustrating Early Christianity: A Review of the Greek Inscriptions and Papyri Published in 1978* (North Ryde: Macquarie University Press, 1983), 24-26. But that offers no support for his case. Most of the discussion has to do with verb forms (ἱλάσκομαι and variants). Only once is a noun form attested (ἐξιλασμόν), and that is from the twelfth century A.D. (p. 24).

covenant and its mercy seat had been lost (perhaps with the destruction of the first Temple), the ritual of the Day of Atonement continued into the Second Temple era as though the ark and the mercy seat were still present, a stone having replaced them.[38] While Gentiles no doubt made up the majority of Christians at Rome when Paul's letter arrived, there were some of Jewish origins there, and together they would have heard the Scriptures read in worship, including the texts assigned for the Day of Atonement. Paul assumes that his readers knew of the OT and its basic contents, since he quotes from it frequently in this letter (more than in any other), draws upon narratives as though they are familiar (e.g., Rom 4:1-25), and speaks to his readers as though at least some of them know the Pentateuch (7:1). If Paul can make allusions to the OT and Jewish institutions when writing to the primarily Gentile Christians at Corinth (cf. 1 Cor 5:7; 10:1-11; 2 Cor 3:6-16), it would seem that he would be able to do so all the more while addressing the mixed community at Rome. It would not have been too much for Paul to expect that his readers would recall the mercy seat of Leviticus 16 at Romans 3:25, especially since the clause also contains the words "by his blood." Moreover, the allusions to the mercy seat in the writings of Philo and the Letter to the Hebrews (9:5) demonstrate that the term ἱλαστήριον as כַּפֹּרֶת was not lost in first-century Judaism and Christianity.

5. It has been said that Paul would not have alluded to the mercy seat at Romans 3:25 because to do so would imply supersessionism, and Paul was not a supersessionist.[39] That need not be the case any more than it does when Paul speaks of Christ as "our paschal lamb" that "has been sacrificed" (1 Cor 5:7) or repeats the eucharistic words concerning a "new covenant" established in the death of Christ (1 Cor 11:25).

Conclusion

For all its difficulties, the interpretation that is most satisfactory is that at Romans 3:25 Paul speaks of the crucified Christ as the "mercy seat," thereby drawing upon the OT imagery associated with the Day of Atonement. It has to be granted that a translation of Romans 3:25 that uses "mercy seat" for ἱλαστήριον is bound to draw objections. With the exception now of the NET, the term has not been used in English versions since the time of William Tyndale (1534). It strikes the ear as strange, and it conjures up a cultic image from the OT that seems so quaint, probably even in Paul's day. But having said that, it

---

38. T. W. Manson, "ἱλαστήριον," 6; and W. D. Davies, *Paul and Rabbinic Judaism,* 238, both citing *m. Yoma* 5.2.

39. S. Stowers, *A Rereading of Romans,* 209.

also provides a theological insight into the meaning of Christ's death that is truly profound. It is precisely in the crucified Christ that God is revealed as righteous, doing a redemptive deed. Whoever wants to see the presence and enthronement of God need look no further than upon the crucified Christ.

BIBLIOGRAPHY

Bailey, Daniel P. "Jesus as the Mercy Seat: The Semantics and Theology of Paul's Use of *Hilastērion* in Romans 3:25." Ph.D. diss., University of Cambridge, 1999.

———. "Jesus as the Mercy Seat: The Semantics and Theology of Paul's Use of *Hilastērion* in Romans 3:25." *TynBul* 51 (2000): 155-58.

Barth, Gerhard. *Der Tod Jesu Christi im Verständnis des Neuen Testaments.* Neukirchen-Vluyn: Neukirchener Verlag, 1992.

Bell, Richard H. "Sacrifice and Christology in Paul." *JTS* 53 (2002): 1-27.

Bengel, Johann A. Gnomon *of the New Testament.* Philadelphia: Perkinpine & Higgins, 1888.

Bluhm, Heinz. *Luther Translator of Paul: Studies in Romans and Galatians.* New York: Peter Lang, 1984.

Breytenbach, Cilliers. *Versöhnung: Eine Studie zur paulinischen Soteriologie.* WMANT 60. Neukirchen-Vluyn: Neukirchener Verlag, 1989.

———. "Versöhnung, Stellvertretung und Sühne: Semantische und traditionsgeschichtliche Bemerkungen am Beispiel der paulinischen Briefe." *NTS* 39 (1993): 59-79.

Büchner, Dirk. "Ἐξιλάσσασθαι: Appeasing God in the Septuagint Pentateuch." *JBL* 129 (2010): 237-60.

Campbell, Douglas A. *The Rhetoric of Righteousness in Romans 3.21-26.* JSNTSup 65. Sheffield: Sheffield Academic Press, 1992.

Carroll, John T., and Joel Green. *The Death of Jesus in Early Christianity.* Peabody: Hendrickson Publishers. 1995.

Cremer, Hermann. *Biblico-Theological Lexicon of New Testament Greek.* 3d ed. Gütersloh: G. Bertelsmann, 1900.

Davies, W. D. *Paul and Rabbinic Judaism: Some Rabbinic Elements in Pauline Theology.* 4th ed. Philadelphia: Fortress Press, 1980.

Deissmann, G. Adolf. *Bible Studies.* 2d ed. Edinburgh: T&T Clark, 1903.

———. "ἱλαστήριος and ἱλαστήριον: Eine lexikalische Studie." *ZNW* 4 (1903): 193-211.

Do, Toan J. "The LXX Background of ἱλαστήριον in Rom 3,25." In *The Letter to the Romans,* 641-57. BETL 226. Ed. Udo Schnelle. Walpole: Peeters, 2009.

Dodd, C. H. "Atonement." In his *The Bible and the Greeks,* 82-95. London: Hodder & Stoughton, 1935; reprinted (and renamed) from his earlier essay, "ΙΛΑΣΚΕΣΘΑΙ, Its Cognates, Derivatives and Synonyms in the Septuagint." *JTS* 32 (1931): 352-60.

Finlan, Stephen. *The Background and Content of Paul's Cultic Atonement Metaphors.* SBLAB 19. Atlanta: Society of Biblical Literature, 2004.

Fitzer, Gottfried. "Der Ort der Versöhnung nach Paulus: Zu der Frage des 'Sühnopfers Jesu.'" *TZ* 22 (1966): 161-83.

Fraade, Steven D. "The Temple as a Marker of Jewish Identity before and after 70 C.E.: The Role of the Holy Vessels in Rabbinic Memory and Imagination." In *Jewish Identities in Antiquity: Studies in Memory of Menahem Stern,* 237-65. Ed. Lee I. Levine and Daniel R. Schwartz. Texts and Studies in Ancient Judaism. Tübingen: Mohr Siebeck, 2009.

Frey, Jörg, and Jens Schröter, eds. *Deutung des Todes Jesu im Neuen Testament.* WUNT 181. Tübingen: J. C. B. Mohr (Paul Siebeck), 2005.

Friedrich, Gerhard. *Der Verkündigung des Todes Jesu im Neuen Testament.* BThSt 6. Neukirchen-Vluyn: Neukirchener Verlag, 1985.

Fryer, Nico S. L. "The Meaning and Translation of *Hilastērion* in Romans 3:25." *EvQ* 59 (1987): 99-116.

Gese, Hartmut. "The Atonement." In his *Essays on Biblical Theology,* 93-116. Minneapolis: Augsburg Publishing House, 1981.

Goppelt, Leonhard Goppelt. *The Typological Interpretation of the Old Testament in the New.* Grand Rapids: Wm. B. Eerdmans, 1982.

Greenwood, David. "Jesus as *Hilastērion* in Romans 3:25." *BTB* 3 (1973): 316-22.

Gundry Volf, Judith M. "Expiation, Propitiation, Mercy Seat." In *Dictionary of Paul and His Letters,* 279-84. Ed. Gerald F. Hawthorne and Ralph P. Martin. Downers Grove: InterVarsity Press, 1993.

Hengel, Martin. *The Atonement: The Origins of the Doctrine in the New Testament.* Philadelphia: Fortress Press, 1981.

Henten, Jan Willem van. "Jewish Martyrdom and Jesus' Death." In *Deutung des Todes Jesu im Neuen Testament,* 139-68. Ed. Jörg Frey and Jens Schröter. WUNT 181. Tübingen: J. C. B. Mohr (Paul Siebeck), 2005.

———. *The Maccabean Martyrs as Saviours of the Jewish People: A Study of 2 and 4 Maccabees.* JSJSup 57. Leiden: E. J. Brill, 1997.

———. "The Tradition-Historical Background of Rom. 3.25: A Search for Pagan and Jewish Parallels." In *From Jesus to John: Essays on Jesus and New Testament Christology in Honour of Marinus de Jonge,* 101-28. Ed. Martinus C. de Boer. JSNTSup 84. Sheffield: JSOT Press, 1993.

Henten, Jan Willem van, and Friedrich Avemarie. *Martyrdom and Noble Death: Selected Texts from Graeco-Roman, Jewish and Christian Antiquity.* New York: Routledge, 2002.

Hofius, Otfried. "Sühne und Versöhnung: Zum paulinischen Verständnis der Kreuztodes Jesu." In his *Paulusstudien,* 33-49. 2d ed. WUNT 51. Tübingen: J. C. B. Mohr (Paul Siebeck), 1994.

Hübner, Hans. "Rechtfertigung und Sühne bei Paulus: Eine hermeneutische und theologische Besinnung." *NTS* 39/1 (1993): 80-93.

———. "Sühne und Versöhnung: Anmerkungen zu einem umstrittenen Kapitel biblischer Theologie." *KD* 29/4 (1983): 284-305.

Hultgren, Arland J. *Paul's Gospel and Mission: The Outlook from His Letter to the Romans.* Philadelphia: Fortress Press, 1985.

Käsemann, Ernst. "The Saving Significance of the Death of Jesus in Paul." In his *Perspectives on Paul,* 32-59. Philadelphia: Fortress Press, 1971.

————. "Zum Verständnis von Röm. 3,24-26." *ZNW* 43 (1950-51): 150-54.

Kertelge, Karl. *"Rechtfertigung" bei Paulus. Studien zur Struktur and zum Bedeutungsgehalt des paulinischen Rechtfertigungsbegriffs.* NTAbh 3. Münster: Aschendorff, 1966.

Klein, Günter. "Exegetische Probleme in Römer 3,21–4,25." *EvT* 24 (1964): 676-83.

Kraus, Wolfgang. *Der Tod Jesu als Heiligtumsweihe: Eine Untersuchung zum Umfeld der Sühnevorstellung in Römer 3,25-26a.* WMANT 66. Neukirchen-Vluyn: Neukirchener Verlag, 1991.

Kümmel, Werner G. "*Paresis* und *Endeixis:* Ein Beitrag zum Verständnis der paulinischen Rechtfertigungslehre." *ZTK* 49 (1953): 154-67; ET, "Πάρεσις and ἔνδειξις: A Contribution to the Understanding of the Pauline Doctrine of Justification." In *Distinctive Protestant and Catholic Themes Reconsidered,* 1-13. Ed. Robert W. Funk. New York: Harper & Row, 1967. The German version is cited in this essay.

Lampe, G. W. H., and K. J. Woolcombe. *Essays on Typology.* SBT 22. Naperville: Alec R. Allenson, 1957.

Liddon, Henry P. *Explanatory Analysis of St. Paul's Epistle to the Romans.* 2d ed. London: Longmans, Green and Company, 1893; reprinted, Grand Rapids: Zondervan, 1961.

Lohse, Eduard. *Märtyrer und Gottesknecht: Untersuchungen zur urchristlichen Verkündigung vom Sühntod Jesu Christi.* FRLANT 64. Göttingen: Vandenhoeck & Ruprecht, 1955.

Manson, T. W. "ἱλαστήριον." *JTS* 46 (1945): 1-10.

Matera, Frank J. *New Testament Christology.* Louisville: Westminster John Knox Press, 1999.

Meyer, Ben F. "The Pre-Pauline Formula in Rom. 3.25-26a." *NTS* 29 (1983): 198-208.

Mollaun, Romuald A. *St. Paul's Concept of ΙΛΑΣΤΗΡΙΟΝ according to Rom III,25: An Historico-Exegetical Investigation.* CUANTS 4. Washington, D.C.: Catholic University of America, 1923.

Morris, Leon. *The Apostolic Preaching of the Cross.* London: Tyndale Press, 1955.

————. *The Cross in the New Testament.* Grand Rapids: Wm. B. Eerdmans, 1965.

————. "The Meaning of ΙΛΑΣΤΗΡΙΟΝ in Romans III. 25." NTS 2 (1955-56): 33-43.

Nickelsburg, George W. E. *Jewish Literature between the Bible and the Mishnah.* Philadelphia: Fortress Press, 1981.

Noth, Martin. *Exodus: A Commentary.* Philadelphia: Westminster Press, 1962.

Nygren, Anders. "Christus, der Gnadenstuhl." In *In Memoriam Ernst Lohmeyer,* 89-93. Ed. Werner Schmauch. Stuttgart: Evangelisches Verlag, 1951.

Rad, Gerhard von. *Old Testament Theology.* 2 vols. New York: Harper & Row, 1962-65.

————. "Typological Interpretation of the Old Testament." In *Essays on Old Testament Hermeneutics,* 17-39. Ed. Claus Westermann. Richmond: John Knox Press, 1963.

Ringgren, Helmer. *Israelite Religion.* Philadelphia: Fortress Press, 1966.

Ritschl, Albrecht. *Die christliche Lehre von der Rechtfertigung und Versöhnung.* 4th ed. 3 vols. Bonn: Marcus & Weber, 1995-2003.

Söding, Thomas. "Sühne durch Stellvertretung. Zur zentralen Deutung des Todes Jesu im Römerbrief." In *Deutung des Todes Jesu im Neuen Testament,* 375-96. Ed. Jörg Frey and Jens Schröter. WUNT 181. Tübingen: J. C. B. Mohr (Paul Siebeck), 2005.

Stanley, David M. "The Atonement as a Manifestation of God's Justice." In his *Christ's Res-*

urrection in Pauline Soteriology, 166-71. AnBib 13. Rome: Pontifical Biblical Institute Press, 1961.

Stökl, Daniel Ben Ezra. *The Impact of Yom Kippur on Early Christianity: The Day of Atonement from Second Temple Judaism to the Fifth Century.* WUNT 163. Tübingen: J. C. B. Mohr (Paul Siebeck), 2003.

Stowers, Stanley K. *A Rereading of Romans: Justice, Jews, and Gentiles.* New Haven: Yale University Press, 1994.

Stuhlmacher, Peter. "Recent Exegesis of Romans 3:24-26." In his *Reconciliation, Law, and Righteousness: Essays in Biblical Theology,* 94-109. Philadelphia: Fortress Press, 1986.

Thornton, T. C. G. "Propitiation or Expiation?" *ExpTim* 80 (1968-69): 53-55.

Vahrenhorst, Martin. *Kultische Sprache in den Paulusbriefen.* WUNT 230. Tübingen: Mohr-Siebeck, 2008.

VanLandingham, Chris. *Judgment and Justification in Early Judaism and the Apostle Paul.* Peabody: Henrickson Publishers, 2006.

Williams, Sam K. "The Meaning of Jesus' Death in Romans 3:24-26." In his *Jesus' Death as Saving Event: The Background and Origin of a Concept,* 5-58. HDR 2. Missoula: Scholars Press, 1975.

Young, Norman H. "'Hilaskesthai' and Related Words in the New Testament." *EvQ* 55 (1983): 169-76.

———. "The Impact of the Jewish Day of Atonement upon the New Testament." Ph.D. diss., University of Manchester, 1973.

The Text of Romans 5:1

Romans 5:1 offers the interpreter one of the most famous and most difficult problems in textual criticism. The 27th edition of the Nestle-Aland Greek NT, like its predecessors, reads: δικαιωθέντες οὖν ἐκ πίστεως εἰρήνην ἔχομεν πρὸς τὸν θεὸν διὰ τοῦ κυρίου ἡμῶν Ἰησοῦ Χριστοῦ (NRSV: "Therefore, since we are justified by faith, we have peace with God through our Lord Jesus Christ"). But an alternative reading (with the key word *italicized*) is: δικαιωθέντες οὖν ἐκ πίστεως εἰρήνην ἔχωμεν πρὸς τὸν θεὸν διὰ τοῦ κυρίου ἡμῶν Ἰησοῦ Χριστοῦ ("Therefore, since we are justified by faith, *let us have* peace with God through our Lord Jesus Christ"). The question is whether the main verb should be read as an indicative (ἔχομεν, "we have") or as a hortatory subjunctive (ἔχωμεν, "let us have").

The external evidence for the indicative (ἔχομεν) consists of the following witnesses: ℵ[1], B[2], F, G, P, Ψ, 0220, 104, 365, 1241, 1505, 1506, 1739c, 1881, 2464, *l*864, *pm*, and vgmss. The external evidence for the subjunctive (ἔχωμεν) consists of ℵ*, A, B*, C, D, K, L, 33, 81, 630, 1139*, *pm*, lat, bo, and Marcion. The former, it should be pointed out, is supported by correctors to ℵ and B and later texts of all text types. But clearly the latter has greater support, including (1) the early Alexandrians (ℵ, B, A, and C), (2) the D text (Western) independently, (3) the early Latin versions (Western), (4) Marcion (Western), and (5) the Bohairic texts (Alexandrian). The fact that both early Alexandrian and early Western text types support it is very strong evidence in favor of the variant.

Although there is no debate concerning the superiority of the witnesses for the subjunctive, interpreters have often opted for the indicative as the preferred reading, as stated in the companion volume to the Nestle-Aland and UBS Greek New Testaments:

> Although the subjunctive . . . has far better external support . . . the internal evidence must here take precedence. . . . Paul is not exhorting but stating

facts. . . . Since the difference in pronunciation between o and ω . . . was almost nonexistent, when Paul dictated ἔχομεν, Tertius . . . may have written down ἔχωμεν.[1]

With few exceptions,[2] the indicative is favored by most commentaries and studies on Romans.[3] And it is the textual basis for most modern English versions that read "we have peace" or a similar expression (e.g., RSV, NIV, NAB, TEV, ESV, NET, and NRSV). There are a couple of exceptions, however. The Moffatt translation reads "let us enjoy the peace," and the NEB has "let us continue at peace."

It is surely possible that a mistake in hearing occurred, in which Tertius should have heard Paul say ἔχομεν but wrote ἔχωμεν at this place. That such a mistake could happen easily can be confirmed by a comparison of the works of later scribes who apparently did not always distinguish between the letters o and ω. A study of verb forms ending in both -ομεν and -ωμεν in the early witnesses (papyri and uncials) throughout the Greek NT has been conducted by Ian Moir.[4] He sought to answer the question whether there are instances in which the indicative form of the verb is altered to the subjunctive form and vice versa. But the results are not conclusive. Although some alterations do appear, they are very few.

One can get the impression, based on the work of major interpreters and the major English versions in use today, that the issue is all but settled in favor of the indicative, but that is actually not so. Early on, the editors of the Westcott-Hort edition of the Greek New Testament wrote that the indicative is not well attested,[5] and their edition of the Greek New Testament has the sub-

---

1. B. Metzger, *TCGNT*, 452. Cf. similar conclusions by K. Aland and B. Aland, *The Text of the New Testament*, 286: "The external criteria yield no certainty here, so that internal criteria become determinative. From the context of Rom 5, as well as from Pauline theology generally, we believe that only the indicative ἔχομεν is possible for Rom 5:1."

2. J. B. Lightfoot, *Notes on Epistles of St. Paul from Unpublished Commentaries*, 284; W. Sanday and A. Headlam, *Romans*, 120; J. Murray, *Romans*, 1:158-59 (n. 1); R. Lenski, *The Interpretation of St. Paul's Epistle to the Romans*, 333-34; O. Kuss, *Römer*, 1:201-2; M.-J. Lagrange, *Romains*, 100-101 (n. 1); W. Schmithals, *Römer*, 149, 154; S. Porter, "The Argument of Romans 5," 662-65; G. Fee, *God's Empowering Presence*, 495-96 (n. 66); and R. Jewett, *Romans*, 344.

3. M. Luther, *Romans*, 43 (having altered *habeamus* ["let us have"] in his Latin text to *habemus* ["we have"]); C. K. Barrett, *Romans*, 95-96; E. Käsemann, *Romans*, 132-33; U. Wilckens, *Römer*, 1:288-89; H. Schlier, *Römer*, 140; C. Cranfield, *Romans*, 257; J. Fitzmyer, *Romans*, 395; P. Stuhlmacher, *Romans*, 79; J. Dunn, *Romans*, 245; D. Moo, *Romans*, 295-96 (n. 17); B. Byrne, *Romans*, 169-70; T. Schreiner, *Romans*, 258; L. Keck, *Romans*, 135; M. Holmes, "Reasoned Eclecticism," 188-90; S. Gathercole, *Where Is Boasting?* 255-56; and F. Matera, *Romans*, 125-26.

4. I. Moir, "Orthography and Theology," 179-83.

5. Brooke F. Westcott and Fenton J. A. Hort, eds., *The New Testament in the Original Greek: Introduction and Appendix* (New York: Harper & Brothers, 1882), 309.

junctive form of the verb.[6] That is also the case with the Tasker edition,[7] in which it is maintained that not only is the subjunctive better attested but that it "carries with it the understanding of the repeated καυχώμεθα, in verses 2 and 3, as subjunctives rather than indicatives, giving a series of three hortative clauses."[8] C. F. D. Moule has suggested: "let us enjoy the possession of peace."[9]

In working toward a conclusion on the matter, there are three items to consider related to syntax.

1. The phrase πρὸς τὸν θεόν. English versions generally translate the preposition πρός as "with" (so "we have peace *with* God"). While that is possible, it is more natural to translate the preposition πρός followed by the accusative as "in reference to,"[10] which works very well *ad sensum* in the present context. That would mean that the believer, being justified, should be at peace in reference to, toward God, laying down any residual hostility. As a translation, however, "peace with God" is appropriate.

2. Some interpreters hold that the words "through our Lord Jesus Christ" fit better with the indicative.[11] Accordingly, it makes more sense for Paul to have said that, being justified by faith, "we have peace with God through our Lord Jesus Christ" rather than "let us have peace with God through our Lord Jesus Christ." Peace with God is thus mediated to us through Christ. But that is not a decisive argument. The phrase διὰ τοῦ κυρίου ἡμῶν Ἰησοῦ Χριστοῦ (or διὰ Ἰησοῦ Χριστοῦ τοῦ κυρίου ἡμῶν) appears eight times in Paul's letters (Rom 5:1, 11, 21; 7:25; 15:30; 1 Cor 1:10; 15:57; 1 Thess 5:9). Romans 5:21; 1 Corinthians 15:57; and 1 Thessalonians 5:9 are clearly instances where the phrase signifies mediation from God through Christ to us. But Romans 5:11 and 7:25 are cases where it refers to mediation from us through Christ to God. It is plausible, therefore, to render Romans 5:1-2 as: "let us have peace in reference to God through our Lord Jesus Christ, through whom we have indeed [καί, not reflected in RSV, NRSV] obtained access to this grace" — i.e., through the mediation he has provided us toward God. That such a manner of expression is possible for Paul — by which Christ is the mediator from us toward God — is

6. Brooke F. Westcott and Fenton J. A. Hort, eds., *The New Testament in the Original Greek* (New York: Macmillan, 1881), 358.

7. R. V. G. Tasker, ed., *The Greek New Testament* (Oxford: Oxford University Press, 1964), 242. This edition of the Greek NT was the basis for the NEB.

8. R. V. G. Tasker, ed., *The Greek New Testament*, 434.

9. C. F. D. Moule, *Idiom-Book of New Testament Greek*, 2d ed. (Cambridge: Cambridge University Press, 1960), 15.

10. LSJ 1498 (πρός, C, III, 2); BDAG 875 (πρός, 3, e, α), citing Matt 19:8; Mark 10:5; 12:12; Luke 20:19; Rom 10:21, etc.; BDF 124 (§239 [6]), citing Matt 27:4; John 21:22, 23.

11. J. Fitzmyer, *Romans*, 396; T. Schreiner, *Romans*, 258; S. Gathercole, *Where Is Boasting?* 255-56.

confirmed by what he says elsewhere, using both prepositional phrases at stake in Romans 5:1 (διὰ τοῦ Χριστοῦ and πρὸς τὸν θεόν). That is at 2 Corinthians 3:4: "Such is the confidence that we have through Christ toward God (διὰ τοῦ Χριστοῦ πρὸς τὸν θεόν)."

3. It has been pointed out that, apart from 3:8 (where Paul quotes his opponents), and setting aside the verbs in 5:1-3 (taking καυχώμεθα as indicative, "we boast"), there are no hortatory subjunctives in Romans 1–9.[12] While that is true, it is necessary to allow Paul freedom in composition. He makes a major shift at 5:1. It is plausible that in consequence of what he has said in 3:21–4:25, he now sets out on an exhortation at 5:1 and following.

Clearly the indicative enjoys the greatest amount of support among commentators — almost universally. Yet the hortatory subjunctive has outstanding support on external grounds. The verb is followed by πρὸς τὸν θεόν, "in reference to God" or "with God." Therefore it makes good sense as a "light exhortation"[13] or bid (as in "let us pray"), rather than as a command. Paul calls upon his readers: "let us have peace in reference to God" or "let us be at peace with God." The problem is not with God (who is at peace with us), but with us! Since we are justified by faith (and have nothing to fear from God), let us be at peace with God. The hortatory subjunctive calls upon the hearer or reader "to possess what is; it does not call into question what is."[14]

That such a reading is not so unusual can be seen by recalling what Origen (ca. 185-254) said in regard to the passage: "By these words [Paul] is very openly inviting the one who has grasped what it means to be justified by faith and not by works to 'the peace of God which passes all understanding.'" He goes on to cite 2 Corinthians 5:20 ("we entreat you on behalf of Christ, be reconciled to God") as a similar invitation from the apostle.[15]

BIBLIOGRAPHY

Aland, Kurt, and Barbara Aland. *The Text of the New Testament: An Introduction to the Critical Editions and to the Theory and Practice of Modern Textual Criticism.* 2d ed. Grand Rapids: Wm. B. Eerdmans, 1989.

Fee, Gordon D. *God's Empowering Presence: The Holy Spirit in the Letters of Paul.* Peabody: Hendrickson Publishers, 1994.

12. M. Holmes, "Reasoned Eclecticism," 190-91 (n. 9).

13. Such is the term used by W. Sanday and A. Headlam, *Romans,* 120.

14. S. Porter, "The Argument of Romans 5," 664.

15. Origen, *Commentarii in Epistulam ad Romanos* 4.8.1; quoted from Origen, *Commentary on the Epistle to the Romans: Books 1-5,* trans. Thomas P. Scheck, FC 103 (Washington, D.C.: Catholic University of America Press, 2001), 279.

Gathercole, Simon J. *Where Is Boasting? Early Jewish Soteriology and Paul's Response in Romans 1–5.* Grand Rapids: Wm. B. Eerdmans, 2002.

Holmes, Michael W. "Reasoned Eclecticism and the Text of Romans." In *Romans and the People of God: Essays in Honor of Gordon D. Fee on the Occasion of His 65th Birthday,* 187-202. Ed. Sven K. Soderlund and N. T. Wright. Grand Rapids: Wm. B. Eerdmans, 1999.

Lenski, Richard C. H. *The Interpretation of St. Paul's Epistle to the Romans.* Columbus: Lutheran Book Concern, 1936.

Lightfoot, Joseph B. *Notes on Epistles of St. Paul from Unpublished Commentaries.* New York: Macmillan, 1985.

Moir, Ian A. "Orthography and Theology: The Omicron-Omega Interchange in Romans 5:1 and Elsewhere." In *New Testament Textual Criticism: Its Significance for Exegesis: Essays in Honour of Bruce M. Metzger,* 179-83. Ed. Eldon J. Epp and Gordon D. Fee. New York: Oxford University Press, 1981.

Porter, Stanley E. "The Argument of Romans 5: Can a Rhetorical Question Make a Difference?" *JBL* 110 (1991): 655-77.

APPENDIX 6

The Identity of the "I" in Romans 7

Within Romans 7:7-25 Paul makes use of the first person singular many times over. The identity of that person, spoken of often with the use of the word ἐγώ ("I"), is a major issue in the study of Romans. The bibliography is lengthy, and extensive surveys can be found in various places.[1] In order to discern the meaning of Paul's use of the expression at this place in Romans, several observations should be made.

1. In spite of all the attention that the "I" deserves, the discussion in Romans 7 as a whole is more about the law than about the self.[2] That should be obvious when one considers that Paul has asserted just prior to this section that the law has authority over a person only as long as that person is alive, but that the believer has died to the law (7:1, 4), has been released from it, and lives by the guidance of the Spirit (7:6). Such assertions about the law require an elaboration in defense of the law. As a person of Jewish heritage, Paul could not leave the impression that the law of Moses was defective from the start or that it causes a person to sin, which could be concluded from what has just been said at 7:5: "our sinful passions, aroused by the law, were at work in our members in order to bear fruit for death." If that is the case, the law seems to be what triggers sin. What follows in 7:7-25 should be seen as having been

---

1. Besides the bibliography in Watson E. Mills, *Romans,* Bibliographies for Biblical Research 6 (Lewiston: Mellen Biblical Press, 1996), 68-76, substantial bibliographies are in J. Lambrecht, *The Wretched "I" and Its Liberation,* 159-65; M. Middendorf, *The "I" in the Storm,* 276-97; and B. Dodd, *Paul's Paradigmatic "I,"* 239-61. An analysis of the views of four major interpreters (K. Barth, A. Nygren, C. Cranfield, and U. Wilckens) has been made by C. Grenholm, *Romans Interpreted,* 19-31, 75-81.

2. Cf. W. Kümmel, *Römer 7 und die Bekehrung des Paulus,* 7-11, 56, 74; C. K. Barrett, *Romans,* 143; K. Stendahl, *Paul among Jews and Gentiles,* 92; G. Bornkamm, "Sin, Law and Death (Romans 7)," 88-89; S. Romanello, "Rom 7,7-25 and the Impotence of the Law," 510-30.

composed in large part as a way of heading off any false conclusions readers might draw from 7:5.

2. Paul uses the Greek pronoun for "I" (ἐγώ) in 7:7-25 eight times (twice in 7:7-13, six times in 7:14-25).[3] His use of the term should not in itself be surprising, since he uses the pronoun 58 times in his undisputed letters regarding himself.[4] But the use of it so often in the space of 19 verses, comprising over 13 percent of the total usage and in a way that appears introspective, is striking. Likewise, he uses the pronouns for "me" (μοί, ἐμοί, and μέ) 13 times in these verses (7:8, 10, 11, 13 [twice], 17, 18 [twice], 20, 21 [twice], 23, 24) out of a total of 117 times in his undisputed letters (amounting to over 11 percent of the total).[5]

3. All the verbs in 7:7-13 related to the "I" (whether the pronoun is used or not; in some cases the first person singular is enclosed within the verb ending) are in the past tense, while all in 7:14-25 are in the present tense with the exception of 7:24, which is in the future tense. One must ask whether there is significance to this or not. Strictly speaking, there is no need to assume that Paul has the same "I" in mind in these two sections.

4. In addition to the difference in verb tenses, the two sections take up and respond to different issues. The first section (7:7-13) takes up the question of 7:7: "Is the law sin?" The second (7:14-25) deals with the problem of being caught between two kinds of slavery, one under the law of God, the other under the law of sin (7:25b).

5. Although 7:13 has been designated here (and in the outline of the letter) as a conclusion to 7:7-13, it is actually a bridge to what follows. To some degree it anticipates what follows by its stress on the way sin assails the law. Yet it more clearly concludes 7:7-13 as a unit because of (1) its past reference to the self (the "I") and (2) its answer to the question whether the law brought death, a question raised in consequence of what is said in 7:9-11.

6. Paul speaks of the law of Moses differently in the two sections. In 7:7-13 the law is seen to have brought knowledge of sin; moreover, the law has been used by sin (as a power) to bring death. In 7:14-25 the law is spoken of as good and as a delight, but the self is not capable of living by its moral precepts, regardless of one's desire to do so. Moreover, it is in this portion alone that Paul speaks of the self as "of the flesh" (7:14, 18).

---

3. The six instances include use of the pronoun in 7:20a, although it appears in brackets in the Nestle-Aland text. The external evidence for inclusion or exclusion is almost equally divided.

4. The word count does not include the use of the pronoun in four OT quotations (Rom 10:19; 12:19; 14:11; 2 Cor 6:17) or the six impersonations of others in 1 Cor 1:12; 3:4.

5. Within this section Paul does not use the other pronoun for "me" (ἐμέ), which he uses 14 times otherwise in his letters. When that term is included, the total is 131, and the percentage for the various forms of "me" in 7:7-25 is 9.9.

7. The second portion of the chapter (7:14-25) builds upon what has been said in the first (7:7-13). Since the law is used by sin as an instrument leading toward death, it is powerless to bring life. Therefore, no one should rely upon the law as a means to righteousness and life.

8. The exclamation of Paul at 7:24, "Wretched man that I am! Who will rescue me from this body of death?" can be understood whether Paul is speaking of Christian or non-Christian experience earlier in the chapter. It is sometimes claimed that only a non-Christian could say such a thing, since the Christian has been delivered already. But when that claim is made, the Christological exclamation of 7:25a becomes somewhat of a problem: "But thanks be to God through Jesus Christ our Lord!"

The fact is that 7:24 can be understood whether it be the outcry of the believer or the non-believer. On the one hand, it is possible for Paul to be impersonating a conscientious non-Christian who is aware of failures to perform the good and cries out in despair. In that case the thanksgiving that follows in 7:25a is a parenthetical remark expressing the joy of the Christian believer who looks for a fleeting moment at his or her own situation over against the plight of the non-Christian. It is then followed by a resumption of describing the human situation apart from the redemptive work of God in Christ in the rest of the verse (7:25b).

On the other hand, it is possible to interpret 7:24 as the cry of a Christian who is committed to doing the good but, alas, knows that it is impossible to do it consistently. In light of that, the person goes on to give thanks for the rescue that has already been made through the redemptive work of God in Christ (7:25a). What follows in 7:25b, after the thanksgiving, is then a restatement of what has gone before, an *inclusio* that recalls what has been said at 7:14, and sums up the situation for the Christian who relies on his or her own resources apart from the redemptive work of God in Christ.

The question whether 7:24 implies the impersonation of a Christian or a non-Christian — as the debate has been framed — has to be considered in light of the larger context of the passage and with an openness to even other possibilities.

The range of possibilities suggested for the identity of the first person singular in this chapter is broad. Surveys exist that identify the various possibilities.[6] To do an adequate survey here, highlighting the nuances between authors, would require more space than is necessary, possible, or desirable. Even to categorize positions (as done here) runs the risk of leaving out nuances among the

---

6. Extensive surveys exist in J. Lambrecht, *The Wretched "I" and Its Liberation*, 59-72; and M. Middendorf, *The "I" in the Storm*, 15-51. Brief surveys appear in the commentaries by C. Cranfield, *Romans*, 340-47; J. Fitzmyer, *Romans*, 463-66; and R. Jewett, *Romans*, 441-45.

various interpreters cited. Suffice it to say that the most widely known and used proposals are that by means of the "I" the apostle Paul: (1) speaks autobiographically of his pre-Christian experience, which could typically be shared by others;[7] (2) speaks autobiographically of his experience as a Christian, which could typically be shared by others;[8] (3) relates the experience of a Gentile who seeks to live by works of the law;[9] (4) describes the experience of anyone (Jewish or Gentile) who pursues "a law-observant religion";[10] (5) speaks of the condition of the unregenerate person individually or of unregenerate humanity collectively since the fall of Adam, which has become clear in light of Christ;[11] (6) depicts the experience of Israel under the law, according to a Christian theological analysis;[12] (7) uses "speech-in-character" to describe "the Gentile majority of the Roman Christian community" indirectly;[13] or (8) uses the "I" as a rhetorical device to make a theological analysis (as a Christian) of the human situation before God apart from grace and deliverance by Christ.[14] It is possible

---

7. W. Sanday and A. Headlam, *Romans*, 186; C. H. Dodd, *Romans*, 104-8; R. Gundry, "The Moral Frustration of Paul before His Conversion," 228; J. Lambrecht, *The Wretched "I" and Its Liberation*, 90; T. Schreiner, *Romans*, 365; C. Talbert, *Romans*, 199-201. According to D. Moo, *Romans*, 431, the "I" is "Paul in solidarity with Israel."

8. Many interpreters have taken the "I" in this way, such as Augustine, *Retractationes* 1.23.1; 2.1.1 (texts in *PL* 32:620-21; 6:29-30); M. Luther, *Romans*, 327-28; J. Calvin, *Romans*, 251-75; A. Nygren, *Romans*, 296-97; C. K. Barrett, *Romans*, 143; C. Cranfield, *Romans*, 344-47 (in reference to 7:14-25 only); D. Zeller, *Römer*, 145-48; W. S. Campbell, "The Identity of ἐγώ in Romans 7:7-25," 61.

9. M. Brice, "Some Reflections on the Identity of the Ego in Romans 7:14-25," 39-47; S. Stowers, *A Rereading of Romans*, 39, 273; idem, "Romans 7.2-25 as a Speech-in-Character," 202 ("Gentiles who had associated themselves with Judaism before coming to Christ, so-called Godfearers"); R. Karris, *Galatians and Romans*, 65; A. Das, *Solving the Romans Debate*, 232. E. Wasserman, "The Death of the Soul in Romans 7," 814-15, supports the view of Stowers, but turns it in a different direction ("an immoral Gentile").

10. G. Burnett, *Paul and the Salvation of the Individual*, 212.

11. G. Bornkamm, "Sin, Law and Death (Romans 7)," 89; idem, *Paul*, 125; D. Catchpole, "Who and Where Is the 'Wretched Man' of Romans 7," 168; J. Dunn, *Romans*, 382-33; H. Lichtenberger, *Ich Adams*, 107-86; L. Keck, *Romans*, 180.

12. N. T. Wright, *NIB (Romans)*, 10:552-53, 568; J. Toews, *Romans*, 196-97.

13. T. Tobin, *Paul's Rhetoric in Its Contexts*, 237.

14. W. Kümmel, *Römer 7 und die Bekehrung des Paulus*, 127-28 *et passim*; E. Käsemann, *Romans*, 192; P. Stuhlmacher, *Romans*, 114-16. Closely associated with this is the view of R. Bultmann, "Romans 7 and the Anthropology of Paul," 147: "The situation characterized here is the general situation of man under the law and . . . as it appears to the eye of one who has been freed from the law by Christ." Cf. also J. Fitzmyer, *Romans*, 465: "unregenerate humanity faced with the Mosaic law — but as seen by a Christian"; H. Hübner, "Hermeneutics of Romans 7," 207: "the pitiable state of the nonjustified as seen by those who are already justified"; H. Betz, "The Human Being in the Antagonisms of Life according to the Apostle Paul," 574: Paul "presents himself rhetorically as an example to demonstrate an insight of self-reflection that applies

also to combine some of these, as some have done,[15] particularly if they allow at least some room for autobiographical experience at all.

In spite of all the complexities and problems with any position taken, the most adequate solution to the question of the identity of the "I" in 7:7-25 is that here Paul speaks of what it means to live under the law in order to be righteous, taking insights from his own life experience in the past under the law as paradigmatic, and seeing all from the perspective of one who is now "in Christ." His major task in this section is to walk the line between affirming the goodness and validity of the law of Moses as divine revelation given to Israel and, at the same time, to maintain that life under the law does not protect a person from being under the power of sin and its effects. It is only through death to the law by incorporation into Christ that one is ultimately free from the power of sin. By faith in Christ one shares his destiny and in the power of the Spirit can walk in newness of life.

What Paul says in the passage would have been determined in part by realities within the Christian community at Rome. In a mixed community where some believers might well continue to maintain prescriptions of the law of Moses and others do not, Paul has to maintain but also clarify various lines of thought that he has developed up to this point.[16] He has celebrated the triumph of ever-abundant grace over sin (5:20-21). He has argued forcefully, however, that that triumph should not be understood in such a way that anyone should continue in sin that grace might abound (6:1). The reason for that is that those who have been baptized into Christ have died to sin (6:2-4) and are free from its

---

to every human being. . . . It is precisely the Christian believer who has the freedom to take a courageous look at the ugly inside at its deepest level."

15. Examples include U. Wilckens, *Römer,* 2:76-78: both the unredeemed (from the Christian viewpoint) and the Christian. C. Cranfield, *Romans,* 342-47: generally of anyone without and then with the law in 7:7-13 but Christian experience plus his own in 7:14-25. G. Theissen, *Psychological Aspects of Pauline Theology,* 201: "What suggests itself most readily is to think of an 'I' that combines personal and typical traits." Later (p. 208) he writes that Paul interpreted his experience on the basis of the model of Adam. M. Middendorf, *The "I" in the Storm,* 171, 224: "Paul himself" in 7:7-11; and "a believer who strives, in accordance with God's law, to refrain from evil and to do good" in 7:14-25. B. Dodd, *Paul's Paradigmatic "I,"* 230: "The 'I' . . . incorporates elements of Adam's story, elements of Paul's experience, and is somehow intended to relate to the experience of Jewish, and perhaps, Christian, believers." E. Lohse, *Römer,* 215-16: both Christians and humanity, seen through the eyes of faith. R. Jewett, *Romans,* 442-43, combines the view that Paul speaks autobiographically of his pre-Christian life, as seen by Paul the Christian, with the rhetorical approach of "speech-in-character." Somewhat similarly, H.-K. Chang, "The Christian Life," 257-80.

16. One should not, then, think of Romans 7:7-25 as an "interlude," as claimed by R. Bultmann, "Romans 7 and the Anthropology of Paul," 153; a "digression," as asserted by C. K. Barrett, *Romans,* 131; or as "a parenthesis" and "a detour from the main road of Paul's argument," as maintained by D. Moo, *Romans,* 424.

bondage (6:14, 22). In fact, he says, believers have also been freed from bondage to life under the law, for they belong to Christ (7:4-6). Even the old sinful passions, which used the law as an instrument for opposing the will of God and led therefore to death, have no power over the believer. For the believer is out from under the law and serves God in the newness of the Spirit (7:6).

All of this could have incendiary effects at Rome. Known by reputation as an apostle who speaks of freedom from the law, it is possible for persons at Rome to conclude that Paul thinks of the law as a malevolent gift from God and that a libertine life is acceptable (cf. 3:8; 6:1, 15). If that conclusion should be drawn, the support for Paul's mission to Spain would collapse. Some theological course correction, even diplomacy, is called for. But being diplomatic cannot be thought of as the sole reason for Paul to write what he does. His claim that the law is holy and good reflected his own convictions about it, based on his upbringing in the Jewish tradition. He could not have thought otherwise. At the same time he could not for a moment, as an apostle of the crucified and risen Christ, think that observing the law of Moses brings justification. Because of sin as an active power in human life, no one should ever expect that he or she can keep the law and thereby be judged as righteous. By way of illustration, Paul says that all one has to do is think of the commandment against covetousness and how it exposes one's sinfulness (7:7-8); in referring to that commandment, Paul refers to the commandment that in some Jewish traditions was considered "the essence and origin of all sin,"[17] indeed, "the sin from which all others flow."[18] Moreover, it is because of the new life in Christ, a life lived under grace, that one is free from the terrors of final judgment and can recognize the truth about oneself. Although from the standpoint of the mind and will one may want to keep the law for righteousness, in fact the indwelling power of sin in one's life prevents one from doing so. Paul says then, in effect, "Look what experience under the law entails; let me tell you about it." He uses aspects of his own life (not in a truly autobiographical sense; see below) as an illustration, which is applicable to anyone else who would observe the law for righteousness.

There are objections to taking this approach. Two are particularly serious and must be discussed. The first is that in the entire passage (7:7-25) the subject (the "I") appears to be a very troubled person under the law. That does not cohere with Paul's own statements elsewhere about his life prior to his calling as an apostle. In those places he speaks glowingly about his life under the law, saying that, by his own estimation, he was "blameless" under it (Phil 3:6) and reveled in it to the extent that he surpassed his peers in zeal for the law (Gal 1:13-17).

---

17. J. Ziesler, *Romans*, 185.

18. J. Ziesler, "The Role of the Tenth Commandment in Romans 7," 44. As references, he lists Philo, *Spec. Leg.* 4.84-94; *Decal.* 28.142, 150-53; 33.173; *Apoc. Mos.* 19.3; *Apoc. Abr.* 24.10.

That objection is important, but it does not finally preclude the view put forth here. First, while Paul may well have thought of himself as blameless under the law prior to his call as an apostle, that does not mean that his life under the law was without struggle. In fact, the very attempt, or even success, at being "blameless" under the law could heighten one's consciousness of the law and of sin. Second, his saying that he was "blameless under the law" does not mean that he had no awareness of sin in his own life.[19] Instead, Paul simply means that, by the usual standards of his day, and within the communities he inhabited, no one could find fault with his degree and manner of observance of the law.[20] That is how he is represented in the Acts of the Apostles, when Paul speaks of himself as being "educated strictly according to our ancestral law, being zealous for God" (22:3) and having "belonged to the strictest sect of our religion and lived as a Pharisee" (26:5). Alternatively, it is possible that Philippians 3:4-6 "reflects the consciousness of the pre-Christian Paul, while Romans 7 depicts a conflict that was unconscious at the time, one of which Paul became conscious only later."[21]

The second obstacle to the view that Paul speaks in this passage about his own experience under the law as paradigmatic for anyone who seeks righteousness by way of the law is his statement: "At one time I was alive apart from the law, but when the commandment came, sin became alive, and I died" (7:9-10). It is difficult to find a place in Paul's life where one could say that he was "apart from the law." No Jew, it can be argued, would ever think of a time in his or her life when such a thing could be said. It is self-evident that one's entire life is to be devoted to the keeping of the commandments. And, once again, since Paul claims that he was considered "blameless" under the law in his earlier years, it seems impossible that he could be referring to himself as having lived at one time "apart from the law."

The expression ἔζων χωρὶς νόμου ποτέ ("at one time I was alive apart from the law"), however, need not be interpreted to mean "at one time the law had no authority over me." Instead Paul can be echoing a familiar Jewish theme of the idyllic youth who has not yet taken on the obligation of the law.[22] According to Jewish tradition, it is not until a boy is into his thirteenth year that he reaches religious and legal maturity, becoming then a "son of the commandment" (bar mitzvah). To be sure, the bar mitzvah ceremony is not documented prior to the fifteenth century, but the tradition that a boy assumes religious and

---

19. Cf. J. Espy, "Paul's 'Robust Conscience' Re-Examined," 163; T. Schreiner, Romans, 365.

20. Cf. F. Thielman, From Plight to Solution, 110; B. Dodd, Paul's Paradigmatic "I," 223.

21. G. Theissen, Psychological Aspects of Pauline Theology, 235.

22. Cf. C. H. Dodd, Romans, 110: Paul "is describing a happy childhood — happier and freer in retrospect, no doubt, than it ever really was." Cf. also W. D. Davies, Paul and Rabbinic Judaism, 24-25.

legal obligations at age 13 is from ancient times, appearing in Mishnaic and Talmudic texts.[23] A classic example is the saying attributed to Judah ben Tema (late second century):[24] "At five years old [one is fit] for the Scripture, at ten years for the Mishnah, at thirteen for [the fulfilling of] the commandments."[25] Moreover, at this place in his letter Paul is more interested in carrying forth an argument, using an illustration at hand, than in providing an accurate report about his earlier years.

The view that Paul is not being autobiographical at all in Romans 7:7-25, as various interpreters have claimed,[26] should not preclude the possibility that he is speaking autobiographically in part. One can agree that this section of his letter is not autobiographical for its own sake, in which Paul shares insights about himself to his readers at Rome. To some extent the first person referent can be called a rhetorical "stylistic form" ("Stilform")[27] or a "fictive I,"[28] or one can say that here we have "an individual painted through speech-in-character."[29] But in his discussion of life under the law as a way to righteousness, which is his main concern, Paul is able to mine insights from his own experience. If Paul is not drawing upon his own experience, "the whole tenor of the passage becomes theatrical and artificial," for the "existential anguish" of the passage is "too real to exclude personal involvement."[30]

BIBLIOGRAPHY

Aletti, Jean-Noël. "Rm 7.7-25 encoure une fois: Enjeux et propositions." *NTS* 48 (2002): 358-76.

Betz, Hans D. "The Concept of the 'Inner Human Being' (ὁ ἔσω ἄνθρωπος) in the Anthropology of Paul." *NTS* 46 (2000): 315-41.

23. Zvi Kaplan, "Bar Mitzvah, Bat Mitzvah," *EncJud* 4:243-44, citing *m. Nid.* 5.6; *b. B. Mes.* 96a. Cf. also Str-B 3:237, citing *Aboth R. Nat.* 16. Kaplan adds that, prior to the thirteenth year, a father was responsible for the deeds of his son.

24. According to R. T. Herford, *Pirke Aboth*, 145, the saying is attributed to Samuel the Small (first century A.D.) in some texts.

25. *M. Aboth* 5.21; quoted from *The Mishnah*, ed. Herbert Danby (Oxford: Oxford University Press, 1933), 458.

26. W. Kümmel, *Römer 7 und die Bekehrung des Paulus*, 7, 76-84, 117-21; E. Käsemann, *Romans*, 192; N. T. Wright, *NIB (Romans)*, 10:552-53.

27. W. Kümmel, *Römer 7 und die Bekehrung des Paulus*, 121.

28. The term is used in reference to the view of W. Kümmel by G. Theissen, *Psychological Aspects of Pauline Theology*, 191-92.

29. S. Stowers, *A Rereading of Romans*, 39.

30. W. S. Campbell, "The Identity of the ἐγώ in Romans 7:7-25," 60. Cf. also W. Sanday and A. C. Headlam, *Romans*, 186; D. Milne, "Romans 7:7-12," 12; J. Espy, "Paul's 'Robust Conscience' Re-Examined," 161-88; G. Theissen, *Psychological Aspects of Pauline Theology*, 201; idem, "Gesetz und Ich," 297-98; D. Moo, *Romans*, 427.

————. "The Human Being in the Antagonisms of Life according to the Apostle Paul." *JR* 80 (2000): 557-75.

Bornkamm, Günther. *Paul*. New York: Harper & Row, 1971; reprinted, Minneapolis: Fortress Press, 1994.

————. "Sin, Law and Death (Romans 7)." In his *Early Christian Experience*, 87-104. New York: Harper & Row, 1969.

Bultmann, Rudolf. "Romans 7 and the Anthropology of Paul." In his *Existence and Faith: Shorter Writings of Rudolf Bultmann*, 147-57. New York: Meridian Books, 1960.

Burnett, Gary W. *Paul and the Salvation of the Individual*. BIS 57. Leiden: E. J. Brill, 2001.

Campbell, William S. "The Identity of ἐγώ in Romans 7:7-25." In *Studia Biblica 1978: Sixth International Congress on Biblical Studies, Oxford, 3-7 April 1978*, 3:57-64. Ed. Elizabeth A. Livingstone. 3 vols. Sheffield: JSOT Press, 1979-80.

Catchpole, David. "Who and Where Is the 'Wretched Man' of Romans 7, and Why Is 'She' Wretched?" In *The Holy Spirit and Christian Origins: Essays in Honor of James D. G. Dunn*, 168-80. Ed. Graham N. Stanton et al. Grand Rapids: Wm. B. Eerdmans, 2004.

Chang, Hae-Kyung. "The Christian Life in a Dialectical Tension?" *NovT* 49 (2007): 257-80.

Cranfield, C. E. B. "Romans 7 Reconsidered." *ExpTim* 65 (1953-54): 221.

Das, A. Andrew. *Solving the Romans Debate*. Minneapolis: Fortress Press, 2007.

Dodd, Brian J. *Paul's Paradigmatic "I": Personal Example as Literary Strategy*. JSNTSup 177. Sheffield: Sheffield Academic Press, 1999.

Dunn, James D. G. "Rom. 7,14-25 in the Theology of Paul." *TZ* 31 (1975): 257-73; reprinted in *Essays on Apostolic Themes: Studies in Honor of Howard M. Ervin Presented to Him by Colleagues and Friends on His Sixty-Fifth Birthday*, 49-70. Ed. Paul Elbert. Peabody: Hendrickson Publishers, 1985.

Édart, Jean-Baptiste. "De la nécessité d'un sauveur. Rhétorique et théologie de Rm 7,7-25." *RB* 105 (1998): 359-96.

Engberg-Pedersen, Troels. "The Reception of Graeco-Roman Culture in the New Testament: The Case of Romans 7:7-25." In *The New Testament as Reception*, 32-57. Ed. Mogens Müller and Henrik Tronier. JSNTSup 230. New York: Sheffield Academic Press, 2002.

Espy, John M. "Paul's 'Robust Conscience' Re-examined." *NTS* 31 (1985): 161-88.

Grenholm, Cristina. *Romans Interpreted: A Comparative Analysis of the Commentaries of Barth, Nygren, Cranfield and Wilckens on Paul's Epistle to the Romans*. Acta Universitatis Upsaliensis, Studia Doctrinae Christianae Upsaliensia 30. Stockholm: Almqvist & Wiksell, 1990.

Herford, R. Travers. *Pirke Aboth*. New York: Schocken Books, 1945.

Hommel, Hildebrecht. "Das 7. Kapital des Römerbrief im Light antiker Überlieferung." *ThViat* 8 (1962): 90-116.

Hübner, Hans. "Hermeneutics of Romans 7." In *Paul and the Mosaic Law*, 207-14. Ed. James D. G. Dunn. Grand Rapids: Wm. B. Eerdmans, 2001.

Jonas, Hans. "Philosophical Meditation on the Seventh Chapter of Paul's Epistle to the Romans." In *The Future of Our Religious Past: Essays in Honour of Rudolf Bultmann*, 333-50. Ed. James M. Robinson. New York: Harper & Row, 1971.

Karris, Robert J. *Galatians and Romans*. NCBC. Collegeville: Liturgical Press, 2005.

689

Kümmel, Werner G. *Römer 7 und die Bekehrung des Paulus.* UNT 17. Leipzig: J. C. Hinrichs'sche Buchhandlung, 1929.

————. *Römer 7 und das Bild des Menschen im Neuen Testament: Zwei Studien.* TBü 53. Munich: C. Kaiser Verlag, 1974.

Kürzinger, Josef. "Der Schlussel zum Verständnis von Röm 7." *BZ* 7 (1963): 270-74.

Lambrecht, Jan. *The Wretched 'I' and Its Liberation: Paul in Romans 7 and 8.* Grand Rapids: Wm. B. Eerdmans, 1993.

Lichtenberger, Hermann. *Das Ich Adams und das Ich der Menschheit: Studien zum Menschenbild in Römer 7.* WUNT 164. Tübingen: J. C. B. Mohr (Paul Siebeck), 2004.

Marin, Brice L. "Some Reflections on the Identity of the ἐγώ in Romans 7:14-25." *SJT* 34 (1981): 39-47.

Middendorf, Michael P. *The "I" in the Storm: A Study of Romans 7.* St. Louis: Concordia Academic Press, 1997.

Milne, Douglas J. W. "Romans 7:7-12: Paul's Pre-conversion Experience." *RTR* 43 (1984): 9-17.

Moo, Douglas J. "Israel and Paul in Romans 7.7-12." *NTS* 32 (1986): 122-35.

Murariu, Cosmin. "The Characters in Romans 7,7-25: A Critique of Stanley Stowers' Thesis." In *The Letter to the Romans,* 739-53. BETL 226. Ed. Udo Schnelle. Walpole: Peeters, 2009.

Napier, Daniel. "Paul's Analysis of Sin and Torah in Romans 7:7-25." *ResQ* 44 (2002): 15-32.

Romanello, Stefano. "Rom 7,7-25 and the Impotence of the Law: A Fresh Look at a Much-Debated Topic Using Literary-Rhetorical Analysis." *Bib* 84 (2003): 510-30.

Russell, Walt. "Insights from Postmodernism's Emphasis on Interpretive Communities in the Interpretation of Romans 7." *JETS* 37 (1994): 511-27.

Schnackenberg, Rudolf. "Römer 7 in Zusammenhang des Römerbriefes." In *Jesus und Paulus: Festschrift für Werner Georg Kümmel zum 70. Geburtstag,* 283-300. Ed. E. Earle Ellis and Erich Grässer. Göttingen: Vandenhoeck & Ruprecht, 1975.

Seifrid, Mark A. "The Subject of Rom 7:14-25." *NovT* 34 (1992): 313-33.

Stendahl, Krister. "The Apostle Paul and the Introspective Conscience of the West." *HTR* 56 (1963): 199-215; reprinted in his *Paul among Jews and Gentiles and Other Essays,* 78-96. Philadelphia: Fortress Press, 1976.

Stowers, Stanley K. *A Rereading of Romans: Justice, Jews, and Gentiles.* New Haven: Yale University Press, 1994.

————. "Romans 7.2-25 as a Speech-in-Character (προσωποποιία)." In *Paul in His Hellenistic Context,* 180-202. Ed. Troels Engberg-Pedersen. Edinburgh: T&T Clark, 1994.

Theissen, Gerd. "Gesetz und Ich: Beobachtungen zur persönlichen Dimension des Römerbriefs." In *Das Gesetz im frühen Judentum und im Neuen Testament: Festschrift für Christoph Burchard zum 75. Geburtstag,* 261-85. Ed. Dieter Sänger and Matthias Konradt. NTOA 57. Göttingen: Vandenhoeck & Ruprecht, 2006.

————. *Psychological Aspects of Pauline Theology.* Edinburgh: T&T Clark, 1987.

Thielman, Frank. *From Plight to Solution: A Jewish Framework for Understanding Paul's View of the Law in Galatians and Romans.* NovTSup 61. Leiden: E. J. Brill, 1989.

Tobin, Thomas H. *Paul's Rhetoric in Its Contexts: The Argument of Romans.* Peabody: Hendrickson Publishers, 2004.

Toews, John E. *Romans.* BCBC. Scottdale: Herald Press, 2004.

Trocmé, Étienne. "From 'I' to 'We': Christian Life according to Romans, Chapter 7 and 8." *AusBR* 35 (1987): 73-76.

Trudinger, Peter. "An Autobiographical Digression? A Note on Romans 7:7-25." *ExpTim* 107 (1996): 173-74.

Voorwinde, Stephen. "Who Is the 'Wretched Man' in Romans 7:24?" *VR* 54 (1990): 11-26.

Wasserman, Emma. "The Death of the Soul in Romans 7: Revisiting Paul's Anthropology in Light of Hellenistic Moral Psychology." *JBL* 126 (2007): 793-816.

———. *The Death of the Soul in Romans 7: Sin, Death, and the Law in Light of Hellenistic Moral Psychology.* WUNT 2/256. Tübingen: Mohr-Siebeck, 2008.

Watson, Nigel M. "The Interpretation of Romans VII." *AusBR* 21 (1973): 27-39.

Ziesler, John A. "The Role of the Tenth Commandment in Romans 7." *JSNT* 33 (1988): 41-56.

The Church as the Body of Christ
in the Letters of Paul

Paul uses the image of the church as the body of Christ at Romans 12:4-5 and at 1 Corinthians 12:12-31. It is possible that the image, and even the complete phrase ("the body of Christ"), was coined by him; opinions are mixed.[1] In any case, in Paul's writings we find the term used for the first time, and it is only in the Pauline corpus that the term is used at all in the NT.

The term "body" had been used to refer to a community prior to Paul's time in Greco-Roman literature. The usage is found already in the writings of Aristotle in reference to the state, and it appears later in the writings of Philo, Dionysius of Halicarnassus, Seneca, Plutarch, and others, including many Stoics,[2] referring to a social unit, the state, or even the cosmos.[3] Yet it is not clear that the common use of "body" to refer to a sociopolitical or cosmic entity would have come naturally to Paul as a term to be used for the church. It has been suggested, therefore, that some other factor must have been at play. One possibility is that the term arose for Paul in connection with eucharistic celebrations. The eucharistic expression, "The bread that we break, is it not a sharing in the body of Christ?" (1 Cor 10:16), is followed immediately by another, and that is an ecclesiological expression: "Because there is one bread, we who are many are one body" (1 Cor 10:17). The common word for a corporate entity is therefore recalled and put to use, the argument goes, for the sake of ecclesiology, based on the eucharistic saying.[4]

---

1. That the term was coined by Paul is asserted by R. Schnackenburg, *The Church in the New Testament*, 77, and H. Conzelmann, *An Outline of the Theology of the New Testament*, 263; reservations are expressed by E. Käsemann, "The Theological Problem Presented by the Motif of the Body of Christ," 105.

2. For texts and discussion, cf. M. Lee, *Paul, the Stoics, and the Body of Christ*, 46-58.

3. For references to many texts, cf. Eduard Schweizer, "σῶμα," *TDNT* 7:1032, 1036-41, 1055.

4. H. Conzelmann, *An Outline of the Theology of the New Testament*, 262; L. Goppelt, *Theology of the New Testament*, 2:146-47.

But that is not the only possible explanation. It has also been suggested that Paul's baptismal theology was the basis for applying the concept of the body to the church. At 1 Corinthians 12:12-13 Paul says that all believers form one body, and then goes on to say that "we were all baptized into one body, . . . and we were all made to drink of one Spirit." It is by means of baptism that persons are incorporated into Christ himself and into his body, the church; and the Spirit, given to those baptized into Christ, links the baptized with Christ and with one another. It is on the basis of this passage that some interpreters have concluded that baptism was the catalyst for Paul's taking up the familiar Greco-Roman image of "the body" as a "corporate" term for the church.[5]

It is not necessary to arbitrate between these two suggestions, or even to discuss further possibilities.[6] What is certain is that the image is used by Paul to exhort his readers to realize their unity, drawing upon their own awareness of their baptismal incorporation into the one body, and reminding them of the unity that they share in partaking of the Lord's Supper. Moreover, his concept of the church as a body goes beyond those uses of "body" as a social, corporate expression in Greco-Roman traditions, in which persons constitute a body through residence in a common *polis*. For Paul, the church is "the body *of Christ.*" That is, it is not simply a body of persons who have a shared locale or interest. Nor is the phrase "of Christ" simply an identifying one. Paul employs a possessive genitive here.[7] The body is Christ's own possession. Members do not create the body. Rather, they are incorporated (a passive verb) by baptism into Christ and into his body and become subject to Christ's lordship.

There has been a long and vigorous debate about whether and to what degree the image of "the body of Christ" should be taken as a metaphor or as something more. There are those, on the one hand, who have maintained that the image is a metaphor and nothing else.[8] On the other hand, there are those who claim that it is more than that in some sense.[9] But can one be more precise?

---

5. R. Schnackenburg, *The Church in the New Testament,* 166-71; W. Kümmel, *The Theology of the New Testament,* 207-12.

6. Various scholars have traced the origins of the image to at least nine different backgrounds, according to the survey by G. Yorke, *The Church as the Body of Christ in the Pauline Corpus: A Re-examination,* 2-7.

7. C. K. Barrett, *A Commentary on the First Epistle to the Corinthians,* 292. Two interpreters who, rightly, claim that the genitive is not to be taken exclusively as a possessive but also as an explicative one (so "the body that is Christ") include R. Gundry, Sōma *in Biblical Theology,* 231, and M. Volf, *After Our Likeness,* 143.

8. E. Best, *One Body in Christ,* 98-101, 112; E. Poteat, "The Body of Christ as Metaphor or Fact," 382-83; R. Gundry, Sōma *in Biblical Theology,* 228, 234; G. Yorke, *The Church as the Body of Christ,* 7-10; M. Volf, *After Our Likeness,* 142; and D. Williams, *Paul's Metaphors,* 89.

9. J. Robinson, *The Body,* 49-51; J. Knox, "The Church *Is* Christ's Body," 62; A. Nygren, "Corpus Christi," 10; idem, *Romans,* 422; E. Käsemann, "The Theological Problem Presented by

Right away two "literal" meanings of the term must be excluded. The term refers to neither (1) the body of the earthly Jesus of Nazareth, which is no longer available to anyone; nor (2) the body of the risen Jesus, by which he appeared to his disciples in the accounts portrayed in the gospels (Luke 24:13-53; John 20:11-29), by which he will appear at his parousia (Phil 3:21), and by which he has an identity distinct from all other persons.

If the term "body" is restricted in meaning to refer to the human body (the "material frame" of a person),[10] it can be agreed that a metaphor is being employed. But the term "body" has taken on other meanings as well, even if they are subsequent to — or even derivative from — it.[11] One can speak, for example, of the main portion of an object as a "body" (e.g., the body of a letter or the body of an automobile), or one can speak in nonmetaphorical ways of heavenly bodies, a body of laws, a body of knowledge, and a "society, association, league, or fraternity."[12] These are all legitimate uses of the term in modern languages, and at least the last of them has ancient, pre-Pauline usage as well. To speak of the church as "the body of Christ" is therefore no more unusual than to speak of it as "the people of God," "the children of God," or "the household of God."[13] The image of the church as "the body of Christ," Ernst Käsemann has written, "is not a metaphorical figure of speech," for Paul asserts that "the exalted Christ really has an earthly body, and believers with their whole being are actually incorporated into it."[14] Likewise, Eduard Schweizer has written that for Paul the image "is more than a metaphor," for "Christ himself *is* the body into which all members are baptized."[15] To be sure, the term lends itself well for metaphorical purposes too, allowing for analogies to parts of the body (1 Cor 12:14-27), but those must be considered secondary. For Paul the body of Christ is first of all the eschatological community of the Spirit, the new creation, which exists already in the present world. Moreover, those incorporated into Christ share his destiny. What God has done in and through Christ's redemptive death and resurrection is theirs. As they have

---

the Motif of the Body of Christ," 104; Eduard Schweizer, "σῶμα," *EDNT* 3:324; P. Stuhlmacher, *Romans*, 191; M. Lee, *Paul, the Stoics, and the Body of Christ*, 129-38.

10. *OED* 2:354.

11. As soon as the meaning of a term is no longer simply transferred from one referent to another, used analogously, it ceases to be a metaphor. Cf. *OED* 9:67 for a definition of a metaphor: a "figure of speech in which a name or descriptive term is transferred to some object different from, but analogous to, that to which it is properly applicable."

12. *OED* 2:355.

13. Contra M. Volf, *After Our Likeness*, 142 (n. 61), who restricts the use of "body" to the human body; anything beyond that is figurative.

14. E. Käsemann, "The Theological Problem Presented by the Motif of the Body of Christ," 104.

15. E. Schweizer, "σῶμα," *EDNT* 3:324.

"died to the law through the body of Christ," so they "belong . . . to him who was raised from the dead" (Rom 7:4).

One of the features of "the body of Christ" image is that, like the word "church," it can refer to either the church universal or the local community of believers. In his own writings Paul can speak of the church as a universal entity (1 Cor 10:32; 15:9; Gal 1:13; Phil 3:6) or as a specific congregation, meaning the church in that place (Rom 16:1, 5; 1 Cor 1:2; 1 Thess 1:1). The situation is more complex in the disputed letters of Paul. In Colossians, as in the undisputed letters, the term "church" can refer to the church as universal (1:18, 24) or local (4:15-16). Within Ephesians, on the other hand, the term "church" always means the universal church (1:22; 3:10, 21; 5:23-32).

As with the term "church," so with "the body of Christ." In Paul's letters it can refer to the universal fellowship of believers in Christ. So he says that all Christians are members of the one body (1 Cor 12:13). In two specific cases it may appear at first glance that he is speaking of the congregation (alone) as the body of Christ, but that is not actually the case. In his words about participating in the Lord's Supper at Corinth, when he writes to his readers about sharing in Christ's body, he can hardly be referring to the Corinthian community alone, for he says that "we who are many are one body," even though he is himself absent (1 Cor 10:17). Another passage that appears to refer to a congregation (alone) is in Romans. When he refers to the church there as "one body" (12:4), Paul includes himself in that company, even though he is absent, and he goes on to speak of gifts of the Spirit within the body, any of which may or may not be present in any given congregation. On the other hand, when Paul speaks of the gifts of the Spirit at Corinth (1 Cor 12:14-26) and concludes with the statement "you are the body of Christ" (1 Cor 12:27) — not "*a* body of Christ" — he is referring in that instance to the local community. Likewise, when he calls upon the Corinthians to "discern the body" at their eucharistic gatherings, he is clearly referring to the local community (1 Cor 11:29). For Paul, it can be said that the local community is an expression of the one body. Putting it in a striking way, one can say that for him the body of Christ is not first of all the local congregation but the whole church; in the final analysis, the members of the body of Christ are not individual congregations but individual believers.[16] So Karl L. Schmidt has written that "the sum of the individual congregations does not produce the total community or the Church. Each community, however small, represents the total community, the Church."[17] Furthermore, he says,

---

16. E. Best, *One Body in Christ,* 113.
17. Karl L. Schmidt, "ἐκκλησία," *TDNT* 3:506.

The fact that individual congregations gradually formed larger organizations leaves an impression of development from the individual to the corporate. But we must not be dominated by this impression. What counts is that the congregation took itself to be representative of the whole Church.[18]

What is particularly striking about the NT communities of faith is that, according to the data we have, they had a sense of belonging to a fellowship that is larger than that provided by the local community. According to Acts, Christian communities arose in Palestine, Syria, Asia Minor, Rome, and elsewhere fairly quickly, and there was a sense of their belonging to a wider fellowship. So Luke speaks of "the church throughout all Judea and Galilee and Samaria" in the singular (Acts 9:31), as though there was one Palestinian church. The church at Jerusalem continued to exert leadership, and therefore to interact with other communities of faith, as long as the "pillar apostles" (Peter, James, and John) were there (Gal 2:9). But going beyond all that, and what has scarcely been noticed in studies of the church in the NT and postapostolic era is that there was a remarkable interconnectedness, a networking, between the congregations, between apostles and congregations, and between ordinary members within different congregations, as the lists of greetings in Paul's letters show. New Testament writings tell of visits by members of one community to another, the sending of financial aid from one to another, and intercessory prayer for the well-being of communities other than one's own.[19] The practice of extending hospitality is noticeably present in the writings of the NT, giving witness to "the presence of God or Christ in ordinary exchanges between human guests and hosts."[20]

The amount of documentation regarding mutual care and interchange among the communities is impressive. There are few analogies in antiquity, if any at all, to the amount of correspondence flowing about among the early Christian communities,[21] which in itself shows how members of these communities had a sense of mutual care and accountability. The correspondence includes the letters of Paul, the deutero-Pauline letters, the Catholic Epistles, the epistolary materials in other books of the NT (Acts 15:23-29; Rev 2:1–3:22), the letters of Clement, Ignatius, Barnabas, and Polycarp, and many items of correspondence quoted or referred to in the *Ecclesiastical History* of Eusebius. Gen-

18. Karl L. Schmidt, "ἐκκλησία," *TDNT* 3:535.

19. All of this originated at least by the time of Paul. Cf. E. Ellis, "Paul and His Co-Workers," 439-52, and R. J. Banks, *Paul's Idea of Community,* 48, who cites such passages as Rom 16:1; 2 Cor 8:11-14.

20. J. Koenig, *New Testament Hospitality,* 2.

21. Cf. R. Williams, "Does It Make Sense to Speak of Pre-Nicene Orthodoxy?" 12, and P. Pokorný, *The Genesis of Christology,* 158-60, 205-6.

erally it can be said that religious associations and cult groups in antiquity had an "inward focus," while the Christian communities had an "international scope."[22] That view concerning early Christianity can be confirmed by the sheer volume of known correspondence alone.

All this suggests that, for the NT communities of faith — to say nothing of early Christianity in general — the church consists of the totality of persons who belong to Christ at the dawn of the new age. Paul's image of the church as "the body of Christ" expresses that same viewpoint. It is an image that he uses to speak of that reality into which one is incorporated through baptism, and it is an image that he can use to emphasize two subsidiary points: the members are to care for the body (Rom 12:3-8), and the body is to care for its members (1 Cor 12:12-26).

BIBLIOGRAPHY

Banks, Robert J. *Paul's Idea of Community.* Grand Rapids: Wm. B. Eerdmans, 1980.

Barrett, C. K. *A Commentary on the First Epistle to the Corinthians.* 2d ed. London: A. & C. Black, 1971.

Barton, S. G., and G. H. R. Horsley. "A Hellenistic Cult Group and the New Testament Churches." *JAC* 24 (1981): 7-41.

Best, Ernest. *One Body in Christ.* London: SPCK, 1955.

Conzelmann, Hans. *An Outline of the Theology of the New Testament.* New York: Harper & Row, 1969.

Ellis, E. Earle. "Paul and His Co-Workers." *NTS* 17 (1971): 437-52.

Goppelt, Leonhard. *Theology of the New Testament.* 2 vols. Grand Rapids: Wm. B. Eerdmans, 1981-82.

Gundry, Robert H. *SŌMA in Biblical Theology: With Emphasis on Pauline Anthropology.* SNTSMS 29. Cambridge: Cambridge University Press, 1976.

Hultgren, Arland J. "The Church as the Body of Christ: Engaging an Image in the New Testament." *WW* 22 (2002): 124-32.

Käsemann, Ernst. "The Theological Problem Presented by the Motif of the Body of Christ." In his *Perspectives on Paul,* 102-21. Philadelphia: Fortress Press, 1971.

Knox, John. "The Church *Is* Christ's Body." *RL* 27 (1957-58): 54-62.

Koenig, John. *New Testament Hospitality: Partnership with Strangers as Promise and Mission.* Philadelphia: Fortress, 1985.

Kümmel, Werner G. *The Theology of the New Testament.* Nashville: Abingdon Press, 1973.

Lee, Michelle V. *Paul, the Stoics, and the Body of Christ.* SNTSMS 137. Cambridge: Cambridge University Press, 2006.

Manson, T. W. "A Parallel to a N.T. Use of *Sōma.*" *SJT* 37 (1936): 385.

Minear, Paul S. *Images of the Church in the New Testament.* Philadelphia: Westminster Press, 1960.

22. Cf. S. G. Barton and G. H. R. Horsley, "A Hellenistic Cult Group and the New Testament Churches," 28-29.

Moltmann, Jürgen. *The Church in the Power of the Spirit: A Contribution to Messianic Ecclesiology.* Minneapolis: Fortress Press, 1993.

Nygren, Anders. "Corpus Christi." In *This Is the Church,* 3-15. Ed. A. Nygren. Philadelphia: Muhlenberg Press, 1952.

Pokorný, Petr. *The Genesis of Christology: Foundations for a Theology of the New Testament.* Edinburgh: T&T Clark, 1987.

Poteat, Edwin M. "The Body of Christ as Metaphor or Fact." *RL* 25 (1956): 378-85.

Richards, George C. "Parallels to a N.T. Use of *Sōma*." *JTS* 38 (1937): 165.

Robinson, John A. T. *The Body: A Study in Pauline Theology.* SBT 5. Chicago: Henry Regnery, 1952.

Schnackenburg, Rudolf. *The Church in the New Testament.* New York: Herder & Herder, 1965.

Schweizer, Eduard. *Church Order in the New Testament.* SBT 32. Naperville: Alec R. Allenson, 1961.

———. "The Church as the Missionary Body of Christ." *NTS* 8 (1961-62): 1-11; reprinted in his *Neotestamentica: Deutsche und englische Aufsätze 1951-1963,* 317-29. Zurich: Zwingli Verlag, 1963.

Volf, Miroslav. *After Our Likeness: The Church as the Image of the Trinity.* Grand Rapids: Wm. B. Eerdmans, 1998.

Williams, Rowan. "Does It Make Sense to Speak of Pre-Nicene Orthodoxy?" In *The Making of Orthodoxy: Essays in Honour of Henry Chadwick,* 1-23. Ed. Rowan Williams. Cambridge: Cambridge University Press, 1989.

Williams, David J. *Paul's Metaphors: Their Context and Character.* Peabody: Hendrickson Publishers, 1999.

Yorke, Gosnell L. O. R. *The Church as the Body of Christ in the Pauline Corpus: A Reexamination.* Lanham: University Press of America, 1991.

House Churches and Communities in Rome

In his undisputed letters — other than his Letter to the Romans — Paul refers to his readers as constituting, or being part of, a "church" (1 Cor 1:2; 2 Cor 1:1; 1 Thess 1:1; Phil 4:15; Phlm 2) or as members of a group of "churches" (Gal 1:2) in scattered communities.[1] In the case of the Philippians he also refers to those addressed as "the saints . . . with their bishops and deacons" (1:1). But in his Letter to the Romans Paul does not address his readers as "the church of Rome" or "the churches of Rome," and he makes no mention of an official leadership of the whole community of Christians in the city. Instead Paul addresses his readers at Rome simply as "God's beloved in Rome, who are called to be saints" (1:7). To this can be added the observation that nowhere else in the letter does he speak of the "church" at Rome as an entity. From this it is often concluded, probably correctly, that there was no one church at Rome, but a number of Christian cells scattered about the city.[2]

On the basis of the evidence of Romans 16, there appear to have been at least three and, more likely, five or more Christian cells at Rome of which Paul was aware.[3] Those of which one can be reasonably certain include: (1) the house

---

1. Additional references to "churches" in a region are at 1 Cor 16:1 (Galatia), 19 (Asia); 2 Cor 8:1 (Macedonia); and Gal 1:22 (Judea). The singular "church" is applied also to the community at Cenchreae (16:1).

2. H.-J. Klauck, *Hausgemeinde und Hauskirche,* 69-70; R. Banks, *Paul's Idea of Community,* 32, 34; P. Lampe, *From Paul to Valentinus,* 359; J. Dunn, *Romans,* lii; P. Stuhlmacher, *Romans,* 7; R. Brändle and E. Stegemann, "The Formation of the First 'Christian Congregations' in Rome," 125; W. Lane, "Social Perspectives on Roman Christianity," 210; R. Gehring, *House Church and Mission,* 146. For a critical response to this view, cf. C. Caragounis, "The Development of the Roman Church," 252-60.

3. There were three Christian cells, according to W. Sanday and A. Headlam, *Romans,* 421; E. A. Judge, *Social Pattern,* 36; V. Branick, *The House Church,* 67; and A. Malherbe, *Social Aspects of Early Christianity,* 70, 100, based on 16:5, 14, 15. P. Lampe, *From Paul to Valentinus,*

church of Prisca and Aquila (16:5); (2) the group associated with Asyncritus, Phlegon, Hermes, Patrobas, and Hermas (16:14); (3) the group of "saints" associated with Philologus, Julia, Nereus, his sister, and Olympas (16:15); (4) those belonging to the household of Aristobulus (16:10); and (5) those belonging to the household of Narcissus (16:11). In addition, fourteen other persons are greeted in the chapter who are not aligned with any of the five explicitly.[4] Since they are greeted separately, it has been proposed that they belonged to one or more other groups within the city.[5] But that may not have been the case. It is equally possible, and finally more probable, that Paul singles out each person not only for a personal greeting but also for a special commendation, for in each case Paul makes reference to the person's significance to himself or to the Christian communities in Rome or adds a term of endearment. Their significance seems not to be in their belonging to other groups within the city but in their special relationship to Paul or the result of their activities, roles, and responsibilities in the Christian community at Rome.

The five groups mentioned would have been organized only in rather informal ways and would have functioned in different ways. The first group can be designated a "house church," a more or less stable community that met for worship in the home of its occupant, who was in effect the patron of the group that met there. Paul refers explicitly to house churches in three places in his letters (Rom 16:5; 1 Cor 16:19; Phlm 2), using the expression ἡ κατ' οἶκον . . . ἐκκλησία ("the church at the house of" someone named).[6] Twice he refers to the house church that met at the home of Prisca and Aquila, which was located at Ephesus when Paul wrote to the Corinthians (1 Cor 16:19) and then at Rome (Rom 16:5). Furthermore, according to Acts, this couple had a home even earlier in Corinth where Paul resided at one time (Acts 18:2-4). The fact that they were community leaders and had homes in Corinth, Ephesus, and Rome indicates that they must have been persons of substantial means.[7] They had been expelled from Rome under the decree of Claudius (Acts 18:1-2), but by the time Paul wrote his letter to Rome, they were back in the city, and they hosted a church in their home.

359, identifies seven at the time Paul wrote the letter, including five referred to in 16:5, 10, 11, 14, 15; moreover, he says, the other 14 persons mentioned would be in two more associations. R. Gehring, *House Church and Mission*, 145-46, speaks of seven different groups. L. White, "House Churches," 119, says that Paul addresses "eight distinct cells in Rome."

4. These include Epaenetus, Mary, Andronicus, Junia, Ampliatus, Urbanus, Stachys, Apelles, Herodion, Tryphaena, Tryphosa, Persis, Rufus, and his mother.

5. P. Lampe, *From Paul to Valentinus*, 359, says that the 14 would have made up at least two additional groups; similarly, R. Gehring, *House Church and Mission*, 146; L. White, "House Churches," 119, concludes that Paul addresses "eight distinct cells in Rome."

6. The expression is also at Col 4:15.

7. L. White, "House Churches," 119.

The "house church" was a gathering (not a building) of persons within someone's home, whether it be a villa or an apartment, that was ordinarily used for domestic purposes. There is no archaeological evidence that rooms, to say nothing of buildings, were ever renovated or constructed during the first century A.D. for worship; instead, rooms used for everyday life would have been put to use for gatherings.[8] It is assumed, for example, that a common dining area would be used for a meal and eucharistic worship at Corinth. Those inclined to eat prior to the arrival of latecomers are told by Paul that they should eat at home (1 Cor 11:20-22). It is customary to make a distinction between the "house church" of the first three centuries and that which came later, the so-called *domus ecclesiae* ("house of the church"). The latter presupposes renovation or even construction of a building used for religious purposes.[9]

The designation of the other four groups as "house churches" requires that the term be used rather broadly, if at all. The difference would be that in the case of Prisca and Aquila there must have been substantial continuity over time for the place of the group's worship, since its hosts are named. In the other cases it is possible that the places of meeting were not regular and permanent. Nevertheless, since their gatherings would have been in domestic settings, those groups can also be designated house churches in a loose sense. The two groups mentioned in 16:14-15 seem to be house churches, since Paul addresses persons by name and others "with them" in each case, as though they are gathered to hear the letter being read at worship. The groups mentioned as belonging to the households of Aristobulus and Narcissus (who, though patrons, are not Christians; see comments on 16:10-11) appear to be intact as well. While it is possible that these two groups can be considered "work groups" of Christians or "house fellowship groups that belonged to house churches somewhere else in the city,"[10] that does not necessarily follow. Paul addresses them as though they are discrete groups that receive his greetings while gathered for worship. Insofar as they were identifiable groups that would have gathered for Christian worship at all, they can be considered house churches in a broad sense.

It is unknown how many persons a house church could accommodate. The number would depend upon the size of a domicile. Some models for early Christian gatherings can be set aside. One example is the "lecture hall of Tyrannus" in Corinth; that was not a meeting for worship but for disputation (Acts 19:9). Another example is the home of Gaius in Corinth at which "the whole church" (ὅλη ἡ ἐκκλησία) of that city could meet (Rom 16:23). The

8. According to J. Petersen, "House Churches in Rome," 265, there is no archaeological evidence prior to the third century to suggest that special rooms were set apart for worship. Cf. also R. Krautheimer, *Early Christian and Byzantine Architecture*, 24.

9. L. White, *The Social Origins of Christian Architecture*, 1:111.

10. R. Banks, *Paul's Idea of Community*, 33; R. Gehring, *House Church and Mission*, 145.

"whole church" most likely refers to the sum of the individual house churches of Corinth,[11] for there is no other apparent reason for Paul to use the adjective "whole" (ὅλη) if the Corinthians met regularly as a whole.[12] Moreover, the various references to different groups (1 Cor 1:11-16) speak in favor of there being several cells of Christians in the city. In any case, the implication is that the home of Gaius must have been rather large and could accommodate a good-sized gathering.[13] But it would not have been a "house church" per se. Then, too, at Acts 20:7-12 there is a scene at Troas where Paul and others met on the first day of the week and broke bread. They met in a room on the third floor of a building. Eight persons are mentioned by name as being present, but how many more have been there is not indicated.

Housing in Rome of the first century varied from grand houses (the *domus*) that could accommodate dozens of persons to apartments within large tenement blocks (called *insulae*).[14] Archaeological remains in Rome and its vicinity indicate an immense variety, including the patrician *domus* with its central atrium surrounded by rooms, villas with agricultural areas appended, smaller houses, and the tenement blocks, which could rise to four or five stories high.[15] Studies based on various methods of investigation lead to the conclusion that most Christians in ancient Rome would have lived in the Trastevere and Via Appia/Porta Capena districts of Rome that were heavily populated by persons of the lower socioeconomic strata and where most people lived in tenement blocks.[16] Not all living in such dwellings, however, were necessarily poor. All but a tiny fraction of the city of Rome lived in tenements, including some who constituted the middle and upper classes.[17] It appears that the housing stock of Rome was "mixed in nature," and "the conventional wisdom that the rich and poor lived apart" has been challenged.[18] The fact that Paul could appeal for support among the Roman Christians for his intended journey to Spain (Rom 15:24) indicates that, at least in his estimation, the Christians at Rome had some financial means to share with him, and were therefore not necessarily poor.[19] Since

11. A. Malherbe, *Social Aspects of Early Christianity*, 97; W. Meeks, *First Urban Christians*, 57.

12. R. Banks, *Paul's Idea of Community*, 32.

13. R. Banks, *Paul's Idea of Community*, 35, estimates that this house could accommodate anywhere from 40 to 90 persons.

14. The former is described by Cicero, *Dom.* 44.116; the latter by Juvenal, *Sat.* 3.190-210.

15. J. Clarke, *The Houses of Roman Italy*, 1-29; A. McKay, "Houses," 1373-84.

16. P. Lampe, *From Paul to Valentinus*, 19-66.

17. Nicholas Purcell, "Houses, Italian," *OCD* 731; A. McKay, "Houses," 1378.

18. A. Wallace-Hadrill, "*Domus* and *Insulae* in Rome," 13-14.

19. For a discussion of scholarship on the socioeconomic status of early Christians, leading to the conclusion that not all were from the poorest strata, cf. R. Gehring, *House Church and Mission*, 167-71. Cf. also F. Filson, "The Significance of the Early House Churches," 111.

estimates of how many persons constituted a particular house church vary (but in general tend to be roughly from one to two dozen persons),[20] and since it is unknown how many Christian cells existed in Rome (perhaps including some unknown to Paul), it is impossible to know how many Christians resided in Rome at the time Paul wrote his letter.

BIBLIOGRAPHY

Banks, Robert J. *Paul's Idea of Community: The Early House Churches in Their Historical Setting*. Rev. ed. Peabody: Hendrickson Publishers, 1994.

Brändle, Rudolf, and Ekkehard W. Stegemann, "The Formation of the First 'Christian Congregations' in Rome in the Context of the Jewish Congregations." In *Judaism and Christianity in First-Century Rome*, 117-27. Ed. Karl P. Donfried and Peter Richardson. Grand Rapids: Wm. B. Eerdmans, 1998.

Branick, Vincent. *The House Church in the Writings of Paul*. Zacchaeus Studies: New Testament. Wilmington: Michael Glazier, 1989.

Caragounis, Chrys C. "From Obscurity to Prominence: The Development of the Roman Church between Romans and *1 Clement*." In *Judaism and Christianity in First-Century Rome*, 245-79. Ed. Karl P. Donfried and Peter Richardson. Grand Rapids: Wm. B. Eerdmans, 1998.

Clarke, John R. *The Houses of Roman Italy, 100 B.C.–A.D. 250: Ritual, Space, and Decoration*. Berkeley: University of California Press, 1991.

Filson, Floyd V. "The Significance of the Early House Churches." *JBL* 58 (1939): 105-12.

Finger, Reta Halteman. *Roman House Churches for Today: A Practical Guide for Small Groups*. Grand Rapids: Wm. B. Eerdmans, 2007.

Gehring, Roger W. *House Church and Mission: The Importance of Household Structures in Early Christianity*. Peabody: Hendrickson Publishers, 2004.

Jewett, Robert. "Tenement Churches and Community Meals in the Early Church: The Implications of a Form-Critical Analysis of 2 Thessalonians 3:10." *BR* 38 (1993): 23-43.

Judge, Edwin A. *Social Pattern of the Christian Groups in the First Century*. London: Tyndale Press, 1960; reprinted in *Social Distinctives of the Christians in the First Century: Pivotal Essays by E. A. Judge*, 1-56. Ed. David M. Scholer. Peabody: Hendrickson Publishers, 2008.

Klauck, Hans-Josef. *Hausgemeinde und Hauskirche im frühen Christentum*. SBS 103. Stuttgart: Katholisches Bibelwerk, 1981.

Krautheimer, Richard. *Early Christian and Byzantine Architecture*. 4th ed. New Haven: Yale University Press, 1986.

20. R. Banks, *Paul's Idea of Community*, 34-36, estimates that voluntary associations of the Greco-Roman world that met in homes had about 30 to 35 persons, but that the house churches would have been smaller than that. Typically a house church would consist of 10 to 15 persons, according to J. Murphy-O'Connor, *St. Paul's Corinth*, 195. It would consist of 15 to 20, according to William L. Lane, *Hebrews*, WBC 47, 2 vols. (Dallas: Word Books, 1991), 1:liii, and P. Lampe, *From Paul to Valentinus*, 192.

Lampe, Peter. *From Paul to Valentinus: Christians at Rome in the First Two Centuries.* Minneapolis: Fortress Press, 2003.

Lane, William L. "Social Perspectives on Roman Christianity during the Formative Years fron Nero to Nerva: Romans, Hebrews, *1 Clement.*" In *Judaism and Christianity in First-Century Rome,* 196-244. Ed. Karl P. Donfried and Peter Richardson. Grand Rapids: Wm. B. Eerdmans, 1998.

Malherbe, Abraham J. *Social Aspects of Early Christianity.* 2d ed. Philadelphia: Fortress Press, 1983.

McKay, Alexander G. "Houses." In *Civilization of the Ancient Mediterranean,* 3:1363-84. Ed. Michael Grant and Rachel Kitzinger. 3 vols. New York: Charles Scribner's Sons, 1988.

Meeks, Wayne A. *The First Urban Christians: The Social World of the Apostle Paul.* 2d ed. New Haven: Yale University Press, 2003.

Murphy-O'Connor, Jerome. *St. Paul's Corinth: Texts and Archaeology.* 3d ed. GNS 6 Collegeville: Liturgical Press, 2002.

Osiek, Carolyn, and David L. Balch. *Families in the New Testament: Households and House Churches.* Louisville: Westminster John Knox Press, 1997.

Osiek, Carolyn, Margaret Y. MacDonald, with Janet H. Tulloch. *A Woman's Place: House Churches in Earliest Christianity.* Minneapolis: Fortress Press, 2005.

Petersen, Joan M. "House Churches in Rome." *VC* 23 (1969): 264-72.

Stark, Rodney. *The Rise of Christianity: A Sociologist Reconsiders History.* Princeton: Princeton University Press, 1996.

Wallace-Hadrill, Andrew. "*Domus* and *Insulae* in Rome: Families and Housefuls." In *Early Christian Families in Context: An Interdisciplinary Dialogue,* 3-18. Ed. David L. Balch and Carolyn Osiek. Grand Rapids: Wm. B. Eerdmans, 2003.

White, L. Michael. "House Churches." *OEANE* 3:118-21.

―――. *The Social Origins of Christian Architecture.* 2 vols. HTS 42. Valley Forge: Trinity Press International, 1996.

General Bibliography

Aageson, James W. *Written Also for Our Sake: Paul and the Art of Biblical Interpretation.* Louisville: Westminster John Knox Press, 1993.

————. "Written Also for Our Sake: Paul's Use of Scripture in the Four Major Epistles, with a Study of 1 Corinthians 10." In *Hearing the Old Testament in the New Testament,* 152-81. Ed. Stanley Porter. MNTS. Grand Rapids: Wm. B. Eerdmans, 2006.

Aasgaard, Reidar. *"My Beloved Brothers and Sisters!" Christian Siblingship in Paul.* JSNT 265. Edinburgh: T&T Clark, 2004.

Achtemeier, Paul J. "The Continuing Quest for Coherence in St. Paul: An Experiment in Thought." In *Theology and Ethics in Paul and His Interpreters: Essays in Honor of Victor Paul Furnish,* 132-45. Ed. Eugene H. Lovering Jr. and Jerry L. Sumney. Nashville: Abingdon Press, 1996.

————. "Finding the Way to Paul's Theology: A Response to J. Christiaan Beker and J. Paul Sampley." In *Pauline Theology,* vol. 1. *Thessalonians, Philippians, Galatians, Philemon,* 25-36. Ed. Jouette M. Bassler. Minneapolis: Fortress Press, 1991.

————. "Unsearchable Judgments and Inscrutable Ways: Reflections on the Discussion of Romans." In *Pauline Theology,* vol. 4, *Looking Back, Pressing On,* 3-21. Ed. E. Elizabeth Johnson and David M. Hay. SBLSS 4. Atlanta: Scholars Press, 1997.

————. *Romans.* Interpretation Commentary. Atlanta: John Knox Press, 1985.

Adams, Edward. "Abraham's Faith and Gentile Disobedience: Textual Links between Romans 1 and 4." *JSNT* 65 (1997): 47-66.

————. *Constructing the World: A Study in Paul's Cosmological Language.* Edinburgh: T&T Clark, 1999.

Affeldt, Werner. "Verzeichnis der Römerbriefkommentare der lateinischen Kirche bis zu Nikolas von Lyra." *Tradition* 13 (1957): 369-407.

Agamben, Giorgio. *The Time That Remains: A Commentary on the Letter to the Romans.* Stanford: Stanford University Press, 2005.

Ahern, Barnabas M. *The Epistle to the Galatians and the Epistle to the Romans.* NTRG 7. Collegeville: Liturgical Press, 1960.

Aletti, Jean-Noël. *Comment Dieu est-il juste? Clefs pour interpreter l'épître aux Romains.* Paris: Editions du Seuil, 1990.

―――. "La présence d'un modèle rhétorique en Romains: Son rôle et son importance." *Bib* 71 (1990): 1-24.

―――. "The Rhetoric of Romans 5-8." In *The Rhetorical Analysis of Scripture: Essays from the 1995 London Conference,* 294-308. Ed. Stanley E. Porter and Thomas H. Olbricht. JSNTSup 146. Sheffield, Eng.: Sheffield Academic Press, 1997.

Althaus, Paul. *Der Brief an die Römer.* 13th ed. NTD 6. Göttingen: Vandenhoeck & Ruprecht, 1978.

Anderson, Janice Capel, et al., eds. *Pauline Conversations in Context: Essays in Honor of Calvin J. Roetzel.* JSNTSup 221. Sheffield: Sheffield Academic Press, 2002.

Anderson, R. Dean, Jr. *Ancient Rhetorical Theory and Paul.* Rev. ed. CBET 18. Leuven: Peeters, 1999.

Ashton, John. *The Religion of Paul the Apostle.* New Haven: Yale University Press, 2000.

Asmussen, Hans. *Der Römerbrief.* Stuttgart: Evangelisches Verlagswerk, 1952.

Aune, David E. *Prophecy in Early Christianity and the Ancient Mediterranean World.* Grand Rapids: Eerdmans, 1983.

―――, ed. *Rereading Paul Together.* Grand Rapids: Baker Academic, 2006.

Avemarie, Friedrich, and Hermann Lichtenberger, eds. *Auferstehung/Resurrection: The Fourth Durham-Tübingen Research Symposium: Resurrection, Transfiguration and Exaltation in Old Testament, Ancient Judaism and Early Christianity.* WUNT 135. Tübingen: J. C. B. Mohr (Paul Siebeck), 2004.

Bachmann, Michael, ed. *Lutherische und Neue Paulusperspektive: Beiträge zu einem Schlüsselproblem der gegenwärtigen exegetischen Diskussion.* WUNT 2/182. Tübingen: J. C. B. Mohr (Paul Siebeck), 2005.

Back, Frances. "Romans as a *Logos Protreptikos.*" In *The Romans Debate,* 278-96. Ed. Karl P. Donfried. Rev. ed. Peabody: Hendrickson Publishers, 1991.

―――. *Verwandlung durch Offenbarung.* WUNT 2/153. Tübingen: J. C. B. Mohr (Paul Siebeck), 2002.

Badenas, Robert. *Christ the End of the Law: Romans 10:4 in Pauline Perspective.* JSNTSup 10. Sheffield: JSOT Press, 1986.

Balch, David L., and Carolyn Osiek, eds. *Early Christian Families in Context: An Interdisciplinary Dialogue.* Grand Rapids: Wm. B. Eerdmans, 2003.

Balz, Horst. "Römerbrief." *TRE* 29 (1998): 291-311.

Banks, Robert. *Paul's Idea of Community: The Early House Churches in Their Cultural Setting.* Rev. ed. Peabody: Hendrickson Publishers, 1994.

―――, ed. *Reconciliation and Hope: New Testament Essays on Atonement and Eschatology Presented to L. L. Morris on His 60th Birthday.* Grand Rapids: Wm. B. Eerdmans, 1974.

Barclay, John M. G. *Jews in the Mediterranean Diaspora: From Alexander to Trajan (323 BCE-117 CE).* Edinburgh: T&T Clark, 1996.

―――. "Paul among Diaspora Jews: Anomaly or Apostate?" *JSNT* 60 (1995): 89-120.

―――, and Simon J Gathercole, eds. *Divine and Human Agency in Paul and His Cultural Environment.* LNTS 335. New York: T&T Clark, 2008.

————, and John P. M. Sweet, eds. *Early Christian Thought in Its Jewish Context.* Cambridge: Cambridge University Press, 1996.

Barcley, William B. *Christ in You: A Study in Paul's Theology and Ethics.* Lanham: University Press of America, 1999.

Barnett, Paul W. *The Birth of Christianity: The First Twenty Years.* Grand Rapids: Wm. B. Eerdmans, 2005.

Barr, George. *Scalometry and the Pauline Epistles.* JSNTSup 261. Edinburgh: T&T Clark, 2004.

Barr, James. "Paul and the LXX: A Note on Some Recent Work." *JTS* 45 (1994): 593-601.

————. *The Typology of Literalism in Ancient Biblical Translations.* MSU 15. Göttingen: Vandenhoeck & Ruprecht, 1979.

Barrett, C. K. *Acts 1–14.* ICC. Edinburgh: T&T Clark, 1994.

————. *The Epistle to the Romans.* Rev. ed. BNTC. Peabody: Hendrickson Publishers, 1991.

————. *From First Adam to Last: A Study in Pauline Theology.* New York: Charles Scribner's Sons, 1962.

————. "The Gentile Mission as an Eschatological Phenomenon." In *Eschatology and the New Testament,* 65-75. Ed. W. H. Gloer. Peabody: Hendrickson Publishers, 1988.

————. "The Interpretation of the Old Testament in the New." In *Cambridge History of the Bible,* vol. 1, *From the Beginnings to Jerome,* 377-411. Ed. P. R. Ackroyd and C. F. Evans. Cambridge: Cambridge University Press, 1970.

————. *On Paul: Essays on His Life, Work and Influence in the Early Church.* London: T&T Clark, 2003.

————. *Paul: An Introduction to His Thought.* Louisville: Westminster John Knox Press, 1994.

————. "Paul: Missionary and Theologian." In his *Jesus and the Word and Other Essays,* 149-62. PTMS 41. Allison Park, Pa.: Pickwick, 1995.

————. *Reading through Romans.* Philadelphia: Fortress Press, 1977.

Barth, Karl. *Christ and Adam.* New York: Collier Books, 1962.

————. *The Epistle to the Romans.* London: Oxford University Press, 1933.

Barth, Markus. *Justification: Pauline Texts Interpreted in the Light of the Old and New Testaments.* Grand Rapids: Wm. B. Eerdmans, 1971.

————, and Verne H. Fletcher. *Acquittal by Resurrection.* New York: Holt, Rinehart, and Winston, 1964.

Bartlett, David L. *Romans.* Westminster Bible Companion. Louisville: Westminster John Knox Press, 1995.

Bartsch, Hans-Werner. "Die Empfänger des Römerbriefes." *ST* 25 (1971): 81-98.

————. "Die historische Situation des Römerbriefes." *SE* 4 ([TU 102] 1968): 281-91.

Bassler, Joulette M. *Navigating Paul: An Introduction to Key Theological Concepts.* Louisville: Westminster John Knox Press, 2007.

————. "Paul's Theology: Whence and Whither?" *Pauline Theology,* vol. 2, *1 and 2 Corinthians,* 3-17. Ed. David M. Hay. Minneapolis: Fortress Press, 1993.

Baum, Gregory. *The Jews and the Gospel: A Reexamination of the New Testament.* Westminster: Newman, 1961.

Baumgarten, Jörg. *Paulus und die Apokalyptik: Die Auslegung apokalyptisch Überliefe-rungen in den echten Paulusbriefen.* WMANT 44. Neukirchen-Vluyn: Neukirchener Verlag, 1975.

Baur, Ferdinand C. *Paul the Apostle of Jesus Christ: His Life and Works, His Epistles and Teachings.* 2 vols. London: Williams and Norgate, 1873-75; reprinted as one volume, Peabody: Hendrickson Publishers, 2003.

Beare, Francis W. "Romans, Letter to the." In *IDB* 4:112-24.

Becker, Jürgen. *Paul: Apostle to the Gentiles.* Louisville: Westminster John Knox Press, 1993.

Beentjes, Pancratius C. "Inverted Quotations in the Bible: A Neglected Stylistic Pattern." *Bib* 63 (1982): 506-23.

Beker, J. Christiaan. "The Faithfulness of God and the Priority of Israel in Paul's Letter to the Romans." In *The Romans Debate*, 327-32. Ed. Karl P. Donfried. Rev. ed. Peabody, Mass.: Hendrickson Publishers, 1991.

———. *Paul the Apostle: The Triumph of God in Life and Thought.* Philadelphia: Fortress Press, 1980.

———. *Paul's Apocalyptic Gospel: The Coming Triumph of God.* Philadelphia: Fortress Press, 1982.

———. "Paul's Letter to the Romans as a Model for Biblical Theology: Some Preliminary Observations." In *Understanding the Word: Essays in Honor of Bernhard W. Ander-son*, 359-67. Ed. James Butler et al. Sheffield: JSOT Press, 1985.

———. "The Relationship between Sin and Death in Romans." In *The Conversation Con-tinues: Studies in Paul and John: In Honor of J. Louis Martyn*, 55-61. Ed. Robert T. Fortna and Beverly Roberts Gaventa. Nashville: Abingdon Press, 1990.

———. *The Triumph of God: The Essence of Paul's Thought.* Minneapolis: Fortress Press, 1990.

Bell, Richard H. *The Irrevocable Call of God: An Inquiry into Paul's Theology of Israel.* WUNT 184. Tübingen: J. C. B. Mohr (Paul Siebeck), 2005.

———. *No One Seeks for God.* WUNT 106. Tübingen: J. C. B. Mohr (Paul Siebeck), 1998.

Berger, Klaus. *Paulus.* Munich: Beck, 2002.

Best, Ernest. *The Letter of Paul to the Romans.* CBC. Cambridge: Cambridge University Press, 1967.

Betz, Hans D. "Christianity as Religion: Paul's Attempt at a Definition in Romans." *JR* 71 (1991): 315-44; reprinted in his *Paulinische Studien*, 206-39. Tübingen: J. C. B. Mohr (Paul Siebeck), 1994.

———. "Paul." In *ABD* 5:186-201.

Bindemann, Walther. *Theologie im Dialog: Ein traditionsgeschichtlicher Kommentar zu Römer 1–11.* Leipzig: Evangelische Verlagsanstalt, 1992.

Bjerkelund, Carl J. *Parakalô: Form, Funktion und Sinn der parakalô-Sätze in den paulinischen Briefen.* BTN 1. Oslo: Universitetsforlaget, 1967.

Black, Matthew. "The Christological Use of the Old Testament in the New Testament." *NTS* 18 (1971-72): 1-14.

———. *Romans.* 2d ed. NCBC. Grand Rapids: Wm. B. Eerdmans, 1989.

Blackman, E. C. "The Letter of Paul to the Romans." In *The Interpreter's One-Volume Com-*

mentary on the Bible, 768-94. Ed. Charles M. Laymon. Nashville: Abingdon Press, 1971.

Blank, Josef. *Paulus und Jesus: Eine theologische Grundlegung.* SANT 18. Munich: Kösel Verlag, 1968.

Bloch, Renée. "Methodological Note for the Study of Rabbinic Literature." In *Approaches to Ancient Judaism: Theory and Practice,* 51-75. Ed. William S. Green, 51-75. BJS 1. Missoula: Scholars Press, 1978.

―――. "Midrash." In *Approaches to Ancient Judaism: Theory and Practice,* 29-50. Ed. William S. Green. BJS 1. Missoula: Scholars Press, 1978.

Bockmuehl, Markus N. A. *Jewish Law in Gentile Churches: Halakhah and the Beginning of Christian Public Ethics.* Edinburgh: T&T Clark, 2000.

Boers, Hendrikus. *Christ in the Letters of Paul: In Place of a Christology.* BZNW 140. New York: Walter de Gruyter, 2006.

―――. *The Justification of the Gentiles: Paul's Letters to the Galatians and Romans.* Peabody: Hendrickson Publishers, 1994.

―――. "Polysemy in Paul's Use of Christological Expressions." In *The Future of Christology: Essays in Honor of Leander E. Keck,* 91-108. Ed. Abraham J. Malherbe and Wayne A. Meeks. Minneapolis: Fortress Press, 1993.

―――. "The Problem of Jews and Gentiles in the Macro-Structure of Romans." *Neot* 15 (1981): 1-11.

Bonsirven, Joseph. *Exégèse rabbinique et exégèse paulinienne.* BTH. Paris: Beauchesne, 1939.

Borgen, Peder. "In Accordance with the Scriptures." *Early Christian Thought in Its Jewish Context,* 193-206. Ed. John M. G. Barclay and John P. M. Sweet. Cambridge: Cambridge University Press, 1996.

―――, Kare Fuglseth, and Roald Skarsten. *The Philo Index: A Complete Greek Word Index to the Writings of Philo of Alexandria.* Grand Rapids: Wm. B. Eerdmans, 2000.

Boring, M. Eugene. "The Language of Universal Salvation in Paul." *JBL* 105 (1986): 269-92.

Bornkamm, Günther. *Early Christian Experience.* New York: Harper & Row, 1969.

―――. *Das Ende des Gesetzes: Paulusstudien.* BEvT 16. Munich: Kaiser Verlag, 1952.

―――. "The Letter to the Romans as Paul's Last Will and Testament." In *The Romans Debate,* 16-28. Ed. Karl P. Donfried. Rev. ed. Peabody: Hendrickson Publishers, 1991.

―――. *Paul.* New York: Harper & Row, 1971; reprinted, Minneapolis: Fortress Press, 1994.

Botha, P. J. J. "Greco-Roman Literacy as Setting for New Testament Writings." *Neot* 26 (1992): 195-215.

―――. "Letter Writing and Oral Communication in Antiquity." *Scriptura* 42 (1992): 17-34.

Bouttier, Michel. *Christianity according to Paul.* SBT 49. Naperville: Alec R. Allenson, 1966.

Bovon, François. *Studies in Early Christianity.* Grand Rapids: Baker Academic, 2005.

Boyarin, Daniel. *A Radical Jew: Paul and the Politics of Identity.* Berkeley: University of California Press, 1994.

Brändle, Rudolf, and Ekkehard W. Stegemann. "The Formation of the First 'Christian Congregations' in Rome in the Context of the Jewish Congregations." In *Judaism and Christianity in First-Century Rome,* 117-27. Ed. Karl P. Donfried and Peter Richardson. Grand Rapids: Wm. B. Eerdmans, 1998.

Branick, Vincent P. *Understanding Paul and His Letters.* Mahwah: Paulist Press, 2009.

Braude, William G. *The Midrash on Psalms.* 2 vols. New Haven: Yale University Press, 1959.

Braumann, Georg. *Vorpaulinische christliche Taufverkündigung bei Paulus.* BWANT 82. Stuttgart: Kohlhammer Verlag, 1962.

Bray, Gerald L., ed. *Romans.* ACCS.NT 6. Downers Grove: InterVarsity Press, 1998.

Brecht, Martin. "Römerbriefauslegungen Martin Luthers." In *Paulus, Apostel Jesu Christi: Festschrift für Günter Klein zum 70. Geburtstag,* 207-25. Ed. Michael Trowitzsch. Tübingen: J. C. B. Mohr (Paul Siebeck), 1998.

Breytenbach, Cilliers. "'Christus starb für uns': Zur Tradition und paulinischen Rezeption der sogennanten 'Sterbeformeln.'" *NTS* 49 (2003): 447-75.

Bring, Ragnar. "The Message to the Gentiles: A Study of the Theology of Paul the Apostle." *ST* 19 (1965): 30-46.

Brock, Sebastian P. "Aspects of Translation Technique in Antiquity." In his *Syriac Perspectives on Late Antiquity,* 69-87. Burlington: Ashgate Variorum, 1984.

——. "The Phenomenon of Biblical Translation in Antiquity." In *Studies in the Septuagint: Origins, Recensions, and Interpretations,* 541-71. Ed. Sidney Jellicoe. New York: KTAV, 1974.

——. "To Revise or Not to Revise: Attitudes to Jewish Biblical Translation." In *Septuagint, Scrolls and Cognate Writings,* 301-38. Ed. George J. Brooke and Barnabas Lindars. SBLSCS 33. Atlanta: Scholars Press, 1992.

——. "Translating the Old Testament." In *It is Written: Scripture Citing Scripture,* 87-98. Ed. D. A. Carson and H. G. M. Williamson, 87-98. Cambridge: Cambridge University Press, 1988.

Brockington, Leonard H. "Septuagint and Targum." *ZAW* 66 (1954): 80-86.

Brown, Raymond E., and John P. Meier. *Antioch and Rome: New Testament Cradles of Catholic Christianity.* New York: Paulist Press, 1983.

——. "Further Reflections on the Origins of the Church of Rome." In *The Conversation Continues: Studies in Paul and John: In Honor of J. Louis Martyn,* 98-115. Ed. Robert T. Fortna and Beverly Roberts Gaventa. Nashville: Abingdon Press, 1990.

——. *An Introduction to the New Testament.* ABRL. New York: Doubleday, 1997.

Bruce, Frederick F. *The Epistle of Paul to the Romans: An Introduction and Commentary.* TNTC 6. Grand Rapids: Wm. B. Eerdmans, 1963.

——. *Paul: Apostle of the Heart Set Free.* Grand Rapids: Wm. B. Eerdmans, 1977.

Brunner, Emil. *The Letter to the Romans: A Commentary.* Philadelphia: Westminster Press, 1959.

Bryan, Christopher. *Preface to Romans: Notes on the Epistle in Its Literary and Cultural Setting.* New York: Oxford University Press, 2000.

——. *Way of Freedom: An Introduction to the Epistle to the Romans.* New York: Seabury Press, 1975.

Buck, Charles, and Greer Taylor. *St. Paul: A Study of the Development of His Thought.* New York: Charles Scribner's Sons, 1969.

Bultmann, Rudolf. *Essays Philosophical and Theological.* New York: Macmillan, 1955.

―――. "Glossen im Römerbrief." *TLZ* 72 (1947): 197-202; reprinted in his *Exegetica: Aufsätze zur Erforschung des Neuen Testaments*, 278-84. Ed. Erich Dinkler. Tübingen: J. C. B. Mohr (Paul Siebeck), 1967.

―――. *The Old and New Man in the Letters of Paul*. Richmond: John Knox Press, 1967.

―――. "Paul." In his *Existence and Faith*, 111-46. New York: World Publishing Company, 1960.

―――. "Das Problem der Ethik bei Paulus." *ZNW* 23 (1924): 123-40.

―――. *Theology of the New Testament*. 2 vols. New York: Charles Scribner's Sons, 1951-55.

Burchard, Christoph. "Glaubensgerechtigkeit als Weisung der Tora bei Paulus." In *Jesus Christus als die Mitte der Schrift: Studien zur Hermeneutik des Evangeliums*, 341-62. Ed. Christof Landmesser et al. BZNW 86. Berlin: Walter de Gruyter, 1997.

Burnett, Richard E. *Karl Barth's Theological Exegesis: The Hermeneutical Principles of the* Römerbrief *Period*. WUNT 2/145. Tübingen: J. C. B. Mohr (Paul Siebeck), 2001.

Byrne, Brendan. "How Can We Interpret Romans Theologically Today?" *AusBR* 47 (1999): 29-42.

―――. "Interpreting Romans: The New Perspective and Beyond." *Int* 58 (2004): 241-52.

―――. "Interpreting Romans Theologically in a Post-'New Perspective' Perspective." *HTR* 94 (2001): 227-41.

―――. *Reckoning with Romans: A Contemporary Reading of Paul's Gospel*. GNS 18. Wilmington: Michael Glazier, 1986.

―――. *Romans*. SPS 6. Collegeville: Liturgical Press, 1996.

―――. *"Sons of God" — "Seed of Abraham": A Study of the Idea of the Sonship of God of All Christians in Paul against the Jewish Background*. AnBib 83. Rome: Pontifical Biblical Institute Press, 1979.

Calvert-Koysis, Nancy. *Paul, Monotheism and the People of God: The Significance of Abraham Traditions for Early Judaism and Christianity*. JSNTSup 273. New York: T&T Clark, 2004.

Calvin, John. *The Epistles of Paul the Apostle to the Romans and the Thessalonians*. Calvin's Commentaries 8. Edinburgh: Oliver and Boyd, 1960.

Campbell, Douglas A. *Deliverance of God: An Apocalyptic Rereading of Justification in Paul*. Grand Rapids: Wm. B. Eerdmans, 2009.

―――. *The Quest for Paul's Gospel: A Suggested Strategy*. Edinburgh: T&T Clark, 2005.

Campbell, William S. *Paul and the Creation of Christian Identity*. LNTS 322. New York: T&T Clark, 2006.

―――. *Paul's Gospel in an Intercultural Context: Jew and Gentile in the Letter to the Romans*. SIGU 69. New York: Peter Lang, 1991.

―――, Peter S. Hawkins, and Brenda Deen Schildgen, eds. *Medieval Readings of Romans*. RHCS 6. New York: T&T Clark, 2007.

Cambier, Jules. *L'Évangile de Dieu selon l'Épître aux Romains: Exégèse et théologie biblique*, vol. 1, *L'Évangile de la justice et de la grace*. StudNeot 3. Bruges: Desclée de Brouwer, 1967.

Capes, David B., Rodney Reeves, and E. Randolph Richards. *Rediscovering Paul: An Introduction to His World, Letters, and Theology*. Downers Grove: InterVarsity Press, 2007.

Caragounis, Chrys C. "From Obscurity to Prominence: The Development of the Roman Church between Romans and *I Clement*." In *Judaism and Christianity in First-Century Rome,* 245-79. Ed. Karl P. Donfried and Peter Richardson. Grand Rapids: Wm. B. Eerdmans, 1998.

Carroll, John T., Alexandra R. Brown, Claudia J. Setzer, and Jeffrey S. Siker. *The Return of Jesus in Early Christianity.* Peabody: Hendrickson Publishers, 2000.

Carson, D. A. *Divine Sovereignty and Human Responsibility: Biblical Perspectives in Tension.* Atlanta: John Knox Press, 1981.

————, Peter T. O'Brien, and Mark Seifrid, eds. *Justification and Variegated Nomism.* 2 vols. Grand Rapids: Baker Academic, 2001-4.

Carson, D. A., and H. G. M. Williamson, eds. *It is Written: Scripture Citing Scripture: Essays in Honour of Barnabas Lindars, S.S.F.* Cambridge: Cambridge University Press, 1988.

Carter, Warren. *The Roman Empire and the New Testament: An Essential Guide.* Nashville: Abingdon Press, 2006.

Cassidy, Richard J. *Paul in Chains: Roman Imprisonment and the Letters of Paul.* New York: Crossroad Publishing Company, 2001.

Cerfaux, Lucien. *Christ in the Theology of Saint Paul.* New York: Herder & Herder, 1959.

————. *The Christian in the Theology of St Paul.* London: Chapman, 1967.

————. *The Church in the Theology of St Paul.* New York: Herder & Herder, 1959.

Chadwick, H. "Florilegium." *RAC* 7 (1969): 1131-59.

Charlesworth, James H., ed. *The Old Testament Pseudepigrapha.* 2 vols. Garden City, N.Y.: Doubleday, 1983-85.

————. "The Pseudepigrapha as Biblical Exegesis." In *Early Jewish and Christian Exegesis: Studies in Memory of William Hugh Brownlee,* 139-52. Ed. Craig A. Evans and William F. Stinespring. Atlanta: Scholars Press, 1987.

————, and Craig A. Evans, eds. *The Pseudepigrapha and Early Biblical Interpretation.* JSPSup 14/ SSEJC 2. Sheffield: JSOT Press, 1993.

Childs, Brevard S. *The Church's Guide for Reading Paul: The Canonical Shaping of the Pauline Corpus.* Grand Rapids: Wm. B. Eerdmans, 2008.

Chilton, Bruce. *Rabbi Paul: An Intellectual Biography.* New York: Doubleday, 2004.

Christophersen, Alf, et al., eds. *Paul, Luke and the Graeco-Roman World: Essays in Honor of Alexander J. M. Wedderburn.* JSNTSup 217. Sheffield: Sheffield Academic Press, 2003.

Clarke, Andrew D. *A Pauline Theology of Church Leadership.* LNTS 362. London: T&T Clark, 2008.

Classen, Carl J. *Rhetorical Criticism of the New Testament.* WUNT 128. Tübingen: J. C. B. Mohr (Paul Siebeck), 2000.

Cobb, John B., Jr., and David J. Lull. *Romans.* CCT. St. Louis: Chalice Press, 2005.

Cohen, Shaye. *Josephus in Galilee and Rome: His Vita and Development as a Historian.* CSCT 8. Leiden: E. J. Brill, 1979.

Cohn-Sherbok, Dan. "Paul and Rabbinic Exegesis." *SJT* 35 (1982): 117-32.

Collins, Raymond. *The Power of Images in Paul.* Collegeville: Liturgical Press, 2008.

Conybeare, William J., and John S. Howson. *The Life and Epistles of Paul.* 2 vols. New York: Charles Scribner, 1852; reprinted, Grand Rapids: Wm. B. Eerdmans, 1980.

Conzelmann, Hans. *Acts of the Apostles.* Hermeneia. Philadelphia: Fortress Press, 1987.

———. *1 Corinthians.* Hermeneia. Philadelphia: Fortress Press, 1975.

———. *An Outline of the Theology of the New Testament.* New York: Harper & Row, 1969.

Coppins, Wayne. *The Interpretation of Freedom in the Letters of Paul: With Special Reference to the 'German' Tradition.* WUNT 2/261. Tübingen: Mohr Siebeck, 2009.

Cosby, Michael R. *Apostle on the Edge: An Inductive Guide to Paul.* Peabody: Hendrickson Publishers, 2005.

Cousar, Charles B. *The Letters of Paul.* Nashville: Abingdon Press, 1996.

———. *A Theology of the Cross: The Death of Jesus in the Pauline Letters.* Minneapolis: Fortress Press, 1990.

Crafton, Jeffrey A. "Paul's Rhetorical Vision and the Purpose of Romans: Toward a New Understanding." *NovT* 32 (1990): 317-39.

Cranfield, C. E. B. *A Critical and Exegetical Commentary on the Epistle to the Romans.* 2 vols. ICC. Edinburgh: T&T Clark, 1979.

———. "Giving a Dog a Bad Name: A Note on H. Räisänen's *Paul and the Law.*" *JSNT* 38 (1990): 77-85.

———. *On Romans and Other New Testament Essays.* Edinburgh: T&T Clark, 1998.

———. *Romans: A Shorter Commentary.* Grand Rapids: Wm. B. Eerdmans, 1985.

———. "St. Paul and the Law." *SJT* 17 (1964): 43-68; reprinted in *New Testament Issues,* 148-72. Ed. Richard A. Batey. New York: Harper & Row, 1970.

Cross, F. M., and S. Talmon, eds. *Qumran and the History of the Biblical Text.* Cambridge: Harvard University Press, 1975.

Crossan, John D., and Jonathan L. Reed. *In Search of Paul: The New Quest to Understand His World and Words.* San Francisco: HarperSanFrancisco, 2004.

Dahl, Nils A. "The Particularity of the Pauline Epistles as a Problem in the Ancient Church." In *Neotestamentica et Patristica: Eine Freundesgabe Herrn Professor Dr. Oscar Cullmann zu seinem 60. Geburtstag Überreicht,* 261-71. NovTSup 6. Leiden: E. J. Brill, 1962.

———. *Studies in Paul: Theology for the Early Christian Mission.* Minneapolis: Augsburg Publishing House, 1977.

Das, A. Andrew. *Paul and the Jews.* LPS. Peabody: Hendrickson Publishers, 2003.

———. *Paul, the Law, and the Covenant.* Peabody: Hendrickson Publishers, 2001.

———. *Solving the Romans Debate.* Minneapolis: Fortress Press, 2007.

Daube, David. *The New Testament and Rabbinic Judaism.* London: Athlone Press, 1956.

———. "Rabbinic Methods of Interpretation and Hellenistic Rhetoric." *HUCA* 22 (1949): 239-64.

Davies, Glenn N. *Faith and Obedience in Romans: A Study in Romans 1–4.* JSNTSup 39. Sheffield: JSOT Press, 1990.

Davies, W. D. "Canon and Christology." In *The Glory of Christ in the New Testament,* 19-36. Ed. N. T. Wright and L. D. Hurst. Oxford: Clarendon, 1987; revised as "Canon and Christology in Paul." In *Paul and the Scriptures of Israel,* 18-39. Ed. Craig A. Evans and James A. Sanders. JNSTSup 83/SSEJC 1. Sheffield: JSOT, 1993.

————. *Jewish and Pauline Studies*. Philadelphia: Fortress Press, 1983.

————. "Paul and the Law: Reflections on Pitfalls in Interpretation." In *Paul and Paulinism: Essays in Honour of C. K. Barrett*, 4-16. Ed. Morna D. Hooker and Stephen G. Wilson. London: SPCK, 1982.

————. "Paul and the New Exodus." In *The Quest for Context and Meaning: Studies in Biblical Intertextuality in Honor of James A. Sanders*, 442-63. Ed. Craig A. Evans and Shemaryahu Talmon. Leiden: E. J. Brill, 1997.

————. *Paul and Rabbinic Judaism*. 4th ed. Philadelphia: Fortress Press, 1980.

————. "Paul from the Jewish Point of View." In *The Cambridge History of Judaism*, 3:678-730. Ed. William D. Davies and Louis Finkelstein. 4 vols. New York: Cambridge University Press, 1984-2006.

————. "Reflections about the Use of the Old Testament in the New in Its Historical Context." *JQR* 74 (1983): 105-36.

Davies, William D., and Louis Finkelstein, eds. *The Cambridge History of Judaism*. 4 vols. New York: Cambridge University Press, 1984-2006.

Davis, Christopher A. *The Structure of Paul's Theology: "The Truth Which Is the Gospel."* Lewiston: Mellen Biblical Press, 1995.

Debanné, Marc J. *Enthymemes in the Letters of Paul*. LNTS 303. New York: T&T Clark, 2006.

Deibler, Ellis W. *A Semantic Structure Analysis of Romans*. Dallas: Summer Institute of Linguistics, 1998.

Deissmann, Gustav Adolf. *Bible Studies*. 2d ed. Edinburgh: T&T Clark, 1903.

————. *Paul: A Study of His Social and Religious History*. 2d ed. New York: Harper & Brothers, 1927.

Denniston, John D. *The Greek Particles*. 2d ed. Rev. K. J. Dover. Oxford: Oxford University Press, 1950.

Dettwiler, Andreas, Jean-Daniel Kaestli, and Daniel Marguerat, eds. *Paul, une théologie en construction*. MdB 51. Geneve: Labor et Fides, 2004.

Dewey, Arthur J. "A Re-Hearing of Romans 10:1-15." In *Orality and Textuality in Early Christian Literature*, 109-27. Semeia 65. Atlanta: Scholars Press, 1995.

Dibelius, Martin. *Studies in the Acts of the Apostles*. London: SCM Press, 1956.

————, and Werner G. Kümmel. *Paul*. Philadelphia: Westminster Press, 1953.

Dinter, Paul E. "Paul and the Prophet Isaiah." *BTB* 13 (1983): 48-52.

————. "The Remnant of Israel and the Stone of Stumbling in Zion according to Paul (Romans 9–11)." Ph.D. diss., Union Theological Seminary, 1980.

Dobschütz, Ernst von. "Zum Wortschatz, und Stil des Römerbriefs." *ZNW* 33 (1934): 51-66.

Dodd, C. H. *According to the Scriptures: The Substructure of New Testament Theology*. London: Nisbet, 1952.

————. *The Bible and the Greeks*. London: Hodder & Stoughton, 1935.

————. *The Epistle to the Romans*. New York: Long & Smith, 1932.

————. *The Meaning of Paul for Today*. London: Allen & Unwin, 1949.

————. *The Old Testament in the New*. London: Athlone, 1952.

Donaldson, Terence L. "The 'Curse of the Law' and the Inclusion of the Gentiles: Galatians 3:13-14." *NTS* 32 (1986): 94-112.

————. "Parallels: Use, Misuse and Limitations." *EvQ* 55 (1983): 193-210.

————. *Paul and the Gentiles: Remapping the Apostle's Convictional World.* Minneapolis: Fortress Press, 1997.

————. "'Riches for the Gentiles' (Rom 11:12): Israel's Rejection and Paul's Gentile Mission." *JBL* 112 (1993): 81-98.

Donfried, Karl P. "Rethinking Paul: On the Way toward a Revised Paradigm." *Bib* 87 (2006): 582-94.

————, ed. *The Romans Debate.* Rev. ed. Peabody: Hendrickson Publishers, 1991.

————, and Peter Richardson, eds. *Judaism and Christianity in First-Century Rome.* Grand Rapids: Wm. B. Eerdmans, 1998.

Doohan, Helen. *Paul's Vision of Church.* GNS 32. Wilmington: Michael Glazier, 1989.

Drane, John W. "Why Did Paul Write Romans?" In *Pauline Studies: Essays Presented to Professor F. F. Bruce on His 70th Birthday,* 208-27. Ed. Donald A. Hagner and Murray J. Harris. Grand Rapids: Wm. B. Eerdmans, 1980.

Dungan, David. *The Sayings of Jesus in the Churches of Paul.* Philadelphia: Fortress Press, 1971.

Dunn, James D. G., ed. *The Cambridge Companion to Paul.* Cambridge Companions to Religion. Cambridge: Cambridge University Press, 2003.

————. *Christology in the Making: A New Testament Inquiry into the Origins of the Doctrine of the Incarnation.* London: SCM, 1980; 2d ed., 1989.

————. "The Formal and Theological Coherence of Romans." In *The Romans Debate,* 245-50. Rev. ed. Ed. Karl P. Donfried. Peabody: Hendrickson Publishers, 1991.

————, ed. *Jews and Christians.* WUNT 66. Tübingen: J. C. B. Mohr (Paul Siebeck), 1992.

————. "The New Perspective on Paul." *BJRL* 65 (1983): 95-122; reprinted in *The Romans Debate,* 299-308. Ed. Karl P. Donfried. Rev. ed. Peabody: Hendrickson Publishers, 1991, and in *The New Perspective on Paul* (next entry), 99-120.

————. *The New Perspective on Paul.* Rev. ed. Grand Rapids: Wm. B. Eerdmans, 2008.

————, ed. *Paul and the Mosaic Law.* Grand Rapids: Wm. B. Eerdmans, 1996.

————. "Paul's Epistle to the Romans: An Analysis of Structure and Argument." *ANRW* 2.25.4 (1987): 2842-90.

————. *Romans.* 2 vols. WBC 38A-38B. Dallas: Word Books, 1988.

————. *The Theology of Paul the Apostle.* Grand Rapids: Wm. B. Eerdmans, 1998.

————. "Who Did Paul Think He Was? A Study of Jewish-Christian Identity." *NTS* 45 (1999): 174-93.

————. "Yet Once More — 'The Works of the Law': A Response." *NTS* 46 (1992): 99-117; reprinted in *The New Perspective on Paul* (see entry above), 213-26.

Du Toit, Andreas B., *Focusing on Paul: Persuasion and Theological Design in Romans and Galatians.* BZNW 151. New York: Walter de Gruyter, 2007.

————. "*Paulus Oecumenicus:* Interculturality in the Shaping of Paul's Theology." *NTS* 55 (2009): 121-43.

Edwards, James R. *Romans.* NIBCNT 6. Peabody: Hendrickson Publishers, 1992.

Ehrensperger, Kathy. *That We May Be Mutually Encouraged: Feminism and the New Perspective in Pauline Studies.* Edinburgh: T&T Clark, 2004.

Ehrman, Bart D. *The Orthodox Corruption of Scripture: The Effect of Early Christological*

Controversies on the Text of the New Testament. New York: Oxford University Press, 1993.

Eisenbaum, Pamela. "A Remedy for Having Been Born of Woman: Jesus, Gentiles, and Genealogy in Romans." *JBL* 123 (2004): 671-702.

Elliott, James K. "Thoroughgoing Eclecticism in New Testament Textual Criticism." In *The Text of the New Testament in Contemporary Research: Essays on the Status Quaestionis,* 321-33. Ed. Bart D. Ehrman and Michael W. Holmes. SD 46. Grand Rapids: Wm. B. Eerdmans, 1995.

Elliott, Neil. *The Arrogance of Nations: Reading Romans in the Shadow of Empire.* PCC. Minneapolis: Fortress Press, 2008.

—————. *Liberating Paul: The Justice of God and the Politics of the Apostle.* Maryknoll: Orbis Books, 1994.

—————. *The Rhetoric of Romans: Argumentative Constraint and Strategy and Paul's Dialogue with Judaism.* JSNTSup 45. Sheffield: JSOT Press, 1990; reprinted, Minneapolis: Fortress Press, 2006.

—————, and Mark Reasoner, eds. *Documents and Images for the Study of Paul.* Minneapolis: Fortress Press, 2010.

Ellis, E. Earle. "Biblical Interpretation in the New Testament Church." In *Mikra: Text, Translation, Reading, and Interpretation of the Hebrew Bible in Ancient Judaism and Early Christianity,* 691-725. Ed. Martin J. Mulder. CRINT II/1. Assen: Van Gorcum/Philadelphia: Fortress Press, 1988.

—————. "Midrash, Targum and New Testament Quotations." *Neotestamentica et Semitica: Studies in Honor of Matthew Black,* 61-69. Ed. E. Earle Ellis and Max Wilcox. Edinburgh: T&T Clark, 1969.

—————. *The Old Testament in Early Christianity.* WUNT 54. Tübingen: Mohr-Siebeck, 1991.

—————. *Paul and His Recent Interpreters.* Grand Rapids: Wm. B. Eerdmans, 1961.

—————. *Paul's Use of the Old Testament.* Grand Rapids: Wm. B. Eerdmans, 1957; reprinted, Grand Rapids: Baker Book House, 1981.

—————. *Prophecy and Hermeneutic in Early Christianity.* WUNT 18. Tübingen: Mohr-Siebeck, 1978.

Engberg-Pedersen, Troels. *Paul and the Stoics.* Louisville: Westminster John Knox Press, 2000.

—————, ed. *Paul beyond the Judaism/Hellenism Divide.* Louisville: Westminster John Knox Press, 2001.

—————, ed. *Paul in His Hellenistic Context.* Minneapolis: Fortress Press, 1995.

Enslin, Morton S. *The Ethics of Paul.* Nashville: Abingdon Press, 1957.

—————. *Reapproaching Paul.* Philadelphia: Westminster Press, 1972.

Epp, Eldon J. "Jewish-Gentile Continuity in Paul: Torah and/or Faith? (Romans 9:1-5)." *HTR* 79 (1986): 80-90.

—————. "New Testament Papyrus Manuscripts and Letter Carrying in Greco-Roman Times." In *The Future of Early Christianity: Essays in Honor of Helmut Koester,* 35-56. Ed. Birger A. Pearson. Minneapolis: Fortress Press, 1991.

Erdman, Charles R. *The Epistle to the Romans: An Exposition*. Philadelphia: Westminster Press, 1925.

Esler, Philip E. *Conflict and Identity in Romans: The Social Setting of Paul's Letter*. Minneapolis: Fortress Press, 2003.

Evans, Craig A. *Ancient Texts for New Testament Studies: A Guide to the Background Literature*. Peabody: Hendrickson Publishers, 2005.

———, and James A. Sanders, eds. *Early Christian Interpretation of the Scriptures of Israel: Investigations and Proposals*. JSNTSup 148/SSEJC 5. Sheffield: Sheffield Academic Press, 1997.

———, eds. *The Function of Scripture in Early Jewish and Christian Tradition*. JSNTSup 154/ SSEJC 6. Sheffield: Sheffield Academic Press, 1998.

Evans, Craig A. and James A. Sanders, eds. *Paul and the Scriptures of Israel*. JSNTSup 83/ SSEJC 1. Sheffield: JSOT Press, 1993.

Fee, Gordon D. *God's Empowering Presence: The Holy Spirit in the Letters of Paul*. Peabody: Hendrickson Publishers, 1994.

———. *Paul, the Spirit, and the People of God*. Peabody: Hendrickson Publishers. 1996.

———. *Pauline Christology: An Exegetical-Theological Study*. Peabody: Hendrickson Publishers. 2007.

Feine, Paul. *Der Apostel Paulus: Das Ringen um das geschichtliche Verständnis des Paulus*. BFTC 2/12. Gütersloh: C. Bertelsmann, 1927.

———. *Der Römerbrief: Eine exegetische Studie*. Göttingen: Vandenhoeck & Ruprecht, 1903.

Feldman, Louis H. *Jew and Gentile in the Ancient World: Attitudes and Interactions from Alexander to Justinian*. Princeton: Princeton University Press, 1993.

Ferguson, Everett. *Backgrounds of Early Christianity*. 3d ed. Grand Rapids: Wm. B. Eerdmans, 2003.

Fitzgerald, John T., Thomas H. Olbricht, and L. Michael White, eds. *Early Christianity and Classical Culture: Comparative Studies in Honor of Abraham J. Malherbe*. NovTSup 110. Boston: E. J. Brill, 2003.

Fitzmyer, Joseph A. *According to Paul: Studies in the Theology of the Apostle*. New York: Paulist Press, 1993.

———. "'4QTestimonia' and the New Testament." *TS* 18 (1957): 513-37; reprinted in *Essays in the Semitic Background of the New Testament*, 59-89. London: Geoffrey Chapman, 1971.

———. "The Letter to the Romans." In *The New Jerome Biblical Commentary*, 830-68. Ed. Raymond E. Brown et al. Englewood Cliffs: Prentice-Hall, 1990.

———. "Paul and the Dead Sea Scrolls." In *The Dead Sea Scrolls after Fifty Years: A Comprehensive Assessment*, 2:599-621. Ed. Peter W. Flint and James C. VanderKam. 2 vols. Boston: E. J. Brill, 1998-99.

———. *Romans*. AB 33. New York: Doubleday, 1993.

———. *Spiritual Exercises Based on Paul's Epistle to the Romans*. Grand Rapids: Wm. B. Eerdmans, 2004.

———. "The Use of Explicit Old Testament Quotations in Qumran Literature and in the

New Testament." *NTS* 7 (1960-61): 297-333; reprinted in his *Essays in the Semitic Background of the New Testament*, 3-58. London: Geoffrey Chapman, 1971.

Flamming, J. "The New Testament Use of Isaiah." *SWJT* 11 (1968): 89-103.

Flebbe, Jochen. *Solus Deus: Untersuchungen zur Rede von Gott im Brief des Paulus an die Römer.* BZNW 158. Berlin: de Gruyter, 2008.

Flesher, Paul V. M., ed. *Targum and Scripture: Studies in Aramaic Translations and Interpretation in Memory of Ernest G. Clarke.* SAIS 2. Boston: E. J. Brill, 2002.

Foakes-Jackson, Frederick J., and Kirsopp Lake, eds. *The Beginnings of Christianity.* 5 vols. London: Macmillan and Company, 1920-33.

Fonrobert, Charlotte E., and Martin S. Jaffee, eds. *The Cambridge Companion to the Talmud and Rabbinic Literature.* New York: Cambridge University Press, 207.

Fowl, Stephen E. *The Story of Christ in the Ethics of Paul: An Analysis of the Function of the Hymnic Material in the Pauline Corpus.* JSNTSup 36. Sheffield: Sheffield Academic Press, 1990.

Fox, Michael. "The Identification of Quotations in Biblical Literature." *ZAW* 92 (1980): 416-31.

Fredricksen, Paula. "Judaizing the Nations: The Ritual Demands of Paul's Gospel." *NTS* 56 (2010): 232-52.

Frey, Jörg, and Jens Schröter, eds. *Deutungen des Todes Jesu im Neuen Testament.* WUNT 181. Tübingen: J. C. B. Mohr (Paul Siebeck), 2005.

Frid, Bo. "Jesaja und Paulus in Röm 15,12." *BZ* 27 (1983): 237-41.

Furnish, Victor P. *Jesus according to Paul.* Cambridge: Cambridge University Press, 1994.

———. *The Moral Teaching of Paul: Selected Issues.* 3d ed. Nashville: Abingdon Press, 2009.

———. "On Putting Paul in His Place." *JBL* 113 (1994): 3-17.

———. *Theology and Ethics in Paul.* Nashville: Abingdon Press, 1968; new ed. NTL. Louisville: Westminster John Knox, 2009.

Gaca, Kathy L., and Laurence L. Welborn, eds. *Early Patristic Readings of Romans.* RHCS. Edinburgh: T&T Clark, 2005.

Gagarin, Michael, ed. *Oxford Encyclopedia of Ancient Greece and Rome.* 7 vols. New York: Oxford University Press, 2010.

Gager, John G. *The Origins of Anti-Semitism: Attitudes toward Judaism in Pagan and Christian Antiquity.* Oxford: Oxford University Press, 1983.

———. *Reinventing Paul.* New York: Oxford University Press, 2000.

Gamble, Harry. *The Textual History of the Letter to the Romans: A Study in Textual and Literary Criticism.* SD 42. Grand Rapids: Wm. B. Eerdmans, 1977.

García Martínez, Florentino, and Gerard P. Luttikhuizen, eds. *Jerusalem, Alexandria, Rome: Studies in Ancient Cultural Interaction in Honour of A. Hilhorst.* SuppJSJ 82. Boston: E. J. Brill, 2003.

Garlington, Don B. *Faith, Obedience, and Perseverance: Aspects of Paul's Letter to the Romans.* WUNT 79. Tübingen: J. C. B. Mohr (Paul Siebeck), 1994.

———. *Studies in the New Perspective on Paul: Essays and Reviews.* Eugene: Wipf & Stock, 2008.

Gaston, Lloyd. *Paul and the Torah.* Vancouver: University of British Columbia Press, 1987.

―――――. "Romans in Context: The Conversation Revisited." In *Pauline Conversations in Context: Essays in Honor of Calvin J. Roetzel,* 125-41. Ed. Janice Capel Anderson, Philip Sellew, and Claudia Setzer. JSNTSup 221. Sheffield: Sheffield Academic Press, 2002.

Gathercole, Simon J. *Where Is Boasting? Early Jewish Soteriology and Paul's Response in Romans 1–5.* Grand Rapids: Wm. B. Eerdmans, 2002.

Gaventa, Beverly Roberts. "The God Who Will Not Be Taken for Granted: Reflections on Paul's Letter to the Romans." In *The Ending of Mark and the Ends of God: Essays in Memory of Donald Harrisville Juel,* 77-89. Ed. Beverly Roberts Gaventa and Patrick D. Miller. Louisville: Westminster John Knox Press, 2005.

―――――. *Our Mother Saint Paul.* Louisville: Westminster John Knox, 2007.

Geer, Thomas C. "Paul and the Law in Recent Discussion." *ResQ* 31 (1989) 93-107.

Gemünden, Petra von. "Image de Dieu — Image de l'être humain dans l'Épître aux Romains." *RHPR* 77/1 (1997): 31-49.

Georgi, Dieter. *Theocracy in Paul's Praxis and Theology.* Minneapolis: Fortress Press, 1991.

Giardina, Andrea, ed. *The Romans.* Chicago: University of Chicago Press, 1993.

Gibbs, John G. *Creation and Redemption: A Study in Pauline Theology.* NovTSup 26. Leiden: E. J. Brill, 1971.

Given, Mark D. *Paul Unbound: Other Perspectives on the Apostle.* Peabody: Hendrickson Publishers, 2010.

―――――. *Paul's True Rhetoric: Ambiguity, Cunning, and Deception in Greece and Rome.* Harrisburg: Trinity Press International, 2001.

―――――. "True Rhetoric: Ambiguity, Cunning, and Deception in Pauline Discourse." *SBLSP* (1997): 526-50.

Glover, Terrot R. *Paul of Tarsus.* New York: George H. Doran, 1925; reprinted, Peabody: Hendrickson Publishers, 2002.

Godet, Frédéric L. *Commentary on St. Paul's Epistle to the Romans.* 2 vols. Edinburgh: T&T Clark, 1880-81; reprinted, Grand Rapids: Kregel Publications, 1977.

Godsey, John D. "The Interpretation of Romans in the History of the Christian Faith." *Int* 34 (1980): 3-16.

Goodenough, E. R., and A. T. Kraabel. "Paul and the Hellenization of Christianity." In *Religions in Antiquity,* ed. Jacob Neusner, 23-68. Leiden: E. J. Brill, 1968.

Goodman, Martin D. *Mission and Conversion: Proselytizing in the Religious History of the Roman Empire.* New York: Oxford University Press, 1994.

Goodspeed, Edgar J. *Paul.* Philadelphia: John C. Winston Company, 1947.

Goodwin, Mark J. *Paul, Apostle of the Living God.* Harrisburg: Trinity Press International, 2001.

Goppelt, Leonhard. *Theology of the New Testament.* 2 vols. Grand Rapids: Wm. B. Eerdmans, 1981-82.

Gorman, Michael J. *Apostle of the Crucified Lord: A Theological Introduction to Paul and His Letters.* Grand Rapids: Wm. B. Eerdmans, 2004.

―――――. *Cruciformity: Paul's Narrative Spirituality of the Cross.* Grand Rapids: Wm. B. Eerdmans, 2001.

―――――. *Reading Paul.* Eugene: Cascade Books, 2008.

Goulder, Michael D. *Paul and the Competing Mission in Corinth.* Peabody: Hendrickson Publishers, 2001.

Gräbe, Petrus. *The Power of God in Paul's Letters.* WUNT 2/123. Tübingen: J. C. B. Mohr (Paul Siebeck), 2000.

Grafe, Eduard. *Über Veranlassung und Zweck des Römerbriefes.* Freiburg: J. C. B. Mohr, 1881.

Grant, Robert M. *Paul in the Roman World: The Conflict at Corinth.* Louisville: Westminster John Knox Press, 2001.

Grayston, Kenneth. *The Epistle to the Romans.* EpComm. Peterborough: Epworth Press, 1997.

Grech, Prosper. "The 'Testimonia' and Modern Hermeneutics." *NTS* 19 (1972-73): 318-24.

Greenman, Jeffrey P., and Timothy Larsen, eds. *Reading Romans through the Centuries: From the Early Church to Karl Barth.* Grand Rapids: Brazos Press, 2005.

Grelot, Pierre. *L'épître de Saint Paul aux Romains: Une lecture pour aujourd'hui.* Versailles: Éditions Saint-Paul, 2001.

Grenholm, Cristina. "The Process of the Interpretation of Romans." In *Society of Biblical Literature Seminar 1997 Papers,* 306-36. SBLSP 36. Atlanta: Scholars Press, 1997.

————. *Romans Interpreted: A Comparative Analysis of the Commentaries of Barth, Nygren, Cranfield and Wilckens on Paul's Epistle to the Romans.* AUUSDCU 30. Stockholm: Almqvist & Wiksell, 1990.

————, and Daniel Patte, eds. *Gender, Tradition and Romans: Shared Ground, Uncertain Borders.* RHCS. New York: T&T Clark, 2005.

————. *Reading Israel in Romans: Legitimacy and Plausibility of Divergent Interpretations.* RHCS 1. Harrisburg: Trinity Press International, 2000.

Grieb, A. Katherine. *The Story of Romans: A Narrative Defense of God's Righteousness.* Louisville: Westminster John Knox Press, 2002.

Griffith, Gwilym O. *St. Paul's Gospel to the Romans.* Oxford: Blackwell, 1949.

Griffith-Jones, Robin. *The Gospel according to Paul: The Creative Genius Who Brought Jesus to the World.* San Francisco: HarperSanFrancisco, 2004.

Gruen, Erich S. *Diaspora: Jews amidst Greeks and Romans.* Cambridge: Harvard University Press, 2002.

————. "Roman Perspectives on the Jews in the Age of the Great Revolt." In *The First Jewish Revolt against Rome: Archaeology, History, and Ideology,* 27-42. Ed. Andrea M. Berlin and J. Andrew Overman. London: Routledge, 2002.

Grundmann, Walter. *Der Römerbrief des Apostels Paulus und seine Auslegung durch Martin Luther.* Weimar: H. Böhlaus Nachfolger, 1964.

Guerra, Anthony J. *Romans and the Apologetic Tradition: The Purpose, Genre, and Audience of Paul's Letter.* SNTSMS 81. Cambridge: Cambridge University Press, 1995.

Güting, Eberhard W., and David L. Mealand. *Asyndeton in Paul: A Text-critical and Statistical Enquiry into Pauline Style.* Lewiston: Edwin Mellen Press, 1989.

Gundry Volf, Judith M. *Paul and Perseverance: Staying In and Falling Away.* WUNT 2/37. Tübingen: J. C. B. Mohr (Paul Siebeck), 1990; reprinted, Louisville: Westminster John Knox Press, 1991.

Haacker, Klaus. "Die Berufung des Verfolgers und die Rechtfertigung des Gottlosen: Erwägungen zum Zusammenhang zwischen Biographie und Theologie des Apostels Paulus." *TBei* 6 (1975): 1-19.

―――. *Der Brief des Paulus an die Römer.* THNT 6. Leipzig: Evangelische Verlagsanstalt, 1999.

―――. "Exegetische Probleme des Römerbriefs." *NovT* 20 (1978): 1-21.

―――. "Der Römerbrief als Friedensmemorandum." *NTS* 36 (1990): 25-41.

―――. *The Theology of Paul's Letter to the Romans.* New Testament Theology. Cambridge: Cambridge University Press, 2003.

Haenchen, Ernst. *The Acts of the Apostles: A Commentary.* Philadelphia: Westminster, 1971.

Hagner, Donald A., and Murray J. Harris, eds. *Pauline Studies: Essays Presented to F. F. Bruce on His 70th Birthday.* Grand Rapids: Wm. B. Eerdmans, 1980.

Haines-Eitzen, Kim. *Guardians of Letters: Literacy, Power, and the Transmission of Early Christian Literature.* New York: Oxford University Press, 2000.

Hanhart, Robert. "Die Bedeutung der Septuaginta in neutestamentlicher Zeit." *ZTK* 81 (1984): 395-416.

―――. "The Translation of the Septuagint in Light of Earlier Tradition and Subsequent Influences." In *Septuagint, Scrolls and Cognate Writings,* 339-79. Ed. George J. Brooke and Barnabas Lindars. SBLSCS 33. Atlanta: Scholars Press, 1992.

Hanson, Anthony T. *The New Testament Interpretation of Scripture.* London: SPCK, 1980.

―――. *Paul's Understanding of Jesus.* Hull: The University Press, 1963.

―――. *Studies in Paul's Technique and Theology.* London: SPCK, 1974.

Harder, Günther. "Der konkrete Anlass des Römerbriefes." *ThViat* 6 (1959): 13-24.

Harink, Douglas. *Paul among the Postliberals: Pauline Theology beyond Christendom and Modernity.* Grand Rapids: Brazos Press, 2003.

Harland, Philip. *Associations, Synagogues, and Congregations: Claiming a Place in Ancient Mediterranean Society.* Minneapolis: Fortress Press, 2003.

Harnack, Adolf von. "The Old Testament in the Pauline Letters and in the Pauline Churches." In *Understanding Paul's Ethics: Twentieth-Century Approaches.* Ed. Brian S. Rosner, 27-49. Grand Rapids: Eerdmans, 1995.

Harrington, Daniel J. "Paul's Use of the Old Testament in Romans." *Studies in Christian-Jewish Relations* 4 (2009): 1-8.

Harris, J. Rendel. *Testimonies.* 2 vols. Cambridge: Cambridge University Press, 1916-20.

Harrisville, Roy A. *Romans.* ACNT. Minneapolis: Augsburg Publishing House, 1980.

Harrisville, Roy A., III. *The Figure of Abraham in the Epistles of St. Paul: In the Footsteps of Abraham.* Lewiston, NY: Edwin Mellen Press, 1992.

Harvey, Graham. *The True Israel: Uses of the Names Jew, Hebrew and Israel in Ancient Jewish and Early Christian Literature.* AGAJU 35. Leiden: E. J. Brill, 1996.

Hatch, Edwin. "On Early Quotations from the Septuagint." *Essays in Biblical Greek,* 131-202. Oxford: Clarendon Press, 1889.

―――. "On Composite Quotations from the Septuagint." *Essays in Biblical Greek,* 203-14. Oxford: Clarendon Press, 1889.

Hay, David M., ed. *Pauline Theology,* vol. 2, *1 and 2 Corinthians.* Minneapolis: Fortress Press, 1993.

————, and E. Elizabeth Johnson, eds. *Pauline Theology,* vol. 3, *Romans.* Minneapolis: Fortress Press, 1995.

Hays, Richard B. "Adam, Israel, Christ: The Question of Covenant in the Theology of Romans." In *Pauline Theology,* vol. 3, *Romans,* 68-86. Ed. David M. Hay and E. Elizabeth Johnson. Minneapolis: Fortress Press, 1995.

————. *The Conversion of the Imagination: Paul as an Interpreter of Israel's Scripture.* Grand Rapids: Wm. B. Eerdmans, 2005.

————. *Echoes of Scripture in the Letters of Paul.* New Haven: Yale University Press, 1989.

————. *The Faith of Jesus Christ: The Narrative Substructure of Galatians 3:1–4:11.* 2d ed. Grand Rapids: Wm. B. Eerdmans, 2002.

————. "Justification." *ABD* 3:1129-33.

————. *The Moral Vision of the New Testament: Community, Cross, New Creation.* San Francisco: HarperSanFrancisco, 1996.

Heil, John P. *Paul's Letter to the Romans: A Reader-Response Commentary.* New York: Paulist Press, 1987.

————. *Romans: Paul's Letter of Hope.* AnBib 112. Rome: Pontifical Biblical Institute Press, 1987.

Hemer, Colin J. *The Book of Acts in the Setting of Hellenistic History.* Tübingen: J. C. B. Mohr (Paul Siebeck), 1989.

Hendriksen, William. *Romans.* Grand Rapids: Baker Book House, 1993.

Hengel, Martin. *Acts and the History of Earliest Christianity.* Trans. John Bowden. Philadelphia: Fortress Press, 1983.

————. *Between Jesus and Paul: Studies in the Earliest History of Christianity.* Philadelphia: Fortress Press, 1983.

————. *Crucifixion in the Ancient World and the Folly of the Message of the Cross.* Philadelphia: Fortress Press, 1977.

————. *Paulus und Jakobus: Kleine Schriften,* Band 3. WUNT 141. Tübingen: J. C. B. Mohr (Paul Siebeck), 2002.

————. *The Pre-Christian Paul.* Philadelphia: Trinity Press International, 1991.

————, and C. K. Barrett. *Conflicts and Challenges in Early Christianity.* Harrisburg: Trinity Press International, 1999.

————, and Anna Maria Schwemer. *Paul: Between Damascus and Antioch — The Unknown Years.* Louisville: Westminster John Knox Press, 1997.

Heyer, C. J. den. *Paul: A Man of Two Worlds.* Harrisburg: Trinity Press International, 2000.

Hill, Craig C. "Romans." In *The Oxford Bible Commentary,* 1083-1108. Ed. John Barton and John Muddiman. New York: Oxford University Press, 2001.

Hillert, Sven. *Limited and Universal Salvation: A Text-Oriented and Hermeneutical Study of Two Perspectives in Paul.* ConBNT 31. Stockholm: Almqvist & Wiksell, 1999.

Hodge, Charles. *A Commentary on the Epistle to the Romans.* Rev. ed. Philadelphia: William S. and Alfred Martien, 1864; reprinted, Grand Rapids: Wm. B. Eerdmans, 1980.

Hodgson, Robert. "The Testimony Hypothesis." *JBL* 98 (1979): 361-78.

Hofius, Otfried. *Paulusstudien.* Band 1. 2d ed. WUNT 51. Tübingen: J. C. B. Mohr (Paul Siebeck), 1994.

————. *Paulusstudien.* Band 2. WUNT 143. Tübingen: J. C. B. Mohr (Paul Siebeck), 2002.

Hollingshead, James R. *The Household of Caesar and the Body of Christ: A Political Interpretation of the Letters from Paul.* Lanham: University Press of America, 1998.

Holloway, Paul A. "The Enthymeme as an Element of Style in Paul." *JBL* 120 (2001): 329-39.

Holmberg, Bengt. *Paul and Power: The Structure of Authority in the Primitive Church as Reflected in the Pauline Epistles.* ConBNT 11. Lund: C. W. K. Gleerup, 1978.

Holtz, Gudrun. *Damit Gott sei alles in allem: Studien in paulinischen und frühjüdischen Universalismus.* BZNW 149. New York: Walter de Gruyter, 2007.

Holtz, Traugott. "Die historischen und theologischen Bedingungen des Römerbriefes." In *Evangelium Schriftauslegung Kirche: Festschrift für Peter Stuhlmacher zum 65. Geburtstag,* 238-54. Ed. Jostein Ådna, Scott J. Hafemann, and Otfried Hofius. Göttingen: Vandenhoeck & Ruprecht, 1997.

———. "Zum Selbstverständnis des Apostels Paulus." *TLZ* 91 (1966): 321-30; reprinted in his *Geschichte und Theologie des Urchristentums: Gesammelte Aufsätze,* 129-39. Ed. Eckart Reinmuth and Christian Wolff. WUNT 57. Tübingen: J. C. B. Mohr (Paul Siebeck), 1991.

Hooker, Morna D. *From Adam to Christ: Essays on Paul.* Cambridge: Cambridge University Press, 1990.

———. "Interchange in Christ." *JTS* 22 (1971): 349-61.

———. "Paul and Covenantal Nomism." In *Paul and Paulinism: Essays in Honour of C. K. Barrett,* 47-56. Ed. Morna D. Hooker and S. G. Wilson. London: SPCK, 1982.

———. *A Preface to Paul.* New York: Oxford University Press, 1980.

———, and S. G. Wilson, eds. *Paul and Paulinism: Essays in Honour of C. K. Barrett.* London: SPCK, 1982.

Horrell, David G. "From ἀδελφοί to οἶκος θεοῦ: Social Transformation in Pauline Christianity." *JBL* 120 (2001): 293-311.

———. *An Introduction to the Study of Paul.* 2d ed. New York: Continuum, 2006.

———. *Solidarity and Difference: A Contemporary Reading of Paul's Ethics.* Edinburgh: T&T Clark, 2005.

Horsley, Richard A., ed. *Paul and Politics: Ekklesia, Imperium, Interpretation: Essays in Honor of Krister Stendahl.* Harrisburg: Trinity Press International, 2000.

Hort, Fenton J. A. *Prolegomena to St. Paul's Epistles to the Romans and the Ephesians.* New York: Macmillan, 1895.

Hubbard, Moyer V. *New Creation in Paul's Letters and Thought.* SNTSMS 119. Cambridge: Cambridge University Press, 2002.

Hübner, Hans. *Biblische Theologie des Neuen Testaments.* 3 vols. Göttingen: Vandenhoeck & Ruprecht, 1990-95.

———. "Intertextualität — Die hermeneutische Strategie des Paulus." *TLZ* 116 (1991): 881-98.

———. *Law in Paul's Thought.* Edinburgh: T&T Clark, 1984.

———. "Pauli Theologiae Proprium." *NTS* 26 (1980): 445-73.

———. "Paulus 1, Neues Testament." In *TRE* 26 (1996): 133-53.

———. "Paulusforschung seit 1945: Ein kritischer Literaturbericht." In *ANRW* II.25.4 (1987): 2649-2840.

———. "Die Rhetorik und die Theologie: Der Römerbrief und die rhetorische Kompetenz des Paulus." In *Die Macht des Wortes: Aspekte gegenwärtiger Rhetorikforschung: Ars Rhetorica 4*, 165-79. Ed. Carl J. Classen and Heinz-Joachim Müllenbrock. Marburg: Hitzenroth, 1992.

———. *Vetus Testamentum in Novo*, Band 2, *Corpus Paulinum*. Göttingen: Vandenhoeck & Ruprecht, 1997.

Hultgren, Arland J. *Paul's Gospel and Mission: The Outlook from His Letter to the Romans.* Philadelphia: Fortress Press, 1985.

———. "Paul's Pre-Christian Persecutions of the Church: Their Purpose, Locale, and Nature." *JBL* 95 (1976): 97-111.

———. "The Self-Definition of Paul and His Communities." *SEÅ* 56 (1991): 78-100.

Hunter, Archibald M. *The Epistle to the Romans: Introduction and Commentary.* TBC 8.6. London: SCM, 1955.

Hurtado, Larry W. *Lord Jesus Christ: Devotion to Jesus in Earliest Christianity.* Grand Rapids: Wm. B. Eerdmans, 2003.

Janowski, Bernd, and Peter Stuhlmacher, eds. *The Suffering Servant: Isaiah 53 in Jewish and Christian Sources.* Grand Rapids: Wm. B. Eerdmans, 2004.

Jeffers, James S. *Conflict at Rome: Social Order and Hierarchy in Early Christianity.* Minneapolis: Fortress Press, 1991.

Jeremias, Joachim. *Jesus' Promise to the Nations.* London: SCM, 1958.

———. *New Testament Theology: The Proclamation of Jesus.* New York: Charles Scribner's Sons, 1971.

———. *Der Schlüssel zur Theologie des Apostels Paulus.* CH 115. Stuttgart: Calwer Verlag, 1971.

Jervell, Jacob. "The Letter to Jerusalem." In *The Romans Debate*, 53-64. Rev. ed. Ed. Karl P. Donfried. Peabody: Hendrickson Publishers, 1977.

———. *The Theology of the Acts of the Apostles.* New York: Cambridge University Press, 1996.

———. *The Unknown Paul: Essays on Luke-Acts and Early Christianity.* Minneapolis: Fortress Press, 1984.

Jervis, L. Ann. *The Purpose of Romans: A Comparative Letter Structure Investigation.* JSNTSup 55. Sheffield: Sheffield Academic Press, 1991.

Jewett, Robert. "Bibliography on Romans." In *Pauline Theology*, vol. 3, *Romans*, 301-29. Ed. David M. Hay and E. Elizabeth Johnson. Minneapolis: Fortress Press, 1995.

———. *Christian Tolerance: God's Message to a Modern Church.* Philadelphia: Westminster Press, 1982.

———. *A Chronology of Paul's Life.* Philadelphia: Fortress Press, 1979.

———. "Following the Argument of Romans." In *The Romans Debate*, 265-77. Rev. ed. Ed. Karl P. Donfried. Peabody: Hendrickson Publishers, 1977.

———. "Honor and Shame in the Argument of Romans." In *Putting Body and Soul Together: Essays in Honor of Robin Scroggs*, 258-73. Ed. Virginia Wiles, Alexandra Brown, and Graydon F. Snyder. Valley Forge: Trinity Press International, 1997.

———. "The Law and the Coexistence of Jews and Gentiles in Romans." *Int* 39 (1985): 341-56.

———. "Major Impulses in the Theological Interpretation of Romans since Barth." *Int* 34 (1980): 1-31.

———. *Paul's Anthropological Terms: A Study of Their Use in Conflict Settings.* AGAJU 10. Leiden: E. J. Brill, 1971.

———. "Romans." In *The Cambridge Companion to Paul*, 91-104. Ed. James D. G. Dunn. Cambridge: Cambridge University Press, 2003.

———. *Romans.* Hermeneia. Minneapolis: Fortress Press, 2006.

———. "Romans as an Ambassadorial Letter." *Int* 36 (1982): 5-20.

Johnson, E. Elizabeth, and David M. Hay, eds. *Pauline Theology*, vol. 4, *Looking Back, Pressing On.* SBLSymS 4. Atlanta: Scholars Press, 1997.

Johnson, Franklin. *The Quotations of the New Testament from the Old Considered in the Light of General Literature.* Philadelphia: American Baptist Publication Society, 1896.

Johnson, Luke T. *Among the Gentiles: Greco-Roman Religion and Christianity.* Anchor Yale Reference Series. New Haven: Yale University Press, 2009.

———. *Reading Romans: A Literary and Theological Commentary.* New York: Crossroad, 1997.

Joubert, Stephan. *Paul as Benefactor: Reciprocity, Strategy and Theological Reflection in Paul's Collection.* WUNT 2/124. Tübingen: J. C. B. Mohr (Paul Siebeck), 2000.

Jowett, Benjamin. "On the Quotations from the Old Testament in the Writings of St. Paul." In *The Epistles of St. Paul to the Thessalonians, Galatians, Romans: With Critical Notes and Dissertations*, 1:401-16. 2d ed. 2 vols. London: John Murray, 1859.

Judge, Edwin A., and G. S. R. Thomas. "The Origin of the Church at Rome: A New Solution." *RTR* 25 (1966): 81-94.

———. *Social Distinctives of the Christians in the First Century: Pivotal Essays.* Ed. David M. Scholer. Peabody: Hendrickson Publishers, 2008.

Jülicher, Adolf. *An Introduction to the New Testament.* London: Smith, Elder and Company, 1904.

Jüngel, Eberhard. *Paulus und Jesus.* HUTh 2. 6th ed. Tübingen: J. C. B. Mohr (Paul Siebeck), 1986.

Käsemann, Ernst. *Commentary on Romans.* Grand Rapids: Wm. B. Eerdmans, 1980.

———. *Essays on New Testament Themes.* SBT 41. Naperville: A. R. Allenson, 1964.

———. "Justification and Salvation History in the Epistle to the Romans." *Perspectives on Paul*, 60-78. Philadelphia: Fortress Press, 1971.

———. *New Testament Questions for Today.* Philadelphia: Fortress Press, 1969.

———. *Perspectives on Paul.* Philadelphia: Fortress Press, 1971.

———. "The Righteousness of God in Paul." *New Testament Questions of Today*, 168-82. Philadelphia: Fortress Press, 1969.

Kaiser, Bernhard. *Luther und die Auslegung des Römerbriefes: Eine theologisch-geschichtliche Beurteilung.* BibSym 9. Bonn: Verlag für Kultur und Wissenschaft, 1995.

Kalin, Everett Roy. "Rereading Romans: Ethnic Issues (or, 'How can I find a gracious community?')." *CurTM* 25 (1998): 461-72.

Kaye, Bruce N. "'To the Romans and Others' Revisited." *NovT* 18 (1976): 37-77.

Kaylor, R. David. *Paul's Covenant Community: Jew and Gentile in Romans.* Atlanta: John Knox Press, 1988.

Keck, Leander E. *Paul and His Letters.* 2d ed. Proclamation Commentaries. Philadelphia: Fortress Press, 1988.

————. *Romans.* ANTC. Nashville: Abingdon Press, 2005.

————. "Searchable Judgments and Scrutable Ways: A Response to Paul J. Achtemeier." In *Pauline Theology,* vol. 4, *Looking Back, Pressing On,* 22-32. Ed. E. Elizabeth Johnson and David M. Hay. SBLSS 4. Atlanta: Scholars Press, 1997.

————. "What Makes Romans Tick?" In *Pauline Theology,* vol. 3, *Romans,* 3-29. Ed. David M. Hay and E. Elizabeth Johnson. Minneapolis: Fortress Press, 1995.

————, and Victor P. Furnish. *The Pauline Letters.* Nashville: Abingdon Press, 1985.

Keener, Craig S. *Paul, Women, and Wives: Marriage and Women's Ministry in the Letters of Paul.* Peabody: Hendrickson Publishers, 1992.

————. *Romans.* NCCS 6. Eugene: Cascade Books, 2009.

Keesmaat, Sylvia C. "Paul's Use of the Exodus Tradition in Romans and Galatians." D.Phil. diss., Oxford University, 1994.

Kerrigan, Alexander. "Echoes of Themes from the Servant Songs in Pauline Theology." In *Studiorum Paulinorum Congressus Internationalis Catholicus 1961,* 2:217-28. AnBib 17-18. 2 vols. Rome: Pontifical Biblical Institute Press, 1963.

Kertelge, Karl. *The Epistle to the Romans.* NTSR 12. New York: Herder & Herder, 1972.

Kilpatrick, G. D. "The Text of the Epistles: The Contribution of the Western Witnesses." In *Text-Wort-Glaube: Studien zur Überlieferung, Interpretation und Autorisierung biblischen Texte: Kurt Aland gewidmet,* 47-68. Ed. Martin Brecht. AKG 50. Berlin: Walter de Gruyter, 1980.

Kim, Seyoon. *The Origin of Paul's Gospel.* 2d ed. WUNT 2/4. Tübingen: J. C. B. Mohr (Paul Siebeck), 1984.

————. *Paul and the New Perspective: Second Thoughts on the Origin of Paul's Gospel.* Grand Rapids: Wm. B. Eerdmans, 2001.

Kinoshita, Junji. "Romans — Two Writings Combined: A New Interpretation of the Body of Romans." *NovT* 7 (1965): 258-77.

Kirk, J. R. Daniel. *Unlocking Romans: Resurrection and the Justification of God.* Grand Rapids: Wm. B. Eerdmans, 2008.

Klauck, Hans-Josef. *Ancient Letters and the New Testament: A Guide to Context and Exegesis.* Waco: Baylor University Press, 2006.

————. *The Religious Context of Early Christianity: A Guide to Graeco-Roman Religions.* Minneapolis: Fortress Press, 2003.

Klein, Günter. "Paul's Purpose in Writing the Epistle to the Romans." In *The Romans Debate,* 29-43. Ed. Karl P. Donfried. Rev. ed. Peabody: Hendrickson Publishers, 1991.

————. "Romans, Letter to the." *IDBSup* 752-54.

Knox, John. *Chapters in a Life of Paul.* Rev. ed. Macon: Mercer University Press, 1987.

————. *Romans.* In *The Interpreter's Bible,* ed. George Buttrick, 9:355-668. 12 vols. Nashville: Abingdon Press, 1955.

Koch, Dietrich-Alex. *Die Schrift als Zeuge des Evangeliums: Untersuchungen zur Verwen-*

dung und zum Verständnis der Schrift bei Paulus. BHT 69. Tübingen: J. C. B. Mohr (Paul Siebeck), 1986.

Koester, Helmut. *Paul and His World: Interpreting the New Testament in Its Context.* Minneapolis: Fortress Press, 2007.

Kolb, Frank. *Rom: Die Geschichte der Stadt in der Antike.* Munich: C. H. Beck, 1995.

Koperski, Veronica. *What Are They Saying about Paul and the Law?* New York: Paulist Press, 2001.

Kraabel, A. Thomas. "Unity and Diversity among Diaspora Synagogues." In *The Synagogue in Late Antiquity,* 49-60. Ed. Lee I. Levine. Philadelphia: ASOR, 1987.

Kramer, Werner. *Christ, Lord, Son of God.* SBT 50. Naperville: Alec R. Allenson, 1966.

Krentz, Edgar. "Meeting Paul Anew: Rereading an Old Friend in a New Age." *Dialog* 39 (2000): 267-83.

Kruse, Colin. *Paul, the Law, and Justification.* Peabody: Hendrickson Publishers, 1997.

Kümmel, Werner G. "Die Botschaft des Römerbriefs." *TLZ* 99 (1974): 481-88.

———. *Introduction to the New Testament.* Rev. ed. Nashville: Abingdon Press, 1975.

———. *The Theology of the New Testament according to Its Major Witnesses: Jesus–Paul–John.* Nashville: Abingdon Press, 1973.

Kugel, James L. *Traditions of the Bible: A Guide to the Bible as It Was at the Start of the Common Era.* Cambridge: Harvard University Press, 1998.

———, and Rowan A. Greer. *Early Biblical Interpretation.* LEC 3. Philadelphia: Westminster, 1986.

Kuhn, Heinz-Wolfgang. "The Impact of the Qumran Scrolls on the Understanding of Paul." In *The Dead Sea Scrolls: Forty Years of Research,* 327-39. Ed. Devorah Dimant and Uriel Rappaport. STDJ 10. New York: E. J. Brill, 1992.

———. "Qumran und Paulus: Unter traditionsgeschichtlichen Aspekt ausgewählte Parallelen." In *Das Urchristentum in seiner literarischen Geschichte: Festschrift für Jürgen Becker zum 65. Geburtstag,* 227-46. Ed. Ulrich Mell and Ulrich B. Müller. BZNW 100. Berlin: Walter de Gruyter, 1999.

Kuss, Otto. *Paulus. Die Rolle des Apostels in der theologischen Entwicklung des Urchristentums.* 2d ed. Regensburg: F. Pustet, 1976.

———. *Der Römerbrief übersetzt und erklärt.* 3 vols. RNT 6. 2d ed. Regensburg: F. Pustet, 1963.

Kuula, Kari. *The Law, the Covenant and God's Plan.* 2 vols. SESJ 72 and 85. Göttingen: Vandenhoeck & Ruprecht, 1999-2003.

Laato, Timo. *Paul and Judaism: An Anthropological Approach.* SFSHJ 115. Atlanta: Scholars Press, 1995.

Lagrange, Marie-Joseph. *Saint Paul: Épître aux Romains.* ÉBib. 4th ed. Paris: J. Gabalda, 1950.

Lambrecht, Jan. *Pauline Studies: Collected Essays.* BETL 115. Leuven: Leuven University Press, 1994.

Lampe, Peter. *From Paul to Valentinus: Christians at Rome in the First Two Centuries.* Minneapolis: Fortress Press, 2003.

Landes, Paula Fredricksen. *Augustine on Romans: Propositions from the Epistle to the*

Romans; Unfinished Commentary on the Epistle to the Romans. SBL.TT 23. ECLS 6. Chico: Scholars Press, 1982.

Lane, William L. "Roman Christianity during the Formative Years from Nero to Nerva." In *Judaism and Christianity in First-Century Rome,* 196-244. Ed. Karl P. Donfried and Peter Richardson. Grand Rapids: Wm. B. Eerdmans, 1998.

La Piana, George. "Foreign Groups at Rome during the First Centuries of the Empire." *HTR* 20 (1927): 183-403.

Larsson, Edvin. *Christus als Vorbild: Eine Untersuchung zu den paulinischen Tauf- und Eikontexten.* ASNU 23. Uppsala: Almqvist & Wiksell, 1962.

Leenhardt, Franz J. *The Epistle to the Romans: A Commentary.* London: Lutterworth Press, 1961.

Légasse, Simon. *L'épître de Paul aux Romains.* LD 10. Paris: Éditions du Cerf, 2002.

Lenski, Richard C. H. *The Interpretation of St. Paul's Epistle to the Romans.* Columbus: Lutheran Book Concern, 1936; reprinted, Minneapolis: Augsburg Publishing House, 1961.

Lentz, John C. *Luke's Portrait of Paul.* New York: Cambridge University Press, 1993.

Leon, Harry J. *The Jews of Ancient Rome.* Ed. Carolyn A. Osiek. Peabody: Hendrickson Publishers, 1996.

Levine, Amy-Jill, and Marianne Bickenstaff, eds. *A Feminist Companion to Paul.* FCNTECW 6. New York: T&T Clark, 2004.

Lichtenberger, Hermann. "Josephus und Paulus in Rom: Juden und Christen in Rom zur Zeit Neros." In *Begegnungen zwischen Christentum und Judentum in Antike und Mittelalter: Heinz Schreckenberg,* 245-61. Ed. Dieter-Alex Koch and Hermann Lichtenberger. Göttingen: Vandenhoeck & Ruprecht, 1993.

Liddon, Henry P. *Explanatory Analysis of St. Paul's Epistle to the Romans.* 2d ed. London: Longmans, Green and Company, 1893; reprinted, Grand Rapids: Zondervan, 1961.

Lietzmann, Hans. *An die Römer.* 5th ed. HNT 8. Tübingen: J. C. B. Mohr (Paul Siebeck), 1971.

Lim, Timothy H. "Eschatological Orientation and the Alteration of Scripture in the Habakkuk Pesher." *JNES* 49 (1990): 185-94.

———. *Holy Scripture in the Qumran Commentaries and Pauline Letters.* New York: Oxford University Press, 1997.

———. "Midrash Pesher in the Pauline Letters." *The Scrolls and the Scriptures: Qumran Fifty Years After,* 280-92. Ed. Stanley E. Porter and Craig A. Evans. JSPSup 26. Sheffield: Sheffield Academic Press, 1997.

Lindars, Barnabas. *New Testament Apologetic: The Doctrinal Significance of the New Testament Quotations.* Philadelphia: Westminster Press, 1961.

———. "The Place of the Old Testament in the Formation of New Testament Theology." *NTS* 23 (1977): 59-66.

Litwak, Kenneth D. "Echoes of Scripture? A Critical Survey of Recent Works on Paul's Use of the Old Testament." *CurrBS* 6 (1998): 260-88.

———. "The Sound of the Trumpet: Paul and Eschatology." *BJRL* 67 (1985): 766-82.

Ljungman, Henrik. *Pistis: A Study of Its Presuppositions and Its Meaning in Pauline Use.* SKHVL 64. Lund: Gleerup, 1964.

Loewe, Raphael. "Jewish Exegesis." In *Dictionary of Biblical Interpretation,* 346-54. Ed. Richard J. Coggins and John L. Houlden. London: SCM, 1990.

Lohmeyer, Ernst. *Probleme paulinischer Theologie.* Stuttgart: Kohlhammer Verlag, 1955.

Lohse, Eduard, *Der Brief an die Römer.* KEK 4. Göttingen: Vandenhoeck & Ruprecht, 2003.

———. *Paulus: Eine Biographie.* München: C. H. Beck, 1996.

———, ed. *Die Texte aus Qumran: Hebräisch und Deutsch.* Munich: Kösel-Verlag, 1964.

Longacre, Robert E., and Wilber B. Wallis. "Soteriology and Eschatology in Romans." *JETS* 41 (1998): 367-82.

Longenecker, Bruce W. *Eschatology and the Covenant: A Comparison of 4 Ezra and Romans 1-11.* JSNTSup 57. Sheffield: JSOT Press, 1991.

———, ed. *Narrative Dynamics in Paul: A Critical Assessment.* Louisville: Westminster John Knox Press, 2002.

Longenecker, Richard N. *Biblical Exegesis in the Apostolic Period.* Grand Rapids: Wm. B. Eerdmans, 1975.

———. *The Ministry and Message of Paul.* Grand Rapids: Zondervan, 1971.

———. *Paul, Apostle of Liberty: The Origin and Nature of Paul's Christianity.* New York: Harper & Row, 1964.

Louw, Johannes. P. *A Semantic Discourse Analysis of Romans.* Pretoria: University of Pretoria Press, 1979.

Lovering, Eugene H., Jr., and Jerry L. Sumney, eds. *Theology and Ethics in Paul and His Interpreters: Essays in Honor of Victor Paul Furnish.* Nashville: Abingdon Press, 1996.

Luck, Ulrich. "Die Bekehrung des Paulus und das Paulinische Evangelium: Zur Frage der Evidenz in Botschaft und Theologie des Apostels." *ZNW* 76 (1985): 187-208.

Lüdemann, Gerd. *Opposition to Paul in Jewish Christianity.* Minneapolis: Fortress Press, 1989.

———. *Paul, Apostle to the Gentiles: Studies in Chronology.* Philadelphia: Fortress Press, 1984.

Lührmann, Dieter. *Das Offenbarungsverständnis bei Paulus und in den paulinischen Gemeinden.* WMANT 16. Neukirchen-Vluyn: Neukirchener Verlag, 1965.

Lütgert, Wilhelm. *Der Römerbrief als historisches Problem.* BFCT 17.2. Gütersloh: C. Bertelsmann, 1913.

Lund, Nils W. *Chiasmus in the New Testament.* Chapel Hill: University of North Carolina Press, 1942.

Luther, Martin. *Lectures on Romans.* LuthW 25. St. Louis: Concordia Publishing House, 1972.

Luz, Ulrich. "Zum Aufbau von Röm 1-8." *TZ* 25 (1969): 161-81.

———. *Das Geschichtsverständnis des Paulus.* BevT 49. Munich: Kaiser Verlag, 1968.

Lyonnet, Stanislas. *Les Épîtres de saint Paul aux Galates, aux Romains.* 2d ed. Paris: Éditions du Cerf, 1959.

———. *Études sur l'épître aux Romains.* AnBib 120. Rome: Pontifical Biblical Institute Press, 1990.

———. *Le Message de l'épître aux Romains.* Paris: Éditions du Cerf, 1971.

Lyons, George. *Pauline Autobiography: Toward a New Understanding.* SBLDS 73. Atlanta: Scholars Press, 1985.

Maccoby, Hyam. *Paul and Hellenism.* Philadelphia: Trinity Press International, 1991.

MacDonald, Margaret Y. *The Pauline Churches: A Socio-Historical Study of Institutionalisation in the Pauline and Deutero-Pauline Writings.* SNTSMS 60. Cambridge: Cambridge University Press, 1988.

Malherbe, Abraham. *Ancient Epistolary Theorists.* SBLSBS 19. Atlanta: Scholars Press, 1988.

―――. *Moral Exhortation: A Greco-Roman Source Book.* LEC. Philadelphia: Westminster Press, 1986.

―――. *Paul and the Popular Philosophers.* Minneapolis: Fortress Press, 1989.

Malina, Bruce J. *The New Testament World: Insights from Cultural Anthropology.* Rev. ed. Lousiville: Westminster John Knox Press, 1993.

―――, and John J. Pilch. *Social-Science Commentary on the Letters of Paul.* Minneapolis: Fortress Press, 2006.

Maly, Eugene H. *Romans.* NTM 9. Wilmington: Michael Glazier, 1979.

Manson, T. W. "Paul's Letter to the Romans — and Others." *BJRL* 31 (1948): 225-41; reprinted in *The Romans Debate,* 3-15. Rev. ed. Ed. Karl P. Donfried. Peabody: Hendrickson Publishers, 1977.

―――. "Romans." In *Peake's Commentary on the Bible,* 940-53. Ed. Matthew Black and Harold H. Rowley. New York: Thomas Nelson and Sons, 1962.

Marrow, Stanley B. *Paul, His Letters and His Theology: An Introduction to Paul's Epistles.* New York: Paulist Press, 1986.

Marshall, I. Howard. *New Testament Theology: Many Witnesses, One Gospel.* Downers Grove: InterVarsity Press, 2004.

―――. "Salvation, Grace and Works in the Later Writings in the Pauline Corpus." *NTS* 42 (1996): 339-58.

Martin, Brice L. *Christ and the Law in Paul.* NovTSup 62. Leiden: E. J. Brill, 1989.

Martin, Dale B. *Slavery as Salvation: The Metaphor of Slavery in Pauline Christianity.* New Haven: Yale University Press, 1990.

Martin, James P. "The Kerygma of Romans." *Int* 25 (1971): 303-28.

Martin, Ralph P. *Reconciliation: A Study of Paul's Theology.* Atlanta: John Knox Press, 1981.

Martyn, J. Louis. *Galatians.* AB 33A. New York: Doubleday, 1997.

―――― "A Law-Observant Mission to Gentiles." In his *Theological Issues in the Letters of Paul,* 7-24. Nashville: Abingdon Press, 1997.

―――. "Romans as One of the Earliest Interpretations of Galatians." In his *Theological Issues in the Letters of Paul,* 37-45. Nashville: Abingdon Press, 1997.

Matera, Frank. *Romans.* Paideia Commentaries on the New Testament. Grand Rapids: Baker Academic, 2010.

Matlock, R. Barry. *Unveiling the Apocalyptic Paul: Paul's Interpreters and the Rhetoric of Criticism.* JSNTSup 127. Sheffield: Sheffield Academic Press, 1996.

Mauser, Ulrich. "Paul the Theologian." *HBT* 11 (1989): 80-106.

McGinn, Sheila E., ed. *Celebrating Romans: Template for Pauline Theology: Essays in Honor of Robert Jewett.* Grand Rapids: Wm. B. Eerdmans, 2005.

McKnight, Scot. *A Light among the Gentiles: Jewish Missionary Activity in the Second Temple Period.* Minneapolis: Fortress Press, 1991.

McLay, R. Timothy. *The Use of the Septuagint in New Testament Research.* Grand Rapids: Wm. B. Eerdmans, 2003.

McRay, John. *Paul: His Life and Teaching.* Grand Rapids: Baker Book House, 2002.

Meech, John L. *Paul in Israel's Story: Self and Community at the Cross.* New York: Oxford University Press, 2006.

Meecham, Henry G. "The Use of the Participle for the Imperative in the New Testament." *ExpTim* 58 (1946-47): 207-8.

Meeks, Wayne A. *The First Urban Christians: The Social World of the Apostle Paul.* 2d ed. New Haven: Yale University Press, 2003.

————, and John T. Fitzgerald, eds. *The Writings of St. Paul: Annotated Texts, Reception and Criticism.* New York: Norton, 2007.

Melanchthon, Philip. *Commentary on Romans.* St. Louis: Concordia Publishing House, 1992.

Merk, Otto. "Paulus-Forschung 1936-1985." *ThR* 53 (1988): 1-81.

Merklein, Helmut. *Studien zu Jesus und Paulus.* WUNT 43. Tübingen: J. C. B. Mohr (Paul Siebeck), 1987.

Metzger, Bruce M. "Formulas Introducing Quotations of Scripture in the NT and the Mishnah." *JBL* 70 (1951): 297-307.

————. *Index to Periodical Literature on the Apostle Paul.* 2d ed. Grand Rapids: Wm. B. Eerdmans, 1970.

————. *The Text of the New Testament: Its Transmission, Corruption, and Restoration.* 3d ed. New York: Oxford University Press, 1992.

————. *A Textual Commentary on the Greek New Testament.* 2d ed. Stuttgart: Deutsche Bibelgesellschaft, 1994.

Meyer, Heinrich A. W. *The Epistle to the Romans.* 2 vols. Edinburgh: T&T Clark, 1873-74.

Meyer, Paul W. "Romans." In *Harper's Bible Commentary,* 1130-67. Ed. James L. Mays. San Francisco: Harper & Row, 1988.

Michel, Otto. *Der Brief an die Römer.* 14th ed. MeyerK 4. Göttingen: Vandenhoeck & Ruprecht, 1978.

————. *Paulus und seine Bibel.* Gütersloh: C. Bertelsmann, 1929; reprinted, Darmstadt: Wissenschaftliche Buchgesellschaft, 1972.

Miller, James C. *The Obedience of Faith: The Purposes of Paul in the Epistle to the Romans.* SBLDS 177. Atlanta: Scholars Press, 2000.

————. "The Romans Debate: 1991-2001." *CurrBS* 9 (2001): 306-49.

Mills, Watson E. *An Index to Periodical Literature on the Apostle Paul.* NTTS 16. Leiden: E. J. Brill, 1993.

————. *Romans.* Bibliographies for Biblical Research 6. Lewiston: Mellen Biblical Press, 1996.

Minear, Paul S. *The Obedience of Faith: The Purpose of Paul in the Epistle to the Romans.* SBT 2/19. Naperville: Alec R. Allenson, 1971.

Mitchell, Margaret M. *The Heavenly Trumpet: John Chrysostom and the Art of Pauline Interpretation.* Louisville: Westminster John Knox Press, 2002.

Moo, Douglas J. *Encountering the Book of Romans: A Theological Survey.* Grand Rapids: Baker Book House, 2002.

———. *The Epistle to the Romans*. NICNT. Grand Rapids: Wm. B. Eerdmans, 1996.

———. "'Law,' 'Works of the Law,' and Legalism in Paul." *WTJ* 45 (1983): 73-100.

Moore, Richard K. *Rectification ('Justification') in Paul, in Historical Perspective and in the English Bible: God's Gift of Right Relationship*. 3 vols. SBEC 50. Lewiston: Mellen Press, 2002-3.

Moores, John D. *Wrestling with Rationality in Paul: Romans 1–8 in a New Perspective*. SNTSMS 82. Cambridge: Cambridge University Press, 1995.

Morgan, Robert. *Romans*. NTG. Sheffield: Sheffield Academic Press, 1995.

Morris, Leon. *The Epistle to the Romans*. PNTC. Grand Rapids: Wm. B. Eerdmans, 1988.

Moule, C. F. D. "Obligation in the Ethics of Paul." In *Christian History and Interpretation*, 389-406. Ed. William Farmer et al. Cambridge: Cambridge University Press, 1967.

Moule, H. C. G. *The Epistle of Paul the Apostle to the Romans with Introduction and Notes*. Cambridge: Cambridge University Press, 1879; reprinted as *Studies in Romans*. Grand Rapids: Kregel Publications, 1977.

———. *The Epistle of St Paul to the Romans*. Expositor's Bible. New York: Armstrong, 1894.

Moxnes, Halvor. "Honor and Righteousness in Romans." *JSNT* 32 (1988): 61-77.

———. "Honor and Shame." In *The Social Sciences and New Testament Interpretation*, 19-40. Ed. Richard L. Rohrbaugh. Peabody: Hendrickson Publishers, 1996.

———. "Honor, Shame, and the Outside World in Paul's Letter to the Romans." In *The Social World of Formative Christianity and Judaism: Essays in Tribute to Howard Clark Kee*, 207-18. Ed. Jacob Neusner et al. Philadelphia: Fortress Press, 1988.

———. *Theology in Conflict: Studies in Paul's Understanding of God in Romans*. NovTSup 53. Leiden: E. J. Brill, 1980.

Moyise, Steve. *Paul and Scripture: Studying the New Testament Use of the Old Testament*. Grand Rapids: Baker Academic, 2010.

———, and Maarten J. J. Menken, eds. *Isaiah in the New Testament*. Edinburgh: T&T Clark, 2005.

Munck, Johannes. *Paul and the Salvation of Mankind*. Atlanta: John Knox Press, 1977.

Murphy-O'Connor, Jerome. *Paul: A Critical Life*. Oxford: Clarendon Press, 1996.

———. *Paul: His Story*. New York: Oxford University Press, 2004.

———. *Paul the Letter-Writer: His World, His Options, His Skills*. GNS 41. Collegeville: Liturgical Press, 1995.

———, ed. *Paul and Qumran: Studies in New Testament Exegesis*. Chicago: Priory, 1968.

Murray, John. *The Epistle to the Romans*. NICNT 6. 2 vols. Grand Rapids: Wm. B. Eerdmans, 1959.

Myers, Charles, Jr. "Romans, Epistle to." *ABD* 5:816-30.

Nanos, Mark D. *The Mystery of Romans: The Jewish Context of Paul's Letter*. Minneapolis: Fortress Press, 1996.

Neusner, Jacob, ed. *Judaism in Late Antiquity*. 9 vols. HO 16, 17, 40, 41, 49, 53, 55-57. New York: E. J. Brill, 1995-2001.

———. *Judaism in the Beginning of Christianity*. Philadelphia: Fortress Press, 1984.

———, and Alan J. Avery-Peck, eds. *Encyclopedia of Religious and Philosophical Writings in Late Antiquity: Pagan, Judaic, Christian*. Boston: E. J. Brill, 2007.

Neusner, Jacob, Ernest Frerichs, Peter Borgen, and Richard Horsley, eds., *The Social World of Formative Christianity and Judaism: Essays in Tribute to Howard Clark Kee*. Philadelphia: Fortress Press, 1988.

Newman, Barclay M., and Eugene A. Nida. *A Translator's Handbook on Paul's Letter to the Romans*. HT 14. London: United Bible Societies, 1973.

Neyrey, Jerome. *Paul, in Other Words: A Cultural Reading of His Letters*. Louisville: Westminster John Knox Press, 1990.

Nickelsburg, George W. E. *Ancient Judaism and Christian Origins*. Minneapolis: Fortress Press, 2003.

———. "The Incarnation: Paul's Solution to the Universal Human Predicament." In *The Future of Early Christianity: Essays in Honor of Helmut Koester*, 348-57. Ed. Birger A. Pearson. Minneapolis: Fortress Press, 1991.

———. *Jewish Literature between the Bible and the Mishnah*. Philadephia: Fortress Press, 1981.

———. *Resurrection, Immortality and Eternal Life in Intertestamental Judaism*. HTS 26. Cambridge: Harvard University Press, 1972.

Niebuhr, Karl-Wilhelm. *Heidenapostel aus Israel: Die jüdische Identität des Paulus nach ihrer Darstellung in seinen Briefen*. WUNT 62. Tübingen: J. C. B. Mohr (Paul Siebeck), 1992.

Noack, Bent. "Current and Backwater in the Epistle to the Romans." *ST* 19 (1965): 155-66.

Nock, Arthur Darby. *St. Paul*. New York: Harper, 1938.

Nygren, Anders. *A Commentary on Romans*. Philadelphia: Muhlenberg Press, 1949.

Oakes, Peter. *Reading Romans in Pompeii: Paul's Letter at Ground Level*. Minneapolis: Fortress Press, 2009.

———, ed. *Rome in the Bible and the Early Church*. Grand Rapids: Baker Academic, 2002.

O'Brien, Peter T. *Gospel and Mission in the Writings of Paul*. Grand Rapids: Baker Book House, 1995.

O'Grady, John F. *Pillars of Paul's Gospel: Galatians and Romans*. New York: Paulist Press, 1992.

Olbricht, Thomas H., and Jerry L. Sumney, eds. *Paul and Pathos*. SBLSymS 16. Atlanta: Scholars Press, 2001.

Ollrog, Wolf-Henning. *Paulus und seine Mitarbeiter: Untersuchungen zu Theorie und Praxis der paulinischen Mission*. WMANT 50. Neukirchen-Vluyn: Neukirchener Verlag, 1979.

Olofsson, Steffan. *God Is My Rock: A Study of Translation Technique and Theological Exegesis in the Septuagint*. ConBOT 31. Stockholm: Almqvist & Wiksell, 1990.

Olsson, Birger, and Magnus Zetterholm, eds. *The Ancient Synagogue from Its Origins until 200 C.E.: Papers Presented at an International Conference at Lund University, October 14-17, 2001*. ConBNT 39. Stockholm: Almqvist & Wiksell, 2003.

O'Neill, John C. *Paul's Letter to the Romans*. Baltimore: Penguin Books, 1975.

Osten-Sacken, Peter von der. "Erwägungen zur Abfassungsgeschichte und zum literarisch-theologischen Charakter des Römerbriefes." *ThViat* 12 (1973/74): 109-20.

———. *Evangelium und Tora: Aufsätze zu Paulus*. TBü 77. Munich: Kaiser Verlag, 1987.

Paillard, Jean. *In Praise of the Inexpressible: Paul's Experience of the Divine Mystery*. Peabody: Hendrickson Publishers, 2003.

Park, Eung Chun. *Either Jew or Gentile: Paul's Unfolding Theology of Inclusivity*. Louisville: Westminster John Knox Press, 2003.

Parker, Thomas H. L. *Commentaries on the Epistle to the Romans 1532-1542*. Edinburgh: T&T Clark, 1986.

Pate, C. Marvin. *The Reverse of the Curse: Paul, Wisdom, and the Law*. WUNT 2/114. Tübingen: J. C. B. Mohr (Paul Siebeck), 2000.

Patte, Daniel. *Paul's Faith and the Power of the Gospel: A Structural Introduction to the Pauline Letters*. Philadelphia: Fortress Press, 1983.

———, and Eugene TeSelle, eds. *Engaging Augustine on Romans: Self, Context, and Theology in Interpretation*. RHCS. Harrisburg: Trinity Press International, 2003.

Pedersen, Sigfried. "Theologische Überlegungen zur Isagogik des Römerbriefes." *ZNW* 76 (1985): 47-67.

Penna, Romano. "Narrative Aspects of the Epistle of St. Paul to the Romans." In *Parable and Story in Judaism and Christianity*, 191-204. Ed. Clemens Thoma and Michael Wyschogrod. New York: Paulist Press, 1989.

Pervo, Richard I. *The Making of Paul: Constructions of the Apostle in Early Christianity*. Minneapolis: Fortress Press, 2010.

Pesch, Rudolf. *Römerbrief*. NEchtB 6. Würzburg: Echter Verlag, 1983.

Peterson, Erik. *Der Brief an die Römer*. Ed. Barbara Nichtweiss. AusS 6. Würzburg: Echter Verlag, 1997.

Petersen, Norman R. *Rediscovering Paul: Philemon and the Sociology of Paul's Narrative World*. Philadelphia: Fortress Press, 1985.

Pfitzner, Victor C. *Paul and the Agon Motif: Traditional Athletic Imagery in the Pauline Literature*. NovTSup 16. Leiden: E. J. Brill, 1967.

Plank, Karl A. *Paul and the Irony of Affliction*. Semeia 17. Atlanta: Scholars Press, 1989.

Plevnik, Joseph. *Paul and the Parousia: An Exegetical and Theological Investigation*. Peabody: Hendrickson Publishers, 1997.

Plummer, Robert L. "Melanchthon as Interpreter of the New Testament." *WTJ* 62 (2000): 257-65.

Polanski, Sandra Hack. *Paul and the Discourse of Power*. GCT 8. Sheffield: Sheffield Academic Press, 1999.

Porter, Stanley E. *Paul in Acts*. Peabody: Hendrickson Publishers, 2001.

———. "Paul of Tarsus and His Letters." In *Handbook of Classical Rhetoric in the Hellenistic Period, 330 B.C.–A.D. 400*, 533-86. Ed. Stanley E. Porter. Leiden: E. J. Brill, 1997.

———. "The Use of the Old Testament in the New Testament: A Brief Comment on Method and Terminology." In *Early Christian Interpretation of the Scriptures of Israel: Investigations and Proposals*, 79-96. Ed. Craig A. Evans and James A. Sanders. JSNTSup 148/SSEJC 5. Sheffield: Sheffield Academic Press, 1997.

———. *Verbal Aspect in the Greek of the New Testament*. SBG 1. New York: Peter Lang, 1989.

———, ed. *Paul: Jew, Greek, and Roman*. PAST 5. Boston: E. J. Brill, 2008.

———, ed. *Paul and His Opponents*. PAST 2. Boston: E. J. Brill, 2005.

————, ed. *Paul and His Theology*. PAST 3. Boston: E. J. Brill, 2006.

————, ed. *The Pauline Canon*. PAST 1. Boston: E. J. Brill, 2004.

————, ed. *Paul's World*. PAST 4. Boston: E. J. Brill, 2008.

————, and Brook W. R. Pearson. "Isaiah through Greek Eyes: The Septuagint of Isaiah." In *Writing and Reading the Scroll of Isaiah: Studies of an Interpretive Tradition*, 2:531-46. Ed. Craig C. Broyles and Craig A. Evans, 2:531-46. 2 vols. VTSup 70. Leiden: E. J. Brill, 1997.

————, and Christopher D. Stanley, eds. *As It Is Written: Studying Paul's Use of Scripture*. SBLSymS 50. Atlanta: Society of Biblical Literature, 2008.

Powers, Daniel G. *Salvation through Participation: An Examination of the Notion of the Believers' Corporate Unity with Christ in Early Christian Soteriology*. CBET 29. Leuven: Peeters, 2001.

Prümm, Karl. *Die Botschaft des Römerbriefes, Ihr Aufbau und Gegenwartswert*. Freiburg im Breisgau: Herder, 1960.

Radermacher, Ludwig. *Neutestamentliche Grammatik*. HNT 1. Tübingen: Mohr-Siebeck, 1925.

Räisänen, Heikki. *Paul and the Law*. Philadelphia: Fortress Press, 1986.

————. *The Torah and Christ: Essays in German and English on the Problem of the Law in Early Christianity*. SESJ 45. Helsinki: Finnish Exegetical Society, 1986.

Reasoner, Mark P. *Romans in Full Circle: A History of Interpretation*. Louisville: Westminster John Knox Press, 2005.

Reed, Jeffrey T. "Using Ancient Rhetorical Categories to Interpret Paul's Letters: A Question of Genre." In *Rhetoric and the New Testament*, 292-325. Ed. Stanley E. Porter and Thomas H. Olbricht. JSNTSup 90. Sheffield: JSOT Press, 1993.

Reichert, Angelika. *Der Römerbrief als Gratwanderung: Eine Untersuchung zur Abfassungsproblematik*. FRLANT 194. Göttingen: Vandenhoeck & Ruprecht, 2001.

Reicke, Bo. *Re-examining Paul's Letters: The History of the Pauline Correspondence*. Harrisburg: Trinity Press International, 2001.

Reid, Marty L. "Paul's Rhetoric of Mutuality: A Rhetorical Reading of Romans." In *Society of Biblical Literature 1995 Seminar Papers*, 117-39. Ed. Eugene H. Lovering. SBLSP 34. Atlanta: Scholars Press, 1995.

Rengstorf, Karl H. "Paulus und die älteste römische Christenheit." In *Papers Presented to the Second International Congress on New Testament Studies Held at Christ Church, Oxford, 1961*, 1:447-64. Ed. Frank L. Cross. 2 vols. *SE* 2-3 (TU 87-88). Berlin: Akademie Verlag, 1964.

Renwick, David A. *Paul, the Temple, and the Presence of God*. BJS 224. Atlanta: Scholars Press, 1991.

Reumann, John. "Romans." In *Eerdmans Commentary on the Bible*, 1277-1313. Ed. James D. G. Dunn. Grand Rapids: Wm. B. Eerdmans, 2003.

Rhys, Howard. *The Epistle to the Romans*. New York: Macmillan, 1961.

Richardson, Alan. *New Testament Theology*. New York: Harper & Row, 1959.

Richardson, Neil. *Paul's Language about God*. JSNTSup 99. Sheffield: Sheffield Academic Press, 1994.

Ridderbos, Herman. *Paul: An Outline of His Theology.* Grand Rapids: Wm. B. Eerdmans, 1975.

Riesner, Rainer. *Paul's Early Period: Chronology, Mission Strategy, Theology.* Grand Rapids: Wm. B. Eerdmans, 1998.

Rigaux, Béda. *The Letters of Saint Paul: Modern Studies.* Chicago: Franciscan Herald Press, 1968.

Robinson, John A. T. *Wrestling with Romans.* Philadelphia: Westminster Press, 1979.

Roetzel, Calvin J. *The Letters of Paul.* 4th ed. Louisville: Westminster John Knox Press, 2009.

————. *Paul — A Jew on the Margins.* Louisville: Westminster John Knox Press, 2003.

————. *Paul: The Man and the Myth.* Columbia: University of South Carolina Press, 1998.

Roosen, A. "Le genre littéraire de l'Epître aux Romains." In *Papers Presented to the Second International Congress on New Testament Studies Held at Christ Church, Oxford, 1961,* 1:465-71. Ed. Frank L. Cross. 2 vols. SE 2-3 (TU 87-88). Berlin: Akademie Verlag, 1964.

Sahlin, Harald. "Einige Textemendationen zum Römerbrief." *TZ* 9 (1953): 92-100.

Sampley, J. Paul, ed. *Paul in the Greco-Roman World: A Handbook.* Harrisburg: Trinity Press International, 2003.

————. "Romans in a Different Light: A Response to Robert Jewett." In *Pauline Theology,* vol. 3, *Romans,* 109-29. Ed. David M. Hay and E. Elizabeth Johnson. Minneapolis: Fortress Press, 1995.

————. *Walking between the Times: Paul's Moral Reasoning.* Minneapolis: Fortress Press, 1991.

————, and Peter Lampe, eds. *Paul and Rhetoric.* New York: T. & T. Clark, 2010.

Sänger, Dieter. *Die Verkündigung des Gekreuzigten und Israel.* WUNT 75. Tübingen: J. C. B. Mohr (Paul Siebeck), 1994.

Sänger, Dieter, and Ulrich Mell, eds. *Paulus und Johannes: Exegetische Studien zur paulinischen und johanneischen Theologie und Literatur.* WUNT 198. Tübingen: J. C. B. Mohr (Paul Siebeck), 2006.

Sanday, William, and Arthur C. Headlam. *A Critical and Exegetical Commentary on the Epistle to the Romans.* 5th ed. ICC. Edinburgh: T&T Clark, 1902.

Sanders, E. P. "Jesus, Paul and Judaism." *ANRW* II.25.1 (1982): 390-450.

————. *Jewish Law from Jesus to the Mishnah: Five Studies.* Philadelphia: Trinity Press International, 1990.

————. *Judaism: Practice and Belief, 63 BCE–66 CE.* Philadelphia: Trinity Press International, 1992.

————. "On the Question of Fulfilling the Law in Paul and Rabbinic Judaism." In *Donum Gentilicium: New Testament Studies in Honour of David Daube,* 103-26. Ed. Ernst Bammel et al. Oxford: Clarendon, 1978.

————. *Paul.* New York: Oxford University Press, 1991.

————. *Paul and Palestinian Judaism: A Comparison of Patterns of Religion.* Philadelphia: Fortress Press, 1977.

————. *Paul, the Law and the Jewish People.* Minneapolis: Fortress Press, 1983.

————. "Paul's Attitude toward the Jewish People." *USQR* 33 (1978): 175-87.

Sanders, Jack T. *Ethics in the New Testament: Change and Development*. Philadelphia: Fortress Press, 1975.

Sanders, James A. "Torah and Christ." *Int* 29 (1975): 372-90.

———. "Torah and Paul." *God's Christ and His People: Studies in Honour of Nils Alstrum Dahl*, 132-40. Ed. Jacob Jervell and Wayne A. Meeks. Oslo: Universitetsforlaget, 1977.

Sandnes, Karl O. *Paul — One of the Prophets? A Contribution to the Apostle's Self-Understanding*. WUNT 2/43. Tübingen: J. C. B. Mohr (Paul Siebeck), 1991.

Schade, Hans-Heinrich. *Apokalyptische Christologie bei Paulus: Studien zum Zusammenhang von Christologie und Eschatologie in den Paulusbriefen*. GTA 18. Göttingen: Vandenhoeck & Ruprecht, 1981.

Schaper, Joachim. *Eschatology in the Greek Psalter*. WUNT 2/76. Tübingen: J. C. B. Mohr (Paul Siebeck), 1995.

Schelke, Karl H. "Kirche und Synagoge in der frühen Auslegung des Römerbriefs." *TQ* 134 (1954): 290-318.

———. *Paulus: Leben — Briefe — Theologie*. EdF 152. Darmstadt: 1981.

———. *Paulus Lehrer der Väter: Die altchristliche Auslegung von Römer 1–11*. 2d ed. Düsseldorf: Patmos, 1959.

Schenke, Hans-Martin. "Aporien im Römerbrief." *TLZ* 92 (1967): 881-88.

Schille, Gottfried. "Dialogische Elemente im Römerbrief." *SNTU* 23 (1998): 153-91.

Schlatter, Adolf von. *Die Botschaft des Paulus: Eine Übersicht über den Römerbrief*. Velbert im Rheinland: Freizeiten-Verlag, 1928.

———. *Luthers Deutung des Römerbriefs: Ein Beitrag zur vierten Säkularfeier der Reformation*. BFCT 21, 7. Gütersloh: C. Bertelsmann, 1917.

———. *Romans: The Righteousness of God*. Peabody: Hendrickson Publishers, 1995.

Schlier, Heinrich. *Der Römerbrief: Kommentar*. 2d ed. HTKNT 6. Freiburg im Breisgau: Herder, 1977.

Schmeller, Thomas. *Paulus und die "Diatribe": Eine vergleichende Stilinterpretation*. NTAbh 19. Münster: Aschendorff, 1987.

Schmidt, Hans W. *Der Brief des Paulus an die Römer*. 3d ed. THNT 6. Berlin: Evangelische Verlagsanstalt, 1972.

Schmithals, Walter. *Paul and the Gnostics*. Nashville: Abingdon Press, 1972.

———. *Der Römerbrief: Ein Kommentar*. Gütersloh: Gütersloher Verlagshaus Gerd Mohn, 1988.

———. *Der Römerbrief als historisches Problem*. SNT 9. Gütersloh: Gütersloher Verlagshaus Gerd Mohn, 1975.

Schmitz, Richard. *Rechtfertigung und Heiligung durch den Glauben: Sünde und Gnade nach dem Römerbrief*. Witten: Bundes Verlag, 1960.

Schnabel, Eckhard J. *Early Christian Mission*. 2 vols. Downers Grove: InterVarsity Press, 2004.

———. *Law and Wisdom from Ben Sira to Paul*. WUNT 2/16. Tübingen: J. C. B. Mohr (Paul Siebeck), 1985.

Schnackenburg, Rudolf. *The Moral Teaching of the New Testament*. New York: Seabury Press, 1979.

Schneider, Norbert. *Die rhetorische Eigenart der paulinischen Antithese.* HUTh 11. Tübingen: J. C. B. Mohr (Paul Siebeck), 1970.

Schnelle, Udo. *Apostle Paul: His Life and Thought.* Grand Rapids: Baker Academic, 2005.

———. *The History and Theology of the New Testament Writings.* Minneapolis: Fortress Press, 1998.

———, ed. *The Letter to the Romans.* BETL 226. Walpole: Peeters, 2009.

Schoeps, Hans-Joachim. *Paul: The Theology of the Apostle in Light of the Jewish Religious History.* Philadelphia: Westminster Press, 1961.

Schrage, Wolfgang. *The Ethics of the New Testament.* Philadelphia: Fortress Press, 1988.

———. "The Formal Ethical Interpretation of Pauline Paraenesis." In *Understanding Paul's Ethics: Twentieth-Century Approaches,* 301-35. Ed. Brian S. Rosner. Grand Rapids: Wm. B. Eerdmans, 1995.

Schreiner, Thomas R. *The Law and Its Fulfillment: A Pauline Theology of Law.* Grand Rapids: Baker Book House, 1993.

———. *Paul, Apostle of God's Glory in Christ: A Pauline Theology.* Downers Grove: InterVarsity Press, 2001.

———. *Romans.* BECNT. Grand Rapids: Baker Book House, 1998.

Schrenk, Gottlob. *Studien zu Paulus.* ATANT 26. Zurich: Zwingli Verlag, 1954.

———. "Der Römerbrief als Missionsdokument." In *Aus Theologie und Geschichte der reformierten Kirche: Festgabe E. F. Karl Müller-Erlangen zu dessen 70. Geburtstag,* 39-72. Neukirchen: Neukirchener Verlag, 1933; reprinted in his *Studien zu Paulus,* 81-106. ATANT 26. Zurich: Zwingli Verlag, 1954.

Schütz, John H. *Paul and the Anatomy of Apostolic Authority.* SNTSMS 26. Cambridge: Cambridge University Press, 1975; reprinted, Louisville: Westminster John Knox Press, 2007.

Schweitzer, Albert. *Paul and His Interpreters: A Critical History.* London: A. & C. Black, 1912.

———. *The Mysticism of Paul the Apostle.* New York: Henry Holt, 1931.

Scott, Ernest F. *Paul's Epistle to the Romans.* 2d ed. London: SCM Press, 1947; reprinted, Westport: Greenwood Press, 1979.

Scott, Ian W. *Paul's Way of Knowing: Story, Experience, and the Spirit.* Grand Rapids: Baker Academic, 2008.

Scroggs, Robin. *Christology in Paul and John.* Philadelphia: Fortress Press, 1977.

———. *The Last Adam: A Study in Pauline Anthropology.* Philadelphia: Fortress Press, 1983.

———. "Paul as Rhetorician: Two Homilies in Romans 1-11." In *Jews, Greeks and Christians: Religious Cultures in Late Antiquity: Essays in Honor of William David Davies,* 271-98. SJLA 21. Ed. Robert Hamerton-Kelly and Robin Scroggs. Leiden: E. J. Brill, 1976.

———. *Paul for a New Day.* Philadelphia: Fortress Press, 1977.

Seeligmann, Isaac L. *The Septuagint Version of Isaiah: A Discussion of Its Problems.* Leiden: E. J. Brill, 1948.

Segal, Alan F. *Paul the Convert: The Apostolate and Apostasy of Saul the Pharisee.* New Haven: Yale University Press, 1990.

Seifrid, Mark A. *Justification by Faith: The Origin and Development of a Central Pauline Theme.* NovTSup 68. Leiden: E. J. Brill, 1992.

————, and Randall K. J. Tan. *The Pauline Writings: An Annotated Bibliography.* Grand Rapids: Baker Book House, 2002.

Shedd, William G. T. *A Critical and Doctrinal Commentary upon the Epistle of St. Paul to the Romans.* New York: Charles Scribner's Sons, 1879; reprinted, Grand Rapids: Zondervan, 1967.

Sherwin-White, A. N. *Roman Society and Roman Law in the New Testament.* Oxford: Clarendon Press, 1963.

Shires, Henry M. *The Eschatology of Paul in the Light of Modern Scholarship.* Philadelphia: Westminster Press, 1966.

Shum, Shiu-Lun. *Paul's Use of Isaiah in Romans: A Comparative Study of Paul's Letter to the Romans and the Sibylline and Qumran Sectarian Texts.* WUNT 2/156. Tübingen: J. C. B. Mohr (Paul Siebeck), 2002.

Siber, Peter. *Mit Christus Leben: Eine Studie zur paulinischen Auferstehungshoffnung.* ATANT 61. Zurich: Theologischer Verlag, 1971.

Simonis, Walter. *Der gefangene Paulus: Die Entstehung des sogenannten Römerbriefs und anderer urchristlicher Schriften in Rom.* New York: Peter Lang, 1990.

Smallwood, E. Mary. *The Jews under Roman Rule: From Pompey to Diocletian.* SJLA 20. Leiden: E. J. Brill, 1981.

Smart, James D. *Doorway to a New Age: A Study of Paul's Letter to the Romans.* Philadelphia: Westminster Press, 1972.

Smiga, George M. "Romans 12:1-2 and 15:30-32 and the Occasion of the Letter to the Romans." *CBQ* 53 (1991): 257-73.

Smith, D. Moody. "The Pauline Literature." In *It is Written: Scripture Citing Scripture,* 265-91. Ed. D. A. Carson and H. G. M. Williamson. Cambridge: Cambridge University Press, 1988.

————. "The Use of the Old Testament in the New." In *The Use of the Old Testament in the New and Other Essays,* 3-65. Ed. James M. Efird. Durham: Duke University Press, 1972.

Snodgrass, Klyne R. "The Gospel in Romans: A Theology of Revelation." In *Gospel in Paul: Studies on Corinthians, Galatians and Romans for Richard N. Longenecker,* 288-314. Ed. L. Ann Jervis and Peter Richardson. JSNTSup 108. Sheffield: Sheffield Academic Press, 1994.

Snyder, Graydon F. "Major Motifs in the Interpretation of Paul's Letter to the Romans." In *Celebrating Romans: Template for Pauline Theology: Essays in Honor of Robert Jewett,* 42-63. Ed. Sheila E. McGinn. Grand Rapids: Wm. B. Eerdmans, 2005.

Soards, Marion L. *The Apostle Paul: An Introduction to His Writings and Teachings.* New York: Paulist Press, 1987.

Soderlund, Sven, and N. T. Wright, eds. *Romans and the People of God: Essays in Honor of Gordon Fee on the Occasion of His 65th Birthday.* Grand Rapids: Wm. B. Eerdmans, 1999.

Song, Changwon. *Reading Romans as Diatribe.* StudBL 59. New York: Peter Lang, 2004.

Soulen, R. Kendall. *The God of Israel and Christian Theology.* Minneapolis: Fortress Press, 1996.

Souter, Alexander. *The Earliest Latin Commentaries on the Epistles of Saint Paul.* Oxford: Clarendon Press, 1927.

———. *Pelagius's Expositions of Thirteen Epistles of Saint Paul.* TS 9. 3 vols. Cambridge: Cambridge University Press, 1922-31.

Spanje, Teunis E. van. *Inconsistency in Paul? A Critique of the Work of Heikki Räisänen.* WUNT 2/110. Tübingen: J. C. B. Mohr (Paul Siebeck), 1999.

Staab, Karl. *Pauluskommentare aus der griechischen Kirche.* Münster: Aschendorff, 1933.

Stanley, Christopher D. *Arguing with Scripture: The Rhetoric of Quotations in the Letters of Paul.* Edinburgh: T&T Clark, 2004.

———. *Paul and the Language of Scripture: Citation Techniques in the Pauline Epistles and Contemporary Literature.* SNTSMS 74. Cambridge: Cambridge University Press, 1992.

———. "The Rhetoric of Quotations: An Essay on Method." In *Early Christian Interpretation of the Scriptures of Israel: Investigation and Proposals,* 44-58. Ed. Craig A. Evans and James A. Sanders. JSNTSup/ SSEJC 4. Sheffield: Sheffield Academic Press, 1997.

———. "The Social Environment of 'Free' Biblical Quotations in the New Testament." In *Early Christian Interpretation of the Scriptures of Israel: Investigation and Proposals,* 18-27. Ed. Craig A. Evans and James A. Sanders. JSNTSup/ SSEJC 4. Sheffield: Sheffield Academic Press, 1997.

Stanley, David M. "The Theme of the Servant of Yahweh in Primitive Christian Soteriology, and Its Transposition by St. Paul." *CBQ* 16 (1954): 385-425.

Starnitzke, Dierk. *Die Struktur paulinischen Denkens im Römerbrief: Eine linguistische-logische Untersuchung.* BWANT 8/3. Stuttgart: W. Kohlhammer, 2004.

Stellhorn, Frederick W. *The Epistle of St. Paul to the Romans.* Columbus: Lutheran Book Concern, 1918.

Stendahl, Krister. *Final Account: Paul's Letter to the Romans.* Minneapolis: Fortress Press, 1995.

———. *Paul among Jews and Gentiles and Other Essays.* Philadelphia: Fortress Press, 1976.

———. "Qumran and Supersessionism — and the Road Not Taken." *PSB* 19/2 (1998): 134-41.

Stirewalt, Martin Luther, Jr., "The Form and Function of the Greek Letter-Essay." In *The Romans Debate,* 147-71. Ed. Karl P. Donfried. Rev. ed. Peabody: Hendrickson Publishers, 1991.

———. *Paul, the Letter Writer.* Grand Rapids: Wm. B. Eerdmans, 2003.

Stourton, Edward. *Paul of Tarsus: A Visionary Life.* Mahwah: Hidden Spring, 2005.

Stowers, Stanley K. "The Diatribe." In *Greco-Roman Literature and the New Testament: Selected Forms and Genres,* 71-83. Ed. David E. Aune. SBLSBS 21. Atlanta: Scholars Press, 1988.

———. *The Diatribe and Paul's Letter to the Romans.* SBLDS 57. Chico: Scholars Press, 1981.

———. *Letter Writing in Greco-Roman Antiquity.* LEC 5. Philadelphia: Westminster Press, 1986.

————— A Rereading of Romans: Justice, Jews, and Gentiles. New Haven: Yale University Press, 1994.

Strack, Hermann L., and Günter Stemberger. Introduction to the Talmud and Midrash. Minneapolis: Fortress Press, 1992.

Strecker, Georg. Theology of the New Testament. Louisville: Westminster John Knox Press, 2000.

Stuhlmacher, Peter. "Der Abfassungszweck des Römerbriefs." ZNW 77 (1986): 180-93.

—————. Biblische Theologie des Neuen Testaments. 2 vols. Göttingen: Vandenhoeck & Ruprecht, 1992-99.

—————. Gerechtigkeit Gottes bei Paulus. FRLANT 87; Göttingen: Vandenhoeck & Ruprecht, 1965.

—————. "Zur Interpretation von Römer 11:25-32." Probleme biblischer Theologie. Ed. H. W. Wolff, 555-70. Munich: Chr. Kaiser, 1971.

—————. Paul's Letter to the Romans: A Commentary. Louisville: Westminster John Knox, 1994.

—————. "Paulus und Luther." In Glaube und Eschatologie: Festschrift für Werner Georg Kümmel zum 80. Geburtstag, 285-302. Ed. Erich Grässer and Otto Merk. Tübingen: J. C. B. Mohr (Paul Siebeck), 1985.

Suh, Joong Suk. The Gospel of Paul. StudBL 56. New York: Peter Lang, 2003.

Suhl, Alfred. "Der konkrete Anlass des Römerbriefes." Kairos 13 (1971): 119-30.

—————. Paulus und seine Briefe: Ein Beitrag zur paulinischen Chronologie. SNT 11. Gütersloh: Gütersloher Verlagshaus Mohn, 1975.

Sundberg, Albert. The Old Testament of the Early Church. HTS 20. Cambridge: Harvard University Press, 1964.

Swete, Henry B. An Introduction to the Old Testament in Greek. Rev. R. R. Ottley. Cambridge: Cambridge University Press, 1914.

Talbert, Charles H. Romans. SHBC. Macon: Smyth & Helwys, 2002.

Tannehill, Robert C. Dying and Rising with Christ: A Study in Pauline Theology. BZNW 32. Berlin: Töpelmann, 1967.

Tasker, R. V. G. The Old Testament in the New Testament. London: SCM Press, 1946.

Taylor, Vincent. The Epistle to the Romans. 2d ed. Epworth Preacher's Commentaries. London: Epworth Press, 1962.

Theissen, Gerd. Psychological Aspects of Pauline Theology. Philadelphia: Fortress Press, 1987.

—————. The Social Setting of Pauline Christianity. Philadelphia: Fortress Press, 1982.

Theobald, Michael. Römerbrief. SKKNT 6. 2 vols. Stuttgart: Verlag Katholisches Bibelwerk, 1992-93.

—————. Studien zum Römerbrief. WUNT 136. Tübingen: J. C. B. Mohr (Paul Siebeck), 2001.

Thielman, Frank. From Plight to Solution: A Jewish Framework for Understanding Paul's View of the Law in Galatians and Romans. NovTSup 61. Leiden: E. J. Brill, 1989.

—————. The Law in the New Testament: The Question of Continuity. New York: Crossroad, 1999.

―――. *Paul and the Law: A Contextual Approach.* Downers Grove: InterVarsity Press, 1994.

―――. *Theology of the New Testament: A Canonical and Synthetic Approach.* Grand Rapids: Zondervan, 2005.

Thiselton, Anthony C. *The Living Paul.* Downers Grove: IVP Academic, 2004.

Thompson, Ian H. *Chiasmus in the Pauline Letters.* JSNTSup 111. Sheffield: Sheffield Academic Press, 1995.

Thrall, Margaret. *Greek Particles in the New Testament.* NTTS 3. Leiden: E. J. Brill, 1962.

Thurén, Lauri. *Derhetorizing Paul: A Dynamic Perspective on Pauline Theology and the Law.* Harrisburg: Trinity Press International, 2002.

Tobin, Thomas H. *Paul's Rhetoric in Its Contexts: The Argument of Romans.* Peabody: Hendrickson Publishers, 2004.

Toews, John E. *Romans.* BCBC. Scottdale: Herald Press, 2004.

Tomson, Peter J., and Doris Lambers-Petry, eds. *The Image of the Judaeo-Christians in Ancient Jewish and Christian Literature.* WUNT 158. Tübingen: J. C. B. Mohr (Paul Siebeck), 2003.

Trobisch, David. *Paul's Letter Collection: Tracing the Origins.* Minneapolis: Fortress Press, 1994.

Trowitzsch, Michael, ed. *Paulus, Apostel Jesu Christi: Festschrift für Günter Klein zum 70. Geburtstag.* Tübingen: J. C. B. Mohr (Paul Siebeck), 1998.

Tuckett, Christopher. *Christology and the New Testament.* Louisville: Westminster John Knox Press, 2001.

Turner, Nigel. "The Preposition *en* in the New Testament." *BT* 10 (1959): 113-20.

Urman, Dan, and Paul V. M. Flesher, eds. *Ancient Synagogues: Historical Analysis and Archaeological Discovery.* SPB 47. 2 vols. Leiden: E. J. Brill, 1995.

VanderKam, James C. *An Introduction to Early Judaism.* Grand Rapids: Wm. B. Eerdmans, 2001.

Vanhoye, Albert, ed. *L'Apôtre Paul: Personnalité, style et conception du ministère.* BETL 73. Louvain: Leuven University, 1986.

Vanlandingham, Chris. *Judgment and Justification in Early Judaism and the Apostle Paul.* Peabody: Hendrickson Publishers, 2005.

Veyne, Paul. *The Romans Empire.* Cambridge: Belknap Press, 1997.

Via, Dan O. "A Structuralist Approach to Paul's Old Testament Hermeneutic." *Int* 28 (1974): 201-20.

Viard, André. *Saint Paul: Épître aux Romains.* 2d ed. SB. Paris: J. Gabalda, 1975.

Vielhauer, Philipp. "Paulus und das Alte Testament." *Studien zur Geschichte und Theologie der Reformation: Festschrift für Ernst Bizer,* 33-62. Ed. Luise Abramowski and J. F. Gerhard Goeters. Neukirchen-Vluyn, 1969; reprinted in his *Oikodome: Aufsätze zum Neuen Testament,* 196-228. TBü 65. Munich: C. Kaiser, 1979.

Vorster, Johannes N. "The Context of the Letter to the Romans: A Critique on the Present State of Research." *Neot* 28 (1994): 127-46.

Vos, Johan. *Die Kunst der Argumentation bei Paulus.* WUNT 2/149. Tübingen: J. C. B. Mohr (Paul Siebeck), 2002.

———. "Sophistische Argumentation im Römerbrief des Apostels Paulus." *NovT* 43 (2001): 224-44.

Wagner, Günter. *An Exegetical Bibliography to the New Testament: Romans and Galatians.* Macon: Mercer University Press, 1996.

Wahlstrom, Eric H. *The New Life in Christ.* Philadelphia: Muhlenberg Press, 1950.

Walters, James C. *Ethnic Issues in Paul's Letter to the Romans: Changing Self-Definitions in Earliest Roman Christianity.* Valley Forge: Trinity Press International, 1993.

Ward, Richard F. "Pauline Voice and Presence as Strategic Communication." In *Orality and Textuality in Early Christian Literature,* 95-107. Ed. Joanna Dewey. Semeia 65. Atlanta: Scholars Press, 1995.

Washburn, David L. *A Catalog of Biblical Passages in the Dead Sea Scrolls.* Text-Critical Studies. Atlanta: Society of Biblical Literature, 2002.

Waters, Guy. *The End of Deuteronomy in the Epistles of Paul.* WUNT 2/221. Tübingen: Mohr Siebeck, 2006.

Watson, Duane F. "Rhetorical Criticism of the Pauline Epistles since 1975." *CurrBS* 3 (1995): 219-48.

Watson, Francis. *Agape, Eros, and Gender: Towards a Pauline Sexual Ethic.* Cambridge: Cambridge University Press, 2000.

———. *Paul and the Hermeneutics of Faith.* Edinburgh: T&T Clark, 2004.

———. *Paul, Judaism, and the Gentiles: Beyond the New Perspective.* Rev. ed. Grand Rapids: Wm. B. Eerdmans, 2007.

Wedderburn, A. J. M. "Like an Ever-rolling Stream: Some Recent Commentaries on Romans." *SJT* 44 (1991): 357-80.

———. "Paul and the Hellenic Mystery-Cults: On Posing the Right Questions." In *La soteriologie dei culti orientali nell'impero romano,* 817-33. Ed. Ugo Bianchi and Maarten J. Vermaseren. EPRO 92. Leiden: E. J. Brill, 1982.

———. "Paul and the Story of Jesus." In his *Paul and Jesus: Collected Essays,* 161-89. JSNTSup 37. Sheffield: Sheffield Academic Press, 1989; reprinted, Edinburgh: T&T Clark, 2004.

———. "The Purpose and Occasion of Romans Again." In *The Romans Debate,* 195-202. Rev. ed. Ed. Karl P. Donfried. Peabody: Hendrickson Publishers, 1991.

———. *The Reasons for Romans.* Edinburgh: T&T Clark, 1988.

Weder, Hans. *Das Kreuz Jesu bei Paulus: Ein Versuch über den Geschichtsbezug des christlichen Glaubens nachzudenken.* FRLANT 126. Göttingen: Vandenhoeck & Ruprecht, 1981.

Wegenast, Klaus. *Das Verständnis der Tradition bei Paulus und in den Deuteropaulinen.* WMANT 8. Neukirchen-Vluyn: Neukirchener Verlag, 1962.

Weima, Jeffrey A. D. "Preaching the Gospel in Rome: A Study of the Epistolary Framework of Romans." In *Gospel in Paul: Studies on Corinthians, Galatians and Romans for Richard N. Longenecker,* 337-66. Ed. L. Ann Jervis and Peter Richardson. JSNTSup 108. Sheffield: Sheffield Academic Press, 1994.

Weiss, Bernhard. "The Epistle of Paul the Apostle to the Romans." In his *A Commentary on the New Testament,* 3:1-146. 4 vols. New York: Funk & Wagnalls, 1906.

Wells, Colin. *The Roman Empire.* 2d ed. Cambridge: Harvard University Press, 1992.

Wenham, David. *Paul: Follower of Jesus or Founder of Christianity?* Grand Rapids: Wm. B. Eerdmans, 1995.

―――. *Paul and Jesus: The True Story.* Grand Rapids: Wm. B. Eerdmans, 2002.

Wesley, John. *Explanatory Notes upon the New Testament,* 358-406. New York: Lane & Tippett, 1847; reprinted, London: Epworth Press, 1950.

Westcott, Frederick B. *St. Paul and Justification: Being an Exposition of the Teaching in the Epistles to Rome and Galatia.* London: Macmillan, 1913.

Westerholm, Stephen. *Israel's Law and the Church's Faith: Paul and His Recent Interpreters.* Grand Rapids: Wm. B. Eerdmans, 1988.

―――. *Perspectives Old and New on Paul: The "Lutheran" Paul and His Critics.* Grand Rapids: Wm. B. Eerdmans, 2004.

―――. *Preface to the Study of Paul.* Grand Rapids: Wm. B. Eerdmans, 1997.

―――. *Understanding Paul: The Early Christian Worldview of the Letter to the Romans.* 2d ed. Grand Rapids: Baker Academic, 2004.

White, John L. "Ancient Greek Letters." In *Greco-Roman Literature and the New Testament: Selected Forms and Genres,* 85-105. Ed. David Aune. SBLSBS 21. Atlanta: Scholars Press, 1988.

―――. *The Apostle of God: Paul and the Promise of Abraham.* Peabody: Hendrickson Publishers, 1999.

―――. *The Form and Function of the Body of the Greek Letter: A Study of the Letter-Body in the Nonliterary Papyri and in Paul the Apostle.* SBLDS 2. Missoula: Scholars Press, 1972.

―――. *Light from Ancient Letters.* Philadelphia: Fortress Press, 1986.

Whiteley, D. E. H. *The Theology of St. Paul.* 2d ed. Oxford: Basil Blackwell, 1974.

Wiederkehr, Dietrich. *Die Theologie der Berufung in den Paulusbriefen.* SF 36. Freiburg: Universitätsverlag, 1963.

Wiefel, Wolfgang. "The Jewish Community in Ancient Rome and the Origins of Roman Christianity." In *The Romans Debate,* 85-101. Rev. ed. Ed. Karl P. Donfried. Peabody: Hendrickson Publishers, 1991.

Wiencke, Gustav. *Paulus über Jesu Tod: Die Deutung des Todes Jesu bei Paulus und ihre Herkunft.* BFCT 2/42. Gütersloh: Bertelsmann Verlag, 1939.

Wilckens, Ulrich. "Die Bekehrung des Paulus als religionsgeschichtliches Problem." *ZTK* 56 (1959): 272-93; reprinted in his *Rechtfertigung als Freiheit: Paulusstudien,* 11-32. Neukirchen-Vluyn: Neukirchener Verlag, 1974.

―――. *Der Brief an die Römer.* 3 vols. EKKNT 6. Neukirchen-Vluyn: Neukirchener Verlag, 1978-82.

―――. *Rechtfertigung als Freiheit: Paulusstudien.* Neukirchen-Vluyn: Neukirchener Verlag, 1974.

―――. "Statements on the Development of Paul's View of the Law." In *Paul and Paulinism: Essays in Honour of C. K. Barrett,* 17-26. Ed. Morna D. Hooker and S. G. Wilson, 17-26. London: SPCK, 1982.

―――. "Über Abfassungszweck und Aufbau des Römerbriefs." In his *Rechtfertigung als Freiheit: Paulusstudien,* 110-70. Neukirchen-Vluyn: Neukirchener Verlag, 1974.

Wilcox, Max. "On Investigating the Use of the Old Testament in the New Testament." In

Text and Interpretation: Studies in the New Testament Presented to Matthew Black, 231-43. Ed. Ernest Best and R. McL. Wilson. Cambridge: Cambridge University Press, 1979.

―――. "Text Form." In *It Is Written: Scripture Citing Scripture,* 193-204. Ed. D. A. Carson and H. G. M. Williamson. Cambridge: Cambridge University Press, 1988.

Wiles, Maurice F. *The Divine Apostle: The Interpretation of St. Paul's Epistles in the Early Church.* Cambridge: Cambridge University Press, 1967.

Wiles, Virginia. *Making Sense of Paul: A Basic Introduction to Pauline Theology.* Peabody: Hendrickson Publishers, 2000.

Wilk, Florian. *Die Bedeutung des Jesajabuches für Paulus.* FRLANT 179. Göttingen: Vandenhoeck & Ruprecht, 1998.

―――. "Paulus als Interpret der prophetischen Schriften." *KD* 45 (1999): 284-306.

Wilken, Robert L. *The Christians as the Romans Saw Them.* 2d ed. New Haven: Yale University Press, 2003.

Willer, Arnold. *Der Römerbrief — Eine dekalogische Komposition.* AzTh 66. Stuttgart: Calwer Verlag, 1981.

Williams, David J. *Paul's Metaphors: Their Context and Character.* 2d ed. Peabody: Hendrickson Publishers, 2003.

Williams, Guy. *The Spirit World in the Letters of Paul the Apostle: A Critical Examination of the Role of Spiritual Beings in the Authentic Pauline Epistles.* FRLANT 231. Göttingen: Vandenhoeck & Ruprecht, 2009.

Wilson, Walter, *Pauline Parallels: A Comprehensive Guide.* Louisville: Westminster John Knox, 2009.

Winger, Michael. *By What Law? The Meaning of Nomos in the Letters of Paul.* SBLDS 128. Atlanta: Scholars Press, 1992.

―――. "From Grace to Sin: Names and Abstractions in Paul's Letters." *NovT* 41 (1999): 145-75.

Winninge, Mikael. *Sinners and the Righteous: A Comparative Study of the Psalms of Solomon and Paul's Letters.* ConBNT 26. Stockholm: Almqvist & Wiksell, 1995.

Winter, Bruce M. *After Paul Left Corinth: The Influence of Secular Ethics and Social Change.* Grand Rapids: Wm. B. Eerdmans, 2001.

―――. *Philo and Paul among the Sophists: Alexandrian and Corinthian Responses to a Julio-Claudian Movement.* Grand Rapids: Wm. B. Eerdmans, 2002.

―――. *Roman Wives, Roman Widows: The Appearance of New Women and the Pauline Communities.* Grand Rapids: Wm. B. Eerdmans, 2003.

Wisdom, Jeffrey. *Blessing for the Nations and the Curse of the Law.* WUNT 2/133. Tübingen: J. C. B. Mohr (Paul Siebeck), 2001.

Witherington, Ben, III. *Paul's Letter to the Romans: A Socio-Rhetorical Commentary.* Grand Rapids: Wm. B. Eerdmans, 2003.

―――. *Paul's Narrative Thought World: The Tapestry of Tragedy and Triumph.* Louisville: Westminster John Knox Press, 1994.

Wrede, William. *Paul.* Boston: American Unitarian Association, 1908.

Wright, N. T. *The Climax of the Covenant: Christ and the Law in Pauline Theology.* Minneapolis: Fortress Press, 1992.

————. *The New Testament and the People of God.* Minneapolis: Fortress Press, 1992.

————. *Paul: In Fresh Perspective.* Minneapolis: Fortress Press, 2005.

————. *Paul for Everyone: Romans,* 2 vols. Louisville: Westminster John Knox Press, 2005.

————. "The Paul of History and the Apostle of Faith." *TynBul* 29 (1978): 61-88.

————. *Romans.* In *The New Interpreter's Bible,* 10:395-770. Ed. Leander E. Keck. 12 vols. Nashville: Abingdon Press, 1994-2004.

————. "Romans and the Theology of Paul." In *Pauline Theology,* vol. 3, *Romans,* 30-67. Ed. David M. Hay and E. Elizabeth Johnson. Minneapolis: Fortress Press, 1995.

————. *What Saint Paul Really Said: Was Paul of Tarsus the Real Founder of Christianity?* Grand Rapids: Wm. B. Eerdmans, 1997.

Wuellner, Wilhelm. "Paul's Rhetoric of Argumentation in Romans: An Alternative to the Donfried-Karris Debate over Romans." *CBQ* 38 (1976): 330-51; reprinted in *The Romans Debate,* 128-46. Ed. Karl P. Donfried. Rev. ed. Peabody: Hendrickson Publishers, 1991.

————. "Reading Romans in Context." In *Celebrating Romans: Template for Pauline Theology: Essays in Honor of Robert Jewett,* 106-39. Ed. Sheila E. McGinn. Grand Rapids: Wm. B. Eerdmans, 2005.

Yarbrough, O. Larry. *Not like the Gentiles: Marriage Rules in the Letters of Paul.* SBLDS 80. Atlanta: Scholars Press, 1985.

Yeo, Khiok-Khng, ed. *Navigating Romans through Cultures: Challenging Readings by Charting a New Course.* RHCS. Edinburgh: T&T Clark, 2005.

Young, Brad H. *Paul the Jewish Theologian: A Pharisee among Christians, Jews, and Gentiles.* Peabody: Hendrickson Publishers, 1995.

Young, Frances M. *The Art of Performance: Toward a Theology of Holy Scripture.* London: Darton, Longman and Todd, 1990.

Young, Maureen W. S. *Faith in Jesus and Paul: A Comparison with Special Reference to 'Faith that can remove mountains' and 'Your faith has healed/saved you.'* WUNT 2/147. Tübingen: J. C. B. Mohr (Paul Siebeck), 2002.

Zahn, Theodor. *Der Brief des Paulus an die Römer.* 3d ed. KNT 6. Leipzig: Deichert, 1925.

Zeller, Dieter. *Der Brief an die Römer übersetz und erklärt.* RNT. Regensburg: Friedrich Pustet, 1985.

————. *Juden und Heiden in der Mission des Paulus: Studien zum Römerbrief.* 2d ed. FB 8. Stuttgart: Katholisches Bibelwerk, 1976.

Zerwick, Max. *Biblical Greek.* Rome: Pontifical Biblical Institute Press, 1963.

Zetterholm, Magnus. *Approaches to Paul: A Student's Guide to Contemporary Scholarship.* Minneapolis: Fortress Press, 2009.

Ziesler, John A. *Pauline Christianity.* Rev. ed. New York: Oxford University Press, 1990.

————. *Paul's Letter to the Romans.* TPINTC. Philadelphia: Trinity Press International, 1989.

Zumstein, Jean, and Andreas Dittwiler, eds. *Kreuzestheologie im Neuen Testament.* WUNT 151. Tübingen: J. C. B. Mohr (Paul Siebeck), 2002.

Zuntz, Günther. *The Text of the Epistles: A Disquisition upon the Corpus Paulinum.* The Schweich Lectures of the British Academy, 1946. London: Oxford University Press, 1953.

Index of Subjects

Index of Modern Authors

Index of Scripture References

Index of Other Ancient Sources